THE AGE OF FEDERALISM

THE AGE OF
FEDERALISM

Stanley Elkins

AND

Eric McKitrick

OXFORD UNIVERSITY PRESS

New York　　　　　*Oxford*

Oxford University Press

Oxford   New York
Athens   Auckland   Bangkok   Bombay
Calcutta   Cape Town   Dar es Salaam   Delhi
Florence   Hong Kong   Istanbul   Karachi
Kuala Lumpur   Madras   Madrid   Melbourne
Mexico City   Nairobi   Paris   Singapore
Taipei   Tokyo   Toronto

and associated companies in
Berlin   Ibadan

First published in 1993 by Oxford University Press
200 Madison Avenue, New York, New York 10016

First isssued as an Oxford University Press paperback, 1995

Oxford is a registered trademark of Oxford University Press

LIBRARY OF CONGRESS CATALOGING-IN-PUBLICATION DATA
Elkins, Stanley M.
The age of federalism / Stanley Elkins, Eric McKitrick.
p.   cm.   Includes bibliographical references and index.
ISBN 0-19-506890-4
ISBN 0-19-509381-x (pbk.)
1. United States—Politics and government—Constitutional period. 1789–1809.
I. McKitrick, Eric L. II. Title.
E310.E45 1993 973.4—dc20
92-33660

1 3 5 7 9 10 8 6 4 2

Printed in the United States of America

To the memory of

Richard Hofstadter

ACKNOWLEDGMENTS

C. Vann Woodward and Richard Hofstadter encouraged us many years ago to undertake this subject. They gave us their friendship many years before that, even before we had left graduate school.

Other friends and colleagues have given us a wide variety of assistance, such as advice in their special fields of competence or helping us to locate out-of-the-way sources; of these persons there have been a great many. By now some may have forgotten what they did, but we have not. They include Edith Abbott, Robert Averitt, Jason Bitsky, Lawson Bowling, Howard Brown, David Cannadine, Elizabeth Capelle, John Catanzariti, Jack Chatfield, Barbara Chernow, Laura Downs, Joseph Ellis, Dorothy Fennell, Eric Foner, Peter Gay, Carl Hovde, Nelly Hoyt, Mary-Jo Kline, Mary McGovern, Diana Meisinger, Mark Nackman, Robert Paxton, Caroline Pierce, Jacob Price, Robert Rutland, David Schuyler, Craig Thurtell, Dorothy Twohig, Leo Weinstein, and Isser Woloch.

Benjamin DeMott, with fine Jamesian perspicuity, insisted that our tale should break off exactly where it now does, and that no tedious "Conclusions" were called for.

R. Jackson Wilson loyally read the entire manuscript, as he has done with much of our previous work, making many valuable suggestions and forcing our attention upon some questions we would otherwise have overlooked.

Mention must be made of two in particular whose combined impact on this enterprise required a whole year for us to absorb and come to terms with in the process of final revision. Kingsley Ervin, Headmaster of Grace Church School in New York, has occupied much of a distinguished career in helping others to know and to say more clearly what they mean. He did this for us, with his scrutiny of every line of our text and jottings on nearly every page—the sum of which, we believe, has made considerable difference in the outcome. Herbert Sloan of Barnard College performed a similar office with the same thoroughness, not only with his own sense of style but through a command of the pertinent literature that is in every way fabulous. He tactfully filled in more than one patch of ignorance on our part and saved us from some real blunders. Our gratitude to both these friends is scarcely expressible.

The authors' families have been—as the stereotyped formula goes—"supportive" and "forbearing"; they have also given some very measurable assistance. Natalie Lamken and Dorothy Elkins read proof; Enid McKitrick took authoritative charge (and with the ocular equivalent of perfect pitch) of computerizing a hopelessly sprawling manuscript. Edyth McKitrick's eye was likewise critical, in both senses. (As one of many such instances, in an earlier version we had Thomas Paine's father as "a mild and rather ineffectual corsetmaker"; her laconic marginal query was: "Do you mean his corsets fell down?")

Fellowships from the John Simon Guggenheim Foundation, the National Endowment for the Humanities, and the Institute for Advanced Study at Princeton allowed us time for attention to some of the most difficult phases of the work; without such assistance the work would have taken even longer than it already has.

India Cooper, whose underground reputation in the New York publishing world was already formidable, showed us that copy editing can be not just an art, but a fine art.

S.E.
E.McK.

CONTENTS

THE AGE OF FEDERALISM

INTRODUCTION

Modes of Thought and Feeling in the Founding Generation

.

This book is an extended encounter with firstness. It begins with the first appearance of the United States as a self-acknowledged nation, at the moment when the nation first put on the organizing structure under which it still functions. But though the structure is still there, the character and substance of what was first contained within it have altered beyond recognition, a process which in fact was in motion almost from the beginning. Our book seeks to recover something of this earlier substance, some measure of what it was like—the difference it made—becoming a "nation" after having been something else, especially in the experience of those persons most directly implicated in bringing this entity into being and setting it afoot. Our scope is defined by the opening cycle of the nation's public life, one we are calling the Age of Federalism. Federalism, as a way of perceiving a society's purposes and guiding its collective affairs, did not have a very long life. We wish to account, to whatever extent is possible, for Federalism's ascendancy, decline, and eclipse, and to discern something of what displaced it.

A familiar way of viewing this historic cycle (which might also, with some justification, be called the Era of Washington) is to think of it as something of a Golden Age. In some sense it may well have been that; but any forceful figure of speech has a way of evoking images which exclude others equally pertinent, perhaps more so. In this case the age of the lawgivers, with its serene echoes of Roman antiquity, is an image that renders its object even more remote than in fact it already is. The remoteness has itself become a major problem, even as one concedes that much of what the lawgivers left has held up tolerably well.

Indeed, well into the twentieth century writers on the subject, whatever the other differences among them, tended to approach the post-Revolutionary era in a spirit that was on balance essentially benign, finding as they did much to respect in the good sense and realism of the founding generation.[1] This habit changed somewhat abruptly in the late 1950s and 1960s, giving way to a decidedly different emphasis. The Federalist period now came to be seen, as Marshall Smelser aptly phrased it, as an "Age of Passion"—a figure of speech which in this case had the salutary effect of chasing most prior images into at least provisional hiding. "American political life during much of the 1790s," asserted John Howe,

> was gross and distorted, characterized by heated exaggeration and haunted by conspiratorial fantasy. Events were viewed in apocalyptic terms with the very survival of republican liberty riding in the balance. Perhaps most remarkably of all, individuals who had not so long before cooperated closely in the struggle against England and even in the creation of a firmer continental government now found themselves mortal enemies, the basis of their earlier trust somehow worn away.[2]

There seems little doubt that it was in fact such a time, and high among our concerns will be to make what we can of the passion that permeated the Age of Federalism and to grasp something of its depth and meaning.

It becomes almost immediately apparent that these currents of feeling had little reference in any primary way to private interests. They arose out of deep anxieties as to the very character the new republic was to assume, the moral direction it would take, and the sorts of men who would give it its predominant tone. They were expressed in the bitterest contentions over the newly established Treasury and its system of public finance, and over the possible consequences— for the complexion of society, the rights of individual states, and the condition of public morals—of a Treasury-dominated central government. They emerged with equal intensity over the state of America's relations with the two leading powers of Europe, powers that were at war with each other throughout most of the 1790s, and the extent to which the American republic ought to attach its sympathies to the fortunes either of revolutionary France or of the former mother country England. The most visible embodiment of the burning ferocity that underlay such questions was of course the colossal enmity that arose, early in that decade, between Alexander Hamilton and Thomas Jefferson.

I

Making Sense of the American Revolution

Still, it is evident—though it has not always been so—that no effort to penetrate the meaning of these passions can go very far without some concern for the manner in which, in those interludes *not* dominated by their passions, the people of that generation did their thinking, on society, government, and the human state. A great deal of study has been made of that subject over the past thirty years: of the patterns of thought that animated these men's understanding of the parts they played in the coming of the Revolution and in the subsequent effort to create a constitutional union. These writings are sufficiently important, having provided succeeding historical scholars with a steadier base of comprehension than anything that was previously there, that they constitute in themselves something of a historical event. We shall have to turn aside for a moment or two and take some account of them. Worth noting, moreover, is that these writings—foremost among them being those of Bernard Bailyn, J. G. A. Pocock, and Gordon Wood[3]—were accomplished in the face of almost unimaginable difficulty. They represent an extraordinary effort of rescue, a retrieval of something which in the course of time had become all but lost.

What that something was, and why lost, is itself an important question, one seldom put into words by most students of the American past. Meanwhile it has been asserted over and over that the most effective and influential portrait ever drawn of this society was Alexis de Tocqueville's *Democracy in America,* published over a century and a half ago. The reasons for the cumulative impact of Tocqueville's work are still being debated.[4] But whatever they all are, the primary one has to be that the extent of what can be recognized in the portrait is considerable. This would almost certainly not be the case with a comparable one from the year 1790, even had it been done by another Tocqueville. It can probably be said that the principal components for a structure of norms and social values most appropriate to the workings of a capitalist, democratic, equalitarian culture were fully in place by about 1830, though not very much before then, and that *Democracy in America* is the first—and perhaps partly for that very reason the freshest—picture of modernity that we have. But it may be doubted whether Tocqueville could have seen and heard what he did, or drawn his conclusions and made his projections with the same confidence and clarity, if he had made his visit (1831–32) even a few years earlier. Probably no subsequent rearrangements of value or transformations in modes of thought and feeling could compare in magnitude to those that occurred in the fifteen years or so prior to 1830.[5]

Thus the mind and sensibility of the founding generation—more inclusively the Revolutionary generation—has been exceedingly difficult to recover: substantial portions of that mentality have long since ceased to strike echoes and resonances. A society in which, for instance, the term "democratic" is not yet one of approval, or in which the significances of "private" and "public" are so inverted from those we attach to them now, is a society sufficiently different from ours that though we may, in a manner of speaking, "see" it, we do not report what we see in the voice of easy recognition.

It is in the face of such obstacles that the work of retrieval has had to proceed, a work not so much of rediscovery and revelation as of painstaking reconstruction of pieces which may have been there all along but whose full pattern had long since disappeared from sight. Such was certainly the case with Bernard Bailyn's *Ideological Origins of the American Revolution* (1967), which set the direction for everything that followed it.[6]

Bailyn's subject was a particular configuration of ideas, a particular way of viewing public events and thinking about them, that had come to be very widespread in colonial America long before the Revolution and long before there was any thought of rebellion and separation. These ideas have as much to tell us about the origins of the Revolution as does the accumulation of grievances, because they served not so much to "rationalize" the grievances but something like the reverse: they gave meaning to the grievances when they appeared, and shaped the sense of how they ought to be responded to. Colonial writers on public affairs who had any degree of education and reading—Bailyn had occasion to meet great numbers of them through the hundreds of pamphlets from the Revolutionary era he examined—had a tendency to cite "authorities" at every step of their arguments, so we have a fair notion of what they read and of those ideas to which they were especially receptive.

They were drawn from a variety of sources, though with a notable degree of selectivity: the ancient classics, especially those relating to the era of the declining Roman Republic (Plutarch, Cicero, Tacitus); Enlightenment rationalism (Locke, Montesquieu, and Rousseau on natural rights and the implicit "contract" between governors and governed); some strains of Puritan covenant theology; and perhaps most fundamental of all, the reform writings, or later adaptations, of the leading radical "Commonwealth" spokesmen of the English Civil War period, Harrington, Milton, Neville, and Sidney. Their leading ideas had been updated and codified early in eighteenth-century England for purposes of opposition to the inordinately long and reputedly corrupt ministry of Sir Robert Walpole. In this form they reached the American colonies in a continuing stream and were read there with an exceptional degree of intentness.

Among Bailyn's most striking achievements was his locating and giving specificity to the principal channels for the transatlantic movement of ideas in the Anglo-American world of the eighteenth century. The opposition polemicists and pamphleteers of the Walpolean age, the voice of the "Country party" attacking "Court" policies, remained for all their bitter persistence a fringe element with little influence within England itself. Their writings were, on the other hand, enormously influential in America. Foremost among them were the essays of *The Independent Whig* and *Cato's Letters,* written collaboratively by John Trenchard and Thomas Gordon, appearing in serial as well as book form beginning in the 1720s, and circulating in the colonies probably more widely than anything else of its kind. Another notable "Country" paper was *The Craftsman,* mouthpiece for the anti-ministerial philippics of Henry St. John, Viscount Bolingbroke. Why these writings should have made so profound an impression in America but not at home is a question whose answer lies somewhere between the nature of the ideas themselves and the self-perception of the provincial society that received them.

The political thought of the eighteenth century began with one governing assumption underlying everything else, a kind of substructural given. The central fact of civic life, by which every political collision and its outcome could be understood, was the irreconcilable antinomy of liberty and power. Power is by its nature aggressive, encroaching, unstable; liberty is passive, exposed, subvertible. The lust for power, left unrestrained, is the most dangerous of human appetites; the safeguarding of liberty (or law, or right) requires unsleeping vigilance, virtue, and will. History abounds with melancholy examples of peoples (Venice, Sweden, Denmark) who through disregard, luxury, and sloth had allowed their liberties to be plucked away and themselves brought under the rod of tyranny.

The English, on the other hand, were a uniquely favored people, the freest in the world. They owed this felicity to the marvelous excellence of their mixed constitution of king, lords, and commons—the one, the few, and the many—marvelous because the aggressive tendencies of any one of these elements were held in check by the other two. It was the resulting balance, inhibiting the incursions of arbitrary power and preventing such tendencies from taking their ultimate form (royal despotism, aristocratic oligarchy, or popular anarchy and mob rule), that served to maintain the liberties of the English nation.

On this much, agreement was all but universal. The never-ending face-off between liberty and power, and the blessings of the balanced English constitution, were axioms more or less accepted on all sides, court and country, metropolis and colonies. But the opposition polemicists drew from them special implications and gave them a special emphasis. They asserted that the balance, though still there, was being insidiously undermined year by year through a deadly process of corruption in high places, a kind of rot spreading into every level of English public life. A power-grasping ministry was already at work to paralyze the independence of Parliament through the arts of bribery, the sale of honors and offices in government and Church, and the control of pocket boroughs, thus giving rise to luxury, extravagance, profligacy, dependence, and servility. The time might not be far off when the ministry, with its legion of parasites, pensioners, and placemen, a subservient Church, a rising and compliant money power, costly wars, ever-heavier taxes and excises, public debts, and eventually an overgrown standing army, would enfold the entire people in coils of oppression and enslavement.

Interspersed with cries of doom were calls for reforms to strengthen the waning vigil and arrest the rot, reforms that were nevertheless scarcely thinkable in Hanoverian England. They included a more equitable suffrage, elimination of rotten boroughs, representation based on population, representatives bound to their constituencies by residence and instruction, full freedom of the press, and the removal of government control over religion.

But what appeared in England to be the utopian ravings of an impotent fringe were in America not utopian at all, but rather the common sense of things. They served on the one hand as a certification of rights and liberties which for the most part the colonies already had, and on the other as a series of warnings of what these free, virtuous, providentially situated, and still-uncorrupted provinces of the English community would do well to watch for in times to come. The mentality of the outsider was being diffused throughout a whole society of outsiders. Thus when in the 1760s the warnings of horrid possibility gave way to what now appeared as horrid reality—taxes of a sort hitherto unknown, a new and augmented corps of placemen in the colonial customs service, the threat of an Anglican church establishment throughout the colonies, and at last the suspension of their assemblies, the closing of their ports, and the quartering of redcoat regulars in their midst—the colonials were in full possession of a language and a grammar to delineate in utmost extent and detail what was revealing itself, a deliberate conspiracy by ministers of the Crown to take away their liberties, step by step, and reduce them to slavery.

The Bailyn paradigm of an eighteenth-century belief system converted to an ideology of revolutionary response has generally served, in the best work subsequently done in and around this subject, as an opening up rather than a delimitation of possibilities.[7] Such work has tended for the most part not to alter the design but to enlarge and extend it. That of J. G. A. Pocock is a conspicuous example.

Pocock's writings, of which *The Machiavellian Moment: Florentine Political Thought and the Atlantic Republican Tradition* (1975) represents a kind of summation, have laid out a much enriched and chronologically lengthened context for viewing the political intelligence of the eighteenth-century Anglo-American community. That intelligence had its birth—or rebirth, considered in the light of its classical ancestry—in the city-states of Renaissance Italy. The rebirth amounted in sum to a revived perception of the collectivity of public life, perhaps even of the thought that there *was* such a thing as "public life," which men might think about and be a part of, and in reference to which individual men might measure their own worth and their own fulfillment.

Pocock out of his great learning has made a place in our vocabulary for certain essences that we can no longer imagine having once done without. He has given currency to a term, "civic humanism,"[8] which provides a kind of synoptic notation and an associative unity to a tradition of thought whose tangled filaments are otherwise all too easy to lose track of. In addition, he has given a fresh insistence to a word—"virtue"—which was central to political thought from the Renaissance through the eighteenth century but whose meaning in modern times has become entirely disjoined from what it was then.

The time of troubles of the Florentine republic in the late fifteenth and early sixteenth centuries confronted a few intellectuals of that time—men of education who were making their way in law, diplomacy, or the state bureaucracy—with a problem of peculiar urgency, one of self-understanding, for the definition of which the categories of medieval Christian thought furnished no satisfactory vocabulary. The Heavenly City was one thing, but it had become imperative to formulate in adequate words what was happening to the earthly republic here and now, or what might happen and why; and how the actions of men, both immediately and over time, could bear on its fate, which required a conception clearer than anything then current not only of an ideal commonwealth and its constituent parts but also of an optimum sphere for the temporal strivings of man himself. The result, seen most prominently in the writings of Francesco Guicciardini, Donato Giannotti, and above all Niccolò Machiavelli, was a reconstruction from Aristotle's *Politics* and Polybius' *Histories* of the mixed and balanced constitution as that kind least unstable, as well as of such a commonwealth's providing the most ample setting for men's own self-realization. Thus the "Machiavellian Moment" was a point in the history of thought at which thought, under strains of temporal experience which reason found no longer tolerable, transformed itself. To the man of reason it presented a model which could be seen as comparable, to some perhaps even preferable, to a life of contemplation upon things eternal and beyond time. It was the model of citizenship, a life of action in the commonwealth, of reason armed against *fortuna* and responsive to contingency and history, to temporal cycles of generation and decay. His arms, if he will take them up, are those of virtue: *virtù,* conceived not simply as "manliness" but as "humanness" at meridian, that quality under which he fulfills the totality of his nature in service to the republic.

Another of Pocock's "Machiavellian Moments" (he can be read as depicting several) was that in which this civic humanism made its way into the thought of seventeenth-century England and effected another transformation there. Foremost among the theorists of the Interregnum was James Harrington, whose *Commonwealth of Oceana* (1656) projected a mixed and balanced republic, very much in accord with the Florentine ideal, and gave an enhanced depth to the more radical side of his contemporaries' social and political awareness. Harrington imported two principles in particular upon which he conceived a fully realized participatory citizenship must rest. One was the right to bear arms in the community's defense, a derivation of Machiavelli's theory of a citizen militia in place of *condottieri* available for hire by any prince or ruler. The other was freehold property as the fundamental safeguard and guarantee of the citizen's independence of judgment, action, and choice.

A final mutation of Renaissance-Commonwealth thought in the early years of the eighteenth century—"neo-Harringtonian," as Pocock terms it—both brought it in line with the logic of the post-Restoration settlement and reshaped it for a rhetoric of opposition in the Walpolean era, defining as it did a new polarity, that of "Court" and "Country." Harrington's ideal constitutional balance, formulated as it was during the Interregnum, had consisted of only two orders, the "few" and the "many" (a kind of rotating "natural" aristocracy of talent, and the people at large) and had not included a royal "one." With the monarchy's return this had to be replaced by the more familiar three. Yet the primary polarities of Renaissance civic humanism—constitutional balance and instability, liberty and power, virtue and corruption—remained in full vigor. "Corruption" in particular, in the writings of Andrew Marvell, Trenchard and Gordon, Bolingbroke, Andrew Fletcher, and Charles Davenant, received a vastly expanded meaning. A generic term not limited to simple bribery, "corruption" embraced the entire range of means whereby the executive power through its ministers and subordinate agents might sap the independent will of Parliament, abet the growth of divisions, factions, and parties, and pervert its collective functions of vigilance and supervision. Members decoyed by the lure of patronage and pensions might give their assent to measures—mounting excises, national debts, standing armies—the disposition of which might run beyond anything Parliament could any longer control. The end-product of corruption would be an end of the balance and an end to liberty.

Such was the lineage and provenance, and such the form, of a political language that had played on the nerves of colonial Americans for a half-century and more before 1776.

The structure of historical understanding erected by Bailyn, then furbished and enlarged by Pocock, was still further extended and brought to a grand completion with Gordon Wood's *Creation of the American Republic, 1776–1787.*[9] Wood's subject was what he saw as a kind of culminating phase in the course of civic humanist thought—or, as he preferred to call it, the Whig tradition of classical republicanism—with the Americans' completion of their revolutionary undertaking and the formation of the Federal Constitution. Wood's contention was that a critical reordering in the categories of political thought had occurred by the end of the eleven-year period during which the Americans endeavored, at first less than successfully, to give specific form to their classical-Whig-republican understanding of what the exemplary commonwealth ought to be. The eventual product, the Constitution, represented a master innovation in the science of politics, while the Framers' perception of what they had done, and their effort to account for it, so transformed political thought as to mark a virtual terminus to the entire tradition in which their political awareness had been shaped.

The deficiencies of the Articles of Confederation formed only a part, and probably the lesser part, of the urgency that had steered them toward this outcome. Decidedly more consequential was the experience, undertaken at the beginning of the Revolution in high optimism and clouded at the end of it in relative disenchantment, of fashioning republican constitutions in the several states and then observing how they worked. The force that had driven the colonies into armed resistance was the conviction that the ancient balance of king, lords, and commons which had hitherto preserved the liberties of Englishmen was being all but fatally destroyed by incursions of executive influence corrupting the rightful functions of Parliament, the embodied guardians of the people's health and safety. The predominant impulse, then, in state after state was to so fashion the new republics, and so rebalance their governing powers, that no such abuses could ever again occur. Governors were rendered little short of impotent, their powers of veto, appointment, and convocation being drastically curtailed from those previously held by the royal governors, while legislative control over the making of laws, functioning of the courts, and disposition of revenue was vastly extended. Provision was made for frequent elections, usually annual, with elective districts and representation proportioned according to population (there would be no rotten boroughs in these republics), all with the two-fold object that the assemblies be as direct a reflection as possible of the character and desires of the people at large, and that governors have little or no scope for manipulating them. As a result, in most of the states the popular assembly had become for practical purposes the supreme sovereign power. And yet these same assemblies, in state after state, began almost at once to wield their powers in capricious, short-sighted, and irresponsible ways.

Out of this experience, received modes of political understanding, "republican" though they might be, came under extraordinary strain. For one thing, it had become apparent fairly soon that the image of the "mixed" constitution under which the differing claims of the social "estates" were held in balance (the one, the few, and the many) was no longer very compelling, no matter which way people might wish to adapt it. Though republican theory had not necessarily ruled out some form of kingship,[10] it was obvious that annually elected governors, whatever their formal powers, could in no way be "sovereigns"; likewise the logic of an upper house could not rest on any approximation of a hereditary nobility, none having ever existed in America. What social orders, then, did the commonalty have to check and balance, other than itself? If balance were to persist as an imperative—as of course it would—in people's thoughts on how a commonwealth governed itself, it would have to materialize in some other way, and in some new form.

Moreover, there began emerging in more and more minds—most notably that of James Madison—the increasingly worrisome question of what had become of virtue itself, anywhere in these scattered republics. There had always been a place in classical theory for a choice few, men out of the common run whose superior talents and wisdom ("enlightened views and virtuous sentiments")[11] were at the commonwealth's service for the just guidance of its affairs. Such spirits now seemed little in evidence, especially with the resumption of peacetime pursuits. The state legislatures, as Madison and many another viewed them, had become a babel of narrow-minded parochial concerns, their members men of selfish interests and untutored understanding, oblivious of minority rights, passing unjust laws (such as legal tender acts whereby debts people owed each other could be paid in worthless currency), and all unchecked by any overriding vision of the public good or what it might consist of. It could even be that virtue was too hard to find, or had too pinched a scope, in small republics. Perhaps it was time to try again, to make a new beginning, to widen that scope and turn this uncertain league of commonwealths into one great Republic.

Wood's crowning achievement was to locate and mark out what appears in retrospect to have been the only course of thought whereby a resolution of all such strains was possible or even conceivable. The ultimate question, at that time still very much an unsettled paradox, was that of sovereignty: what sovereignty was, where it lay, and how people ought to think about it. The sovereignty of the people was not in itself a new idea, having been present in Whig theory from the time of the English Civil War. But it had always been something of a platitude, conveying little practical meaning. In the normal course of things the people's "sovereignty" lay dormant, being exercised in full directness only in extreme instances of rebellion against tyranny. Meanwhile the supreme authority of the realm, the operative sovereignty, from which there could be no appeal, lay in Parliament—"Parliament" conceived for the purpose as "king-in-Parliament," or more precisely, king, lords, and commons. Nor was sovereignty divisible. There was no province of government from which Parliament's authority could be excluded; and sharing any portion of it with any other body would be *imperium in imperio,* a solecism, a logical absurdity.

The debates of the 1760s and 1770s over what Parliament rightfully could or could not do to the colonies were at best inconclusive on the question of sovereignty. Whereas sovereignty in theory may have been indivisible, and the Americans were never quite able to say it was otherwise, still, it had somehow seemed in practice as though it *could* be divided and had been all along—that Parliament in practice exercised one portion of it and their own assemblies another—but they had no vocabulary for saying so. With independence, of course, the idea of popular sovereignty took on an immediacy it had never previously had. Yet the full logic of sovereignty—how it might be divided, or parceled out, or delegated, or even whether it could be—remained as indeterminate as ever. Especially since, if sovereignty were now seated in the several states, as seemed to be generally taken for granted, it was a real question whether the Continental Congress could claim any of the attributes of sovereignty at all.

A diversity of factors—at one end, the extension and heightened intensity of participatory action in community life during the Revolution, and at the other, the perplexities and discontents of the 1780s—made for an emerging awareness that sooner or later the whole question of sovereignty would have to be asked in a new way. For one thing, it was evident from a variety of out-of-doors doings, ranging from vigilante action to *ad hoc* conventions, that the people's sovereignty was anything but an inert and dormant quantity. It was further evident that the scope of such sovereignty was not confined to the formal agencies of government, and that perhaps it ought not be thought of as residing in government at all, or even as having been transferred or delegated there: that sovereignty, without moving from where it lay, could retain full control of its forces and powers while deploying them in any direction the people might choose. And it was obvious in still a further way, with the people turning out to be just as suspicious of their own elected representatives as they had ever been of royal governors, judges, and magistrates, that there was something wrong with the idea of an unfettered assembly as a fully adequate reflector of the people's will, and that the sovereign mind was having its second thoughts about the allocation it had made of sovereignty's instruments.

The outcome was a new synthesis, probably most clearly articulated by James Wilson, out of which was drawn the formula whereby defenders of the Federal Constitution in 1787–88 could counter every objection its opponents could bring against it. The sovereignty of the states, the Antifederalists claimed, had been invaded on behalf of a consolidated government which now had executive powers that were shockingly great, and which had been brought about by illegally circumventing the Articles of Confederation, no part of which could be amended except by unanimous consent of the state governments. The reply was that state sovereignty was not being invaded because sovereignty had never resided there. Sovereignty resides not in rulers or magistrates, nor in state governments, nor indeed in governments of any kind, but in the whole body of the people, who can never allow it to be taken anywhere else. And such is the supreme authority of the people that although the people may not, indeed cannot, part with any portion of that sovereignty—which is to say that sovereignty is in some final sense indivisible after all—they may still distribute its functions in as many ways as they choose, and yet again revoke them should prudence so advise it. And should the people still further conclude, through conventions chosen for the purpose by themselves, that the powers of sovereignty ought to be balanced in a new way—not, say, between social orders but among departments of government—and should majorities of them consent, the people would thereby be obeying no other ruler, no prior laws or charters, no higher power than themselves. The argument, at least in that form and for the time being, proved unanswerable.

2

"Court" and "Country" Mentalities
in Eighteenth-Century England

The writings just discussed—those of Bailyn, Pocock, and Wood—have invested the concept of ideology with a refinement it did not previously have, and have fashioned that concept into a device exceptionally useful for illuminating sequences of political action and cycles of historical change. Ideology, here conceived as a shared body of reference—a configuration of more or less formal abstract ideas, unified through conviction and held in place by the hopes, fears, anxieties, and prejudices that normally accompany them—is nevertheless not to be thought of as a "cause" for the actions people take. Nor ought it be seen primarily as a "justification" for actions they have already taken. Ideas may exert a great deal of influence on the direction in which such actions go; they may also be highly useful in "rationalizing" them afterward. But that is not quite the point. The true relation is closer still: ideas are simply *there;* they inhabit the same field of force in which any action occurs, and in reality are never absent from it. People do not, indeed cannot, act in any concerted way without some conception of a meaning for what they do; ideology, expressed in acts of thinking, speech, and writing, may be seen as the medium whereby they reach for it.

These ascriptions of meaning, then, must in the most basic sense be fashioned out of what is already there. The clusters of ideas, the values attached to them, and the modes whereby they are put into words must be drawn from some common reservoir; otherwise there can be no echoes, no recognition, no meaning. To quote Pocock's now-famous phrase: "Men cannot do what they have no means of saying they have done; and what they do must in part be what they can say and conceive that it is."[12]

Thus ideology, whatever its "rationalizing" function, has a limiting function as well. The language people draw upon sets bounds to the range of action they can imagine; they are never quite free to do whatever they might please or to fashion any language whatever to justify it—or, more precisely, to give it meaning.

This principle is certainly not without its paradoxes and perplexities, which meet us at more than one point in the public life of the eighteenth century, both in England and in America. People might take sharply adversarial positions on fairly basic issues and still find their meanings within essentially the same structure of ideas and values, the same body of reference.[13] Or, to turn the case around, overwhelming numbers of them might support the same cause—say, the American Revolution—from a variety of divergent individual motives and interests, yet still be drawing upon the same enveloping tradition of thought for whatever community of purpose and meaning they might reach.[14]

The "Court" and "Country" contentions of Hanoverian England give a sharp sense of this paradox, of how mutually acknowledged values might be put to very different, indeed opposing, purposes. The party divisions that had vexed English politics in the closing years of the seventeenth century and opening years of the eighteenth (though Whigs and Tories cannot quite be thought of as "parties" in any modern sense) had become substantially dimmed by the time of Walpole's rise to power in the 1720s and with the consolidation of a predominantly Whig interest in Parliament. These former divisions were now replaced, or at least overlaid, by something more elemental in character: the suspicions and resentments of an outsider state of mind, a Country viewpoint with its vocal center in the landed gentry, leveled against the Court establishment of an entrenched executive ministry in alliance with the emergent powers of money and exchange in the City of London and upheld in Parliament through a selective distribution of Crown patronage. This Court-Country polarity is of special interest to us for several reasons. Not only did it define the predominant temper of a half-century and more of English politics, but a strikingly similar counterpart of it would reappear in the America of the 1790s. Moreover, the words reached for to invest it with meaning were drawn from a substantially shared vocabulary: so much so that the two sides—in England at least—may even be said to have functioned, as more than one writer has put it, in a kind of "symbiotic relationship."[15]

The "Financial Revolution" of the 1690s marked a profound turning point in the history of both the economic and political life of England, inaugurating as it did a new and essentially modern conception of the mobilization and management of government resources, and bringing into existence two formidable new institutions—a funded public debt and a large central bank with quasi-public functions. The system of public finance which thus had its birth during the reign of William III was subsequently brought to a state of considerable maturity and stability by the ministries of Walpole and Henry Pelham under the first two Georges. But it also provided a key term in the emerging tensions of Court and Country: "government by money."

William III's policy of war against the France of Louis XIV, while it had the public's general support, proved vastly more expensive than anything of the sort the nation had previously undertaken. With current taxes and *ad hoc* private loans clearly inadequate to meet unprecedented and continuing costs, William's Treasury officials arranged with a group of London's wealthiest merchants for the first of a series of exceptionally large loans, to be secured by specific future taxes, in return for which the financiers would be granted a charter with monopoly privileges for certain forms of banking. The resulting Bank of England (1694) would handle government deposits, assist in organizing future borrowing by government, do private commercial business, and issue notes which could circulate as public currency. (Two other great chartered monopolies, the East India and South Sea Companies, would also, for a time, handle large portions of the public debt.) This transformation in public finance brought long-term consequences in two broad spheres, one in the nation's business life and the other in the workings of government itself. A financial revolution on this order had of necessity to be accompanied by an administrative revolution.[16]

Extended periods of war, which would recur at more or less regular intervals throughout the eighteenth century, together with the growing public debt needed for maintaining them—a debt which nonetheless would prove more than adequately supportable by a very sound base of government credit—combined to bring into being a vastly expanded money market, new forms of investment, and a substantially new trading class concerned primarily with the movement of public securities and allied varieties of negotiable paper, and with the kinds of transactions which made them profitable. Meanwhile these same factors—an intermittent war footing and greatly increased sums available for expenditure by government—required a much expanded bureaucracy in the Treasury, Admiralty, and War offices for handling them. The purposeful allocation of this patronage and other forms of royal preferment in such a way as to assure government of dependable majorities for its policies in the House of Commons was brought to something of a fine art by Sir Robert Walpole.[17]

To the extent that the resulting Country opposition had a community of sentiment and purpose, it derived from a somewhat indeterminate mixture: a sense of exclusion, suspicion of the new kinds of power and new ranges of influence that money seemed to be opening up in London and Westminster, and hostility to men who appeared to be threatening the standards and values of which rural squires had customarily seen themselves as the hereditary custodians. The Country voice, to which were added those of a variety of literary types, was loud in judgment.

A perilous new era, as the Country saw it, had arrived, one in which the decisions and choices that most affected the nation's liberties, well-being, and morals were more and more removed from the hands in which they had traditionally been safest—from the body, that is, of the nation's landed proprietors—and were now lodged elsewhere and out of reach. Though the Glorious Revolution of 1688–89 had supposedly blown away the last traces of the divine right of kings, the Crown's executive power had nevertheless taken on a new weight, exercised in new ways, and now appeared more pervasive and menacing than ever. The houses of Parliament could no longer be seen as an independent force in government or as the guardians of liberty and virtue in the nation's life, because the base upon which virtue in public service was presumed to rest—landed property and freehold tenure as the safest guarantee of independent judgment and action—was being sapped by the power of money. While the burden of a rising national debt and the costs of continuing wars were being principally borne by the gentry through the land tax and the excise,[18] men in the City whose wealth was based not on the real value inherent in land but on the ephemeral values of paper and credit were enriching themselves at the nation's expense. Meanwhile the royal ministry, with its enhanced latitude of initiative and action, and with this new class at its beck and call, was perverting the independent will of Parliament and purchasing its subservience to the Crown's own will through offices, honors, and perquisites. The sacred balance of the constitution, the venerable equilibrium of king, lords, and commons, was teetering over an abyss of corruption.

Consequently the direction assumed by the Country opposition might be taken as either the impulse of reform or resistance to change, or both. Looking back to a time when the king supposedly "lived of his own" but was obliged to consult Parliament each time on anything, such as an occasional foreign venture, that went beyond routine expenses, Country spokesmen sounded a continuous call for a return to cheap, simple, and honest government. They attacked the excise and land tax as impoverishing the nation, wars and funded debts for the same reason (and because both the burdens and the profits fell on all the wrong people), the standing army because of what it boded for the nation's liberties, and all these things because of their potential for corrupting the nation's virtue. Meanwhile, in defense of the balanced constitution and genuine mixed government they kept bringing up Place Bills to limit the Crown's patronage powers and to keep down the numbers of pensioners and placemen sitting in Parliament, and they called for more frequent elections in order to check the range of temptations laid before a too entrenched membership in the House of Commons. There was even some talk of reforming the vote, though nothing of a "democratic" tendency, neither Court nor Country having the least interest in extending the franchise to the unpropertied. (If anything they would have liked to raise the qualification rather than lower it.) It was more a question of adjustments in representation and electoral practice that would give more weight to the landed interest and less scope for courtiers and stock-jobbers to buy their way into Parliament. In short, every argument the Country made, for or against change of any kind, referred back in some way to the swollen power of the Court, the threat to the balanced constitution and civic virtue, and behind it all the corrupting power of money.

The response of Court-minded—or non-Country-minded—publicists to the Country polemics was not made in a language that challenged in any fundamental way the principles the Country stood for. Indeed they professed, by and large, to hold all the same principles, other things being equal. They put their emphasis, however, on the practical and technical considerations in government, foreign relations, and economic life that must modify a too literal construction of those principles.

England's mixed and balanced constitution, as all proclaimed, was beyond doubt the best in the world. But the parts could in no strict sense be independent of each other; the balance would actually be upset if they were. There must be a balance of liberty and authority, also an equilibrium of all the most important and powerful interests in the state. These included not only the landed but the commercial, moneyed, professional, and religious interests as well, all of which government must both represent and reconcile. King, lords, and commons were all combined in one supreme authority, yet this too involved a balance, which required harmony rather than separation. The Crown—the executive side—must have its own part in maintaining that balance, and could not do so without the Crown's positive and purposeful exercise of those prerogatives still remaining to it: control of foreign policy and, most especially, of conferring office and honors.

Neither harmonious relations nor informed debates were possible unless the executive had its spokesmen in the legislature, just as the Commons must have theirs at court. Nor was it fair to claim that giving a man a place automatically corrupted his conscience. How otherwise were merit and loyalty to be given recognition? Place Bills could actually be said to strike at the principle of virtue itself: if the king chose men of quality and talent to be his servants and such men were thereby excluded from the Commons, or if as members of Parliament they were forced to choose and elected to remain where they were, one or the other—Crown or Parliament—would be deprived of a prime source of virtue in the public service.

Court supporters could be as ready as anyone to deplore the burdens of war, to admit the possibility of the debt getting out of hand, or to acknowledge that standing armies needed watching, or to concede that money, commerce, and virtue did not always go together. Nevertheless the world of the eighteenth century had become immensely widened in scope for the interests of the British nation. A far-flung network of overseas trade, a colonial empire, and a due weight in the power relations of Europe all required an active foreign policy and a professional military and naval establishment for giving effect to it. Moreover, such commitments and responsibilities would scarcely even be thinkable without a dependable system of public finance to support them.

Thus while such received civic humanist values as those concerning luxury, corruption, and virtue may not have been exactly repudiated, Court language certainly showed a decidedly revised slant on them. For instance, whatever the virtue once inherent in citizen militias in preference to standing armies, it was now out of the question to send off such a body to be destroyed in France or anywhere else. As for the public debt, the very size of it and the sound credit of the government on which it rested could be seen as testimony to the patriotism and good faith of the class willing to invest their money in it. And as the nation prospered and commerce flourished, luxury itself need not be thought of as leading to certain corruption if it brought refinement and amenity to the common life. So the emergent financial system, the government structure that administered it, the men of affairs who both supported and profited from it, and the beneficent consequences for the nation that could be claimed to flow from it were all defended in strong accents against the prophecies of doom from the Country.

With regard to the basic arrangements of English society and the management of its public affairs, the preponderance of sentiment in the political nation by the middle years of the eighteenth century had come to rest heavily on the Court side. And as time went on, more and more circumstances combined to make the issues between them appear, for all their rhetorical stridency, as matters somewhat short of life and death. For one thing, the political nation itself—the governing class and its voting constituency—was still relatively small in relation to the population at large, and most elements within it had a strong common interest in keeping it that way. Moreover, anyone, Country-minded or otherwise, with more than a passing acquaintance of life at the center of things knew that the world of high affairs, either of government at Westminster or of trade and exchange in the City, had long since taken a course that was not likely to be reversed. The British structure of government finance under Walpole and his successors, for all its perplexing intricacies, had emerged as stronger, stabler, and more advanced than that of any other country—in marked contrast, say, with Bourbon France, whose antiquated financial patchwork would be in a state of collapse on the eve of the French Revolution. Meanwhile the interconnections of private facilities for credit, insurance, and exchange radiating outward from the commercial houses of London were infinitely more sophisticated than those available anywhere else. (This had more than a little to do with the prosperity of the American colonies.)

There were a fair number of limits, then, on what the Country could imagine itself doing to alter any of this, or even wanting to. And not the least of them was a set of assumptions that permeated all levels of political life with regard to the propriety of a permanent, formed opposition. Virtually nobody was yet prepared to argue that regular parties might be a good thing; Court and Country each charged the other with stirring up faction; and many a country gentleman, true to his picture of his own independent self, shied away from joining in any sustained and systematic effort to discredit the Court's established policies and drive the sitting government out of office. Whatever the dissenters said and did, they must be seen to stand on the most elevated ground without thought of profit for themselves, warning the king from time to time against the designs of wicked councillors, and always with their foremost care being for the safety of the constitution and the soundness of the nation's moral health.

All in all, the interests and associations which Court and Country held in common probably counted for more than did those dividing them. In 1740 James Thomson, a Court pensioner who wrote Country poetry, composed an ode which was set to music in that same year by Thomas Arne, a London singing master and sometime impresario who longed for royal preferment but never quite got it. Yet the ode was a tremendous success everywhere, one in whose haughty cadences all voices could join, and did: "Rule Britannia."

3

"Court" and "Country" in the New American Republic

Returning now to the subject of this book, the America of the 1790s, one is presented with what seems—at least at first glance—an extraordinary repetition of historical experience. There appears to be a striking parallel between the Court-Country divisions of Georgian England and those that subsequently appeared in Washingtonian America.

The principal concerns of the Country viewpoint in England, as Lance Banning has asserted, re-emerged with an exceptional degree of similarity in the new republic and gave form at virtually every turn to the opposition temper which developed in very short order in response to the policies and actions of the new federal government. The anxieties and apprehensions, though at first muted, were nevertheless all there, ready and waiting from the start. With the government barely weeks old, Elbridge Gerry, for one, was opposing a single head for the Treasury, the Treasury being the customary base for power-grasping British prime ministers. As early as July 1789 William Maclay thought he discerned the makings of a "court party" scheming to bring about through ministerial influence and the arts of corruption a consolidated government which would swallow up the states and destroy republican virtue. "The fuse was laid. And Alexander Hamilton was ready with the match."[19] As the Hamiltonian program revealed itself over the next two years—a sizable funded debt, a powerful national bank, excises, nationally subsidized manufactures, and eventually even a standing army—the Walpolean parallel at every point was too obvious to miss. It was in resistance to this, and everything it seemed to imply, that the "Jeffersonian persuasion" was erected.

Not only may the Court-Country parallel be taken as a key term for penetrating the logic of opposition; it could also be extended, as Drew McCoy has done, well beyond its more obvious political and constitutional implications. McCoy sees the Jeffersonian and Madisonian response as more than simply reactive; it consisted rather of an already well articulated alternative conception of the republic's economic and moral future, to which Hamilton's system appeared as a mortal challenge. Theirs was a particular version of political economy as well as one of republican government. "Political economy" as understood in the eighteenth century was something quite different from the largely value-neutral science of "economics" that would eventually displace it, not only referring to the management of a state's economic affairs but embracing as well the entire range of relations between government and the social and economic order, and having a clear moral component.[20]

Enlightenment thought in this realm was not, generally speaking, an undifferentiated depiction of social progress. There was a distinct strand in it, to which the Jeffersonians were highly sensitive, that took for granted a kind of cyclical movement from youth to age, and that all civilizations must eventually reach a stage of decline and decay. The problem for political economy was that of prolonging the stage of youthful vigor and making the onset of decay as remote as possible. A master variable, moreover, was assumed to be the pressure of population growth, well before Thomas Malthus produced his celebrated essay on that subject toward the close of the century. A predominantly agricultural society was seen as the kind inherently most virtuous, the freest from corruption, the kind best constituted for resisting decay, and the one most to be desired for the American republic. Its growth and expansion, the Virginians believed, should occur across space rather than through time; its vigor might best be retained, its decline postponed, and time thus be thwarted, as long as its surplus population could keep moving into virgin land and as long as such land remained abundant.

The counter-picture, which stood as a kind of warning, was the example of Great Britain. Here was a society sufficiently advanced—or rather sufficiently aged, far enough along in the process of decay—that, with its open land gone, found itself with an ever-expanding population which could no longer be supported in agriculture and was spilling into the cities, kept alive at worst by beggary and at best through employment at bare subsistence in manufacturing establishments producing luxuries for the aristocracy, great amounts of which also went out for export, and swollen wealth for their owners. One part of society was sinking in venality and luxury, the other in poverty and brutishness. Meanwhile a misconceived system of political economy—the term for it was "mercantilism"—took for granted that the nation's prosperity could only be advanced through a structure of privileges and monopolies for its domestic commerce, while giving the law to the rest of the world with elaborate trade regulations for protecting a far-flung network of overseas markets. An all-pervading government thus sought to dominate the channels of international trade and support an overextended series of foreign involvements through naval power, standing armies, and a growing burden of debt, while the nation's true wealth was being perverted to the unnatural enrichment of its moneyed and commercial classes. The entire society was being recklessly propelled toward a final stage of degeneration, corruption, and collapse.

Yet for all such warnings and dangers, the Americans knew they could not conceive their republic simply as a continuously expanding agricultural utopia in a state of primitive Spartan virtue. Despite an inherent disjunction between virtue and commerce, and though "commerce" must forever be a figure of suspicion, never possessing in itself the kind of liberating force ascribed to it by such as Hamilton, they were nevertheless acutely aware that they could not do without it. Nor could they do without some form of manufacturing. Yet they were still free, they thought, to make a series of vital distinctions through which their republic might for an indefinite term be spared the consequences they feared from the example that was before them. There must be commerce and there must be manufactures. But these could be, and must be, of the right kind. For the well-being of the nation's agriculture, a commerce functioning primarily as carrier of its surplus produce to worldwide markets was indispensable. As for manufactured goods, the wrong kind, the kind a republican people did not need, were the superfluous luxuries turned out in the great industrial workshops of England. The right kind, those fully adequate to an existence of modest comfort, could be produced at home through household industry or artisan enterprise. To be sure, the line drawn by such a mind as James Madison's between luxuries and necessities arriving in British cargoes was always apt to be a bit blurred. Madison tended to talk of laces and silver buckles, even as his compatriots were buying woolens, cottons, cutlery, tools, and pottery in grades and quantities to be had from no other source.

Still, what was above all to be avoided was an unholy alliance of commerce, manufacturing, money, and public credit, fostered by an intrusive and interfering government. The right kind of commerce *could* flourish, in a world of free trade such as that envisioned by Adam Smith in his famous indictment of mercantilism. Such a world, as the Americans knew all too well, did not yet exist. Yet it *could* be brought into being with the right kind of foreign policy, one that required no wars, military forces, or great funded debts and excises to sustain it. The masses of Great Britain and Europe, they imagined, needed our foodstuffs, and their merchants and manufacturers needed our raw materials, more than we needed their luxuries. Upon that need might be fashioned a policy of peaceable coercion, of discriminatory duties and other sanctions on their trade, an instrument of potential use for persuading them to do justice to ours and to allow it and that of the rest of the world to flow in their "natural" channels. Both Jefferson and Madison were strongly attached to such a policy, and would in fact begin efforts almost at once to get some form of it enacted into law.

A final way of viewing the Court-Country polarity, as proposed by John Murrin, would be to make a direct comparison between the two societies, America's and Britain's, in which "Country" challenged "Court," to observe how the challenge was resolved, and then to consider what kind of parallel — and how much of one — it really was. It would then be seen that while the vocabularies may have been strikingly similar, the outcomes were drastically different. Murrin's own comparison is made in the context of the respective "Revolution Settlements": England's in the thirty-year period subsequent to the Glorious Revolution of 1689, and America's in the two or three decades following its War for Independence. In both Britain and America the Court-Country tensions were an accompaniment to the process whereby each society reached its Revolution Settlement and acquired the rough shape of its eventual modernity. But for England it was beyond question a "Court" settlement; for America it was clearly and definitively a "Country" settlement. In Britain political, social, and economic change were all bound up together, eventuating in a centralized state and an integrated economy destined to become with all its worst and best consequences the most dynamic in the world, having its center in London along with a government whose own character had been shaped in part by what it saw, mistakenly or otherwise, as the nation's vital requirements. A comparable degree of economic integration in the United States would not be reached until the middle third of the nineteenth century, and political supervision would have little to do with it. By that time the republic's political arrangements had long since been so fixed — its Revolution Settlement completed — as to rule out anything like a Court option. Such an option had, to be sure, appeared as briefly thinkable in the troubled times of the republic's birth and earliest life. But with their successful challenge to Federalism in 1800, and with Country principles as their index of meaning, the Jeffersonians would proceed for practical purposes, as Murrin puts it, simply to detach national politics and government altogether from the "larger patterns of economic and social change."[21]

A central question for this book will be that of exactly how the "Court option" — the Federalist version of a republican future — was smothered in the 1790s, and the degree to which it smothered itself.

4
The "Court" Persuasion in America, and Other Questions

What, then, did the Court option consist of; what *was* the "Federalist persuasion"? Actually there would be two versions of it, one at the beginning and the other at the end, though most accounts tend to blur them by lumping it all together. But in neither form did it have the rootedness, nor indeed the self-assurance, of the Country view, while its initial acceptability rested on a premise that would prove to be somewhat tenuous. One side of the premise was that the work done at Philadelphia, at a historical moment both portentous and uncertain, might open the way for a stable and spacious though as yet unspecified national vision. The other was that Federalism could accommodate a range of values and expectations not out of keeping with those generally supposed to have been tested and certified in the Revolution. And indeed it might have appeared for a moment as though all this were true. But that aspect was shortly to be transposed into something not wholly expected, something novel and idiosyncratic that seemed not quite to fit, and no one individual did more, or nearly as much, to impart this altered face to Federalism than Alexander Hamilton.

The initial version, logically enough, was *The Federalist* itself, that remarkable sequence of numbered statements designed to convert doubters objecting to the new Constitution. The extent to which *The Federalist* actually performed this function cannot of course be measured, and was in any case largely limited to the state of New York. But more important is that these same papers represent in aggregate the outer bounds as well as the central substance of what their authors conceived was the claim they could make—the object being above all persuasion—on their readers' experience, aspirations, and habits of thought. Read in this way, the papers are a striking reflection not so much of points being debated as of values either negotiable or held more or less in common. It is obvious, for instance, that the world in which they all functioned was hardly a "democratic" world (likewise the case between Court and Country in England) but an elite one, and that the pseudonymous collective author "Publius" (Jay, Madison, and Hamilton) was unaffectedly candid about this. A key theme was public service by men whose special merits an expanded commonwealth might make more available than they currently seemed to be. References to "virtue" abound, with great deference of course to that which resided in the people. But it seems that the people's virtue was still primarily to be thought of as their capacity less to act than to choose wisely, "to obtain for rulers," as Madison put it in Number 57, "men who possess most wisdom to discern, and most virtue to pursue the common good," men so preferred as "will be somewhat distinguished also, by those qualities which entitle them to it. . . ."[22]

Other, more focused, aims were held up, and about these too Publius was honest and straightforward. "Energy" in government was something each of the Publiuses talked about, taking for granted that such energy was mainly to be welcomed after the irresolution and drift of the years just preceding, in order to evoke the respect of foreign powers as well as that of the people's own national self. Each pointed to the military weakness of the ancient confederacies. Nor was Madison the only one to make the argument for a large republic, as he did in his famous Number 10, nor even the first. Jay and Hamilton had already done this in the preceding numbers. The importance of a sound public credit was repeatedly referred to, as was the paramountcy of the government's uncontested freedom to tax. None believed that government's power to raise military or naval forces in peacetime should be essentially impeded or qualified either. Hamilton even went so far as to question directly the traditional argument against standing armies. His essays on this subject were referred to elsewhere by Madison in support of his own views.[23]

But as with any exposition of first principles, these were essentially abstractions. There was little if anything in *The Federalist* that gave any real hint of the specific shape and detail Federalism would shortly take on with the issuance of Hamilton's Treasury papers on public credit, taxation, a national bank, and a program of government-encouraged manufactures. And when it did, a strikingly patterned response was activated which may have been as unsettling to Hamilton as to anyone else. What he had presented, though some details of it could doubtless have been predicted, was a comprehensive design for which few were quite prepared, least of all his erstwhile co-author Publius-Madison. For when it was fully unrolled, many of them thought they were standing before a sinister exact copy of post-Walpolean British mercantilism, a transplanted system of Court influence, corruption, and government by money. Whereupon sprang into existence an exact copy, or seemingly so, of the Court-Country face-off in which the Court had overwhelmingly prevailed and could, for all anyone knew, prevail here, especially with the final piece at the end, a potent military force.

Yet in America it would all work otherwise, and in reality was no "copy" at all. The two situations were altogether different.

Actually both the "Court" and "Country" positions in America were abstractions, even at the point of highest articulation, having none of the context of direct experience and time, or accommodations forced by the density of life and affairs in metropolis and empire, or the self-awareness of a thick social fabric, that had characterized their counterparts in Britain. Here the Country case, the older of the two, had been abstracted from something out of sight and at a distance, which gave it a symmetry not encumbered by an excess of known facts or by the knots and snags of circumstance, though it had already served with great force as a glossary of meaning for the most efficient and least wasteful revolution in history.

And yet much of the same abstractness could be said to characterize the Court option as well, such as it was, when it took the form Hamilton gave it. Hamilton, with an imperiousness scarcely matched by any American statesman to succeed him, had fashioned his design for national greatness, also at a distance, out of what was then the most advanced system of political economy in the world, the product of a century of trial and evolution, and presumed to set this British model down in an environment which could provide little or no context for receiving it, and with no base, either in experience or in prepared resources, material or human, on which it might rest. Still, it too could claim to have had, in an earlier form, a test of sorts in the Revolution. The first germ of the Federalist vision was a product of what might be called the "Continentalist" side of the war effort, a side most sharply perceivable from the vantage point of Washington's staff, or of the diplomatic missions, or of the war committees of the Continental Congress, rather than that, say, of the state and local governments. This was the side so placed as to be most driven by the urgency of a common purpose, of coordinating thirteen separate revolts against a common enemy and against the cross-purposes of local authorities and local populations. It was here, and in the experience of those most associated with this side of the endeavor, that a nationalist vision could exert its greatest attractions.[24] Yet this Continentalist side was in most ways the lesser side in contrast to the localist one, most people's perceptions of the Revolution being shaped by what went on more or less in front of them, in their own states and neighborhoods. Aside from a universal veneration for the Commander-in-Chief, which would of course persist long after Federalism was gone, Federalist values and their acceptance probably reached their meridian with the form they took in *The Federalist*.

The Country persuasion was an ideology of suspicion and resistance, tough and serviceable for purposes of revolution, though less of an asset when it came to nation-building. Still, when it rose up almost at once in challenge to Hamilton's variant projection of a national future, and was applied with the kind of literal-mindedness which is possible with unqualified abstractions having widespread currency, it operated somewhat as a contagion against which there is no adequate immunity system. The Court and its adherents had little in the way of defense that was at all comparable to the resources on which the Court in England could draw, the self-possession that could come from assured support, long experience, and prior results.[25] The choices individuals thereupon felt they had to make became within a very short time quite stark. They had to choose one abstraction or the other, and soon found themselves forming parties, in spite of themselves. They did so in the face of an inherited value-system which took for granted that party and faction were in all ways bad, and to which they themselves continued to subscribe. It was this—the emergence of parties—that proved to be the true novelty of the age, though the unacknowledged evasions inherent in the first steps make for a great deal of ambiguity in any effort to trace a pattern in the political passions, and the charges of plots and conspiracies, that ran through it. In any event the response of Federalism was that of righteousness under siege, and amounted to little more in the end than a sterile defense of constituted order against the forces of insubordination and sedition. What had become of Federalism by then did not make a pretty picture.

True, in the beginning there were clear interests at large in the society, each with its own particular version of what the future ought to hold for it, and for each of which Federalism in some form might make a difference. There were private interests and a variety of public ones as well. A number of state governments had something substantial to gain by way of rescue from a sea of troubles. There were states hemmed in by the commercial regulations of neighbor states, others with exposed and threatened military frontiers, still others with burdens of debt no longer supportable by their own taxes. Of the private interests, some were straightforward enough: merchants with disposable capital who had invested in the war debt, and for whom any central government with the power to honor its obligations was reason enough for supporting it; or merchant shipowners who could see any measure of national power as a better guarantee for the safety of their voyages than any they currently had. As for the "agricultural interest," once seen as a natural salient against Federalism everywhere,[26] much depended on local circumstances for a Federalist direction to imply either benefit or injury, or neither. The great planter interest of South Carolina embraced Federalism for one reason; the great planter interest of Virginia repelled it for another reason. In rural western Massachusetts, where widespread debt and foreclosures had brought on Shays's Rebellion, the weight of the state's tax structure was much eased by the federal assumption of state debts, and in the aftermath that same region would emerge as the solidest and most persistent bastion of Federalism in all of New England, indeed anywhere.

Nevertheless when the entire design of Federalism was eventually in place, there was not enough in it for any of them, or else the claim any particular interest could make on the others was too tenuous, so that for any lasting or positive purposes the design never quite added up. For some it was a downright rude awakening. Such was evidently the case for the community of city artisans, who at first saw in Federalism a saving force to which they might look for protection against foreign competition, and who in New York City had paraded in a body to celebrate the new Constitution with a great float inscribed HAMILTON. They seem to have undergone a certain disillusionment as it dawned on them that when Hamilton himself later talked of "manufactures," what he had in mind was not the kind they made. Few groups thereupon did more, according to Sean Wilentz, to fashion the language of American republicanism: "country" thoughts, as it were, in a city voice.[27]

Still, there remains the question of exactly how all this is to be charted—the motions, that is, whereby thought and feeling came to be either hardened or loosened, or altered, transformed, or turned around—in the course of that historical cycle we are calling the Age of Federalism. We find that the categories of "intellectual history," indispensable as they have been in preparing the entire subject for our own understanding, cannot quite contain it here. Nor, it seems, can any one formal mode of inquiry; all may be necessary, none is sufficient. One name for the process being traced, if there has to be one, is "political," and politics can be assured of a great deal of attention. But so also must diplomacy, economic affairs, and matters of military concern, each in some places to a degree of unavoidable technical depth. What may perhaps be seen running through all of it is something almost requiring a literary sense to penetrate: the makings of a cultural settlement, not entirely unmediated by those who had a hand in it, that would give "national civilization" a different meaning in America from what it has, or has had, anywhere else.

The process must in some way be shown happening, to whatever extent our capacities can control it, and not in one way but many. There must be some view of actual experience, an occasional grasp of what things may have looked like on a given day, the behavior of groups and of individuals in their encounters, what they said to each other and how we might know or guess they felt about it or did about it afterward. Some individuals, perhaps two or three, should come off passably well. Very few others will get through a scrutiny, detached though we may presume it to be, without something or other to answer for. Readers attracted to Great Men may get either less or more than they are prepared for. Two of the figures they are to meet—Hamilton and Jefferson—will appear in all the scale we believe anyone supposes they deserve, but each touched with a dimension of almost tragic irony, a self-deceiving obstinacy that had many a consequence for the whole temper and tendency of their times. As for the generality of Federalists, Hamilton among them, one sees them doing a surprising number of things right, at least from day to day, and leaving a surprisingly tidy house for their successors to move into. But how this is to be read, in view of the shambles of spirit they made of their own mission, is a question perhaps not to be ventured until after one follows them through it.

Moreover, we have encountered a number of gross phenomena that seem scarcely classifiable at all, almost one of a kind, not reducible to more general categories and not to be seen in any other setting than this one. We might mention a few of them.

One is an "interest" that seems to fall outside any of the others, in some ways more compelling than all of them combined. It might be thought of on one level as the interest of a relatively small number of individual careers, converging at a point of exceptional possibility for each of them. But the level is raised to a point scarcely conceivable if such possibility is seen by those affected, in pride or humility, as something not unlike immortality. Those present at a moment evidently occurring once in an age must, however they do so, rise to it, lay hold of it, and make it their own before it slips away. The "young men of the Revolution," as we have elsewhere referred to them, who appeared at Philadelphia in the spring of 1787 were certainly such a company.[28] Their picture of themselves, of their own capacities and worth, had to rest on the view to be taken of what they did there by those who came after them, and on how this would define *them*. Opportunity, profit, and reward have knowable meaning in such a setting only if such opportunity—of having a hand in nation-building—can in any way be measured against the lure of lesser ones. By far the preponderance of the men gathered there, as well as those who journeyed to New York for the First Congress, became Federalists and remained so, in their own eyes a special elite, a chosen few.[29] Little of their behavior, there or thereafter, is quite separable from their sense of their own firstness. In this respect no courtier in England, of origins however ancient or noble, had ever experienced such an event, or felt such a weight.

But to this phenomenon should be added another which might, for want of a better term, be called the "Virginia principle." Here was another elite, also of a special sort, of men out of a special setting whose talents, experience, and standing disposed them to see everything in what can only be called, perhaps helplessly, a Virginia way. By far the greater part of them—with a few such exceptions as Washington, Marshall, certain of the Lees, and not many others—would very shortly come to feel themselves and their sort left wholly out of the Grand Design. Their leading spirits, Jefferson and Madison, would do more than any two other individuals to shape the opposition, set its tone, and define the enemy. Of the only high officials of the first administration to become disaffected from it, all three were Virginians.[30] Further features will appear in the following pages that seem to leave little choice but to allow for "Virginia" a singular classification.

One of them was a passion that served in one way or another to underlie or overrule almost any other category of thought and most other considerations of high policy as seen through Country eyes. This was an anglophobia that could make "England" a word capable of tainting almost anything. Few other individuals were more propelled by it in all they thought, said, and did than Jefferson and Madison, and nothing was more of a constant than this same anglophobia in the hostility to Hamiltonian Federalism, which depended for its very life on a prosperous commerce with England, or to give body to the wild francophilia — or "Gallomania" as the Federalists sullenly called it — that persisted throughout the 1790s.

Still another phenomenon, which owed everything to its Virginia genesis and to the anti-metropolitanism that permeated it, was the choice of a location in which to set the capital of the new republic. Placing it on a stretch of uninhabited wasteland on the Potomac and thus keeping it out of a central city, as a trade-off for the votes Hamilton needed for the assumption of state debts in 1790, may have had more implications for the cultural future than anything else the Virginians did. A fragmented, polycentric, and essentially provincial culture, peculiarly innocent of a detailed and intricately shared sensibility, may well have been a consequence not wholly separable from this initial act of choice. Culture too, like government, needs a focus of authority, and cultural authority to be effective needs to function in close proximity with political, economic, and other kinds. In most civilizations that have flourished, the leading edges of each kind have been gathered in the same place, and have worked upon each other. Moreover, people have actually lived there, and in such a place government itself will take some part in conferring what legitimacy there is, in the society's system of values, on the satisfactions and worth of urban life. American civilization has had to do its flourishing without that kind of legitimacy.

The Country persuasion, then, was the one that prevailed. It might appear that the principal substance of the Country option, Jeffersonian Republicanism, was a kind of extended localism and parochialism, and little more — just as Federalism ended up as little more than a kind of strident exclusivism. But that would stop well short of its full meaning for the American future. The Jeffersonian ascendancy was to have at least two latent functions, or unanticipated consequences, which would not be entirely evident until some time after the point at which the present study closes. For all its anti-commercial rhetoric — certainly from Jefferson himself — it was Jeffersonian Republicanism and not Hamiltonian Federalism that would provide the political opener for the emergence and growth of nineteenth-century middle-class capitalism in America, and for the values that accompanied it.[31] The ambitious young men who in one commercial town after another formed the Jefferson committees early in the new century did not do so under the inspiration of any elaborate economic ideology, but in consequence of something else, which might simply be called the politics of inclusion.[32]

Whatever its elite sources, this other latent function of Jeffersonianism had been made necessary, and no doubt inevitable, by the earliest exigencies of opposition: a politics of recognition and welcome to all comers for which Federalism, situated as it was, could have little or no room. Here too the comparison with Great Britain, which begins with an illuminating parallel, must end with the vast differences in the reaching of our respective Revolution Settlements. The effective political nation in Britain was small and manageable; in America it was for most practical purposes universal, and manageable only in ways yet to be found. The Jeffersonians themselves did not form such a political nation, nor had they anything to do with determining its size. It was already there, waiting for them at the time of the republic's birth.

The conditions for it, indeed, had been present in the very beginnings of the American colonies, in two institutional devices. One was the individual freehold, widely distributed; the other was the representative assembly, of which there was one in every colony. They resulted from choices made in England as to how to populate and run the colonies most cheaply, in preference and sharp contrast to those made by Spain, the other great colonizing power in the New World. It is true that provincial assemblies as well as local governments remained under the control of small and fairly stable cohorts of notables everywhere down to the Revolution, and that habits of deference tended to govern most of the relations between them and their constituencies. Nevertheless beneath all this—whatever the *de facto* distance between the dominant figures in any provincial government and the most obscure members of any assembly, or between the selectmen of any town meeting and the householder who could speak his mind there if he insisted on doing it, or between the grandees on Court Day in any Virginia county and the yeoman freeholders whose votes they courted with rum punch—there was a kind of *de jure* continuum that included them all, one that had been established by these two earliest institutional conditions. In the Revolution the continuum was exposed for what it potentially always was, on the one hand by the reduction of any local elite of which Loyalists had composed a part, and on the other by the flood of problems that any wartime community faced, with the claims in participation that they made on everyone. Politically those communities in 1790 were no longer quite as they had been in 1775.[33]

What the Jeffersonians and their successors did to those communities—perhaps more pertinently, what the communities and the political nation did to them—would constitute the true basis for the Revolution Settlement and all that followed it. Politics itself became an "interest." It would have its own logic, distinct from and on a par with any other interest. Or to put it another way, when "party" and "faction" were at last scrubbed of their illegitimacy and put to more or less constructive uses, the Settlement would be complete.

With this would come a final transformation of the civic humanist conception of virtue, and a tolerable resolution of the classical antithesis of liberty and power.

The resolution would be of the need for something more than simply checking men's insatiable appetite for power, but rather for a way of directing it in the most benign and least destructive channel to be found for it, for containing and regularizing contention and faction, and for conceding, in a political nation of this magnitude, a place for the appetites of anyone, high or low, who dwelt lawfully within it. This channel would not be fully conceded, as we have said, until after the time marked by our final pages. It would be a precondition for the full satisfaction of all the other interests, admirable or otherwise, that this society would come to define for itself. And only when it was so found and conceded could it be said that "democracy" had become that society's predominant abstraction and governing value.[34]

Meanwhile what we attempt here is to catch the first glimpses of the forces that would push this tendency forward, and at the same time to take due account, give due weight, and accord due justice to the forces holding it back.

CHAPTER I

Legitimacy

The Continental Congress did its last business on October 10, 1788, and went out of existence forever.[1] The change was not "revolutionary" in any obvious sense; it had occurred without upheaval. There were no political prisoners, no bloodshed, and few of the aspects of *coup d'état* which characterized even the succession of republics in post-Napoleonic France, to say nothing of many other states in the two hundred years between that time and now. But time flattens out everything, and this orderliness could be taken somewhat more for granted than it ought to be. It was only achieved in the face of resistance, and not without great exertions.

The first phase of the movement for a new federal constitution had contained many elements of conspiracy, subversion, and illegal manipulation. In view of popular inertia, and inasmuch as the only effective power in the country was dispersed and located in the several states, controlled by ruling groups not at all anxious to see that power diminished, it could not have been otherwise. Initially, the energy of the movement was the energy of determined individuals rather than that of popular support and consent. The latter was not automatic, and not to be achieved in a single step. It had to be sought, cultivated, and labored after. The steps themselves could not be announced in advance, nor could they be taken more than one at a time. The initial call for a constitutional convention had been represented as being merely "for the sole and express purpose of revising the Articles of Confederation,"[2] not of doing away with them. When the Convention did meet, its sessions were conducted in utter secrecy, by delegates from twelve of the thirteen states. The procedure for ratifying the new Constitution was cleverly devised and quite outside legal boundaries, as the law then stood. It could go into effect after nine states had accepted it, as opposed to the unanimous consent required by the Articles. The machinery for "consent" was not a popular referendum. Nor was it to be given through the state legislatures, several of which would either have refused outright or strewn obstacles in its way, but rather through conventions of more or less uninstructed delegates. Two of the states did, in fact, fail to ratify; in four of the others the fight was hard and close; in all but three there was a formidable Antifederalist opposition.

By the time the ninth state had ratified, as New Hampshire did on June 21, 1788, the new organic law had nominally superseded the old. But even when the tenth and eleventh—the powerful states of Virginia and New York—accepted it within the next five weeks, there was still, as yet, no New Republic. On paper, the new frame of government certainly looked stronger than the old, and ratification had made that strength at least potential. But in fact it had as yet no more power than the former one. It could not as yet make anything happen, nor could it yet restrain or coerce anyone.

Not that the new Constitution was "unpopular," once its contents became generally known and more and more people had thought about it. By the end of the summer of 1788 it had probably through one means and another come to be supported, at least in an anticipatory way, by a majority of the public. But was this enough? Such support still had to make itself fully evident, acted out in the sight of all. The Federalists—the supporters of the Constitution—had been more deeply committed, had cared more, and had outmaneuvered the less energetic opposition. But the Antifederalists were still there, and the depth of their disgruntlement remained unclear; nor was it clear what, or how much, was needed to conciliate them and to neutralize the "country-party" sentiments they represented. The Constitution contained no bill of rights, and this had been a grave obstacle to ratification. One or more states might still change their minds. A legislature or two might try to undo the work of their ratifying conventions. A coalition of states might insist on a series of crippling amendments. There had even been talk of calling a second constitutional convention. And finally, if the fall elections of 1788 were to register less than wholehearted enthusiasm for the new model of national government, producing less than a decisive Federalist majority, then the new government stood little more chance of survival than the old.

The problem, in short, was not simply that of acceptance, but the more fundamental one of legitimacy. It was a problem whose resolution ought to begin even before the new government was organized, and could not be seen as complete until some time after it had begun to function. This new government must have competence, authority, and respect, and all this must be *believed*. Meanwhile each step it took would be taken for the first time, and would thus be weighted with a double significance, symbolic as well as practical. Each of these acts, depending on how performed, would have a special bearing on the achievement of legitimacy.

True, deep discords were shortly to reveal themselves within American society and within the circles of American government. But these discords would for a time be remarkably muted. The first year of the New Republic—which should for present purposes begin not in the spring of 1789 but in the fall of 1788, and extend to the fall of 1789—was to be a record of strikingly consistent success. It could be said that the key to its successes, which included virtually every decision it made and every step of any consequence taken during that year, is that they were the successes of legitimacy.

The first elections to the new Congress would return heavy Federalist majorities. Yet since this outcome could hardly be taken for granted before it happened, the friends of the Constitution once again made great exertions. They met opposition in every state except Georgia. Nor was it apparent until after the first of the year that they would be generally successful, since all the state legislatures had to enact new electoral laws and were slow in doing so; some of the elections were not held until February and March 1789. Indeed, in the strongly Antifederalist state of New York, senators were not elected until July, owing to the paralysis of a divided legislature there, and presidential electors from that state were not chosen at all. Virginia, New York, Massachusetts, and South Carolina had Antifederalists in their congressional delegations. And yet viewing the Congress as a whole after the returns were finally in, the Federalists had reason to be relieved. There were no more than eleven Antifederalists out of fifty-nine representatives, and only two out of twenty senators. St. John de Crèvecoeur, writing to Thomas Jefferson from New York in November 1788, could worry over "how rankly antifederal" the Assembly of Virginia had become, but as early as October 20 he had felt guardedly optimistic about most of the other states. "The murmurs of partial discontent, cloaked under what is called here antifederalism," he said, "seems now greatly to abate; there remains but one wish, which is, that those country partys may not preponderate in the choice of federal Senators and Delegates; if a majority of federalists can be obtained in those two bodies, every thing will go smoothly on."[3]

In the work of persuading the public, the friends of the Constitution had shown considerably more energy than their opponents. But Federalist energy and Antifederalist inertia can explain just so much. Alongside their efforts must be placed an event which required no effort at all to bring about, the unanimous election of George Washington as first President of the United States.

The Continental Congress in September had directed that presidential electors be chosen on January 7, 1789, which meant that the issuing of proclamations by state governors, the summoning of legislatures to write new electoral laws, the bringing forward of candidates, and the voting all had to take place within a very short time. These electors were chosen by popular vote in five states; in the remainder they were appointed by the legislature or, as in New Jersey, by the governor and council. Yet however chosen, each group of electors, meeting in their respective state capitols on the same day (February 4, 1789) with no direct knowledge of what any of the other delegations were doing, cast unanimous ballots for Washington. Federalist or Antifederalist, no one thought of any other person. John Adams, who was elected Vice-President, received less than half the number of votes given to Washington, the remainder being scattered among ten other candidates.[4]

The general expectation that Washington would be the first President, which was not seriously disputed anywhere, dated back at least to the completion of the Constitution in September 1787, and probably before. This expectation thenceforth underlay almost every notion that might arise regarding the great changes about to be embodied in a new national government, and it must have accounted in great part for the heavy Federalist successes in the first congressional elections. Even before that, the very process of ratifying the Constitution had been incalculably advanced—perhaps even made possible when it would otherwise not have been—by something more than simply Washington's support: the assumption that he and no other would preside over the republic created by it.

But why this unquestioning unanimity? Why should the only thinkable candidate have been George Washington? He was the country's most preeminent military figure, but military figures as such were not accorded automatic deference in the ideology of the Revolutionary generation. They were just as likely to be objects of suspicion. Nor was Washington to be seen simply as an august figurehead, brought forth from retirement as a cover for the purposes of other men. It was rather that Washington's person—more pertinently, his prior career and what was known of it—represented much that was most essential not only to legitimize a republic but also to conciliate the fears, passions, and prejudices of a republican citizenry. Washington had been much more than commander-in-chief of the Continental Army. Since 1775 he had been performing executive functions for the states in combination, and thus for the country as a whole, not simply in a military capacity but in one which was civil and political as well, and in a range and scope exceeding that undertaken by any other individual. These functions, moreover, had been dependent at virtually every point on a high degree of voluntary consent—the Revolution could not have been sustained otherwise—and Washington's actions were a continuing demonstration of how he was governed by this principle. He had also taken for granted that whatever powers he exercised both began and ended through the sanction of the legislative authority, and he had shown himself willing in 1783 to surrender those powers in a manner that was to all intents and purposes final. As a result Washington's authority, both direct and symbolic, had been growing for nearly fifteen years. He had in a certain sense been acting as President of the United States since 1775.

I

George Washington, Republican

The reasons which made the choice of George Washington as commander-in-chief appear so logical even in 1775 were quite comparable to those which made a similar choice so logical in 1789. They were based in both instances on what he had made of his career prior to that time, a career exposed in an exceptional way to public scrutiny. There were elements in it which made it both representative and special, and could probably not have existed anywhere but in the province of Virginia.[5]

A sharp turning point, probably in some degree fortuitous, occurred in Washington's very early manhood. It had to do with his military aspirations, which were considerable, and it perhaps did as much to determine the quality of his subsequent life, as well as his own conception of himself, as a casual circumstance could do.

We do not ordinarily recollect that Washington's achievements in the frontier warfare of the 1750s against the French were a matter of general knowledge throughout the colonies, or that his name was personally known to King George II when Washington was still in his early twenties. Distinction for bravery at Laurel Mountain and Fort Necessity, and gallant behavior as Braddock's aide-de-camp at Fort Duquesne, were already behind him by the time he had become, at twenty-three, commander-in-chief of Virginia troops with the rank of colonel. It was his responsibility to protect the entire exposed line of the Virginia frontier, 350 miles long. From this time until 1758, when the French finally abandoned Fort Duquesne, permitting the British to erect Fort Pitt on its ruins, Washington's latent administrative capacities had much ungrateful material on which to test themselves. He had to deal with problems of recruitment, supply, and personnel under conditions of frustration not dissimilar to those he was to face again twenty-five years later. And yet just as important for the future was that by the end of 1758 George Washington, at the age of twenty-six, had turned away from a military career, to all intents and purposes forever, and begun what was in many ways an entirely new one. He was elected to the House of Burgesses, where he would serve for fifteen years; he resigned his commission; through the provisions of his brother's will he came into full possession of Mount Vernon; and shortly after the New Year he married Martha Custis, an amiable young widow with substantial property and two children.

During the five-year period between his coming of age and his assuming the life of a gentleman planter and man of public affairs in a civilian capacity, George Washington had been intensely ambitious. He remained so, but the character and quality of his ambition henceforth underwent transformations of an intricate and interesting kind.

Rather than remain an officer in the Virginia militia, Washington originally had very much wanted a regular commission in the King's forces, and had done everything within the limits of propriety to obtain one. But his claims had some-how got themselves buried in the mysterious recesses of the mid-eighteenth-century British patronage system, and with them his hopes of royal preferment. Yet Washington managed also to bury his own disappointment, and apparently with-out the sort of strain that might be expected in a man of normal egotism. He continued to be greatly concerned with his reputation. Yet this was now to be supported not by feats of glory but rather by the good opinion of his Virginia neighbors. Closely related to this shift in Washington's sense of what nourished a man's reputation was another shift, having to do with his grasp of just where ultimate authority was really located, in fact if not in theory, for the particular world in which he moved. It may have been mostly a change of emphasis, occur-ring without his fully realizing it. But the direction, in any case, would be from the throne of Great Britain, where the emphasis had once rested, to the Assembly of Virginia. We shall return to this point.

Meanwhile another form of ambition, and a very consuming one, had been driving the young Washington even before he was out of his teens and well before his taking over Mount Vernon. He was obsessed with the idea of amassing land in the West, tremendous amounts of it, putting it all under cultivation and bringing commerce and people there. This cycle of acquisition and development began very much as the expression of a "private" self, of private ambition and private interest. He was fully determined that it should bring him wealth, possessions, and status. He would in fact expend much time and effort on this, revealing considerable executive capacities in the course of it, while some of his dealings — especially with men who seemed to get in the way of his projects and ambitions — were exceedingly sharp and even ruthless. During his military service, having already used his earnings as a surveyor to acquire several thousand acres on the Virginia frontier, he got his first sight of the rich bottom land along the rivers of western Pennsylvania. He subsequently bought fifteen thousand acres of it in the Fort Pitt area. Eventually he badgered Governor Botetourt of Virginia into making good on promises of land to the veterans of his former regiment, whereupon he proceeded, through swift action, advance surveys, and purchases of other men's bounties added to his own, to engross an inordinate amount of it — over forty thousand acres — for himself. Meanwhile his mind brimmed with designs of access and transportation by land and water, ever more extensive and detailed, which to be successful would require an ever-widening network of cooperation from neighboring communities, for opening up the western country.[6]

This cycle of private ambition, however, would terminate quite differently from the way it began. Time and circumstances would bring Washington to see that the rich returns he had once imagined for himself were not to materialize. Moreover, he was acquiring, layer by layer, an additional self. It was one that would preoccupy him in a multitude of other ways, even while his vision of the West, on quite another plane, remained undiminished.

The two questions mentioned above, that of reputation and that of authority, with their implications, may impart a special logic to the direction George Washington's career was taking in the 1760s and 1770s. In addition to continuous service in the Virginia House of Burgesses, which should be reckoned as a key constant, he served also as justice of the peace for Fairfax County, vestryman and later warden of Pohick Church in Truro Parish, and chairman of the meeting which adopted the Fairfax County Resolves of 1774. Meanwhile, as master of Mount Vernon, he accepted a status in his neighborhood which was itself quasi-public in nature. In addition to building up with considerable patience and labor what had been a depleted estate, supplementing his tobacco crop with wheat, building a flour mill, exporting fish caught in the Potomac, and adding to his holdings in the West, he took on a range of small and not-so-small responsibilities on behalf of those near and about him. They might regularly include such matters as executing a will, qualifying as guardian for a neighbor's son, counseling a tenant on problems touching the law, lending money (which for all the prudence he observed in his own handling of money, he did freely and continually), and so on. Since he had become, moreover, the most successful of the Washingtons, Mount Vernon became the base and center of all that family's many affairs and concerns. It was thus a man of both substance and experience, as well as the object of wide respect, who went as a delegate to the first Provincial Convention at Williamsburg in August 1774. There he was elected to go to the First Continental Congress. He went, attended the sessions faithfully, and impressed the other delegates by the unobtrusive soundness of his judgment when he chose to give it. He was elected again, and went to the Second Continental Congress in 1775. It was this body, choosing one of its own members, that elected Washington commander-in-chief of the Revolutionary forces, and the choice was unanimous.

In view of the place which Washington came to occupy in the tablets of history, and in view of the man's own reserve, the question of his character, his personality, his essential being, has induced endless crises of mind in most of his biographers, especially those of the present century. The most distinguished of them, Douglas Freeman, toward the close of many years of work tempered by a restraint in keeping with the subject itself, admitted somewhat helplessly that so far as he could discover George Washington was, and had been all along, almost exactly what he appeared to be. The face in the Charles Willson Peale portrait of 1772, as Marcus Cunliffe has said, is that of an "upright man," "at peace with the world," "the master of himself and his surroundings." So he was seen, with hardly a known exception, by the other men of his time. But the differences between that time and our own, regarding both the formation of personality and the manner in which such matters were thought of and defined, are considerable. This applies to the entire world of the eighteenth century, but perhaps with a special pertinence to that of pre-Revolutionary Virginia.

A point of some interest is the use that was made of the noun "character" as something objectively visible, and as something both different and more inclusive than the same term today. Washington, when he became President, would announce his intention to appoint, if possible, only "the first Characters" to high public office. The word meant either an individual or something he possessed. It still does, but the application in both senses has changed significantly. In Washington's day "character" had essentially a public meaning; it was virtually synonymous with "reputation." It also had its private side, as it does now, but the distinction between that and the public side was considerably more vague: the term "personality" was hardly needed then, and was seldom used.[7]

It is in this sense that the character of George Washington might not have to be regarded as quite such a mystery. The sum of what the man was could be plainly seen in the appearance he made and the acts he performed. And by the same token, "reputation" had as much to do with his own judgment of himself as with that of his community. Thus for a representative man of Washington's world and time, the allocation of energies between the private and public sides of his being seems to have been weighted a good deal more heavily toward the latter than may seem "natural" today. Among other things this may account for the greater formality of that age, as well as for the fact that two generations later, the emergence of "individualism" as an acknowledged value had to be accompanied by something of a psychic revolution.

If a man was to count for anything in mid-eighteenth-century Virginia, he had to assume responsibility for a range of concerns and people. The society itself, as well as the aspirations available in it and the rewards it conferred, was so organized that his "private affairs" were not really private. They touched on the affairs of too many others. A wealthy planter of Washington's class presided over a domain all of whose members from the slaves on up—tenantry, neighboring yeomanry, and an extended group of kinship and cousinage—were in some way attached, directly or indirectly, as dependencies. But equally significant was that although such a man stood at the top of the social scale, he was not part of a hierarchy. Or rather, the hierarchy was peculiar in that it had no apex. His membership was in a community of peers, and for his ultimate sanctions, of whatever nature, he looked not upward but laterally. The embodiment of this system was a collectivity, the House of Burgesses, and the Burgesses in their corporate nature ratified a man's reputation. And yet before he could be one of them, he had to be elected—not by his Burgess-peers but by his neighbors, large and small, and to this extent he depended upon his dependents.[8]

With the culmination of the revolutionary crisis in the 1770s, all the colonies embraced the idea of republicanism in a way that now seems almost automatic, and not to be explained without reference to an already long history of representative government. But it appears to have been more automatic, and in many ways more natural, in some colonies than in others. One may wonder why it is that Virginia—of all places—should have emerged so plainly as the very model of a republican commonwealth, more emphatically even than others whose social and political life was in practice more "democratic." Why should the political, the military, and the doctrinal leadership of revolutionary republicanism have been drawn so prominently from Virginia? And why should a republican character have been adopted with such relative swiftness there, with such comparative unanimity, with so little strain, and without the opposition—as in so many of the other colonies—of a Tory class of any standing or importance? Again the answer points to the House of Burgesses, and what it represented in Virginia life.

The Burgesses as a group represented the social, economic, and political elite of Virginia, and its members ran the affairs of the province. They could do so in the conviction that they acted in the interests of the whole people, a conviction that appeared to be regularly ratified by elections in which a substantial proportion of the freeholders voted. Exclusively a planter elite, this group had a homogeneity of interest not found in any of the northern colonies, and of the various southern elites it was easily the oldest and stablest. This stability was reflected within the House itself in a remarkable continuity of membership, while the speakership, clerkship, and chairmanships of the standing committees were held by the same men over long periods of time. Factionalism over matters of either interest or influence was seldom the problem in the Burgesses that it often was elsewhere. But though the internal structure of the House was stable, it was certainly not rigid. Its considerable *esprit de corps,* made possible by security of tenure and power, created a setting in which talent could be recognized, developed, and rewarded. From time to time young men of ability might be placed on important committees, and even in chairmanships, relatively soon after their first appearance in the House, and over the heads of colleagues more senior in service. Thus for a variety of reasons a successful career, promoted as it had to be from within the Virginia planting gentry, required a man to win the respect and support of a company of equals. Alternative paths to success, either (as with the elite of New York) through other callings or through English connections, were relatively few in Virginia.[9]

As with the other colonial assemblies in the period prior to about 1760, the House of Burgesses had steadily acquired and assumed a range of prerogatives and powers having to do with finance, military policy, appointments, elections, districting, and public works. Concurrently it had built up an enormous sense of its own dignity and privileges. The result was that when those privileges and powers were challenged—as they began to be at a number of explicit points by the Crown and Parliament in the years after 1763—the response could occur with a remarkable unity of spirit. The Stamp Act drew resolutions of resistance from the Burgesses and from all over Virginia, and the man who had been appointed as stamp distributor was forced to declare before an angry mob at Williamsburg that he would proceed no further in his work "without the assent of the General Assembly of this colony." When the Burgesses asserted, in a petition of protest over the Townshend Acts in 1768, "the right of being governed by such laws only, respecting their internal Polity and Taxation as are derived from their own Consent," the Governor dissolved them. They thereupon met illegally and adopted an agreement of non-importation, which was observed throughout the colony. After the Coercive Acts of 1774, the Burgesses ordained a day of fasting and prayer "to give us one heart and mind firmly to oppose, by all just and proper means, every injury to American rights." Each of these actions was a response to what these men, individually and collectively, could see as a challenge—a challenge in a very immediate way, to *them*. As was not fully the case in many other colonies, the doctrinal radicalism of, say, a Patrick Henry—who was of course a member of this same elite—could be absorbed by a variety of temperaments with a minimum of disruption. There was thus a logic to the process whereby all this could be converted into explicit republican principles, to be spelled out eventually for all the colonies by another member of this elite, Thomas Jefferson. A challenge to a representative assembly, acting for the people of Virginia, could be generalized into a threat to all the liberties of the commonwealth.[10]

George Washington, in the very midst of this, never questioned the necessity of resistance. Washington made something of a contrast to Patrick Henry, who spoke often, was not the best of listeners, and had a tendency to laziness. Yet his and Henry's had been essentially the same experience, and their responses, each in its way, moved to the same end. Moreover, for neither man could a setting have been more aptly designed to form the implicit, and then explicit, conviction that there could be no legitimate claim to power and obedience which did not rest upon the final sanction of legislative authority.

Washington went to the First Continental Congress in 1774 in company with Patrick Henry, Peyton Randolph, Richard Henry Lee, Benjamin Harrison, Richard Bland, and Edmund Pendleton. Henry fired the hearts of all with his declaration "I am not a Virginian, but an American." Washington, as always, said little but listened carefully to this and all the other proceedings. He heard long debates, and observed the mutual suspicions and clashes of interest that would have to be reconciled before a common effort was possible, but unlike a number of others he betrayed no irritation or impatience. When the Second Congress met shortly after Lexington and Concord in the spring of 1775, Washington, again elected as a delegate, attended the sessions in his military uniform. This seems not to have been seen as anything beyond a symbol of his conviction that a general resort to arms was probable, and that he was ready for it. He assumed that he would command the Virginia militia. He was placed in charge of two committees and made a member of a third, all having to do with matters of defense and military stores. His judgment proved consistently good; his talent for making sound choices among a variety of alternatives showed to advantage, and he was obviously better informed on military questions than his colleagues. It quickly became apparent that if the large forces then gathering for the relief of Boston—mostly from New England but from other colonies as well—were to be kept together, Congress would have to take charge of them. And the best guarantee of support from the southern colonies would be to put a Virginian in command of them. Washington was not anxious to take the command, did not believe his abilities equal to it, and refused to accept any pay.[11] But the logic of it, concerning as it did a man whose qualities everyone by then had come to know quite well, was fairly self-evident. The nomination was made by John Adams of Massachusetts, seconded by his cousin Samuel Adams, and accepted with little or no opposition. Meanwhile Washington's own acceptance rested on a curious balance consisting of his "full intention," already privately expressed, "to devote my life and fortune in the cause we are engaged in," his abhorrence of any public honor which might be open to the least suspicion of his having sought it (his reason for taking no pay), and his equal abhorrence of what his "character" might suffer from refusing to do his duty.

In the early stages of Washington's experience as commander-in-chief there was something of a reversion to his youthful relish for martial exploits. He took for granted that military success required pugnacity, and assumed that the primary mission of an army was to give battle to the enemy. His conception of strategy and tactics was not overly refined; his actual training was minimal. Thus he had to depend heavily on his innate capacities of judgment, which were on the whole reliable, but did not always save him from error, even occasional rashness. Twice during the remainder of 1775 he was for throwing a direct assault against occupied Boston; both times his subordinates persuaded him otherwise. The town was eventually reduced by siege. He wanted to fight it out with Howe on Long Island in 1776, but in leaving his left flank unprotected, and then reinforcing his lines after it was too late instead of evacuating them, he nearly lost his army. His defeats at Brandywine and Germantown might have been less costly had they been fought with more caution.

Yet Washington was chastened again and again by the intractable realities of both inferior strength and unpredictable support. In his military capacity he came to see very early that a revolutionary strategy required above all that he keep an army in being, which meant avoiding general engagements. The one exception was Yorktown, which had been carefully planned, massively organized, and fought with forces heavily superior to those of the enemy. But Washington's role was in the last analysis only partially that of a leader of troops. "He was," according to Freeman, "one-tenth field commander and nine-tenths administrator." Even this does not do justice to the variety of functions he was called upon to perform. The very nature of the Revolution, an undertaking prosecuted in varying ways by thirteen separate governments, made for an inevitable vacuum in executive presence whenever it was a question of almost any kind of concerted effort. Since Washington's army was the pivot upon which the entire effort must ultimately turn, its commander found himself in a role whose requirements went far beyond the tactical, or even the administrative. It was political as well, executive in the broadest sense.[12] It even included functions of foreign as well as domestic diplomacy. He had to overcome his own provincialism. He repressed his initial distaste for the Yankee ways of his predominantly New England troops, and at the same time built a staff of bright young men from every colony. This may have had the effect of personalizing his own commitment to what was still for most people rather an abstraction, the "United States." The volume of his paperwork was enormous. He had to deal with a flood of problems involving recruitment, supply, clothing, food, and pay for his troops—which in turn required endless negotiations with committees of Congress, state governors and legislatures, and the leaders and populations of the states within which his army operated.[13] In preparing for Yorktown he even had to negotiate, successfully as it turned out, for the services of the army and navy of Bourbon France.

Congress, itself recognizing the executive vacuum which the revolutionary crisis made so manifest, voted Washington what amounted to dictatorial powers for a six-month period late in 1776. But these could not really be used in a dictatorial spirit, so in that sense they had little meaning. Few of the dealings Washington had with local, state, or congressional authorities, with suppliers, or even with his own troops could be realized on terms that did not involve a high degree of voluntary consent. It was the perpetual awareness of this that did as much as anything to set the limits within which Washington operated all through the war, and it formed an essential element in the restraint and self-discipline that characterized most of what he did during those years. On the other hand, the deference he showed to Congress was probably largely unforced. Respect for legislative authority had been a part of his training long before, at least since the days when he himself had been a legislator and had himself been accustomed to receiving that same respect.

Moreover, Washington's actions were subjected to repeated investigations, and were more or less constantly open to public view. The opinions people formed of him and his merits, as time went on, could at least be formed from a growing body of publicly available evidence. And it was probably inevitable that Washington's very person should eventually take on a symbolic character; his personal example came both to symbolize and to reinforce a determination by a significant part of the population to see it all through to the end. The self-pride of people everywhere came to be bound up with a figure whose stature had grown, nationally and internationally, as the stature of the country and its cause had grown. The praise heaped upon Washington by his royal and noble French allies must have been deeply satisfying to any provincial American who read or heard it. "I mark, as a fortunate day," wrote one of Rochambeau's officers, "that in which I have been able to behold a man so truly great."[14]

Washington's restraint failed him at least once, after it was all over, when he had to take leave of his officers at Fraunces Tavern in New York. It was a scene which those present remembered all their lives. No speeches were made. The Commander-in-Chief, after trying to eat some of the food and to drink the wine that had been laid out for the company, asked each of them to come up and take him by the hand. The huge Henry Knox, his chief of artillery, a onetime Boston bookseller who had been with him from the beginning, was the first. It was here that Washington's emotions, almost never displayed, seem to have got the better of him. Blinded with tears and unable to part with a mere handshake, he put his arms about Knox and kissed him. He did the same with the others, none of whom could speak; he thereupon turned, walked out the door, and strode down the wharf to Whitehall, where a barge was waiting to take him across the river. At Powles Hook he took horse for the first stage of his journey home. When he reached Annapolis, where Congress was then sitting, he presented himself briefly to that body and returned his commission. He arrived at Mount Vernon on Christmas Eve 1783.

By this time, Washington's influence and renown had become immense. And yet one thinks of other societies so constituted that leadership in them can assume a character decidedly different from that of this particular career. The name of Simón Bolívar, the "Liberator," has often been linked with that of Washington. Bolívar was "the Washington of Latin America"; each man was the "savior of his country." But in reality these two present an extraordinary antithesis, and the contrast lies in the way each man conceived his own relationship to authority. Bolívar was an aristocrat, but hardly in any "Virginian" sense: he drew few if any of his social or political sanctions from his peers. All authority, and all glory and preferment, descended from the person of the King. With Napoleon's invasion of the Spanish peninsula the power of the Crown was swept away, which meant that in the New World colonies a man of towering ambition, as Bolívar was, could suddenly make his own glory and his own authority. He could fashion the role all by himself, depending solely on personal "charisma" (a term that has been applied mistakenly, and somewhat clumsily, to Washington). Like Bonaparte, whose motives and inner drives his own so much resembled, Bolívar through his military exploits made himself a king in all but name. He had the conquistador's impulse to fling aside the law, and then to redeem his acts through conquest. He treated *cabildos* and other legislative bodies with lofty contempt. He wrote and promulgated his own constitutions. Though he was capable of strong affections, his personality was actually quite self-sufficient; thanks to his egotism it had little need to depend upon others, a principle that applied to all his military and political subordinates as well as to his mistresses. He recognized no peers, least of all the other great revolutionary leaders of Latin America. He detested San Martín, the liberator of Peru, who was doing all the same things there that he himself had done in Venezuela, and it was Bolívar who delivered Miranda over to the Spaniards. Truth served him in much the way it served Bonaparte. He pretended to be a republican while hoping to reconstitute the Empire under himself. "Have no fears about the colored people," he once told a confidant. "I flatter them because I need them; democracy on my lips, and"—pointing to his heart—"aristocracy here." In the relationships that define authority, the two "Washingtons" were as far apart as were the two worlds in which they moved.[15]

Even after Washington's "retirement," which followed his having divested himself of all formal authority, he continued to function as a kind of moral executive. Mount Vernon swarmed with visitors of all ranks, seeking his opinions and soliciting his advice. As early as the spring of 1784 he found himself once more involved in an affair of national concern. Bitter attacks on the Order of the Cincinnati—the recently formed society of Revolutionary officers—as a "foreign conspiracy" (because of its French members) and as a "perpetual aristocracy" (because of its hereditary membership), led Washington as president-general to recommend sweeping changes in its structure and rules so that all causes for offense might be removed.[16] Then, a visit to the headwaters of the Ohio in the fall of 1784 to look into the state of his landholdings in that area proved to be the first in a chain of events which culminated less than three years later in his presiding over the Constitutional Convention at Philadelphia.

Once again, private concerns found themselves almost unwittingly absorbed into public ones as Washington's interest was drawn first to problems of water transportation to the West, and eventually to the entire range of limitations which prevented the Confederation government from doing anything effective in categories of action of which commerce was but one. Plans for improving the navigation of the Potomac, first undertaken in Virginia under Washington's direct inspiration, broadened to include the participation of Maryland. An agreement upon such lines was concluded in the spring of 1785 at Mount Vernon. This in turn led to the Annapolis Convention of September 1786, called to discuss matters of common commercial concern, and attended by delegates from five states. It had been hoped that all thirteen would be represented. The impotence of the Confederation had by this time become apparent, and the report of the Annapolis meeting, drafted by Alexander Hamilton, included a proposal for a general convention to revise the Articles of Confederation. A year before, Washington had already written: "Illiberality, jealousy, and local policy mix too much in all our public councils for the good government of the Union. In a word, the confederation appears to me to be little more than a shadow without the substance. . . ."[17] This judgment seemed more than confirmed in the winter of 1786–87 by Shays's Rebellion, the debtors' uprising in western Massachusetts which convinced Washington that a government unable either to redress popular grievances or to maintain civil order was no government at all.

Washington did not want to go to Philadelphia in May 1787, and finally did so only with the greatest reluctance. He is sometimes pictured as having been pushed into it by the leading spirits of the constitutional movement, among whom Hamilton and Madison were prominent, playing upon his fears of anarchy in New England. But this somewhat misrepresents Washington's own initiative, and the public implications of virtually every move he had made since relinquishing his commission. There were actually two lines of effort, ending at Philadelphia but having in effect merged well before. The better-known one is that with which the names of Hamilton and Madison are primarily associated, the single-minded determination to set up an entirely new frame of government. The other was the movement to extend inland water transportation westward, of which the leading exponent was Washington himself. The major steps taken in this direction—the passage of legislation, the chartering of stock companies, the calling of conventions—were taken on Washington's initiative and in deference to his known desires. They could probably not have been taken otherwise. "The earnestness with which he espouses the undertaking is hardly to be described," wrote Madison to Jefferson in January 1785, "and shows that a mind like his, capable of great views, and which has long been occupied with them, cannot bear a vacancy."[18] Back of all this was the extent to which Washington's "character"—in the word's special eighteenth-century meaning—had been committed by eight and a half years of public toil to the success of the Revolution and of a united country. It was as though any sign that things were not as he had conceived they ought to become—any indication of fundamental discontent, of tumults, of unwillingness or incapacity to promote designs for the common benefit—somehow reflected on him, and was in some way his responsibility. In this sense Washington never "retired" at all. He never relinquished his leadership, and though it would not do to represent each of the steps toward Philadelphia as having been taken first by Washington, it would hardly be wrong to say that most of them had been marked out by his example, and taken under his aegis. When the moment arrived, he was universally assured that success was not thinkable without his presence. For all his reluctance, he could give himself no satisfactory reasons for staying away. When he arrived, he was unanimously elected president of the Convention.

The emergence of the American presidency under George Washington as an effective executive force—considering the grasp of the role which Washington himself was to show, as well as the disorganization and suspicion that characterized the country just prior to his assuming it—may contain an element of the fortuitous. Yet it seems rather less so in view of Washington's extraordinarily long preparation for the role—much longer, and more thorough, it would appear, than that of any of his successors. The final rehearsal came at Philadelphia. There, for four long months, the best minds in the country spelled out for Washington in great detail what the country thought it needed in the way of executive authority, the limits on that authority which the country might be expected to insist on, the range of alternatives that were open as well as of those that were not open, and the theoretical and historical principles which might justify the right choices as well as warn against the wrong ones. Washington, listening intently as always, was given as comprehensive a course of lectures on all these matters as could be obtained at another seat of learning anywhere, at any time.[19]

Yet for Washington this was not simply a matter of instruction. Much of it was in the nature of a reminder as well, a codification both of what he already knew and of what he himself had already done. For most of the delegates were aware, even as they spoke, that the man whose theoretical attributes they were defining was in fact sitting before them. Most of them assumed, even then, that Washington would be the Executive. The balance they struck was almost certainly arrived at with reference—other than George III, they had no point of reference—to what they already knew of Washington. What they decided, in short, was whether the strength they wanted, as well as the restraint, were to be found in Washington, and whether the weakness they feared, or the despotism they abhorred, were likely to appear under Washington's hand. The executive powers, Pierce Butler wrote, would probably not have been so great "had not many of the members cast their eyes toward General Washington as President; and shaped their Ideas of the Powers to be given to a President, by their opinions of his Virtue."[20]

Washington's journey from Mount Vernon to New York in the spring of 1789 for his inauguration, despite his own efforts to make it as unostentatious as possible, proved to be a stirring eight-day processional, in the course of which the people of six states symbolically witnessed and ratified what they and their representatives had done. The General departed by coach on April 16, was given a civic dinner at Alexandria, crossed the Potomac, and was escorted into Baltimore by the First Maryland Infantry and given the honors of the city. Further honors met him at Wilmington. At the Pennsylvania line he was greeted by a delegation headed by the chief executive of the state, and after another grand dinner and parade at Philadelphia he was accompanied to Trenton by the City Troops of Horse. The bridge over Assunpink Creek, where he and his Continentals had resisted the British advance in January 1777, was now decked in greenery, and its approaches were lined with young women in white costume strewing flowers in the hero's path and singing an ode composed in his honor. There were civic ceremonies at Princeton, New Brunswick, and Elizabethtown. The booming of cannon signaled his approach to every town along the way, and at several of them the General had to quit his coach and mount a handsome horse that had been put at his disposal for the occasion. (He made a good figure, being one of the best horsemen of his day.) On the 23rd a decorated barge brought him across Newark Bay and into New York Harbor. There salutes were fired, and upon that signal every vessel in the harbor broke out flags. The city had stopped work amid the ringing of bells, and the waterfront was packed with thousands of cheering citizens. "All ranks and professions expressed their feelings, in loud acclamations, and with rapture hailed the arrival of the Father of his Country." The day ended with a dinner at the house of the Governor.[21]

Washington, emotionally spent, had just been the central figure in an extended rite, eight days long and spontaneously performed, of legitimacy. A week later at Federal Hall, on an open portico overlooking Wall Street, he underwent another.

Robert R. Livingston, Chancellor of the State of New York, administered the oath of office. When he had finished, the Chancellor turned to the people with a wide, exulting gesture of his arm and cried: "Long live George Washington, President of the United States!"

2

Roman Simplicity

For about three weeks, beginning with the day of Washington's arrival in New York, the attention of the Senate and House of Representatives, and to some extent of Washington himself, was occupied with a problem which caused no little stir at the time, but which has not agitated any subsequent American government. This was the general question of titles, ceremony, and official etiquette. By the middle of May 1789, most aspects of it had been settled with such finality that they never needed to be reopened. Yet the warmth that attended these discussions and debates was such that they came to occupy a peculiar place in nearly every history of the time that has since been written. The proportion which the episode properly ought to have thus remains something of a question. The proportion which it does have, on the other hand, would not be what it is were it not for the influence of two specific individuals, both very strong-minded, one of them being John Adams, the Vice-President, and the other William Maclay, the senator from Pennsylvania. The two men quarreled publicly over titles and other matters of style and procedure. Most of the evidence on the quarrel comes from one of the participants, the fullest record we have of it being the personal journal of Senator Maclay.

Neither of the two shows to good advantage here. In insisting on the propriety of titles, Adams laid himself open to charges, which he never fully lived down, of secretly favoring monarchy. As presiding officer of the Senate, and thus to some degree responsible for the etiquette and procedure with which the President-elect was to be received and the affairs of government set in motion, Adams somewhat resembled a nervous hostess anxious that everything should be just so. Moreover, he appears to have abused his prerogatives to the point of breaking in frequently upon other members with his own views, which he gave in the form of little lectures. Maclay was equally trying. He too was something of a hair-splitter; and being from the frontier region of Pennsylvania he tended to be suspicious on principle of seaboard influence, particularly that of Massachusetts. He was one of those, to be met at almost any meeting, who are always rising to points of order. He and Adams between them took up a large share of the Senate's time, and one clue to the senators' votes during this interlude may very well be simply the balance of their irritation with the one and indulgence with the other as it shifted back and forth.

On April 23, upon Adams's instigation, the Senate appointed a committee to confer with the House on "what style or titles it will be proper to annex to the office of President and Vice President of the United States," and how the forthcoming inauguration ceremonies ought to be conducted. The next day Maclay tried to get the part about titles thrown out, but was voted down. Adams wanted to know whether the Speaker of the House should be addressed as "Honorable"; the Senate voted No. On the 25th Adams asked the Senate in which of his capacities—as President of the Senate or as Vice-President of the United States— he ought to receive the President. Nobody was certain, and Maclay heaped ridicule upon Adams in his diary. Whether he did so publicly is not a matter of record, though he noted, "I was up as often as I believe was necessary." On April 30, the day of the inauguration, Adams was in a great fret. "The President will, I suppose, address the Congress. How shall I behave? How shall we receive it? Shall it be standing or sitting?" It was apparently decided, after some confusion, that they should stand while the President addressed them. When Washington finally appeared, the Vice-President stumbled over his phrases of welcome, and even forgot for a moment what he had planned to say. Maclay was pained by the President's own awkwardness in delivering his inaugural remarks. When the ceremony was over, a Senate committee was appointed to prepare a reply.[22]

When the minutes were read next morning, Maclay—since the other members seemed less than fully attentive—thought he should as a matter of principle object to the words "his most gracious speech," and did so strenuously. He insisted that these words (which Adams had directed the secretary to use) were the same as those customarily applied to a speech from the British throne. Adams, greatly displeased, saw nothing objectionable in them, but after some argument the Senate decided to strike them out. Another question that had been agitating both houses was the manner of transmitting messages back and forth between them, and whether the messenger should make "obeisances" coming in and going out. A Senate resolution of the 23rd had specified that he should, but the House in derision struck out the obeisances. The Senate did not insist. Meanwhile President Washington had been trying to decide how to draw the line between his public and private social life, and had been making somewhat furtive requests for advice. (Senator Maclay, already notorious for his tirades against pomp and ceremony, was delicately sounded out on this point by General Arthur St. Clair, acting on behalf of the President.) Then in a debate on May 7 over the Senate's proposed reply to the President's speech, Maclay moved to strike out a reference to the "dignity and splendor" of the government. The Senate voted to leave it in, while Adams exulted. And it was during these same few days that the whole question of titles was brought to a head.[23]

On May 5 a joint committee of the House and Senate reported that it was "not proper to annex any style or title to [those] expressed in the Constitution." The House immediately accepted the report, but on the 8th the Senate rejected it and began a lively debate which went on until the 14th. The Vice-President and Richard Henry Lee of Virginia were the strongest exponents of titles, Lee insisting that "all the world, civilized and savage," had to have them. Maclay was up constantly, declaring that it was "impossible to add to the respect entertained for General Washington," and that the President of the United States needed no other title. Adams, in one of his many interruptions from the chair, sourly

remarked that the mere word "president" made him think of the president of a
fire company or a cricket club, and that dignity required something more. A new
Senate committee on titles was thereupon appointed, which promptly reported
in favor of the title "His Highness the President of the United States of America,
and Protector of their Liberties."[24]

The Senate asked the House for a conference committee to take up the question anew, and on the 11th, after debate, the House agreed. But when the committee met, the House members would still have nothing to do with titles. Thus
on May 14 the Senate, "desirous of preserving harmony with the House of Representatives," finally voted that "*'To the President of the United States,'* without
addition of title," should be the proper address. At no point during the entire
affair had Washington himself given any hint of his wishes (if he had, Maclay
observed in his journal, "I would have heard it"), but he did unburden himself
about it afterward. "The truth is," Washington wrote in a private letter,

> the question was moved before I arrived, without any privity or knowledge of it
> on my part, and urged after I was apprized of it contrary to my opinion; for I
> foresaw and predicted the reception it has met with, and the use that would be
> made of it by the adversaries of the government. Happily the matter is now done
> with, I hope never to be revived.[25]

It was, in fact, never revived. Nor was the outcome, for all the momentary
see-sawing, ever in much real doubt. What had governed just about everyone was
a principle which gave a strong accent to the ideology of the Revolution: the
austere simplicity of the Roman Republic. The imagery of the Latin classics had
penetrated their lives, words, thoughts, and acts in endless ways ever since they
could remember. The almanacs of the day, with lines from Horace, Virgil, and
Ovid, had sung the praises of virtuous husbandry. The chief propagandists of the
Revolution had been classical scholars, and had signed their tracts with classical
pseudonyms. The non-importation agreements had been supported by the symbolism of Roman frugality and abstinence. The entire literature of the Revolution
was permeated with the imagery of republican Rome menaced by the approaching
shadow of the Caesars, and it was thus appropriate that in the Constitutional
Convention appeal should repeatedly be made to the history of the ancient republics. The very nomenclature of government—"president," "senate," "congress"—
as well as the official iconography, the mottoes of state, even the architecture,
would all be heavily Roman. Somehow their behavior ought to be Roman too.
James Madison (whose expression, according to one observer, "was that of a stern
Censor") said on the day titles were debated for the last time in the House of
Representatives, "The more simple, the more Republican we are in our manners,
the more rational dignity we shall acquire."[26]

The epitome of the Roman citizen, logically, was Washington himself. He was
hardly unaware of this, having in fact been playing the role for years. By this time
the parallels between Washington's own life and those of the great heroes of the
Roman Republic, Cincinnatus, Fabius, and Cato, had been proclaimed again and
again. In his youth he had read Addison's *Cato* with Sally Fairfax; years later he

had the play performed for his troops at Valley Forge; by then, people were saying he *was* Cato. It was the military tactics of George Washington that first brought the adjective "Fabian" into the English language. And when the war was over he became Cincinnatus, and returned to his plough. "You have often heard him likened to Cincinnatus," wrote Brissot de Warville after a visit to Mount Vernon in 1788; "the Comparison is accurate. This famous general is now merely a good countryman entirely devoted to the care of his farm. . . ." Three years later the young Chateaubriand met Washington, after having caught a glimpse of him out driving with a coach and four, and wondering whether that was quite the proper transportation for Cincinnatus. "However, when I presented to him my letter of introduction I recognized the simplicity of the old Roman."[27]

In addition to simplicity, the personal style of the Executive had to allow for both dignity and duty. Finding the right balance was perplexing, and Washington thought it prudent to make some private soundings before he finally struck it. Should he appear at parties? Make visits? Give entertainments? Receive calls? Under what circumstances, and how often? How was he to protect his working time? During the opening days, he said, "I should have been unable to have attended to any sort of business unless I had applied the hours allotted to rest and refreshment to this purpose." Perhaps he ought to give no invitations at all, nor receive any. "But to this I had two objections: . . . first the novelty of it I knew would be considered as an ostentatious show of mimicry of sovereignty; and secondly that so great a seclusion would have stopped the avenues to useful information from the many, and make me more dependent on that of the few; but to hit on a discriminating medium was found more difficult than it appeared to be at first view. . . ." He finally decided to make no calls, accept no invitations, and give no large entertainments, but to go to the theater occasionally and to hold one hour-long levee a week, asking a few of the guests each time to remain for dinner. A contemporary account of one of these levees—which seem to have been rather grave affairs—describes the President as dressed

in black velvet; his hair in full dress, powdered and gathered behind in a large silk bag; yellow gloves on his hands; holding a cocked hat with cockade in it, and the edges adorned with a black feather about an inch deep. He wore knee and shoe buckles; and a long sword, with a finely wrought and polished steel hilt, which appeared at the left hip; the coat worn over the sword, so that the hilt, and the part below the folds of the coat behind, were in view. The scabbard was white polished leather.

He stood always in front of the fire-place, with his face towards the door of entrance. . . . He received his visitor with a dignified bow, while his hands were so disposed of as to indicate, that the salutation was not to be accompanied with shaking hands. This ceremony never occurred in these visits, even with his most near friends, that no distinction might be made.

As visitors came in, they formed a circle around the room. At a quarter past three, the door was closed, and the circle was formed for that day. He then began on the right, and spoke to each visitor, calling him by name, and exchanging a few words with him. When he had completed his circuit, he resumed his first position, and the visitors approached him in succession, bowed and retired. By four o'clock this ceremony was over.[28]

In addition there would be a period in each day when callers might see the President on official business. With this regime, as Freeman puts it, "he did not seek the glorification of his office but the simplification of his work."[29]

Thus the Roman standard in public conduct required both *simplicitas* and *dignitas,* and here there was no disagreement on fundamentals.[30] Even in the debate over titles, both sides had used "Roman" arguments, one claim being that the Romans had not used titles, the other that they had. What about *Vir amplissimus, Vir Clarissimus, Vir amplissimus Consul, Vir Summus?* "These," expostulated John Adams, "were familiar among them in the simplest times . . . [and] I say farther that Patres Conscripti was an higher Title than my Lords. . . ."[31]

So everyone was more or less Roman. George Washington ranked first, and John Adams was the next Roman below him. Adams "always wrote for the public," according to Howard Mumford Jones, "as if he had a toga on." It was just that John Adams, like a fair number of others, was not as yet certain how long this particular republic would last. Some visible mark of distinction, conferred upon a few of its leading officers, might cause the people to accord it greater veneration. A majority of those who considered it, however, seem to have decided that the legitimacy Adams was reaching for would have to be achieved in less direct ways.[32]

3
The Executive Establishment

In the beginning there were no executive departments—no Treasury, no State Department, no War Department, or any others—nor was there any clear idea what such departments might be like once they were organized, or who would really control them, or to whom they would be finally responsible. The Constitution had said nothing about any of those questions, and there was no automatic way of settling them. Before Congress had confronted them and debated them, before specific enactments had been made, and before clear standards had been established for appointing anyone to office, the pervasive suspicions of the Revolutionary era—rooted in what the Americans had known of British politics— might have overflowed and caused the problem to be settled in any of several ways. Fears of executive power, and especially the corruptions of the British patronage system which had undermined the virtue of the English nation, were at the core of what had seemed to make the Revolution necessary. Such questions, facing the Americans all over again, were therefore not to be disposed of lightly. Moreover, the principles upon which they were finally settled would not have had the clarity they were eventually given were it not for the intellectual and parliamentary leadership of James Madison, the thirty-eight-year-old congressman from Virginia.

It is sometimes assumed that the initial decision to define cabinet officers as the President's assistants, responsible to him and for whose acts he in turn took responsibility—rather than as ministers whose functions to some extent rivaled his own—was simply up to Washington, and was made by him. This is only partially true. The departments first had to be established, and it was up to Congress to decide at whose pleasure, and under what conditions, the head of each of them would hold office. Meanwhile the departmental officers of the old Continental Congress of the Confederation—John Jay as Secretary of Foreign Affairs, the members of the Treasury Board, and Henry Knox as Secretary of War—would have to carry on *ad interim* as holdovers. They would do this until September 1789, and in one case until March 1790.

On May 19, 1789, Representative Elias Boudinot of New Jersey, after an extended debate on the tariff, proposed that Congress establish a Department of Finance. Egbert Benson of New York shifted this to the prior question of all the departments, and of which ones ought to be established. He suggested Foreign Affairs, Treasury, and War. It was at this point that Madison took charge of the question. He agreed that all the departments should be organized. But knowing exactly what he wanted, and realizing that to discuss the Treasury first would be to open the debate on the most potentially controversial of any department, Madison opened with a proposal for a "Department of Foreign Affairs, at the head of which there shall be an officer, to be called the Secretary to the Department of Foreign Affairs, who shall be appointed by the President, by and with the advice and consent of the Senate; and to be removable by the President." The phrase "removable by the President," as Madison well knew, was the key to everything else. If the Senate's advice and consent were required for removal as well as for appointment, or if the only other way was by impeachment, then the entire relationship of the President to the heads of departments would be profoundly altered. Madison argued, moreover, that the President's removal power should not be regarded as having been conferred by legislative grant, but simply acknowledged, since it had been there all along, already inherent in the Constitution.[33]

After long debate, Madison carried his point. But the matter did not end there. In the Senate, the question was complicated not only by the usual suspicions of executive power but also by jealousy of the Senate's own prerogatives and a feeling that the House was bent on cutting them down. (There had already been a touch of this in the fight over titles.) Maclay was convinced that Madison was at the head of a plot to control the Executive himself and to "exalt the President above the Constitution, and depress the Senate below it." The Senate's vote on the removal power, which could not be taken until July 16, resulted in a tie. Much to Maclay's chagrin, it was broken by the casting vote of the Vice-President, and the House's position was sustained.[34]

The same battle, in more complicated form, occurred over the organization of the Treasury. There was the question of whether that department ought to be headed by a single person, or by a board as had been the previous practice. There was also the problem, more acute than in the case of foreign affairs, of how extensive the Treasury's functions, power, and authority should be, if exercised by one man, in a realm that included the nation's finances, revenues, and credit. Madison again took the lead in urging that the department, under a single Secretary, be allowed the maximum power and energy consistent with the President's ultimate control under the removal power. He won his point that a treasury board would divide responsibility and dilute energy, but there were vigorous objections to the proposal that the Secretary should "digest and report plans for the improvement and management of the revenue, and the support of the public credit," that being a power rightfully belonging to Congress. But the eventual compromise — that the Secretary would "digest and *prepare*" such plans — turned out to be not very different. Once more the Senate showed its intransigence. It wanted, as before, to limit the President's removal power by its own advice and consent; Madison, in announcing this to the House, recommended that the House refuse the change, which it did; and on August 25 the Senate reluctantly agreed. Again the vote was a tie, and again the tie was broken by Vice-President Adams.[35]

At what point Madison knew that his friend Alexander Hamilton would be the first Secretary, and to what extent, if any, Hamilton himself had a hand in this legislation, is unknown. But Madison had in any case won at every point, and Hamilton, in retrospect, gives every appearance of having been the man the post was designed for. He was nominated by the President on September 11, 1789, was confirmed by the Senate on the same day, and assumed the duties of office immediately. The next day the nomination of Henry Knox, who had been reappointed as Secretary of War, was also confirmed. Thomas Jefferson, Washington's choice to be Secretary of State (that department's functions had been enlarged, and its name changed from "Foreign Affairs"), was nominated on September 25 and confirmed on the 26th. In Jefferson's case, it was not to be until March 22, 1790, that the new Secretary would assume charge of his department. With respect to the President, another ambiguity left over from the Philadelphia Convention had been clarified. The Constitution had already provided for a strong and independent Executive. Now, once his Secretaries had been appointed and approved, he was to have full control over them. They were to be unquestionably "his."[36]

The next stage in legitimizing his administration — of so filling the various positions therein as to win for it the support of the country at large — was now up to him. Here too, there was more than one way he might have gone about it. Standards for the making of appointments were neither automatic nor self-evident. They had to be consciously chosen.

One visible precedent was to be found in the history of eighteenth-century England. Seventy-five years earlier, Sir Robert Walpole had deliberately and successfully used the royal patronage to bring a high degree of stability to English political life. Patronage involved money and perquisites; more important, it involved power and influence. By a purposeful distribution of offices, the precise value of each of which could be measured, graded, and thus generally understood, Walpole in the 1720s and 1730s did much to bring an end to the debilitating struggles for power between Whig and Tory aristocracy that had kept English politics and government in a chronic state of disruption for some years after the Glorious Revolution. The interlocking system of status, place, and power among the aristocracy and gentry which he created by this means came ultimately to be known as the "Establishment," the governing class of England, something that had never existed before on quite so orderly a basis. The offices used in its formation—everything from doorkeeperships, stewardships, Church deaneries, army and navy commissions, baronetcies, and colonial governorships to membership in the Privy Council—enabled Walpole to stabilize political behavior both in the local constituencies and at court, and thus to guarantee stable majorities year after year in the House of Commons.[37]

This was well and good, except that it also created, as we have seen, around the outer fringes of politics and beyond the pale, the Country mentality, the psychology of the outsider. Disaffected Tory squires, "independent Whigs," habitués of the London coffee-houses—all despised the "Robinarchy" and denounced its corruption, its luxury, its rotten boroughs, and its armies of placemen, relatives, and parasites. It was a mentality, meanwhile (as we have also seen), to which the American colonies were peculiarly susceptible: by and large, the fundamentals of their own political understanding rested not on the Court but on the Country attitude.[38]

From out of their past experience, therefore, "patronage" to Americans was a highly sensitive subject. At almost every point where the British patronage system—so inscrutably sinister in its mysteries—touched their affairs, as it did with royal governors, customs officials, and military garrisons, there was built-in trouble. In their experience, patronage appeared always as something that was controlled by somebody else, over whom anyone *they* knew was powerless; and in their imagination the power that could, in turn, be wielded through patronage was all but limitless, and mostly evil. It was against this background, and all the prejudices and suspicions created by it, that George Washington in 1789 had to decide how to distribute offices in the Federal Republic.[39]

He could, of course, go to the opposite extreme, and use his power of appointment not to reward friends and punish enemies, but to place the ablest men he could find in each office at his disposal. In one sense this is what he did, or tried to do, and he would in fact defend his practice on just such grounds. But Washington's alternatives may not be conceived in terms so simple, and he himself did not so regard them. The standard of expertise, of pure technical competence, individual training and individual ability—the "merit system" as seen by the civil service reformers of a later day—still fell a good deal short of what Washington required of his appointees. He wanted more than simply "merit" in this sense; he most typically referred not to the "best men" but to the "first Characters." These were not incompatible, but they were not the same either.

In one sense Washington's problem was really not so different from Walpole's, in that his appointments too had to serve broader purposes going beyond the simple filling of an office, and being essentially political in nature. He, too, was concerned with the manner in which his patronage might or might not bind loyalty to his government. But the materials with which he had to work in effecting this purpose were altogether different. The basic units of power with which he had to deal and make terms were not leading families, but local communities. "First Characters" were men who by virtue of their abilities and records of public service stood first, as it were, in the respect of their neighbors.

Washington in effect had to deal with a set of quasi-autonomous republics, and republics within republics. Until the officials appointed to function in a given community should be acceptable to that community—as measured by the reputation they had already made there, and thus by claims superior to those of other candidates—the federal government itself would not have attained full legitimacy in these places. "It is the nature of Republicans, who are nearly in a state of equality," Washington wrote,

> to be extremely jealous as to the disposal of all honorary or lucrative appointments. Perfectly convinced I am, that, if injudicious or unpopular measures should be taken by the Executive under the New Government with regards to appointments, the Government itself would be in the utmost danger of being utterly subverted by those measures. So necessary is it, at this crisis, to conciliate the good will of the People: and so impossible is it, in my judgment, to build the edifice of public happiness, but upon their affections.

Two years later, Washington's Postmaster-General observed: "An office which in its execution is confined to a particular state, ought to be exercised by a citizen of that state. In like manner an office which especially regards a county or a town, should be held by an inhabitant of such county or town—if it afford a person qualified to execute it. This principle has evidently governed the President of the U. States in his appointments."[40]

A geographic distribution of the higher offices, Supreme Court and cabinet, was adhered to with some nicety. The balance of Massachusetts, New York, and Virginia in the cabinet gave general satisfaction, as did that of six states on the Supreme Court, whose first Chief Justice was John Jay of New York. But in all the offices—these and the 350-odd others Washington filled—the fundamental standard was that of "first charactership." Presumptive evidence for it was to be found in personal merit, talent, and prior public service—in the same office under the Confederation, in elected office, or in some capacity, military or civil, during the Revolution—all of which added up to what Washington most wanted for his appointees, the esteem of their fellow-citizens. It was summed up in the reasons he gave for nominating as Naval Officer of the Port of Savannah a certain Benjamin Fishbourn, who, he told the Senate, "must have enjoyed the *confidence* of the militia Officers in order to have been elevated to a military rank; the *confidence* of the Freemen to have been elected to the Assembly; the *confidence* of the Assembly to have been selected for the Council; and the *confidence* of the Council to have been appointed Collector of the Port of Savannah." [41]

Thus it was that the ties of family—which had been vital in binding the British system together—would be of limited value in constructing the far more tenuous web of loyalty that would have to do in America. No primary claims could be made upon such ties; quite the reverse; these were actually to be avoided in the making of appointments, and were thus a downright liability. Washington's nephew Bushrod discovered this for himself in the summer of 1789 when his uncle informed him:

> You cannot doubt my wishes to see you appointed to any office of honor or emolument in the new government, to the duties of which you are competent; but however deserving you may be of the one you have suggested, your standing at the bar would not justify my nomination of you as Attorney to the Federal district Court in preference of some of the oldest, and most esteemed General Court lawyers in your own State, who are desirous of this appointment. My political conduct in nominations, even if I was uninfluenced by principle, must be exceedingly circumspect and proof against just criticism, for the eyes of Argus are upon me, and no slip will pass unnoticed that can be improved into a supposed partiality for friends or relatives.[42]

Forty-eight years before, an outraged Sir Robert Walpole had exclaimed in the House of Commons:

> Has my conduct been different from that which others in the same station would have followed? Have I acted wrong in giving the place of auditor to my son, and in providing for my own family? I trust that their advancement will not be imputed to me as a crime, unless it shall be proved that I placed them in offices of trust and responsibility for which they were unfit.[43]

Washington had protected himself from all this; indeed, his protection was already there, in his having to deal with a political community quite different from that of Walpole. Here, old Roman republican standards were not only appropriate; in a way they were unavoidable. His favors were to be bestowed on the basis not of *noblesse oblige* but of civic virtue.

4

Advise and Consent

On Saturday, August 22, 1789, President Washington appeared in the Senate chamber, accompanied by Secretary of War Knox, to ask the Senate's approval for the project of a treaty he wished to negotiate with the Southern Indians. Senator Maclay in his journal gives the impression that this was done precipitously, on less than a day's notice, that the effect of it was to embarrass and overawe the senators, and that he, Maclay, rescued them from their discomfiture by insisting that the matter be deferred until they could give it mature and uncoerced consideration. Washington, his dignity affronted, left in a state of high displeasure, having been balked of his intention to "tread on the necks of the Senate." According to another story, the President "said he would be damned if he ever went there again."[44]

The truth of the first story is partial; for the second, the evidence is dubious. But the incident did occur. It occurred, however, after the President and the Senate had each been considering for more than two weeks the entire question of oral communication between them, and had fully agreed upon a procedure. During these same two weeks the Senate had been in full possession of the facts regarding the Indian troubles, and was fully aware that a treaty was being contemplated. Moreover, Washington did go back again, at which time (two days later) the Senate agreed to everything he had asked for, though it is true that such a method of consultation was abandoned after that. Still, the affair is instructive, whatever its exact details, because of its nature as both a positive and negative precedent. Some procedures need to be acted out before their unworkability becomes fully apparent, and the unintended consequences then become themselves a kind of precedent. In this case a new clarity was given to the idea of the Senate's "advice and consent," and a new depth of refinement not only to the nature of executive-legislative relations but also to the nature of the presidency itself. The President was not to be precisely a sovereign, but even less was he to be a prime minister.[45]

Washington at this time still assumed that he ought to seek the Senate's advice and consent *before* embarking upon any diplomatic negotiations which would result in the making of a treaty. That was what the wording of the Constitution seemed to require. How it should be done, however, remained unclear, and it was the Senate that took the first steps to explore the question. On August 6 a committee was appointed to "confer with [the President] on the mode of communication proper to be pursued between him and the Senate, in the formation of treaties, and making appointments to office." The committee met twice with Washington, who, between times, asked Madison for advice on what position he ought to take. At the first meeting, he felt that oral communications were "indispensably necessary; because in these treaties a variety of matters are contained, all of which not only require consideration, but some of them may undergo much discussion; to do which by written communications would be tedious without being satisfactory." At the second meeting, he was less sure. Perhaps they should sometimes be oral, at other times written. The committee was quite satisfied to do it any way the President wished, and its report to this effect was agreed to by the Senate. It was against this background that Washington on August 21 sent his message announcing that he would "meet the Senate, in the Senate Chamber, at half-past eleven o'clock to-morrow, to advise with them on the terms of the treaty to be negotiated with the Southern Indians."[46]

When the President and General Knox duly appeared, and all had taken their places, it quickly became apparent that something was wrong. For one thing, it was hard to hear much that was said, since there was considerable noise outside from carriages clattering up and down the street. Washington had put a great deal of work into his presentation, and thought he had digested it all into the simplest possible terms, in the form of a short paper containing the background of the Indian problem, together with seven questions upon which he wished the Senate's advice and consent. It was read to the Senate by Vice-President Adams, who seems to have gone through it with undue haste. Robert Morris thereupon apologized for not having heard it all, because of the noise in the street, and asked that the paper be read again. So it was read again, after which the Vice-President immediately re-read the first question (making this the third time) and concluded by putting the question, "Do you advise and consent, etc.?"

There was a dead silence, nobody knowing quite what to say. Nerves must have been frayed enough already when Senator Maclay, who could always be counted upon to make difficulties, rose from his seat and asked for a reading of all the prior treaties and other related documents. "It is our duty," he announced, "to inform ourselves as well as possible on the subject." This took up more time. When it came around again to the first question, which was about the Cherokees (this was now the fourth time it had been read), someone suggested that a messenger from that area, expected momentarily, might provide more information. At this point Washington, with what patience he could muster, said he had no objection to that question's being postponed.

They got no farther than the second question, when a long and laborious discussion arose over whether they were really going about the business in the right way after all. Though some members had already begun to grumble, Maclay nevertheless made another speech, in which he argued that it should all be referred to a select committee, who would then make a report. By now Washington had had enough.

> As I sat down [Maclay wrote], the President of the United States started up in a violent fret. *"This defeats every purpose of my coming here,"* were the first words that he said. He then went on that he had brought his Secretary of War with him to give every necessary information; that the Secretary knew all about the business, and yet he was delayed and could not go on with the matter.

He then cooled down, and said he would be satisfied to have the question postponed until the following Monday. Nothing more was said about a committee; the President and Secretary Knox withdrew, and the Senate adjourned for the weekend. On Monday morning he reappeared, this time relaxed and serene, and the Senate agreed to all the remaining points of his project. But no further sessions of this sort were held, either by Washington or by any succeeding President.[47]

The full implications of this episode were latent, and not immediately discerned. In retrospect, one of the more obvious ones was that this was a first step in discovering the drawbacks of open prior consultation, on any terms, in matters of diplomacy. Washington would continue for a time to communicate in writing with the Senate before making treaties, but this too was eventually abandoned when, in the delicate state of international affairs which emerged in the 1790s, secrecy of negotiation came to be seen as indispensable. This difficulty would have emerged in any case. But it was already becoming apparent that the operative term was "consent," not "advise," and that the latter term constituted little more than a legal formula. It had been so, indeed, with legislative enactments in England since the time of Henry VII, and the American Constitution-makers had probably copied the formula without giving much thought to the distinction.

Another implication, strongly conveyed by Maclay, was that the Senate's dignity was being affronted by the President's appearing before them to assert the force of his majesty, and that the senators' response was such as to discourage him from doing it again. But there is not much evidence that this was the way the rest of the Senate saw it. In this case it is more likely that the senators' embarrassment reflected not so much resentment as an acute sense of the constraints that operated upon Washington himself as well as on them.

The episode was not in the last analysis a challenge to Washington's authority but a dramatic confirmation of it, and the legitimacy of the presidency—in the peculiar form given it by the American Constitution—was thereby deepened rather than lessened. That is, Washington's restraint in following what he regarded as the letter of the Constitution in *not* assuming full initiative in treaty matters was shown in the sight of all to be impracticable. He was appearing, as a prime minister might do, to present his case to a legislative body, and was being told, by the response that greeted him, that he was more than a prime minister, and did not need to lay his prestige on the line in any such way.

There would, in the future, be consultations. But they would occur in private. The Executive would defend its actions and policies to the Senate, but it would be done informally. The Secretary of State, not the President, would do it, and it would take place not in the open Senate but in closed committees, and sometimes through channels less formal than that. The "advice" aspect, in short, was to become almost wholly unofficial.

It might be said that all such implications were "inherent" right along. But the subtleties were such that a test of some sort was probably required to show that they *were* inherent. When it occurred, a direct confrontation of the executive and legislative branches on such a level—the level of formal argument—was shown to be so disruptive, from a variety of causes, as to be henceforth out of the question.

5
A Bill of Rights and a Judiciary System

The Constitution of the United States in the course of its history has seldom if ever been amended lightly. After the adoption of the Twelfth Amendment in 1804, sixty years were to pass before there would be another, and the Fifteenth and Sixteenth Amendments were separated in time by forty-three years more. Only five amendments would be added to the Constitution between 1798 and 1913, a total span of 115 years. Moreover, every amendment beginning with the Eleventh has been framed with a very specific object, in response to what was seen as a substantive need. It may well be wondered, then, why the first ten—familiarly known as the Bill of Rights—should have had so different a character from the others, and why they should have been framed in what seems, in retrospect, inordinate haste, the federal government being scarcely six months old when they were completed. There was little in them that was specific, in the sense that later ones would be; they were broad, general, and diffuse, and most of them did little more than state what was already clearly present in existing common-law practice. In order to frame them, moreover, it had been necessary for Congress to delay a mountain of business that was exceptionally urgent and that many regarded as more immediate. The reasons for this haste are not to be found in any need for which the amendments provided a specific remedy. The need was general, being of a political rather than legal nature. It involved, as did so much else that was done during that first year, the legitimacy of the government itself, and of the very Constitution under which it functioned.

Washington, ever sensitive to the possibility that he might be accused of overstepping his powers (such as in presuming to initiate legislation), forbore in his inaugural address from telling Congress what measures he thought it ought to take—with one exception. His single recommendation was that the amending power of the Constitution be used to make certain that "the characteristic rights of freemen" might be "more impregnably fortified." Behind this proposal for a bill of rights—deferentially and indirectly stated but unmistakably desired—lay a year and a half of tension and open political strife. This tension had been clearly present since the adjournment of the Constitutional Convention in September 1787, and had by no means disappeared when Washington in his Inaugural referred to the "objections which have been urged against the System" and "the degree of inquietude which has given birth to them" on April 30, 1789.[48]

In the closing days of the Philadelphia Convention, after all the major compromises had been made and the form essentially set, George Mason of Virginia had proposed that the new Constitution be prefaced by a bill of rights. This was voted down, mainly because the delegates, who had toiled all through a warm summer, were anxious to wind up their work and had no heart for the delays that would most certainly be incurred in opening up an entirely new issue. In minimizing the urgency of a bill of rights, however, they were to some extent the victims of their own impatience. On the other hand, in not making his proposal earlier, Mason left himself open to suspicions of sabotage. A number of his ideas on other matters had been disregarded by the Convention, and he had by this time become disaffected on general grounds. A day or so before adjournment he drafted a set of "Objections to this Constitution of Government," at the head of which was the statement that the document contained no bill of rights. He then left ("in an exceeding ill humour," according to Madison) without signing. Mason's "Objections" were subsequently printed and circulated through all the states, and the absence of a bill of rights thereupon became a rallying point for any who had reason for opposing the Constitution. "To alarm the people," Washington wrote exasperatedly, "seems to be the groundwork of his plan."[49]

In the battle over ratification during the months that followed, the Federalists found again and again that the point at which they were most vulnerable was their neglect of a bill of rights. It was principally because of this that North Carolina and Rhode Island failed to ratify. A demand for amendments that would guarantee personal rights threatened to block ratification in all but three of the other states. There were several devices the Antifederalists tried to get their conventions to adopt. One was that of "previous amendments": a state would prepare a series of proposed amendments and then announce that until these had been substantially adopted it would withhold its ratification. (This was what Patrick Henry and his supporters tried to do in Virginia.) Another device was "conditional ratification": a convention would ratify, but upon condition that the state might withdraw if within a specified time the changes it desired had not been made. A move of this sort—which, as Madison pointed out, would be no ratification at all and "worse than a rejection"—was narrowly defeated in New York. Still another was the plan of calling a second federal convention to amend the Constitution. Such a plan was still being discussed in New York and elsewhere as late as the spring of 1789, and must have been very much in Washington's mind as he considered his pending Inaugural. The compromise whereby these potential obstacles had for the moment been avoided was that hit upon by Massachusetts and adopted by other conventions, which was to ratify without conditions but to accompany the ratification with a list of recommended amendments. Meanwhile a number of the religious sects, most prominently the Baptists, were expressing strong doubts. A Baptist convention in Virginia had considered whether the new Constitution "made sufficient provision for the secure enjoyment of religious liberty; on which, it was agreed unanimously, that . . . it did not." Such in brief was the state of things when Congress took up the question of amendments in June 1789.[50]

In this, as with most of the other measures of the first session, the dominating voice was that of James Madison. Madison had at first been among those who felt that a federal bill of rights was unnecessary, such rights being already provided for in most of the state constitutions. The amending power, moreover, might become a great force for mischief if resorted to before the Constitution went into effect. Many of the advocates of amendments clearly wanted to go beyond bills of rights and to limit federal powers in ways that would make the Constitution something quite different from the instrument that had been adopted, with its many fragile compromises, at Philadelphia. But as for the principle itself of enumerating the rights of citizens, Madison had already begun to change his mind (as had Washington) by the time of the Virginia convention, and to concede that such an enumeration ought to be added to the Constitution soon after the new government was in operation. The vindictive Henry, playing upon local suspicions, had successfully worked to prevent Madison's being elected to the Senate. These suspicions might have cost Madison a seat in the House of Representatives as well, had he not in the meantime given clear promises. He declared his "sincere opinion that the Constitution ought to be revised, and that the first Congress meeting under it ought to prepare and recommend to the States for ratification, the most satisfactory provisions for all essential rights, particularly the rights of Conscience in the fullest latitude, the freedom of the press, trials by jury, security against general warrants &c." He thought this would provide "additional guards in favour of liberty," but his primary purpose was that of "satisfying the minds of well meaning opponents" of the Constitution. It was in this spirit that Madison on May 4, 1789, gave notice that he intended three weeks hence to open debate on the subject of amendments to the Constitution.[51] The House was not able to get to the question until June 8, and would not have done so then but for Madison's persistence. Having to contend with a number of opposing difficulties, Madison managed his campaign with considerable skill, and was almost solely responsible for the eventual success of it. A number of strong Federalists wanted no amendments at all, and complaints over the delaying of pressing business in order to consider them were heard from Federalist and Antifederalist alike. But Madison wanted it done as soon as possible, and in Congress rather than in another convention. Public opinion, moreover, now seemed to be on his side. He had taken care to announce his intentions in advance and to make his position widely known. His views were embodied in a series of proposals which he read to the House on the first day of debate, and most of them—in a number of cases with Madison's own phraseology—eventually found their way into the Constitution.[52]

As to their nature and extent, here again Madison had to contend with both strong Federalist and Antifederalist pressures. The total number and variety of amendments proposed by the various states had been enormous. Moreover, a good many Antifederalists, especially those powerful in their respective states, were inclined to lump state rights with personal rights, and to regard the former as equally if not more important. Most Federalists, on the other hand, wanted nothing that would threaten the authority and energy of the government, a concern which Madison still shared, but many would have been glad to avoid such a threat by staying away from amendments altogether. Madison's solution was to concentrate on personal rights, avoid everything that encroached on federal power, and emphasize general principles rather than detailed provisions.

The result—involving freedom of speech, press, and conscience, trial by jury, security of person and property, and various other rights—was referred to a committee, whose report underwent many delays and much debate. On August 24 it was sent to the Senate in the form of seventeen proposed amendments. They came back on September 10 reduced in number to twelve, and by September 25, having been put in final form by a joint conference committee, they were finally approved by both houses. In the subsequent process of ratification, two of the proposed twelve amendments—one concerning the basis of representation and the other the salaries of members of Congress—would be lost by the wayside, and the remaining ten incorporated as the Bill of Rights.[53]

A year before Madison completed his work, and when he was just beginning to change his mind, he had begun by conceding that a bill of rights, properly framed, would do no harm. But in the course of time he had found more positive grounds. Believing as he did that the greatest likelihood of tyranny and the true danger to liberty lay in abuses by the majority rather than by the government (the government being but the majority's instrument), Madison reasoned that a bill of rights would function not so much as a specific set of rules but as a kind of public standard. Its benefits were of a sort that would accrue over time, the values which it embodied being gradually internalized by the whole society. "The political truths declared in that solemn manner acquire by degrees the character of fundamental maxims of free government, and as they become incorporated with the national sentiment, counteract the impulses of interest and passion." Then if, on the other hand, liberty should from time to time be endangered by government, such a standard would be "a good ground for an appeal to the sense of the community." And, as Jefferson wisely reminded him, there was a "legal check which it puts into the hands of the judiciary."[54]

Even so, it was not the long-term benefits that Madison had primarily in mind in his urgency to get a bill of rights through. He was concerned first of all with legitimacy and acceptance. He knew that a bill of rights would be the most dramatic single gesture of conciliation that could be offered the remaining opponents of the government, and would provide the most convenient possible formula whereby they might change their minds. The proof would soon be at hand. Washington was informed by the Rhode Island legislature in September that the amendments had "already afforded some relief and satisfaction to the minds of the People of this State," and there was similar news from North Carolina. That state joined the Union in November 1789, and Rhode Island would do so the following spring.[55]

With the Constitution now completed to the satisfaction of most, the question remained as to the nature and form of the judicial system that would interpret it as law. That question had been to all intents and purposes wide open when the senators who framed the Judiciary Act of 1789 began their work in the spring. Article III of the Constitution had given them virtual *carte blanche:*

> The judicial power of the United States shall be vested in one Supreme Court, and in such inferior courts as the Congress may from time to time ordain and establish. . . .
>
> The judicial power shall extend to all cases, in law and equity, arising under this Constitution, the laws of the United States, and treaties made, or which shall be made, under their authority. . . .

Had they fully put their minds to it, they might have fashioned under these sanctions, and at this critical juncture, one of the most effective of all conceivable instruments of nationalization. They might have established a system of courts sufficiently numerous and widely enough distributed as to be conveniently accessible everywhere, and then given them the widest jurisdiction allowed under the judiciary article of the Constitution, common law as well as statute law. This would have enabled the Supreme Court in effect to supervise the court systems of the states, through ready appeal and through the body of precedent that would thus quickly accumulate. The result would be to create, in time, a fully unified system of national law and judicial procedure. The framers of the Act did not do this, and so no such result followed. The Judiciary Act of 1789, completed in September of that year, was to lay down the basic terms and assumptions upon which federal justice has operated ever since, and there never has been a consolidation of state and federal law into a unified body of national law. But then the framers had other things to contend with besides the desirability of a rational, nationwide system of law. The same need to conciliate, to secure acceptance, operated upon this set of decisions as it had upon most of the others of 1789.

The Special Judiciary Committee appointed on April 7, with Oliver Ellsworth as chairman, consisted of ten members, one from each state as the Senate was then constituted. In view of this geographic distribution, and since there were men with strong state-rights and even Antifederalist leanings included (notably Richard Henry Lee of Virginia), it became likely that most of the gross differences of view would be adjusted within the Committee, and before its proposals reached the floor of the Senate. This, with certain exceptions, seems to have been what happened.

In principle, the strong Federalist broad-construction view was that the Constitution had given wide powers to the federal courts and that Congress, once it had established such courts, was not entitled to withhold any of these powers from them. On the other hand, a strong strain of the Antifederalist criticism of the Constitution, ever since the Convention, had concentrated on this very point. The critics either wanted no inferior federal courts at all, or else wanted to give such courts as little jurisdiction as possible. They wanted original jurisdiction in most federal questions given to state courts, subject only to the appellate power of the Supreme Court, and it was in this direction that a number of the proposed constitutional amendments had looked. Neither side fully had its way, and Chairman Ellsworth, himself a good Federalist, seems to have assumed from the first that this would be so. But even Ellsworth had probably not anticipated how restrictive his committee's bill would in the end turn out to be. In any case, when the Act reached its final form—proceeding from Ellsworth's earliest ideas to the Committee's draft bill, and from there through the Senate's amended version and to the bill that was eventually reported by the Senate-House conference committee—it became apparent that the nation's system of courts had been shaped less by the sanctions of the Constitution, literally read, than by the requirements of a political compromise.

The Act did provide for a six-member Supreme Court and a system of federal district and circuit courts, as contemplated by the Constitution, and in the face of some opposition with regard to the inferior courts. But the districts were very large, and the courts within them were few in number, confined to one or two points within each state. Their accessibility and convenience, in comparison with similar state courts, was thus limited. The Supreme Court justices, moreover, were required to hold two circuit courts a year in every state under primitive conditions of transportation, which made for delays, postponements, and much general inconvenience. As for the broad grant of jurisdiction which the Constitution had apparently made to the national courts, extending "to all cases, in law and equity, arising under this Constitution, the laws of the United States, and treaties made, or which shall be made, under their authority," such jurisdiction was defined in a relatively narrow way.

Though the Act granted the right of appeal to the Supreme Court from the highest state courts on all federal questions, original jurisdiction in the great bulk of civil cases involving such questions was given to the state courts. The federal courts, moreover, had no common-law jurisdiction except for criminal offenses against the United States. Federal jurisdiction in diversity cases—those involving parties of different citizenship, either of another state or of a foreign country—was similarly limited. The matter in dispute had to be greater than five hundred dollars in value, and—far more important—one of the parties had to be a citizen of the state in which the suit was brought. This, plus the provision in Section 34 that "the laws of the several states . . . shall be regarded as rules of decision in trials at common law in the courts of the United States," would in effect prevent the development of a body of national common law. Consequently the nationalizing potential of a federal judiciary system would henceforth be limited in scope by a variety of local systems.[56]

It has been argued that all this represented a very long departure from the intentions of those who wrote the Constitution.[57] So it might appear, yet appearances in this case may be deceiving. Evidence that the judiciary branch raised issues of absorbing importance is actually rather sketchy. The amount of attention and discussion given to the judiciary in the Constitutional Convention was only a fraction of that devoted to the executive and legislative branches. The resulting article was broadly worded, making wide grants or narrow grants of power equally possible, and this had been one of the arguments used in the Convention for so wording it. Indeed, the Federalists' main concern was simply that the authority of the United States be judicially enforceable, and that there be some ultimate guarantee of appeal in disputes between the United States government and those of the states, or between the states themselves. This had not in principle been seriously questioned in the Convention, and was in fact amply provided for in the Judiciary Act of 1789. Perhaps a few Federalists like Alexander Hamilton or Gouverneur Morris may have imagined a powerful and highly articulated system of national courts and national law. But even they did not think very specifically or concentratedly about this particular problem, being preoccupied with others, and Federalist thought in general never showed the degree of unity or focus on judiciary matters that might have been expected.[58]

The fact was that a national judiciary as a branch of government was still something of an abstraction, substantially less real than were the other two. Far more real to Federalist and Antifederalist alike were the already existing legal institutions of the states, going well back into colonial times and having been little altered by the Revolution, and the strong vested interests they had accumulated through time and tradition. Thus when it became a question of spelling out a federal system in detail, efforts to protect those interests and to resist encroachments upon state authority were only to be expected. Even the most thoroughgoing Federalists had little inclination to resist them, even assuming the alternatives to be self-evident, which apparently they were not. The natural drift, therefore, was toward conciliation.[59]

6

Revenue, Tariffs, and Tonnage

On the face of it, one of the most neutral and matter-of-fact of all the questions Congress had to deal with in its first session was that of revenue. All agreed that a federal revenue act was essential for meeting the expenses of government. All further agreed that most of the revenue would, as a matter of course, have to be provided through a federal impost, a tariff on goods imported from foreign countries. Such an impost had already been proposed during the Confederation period, and although the rule of unanimity which then prevailed had obstructed it from going into effect, the fact was that every state but one had accepted it. So there should have been no reason to expect trouble in 1789, especially inasmuch as James Madison proposed, as the very first order of business after organizing the House, that the impost of 1783 simply be enacted now.[60] And yet Madison would not quite let it go at that, and there *was* trouble. The provision for tonnage duties which he added to this otherwise straightforward proposal would have had the effect, as he well knew, of striking at the shipping of Great Britain. The resulting debates went well beyond matters of revenue. They touched upon the deepest feelings that had been left over from the Revolution, and foreshadowed one of those crises of spirit in the life of a new nation in which the supposed harmony between its material interests and its ideological convictions becomes highly uncertain.

The opening phase of debate on the Tariff of 1789 was somewhat misleading. It concerned the nature and amount of import duties—the tonnage aspect would come later—and it was characterized by some colorful oratory and a good many sharp words. And yet this phase, for all its warmth, was more like a kind of bargaining forum than a basic struggle over first principles. It was contained; the boundaries were more or less clear; the objects and interests were immediate and measurable; and there was a minimum of hard feelings.

The first feature in Madison's proposal of April 8 was an *ad valorem* tax of 5 percent on all imports, exactly following the 1783 impost. To this there was no objection. The second was a short list of enumerated articles (rum, wine, tea, molasses, and the like), to be taxed by duties of a specified amount. This too had been a feature of the 1783 impost, and the list of articles offered by Madison was virtually the same, item for item, as that proposed in 1783. Though he had left the amounts blank, to be filled in by Congress, Madison nonetheless felt that the wisest course for the moment would be to adopt more or less the same schedule that had been agreed to before. This would be the simplest way to get a revenue measure passed at once, and to take fullest advantage of the spring imports. All of this made excellent sense, and a more permanent and comprehensive system, if needed, could be worked out later.

But the enumerated list was not to get by so quickly, even as a temporary measure. Changes had occurred in the country's business life since 1783, and the free-trade assumptions generally prevailing at that time—tariffs being regarded only as a device for obtaining revenue, and not for the protection of home industry—had likewise changed. Domestic manufactures that had developed during and after the Revolution were adversely affected by the influx of cheap British products in the mid-1780s; a number of states, meanwhile, had erected their own impost systems in order to service their state debts; and it was thus logical that the revenue aspects of these systems should be combined with experimental efforts to protect industries that had grown up within the state and that had suffered most from outside competition. At any rate, a taste for protection had already been implanted, local vested interests were already in evidence, and no sooner had debate begun on the Tariff of 1789 than Madison's list of enumerated articles began to grow. As the list mounted, the vivacity of the haggling over individual duties mounted also.[61]

Thomas FitzSimons of Pennsylvania, for example, gave a good foreshadowing of what that state's behavior would be throughout a century and a half of future tariff history. FitzSimons, a worthy precursor of "Pig-Iron" Kelley, wanted taxes systematically laid upon nails, spikes, tacks, brads, slit iron, rolled iron, iron castings, and steel in all forms, not to mention saddles, shoes, hats, gloves, carriages, and a host of other items, all of which happened to be produced in respectable quantities in the state of Pennsylvania. FitzSimons, on the other hand, was prepared to be reasonable. "When we come to consider them, article by article . . . , gentlemen will be at liberty to object; and if they offer good reasons for it, they may get them struck out. . . ." (He later proved willing to have tacks and brads struck out.) Thomas Tudor Tucker of South Carolina, like future South Carolinians, would have been glad to eliminate the enumerated articles altogether, believing that most of the duties would bear heavily on his state, which did little manufacturing. He repeated these sentiments nearly every day. But he also conceded that "if gentlemen are content with *moderate* duties, we are willing to agree to them. . . ." (Tucker's colleague Aedanus Burke, meanwhile, urged a duty on hemp, to encourage the production of that item in South Carolina.) Probably the choicest language of the entire debate was that used by Fisher Ames, the young and talented member from Massachusetts, in his zeal to prevent a high tariff being laid on molasses. Enormous amounts of molasses were imported annually into the state and used for the widest variety of purposes (including the manufacture of rum), the purchase of it being financed in large part by exports of fish. Higher prices for molasses, Ames ominously warned, would bring ruin to the fisheries and melancholy to all classes of the Commonwealth. "No decent family," he said, "can do without something by way of sweetening. . . . Mothers will tell their children, when they solicit their daily and accustomed nutriment, that the new laws forbid them the use of it, and they will grow up in a detestation of the hand which proscribes their innocent food and the occupation of their fathers. . . ." Ames's energy was rewarded. "Another molasses battle has been fought," he wrote briskly to his friend George Minot afterwards. "Like modern victories, it was incomplete, but we got off one cent."[62]

But although much time was spent in this fashion, the arguments were based largely on local interest rather than on doctrinal convictions regarding free trade or protection. Such convictions at this stage were still quite fluid. Although the principle of protection was certainly discernible in the Act which finally emerged, it was balanced throughout by the primary consideration of revenue and of what the government in any given case might reasonably hope to collect. Madison, for example, thought that generally speaking "commerce ought to be free" (Fisher Ames thought one of his speeches had been taken right out of Adam Smith), yet Madison found it no strain to make any number of exceptions in favor of protection. Ames, on the other hand, whose major effort might have been read as a free-trade polemic, admitted that "the navigation and manufactures of America cannot well be too much encouraged." The Tariff of 1789, in short, was mildly protective, in the sense that most interests with a reasonable claim to protection received at least a token of it, consistent with the government's claim to revenue.[63] The debate on tonnage, however, which followed that on tariffs, would be a very different matter. One side, at least, of *that* debate would be founded not so much upon interest, narrowly conceived, as upon deeply felt doctrines of national independence dating from the Revolution.

The third feature of Madison's April 8 resolution on revenue—in addition to those on the *ad valorem* tax and the tariffs on enumerated articles—was introduced by him in a deceptively off-hand and deprecating way as "a clause or two on the subject of tonnage." In reality, it was to this feature that Madison was more tenaciously committed than to any of the rest, and it was probably for this reason that he tried at first to underplay its importance. His proposal was that all ships bringing goods of any kind into American ports be taxed according to tonnage, and that such taxes be levied upon three categories of vessels. American-built and -owned ships would pay the lowest duties; ships of nations with which the United States had commercial treaties would pay a somewhat higher duty; and ships of all "other powers" would pay the highest duties of all. What this specifically meant was that, since the United States had a treaty with France and none with England, the American government would in effect be adopting a policy of systematic discrimination against British shipping in favor of French.[64]

The discriminatory features of the tonnage measure (which was eventually written up as a separate bill) did not at first provoke heated debate. Or rather, the debate was slow in coming to a focus, even when Madison made it quite clear that his principal target was Great Britain. The first outbursts of opposition, indeed, came from a minority quarter—South Carolina and Georgia—and were directed not at the discrimination between other countries and England but at any principle of discrimination, between all foreign shipping and American, which would result in higher freight charges on southern produce carried in foreign vessels. This aspect of the bill, on the other hand, found favor with most of the other members, especially those from New England, since it offered solid advantages to American shipping as well as incentives for its future growth. A thirty-cent duty per ton on ships of nations with whom the United States had treaties, a fifty-cent duty on all others, and only a six-cent duty on American ships represented a differential which, on the face of it, any American shipowner could only welcome. Even the discrimination against England was in principle hardly unreasonable. American shipping was itself already discriminated against by the British policy of excluding American vessels from the West Indies and of allowing them to carry none but American goods in the direct trade to England, and this had caused intense irritation in every shipping center on the Atlantic seaboard. The result was that Madison, arguing his case with great cogency as always, got his tonnage bill through the House by a good majority. Only a flash of outright opposition from New York and some murmurs of misgiving from New England could have foreshadowed what was to happen to the bill in the Senate.[65]

Between May 7, when the House took its vote, and June 17, when the Senate sent back its amended version of the bill with the special discriminations struck out, there had been a welling up of resistance against any policy that might provoke commercial hostilities between the United States and Great Britain. Precisely how this resistance developed is not a matter of record, but that it originated among mercantile groups in the seaport cities—probably first among those in New York—seems fairly clear. It represented the first serious impasse of principle to appear within the new government, one upon which, as it turned out, no compromise was possible, and in the face of which one side or the other would have to back down. Twice the House, as Madison labored to prevent his votes from slipping away, refused the Senate's amendments, while the Senate as adamantly refused to recede from them. Even as the House gave in, which it finally did on July 1, Madison, normally the conciliator, took the result in stubborn bad grace and made it clear that he would try again as soon as the chance arose.[66]

Madison's position, which he insisted was one involving "the common good" and "the vindication and support of our national interest," certainly had a historical basis. There was a kind of self-evidence in the assumption that freeing America's commercial life from the arbitrary pleasure of Great Britain had been one of the objects of the Revolution, and that keeping it so should be the constant care of the new federal government. Nor could there be any better perspective from which to view the arbitrary side of British mercantile practice than the experience of Virginia, more or less passively dependent as its planters had been for decades upon an outsider class of Scottish middlemen. These convictions and this experience led to one clear version of what form national policy should take, and one way, indeed, of visualizing the whole national future. But it was not necessarily the only version, or the only way. In the northern cities, where commercial relationships with the mother country had historically been direct rather than indirect, intricate and predictable rather than simple and arbitrary, a new era of well-being had by 1789 already begun. Old connections had been reknit, new ones had been formed, and expectations were justifiably on the rise. Herein were the makings of a variant version of "the common good" and the "national interest," and a consequent reluctance to take steps that might conceivably threaten them. Herein also were the makings in embryo of a conflict not simply of interest but of principle.

An incipient ideological divergence, involving in its simplest form the question of American behavior toward foreign powers, had made its appearance. It would, in the course of its growth, acquire a variety of forms, of which the original was but one, and embrace any number of aspects of the national life.

Madison's plan of discrimination on tonnage, implying as it did a distinct line of policy in foreign relations, was no spur-of-the-moment inspiration. It was rather the product of reflections and experience that went back five years or more, to the time when Madison's close friend Thomas Jefferson first went to Europe in 1784 to negotiate commercial treaties for the Confederation. Jefferson, who had gone to join Adams and Franklin as a member of a commission formed for that purpose, had then succeeded Franklin as United States minister to France, and would remain at that post until September 1789. His major concern all during this period had been commerce, and he had not had an easy time of it. In proportion to the hopes he had entertained and the considerable efforts he had expended, Jefferson's achievements had been minimal. And yet in the course of his stay he developed a number of very strong opinions about the nature of commerce, and on the uses to which commerce ought to be put as an instrument of national policy.[67]

The gross fact upon which everything had to turn was the virtual monopoly of American trade possessed by Great Britain. Meanwhile, within this orbit of trading relationships, many limits had now been placed upon the Americans' freedom of action by England's reimposition of the old navigation system. Under that system they had once enjoyed many advantages as English colonials, but it applied to them now as citizens of a foreign nation, and was full of odious restrictions. The principal ones were their exclusion from the lucrative West Indies trade and the limitation of their direct trade with England to goods produced in America. During the peace negotiations there had been a moment when the liberal-minded Earl of Shelburne considered a kind of commercial union, under which the shipping of each country would be accorded special privileges by the other. Shelburne himself, however, came to realize that his government would never tolerate such an arrangement, and nothing came of it. The British attitude was made only too clear by the Earl of Sheffield in his *Observations on the Commerce of the United States,* published in 1783. There was no reason, Sheffield argued, for England to grant any particular concessions to American trade; there was, indeed, every reason for not doing so. Great Britain already had as much of the American states' trade as her interest required, and now without the expense of governing them. The Americans' interest, moreover, was well enough served in their own view that they would continue to carry on the bulk of their trade with England whether their government liked it or not. Given the credit facilities extended in London and available nowhere else, and given the superior development of British manufacturing and the cheapness and quality of British goods, they had no choice. On the other hand, England would be acting directly contrary to her own interest in granting the Americans access to the West Indies. Allowing them thus to expand their shipbuilding and carrying trade would be at the direct expense of British merchants, British shipowners, and—in view of the inducements to British seamen—the British navy. "The Navigation act, the basis of our great power at sea," Sheffield insisted, "gave us the trade of the world: if we alter that act, by permitting any state to trade with our islands, or by suffering any state to bring into this country any produce but its own, we desert the Navigation act, and sacrifice the marine of England." With the British Order in Council of July 1783, whereby the principles of the Navigation Act were reaffirmed in all their vigor, the British government in effect followed Sheffield's advice.[68]

Dealing directly with England in an effort to work out mutual arrangements was no part of Jefferson's plan or wish. His great vision was that of a world in which America's dependence on a hostile power might be ended altogether, and his great instrument was to be the attractions of American trade to the other nations of Europe. A series of commercial treaties with them would in effect create a free-trade community which Great Britain could no longer monopolize, and in the presence of which she would be forced to alter her policies. Unhappily, the commission's efforts to conclude such treaties proved almost wholly fruitless. Most countries were indifferent to them; the others did not have colonial possessions; and none was in the least willing to grant special privileges beyond the "most favored nation" formula, which in the Europe of the eighteenth century meant very little in the way of real advantages. When the commission's term expired, its members had next to nothing to show for their work.

Jefferson's next thought, as he took up his new duties at Paris in May 1785, was to concentrate upon France. He reasoned that if free trade was for the moment out of the question, then the next best thing would be to divert as much American trade as possible away from America's chief enemy to America's chief ally. The ministry of Vergennes, which had its enlightened side, was not unreceptive to Jefferson's argument that the French must provide markets for American goods if they expected Americans to buy French goods, that French merchants ought to be more flexible in their willingness to extend credit, and that French manufacturing ought to adjust to the tastes and requirements of the American market. The negotiations did, indeed, achieve some successes. The market for whale oil was granted exclusively to the American fisheries, and a number of French mercantile firms were persuaded to import quantities of Georgia and Carolina rice. The tobacco trade to France from America had been engrossed by monopolies in both countries, and although nothing could be done about the monopoly held by the Farmers-General on the importation and sale of tobacco in France, the one that had been granted to Robert Morris on the sale of tobacco from America to France was dissolved. Through these and a number of lesser concessions, the French market by 1789 was open to American trade—at least in theory—to a greater degree than ever before.

Yet none of this could make much of an imprint on the real patterns of American trade, with either France or Great Britain. That with France remained about the same as it had been, whereas in England a cycle of unprecedented expansion in manufacturing, both in efficiency and in quantity of output, pointed to an even greater volume of exports, to America as well as elsewhere, than had been the case before. Indeed, British success in the American market had been and would continue to be the product of a series of advantages that were irresistible. They included a detailed knowledge of that market based on long experience; a close network of trading relationships; and a generous reservoir of credit, for which those very elements of knowledge and experience gave the security. They included, moreover, a vast trading center at London, an emporium in which an American merchant's agent could exercise a wide range of choice in making up return cargoes as well as disposing of those his ships had brought in. They included, finally, the most advanced manufacturing techniques in Europe. The result was that the bulk of the hardware, cutlery, iron and steel manufactures of all kinds, earthenware, glassware, and woolens used by Americans was British-made, and 87 percent of America's import trade in manufactures between 1787 and 1790 was done with Great Britain.[69]

By contrast, America's trading relationships with France were simple, sketchy, and few. They were clouded with mutual suspicions and ignorance, and there was little of substance—beyond a certain benevolent courtesy in high places—on which they might be nourished. Of what there was, the Yankees had all the better of it. Neither the state of French manufacturing, the mentality of the French bourgeoisie, nor the condition of the French economy as a whole could provide the least basis for theorizing that France was America's "natural" trading partner, or even that France might become, in the foreseeable future, a major commercial power. For one thing, the French had had very limited experience with the American market, almost all of it bad. The increased numbers of French cargoes coming into American ports immediately after the Revolution represented, for the most part, a disaster to their owners, who had very little knowledge of the people they hoped would buy them. Made up ineptly and with considerable guesswork, they consisted of products that were either badly packed, inappropriate to the season, unsuited to the tastes of the public, or else inferior to similar goods furnished cheaper and better by the British. Unable or unwilling to extend credit, requiring quick payment, in constant fear of being cheated, and having few established connections, the owners—or rather the ship captains or supercargoes they often used as their agents—in case after case were constrained to dispose of these lots hastily and at a loss in order to get rid of them at all. The terms of trade, moreover, heavily favored the Americans. The French had opened several of their West Indies ports in 1784, and American trade with them was far greater than with metropolitan France, where the imbalance was as much as five or six to one. Basically, Americans were not interested in French goods. Between 1784 and 1790 their imports from France amounted to no more than a twentieth of those they took from England. They consisted mainly of luxury items, such as brandies, wines, Mediterranean fruits, and women's finery. As for the balances earned on American products sold to France, they would almost invariably be taken straight to England, and spent for English manufactures.[70]

Nor was there much encouragement for French manufacturing to be roused from its sluggish inefficiency, in view of France's antiquated structure of internal tariffs, export duties, and excise taxes, which meant that French products had to compete with the burden of roughly a 15 percent surcharge already upon them. Thus when the royal ministers in a burst of misguided enlightenment concluded a limited free-trade agreement with England in 1786, the results were calamitous.

As they ought to have foreseen, their own manufacturers were drowned in the ensuing flood of British goods. The final element that effectively prevented the formation of external trading patterns in any way comparable to those of Great Britain was the conservatism of the French merchant class itself. Its mentality tended more toward that of the *rentier* than of the *entrepreneur,* concerned mainly with protecting and stabilizing what they already had rather than with reaching out for new fields of enterprise. The chambers of commerce in the port cities of France accordingly resisted concessions to American trade at every turn, since such concessions could only invade and disrupt in some way their own engrossment of France's internal market.[71]

Thus the climate in which Jefferson conducted his talks with French ministers and aristocratic intellectuals in the years just before the French Revolution had about it a certain benevolent mistiness. The French were certainly well disposed, though somewhat dilettantish, being not much attuned to the realities of French economic life. The Physiocrats, under whose influence the 1786 Eden Treaty with England was concluded, were so doctrinaire in their attachment to free-trade theories that they had little idea what a bad bargain they were making. With regard to America, it was thought by Lafayette, Condorcet, and Jefferson's other friends that expanded trade relations would be an excellent thing. But they never appreciated that the benefits could in no sense be really mutual. Jefferson did have some success in securing entree to French markets not previously open, but the Americans in practice failed to reciprocate. They tended to spend their money not in France but in England, and for things they could get nowhere else. Jefferson did as the rest. Once, having looked vainly all over Paris for oil lamps of a model lately invented, he found just what he wanted on a visit to England. Another time, he apologized somewhat helplessly to Lafayette for buying English harness:

> The reason for my importing harness from England is a very obvious one. They are plated, and plated harness is not made at all in France as far as I have learnt. It is not from a love of the English but a love of myself that I sometimes find myself obliged to buy their manufactures.[72]

In any event, neither Jefferson nor the Ministry had much contact with the French bourgeoisie, and judging from what they did, the latter's complaints must never have seemed fully real to them. The time was shortly to come when the bourgeoisie would itself have something to say in the councils of state, whereupon this official good will on questions of commerce would come to an abrupt end. With the French Revolution and the ascendancy of the Jacobins, there would be no more talk of free trade. The official policy would thenceforth be one of rigid economic nationalism.[73]

In the America of the mid-1780s, languishing in depression, resentment against England for reimposing the Navigation Act was fairly general. Alexander Hamilton wrote of retaliation. The merchants of Boston in 1785 voted to "do all in our power" to prevent further commercial relations with British agents resident in that city. John Adams thought it might be necessary for Americans to have their own navigation act. The correspondence of Jefferson and Madison all during the Confederation period bristles with hatred of England and all things British. And yet united in resentment as most of them were, there was an underlying divergence. From the viewpoint of New York and New England, of Hamilton and Adams, the principal object of policy was to persuade England to ease and modify. For Jefferson and Madison on the other hand, the object, ideally, was nothing short of detaching America altogether from commercial dependence on Great Britain.[74]

By the summer of 1789 the divergence was more or less in the open. Prosperity had returned, American traders were discovering new outlets, and expectations were on the rise. Specie balances for use in the direct trade with England were being replenished to the point where it was once more the benefits, rather than the constraints, of that trade that seemed to make the greater difference. The first ventures in the China trade had already begun, and increasing numbers of American vessels were appearing in the Russian ports of the Baltic. More important, the British West Indies, though closed by law, had in fact again become remarkably accessible to enterprising American shippers. With the connivance of local planters, governors, and customs officials, through forged papers and other stratagems, virtually regularized, the wants of the sugar islands were being almost as well supplied as ever by 1789, despite all the efforts of Nelson's squadron on the Caribbean station. And finally, Jefferson's own work in France, influencing as it did the widening of American privileges in the French islands, contributed in spite of itself to the same overall end, the revival and renewed prosperity of Anglo-American commerce. Thus although the same bellicose formulas of a few years before were still being voiced in 1789, it was no longer with quite the same depth of conviction. "I feel the necessity of having a more equal and reputable trade with the British," wrote the Boston merchant Stephen Higginson to John Adams, "but I am not yet satisfied that we can either compel or conciliate them to more reciprocal terms—the latter however at present is, in my mind, more eligible and promising."[75]

When James Madison, with his tonnage proposals in the spring of 1789, declared himself for discrimination against Great Britain, he offered several leading arguments for it. The channels through which American commerce with Great Britain flowed were "artificial," and gave that country "a much greater proportion of our trade than she is naturally entitled to." Moreover, the British needed our trade more than we needed theirs; most of the manufactures presently being imported from them would soon be produced in the United States. And finally, after reciting the various ways in which American commerce was being favorably regarded by France, Madison declared that "our policy . . . ought to be calculated to give it that impulse which nature directs." Senator Maclay remarked that Madison was thought to have "labored the whole business of discrimination in order to pay court to the French nation through Mr. Jefferson, our Minister to Paris."[76]

Madison was challenged by Representative John Laurance, a merchant of New York City, who insisted that such a policy could only lead to ruinous commercial warfare, that there was no need for it, that the United States could better achieve its ends by moderation, and that Great Britain had far greater capacity to injure

America than America to injure her. Still, the hostile response was slow in crystallizing, and Madison's position was upheld in the House. Fisher Ames of Massachusetts was beginning to have some misgivings about Madison. "Very much Frenchified in his politics," he noted on May 3, and two weeks later: "I think him a good man and an able man, but he has rather too much theory, and wants that discretion which men of business commonly have."[77]

By the time the tonnage bill reached the Senate, the mercantile community had taken alarm. Their predictions of the evils to which discrimination might lead seem to have been convincingly impressed upon leading senators, inasmuch as the Senate moved with virtual unanimity to strike that feature from the bill. When it passed in final form on September 19, the duty had been fixed at six cents a ton on American shipping and fifty cents on that of all other countries, regardless of whether they had commercial treaties with the United States. Ames, who meanwhile had made up his own mind, was much relieved. "The Senate . . . as if designated by Providence to keep rash and frolicsome brats out of the fire, have demolished the absurd, impolitic, mad discrimination of foreigners in alliance from other foreigners."[78]

The issue was thus laid to one side, but only temporarily. It would remain in some form to shape and to polarize virtually every other theme in American political life for the next twenty-five years.

7

Legitimacy Ratified

The first session of the First Congress was adjourned on September 29, 1789. Any tensions which may have arisen in the course of it—and which could not yet be said to have produced serious divisions or factions—were thereupon dissipated. Until the first Monday in January, the national government had in effect reverted to the Executive. Washington, though ever a grave and cautious man, could have much reason for satisfaction, and almost for the first time felt he could afford to breathe a little. But he was also curious to know whether his own guarded optimism as to the success so far of the new government was justified by the spirit and sentiment of the country. He thereupon decided to make a personal sounding, in the form of a visit to New England. Six months before, his reception on the inaugural trip from Mount Vernon to New York had been an overwhelming expression of favorable expectations, of confidence in the future. A similar trip now would be to some degree a test of things already done. He departed from New York on October 15, and was gone about a month.

The results were all Washington could have wished. As before, there were receptions, parades, dinners, and joyous throngs of citizens everywhere. Perhaps the climax came with the welcome he was given at Cambridge, where he had first taken command of the Continental Army in 1775, and in Boston, where decorated arches commemorated the relief of that city in 1776. Washington's diary, normally very dull, almost comes to life as the delighted President notes the cheering, the music, and the "vast concourse of people." He was carrying the government in person into New England—where he had not as yet been in his presidential capacity—and most particularly into Massachusetts, the key not only to New England but to so much else that concerned the well-being of the new Republic.[79] (A similar visit to Rhode Island the following spring—that state having by then finally ratified the Constitution—would produce similar results.)

After his New England tour, and as he prepared to do business with the returning Congress early in the new year of 1790, Washington for the first time in many weeks found enough leisure to write a lengthy private letter. It was addressed to Catharine Macaulay Graham, an Englishwoman who had once been a guest at Mount Vernon. He touched on various subjects, but the central theme— his satisfaction over the events of the year just past—was almost luminous.

> That the government, though not absolutely perfect, is one of the best in the world, I have little doubt. . . . It was indeed next to a miracle that there should have been so much unanimity, in points of such importance, among such a number of Citizens, so widely scattered, and so different in their habits in many respects as the Americans were. Nor are the growing unanimity and encreasing goodwill of the Citizens to the Government less remarkable than favorable circumstances. So far as we have gone with the new Government (and it is completely organized and in operation) we have had greater reason than the most sanguine could expect to be satisfied with its success.[80]

The tone, for the opening of the year 1790, was undoubtedly justified. But Washington would never again, in a comparable buoyancy of spirit, write another such letter.

Finance and Ideology

Of all the events that shaped the political life of the new republic in its earliest years, none was more central than the massive personal and political enmity, classic in the annals of American history, which developed in the course of the 1790s between Alexander Hamilton and Thomas Jefferson. The struggle ensuing from it derives its classic proportions from classic circumstances. It was in one sense personal, quickly progressing from caution to suspicion, and then to a mutual hatred that gave little quarter, but it mattered greatly that this hatred was one subsisting between the two highest officers of Washington's government. It would in time attach to itself two rival hosts of followers and form the basis for two political parties professing two rival sets of principles. The character and quality of national life in the 1790s are thus not to be understood aside from the warfare of Hamiltonian Federalists and Jeffersonian Republicans. Worth noting, however, is that the groundwork for Jefferson's side of it was laid not by Jefferson himself, but by his friend and fellow Virginian, James Madison. It is to James Madison's estrangement from *his* friend, Alexander Hamilton, that one must go as a first step in plumbing the political passions of the 1790s.

To contemporaries, the Hamilton-Madison rupture and its consequences would not have seemed predictable in any obvious way, though historians in long retrospect have offered rationalizations which make it appear as part of a certain unerring drift. The Federalist-Republican polarity which was the outcome of that rupture has been seen on one level as the expression of a basic conflict between the interests of commerce and money on the one hand, and of agriculture on the other. On another level, it seems to range the supporters of a powerful national government against those of state rights. And on still another, the forces in conflict are no less than those of elitism and those of an incipient democracy. None of these versions is wrong; each provides a way of understanding the problem at long range. And yet on a more immediate and more human level, they do not begin to account for the explosion which shattered a friendship between two men whose ideas and interests, in the things that mattered most to them, had been at one time harmonious.

What sets the men of this generation apart from those of any other in American history is that their every response to virtually every question of a public nature was conditioned by their having just been through a revolution. We have long since turned our revolutionaries into "Founding Fathers," a title which may be the real measure of their success. But such an ascription is also a measure of how difficult it has become to see their motivations in terms that are psychologically believable, or to imagine these "Fathers" as anything but "rational." Any view we take of these men and their actions must allow for the revolutionary's volatile sense that his very next step, or anyone else's in the historical movement which he has had a part in fashioning, could affect the destiny of future generations.

A by-product of the revolutionary movement had been a republican ideology. But in imposing an ideological order on all matters concerning government, society, liberty, and authority there emerged—especially for those at the center of things—an intensely personal side. With the enlargement of a man's view of the world came an enlargement in his own consciousness of the difference *he* made in his power to characterize that world, to impress upon others that it operated in such and such a way, and to prescribe that its health and welfare be sought in this direction rather than that. There was thus a sense in which the personal attributes of leading men, their thoughts and actions as individuals, and the everyday relations between them, had more than a casual bearing on the society which they were in the act of re-creating. Their commitment to that society was not limited to mechanical categories of "interest." It was total: they had identified their very personalities with a particular understanding of it, and thus a challenge to that understanding would be a fundamental challenge to *them.*

The energies that could be generated in such a setting were prodigious, as the careers of some of these men clearly show. Commitments formed in the Revolution were reinforced and intensified by the experience of remodeling the government once more, four years after the Revolution was over, and of persuading the country to ratify what they had done. Throughout all this, the necessity of "first things first" had maintained a certain singleness of purpose and a rough ideological unity. But once the new government was in being and its legitimacy established, a new kind of ideological problem, hitherto not of the first urgency, became insistent. The Revolution had made the United States republican, and now it had been determined that these states were no longer a republican confederation, but a republican nation. But what else? Beyond the words of the Constitution and the republican values represented by General Washington, what was to be its character? At the beginning of 1790, the answer still lay very much in the future. Now that it lies in the past, we find it hard to imagine how heavily this question could have weighed upon the leaders of the time.

A primary stress in the emotional and ideological life of new nations in the twentieth century has been the problem of national self-definition. What sort of face, or character, the nation is to exhibit to the rest of the world; in what manner its economic life should be organized, how extensively and with what degree of independence; the quality of its ties with other nations; and above all, the way in which it defines itself with reference to the former mother country: such questions have generated tensions and even upheavals in the world of today that have seemingly rested on no "rational" basis. Problems of national economy have been addressed by some societies in ways that appear to bear only indirectly upon their true material interests. The bitterest of ideological factionalism has erupted over differences in cultural orientation which to outsiders seem almost unreal.[1] Like most other nations founded upon revolution, America did not escape such strains. It was in fact no less a problem than this that wrecked the personal and political relations between James Madison and Alexander Hamilton.

I

James Madison: The Political Economy of Anglophobia

From the most constructive period of Madison's career, that spanning roughly the decade between 1780 and 1790, there remains a picture of the man that has become more or less traditional. It is the picture of the modest conciliator, the statesman of compromise. James Madison comes to us as the man of sagacity and intelligence, of great learning in the realms of history and political science, who nevertheless does not insist upon himself. He is the quiet builder, mindful of other men's ideas and feelings, willing both to channel their energies and to allow them the credit. He is self-effacing, resourceful, and tireless, his accomplishments being due in no small part simply to his willingness to remain at work long after others had gone to bed. It is thus James Madison who, almost in spite of himself, emerges as the chief architect of the United States Constitution.

There is only one aspect of this picture that does not belong. But add a touch or two, and even with all the rest remaining the whole effect is somehow altered. James Madison was not really a compromiser. He was a revolutionary; his ideological presuppositions, down deep, were immovable; despite all appearances to the contrary, he was one of the most stubborn and willful men of his time. In what to him was fundamental, he was quietly, implacably determined to have his way.

From the present distance, one penetrates the essential Madison just so far. But watching him always with reference to certain fixed points in his personality and career does help us around some of the paradoxes. Probably the most important of such points is the man's almost paralyzing shyness. All his other attributes—some of them quite incongruous, such as his ambition, his talent, his tenacity, and his intellectual authority—had somehow to be arranged about and adjusted to this, in the course of his development and growth. This process of psychic adjustment had some intriguing by-products. He managed to have his talents recognized at an early age, even though it was not until he was thirty that he could bring himself to take the floor at a public gathering. Personal references in his correspondence are maddeningly few, and when in later life he arranged his papers for eventual publication (not to occur until after his death), he appears to have systematically suppressed virtually everything of a "private" nature, though it is not likely that such material had ever really abounded in the first place. For this and other reasons, James Madison's humanity is harder to reconstruct than that of any comparable leader of his time.

Ideas were of consuming importance to him, and some of the most striking ones in the history of American constitutional thought are his. But pride of authorship in the ordinary sense was something he learned to renounce very early, if indeed he ever had it. The cause, the idea, was the vital thing, and time after time he would attribute an origin to someone else rather than claim it for himself, which made for a special kind of delicacy in a man not otherwise given to large gestures of open generosity. Anonymity was far more comfortable than the glare of the limelight. "Madison," as one writer has put it, "was made small enough (five foot six) and sufficiently diffident as not to excite the suspicion of men that he would be in competition with them for anything. . . ."[2] He could go to some lengths to assist in the saving of face, and he had a well-developed sense of how to achieve the measures he sought without making other men angry. And yet this flexibility, as we shall see, was hardly unlimited. It must in any case be remembered that everything he did was done by a man both timid *and* stubborn.

In addition to his extreme personal diffidence, there is a related element in the *modus operandi* of James Madison that is important for an understanding of his career as a whole. Unprepared to confront his environment alone, through direct force of personality—as many men of his time, such as Patrick Henry, could and did do—James Madison always functioned, when he did so effectively, under some kind of "cover." As a rule it was only in the setting of the committee, rather than that of the forum, that he could have an operative public self. The rule had few exceptions. Even the Constitutional Convention, which was the peak point of Madison's career, was in many ways a kind of closed committee, whose actual proceedings were not made public for more than fifty years and then only when he himself chose to do it. Then there was another form of "cover" that Madison maintained in constant repair. He would enter upon no question of policy or law without the most massive prior preparation, which meant that he would almost always know at least twice as much about it as anyone else present. So it is not so much the image of a man, but of the man's knowledge and intelligence with a life of their own, that has left its impress upon history. The "cover" principle even operated, in an odd sort of way, in the sphere of his social relations. Depending on the witness, accounts of Madison's social presence could vary between the most perplexing extremes. One might find him charming; another could think him a "gloomy stiff creature." It was Margaret Bayard Smith who may have hit it closest: "this entertaining, interesting and communicative personage, had a single stranger or indifferent person been present, would have been mute, cold and repulsive."[3]

James Madison was born in 1751 and grew up at Montpelier, a plantation in the Virginia piedmont near the Rapidan, an upper branch of the Rappahannock. Of his forbears he wrote, "They were planters and among the respectable though not the most opulent class." Nevertheless his father, Colonel James Madison—county lieutenant, justice of the peace, large landowner, and vestryman of St. Thomas Parish—was probably the most important man in Orange County. Colonel Madison, who did not have all the learning he would have liked, was determined that his son should receive the best education available. James junior attended a preparatory school at Dunkirk in King and Queen County conducted by the able Scottish pedagogue Donald Robertson. There, and later through a season of tutoring at home, he studied Latin, Greek, French, Spanish, logic, mathematics, and geography, and developed an interest in political philosophy through the reading of Montesquieu and Locke. He entered the College of New Jersey at Princeton in 1769 and completed the course of four years in a little over two. He received the bachelor's degree in September 1771.[4]

Princeton, in addition to its high intellectual élan during the years Madison attended, was already penetrated by an all-but-open republicanism, and the college vibrated with revolutionary sentiments as time went on. Such sentiments were shared, and even abetted, by the president. John Witherspoon was a burly, vigorous, and irrepressible Presbyterian cleric recently arrived from Scotland, where the most advanced ideas of the age in moral and political philosophy were being generated. "The Doctor," as Witherspoon was fondly known to his students, would himself be a signer of the Declaration of Independence and a member of the Continental Congress. In 1770, when the merchants of New York went back on their agreement to maintain non-importation, a copy of their self-justifying letter to the Philadelphia merchants was burned at Princeton in the college yard by the public hangman, hired for the purpose by the students, "all of them appearing in their black Gowns & the bell Tolling."[5]

Though both law and theology were among Madison's many intellectual interests, neither the bar nor the ministry seems ever to have been seriously considered by him as a career, in view of his weak voice and personal shyness. Of the latter failing he was apparently quite conscious, judging from the frequent entries in his youthful commonplace book on timid men and their behavior, culled from the maxims of Cardinal de Retz and others. At Princeton he was among the founding members of the American Whig Society. Little is known of the early activities and purposes of American Whig and its rival society, Cliosophic, except for the so-called paper wars between them, but in these James Madison first found a vehicle of public expression which did not constrain him. Members of each society wrote lampooning ditties about those of the other; these satires would then be read in open hall by a designated spokesman before the entire student body, while the actual authors—notable among whom was Madison—remained anonymous. Madison's verses were a bit on the ribald side, which somewhat relieves the picture we have inherited of him as a man of no wit. Among Madison's fellow Whigs were Hugh Henry Brackenridge, William Bradford, and Philip Freneau; Aaron Burr was a Clio.[6] At commencement, each graduate was expected to deliver an oration. Madison, though a shining student and well enough at the time, could not do it, and was excused. Upon his return home he suffered a breakdown in the form of epileptoid hysteria, an ailment connected with "overstudy, daydreaming, hypochondria and a sense of physical inferiority," and among whose victims, as Breuer and Freud later wrote, "one may meet persons of the clearest intellects, the strongest wills, greatest principles, and of the subtlest minds." For a time Madison kept his friend Bradford in a state of some alarm with letters gloomily predicting his own early death, but seems to have recovered himself through exercise and by temporarily easing up on his reading. Within a year he was back in health.[7]

Early in 1774 five or six Baptists were jailed in Culpeper County for preaching without licenses, and this drew from James Madison an exceptional flare-up of feeling, plus his first words and acts of a public nature. "I have neither patience to hear talk or think of any thing relative to this matter," he wrote to Bradford, "for I have squabbled and scolded abused and ridiculed so long about it, to so little purpose that I am without common patience." It is not clear precisely what he did, but he seems to have exerted some influence on behalf of the dissenters, and the Baptists were to support him in his home district from that time on. The approach of the Revolution in effect opened to the twenty-three-year-old Madison his true career. "On the commencement of the dispute with Great Britain," he later wrote in his "Autobiography" (characteristically referring to himself in the third person), "he entered with the prevailing zeal into the American Cause. . . ." This seems to have occurred to some extent under his father's aegis. At the meeting of freeholders which chose James junior as a member of the Orange County Committee of Safety in 1774, Colonel Madison was elected chairman. Father and son were likewise elected to the Convention of 1776 which was to devise a new government for Virginia. During the adoption of the Declaration of Rights at that convention, the young man once again put himself on record for religious liberty. In committee, he succeeded in having George Mason's article on that point amended from a guarantee of "toleration" to the more ample "free exercise" of religion. He was defeated for a seat in the newly constituted House of Delegates, presumably because he refused to treat the voters to liquor. But his talents were already sufficiently evident to the members of the House that they elected him to the Council of State, where he served under the first two elected Governors of Virginia, Patrick Henry and Thomas Jefferson. Late in 1779 he was chosen to go to the Continental Congress, where he remained until October 1783. By the time he left, his biographer says, he had made himself "the acknowledged leader in every activity that bulwarked independence and pointed toward a strong, firm national union of the states."[8]

Madison's preeminence in Congress came not primarily from speechmaking but from his tireless committee work and the writing of letters, instructions, and reports. He was directly concerned with a range of business that included defense, military finance, revenue, commerce, diplomacy, and western lands. The very intensity with which he committed himself to this work, rarely missing a day's session, made it virtually inevitable that he should also commit himself in the course of it to a broad continental view of the Revolution which had little room for narrow sectional or local interests. It was during this period that he first met Alexander Hamilton, who entered Congress in 1782. The two saw eye to eye on almost everything, and quickly became friends and allies.

Side by side with Madison's nationalism grew a bitterness toward England which was greatly intensified by the British campaign in the South. "Negroes, Horses, Tobacco &c," he wrote to Philip Mazzei, "not the standards and arms of their antagonists, are the trophies which display their success." His reaction to these depredations, says Irving Brant, "deepened an Anglophobia which ruled his mind and emotions for years to come." Madison's mind, whose judicious and rational side may be the more prominent, is nevertheless not at all comprehensible unless this anglophobia is seen as a significant force in its workings.[9]

Still, it is principally to Madison's nationalism that one looks for the energy which propelled his actions from the end of the Revolution through the framing and ratification of the Federal Constitution—through two more terms in the Virginia Assembly, membership in the abortive Annapolis Convention, a return to Congress, a seat at Philadelphia in 1787, and another in the ratifying convention of Virginia in 1788.

Madison's great contribution to the Philadelphia Convention consisted not of compromises—these were for the most part worked out by others—but rather of a master theory and a master plan. The theory—to be known as "Federalism"—was one which rationalized a large republic in the face of the prevailing idea that only small ones could function; it was also one which justified a strong central government in the face of fears in the several states that central power meant tyranny. The plan—to be known as the "Virginia Plan"—specified a series of key arrangements which to Madison were indispensable if Federalism was to work. Most of them were enacted, thanks in great part to the persistence of Madison himself. Two of them, however, were not, despite Madison's every effort to save them. Stubbornly opposed to state encroachments on national power, he resisted state equality in either branch of the national legislature. When the great compromise was reported whereby representation in the lower house was made proportionate to population and that in the Senate made equal, Madison, according to his own words, "was not only fixed in his opposition to the report of the committee but was prepared for any event that might follow a negative of it."[10] It was only with deep disgust that he finally gave in. The other provision he had his heart set on but lost was a sweeping veto by the national government on all state laws. The authority of the federal judiciary was not in his view an adequate substitute. Yet most of Madison's views on national supremacy were in fact embodied in the completed Constitution, even though the powers of the national government would have been still greater if he had fully had his way.

The following year he and Hamilton, with the assistance of John Jay, defended the work of the Convention and the logic of the Constitution in *The Federalist*. In Madison's case it was logical that the thoughts that went into these papers, and into the work he had done at Philadelphia, should have received a fair portion of their shape from Madison's prior intellectual experience.

The Princeton of Madison's day furnished nine delegates to the Federal Convention—more than any other college, and one more than the combined total of Princeton's two closest competitors.[11] For Madison the choice of Princeton, rather than the more convenient William and Mary, was itself that of an at-least-partially prepared mind. Madison's initial revolutionary impulses had already taken the form of strong opposition to the Anglican establishment in Virginia and to the movement in England for sending a bishop to America. Though the Madisons themselves were Anglicans, both father and son seem to have been suspicious enough of Church of England influence at William and Mary that they preferred Presbyterian Princeton, already known for libertarian sentiments and already "talking as if she was to be a bulwark against Episcopacy." Religious liberty was insisted upon there, and the subject was frequently debated. A major premise of Madison's Federalist Number 10 — that a multiplicity of interests may function as a guarantee of political stability and against majority despotism — had grown very logically out of Madison's earliest responses to the ecclesiastical situation in Virginia and to his own peculiar determination all through the 1770s and 1780s to pull down the Anglican Church's privileged position there. "If the Church of England had been the established and general Religion in all the Northern Colonies as it has been among us here," he wrote to William Bradford early in 1774, ". . . it is clear to me that slavery and Subjection might and would have been gradually insinuated among us." The shape of the thought is that of Voltaire, whom Madison and his fellow-students read at Princeton. He was fond of quoting Voltaire's quip that if only one sect were allowed in England, "despotism might be apprehended; if two only, they would seek to cut each other's throats; but as there are at least thirty, they live together in peace and happiness."[12]

Enlightenment thought was accessible not only at Princeton but at colleges and academies everywhere in the colonies: the works of Locke and Montesquieu, Vattel and Burlamaqui, even Rousseau and Voltaire, were more or less basic equipment for anyone intellectually concerned with public questions. But the setting at Princeton still seems to have contained a certain extra something, and many writers have tried to account for the special vitality of that setting during the period at which James Madison and his contemporaries studied there. Various elements appear to have intersected in a felicitous way to produce it. The prestige of the college had risen vastly with the trustees' success in persuading the distinguished Witherspoon to take over its leadership, and the excitement generated by Witherspoon's vigorous reorganizing was still new when the young Madison first arrived less than a year later.[13]

It was of considerable importance, moreover, that Witherspoon was fresh from Scotland and that Edinburgh, where he had been trained, was then the most vital intellectual center of the English-speaking world. The English universities of that same period, placidly mired under Establishment control and whose chief professional product was candidates for the Anglican clergy, were moribund. The Scottish universities, on the other hand, were full of energy. It was energy of a contentious and restless sort, and the restlessness was a feature of Scottish society as a whole, in which there were many strains. For a very poor country, the Union of 1707 had opened the way for an economic development which would at least be complementary to, rather than competitive with, that of England, but the advance of prosperity that resulted from it was by no means quickly or evenly achieved. Meanwhile Scots showed themselves willing to talk, at least, about remedies for almost anything. They both considered and achieved reforms in land tenure and agriculture, developed Scottish commerce, and made scientific advances in industry. They discussed electoral reform endlessly, though with fewer results. Even the frequent spasms of emigration (mostly to America) and the Jacobite rebellions of 1715 and 1745 reflected tensions that were salutary as well as disruptive. There was great popular enthusiasm for education. An act of 1696 had provided for the establishment of a school in every parish, as a result of which the Scots in the eighteenth century developed a better system of education than that of any country in Europe. Scottish boys with talent but no money could find their way into the universities to an extent unthinkable in England. The universities themselves catered to a range of intense professional ambition, in public law, science, and medicine as well as theology, and one of their unique features was unofficial student debating societies to whose meetings professors came only on invitation, and in which contention was heated and vigorous. Moreover, the cultural tension between England and Scotland, replete with both attractions and repulsions, imparted still another special element to Scottish intellectual life. On the one hand, English dissenters and nonconformists were welcome at Glasgow and Edinburgh but not at Oxford and Cambridge; on the other hand, the Scot who ventured into the literary world of London was never allowed to forget his provincialism. In conservative eighteenth-century England, the mentality of the outsider—of opposition, of criticism, of reform, of the "Country party"—had few formal or stable vehicles of expression. In Scotland, all this was more or less institutionalized in the universities.[14]

Such, in short, was the setting of the "Scottish Renaissance" of the eighteenth century. It produced a formidable group of luminaries: David Hume, Adam Smith, Francis Hutcheson, Thomas Reid, Adam Ferguson, John Miller, William Robertson, and Lord Kames. They were contemporaries, all knew each other, and all were known to John Witherspoon by the time he left Scotland in 1768 to take up his new station in America.

What Witherspoon gave to his students, and what made him the greatest teacher of his day in America, did not primarily consist in creating bonds of discipleship. He did something better; he brought them the news of ideas, a good many of which, as it happened, he had little use for. In their own management of ideas, however, Witherspoon by his personal example encouraged them, almost in spite of himself, to be selective. Intellectually he was pugnacious, dogmatic, and arbitrary. One of his favorite targets was the moral philosophy of Francis Hutcheson, which he saw as deplorably superficial. On the other hand, the political dimension of Hutcheson's moral system included the first specific discussion of the conditions under which colonies and mother country ought to separate— a doctrine which Witherspoon fully endorsed in both thought and deed. In his lectures on moral philosophy he thundered against David Hume as an "infidel"; in his lectures on eloquence Hume became "sagacious" and possessed of "great reach and accuracy of judgment in matters of criticism." It seems to have been a working principle with Witherspoon that if persons suspected a thing of being pernicious, "they ought to acquaint themselves with it; they must know what it is, if they mean to shew that it is false." His list of what the students ought to read embraces the choicest works of the Enlightenment, pernicious or otherwise. The evidence suggests, moreover, that all, or nearly all, were devoured by the young Madison.[15]

James Madison's theory of the extended republic and of the nature of political man is probably seen in its most compressed form in Federalist Number 10. The assumptions behind it, the particular spirit of inquiry implicit in it, and even certain of its leading ideas—as Douglass Adair has shown[16]—take on additional meaning when viewed with reference to the special edge given to Enlightenment thought by the Scots. The "utopianism" of Enlightenment thinking amounted to more than mere constructs of reason. It had little room, on the other hand, for assumptions such as those of Burke that governments and constitutions were the product of slow organic growth, and that changes in them could only occur in the same way. Nor, at the same time, did it have much in common with one of the central beliefs of nineteenth-century Romanticism, that all discourse on matters of government and society must take for its starting point the unique character and needs of a given people and a given national state. The political philosophers of the Enlightenment tended to be universal planners; they made endless projections into the future. But they also insisted that such projections be based not simply on reason but on experience and evidence, and herein lay both a certain freedom and a certain psychological protection. Behind an attitude of "realism"—a kind of *a priori* skepticism toward any proposed system, and a judicious pessimism about most aspects of human nature—they felt free to inquire into the ways whereby people might still predict, plan, and promote their own progress.

In Scotland this state of mind was brought to a focus probably sharper than occurred anywhere else. It has been conceded that the Scots—Hume, Smith, and Ferguson in particular—are as entitled as any to be called the founders of empirical social science. A basic premise they all shared was that the behavior of people in society occurs in patterns that are more or less uniform in virtually all times and places, and that human nature itself is not subject to very great change. A dependable science of politics and government, with principles of predictability that are applicable anywhere, is therefore possible if those principles are based on experience and observation. It further follows that the materials of experience are to be found in the study of history—the history both of ancient republics and of modern states. (It was for such reasons that John Witherspoon first introduced history to the curriculum at Princeton.) State-making and the forming of commonwealths must thus be guided by the scientific reading of history's lessons—bearing always in mind, of course, that those lessons might be read in more than one way.[17]

Douglass Adair has pictured James Madison writing the Tenth Federalist with the *Essays* of David Hume lying open on his table. There are certainly parallelisms that make this plausible. Hume in 1752 had hoped that an opportunity might some day be afforded for reducing to practice the "Idea of a Perfect Commonwealth," "either by a dissolution of some old government, or by the combination of men to form a new one, in some distant part of the world."[18] Madison in 1788 was justifying in theory, with Hume's assistance, what he had just helped to bring about in practice. Both assumed that among the worst of all perils in a free government was that of faction. A great inspiration for Madison was Hume's insistence that such perils were more easily controlled in a large republic than in a small one, despite Montesquieu's widely believed doctrine that only small states were governable as republics. Each took for granted that factions and parties— they used the terms more or less interchangeably—were evil. A faction, according to Madison, was any group, a majority or minority in the commonwealth, actuated by some "passion, or . . . interest" adverse to the public good or to the rights of the whole. The designs of a minority faction might be thwarted by the republican principle of majority rule. But where was the remedy if the faction should embrace a majority?

The causes of faction, Madison asserted, are "sown in the nature of man."[19] Like Hume, he allowed that there could be any number of occasions for forming factions and all manner of differences—of class, religion, property, and what not—on which they might be based. There has been some conjecture by modern writers as to just what sorts of divisions Madision thought most susceptible to faction. But whatever the answer may be, of one thing he seems to be certain: if factions are not formed on one pretext they will be formed on some other. Men commit aggressions upon one another because—tautology though it may be—it is in man's nature to be aggressive.[20] And yet the remedy for faction is not to remove its causes, because that is impossible; nor is it to take away the liberty without which factions cannot be formed, since to take away liberty is to take away all. Such a cure would be "worse than the disease." The true remedy is not to strike at the causes, but to control the effects.

Small republics, said Hume in the "Idea of a Perfect Commonwealth," are "frail and uncertain," because the close habitation of the people makes them more susceptible to sudden currents of popular passion and facilitates the formation of tyrannical majority factions. Hume then declared that

> in a large government, which is modelled with masterly skill, there is compass and room enough to refine the democracy, from the lower people . . . to the higher magistrates, who direct all the movements. At the same time, the parts are so distant and remote, that it is very difficult, either by intrigue, prejudice, or passion, to hurry them into any measures against the public interest.[21]

It was just such a government as this, Madison thought, that had in fact been formed in America, and it was under just such a government, he argued, that the rights of all would be most secure. In this large and extended republic, there would be a wider choice of representatives, a "greater variety of parties" which would prevent any one party's "being able to outnumber and oppress the rest"; and although "factious leaders may kindle a flame within their particular States, [they] will be unable to spread a general conflagration through the other States. . . ." And so, he concluded, "in the extent and proper structure of the Union . . . we behold a Republican remedy for the diseases most incident to Republican government."[22]

The Tenth Federalist was the first of the series that Madison wrote, and it represented the compressed essence of several years' reading and thought as developed in more diffuse form through his correspondence, in the two papers he had written prior to the Convention, "Vices of the Political System of the United States" and "On Ancient and Modern Confederacies," and in the speeches he had made in the Convention itself. Among the ways in which the Tenth Federalist has been read in modern times is as an outline for "brokerage politics," the arts of compromise, the "politics of privacy."[23] Yet in fact such a realm hardly existed in 1789, certainly not for James Madison. The philosopher, the system-builder, is not the man most likely to be found playing the role of compromise broker for other men's "private opportunities," and even less for other men's systems. The "politics of privacy" had virtually no room for the choices and opportunities of a James Madison, because he could not have them in the sense that ordinary men could. His most valued private choices could not be private at all. They were made in the realm of ideas and systems; his opportunity was the public good. He was, when Fisher Ames first observed him in 1789, wholly a public man: he "was bred to it, and has no other profession."[24] He could thus have no clear way of perceiving when those choices might—to use his own definition—become strongly, even dangerously, "factious."

Madison and his friend Hamilton might agree on the structure of the republic, on the extent of its powers, on its need for a strong Executive and a generous revenue, and even on its need to coerce the states. And yet on the republic's character, its moral texture, the face it presented to the rest of the world—matters that almost defied thought—the two could never agree, though they did not as yet know it. The moral weather of James Madison's republic must never be tainted by the least shadow of dependence on Great Britain. This was fundamental; he could go no deeper. And though he may have been thinking thoughts of continental breadth, the eyes through which he saw his republic were still, with all said and done, those of a Virginian.

The intensity with which Madison promoted his plan of discrimination against British commerce in the spring and summer of 1789 was the product of convictions already formed before the new government was organized, convictions he was determined to put into practice as soon as possible. A uniform tonnage duty on the vessels of countries with whom the United States had commercial treaties (specifically, France), and a higher duty on those of countries with whom we did not (specifically, England) had as its primary object neither increased revenue nor advantages for American shipping. These could be achieved just as well or better by duties that would be the same for all. Nor was the plan simply one whereby a bargaining instrument might be fashioned to extract concessions for American trade with the British West Indies. Madison hardly pictured himself as a spokesman for the interests of American merchants. Indeed, when merchants objected to his plan, he turned his hostility upon them, charging that they were unduly subservient to British influence. His was no less an object than the dignity of his republic, which Great Britain might be expected to debase in any way she could. Her instrument now was commerce, and as long as the mother country held "a much greater proportion of our trade than she is naturally entitled to," she retained that instrument. The true remedy would be to alter the channels entirely, if possible, and redirect them toward France. For several years past, Thomas Jefferson had worked toward this aim through diplomacy; Madison now hoped to achieve it through lawmaking.[25]

James Madison was not normally a man of passion, and Fisher Ames found himself "unable to account for Madison's passionate attachment to the discrimination."[26] But if Ames had been a Virginian rather than a New Englander, holding Virginia values and seeing the world as Virginians saw it, it would have been evident to him that Madison was acting not upon "interest" but on principle. He might then have responded as Virginians did to what they saw as the moral hazards of commerce, the moral status of debt, and the moral influence of Great Britain in fashioning these into instruments of corruption.

Madison's first election to the Continental Congress was in December 1779, but on account of heavy snows he had been obliged to remain in Virginia until early in March. One of the most critical problems then facing Congress was that of Revolutionary finance, and Madison used the interval to prepare himself for his new duties by writing a treatise on money. Twelve years later, in 1791, he would have the same treatise published in Philip Freneau's newspaper in Philadelphia, on the ground that its argument was as valid then as it had been when he wrote it. Though its economics was debatable, the paper was nonetheless intelligent, reasonably technical, and informed. But it is of special interest for the attitude it reflected on the subject of debt. It was an attitude which had permeated the atmosphere of Madison's boyhood, and would remain with him throughout his life.[27]

The financial crisis of 1779–80 had been occasioned by excessive issues of Continental paper currency which were now in an alarming process of depreciation. Various remedies were under consideration—devaluation, increased taxes, and redemption for interest-bearing certificates of indebtedness—and, as it turned out, Congress was to try a mixture of them all. But the common-sense assumption behind each was that depreciation had occurred principally because the quantity of currency in circulation had become inordinate, and should therefore be reduced with the object of stabilizing its value. It was this "quantity theory" of money that Madison challenged. He argued that the major variable affecting prices was not the quantity of currency in circulation (in relation to the amount of goods and services available), but rather the confidence of the public in its redeemability, whatever might be the amount of it. As an intellectual exercise the treatise is curious, because on the one hand Madison offers no specific remedies of his own, and on the other he constructs an ingeniously elaborate attack on the one remedy he is against, that of a funded debt. He says nothing about the need for taxation (though he perceived it, as his correspondence certainly shows, and he strongly advocated it in Congress), but he has narrowed the ground upon which taxation or any other expedient may be justified. For example, it would not be to reduce the quantity of currency that taxes should be levied, but rather to assure the public that government revenues were adequate to fulfill its obligations. (This had been Virginia's technique for financing its colonial wars: to issue paper money and then to commit a proportion of the taxes toward its redemption.) But the most pernicious remedy for depreciation, the one least rational and most to be avoided, was public loans in any form. By adding the interest charges which these entailed, "we invent new expenditures. In order to raise the value of our money, which depends on the time of its redemption, we have recourse to a measure which removes its redemption to a more distant day. Instead of paying off the capital to the public creditors, we give them an enormous interest to change the name of a bit of paper which expresses the sum due to them. . . ." James Madison was the last man to deny that the public debt was a sacred obligation. Quite the contrary; the government's solvency and credit were among his most intense concerns throughout the period of the Confederation. But he was certainly the last man to think of a public debt as a public blessing. Indeed, a special mentality with regard to debt of any kind was the heritage of almost any Virginian, running in the borderland between thought and feeling.[28]

The economic life of colonial Virginia had been so organized that most of what Virginians knew about business, credit, finance, and trade had been taught them by the British. These lessons could well have been salutary ones, inasmuch as British experience and techniques in all these realms were probably more sophisticated and advanced than any others in the world. But the Virginians' very location in the network of production and trade of which they were a part necessarily rendered any role they might play in the shaping of it a relatively passive one. It was this psychic immobilization, rather than the question of how well the system did or did not function over the long cycle, that made the main difference in their behavior. To be dependent on it was one thing; to identify themselves in a positive way with the well-being of the system as a whole, and to internalize its values, was quite another. They were bound to see any fluctuations in it, whether to their advantage or not, as the work of outsiders and of forces beyond their reach; a sense of real creativity in molding its standards, processes, and operating norms was by the nature of the case denied them. For its benefits, they need thank only themselves and their own industry. For its shortcomings, they could look to a chain of British middlemen, manipulating invisible values, weaving snares of credit and debt, wielding invisible instruments, and slicing off shares of a Virginian's rightful profits at every step of the way. It was in such a pattern that most Virginians of that day formed their habits of mind.[29]

Some historians have intimated that a strong motive impelling the planter class of Virginia into the Revolution was a desire to repudiate debts owed to British merchants. Though that case has been shown to be overdrawn, what is obvious beyond much doubt is that the heaviest shadow hanging over Virginia life by the 1760s and 1770s was the shadow of debt. Virginians owed more money to British creditors on the eve of the Revolution than did those of any other colony, and almost as much as all the rest combined. Reluctance to alter a steadily rising style of life in the face of sharp drops in tobacco prices in 1763 and 1773 accounted for deep crises in most of Virginia's leading families.[30] A man in such straits, wrote George Washington, ought to retrench, but then "how can I, says he, who have lived in such and such a manner change my method? I am ashamed to do it; and besides such an alteration in the system of my living, will create suspicions of a decay in my fortune, and such a thought the World must not harbour. . . . This I am satisfied is the way that many who have set out in the wrong tract, have reasoned, till ruin stares them in the face." When Treasurer and Speaker of the House John Robinson died in 1766, it was discovered that he had lent out over £100,000 in public funds to straitened planters, and the list of debtors to the Robinson estate included the greatest names in Virginia.[31]

The Robinson affair occasioned much gloom (some of which must have penetrated the Madison household, since Edmund Pendleton, the estate's co-administrator, was a close friend of the family, and Pendleton's ward, the future "John Taylor of Caroline," was a schoolmate of James junior), but the public reaction to it seems to have been rather muted. Robinson's own name escaped the kind of dishonor that might normally have been expected in such circumstances because of his "Compassion for Persons in Distress."[32] The fact was that the exigencies behind these desperate transactions were too much a feature of everyone's experience to make of the episode a far-flung scandal. Instead, this and a whole series of less spectacular but equally oppressive stringencies in the economic life of the gentry during this period made for a more diffuse moral crisis. They began accusing themselves of falling prey to the corruptions of sloth and luxury. "Extravagance," lamented William Nelson, "hath been our Ruin," and, according to Nathaniel Savage, the only "Recipe that can be prescribed at this juncture, is Frugality and Industry, which is a potion scarcely to be swallowed by Virginians brought up from their cradles in Idleness Luxury and Extravagance."[33] A gentleman, however, paid his debts, or tried to. Of that there was no doubt in the Virginia code, and repudiation was never a threat to the public morality even at the height of the revolutionary crisis. Thomas Nelson, Jefferson's successor as governor, was as heavily entangled as any, but he publicly declared, "By God, I will pay my debts like an honest man."[34] Considering the economic arrangements under which the tobacco-planting gentry functioned, debt was a fact of existence and a necessary evil. But that it was anything but an evil, an evil that led to countless other evils, and that this was its overriding feature, few Virginians were capable of imagining.

But to suppose that the Virginians would not find a ready scapegoat would be expecting too much of them. The real author of all these evils was the British merchant, whose very profession, Landon Carter declared, "kicks Conscience out of doors like a fawning Puppy," and whose broker "is a villain in the very engagements he enters into." Such villainy was at the heart of Thomas Jefferson's explanation of the disproportionate balances owed by Virginians to Great Britain:

> The advantages made by the British merchants on the tobaccoes consigned to them were so enormous that they spared no means of increasing those consignments. A powerful engine for this purpose was the giving good prices and credit to the planter, till they got him more immersed in debt than he could pay without selling his lands or slaves. They then reduced the prices given for his tobacco so

that let his shipments be ever so great, and his demand of necessities ever so economical, they never permitted him to clear off his debt. These debts had become hereditary from father to son for many generations, so that the planters were a species of property annexed to certain mercantile houses in London.

Jefferson, who was himself never able to live within his means, was in no position to perceive that the merchants were as dependent on the planters—many of whom had in effect been supported by them for ten or fifteen years prior to the Revolution—as the planters were upon them, since a merchant who tried to limit one man's credit risked alienating all his other customers, most of whom were related. But there is no way of settling the final "justice" of a whole society's view of its own experience. What is certain is that for a Virginian, the ideological consequences of this particular experience went very deep. Debt and the very idea of debt, merchants and the very idea of a mercantile way of life, were inseparable from the anglophobia of the Revolution.[35]

A term of which James Madison made frequent use in his writings was "the national character." And for him, if the lessons of Virginia meant anything, it was that a further dependence, in any form, on the mother country could have no other effect on the purity of the national character than to debase it. With this as a kind of first principle, much in Madison's words and actions throughout the remainder of his public life becomes understandable.

2

Alexander Hamilton and the Mercantile Utopia

At some point the careers and outlook of both James Madison and Alexander Hamilton took what might almost be called a reactionary turn, in the sense that in the fluid phases of any revolutionary cycle there is always a certain openness of mind and spirit, and a shared broadness of aim, which cannot be permanent and which is bound to alter with the passing of time and with the consolidation of the revolution's achievements. At the moment of these two men's collaboration in the writing of *The Federalist,* the phase of openness, of promise and possibility, was evidently at its meridian. The consistency of aim and intention throughout most of those essays is decidedly more impressive than the numerous internal variations, and it is easy to imagine the Publius who put his name to each paper being animated by the same spirit and largely the same thoughts throughout. And yet while Publius remained forever open, it would be no more than two or three years before James Madison and Alexander Hamilton would close, harden, and drift away from the Publius who had represented the union of their energies and talents, and become enemies. One ought to see and know these men as they were before, as well as after, this happened. In certain important ways it changed them both, and in neither case is this drift quite comprehensible without the influence and contribution of the other.

This would not be quite the problem that it is, were it not for a certain perennial urge to locate the "blame." Hamilton, for various reasons, seems to have absorbed much the greater share of it, and it is easy to see why, if one begins with their respective temperaments and moves outward. Hamilton's vivacity, self-insistence, and gross visibility wherever he was—contrasted with all the opposite qualities in Madison—would seem to contain in themselves all the makings of a sharp personality clash. But if so, it was certainly delayed for quite a few years, during which time the two were good friends with occasion enough for each to discover what the other was like. Perhaps there was more to it. A variant explanation has had to do with a craving for power on Hamilton's part and a calculated drive to lay his hands on as much of it as he could, to the dismay of his less forward co-worker. Each, however, was fascinated by power and preoccupied with it, as revolutionaries generally are; at the same time, Hamilton, when we look closer at him, turns out to be a good deal less "calculating" than he has often been represented—probably, indeed, less so than Madison. True, a power contest of sorts does seem to have occurred between them. But it takes two to make a contest. It may be imagined that Madison, in the spring and summer of 1789, found his position very satisfying. As the most trusted advisor of Washington, his fellow-Virginian, and having had things so largely his own way in framing the basic legislation, Madison could not have viewed the sudden incursion of Hamilton's influence, and that of Hamilton's Treasury which he, Madison, had created, without some degree of fretfulness. When Hamilton, with his grand system of finance, usurped so large a share of Congress's attention as well as of the President's ear, there were two powers in the field where there had previously been one.[36]

Still, something more subtle was at stake than simple power. It may have been no less than Hamilton's grand design itself, its very self-contained massiveness, that repelled Madison and caused him to exert all his strength in opposing it. It has been said that Hamilton's determination to enact the whole of his utopian financial system—the funding plan, assumption of state debts, national bank, and the rest—was the primary cause of the rupture, and that a rigid refusal to compromise, to accept any alterations, was what made wreckage of a former unity. The plan, which had been thought out at great length, was indeed "utopian." But it was hardly less so than those which Madison himself had devised, also at great length, for the political as well as economic arrangements of the republic, and which he had promoted with equal stubbornness, equally reluctant to compromise, both in the Convention and in the legislative session of 1789. It was rather that with Hamilton's plan there were now two utopias where previously there had been one. It was not primarily men that clashed, or even interests, but visions.[37]

If his career had somehow ended just before the rupture with Madison, Alexander Hamilton might well have come down to us as one of the most attractive and dashing figures in American history. The stresses that came to fix the picture we do have were for the most part introduced after that time; in any case the perpetual romantic youth, grandly certain of his prowess and forever touchy about his public honor, does not as a rule age gracefully. But the first thirty-four years of Hamilton's life give some proof of the other rule that the youthful prodigy, abounding in charm, good looks, talent, and energy, is not unreasonable in expecting that the world—that part of it whose approval he values—will lay its heart at his feet.

The circumstances of his origin, being cloaked in just enough tropical shadow to arouse the most fanciful reveries, would have done justice to one of the heroes of Stendhal. It is supposed that he was born January 11, 1755, illegitimately, on the island of Nevis in the British West Indies; it is known with more certainty that he grew up on the neighboring island of St. Croix. His mother, Rachel Fawcett Lavien, was an unhappy beauty whose distracted ardors eventually led her cuckolded husband to divorce her for adultery. Legally unable to remarry, the girl had meanwhile found refuge with James Hamilton, an agreeable young Scotsman whose family had held lands and a seat in Ayrshire for centuries. But being a fourth son, James had had to strike out for himself and had come to the West Indies at an early age. He was never successful. An agent for various merchant firms, he drifted from place to place and may have abandoned Rachel and their two sons, James junior and Alexander, on St. Croix about 1765. Rachel, maintaining a store at Christiansted, proved a better provider than he, though she died of a fever three years later, leaving the boys for practical purposes orphans. Even so, James Hamilton senior for some reason never forfeited his sons' affection. They got news of his whereabouts some years later, and Alexander would henceforth send him money and remain in touch with him, off and on, until his death at the age of eighty-one.[38]

How Alexander received his early education is unclear, but of its efficiency there appears little doubt. As a boy he read everything within reach—his favorite authors being Pope and Plutarch—and was bilingual, having learned to speak, read, and write French from his mother. His penmanship, adeptness at arithmetic, and capacity to express himself in writing with both precision and force all combined to make him a wonderful asset to the St. Croix merchant firm of Beekman and Cruger, into whose employ he entered as a clerk at about thirteen.

The young Hamilton, despite his lack of fortune, was peculiarly situated to absorb the values, standards, habits of mind, and cosmopolitan outlook of the world of commerce under the most favorable possible circumstances. Though in a nominal sense he had no prospects, his ambitions were in fact warmly encouraged, and he was treated with every consideration both by his employers and by other members of the St. Croix community who knew him. Nicholas Cruger was a kindly and upright man who quickly recognized the youth's exceptional abilities, befriended him, and allowed him a large degree of responsibility and discretion in the affairs of the firm. When Hamilton was seventeen, a substantial fund was raised by the leading men of the island, Cruger probably subscribing the major share of it, to send him to North America for a college education. Cruger, who had good New York connections (his uncle was first president of the Chamber of Commerce), established an account there for the youth's maintenance. Those to whom the newcomer presented himself in New York, and who took responsibility for his welfare, were mercantile men. The world of commerce and mercantile affairs, in short, was one he had known from early boyhood, and he must have seen it very differently from one who—like his future friend James Madison—knew it only from the outside. To such as himself, its ways were orderly, honorable, and essentially benevolent, judging from the men who were giving him his start in life.

Among the most striking traits of Hamilton's personality was one that flashes forth in the earliest glimpses we have of him, fleeting though they are. This was an intense need to lay hold of whatever operation he had any connection with, either to run it himself or to instruct others how it ought to be done. The spectacle of the person who is certain he knows how to do almost anything better than anyone else is normally irritating. So it would be on more than one occasion with Alexander Hamilton. But most of the time such a trait in his case was not the defect it might have seemed in others, but a clear asset, since he generally *could* do it better. This was because he had both a penetrating intelligence and a great fund of energy, together with a passion for seeing a thing done right. He could accomplish huge amounts of work in short spaces of time, and was willing to take responsibility, make arrangements, oversee details, and anticipate contingencies.

We see all this in him at sixteen, when Nicholas Cruger went on a five-month voyage, leaving the St. Croix end of the business entirely in the boy's hands. Though he was furiously busy, young Hamilton's correspondence pops with a kind of staccato zest. He collects sums due the firm ("Believe me Sir I dun as hard as is proper"), urges Cruger's trading partners in the other islands to keep him promptly informed on the state of their accounts, and crisply notes mistakes in their addition. He shifts the firm's legal affairs from one attorney to another because the first, as his employer would later comment in approving the step, "was very negligent in them and triffled away a good deal of money to no purpose." He advises Tileman Cruger, Nicholas's brother in Curaçao, to give very explicit instructions to the captain of the firm's sloop ("I think he seems rather to want experience in such Voyages"); and in his own instructions to Captain Newton, the youth admonishes him to "reflect continually on the unfortunate Voyage you have just made and endeavor to make up for the considerable loss therefrom. . . ." This was after Newton had brought in a cargo of sick mules, most of which Hamilton had managed to save through swift arrangements for pasturage, but had to sell at a reduction. He suspects that Tileman Cruger will not take the trouble to arm the sloop for defense against the coast guard launches in the Spanish Main (a hunch that would prove correct), so he orders Captain Newton to do it himself, after having already determined the rate of hire for the guns. And finally, he makes decisions on prices and other matters that had to depend on somewhat complex variables, such as how worthwhile it would be, considering unloading delays and the number of round voyages possible before crop time, to take off portions of a carelessly stowed cargo to sell at Christiansted rather than sending it on to Curaçao. Eighteen years later he would be writing letters in the same tone and spirit to the revenue officers of the United States Treasury.[39]

To give himself the preparation in classics necessary for college, Hamilton entered the academy at Elizabethtown, New Jersey, in the fall of 1772 and raced through the course in about a year. While there, he was under the sponsorship of Elias Boudinot and William Livingston, to whose care he had been commended by Hugh Knox, a Presbyterian minister and Princeton graduate who had been one of the boy's patrons in St. Croix. Both were lawyers and men of affairs, cultivation, and good Whig principles; both gave him their warmest friendship. His first choice of a college was Princeton, reportedly "because it was more republican." He visited Dr. Witherspoon, who was impressed with his preparation, but the Doctor was later obliged to inform him with regret that the trustees could not grant his request to proceed from class to class at his own speed. (They may have remembered two cases of overwork a short time before when a similar arrangement had been permitted, those of Joseph Ross and James Madison: one had died within a year of graduation, and the other had suffered nervous exhaustion.) Hamilton returned to New York in 1773 and entered King's College, where he seems to have been enrolled in a special course of study, individually arranged.[40]

As to exactly how long Hamilton remained in college—perhaps a little over two years—the record is unsatisfactory; nor is it clear exactly what he studied. But the evidence does suggest that in his energetic reading habits he was not so much passively complying with standards set by others as he was laying hold of everything that might be of use to him at a time of rapidly expanding political consciousness everywhere around him. For it is clear that the youth plunged into the Revolution with ardor while still a student, bringing himself and his polemical talents to the favorable attention of the New York Sons of Liberty as well as to that of influential Whigs throughout the community.[41]

His remarkable pamphleteering bout with the Anglican clergyman Samuel Seabury, the most powerful Tory voice on the scene in the winter of 1774–75, was undoubtedly exhilarating. The question of New York's support of the First Continental Congress and its boycott of British goods, following the Boston Tea Party and Britain's retaliation for it, was very much in doubt and would remain so up to Lexington and Concord. Meanwhile such Tory blasts as Seabury's anonymous "Letters of a Westchester Farmer" appear to have been disconcertingly influential. In *Free Thoughts on the Proceedings of the Continental Congress,* addressed to the farmers of New York, Seabury denounced the acts of the "illegal, tyrannical Congress," accused the New York merchants of a plot to profit from the swollen prices that were certain to follow non-importation and the attendant scarcity of goods, and predicted ruinous consequences, especially for the farmers, who would be unable because of non-exportation to sell their surplus produce. The British, he insisted, could easily take their trade elsewhere, and if the dispute should reach the point of arms, they could devastate the colonies in a single campaign. Seabury therefore urged New Yorkers to reject the pretensions of Congress, refuse to submit to the self-denials Congress demanded of them, and look to the lawfully constituted authorities for redress of any grievances they might have. The nineteen-year-old Hamilton was moved to produce an anonymous pamphlet of his own. In *A Full Vindication* he challenged the "Farmer's" contentions and sharply defended the measures of Congress as the only way in which free men could uphold their liberties after seeing their petitions treated with contempt. He also defended the honor of the merchants, cautioned the farmers to resist such appeals to their selfishness, and twitted the "Farmer" for being no farmer at all but a tool of the ministry in disguise. Seabury, having no notion of who his opponent was, prepared a long reply, full of violent language, in which the entire Tory case for parliamentary supremacy was fully set forth. Hamilton rose to the occasion with a second pamphlet, noticeably superior to his first. In *The Farmer Refuted,* there is now a view of the young man's powers fully engaged, and more than a glimpse of both his own and his country's future.[42]

The Farmer Refuted, an eighty-page tract published shortly after its author's twentieth birthday, contains several striking elements. One is that it covers virtually the entire ideological range within which the Americans were to justify in a theoretical way what they would shortly do. Here one sees each of the major Whig arguments on natural law and the nature of representation. The apprehensions of ministerial conspiracy are all there: the growing design to constrict the liberty of Americans, to make free with their lives and property by forcing them to support standing armies and legions of pensioners, placemen, and parasites. Another feature of the pamphlet is a remarkable grasp, based on an already formed mercantile world-view, of the conditions upon which national prosperity depends. Hamilton's knowledge of Great Britain's national debt and the state of British foreign trade is clearly beyond Seabury's, and his discussion of the West Indies and their dependence on American supplies, based on his own experience, is devastating. There is also a projection of the military and diplomatic odds which Great Britain would have to face in any effort to subjugate the colonies by force, and of the sort of war which the Americans, in such circumstances, were most likely to wage. The predictions would prove in all respects sound, and a good deal more realistic than Seabury's.[43]

Perhaps the most pervasive feature of Hamilton's *Farmer Refuted,* noticeably absent from Seabury's work, is the way in which those habits of mind most characteristic of the Enlightenment—especially the Scottish—are reflected throughout most of its pages. There is the conviction, at once hard and utopian, that both one's learning and one's experience may be used instrumentally, to lay hold of the future and shape it. Hamilton's use of Hume—the same essays upon which his future friend Madison would draw in composing the Tenth Federalist— foreshadows the Publius who would take it for granted that no successful constitution of government was contrivable that did not provide for the harnessing of private interests in order to promote the public good. He takes what he needs from Locke, Montesquieu, Grotius, Pufendorf, Burlamaqui, Coke, and Blackstone on law and politics, and from Postlethwayt and the *Lex Mercatoria* on trade and commerce. The lessons that history teaches—those of the colonial charters, the wars of Charles XII and Peter the Great, the oppression of the Roman provinces— he assumes to be universal. And from the view he projects of America's latent power and limitless resources it is easy to picture him, in his own fancy, taking a hand in directing their use for some future greatness.

Plunging into the military phase of his career, Hamilton displayed in redoubled form the energy that had been evident in his pamphleteering, to which quality were added those of vivacity, dash, quick judgment, and a physical courage verging on the reckless. He and a number of his fellow-students began drilling every morning at St. George's churchyard early in 1775. One night in August of that year, Hamilton and others of his volunteer unit succeeded, under fire from a warship in the harbor, in removing some twenty cannon from the Battery to prevent their falling into British hands. In January 1776, when he learned that the New York Provincial Congress had ordered the raising of an artillery company, he set about, with the support of the leading radical Alexander McDougall, to obtain the command of it. He learned enough gunnery in the meantime to be examined and judged qualified, and was awarded the commission in March. He was brisk and efficient both as an administrator and as a trainer of troops. He took part in the retreat of Washington's army across New Jersey, acquitting himself with merit at New Brunswick, Trenton, and Princeton. Sometime after the first of the year Washington, having been impressed by the young officer's skill and intelligence, invited Captain Hamilton to join his staff as an aide-de-camp. It was "absolutely necessary," Washington had written, "for me to have persons who can think for me, as well as execute orders." Hamilton's formal appointment, at the rank of lieutenant-colonel, was dated March 1, 1777, seven weeks after his twenty-second birthday.[44]

As a staff officer Hamilton revealed a capacity to perform great stints of work, and made himself immensely valuable to his commander-in-chief. He did "think" for the General. He did much more than simply copy Washington's letters and dispatches; in many an instance, with little to go on but a few broad guidelines, he virtually framed them himself. Washington's reports to Congress, orders to other commanders, and campaign plans bear many a touch of Hamilton's mind as well as of his hand, and much of the information upon which Washington acted was gathered, assessed, and organized by his young aide. In the execution of orders, Hamilton could add flourish through the exercise of personal initiative. In charge of destroying flour in the path of Howe's advance on Philadelphia in September 1777, he and his detachment drew fire, whereupon Hamilton escaped across the Schuylkill, warned Congress out of the city, and in less than two days supervised the impressment of provisions from reluctant Philadelphians and managed to move most of the available military stores in vessels up the Delaware and out of British reach. After the battle of Saratoga in October 1777, Washington entrusted him with the delicate mission of journeying to Gates's headquarters at Albany and extracting as many reinforcements from his army as that vain and recalcitrant general would part with. Despite all arguments, Gates would agree to no more than one brigade of the three Washington wanted, but when Hamilton discovered that it was the poorest of the three he took it upon himself to order Gates in Washington's name to deliver up another. Gates grumblingly capitulated. The following year Hamilton undertook, both through Washington and on his own account, to smooth over the dangerous ill feeling that General John Sullivan had aroused with his loud complaints at the French fleet for not having remained at Newport to assist Sullivan in his attack on Rhode Island. Admiral d'Estaing seems to have been highly gratified by Hamilton's efforts at mutual conciliation. And at the critical battle of Monmouth in June 1778, he was everywhere at once.

In the saddle for four days beforehand gathering intelligence and acting as liaison between widely dispersed units, Hamilton made the line between report, tactical recommendations, and outright command a very blurred one, and played no small part in coordinating the action on the day of the battle. He "courted death," had his horse shot from under him, and seemed, according to the jaundiced General Charles Lee, in "a sort of frenzy of valor."[45]

Hamilton was certainly a loyal subordinate. At the same time, he was brimming with ideas on how to run everything. In the late summer of 1776, even before he joined Washington's staff, he worked out a plan for evacuating the outnumbered Continentals on Long Island, which he transmitted to Washington anonymously. Hamilton and his South Carolinian friend and fellow-aide, John Laurens, both of whom detested slavery, devised a scheme for enrolling South Carolina slaves in the army, and in urging it upon John Jay, then President of Congress. Hamilton wrote: "An essential part of the plan is to give them their freedom with their muskets. This will secure their fidelity, animate their courage, and I believe will have a good influence upon those who remain, by opening a door to their emancipation." The South Carolina legislature, as might have been expected, would not hear of it. Hamilton also gave advice to the New York Convention on such matters as how to punish Tories and how to avoid jealousies between troops from different parts of the country; he schoolmastered Governor George Clinton on irregular seizures of property for military use and expounded to him the importance of the state's sending its best men to Congress. To Congress itself he made various helpful suggestions. Through William Duer he urged a consolidation of the military structure, through Elias Boudinot an enlargement of the powers of the inspector-general, and through Jay a militia draft in the Carolinas.[46]

Nor did he confine himself to military matters. Amid all his regular duties at headquarters he somehow found time not only to read extensively but to compose a series of what can only be called state papers, substantial little treatises that dealt with nothing less than the health of a future American nation. In this category were a seven-thousand-word letter to James Duane in 1780 with a plan for overcoming the "want of power in Congress," a longer one to Robert Morris in 1781 outlining a complete system of national finance, and a series of six essays entitled *The Continentalist,* published in the *New York Packet* in 1781 and 1782, giving a whole set of political and economic prescriptions for imparting strength and energy to the Confederation.[47]

There was no question of Alexander Hamilton's immense ambition, his pride, his acute sense of personal honor, or his propensity for sweeping plans which nobody quite knew better how to execute than himself. He was fascinated by power and the uses of power. And yet one cannot quite project from this a picture of Hamilton as the calculating schemer. The cold Machiavellian, the crafty plotter, the man whose eye is on the main chance—this, for better or worse, was no part of Hamilton's character.[48] The sheer ardor of the man, the impatience, the impulsiveness, the need to keep moving, all served to inhibit that calculating prudence which might have made a very different person of him. Thus his rupture with Washington in February 1781, the upshot of which was his departure from the

General's staff, was the result of little more than frayed nerves, short temper, and Hamilton's growing fretfulness at not being in the field. Had it not been for Washington's own forbearance and his real appreciation for his aide's exceptional talents, the break might well have been permanent; it could even have cast an early eclipse over Hamilton's career. Nor does Hamilton's courtship of Elizabeth Schuyler at Morristown in 1780, for all the incidental advantages it may have brought him, seem very "calculated" an affair. The fatuities of the true lover still shine forth from his letters, while Philip Schuyler from the first was delighted with his brilliant son-in-law. Hamilton's personal relationships with Lafayette, Laurens, and other male contemporaries were imbued with impulse, affection, and fervor. And it was his pure urge for glory, his contempt for danger, and his weakness for the *beau geste* that made Hamilton the hero of one of the key actions at Yorktown. Two strongly held British redoubts near the York River had to be taken before the Allies could establish their siege lines on Cornwallis's left. Hamilton, having at last badgered Washington into giving him an independent field command, now insisted that he should be the one to lead the assault on one of the redoubts, and the feat was accomplished with éclat. Not until afterwards did "prudence" reassert itself. "Two nights ago, my Eliza," Hamilton wrote to his bride,

> my duty and my honor obliged me to take a step in which your happiness was too much risked. I commanded an attack upon one of the enemy's redoubts; we carried it in an instant, and with little loss. You will see the particulars in the Philadelphia papers. There will be, certainly, nothing more of this kind; all the rest will be by approach; and if there should be another occasion, it will not fall to my turn to execute it.[49]

Less than a week after the British surrender at Yorktown, Hamilton resigned his commission, left the army, and hastened back to Albany to rejoin his family and prepare himself for the profession of law. His studies were completed in a matter of months. He was admitted to practice as an attorney in July 1782, and as a counselor in October. He had meanwhile been appointed by Robert Morris as Receiver of Continental Revenues for the State of New York. In his representations before the legislature that the state ought to meet its responsibilities, Hamilton made a vigorous impression, as a result of which he was elected to Congress in July 1782. He was now twenty-seven. He took his seat in November, and it was here at Philadelphia that he first met James Madison. The two seem to have recognized each other immediately as allies.[50]

Like James Madison, Alexander Hamilton had been almost exclusively concerned with the continental side of the war effort. He too was obsessed with nationality and nationhood; he too was preoccupied with "the national character." All of this had been painfully sharpened by the view from headquarters. In his private letters during this period, Hamilton had frequently given vent to feelings of humiliation and despair over the failure of the states to rouse themselves for the common cause. The people were "determined not to be free," and through selfishness, private interest, and parochial prejudice the army was kept perpetually in want of men, clothing, and provisions. There was no adequate national government; the "fundamental defect," he had told Duane, was "a want of power in Congress." For this there were three causes. One was the states' "jealousy of all power not in their own hands"; a second was Congress's own timidity and indecision about exercising the power it rightfully had; and the third was lack of an adequate revenue or of sufficient vigor to levy it. During Hamilton's eight months' service in Congress it was this problem of an adequate national revenue, without which no government could have either authority or self-respect, that absorbed almost the whole of his attention and effort.[51]

He immediately joined Madison in the leadership of this movement, the eventual failure of which would lead the two into fresh efforts at the highest reaches of state-building. A 5 percent impost—the minimum needed by the government for a guaranteed income and the means for making some sort of progress on the payment of its debts—had been agreed to by all the states except Rhode Island. Efforts by Congress to exert special pressure on Rhode Island during the winter of 1782–83 broke down completely when the legislature of Madison's own state of Virginia reversed itself and repealed its former acceptance. Behind this resistance to the impost was the fear that any power to lay duties or taxes on the people other than through their own legislatures undermined state sovereignty, and that this would be only the beginning of an oppressive system of federal taxation, high finance, and the growth of a permanent moneyed interest. Hamilton and Madison thereupon set to work to reinstate the impost on terms that would quiet the states' worst suspicions, at the same time devising other forms of revenue sufficiently circumscribed to be both acceptable to the states and adequate to the government's needs. This proved to be impossible. The best they could manage was a compromise which limited the impost, to be collected by agents appointed by the states themselves, to twenty-five years, together with a new requisition on the states of $1.5 million annually, also limited to twenty-five years. Hamilton could not even vote for the plan he had helped to frame, though after it was passed he strongly urged his state to accept it as better than nothing. He knew the debt could never be extinguished within such a time limit, that requisitions were worthless, and that on such a precarious tax base the public securities could never serve as a circulating medium. Madison was not satisfied with the plan either, but he wrote a vigorous address to the states in support of it. But since unanimous consent was required and, as things turned out, was never achieved, for the remainder of the Confederation period Congress would have nothing in the way of a regular income. In July 1783, Hamilton quit Congress in disgust. One of his last acts was to prepare a series of resolutions for the calling of a constitutional convention to amend the Articles of Confederation. They were "abandoned for want of support." Madison himself left in October and went back to Virginia.[52]

Two little incidents of Hamilton's term in Congress show him chafing violently under the mortifications of impotence, and serve once more to highlight an impulsive impatience which was forever verging on the indiscreet. One occurred during a debate over the collection of federal revenues, at a time when it was of the utmost importance to soothe the delegations of Rhode Island and Virginia over the specter of outsiders coming in to interfere with the liberties of their citizens. Hamilton blurted out that what *he* wanted to see was a corps of federal revenue officers, appointed and paid by Congress to motivate their support of national authority, for the purpose of "pervading and uniting the States." Madison actually wanted the same thing, but he must have skipped a heartbeat when he saw the opponents of the impost smiling among themselves at this revealing outburst, and he hastily diverted the argument to other channels. The other incident involved the presence of an unpaid and near-mutinous army, more and more restless at the camp around Newburgh, and with officer representatives at Philadelphia waiting upon Congress demanding a just settlement of accounts. It struck Hamilton, wild over the frustrations he himself was undergoing, that a discontented army might be used to excellent advantage at this juncture, that Congress under such a spur might see the light and enact a truly adequate financial system, and that Washington might well take charge of such an effort. He suggested as much to Washington, and told a gathering of his congressional friends, including Madison, that he had done so. We do not know what Madison thought of this idea, inasmuch as he recorded it without comment. Washington, however, would emphatically have nothing to do with it. The army, he said, "was a dangerous instrument to play with."[53]

The two young state-builders resumed their collaboration at the Annapolis Convention in September 1786. Though that meeting was abortive in its immediate purpose of devising a more orderly system of commercial regulations, it proved to be the instrument for calling the Constitutional Convention of 1787. The address was written by Hamilton. As a delegate to the Philadelphia Convention, however, Hamilton, for a number of reasons, was not nearly as effective as Madison. One of them was that he was hemmed in by his two fellow-delegates from New York, Yates and Lansing, intrepid Antifederalists who canceled him out on virtually every vote. Nevertheless he threw himself headlong into the fight for ratification immediately afterwards. It was Hamilton who conceived the *Federalist* project and saw it through the press, writing fifty-one of the eighty-five papers to Madison's twenty-nine and John Jay's five. All were produced at desperate speed. They were published in four New York papers between October 1787 and May 1788, and were brought out in book form in the spring of 1788. Ratification in both Virginia and New York was doubtful, and required in each case great exertions. Chiefly responsible for achieving it in the Virginia convention was Madison, while success in the heavily Antifederalist New York convention was due principally to the efforts of Hamilton. Probably the closest Alexander Hamilton ever came to popular acclaim was at the great civic celebration held in New York City on July 23, 1788, after enough states had ratified to make the new Union a certainty. He himself could not be present, since the convention at Poughkeepsie was not quite over, but he was the hero of the day. The grand parade, participated in by all ranks and trades, had as its chief feature the model of a frigate ship drawn through the streets on wheels, christened HAMILTON.[54]

None of this is very helpful in foreshadowing the deep rupture that would so soon reveal itself between Alexander Hamilton and James Madison. For some historians, the need to uncover its origins has been so urgent that they have looked to *The Federalist* itself for clues. What they find there persuades them that the authors, despite their immediate common object, are not in a state of true harmony after all. Publius is in fact divided against himself; he is of two minds, and has two voices.

The claim that Publius is a "split personality" takes as its inspiration a remark made in 1836 by John Quincy Adams that Hamilton's Ninth Federalist and Madison's Tenth were "rival dissertations on faction and its remedy." But whereas Adams meant only that the two essays were variant efforts to establish a common point—that a large republic did have the resources to absorb the evils of faction—some modern writers have taken the statement as the basis for postulating a divergence of view in the most fundamental respects between the Publiuses of New York and Virginia. Madison's emphasis in Number 10, repeated in Number 51, is a pluralistic one: that factions arise from divisions in the community that are in large part shifting and diverse, and that this diversity in a large state is the very key to their control. They are thus contained, and may be counted upon to check and balance one another. Hamilton, on the other hand, seems to take for granted in Number 9 that faction is to be simply "suppressed," and goes on in other papers to emphasize not pluralism but power. A strong authoritarian note is discernible throughout his work. He stresses an independent Executive with sufficient vigor and energy to check the excesses of both legislature and people, announcing at one point the Rousseauean maxim that although "the people commonly *intend* the PUBLIC GOOD," they do not "always *reason right* about the *means* of promoting it." He holds up a judiciary with indefinite tenure that can serve as a balance against both state and national legislatures and manifest "the majesty of the national authority." He celebrates a consolidated national system to subordinate the states, whereas Madison is more attentive to the divisions of power between states and nation. Hamilton emphasizes those powers of the national government that are "unconfined" and extensive, while Madison reminds his readers that such powers are "few and defined."[55]

But it is Hamilton's speech of June 18, 1787, at the Philadelphia Convention, so it is argued, that reveals the true character of Hamilton's Publius and shows the true depth of his divergence from Madison. In this long and impassioned harangue, Hamilton made a number of his real convictions clear. His notion of faction was not something shifting and diverse, as with Madison, but something durable and permanent: the few and the many, the rich and the poor, the debtor and creditor. Being themselves permanent, these interests should be more or less permanently represented in government as forces of balance. In addition to a representative lower house there should be an elected Executive with indefinite tenure, a sort of republican "monarch," and a Senate elected for life, a kind of aristocracy. The best possible model, he insisted, was the government of Great Britain. Even the much-reprobated "corruption" in the hands of the British Executive—the bestowal of offices, honors, and emoluments—was not at all a bad thing, because it enabled the Executive, through the loyalties he thus attached to himself, to maintain "the equilibrium of the Constitution."[56]

The reasoning has its plausible side. Yet no study of *The Federalist* itself, on its own merits, will reveal divergencies of any such magnitude. These must be read into *The Federalist* from utterances made by Hamilton and Madison at other times in their public careers, while in their *Federalist* papers the parallelism of ideas and aims is far more evident than are any variations that might be worth pointing out.[57] The same parallelism may be seen in their endeavors before they joined their talents as Publius, and there are many examples of it in their respective doings throughout the 1780s. Hamilton's long letter to Duane insisting on the implied power of Congress to coerce the states is paralleled by one from Madison to Jefferson a few months later insisting on the same thing. Assumption of state debts by the national government—a feature of Hamilton's 1790 Report on Public Credit, and a point upon which the two would subsequently differ—was also a feature of Madison's own report of March 1783 on the same subject. The same was true of the important principle of not discriminating among different classes of the public creditors. That principle too was favored by Madison in his Address to the States in April 1783. The strong reply to Rhode Island in December 1782 on the indispensability of a national revenue, collected and administered by the national government, could have been written by either man. As it happened, Hamilton wrote it and Madison supported it. Hamilton's *Continentalist* of 1782 and Madison's *North American* of 1783 may be read interchangeably, both being pleas in the strongest terms for national power.[58]

In short, these men were united in aim throughout the period of the 1780s by strong national feelings which had little room for fine discriminations. They shared an intense concern for a stable national revenue, a contempt for the impotence of Congress, and an impatience with the narrow parochialism of the state governments, all of which drove them to the liveliest exertions. No two men were more energetic in the movement to bring the Constitutional Convention about beforehand, or to have its work ratified afterward.

Much has been written about Hamilton's extravagant speech of June 18, 1787, at the Convention. Many have deprecated it, some have tried to explain it away. Sympathetic writers have suggested that he was making it for a deliberately calculated purpose, that of establishing an extreme nationalist position for purely tactical purposes, knowing that his own plan, in itself, would receive no serious consideration. But this is doubtful, even though it is true that he did not expect anything to come of it. It is quite likely that to him the speech was almost an end in itself, and it is probably not to be understood without reference to yet another aspect, hitherto not stressed, of his own personality. The other side of Hamilton's impulsiveness and impatience, especially when he could not be managing things, was his frequent susceptibility to black despair and blue funks, to which he gave way on more than one critical occasion during his life. The immediate context of this particular speech is not very difficult to reconstruct. He had sat virtually silent for three weeks, nursing a wildly mounting desire for a strong Executive, the stronger the better, stronger than anything being talked of on the floor, and was all but ready to propose the Grand Turk himself if that could avoid the imbecilities of the recent Confederation. There had been too much quibbling over the Virginia Plan, which he had no part in devising, and then over the New Jersey Plan, which would have reinstated most of the same old weaknesses that had already wrecked the Confederation. The great opportunity seemed once more to be slipping away, and he was the only one, as usual, who really appreciated the awesome pass to which things had come. Moreover, Hamilton had been isolated in his own state delegation by Yates and Lansing, who were there expressly to check his nationalist ardors and see that he did not accomplish anything. To have a say, to get in with a plan, his plan, no matter what happened to it, had become an utter necessity.[59]

After he had made his speech—which lasted most of the day, was well prepared, and, though animated, leaned rather on the pedantic side—he seems to have felt somewhat better. He was warmly applauded, and the next day the Convention resumed exactly where it had left off. He did not really expect to be taken seriously, and had said so. Hamilton was never fully satisfied, and still brooded, but after an absence to look after his affairs in New York he returned and made little trouble from then on. He did not have much influence on the shaping of the final document, but he assisted in various small ways to wind matters up, and at the end strongly urged everyone present to sign. And when it came to organizing the *Federalist* project—something he himself was to be in charge of—he really brightened up. Despite the pressures of a full-time law practice, the virtues of a federal republic were enumerated in thousands of ardent words turned out at feverish speed over the next several months, and it seems fair to assume that he meant all of them.

The intellectual context in which Publius wrote was suffused by the Scottish Enlightenment; and the governing assumptions under which both Hamilton and Madison proceeded were largely those of David Hume. A "science of politics" *is* possible from which correct principles for promoting it may be derived; people can, through their own efforts, devise new instruments and institutions of government and put them into being, without having to submit to caprice, custom, or circumstance. They can do it by reason brought to bear upon experience. A vital component of experience is history—other people's experience—since in comparable circumstances men's behavior in all places and ages proceeds in roughly predictable patterns.[60]

Within these general principles Hamilton and Madison found a broad area of agreement. Both appeal to the lessons of history, of modern and ancient leagues, as well as the lessons of recent experience—that of the Confederation—to show that it had been both just and necessary to try again. Both are emphatic about men's inherent frailties, the evils of faction, and the need for strengthened instruments of government. Both distrust majorities; both are suspicious of state governments; both accept the doctrine of implied powers—the classic statement of which comes not from Hamilton but from Madison. "No axiom is more clearly established," Madison declares in Number 44, "than that wherever the end is required, the means are authorized; wherever a general power to do a thing is given, every particular power necessary for doing it is included." But finally, for every power that either writer chooses to stress in one place, there will be another place at which the same writer will qualify that power and point out the means whereby it is checked. Thus while Hamilton and Madison check and balance each other, Publius, in the person of each, does the same with himself.[61]

Still, to say that there are few intellectual differences between Hamilton and Madison, even at this period, is in another sense misleading. The focus of creative energy simply does not fall in the same place for each. One sees this difference through the ways in which they respond and adjust to political theory. It is not that their ideas are so very different; they draw from the same sources. It is rather that when it comes to the theory of government Hamilton's responses are coarser; his imagination is more mechanical; the pitch and span of his attention are less acute. In their handling of "faction," both take for granted—following Hume—that this is a major problem. But Hamilton responds in rather a conventional and routine way, especially in the June 18 speech, using the commonplace theoretical categories of "mixed government" and "balance" without quite taking the final step to fit them fully to the American political environment. Madison too uses the language of "balance," as everyone did, but in a bold and original manner. *His* use of Hume on faction is a peculiarly sensitive adaptation to American requirements, and the result is Federalist Number 10.

Even more pertinent is Hamilton's notorious comment on "corruption"; Jefferson, a few years later, would profess to be scandalized when Hamilton repeated it in his presence. This too had come directly out of Hume, and was itself something of a commonplace. But in Hume's hands, the idea had been managed with a certain subtlety. "Corruption" was simply the catch-name for the Executive's power of appointment, and Hume's interest in it had to do with the conditions under which the king could maintain his independence in the face of Parliament. Hamilton, for all his ardor for a strong Executive, was not nearly so alert to the implications of this Humean perception as was Madison, and but for Madison, he might well have let the lesson slip away. Hamilton had rather carelessly said in Federalist Number 77 that the Senate would have to approve not only the Executive's appointments but also his dismissals. Madison perceived that the Executive's independence, as well as his control of his own establishment, would be greatly reduced were the removal power not in his hands, and in his alone. And in order to make this point, Madison had to do a great deal of very urgent talking in the spring of 1789 while the executive departments were being established, and in the face of considerable opposition. It was thus he, and not Hamilton, who saw the full advantage of Hume's "corruption," and had the perception to adapt it to an American setting.[62]

But there was another realm in which the relative qualities of the two men's imagination were almost directly reversed. This was the realm of political economy. Here, it is Madison who is not very imaginative. Madison, indeed, shows something of the same literal-mindedness and sluggishness of response in this area that Hamilton occasionally betrayed when dealing theoretically with government. And here, conversely, the alertness, the sense of implication, the readiness to adapt, are all Hamilton's: in political economy he would transpose and domesticate foreign ideas just as creatively as Madison had done with ideas on government in Federalist Number 10. Hamilton scholars have, to be sure, clearly identified the influence of such writers as Adam Smith, Jacques Necker, James Steuart, and Malachai Postlethwayt in the evolution of Hamilton's thought.[63] But what is generally missed is that in economic thought, to a greater extent, even, than in political thought, for Hamilton the most congenial mind seems once again to have been that of David Hume.

The question of why Hume's influence on Hamilton's economic thought should have been somewhat overlooked is probably connected with another question, that of Hume's own standing as an economic thinker in relation to his friend and pupil Adam Smith. The preeminence of Smith as the "father of classical economics" has coerced the historian's habits of mind in more than one way. Hamilton certainly read Smith with profit, and gave much attention to his ideas; he also differed from Smith at a number of critical points. As a result, most analyses of Hamilton's economic thought—Smith and his challenge to mercantilism having usurped the major categories of historical bookkeeping—tend to center on the problem of whether he was or was not a "mercantilist."[64] The reputation of David Hume, meanwhile, is itself somewhat anomalous. Not taken seriously by most academic philosophers prior to the 1930s, Hume has since come to be regarded as "the greatest of British philosophers."[65]

Hume's economic writings occupy but a minor place in the whole body of his work. Yet a revival of interest in those writings has revealed them to be the product of a mind just as subtle in its way as that shown in his other work. Both their fragmentary nature and Hume's having been Smith's "predecessor" have heretofore obscured this. But there is another obscuring factor as well. The real difference between Hume and Smith is not the difference between mercantilism and laissez faire, or even between an embryonic version of laissez faire and a fully articulated one, but something else, to which economists have only recently begun to give systematic attention. Smith was interested not in the conditions that produce incentive, but rather in identifying the general "laws" under which economic life is carried on in societies where both incentive and the conditions supporting it are taken more or less for granted. Hume, on the other hand, would not take these things for granted; he put them in his foreground, and concerned himself with what might be called the sociology of economic development.[66] So also did Alexander Hamilton, which accounts for the "modernity" some economic writers have seen in his work.[67] Hamilton read Hume very early, and whereas his letters and reports contain numerous references to Smith, Colbert, and Postlethwayt—he picked and chose whatever he found useful—the affinity of his thoughts, paragraph by paragraph, to those of Hume is striking.

In the economic essays of David Hume, published in 1752, one finds a theoretical projection of the optimum conditions for economic development: a rudimentary but shrewd forerunner of what would in our own day come to be called developmental economics. One also finds a reflection of conditions that were unfolding in Scotland at the very time Hume wrote. Scotland as a depressed, poor, and backward country was very much within Hume's memory. But from the 1720s to about 1750 there occurred a period of transition in which Scottish society experienced a steady growth in foreign trade, manufacturing, and improved techniques of agriculture. These advances were all a matter of keenest interest in intellectual circles, and in fact the intellectual efflorescence of the time—the so-called Scottish Enlightenment—is not unconnected with the heightened level of vitality in the society at large.[68] (It is no accident that Hume's "Of Refinement in the Arts" must be classed as the keystone of his economic essays.) Scotland seems to have played a role in Hume's projections of economic development not unlike that which would later be played by America for Tocqueville's forecasts on the future of democracy. The observer in each case had the advantage of being poised between two states of existence and being thus able to perform an imaginative act of comparison, and in each case the line between theory and description would be richly ambiguous.

In all likelihood these changes in Scottish life would have represented somewhat more of an intellectual challenge to a man of Hume's generation than to one of Smith's, for all the real novelty of Smith's work, and by the same token the future in 1750 would not have seemed so certain as it did in 1776 when *The Wealth of Nations* was published.[69] By then, the Scottish economy was much more firmly fixed on its path of expansion, and Smith could universalize what he had come to take for granted around him. He could not only see "a Scotsman in every man," as Walter Bagehot would later put it, but also formulate laws of economic behavior that might be regarded as axiomatic only in fully developed societies. And yet there had been a time when the Scottish character would not have appeared as it later did, and when it could not be taken for granted that man's essential instinct was to "truck and barter." *The Wealth of Nations* tends to assume a mechanical economic psychology—the propensity to enterprise as being more or less innate—whereas Hume is concerned with the satisfactions of work, creativity, and innovation as being relative to the varying states of a society's economic life.[70] Smith's is an extensive and systematic treatise on principles assumed to be universal, but its guiding formula—free trade—is peculiarly designed for the well-being of Great Britain, then the strongest commercial power in the world. Hume, using the essay form, was less systematic and less thorough but perhaps imaginatively more mobile. Being able to look both ways—backward to the sloth and poverty of Scottish life in the early part of the century, and forward to an energetic society of merchants, manufacturers, farmers, and artisans—he could appreciate with a special sensitivity the implications of transition. Moreover, with the lumpish conservatism and inertness of the rural Scot as an image that had still been dominant at the time of his youth, Hume was quite unwilling to celebrate the virtues or assume the moral superiority of rustic existence. Vitality and refinement, for him, were to be found above all in cities, and the good society was one in which commerce was preeminent. All of which would exactly fit the temperament and ideas of Alexander Hamilton. Hamilton nursed the vision of a great nation, and fully shared the Enlightenment faith that people might rationally design institutions and arrangements capable of reaching their society's inner spirit—and in this case, of galvanizing the American people into exploiting the enormous bounty that lay before them. The inspiration could come through a major effort to confer peculiar dignity and favor upon trade and industry. For this, David Hume's essays on political economy offered both the design and the justification.

Hume's opening essay, appropriately enough, was entitled "Of Commerce,"[71] and its principal concern was the relation between commerce and national power. A society predominantly agricultural, with small commerce, tends to produce at a level little beyond that required to maintain itself. With few luxuries ("consumer goods" we would call them) to be had, the incentive to work harder to raise a surplus is limited. It is this kind of society, whatever pastoral poets may say, that creates sloth and indifference. In times of crisis, moreover, such a society would demand extraordinary hardship and sacrifices. The state in these conditions would have few resources to support an army, and the very act of raising one would entail the removal of essential labor and thus force the economy below the edge of subsistence. This principle may seem to have its disproof, Hume concedes, in the examples of early Rome and classic Sparta, whose rustic simplicity did not prevent them from raising and maintaining enormous armies which subsisted on booty. But to take such states as models would be to exact an inhuman level of patriotism and self-denial, nourished by a perennial environment of menace.

A prosperous commerce and industry, on the other hand, could create the same kind of strength without making comparable demands. With the promise of luxuries and amenities, people in time of peace are encouraged to exert themselves, thus instituting a cycle of increasing energy, enterprise, and efficiency both in commerce and in agriculture. Eventually a substantial portion of the population would find itself engaged in the production of goods and services that fulfill wants beyond those of subsistence. Farmers as well as artisans could increase their efforts until the basic needs were provided by a fraction of the labor force, while the entire population accustomed itself to sharing in the general affluence. Thus in time of emergency that portion engaged in the production of luxuries represents a surplus asset that can be tapped. In a money economy such a surplus can be drawn upon quickly and efficiently through taxes that cut sharply into the demand for luxuries, leaving both men and resources available to a government with the funds to hire and purchase them, and making it possible to distribute the sacrifices both justly and equitably.

This would prove to be a very fair prediction of how Great Britain would wage the wars of the French Revolution, and to Alexander Hamilton, a quarter-century before, it made immediate sense. He had already perceived, in his *Farmer Refuted* of 1775, the vast potential of America both in present wealth and future resources. He had also discovered through bitter experience at Valley Forge that the instruments for tapping them were not at hand. Americans might picture themselves as spiritual heirs of the Roman Republic, but American farmers sold supplies for British gold while other Americans were close to starving, and in such a setting neither Roman virtue nor Spartan patriotism had been enough.

Hume's case for a commercial society goes well beyond simply the argument for national strength. In "Of Refinement in the Arts" he insists not only that such a society allows a nation to be strong in times of crisis but that it is, by its very nature, a good society. With its promise of affluence and activity, it is a prosperous commercial state rather than a pinched and rustic one that produces a humane, sociable, and virtuous people. Luxury need not be regarded in and of itself as bad, if it is the reward of enterprise and the interlude to useful work. A man is happiest when his life consists of an appropriate balance of action, pleasure, and repose, and the most auspicious setting for it is one in which "industry and the arts flourish." Men relish both action and the pleasures that are its reward, and rest ("indolence") as a respite from action is not demoralizing but restorative. "The mind acquires new vigour; enlarges its powers and faculties; and by an assiduity in honest industry, both satisfies its natural appetites, and prevents the growth of unnatural ones, which commonly spring up, when nourished by ease and idleness." Moreover, refinement in the mechanical arts generally produces refinement in the liberal arts. "The same age, which produces great philosophers and politicians, renowned generals and poets, usually abounds with skilful weavers, and shipcarpenters." And the more the refined arts flourish, the more sociable people become.

> They flock into cities; love to receive and communicate knowledge; to show their wit or their breeding; their taste in conversation or living, in clothes or furniture. Curiosity allures the wise; vanity the foolish; and pleasure both. Particular clubs and societies are everywhere formed: Both sexes meet in an easy and sociable manner: and the tempers of men, as well as their behaviour, refine apace. So that, beside the improvements which they receive from knowledge and the liberal arts, it is impossible but they must feel an encrease of humanity, from the very habit of conversing together, and contribute to each other's pleasure and entertainment. Thus *industry, knowledge,* and *humanity,* are linked together by an indissoluble chain. . . .[72]

This "industry, knowledge, and humanity" constitutes not only a private benefit but a public good. Not only does an increase in the consumption of all commodities create a fund of surplus labor that can be drawn upon in time of emergency, but orderly ways and habits of industry will be the best influences for making a government and its laws more moderate, humane, and rational. Hume has no patience with the argument that poverty and rusticity made the Romans virtuous, or that it was the luxury of their conquered provinces that eventually corrupted them. What corrupted them was "an ill-modelled government, and the unlimited extent of [their] conquests." And a modern society such as Poland, without commerce, can produce only two classes, those of tenant and proprietor, of peasant and noble: the one fit only for subjection and the other to function as a petty tyrant, and with no class in between to cherish liberty or promote equality of laws. It is in just such a society that ignorance, brutishness, and "meanness of spirit" abound, and in which all pleasure and sloth are forever verging on the vicious.

Here, then, was a very strong case for an urban, commercial society. Its common man of virtue was not the yeoman farmer but the skilled city artisan, and

were reduced only very slowly, which was probably what Hamilton had in mind—the taxes for supporting it would constitute a steadily diminishing burden on a population growing both larger and richer. How, then, could a public debt *not* be seen as a public blessing?

Hamilton's long letter to Robert Morris written from headquarters in 1781 was in effect the first of his state papers on political economy and finance. One of the books he is known to have borrowed for assistance in preparing it was the *Essays* of David Hume. By 1786 or so, his emerging ideas on public credit and the particulars of funding had been given an added infusion of specificity by a study of Jacques Necker's writings on that subject, and no doubt by the works of various other authorities as well. His synthesis of all of them was more or less complete by the time he took office, and his own grand vision was fully before him as he began to draft the first of his Treasury reports in 1789.[75]

So central, indeed, was the public credit to the country's well-being, as Hamilton saw it, that every means must be taken to protect it. A war with any country would threaten that credit; another serious dispute with Great Britain would ruin it. Out of our commercial relations with that country came our wealth in its most liquid form, and without the revenues—public and private—from that commerce the national debt could not be supported. Another way of putting this would be that America's prosperity and that of Great Britain were inseparable.

These principles did more than constitute the theoretical basis for Hamilton's plans as he took up his official duties in September 1789. They would form the core of an entire ideological configuration, a world-view which—by its very totality, rather than because of any one part of it—would doom his friendship with James Madison. It was not that their views on government were materially different, or even that they were not in fair agreement on the indispensability of securing both the national revenue and the public debt. It was rather that Madison too had a world-view, at the core of which was the deepest anglophobia, and the elements which these two ideological nuclei would gather about them would add up to two massively different ways of organizing the nation's values and defining its moral future. Only when Hamilton's grand design was fully put together would James Madison, upon his return from Virginia in January 1790, receive its full impact and sense its full implications.

The two must already have become a little wary of each other by the time Hamilton took office. Hamilton was certainly aware of Madison's discrimination schemes against British shipping, and Madison must have known Hamilton was opposing them. In their last exchange of letters there is something attenuated; in their solicitude they are almost too polite. They lend each other books, and reaffirm the usual sentiments of warmth. Hamilton professes chagrin at discovering too late that Madison had remained in New York without his being aware of it for a time after the session of Congress adjourned; he had supposed the other would return to Virginia immediately. Had he known otherwise, they might have had a good long talk. He also professes to desire any thoughts Madison might have on the revenue and public debt. But between these lines there is much to be read; the two had not exerted themselves of late to see much of one another.

Perhaps the last time they ever met in friendship was in that summer of 1789, when they took, no doubt, a number of rambles together about the city. Many years later, perhaps a half-century or more, an old lady would recall how as a girl, long ago, she had seen them "talk together in the summer, and then turn, and laugh, and play with a monkey that was climbing in a neighbor's yard."[76]

3

The Projection

Summer was on the wane, and there were probably touches of fall weather already by the time Alexander Hamilton took office as Secretary of the Treasury. The members of Congress would shortly be quitting the city, and not long after that the President himself would leave on his tour of New England. There would thus be a spell of time in which the Secretary would have things pretty much to himself. We may imagine the setting at that place, and that particular period of the year, to have been one peculiarly congenial to the energies of a highly energetic man. The rhythm of daily existence in those times was adjusted to take maximum advantage of daylight; people arose at dawn, got to bed earlier, worked longer hours, and took their meals at times of the day altogether different from those of a later era. This may have had something to do with the amazing amounts some public officials managed to accomplish in the course of a day's work, even with no more than a clerk or two to assist them. In the New York of 1789, moreover, officers of the United States government could find almost everything within a few minutes' walk of everything else. Coming out of his house on a morning, say, in late September, Alexander Hamilton would have walked up Wall Street, past Federal Hall to Broad Way, a block beyond, where the Treasury Office stood a little below Trinity Church. From there he could have looked down to the Bowling Green, and beyond it to the sea; a morning stroll in that direction would have taken him around the Battery and back. The leaves would have just begun turning color, trees being still everywhere in the Manhattan of those days. We may be certain that as he walked among them, his head was full of plans.[77]

Hamilton was appointed on September 11 and confirmed by the Senate on the same day. This was on a Friday, and it might be supposed that he could have waited at least until Monday morning before taking up his duties. But he was at it immediately, and spent all day Sunday at the office in an outpouring of activity. Having determined the day before that he needed $100,000 instantly for the government's operating expenses, he had arranged for the loan of half of it from the Bank of New York (located in Queen Street, just around the corner from where he lived in Wall Street), and he now shot off a letter to the president of the Bank of North America in Philadelphia with a brisk request for the other $50,000. He would put it in the hands of a special messenger, he explained, because he wished no delay in the matter. Letters to his newly appointed assistants made it clear he wanted them on the ground at once. He had a talk with the French minister, Comte de Moustier, about the servicing of the American debt to France. From one of the commissioners who had been appointed to settle the public accounts dating from the Revolution, he wanted information on the entire state of those accounts. All of which meant in effect that Alexander Hamilton was addressing himself to matters of both short-range and long-range importance virtually the instant he stepped inside the Treasury. On the one hand, he was taking personal charge — setting the office in order, seeing to details, and making things hum — just as he had done at St. Croix in the absence of Nicholas Cruger eighteen years before. On the other, he was already taking steps toward the fashioning of an overall financial system for the United States. During the days to come, Hamilton would busy himself with immediate requirements, issuing instructions to revenue officers and preparing two major reports desired by Congress, one on estimated civil and military expenditures and the other on warrants issued by the former Superintendent of Finance, each completed within two days of its being requested. But he also set to work collecting information: from the governors on their states' indebtedness, and from various prominent citizens on trade, shipping, and anything else that might be of assistance in the formulation of his grand design.[78]

The principal features of Hamilton's design, which would assume its completed form in the Report on the Public Credit of January 9, 1790, were probably settled in his mind during the six weeks or so between the departure of Congress at the beginning of October and President Washington's return in mid-November.[79] As to how it evolved, the process may perhaps be pictured as going on at two levels. One was the level of theory and imagination, that of the conception in its total sweep. The other was that of practical detail and of specific choices.

There is a characteristic device of Hamilton's mind which is discernible at almost every stage of his reasoning, and seems also to furnish the key to certain of his critical choices in the translation of theoretical predilections into practical policy. The device is that of the projection: an ordering of facts and circumstances into patterns which present conditions have not as yet made actual but which future ones will. On the very highest plane, Hamilton's imagination was dominated by a projection of what America could and ought to become. It was a vision upon which he had been dwelling in one way or another ever since *The Farmer Refuted*, his youthful polemic of fifteen years before, a vision of economic growth and economic development. The *potential* for growth — an expanding population, limitless natural resources, vast tracts awaiting tillage, a vigorous people — was most certainly there. The problem was one of execution, of how the potential was to be made real. Up to this time there had been two massive difficulties. One was political in nature, the question of a government with the power to act. This had been for the most part solved, and Hamilton's own efforts had had much to do with bringing such a government into being. The other difficulty was economic. It was this challenge — that of how the economic energies of the people might best be mobilized — that Hamilton now intended to meet, to the extent that the initiative of the United States Treasury could shape the result.

In Hamilton's scheme of things the dynamic force was beyond doubt the merchant class. These were the men who could and would use capital to create more capital—who would build the ships, develop the markets, provide the goods, and make the decisions that affected the uses to which the community's resources would be put. As a definition, "merchant" in the eighteenth century embraced a variety of forms of enterprise, while enterprise itself, in practice, had not yet become nearly so sharply differentiated as would be the case in later times. There was thus an intellectual implication: the merchant knew, and had to know, a great deal about the world and its affairs. Thus Alexander Hamilton's faith in the capacity of the merchant class to perform a creative role in the nation's life could rest on a persuasion that this class was the receptacle for a wide variety of knowledge, experience, and ideas. He was in any case determined to provide for these men a national economic context in which their energies could function. That context should include capital in mobilizable form, readily accessible credit both foreign and domestic, a stable currency for the transaction of business, and government encouragement for the kinds of enterprise that would be of greatest benefit to the entire community.

Parallel with Hamilton's projection for America as a society was one for the United States as a government. The government required a sound system of taxation, undoubted stability of credit both national and international, an orderly funding of the several complicated layers of public indebtedness that had grown out of the Revolution, and a banking institution to provide a dependable circulating medium and to manage the government's day-to-day fiscal affairs. The carrying through of both these projections would result in a nation strengthened in every possible way. Prosperous and flourishing in peace, and able to defend itself if war should require it, such a nation would be rightly equipped to fulfill a great destiny.

On this level, then, that of theory and vision, Hamilton's mind had long been formed. It was upon the level of practical choices that he now proceeded as he worked out the details of his plan for managing the public debt. One thing was given. There was at last an assured specie income, and from this it was certain that the debt would be paid. The new government would fund—that is, refinance with a specific commitment of future taxes to support it—on a uniform and simplified basis the entire Continental war debt, with a new issue of its own securities in exchange for those issued over the years and under fluctuating conditions by the Continental Congress. With the new tax revenues, interest payments were in effect guaranteed. It was this national debt that Hamilton could see functioning, under proper safeguards, as "a national blessing." Debts must eventually be repaid. But in the meantime such a debt, properly funded, meant the use of a large pool of liquid capital—in effect, the taxing power of the United States was being capitalized in order to make it available—with which the merchant class, the chief holders of it, might develop the country. Such had been a long-term effect, as Hamilton knew, of the Financial Revolution in England.[80]

So the debt would be funded, but on what terms? Should it be funded at par—that is, on exactly the same terms of interest as the Continental debt? Should any discrimination be made between original and current holders of Continental securities? What should be the status of accrued interest on the old debt? Having preempted the major sources of revenue—tariff duties—should the federal government assume the remaining war debts of the states? How was the value of the new securities to be maintained? What specific steps should be taken to establish a sound currency? Was there a specific way to encourage domestic manufacturing?

Certain of the decisions were made very quickly. There would be no discrimination between original and current holders, despite a predilection in some quarters for just such a policy, and on this point there had probably never been any doubt in Hamilton's mind. It was true that a persuasive argument could be made on grounds of equity for a plan whereby secondary holders of Continental securities would be required to share the profits of funding with the original holders who had sold them at depreciated prices. According to such a plan, they might be given in new securities no more than, say, the going market value of the old, plus interest, while the remainder (the difference between market and face value) went to the original owner. Many veterans of the Continental Army, having received such securities in lieu of back pay, had in their stringency disposed of them to speculators for a fraction of their denominated value. It was thus felt that they were entitled to some of the benefits of their country's new solvency; speculators, so it was urged, should not be allowed to reap them all.[81]

Hamilton would have none of this argument. In the first place, discrimination, being a breach of contract, was an act of injustice to the individuals concerned. The public had contracted to pay face value to the holder or assignee, and the intent of the contract, in making the security assignable, had been to allow the owner "to make use of his property, by selling it for as much as it may be worth in the market, and that the buyer may be safe in the purchase." Second, the principle of discrimination was subversive of the public credit because it impaired the liquidity of the public securities—their capacity, that is, guaranteed by security of transfer, to pass as money.[82] Then there was a final reason Hamilton had for opposing discrimination, one which was interwoven in the very texture of his thought and which in its way underlay all the others. He did not want holdings in the public debt widely dispersed. He wanted the resources which they represented concentrated as much as possible in the hands of a particular class of men, because he wanted those resources maximally available for productive economic uses.

The absolute soundness of the public credit was a prerequisite to everything else. Hamilton was intensely aware of the advantages this would bring for the immediate prestige and future security of the United States as a sovereign nation, and remembering that the principal weakness of the Revolutionary government had been its inability to raise money, he was perhaps over-obsessed in his determination that this should never happen again. But to enhance the standing of his government was only one of his ends; Hamilton was convinced that a funded debt—though only through an impeccably stable public credit—could serve as capital in a capital-poor country. And from this it followed that the sort of men who held this debt, and what they did with it, should constitute a question of the utmost concern. He had no use for speculation as an end in itself; this could be a cause as well as a symptom of instability in the public credit. Once that credit was established, speculation should logically cease; if conditions arose in which it threatened to recur, he would take every measure to discourage it. But activity of a speculative nature at the stage prior to funding, though incipiently pernicious, was not without its uses in accomplishing two things with which he could hardly quarrel. It was part of the process whereby the debt was being not only brought toward par in value, but also concentrated.[83]

Capital dispersed about the country in modest amounts would not really act as capital, not being readily mobilizable for economic development. It would do little more than raise prices as people spent it. Indeed, it was just such an infusion, from British purchases and French subsidies during the Revolution, that had resulted first in a sharp rise in the consumption by Americans of foreign luxuries, and then in an abrupt depression in the later 1780s when their credit ran out. For the capital created by a funded debt to become *"an accession of real wealth,"* rather than merely *"an artificial increase of Capital,"* it must serve "as a New power in the operation of industry," and this would occur only if it went through the hands of men who would use it to build ships and factories, launch business ventures, and augment commerce. Directing it toward an undifferentiated mass of farmers and veterans, on the other hand, was not unlike Hume's example of what would happen if "every man ... should have five pounds slipt into his pocket in one night." Such money, "however abundant, could never gather into sums; and would only serve to encrease the prices of every thing, without any farther consequence."[84]

Having disposed of discrimination, Hamilton then considered his choices on whether to fund at par and whether to assume the state debts in addition to the Continental debt. The two choices were interconnected. He made up his mind on assumption first, probably by the end of October, deciding that it could and should be done. His reasons were both economic and political, but the political reasons were the more immediate and much the more complex.

One of the things Hamilton wanted to effect with assumption was to unite into one group all the creditors of both the national and the state governments. He wanted them all dependent on, and giving their support to, the federal government, and he was very anxious that they not constitute the divisive influence upon public finance that would be created by two opposing classes of financial interest. A further objective, which he would urge in his report under the heading of convenience, was to avoid having the states and the federal government competing for the available sources of tax revenue. Any state government, pressed by a heavy structure of indebtedness, that sought to support its debt by laying an excise, say, on whiskey, would present the federal government with a serious dilemma. If the federal government wanted to levy a whiskey tax for its own purposes, it would now face the disagreeable choice either of placing an intolerable burden on the distillers of that particular state or of foregoing one of the most logical and desirable sources of national revenue. In short, the decision of a single state to tax a given item might well foreclose a source of federal taxes on that same item from all the rest, and if more than one state had substantial debts to service, the dilemma would only be worse compounded. Hamilton's impulse, therefore, in assuming all outstanding state debts was to avoid unnecessary and destructive competition between state and federal governments, and at the same time to preempt the best sources of revenue for the United States Treasury.[85]

But the most complicated of all the political factors bearing on the desirability of assumption had to do with the question, still pending from the Confederation period, of settling the Revolutionary accounts. The problem of the state accounts and that of the state debts, though closely related, were by no means identical, and the distinctions between them are important for making sense not only of what Hamilton intended to accomplish through assumption but also of the debates which the issue of assumption would subsequently provoke.

From the very beginning there had been the understanding, which was written into the Articles of Confederation, that the costs of the Revolution were to be borne by the United States in its character as a national government and not by the several states acting individually. In practice, however, since the Continental Congress had no independent power to tax, the financing of the war effort had had to be accomplished by loans and by contributions from the states, through their state governments, to the "common charges." There was a considerable extent to which the states had had to run their own war efforts and manage their own expenditures, though such expenditures, to qualify as a contribution to the "common charges," needed to be authorized by Congress. As for a principle whereby each state's contribution was to be apportioned (varying as they did in population and resources), no absolute rule could be fixed as long as the war was still in progress. Though a standard based on population was Congress's rule of thumb in making direct requisitions, only with a final accounting and the weighing of many circumstances could this or any other rule be invoked with assurance in determining which states in the last analysis had, and which had not, contributed their due share.[86]

The task of accounting would be formidable. The tangled circumstances made a just final settlement difficult at best, and to insist upon strict and uniform accounting procedures would be hopelessly impracticable. In case after case the line between expenditures authorized by the Continental Congress and those not so authorized could not be maintained. Some states had spent money on expeditions that were not authorized but turned out to be very useful; others had assumed expenses that properly belonged to the Continental government; many of the southern states—Virginia in particular—had either failed to keep proper records or else had lost them as a result of British invasions. Finally, the size of the expenditures as well as the mode of financing them had varied considerably from state to state. Massachusetts, Virginia, and South Carolina all claimed very large expenditures. Massachusetts had kept careful records but wanted credit for a major undertaking, the Penobscot Bay expedition, which had not been authorized. South Carolina also had good records but had assumed the unliquidated claims of her own citizens against Congress by absorbing them into the state's debt before they had been properly reviewed by Continental commissioners. Virginia could show little evidence for what that state had expended in its struggle to repel the British invasions of 1779–80. To make matters still more complex,

Virginia had by 1789 paid off a large part of its state debts while South Carolina and Massachusetts were still burdened by huge debts which they had no wish to scale down but which, with their limited tax resources, they could not continue to support.

Ideally there ought to have been a way to settle all these difficulties equitably. A General Board—such a Board was in fact established in 1787—would add up the expenditures of all the states together, after eliminating those that could under no rule be called authorized. Applying some standard of apportionment (that of population, even with its defects, was probably the least inequitable) to this sum, the Board would then determine state by state whether each one had contributed more or less than its share to the "common charges." It would determine, that is, which states were the creditors and which the debtors, whereupon the debtors would make up their deficiencies by compensating the creditors, and the accounts would by definition be closed. But such an "ideal" solution had virtually no chance of coming to reality, nor was it especially desirable that it should. In the first place, it was unlikely that any state which might be found to have spent less than its share would be willing to compensate those which had spent more, and indeed, this was more or less generally accepted already. It was tacitly supposed, now that the new Constitution had established a federal government with the capacity to make itself solvent, that that government would assume the balances due the creditor states in any case. Yet even so, the completion of the accounting process would take several years under the best of circumstances, and the delay itself created a situation inherently volatile and potentially dangerous, in view of various unresolved dissatisfactions. For example, such states as Virginia, convinced of having made disproportionate sacrifices but without the full records to prove it, were obsessed by the fear that the General Board would never do them proper justice. Such states as Massachusetts and South Carolina, on the other hand, staggering under state debts that represented sacrifices both disproportionate and authenticated, were crying for immediate relief. Such, in short, was the situation for which Hamilton now sought a remedy.

He proposed to cut the Gordian knot in two relatively simple steps. One was to assume all outstanding state debts, which would instantly relieve Massachusetts and South Carolina. The other was a basis for a final settlement of accounts by which no state could lose. They would be credited "for all monies paid and articles furnished to the United States, and for all other expenditures during the war, either towards general or particular defence, whether authorized or unauthorized"; they would be debited for all obligations assumed by the federal government; they would have their share of the total of these balances computed "according to some equitable ratio, to be devised for that purpose"; and those which still turned out to be creditors would receive a final compensation from the federal government.[87]

The plan whereby Hamilton tied assumption to a final settlement of accounts thus had several significant characteristics. One, obviously, was its generosity. In his effort to inhibit divisive tendencies within the Federal Union, he had put something in it for everyone. Another was its nature as an unstated projection.

He was predicting—with no more than partial evidence, since the full returns would not be in for some time—that the states with the heaviest war debts would turn out to be the very ones that had made the heaviest sacrifices and would emerge in the final accounting as "creditors." Meanwhile, of course, the debts of the "debtor" states would also be paid in the process of assumption, which meant that the federal debt would be considerably expanded. The economic advantage of this, in addition to all the political ones he hoped for, and in view of his total scheme of thought, was simple enough. It would provide another solid increment of development capital.

With assumption, roughly $25 million was being added to a public debt already calculated at something over $54 million, which led directly to the related choice on interest—the question of how to set the terms upon which this $79 million debt would be funded.[88] Doing so at par—principal at 6 percent, payable in specie—was conceivably possible, but it would have strained the resources of the Treasury well beyond any point the Secretary could contemplate with comfort. Some kind of adjustment was clearly called for. As Hamilton considered his alternatives he was favored with various kinds of advice, and two of the letters he received at about this time may be selected as representing the permissible range within which he had to work.

Stephen Higginson of Boston and William Bingham of Philadelphia were both merchants, both good Federalists, and both earnestly concerned with the integrity of the public credit. But while the concern of the one seemed marked by a sense of public responsibility, that of the other, though plausibly expressed, reflected unmistakable overtones of self-interest. Rather piously, Bingham took the ground that anything short of 6 percent would be unthinkable, a breach of faith to the public creditors, and that even at 6 percent the market value of the debt would require considerable time to reach par. When it did, the debt might then be renegotiated at a lower rate. Higginson, on the other hand, warned that to tax the people in order to pay a full 6 percent in specie to men a good many of whom had bought up their holdings at no more than two or three shillings in the pound would be asking for trouble. There were other ways, he thought, of keeping faith with the public creditors "without hazarding the peace of Society, or endangering Government." He suggested a plan whereby the debt might be funded nominally at 6 percent, only half of which, however, would be paid in specie, the other 3 percent being paid in notes. He too believed that a new loan might eventually be floated after the government's credit had been stabilized; he too, like Bingham, guessed that the eventual cost of funding would average out to a little over 4 percent.[89]

Hamilton accepted neither plan. Or rather, by means of a simple projection he devised a combination of both with none of the awkward features of either. Both Bingham and Higginson anticipated an eventual solidification of United States credit; he himself never had any doubt of it. And like them, he too had calculated that future conditions (which included a sound public credit) would bring about a rise in the country's productivity and enterprise, together with a general drop in interest rates, which would in turn allow the United States to pay off its debt ultimately at something closer to 4 percent than to 6. But if a fair basis for such expectations existed already, why not build them into the system from the start? Hamilton's own proposal, accordingly, was one whereby the public debt would be funded from the outset at 4 percent, and one that guaranteed it would remain at that rate throughout its existence.

Both Bingham's and Higginson's projections were partial, involving a linear series of consequences which would only materialize step by step; Hamilton's projection was total. The very act of funding itself, the clear manifestation of the government's intention, would bring all those consequences sufficiently into view that people would begin at once to act with reference to them as though they already existed. "Probabilities," he observed, "are always a rational ground of contract." Bingham wanted a sweeping program of taxation and then a mortgage on those resources, a specific pledging by law that the first charge on such revenues would be the punctual payment of interest; otherwise, he insisted, the debt would depreciate in value. Hamilton did not believe such a mortgage was necessary, and although he was quite aware that America was undertaxed in proportion to its resources, he seems to have shared some of Higginson's sense of limits regarding what public opinion was likely to tolerate. Bingham also argued that even a 6 percent funded debt, with maximum security, would still be worth initially only about 60 percent of face value in the open market, and that a large number of the public creditors would refuse to subscribe at anything less than 6 percent. Hamilton, with a keen sense of the country's true potential, took neither of these predictions seriously. Bingham believed that the government might take advantage of the eventual drop in interest by renegotiating the debt at some future time at a lower rate. But this would require that it be redeemable at the government's pleasure. Hamilton proposed instead to guarantee that no more than a specified fraction would be retired annually, and that a sinking fund be established for that purpose. The creditors would thus know from the outset exactly where they stood, and Hamilton took for granted that they would also see how well.[90]

Meanwhile Hamilton was offering them a number of options. These ranged from a plan whereby each creditor would receive two-thirds of his principal in securities at 6 percent and the remaining third in public lands at the very favorable rate of twenty cents an acre, to one whereby all his securities would bear 6 percent but, for one-third of them, only after ten years. The immediate specie cost to the government in virtually every case would be something over 4 percent.[91]

Hamilton's argument on interest was both precise and succinct. There was "good reason to believe," he announced, "if effectual measures are taken to establish public credit, that the government rate of interest in the United States, will, in a very short time, fall at least as low as five per cent. and that in a period not exceeding twenty years, it will sink still lower, probably to four." He then explained that there were "two principal causes" which were "likely to produce this effect." One was so self-evident that we may suspect William Bingham—who omitted any mention of it from his own argument—of ignoring it for ulterior motives. This was "the low rate of interest in Europe." With 3 to 4 per cent "deemed good interest" in some parts of Europe and a still lower rate deemed so in others, it ought to follow that in view of America's favorable location, removed from European conflicts, and of America's obvious tax resources, there existed the most solid security and the most powerful attractions for foreign capital. "The advantages of this situation have already engaged the attention of European moneylenders, particularly the Dutch."[92]

Hamilton's other explanation for a lowering of interest was simply "the increase of the monied capital of the nation, by the funding of the public debt." The key term was "capital," not merely money, and here, once again, his mind reflected the lessons it had absorbed from Hume. Though he could not be very explicit about it to a nation full of farmers, there can be no doubt that once more he was thinking of concentration. "It is only requisite," Hume had written, "that the property or command of that quantity, which is in the state, whether great or small, should be collected in particular hands, so as to form considerable sums, or compose a great monied interest. This begets a number of lenders, and sinks the rate of usury. . . ."[93]

Such, then, was Alexander Hamilton's grand design. The Continental debt, though originally set at 6 percent, would be funded at 4, but it would be done in such a way that the soundness of the public credit would be all but self-evident from the start. There would be a solid tax base—the federal impost supplemented by a new excise law, drafted by himself, on domestic and imported spirits—for insuring the regular payment of interest. A sinking fund would be established from the revenues of the Post Office, to be used for retiring a portion—5 to 6 percent—of the principal every year and for stabilizing its value by purchases from time to time in the open market. Certificates of accrued interest on the old debt, known as indents, would be treated as principal, and funded on the same terms as the rest of the debt.[94] The Revolutionary debts of the states would be assumed by the federal government, tied to which was a plan for a final settlement of the Revolutionary accounts sufficiently generous that every state would benefit. A national bank would provide a dependable circulating currency and would manage the financial transactions of the Treasury; the Secretary would soon submit, he promised, a separate report on that subject. As for his dreams of industrial development, so logical an extension of all his thinking on public finance, no fully articulated plan was as yet forthcoming. But it is evident that the theoretical basis for the ideas he was to set forth two years hence in his Report on Manufactures was already in place by the fall of 1789.

4

The Political Economy of Anglophilia

There was another aspect of things so fundamental to the success of Hamilton's plan that it was necessary all but literally to build it into the plan itself. This concerned the basic footing of the United States vis-à-vis Great Britain, which at this time was anything but settled. The plan was predicated on a stable revenue. Although Hamilton hoped to broaden the sources of income to include excises, the fact remained that the essential source, the one easiest to collect and least objectionable to the taxpayer, would be the impost, a system of duties on goods imported from abroad. Tied as it was to the volume of overseas trade, moreover, the very nature of the impost was such that the government would be able to collect ever-increasing revenues from it with the expansion of the domestic economy. The fatal danger, therefore, would be a disruption of American commerce with Great Britain. With the primary basis for solvency being receipts from the tariff on imports, 90 percent of which were coming from Britain, a trade war with that country would almost certainly destroy the entire system. The extent to which this conditioned Hamilton's total mentality was prodigious. Not only did he see it as indispensable to avoid hostilities of any kind, but he was further convinced that the closer the two countries could approach a relationship of positive cooperation and understanding, the more secure the whole system would become. He might be expected, consequently, to be very much on the alert for signs. And fortuitously, less than three weeks after his assuming office as Secretary, came an occurrence that seemed to bear all the marks of a golden opportunity. This was the appearance in New York toward the end of September of an informal spokesman of the British ministry. He was Major George Beckwith, aide-de-camp to Lord Dorchester, the Governor-General of Canada, and he had, as it happened, come straight from London.[95]

Major Beckwith's business was very simple. The Ministry had been disturbed over the discriminatory tonnage measures discussed in Congress during the spring and summer; Beckwith had come to inform persons of influence in the United States government that such measures, if enacted, would be met by retaliation. Besides there being as yet no regular diplomatic channels between the two countries, Beckwith had good qualifications for his mission. An able and discreet officer, he had handled British intelligence activities in New York for General Sir Guy Carleton during the later years of the Revolution, and when Carleton—now as Lord Dorchester—became Governor of Canada, Beckwith accompanied him to Quebec. Then in 1787 and 1788 he spent time in America as Dorchester's confidential agent, observing conditions and making many acquaintances, especially among persons well disposed toward Great Britain. "There is a general growing British interest in the states," he wrote in 1788, "and it will be good policy to hold a friendly language to that country, and to show a disposition to make a treaty of commerce with them, whenever they shall have established a government and shown that they have something solid to bestow in return." Though his demeanor was circumspect, Beckwith's own disposition was amiable, and he seems to have been well regarded by all with whom he dealt.[96]

Beckwith was home in England on a visit in the summer of 1789 when the news arrived of the American debates over tonnage. His familiarity with the American scene was known to several members of the Ministry, and as he prepared to return, the Secretary of State for Home Affairs, William Wyndham, Lord Grenville, made him "the bearer of a message from his Lordship, to The Executive Government of The United States." He would report the results to Lord Dorchester, who would in turn communicate them to Grenville. Beckwith landed in

New York on or before September 30 and spent a week or ten days there before proceeding to Quebec. He communicated his message to Senators William Samuel Johnson of Connecticut and Philip Schuyler of New York, and Schuyler, after his interview, arranged a meeting between Beckwith and his son-in-law, Alexander Hamilton.[97]

Hamilton seized the occasion to set forth for Beckwith his version of an arrangement that would be to the advantage of both countries. He wanted above all, he said, a commercial treaty "to every extent, to which you may think it for your interest to go." Ideally this would be on the liberal principles proposed by Lord Shelburne at the close of the Revolution, though Hamilton recognized that the spirit reflected in the subsequent navigation and regulatory acts, as well as in the writings of certain English publicists, now made such liberality unlikely. Still, he thought, the British might at least let our ships into the West Indies "under certain limitations as to size of vessels"; this would be better than "a rigid adherence to your present plan to produce a system of warfare in Commercial matters." Trade with France, moreover, brought few of the benefits to America of that with England; "what she can furnish, is by no means so essential or so suited to us as your productions, nor do our raw materials suit her so well as they do you." When Beckwith raised the matter of tonnage discrimination and the efforts that had been made to adopt such a policy (this being the topic he had been sent to sound warnings on), Hamilton assured him: "Whilst the Revenue and Tonnage Bills were under discussion, I was decidedly opposed to those discriminating clauses, that were so warmly advocated by some gentlemen." Beckwith said he had been surprised to find the name of James Madison among these persons, he being "a man, from whose character for good sense, and other qualifications, I should have been led to expect a very different conduct." Hamilton confessed that he was "likewise rather surprised at it."

> The truth is, that although this gentleman is a clever man, he is very little acquainted with the world. That he is uncorrupted and incorruptible I have not a doubt; he has the same end in view that I have, and so have these gentlemen who act with him, but their mode of attaining it is very different.[98]

In sum, the principal point Hamilton wished to make with Beckwith was that "I have always preferred a connexion with you, to that of any other country, *we think in English,* and have a similarity of prejudices and of predilections." What he had in mind was a commercial treaty; he even hinted at another point in the conversation—though no more than vaguely—that this might some day extend to "political friendship" as well. He assured Beckwith, moreover, "that the ideas I have thrown out, may be depended upon, as the sentiments of the most enlightened men in this country, they are those of General Washington, I can confidently assure you, as well as of a great majority in the Senate."[99]

All in all, this was stretching matters, though just what Hamilton's indiscretion consisted of in this interview, and at such a time, is less than self-evident. Probably the mode of communication in itself would not have been found objectionable.

Though Major Beckwith had no official capacity, it would be too much to say that he was acting here as a British spy, or even as a "secret agent." His presence in New York was certainly known; he had attended one of Washington's levees, and he had even had some conversation with the President concerning a piece of business which the latter had recently initiated with Lord Dorchester. And Hamilton, given his own ends, might be expected to grasp his opportunity when he saw it. The real stretch, rather, consisted in Hamilton's representation of Washington's views. He may not have misrepresented their letter, but he hardly conveyed their spirit.[100]

Relations with Great Britain were indeed very much on Washington's mind. He too would undoubtedly have been pleased if those objectives which Hamilton had outlined to Beckwith could be achieved, other things being equal. But other things were not equal. Washington's priorities and those of Hamilton were perceived quite differently, and for Washington a comprehensive connection between the two countries was certainly not at the top of the list. Some serious difficulties would need to be settled before "friendship" of any but the most perfunctory kind was even thinkable. Foremost among these was the British failure to evacuate the frontier posts in the American Northwest which they had continued to occupy in disregard of the Peace Treaty of 1783. Directly related to this was the continued hostility of the Indian tribes throughout the Northwest. Given the inadequacy of American military power, efforts to pacify that area and to promote settlement through the making of treaties were facing grave impediments, which would continue as long as British garrisons held the posts. By the same token, the authorities in Canada had the most compelling motives, both economic and strategic, for retaining them. The fur trade, operated by British merchants whose depot was Montreal, was "the greatest and most profitable single industry in North America."[101] The Indians who supplied the furs lived for the most part south of the American border, and they themselves were dependent on supplies and protection from the occupied posts. For the British to give up the posts, therefore, was to abandon control not only of the fur trade but of their Indian allies as well, with consequences for the military security of Canada that the governors dreaded to contemplate. The force of these considerations had made itself felt at Whitehall almost as soon as the Peace Treaty was completed. Thereafter the impotence of the Confederation Congress to prevent state legislatures from obstructing collection of British debts and harassing former Loyalists—contrary to Articles IV, V, and VI of the Treaty—became the settled excuse for not delivering up the posts. What this further implied was a set of severe strains upon the allegiance of settlers in the Ohio Valley to the United States. These communities required security as well as free navigation of the Mississippi for their produce; they enjoyed neither; in the case of Kentucky, and elsewhere as well, their discontents were being played upon by British intrigues to encourage separationist tendencies. The interconnectedness of all these factors was well understood by the President.[102]

There were further difficulties. Another issue arising from the Peace Treaty was the failure to return or make restitution for the slaves carried off by the British army during and after the Revolution, contrary to the provisions of Article VII.

Then there was the affront to American sovereignty implied in the British government's neglect to establish a legation and send a regular minister to the United States. The American minister in London during the 1780s, John Adams, had been virtually ignored, and until that government showed a disposition to exchange representatives in good faith, Washington was not inclined to appoint another. And finally there was, of course, the problem of trade with the British West Indies.

It was not that Hamilton, in his talk with Beckwith, had ignored these matters. Except for the question of exchanging ministers, he had been careful to touch on them all. But Alexander Hamilton in his state of urgency was overlooking those basic conventions which must govern the conduct of any diplomacy, at any level. Hamilton desperately wanted friendship, and he had placed his entire case upon that basis. But diplomacy, even if one of the ends is friendship, requires for its own protection an adversary setting; this was not a negotiation but an appeal. To be sure, neither Hamilton nor Beckwith had any powers to conduct a negotiation. But there was nothing to prevent their rehearsing one, and in this time of flux every rehearsal mattered.

But again, Hamilton was making a projection. And characteristically, it was the sweep of the projection, rather than the immediate problems and inconveniences of diplomacy, that engaged his imagination. We see his mind moving in much the same way here as it was doing concurrently with respect to national finance. "Probabilities are always a rational ground of contract": why not act upon them now? If we move rationally (he told himself and Beckwith), a commercial understanding becomes inevitable; then given close commercial relations, an even closer understanding—perhaps extending to an actual alliance—would appear perfectly logical. (History would, of course, bear him out, though the century or so that this would require involved more than an inconvenience.) Thus the temptation to include Washington himself in this projection—to project something as being true that was not true yet but presumably would be in the future—must have been overwhelming. Especially so, in view of something else Hamilton told Beckwith which already was true. He told him that a special mission to England would shortly be appointed in order to sound out the Ministry on the very matters they themselves had been discussing. Washington had, in fact, been considering just such a move, and he had probably made up his mind already that the clever Gouverneur Morris—then in Paris on private business—should be the man to carry it out. He would, within a few days, complete a set of instructions to Morris together with a letter of credence, and send them off before departing on his tour of New England.[103]

It was logical that James Madison should not favor such a mission—certainly not yet. When Madison took his leave of Washington on October 8 before setting off for Virginia, the President asked his opinion on it, and Washington afterwards recorded in his diary that "with respect to the private agent to ascertain the disposition of the British Court with respect to the Western Posts and a Commercial treaty, he thought if the necessity did not press, it would be better to wait the arrival of Mr. Jefferson, who might be able to give the information wanted on this head. . . ."[104] James Madison, author of the tonnage discrimination plan, faced with what might from his viewpoint be a premature accommodation with England, was temporizing. He did not want the options on his plan foreclosed, especially insofar as they might affect American relations with France. His notions and those of Hamilton on the indispensability of such an accommodation were obviously quite different.

But for Washington evidently the necessity did press, and for reasons more immediate than those of either. Hamilton wanted a commercial understanding which would, among other things, block discrimination; Madison wanted no such understanding until it could be seen what discrimination might do to effect it; Washington wanted a settlement of differences through the processes of diplomacy, and he wanted to begin at once. No one knew when Jefferson would arrive, Jefferson himself did not yet know of his nomination as Secretary of State, and there was no certainty at all that he would accept it when he did. As for the question that concerned Washington most—the state of affairs on the northwest frontier—he already had all the information he needed to convince him of its urgency.[105] It may be supposed that before leaving for New England the President wanted to leave a clean desk.

A clear by-product of all this, for Alexander Hamilton, was the makings of a very special attitude toward England. An anglophile position on virtually everything was a basic component in what Hamilton would come to stand for ideologically, and it would be of extraordinary importance in the political divisions of the future.

Such a predilection was organic to Hamilton's entire experience and temperament. Not only did he see his financial plan as depending in the most fundamental way on a close understanding with Great Britain, but the plan itself was overwhelmingly "British" in character. It was a reordering of British ideas and British experience, without which it would hardly have been thinkable. The closest thing to a model for Hamilton's new society was Great Britain's—or at least those aspects of British society that had most affected America, those having to do with trade, manufacturing, and overseas commerce. The primacy of trade; the prominence and pervasiveness of credit, not as an interim resort but as a way of life; banks; funded debts; large-scale money transactions: all those images that were most negative and odious to James Madison, the Virginian, were to Alexander Hamilton positive, dynamic, and creative. This very configuration, so full of promise to him, had made Great Britain and all its influences hateful to the Virginians. Their picture of separation had always been a total one. It was a separation not only political but economic and—above all—moral as well, and from all appearances they were not yet done. With Hamilton, on the other hand, the basic fact was the one he laid on the line to Beckwith: *we think in English.*

This predisposition toward Great Britain and British ways of doing things reached so far back into Hamilton's experience that in certain respects even the Revolution did not really affect it. Many elements had gone to make it up, and his life in the West Indies may well have been the most decisive one. The community there may have been a planting community, but it was the merchant who brought it to life and gave it whatever touch it had with the outside world. (It was this class of men, moreover, that had first recognized the talents of Alexander Hamilton.) In no setting, probably, could the cosmopolitan character of the eighteenth-century merchant have been more sharply appreciated.

Then there was Hamilton's oft-repeated regard for the English constitution. His words at Philadelphia in praise of the British government as "the best in the world" gave him a reputation in later years as an advocate of "monarchy," which he would spend the rest of his life denying. But above all he wanted energy in government, and there could be no energy without a vigorous Executive. "The English model [is] the only good one on this subject," he declared, the only one "which unites public strength with individual security." With energy went order, which was his other passion, and this too was to be found in its aptest balance under the English constitution. With this guide, he believed, "we ought to go as far . . . to attain permanency and stability, as republican principles will admit."[106]

This passion for order included everything from Hamilton's immediate surroundings to society at large, and it had been with him from the first. He loathed disarray in his own affairs, and he detested anarchy in society, which made it fully in character that the youthful Hamilton, ardent Whig though he was, should have acted so swiftly to protect Myles Cooper, the Tory president of King's College, from the ire of a Patriot mob in 1775, or that as a rising lawyer in the 1780s he should have defended former Loyalists against the legal harassments put upon them by a vengeful public. It might even be said that Hamilton's very pride, his acute sense of both personal and public honor, had strong "English" implications. His country needed to establish its claims to nationhood; revolution or not, he wanted it done right, and given that, the first nation with which it had to make its terms was the very one against which the struggle had been made. He was jealous of his country's honor; it should stand well, especially with its former parent. Indeed, his willingness to take up arms could itself be considered as a matter not so much of rage as of honor, and on those grounds he would have done it again, even against England. Thus if his country in the process of asserting its claim should do anything petty, he would take it as a personal humiliation, and various of his acts and utterances may be read in this light. In the celebrated *Rutgers* v. *Waddington* case of 1784, he argued against the award of punitive damages to the owner of a New York City brewhouse whose property had been occupied by a British merchant during the war, and he did so on grounds of international law and international honor. In 1782 he pleaded for the life of Charles Asgill, a nineteen-year-old British officer who had been selected by lot to die in retaliation for the hanging of an American prisoner. Such an act, he thought, was beneath our dignity. He argued that "if we wreak our resentment on an innocent person, it will be suspected that we are too fond of executions," and that it would have "an influence peculiarly unfavorable to the General's character." (James Madison, then sitting in Congress, had voted to approve the execution.) And it was for reasons of honor, among others, that Hamilton in 1780 had urged the granting of Major André's petition that he be shot rather than hanged.[107]

In any event, a variety of influences from the past were now being given new impetus by the commitments Alexander Hamilton was undertaking in the fall of 1789.

But how real were Hamilton's picture of England and his hopes for an early accommodation? What were the chances of his making happen what he so desperately wanted to happen? His contacts with Major Beckwith—he would have several more during the coming months—were on the whole encouraging. Beckwith was congenial; the two appear to have got on well. Yet it cannot be assumed that the impressions Beckwith gave Hamilton reflected with full precision the spirit of the Ministry in London, because the interests of Canada and those of the Ministry vis-à-vis the United States diverged in at least one important respect. In the eyes of Lord Dorchester and of his aide, the security of the Canadian frontier was a problem sufficiently absorbing as to make an accommodation with the Americans on the West Indies trade at least worth considering. Thus Beckwith's own wishes may have had something to do with the impressions he would give, and at which Hamilton would grasp.[108] These, as it turned out, would have no basis, and would come to nothing.

Another consideration, however, involved the enlightened sentiments of Pitt and Shelburne as manifested directly after the Revolution, which ought to have counted for something. They had contemplated a favorable arrangement with America which might have extended so far as full privileges of the Empire regarding trade with the British colonies. Pitt was a man of reason, and back of his conception of commerce stood the rational intelligence of David Hume and Adam Smith, whose thoughts had greatly influenced his. Yet this side of the British mind was hardly the dominant side by 1789, nor was it even any longer the dominant side of Pitt's own. The idea of accommodation with America in matters of trade had flickered briefly and at best half-heartedly, and it was not long after Shelburne's departure from office that the conciliatory projects of both Pitt and Fox were abandoned by their authors once and for all, and with few regrets. The heavily dominant side of the question was that represented intellectually by Lord Sheffield and politically by the unreconstructed mercantilist Lord Hawkesbury. By 1789—indeed, well before then—it had come to be fully shared for practical purposes even by such onetime "friends" of America as Pitt and Fox themselves. They too, with most others, were by now strongly disposed to think that the best of all possible footings with regard to America was the status quo.[109]

A further question, however, is that of whether the alternative envisioned by James Madison was a real one. The basic assumption behind any proposal Madison had made, or would make, was that the United States had both the power and the will either to coerce England into adopting a policy of reciprocity, or, failing that, to do without her trade entirely and establish new patterns of commerce elsewhere. There was no evidence, then or subsequently, for such an assumption. Sheffield had made his case, and the result was a settled commitment to the Navigation Laws rooted in the conviction that they were essential to Great Britain's maritime strength. It was fairly clear that the initial reaction to any hostile act would be retaliation, beginning with the elimination of all special privileges which American shippers already enjoyed, of which there were a number—all loss, since of course the opening of the West Indies would be farther away than ever. Madison did understand that to coerce England effectively it would be necessary both to cut off the raw materials exported from America in British ships and to block the admission of British manufactured goods into American ports, and he was preparing to advance these very ideas in the next session of Congress. This would eliminate the bulk of Anglo-American commerce and amount to a virtual embargo. A very nice question was thereupon that of which side would break first. The British, to be sure, had a great deal of commerce at stake, roughly a sixth of their total, and the distresses would certainly not be negligible.[110] But for the Americans the stake was about three-fourths, and the costs of undertaking to do without it had to be reckoned in categories that embraced the country's very political stability. It would undercut all current efforts to settle the national finances and would risk a collapse of American credit abroad. The new government, moreover, still engaged as it was in consolidating the loyalty of its citizens, would now find itself required to demand from them a series of extraordinary sacrifices—a dwindling market for food crops, a serious strain on the entire mercantile and maritime community, and removal of the first taste of prosperity Americans had known in some years—all for an object whose value might well seem abstract in view of the price being asked. The ostensible object was the opening by formal treaty of a West Indies trade much of which was already accessible informally. As for the supposed alternative, a whole new pattern of trade: whether this could be more than a theoretical construct was a question that had already been tested, with dismal results.[111] In any case, the policy had now been so formulated that a contest of wills became the precondition for any outcome, whatever its nature, and whether Madison had ever actually tried to project the steps, or think through the implications, is doubtful. Here, in short, was the first instance of a dilemma the lessons of which Americans in all their history have never been quite willing to learn: the extreme difficulty of coercing another country, and the self-discipline and sacrifice that are required in order to undertake it.

But there was a final factor bearing on the question of any British action, either hoped for or feared, with regard to America, and it was one which set both the Hamiltonian and Madisonian views on a more or less equal plane of unreality. This was the factor of sheer inattention. The claims that any American could make on English attention for any purpose, and the degree of attention a British ministry was inclined to spare for any version of American policy, were minimal. By the same token this was the last factor the Americans—the center of whose universe was naturally themselves—could bring themselves to perceive. Gouverneur Morris, arriving in London in the early spring of 1790, would be kept waiting a month before the Foreign Secretary troubled to answer his initial inquiries, and then would get nowhere.[112] Such neglect had been the rule for the previous seven years, and would continue to be so for the indefinite future. There would be apparent exceptions, but there is another rough rule which might be useful in gauging them. Any flutter of concern the British authorities might show for American affairs was in direct proportion to whatever effort was needed for enabling them to resume what they had been doing about those affairs since 1783, which was nothing.

The Divided Mind of
James Madison, 1790: Nationalist
Versus Ideologue

James Madison was absent from New York from October 9, 1789, to January 20, 1790. He was beset by bouts of illness at either end of his round journey, and in between, his mind was occupied by a variety of problems. Added up, they represented among other things the dilemma of what it meant to be both a leading Federalist and a leading Virginian. The search for a resolution of that dilemma would turn out to claim virtually the whole of James Madison's energies throughout the congressional session of 1790.

Madison, aware that his friend Jefferson was on his way home from France, had lingered an extra week or so in New York in the hope of welcoming him there. At length he set off southward. But he stopped at Philadelphia and waited in that city for nearly three weeks more, still hoping for some news of Jefferson's arrival. None came, but while there he chanced to run into Robert Morris, the senator from Pennsylvania, and the two had a lengthy conversation on the question of where the national capital should eventually be located.[1] This issue had already been debated extensively in the session of 1789 just completed, and had occasioned tortuous maneuverings both open and covert. Bargains had been made and remade, understandings reached and then repudiated, and the matter had been left in a state of volatile non-resolution at the time of adjournment. Robert Morris had been heavily involved throughout, as had Madison.

Two factions, generally speaking, had been in contention, with a third holding the balance of power. For years it had been the dream of Jefferson, Madison, and Washington himself that the capital might some day be located on the banks of the Potomac, and for this design the Virginians now had the support, other things being equal, of the other southern states. Then there was a Pennsylvania bloc, in which Morris was prominent, whose members were interested in one or more of three possible locations in Pennsylvania. They were Philadelphia and Germantown, both on or near the Delaware, and some site as yet unspecified on the Susquehanna. The Pennsylvanians, from varying internal interests, were not always united, and the nature of their support from neighboring states likewise fluctuated. (Maryland, for example, naturally preferred the Susquehanna, while Delaware and New Jersey inclined to the Delaware.) Finally, there was a third group consisting of New York and the other northern states of New England. They would have liked New York above any other place, but they realized that in view of the universal desire for geographic centrality the most they could hope for New York was that the capital might be kept there temporarily for a few years longer. But of all possible other locations, the one the Northerners found least acceptable was the Potomac.

Thus among these three groups there were really two issues, not simply one; the temporary capital as well as the permanent capital. In a practical sense they were of equal importance, constituting two bargaining items that could be played off one against the other. There was a generally unspoken assumption that the permanent capital would probably be located at a place not yet developed—a village or less, rather than an existing large city—which meant that the site, wherever it might be, would require a period of preparation, and that consequently the seat of government could not be transferred there at once. It was likewise assumed that the temporary capital would meanwhile reside in one or the other of the country's two largest cities, in New York or in Philadelphia. The importance of this as a bargaining item was the beckoning hope, also unspoken, cherished by the respective supporters of these two cities that once the capital were settled *ad interim* in either of them, a way might subsequently be found to keep it there. And behind all the bargaining, there had been and would continue to be two sets of motives, those of geographic convenience and those of local self-interest. It was thus in the nature of the case that a kaleidoscopic variety of combinations was possible, that no single resolution could be counted on as the "logical" one, and that in the meantime—thanks to the profusion of interests involved—various acts of minor treachery were to be expected down to the end. All this was perfectly understood, and indeed taken for granted, by everyone.[2]

What Morris now proposed to Madison was a bargain between Pennsylvania and the South, whereby the temporary capital would be moved to Philadelphia and the permanent one located on the Potomac. But the same arrangement had been struck before, and it was Robert Morris himself who had sabotaged it. (Morris wanted above all else a site in the Germantown area, having valuable lands there.) Madison had no doubt he would do it again if he could, meanwhile using such a bargain merely as a threat under which the Northerners might agree to any Pennsylvania location in order to remain in New York for the time being and keep the permanent capital away from the Potomac. So when Morris said he intended to "speak seriously to the S. States," Madison was skeptical, and said so. "I told him they must be spoken to very seriously, after what had passed, if Penna. expected them to listen to her. . . ." Shortly after his talk with Robert Morris, Madison took to his bed and was confined to quarters for about two weeks, probably with dysentery, and did not arrive at Montpelier until the first week in November.[3]

In addition to the question of the national capital, his impressions of which he promptly reported to Washington, Madison during this interim was beset with two major concerns. One had to do with the recalcitrance of his own state of Virginia in ratifying the bill-of-rights amendments which he himself had fashioned, and the other involved the future role to be played in the affairs of the Republic by Thomas Jefferson.

"The enmity to Govt. is I believe as strong as ever in this State," Henry Lee wrote Madison late in November. "Indeed I have no doubt of this fact if the assembly be considered as a just index of the feelings of the people." Madison had rather more confidence than Lee in Virginia's loyalty to the United States, yet it was obvious that Antifederalism was still very strong there, and that a variety of stratagems was being resorted to in the legislature to prevent the amendments' being ratified. To the ones immediately before them, the Virginians had little objection. But they wanted more, and they were as much concerned with state power as with individual rights. "It is impossible," Virginia's two senators had written, "for us not to see the necessary tendency to consolidated empire in the natural operation of the Constitution if no further amended than as now proposed. . . ." The opponents feared that if the present amendments were approved, the sense of urgency needed to bring about a general convention for proposing further ones would have been drained off. The chief object they had in mind was to do away with Congress's power of direct taxation. The theme of direct taxation was to recur in the public discourse of Virginia again and again in the years to come, and Madison must have realized that the touchiness of Virginians about being taxed for anything—going back to the days of Charles Townshend and Lord North—was something to be borne in mind for the immediate future, especially as it might concern provision for the public credit. Anything beyond the bare essentials in that respect was sure to meet resistance from Virginia. "Can you not," asked Henry Lee, "make your W. lands equal to the support of your domestic debt Note redemption. This being done will the revenue arising from commerce be sufficient for the support of govt. & the payment of interest on the foreign debt. I hope so, for indeed if it is not I am at a loss to see what you will or can do."[4]

At any rate, enough obstructions were devised in the Assembly that for the time being no action was taken on the amendments, and Virginia, though "one of the first states to consider ratification," according to an authority on the Bill of Rights, "was the last (of the necessary eleven) to approve them."[5]

Madison's other preoccupation was with whether or not Jefferson could be prevailed upon to accept Washington's nomination as Secretary of State, a question which gave him no little anxiety. The day before Madison's departure for Virginia, Washington had told him of his plans for the Gouverneur Morris mission, and Madison could not have helped sensing in this piece of news some vague threat to his own version of the line that ought to be taken toward Great Britain. He hoped Washington would delay his decision until Jefferson's return. But when the President went ahead with his plans, sending on to Madison at Montpelier a copy of his instructions to Morris, Madison wrote out a memorandum on the subject in which he made three main points. One was that England should honor the treaty already concluded before the two countries made any other treaties; another was that his own plan for commercial discrimination against England had failed not because it was "wrong in its principle" but because some had thought it "defective in energy"; and the third was Madison's conviction, once more expressed, that there would be much advantage in awaiting Jefferson's arrival before doing anything with regard to negotiations with England. Indeed, on the very day he was told of the Morris mission, Madison had written to Jefferson in tones of some urgency:

> I wish on a public account to see you as soon as possible after you become informed of the new destination provided for you. It is of infinite importance that you should not disappoint the public wish on this subject. Be persuaded of the truth, with proper opportunity it can be demonstrated to you. Let me particularly intreat you not to yield hastily to objections. . . . Drop me a line the moment you get on shore.[6]

Jefferson landed at Norfolk on November 23, where he first heard the news of his appointment. He was not inclined to accept, and his acknowledgment to Washington was equivocal, one of his reservations having to do with the domestic burdens of the secretaryship in addition to those of foreign affairs. Late in December Madison rode over to Monticello for a reunion and a good talk, with further urgings and assurances that the domestic duties would be light. He reported hopefully to Washington that some of his friend's doubts had been overcome, and that things now looked more favorable. Madison did not arrive in New York in time for the reconvening of Congress on January 4, having been detained in Virginia first by his mother's illness and then by his own. Another attack of dysentery immobilized him some time at Georgetown, and he finally reached New York on January 20. A few days before that, the Secretary of the Treasury's Report on Public Credit had been distributed, and Madison had not had time to give it full study when he sat down to write once more to Jefferson. He gave Jefferson a final nudge on the Secretaryship of State, though it seems to have become reasonably clear by then that he would accept, as he eventually did three weeks thence. A new concern by now had made its way into Madison's mind. It regarded a breed of men whom everything in his training and background had predisposed him to detest, men currently engaged in speculation in the public securities. In that same letter to Jefferson he remarked, relative to Hamilton's report: "Previous to its being made, the avidity for stock had raised it from a few shillings to 8/ or 10/ in the pound, and emissaries are still exploring the interior and distant parts of the Union in order to take advantage of the ignorance of holders."[7]

I

Madison on Funding

James Madison's unexpected attack on Hamilton's proposed system—on funding, through his plan of discriminating between current and original holders, and on assumption of state debts, through counter-proposals almost certain to make assumption unacceptable—continues to raise puzzling questions. Madison's own schemes, if enacted, would have increased the debt considerably, and his plan—if such it may be called—would thus have cost the public substantially more than Hamilton's. Madison in the Confederation Congress had favored assumption and opposed discrimination, the very reverse of the stand he was now about to take; he had been a tireless advocate for sound support of the public credit, and he himself had recently taken the lead in creating a strong Treasury Department. And here he was, early in 1790, preparing to mount the most determined opposition to the work of his former close associate and friend Alexander Hamilton. Hamilton was shocked, and never would fully understand it. How is the turnabout to be explained? And indeed, considering the curiously high value Madison seems to have placed on consistency, how much of a turnabout really was it?

In the light of the outcome, the leading authority on this era of national finance suspects Madison of a certain knowing deviousness, all primarily directed toward caring for the material interests of Virginia. But in view of the man's probity as well as his stubbornness, we might do well to begin, at least, with Madison's own explanation for the course he took. According to him, it was not he but the problem itself that had changed. He and Hamilton had a final talk shortly before the debates on funding began, in which he admitted to Hamilton what he was about to do. As the latter recalled it, Madison "alledged in his justification that the very considerable alienation of the debt, subsequent to the periods at which he had opposed a discrimination, had essentially changed the state of the question." Madison was referring, in short, to the dramatic emergence of speculators and speculation as a gross visible fact. There is much reason to take him at his word, and to conclude that he was, after all, basically animated by principle. But what sort of principle? If Madison's grasp of business affairs was in any way competent, as presumably it was, why should speculation have been so shocking to him and not to Hamilton? The answer may well lie, as with so much else in James Madison's behavior, in the sociology of his being a Virginian; it may also be that his understanding of financial affairs, full as it may have been in its way, was of a qualitatively different order from that of a man whose experience had been entirely interwoven with such affairs.[8]

The fluctuation in market value of the various categories of the domestic debt, and the process whereby holdings in it were transferred and concentrated, had a history that went back nearly a decade. Three general categories of paper—four, if state debts are included—should be distinguished in this connection. The solidest category consisted of about $11 million in "loan certificates," representing money lent directly to Congress during the war by citizens of means. Interest had been regularly paid on these notes until 1782. After that time their market price settled down to between twenty and twenty-five cents on the dollar, and so remained until 1788. A second category was that of "final settlement certificates" in the amount of $17 million, issued in 1783 to soldiers in payment for military service and to civilian creditors for supplies and services rendered to the army. By far the greater part of these certificates, especially those received by soldiers, were sold soon after being issued. They went at a great discount, and the market rate of ten to fifteen cents on the dollar generally held until about the time the new federal government went into operation. A third category was indents, or certificates of accrued interest, the face value of which came to approximately $13 million. These were even more highly speculative, owing to uncertainty as to whether they would be funded on equal terms with principal, and their market price had probably never gone above ten cents on the dollar prior to 1789.[9]

All categories of securities had begun to appreciate in value as soon as it became clear, the requisite number of states having ratified the Constitution, that a new federal government was a certainty. The rise in prices became especially sharp during the final quarter of 1789, when those men most heavily engaged in speculative activity were doing their best to predict the form Hamilton's forthcoming recommendations would take. For example, loan certificates, the steadiest category of the debt, were being quoted in December 1789 at fifty cents on the dollar, having virtually doubled in value since mid-year. But the best speculative opportunities by this time were seen to lie in the realm of state debts, the securities of which could still be had for prices ranging from ten cents to twenty cents on the dollar, together with indents, whose price remained similarly low. It was speculation in state debts that Senator Maclay referred to in his diary when he wrote of vessels and "expresses with very large sums of money" heading southward to buy up certificates; Madison, writing to Jefferson of emissaries "still exploring the interior and distant parts of the Union in order to take advantage of the ignorance of holders," was referring to the same thing. Meanwhile the larger part of the domestic debt had long since passed from its original holders, and had become concentrated in relatively few hands. $12.3 million in Continental securities for which there are specific records was held by 3,300 individuals, 100 of them holding $5 million of it, and another 170 holding $2.6 million more. In state debts the concentration was even more striking. Seventy-two percent of the North Carolina debt, for example, was held by a group small enough to have met in one room.[10]

This furious speculative activity, it was alleged, owed much to inside information gained prior to publication of the Secretary's report. That there was such information is more than likely, though neither the extent of it nor the amount of difference it may have made at this point can be known with any certainty. Hamilton himself seems to have been quite circumspect. To one friend who tried to draw him out he replied: "I am sure you are sincere when you say you would not subject me to an impropriety. . . . But you remember the saying with regard to Caesar's Wife." On the other hand, among those with whom Hamilton sat at various New York dinner tables during this period were men whose interests required that they be endlessly sensitive to every nuance, however guarded, of the Secretary's conversation. One such was Andrew Craigie, of the mercantile firm of Craigie and Constable. Craigie could not be absolutely certain, but he knew how to put two and two together, and after one of these occasions he predicted that Hamilton would recommend both the equal funding of indents and the assumption of state debts. He turned out to be right on both counts. At the Treasury itself, moreover, Hamilton had as his assistant a man in whom private and public interest were richly intermixed. This was the ineffable William Duer, strong neither in scruple nor discretion, whose own speculative enterprises would finally bring him to disgrace. That Hamilton could have kept all his secrets to himself amid such circumstances is very doubtful. Meanwhile the market crackled with excitement both at home and abroad; for American merchants and Dutch bankers alike, United States public securities were the best thing in sight.[11]

But the question remains: what is there about the picture of speculation that can drive a man mad? Much depends on the man and how he happens to be situated, and we ought to have a nice sense of this in order to take a man like James Madison, at this phase of his career, seriously. For Madison's biographer, Irving Brant, it is no problem at all. In Brant's pages we follow the virtuous Madison in his earnest assault upon the speculators, who self-evidently represent the forces of darkness, in a drama of good and bad curiously lacking in tension. In E. James Ferguson's *The Power of the Purse,* on the other hand, the thing is seen as somewhat less simple. Assuming Madison to have been well acquainted with the facts of life, Ferguson regards his moves during the funding debates as "dictated by political expediency rather than a concern for the common man." That is, by making the Continental veterans partial beneficiaries of a funding scheme which would so increase the debt as to make assumption of state debts insupportable, Madison could have things both ways. He could in any case establish "an impeccable moral position," and if his plan were actually accepted it would rule out assumption, to which Virginia was stoutly opposed. It was, in short, "the opening move in a resumption of state-oriented politics."[12]

There is enough truth in such a view to give it a rough serviceability in mapping the turns which were beginning to occur in James Madison's public actions. Certainly the form and tactics would be clothed with considerable sophistication, as might be expected of a man who had always known that his talent for influencing events depended almost wholly on a parliamentary setting. And the result would, indeed, draw Madison closer again to his Virginia origins. But this still does not quite touch the finer vibrations of the man's character, which need not always be gauged by rationalistic criteria. Several considerations should be placed prior to all else. One is that there was no stronger nationalist, on the question of a government's paying the full value of its rightful debts and keeping its credit spotless before the world, than James Madison. Madison's view had more than once opposed itself, in this and other matters, to the parochial prejudices of Virginia. Another, however, is that with regard to the everyday world of trade and finance no Virginian, Madison included, could really experience the "facts of life" or apprehend them in the same way as a Philadelphian or a New Yorker. Thus how could he not be shocked by doings the most obvious analogy to which, in his own world, was hoggish gambling? And finally, there was the enormous stake that he, James Madison, already had in the tone and character of the new Republic. After everything he himself had personally given to the shaping of it, influences were now emerging which he might have foreseen with his mind but not with his viscera: they were being wielded by men whose ways he simply did not know, men who were not of his sort.

Perhaps the most distinctive feature in any business community's life is a fixed and unwavering attention to the complex set of variables that govern the price of any commodity. There is a certain respect, howbeit grudging, for the person who can manipulate these variables, make true predictions from them, and take advantage of such predictions. Something of the sort, to be sure, occurs in agriculture as well. But there, the true opponent is nature; "honesty" is not an issue, and one is not necessarily engaged in outmaneuvering the rest of mankind. There, one somehow does not think of "killings." The business world, however, does have its special morality. The risks involved in any projection are all part of it, and with the possibility of loss in any man's operations one is not prepared to deny him the rewards of his risks. In that sense, the honest and the dishonest trader partake of the same morality; and in a not dissimilar sense, moving from normal activity into speculation is to cross a line that may not be invisible but is certainly very blurred. Wherever the market fluctuates in either direction, which is most of the time, speculation hovers; it is very much a matter of degree.

And so it was with the market for the federal debt in 1790. On the one hand, speculation—most especially in these circumstances—had been inevitable, though the average speculator at this point was operating not against widows and veterans but against other speculators. On the other hand, it was this very process of speculation that was bringing the debt toward par. The friends of funding argued, with a certain common sense, that the sooner it did so the better, and that when it did, speculation would cease. And there, indeed, was the irony: the work of no man, from the early 1780s on, had been more critical to the entire process of speculation than that of James Madison. Speculation had a life of its own throughout this period, being affected by only one gross factor, the question of whether eventually there would or would not be a government competent to honor its engagements. Meanwhile a community of speculators remained acutely sensitive to every piece of news that might affect the price of securities. James Madison, fighting for a specie income, going on record as opposed to discrimination and favoring assumption, laboring at Philadelphia for a constitution, speaking in Richmond and writing in New York on behalf of its ratification, drafting the first tariff act, and organizing the Treasury Department, had probably been more important in the making of that news than any other individual.

Yet the basic fact remains that James Madison did not come from a community in which mercantile affairs was a highly developed concern. Consequently a sense of the relationship between such affairs and the affairs of government, which was second nature in all the cities of the seaboard, was in no real way organic with him. The lore of those places was no part of his experience, and the men who lived there, merchants and speculators, were a breed apart, "steeped in Anglicism." The Virginia gentry themselves constituted a very special community. With a psychology long adjusted to its own experience of insidership and control, it could be a very volatile quantity at those times when initiative and control seemed to have migrated elsewhere. And the public debt—flatly denounced by James Madison as "a public curse"—was one of those items with which Virginians had little to do. It was owned by other insiders, in other places, by men whose ways and doings were objects of suspicion, hostility, and contempt. Henry Lee, for one, was forcibly reminded of this when he requested of his old wartime friend Alexander Hamilton a bit of inside information for himself. He received, instead, Hamilton's little homily about "Caesar's Wife." And it was not so long thereafter that the same Henry Lee was writing wrathfully to Madison that he would rather do almost anything than endure "the rule of a fixed insolent northern majority." The only remedy for that, he thought, was moving the seat of government to the Potomac and doing away with "gambling systems of finance."[13]

We cannot know with precision just how quickly Madison made up his mind on funding, nor fully penetrate the process whereby he did it. The report was not available in print until about January 20, 1790, the day he arrived in New York. His initial response to it, judging from what he wrote to Jefferson four days later, was cautious and guarded.[14] He would not enter the debate immediately. But when he finally rose to make his opening statement on February 11, the range of possible positions had by then been established; he had already heard and considered the various arguments.

The bitterest opponent of the entire scheme—aside from provision for the foreign debt, which no one questioned and which was promptly adopted—had been James Jackson of Georgia. The brawling Jackson, a fundamentalist in anything involving fiscal complexity, would probably have been as glad if a way could be found not to pay the debt at all. He brought the issue of the speculators— "rapacious wolves seeking whom they may devour"—immediately into the open. Charging that these men "had an access to the information the report contained," he wished the seat of government had been "at any place in the woods, and out of the neighborhood of a populous city; all my unsuspecting fellow-citizens might then have been warned of their danger, and guarded themselves against the machinations of the speculators." At the very least, Jackson insisted, there should be some provision to benefit "the gallant veteran," from whom the speculators had "drained . . . the pittance which a grateful country had afforded him, in reward for his bravery and toils." Every one of these sentiments found some counterpart in the bosom of James Madison. But Jackson's plea for a long delay before taking up the report—obviously in the hope of rousing up as much resistance to it as he could—and then his emotional attack on the entire idea of a funded debt, added up to a position too baldly repudiationist for Madison to take very seriously.[15]

Nor did he find arguments for scaling down the debt morally palatable either. Such an argument was made by Samuel Livermore of New Hampshire. Livermore saw no reason for paying the full 6 percent originally offered on a debt "not incurred for efficient money lent, but for depreciated paper, or services done at exorbitant rates, or for goods or provisions supplied at more than their real worth." Otherwise it would be just as logical to pay face value on the Continental currency itself, which Hamilton had recommended retiring at the ratio of forty to one. Livermore agreed that the Secretary's 4 percent already represented a reduction of interest on the debt, but it was not enough of a reduction; something closer to 3 percent would be better. But whereas Madison may have appreciated some of the logic, the remedy was too crude for his taste. Neither unilateral action, with no pretense at negotiation, nor arbitrary cheese-paring quite comported with his idea of the public dignity. Hamilton's case for 4 percent, tied as it was to predictions of a gradual drop in interest rates generally, had at least the merit of rational consistency. (Nor could Madison have been much impressed by Livermore's effort to equate the debt with the emissions of paper money, which, unlike loan certificates, had never commanded anything resembling specie value.) Senator Maclay, about this time, tried to interest Madison in his own plan for scaling down the debt at 3 percent. Madison handed back Maclay's paper without bothering to read it. "His pride," Maclay fumed, "seems of that kind which repels all communication."[16]

Meanwhile strong arguments for upholding the public faith and public credit were being made by Representatives Elias Boudinot of New Jersey, John Laurance of New York, William L. Smith of South Carolina, and Fisher Ames of Massachusetts. Smith announced: "[W]e are not in a situation to determine whether we will or will not have a public debt. We have it already. . . . [I]t follows, of consequence, that we must pay. . . . The only question that can come before us is, the mode of doing it." Ames likewise insisted there was no choice: "If, then, the public contract is a solemn obligation upon us, we are bound to its true and faithful performance." "Shall it be said," Ames demanded, "that this Government, evidently established for the purpose of securing property, that, in its first act, it divested its citizens of seventy millions of money, which is justly due to individuals who have contracted with Government!" The nation's credit would evaporate, "and all this risk is to be run for the sake of—what?" But James Madison needed no convincing here. He himself had been arguing public faith and sound public credit for the better part of a decade. He could not have reversed himself on these grounds even if he had wanted to.[17]

Thus the only device left which would allow him to strike at the speculators, yet not impair the face value of the debt, was to discriminate between current and original holders on grounds of equitable justice. One such scheme had been advanced by Thomas Scott of western Pennsylvania, but it was so devised that the total capital value of the debt would be reduced. Aedanus Burke of South Carolina proposed a motion in general terms for discrimination, only to withdraw it the following day on the ground that he had not actually intended to vote for it.[18] Madison must have found this somewhat embarrassing. Thus, preparing to rise for the first time on February 11, Madison could hardly have expected to stand on the solidest of ground.

But before he could do so, there came a very disagreeable and inconvenient interruption. A petition from the annual assembly of Quakers at Philadelphia was presented, praying for abolition of the slave trade, and the episode produced a sudden flare-up in the House. It revealed, among other things, a measure of James

Madison's nationalism, which was still very strong, as well as the limits of Madison's willingness to exploit any issue that might seriously estrange the northern and the southern states. The members from Georgia and South Carolina erupted with wrath, and the vigorous Jackson, who two days before was deploring that "the honest and hard-working part of the community will promote the ease and luxury of men of wealth," now turned his thunder upon the honest and hard-working Quakers. "Is it to them we owe our present happiness?" Let them consult their Bibles, and "they will find that slavery is not only allowed but commended." The Southerners demanded that the petition not be referred to committee, because it asked for action by Congress that was unconstitutional and because, as Burke put it, "the rights of the Southern States ought not to be threatened, and their property endangered, to please people who would be unaffected by the consequences." The Northerners, on the other hand, insisted that it should be so committed, in order that due consideration might be given to how far Congress's powers did in fact extend with regard to (in Laurance's words) "a traffic which is a disgrace to human nature." Madison was alarmed. Remonstrating that "the question before the committee was no otherwise important than as gentlemen made it so by their serious opposition," he assured them that they might "vote for the commitment of the petition without any intention of supporting the prayer of it." The House, dividing on sectional lines, voted to commit, Madison voting with the Northerners.[19]

Turning now to the public debt, Madison began his remarks in a characteristically modest and deferential key. He had remained silent so far, he said, in order to keep his mind open and to benefit from the thoughts of others. But the time had finally come for setting forth a few thoughts of his own. The first was that whatever anyone said, the debt remained an inviolate national obligation, the same now as when it was contracted. He flatly rejected, moreover, any notion of cutting it down in either principal or interest, the amount of it continuing to be exactly what the United States had originally promised to pay: "a certain sum in principal, bearing an interest of 6 percent." "No logic," he declared, "no magic, in my opinion, can diminish the force of the obligation." So far, this was taking the highest possible ground. The solemn insistence on 6 percent was an especially shrewd cut at Hamilton, who had recommended that the debt be funded at less. If we are to pay our debts, Madison was in effect saying, let us really pay them.

So there was no doubt as to the debt's being owed. But the real question was, to whom? The original holders and the current holders, he argued, each had legitimate claims. "To pay both is perhaps beyond the public ability; and as it would far exceed the value received by the public, it will not be expected by the world, nor even by the creditors themselves. To reject wholly the claims of either is equally inadmissible. . . ." The only honorable alternative would be a compromise: "let it be a liberal one in favor of the present holders, let them have the highest price which has prevailed in the market; and let the residue belong to the original sufferers." This might not do "perfect justice," but it would do "more real justice" than anything yet proposed. The current holders, most of whom would still make a profit, could have no ground for complaint, while the original ones, who had been forced to take depreciated securities and then to sell them for whatever they could get, would at least receive "a tribute due to their merits." He would not normally think of interfering with a contract. But in the present case, with "a fluctuation amounting to seven or eight hundred per cent," the "ordinary maxims" did not apply. Madison was, in the last analysis, haunted by the specter of windfall gains for gamblers.[20]

Madison actually did not have much support for his position, and from Smith, Laurance, Sedgwick, and Ames came a barrage of objections. No fraud had been committed upon the original holders, and no kind of justice would be done by confiscating one person's property and giving it to another. Discrimination would seriously impair the public credit both at home and abroad; it was the very transferability of the debt—now being called into question—that had permitted it to rise in value. And finally, the work of tracing the original creditors would be an administrative nightmare, filling the land "with discontent, corruption, suits, and perjury." Fisher Ames implored the gentleman from Virginia to bethink himself. "That gentleman helped to frame the constitution. I have no doubt it is the better for his eminent abilities; I hope that the love of his own work, and his zeal for the cause which he has so ably supported, will induce him to abandon a measure, which tends so fatally to disappoint the first wishes of his own heart, and the hopes of his country."[21]

Madison was stubborn, argumentative, and angry. "He must renounce every sentiment which he had hitherto cherished, before his complaisance could admit that America ought to erect the monuments of her gratitude, not to those who saved her liberties, but to those who had enriched themselves in her funds." He repeated that soldiers and suppliers had been forced to accept depreciated paper for their services, that Congress should "consider not the form, but the substance—not the letter, but the equity" of the question, that discrimination need not be impracticable, and that with prompt payment of interest there need be no undermining of the public credit. But when the vote was taken on February 22, Madison's motion was overwhelmed. The count was 36 to 13, nine of the thirteen being Virginians. "The obstinacy of this man," wrote Maclay, "has ruined the opposition."[22]

Much heat had been generated over the merits and demerits of discrimination. As a matter of practicability, tracing the original holders would have been very complicated but not impossible, since records did exist. As to whether such an operation would have injured the public credit, there are no precise technical terms in which such a question can be answered. But in all probability it would have. To adopt Hamilton's plan would be to place the government's credit beyond doubt; to adopt Madison's would be to introduce uncertainty, and a business community does not respond well to uncertainty. Theoretically the United States, having paid face value on its securities at the full 6 percent as Madison proposed, would have had every right to expect an unimpeachable credit. But in fact the men upon whose actions credit was established and defined—men with capital—would be badly disappointed by such an arrangement; foreign investors would be injured by it; and this together with continued confusion in American public finance would probably have resulted in a significantly weaker credit at a higher cost. It need not be suggested that only by keeping businessmen contented can public credit be secured. But to alienate them *en masse,* as James Madison was threatening to do, would undoubtedly have led to difficulties. In any case, by insisting that the public credit would not suffer under a system of discrimination, Madison was in effect venturing predictions about these men's behavior. Yet in reality he was not making predictions at all. He was telling the world, and them, not how they *would* behave but how they ought to behave.

As to James Madison's motives, it has to be concluded that there was really nothing very devious about them. True, his letter of the previous November in response to Hamilton's request for suggestions had contained no hint of discrimination.[23] True, the transactions by which the soldiers had alienated their securities were not recent but had occurred years before, and thus Madison's own explanation for his change of mind—the recent fever of speculation—might at first seem dubious. But James Madison had had other things on his mind up to the time he had left New York early in October, and the really dramatic speculative activity had occurred between September and January. Nor could its full impact have struck him until his return. He must have realized from the start that he occupied a minority position in the House. But it would not be quite fair to suggest that he took it with less than full seriousness. To be sure, he might have hoped for indirect benefits, but his stand was certainly consistent if his motives were what he said they were. A major share of the speculation was by this time being carried on in various state debt securities, which meant that he might strike at the speculators in ways other than through the Continental veterans. The stakes were high, and the effort worth making. That is, the cost of funding the Continental debt on the terms Madison proposed, at 6 percent interest and with discrimination, would have ruled out the assumption of state debts and thus made havoc on a very rich field of speculation. Even taking into account the slim chances of success on discrimination, he might have exploited whatever support he had aroused on that issue to defeat assumption on some other ground when it came up for consideration, as it shortly would.

In any event James Madison believed in what he was doing, and the primary ground for his doing it was speculation. No hidden motive appears in the letter he wrote to Jefferson in the midst of the debate, insisting that the speculators should be allowed "the highest market price only," and that "the balance be applied to solace the original sufferers." And shortly thereafter to Edward Carrington, a Virginia correspondent of many years who had raised objections to his views on discrimination, Madison retorted that "there must be something wrong, radically & morally & politically wrong, in a system which transfers the reward from those who paid the most valuable of all considerations, to those who scarcely paid any consideration at all."[24]

2

Madison on Assumption

The struggle in the United States Congress over assumption of state debts in 1790 constitutes something more than just another block that has to be set in place to complete the early annals of the republic. Every major issue, and the mode of its disposal, in those first years was bound to have disproportionate consequences for the republic's future, and in no case more so than with assumption. Technically abstruse and more difficult to understand than funding, at the same time full of delayed and not-so-delayed ideological fuses, assumption must be considered with care. Before it was finally settled late in July 1790, it had been impinged upon— or had its path crossed—by a series of other issues each of which had some bearing on the outcome. They concerned not only national finance but maritime policy, relations with France and Great Britain, slavery, the rights of states, and the location of the national capital.

The principal forces that pulled on Madison throughout were those of ideology and those of nationalism. For him these no longer coincided as they once had; now, they were most of the time in a state of incipient conflict. There was, on the one hand, a particular version of a rightly ordered world retained by a very particular Virginian; there was, on the other hand, the need felt by that same Virginian to hold together in nationhood a variety of inconveniently disparate elements, by no means all Virginian and some perversely un-Virginian. For a peaceful resolution of assumption, Madison would permit his nationalist side to prevail. But he would do it grudgingly, and, given both his diffidence and his stubbornness, the grudge would remain.

Madison tried to block assumption, using tactics far less direct, with objectives more mixed and probably more diffuse, than had been the case with his approach to funding. It is this very diffuseness, together with the complexity of the issue itself and the artfulness of Madison's tactics, that makes it difficult to penetrate the workings of his mind. Each step of the process discloses something important, and each step was more or less rationally taken. To assume an utter rationality for the entire pattern, however, may be to leave something out. There is a certain impression that remains after the whole sequence is traversed and the variables arranged in every possible combination, which we would do well not to dismiss. It is that James Madison did what he did because of a spreading repugnance within himself to the entire system of which assumption was a part, that the more he saw of it and its layers of implication the less he liked it, and that—*within certain limits*—he would strike out at it in any way he could. He wanted somehow to render it less of a perfect total entity than that which had sprung from the mind of Alexander Hamilton, a mind whose overall purposes he no longer trusted and whose designs were revealing themselves as more and more of a piece. In this, it was Madison's ideological side that drove him on.

Those limits, however, were in the end decisive. On the one hand, he had never doubted that the national honor required an unassailable national credit. And on the other, he was finally convinced, from the tenacious fury with which the debt-ridden states of Massachusetts and South Carolina insisted upon assumption, that any provision for the public credit might well be wrecked and the Federal Union itself threatened if they did not get it. He thereupon settled for the best possible terms—having to do with the Revolutionary accounts as well as other matters—that could be had for the state of Virginia. And such was the man's perspicacity that all these alternatives and considerations were undoubtedly present in his mind, and held in a mixed state of suspension there, from the very first.

As to who wanted what, four or five categories should be distinguished among the friends and opponents of assumption. The position of Hamilton himself, as has been seen, was clear enough. His object was to unite all the public creditors, state and national, into a single body, thereby removing potential conflicts of interest between them and guaranteeing for the new government a solid basis of support from a united financial community. This would also reduce competition between state and federal governments for available sources of taxation. Moreover, by tying assumption to the related problem of a final settlement of Revolutionary accounts, the federal government would provide a formula whereby those states hardest pressed with Revolutionary debts would obtain immediate relief through assumption, and in the subsequent final settlement the claims of all would be generously interpreted. The $25 million so added to the public debt would thus—though the premise was not explicitly stated—constitute an additional increment of solid investment capital for economic development.[25]

The states with the heaviest burden of debt—Massachusetts and South Carolina being the outstanding cases—strongly desired assumption. In accepting the Constitution they had surrendered their best source of revenue, the impost, and could no longer service their debts. Theoretically a final settlement of accounts would lift this burden whether assumption were enacted or not, since their huge debts were a presumptive indication of these states having contributed more than their due share to the war effort. That is, they would turn out to be creditor states and thus entitled to compensation. But they were unwilling to wait for this, and wanted assumption now. A final settlement could not in any case occur immediately, if only because of the time required for the commissioners to complete the audit. Moreover, as long as legislation on the mode of final settlement remained unwritten, there was no security for these states that it would ever take place at all. The potential debtor states might find some way of sabotaging it. They could not be certain the commissioners would treat their claims reasonably, nor could they be sure what might be done to inflate the claims of other states, Virginia in particular, which would operate at the direct expense of their own. There was thus every reason for Massachusetts and South Carolina to want theirs at once in the form of assumption, and in that way the purposes of a final settlement, for them at least, would have been in effect accomplished. But meanwhile their own creditors remained a dangerously uncertain quantity. Their passivity could hardly be counted upon in the face of what appeared to be preferential treatment of Continental creditors while they themselves had to wait.

Still another category of interest was represented by such states as Virginia and North Carolina, which opposed assumption. Their motives were very complicated. A thread of ideology ran through them, but it was ideology overlaid with some very specific considerations of state interest. These states' response to assumption is usually explained by the half-truth that having already discharged most of their own debt, they were unwilling to share the burden of taxation required for assuming the debts of the others. They did indeed begrudge their taxes and said so, which is as far as many historians have followed them. But there was more to it. They had indeed paid some of their debt, but by no means all, and they wanted a final settlement to occur before assumption rather than after, if assumption were to occur at all. Virginia in particular nourished extravagant expectations from the final settlement, which she believed would bring her far greater benefits than would assumption. That is, if assumption followed rather than preceded a final settlement, the total amount of all state debts assumed would be smaller—since the states emerging as deficient in their contribution to the common charges would be shown as entitled to no compensation—and Virginia's share of the creditor balance would be proportionally larger. Whereas if assumption occurred immediately, the final settlement might not occur at all. For states with large debts already assumed, there would be little incentive to support a generous final settlement and every reason to delay it, especially considering the difficulties that might be raised about the chaotic state of Virginia's financial records. For both Virginia and North Carolina, therefore, an early final settlement would achieve the same purposes that for other states would be achieved by assumption, and for them there was every advantage in delaying assumption as long as possible if not in killing it altogether. This would both discourage a sharp rise in the value of state securities, their own being mostly in the hands of out-of-state speculators anyway, and leave open various options for liquidating that debt themselves and on their own terms. From their viewpoint it would be a pity to use good money received in a final settlement merely to enrich speculators. And it was probably for this very reason that the speculator issue would be kept out of the arguments against assumption; there was no need to risk charges of repudiationist motives.[26]

A final category—though in various respects overlapping the others— consisted of the security-holders themselves. The holders of state securities (who could be pictured from a Massachusetts viewpoint as upright and deserving citizens of Massachusetts but from a Virginian one as undeserving outside speculators) obviously had every reason to want these holdings assumed by the federal government, and the sooner the better. On the other hand, investors whose portfolios were principally in Continental rather than state securities were by no means disposed to see assumption as a blessing. Quite the contrary: it was very important that federal tax resources not be strained by assuming too large and unwieldy a public debt, thus weakening the value of their own holdings. The financial community itself, in short, was not of one mind on assumption, and the opposition within that community tended to come from the more conservative sector of it.[27]

Such, then, was the spectrum of interests. The supporters of assumption would again and again—besides echoing Hamilton's insistence that federal resources were equal to it—assure members from the doubting states that any remaining inequities which assumption might create would be removed once and for all by the final settlement of accounts. That is, the assumed debt of a given state would be charged against that state's account, and in the settlement she would simply receive that much less in final compensation for her war expenditures. All of which was well and good, but what if, after the commissioners had totaled up the common charges and computed the excess or shortage of each state's contribution to them, that particular state should emerge as a debtor? Should this turn out to be the case, for example, with New York (as in fact it did), the federal government would have assumed that state's debt but with no way to force her to make good the debit against her account. Six years later, after the final settlement had been made, Albert Gallatin would touch on this and related difficulties in a closely reasoned paper on public finance. Gallatin would grant that, as eventually worked out, assumption together with the final settlement had come very close to equity. But if the federal government had awaited the final settlement, he argued, and then undertaken assumption, the very same degree of equity could have been achieved at half the cost. Gallatin was, however, arguing from hindsight. The final condition of the accounts, which was known to him in 1796, was not known to anyone in 1790, being still in the future. Nor were certain other things known either. There was no way of predicting what might be the behavior of states presently convinced that either their credit or their tax structures would crack if their debts were not lifted forthwith.[28]

The debate on assumption opened on February 23, it having been settled the day before with the defeat of Madison's motion that the public debt would be funded without discrimination. This time Madison waited only a day before getting into it, and the skill with which he proceeded remains something of a model in technique. The course taken by the debates was largely a matter of his initiative, the turn he gave things, and the psychology he created. The first thing he did was to shift the focus of attention from assumption to the question of a final settlement. He did not say he was against assumption. But he did propose, as an amendment to the pending resolution, "that effectual provision be, at the same time, made for liquidating and crediting, to the States, the whole of their expenditures during the war . . . and, in such liquidation, the best evidence shall be received that the nature of the case will permit." He was giving notice, in other words, that so far as he was concerned assumption would not proceed very far unless and until clear provision should be made for a final settlement, that in such a settlement evidence for state claims should be more liberally construed than was now being done by the commissioners under the current regulations, and that Virginia in particular should have additional time to present her claims more fully. The friends of assumption rose nicely to the bait, assuring Madison that they would not agree to assumption without a clear guarantee of a just final settlement. His motion was passed unanimously.[29]

Madison now altered his tactics and gave the screw another turn. If the federal government were to be responsible for all wartime debts, he asked, why should it not in justice assume those that had already been paid, as well as those that remained unpaid? Madison's motion to this effect might well be regarded as preposterous, adding as it would another $15 million to the $25 million already estimated in the Secretary's report as the cost of assumption. But for Madison it had a very good logic. On the one hand, such a scheme would actually have been substantially cheaper for Virginia, because the income from the federal securities which the state would receive for the paid portion of her debt would enable her to reduce or eliminate state taxes, and would more than offset the additional federal taxes Virginians would have to pay in order to support the increased federal debt. On the other hand, by proposing an alternate version of assumption based on a wider definition of justice, Madison was blurring the moral case for Hamilton's version and thus rendering a little less certain the convictions of those inclined to support it. If true justice should cost this much, perhaps in the end a sufficient number might persuade themselves that assumption was not even necessary.[30]

Massachusetts and South Carolina were wild with anxiety to get assumption nailed down; and to hush Madison, Fisher Ames offered to spell out in detail a generous plan for a final settlement. Madison permitted himself to brood aloud. "I am afraid, I confess, that notwithstanding every step which may be taken, there will be unforeseen difficulties in the final liquidation and adjustment of the accounts; and I am persuaded if that measure should miscarry, the assumption of the existing State debts would work indeed an enormous injustice." On the other hand, he added, "if we can reduce that event to a moral certainty, and be sure that it will speedily take place, we may delay the assumption, with great propriety, until its accomplishment." With this, he could both sow further doubts and steer back toward the position expressed in an earlier unsuccessful motion by his Virginia colleague, Alexander White, that if assumption were to be enacted at all, the final settlement really ought to come first. Smith of South Carolina, recognizing Madison's effort to delay assumption, tried to discredit his position with an amendment to include interest as well as principal on all state debts paid and unpaid, which would have made the additional costs not $15 million but $27 million. Thus amended, Madison's motion failed. But the margin was uncomfortably close (28–22), even with Smith's outlandish proviso, and it was now obvious that a delay on assumption was looking more and more attractive.[31]

Every effort was now exerted by the friends of assumption to bring the measure to a vote. On March 9 absentees were rounded up and even sick members borne in, and the original resolution to include assumption in a funding bill was carried 31–26. But the margin had now become even closer, and support for assumption was becoming very shaky. The new members from North Carolina — all of them opposed to assumption — were appearing to take their seats, and their leading spokesman, Hugh Williamson, wanted more time to debate the subject of public credit even though the ground had been exhaustively covered already. Williamson's motion was denied, but the House on March 29 did vote, 29–27, to recommit the proposition on assumption. In effect, the vote of March 9 had been reversed. And when assumption was brought out once more for a vote on April 12, there was at last enough opposition to defeat it, 31–29. Should this new majority hold, it would mean that a funding bill, when completed, would contain no provision for the assumption of state debts.[32]

So Madison had won, or so it appeared when the House finally voted on April 26 to end its debate on assumption.[33] But how much was his victory worth, and was he prepared at any price to insist on it? Madison was still the nationalist, the Revolutionary patriot, and his hopes for a united nation were not so secure now as they had seemed at the beginning of the year. Things had happened during the past few weeks that must have muted whatever elation he may have felt over the blocking of assumption, and left him with certain forebodings.

One of them was the reintroduction of the issue of slavery. On March 16 a House committee brought in its report on two antislavery petitions, the one first presented on February 11 from the Quakers and the other received the following day from the Pennsylvania Society for Promoting the Abolition of Slavery. The latter petition, urging Congress "that you will promote mercy and justice towards this distressed race, and that you will step to the very verge of the power vested in you for discouraging every species of traffic in the persons of our fellow-men," had a certain historic significance. It had been signed and transmitted by the Society's president, the venerable Franklin, in what was to be the final public act in a career which had embraced service in the Continental Congress, the signing of the Declaration of Independence, responsibility for concluding the wartime alliance with France, virtual authorship of the peace treaty with Great Britain, membership in the Philadelphia Convention, and the signing of the Federal Constitution.[34]

The committee reported that the petitions had led it "to examine the powers vested in Congress, under the present Constitution, relating to the Abolition of Slavery." Its conclusions were that Congress had no power to prohibit the slave trade before 1808, or to emancipate any slaves born within or imported into the country prior to that year, or to interfere in the states' "internal regulations" with regard to slavery. Congress could, however, regulate the slave trade and levy the ten-dollar importation tax referred to in the Constitution; by implication it might have cognizance over emancipation and other matters after 1808; and it should encourage state legislatures to "revise their laws from time to time, when necessary, and promote the objects mentioned in the memorials." The report concluded "that in all cases to which the authority of Congress extends, they will exercise it for the humane objects of the memorialists, so far as they can be promoted on the principles of justice, humanity, and good policy."[35]

The violent outbursts of the Southerners in response to this were deeply dismaying to James Madison, who could see, if they could not, the light in which they appeared to their northern colleagues. Aedanus Burke denounced the Quakers as spies, traitors, and suppliers of the enemy until he had to be called to order. Smith of South Carolina insisted that to accept the report in its present form "would excite tumults, seditions, and insurrections." Smith then proceeded upon a harangue that included virtually every item that would characterize the South's proslavery argument for the next seventy years: the economic indispensability of slavery, the unfitness of blacks by nature for any other state, the horrors of miscegenation, the benevolent sanctions of history and Scripture, and the manner in which slavery supported a society of culture, refinement, and valor. The report was thereupon stripped by successive amendments of everything that could give offense to slaveowners, and adopted by a single vote. Madison, who had confided to Edmund Randolph that the debate had been "shamefully indecent," moved that the original as well as amended versions of the report be entered in the House Journal. His motion was carried by a margin of 29 to 25. Both times, Madison had voted with the northern members.[36]

James Madison, the Southerner, believed that "the true policy of the Southn. members [should have been] to have let the affair proceed with as little noise as possible, and to have made use of the occasion to obtain along with an assertion of the powers of Congs. a recognition of the restraints imposed by the Constitution." James Madison, the nationalist, deplored that the issue had been raised at all—less because he was unwilling to risk slavery than because he was unwilling to risk the Union. He was discovering, however, that the price of nationalism was toleration of extremists, which required a highly ambiguous effort to counterbalance them on the one hand and mollify them on the other.[37]

Benjamin Franklin died on April 17, 1790, in the eighty-fifth year of his age. To the Burkes and Jacksons of the day, Franklin's life and doings may no longer have mattered very much, but they still lay very deep in the awareness and conscience of James Madison. Madison rose in the House on April 22, spoke feelingly on the services of Franklin to humanity and to his country, and closed by offering the following resolution:

> The House being informed of the decease of BENJAMIN FRANKLIN, a citizen whose native genius was not more an ornament to human nature, than his various exertions of it have been precious to science, to freedom, and to his country, do resolve, as a mark of the veneration due to his memory, that the members wear the customary badge of mourning for one month.[38]

The other instance of extremism that alarmed Madison during these same weeks was the desperate language which issued from the frustrated proponents of assumption. "I confess, Sir," announced Jeremiah Wadsworth of Connecticut on April 1, "I almost begin to despair of the assumption of the State debts, and with that I shall despair of the National Government." Theodore Sedgwick of Massachusetts made a violent speech on April 12 during which he was called to order by one of the Virginia members. Roger Sherman of Connecticut brought forward a proposal on April 21 which tried to bring back assumption in a somewhat modified form, whereupon Madison spoke a piece which echoed some of his own inner conflicts. He still very much wanted his way, but he hoped the consequences would not be ruinous. He wished the assumptionists would not press "a matter of such peculiar importance and delicacy, by a bare majority."

(His own majority was hardly overwhelming.) He concluded by imploring them to "forbear those frequent assertions, that if the State debts are not provided for, the Federal debts shall also go unprovided for; nay, that if the State debts are not assumed, the Union will be endangered." But a few days before, he had written to James Monroe: "We shall risk their prophetic menaces if we should continue to have a majority."[39]

3
The Resolution

Madison the Virginia ideologue emerged in sharp focus once more on another issue during the second week in May. In February he had struck at Hamilton's master plan through a substitute scheme of his own on funding, but without success. He had done so again regarding assumption, but success here, though it looked more likely, could not be certain until the entire subject was settled by a bill with support enough to pass both houses. Now came an opportunity to strike at the system at still another point, that aspect of it which presupposed close maritime connections with Great Britain. Madison brought forward once again the design he had vainly promoted the year before of depriving Great Britain of as large a share of American trade as possible, and diverting it to France, through discriminatory duties against British shipping. In this he had the eager encouragement of the new Secretary of State, Thomas Jefferson.

The opportunity came through a petition from the merchants of Portsmouth, New Hampshire, requesting government protection for their shipbuilding industry. In its report on the petition, a House committee recommended an increase of the current tonnage duties from fifty cents to a dollar per ton on all foreign-built vessels arriving in American ports, and the report was taken up on May 10. Madison seized the occasion to widen vastly the scope of the committee's proposal by offering an amendment which would lay such a duty "on all foreign-built bottoms belonging to nations not in *commercial treaty with the United States.*" The implications of the measure thus amended went well beyond American ship-building; they now embraced the entire range of American commerce and foreign relations. On the one hand, the plan exempted (and thus favored) France, with whom we did have a commercial treaty. Madison painted a cheerful picture, based more on desire than on fact, of the prospects for Franco-American commerce: it would not be long before "the trade of France will probably be of three times the benefit to the United States [as is] that of any other commercial country whatever." And on the other hand, of course, his plan discriminated against England. Madison's fixed dogma here, again more prescriptive than predictive, was: "We can do better without Great Britain than she can do without us; articles of luxury can be retrenched with advantage."[40]

Madison's amendment carried, and the next day he pulled it a notch tighter with another amendment. Not only should increased tonnage duties be levied on the vessels of countries not in treaty with us, but the same vessels should be prohibited from carrying any produce or raw materials of American origin. To this there were sharp objections. "It is a useless declaration of passion," protested Theodore Sedgwick, "not dictated by the understanding. . . ." Madison retorted that it was not a declaration of passion at all but a "cool as well as a proper measure"; with the existence of the West Indies and the prosperity of Great Britain depending as they did on American trade, "it would be madness in her to hazard an interruption of it." Again his amendment carried, after the addition of a proviso exempting "any nation which permits the importation of fish, or other salted provision, grain, and lumber, in vessels of the United States." (A hopeful bribe to the British to open the West Indies.) A bill was ordered to be brought in, and Madison now had everything he wanted. Jefferson wrote jubilantly to his new son-in-law: "The tonnage bill will probably pass, and must, I believe, produce salutary effects. It is a mark of energy in our government, in a case where I believe it cannot be parried."[41]

But then things began to happen, and—as in 1789—mysterious resistances arose which had the effect of melting away Madison's majority. In principle, everyone would have liked to see the British relax their commercial restrictions, and no one would have objected to any means that held a fair promise of inducing them to do so. But a combination of strong misgivings, second thoughts, and various kinds of private persuasion—in which Hamilton, as before, undoubtedly played a part—brought a number of members to change their minds about this particular means. Southerners believed it would leave them with insufficient shipping and higher freights for their produce, "taxing South Carolina and Georgia, to give bounties to Massachusetts and New Hampshire." Northerners believed that the British could hardly be expected not to retaliate and that a trade war would ruin American commerce altogether. As a result, by June 23 the discriminatory clauses had all been separated from the bill and the tonnage rates reduced, and anything that now passed would do no more than re-enact the tonnage law of 1789.[42]

Meanwhile Jefferson, who had been seeing to the publication in local newspapers of letters he had received or solicited urging discrimination, received a report from Gouverneur Morris in London:

> I have some Reason to beleive that the present Administration intend to keep the Posts, and withhold Payment for the Negroes. If so they will color their Breach of Faith by the best Pretexts in their Power. I incline to think also that they consider a Treaty of Commerce with America as being absolutely unnecessary, and that they are perswaded they shall derive all Benefit from our Trade without Treaty. It is true that we might lay them under Restrictions in our Ports but they beleive that an Attempt of that Sort would be considered by one Part of America as calculated by the other for private Emolument, and not for the general Good.

This must have infuriated both Jefferson and Madison, not only for the news it contained but also for the ministry's all-too-accurate predictions about the behavior of Americans and their unwillingness, not to say their incapacity, to take united action.[43]

Refusing to give up, Madison made one more try on June 30. Since the idea of discrimination had been rejected, perhaps the "principle of reciprocity" might be more agreeable. Reciprocity, he explained, did not exist in the current state of Anglo-American trade, and he now proposed a way of seeing that it would. Nations that did not allow American ships to carry a given article to or from the United States would be prohibited from carrying that same article in their own ships. Madison's stubbornness had finally brought James Jackson to the end of his patience. "He thought it extraordinary that the gentleman from Virginia should come forward with one exceptionable proposition after another; the gentleman having lost one favorite proposition, so tenacious is he of his object, that he now brings forward another, in my opinion, fully as exceptionable." No more was heard that session either of discrimination or "reciprocity."[44]

According to Thomas Jefferson, the two most fundamental issues of the year 1790—the assumption of state debts and the location of the national capital— were resolved in an understanding reached at his dinner table some time in June, with himself presiding, between James Madison, acting for the proponents of a site on the Potomac, and Alexander Hamilton, representing the forces for assumption. The House of Representatives had passed a funding bill on June 2 which contained no provision for assumption, and whatever the Senate might do, Hamilton's plans were blocked unless the House could somehow be brought to reverse itself. Hamilton was in despair. "Going to the President's one day," wrote Jefferson,

> I met Hamilton as I approached the door. His look was sombre, haggard, and dejected beyond description. Even his dress uncouth and neglected. He asked to speak with me. We stood in the street near the door. He opened the subject of the assumption of the state debts, the necessity of it in the general fiscal arrangements and it's indispensible necessity towards a preservation of the union: and particularly of the New England states, who had made great expenditures during the war . . . [and who] would make it a sine qua non of a continuance of the Union. That as to his own part, if he had not credit enough to carry such a measure as that, he could be of no use, and was determined to resign. He observed at the same time, that tho' our particular business laid in separate departments, yet the administration and it's success was a common concern, and that we should make common cause in supporting one another. . . . On considering the situation of things I thought the first step towards some conciliation of views would be to bring Mr. Madison and Colo. Hamilton to a friendly discussion of the subject. I immediately wrote to each to come and dine with me the next day, mentioning that we should be alone. . . . They came. I opened the subject to them, acknoleged that my situation had not permitted me to understand it sufficiently but encouraged them to consider the thing together. They did so. It ended in Mr. Madison's acquiescence in a proposition that the question should be again brought before the house by way of amendment from the Senate, that that he would not vote for it, nor entirely withdraw his opposition, yet he should not be strenuous, but leave

it to it's fate. It was observed, I forget by which of them, that as the pill would be a bitter one to the Southern states, something should be done to soothe them; that the removal of the seat of government to the Patowmac was a just measure, and would probably be a popular one with them, and would be a proper one to follow the assumption. It was agreed to speak to Mr. White and Mr. Lee [of Virginia]. . . . This was done. Lee came into it without hesitation. Mr. White had some qualms, but finally agreed. The measure came down by way of amendment and was finally carried by the change of White's and Lee's votes. But the removal to Patowmac could not be carried unless Pennsylvania could be engaged in it. This Hamilton took on himself, and chiefly, as I understood, through the agency of Robert Morris, obtained the vote of that state, on agreeing to an intermediate residence at Philadelphia. This is the real history of the assumption. . . .[45]

History, reassured by subsequent events, has generally declared itself satisfied with Jefferson's story of the bargain. But since the symmetry of Jefferson's version has at last been challenged, some further reflections on it may be in order. Such a bargain on the scale claimed by Jefferson, according to Jacob E. Cooke, could never have occurred, nor could anything that may have been said at that dinner meeting have been responsible for the passage of the funding and residence acts in the form they finally took. The two were for the most part unconnected, and though bargaining certainly occurred, the critical bargains were those involving each measure separately. The one on "residence," as the capital question was called, was negotiated between the Virginia and Pennsylvania delegations and was completed before the June 20 dinner took place, while it would have required more than two Virginia congressmen to complete the one on assumption. For the rest, not a little must be ascribed to chance: "fortuity is perhaps as often responsible for the course of events as hidden causes or conspiracies."[46]

Well and good, but history is recalcitrant, and in this case a full re-reading of the evidence prompts the conclusion that all things considered there is really no better shorthand for what happened than the story told by Thomas Jefferson. True, the essential understandings on the residence issue had been reached by the time this episode occurred; true, the working out of particulars on each bill was done in large part without reference to the other. But the fate of neither was as yet certain, nor would it be until the last moment. Majorities throughout were highly unstable, and bargains on residence had been made and unmade with nervewracking frequency for over a year. For any such bargain to be final, some broader understanding—not only for arriving at it but also for making it stick— was essential. True, Jefferson, Madison, and Hamilton could not themselves impose a final resolution. But a fair guess, considering the circumstances, is that no settlement *not* acquiesced in by them was likely to occur. One might assume that what they agreed upon at that quiet dinner provided the moral cement needed to make the arrangement cohere until passage and—since there would still be ten or fifteen years in which anything might happen to it—to guarantee that it would continue to hold afterward. And if the occasion achieved nothing else, it secured an asset of crucial value to the assumptionists, the silence of James Madison.

The objectives involved in the residence question were two. One was geographic accessibility (argued as "convenience" if one was a New Yorker and as "centrality" if one was a Virginian); the other was state and local self-interest. The pull and counter-pull of these considerations made it likely that the permanent capital would come to rest at a point more or less centrally located (either on the Potomac or somewhere in Pennsylvania), and that local jealousies would only be circumvented by a site having most of the characteristics of *tabula rasa*. All of this meant there would have to be a temporary residence somewhere while the permanent one was being prepared, and the two likeliest places were New York and Philadelphia, though Baltimore was also mentioned. In the presence of all these elements the variety of shapes that a final arrangement might theoretically take was almost infinite, and by the same token the possibility of a deadlock—the incapacity to make any bargain—was considerable. Such in fact had been the case when an attempt at settlement was made in the session of 1789.[47]

There were as many local interests as there were localities, but the strongest single local-interest blocs were those of New York and Philadelphia. Each, however, restricted its strategy to making its city the temporary capital, with the covert hope that time and circumstances might conspire to make it the permanent one. Then there were roughly three regional blocs, though with little more than superficial cohesion. One was the entire group of southern states, preeminent among which was Virginia. Its object was to place the permanent seat on the Potomac, on which there was general accord among them, but there was serious division on tactics with respect to the temporary capital. South Carolina preferred New York, while the Virginians were inclined to think that the best way of getting what they wanted was to make a bargain that included Philadelphia. A second bloc consisted of the northern states of New England and New York, whose main desire was to keep the capital away from the distant Potomac, and to retain it temporarily if possible in New York City. A third, and pivotal, bloc consisted of the House and Senate delegations of Pennsylvania. Unlike any other state, Pennsylvania was in serious contention for both the temporary and permanent capitals, the likelihood of their getting one or the other—perhaps even both—having been present from the first. By early in the 1790 session, however, the Pennsylvanians because of internal disagreements had all but abandoned any serious effort to promote a Pennsylvania site for a permanent capital, and had begun to concentrate most of their energies on moving the temporary residence to Philadelphia. Thus as early as February the Pennsylvanians were preparing themselves to go to the Potomac, if forced to, in exchange for a temporary stay in Philadelphia.[48]

This emergent logic received its testing during the last week in May and the first two weeks of June. The doings of that period may be thought of as the final struggle between New York and Philadelphia for the temporary capital, these being the two poles around which all other forces arranged and rearranged themselves. The Pennsylvania strategy was to try first for an adjournment to Philadelphia for the next session without a commitment on the permanent capital. The

New York strategy was first to propose a permanent seat on the Potomac, in exchange for a few years more in New York. (Unlike the Philadelphia backers, the New York men saw they had little chance of success without an immediate *quid pro quo.*) In this elaborate ballet each participant seems to have had a nice sense of the attractions and forces that operated on all the others. Robert Morris, unable to persuade anyone else to introduce the Pennsylvania motion in the Senate, finally did so himself. On May 26, as he and Rufus King, the senator from New York, eyed one another, a jovial little scene unfolded while Morris, up and down several times, called for the question on his motion. He began with a chuckle, King chuckling back and others joining in; each time the portly Morris rose he laughed more heartily and was answered the more heartily by the portly King; and eventually, except for the bleak Maclay, the entire chamber rocked in harmless transports of hilarity.[49]

Morris's motion lost by two votes in the Senate, but the next day FitzSimons of Pennsylvania introduced the same proposal in the House. It was carried on May 31, 38–22, despite strong resistance from South Carolina, New York, and New England. Meanwhile the New York effort in the Senate came under the management of Pierce Butler of South Carolina. Butler brought in a bill on May 31 to take the permanent capital to the Potomac, the understanding being that the temporary one would remain in New York, and succeeded in keeping the House's Philadelphia resolution bottled up in committee pending the expected arrival of the senators from Rhode Island. But the Virginians and Carolinians were at odds on this move, even though both wanted the Potomac. The Carolinians were convinced that the best strategy was to support New York as the temporary capital because New York would have less chance than Philadelphia of keeping it there. But the Virginians had come to believe that the only route to the Potomac was through Pennsylvania. True, the Pennsylvanians were not to be trusted, but the New Yorkers' reliability was even less. Both would of course try, once having got the temporary residence, to keep it, but in case of failure the New Yorkers would resist going south more tenaciously than would Pennsylvania, and they might make a bargain with Pennsylvania to place the permanent residence somewhere other than on the Potomac.[50]

The fate in the Senate of the two measures, the one for Philadelphia and the other for New York, created an anomaly in the House. On June 8 the Philadelphia resolution was again defeated in the Senate, and the Potomac resolution was also defeated when the Philadelphia supporters agreed to vote against any permanent site on the ground that the measure had been concocted by their enemies in order to divide them, and that if they let it through they might lose everything. Thereupon the Philadelphia men in the House decided to insist on the House's previous vote and tried to repass the Philadelphia adjournment motion. But they were headed off by an amendment substituting Baltimore for Philadelphia, which passed by three votes. The anomaly was Baltimore, support for which was minimal. Three Baltimore adherents had joined the anti-Philadelphia coalition, and the amended bill passed because of parliamentary confusion and because the

House rules forbade the reinsertion of Philadelphia. But the Senate would never accept Baltimore, as repeated votes had already shown, and some sort of compromise now became imperative. Both Hamilton and Jefferson, acting separately, perceived this.[51]

Hamilton, distracted over assumption, met Robert Morris on June 12. If Morris could garner five votes in the House and one in the Senate for assumption, Hamilton would undertake to persuade the New Yorkers to support a permanent capital on the Delaware. Morris told him the bargain would have to include Philadelphia as the temporary seat as well; he probably said this because although he himself supported assumption and could not resist the Delaware site in view of his own landholdings there, he knew that since a majority of the Pennsylvanians preferred the Susquehanna and were against assumption, without Philadelphia he stood no chance of persuading them. But nothing came of it in any case. The Pennsylvanians turned Morris down, and the New Yorkers, unwilling to give up the temporary residence, turned down Hamilton.[52]

Morris was also approached on June 14 by Thomas Jefferson, with an offer to move the capital to Philadelphia in exchange for a permanent seat on the Potomac. Virginia congressmen, alarmed by the vote on Baltimore, had been making similar approaches to the Pennsylvania delegation. Both groups had now come to see such an exchange as the best hope of securing their ends, and an understanding to that effect had already been reached by the time of Jefferson's subsequently famous dinner meeting with Hamilton and Madison on June 20.[53]

But the question recurs: why should this dinner be regarded as so important, and why indeed should it have been held at all? Jefferson and Madison presumably knew that the Potomac was already within sight, having themselves participated in the goings-on between Virginia and Pennsylvania; Jefferson by now was already prepared to give in on assumption, as apparently was Madison, both fearing the consequences of standing fast.[54] Why, then, should they have troubled to have anything to do with Hamilton? To some extent we must trust the principals themselves, who between them knew as much as anyone on the ground, in their conviction that a further understanding was essential. And this in turn prompts a thought or two on what a "bargain" means when it occurs at the highest level of statesmanship.

For the Virginians, an understanding with Hamilton would commit him to the Potomac in return for something they were already prepared to concede, and it would provide the private moral sanction for their ceasing to oppose assumption. As for Hamilton, though he certainly knew Jefferson and Madison could not actually "deliver" assumption, there were certain things an agreement could achieve. It could convert two Virginians in the House, and it could provide an implicit appeal to the Southerners' sense of justice: having secured the Potomac, they ought to be reasonable about assumption. And the most important assurance of all, of infinite value to Hamilton, was the withdrawal of James Madison, hitherto assumption's most resourceful opponent. Hamilton was, to be sure, deserting his fellow New Yorkers on the residence question. As he explained to Rufus King two days later, "the project of Philadelphia & Potomac is bad, but it will insure the funding system and the assumption: agreeing to remain in New Yk will defeat it." Hamilton himself was meanwhile prepared to allow his allies in the Senate to make the necessary compromises on details in order to bring forth an acceptable bill on funding that would also include assumption.[55]

In short, a bargain at this level is not to be judged on simple mechanical criteria, so many votes this way or that, because if the necessary elements for consummating it are not already in view, it cannot be made at all. But not only is it still worth making, it is imperative to make it. It is thereupon ratified and given whatever legitimacy it can have by the most important persons concerned, who are able, if no one else is, to give their word of honor that it will be kept. This in effect was why Thomas Jefferson, Alexander Hamilton, and James Madison did what they did on the evening of June 20, 1790.

By mid-July a residence act had been passed, and a funding bill, complete with assumption, was well on its way to completion. The key votes on residence occurred in the Senate on June 29, and the critical switches from New York to Philadelphia were made by senators from Massachusetts and South Carolina, those states most anxious for assumption.[56] The working out of an acceptable funding bill was also done in the Senate, which had all along been more receptive to assumption than was the House. Assumption was limited in advance to stipulated sums, while certain states—notably Virginia, North Carolina, and Georgia—received extra allowances. As for the final settlement of accounts, the evidence for a state's expenditures would be very liberally interpreted. Indents would be funded at the reduced rate of 3 percent, the persisting demands for a full 6 percent on the whole debt were quietly squelched; and provision was made to retire the Continental currency at 100 to 1 instead of the recommended 40 to 1. For all the importance of these compromises, they represented for Hamilton no extraordinary sacrifices of principle, and were probably in no case grossly short of what he was prepared at any time to accept. The bill was reported from committee on July 12 and passed the Senate on the 16th. On July 26 it passed the House. There, the votes of the two Virginia congressmen may not have been sufficient, but the bill would have had very hard going without them.[57]

One of those congressmen was Richard Bland Lee, who had made a speech earlier that month as the House was preparing to take its final action on the residence bill. It contained certain broad hints, the essence of which was that the South would accept no capital other than the Potomac, but if the North conceded that, the South would accept assumption. On the same day, July 6, another speech was made by James Madison, who never said anything he had not previously thought about. It was well known that the Pennsylvanians, who were about to receive a ten-year stay for the national capital in the City of Brotherly Love, would remain very much alive to any opportunity for keeping it there forever. But they, and other Northerners as well, would simply have to be trusted. "Our acts," said Madison, "are not like those of the Medes and Persians, unalterable. A repeal is a thing against which no provision can be made. . . . But I flatter myself that some respect will be paid to the public interest, and to the plighted faith of the Government."[58]

The diplomacy of the phrase "plighted faith of the Government" had a nice touch. When the laws of the Republic are made, it becomes the duty of the Executive to see that they are carried out, and in this case the Executive, shortly to receive his heart's desire, would have every reason for doing so forthwith.[59] To the fulfillment of this end, moreover, his Secretary of the Treasury and his Secretary of State, though not much liking the rest of what they were settling for, had given their word.

CHAPTER IV

The Republic's Capital City

A small but significant number of those who experienced the Revolution cherished a tremendous vision of what the Revolution and its outcome promised for America's cultural future. As Joseph Ellis has described it, these Americans now possessed—or imagined they did—the one essential element, hitherto lacking, for releasing the creative energies of an already favored people. This was individual and civic liberty. An all-but-miraculous force, liberty would give wings to every conceivable endeavor. All other obstacles were negligible, now that the main one—dependency—had been swept away. Not only would there be prodigious advances in agriculture and industry, there would also be such a flowering of the arts, literary and all other kinds, as the world had not yet seen. In addition to the "Painting, Sculpture, Statuary," and "greek Architecture" envisioned by Ezra Stiles, John Trumbull announced that

> This land her Steele and Addison shall view,
> The former glories equal'd by the new;
> Some future Shakespeare charm the rising age
> And hold in magic chains the list'ning stage.

The dream was that of "an American Athens."[1]

The dream would prove a mirage. The expected renaissance did not occur; the American Athens failed to materialize. That first generation would slip into a disillusioned old age still wondering what had happened—or rather not happened—and subsequent generations have been wondering ever since. With reference to the original meaning of "culture"—making things grow in the earth—the fields of post-Revolutionary America would of course be ever more bountiful. But under culture's later meaning, most of the country remained something of a wasteland for many years to come. We are still far from certain what all the reasons may have been.

One aspect of the imagery employed by those of Trumbull's generation lingers as a curiosity. The "Athens" they projected was not really a "place" at all; it was simply a non-specific metaphor for the artistic and intellectual outpouring about to occur all over America. They somehow did not think of their Athens as an actual city, a metropolitan center where special things occurred for special reasons and were unlikely to occur anywhere else. If enough of them had, things might (one can only guess) have turned out differently.

I
Theories of Culture

The term "high culture" was very possibly first coined in America, older civilizations having apparently felt no great urge to formulate that sort of distinction.[2] This may seem odd, inasmuch as the United States for at least the first hundred years of its national existence undoubtedly had less of it, as "culture" has since come to be understood, than any other of the world's leading national societies. Much thought has been given to the question of how to account for this lack, and of just what was missing. Literature is the case that has come in for the most attention, though a parallel impoverishment during that same period could be claimed, and has been, for the other expressive arts in America as well.[3]

It was this very barrenness that came to be seen early in the nineteenth century as the primary fact of the American cultural landscape. A body of symbolic notation adequate for mirroring the acuteness of felt or observed experience somehow did not exist. What served as a substitute language—an idiom of "refinement" and "elevation"—did not originate at home but had to be imported from other places, even from other times. That language did not seem to have many resources for depicting the contrarieties of the common life, high or low, or for taking nourishment from either great or small happenings. It might have been expected otherwise, Ralph Waldo Emerson observed in 1838. "But the mark of American merit in painting, in sculpture, in poetry, in fiction, in eloquence, seems to be a certain grace without grandeur, and itself not new but derivative, a vase of fair outline, but empty. . . ."[4]

There appeared to be an all-but-unbridgeable distance between the vocabulary of refinement and that of everyday—and even not so everyday—comings and goings. Such a disjunction in fact forms the central premise of two of the most influential statements since made on the subject, both in the opening years of the present century. George Santayana delivered a subsequently famous address in 1911 whose title contained a phrase—"The Genteel Tradition"—which everyone now knows and of which few critics of the American cultural past have since failed to make some sort of use. America, Santayana announced, was not simply "a young country with an old mentality"; it was "a country of two mentalities, one a survival of the beliefs and standards of the fathers, the other an expression of the instincts, practice, and discoveries of the younger generations." This younger temper, he said, "is all aggressive enterprise; the other is all genteel tradition."[5] Four years later, in 1915, the young Van Wyck Brooks said much the same thing. The mind and voice of American life, Brooks asserted, had been divided between two opposing types. He therewith gave currency to a celebrated antinomy—"Highbrow" and "Lowbrow"—which has remained in the American vocabulary ever since. Between the two worlds these types inhabited there was "no community, no genial middle ground."[6]

Literary art, for both Brooks and Santayana, was the test for most of their ideas about culture in America. Part of the American mind, as Santayana put it, "has floated gently in the back-water," and even that part, according to Brooks, has tended "to suppose that a writer belongs to literature only when he is dead; living he is, vaguely, something else."[7] True, there had been a time at about mid-century (Santayana again) when

> New England had an agreeable Indian summer of the mind; and an agreeable reflective literature showed how brilliant that russet and yellow season could be.... But it was all a harvest of leaves; these worthies had an expurgated and barren conception of life; theirs was the purity of sweet old age. Sometimes they made attempts to rejuvenate their minds by broaching native subjects ... [such as] "Rip van Winkle," "Hiawatha," or "Evangeline"; but the inspiration did not seem much more American than that of Swift or Ossian or Chateaubriand.... Their culture was half a pious survival, half an intentional acquirement; it was not the inevitable flowering of fresh experience.[8]

In short, whatever movement American writing could show was more a matter of lineal descent than of lateral outreach, a culture that was "European without the corresponding pressure and responsibility of the European mind." In the rush of contemporary life, repelled by the brute energy of a society absorbed in the pursuit of money, literature expended an excessive share of its resources simply in avoiding contamination. Not that Americans were unwilling to accord respect, of a sort, to "culture." But it was a segregated respect, not unlike that between Sundays and weekdays, and was to a significant extent prompted and even taken charge of by women.[9]

As to what this lineal descent consisted of, neither Brooks nor Santayana was able to be very circumstantial. Each perceived a gulf of abnormal proportions between the active and the contemplative sides of the American mind; each rightly saw the latter as isolated, derivative, and insubstantial. Each then attempted to locate the origins of this disjunction in the Puritan heritage, in the disembodied abstractions and "agonized conscience" of Calvinism; and a number of other writers have taken a similar line. (The early Puritans, it seems, have had a great deal to answer for, including a perverse preference by their descendants for European models.)[10] But a genetic account, whatever its merits, may not quite do as a causal explanation. The cultural state to be explained appeared in full form after the force of the Puritan way had been largely spent. The problem may have been less one of intellectual history than of cultural sociology, of the environment in which the literary artist has functioned and of those conditions which—as most critics have tended in principle to agree—have served to cramp and inhibit the fulfillment of his work.

A companion theory is one that pictures commerce as the great destroyer. Federalist literary aspirants sounded this note very early. Winthrop Sargent wrote in 1805 that the "national maxim" was "to *get money*." "When this is the predominant passion of a nation, nothing can be expected but its concomitant evils.... In such a country genius is like the mistletoe on the rock; it seems to exist ... only by its own resources, and [by] the nourishment it receives from the dews of heaven. The progress of literature has therefore been very slow...." The lesson of Mark Twain's career, Van Wyck Brooks flatly asserted in 1922, was that "the acquisitive and creative instincts are ... diametrically opposed," that Mark Twain was induced to betray his talent by the commercial values of his society, and that the artist in any writer—as in Twain's case—is bound to be stifled by "the pursuit of worldly success." Emerson undoubtedly had something of this sort in mind when he counseled that the scholar and poet "must embrace solitude as a bride," and that "if he pines," "hankering for the crowd ... , his heart is in the market; he does not hear; he does not think." Yet a contrary theory could well say, with the examples of Dickens, Hugo, Stendhal, Balzac, and most of the other great novelists of nineteenth-century Europe, that a direct acquaintance with money, power, and the crowd is itself the very thing the writer most needs for the nourishment of his art.[11]

Others have pointed to the absence of any recognized system of patronage for things of the mind and spirit in America, official or otherwise. Robert Southey, shortly to become the poet laureate of England, wrote in 1809 that the American government was itself to be blamed "for the little encouragement it holds out to literature." Southey thought it incumbent on this nation "to set other countries an example by patronizing and promoting those efforts of genius which all civilized nations consider as their proudest boast, and their only permanent glory." Margaret Fuller in 1844 lamented, "When an immortal poet was secure only of a few copyists to circulate his works, there were princes and nobles to patronize literature and the arts. Here is only the public...."[12]

No princes and nobles, no leisured aristocracy for the support of high culture: perhaps that was the fatal deficiency. Henry James might be read as having intimated something of just this sort in his famous catalogue of everything Hawthorne lacked for the completion of *his* talent: "no sovereign, no court, no personal loyalty, no aristocracy." But it is evident from the remainder of the list ("no political society, no sporting class, no Epsom nor Ascot," and so on) that James actually meant something quite different, that "support" was not primarily what he had in mind. His great point, stated at the very beginning of his essay on Hawthorne, was simply "that it needs a complex social machinery to set a writer in motion."[13]

A more recent statement, illuminated by the added dimension of modern feminist thought, contains more of the elements required of a rounded theory than do any of those so far noted. Ann Douglas's *The Feminization of American Culture* undertakes to account for the prominence attained by numbers of educated middle-class women in nineteenth-century America in the province of culture, especially literature, and in contrast to the relative powerlessness of women in other realms of American life. Douglas thus takes seriously a theme which for Santayana was largely marginal, and which he handled with a certain patronizing irony.

One of the most extraordinary psychic transformations in the entire American experience occurred within a surprisingly short stretch of time during the first third of the nineteenth century. The disparate voices of an entire society seemed to converge out of almost every corner to define those attitudes of mind, habits of work, social values, and differentiations of function most appropriate to the race about to be run, to the optimum workings of an emergent capitalist order. The new roles allotted to women — as administrators of the household and guardians of family morals, or else as teachers and missionaries — undoubtedly had some indirectly liberating consequences. But the net outcome for the generality of women was stifling and stultifying. It codified a special kind of isolation for women's lives, a sort of spiritual walling off of both aspiration and experience, that had no counterpart, of such completeness, in European society. Within their delineated "spheres" of domesticity and preceptorship women could, through persistence, force of character, and a degree of subversion, achieve a substantial measure of authority. But though the spheres might be widened, neither their separateness nor their boundaries were to be challenged, and they seldom were.[14]

One of the few modes whereby an educated woman might reach for some expression of both her human and feminine nature was literature. The output of such literature written by women, beginning in the 1820s, was in fact considerable. This was the one commodity women might produce which could serve the wants of a consumer market, reinforce the values of the age, and be made profitable. But the expression could seldom go very deep, and the product must make no great demands on its readers. The books and periodicals, the novels, verse, and didactic pieces of various sorts, were aimed principally at a female audience. Their tone was predominantly sentimental; they were permeated by a religiosity that tended to be long on feeling but short on doctrinal substance; and they did not resist but in fact celebrated the sacred functions that had been assigned to the women of the American republic. Either through a socialization process of extraordinary efficiency or in the absence of recognized alternative models of sensibility, American literary women found themselves contributing voluntarily to the definition of their own confinement.

Moreover, given what then passed for a critical temper, and in view of a reading public consisting more and more of women ("It is the women," wrote Nathaniel Willis, "who give or withhold a literary reputation"), this sentimentalization of literary culture could not fail to have its effect on male authors as well. Few were disposed to be venturesome, and those who were had relatively few readers.[15]

The comparative widening of the middle-class woman's visibility, as well as the style which made it allowable, are given additional persuasiveness with Douglas's description of a remarkable alliance with the liberal protestant clergy, who no longer possessed the civic and ecclesiastical authority of their Calvinist forbears. Increasingly, "the nineteenth century minister moved in a world of women." He needed their support; they needed his attention. As clergymen, these men courted and encouraged women. But as men, they did as much to keep women in their restricted sphere as did any contingent in American society. "Stay within your proper confines," they said, "and you will be worshipped . . . ; step outside and you will cease to exist." The required note of sentimental uplift accordingly sounded forth in most of what these women did as parishioners, teachers, missionaries, guardians of the home, and authors and keepers of culture.[16]

This account says something important about how the American sensibility came to be organized in the particular way it was, and about how art and expression could have become so attenuated amid the central currents of American life. It gives a resolution to previous efforts, and makes a "genteel tradition" newly plausible. Returning to the eighteenth century, and to our opening point, we might venture a corollary.

At the time of the republic's founding there was little room in the American imagination for the idea of a metropolis as the mirror of a national civilization. On the contrary, the anti-urban, anti-metropolitan component of the Revolutionary mentality would prove to be one of its most persistent and durable features. The colonial phase of their history had given Americans no experience of a metropolis other than the worst kind: the metropolis was London, a place out of sight and out of reach, where corruption permeated everything, and where, as everyone knew, all the schemes for abridging colonial liberties had been hatched. One of the earliest decisions by the fathers of the new republic was made with the more or less clear purpose not to have that kind of metropolis in America.

Less clear would be the consequences for the nation's cultural identity, consequences that have remained problematical to the present day. The growth of cities in nineteenth-century America would proceed without clear models in the American spirit for the pleasures and compensations of urban life; by the same token, a metropolitan capital as the matrix for the growth of a national society's self-knowledge was not available either. London or Paris did not, perhaps could not, serve as the model. But if they had, the result would have contained at least three lines of force, all intersecting in the same place: those of political authority, of commerce and money, and of art and intellect. The daily transactions among the men and women associated with these disparate fields of energy—transactions trivial as well as official, corrupt as well as virtuous, after dark as well as in daylight; the things they said and did in their marketplaces, their cloakrooms, at their dinner tables, on their promenades, in their back alleys and even in their bedrooms— would not have occurred in quite such "separate spheres," and would have constituted the body of fact, perception, and feeling with which culture makes its terms and through which culture, in a variety of forms, is reflected.[17]

In early nineteenth-century America, unlike the case in England and France, the foremost talents in politics and government, in the nation's economic life, and in the life of thought and artistic expression had no specific setting in place or time in which they could act upon each other (as a "complex social machinery") in quite this way. Each would thereupon function to most intents and purposes on a plane detached from the other two, and culture would make its terms and work out its forms without the example or authority of a metropolitan capital that was the acknowledged center of the nation's life.

That the seat chosen in 1790 for the federal government would not be such a center was evident almost from the first. In this determination, the leading spirit was no less a figure than Thomas Jefferson.

2
Jefferson and the Federal City

Thomas Jefferson's role in the final resolution of the residence-assumption issue in June 1790 was, as we have seen, a critical one. But the part he took then was only the first in a sequence of actions having to do not simply with the national capital's location but also with the planning whereby the capital city itself would be brought into being. The subject was one that had already occupied his mind for many years previously, and addressing it now was in certain respects Jefferson's first major effort of statesmanship in his new position as a member of the first administration. He subsequently gave more of his time, energy, and thought to that problem than did any other officer of state, and the consequences may be seen as having much symbolic bearing on the way Americans came to think about seats of government, and about cities in general.

Actually Jefferson's deep preoccupation with the Federal City was not without precedent. He had been similarly engaged in the state of Virginia. It was Jefferson who in 1777 sponsored a removal of the state capital from Williamsburg to Richmond—then a village of about 1,800—on grounds of greater security and centrality. The Assembly very reluctantly consented just after his election as governor in 1779. "As grandly conceived by Jefferson," writes one of his biographers, "the new capital was to occupy six large public squares, each with a handsome edifice of brick brilliantly porticoed." The first public building to be specifically designed for a republican government was the classical capitol at Richmond. It was based on the Roman Maison Carrée at Nîmes, and built from a design which Thomas Jefferson had prepared.[18]

The prestige of George Washington and the knowledge of Washington's long-cherished desire to have the capital of the Republic seated on the banks of the Potomac had had no little to do with the Virginians' eventual success in putting it there. There is no doubt at all, moreover, that the weight of Washington's moral authority was a major factor in making the decision stick. The Chief Executive lost no time in implementing the Residence Act of 1790 and setting in motion those steps whereby the site might be made ready for its occupancy ten years hence. Washington's chief coadjutor in this work was his Secretary of State, and Thomas Jefferson's involvement with it, regarding both general conception and immediate detail, seems to have been far greater than that of Washington, and would so continue as long as he remained in office.

Jefferson's concern over the federal capital dated at least as far back as the fall of 1783, when he proposed to the Virginia Assembly that Virginia and Maryland purchase land on the Potomac, erect public buildings there, and then "tender the said buildings to Congress." He also expanded a set of notes left him by Madison, in which every advantage of the Potomac site that could be thought of was carefully listed.[19] For the time being, of course, nothing came of any of this. But while the seat of government migrated several times during the 1780s—residing variously at Philadelphia, Princeton, Annapolis, Trenton, and New York—Jefferson's dream remained undiminished. When success came at last in 1790, he drew up a memorandum for Washington concerning the speedy and efficient implementation of the Act, and assumed at once the role of Washington's principal advisor in all matters concerning the Federal City. He helped supervise the work of Major L'Enfant and the Commissioners and offered a wealth of assistance to them and to Washington on the choice of the site, the layout of the city, and the design of the buildings. The Federal City on the Potomac, in short, was one of Thomas Jefferson's dearest undertakings, and he did everything he could to make certain that Congress actually would take up its residence there when, at the end of the ten-year interim established by law, the time came to move.

Like the Philadelphians and New Yorkers with respect to their cities, Jefferson was not unmindful of the local benefits which might accrue to the Potomac area. But these did not preoccupy him, or even greatly interest him. His was not the spirit of the urban booster; his vision of the future city extended far beyond commercial advantage. Indeed, he actually hoped the new capital would remain "a secondary place of commerce," and recommended "leaving Norfolk in possession of all the advantages of a primary emporium." Rather, when Jefferson thought of the benefits to be had from locating the Federal City in Virginia he tended to conceive them in the broader categories of moral influence: the capacity of Virginia to impose its own special character on the character of the new republic. The capital would be placed amid predominantly rural surroundings, far from the corruptions "of any overgrown commercial city." Virginians, moreover, would be preferentially situated for service in the federal government and for creating "a favourable biass in the Executive officers." To be sure, such a site might also serve as the gateway to the West, and the Potomac as a highway to the interior, a vent for the agricultural surpluses which the western population might want to market in Europe and through which they might receive foreign goods in return. But the particulars of how this was to work were never very immediate in Jefferson's mind, nor did they form a very prominent aspect of his thinking. This too, when he thought of it, seems to have been largely a matter of influence: the influence Virginia might have on all activities and movements, of which commerce was only the immediate expression, wherein the new agricultural West was in any way concerned.[20]

Moreover, Jefferson was fascinated by the opportunities which a capital built *de novo* would offer for giving physical form to his vision of what the new republic should be, insofar as its spirit could be embodied in its center of government. Building codes could be established in advance to assure a tasteful uniformity in the city's domestic architecture. There could be boulevards and broad avenues; generous provision could be made for spacious parks and open squares. Public buildings could be designed with imaginative sweep and nobility of scale. Thus by laying out the whole rationally and in accordance with a master plan, and insisting on both republican dignity and elevation of spirit in every phase of design and construction, the builders could make the Federal City a fit expression of America's aspirations. The City could serve, in its carefully articulated perfection, as a kind of physical counterpart to the Constitution.[21]

The plan submitted in August 1791 by Major Pierre Charles L'Enfant, the zealous French engineer who had pressed his services upon Washington, was much more ambitious than the rather simple preliminary sketch Jefferson himself had given Washington in March. It was nonetheless quite in line with Jefferson's own hopes and expectations. L'Enfant had superimposed a radial system of avenues on Jefferson's grid street design, "at the same time preserving," according to Fiske Kimball, "the general arrangement of the main elements which Jefferson had suggested." L'Enfant's "Grand transverse Avenues" would be 160 feet across, with thirty-foot-wide tree-lined walks on either side of an eighty-foot carriageway. There would be great public squares, "five grand fountains intended with a constant spout of water," extensive parks and gardens, and the public buildings so placed as to take fullest advantage of the splendid vistas across the Potomac. It was L'Enfant's claim that the plan was wholly the product of his own original genius. But one of the most noteworthy aspects of it—quite aside from the elements he took from Jefferson—was its striking correspondences with the royal French seat of Versailles. "The cardinal features of L'Enfant's plan," writes Charles Moore, "the long vista from one focal point to another, the radiating avenues, and especially the conception of the entire city as a well-articulated unity—these ideas and ideals were already realized in Versailles, planned as the capital of France, the city in which L'Enfant's early years were spent."[22]

Yet the correspondence with Versailles, at first glance inspiring, may now be seen as a bad omen. Considering the train of evils shortly to follow, it is no wonder that the city of Washington should be fated not to rouse itself from its boggy squalor for the next hundred years. Versailles was grand indeed, though it had taken the will of an absolute monarch to impose such a prodigy on the open fields of the Isle-de-France. Yet the King of France and forty thousand men had not been able to make it a capital, or even a city. At the very moment L'Enfant was projecting a republican Versailles in America, the original Versailles was ceasing to be the capital of France, and would shortly thereafter become little more than a museum of the *ancien régime*. It had been steadily losing its influence to Paris for nearly half a century before the Revolution which gave it its final coup, Paris being the center not only of commerce and finance but of art, intellect, and every kind of talent. The King might command a small legion of courtiers to attend upon him at Versailles, but it was a dreary captivity; meanwhile the most gifted, most ambitious, most influential men in France were being drawn, steadily and inexorably, to Paris.[23]

In any case, it was to be at least a century before L'Enfant's grand conception would even begin to fit the requirements of an American capital city. During that very long interim, few places in Christendom or elsewhere would be so fervently reviled or broadly derided as Washington on the Potomac. Jean-Jacques Ampère, visiting there in 1851, still saw "streets without houses," "houses without streets," all giving "striking proof of this truth, that one cannot create a great city at will." By the early years of the twentieth century L'Enfant's plan had at last begun to appear feasible, at least in the eyes of the Park Commission of 1901 which resurrected it and proceeded at great expense to carry out various of its principal features. Though it might be suspected that any plan which takes a hundred years to implement is by definition a bad plan, the beautifications of the Theodore Roosevelt era had the effect of restoring, indeed of monumentalizing, the reputation of Pierre Charles L'Enfant. Thus it remains, more or less undisturbed, to the present day. Even so, the daughter of another American President could still refer to Washington, D.C., another half-century after that, with reference to the things that mattered most to her, as little more than a country town.[24]

What had gone wrong? The first clue may be the sea of troubles that awaited Thomas Jefferson as he turned his attention to the problems of the Federal City in 1790.

At the outset, all seemed reasonably auspicious. The Act of 1790 had given the President authority to locate the ten-mile square Federal District at any point within a specified range of some eighty miles along the Potomac. After a personal reconnaissance in the fall, and upon consultations with Jefferson and Madison, Washington announced his choice on January 24, 1791, in a proclamation which Jefferson had drafted. (Congress was by this time sitting at Philadelphia, having left New York forever on August 12, 1790.) It was to be a diamond-shaped area just above the Eastern Branch, and would include land from Virginia on one side of the river and from Maryland on the other. Within it, the only settlements of any account were the villages of Alexandria and Georgetown.[25]

Washington may have made up his mind on this as early as August 1790, inasmuch as the memorandum of procedure drawn up for him at that time by Jefferson was predicated on that same location. In this memorandum Jefferson laid down two general principles, one concerning the President's authority and the other with regard to financing, and these were to form the basis of all policy thereafter. He urged the fullest exercise of executive authority over the entire proceeding. This should include, first, the acquisition of land within the District. The Act ought to be construed liberally, so that land might be acquired sufficient not merely for the public buildings but for the entire Federal City. (The whole thing should be planned.) The President's authority should include the plan itself: the layout of streets, the design of the public buildings, and regulations on the construction of private houses. (Jefferson had ideas of his own on all these matters, a number of which he mentioned here.) And it should include, finally, the three Commissioners who were to have general supervision of the undertaking. The Commissioners should be appointed by the President and "be subject to the President's direction in every point." They should, moreover, "have some taste in architecture." As for the other element of general policy, that of financing, the main reliance for funds should be upon sales of lots from land ceded or otherwise acquired from the current owners. It would be best not to depend on grants of money from the states of Maryland and Virginia, though as it happened, such grants—$72,000 in one case and $120,000 in the other—had already been promised. Congress must not be counted on at all. Asking Congress for an appropriation, or for any other kind of assistance, might reopen the entire question of the residence. Herein lay the fatal weakness of the whole conception.[26]

Thus in January 1791, Washington issued his proclamation, appointed his three Commissioners, and designated Major Andrew Ellicott as surveyor. It was further understood that Major L'Enfant would make a plan of the city, design the buildings, and be in charge of the construction. Ellicott began his work during the second week in February; he was followed not long thereafter by L'Enfant, who had received his initial instructions from Jefferson early in March. L'Enfant was to reconnoiter the best sites for public buildings and make drawings of the ground; Jefferson himself, meanwhile, was brimming with visions. He thought the capitol should be of classical design and the President's house modern. He sent the Major some two dozen plates of "the handsomest fronts of private buildings" which he thought might be engraved and distributed free to the local inhabitants to educate their taste. He also forwarded a number of city plans which he had collected on his travels in Europe.[27]

At the end of March 1791, Washington met the landholders of the locality in which he had decided the city itself should be placed—the east bank of the Potomac—and made an agreement with them. They would cede to the United States a stretch of some three to five thousand acres between Rock Creek and the Eastern Branch, and upon its being laid off in lots the proprietor of each tract would retain every other lot. Such land remaining in private hands as might be taken for public purposes (excluding streets) would be paid for at a stipulated rate. The benefit to the proprietors, of course, was that the land they retained would be steadily enhanced in value with the unfolding of a golden future. L'Enfant, meanwhile, was completing his plan. After having made various alterations suggested by Washington and Jefferson, he had it finally ready by summer. It was magnificent. Jefferson saw it at the end of August and was "well pleased."[28]

A meeting of the Commissioners was held at Georgetown on September 8, with Jefferson and Madison present, at which it was decided that the city should be named "Washington" and the Federal District "Columbia." The other decisions reflected the general principles laid down by Jefferson in his memorandum of the previous year. There should be a sale of lots as soon as possible, on the site. (Washington and Jefferson had already scheduled an auction for October 17 which the President, the Secretary of State, and Congressman James Madison would attend.) It would not be prudent to start borrowing money, at least until a sale should determine the value of the lots, and not without legislative authority. The proprietors should not be paid for public squares taken out of their property until the money for it should be raised from the sale of their own lands. Various restrictions were placed on private buildings; there should be no wooden houses, no projections into the streets, and no house over thirty-five feet high. The digging of earth for brick for the public buildings should begin at once.[29]

It was at about this point, however, that everything began falling to pieces, a structure of circumstances having by now been created which made such a collapse virtually inevitable.

The basic problem, which had been there from the first, was the extreme thinness of the commitment itself. The nation's capital, in being removed from the scene of any of the nation's major activities, had been stripped to an abstraction. About all the commitment consisted of was the very tenuous adherence to an agreement made by a bare majority of the First Congress—now out of existence—to move to the Potomac in 1800. On the one hand, every effort was being made by the Pennsylvanians, as expected, to undermine it. Movements were afoot in their legislature to appropriate money for federal buildings in Philadelphia; funds were also being raised to build a house there for the President. Washington brooded constantly over all these machinations, and when the house was finished he would flatly refuse to live in it.[30] On the other hand, Pennsylvanians or no Pennsylvanians, there was bound to be a limit to how much the imagination, sense of nationality, and patriotism of the society as a whole could be commanded in behalf of a blank space. So, short of forcing people to go there—as Louis XIV and Peter the Great could and did do with respect to their own self-created capitals—the only thing left was to engage their speculative cupidity, which in effect was what the policy-makers did. The financing of the Federal City was organized as a venture in real estate speculation. But even real estate ventures of this sort require a visible urban base, which did not exist, and must attract urban money, which became unlikely when no effort was made to hold the sales in centers of commerce and finance.[31] Out of this thinness of commitment arose two gross elements of liability, one of finance and the other of authority, and together they formed a kind of closed circle from which there was no escape.

Endemic to the entire undertaking was lack of money. The decision to rely principally on land sales was in effect to restrict the source of funds from the outset to a mere trickle. It would in turn be necessary to deceive Congress in reporting progress, in order to inhibit the spread of damaging rumors and to avoid depressing the confidence of the potential buying public. All of this meant formally committing the Executive and the entire government to a policy of minimal financial support. Thus the Executive, should he subsequently want to try reversing that policy and ask Congress for money, would incur a full review and risk a jettisoning of the entire enterprise.

Of profounder seriousness was that lack of money meant lack of authority. It meant impotence to command resources, manpower, or even loyalty—even within the tiny organization directly engaged in the work. With Congress in effect out of it, by necessity as well as design, all the personal authority of the President, fully supported at every point by his Secretary of State, would not be sufficient to command the structure that remained, or even to hold it together. The prime symbol of all this was Pierre Charles L'Enfant, who in a peculiar sense was the only man on the scene to act with full consistency. L'Enfant had been commissioned to do a thing; he could not get it out of his head that somewhere, somehow, the authority must exist whereby he might carry out his commission, and he proceeded accordingly. He was thus virtually bound, whatever the state of his famous temper, to be the first casualty. He would in fact be gone by the end of February 1792, having been at work not quite a year.

L'Enfant remained from first to last bitterly opposed to local land sales, having warned Washington in August—two months before the first one was held—that they would fail because the lots had as yet little value, that this policy and his plan were totally inconsistent, that the whole scheme was beneath the government's dignity, that the work should proceed on all fronts simultaneously, and that the only way to effect this was through the floating of substantial loans. Washington and Jefferson, fully committed to the L'Enfant plan but unwilling or unable to face the implications that went with it, pushed ahead with their policy, and L'Enfant's predictions proceeded to unfold.[32]

The first sale was a dismal affair, despite the presence of the nation's two highest dignitaries and the leading congressman from Virginia. Out of ten thousand lots in the government's possession only thirty-five were sold, four of them taken by the Commissioners themselves in order to keep up the bidding; and the actual cash receipts came to little more than $2,000. Trapped by his own policy, Washington in his annual message to Congress referred to the affairs of the Federal City in a manner that was anything but candid. "And as there is a prospect," he announced, "favoured by the rate of sales which have already taken place, of ample funds for carrying on the necessary public buildings, there is every expectation of their due progress."[33]

A second sale was held a year later, on October 8, 1792. It too was a failure, and Washington knew it. But he thought there ought to be another; he fidgeted over suggestions that he send an agent from city to city ("which rather appears to me to be hawking the lots about"); and in his annual message that year he told Congress nothing. The third sale was held on September 17, 1793, after great preparations had been made to render the occasion auspicious. The President came to lay the cornerstone of the Capitol, and there was a procession which included two brass bands, a company of Virginia artillery, and members of nearby Masonic lodges. In their colorful costumes they all paraded through the woods toward Jenkins's Hill (renamed Capitoline Hill), broke ranks at Goose Creek (renamed the Tiber), and clambered across by means of a log and "a few large stones." Though the cornerstone was laid without mishap, the auction fared even worse than had the previous two. After this mortification, Washington suspended all further public sales. Again, not a word to Congress, but in a long letter to the English agriculturist Arthur Young, Washington referred glowingly to the Federal City. "It is encreasing fast in buildings, and rising into consequence; and will, I have no doubt, from the advantages given to it by nature, and its proximity to a rich interior country, and the western territory, become the emporium of the United States." This (alas for the veracity of our first Chief Magistrate) was simply not true.[34]

Major L'Enfant, somehow trusting that the President and his advisors would any day be overcome by the logic of his case, had long since plunged headlong and uncompromisingly to his doom. The engraver had no copies of the city map ready for distribution at the first sale of lots in October 1791, and the evidence suggests that sabotage by L'Enfant himself was the main cause, the Major having actually refused the Commissioners the use of his own map on the same occasion.[35] The following month he and the Commissioners came into direct collision when, despite orders to desist, he had his workmen demolish a house being built by a local landowner because it projected into his proposed New Jersey Avenue. Washington, in patching this up, had Jefferson warn L'Enfant that he must conduct himself "in subordination to the authority of the Commissioners." Then while L'Enfant was in Philadelphia completing an extended report on forthcoming operations, having left instructions with his assistant Isaac Roberdeau for the winter's work, the Commissioners decided to suspend that work until spring because of limited funds. Roberdeau, believing himself bound by his master's orders, refused, whereupon the Commissioners discharged the seventy-five workmen and had Roberdeau imprisoned for trespass. Washington's final effort to reconcile L'Enfant and the Commissioners, and to force the Major to put himself under their orders, was a failure.[36] The furious Frenchman declared that he would "renounce the pursuit of that fame, which the success of the undertaking must procure, rather than to engage to conduct it under a system which would . . . not only crush its growth but make me appear the principal cause of the destruction of it," and that with regard to the Commissioners he was determined "no longer to act in subjection to their will and caprice." Jefferson thereupon wrote to him on February 27, 1792: "I am instructed by the President to inform you that notwithstanding the desire he has entertained to preserve your agency in the business, the condition upon which it is to be done is inadmissible & your services must be at an end." L'Enfant immediately predicted that no one who succeeded him would fare any better, and once again, events were to prove him right. Andrew Ellicott and Samuel Blodgett, who followed L'Enfant, would meet a similar fate.[37]

The Commissioners themselves should probably not be blamed for this. They were men of standing and ability, personally known to Washington, and were serving without salary. Not being local residents, they were unable to meet oftener than about once a month. It is true that by this time they were held in contempt throughout the District, but theirs was inherently an impossible position. They were belabored from every side. To L'Enfant they had been men of "confined ideas," "ignorant and unfit," and "little versed in the minutiae of such operations." From Washington himself they heard that "if inactivity and contractedness should mark the steps of the Commissioners . . . whilst action on the part of this State [Pennsylvania] is displayed in providing commodious buildings for Congress &ca. the Government will remain where it now is." Washington warned that although such sentiments were not his own but those of the enemy, the best antidote to them was "perseverance, and vigorous exertion."[38]

The Commissioners' most persistent headaches were created by the local landowners. They had been an unruly lot from the outset, though it was the very circumstances of the case that made them so. Before the exact site of the city was revealed, they had been thrown into agitation by simultaneous surveys deliberately intended to mislead them and to inhibit speculation. Bringing them into subsequent agreement required Washington's own presence. When several backed out because of uncertainty over the boundary, the President once more had to appear in person to get them back into line.[39] Further discords were created by the emergence of a pro-L'Enfant party at the time of the Frenchman's dismissal. Captivated by the noble plans which promised so much for property values, the proprietors vainly besieged Washington and Jefferson with pleas for his reinstatement.[40] Anything the Commissioners undertook in one part of the District, such being the piecemeal way in which they had to proceed, was bound to antagonize somebody in some other part. An example was the bridge they tried to build across Rock Creek, which was denounced as an act of favoritism toward Georgetown. But then the hapless builder, one Harbaugh, turned out to be not very experienced in designing arches, and the entire matter was in a way resolved when the bridge fell down. By August 1793, two of the Commissioners, Thomas Johnson and David Stuart, had had enough and asked to be relieved. They were obliged to remain more than a year thereafter because Washington could find no one to replace them. The third, Daniel Carroll, resigned in 1795, worn out from his labors, and died the following year.[41]

This general lack of cohesion and control was even to be seen in the design and execution of the two main buildings, the President's house and the Capitol. Bereft of L'Enfant's services, Jefferson advertised in the newspapers for plans. Three months passed before a single response came in. For the President's house only two designs were offered, and the one chosen was the work of James Hoban, an Irishman from South Carolina. It was for a stately building with wings at either end, inspired by the residence of the Duke of Leinster in Dublin. The center portion, a kind of large box, was the only part that went up, and even this would be no more than partly completed when Jefferson himself moved into it in 1801. It was still not completed when the British burned it in 1814. Not until 1833, more than forty years after it was begun, would an American President have a finished house to live in.[42]

As for the Capitol, the cornerstone of which was laid before anyone knew for certain what it would finally look like, there were even greater difficulties. In this case the prize was awarded to a Dr. William Thornton, whose principal achievement was a method of teaching oral speech to deaf mutes, and whose knowledge of architecture consisted of a hasty scanning of whatever books he could collect just prior to preparing his design. In the meantime another man, Stephen Hallet of Philadelphia, who did know something about architecture, had been encouraged to believe the prize would go to him. Hallet had been at work for some time trying to realize the various suggestions with which he was besieged by Jefferson. He struggled unsuccessfully with the Roman temple form, which Jefferson had persuaded the authorities at Richmond to adopt, and then with something on the order of the Pantheon, of which Jefferson had made a sketch of his own. Hallet was still at it when Thornton's design—projected on similar lines—came in, and the Thornton plan, "simple, noble, beautiful," according to Jefferson, "captivated the eyes and judgment of all."[43]

But Dr. Thornton had no qualifications or experience in making working drawings, so that chore was turned over to none other than "poor Hallet," his disappointed competitor. Hallet duly reported that in consideration of time, practicality, and expense, serious modifications would be necessary. Jefferson had to supervise these matters in Washington's absence, Washington helplessly observing from Mount Vernon that it was unfortunate they had not done this figuring before they took the plan. But by now Washington was ready to settle for almost anything: "a Plan must be adopted; and good, or bad, it must be entered upon." He informed the Commissioners that what Jefferson and a conference of architects now recommended was a "plan produced by Mr. Hallet, altho' preserving the original ideas of Doctor Thornton, and such as might, upon the whole, be considered as his plan [Thornton's]," but which "according to Mr. Hallet's ideas would not cost more than one half of what it would if executed according to Doctr. Thornton's." With various details still unsettled, such as whether or not to have a portico or a recess at the east front, the cornerstone was laid on September 18, 1793. These ambiguities seem to have remained, inasmuch as Hallet as superintending architect was discharged the following year for persisting in his own plans rather than Thornton's. Hallet's successor, George Hadfield, fell into similar errors with similar results, Dr. Thornton having meanwhile become one of the Commissioners. The Capitol would be completed, after various other modifications, in seventy-one years.[44]

Thus lack of cohesion, lack of control, and lack of money all came to the same thing. Most of what was used for operating expenses had had to come from the original grants by Maryland and Virginia. Sales of lots languished, and the Commissioners with Washington's approval furtively began borrowing money, or rather trying to borrow it, though not authorized by law to do so. A syndicate was formed by three men of acknowledged standing in financial circles, James Greenleaf, John Nicholson, and Robert Morris. The syndicate was to purchase several thousand lots, pay for them in seven annual installments, sell a portion to private buyers at the enhanced prices which would presumably be created by their activities, provide the Commissioners with a monthly sum for operating expenses, and negotiate a large loan abroad, using the lots (title to which had been transferred to the syndicate before they were paid for) as collateral. The promoters, however, could not sell their lots, could not meet their installments, and could not interest any investors, foreign or domestic, in a loan of any such nature. Their entire structure collapsed, and by the fall of 1797 all three were in debtor's prison. Meanwhile the industrious Samuel Blodgett, who served for a time as superintendent of construction in the District, organized a grand lottery with the blessing of the Commissioners. It too came to a bad end, complete with the imprisonment of Blodgett.[45]

With the Commissioners forced to carry on operations with local bank loans on their own notes, Washington—no doubt with many inward groans—finally faced the bitter choice early in 1796 of asking Congress for authority to borrow money openly on the security of public property. His message was a true masterpiece of evasion. He transmitted a memorial from the Commissioners praying that an act to this effect be passed, and he told the House and Senate that in such an enterprise as the building of a capital "difficulties might naturally be expected: some have occurred; but they are in a great degree surmounted, and I have no doubt if the remaining resources are properly cherished, so as to prevent the loss of property by hasty and numerous sales, that all the buildings required ... may be compleated in season, without aid from the Federal Treasury." But Washington and the Commissioners understood full well that what they were asking for was not really a loan after all, but "aid from the Federal Treasury," and the reason was the same as that for which all the other schemes had failed. The key phrase in the memorial was the final one: "that, in case the property so pledged shall prove inadequate to the purpose of repayment, the United States will make good the deficiency." That is, the lots may not have been quite worthless, but they certainly were "inadequate to the purpose of repayment," because few really believed anything would come of the Federal City. The question was dragged out four months before a loan of $500,000 was finally authorized.[46]

Even so, a loan authorized was not the same as a loan in hand. Even this guarantee, that "the United States will make good the deficiency," was not enough to attract subscribers. It was only when the state of Maryland came to the rescue with $100,000 that the Commissioners were enabled to keep things going, and then on a very thin shoestring. Nor, obviously, was the problem that of "loss of property by hasty and numerous sales." The Commissioners had done everything they could, not to "cherish" such property but to persuade people to buy it and build houses there. The building code had long since been abandoned. But all was in vain, and when the government moved to the City of Washington in 1800, President Adams's Secretary of the Treasury found to his dismay that there were "but few houses at any one place and most of them small miserable huts." Many years later, one of the original proprietors was offering "to give lots away in certain sections of the city if people would come and build on them."[47]

And yet no factual account of the founding of Washington, however melancholy its details, can begin to plumb the implications of what was done, and not done, at that time and place. L'Enfant, the author of the grand plan, had acted in a spirit fully in keeping with the plan's requirements and scope. But what of the plan itself? Either in form or in function, as Lewis Mumford has stated, it had little to do with republican government. It was a plan for a baroque city—the essence of baroque being absolutism, regularity, and display.

The ruling principle of the baroque design, as Mumford observes, is the abstract geometrical figure, the execution of which no obstruction can be allowed to spoil. The plan has for its focal points those edifices and other monuments which are the visible symbols of majesty and authority. Its lines of access and communication, its avenues and boulevards, are designed almost exclusively for the requirements and convenience of the nobility. There is no real place in it for work: no provision for the common life of the community, or for the way in which its people get their living. All of this is kept out of sight, and in a sense out of mind. The plan, moreover, must be executed at one grand stroke or it cannot be executed at all. It is thus—as with Versailles—frozen in time, with no allowance for future growth, except insofar as growth will mar and violate its very perfection. And finally, the stroke whereby the baroque plan is imposed must be an act of despotism.[48]

As a baroque conception, L'Enfant's plan certainly had its elements of technical virtuosity. The artist-engineer began not with the street system but with the principal public buildings and squares, and these served as the cardinal points which gave the law to everything else. He made the most of a difficult site, and his inspiration, for example, of having a cascade, using water from the Tiber, flowing down Capitol Hill was, in Mumford's words, "worthy of Bernini himself." What L'Enfant brought forth had all the surface aspects of "a superb baroque plan: the siting of the public buildings, grand avenues, the axial approaches, the monumental scale, the enveloping greenery."[49] But as an American community, as the center of a republican nation's life, what did it mean?

The "grand avenues" may serve as the central anomaly. These avenues, 160 feet in width, took up with their tributaries a total of 3600 acres, more than all the remaining land that was available for private residences and public buildings together. A population of half a million would have been required to justify them, whereas in fact they left room for a population of little more than a hundred thousand. To pave them would have required a sum equal to perhaps a quarter of the entire national debt. Two assumptions with regard to avenues lurked behind all baroque planning. One was that width and linear straightness—neither of which had been typical of medieval or Renaissance cities—were ideal, and indeed indispensable, for the fast-moving carriages and spirited horses of the aristocracy in their daily comings and goings. Thus one of the most compelling spectacles in the life of the baroque city, gaped at from the sidewalks by the common herd, was "the daily parade of the powerful." The other assumption was that such avenues, for the same reasons, were ideal for military display and columns of marching men.[50]

Conceivably something might have been said for putting the streets of Washington to either of these uses, though Thomas Jefferson, for one, would have been horrified at the least thought of it. But there was of course no danger; such streets required the invention of the internal combustion engine before they could make any sense at all, and the reaching of that point would itself be the beginning of their obsolescence.

But far more fundamental than the street system was the question of what, besides the activities of government, was to sustain the city's life. This was never L'Enfant's main concern, nor was it really that of anyone else. The central drama of the baroque city was that not simply of government in itself, but of majesty — physically embodied in its court, its display, and its monuments. But what of the daily life behind all this? What was to bring people, resources, prosperity, refinement, and vitality to this place? What sorts of people? Why should they come at all, and what were they to do?

In the "Observations" and "References" attached to L'Enfant's plan there is much about "grand fountains," "grand edifices," and "grand avenues," but not a word about works for the facilitation of commerce, except for mention of an arcade under which "shops will be most conveniently and agreeably situated." In his plan L'Enfant did provide for a canal from the Eastern Branch across part of the city, but judging from his reports it seems that what he had in mind was a facility not so much for making the place a commercial entrepôt as simply for supplying the city itself. Indeed, the idea of the Potomac as an artery of navigation to and from the West had been a piece of wishful thinking all along, probably subordinate to the urge simply to place the capital in Virginian hands. The river, with its five major falls and shallow channel, was a dubious proposition from the outset, and all efforts to reach the Ohio through canals, dredging, and the building of locks — all dragged out over many decades — were to end in failure. Commerce at the port of Georgetown, at best amounting to no more than two or three ships a month, actually began to decline during the 1790s. Out of the four commercial enterprises that were founded in Washington during its first decade, only a brewery survived.[51]

> In consequence, there was "not a single great mercantile house" in the District of Columbia, observed a foreign dignitary in 1811–12; "no trade of any kind" (1828); a "total absence of all sights, sounds, or smells of commerce" (1832). "The greatest and most respectable business that is done in Washington," read a handbook for newcomers in 1829, "is keeping boarding houses."[52]

It was not even possible to attract with wages enough men to work on the public buildings. Thus a considerable portion of the labor was performed by slaves, which was the only element of baroque, the only aspect of despotism, that the city saw. One thing that Washington and St. Petersburg did have in common, as John C. Miller has remarked, was that both were largely built with unfree labor. As for the government establishment itself, the court and nobility, as it were, who would reside there and display themselves on the grand avenues, there would be an unhappy total of less than three hundred persons straggling into the woods and marshes of Washington in 1800. The local population that greeted them were a disquieting lot. Drifters, vagabonds, and adventurers, these birds of passage did little for the tone of the place except to depress it still further. "The people are poor," observed Oliver Wolcott, "and live like fishes, by eating each other."[53]

3
The Idea of a City

The failure of Washington was certainly a failure of execution; it could also be seen as a failure of the plan itself, full of anomalies as the plan was. But one may well wonder what the alternatives were. Would some other plan have been any better? Would another design have been more suited to a successful execution? Judging from historical precedent, one is inclined to doubt it.

Historically it seems that cities—capital cities or any other kind—have not been "created" at all; they have germinated and grown. Not that such growth has been uncontrolled, or even unplanned. But with the cities of medieval Europe, the "planning" that went into them tended to consist first of a rudimentary initial layout—an ecclesiastical seat, a military garrison, a market—and then of civic supervision, under civic standards, of piecemeal expansion over time. The energy behind such planning and supervision was a reflection of clearly recognized needs, and of the values inherent in what was already there. Therein lies a major difficulty with regard to the city of Washington. That enterprise was in the hands not of a nascent communal body but of men who had no feeling for cities at all, little sense of what a city was, and little experience of what urban life meant.

The emergence of the towns and cities of the Middle Ages is itself a subject in whose intricate fascinations it is easy to lose oneself. Yet even a casual survey discloses a truism: that the indispensable term in accounting for these places is commerce. (Henri Pirenne went so far as to say that without a market one could not speak of a city.) Other functions, military or ecclesiastical, seldom existed independently of the town's commercial life. Even the Norse invaders, as the old chronicles go, came to plunder and stayed to trade. The counts of Flanders, in making their regions defensible in the eleventh century, intentionally created the conditions for a peaceable commerce; "they stimulated town and country alike," as John Mundy has written, "by building fortified bourgs and by draining marshes." The Church did even more, mobilizing vast amounts of capital and at the same time, with the celebrated laws on usury, making great exertions to police its employment.[54] In the earliest known writing, as Robert S. Lopez has pointed out, the hieroglyph for "city" is a cross within a circle. The cross stands for converging roads which bring in and redistribute people, merchandise, and ideas. The circle indicates a moat or wall—morally if not physically present—which serves to bind the citizens together, shelter them from the world without, and fortify their pride in being members of a community. "The city," as Richard L. Meier puts it, "is not only a crossroads, a place for outsiders to meet and trade, it is a living repository for culture—high, low, and intermediate." Cities exist "to promote access, under conditions of relative security . . . , not only to people, artifacts, and services, but also to accumulated stores of information."[55]

The expansion of commerce and its corollary features in the late Middle Ages—more sophisticated legal forms, modes of economic organization such as guilds and trading companies, new political forms for acquiring local control of urban communes, and such newly recognized social classes as merchants and artisans—made for the emergence of an urban culture strikingly distinct from that of the peasant countryside. People saw more outsiders, saw more of each other, traveled more, and talked more. Education became itself a commercial commodity, indispensable in such trading centers as, for example, Genoa, where illiteracy was virtually unknown.[56] And it was in the cities and towns, not the country, that the medieval universities grew. All of this made for a pattern of social existence that had taken on complexity, diversity, and energy.

Such a mode of life generated many strains. But it also developed a set of values and loyalties whose force depended on the city's character as a corporate entity, and on the recognition that it gave its citizens benefits which they could claim only in their capacity as a civic body. It is remarkable how much of the building, public and private, during the Middle Ages and later was carried out under municipal control. The important guilds were represented in the town councils, and again and again projects of planning and construction would be supervised by master builders who were also acting as municipal officials. "From the thirteenth century onwards," writes Fritz Rörig, "it was a municipal building committee which constructed the whole of Bruges in the subsequent centuries. It fixed the rows of buildings with a deliberate, even exaggerated stress on differences in balustrades; it looked after the paving of the roads and the water supply of the town; it encouraged the replacement of thatched roofs in favour of tiled roofs through a kind of bonus system; and in short it intervened in everything."[57]

An invariable element of such planning was its explicit recognition of sociability. The prime example is the *piazza* of the Italian Renaissance city. The *piazze* of Florence, Siena, Pisa, and Venice served a wide variety of communal uses. The square, lined with shops where the craftsmen worked subject to the inspection and criticism of the passersby, with restaurants and tables along the *trattorie* and the church at one end, was at once a marketplace, a playground, a promenade for lovers, a place to meet, mingle, and gossip, and an *al fresco* stage for civic pageants and religious processions. The *piazza* was the mirror of the city's being.[58]

The very tangled diversity of urban life provided a setting for the most diverse and complex urban personalities. Florence, for example, while producing and trading tons of cloth over the centuries, also produced Dante, Boccaccio, Savonarola, Giotto, Donatello, Ghiberti, Brunelleschi, Michelangelo, da Vinci, Masaccio, Fra Angelico, Fra Lippo Lippi, Alberti, della Robbia, del Sarto, Ghirlandaio, Machiavelli, Cellini, and Galileo, not to mention the Bardi, the Pitti, the Medici, and the legendary Buondelmonte, whose picturesque murder is said to have given history the Guelfs and the Ghibellines. For a man who appeared and flourished under such circumstances, his city, for good or ill, was inseparable from both his inner and outer self. Dante, exiled from Florence, saw himself as ceasing to exist.[59]

In the America of the late eighteenth century, there was none but the palest reflection of the city as any such idea as this: as a corporate body, a cross in a circle, a living community. This was a concept either unknown to or hardly felt by the planners of what was intended as America's first city.

4

The Idea of a Capital

One may say (at the risk of circularity) that most of the world's great cities have grown out of something that was already there. A similar logic applies to capital cities: these are not created at will; it is all but impossible to make them appear out of nothing.

But there have been exceptions. A delightful example is that of St. Petersburg, built early in the eighteenth century by Peter the Great and substantially completed during Peter's own lifetime. The case even contains certain parallels to that of Washington. The site which Peter personally chose was hardly auspicious, the estuary of the Neva being an inhospitable wilderness—foggy, unhealthful, and marshy—and virtually nobody in all Russia wanted to go there but the Tsar himself.

But the Tsar was no ordinary man. Peter Romanov was nearly seven feet tall, massively built, and bursting with demonic energy. He could never watch craftsmen at work without wanting to master the craft himself, which in instance after instance he did: stonemasonry, blacksmithing, carpentry, printing, and even watchmaking. The Russians of his day knew absolutely nothing about ships, navigation, or shipbuilding; Peter, with the assistance of foreigners, taught himself everything that could be learned about each of these mysteries. He even took a small retinue to England in 1698, occupied a house at Deptford on the Thames next to the royal docks, worked in the shipyards by day, caroused by night, and left the house a shambles. It was Peter who, almost single-handedly, created the Russian navy. He was a man of great charm, also of ferocious will and volcanic rages. The occasional uprisings of the *streltsi*—a professional military class bearing some resemblances to the *condottieri* of Renaissance Italy—would be suppressed by Peter with hair-raising brutality amid scenes of mass rackings, disembowelings, and gibbetings. Such was the father of his people, Autocrat of the Russias, the man who built St. Petersburg and named it after his patron saint.[60]

Peter wanted a capital; he also wanted a great commercial center with a port and naval base on the Baltic whereby he might turn Russia economically, politically, and culturally toward Europe. In his mind, in fact, the "window to the West" idea had preceded that of a capital. When work began in 1703, Peter was on the ground in person, staying in a small house that had been built for him there in two days' time. The initial undertaking was the fortress of Saints Peter and Paul on Yanni-Saari, or Hare Island; it consisted of six great bastions, the construction of one of which Peter supervised himself. Earth being scarce and wheelbarrows non-existent, long lines of laborers had to carry loads of earth in the skirts of their tunics or in bags made of old mats. The technology was somewhat primitive.

For labor, men were arbitrarily conscripted from all parts of the empire to the amount of some forty thousand a year. (One of Peter's earliest levies was for "several thousand thieves": criminals sentenced to Siberia were to go to the Neva instead.) The mortality—from dysentery, plague, malnutrition, exposure, and overwork—was frightful. Through it all, the ebullient Peter in sending out his letters headed them "From Paradise."

He employed foreign architects, the two principal ones being men of exceptional ability. Domenico Trezzini was responsible for a large number of the more imposing public buildings, including the Peter and Paul fortress, and it was Trezzini's authority that directed the design of the several classes of dwelling houses. Alexandre Jean-Baptiste Leblond was the man who designed and set into execution the baroque street plan, which included two grand *prospekts,* the Nevsky and the Vosnesensky. Nevsky Prospekt, two and a half miles long, was paved in stone by Swedish prisoners, who also had to clean it every Saturday. Leblond, who had studied under LeNôtre, the landscape architect of Versailles, built grottoes and fountains in the Tsar's garden, using water from the Fontanka canal for his cascades. He was given a very free hand.

Since few would have dreamed of settling in St. Petersburg of their own free will, Peter blithely populated his city by force. According to one of his ukases, a thousand of the leading noble familes were to come and build houses along one side of the Neva; five hundred merchants and five hundred traders would do the same on the opposite bank; and two thousand artisans of every sort "must settle themselves on the same side of the river...."[61] Fires being a constant danger, Peter decided (like Jefferson some eighty years later) that houses should all be built of brick or stone, and he issued another ukase to that effect. He also specified that meanwhile no stone edifices were to be erected anywhere else, to make sure that every mason in the empire would be available, if and when needed, for the work at St. Petersburg.

Peter gave endless attention to the city's commercial and port facilities. He built extensive wharves and shipyards on the left bank of the Neva, and for protection of the sea approaches he established a fortress on Kotlin Island, later called Kronstadt. (He prepared the drawings himself, after personally taking the channel soundings around the island.) For access from the interior he began the building of a direct road to Moscow, and supplemented it by a canal around Lake Ladoga linking the Volga and the Neva. This remarkable canal was begun in 1718 and completed shortly after his death. The Tsar went to great lengths—including the reduction of port dues and the offering of bargain prices on various Russian products—to induce foreign merchantmen to call regularly at St. Petersburg. When the first one arrived in 1703, the jubilant Peter sailed out incognito, piloted the ship into port himself, and presented the dumfounded master a purse of five hundred ducats, together with gifts for the entire crew.

Despite the fervent prayers of Tsarevna Maria that St. Petersburg might once more become a desert, the place grew and prospered. The imperial family and all the agencies of government took up permanent residence there in 1710; foreign trade increased year by year; and a building census of 1714 reported—perhaps with some exaggeration—that houses of all kinds totaled 34,550 in number. At any rate by 1725, the year of Peter's death, the city had a population of a hundred thousand.[62]

St. Petersburg is the only case known to the Western world of a created city that successfully served all the functions of a true capital.[63] A society's "capital" in the fullest sense consists not only of its political center but of its economic and its cultural center as well; only the power and the will represented by a Peter the Great could successfully bring all three out of nothing and make them survive. Aside from this extraordinary example, which even Louis XIV could not duplicate, the most organic expressions of national civilization have been such capital cities as London and Paris, where the elites of government, of money and trade, and of intellect and art have regularly met and intersected for centuries. "The kings might prefer Winchester," Denis Brogan has written, "but the nature of things preferred London." By Edward III's and Geoffrey Chaucer's time in the fourteenth century, the kings preferred it too. London by then was being referred to in royal documents as "a mirror to all England."[64]

5

An Imaginary Capital City

Washington, D.C., remained a slatternly miserable village throughout much of the nineteenth century, hardly endurable even in the barest physical sense, and it has never had, even in our own day, any of the characteristics of those capitals selected by "the nature of things." In the humiliations and failures of Washington and Jefferson, we have already seen something of the price of imagining that a selection could be made with impunity on some other basis.

Perhaps an inkling of it might be gained by venturing a counter-factual projection. The choice that was actually made in 1790 could be seen as altogether arbitrary; conceivably the "nature of things" pointed in a different direction. What might have been the consequences if in 1790 the capital had simply been allowed to remain where it was?

As a matter of record, New York was an older city than either St. Petersburg or Versailles. Peter Minuit's famous purchase of Manhattan in 1626 followed rather than preceded the first settlement and planning of the Dutch post of New Amsterdam. Since Hudson's explorations of 1609, trading companies had been making voyages up the river and around its mouth, erecting buildings on Manhattan for temporary headquarters. (In fact, a century before Minuit's time Verrazano had described the place enthusiastically to Francis I after his own reconnoiterings of 1524, and a map of unknown authorship exists in Paris, dated 1570, which shows the topography of the area in considerable detail.) In any case, the Dutch West India Company's plans had been completed by 1625, and the instructions to the Company's engineer for laying out the fort bear a date of that year. With its great natural advantages New Amsterdam was an immediate success as a trading center, though the Company's conception of it was not very imaginative, and its initial intentions were rather limited. The emphasis was on trade and military protection rather than the development of a colony, and this tended for some years to keep the population lower than it might otherwise have been. Nevertheless, the cosmopolitan and polyglot character of the town seems to have emerged quite early; Father Isaac Jogues reported eighteen languages spoken there and in the vicinity when he visited it in the 1640s. When the British took it over in 1664 they found a bustling mart of commerce, with wharves, warehouses, brick buildings, and cobblestoned streets. These streets, established along the natural paths taken by people and animals in their earliest comings and goings, made an irregular pattern that survives in some measure to the present day. Beyond the north line of fortification across the island (a line to be known, logically, as Wall Street) were various hamlets, such as Bowery Village and Harlem, which would eventually be absorbed in the city's growth. Travelers in the mid-eighteenth century invariably commented on the exceptional cleanliness of the town, with its gabled houses, neatly paved streets, and flatstone sidewalks. Its population on the eve of the Revolution was about 25,000.[65]

In the face of the British occupation, New York's population dropped to about 5,000; it rose again with the subsequent influx of Tory refugees and British soldiers; and it dropped once more with the British evacuation in November 1783, when it amounted to between 10,000 and 12,000. But in the next three years the population more than doubled, and in 1786 it stood at 23,614. New York's remarkable expansion in commerce as well as population during these years made it seem more than likely that the city would eventually pass Philadelphia in both, as in fact it shortly did. The census of 1790 gave New York 33,131 and Philadelphia 28,522, though prematurely: if the adjoining "liberties" of Philadelphia had been properly counted, New York would not have moved ahead until shortly after 1810. But its special advantages over Philadelphia for commerce were already apparent in the 1790s, and were clearly perceived by such visitors as Talleyrand and La Rochefoucauld-Liancourt. New York, already ahead in enrolled tonnage used in the coasting trade in 1789, passed Philadelphia in total tonnage in 1794, in the value of imports in 1796, and in exports in 1796–97.[66] By 1800 New York could already imagine itself becoming what it would in fact become during the nineteenth century, the greatest port in the world. Were New York to become America's political as well as its commercial capital, it would do so under a certain historical logic.

As soon as Congress voted in December 1784 to move to New York, civic groups and associations of individuals began exerting themselves to the utmost in plans and projects for accommodating the government. It was determined to transform City Hall into Federal Hall through extensive alterations and rebuilding, and the Chamber of Commerce brought incessant pressure on both municipal and state authorities for hurrying up the work. Money was appropriated; immediate cash was borrowed from public-spirited citizens; and the work was carried out in accordance with plans prepared by Pierre Charles L'Enfant. The final cost of $65,000 was twice as much as had originally been appropriated, but the city was vastly proud of the result. Under a city-appointed commission, work was also begun in May 1790 on a house for the President on the site of Fort George, just below Bowling Green and overlooking the Battery. It was a fine structure, completed the following year, though by then the government had departed. Still, there had been great hopes and great plans, one group of promoters having even worked out a scheme for erecting a kind of great Acropolis for the government atop Brooklyn Heights.[67]

What all this represented was a concentration of energy, money, public spirit, and civic pride that could be of immense benefit to a new and groping federal government in establishing the appropriate setting, consistent with its own future dignity, in which to conduct its business. The most obvious and immediate expression of this civic energy would be found in the physical appurtenances of the government's capital city. But there would be less tangible ones as well. As with Paris and London, the resources of an ascendant city were there to be combined with those of government, and the product could well exceed the sum of their parts.

In addition, it would be an *available* capital: available not only to the members of Congress, officers of state, and employees of government, but available to the people of the entire country. The "centrality" argument for the Potomac, heard so often during the debates on the residence question, was an abstraction, even in 1790. It was based not on population (though the Virginians insisted that the growth of the Southwest would some day make it so) but rather on geography. And yet even with centrality argued on that basis, the operative variable was logically not a place on the map but speed and convenience of travel. Readily accessible by water from everywhere along the Atlantic coast, and by river from upper New York and western New England, and with more coasting ships moving in and out than was the case with any other port, New York City was already in 1790 probably easier to reach from more points than was any other place in the country. This was true even for the South. One could reach New York from New Orleans—or indeed, from anywhere in the Mississippi Valley—more quickly and easily than one could reach Washington. Even from Charleston, Washington was less convenient than New York.

Still, the real meaning of "centrality" does not lie in geography at all, or even in convenience of travel. Centrality in the last analysis concerns the place to which more people have more different and various reasons for going than they do to anyplace else. For the people of the United States, including a steady flow of southern planters coming north for their annual shopping, New York, even without its being the center of government, would increasingly take on this character in the course of the nineteenth century.[68]

And a capital of that sort could do some remarkable things for the federal government itself. It would bring the government into contact with the nation at the peak point of the nation's visibility, possible only at a real crossroads. It would be the place from which the people's chosen representatives might return home wider in sense and spirit than when they came—supposing they were offered at the very least a life of some grace and civility while there. Even this was to be denied them in the barracks-like, company-town, celibate existence of nineteenth-century Washington, where congressmen "lived like bears, brutalized and stupefied."[69] But a real capital would represent a great deal more than a decent existence for congressmen. The people's deputies would be surrounded by forces, other than simply one another's company, for enlightening them as to what the character of their country was. Their capital could serve them as "a mirror to all America."

We are thus brought back to the question of culture, and to what it is that relates a nation's capital to a nation's culture. If culture is perceived simply as objects of art on display, then it is easy enough to set up "culture" almost anywhere. Yet if culture is seen as what brings the objects themselves into being, it becomes a very complicated subject indeed. Perhaps culture may itself be thought of as a kind of mirror, held up to us at critical moments by our wisest or most agitated spirits. In it we are allowed glimpses of important knowledge: of who and what we are, and of the powers by which we rule ourselves. Those who hold the mirror up need to be standing in some sense at the crossroads of our corporate life. We then see ourselves, our customs, aspirations, and delusions, our houses, cities, and countryside; we even see a little more clearly those whom we choose to govern us, government itself being an item in culture. So a fair fraction of the artists and thinkers who define a society's visions ought to be located at the center of things, while those who embody authority must be there too, and must take account of *them*.

The structural support of culture—the social, and indeed the downright physical, context in which a republican society's cultural resources are husbanded and renewed—seems to be a subject we do not know very much about. But judging from what we do know, without a legitimate capital city the process has been at best a very erratic one. The early experience of New York—in which many of the elements for a focusing of national culture were present, but from which, on the other hand, certain critical elements were missing—may offer a few clues to how it might or might not have worked.

A nice case of cultural logistics is that of the New York theater, which seems to have enjoyed a clear preeminence over that of other American cities from the first. Yet this preeminence, seen as the intersection of certain influences occurring at a critical time, cannot have been altogether accidental. In 1785 Lewis Hallam, whose father's American Company had opened the John Street Theater a few years before the Revolution, returned to New York and revived the company at the same theater. There they played a repertory of Shakespeare, Sheridan, Addison, and Goldsmith, and in 1787 they brought out Royall Tyler's *The Contrast.* Tyler thus became the first American playwright to have his work performed professionally. Tyler's success was directly responsible for the decision of William Dunlap, a rather remarkable young man just returned from a sojourn in England where he had studied painting under Benjamin West, to try his own hand at playwriting. Dunlap's comedy *The Father, or American Shandyism* was performed in 1787, also with success.[70]

But the New York theater was itself the object of considerable social opposition. The home-front morality of the Revolution had frowned heavily on frivolous amusements. Stage plays continued to be denounced by the clergy and many others, and a number of petitions to the Common Council and the state legislature urged that such spectacles be suppressed. No action was taken, but a good number of New Yorkers in 1789 remained in some uncertainty as to just how they ought to think about such matters. The decisive cues were given by the President of the United States. Washington loved the theater; he got up theater parties during the season of 1789 and took various high dignitaries and members of Congress with him. John Street on November 24, 1789, had the fullest house ever seen, according to the *Daily Advertiser,* "owing to the President and Lady being there, and its being previously known." The piece being played happened to be a new farce by William Dunlap, *Darby's Return,* and this is said to have been the only public occasion at which George Washington was observed to laugh. William Dunlap (1766–1839) thus began a career as author, translator, impresario, and manager that would, by the time it closed fifty years later, establish his reputation as "the father of the American theater." Dunlap was a man of extraordinarily wide interests. Since his theater ventures kept him in chronically poor financial straits, he made ends meet through his second profession, which was painting. (He had done pastel portraits of General and Mrs. Washington in 1783, when he was only seventeen.) He seems to have known everyone in town, was very kind to young writers and artists, and had a wide circle of friends in the world of letters, painting, theater, and commerce. Two of Dunlap's books, *The History of the American Theatre* (1832) and *The History and Progress of the Arts of Design in the United States* (1834) remain valuable sources to this day.[71]

Among the painters Dunlap knew who lived and worked in New York were Gilbert Stuart, John Vanderlyn, Edward Savage, John Trumbull, Thomas Cole, Asher Durand, Samuel F. B. Morse, and John Wesley Jarvis. The fame of these men, with the exception of Cole and Durand, rested largely on their portraits of statesmen. But statesmen, to be painted, have to be there; otherwise the painter has to follow them about. Gilbert Stuart, for one, simply closed his New York studio and moved to Philadelphia in 1794. It was there that Stuart executed his best-known portraits, foremost of which were those of Washington.[72]

A decade and a half after William Dunlap's death, New York was visited briefly by the Edinburgh publisher William Chambers. "Without a court," Chambers wrote, "and not even the seat of the state legislature, New York cannot be described as the place of residence of a leisurely or a numerous literary class." Chambers was simply taking for granted the intimate relationship between literature and political power, and the consequences of a serious disjunction between them. Conceivably such a connection should have been especially urgent in America, whose culture since at least the 1760s had been so specially political, and where so much of the society's creative energy had been put to purposes political in nature. "When the United States began its national existence," Richard Hofstadter has written, "the relationship between intellect and power was not a problem. The leaders *were* the intellectuals." Why, he asks, should politics and intellect then have gone their separate ways? No doubt there were a number of reasons. But sheer physical separation—not having a capital city where writers as well as politicians could function, and in which they would want to live—has to be counted as one of them.[73]

Actually the leading literary figures of William Dunlap's New York—Washington Irving, James Fenimore Cooper, and William Cullen Bryant—never suffered from obscurity. For holding up the mirror to whatever extent their talent allowed them, each was probably as well rewarded as any man of letters could have expected in the America of that time. Each of the three, moreover—Federalists in their youth and Jackson Democrats in maturity—was well acquainted with figures of power. Irving (who as a small boy had been blessed on Broadway by General Washington) acted as secretary to the American legation in London and was for a time in charge of it; he was a good friend of Martin Van Buren, who wanted to make him Secretary of the Navy when he became president; and he served for several years as United States minister to Spain. Cooper's father was a prominent upstate landholder and a member of Congress. His family and that of John Jay were very close, and it was in fact Jay who had told Cooper the story upon which *The Spy* was based. Cooper was active politically for DeWitt Clinton, and he wrote extensively on political questions. The memorial gathering which was held in New York at the time of his death was presided over by Daniel Webster. Bryant was bound up in politics all of his life. He too was a friend of Van Buren, whom he supported for the presidency. From the editorial throne of the New York *Evening Post,* which he occupied for half a century, Bryant himself received the homage of all the leading political figures of the day. It was Bryant, by then a patriarch, who introduced Abraham Lincoln at Cooper Union in 1860.[74]

Such were among the conditions that sustained them; other conditions kept their company very sparse. It could even be guessed that had there been more such company, these particular three would not have been as consequential as they were.

For the stream of foreigners who began entering the national life from the beginning, New York was the major port of entry. This was undoubtedly the chief factor in the early ascendancy of New York's musical life over that of other cities. For example, the influence and presence in New York of Lorenzo da Ponte, who had given Mozart his libretto for *Don Giovanni* and who would end his days as professor of Italian at Columbia College, was responsible for initiating the performances of Italian opera which would occur more or less regularly from the mid-1820s on. Much of the impetus for the founding of the Philharmonic Society in 1842 came from Daniel Schlesinger, a pianist who had been trained by a pupil of Beethoven and who was the best musician in town. The success of the Society's orchestra, moreover, was largely due to its corps of German musicians.[75] In this there was nothing unusual for a cosmopolitan city; the musical life of London was by no means all English, nor that of Paris all French. With immigration destined to be a highly significant element in the national experience, New York as a capital as well as a cosmopolitan city might have made that experience a good deal more vital than it actually was. There was a time when the republican myth of America served as an inspiration for half of Europe, and the promise of a great capital might have drawn steady and substantial numbers of the most creative spirits of European culture.

One of George Washington's fondest hopes for his federal seat was a national university. The hope was shared by Thomas Jefferson, who had the happy thought that the entire faculty of the University of Geneva might be brought over and reinstalled on the banks of the Potomac. Nothing ever came of these fancies, nor was anything resembling higher education to appear in Washington for a long time to come. In New York on May 6, 1789, a week after his inauguration, President Washington attended the annual commencement of Columbia College, where his stepson had once studied briefly but which was not at that time an institution of great consequence. But it had at least one thing upon which futures are built, a prior existence. It already had a tradition of sorts that went back thirty-five years, a small endowment from Trinity Church and other sources, and among its alumni were men of some influence. They included the Chief Justice, the Secretary of the Treasury, the delegate who had penned the United States Constitution, and the Chancellor of the State of New York. If the support given in the 1790s by the city and state, which was not inconsiderable, had been continued into the nineteenth century, and if to this had been added no more than the moral support of the federal government, Columbia might indeed have become a national university, and one of the world's leading centers of learning, well before it in fact did.[76]

Things done for the first and only time exert, by definition, the most coercive weight as precedents. Such was the case with virtually all the precedents set in the first year or so of the federal government's existence, and none more so than with the decision made in 1790 to remove the capital from New York and subsequently from Philadelphia. That decision entailed a renunciation of whatever moral authority the national government might have had over the public imagination in matters of urban development and design. By that choice, made at a critical moment, a quasi-official benediction was in effect laid upon a set of values which had no real place in them for cities. This would not have occurred if the government had committed itself to an existing city at the outset and had concerned itself, as it would in some sense have been forced to do, with its future welfare and growth. Henceforth there would be few models and few standards, except for negative ones. Cities were not destined to be defined as publicly supervised emplacements of civilized life. Henceforth cities as anything but excrescences, necessary evils free to grow unchecked however they might, were to have little standing in America's official folklore.

The alternative fabric of values which the Founders bequeathed to the nation, though it would have the effect of rendering culturally odious the very idea of the city, was nevertheless not an unpleasing one. Permeated by an agrarian imagery and an ideal of rural prosperity and peace, it certainly had its attractive side for most of the people of that day. In many a sense it still does. It was fully harmonious, moreover, with those ideological aspects of the Revolution which had been inspired by the classical tradition: the Roman Republic, Cincinnatus, Cato, the Sabine farm.

In the nation's cultural memory this rural vision is referred back more often to Thomas Jefferson than to any other of the Founders' generation. And rightly so, for in Jefferson it receives its most complete and most compelling expression.

CHAPTER V

Jefferson and the Yeoman Republic

"Those who labor in the earth," wrote Thomas Jefferson in 1783, "are the chosen people of God, if ever He had a chosen people, whose breasts He has made His peculiar deposit for substantial and genuine virtue." This might be read, as it frequently is, simply as a benign ceremonial affirmation in praise of husbandry. But in view of the thoughts that follow, it cannot be left it at that. The existence of that virtue which resides in agriculture and in its practitioners seems to depend, in an almost mathematical way, on a corresponding lack of it in everything and everyone else. That is, "generally speaking, the proportion which the aggregate of the other classes of citizens bears in any State to that of its husbandmen, is the proportion of its unsound to its healthy parts, and is a good enough barometer whereby to measure its degree of corruption." The point is an arresting one, and needs pursuing. Had Jefferson the ordering of things, he would have no more to do with commerce or industry than he could help ("let our workshops remain in Europe"), and he reaches the climax of this train of thought with a passage on cities which borders on the visceral. "The mobs of great cities add just so much to the support of pure government, as sores do to the strength of the human body." Thomas Jefferson's view of the city—here expressed in the only formal work he produced—as embodying forces which were foreign, unnatural, and corrupting to the morals of his fellow-citizens—was one to which he would hold throughout the remainder of his life. It was, moreover, a formulation that would exercise a special influence on both popular and intellectual culture in America, long after the passing of its most distinguished exponent.[1]

There is every reason for taking these sentiments at face value, and a review of Jefferson's career as a whole can strengthen rather than weaken the conclusion that he meant, and would continue to mean, exactly what he said. But the career itself may be read in more than one way, and the many contradictions and ambivalences in it have created a variety of obstacles to finding the most plausible one. With regard to the instance just noted, an inordinate number of Jefferson's most keenly savored pleasures were found in cities. It might even be said that he did like cities in practice—rather in spite of himself—but detested them in theory. Williamsburg was a major awakening force when he arrived there as a youth to attend college and to partake of the social rounds. But Williamsburg, though hardly a city, nonetheless served him in ways that were more analogous to the functions of a city than to those of a country village; and as the center of provincial culture and meeting place of Virginia's elite, Williamsburg, small though it may have been, was more of a "capital" than Washington ever became in his lifetime. His years in Paris were full of delights: good books, good music, good wines, and good company. But they were ambiguous delights, part of a dialectic of attraction and repulsion. Direct acquaintance only confirmed his conviction that Europe was the breeding ground of all vice; Paris, in so many ways the quintessence of all Europe, was through her very charms the temptress herself. Not to him, perhaps, but to all other provincials. A letter in response to a friend's inquiry about the best place in Europe for a young man to study was turned into an agitated sermon not upon Europe's many opportunities but upon its many perils. The sexual imagery is insistent (the youth "recollects the voluptuary dress and arts of the European women and pities and despises the chaste affections and simplicities of those of his own country"); in effect Jefferson's prescription for young Americans is that for their own protection they had better be kept at home.[2]

It would appear that however secure from such temptations Jefferson may have considered himself, he had no stable frame of reference in which he could take his pleasures wholeheartedly. They had to be taken somewhat on the outer margins of permissibility. Even Philadelphia he regarded with a stern eye. He called it "the old Babylon," and could seize the occasion of an epidemic to tell his friend Benjamin Rush that the yellow fever was really a blessing in disguise since it would "discourage the growth of great cities as pestilential to the morals, the health and the liberties of man." Yet Jefferson himself relished the refinements of Philadelphia, the Philosophical Society, and the company of cultivated spirits he found there. And when the seat of government was moving about in 1783 he was determined, no matter where Congress went, to place his daughter Martha in Philadelphia for her education, and he "canvassed the city for the best instructors in French, music, dancing, and drawing."[3]

The aspect of contradiction and ambivalence in Jefferson, which more than one writer has commented on and tried to deal with,[4] should be taken not so much as a defect but as a distinctive quality of his mind. In charting this quality one might begin by referring to it as "disjunction," an open space in his mental habits between the general and the particular which could sometimes assume dramatic proportions.

Jefferson was not a systematic theorist, nor indeed a system-builder of any kind. He produced no fusions of theory, experience, and necessity comparable to Madison's theory of the extended republic or Hamilton's system of public finance. His many legislative achievements in Virginia as well as his innumerable practical inventions, tabulations, and measurements attest to an exceptionally wide-ranging mind. But it was a mind that habitually worked on two quite different levels. One was that of broad general statement, the other that of specific technical detail. He was both a utopian and something of a gadgeteer.

He could be very effective as both. The force of the Declaration of Independence, with its majestic abstractions, as one of the world's most inspired manifestoes has been acknowledged everywhere. But Jefferson could be similarly proficient in the realm of the specific and immediate. It may be misleading to equate his legislative draftsmanship in Virginia with his inventions and the numerous appurtenances and installations at Monticello, but there is a quality they have in common. All show a striking capacity for absorption with detail. But though Jefferson's powers in the domains of both the general and the particular were considerable, he could rarely manage to work on both levels at once. We do not see them interacting; the one seldom modifies the other in any visible and developing way. It is hard to find a truly complex problem that Jefferson, for all the time he spent at it, fully thought through from top to bottom.

Those of his legislative innovations that were clearly successful—the abolition of primogeniture and entail, the revision of the Virginia Code, the Statute of Religious Liberty—involved creative imagination and a good deal of persistent effort. But they also represented the liberalization of an existing system at points already more or less prepared, without essentially changing or even challenging it. One notes an *a priori* quality about all Jefferson's reform thought, in the sense that failure, and the functional grounds on which failure might occur, were never actually built into his thinking. For the most part he seems to have made up his mind quite early as to what the world ought to look like, and setbacks meant not re-evaluating his assumptions but simply trying again. He could tell a correspondent "that the ground of liberty is to be gained by inches, that we must be contented to rescue what we can get from time to time, and eternally press forward for what is yet to get. It takes time to persuade men to do even what is for their own good."[5] The reformer is the person who already knows essentially what there is to know about what is good for people; meanwhile it is only their own stubbornness that prevents them from seeing what it is. But something more in the way of operating principles would seem to be called for in traversing the steps by which one arrives at, say, a theory of federalism or a system of public credit.

This disjunction in Jefferson's thinking between the general and the particular, the long range and the short, and between broad conception and concrete realization, might seem belied by his historical reputation for "pragmatism." He was quite aware that hard facts frequently got in the way of his ideal constructs and his spacious schemes for human improvement, and he could make concessions. When his basic convictions were challenged by men and circumstances on such questions as banks, commerce, and manufacturing, he was certainly capable of adjusting. He could admit that although Americans ought to limit themselves to furnishing Europe with raw materials and food, the public servant was not free to act on such a theory because "our people have a decided taste for navigation and commerce"; or he could concede that the Hamiltonian system, though "radically vicious," was law and must be upheld. But such cases were, as A. Whitney Griswold puts it, a matter "of expediency rather than of principle."[6] He could do this, in short, without altering the convictions themselves. True "pragmatism" consists not simply in adjusting one's actions but also in adjusting one's mind; indeed, an odd thing about a man who lived as long as Jefferson is that he seldom changed his mind about anything.

A further test of this disjunction might be found not in the reforms that succeeded but in those that failed. Jefferson's 1778–79 proposal for the distribution of land in small parcels at nominal prices, based on his conviction that the yeoman farmer was the ideal citizen of an ideal republic, was cut to pieces by the Virginia Assembly. The controlling forces of Virginia life were concerned not for a society of small farmers but for one of large estates. The implications of this for the settlement of the West—not the Northwest but the Southwest, the region into which movements from Virginia were most likely to go—Jefferson never fully faced. It would not be a society of small farmers; it would be one of small farmers overshadowed by great planters, just as it was in Virginia. His "Bill for the More General Diffusion of Knowledge" contemplated a system of public education not unlike that of New England. It was defeated for a variety of reasons. The costs and difficulty of administering it in sparsely settled country would be considerable; the projected new administrative units seemed to threaten the jurisdiction of the county courts; and there were various religious difficulties, in that on the one hand, the whole scheme looked dangerously secular, and on the other, the non-Anglicans distrusted the influence of William and Mary College, which was intended to stand at the top of the system. And yet the basic problem was simply that the Virginia elite, on whom the bulk of the taxation would fall, had no intention of paying for the education of their poorer neighbors' children. That pattern was to hold throughout the South for the next ninety years. Then there was Jefferson's plan for gradual emancipation and the encouragement of private manumission of slaves. Nothing came of the plan, conceived in the course of his work in revising the colonial slave code, and Jefferson himself did not press it. "It was thought better that this should be kept back," he explained, "and attempted only by way of amendment, whenever the bill should be brought up." Much as Jefferson abhorred slavery, the implications of its being an integral part of Virginia life, and likely to remain so, constituted a problem to which he was in no way prepared to address his whole mind.[7]

The disjunction in all this was between a series of very wide-ranging reforms and the graded projections, practical and theoretical, whereby their enactment might be visualized—or their failure predicted, which conceptually would come to the same thing. Jefferson was an example of what Marx and Engels would have in mind when they wrote about the inability of a class to challenge effectively, or even to understand, the basic conditions of its own survival. There are minds that can free themselves from those particular aspects of their social location which block their view, but Jefferson's was not one of them. Jefferson was in one sense a man of truly radical ideas, for which some of his political enemies later on would give him full credit. But this was true only up to a point; others would taunt him with being a "closet philosopher," which was a coarse way of saying that these "radical" ideas were not radically prosecuted, and were in many cases not prosecuted at all. To have done so would have required a temperament—more fundamentally, a mind—quite different from Thomas Jefferson's. Such a mind would have measured the proportions of the challenge it was throwing down and the character of both its constituency and its opposition; it would not have been content with reassurances that the problem would solve itself through enlightenment and time, during which the ground might be "gained by inches"; and it would have known that on a matter of deep import the opposition was not to be gently maneuvered "by way of amendment." Thomas Jefferson, on the other hand, could seriously persuade himself that the difference of one vote by a New Jersey delegate in the Confederation Congress on the Ordinance of 1784 would have kept slavery out of the territories forever.[8]

The basic reference for Jefferson's social views is, of course, his *Notes on the State of Virginia*. The work is not a systematic treatise, not a theoretical statement on the nature of man, society, and government, nor was it so intended. Thus Jefferson cannot be held to the standards customarily applied to theoretical systems. On what formal plane, then, should it be considered, and what level of importance had it assumed in Jefferson's own mind to warrant his decision to prepare it for publication? Whatever the complete answer may be, the *Notes*, despite its apparent lack of system, does constitute a very comprehensive statement on the level of ideology. It is a world-view couched in a medium—a loose sequence of "Queries" propounded by the secretary of the French legation, Barbé-Marbois, and Jefferson's responses to them—which he found congenial for what he wanted to say. Here one sees, in language impossible to mistake, Jefferson's conviction that whatever his countrymen might do, and whatever concessions he himself might have to make, the United States ought to remain a rural society. The view is advanced not for mere utilitarian reasons—that because of vast stretches of untilled land together with a sparse population, concentrating on agriculture would make the most economic sense—but for ideological ones. Whatever economic expediency might seem to dictate either way, a society of yeoman farmers was inherently more stable, more virtuous, and more republican than any other. Nor is it difficult to see this world-view as guide and touchstone to almost all Jefferson's reform schemes and notions of public policy from first to last. It applies to the questions of primogeniture, entail, education, and slavery, to his land bills, to the Ordinances of 1784 and 1785, and to his attitudes on commerce, manufacturing, and cities. And it applies not least to his feelings about England, where commerce was being used as an instrument to corrupt America, and against whose commerce America ought to strike to cleanse herself of those corruptions.

It will not do to explain Jefferson's rural utopia as an expression of class interest one way or the other, though class interest is clear enough in the case of the Physiocrats, to whose writings Jefferson was certainly attracted. In the Physiocrats' preoccupation with large-scale scientific agriculture there was hardly much concern for the agricultural laborer or the peasant proprietor. But Jefferson was a liberal idealist, which is what has made him so perennially attractive a figure in American culture. It has been suggested that Jefferson's yeoman republic was simply Virginia writ large. There is some truth in this. It is appropriate that such

a vision as Jefferson's should have come out of Virginia, if only for its incorporation of various Virginia prejudices, and it is even fair to grant that it was the
Virginia yeomanry that served as Jefferson's model. But his ideal version of the
Virginia yeomanry was not necessarily the only one. Indeed, those very attributes
of the Virginia yeoman that attracted him were made possible by conditions he
was unwilling to write into his ideal equation. That is, the good yeoman, deferential and willing to take his cues from above, was in fact ringed about by influences (a slaveholding planter elite) which contained him and made him agreeable
to a man of Jefferson's benevolent views and social location. Jefferson seems not
to have projected how the farmers of this class might have looked once they got
out from under—when they moved into Kentucky, say, and became the brawling,
exploitative lot that they did.[9] Jefferson's yeoman republic may best be understood
as the moral, ideological, and literary construct of a humane and cultivated Virginia gentleman.

As for the literary sources of Jefferson's ideas and convictions, the work of
Leo Marx is especially illuminating. These ideas owe a clear debt, as Professor
Marx points out, to some of the main currents of eighteenth-century thought. The
popularity of rural images in English and French culture had several components.
One was the development and transformation of ideas about landscape, which
was to have its reflection not only in painting but also in poetry, gardening, and
architecture. Addison, for example, rejecting the rigid geometry and bounds of
the formal English garden for "an agreeable mixture of garden and forest," tended
to generalize this mixed or "middle" landscape over the entire rural scene. At the
same time, the older stylizations of pastoral poetry gave way to a similar readjustment of the balance between wild nature at one extreme and the over-for-
malized landscape or the denatured city at the other, in such works as James
Thomson's "The Seasons":

> Now from the town,
> Buried in smoke, and sleep, and noisome damps,
> Oft let me wander o'er the dewy fields,
> Where freshness breathes....

The young Jefferson eagerly copied these lines, together with many more from
the same source, into his commonplace book.[10]

Another component was the writings of the political economists—both the
Physiocrats and Adam Smith—on the primacy of agriculture. Though Smith's
principal influence was not exerted in this direction, Smith did assert that the
wealth of nations, whatever its sources, had to have a solid agricultural base. A
final element, paralleling the others, came out of the various debates of the period
regarding the nature of man. The most satisfactory resolution was an eighteenth-
century version of the "middle state" doctrine—man as the middle link between
the animal and intellectual states of being—the origins of which went back to
antiquity. Even Rousseau realized that the "noble savage" needed some modification, up to a point. The husbandman, clearly, was the perfect middle-state
figure. The main elements of the middle state and the middle landscape were

explicitly fused in the work of the Scotsman Hugh Blair, whose *Lectures on Rhetoric and Belles-Lettres* became very popular in America, and were familiar to both Madison and Jefferson.

Still, in Europe all this rural enthusiasm was to a large extent an aristocratic fashion, an esthetic convention to be taken somewhat short of literally.[11] Many who embraced it did so out of a fastidious distaste for that same commercial spirit which David Hume had seen as a civilizing influence, and the sturdy farmer who inhabited their middle landscape was a figure with whom they were acquainted only at a becoming distance. Meanwhile they could and did pass the winter season not in the tranquility of the middle landscape but amid the social whirl of London or Paris. For Thomas Jefferson, on the other hand, the rural ideal amounted to something rather more serious. It was central to the whole vision which the Revolution, as he saw it, had opened up for America's future.

Jefferson's love of amenities—physical amenities as well as cultural ones, books, music, pictures, and the rest—was an essential part of his being. At the same time his own country, as he gazed down upon it from his mountaintop at Monticello, was a composite of the primitive, the innocent, the untutored, and the uninstructed—but there it all was, vast limitless tracts of it, waiting for seed and cultivation. And here was a cultural mode, the middle landscape, capable of accommodating both him and it. It provided a legitimate and sanctioned esthetic framework for refinement, sensibility, enjoyment, and gentility; it also offered a moral outline for his country's destiny. The picture of virtue, simplicity, and honest toil, of republican freedom amid rural surroundings, was one he found supremely agreeable to contemplate for his fellow-citizens. He may have been somewhat removed from them in fact, but he was generously with them in spirit. A sturdy yeoman population, a fallow and untenanted West: the materials were all there; the best aspects of the Enlightenment could be objectified if all would but share his vision, and a literary convention might be made real.

Jefferson's love of good things did nonetheless have certain special consequences for his mind. A number of oddities come together at this point: not only the books, the wines, and the French cuisine, but much of the endless gadgeteering at Monticello: the dumbwaiter, the special serving-shelves, the cunningly submerged servants' quarters, the fabrics he himself designed for the curtains, the preposterous eight-day clock. The striking thing here is the minute attention he could lavish on *all* these items; he could scurry about endlessly to see that everything might be just so. (Much the same quality is evident in his micromanagement of Latrobe with regard to the Capitol.)[12] He was concerned, in short, for a total effect. He wanted a total effect for his America, just as he did for Monticello, and he would have liked nothing better than to lay on any number of the touches himself. But this kind of impulse breeds certain idiosyncrasies, and it may be that a man willing to fret over details and effects will do so at a greater expense to his synthesizing energies than he realizes.

The formative experience of Thomas Jefferson adds still further clues to the world-view with which one associates him. That experience may well have had for him the effect both of highlighting the attractions of his rustic ideal and of blurring its incongruities.

He was born in 1743 in Goochland County—later called Albemarle—in the Virginia piedmont, on the very western fringe of settlement. His "first wails," says Dumas Malone, "could have been echoed by the howling of the wolves." His father, Peter Jefferson, was a dominant symbol in his life. A man of great stature and strength, Peter had been one of the earliest settlers in the Rivanna region, and was said to have entertained Indians at his house. He helped to survey the western boundary, and his expeditions through the wilderness, with their perils and hardships, became a part of the family lore. It was said that on the frontier he associated with men of rough virtues and was indifferent to the niceties of social rank. All this seems to have been a source of pride and satisfaction to Thomas Jefferson. "My father's education," he observed in later life, "had been quite neglected"—adding, however, that "being of a strong mind, sound judgment and eager after information, he read much and improved himself."[13]

But with this remarkable father Thomas Jefferson could have it both ways. Peter Jefferson was no Daniel Boone, and it would even be leaving something out to call him a self-made man. He was, and had been since early adulthood, a solid member of the Virginia ruling class, as had his own father before him. Indeed, there had been Jeffersons in the province almost from the first, a John Jefferson having arrived in 1619 as a member of the Virginia Company. Thomas Jefferson's great-grandfather, Thomas Jefferson I (d. 1697), owned several slaves and was "a man of respectable estate"; his grandfather, Thomas Jefferson II (1677–1731), was a justice of the peace of Henrico County for twenty years as well as sheriff and captain of militia. Peter Jefferson at the time of his death at forty-nine was the first citizen of Albemarle County. He had served as justice of the peace and sheriff of Goochland, and in Albemarle he was a justice of the peace and judge of the court of chancery, lieutenant-colonel of militia, county lieutenant, and a member of the House of Burgesses. He married into the Randolph family, whose pedigree (though Thomas professed to hold it lightly) "went far back in England & Scotland." At his death Peter's property—none of which came from Jane Randolph—amounted to some sixty-odd slaves and about 7,500 acres, two-thirds of which would go to Thomas as the first son.[14]

Nor was Thomas himself ever subjected at first hand to the rigors of the frontier. By his time it had melted into the middle landscape. His early years were spent at Tuckahoe, the estate of his father's closest friend, William Randolph, who died when Thomas was two; as his friend's loyal executor, Peter would manage the place for the next seven years. It seems that the infant Thomas was carried there on a pillow by a mounted slave. There he was educated with the Randolph children by private tutors, and when he returned to the Jefferson plantation, Shadwell, he was sent to learn Greek and Latin at the school of the Reverend James Maury a few miles off. Long and earnest application to study was always his greatest surcease and delight, and he remained grateful to his father for providing him with good instruction. But the symbol of his father was something of an ideal construct; the son never really saw much of him. It often happened that when one was at home the other would be away; Peter died, moreover, when his son was only fourteen. Three years later Thomas enrolled at the College of William and Mary. When he arrived at Williamsburg it was the first time he had ever seen a town of that size or importance.[15]

At Williamsburg the young Jefferson came under the spell of the two best-trained intellects in Virginia, those of William Small and George Wythe, who gave him both friendship and special attention. Small, a Scotsman, was the professor of mathematics and natural philosophy. His religious opinions were not orthodox; and he introduced Jefferson to the wonders of science in a wholly secular and rationalistic way, instructing him also in logic, ethics, rhetoric, and belles-lettres. Jefferson stayed in college two years and then commenced the study of law under Wythe, a classical scholar himself and the most learned man of the Virginia bar.[16]

If one of the potent symbols of Thomas Jefferson's early life was Peter Jefferson, very possibly the other was the royal governor, Francis Fauquier, who with his urbanity, intelligence, and manners was the first living embodiment of the culture of Europe he had ever laid eyes on. Fauquier, acknowledged by Jefferson as the ablest man ever to fill the colonial governorship, had both wit and charm, and was a discriminating amateur of art, science, music, and literature with something of a taste for things French. Fauquier, Small, and Wythe were close friends and congenial spirits, and at some point the young Jefferson was adopted into their circle. He never forgot the intimate dinners à quatre at the governor's palace where, he recalled, he "heard more good sense, more rational and philosophic conversations than in all my life besides." Jefferson, who had taken up the violin, was also recruited to perform in quartets at the Governor's weekly musicales. He knew very early what it was to be an insider.[17]

He would never, in fact, be anything but an insider. His rise was swift and smooth as leaders of the provincial elite quickly recognized his abilities and in effect brought him into the ruling group while still in his mid-twenties. He was admitted to practice before the highest court at twenty-four, and went to the House of Burgesses at twenty-six without first serving the customary apprenticeship on his county court. In 1769 he began the building of Monticello, with himself as architect, and in 1772 married Martha Wayles Skelton, a young widow whose father, John Wayles, had a large fortune. Wayles died the following year, and with Martha's share of the estate, Jefferson's property was thereby doubled. Even after selling off over half this legacy to pay Wayles' creditors, he now had an estate of ten thousand acres—three large plantations and several smaller ones— with 180 slaves. Meanwhile he had been made county lieutenant and county surveyor in Albemarle, and in the Burgesses he was given important committee assignments, where his powers of draftsmanship were perceived and made use of. He found himself increasingly committed in the mounting struggle against royal authority, as the entire ruling class moved in the same direction. Jefferson's tract *A Summary View of the Rights of British America* (1774) gained wide currency. The logical next step was selection by his peers as a delegate to the Continental Congress. By this test he had become at the age of thirty-two—in company with

Washington, Lee, Pendleton, and Henry—one of the eight or ten leading men in Virginia. Four years later, in 1779, he would be elected governor.[18]

The coercions of this insidership were undoubtedly considerable. The system had given him everything he could have asked for: wealth, social position, the fullest opportunity to engage his talents, and general recognition. He was thus allowed the luxury of determining which of these things he valued most, and which least, without having to give up any of them. Such being the case, the likelihood of his offering a basic challenge to that system, whatever the defects he might decide needed remedying, was not very great. He might suppose himself viewing it with detachment, but he would never do so from the outside.

What we know of Jefferson's temperament and personal characteristics may add a further increment to an understanding of his mind and the way he used it. He never had to worry a great deal about his health: he was tall and raw-boned, with a good constitution and excellent digestion. He did not have much physical grace, being rather awkward, but if he lacked the natural coordination seen in athletic types, he could use his hands with considerable skill. Unlike many men of his time, he had no military inclinations whatever, in either an active or a theoretical way. He was the titular first military officer of his county, with the rank of colonel, but he never took the field, and for all his many interests his mind was never engaged by either the strategy or the technology of warfare on land or sea. He frequently declared himself to be a man of peace.[19]

Jefferson had an agreeable enough exterior presence, though he was not very ardent in personal relationships. He was entirely accessible but always fastidious and a bit distant; he could occasionally even exhibit—though shrinking from open hostility—a touch of the cold fish. But for the most part he was quite amiable, especially in small groups, where his shyness left him; knowing a great deal about a great many subjects made him endlessly interesting. And, allowing for that imperceptible shade of distance, he was always regarded in Virginia as a good neighbor. As patron and aegis to bright young men, moreover, he was unfailingly generous. There was always something of this element, for example, in his friendship with James Madison, whom he came to know in the mid-1770s. One imagines that he would have been all but ideal as a professor.

He was notably industrious, almost compulsively so. He abhorred licence and idleness (especially gambling), and was obsessed, perhaps a little primly, with the virtuous uses of time. He seems to have been somewhat agitated by the spectacle of confusion. "His whole tendency," observes Merrill Peterson, "was to combat the chaos of experience and submit it to the dictates of reason. . . ." He was often wont to occupy himself, perhaps because it kept his spirits calmed, with drawing up plans for something. He liked to prepare schedules, especially for his children, which he would accompany with rules of conduct. His daughter Martha, an unusually serene and even-tempered girl, took a fair amount of this, mostly in stride, and during her stay in Philadelphia did what she could with a day which began at eight with practicing music and ended with "read[ing] English, writ[ing] &c." from five to bedtime, and in which her absent father had (inadvertently, no doubt) left no time for meals. Still, one wonders what she must have

thought when he told her, in one of his epistolary lectures about keeping herself
and her clothing clean, that "nothing is so disgusting to our sex as a want of
cleanliness and delicacy in yours."[20]

Jefferson was hardly a combative man. He was repelled by face-to-face controversy and would go to some lengths to avoid it. True, he could be callous and
even bloodthirsty on paper or at a distance, but not directly. He held the most
advanced ideas, as Richard Hofstadter has remarked, "but he was not in the habit
of breaking lances to fulfill them." He sat mostly silent in the Continental Congress, having no gift for debate, and in court he was at a disadvantage at those
times when extemporizing was called for. Without careful notes, he was lost. He
was once thrown into something of a panic when his notes for a series of impending cases were accidentally burned, and petitioned for a postponement. As soon
as he could, he confined himself to appellate work in the General Court, where
he did not have to face juries. Thomas Jefferson was not a man who could
improvise easily, least of all under pressure.[21]

But because of his essential optimism Jefferson seldom felt it necessary to
break lances. He believed, and often in effect said, that all would come right with
time. And so it may have been his sanguine temper, as well as his *a priori* mental
habits and the faith he put in reason, that made so many of his schedules, his
rules, his plans and sketches of the world, a reflection of how he wanted things
to look rather than the way they happened to be.

At the same time, his abhorrence of disagreeable things made him very thin-
skinned and touchy at the smallest impeachment of himself. He could not bear
censure, and the very anticipation of it could call forth spasms of self-justification
which tended to arrest the normal processes of his mind. Nor, finally, did he have
very much humor. There was little sense of irony in him, least of all toward himself.
There seems no other explanation for his frequent homilies on frugality, both to
his country at large and to young men "unacquainted with the practices of domestic economy necessary to preserve [them] from ruin,"[22] while he himself—with
his books, chefs, retinues of servants, and extravagant trappings—could never
manage to live within his own income, and in his movings-about would insist on
extensive remodelings of every house he stayed in, no matter how briefly. Always,
of course, in accordance with elaborate plans, busily prepared by himself.

Actually there were very few points in the course of Jefferson's long life at
which most of these characteristics did not function as assets, or at least not as
liabilities. But there were exceptions, and one of the most nightmarish was his
Revolutionary war governorship of Virginia. After it was over, though a movement
for censuring him was dropped, a number of questions were raised in the Assembly about Jefferson's behavior in the face of Benedict Arnold's invasion of the
state in 1780–81. The Governor was not a very warlike figure, though such were
the limited powers of the Virginia executive that no one in that role could have
assumed too many martial airs without arousing suspicion. The fact remains,
however, that war governors in other states with powers no greater than Virginia's
used them a good deal more aggressively. Jefferson was certainly an industrious
governor, the most impressive evidence of which was the volume and meticu-

lousness of his paperwork. But Jefferson had a fixed conception of Virginia's role in the war—as the main supply and support base for the fighting in the Carolinas—which had little room in it for the possibility of a British invasion. Thus he was quite unable to adjust when Arnold's incursion actually began, and did not want to believe it even when the signs could not be mistaken. He suspended judgment for two days while the enemy made their way up the James, and finally called out the militia, who did not arrive in time to do any good. After occupying Richmond and committing various acts of destruction, Arnold withdrew southward.

The possibility of a repetition, perhaps even with the entire British southern army, ought to have been fairly clear. But Jefferson still shrank from its implications, and from such unpleasant measures as using the militia on fatigue or conscripting labor to work on the fortifications. He doubted, he said, whether such measures were legal. Actually this was the very point, short of massive resistance from the Assembly, at which a governor might have improvised most freely. But Jefferson's real collapse came with the invasion by the main army. The glimpses we have of him from this point on—the insistence on calm, measured deliberateness—have a somnambulist quality not unlike the behavior of the French general staff as the Germans advanced in 1940. But as the disorganized government moved from Richmond to Charlottesville and then, with Tarleton's raid, set off for Staunton, Jefferson did not offer to follow. He had been silently counting the days until the end of his term, and when June 2 arrived, though the legislators were in midflight and a successor had not as yet been named, he divested himself of the whole dreadful business. Later, when he received news of the censure movement, the mortified Jefferson went into a deep sulk for months.[23]

The disjunction between theory and practice, between plan and execution, which Jefferson always seemed able to accommodate somewhere in his mind, and to live with, is revealed—either as a rare burst of candor or as a pre-Freudian slip—in a letter he wrote to the irascible Baron Steuben during the thick of the confusion. Steuben had exploded in frustration over all that had somehow gone wrong with Virginia's measures of defense. "We can only be answerable," Jefferson replied, "for the orders we give, and not for their execution."[24]

And yet neither Jefferson's political reputation nor his personal honor seems to have been severely damaged by the ordeal of his war governorship. Washington's great victory at Yorktown in October provided the atmosphere in which censorious spirits might quickly calm down, especially inasmuch as some of them had found the zeal of Thomas Nelson, Jefferson's successor, a bit on the highhanded side. Virginians could reflect that Governor Jefferson had, after all, worked hard in the face of crushing difficulties, including a currency depreciated almost to worthlessness, and that he had nonetheless been endlessly scrupulous about legality and private rights. He had done his best, and in view of the sacrifices he had made in the public interest, not only in his two years as governor but from the beginning of the Revolution, the Assembly by the end of the year was more than willing to tender him a unanimous resolution of thanks.[25] Jefferson, who had continued to believe in the rightness of his acts and decisions, had thus gained vindication. What he may have gained in the way of self-knowledge cannot of course be known.

And Jefferson had continued to contribute in a creative way, even with his war governorship, to the tradition of American liberalism with which his name is more pervasively associated than is that of any other statesman. The liberal tradition may not provide the most precise of all possible standards for national self-scrutiny or for assessing the true price of things, but it does provide other standards which are not without value. Something has to be accorded its essential mildness: its peaceability, its good intentions, its eager faith in knowledge and reason. By word and example, Thomas Jefferson did as much as anyone to make it a more or less official sanction that a government ought not to be coercive. While in the course of time this may also have become the sanction for a good deal of private coercion and private violence, the American government itself has for the most part not felt compelled to maintain its dignity by an exercise of force against its citizens.[26]

Thomas Jefferson, then, is properly regarded as the reflector and embodiment of a tradition. Among other things it includes, as already noted, a set of values bearing positively on the countryside and negatively upon cities. A final note might be that it also includes a peculiarly American attitude about capitals. There has been no real impulse in American life for regarding a capital as anything but a "seat of government."

When Jefferson sponsored the move from Williamsburg to Richmond in 1780, a clear precedent was set for a number of similar movements of other state capitals in the years that followed. Among them were those from New York City to Albany, from Philadelphia to Lancaster and then to Harrisburg, and from Charleston to Columbia. Indeed, virtually every state underwent some variation of this process. The pattern was invariably one in which the capital ended up in a more or less centrally located place, and not in the state's principal city. Any lingering commitment to the idea of a capital as a cluster of economic and cultural as well as political resources had at some point been left behind once and for all, which meant that there were few inhibitions against either moving the capital around or building one *de novo*. It was thus made available as an item for political deal-making, in which the variables included local ambitions, the desire of outlying districts for accessibility to government, and whatever the more thickly settled areas might want or accept in return for giving up claims to a capital they could not have anyway.[27] The results have been curious. Not only did the country at large, by going to the Potomac for its capital, fail to acquire a focus for the national culture, but it would develop few distinctive focuses for regional cultures either. It is Albany, for example, that has prevented New York from being in the fullest sense the "Empire State." It is no accident, on the other hand, that Boston— which for various reasons resisted this trend—came closest to functioning as a true provincial capital. Boston, with its State Street, its State House, its churches,

Harvard, and Faneuil Hall, had been the "capital" of New England from the beginning, and in a sense never ceased being so. This would make some difference in the cultural and political history of nineteenth-century America.

The implications for the national culture would be deferred during the decade in which the national government resided in Philadelphia. That city at this period was plausibly as good a choice as New York, and for all anyone knew perhaps a better one. Thomas Jefferson, in the years he was to spend there between 1790 and 1800, would continue to believe in the pernicious effects of cities and to deplore what he saw of their commercial character. He would nonetheless be tolerably compensated by the varied amenities of Philadelphia life.

CHAPTER VI

Jefferson as Secretary of State

An event of great significance in defining the foreign policy which Thomas Jefferson was to follow as Secretary of State had occurred at the very moment of his first entry into public life, over twenty years prior to his joining Washington's cabinet. This was the Association of 1769, the non-importation agreement entered into by members of the Virginia Burgesses as a protest and counter-measure against the Townshend Acts. Similar agreements had been concluded by groups of leading men in all the northern colonies. Inasmuch as all the Townshend duties were subsequently repealed except for the tax on tea, the Association had accomplished substantially what it set out to do. On Jefferson, the impression of this experience of successful commercial pressure would be lifelong.[1]

It was understandable that he should have found this form of coercion so attractive. It was a mode of action that did not require bloodshed. Moreover, viewed from the perspective of Virginia the experience seemed to show that the sacrifices could be borne, despite the inconveniences, without permanent damage. Virginia's rural life was so organized that the impact of a trade stoppage could be absorbed and diffused; consumption of luxuries and manufactured goods could be postponed, with no need in the meantime of anyone's starving. As a matter of record, Virginia's compliance with the Association was not as thorough as that of northern merchant groups, though the absence of a central port and the consequent temptations to smuggle undoubtedly had something to do with this. But perhaps the only real difficulty anywhere was that of voluntary compliance. This would be largely overcome if non-importation or some other form of commercial coercion were to become the law of the land.

All of this may well have strengthened Jefferson's convictions as to the relatively circumscribed function of commerce, and further limited his sensitivity to the impact such a policy might have on a community largely dependent on commercial pursuits. The above influences, together with the deep anglophobia which peace did little to abate, had provided Jefferson his ideal formula for addressing the various problems stemming from America's new relationship with Great Britain. From 1790 to the end of his secretaryship in 1793, he continued to believe that the range of difficulties created by exclusion of American ships from the British West Indies and British non-compliance with the Peace of 1783 would have yielded more readily to commercial coercion, purposefully applied, than to any other proceeding.

The obverse of Jefferson's anglophobia was his predilection toward France. Here the counterpart to his experience with the Association in shaping his ideas on foreign policy was his mission in Paris from 1785 to 1789. His major preoccupation during this period had been with cutting down Great Britain's monopoly of American trade, his intended instrument being expanded trade relations with France. A previous plan had envisioned the constricting of this monopoly through the creation of a great free-trade community which would include America and the other nations of Europe. The device would be reciprocity: a series of trade treaties with each of these other nations, the result of which would be to force England to revoke her restrictions against American commerce and thus in effect to fall in line with the others. The undertaking was abandoned when the intended parties proved not to be interested. Jefferson thereupon reasoned that the best way to work toward the desired object was to concentrate on France alone. Through agreements with the French government he would do everything possible to widen Franco-American trade, on the premise that the more this increased, the less would be the volume and importance of American commerce with Great Britain. Trade developed with the French meant trade diverted from the British.[2]

For Jefferson the attractions of France and the French were considerable. Basic to these, of course, were the ties created by the wartime alliance against the common enemy, and the generous sentiments of that connection were shared in some form by most Americans. But for Jefferson a special color was imparted to them by the friendships he formed during his years in France, for which—though he visited London more than once during that same period—he found no counterpart in England. Such men as Lafayette, Condorcet, La Rochefoucauld, and DuPont de Nemours had considerable official influence, and their concerns were similar in many ways to Jefferson's own.

For one thing, they had much to do with establishing the point of view from which Jefferson would regard the onset of the French Revolution. As members of the liberal nobility, these men were all warmly pro-American, inspired by the Americans' example, and all anxious to bring about a liberalization of the Bourbon monarchy. And though Jefferson could observe at first hand the succession of events from the Assembly of Notables in 1787 to the occurrences of 1789, it was unlikely—surrounded as he was by such liberal spirits—that he could have seen these events in truly apocalyptic revolutionary terms. It must have seemed rather like revising the Virginia Code. "I think it probable," he wrote enthusiastically to James Monroe in 1788, "this country will within two or three years be in enjoiment of a tolerably free constitution, and that without it's having cost them a drop of blood."[3] Of the murderous passions of the bourgeoisie in their drive for equality he could have had little direct acquaintance.

Another element in his association with these friends which undoubtedly had its misleading side was the cordial encouragement they gave to his trade schemes. The influence among them of large agriculture and Physiocratic doctrine was very strong, and none of them had any connections with French commerce or manufacturing. They were nonetheless quite willing to instruct French businessmen as to where their true interests lay, and even on occasion—as with the ruinous free-trade treaty of 1786 with England—to play fast and loose with them. In any case, Jefferson was not so situated that he could make any genuine accommodation in his theories for the mentality of the French bourgeoisie, which was one of reactionary mercantilism. This, under Jacobin leadership a few years later, would be translated into national policy.[4]

Thus despite having arrived at understandings in a few limited areas, Jefferson's efforts to broaden Franco-American trade came to very little. But the lessons he chose to draw, as he sailed away in the fall of 1789, were drawn not from those aspects of his policy that had failed, which meant by far the greater part of it, but rather from the degree, minimal though it may have been, to which it had succeeded. Continued exertions might yet do it (the ground might be "gained by inches"), and it was in this spirit that he would give his earnest support to Madison's projects of tonnage discrimination in 1789, 1790, and every subsequent year he brought them forward.

Inherent in these views, and in his related distaste for the corruptions of speculation and commerce, were the makings of a jarring collision with Hamilton. This was virtually bound to occur, almost without regard to the two men's personalities. For Jefferson, questions of foreign and domestic policy would be inseparable, just as they were for Hamilton, and neither would be able to avoid repeatedly invading the other's department. On the one hand, Jefferson's ideal foreign policy threatened to play havoc with Hamilton's domestic policy. On the other, Hamilton's system—shortly to be augmented by a national bank, which Jefferson would strenuously oppose—committed Hamilton to an anglophile foreign policy which Jefferson despised. Well before Jefferson left office this fundamental divergence had created an ideological impasse so great, and a partisanship so intense, that it would color every action, foreign and domestic, which the Administration took.

Secretary Jefferson, then, was convinced that the only way the United States might resolve its difficulties with Great Britain was to expose Britain's dependence on American markets and American supplies through the standing threat of commercial coercion. He was not to have the opportunity, however, to consummate this policy or to realize its fruits. The outstanding points of conflict—trade with the West Indies, unpaid debts to British creditors, British spoliations, and continued British occupation of the western posts—would continue unresolved as long as he was Secretary of State. With the eruption of war in Europe, irritations growing out of them would bring the two nations to the verge of war in the winter of 1793–94, making a settlement imperative. But Jefferson did not remain to preside over it. Despite the entreaties of Madison he resigned in December 1793, and by the time the Jay Treaty was concluded—which would stabilize Anglo-American relations for another decade, though hardly in the way Jefferson desired—he would be rusticating once more in the tranquility of Monticello.

I

The Nootka Sound Affair, 1790

It may not seem wholly logical to line out the first phase of Jefferson's secretary-ship — in his capacity as the United States' foreign minister — with reference to an episode in European diplomacy which implicated the United States no more than marginally. But it may still be instructive. The Nootka Sound crisis, which kept England and Spain on the edge of war throughout a good part of the spring and summer of 1790, represented a chapter in Pitt's foreign policy which was of much importance in the affairs both of England and of the Continent. This in turn corresponded in point of time with the United States' first opportunity to test its own relations with Great Britain. The dealings that occurred about the fringes of this crisis exhibited for practical purposes all the elements that would govern Anglo-American relations for the next four years.

There had certainly been nothing official about the exploratory interview between Alexander Hamilton and Major George Beckwith in the fall of 1789; there is no evidence that Hamilton even told anyone about it. Their talks would resume in 1790, but even then — even when carried on with Washington's and Jefferson's knowledge — they could hardly be regarded as true diplomatic exchanges. But the mission of Gouverneur Morris was a different matter. The United States government during the year preceding Morris's arrival in London had given evidence of its stability, and although Morris was not a fully accredited minister, he bore a letter of credence from the President which gave him the status of an authorized special envoy. When he presented his letter on March 29, 1790, the British ministry presumably had reason to be satisfied that it could now deal with the United States on solid grounds and on an amicable footing. From the American viewpoint, moreover, Morris's position might be seen as tolerably strong, inasmuch as England was on the verge of an international crisis from which the United States might extract some advantage. On the face of it, things should have augured well for the Morris mission.

But the British response to Morris did little to bear out such hopes. They seemed to feel little urgency about dealing with him, and in the four interviews he was able to obtain during the nearly six months he spent in London, they did not even seem certain what they should do with him. There did appear to be at one point a brief possibility of opening real negotiations. But Morris asked for more than the British were willing to give; they remained amiably non-committal, and the mission ended without Morris's having accomplished anything.

As to why this should have been, and whose fault it was, there are several plausible explanations. One is simply the intransigence of the Ministry: a narrow-ness of view and rigidity of mind that prevented the emergence of anything resem-bling creative diplomacy. Another is that Morris — who was himself rather a prickly sort, and sometimes too clever by half — overplayed his hand, and thereby missed the chance to open a new era of reason in 1790. Still another is that Hamilton, pursuing on his own account a line of policy sufficiently divergent from that of Jefferson, undercut official policy and prevented the United States from speaking with one voice.

Something can be said for each of these cases. But the reason for what did and did not happen between the United States and Great Britain in 1790 and for some years thereafter may go deeper. The very conventions of diplomacy itself, as well as the way in which the annals of diplomacy have to be recorded, may be more of a hindrance than a help in discovering what it is. Diplomacy is conducted between sovereign powers, which means that the formal ratio between them, at least at the point of contact, has to be something approximating one to one. But it was very apparent that here the ratio was in reality not one to one. What, then, was the true proportion?

Nearly all who have written about this particular sequence of Anglo-American diplomacy have been Americans. They have had to view it, moreover, through the eyes of the Americans of that time—Morris, Washington, Hamilton, and Jefferson—because most of the source material is itself American. Relatively little is to be found on the British side. This very paucity may be a clue in its own right, and should itself be seen as part of the evidence.

The vast disproportion in power between Great Britain and America in the early years of the republic is well enough recognized, debates on this score tending rather to focus upon the ways in which the United States might or might not have brought what power it did have into the scale of diplomacy to effect its ends. But the most baffling of all to assess and measure is something that goes deeper. It has to do not so much with power but simply with the extent of the claim— relative to their various preoccupations as well as their power—that each side is able to make on the other's attention. The problem, as mentioned earlier, is the enormous disparity between the level of American attention upon Britain and that of Britain upon America.

Perhaps the most useful way to address this particular sequence is to let Pitt's foreign policy and his manner of conducting it serve as the governing context. From this it becomes evident that whatever the Pitt ministry was prepared to do, or not do, with respect to the United States would be motivated by the object of maintaining the status quo—which, as worked out over the previous seven years, had come to be regarded as generally satisfactory. Consequently the ability of the Americans to make any imprint on this attitude, from whatever angle of approach, was extremely limited. And since the status quo was what most Americans— anglophile or anglophobe—wanted to alter, all were in the last analysis facing the same impasse, with little to choose from in the way of instruments, and with the chances of failure about equal for all. To say that the actions they took made little difference is not necessarily to say that they made no difference at all. But that is about the margin we have to work with. If any modification of the status quo was possible in 1790, the Americans had to be prepared to give the British something they wanted from the United States which they could not have obtained otherwise. This might have included the American government's assuming responsibility for individual prewar debts to British creditors; it might also have included a stop to all further efforts to discriminate against British shipping. But however it might work, nobody was likely to get anything for nothing.

A scholarly biography of William Pitt the Younger, published in 1911, describes the entire Nootka Sound crisis without so much as a single reference to America. A new life of Pitt (still generally regarded as England's greatest Prime Minister) redresses the balance somewhat, though not by much.[5] The crisis may nevertheless still be worth seeing for a moment as Pitt and England saw it.

At the time Pitt became Prime Minister in 1783 at the age of twenty-four, England had come to be regarded in the courts of Europe as having fallen, as Emperor Joseph II of Austria put it, "to the rank of a second rate Power." Seven years later all that had changed. By then, English standing in European diplomacy had been completely restored, largely at the expense of France, under a foreign policy of which Pitt had taken personal charge, and Pitt's own prestige was at meridian. The rise began in 1786 when Pitt interested himself in the extremely unstable political situation in the Dutch Netherlands and the growing French interest there. To keep this deterioration from reaching such a point as to make Holland entirely dependent on France, he set carefully to work building up British influence and bringing in Prussian assistance. By the time civil war appeared imminent in the late summer of 1787, Pitt felt himself in a position, having persuaded cabinet and King to approve military and naval preparations, to inform the French government that England could not "remain an indifferent spectator of the armed interference of France" in Holland. The French thereupon disclaimed all intention of interfering; the House of Orange was firmly re-established; the British diplomatic corps was jubilant; and it was widely regarded as a triumph for Pitt. William Eden, who had disapproved of the enterprise, nevertheless "shuddered at his courage." This led to the fashioning of the Triple Alliance with Holland and Prussia, completed in the course of the following year. An outbreak of war in central Europe was prevented in 1790 through the efforts of the Alliance powers, and the leading influence was British.[6]

The first intimation of trouble with Spain came in January and February 1790, with news of the seizure of two British merchant vessels by a Spanish naval officer at Nootka Sound (later Vancouver), which led to protests and counter-protests. The Spanish ambassador, declaring that a British ship had tried to "take possession of Nootka Sound in the name of the British King," insisted that the action be punished and that similar ones be prevented in the future. The British demanded release of the ships before there could be any discussion of territorial rights. But neither was as yet anxious to provoke hostilities, and the matter remained more or less in suspension until about mid-April, when John Meares, the owner of the seized ships, arrived home in England to tell his story. Meares reported to the Ministry that he had erected buildings at Nootka and established a permanent settlement there, that he had explored and traded up and down the northwest coast, that the crews of the captured ships had been badly treated and imprisoned in Mexico, and that the Spanish had formally proclaimed their possession of the entire area. This claim, plus Spain's other pretensions, rested on the authority of the historic papal bull of 1493 which had bestowed most of the New World on Spain.[7]

Pitt now determined that the occasion warranted decisive action, not simply in satisfaction for an insult but to achieve a general settlement over a range of principles, problems, and interests which had been emerging from British explorations, trading enterprises, and whaling activities over the previous ten or fifteen years. The full weight of British power, moreover, should be in readiness to insure against failure. On April 30 Pitt asked and received authority to fit out a squadron of ships of the line; on May 3 a press of seamen was ordered for the night of May 4–5; and on May 5 the whole affair was for the first time disclosed to an excited public. Pitt's plan was to proceed in two stages. The first was to require immediate restitution and compensation, with the understanding that this would be followed by a negotiation of the broader questions. The second was to proceed to a general understanding with regard to trade and sovereignty in the unoccupied areas of North America and the Pacific.

On July 24 Spain very unwillingly acquiesced to the first stage of Pitt's demands, thanks to the obvious vigor of England's preparations. The naval mobilization was especially efficient: of a total of ninety-three ships of the line, forty were being fitted out, and twenty-five of these were at sea by the end of June. Most of the remainder would be ready by the end of summer. Strategic dispositions were strengthened at Gibraltar, in the Caribbean, and in India—the last in preparation for an attack on the Philippines. The Triple Alliance held nicely; both Prussia and Holland confirmed their readiness to meet their obligations if required, Prussia on land and Holland at sea. Pitt even held secret talks with the Latin American patriot and soldier Francisco Miranda, against the possibility that an uprising in that quarter might provide an opportunity to strip Spain of all her New World colonies. Spain's principal reliance, on the other hand, lay in the Bourbon Family Compact with France. Louis XVI still held his throne, but the willingness of the National Assembly to honor the expenses of a naval mobilization was very doubtful. The Compact proved unequal to the strains put on it, and by October Spain was ready to give Pitt substantially what he wanted. By the Convention of October 28 the British occupation of Nootka was confirmed and recognized, and the entire question of territorial and maritime sovereignty in the Pacific was comprehensively redefined. For Pitt, Nootka was in certain respects the peak point in his diplomacy.[8]

Inasmuch as Gouverneur Morris appeared on the scene late in March—before the crisis became public—the manner of the Ministry's handling of foreign affairs is of some interest insofar as it concerned America. The main business with Spain was being handled not by the Foreign Secretary but by Pitt himself, which was rather unusual. Lord Carmarthen, recently become the Duke of Leeds, occupied that office but was not carrying much weight, and felt keenly the light estimate Pitt held of his capacities.[9] On the other hand, Pitt felt little or no concern for American affairs during this period, and left all dealings with Morris up to Leeds. As for those aspects of American affairs which involved commerce, that subject had long since been delegated to the Privy Council Committee of Trade, of which the arch-mercantilist Lord Hawkesbury, a man of considerable ability, had been chairman since 1786. Pitt's own mind had been fairly well settled on this question; he was quite content to accept Hawkesbury's definition of it, and there was no likelihood of this changing in the then foreseeable future. There might be a disposition to adjust some trivial matters involving charges and privileges in each other's home ports, but nobody was prepared to alter the state of the West Indies trade, which was the Americans' chief concern. (Hawkesbury, indeed, would have liked to retaliate against the American tonnage duties already in existence, even though they were not discriminatory.)[10] And finally, communication with Canada was being handled by William Wyndham Grenville—shortly to become Lord Grenville—as Secretary of State for Home Affairs. Information about the frontier situation, as well as about legislative activity in America looking to discrimination, was coming through this channel. These several lines of communication were connected, though somewhat casually. They did not need to be very purposefully coordinated, inasmuch as they served for information rather than negotiation. The British were not anxious to negotiate in any case, which was the main reason for their being in no hurry to exchange ministers.

Gouverneur Morris was instructed to sound the Ministry on three principal questions. He was to begin by observing that with the establishment of the United States' new government and system of courts there should be no further objections on England's part to fulfilling her remaining engagements under the Peace Treaty by delivering the frontier posts into American hands and making compensation for slaves carried off during the war. (These "objections" had been based on the great difficulty being experienced by British creditors in collecting prewar debts owed them by individual Americans and the general disinclination of the state courts during the Confederation—despite Article IV of the treaty—to assist them in doing so.) A second question was whether the British contemplated a treaty of commerce with the United States, and on what terms. The opening of the British West Indies to American ships was a *sine qua non;* Morris was "not to countenance any idea of our dispensing with it in a treaty." And finally, he was to ask their intentions about a minister, remarking that their prior failure to send one "did not make an agreeable impression on this country." Morris presented these matters in his opening interview with the Duke of Leeds on March 29.[11]

The Duke was very cordial but distressingly vague, and Morris's account of the conversation is somewhat amusing. "I assure you," said the Foreign Secretary, "it is very much my Wish to cultivate a friendly and commercial Intercourse between the two Countries, and more, and I can answer for the Rest of his Majesty's Servants that they are of the same Opinion." With regard to what they intended to do about the posts and slaves, "he [Morris reported] does not exactly know the Situation. As to the last, he had long wished that Something had been done but Something or another had always interfered. He changes the Conversation which I bring back and which he changes again." When Morris brought up the matter of a minister, the Duke said, "I wished to send you one, but then I wished to have a Man every Way equal to the Task ... but it was difficult; it is a great Way off." ("He again changes the Conversation.") Morris suggested that the Duke might wish to think these matters over and inform himself more fully on them, and then make his reply in writing. Leeds happily embraced the suggestion and, bowing Morris out, promised to be prompt.[12]

Morris waited a month, and only after two reminding notes did he receive the very briefest reply to his questions. During this period the Ministry had been furiously busy, still behind closed doors, with the Nootka crisis. Leeds apologized on account of illness and "a multiplicity of engagements" for not having written sooner, and then informed Morris that Great Britain could not fulfill those points of the treaty that still depended on her until British subjects should receive redress or just compensation for their losses. As to commerce: "I can only say, that it is the sincere wish of the British government to cultivate a real and bona fide system of friendly intercourse with the United States. . . ." Morris reported to Washington that the British did not intend to treat with them. "Perhaps there never was a Moment," he said, "in which this Country felt herself greater," though he believed the feeling to be "fallacious." Nonetheless it seemed to him that Great Britain would "rather keep Things in Suspense with us."[13]

The most visible problem remaining from the Peace Treaty was that of the Northwest posts, the history of which went back seven years. As seen by the authorities in Canada, both economic and strategic considerations had made retention of them highly desirable. The posts were useful in protecting the fur trade south of the Canadian border and in retaining the good will of the Indians in the Ohio Valley, though Canadian officials had been generally careful to refrain from inciting these tribes against the Americans. Meanwhile they had been quite satisfied to let the question of debts and American treatment of Loyalists serve as an excuse for retaining the forts. During the disturbed years of the Confederation this had come to be more or less the settled policy in London.[14]

As for the Americans, the posts represented not only a matter of national honor but a serious impediment to the peaceful settlement of the Old Northwest and the Ohio Valley. Such settlement was naturally being resisted by the Indians, who, they suspected, were being covertly encouraged by the British. Closely connected with this was the strong desire of Americans in the western settlements for access to the Mississippi as an outlet for agricultural produce, still closed to them by Spain. This grievance, together with the unsettled and warlike state of the Indians, made the Westerners restless and receptive to any separatist movements which the British, or even the Spanish,[15] might be disposed to abet. Thus it was that Indian problems had been on Washington's mind for some months, and at this very moment—the spring of 1790—military preparations were being made for a campaign in the Ohio country against the Shawnees.

A third view of the frontier question, not coinciding in all ways with the Canadian view, was that of the Ministry in London. By this time there seems to have been some loosening of conviction about how necessary it was to keep the posts, Grenville having recognized that they would probably have to be given up someday.[16] But the question of the prewar debts was itself not a trivial one, and should probably be regarded as something other than a mere pretext for keeping the posts. The Pitt ministry had been bedeviled for years by complaints from British merchants with unsatisfied claims, and it had clearly reached the point of concluding that this was a matter for which the American government might well assume some form of direct responsibility. The American government itself, as was clear from Morris's instructions, had by no means reached a similar conclusion. The letter of the treaty was "that Creditors on either Side shall meet with no lawful Impediment," and now that a stable government was in existence the Americans had taken the position that this was a sufficient guarantee in itself. The debts nevertheless remained, and when the question was finally liquidated between the two governments some years later, they would be discharged by a payment of some $2.6 million.[17]

When the Nootka crisis became public on May 5, whatever concern the Ministry may have felt about America's attitude in the event of war was not reflected in any effort to reopen communication with Morris. Pitt was already determined upon war if that should become necessary; the preparations were sufficiently extensive and the stakes sufficiently high that the policy was not likely to be much influenced, if at all, by anything the United States did. Still, Grenville naturally wanted to be satisfied that all was well with Canada. On May 6 he wrote to the Governor, Lord Dorchester, and took up a number of matters. He thought it "extremely improbable" that Spain would make an attack on the British dominions in North America. The United States, on the other hand, might be encouraged to demand the posts, and for that reason Spain, in the event of hostilities between herself and Great Britain, might possibly induce the Americans to take an active part in the war. No reinforcements for Canada were at the moment contemplated, so Dorchester was advised to postpone the leave he planned to spend in England in order that he might oversee the embodying of Canadian militia in case of need. Grenville also told Dorchester about the Morris mission. He said that it had been necessary to be firm with Morris on account of America's "non execution of the Treaty," but that it might be a good idea through informal means to cultivate "a greater degree of interest than we have hitherto had in that country" and to find out as much as possible about the state of opinion there with regard to an Anglo-Spanish war. The Americans might be persuaded that they could more easily gain their object of access to the Mississippi with the help of Great Britain against Spain than they could acquire the posts by joining Spain against England.[18]

Grenville took up still another subject in the same set of dispatches, making various suggestions about attaching Vermont, still an independent state, to the British interest. This was in connection with the quiet encouragement then being given in London to the Allen brothers, who were themselves intriguing against groups in their own state who hoped soon to bring Vermont into the Federal Union. Levi Allen was at that moment trying to negotiate a separate commercial treaty with the British and to obtain British recognition of Vermont's independence; he seems also to have had in mind an eventual political union with Canada. The British were at the same time carrying on covert communications with similar groups in Kentucky.[19]

It might seem that the idea of joining forces with the United States against Spain, on the one hand, and encouraging separationist movements at the expense of the United States, on the other, involved the British in two diametrically opposed and mutually exclusive policies. And so it did—or rather would have, if these had really been "policies." But it is doubtful whether either one was being taken very seriously. These tentative dabblings were all kept in a state of sufficient vagueness that they could be completely disavowed if they became inconvenient, as in fact they very shortly would.

Morris had another interview with Leeds on May 20, this time through his own initiative and on another subject. He had taken it upon himself to intercede on behalf of a number of American seamen who had been taken in the press of May 5 and in others that had followed it. The Duke apologized, promised he would take the matter up with the proper persons, and invited Morris to come back the following day. When Morris arrived, he found the Foreign Secretary closeted with the Prime Minister. The three discussed impressment, managed to get that question adjusted in short enough order, and then turned the conversation to Anglo-American relations in general. Pitt repeated Leeds's prior assurances about his government's willingness to consider a treaty of commerce. Morris, somewhat in high feather, retorted that it was "idle to think about making a new Treaty until the Parties are satisfied about that already made." Pitt remarked that great injury had been caused by the American delays in complying with the Treaty of 1783, whereupon Morris declared that "the injury was much smaller than was imagined." Pitt wondered whether the subject might be considered in such a way as to "see if, on general ground, some compensation could not be made mutually." (He seems to have had in mind a simple trade: the posts for the debts.)

> I immediately replied, "if I understand you, Mr. Pitt, you wish to make a new treaty instead of complying with the old one." He admitted this to be *in some sort* his idea. I said that, even on that ground, I did not see what better could be done, than to perform the old one.

Morris, reporting all this to Washington a week later, was by now putting a great deal of faith in the likelihood of war, and predicting that "they will give us a good price for our neutrality." Pitt and Leeds had "promised to consult together, and give me the result of their deliberations." But the two must have decided (unless they forgot all about it) simply to do nothing, inasmuch as Morris waited for the next four months without a word from either. No further communication was to approach the ground—little advanced though it may have been—that was reached in the interview of May 21.[20]

Back in America, meanwhile, Dorchester had already sent Beckwith on a visit to New York (well before Grenville's May 6 dispatches had even been written), where he spent two or three weeks finding out what he could about American military movements in the Northwest. While there, Beckwith saw Hamilton and others and reported to Grenville that these movements were indeed directed against the Indians, that there were no indications of an intention to attack the posts, and that there was "a wish to cultivate a connexion infinitely Important, in my humble apprehension, to the genuine interests and future prosperity of this country."[21] He made a second visit in July, after Dorchester had received the dispatches of Grenville that had been prompted by the war crisis, and again his principal informant was Hamilton. He was instructed to express the hope that the possibility of war would not affect America's friendly disposition toward Great Britain, and to hold out the suggestion—which Hamilton would make a great deal more of than Beckwith's vague language warranted—that the United States might profit from a British connection in case of a war with Spain. Beckwith also repeated Grenville's apologies for the delays in seeing Morris, delicately hinting that among the reasons for things not being farther along was America's "non execution of the Treaty." This conversation was held on the morning of July 8, and Hamilton reported it to Jefferson and Washington the same day.[22]

Washington, who had just received Morris's initial report of his doings up through May 29, was already annoyed, and this new communication did little to calm his state of mind. What the British seemed to be saying, he wrote in his diary, was:

> We did not incline to give any satisfactory answer to Mr. Morris, who was *officially* commissioned to ascertain our intentions with respect to the evacuation of the Western Posts within the territory of the United States and other matters into which he was empowered to enquire until by this unauthenticated mode we can discover whether you will enter into an alliance with us and make Common cause against Spain. In that case we will enter into a Commercial Treaty with you and *promise perhaps* to fulfil what [we] already stand engaged to perform.

So far as Washington was concerned, until something was done about the posts things were at a standstill. Hamilton was told that in future talks with Beckwith he should treat the agent with courtesy but give him to understand that he had no official status. He was to extract as much information as he could, and make no commitments. Further talks were in fact held, and in them Hamilton strove mightily to keep alive the project of an alliance, which he now wanted very badly. But his efforts were disheartening. His own government was not interested, and Beckwith could offer none but the vaguest encouragement because his government was not really interested either. Whatever glimmer of reality the idea had, which was faint at best, would disappear altogether with the settling of the Nootka crisis.[23]

It should be noted that during this period—the summer of the assumption-residence settlement—Hamilton and Jefferson worked in relative accord on most objects of American interest. Both were fully aware of the importance of repossessing the Northwest posts and of England's sending us a minister. Both fully supported Washington's movements against the Indians in the Ohio country. They were equally impatient for Spain to yield the navigation of the Mississippi. Hamilton told Beckwith, "We must have it," and Jefferson wrote the American chargé in Madrid that we would get it one way or the other: "It is *necessary* to us." Both, moreover, looked with great disfavor on any British movement to seize New

Orleans—also in Spanish hands—because the United States wanted that too. Washington, who believed for a time that the British might actually be considering such a movement, asked both Jefferson and Hamilton for their opinions as to what the United States should do in case the British asked permission to cross American territory. Jefferson advised not replying, but if a reply became necessary he would permit the passage; Hamilton would permit the passage, because if it were refused and the troops passed anyway, the country's honor would oblige it to fight.[24]

Nevertheless, Hamilton already had reason to be wary of Jefferson. When the United States and Great Britain exchanged ministers, which he hoped would be soon, official negotiations might then begin in earnest at the American seat of government. He was anxious that nothing occur to prevent them from going smoothly. "Mr. Jefferson our present Secretary of State," he said to Beckwith in one of their talks,

> is I am persuaded a gentleman of honor, and zealously desirous of promoting those objects, which the nature of his duty call for, and the interests of his country may require, but from some opinions which he has given respecting Your government, and possible predilections elsewhere, there may be difficulties which may possibly frustrate the whole, and which might be readily explained away.

Should such difficulties come up, Hamilton was saying, he would be glad to be kept informed of them. He could thus be sure that "they are clearly understood, and candidly examined."[25]

Gouverneur Morris, after waiting about London all summer, finally wrote Leeds another note deploring the four months of silence and intimating that he could not remain much longer. He supposed that the Duke's failure to specify the sort of redress expected on the points of the treaty was to be "construed into unconditional Refusal" to perform England's part of it. The Duke replied that he would be happy to see Morris before he went back to America. (Morris had said he was going back to Europe, not to America.) Morris called on September 15.

Leeds repeated the usual sentiments, "that he was earnestly desirous of a real bona fide connexion," and told Morris that he "hoped soon to fix upon a minister to America." All efforts to fish out further intentions relating to trade, the posts, and the Nootka crisis drew the usual vague answers.[26]

Thus it might be concluded that the British had no further use for Morris, now that Nootka had ceased to be a menace. The affair was not yet settled, but Spain's first capitulation had made it a good possibility that there would be a second, as indeed there was the following month. But the coincidence of events is misleading; the British never had had much use for Morris. Nor was this because of his having become *persona non grata,* as some have suggested. At the beginning of his London sojourn Morris had revealed the nature of his mission to the French minister, and had been seen once or twice in the company of the opposition leader Charles James Fox; these indiscretions had given rise to some disapproving comment. But it may be doubted whether this had much to do with the Ministry's keeping him at arm's length; if the authorities had believed there was anything to be gained by dealing seriously with Morris, it would have required more than "indiscretions" of this sort to prevent it.[27]

It may be concluded, then, that so far as the British were concerned the principal function of these various exchanges was to provide them with information which would confirm them in their disposition to exert themselves as little as possible in the direction of America. The most that might have been accomplished was a settlement on the debts and the posts, though this was by no means a trivial prospect. Pitt, occupied as he was with the numerous details of the European crisis, appeared willing to consider disposing of this particular matter if by so doing he could get the aggrieved British creditors off his neck, while Grenville had satisfied himself that the posts could be given up if some arrangement acceptable to the Indians—a kind of buffer area—might be worked out for peace along the frontier.[28] But Morris's instructions would admit of none of this, and the British did not feel strongly enough to press it. It might even be doubted whether such a trade at this time would have been a good thing for American interests anyway, since these items would then not be available as counters for a general settlement later on.

A commercial treaty which would be to the Americans' taste required admission to the West Indies, as Morris's instructions also made clear. At no time was there any indication that the British were willing to discuss this. Indeed, not until the report of Hawkesbury's Committee of Trade—which would be ready in January—was before the cabinet would they even decide what *could* be discussed. This in turn was tied to the question of a minister: the man appointed would go with instructions based on the report.[29]

A final question concerns the way in which Hamilton's role, and his talks with Beckwith, ought to be evaluated. The negative assessment is familiar enough.[30] By assuring Beckwith that there was a substantial element in the country favorable to Great Britain, and opposed to the use of discriminatory regulations against British shipping, Hamilton thereby undercut American aims and interests by assisting the British to settle their minds and resume their intransigence. But this line loses some of its impressiveness when it is seen that the behavior of almost every American who came within the British ken contributed in its way to the same result, the settling of the British mind. That is, Washington and Morris, with their position on the non-negotiability of the Northwest posts question; Hamilton and those sharing his views, with their assurances of a contingent in America friendly to England; and even the Allens and their ilk, with their separationist schemes, all helped the British to conclude that there need be no great hurry about making new terms with the United States.

One scholar has suggested a more positive way to look at Hamilton's dealings with Beckwith: as having actually helped to keep the way open for friendly relations and a future rapprochement, assuming such an aim to have been desirable.[31] Something might be said for this argument, novel though it is; presumably there ought to have been some way to maintain a pro-British position in the American republic. The evidence suggests, moreover, that George Beckwith—who was not a wooden robot but a man with some independence of judgment—was to a considerable degree converted to Hamilton's vision. Beckwith would shortly urge upon Grenville in the strongest terms policies well beyond what the Ministry had in mind, in the face of rising sentiment for discrimination in 1791. It might also be said that Hamilton, by maintaining his credibility with Beckwith as spokesman for the pro-British interest in America, was able to point out to the British themselves the line beyond which they could not go. He did this with regard to the posts, the navigation of the Mississippi, the separationist movements, and New Orleans, and when Beckwith broached a hint of Grenville's buffer scheme, Hamilton would emphatically not hear of it.[32] Hamilton's alternative might have been to slur over the real divisions within the United States government and make Beckwith believe that it stood as a unit behind any action the discriminationists might take. But Beckwith knew otherwise, and had the sources to confirm it.

On this question, then, there is a real balance. And yet the conclusion has to be that if the balance was this precarious—if even America's Canadian advocate was not listened to back home—Hamilton's efforts did not much matter one way or the other.

After the United States government transferred its offices to Philadelphia in August 1790, Secretary Jefferson went home for a six-week stay at Monticello, accompanied on his eighteen-day trip to Virginia by his friend James Madison. When he returned to Philadelphia he wrote up his report on the Morris mission and submitted it to the President. "Mr. Morris's letters," he declared, "remove any doubts which might have been entertained as to the intentions and dispositions of the British cabinet." He recommended that no further demands be made "till we are in readiness to do ourselves the justice which may be refused."[33] With this, he was coming back to the object—commercial coercion—which had never been absent from his mind and for which he would make every exertion, within the bounds of his office, during the session to come.

2

The Bank

Jefferson and Madison had ample opportunity on their way home to Virginia in September 1790, and on their way north to Philadelphia two months later, to talk things over and to consider plans. The session of Congress just concluded had been full of events. The Virginians had succeeded in securing the national capital, though they had had to give way on the assumption of state debts. In no important particular had they effected any modification in Hamilton's arrangements for the public credit. They had been blocked once more on tonnage discrimination. And they had been given new proofs, through the Morris mission, of the immovability of the British with regard to American desires, demands, and interests.

Jefferson and Madison probably still regarded the bargain over assumption and the capital as a tolerable settlement, though they heard a great many complaints in Virginia about assumption.[34] Nor did they doubt that the Pennsylvanians would do everything in their power to keep the capital at Philadelphia and thus frustrate, if they could, Virginia's visions of a future seat on the Potomac. Nonetheless their chief preoccupation was not with these matters but with foreign affairs: with the dignity of the new republic and the character they wanted it to present to the rest of the world. They were determined upon another effort to bring the country to assert itself, and to shake England into taking some account of America. Their instrument, once again, would be the country's commerce.

The coming session, however—the short one beginning December 6 and ending March 3, 1791—would further underscore the interconnectedness of foreign affairs and domestic fiscal policy. The efforts of Jefferson and Madison toward the enactment of tonnage and navigation laws would be crowded aside by the next major block in Hamilton's system of public finance, the creation of a national bank. The most prominent supporters of the bank, or so it seemed to them, were the same men—the northern and seaboard forces of speculation and commercialism—who constituted the "English interest" and who appeared to be undermining every endeavor they themselves made to bring the English to reason. A web of subservience was thus being woven, all part of an emerging system the spread of which they viewed with growing suspicion.

Both Jefferson and Madison contributed a major share to the effort which was made, though unsuccessfully, to block the bank. But Madison's was the more extended. Such were the ideological compulsions now upon him that he would repudiate the arguments of *The Federalist* for a strong national government. He would thereupon make the first major statement of a new doctrine, broached before but by no one of Madison's eminence: strict construction of the Constitution. And when that failed, he and Jefferson would do something else that was new. They would take the first random and haphazard steps—themselves scarcely realizing or understanding the implications of what they were doing—toward organizing a political opposition to their own government. Or rather, to those influences in the government which they were beginning to view as deeply dangerous to their own vision of a happy Republic.

The Virginians' plans to set the stage for legislative action against England were carefully laid. Madison submitted to Washington a draft of recommendations to be included in his opening message to Congress. "I recommend to your serious reflexion," he had Washington say, "how far and in what mode, it may be expedient to guard against embarrassments . . . by such encouragements to our Navigation as will render our commerce less dependent on foreign bottoms. . . ." He had in mind a navigation act which would cut into the British carrying trade, special encouragement for the American fisheries, and measures to protect American trade in the Mediterranean. When this message reached the House it was Madison who wrote the reply, in which he heartily agreed with his own words, and when Washington received it he asked Madison to draft an acknowledgment for him. "I look forward," said Madison, acknowledging his own reply to himself, "to the happiest consequences from your deliberations during the present session."[35]

Jefferson meanwhile set to work on a series of reports on these subjects, each designed to assist in promoting the ends Madison was pursuing in the House. His report of December 15 on the Morris mission, describing in tart language the equivocations of the British regarding American demands, recommended that negotiations not be reopened until America could enforce those demands herself. A report on the Mediterranean trade was submitted two weeks later, together with another of the same date on Americans held captive by the pirate state of Algiers. It recommended steps for reopening the Mediterranean and freeing that area from the depredations of the Barbary powers. The notorious example of Great Britain and other nations in purchasing peace with these states—and thus discouraging independent efforts to force them to terms—might be counteracted by cooperative arrangements with the smaller Mediterranean powers to use naval force in keeping the ports open. Jefferson's Report on the Tonnage Law, dated January 18, 1791, proposed a somewhat less formal kind of tonnage discrimination in favor of France than that unsuccessfully promoted by Madison in the two previous sessions. The French government had complained that American tonnage duties on foreign ships contravened the wartime treaty of amity and commerce between the two countries. Jefferson, while believing that the French did not have a legal case on this point, nonetheless felt that the law might be relaxed to give them various special concessions in the light of friendship and of the favors they themselves had granted to certain American products. And finally, his Report on the Cod and Whale Fisheries of February 1, 1791, noted that the failure of the American fishing industry to recover from its wartime prostration was due mainly to England's policy of either placing high duties on its products or excluding them altogether, in contrast to the friendly attitude of France. He recommended a series of specific encouragements, such as lowered duties on items used in the fisheries, together with a navigation act aimed at Great Britain's carrying trade and favoring our own. The revived fisheries would create a "nursery of seamen" for an expanding merchant marine.[36]

Nothing at all, however, was done about any of these matters throughout the session. The House committee appointed to report a bill for the encouragement of American navigation failed to do so, and was discharged on February 12. No action was taken on any of Jefferson's reports. Jefferson finally persuaded Washington on January 14 to release the one on the Morris mission—that report having been submitted to the President rather than to Congress—and he himself drafted Washington's covering message for it, urging action. A new House committee was thereupon appointed, of which Madison was a member, and on February 21 it reported by a majority of one a bill fashioned after the navigation laws of England. But the session was by then drawing to a close, and the bill's supporters were unable to get it to the floor of the House. It was thereupon referred to the Secretary of State, who was directed to prepare a report on the entire state of America's foreign commerce and to recommend whatever measures he might think appropriate for its improvement.[37]

The principal reason for this lack of zeal was Congress's preoccupation during most of the session with two new Hamiltonian proposals, one for a system of excises and the other for a national bank. In August 1790 Hamilton had been instructed to prepare reports on whatever further measures might be needed for the support of the public credit. By December he had them ready, and they were submitted to Congress on the 13th and 14th of that month.[38]

In the first, he recommended a new schedule of taxes on spirits in order to raise the additional revenues required to begin paying interest on the public debt. Madison did not oppose this, knowing that such revenues were necessary; he himself had proposed a similar tax the year before. There was a fair amount of debate on the measure, but at no point was there any danger of its not succeeding. It passed the House on January 27 and the Senate on February 26, and with it the first phase of Hamilton's financial program was complete.[39] The federal government now had an income sufficient to cover current expenses and to pay full interest on the entire debt. This meant that the tax potential which had long impressed European financiers was no longer a projection but a fact, and as Hamilton's predictions about the Treasury's ability to meet its obligations without undue strain were borne out, the price of federal securities would continue to move toward par. They would thus be less and less viewed as an item for speculation. The debt would come to represent—given its relative concentration, and in view of the many opportunities for profitable investment in the United States—a pool of liquid capital for economic development.[40]

A further step was essential, however, for rendering this capital fully operative. There ought to be an arrangement whereby it should be to the advantage of individual security-holders to place both securities and specie at the disposal of a public institution—thereby achieving a new level of concentration—that could make these resources accessible to the entire mercantile community. This, Hamilton believed, could be achieved by the creation of a large national bank.

The bank Hamilton proposed in his report of December 14, 1791, thus represented the second phase of his program. It was designed to provide a number of important services both to government and to the world of business. It would serve as the government's chief fiscal agent, assisting in the collection of taxes, the disbursement and transfer of funds, and the provision of immediate short-term credit whenever needed. A ready source of funds, moreover, would be present in time of national emergency. The bank's notes would provide a universally acceptable and convenient currency for an economy traditionally short of specie. Of special importance, however, was that by means of its capital base of specie and federal securities—and inasmuch as it would be allowed to carry on commercial operations—the bank could provide to the mercantile community a large, dependable, and convenient source of credit for expanding business projects. Finally, by no means unimportant to the public credit was that by making it possible to use government securities at face value in purchasing shares in the new bank—payment would be three-fourths in securities to one-fourth in specie—the price of all United States securities would be given yet another strong push toward par.

The bank's total capital was to be set at $10 million, more than that of all existing American banks combined. Of this, $2 million would come from the federal government. The remaining $8 million—one-fourth in specie and the remainder in federal securities—would be the price of shares subscribed by private investors. The note circulation would be set at $10 million, a potential fivefold expansion of the $2 million in specie which the private investors were to supply.[41]

We cannot account with final precision for all the origins of Hamilton's bank plan, though certain of the main sources are clearly enough identified. In this instance, unlike that of his first Report on Public Credit, Hamilton's direct theoretical inspiration did not come from David Hume. Hume recognized that banks could be useful in providing credit for an expanding economy, but he also believed that they were an inflationary influence and that they encouraged unduly the export of specie. Hamilton could look, however, to a number of recognized authorities, such as Postlethwayt and Adam Anderson, for a favorable theoretical exposition of banks and their functions. He made considerable use of Adam Smith. His vivid account of the process whereby specie deposited in a bank, and serving as the "basis of a paper circulation," is transformed from "dead Stock" to productive capital was directly appropriated from *The Wealth of Nations.* There was a very close correlation, moreover, between Hamilton's final plan and the charter of the Bank of England, and in all likelihood he worked with a copy of the British statute at his elbow. Yet there were significant differences between them, chief among which was the stipulation that only three-fifths of the bank's total capital should consist of government securities, rather than all of it as was the case with the Bank of England.[42]

The report was written to persuade; it was lucidly successful in that respect and still remains so. Hamilton was sufficiently informed, through reading and experience, about both the theory and the practice of banking that he could with assurance use his authorities selectively. The Bank of the United States was designed to meet the special needs of the American economy as Hamilton understood them, the chief ones being a dependable source of credit and a substantial circulating medium based on a minimum of scarce specie.

But though Hamilton had far too much imagination to follow slavishly any given authority, it is hardly without significance that his precedents were so largely British. There was one "authority," moreover, whom he could not very well cite in his footnotes but whose example somehow hovered over everything he did. That was William Pitt himself. It may well be that Pitt's example was so pervasive an influence that it operated not so much as a series of specific policies (though Hamilton did appropriate a number of such policies)[43] but rather as the model of a career. The office of prime minister by Pitt's time was certainly a functioning one, but the title itself had not yet become official. Pitt's manifest role was that of finance minister, and his official designations were those of Chancellor of the Exchequer and First Lord of the Treasury.[44]

When William Pitt took office in December 1783, England was burdened with a debt of £243 million, almost double what it had been on the eve of the American war. Simply servicing this debt involved an annual charge of £6.8 million out of a total revenue of between £12 and £13 million, which meant that roughly two-thirds of Great Britain's tax income would have to be devoted to paying interest on the debt, compared to about one-fourth in 1774. Many Englishmen were convinced that the nation was on the verge of bankruptcy.[45]

But Pitt, like Hamilton after him, sensed the underlying strength of his country's economy. He saw that the need was for a series of measures which would re-establish England's confidence in its own future by demonstrating the government's ability to manage its debts and eventually to reduce them. He thereupon launched a program of reforms which included a tightening of customs procedures to prevent the perennially huge losses of revenue to smugglers, a selective increase in taxes to establish a small surplus, a funding of the floating debt on terms as favorable as could be found, and the establishment of a sinking fund which would begin the process of eventual repayment. By February 1792, when he made his celebrated report to Parliament, Pitt could announce what approximated total success. A steady increase in tax income had enabled the government to cover all its expenses, increase its contribution to the sinking fund by about a quarter-million pounds, and cut taxes by about the same amount. In the preceding decade, moreover (during most of which he had been Prime Minister), British imports had risen from £9.7 to £19.1 million, and exports and re-exports from £12.2 to £20 million. Actually the success of Pitt's efforts was clear well before 1792. Hamilton had been closely informed on them from the beginning of his own secretaryship in 1789.[46]

Moreover, the assurance with which Pitt could proceed in the Nootka affair of 1790 was directly related to all this. British finances were by then sufficiently stable that the nation could undertake an expensive program of naval armament in support of its claims against Spain. The country's foreign affairs and domestic policies, in short, were intimately connected, and Pitt, concerning himself with each, had brought off impressive successes in both. Beckwith had told Hamilton that Pitt's policy was "to hold the Nation high, in the opinion of the world," and it may be imagined how satisfying Hamilton himself would have found it to be able to act in the same way. Hamilton could do what Pitt had done, and could in many respects do it better—having the advantage, as Pitt had not, of starting with *tabula rasa*. If, that is, he had the imagination and audacity to view himself as something more than simply another cabinet minister. And there is every indication that he did.[47]

The bank legislation was well planned, organized, and managed from the outset. Its supporters outnumbered its opponents by about two to one in the House and three to one in the Senate. As soon as the report was received it was printed for the use of the members; copies were released to the newspapers and full texts were published a few days later. The decision was made by the House, through a process now unknown, to let a bill originate in the Senate. There a committee of five was appointed, four of whom had been members of the Philadelphia Convention, to draft a measure which was reported on January 3, 1791. It was debated in the Senate over the next two and a half weeks, passed on January 20, and sent to the House for concurrence. There it proceeded through three readings, no amendments being offered, and on February 2 debate began on the question, whether the bill should pass.[48]

The bank's opponents were at a disadvantage throughout. This did not make them any the less opponents, but the character of their opposition as well as the reasons for it tended to be diffuse. One element, of course, was simply suspicion of banks, and there was a good deal of this. "This bank," said Stone of Maryland, "will raise in this country a moneyed interest at the devotion of Government; it may bribe both States and individuals." Jackson of Georgia thought it was "calculated to benefit a small part of the United States, the mercantile interest only. . . ." He called it "a monopoly . . . of the public moneys for the benefit of the corporation to be created." But the kind of country-party fundamentalism with regard to banks that was to become so prominent in the politics of a later generation was not nearly so sharp here. Men were against it but were not entirely sure why. Stone "said it was one of those sly and subtle movements which marched silently to its object; the vices of it were at first not palpable or obvious. . . ." Maclay noted that the bank's opponents had "no system, no plan or calculation."[49]

A somewhat more specific motive for opposition, not openly acknowledged but apparently real enough, was anxiety about the national capital. The bank was to be established at Philadelphia, and the presence and influence of such a powerful agency there, so it was feared, would operate as a force for preventing removal to the Potomac in 1800. James Madison seems to have been among those so motivated. Madison is reported to have approached the Pennsylvanians with a plan for reducing the period of charter from twenty to ten years, so that it would expire at the time the government itself was to leave Philadelphia. The future national capital, on the one hand, was one of the most visible remaining symbols of Virginia influence; the bank, on the other, constituted one more block in a system which was threatening to be less and less amenable to Virginia control. When this move failed, the only device that remained was to oppose the bank on grounds of constitutionality.

The leader of the forces here was Madison himself, and the case he made was the case for strict construction.[50]

Madison began his attack with a discussion of the advantages and disadvantages of banks. He conceded their utility, both to the mercantile community and to the government, for expediting business. But first among the disadvantages was that the circulation of banknotes would accelerate the exportation of precious metals. Adam Smith's answer to such a contingency had been that the specie would be used to import tools and other goods which would increase a nation's productive capacity. But Madison "doubted whether, in the present habits of this country, the returns would not be in articles of no permanent use to it." In other words, our specie would be increasingly shipped off to England in return for unnecessary goods, a trade which James Madison, on another level, was at that very moment doing everything he could to discourage. This bank, moreover, was not a good bargain to the public. It discriminated among the public creditors by making only certain classes of securities receivable for stock subscriptions, and by making the subscription period unduly short it discriminated against those residing at a distance. He thought that because of the country's extent, together with the possible evils of a run on one bank, the advantages might be better realized "by several banks, properly distributed, than by a single one." (As it turned out, these objections would all be met in some fashion by a supplementary act.) Madison also denied that the value of the public debt as a whole would be raised; this would occur, he said, only with the value of those securities actually subscribed. This prediction would in fact turn out to be wrong.[51]

But the main body of Madison's argument was placed on constitutional grounds. Congress did not have authority under the Constitution to incorporate a bank, because of "the peculiar manner in which the Federal Government is limited." The Constitution was not a general grant, with specified exceptions of particular powers, but rather the reverse. It was "a grant of particular powers only, leaving the general mass in other hands." This meant that none of the clauses in Article I under which the power of erecting a bank might be pretended—the power to "lay and collect Taxes . . . to pay the Debts and provide for the common Defence and general Welfare," to "borrow money on the credit of the United States," or to make all laws "necessary and proper" for carrying out the powers granted by the Constitution—was applicable, because the enumerated powers subjoined to those clauses did not include it. The bill in question laid no taxes and borrowed no money; nor did the "necessary and proper" clause give Congress discretion to add anything to the Constitution that was not already there.

The doctrine of "implication" and "construction," Madison declared, was infinitely dangerous; with it could be formed a chain that would reach all objects whatever. "The latitude of interpretation required by the bill is condemned by the rule furnished by the Constitution itself," in which no important power was left to implication but was explicitly spelled out. Armies, for example, were far more incident to the power to declare war than incorporating banks was to that of borrowing money, yet under the war power raising armies, making rules for their governance, and the regulating and calling out of militia were not merely implied but expressly enumerated. Nor, Madison asserted, was the proposed bank even necessary; "at most it could be but convenient." These rules of construction (which "exclude the latitude now contended for") had been understood by the Framers and reasserted in the Ninth and Tenth Amendments.

Madison had been standing on very unsteady ground throughout, as he must have sensed, especially when such supporters of the bank as Ames, Gerry, Sedgwick, and Boudinot had finished reviewing his arguments. "It seems to be conceded within doors and without," said Ames, "that a public bank would be useful to trade, that it is almost essential to revenue, and that it is little short of indispensably necessary in times of public emergency." Proceeding to the constitutional question, Ames observed that if Congress could exercise no powers but those expressly set forth in the Constitution, then it was "rather late in the day to adopt it as a principle of conduct," because hardly a law had been made in the previous two years that did not require the doctrine of implication and construction. He did not see why negative construction should be any safer than positive construction. "Not exercising the powers we have, may be as pernicious as usurping those we have not." Raising armies would still be implied under the war power even if not expressly stated: if the country were invaded it could hardly be argued that the safest course would be *not* to raise one. As for the "necessary and proper" clause, Ames did not "pretend that it gives any new powers; but it establishes the doctrine of implied powers." "That construction may be maintained to be a safe one which promotes the good of the society, and the ends for which the Government was adopted, without impairing the rights of any man, or the powers of any State." This certainly applied to the right of incorporating a bank, which was "a necessary incident to the entire powers to regulate trade and revenue, and to provide for the public credit and defence."[52]

Gerry asserted that the rules of interpretation expounded by the gentleman from Virginia were not those commonly in use, nor used by Congress in the past, nor those understood by the Convention, but were "made for the occasion." He read Madison an extended lecture out of Blackstone on interpreting the will of the legislator, which was to be construed "either from the words, the context, the subject matter, the effect and consequence, or the spirit and reason of the law." Sedgwick reminded Madison of the argument he himself had made in 1789 for the Executive's power to remove his own appointees if he wished: that power "was, by construction and implication, vested in the President; for there could be no pretence that it is expressly granted to him."[53]

All of these arguments, indeed, were to be found in Federalist 44, excerpts from which Boudinot read at some length. Publius had said:

> Had the Convention attempted a positive enumeration of the powers necessary and proper for carrying their other powers into effect; the attempt would have involved a complete digest of laws on every subject to which the Constitution relates; accommodated too not only to the existing state of things, but to all the possible changes which futurity may produce: For in every new application of a general power, the *particular powers,* which are the means of attaining the *object* of the general power, must necessarily vary with that object; and be often properly varied whilst the object remains the same.

Publius had also said that to forbid Congress from using any power not expressly granted would be "to disarm the government of all real authority whatever"; that no important power could be exercised "without recurring more or less to the doctrine of *construction* or *implication*"; and that the Constitution never intended the dilemma of choosing between "betraying the public interest by doing nothing; or of violating the Constitution by exercising powers, indispensably necessary and proper; but at the same time, not *expressly* granted." And his most sweeping assertion of all: "No axiom is more clearly established in law, or in reason, than that wherever the end is required, the means are authorised; wherever a general power to do a thing is given, every particular power necessary for doing it, is included."[54]

It was a moment of some irony. The authors of *The Federalist* were still unknown, but rumor had it that the author of this particular number was Hamilton, and Boudinot supposed himself to be reading Hamilton's words. But those words had in fact been James Madison's, and one may wonder what went through Madison's mind as he listened to them. (So far as is known, he did not set Boudinot straight as to their real authorship.) In any case Madison's final argument, though stubborn, was not very convincing. He repeated his constitutional points and his specific objections to the bill itself, "recapitulated" his reasons for support of the President's removal power in 1789 (though the reporter does not say what they were), and then called for the question. The bill passed, 39–20. Madison seems to have recognized all along that there was no chance of defeating it, and he was directing his strategy toward one of two objects. The minimum was to make possible subsequent amendments; the maximum was to present a case to Washington in support of a veto. Indeed, he and Washington "held several free conversations" on that subject in which the President listened attentively to Madison's view of it. He even asked Madison to prepare a message in case he should decide to veto the bill.[55]

Washington was genuinely perplexed. He had never used the veto before, and he must have been disturbed by the constitutional arguments propounded by a trusted advisor in an area where he did not have much faith in his own unaided judgment. He requested opinions of three others besides Madison before he finally made up his mind. One was his Attorney-General, Edmund Randolph; another was Secretary of State Jefferson; and the third, whom he did not consult until after hearing from the first two, was Hamilton.

Randolph in two rather rambling papers advised Washington that the bill was unconstitutional because there was no way of construing the incorporation of a bank from the Constitution's enumerated powers. He said that the Preamble was not in itself a source of power (if it were, the main body would be superfluous); that the "necessary and proper" clause did not expand the government's authority; and that the Tenth Amendment explicitly limited it to enumerated powers.[56]

Jefferson also cited the Tenth Amendment, and argued that to "take a single step beyond the boundaries thus specially drawn around the powers of Congress, is to take possession of a boundless field of power, no longer susceptible of any definition."[57] Hamilton's opinion was more thorough and comprehensive than the arguments by the bank's supporters in Congress, and was better thought through on constitutional as well as technical grounds than any of the adverse opinions. He had the advantage of having the others laid out before him;[58] he also knew more about the subject than anyone else. The result was another of Hamilton's great disputations, quite in the line of *The Farmer Refuted* and *The Federalist*. In it, he made the case for implied powers.

His opening point was on sovereignty. A general principle inherent in the definition of government was "that every power vested in a Government is in its nature *sovereign*, and includes . . . a right to employ all the *means* requisite, and fairly applicable to the attainment of the ends of such power; and which are not precluded by restrictions & exceptions specified in the constitution; or not immoral, or not contrary to the essential ends of political society." That the powers of sovereignty in the United States were now divided between national and state governments did not mean that each of the powers delegated to one or the other "is not sovereign with *regard to its proper objects*," only "that each has sovereign power as to *certain things,* and not as to *other things.*" The power that could create "the supreme law of the land" in any given case, as the Constitution did, must certainly be regarded as sovereign with regard to that case. It is true, he said, that the power to erect a corporation was not expressly stated in the Constitution. But a corporation is not an end in itself but a means; Congress cannot form a corporation to regulate the police of Philadelphia because it has no power to regulate the police of that city. Yet it could form one—as in the case of the bank—if a corporation happened to be one of the natural and logical means for achieving ends over which Congress did have power.

Hamilton made short work of Jefferson's narrow interpretation of "necessary." The Secretary of State seemed to prefix "absolutely" and "indispensably" to a term which in both grammatical and popular usage meant no more than *"needful, requisite, incidental, useful, conducive to."* Few measures could stand Jefferson's rigid test, and in any event the degree to which a thing was necessary—since that was a matter of opinion—could not very well be a test of the legal right to do it. Hamilton went on to dispose of Jefferson's argument in detail, spelling out the logical relation between the proposed bank and the delegated powers of the Constitution. Washington received the opinion on February 23, and signed the bill two days later.[59]

It has generally been conceded that Hamilton's opinion was good law, and that those of Jefferson, Randolph, and Madison were bad law.[60] But a question remains as to why, and as to how the strong quality of Hamilton's paper is to be accounted for. The merits of broad construction over strict construction may not be quite the start for an answer; those merits depend rather on the contexts— which are very different—in which these respective arguments tend to be made. One might better consider why, being on the offensive, expounding the positive side of any argument, dealing with positive innovations, and being on top of one's subject all have more than a casual relation both to the energy of a person's convictions and to the effectiveness with which the case is made. Having thought extensively about the ends to be gained and the means required for achieving them is a wonderful stimulant to ingenuity. And in a case such as this, one will argue broad construction when convinced that a generous use of the government's powers will have a positive and salutary effect on the community, and a broad-construction opinion is likely to be of high quality when behind it is a sense of urgency about taking some kind of action. Under such conditions one is enabled to perceive a range of implications—social, economic, and political—of reading the Constitution liberally, which has a tendency to enhance comprehension rather than limit it. Both Hamilton and Madison had found themselves in precisely this position when they were writing *The Federalist.*

Thus a question of equal interest is that of what had happened to James Madison since that time. Jefferson could move into strict construction with rather less strain than Madison, his commitment to the Constitution having never been on the order of Madison's. But Madison's position was now fully reversed. In denying Publius, he was denying an earlier version of himself.

The reaction in Virginia against assumption was more hostile than he had expected. But that was only a part of the difficulty. The bank proposal both threatened the Potomac capital and completely usurped the stage from something else—striking at England—which he and Jefferson had been deeply determined to do. The sheer momentum of Hamilton's schemes was an indication that his system might well become the dominant preoccupation of the federal government, to the exclusion of all else and preempting all manner of alternatives. The world that was materializing before him—one dominated by moneyed men and merchants subservient to the interests of England and a British system—bore little resemblance to the one he had originally envisioned. He had reached the point of concluding that only on the highest possible ground—that of the Constitution itself—was there any hope that this tide might be stopped. But by the same token, matters had reached the point where the Constitution was not really the highest ground after all. Madison's picture of an ideal world—of which the Constitution, to be sure, had been a prominent feature—was now gravely threatened, and when that happened, he could no longer feel bound even by his own previous version of the Constitution.

Strict construction, then, is in a special sense the resort of persons under ideological strain. It represents a willingness to renounce a range of positive opportunities for action in return for a principle which will inhibit government from undertaking a range of things one does not approve of. It marks the point at which one prefers to see the Constitution not as a sanction for achieving one's own ends but as a protection against those designs of others which have come to be seen as usurping and corrupting. Thus James Madison, confronted by Federalist 44, now might truly and consistently have replied that he had never anticipated the extent to which others would exploit the opportunity which broad construction offered them to pervert what he assumed to be the true ends of government. While he waited in suspense for Washington's action, he listened to what the other side, in equal suspense, was saying. The "licentiousness of the tongues of speculators and Tories," he told Jefferson bitterly, "far exceeded anything that was conceived."[61] The term "speculators and Tories," freighted with the most infamous associations, now encompassed in a bald phrase the world both of them feared and hated.

As to when Thomas Jefferson began to hate Hamilton personally and to treat him as a personal enemy, that moment was not yet quite at hand. The two were still treating each other civilly with regard to the question of a mint, which came up during this same period. Their dealings on that question are not without interest. Even the subject of a mint, it appears, had a certain ideological undercurrent, and is another illustration of the differences in the workings of their two minds.

Jefferson's own interest in matters of coinage went back many years. In 1784 he had proposed a system of decimal coinage with an American equivalent of the

Spanish dollar as its basic unit. The plan was perfectly rational; it avoided the clumsy English system of pounds, shillings, and pence and substituted one with fractional coins (tenth, double tenth, five-copper piece, and penny) which would be decimal in nature and would at the same time coincide in weight and value with the foreign coins (Spanish bit, pistareen, half-bit, and copper) currently in circulation. The Confederation Congress adopted Jefferson's plan in 1786 with very few changes, though its implementation was postponed to a later time, and provided that the American dollar should contain 375.6 grains of pure silver.[62]

Subsequently Jefferson, in preparing a report on weights and measures in the spring of 1790, tried to devise a set of standards—also measured in decimal units—which would be directly tied into decimal coinage in one grand system. By virtually pure coincidence it had turned out that Jefferson's ideal ounce (the standard for which would be a thousandth of a cubic foot of rainwater) and the dollar he had proposed in 1784 would weigh almost exactly the same. He took this as an all-but-miraculous sign that there was a kind of universal symmetry in nature which extended itself to matters of coinage. Jefferson would thus await with considerable interest the Report on a Mint—and on the actual implementation of a decimal coinage system—which Congress had requested from Hamilton at about the same time he himself had been directed to prepare his Report on Weights and Measures. Meanwhile he passed on to Hamilton a report from the French National Assembly about a new alloy used in minting, and closed his covering letter by saying: "This information he [the Secretary of State] submits to the better judgment of the Secretary of the Treasury, & hopes he will consider the liberty taken as an advance towards our unreserved communications for reciprocal benefit." Hamilton, still concerned to give no undue offense to Jefferson, and at the same time aware that his own conclusions on coinage did not coincide with those of his colleague, took care to show Jefferson an advance copy of his own report before it was released.[63]

What the two reports represented were two contrasted modes of thought and two very different ways of addressing a problem. Jefferson's was essentially *a priori*, Hamilton's flatly empirical; Jefferson's was based on the principle of symmetry, Hamilton's on the existing practices of a world community in which the nation's coin would circulate. The problem as Hamilton saw it was to determine what the weight and silver content of the new dollar should be, to establish a ratio with gold that would enable both silver and gold coins to circulate simultaneously, and to decide how best to establish the costs of mintage. He spent much time in factual research and in considering the many painfully complicated variables, which was why the report took him so long to prepare. He had to determine the actual weight and silver content of coins then circulating in the United States, the market ratios of gold and silver under varying trade conditions, and the differing experience of European countries with mintage fees. His aim was to strike some sort of reasonable balance among all these things, so that by definition his would hardly be an ideal system.[64]

The basic point of difference between himself and Jefferson was the weight of the dollar. Subsequent to the old Congress's decision to establish a dollar containing 375.6 grains of silver, based on what was then thought to be the content of the Spanish dollar, it had been discovered that Spanish dollars actually varied in weight between about 377 and 370 grains, the lighter coin being that of most recent issue and the one now most commonly in use in the United States. Adhering to the decision of 1785 would mean a coin some five grains heavier than corresponding ones currently circulating, thus enormously complicating problems of exchange. Hamilton therefore proposed a dollar of 371.25 grains of pure silver or 24.75 grains of pure gold. This would establish a ratio of fifteen to one between gold and silver, which was approximately the ratio then existing in the London and Amsterdam markets. Then after an extended consideration of various ways of handling the costs of minting, he proposed as an experiment a mintage charge of one-half percent.[65]

Jefferson was indeed nettled. His own system of abstract ideality was being set aside in favor of one based on the practices of merchants and men of money. Actually his 1784 proposal of a 375.6-grain dollar had itself originally been advanced in order to coincide with the Spanish dollar. He was now adhering to it on different grounds entirely, those of symmetry, even though there was no other reason why a dollar should weigh exactly an ounce, or why weights and measures need be connected in any way with coinage. He argued that the "incertainty" about the dollar's value had been removed when Congress declared it to contain 375.6 grains (ignoring the fact that regardless of what Congress had said, the actual coins in circulation were still five grains lighter) and that Hamilton had no right to change it.[66]

No action would be taken until the following session, that of 1791–92. At that time, Madison tried to edit Washington's annual message so as to juxtapose the recommendations on weights and measures with those of coinage in such a way, according to Hamilton, that it would look as though the President wanted the unit of weight and the unit of coinage to be the same. Hamilton, who saw the draft before Washington put it in final form, pointed out the implication. Washington said he had intended no such implication, and in the finished version of the message the two recommendations appeared separately. The proposal for a mint would be adopted into law in April 1792. Jefferson's Report on Weights and Measures was never to be acted on at all.[67]

Written communications on this and other matters between Jefferson and Hamilton during the winter of 1790–91 were subscribed with "affection." But this shortly stopped, and the customary word now became "esteem," or simply "respect."[68] Jefferson seems to have been the first to change, and probably Hamilton was at first unaware of Jefferson's rising hostility to him. The final transition apparently occurred during January and February 1791. Everything went wrong, from Jefferson's viewpoint, during that period. Madison's proposed navigation act was buried, none of Jefferson's several reports was acted on, the Hamiltonian program—Excise, Bank, and Mint—seemed headed for total victory, and on questions of national import Washington now seemed more inclined to take Hamilton's advice than that of Jefferson and Madison.

For the Virginians it was all emerging as more and more of a piece, and the "enemy" was assuming a more and more definite—and at the same time more simplified—shape in their minds. One of the phenomena that emerged during this very time in the language of Jefferson and Madison was the use of tag-words, of formulas that seemed to tie all these suspected men and their principles together in a system of ready reference. Madison's "speculators & Tories," which lumped all his opponents on domestic and foreign matters alike into one, is a striking example. Another is the tag-formula which set "monarchists" and "aristocrats" off from "republicans." The "aristocrats" tended to be those of money rather than of land, and the "monarchists" were in practice those who favored English monarchy rather than French. "Republican," too, meant something special. A man might technically be a "republican" but not of the right kind, in which case he was not a real republican at all.

Something at any rate needed to be done to combat the influence of these men, and it was under this urgency that Thomas Jefferson began writing letters of at least proto-political significance. In his correspondence of this period we see Jefferson's first tentative efforts to identify, and perhaps to establish, future sources of support. To George Mason he suggested that "the only corrective of what is corrupt in our present form of government will be the augmentation of the numbers in the lower house, so as to get a more agricultural representation, which may put that interest above that of the stock-jobbers." He also warned Mason that the success of the present French government was "necessary to stay up our own, and to prevent it from falling back to that kind of Half-way house, the English constitution." He urged James Innes of Kentucky to run for Congress, having "such confidence in the purity of your republicanism, that I know your efforts would go in a right direction." The government needed "examples," he told Innes, "which may fence us against future heresies preached now, to be practiced hereafter."[69]

With at least one of the letters Jefferson wrote during this period he overstepped himself, and gave serious offense to a very old friend, John Adams. Sometime in April 1791 John Beckley, the Clerk of the House, had obtained a copy of Thomas Paine's new pamphlet, *The Rights of Man,* which was a direct attack on Edmund Burke's highly critical and pessimistic *Reflections on the Revolution in France.* Beckley had lent it to Madison, who in turn lent it to Jefferson, who was then asked to pass it along when finished to the Philadelphia printer who planned to bring out an American edition. Jefferson was delighted with this anti-British polemic, which approvingly linked the French Revolution (still in its relatively peaceful constitutional-monarchy phase) with the American Revolution. In a covering letter to the printer he wrote, among other things, "I am extremely pleased to find it will be reprinted here, and that something is at length to be publickly said against the political heresies which have sprung up among us." From the context it was obvious that the "heresies" he had immediately in mind were those of Vice-President Adams, who had been publishing in the *Pennsylvania Gazette* a long and dull series of essays called *Discourses on Davila* in which he, like Burke, commented disapprovingly on events in France and tried to vindicate his own belief in the need for forms, titles, and distinctions in all societies, republican included. Professor Malone doubts that Jefferson actually read these essays, but the fact was that they had caused no little public stir inasmuch as American opinion was still heavily favorable toward the French Revolution, and the fuss over titles in the spring of 1789 had led to Adams's being stigmatized in some quarters as a "monarchist." It seems to have been enough for Jefferson that the essays themselves were derided as monarchist, Tory, anglophile, and unrepublican.[70]

But Jefferson was appalled to discover, when the American edition of *The Rights of Man* came out early in May, that his own note to the printer had without his permission been included as a preface. Readers saw Jefferson's allusions for what they were, the affair was taken up in most of the newspapers and the letter reprinted, and it seems to have been this stir that made the occasion for Jefferson's and Hamilton's final open break.[71] Meanwhile the mortified Jefferson tried to explain himself to President Washington. "I am afraid the indiscretion of a printer has committed me with my friend Mr. Adams, for whom, as one of the most honest & disinterested men alive, I have a cordial esteem, increased by long habits of concurrence in opinion in the days of his republicanism; and even since his apostasy to hereditary monarchy & nobility, tho' we differ, we differ as friends should do." His own words to the printer had been intended only "to take off a little of the dryness of the note," and although he was indeed referring to Adams's *Discourses,* "nothing was ever further from my thoughts than to become myself the contradictor before the public." When the furor failed to subside, Jefferson finally wrote to Adams himself, with similar explanations. "That you and I differ in our ideas of the best form of government is well known to us both; but we have differed as friends should do, respecting the purity of each other's motives, and confining our differences of opinion to private conversation." Adams replied that he was glad to have the explanation but was unaware that they had "differed" at all:

> I know not what your Idea is of the best form of Government. You and I have never had a serious conversation together that I can recollect concerning the nature of Government. The very transient hints that have passed between Us have been jocular and superficial, without ever coming to any explanation. If You suppose that I have or ever had a design or desire, of attempting to introduce a Government of King, Lords and Commons, or in other Words an hereditary Executive, or an hereditary Senate ... you are wholly mistaken. There is not such a Thought expressed or intimated in any public writing or private Letter of mine, and I may safely challenge all Mankind to produce such a passage and quote the Chapter and Verse. If you have ever put such a Construction on any Thing of mine, I beg you would mention it to me, and I will undertake to convince you, that it has no such meaning.

Jefferson, unwilling to let the matter drop, insisted on exculpating himself still further and blamed the whole uproar on "Publicola," the pseudonymous writer who had come to Adams's defense in the newspapers and whose identity—he was Adams's own son John Quincy—Jefferson certainly must have suspected.

With this (and having taken no notice of Adams's explicit disavowal of being a "monarchist"), Jefferson had added one touch too many. Adams did not reply, and the correspondence lapsed. Meanwhile Madison relished the whole affair, insisting that Adams in view of his "anti-republican discourses" should have no reason to complain. The case of John Adams, complicated though it may have been in fact, could now be disposed of in tag-words.[72]

Another individual who came into Jefferson's life about this time was Philip Freneau, himself rather a Paine-like spirit and a man in whom the vigorous employment of tag-words had become, so to speak, second nature. Pamphleteer, poet, quondam journalist, and a former schoolmate of Madison's at Princeton, Freneau had knocked about the world and was currently somewhat down on his luck. Jefferson and Madison expended a great deal of time and care during the spring and summer of 1791 trying to persuade Freneau to put his journalistic talents at their service in combating what they saw as the forces of monarchy, anti-republicanism, and anglomania. They would ultimately succeed, though not without much wooing and attention, Freneau's appetite for which was all but insatiable.

Some time later, when Philip Freneau had become perhaps the most controversial editor in the country, Thomas Jefferson would solemnly deny that he exercised any control or influence over his sayings and doings.[73] This was technically true, inasmuch as Freneau was not the sort to be held in check by anyone. But when Jefferson and Madison determined to do their best to bring Freneau to Philadelphia, they knew their man and knew very well what any paper under his editorship would be like. Freneau's ferocious anglophobia, his violent hostility to moneyed men, his country-party temperament, and his penchant for editorial brawling were as well known as his dexterity with language and his modest reputation as a popular poet.

Born in 1752 of Huguenot extraction and raised in the New Jersey countryside around Monmouth, Philip Freneau was almost the same age as James Madison. He came from a lineage of near-misses: both father and grandfather, after promising beginnings in business, had eventually been overwhelmed by creditors and died insolvent, and something similar occurred with all his uncles. Despite their uncertain financial condition, however, the family managed to send Philip to Princeton, where he fell in with Madison, Hugh Henry Brackenridge, and William Bradford. He subsequently abandoned his earlier plans of entering the ministry; on two occasions he took positions as a schoolteacher which ended in unexplained flight each time; and he wrote a fair amount of poetry as he moved from place to place. As member of the ship's company on board a privateer during the Revolution, Freneau was captured and spent six weeks in a British prison ship amid inhuman conditions. His verses about the British ("gorged monsters") and the "hell-born Tories" thereupon became "hymns of hate," according to his biographer: "Vague humanitarian impulses were transformed to one mighty resolution—the extermination of English influence from America forever."[74]

Engaged by the Philadelphia publisher Francis Bailey in 1781 as editor of the *Freeman's Journal*, Freneau developed his newly discovered gifts for invective in prose and verse, and soon widened them to include not only Tories and English-men but selected figures in state politics as well. In rehearsal for his Antifederalism of a few years later, he heaped every kind of slander and abuse on John Dickinson and his followers in the mercantile community for wanting to change Pennsyl-vania's constitution, do away with its all-powerful unicameral legislature, and substitute a government of checks and balances with an upper house and an independent executive. When a rival paper defended them, Freneau hissed:

> Vile as they are, this lukewarm tory crew
> Seem viler still, when they are praised by you.

The *Freeman's Journal* came to be known as "Bailey's Chamber Pot."[75]

Freneau shortly drifted off to other things, including a stint as captain of a coasting vessel and seeing through the press two more volumes of poetry. These were reasonably successful, though he did not think he received the recognition he was entitled to. By 1790 he was back in journalism again, this time as regular contributor and editor of the *Daily Advertiser,* New York City's leading Antifed-eralist newspaper. He lashed out at speculators enriched by Hamilton's funding system. John Trumbull, David Humphreys, and Joel Barlow were other poets of the day whose work was being favorably received; Freneau, his envy aroused, publicly attacked them for sycophancy before famous persons and for bribing the London reviewers. He wrote an ode on Paine's *Rights of Man,* whose theme was

> A vast republic, fam'd thro' every clime,
> WITHOUT A KING, TO SEE THE END OF TIME.[76]

On February 28, three days after the President had signed the Bank bill, Jefferson wrote Freneau offering him the post of translating clerk at the State Department. This was part of his and Madison's scheme for establishing Freneau in Philadelphia in order to set up a newspaper there which would counteract the "doctrines of monarchy, aristocracy, & the exclusion of the influence of the peo-ple" currently being disseminated by John Fenno's *Gazette of the United States.* Freneau, enjoying these solicitations and not averse to stringing them out, kept Jefferson and Madison on tenterhooks for a good part of the spring and summer while making up his mind whether he wanted to go to Philadelphia, not being certain of financial support, or retire to the country. But increasing the induce-ments—a promise of public printing, inside news of foreign affairs, and the influ-ence of Madison and others in collecting subscription lists—they finally bagged their prize late in July 1791. The *National Gazette,* edited by Philip Freneau, would begin publication by the end of October.[77] Meanwhile the postmaster-generalship had fallen vacant, and Jefferson hastened to press as his candidate for that position Thomas Paine himself. Paine and Freneau would have made a colorful pair in Philadelphia, and there would perhaps have been lively scenes in the Senate over Paine's confirmation. Washington may have sensed something of this, inasmuch as nothing further was heard of it.[78]

Still another letter Jefferson wrote in the early months of 1791 was to have some bearing on the subsequently famous "botanizing tour" taken by him and Madison late in the spring through New York and New England. It was addressed to Robert R. Livingston, the landed magnate of the upper Hudson. In it, Jefferson gracefully touched upon various neutral topics, matters of mutual interest between gentlemen farmers. Then, abruptly: "Are the people in your quarter as well contented with the proceedings of our government, as their representatives say they are? There is a vast mass of discontent gathered in the South, and how and when it will break God knows." Livingston responded in a similar spirit. He too moved casually from topic to topic, and though he had to admit that things were fairly prosperous in his part of the country, he eventually said what Jefferson hoped he would say: "Our delegates deceive themselves if they believe their constituents are satisfied with all the Measures of Government."[79]

Jefferson's and Madison's vacation trip lasted from May 17 to June 19, 1791. They started from New York City, journeyed up the Hudson to the Lake George–Lake Champlain region, and returned southward through western New England. Along the way they fished, collected specimens, and feasted their senses on the beauties of what is still one of the most attractive sections of the United States. But ever since Claude Bowers nearly seventy years ago offered his portrait of Thomas Jefferson as the "master politician," "the original 'Easy Boss,'" there has been an urge to regard this expedition as part of a purposeful course of political organizing, and as the occasion for forming what was to emerge as the Virginia–New York "axis" with Livingston, Aaron Burr, and Governor George Clinton. This may be somewhat anachronistic. The evidence, though hardly non-existent, is sketchy; more important, there were as yet no precedents for this sort of "organizing," and indeed, all the values of the age were sternly against it. Jefferson and Madison, no less than other men of their time, abhorred the evils of "party" and "faction" and were not likely, at least not knowingly, to set about forming one themselves. Politics, in the overt form that would come to be taken for granted in the nineteenth century, was as yet unknown.[80]

On the other hand, there was certainly something. Both men were now thoroughly agitated by impulses which a later age would not hesitate to characterize as "political," even though a recognized form for embodying them did not yet exist. It is virtually certain that the two did stop on their way through the city for a visit with Livingston, who was currently holding a court term there; they may also have seen Burr, and at some point perhaps even Clinton, though the last is less likely.[81] It is quite logical, moreover, to picture them discussing those aspects of public affairs which most disturbed them, especially with persons whom they knew to be generally like-minded.

Perhaps a more suggestive analogy than "politics"—in the more familiar nineteenth-century sense—would in this case be that of diplomacy. Jefferson's dealings with Robert Livingston, for example, rather resemble the diffusely graded process, formal and informal, whereby two major powers make themselves accessible to one another in the stages preliminary to what might later become an entente. Jefferson and Livingston might be expected to take satisfaction in comparing notes on agriculture in their respective domains. They might also discuss improvements in mill machinery, and as men who cultivated scientific interests they would undoubtedly be pleased to find themselves seeing eye to eye on a range of matters touching weights, measures, and coinage. And then if it should happen that they held certain sentiments in common with regard to particular men and measures of government, there might be the makings of a real understanding—eventually, perhaps, even an alliance.[82]

In any case, the personal circumstances of Robert R. Livingston at this time were such as might have made him more than ordinarily receptive. Chancellor of the State of New York and lord of Clermont, the vast family estate in Columbia County on the east bank of the Hudson a little above Rhinebeck, Livingston had a due sense of his own eminence. He had been John Jay's predecessor as Secretary of Foreign Affairs under the Confederation, and he would have liked an appointment to federal office in 1789; he even so far overlooked his dignity as to ask Washington for one. Chief Justice, Secretary of State, or Secretary of the Treasury: inasmuch as any of these would have been acceptable, Livingston was much mortified when none of them materialized. It seems that Alexander Hamilton and his father-in-law, Philip Schuyler, had had something to do with blocking them. A coolness fell over his old college friendship with John Jay about the time Jay was appointed Chief Justice, and not long thereafter Livingston began attacking Hamilton's funding system and "the spirit of stock Jobbing." (His biographer explains that "as a landowner he was afraid of the rise of a consolidated moneyed interest.") He did not like Hamilton's Mint Report either. Nor was this all. He was francophile in his foreign sympathies; he detested England, and took to calling Hamilton, Jay, and Schuyler "Anglocrats." In January 1791 he joined his influence with that of Governor Clinton in a movement to have the Assembly oust Schuyler from his Senate seat by electing in his place the moderate Antifederalist Aaron Burr. The movement was successful, and its outcome gave Livingston much satisfaction.[83]

Of what was said during the first exchanges in the New York–Virginia diplomacy there is no record. But Hamilton's friend Robert Troup doubtless had some basis for reporting: "There was every evidence of a passionate courtship between the Chancellor, Burr, Jefferson & Madison when the two latter were in Town." Meanwhile George Beckwith in Philadelphia and Sir John Temple in New York were convinced that the real motive of the Virginians' excursion was to promote anti-British policy and "to proselyte as far as they are able to a commercial war with Great Britain." "Delenda est Carthago [Carthage must be destroyed] I suppose," Troup told Hamilton, "is the Maxim adopted with respect to you."[84]

The scenes that occurred in Philadelphia when shares of the new Bank were placed on sale early in July were all that was finally needed to goad Jefferson and Madison into shudders of loathing.

When subscriptions for Bank stock were opened on July 4, 1791, they were filled within one hour. The arrangement was that a subscriber would pay one-fourth in specie and three-fourths in government securities for each $400 share of stock. But not immediately: at the time of subscription he paid $25 down for each share to be delivered, for which he received scrip—certificates of option entitling him to purchase so many shares which he would pay for in four semiannual installments. But although subscriptions were filled immediately, what ensued was the most furious speculative activity in scrip, the scrip being of course transferable.

What was it that made the stock so attractive, and what accounted for this speculative "scrippomania"? For one thing, the government securities in anyone's possession were by definition raised to par when used to pay for Bank shares. The security of that investment in turn depended on the success of the Bank itself, but there was every reason to think—in view of the Bank's monopoly on government business and its having been organized on sound principles—that it *would* be a success, and that its dividends would be substantial. They might amount to 8 percent or better. Consequently, not only was there the liveliest trading in Bank scrip, but the market activity in federal securities themselves throughout the summer exceeded even Hamilton's expectations. By August 1 they actually reached par, and would never again drop below.[85]

This represented the success of Hamilton's entire system of public credit. Its continued success, as well as that of the Bank, required that the government continue to enjoy a dependable and undisturbed income from tariff receipts. And the problem of protecting that income, as Hamilton saw it, was in turn bound up in the closest way with the stability of the country's foreign relations.

How Jefferson and Madison, on the other hand, saw all these same questions and events may be inferred from their correspondence during the months of July and August. "It is impossible to say," Jefferson told Monroe, "where the appetite for gambling will stop." Jefferson, largely innocent of theoretical knowledge about banking or money, had hit upon the idea "that we shall be paying 13 per cent. per ann. for 8 millions of paper money instead of having that circulation of gold & silver for nothing." (The difficulty with this theory was that its parts were in no way related; the circulation of gold and silver, chronically scarce, did not come to a fraction of this amount, whereas the circulation of this same "paper money" was in fact costing the public nothing.) "As yet the delirium of speculation," Jefferson wrote to Edmund Pendleton with perhaps unconscious irony, "is too strong to admit of sober reflection." Meanwhile he confided to Madison on July 24 that "several merchants from Richmond (Scotch, English &c.) were here lately. I suspect it was to dabble in federal filth."[86]

Madison was possessed with a cold fury which was perhaps even more intense than Jefferson's. The whole business, which he regarded as "shameful," was "a mere scramble for so much public plunder." "In fact," he reported from New York, "stock-jobbing drowns every other subject. The Coffee House is in an eternal buzz with the Gamblers." He too had his theories. When federal securities reached par early in August, he refused to see this as a movement from visibly logical causes; rather it was an artificial bubble created by a conspiracy of insiders, and would collapse as soon as they got their own money out. He could not get it through his head that federal securities now had a life of their own. He was also ready to believe that Hamilton was planning to refund the deferred debt in order to make interest on that part of it payable immediately, thereby feeding the gamblers' appetite, as Jefferson had expressed it, "by throwing in . . . new aliment." (Such a preposterous scheme would have increased government obligations by 20 to 25 percent.) It was all part of a wider plan whereby the speculators would soon seize control of the country: "my imagination will not attempt to set bounds to the daring depravity of the times." "The stock-jobbers," Madison insisted, "will become the pretorian band of the Government, at once its tool & its tyrant; bribed by its largesses, & overawing it by clamours & combinations."[87]

Jefferson summed up all the issues in a letter to Edward Rutledge in which he undertook to remind the wayward South Carolinians where their true interests lay. ("Would to God yourself, Genl. Pinkney, Maj. Pinkney would come forward and aid us with your efforts.") He deplored what had happened to the plans put forth "for the purpose of bringing Gr. Brit. to reason," and was "sorry to see that your state has been over-jealous of the measures proposed on this subject." As for the current madness of "scrippomany," Jefferson declared that "the tide of public prosperity almost unparalelled in any country, is arrested in it's course, and suppressed by the rage of getting rich in a day." The newspapers, to be sure, with their talk of "public felicity," told a different story, but that was "because our papers are under the orders of the scrip-men." Turning to the latest news from France, Jefferson still ventured to hope that "the French revolution will issue happily." He felt "that the permanence of our own leans in some degree on that, and that a failure there would be a powerful argument to prove that there must be a failure here." And finally, he acknowledged that the British might be about to send a regular minister to the United States after all. But it was obvious that the prospect gave Jefferson no pleasure, and that he did not expect — or perhaps even want — anything to come of it. He had made up his mind that the British had "no serious view of treating or fulfilling treaties."[88]

3

Jefferson and Hammond

On October 20, 1791, two attractive young men arrived at Philadelphia, having traveled in each other's company all the way from England. Each was on the threshold of a career, and each was full of high hopes. One was George Hammond, the newly appointed British minister to the United States, who was twenty-eight years old. The other was the secretary of legation, Edward Thornton, who was even younger, being only twenty-five. The talents and training of each were unexceptionable. Hammond was a Master of Arts and Fellow of Merton College, Oxford; Thornton had a Bachelor of Arts from Pembroke, Cambridge, and had been third wrangler there. The case was auspicious; the prospects of both were excellent. Much depended, of course, on whether their American mission were a success; both, understandably, had every motive for desiring that it should be.

Nothing approaching a rounded character portrait of George Hammond exists, and the episodic nature of his history has tended to fragment still further the little we do know of what he was like. Phineas Bond, the British consul at Philadelphia, being Hammond's junior in rank though fourteen years his senior in age—and with distinctions in English official and social life being what they were—had every reason to await his arrival with dread. To his vast delight, the young minister treated him with consideration, and the two would henceforth be on terms of the utmost warmth and cordiality. Edward Thornton, for his part, confided to his patron back home that "Mr. Hammond, whom I admire more and more every day . . . , behaves with exceeding great attention to me." Evidence abounds that the "rosey-faced" Hammond was highly industrious, and his assiduity to business did not permit him to accept all the invitations that were showered upon him. But he was a bachelor and hardly reclusive; it was not long before his heart was captured by Margaret Allen, a Philadelphia young woman of unusual beauty. They were married during the second year of his mission. Young Thornton, meanwhile, plodded away. His unflourishing but forthright hand copied all the Minister's dispatches in duplicate, and such was the sober neatness of his work that they may still be read today without difficulty. The secretary seems to have earned his keep.[89]

But the mission was not a success. Despite George Hammond's efforts to make himself agreeable to Philadelphia and to the American government, things began to happen almost at once to put a chill upon his hopes for an accommodation between the two countries, things he took to be deliberate provocations. It was not long before he came to regard himself as rather put upon, and he retreated behind a facade of stiffness which helped matters not at all. His efforts to negotiate were fruitless. Meanwhile the cross-pressures he had to endure—the anglophobia of those with whom he had official dealings, the touchiness of Canadian authorities forever apprehensive over conditions on the frontier, and a home government so little able to keep its mind on American affairs that its instructions were sometimes worthless as a realistic guide to action—eventually wore him down. By 1795 he had had his fill of America. When he departed with his bride in August of that year, it was never to return. Shortly thereafter, Robert Liston was asked to go as Hammond's successor. Liston supposed he would have to do it, but confided to a friend with sinking heart, "I would much rather go anywhere else. A severe climate, hard work and the being surrounded by ill-disposed Yankee doctrinaires will, at my time of life, probably finish me off in a year or two."[90]

George Hammond never quite fulfilled his early promise, though he was to have a decently rewarding and honorable career. He served for many years as an undersecretary at the Foreign Office; he enjoyed the friendship of Grenville and later of the brilliant George Canning, in whose literary circle he played some part. Edward Thornton, considering his more modest origins—he was the son of an innkeeper—would do somewhat better. Thornton made himself less conspicuous in America and lasted a good deal longer there in various consular and subministerial capacities. He subsequently received diplomatic appointments to several European countries and ended his career as a K.C.B. Whatever effect their American experience may have had on the subsequent career of either, the two would manage to establish a precedent of sorts. Their example would serve as a warning to aspiring British diplomats for some time to come that a tour of duty in the United States was likely to bring them little luster.

How George Hammond might have been remembered in America had things gone a little better can only be guessed. We have a glimpse of him on shipboard as the young couple came within sight of England:

> Dearest Papa [wrote Margaret], our long voyage is nearly over and I shall send this letter to you the moment we land. . . . George has been so attentive; you will hardly realise how happy I have been in his company. Ever since we left America he has been so changed. His cold, formal manner, not only with strangers, has been thrown off and everybody observes how agreeable he is in company. And he is so tender towards our darling baby. . . . I don't think you ever saw him at his best in Philadelphia. I think we shall be very happy together.[91]

But what were the circumstances which could lead to the eclipse of so promising a mission? Ever since the end of the Revolution the British had been intending to send a minister to America, but for one reason or another they did not get around to it until the summer of 1791. During most of that period the matter had been regarded as something less than vital. Moreover, there was some truth behind the excuses the Duke of Leeds had made to Gouverneur Morris: "I wished to send you one, but then I wished to have a Man every way equal to the Task . . . but it was difficult; [America] is a great Way off." That is, a man suitable and qualified and a man willing to go was not the easiest combination to find. Conjectures have been made as to what it was that finally moved the Foreign Office to action. Reports from the consuls had urged it; continued threats of commercial discrimination may have been a stimulus; Washington's message in February 1791 on the Morris mission may have been another. But there is no evidence that it was any one thing in particular. It was rather like one of those troublesome standing obligations that require just enough extra effort and attention that one tends to put them off until prodded by the rising sharpness of the reminders.[92]

After Lord Hawkesbury's Report of the Privy Council Committee for Trade on the state of commerce between Great Britain and America was presented in January 1791, little excuse for procrastination remained. This report, with its complacent mercantilist assumption that Great Britain's navigation system had been vindicated since the war, and that the fewer alterations made in it the better, would serve in large part as the basis for any instructions which a minister-designate would take with him. Hawkesbury was in fact requested by Foreign Secretary Grenville to prepare a draft for the instructions to be given George Hammond. This draft, confined to commercial questions, reflected in considerable measure the report Hawkesbury had just submitted, and refers to the report as the guideline to be followed in any commercial negotiations.[93]

Hammond's final instructions, as prepared by Grenville himself, were rather more extended in scope, emphasis, and detail than Hawkesbury's version, and embraced the entire range of differences outstanding between the two countries as viewed from London. As a whole they reflect, in about as reasonable a form as was then to be found, the official state of mind regarding America. There was, on the one hand, a current of deep annoyance over the Americans' continued unwillingness to settle the issue of unpaid prewar debts, and a consequent tone of self-righteousness regarding continued British occupation of the Northwest posts. There is a clear recognition, on the other hand, that sooner or later the posts would have to be evacuated.

Hammond's "first and leading Object" was to press for full execution of Articles IV, V, and VI of the Peace Treaty of 1783, those relating to debts and the treatment of Loyalists. He was also to make it known that if there were "a real disposition to meet the just expectations of this Country in that respect," Great Britain was prepared to make "some practicable and reasonable Arrangement on the Subject of the Posts." Lord Dorchester was shortly expected home on leave from Canada, and there would be fuller instructions on this point after his arrival. Hammond was further to exert himself, "if any opportunity should occur," to contribute to peace in the West between the Indians and the Americans, and "to disclaim in the most unequivocal manner any Idea of Lord Dorchester's having encouraged the measures of hostility taken by the Indians." Finally, he was empowered, if the Americans took the initiative, to open negotiations on a trade treaty based on reciprocal benefits, "on the terms of the most favoured nation." All commercial questions must be referred back to England before being embodied in a treaty. As for American trade with the British West Indies, Hawkesbury had wanted it explicitly stated that "this Proposition cannot be admitted even as a Subject of Negociation." Grenville apparently preferred not to seem quite this rigid, and omitted that point from the final instructions.[94]

Hammond's freedom of action was not very wide. But he was determined to make maximum use of what latitude he had, and to make his mission a success through a general settlement as satisfactory to all parties as possible. There were at first some grounds for optimism. There were many indications that a fair number of influential persons in America wanted good relations with England, and that he might count on the assistance of this "English interest" to bring them about. In settling the question of the debts, and perhaps of the Loyalists as well, Hammond had something valuable to offer in return, the evacuation of the Northwest posts. The British case on the debts was not unreasonable; few Americans were prepared to deny that the British creditors had good cause for complaint. Hammond was aware of the benefits to America of British trade, and he must have understood, as Beckwith certainly had, that it was in view of this that the American financial system required a period of peace in which such trade might proceed uninterrupted.[95] The Americans could expect little or nothing on the West Indies. Still, the "terms of the most favoured nation" might make possible various accommodations which would be to the two countries' "reciprocal advantage." The Americans already received various advantages enjoyed by no others, of which Hammond was prepared to remind them, and it was also in England's power to retaliate should they do any more experimenting with measures of discrimination. Hammond knew about the Secretary of State's hostility to all things British. But he did not believe Jefferson's views to be widely shared in official circles, and he hoped that with tact and good management any difficulties arising from them might be overcome. Things seemed to get off to a good start when Hammond, to avoid giving offense to the Americans, stretched his instructions somewhat by presenting his credentials without awaiting an official announcement that the American government had appointed a minister to England. He was thereupon accorded an "audience" with President Washington, and afterward reported that he had been received with "the utmost politeness and respect." Similar "politeness and respect" were forthcoming from other "persons of consideration."[96]

But then when it came to the opening of discussions, Secretary Jefferson moved immediately to paralyze most of the young minister's hopeful anticipations and to place him on the defensive. He told Hammond that their business should be conducted in writing; he then began it himself by addressing to him two questions in what Edward Thornton regarded as an "abrupt and I may say rude style." He wanted to know what Hammond's government intended to do about carrying out Article VII of the treaty (regarding the posts), and whether Hammond himself was authorized to negotiate a treaty of commerce.[97]

A strong note of badgering on Jefferson's part characterized the exchange that followed. Hammond replied the following day, saying that execution of Article VII had been suspended in view of non-compliance by the United States with Articles IV, V, and VI, and such was the interconnectedness of these questions that they could not be separated in any discussion of them. He was, however, fully prepared to discuss all measures, on both sides, for carrying out the provisions of the treaty. As for Jefferson's other question, Hammond assured him that his government was "sincerely disposed to promote and facilitate the commercial intercourse between the two countries," and that he was ready "to enter into a negotiation for establishing that intercourse, upon principles of reciprocal benefit." Ingratiatingly, he closed with appreciation for "the obliging expressions of personal regard" which had been shown him, adding "that it would be the highest object of my ambition, to be the humble instrument of contributing, in any manner, to fix upon a permanent basis the future system of harmony and good understanding between the two countries."[98]

Jefferson replied a week later. He took no notice of Hammond's response to his first question, and as for the second:

> Where you are pleased to say that you are "authorised to communicate to this government his majesty's readiness to enter into a negotiation for establishing that intercourse upon principles of reciprocal benefit," I understand that you are not furnished with any commission or express powers to arrange a treaty with us, or to make any specific propositions on the subject of commerce; but only to assure us that his Britanic majesty is ready to concur with us in appointing persons, times and places for commencing such a negociation. Be so good as to inform me if there be any misapprehension in this. . . .[99]

Hammond tried again. He wrote the next day saying, "I am not as yet empowered to *conclude* any *definitive* arrangement, with respect to the commercial intercourse between the two countries, [but] I am fully authorized to *enter* into a negotiation, for that purpose, and into the discussion of such principles as may appear best calculated to promote that object, on a basis of reciprocal advantage."

Another week went by, and Jefferson then wrote as though Hammond had told him nothing: "where you say that you are fully authorized to enter into a negotiation, for the purpose of arranging the commercial intercourse between the two countries, I have the honor to inform you, that I am ready to receive a communication of your full powers for that purpose, at any time you shall think proper, and to proceed immediately to their object." Hammond immediately replied, though in some discouragement, "I can only repeat what I have before stated, . . . that I have no special commission, empowering me to *conclude* any *definitive* arrangement, upon the subject of the commercial intercourse between Great Britain and the United States; but that I conceive myself fully competent to enter into a negotiation with this Government, for that purpose. . . ." He appealed to his "general *plenipotentiary* character," and to "the President's recognition of me in that character."[100]

By now Hammond's apprehensions were fully aroused. Jefferson's motives for addressing to him "questions so pointed and categorical," he feared, were to obtain proof "that I was either unwilling or unauthorized to enter into any discussion" of a commercial arrangement. He had consequently tried, he explained to Grenville, "not to leave . . . any thing equivocal, undefined, or that could excite any doubt of his Majesty's disposition to suffer this question to be fairly and candidly investigated." But Jefferson's letter of December 13 casting doubts on his powers "really surprized me," he said, until he learned through others that the Secretary of State had been trying to establish "in council" a distinction between the powers required to begin negotiations over an existing treaty and those needed to begin negotiations for a treaty of commerce. "By what mode of reasoning he will support this distinction, I cannot easily conjecture."[101] Nevertheless Jefferson succeeded in spreading the impeachment all over town. "I will tell you what, Hammond," taunted one of Jefferson's friends at a dinner party, "it is conjectured here that there is some defect in your powers, and that in consequence, the result of your visit will not be productive of any good." To which the Minister could only protest, "I have full and ample powers, upon my honour."[102]

Jefferson could have discussed commerce with Hammond to his heart's content if he had so wished, but this was evidently the last thing he did wish, and he seems to have concluded that their exchanges of November 29 through December 14 were enough to make up his case for setting that question aside and never bringing it up again. The case had in fact been largely made up already, and meanwhile the Minister's very presence was something of an embarrassment after Jefferson had encouraged the opinion everywhere that the British would never send one. Back in February Jefferson had been directed by the House of Representatives to prepare a report on foreign commerce, and in it he planned once more to urge commercial discrimination against England on the basis of that country's having no wish or intention to negotiate commercial questions with the United States. But now with a British minister actually appointed and on the ground, the expediency of issuing such a report became dubious. Jefferson was persuaded in cabinet to withhold it for the time being. Nevertheless he was not much inclined to seek new evidence which might alter his convictions. On the one hand, he knew the contents of the Hawkesbury Report; on the other, he was in daily wait for new commercial proposals from France which would show how much more generously disposed the French were than the British.[103]

By this time Jefferson had his next blast ready, and he gave it to Hammond on the 15th. He proposed that "in order to simplify our discussions," they should "begin by specifying, on each side, the particular acts which each considers to have been done by the other, in contravention of the treaty." "I," he added, "shall set the example." He thereupon set forth, with many accompanying documents, his indictment of Hammond's government for its violation of Article VII of the treaty by failing to evacuate the posts and by carrying off large numbers of American slaves at the close of the war. Hammond politely acknowledged receipt of this communication and promised to submit a similar one as soon as he could get the pertinent materials together.[104]

Meanwhile an event had occurred in the West, news of which reached Philadelphia about this time, which would prove to be of considerable significance. This was the total defeat by the Indians of an American force operating in the Ohio country under the command of Major General Arthur St. Clair.

In the face of the refusal by many of the western tribes to recognize American sovereignty within the treaty line of 1783 and to make peace, a military campaign in the Maumee Valley under Brigadier General Josiah Harmar had already been undertaken in 1790. Harmar's force of between fourteen and fifteen hundred men, mostly militia, managed to destroy a few villages and a fair amount of grain but accomplished little else except to inflame the Indians still further. A much larger force was thereupon organized by St. Clair, Governor of the Northwest Territory, who took command of the small regular army augmented by militia to the number of some six thousand men in all, and prepared to move against the Indians in 1791. St. Clair's ill-supported and incompetently officered force subsequently proceeded northward from its base at Fort Washington, not far from where Cincinnati now stands, penetrating about ninety miles to the neighborhood of present-day Fort Wayne. There, on November 4, 1791, they were descended upon by a body of Indians who slaughtered over nine hundred of them.[105] The humiliation of this defeat—far worse than that of Custer eighty-five years later—together with the implications of what would be required in expense, military involvement, and reorganization to rectify its effects, would henceforth hang heavily over the public mood and preoccupy attention at all levels of government for some time to come. On the one hand, for the Americans this made the question of the posts more acute than ever; on the other, the ever-increasing volatility of conditions on the frontier aroused new anxieties among the authorities in Canada. All of this would incline Grenville in London toward remedies and safeguards which would have the effect of greatly raising, to the Americans, the price of an evacuation of the posts.

Another event of some importance to the Hammond mission was the establishment of a good understanding with the Secretary of the Treasury, in that this gave Hammond a more accurate index than he would get anywhere else of the price both sides would have to pay for what they wanted. Hammond had his first occasion to take Hamilton's measure some time in mid-December 1791, and he liked what he saw: "the opinion, I had entertained, of that Gentleman's just and liberal way of thinking was fully confirmed." In the course of it Hamilton gave the Minister to understand that a formal offer of mediation by England between the Indians and Americans — an idea Whitehall had toyed with before — would not be acceptable. (He had already made the same point to Beckwith.)[106] In another interview shortly thereafter, Hamilton went over with Hammond all the points at issue between the two countries and gave him a clear picture of what America interests were, what it wanted, and some idea of what he thought was reasonable in the way of equivalents — a point that Jefferson, with all his voluminous letters, would never actually reach.

Regarding the posts, Hamilton saw this as clearly the most serious issue — here he had no disagreement with Jefferson — and so far as he was concerned there was little likelihood that the United States would "consent to a dereliction of any part of its territory acquired in the Treaty." He did, however, intimate that evacuation of the posts need not preclude some arrangement to protect the interests of the Canadian fur traders operating in those areas. The issue of slaves liberated by British authority, Hammond had maintained, should not be regarded as a vitally important one, and Hamilton — whose repugnance to slavery was strong — "seemed partly to acquiesce" in his reasoning. On the debts, Hamilton admitted that the British creditors had a good case, and regarded this question "as the chief ground of complaint on the part of Great Britain." But he did believe that the operations of the federal courts would in time completely remove this ground. As for "other contraventions," which presumably included the treatment of Loyalists, he doubted whether any workable mode of compensation could be devised, but he believed the American government "would consent to any reasonable or practicable method of settling this point, if any such could be proposed." The same principle, conceivably, should apply to the debts: in the last extremity something could surely be worked out short of the federal government's disclaiming any and all responsibility for their settlement. And finally, there was the question of American trade with the British West Indies, a point Hamilton argued "with much force and emphasis." He urged the expediency of granting the United States at least some share in the carrying trade, subject to whatever restrictions on size and tonnage might be required to "prevent the ships of the United States from interfering in the exportation to Europe of the productions of the British West India Islands." Hammond, however, was careful to report to Grenville that he himself had dropped no hint which might be construed as encouragement on this point.[107]

Hamilton has been accused of preempting Jefferson's functions as Secretary of State, which in its way is true enough. If such a man as Hamilton were convinced that the Secretary of State was not fully performing his own functions, or was doing so in a manner flatly opposed to what *he* saw as the public interest and to what he himself had done in behalf of it, he was not likely to hold his tongue in the face of a threat to his own work. At the same time, if any kind of settlement were to take place, it would appear that the terms Hamilton spelled out for Hammond came closest to what was actually possible. He was uncompromising on the posts, flexible on the fur traders and the debts, and anxious for some kind of limited entry into the West Indies. Nor was he inclined to make much of the slave issue, meanwhile giving Hammond a fair cue on what the British might expect regarding the Loyalists, which was not a great deal. To be sure, the news of St. Clair's defeat had done nothing to improve the United States' already limited bargaining power; nevertheless these terms, as Hamilton saw it, were the only logical alternative to the commercial warfare which the two countries might otherwise blunder into. These points did in fact prefigure with some accuracy the Jay negotiations of 1794.

For the time being Hammond had no choice but to meet Jefferson on his own ground. He professed to welcome Jefferson's mode of procedure, inasmuch as the facts appeared to favor the British case on treaty infractions. He and Bond prepared the case with considerable care, and on March 5, 1792, it was presented to Jefferson in a lengthy communication.

Its weakest point, as a matter of logic, was its justification of the British decision to retain the posts. It had been done, he said in effect, in view of prior infractions by the Americans. This was in fact not true; the authorities had made that decision immediately, for reasons which had primarily to do with British interests on the frontier. A similar claim in reverse would be made by Jefferson — that failure to evacuate the posts justified and accounted for actions by the states to hold up the satisfaction of claims — and this was not true either. There too, alleged cause and effect had little connection. Each side probably required some such preliminary formula, simply to account for conditions as they then stood, preparatory to negotiations. If each adhered to it rigidly, however, the only result would be stalemate and recrimination. This was by no means Hammond's intention.

The rest of his paper was carefully and ably presented, and was not provocative in nature. He cited a long series of acts by the states which had had the effect of impeding the collection of debts owed to British creditors, and pointed out that the states had paid little attention to the recommendations of Congress in accordance with Article V of the treaty on restitution of Loyalist property confiscated during the war. He had made every effort, he said, to see that his information was accurate, and though he was conscious of no errors, if such should turn up he would be "extremely solicitous to have them explained and corrected." But whatever the injuries that had been inflicted, Hammond reiterated his government's "sincere desire to remove every occasion of misunderstanding" and "readiness to enter into a negotiation with respect to those articles of the treaty, which have not been executed by the two countries, respectively, and to consent to such arrangements upon the subject, as, after due examination, may now be found to be of mutual convenience, and not inconsistent with the just claims and rights of his [Majesty's] subjects." In short, the paper was intended as the basis for a negotiation, and was the work of a man who wanted to succeed in what he was engaged in. Hammond wanted a settlement, not a debate.[108]

Jefferson's reply took nearly three months to prepare. It was a formidable disputation. One authority has called it "a document of uncommon power" and a "stunning reply"; another refers to it as "a brilliant piece of advocacy." Professor Malone believes it was the greatest paper Jefferson ever wrote as Secretary of State. In any case the paper made it apparent that negotiation in the accepted sense was not what Jefferson had in mind. The primary intention was to demolish Hammond's case beyond salvage, though what was to come after that—short of Hammond's simply abandoning it—he seems not to have thought through. The paper was very long (five or six times the length of Hammond's); it was obviously the product of great industry and was accompanied, as Jefferson's biographer says, by "beautiful tables."[109]

Jefferson disposed of the Loyalists by declaring that all Hammond's charges of actions against such persons had occurred before the treaty, and that those which followed it involved legislation to deal with confiscations and other measures already taken. He insisted that the retention of the posts and the carrying off of slaves constituted prior infractions, that these had contributed to removing the means whereby individuals might discharge their debts, and that the United States would have been perfectly justified, had it so wished, in dissolving the entire treaty because of them. Much space was devoted to discussion of the debts. Each case cited by Hammond was taken up and minimized in some way, as often as not to the effect that Hammond's information was undependable, besides which the measures taken by various states in favor of their own citizens to "modify" the recovery of debts could not be regarded as wrongdoing in view of British infractions. The courts, moreover, were now open and were, generally speaking, favorably disposed. In short, the United States had already fulfilled its part of the treaty, and having demonstrated this so fully, he trusted there remained no further reason for delay on the part of Great Britain.

Jefferson had shown his paper to Madison, Randolph, and Hamilton before submitting it to the British minister. Madison suggested a few alterations; Randolph saw a "peculiar asperity" in it; and Hamilton tried to tone down some of its violence. Hamilton did not see the point of getting into an argument over the right and wrong of the war itself, which was one of the paper's features; he also thought that placing beyond discussion all acts done prior to April 11, 1783 (when official news of the treaty was received), was going too far; and he questioned "the expediency of so full a justification of the proceedings of certain states with regard to Debts." He thought "*Extenuation* rather than *Vindication* would seem to be the desirable course." And finally, he doubted that anything could come of an argument based "on the supposition of either of the parties being in the *wrong*. . . . The rule in construing Treaties is to suppose both parties in the right, for want of a *common judge* &c." Jefferson accepted some minor modifications, but changed nothing of importance.[110]

Hammond was both dismayed and deeply discouraged on receipt of this communication. He himself, he thought, had done as much as he could; little further in the way of facts was likely to be scraped up by either side; and he did not see what was to be gained by continued arguments and recriminations. He decided that the only thing he could now do was to refer Jefferson's letter back to London for further instructions. He had been struck by the "great quantity of irrelevant matter contained in this paper, the positive denial of many facts, which I had advanced upon the authority of the British agents and of other respectable persons in this country, the unjustifiable insinuations thrown out with respect to the mode of prosecuting the war, and to the conduct of his Majesty's ministers subsequent to the peace, and the General acrimonious stile and manner. . . ." In communicating to Jefferson his decision to refer it to his government, he said that if there were any points on which he had been misinformed he would "most readily acknowledge [his] error." But since the exceptions taken seemed to be so sweeping, he owed it to himself "to vindicate the purity of my sources"; he could only recur to the same ones for amplification, and trust that such amplification would "protect me from the imputation of negligence, or the suspicion of intentional deception." Hamilton, to whom he had gone upon receipt of the paper, could offer him little consolation except to lament "the intemperate violence of his colleague," and to assure Hammond "that this letter was very far from meeting his approbation, or from containing a faithful exposition of the sentiments of this government." Washington, having just returned from Virginia, had not had time to read it himself, and had taken Jefferson's word for its having met the general agreement of the others.[111] The question of Anglo-American relations was thus placed in a state of suspension for the remainder of Jefferson's secretaryship.

What George Hammond had sought all along was a general settlement, a hope in which he had been encouraged by Hamilton. The achievement of such a settlement by definition required that the various issues be kept tied together in order to be negotiated as part of a comprehensive arrangement. Jefferson, on the contrary, did not want a general settlement, and he did everything he could to detach each issue from every other. He separated the commercial question from the others at the outset; he then separated the issue of the posts from that of the debts. He might argue that the federal courts had so far acted in a favorable way toward the British creditors, which was technically correct, but the fact remained that in Virginia, where the greatest concentration of unpaid debts existed, no federal cases had been adjudicated at all.[112] His paper, unlike Hammond's, could not have been intended as a basis for negotiation; it is, indeed, a remarkable example of the "double or nothing" element that would characterize Jeffersonian diplomacy throughout his public life.

What it came down to was that Jefferson could not conceive the ordinary arts of diplomacy as applying to anything he wanted from England. He did not want a commercial arrangement, because he thought the United States could force its own terms upon England later on, through some form of coercion and perhaps a favorable treaty with France. He certainly wanted the posts, and it was especially important to his country at this particular time that he should get them, but he seems to have persuaded himself that the only honorable way of going about this was to convince the adversary of how wrong his home government was; the United States by right ought to have them without paying any kind of price. He was currently taking a similar line toward Spain, his basis for claiming the free navigation of the Mississippi and other objects being the law of nations, "written in the heart of man."[113]

A little scene with Hammond early in June was symptomatic. Hammond had replied to his long letter of May 29 courteously enough, but had allowed himself to bristle at certain of Jefferson's insinuations regarding his facts. Jefferson thereupon hastened to seek him out, invite him to dinner, and explain that he only wanted to show "that my information upon several points had been inaccurate." According to Hammond their long talk ended in stalemate; they discussed the differences between their respective statements with regard to facts, and "a discussion of this sort, turning upon information of an opposite tendency, communicated from different quarters, was not calculated to effect conviction on either side." Jefferson terminated by asking whether, inasmuch as the United States had already carried out its part of the treaty, he was authorized "to shorten the discussion by consenting to the execution of it on the part of my sovereign." Hammond, as Jefferson later told it to Madison, "smiled at the idea," as well he might, but Jefferson also reported him as having "acknoleged explicitly that his court had hitherto heard one side of the question only, & that from prejudiced persons, that it was now for the first time discussed, that it was placed on entirely new ground, his court having no idea of a charge of first infraction on them, and a justification on that ground of what had been done by our states, that this made it quite a new case to which no instructions he had could apply." That Hammond actually acknowledged any such thing is inconceivable. It is plausible, however, that Jefferson could persuade himself that he had.[114]

As for whether Hamilton was undercutting Jefferson's negotiations, there is not much ground for judgment; the kind of diplomacy Jefferson was engaged in virtually guaranteed that there would be no negotiations at all. Hamilton recognized this, and in his usual style stepped in, at which point the only thing approaching negotiations — assuming the aim to be something beyond a test of strength, a show of rectitude, or a stalemate — was being carried on through him. At one point in particular he represented American interests far more effectively than Jefferson. St. Clair's defeat had revived in the British ministry thoughts of mediation and the creation of an Indian buffer state, and Hammond in May received new instructions to broach this idea. Hammond was certain that such a thing was out of the question, but decided to "risque an experiment." He tried it out on Hamilton, who "replied briefly and coldly, that he wished me to understand that any plan, which comprehended any thing like a cession of territory or right or the allowance of any other power to interfere in the disputes with the Indians, would be considered by this government as absolutely impracticable and inadmissible."[115] When the British minister wanted to know whether a thing was or was not unreasonable, he found the Secretary of the Treasury a better guide than the Secretary of State.

Back in London, the British government's concern with the United States was, as usual, no more than marginal. The Indian buffer scheme, for example, was one of those inspirations, whereby all inconveniences might be made to vanish, which sometimes occur to officials when their level of concentration is not very high.

For the rest, it was hardly the policy to place impossible obstacles in the way of a settlement, but the Ministry certainly intended to have a *quid pro quo* before turning over the posts. As for the Jefferson-Hammond exchange, this has often been viewed as a duel of skill, with high marks for Jefferson. But the question remains: to what purpose? For what object were these letters written, and what were they intended to accomplish? Jefferson's were designed not for negotiation but for breaking negotiations off, and this was how the British understood the case when it was referred back for study in the summer of 1792. No reply would ever be made. Meanwhile Great Britain was to find herself totally absorbed elsewhere, with the outbreak of war in Europe.[116]

A decade or so later, Oliver Wolcott would pass a number of observations upon the entire episode. "It being evident," he wrote,

> that the non-execution of the Treaty of Peace, was an obstacle to a sincere reconciliation between the *United States* and *Great-Britain*, Mr. JEFFERSON proposed to Mr. HAMMOND an exchange of Notes, in which the mutual complaints of the two countries should be *specifically* detailed . . . and instead of settling a dispute, the two ministers, by the address of Mr. JEFFERSON, were employed in the hopeless undertaking of writing a history of the war, in concert.[117]

The Emergence of Partisan Politics:
The "Republican Interest"

The twelve-month period from the fall of 1791 to the fall of 1792 was marked by the emergence of what could for the first time be clearly discerned as an opposition. The opposition impulse was in reaction to the rising influence of the Treasury over Administration policy, and to the fierce urge of Jefferson and Madison to prevent the completion of Hamilton's grand design. They would partially succeed, and in the course of their efforts all the hostilities that had been accumulating since Hamilton's plans first began unfolding late in 1789 would burst fully into the open in bitter partisan warfare.

But as Hamilton himself viewed the future in the autumn of 1791, he had every reason to hope that the program of national development he had projected two years earlier would be fully enacted into law by the end of the coming session. Except for the temporary impasse over assumption and the brief financial panic of the late summer, he had experienced nothing but success since taking office in 1789. Madison's attempt to prevent the establishment of a national bank had been no more fruitful than his effort to discriminate between original and current holders of Continental securities or his campaign to kill assumption. Moreover, the predictions of Hamilton's critics that the nation's credit would collapse under the huge debt it had assumed were dramatically disproven, first by the sharp improvement of American credit abroad and then by the rapid rise of federal securities at home. And finally, the minister from Great Britain who was about to arrive might well be the instrument for bringing the two countries a step closer to the hoped-for accommodation. Hamilton, of course, had as yet no idea of the frustrations George Hammond would encounter at the hands of Secretary Jefferson.

Only two major items remained to complete Hamilton's program. One was congressional approval of a plan for direct assistance to domestic manufacturing through a system of tariffs and bounties. The other was the establishment of a model manufacturing corporation—financed and organized on a sufficient scale that it might take full advantage of government bounties and new labor-saving machinery, and compete successfully with European manufacturers. Such a corporation, Hamilton reasoned, could furnish inspiration and example to future American industrialists.

I

Hamilton's Industrial Vision

Hamilton's subsequently famous Report on the Subject of Manufactures was submitted to Congress on December 5, 1791. The immediate occasion for it had been an Order of the House, following a recommendation from the President, requesting that the Secretary prepare a plan "for the encouragement and promotion of such manufactories as will tend to render the United States independent of other nations for essential, particularly for military supplies." Whether the original suggestion came from Hamilton or from Washington—who had been keenly interested for some time in the problems of manufacturing—is of minor significance, since the subject itself was an integral part of Hamilton's total design.[1] Hamilton took the occasion to prepare a major policy statement, a labor which occupied him for well over a year. As much a work of theory as a series of particular recommendations, the Report on Manufactures was intended to establish the ground for a systematic fostering of industry by government.

In its theoretical dimension, the report drew upon a variety of elements in contemporary economic thought. But in synthesizing these elements with reference to the American situation, in so many ways without precedent in Western experience, Hamilton's work exhibits certain clear aspects of novelty. In his commitment to the advantages of a mixed economy, together with his concern for the productivity of the nation as a whole, there is a ring of modernity. The one writer of the eighteenth century whose experience and perceptions were in certain ways analogous to Hamilton's was David Hume. Hume had had the advantage of witnessing the process of development in Scotland at a critical point in that country's emergence from an almost total preoccupation with agriculture, and of sensing its implications with somewhat more immediacy than was possible for his successor Adam Smith. Hume's thought, as we have seen, had already made a considerable impression on Hamilton's mind. The Report on Manufactures, with its acute sensitivity to the many benefits that increased manufacturing might bring to an overwhelmingly agricultural economy, is in some respects the most Humean of all Hamilton's papers.

Hamilton was convinced, moreover, that a series of factors had now combined to make the year 1792 an auspicious one in which to launch the final major element of his program. One was the restrictions of foreign countries on American trade; another was the rising threat of war and civil disturbance in Europe. And finally, there was the striking success of funding and assumption and the excellent state of American credit abroad. All of this offered strong attractions to European investors who might be looking for secure fields in which to place their capital.

The report opens with the assertion that restrictions on American trade abroad, together with many indications of rising vitality in manufacturing enterprise at home, not only made the future of American manufacturing much more promising than it once seemed, but also rendered the need for further encouragement of it the more urgent.[2]

"There still are, nevertheless, respectable patrons of opinions, unfriendly to the encouragement of manufactures." Some believed (following the Physiocrats) that agriculture was the most productive form of economic activity under all circumstances; others argued, more sophisticatedly (following Adam Smith), that support of manufacturing would actually subtract from the total wealth of the community. That is, a nation should concentrate on those undertakings in which it had "natural" advantages; otherwise the interests of its most efficient producers would be sacrificed in supporting its less efficient ones. America, in short, should stick to agriculture and let both herself and Europe do what they could do best.[3]

Hamilton allowed Adam Smith to assist him in refuting the Physiocratic side of the argument before turning to question Smith's own doctrines on free trade and laissez faire. He conceded that agriculture had "intrinsically a strong claim to pre-eminence over every other kind of industry," but insisted that this could hardly be justified as a universal rule. To set his theoretical basis, he listed a series of circumstances in which manufacturing establishments might clearly be seen to increase a society's general productivity. The first was Smith's own division-of-labor principle, which in separating "the occupations of the cultivator, from that of the Artificer," results in the saving of time and perfecting of skills, and "augmenting the productive powers of labour." Another is the use of machinery, which saves labor and can be much more widely applied in manufacturing than in agriculture. Still another is the capacity of industry to provide employment to classes of persons who might otherwise be idle, and to others—such as women and children—not normally suited to agricultural labor. Industry might also serve as a stimulus for attracting new and useful classes of immigrants, skilled artisans in particular. A further circumstance—more subtly conceived, and more in the spirit of Hume than of Adam Smith—is the enlargement of scope that industry provided for the diverse talents in society, and yet another is the way in which a more ample field for enterprise stimulates greater exertion. And finally, industry creates a domestic market for agricultural surpluses, which both maintains the farmer's energy and protects him from the uncertainties of foreign markets.[4]

Turning to the argument that under a system of free trade there was no need for a mixed economy, and that America would find it more efficient to keep her workshops in Europe, Hamilton asserted in effect that such a world was not the one in which Americans lived. The real world was one in which foreign restrictions persisted, and in which American demand for foreign manufactures was constant and increasing while foreign demand for American products was fluctuating and unstable. America, therefore, remained under an inherent and chronic disadvantage.[5]

An allied argument, central to the doctrines of Adam Smith, was that "industry, if left to itself, will naturally find its way to the most useful and profitable employment," removing any need for government encouragement. But such an argument overlooks the deadening force of habit and custom. People do not easily make a "spontaneous transition to new pursuits," nor are "cautious sagacious capitalists" normally disposed to sink their money in uncertain ventures. Thus the "incitement and patronage of government" were needed both to overcome old habits and to embolden reluctant investors. It was necessary, moreover, to help manufacturing enterprises over their initial obstacles, which in the present case were the more exaggerated by the assistance which foreign competitors were receiving from their own governments. Adam Smith's principles, in short, tended throughout to rest on assumptions of "other things being equal," while Hamilton persistently stressed the ways in which things were generally not equal.[6]

The theoretical section of the report reaches its culmination with Hamilton's effort to show that scarcity of capital is not a valid objection to a wide-scale launching of industrial enterprise. Among the remedies are the introduction of banks, with their "powerful tendency to extend the active Capital of a Country," as well as the attractions of America for foreign investors, both having already been demonstrated by experience. Hamilton's principal counter-argument, however, is a defense of the funded debt, the existence of which "relieves from all inquietude on the score of want of Capital." He insists that the funded debt, though not in itself an augmentation of the country's real wealth, is nonetheless a powerful instrument for bringing such augmentation about. The taxes required for servicing the debt may, if the debt is not excessive, serve as a stimulus to greater exertions throughout the community. The public debt, moreover, can be a medium—freely transferable as it is—for making foreigners invest indirectly in American manufacturing when they might not be persuaded to do so directly. That is, the debt itself is a profitable investment, but a bond sold in Europe is an importation to America of specie which, invested in machinery, will ultimately bring profits greater than the interest on the bond. The funded debt, in short, functions for the entire community "in like manner as money borrowed by a thrifty farmer, to be laid out in the improvement of his farm may, in the end, add to his Stock of real riches."[7]

Hamilton now makes the general assertion—which in a modern developing state would be taken as a matter of course—that a mixed economy is "more lucrative and prosperous" than a purely agricultural one. The demand for its agricultural products is more stable than it would be in the case of exclusive dependence on foreign markets. It offers a more diversified, and therefore more attractive, market for foreign customers. It is less vulnerable to, and less likely to be injured by, market fluctuations. The balance of trade normally favors a mixed economy over an agricultural one, since "importations of manufactured supplies seem invariably to drain the merely Agricultural people of their wealth." Nor does encouragement of a country's manufacturing necessarily operate at the expense of its agriculture. Particular encouragements to particular manufactures may appear to "sacrifice the interests of landholders to those of manufacturers" (Hamilton was thinking of a possible conflict of interest between North and South in the United States); but "the aggregate prosperity of manufactures, and the aggregate prosperity of Agriculture are intimately connected."[8]

Hamilton concludes by recommending a combination of tariffs, bounties, and premiums on specific manufactured products. The proposals themselves were modest, but the overall intention was an explicit policy of active government support of industrial growth for the benefit of the entire country.[9]

Hamilton was certainly impressed by Adam Smith's case for releasing the energies of the merchant-entrepreneur, but whereas Smith was concerned that the entrepreneur not be hampered by "unnatural" restrictions, Hamilton also sensed that he had some very "natural" inhibitions, and that to overcome them he needed in the beginning not only freedom but positive encouragement. It would be misleading, on the other hand, to picture Hamilton as conjuring up a kind of "neo-mercantilism." Mercantilism was a conscious policy of controlling the economy for purposes of state; Hamilton's purpose was a temporary stimulation of key sectors in an effort to mobilize the energies of the entire community—which made his primarily an economic rather than a political conception. It would be equally misleading to connect Hamilton too closely with the protective-tariff theorists of the early nineteenth century, much as they may have looked to him for inspiration. His ends were more complex than theirs, and went well beyond simple protection. (Indeed, a nineteenth-century Hamilton would in all likelihood have been a free trader: he did not think it well that any interest should become too settled and comfortable.) More illuminating are the mid-eighteenth-century writings of David Hume, who was very sensitive to the energizing functions of urban and industrial expansion, and was less willing than Adam Smith to leave such growth to the workings either of people's natural reason or of impersonal "laws."[10]

But even Hume's thought, valuable though it is as a touchstone for Hamilton's, operated within certain limits. Hume certainly appreciated the effect of mercantile energy upon a lethargic agricultural community, and understood its workings as a sociological phenomenon rather than as the movements of an invisible hand. But an undeveloped continent of vast resources, with no limits on the production of food, was never the immediate reality for him that it was for Hamilton, nor was he historically situated, as Hamilton was, to influence events.

A basic assumption of traditional economics was always a kind of equilibrium of resources, within which the key problem was their most effective distribution. Only recently, as Peter Drucker has put it, have "proper economists accepted the purposeful creation of dynamic disequilibrium as possible and meaningful." In the Report on Manufactures, and in his hopes for an industrial complex at the falls of the Passaic, such "dynamic disequilibrium" was exactly what Hamilton had in mind. That is, the appearance of substantial manufacturing enterprises would not only function as salutary examples; they would summon into being enterprises yet more highly differentiated, call upon unused resources, create hitherto unsuspected demands, and give new directions to old pursuits. Thus, Hamilton declared, "the bowels as well as the surface of the earth are ransacked for articles which were before neglected. Animals, Plants and Minerals acquire an utility and value, which were before unexplored."[11]

The Society for Establishing Useful Manufactures was to be the practical embodiment of Hamilton's theoretical projection. The Society had in fact come into being a little before the report itself was issued, its initial organization having occurred between July and November, when an act of incorporation was passed by the New Jersey legislature. The actual promotion was undertaken by others, but the plan itself was primarily the work of Hamilton, who probably both wrote the prospectus and drafted the chartering bill. He was zealously aided in the details by his Assistant Secretary of the Treasury, Tench Coxe.[12] Though Hamilton was never an official of the corporation, or even a shareholder in it, the Society was nonetheless the synthesis of his most cherished hopes, and the time, attention, and support he devoted to it were considerable.

The immediate objects of the Society were to purchase land (seven hundred acres would shortly be acquired along the Passaic River); to lay out a town; erect buildings, both for dwelling houses and for "manufactories"; set up machinery; engage skilled artisans and other workers; and begin operations as soon as possible. Among the articles to be manufactured were paper, cardboard, sailcloth, cottons and linens, printed cloth, blankets, carpets, thread, ribbons, stockings, women's shoes, straw hats, pottery and earthenware, and brass and iron wire. There might also be "a brewery for the supply of the manufacturers." Such an extended establishment, if it prospered, would have no end of lively consequences for future enterprise everywhere.[13]

The authorized capital stock was set at $500,000, with the liberty of subsequently increasing it to $1,000,000. There was an initial capital subscription of $100,000 in July and August 1791, and when the books were opened to the public in late September the remainder was subscribed in a matter of days. Among the leading subscribers were Elias Boudinot, Nicholas Low, William Constable, Matthew Clarkson, Andrew Craigie, Alexander Macomb, John Pintard, Jonathan Dayton, Richard Stockton, Brockholst, Henry, and Philip Livingston, and the highly influential William Duer.[14]

The next step was to persuade the New Jersey legislature to grant the Society a generous charter; this too was accomplished with gratifying success. On November 22, 1791, Governor William Paterson signed the bill that would establish a new town, named in his honor. Directors were chosen, and Colonel Duer was elected "governor" of the corporation. Hamilton himself was commissioned by the group to secure the services of skilled foreigners to superintend the various branches of manufacture.[15]

Thus amid the cheer of the Christmas season, things must have looked exceedingly bright to Alexander Hamilton. His formidable report, on which he had worked so long and assiduously, was finished and had been presented to Congress. The Society for Establishing Useful Manufactures—the S.U.M. for short—had been triumphantly set in motion. The temporary financial disturbances of August were a distant memory, as federal securities continued to rise in value along with

Bank stock and the scrip of the S.U.M. Indeed, by January S.U.M. scrip, having originally sold for \$19.91 per share, would reach \$50.00.[16]

And yet the new year of 1792 was to bring a melancholy harvest of disappointments. Probably unknown to Hamilton, a number of the S.U.M.'s leading promoters — including its own governor, William Duer — were by this time already unloading part or all of their subscriptions at a snug profit. This was the very class of men whose imagination and energy Hamilton most counted on to bring his own vision to fulfillment. But while Hamilton dreamed of broad economic development and expanding national wealth, their concerns turned out to be limited to scarcely more than immediate speculative gains. By the early spring of 1792, their doings would constitute for the Secretary of the Treasury an oppressive burden. Meanwhile Hamilton faced a threat even closer at hand: the purposeful movements, directed at himself and all his policies, of Thomas Jefferson and James Madison.

2
Madison Revises *The Federalist*

The emergence of so many new national states in the second half of the twentieth century — in a number of cases amid revolutionary circumstances — has made for a new sensitivity to problems of national economic development. But there has arisen a parallel interest, as Richard Hofstadter has observed, "in the general phenomena of political development" as well. The pertinence of both questions to our own early history is clearer now than it once was; it might even be said that not until recently have the questions themselves been formulable in any broad general way, and this is nearly as much the case in the political realm as in the economic.[17]

Though there has been a tendency in the past to take opposition parties as being inherent, it is now obvious that in a revolutionary state such parties do not emerge without severe resistance. The experience of the United States, moreover, represents the first major instance of this principle in modern history. And the uncertain future of the new republic, reared as it was upon revolution, was not the only factor that made for powerful inhibitions against the forming of parties. Such inhibitions were also supported by a whole system of political beliefs and doctrine that long antedated the Revolution, reaching well back into early eighteenth-century England, in which party and faction in any form were seen as disruptive, subversive, and wicked. Consequently, any public man of probity and conscience in the America of the 1790s who engaged in factional politics would have had to persuade himself, not to say others, that what he was doing in practice did not controvert a theoretical view to which everyone, himself included, subscribed. Such was the dilemma faced by James Madison, and Madison's response to it resulted not only in certain shocking new elements of political practice, but also in a minor — though highly significant — modification of theory.

Madison and Jefferson had spent much of the spring and summer of 1791 laying the basis for a systematic effort to obstruct Hamilton's program and to curtail his influence with Congress and the President. Madison himself was prepared to continue his arguments in the House against a constitutional interpretation so broad that under it Hamilton might do anything he pleased. But his and Jefferson's activities went well beyond those appropriate simply to opposing specific measures in Congress. They had tested the political sentiments of various notables throughout the country, with an eye to possible regional alliances. They had expended much anxious effort in persuading Philip Freneau to come to Philadelphia and establish a "republican" newspaper there which might have a national circulation, and had then been active in soliciting support for Freneau's paper, which began publication on October 31, 1791, as the *National Gazette*. These were movements—at least by hindsight—that were preliminary to, and characteristic of, the formation of a political party.

"The idea of a legitimate opposition—recognized opposition, organized and free enough in its activities to be able to displace an existing government by peaceful means—is an immensely sophisticated idea," as Professor Hofstadter has written, and it was for practical purposes not even in existence at the time of the republic's founding. On the contrary, the "root idea" one finds regarding the place of parties in eighteenth-century Anglo-American thought "is that parties are evil." It was believed that society should be as much as possible an organic whole, characterized by harmony and like-mindedness; parties created unnatural conflicts and aggravated natural ones; and the disruptions they caused in the political order could lead successively to instability, anarchy, and tyranny. Parties and factions— the words were used interchangeably, though "faction" was an even worse form of "party"—were denounced from both left and right. Attacks came not only from such radical Whigs as Trenchard and Gordon in the 1720s, but also from Lord Bolingbroke's "Patriot" resistance to the Walpole regime in the 1730s. The simplest and most orthodox view was associated with Bolingbroke, whose *Idea of a Patriot King* pictured a transcendently benign ruler above petty considerations of party who could, without resorting to tyranny, subdue the spirit of party through wise and disinterested statecraft. In America Bolingbroke made quite an impression on a number of the Founders, Madison included.[18]

But in the Bolingbrokean view the hope was still cherished that party might somehow, though admittedly only in an ideal setting, be eliminated; whereas there was a variant view that impressed Madison even more. This was David Hume's "necessary evil" version of parties. Parties and factions are bad, but in a free state they are inevitable and not to be destroyed without destroying liberty itself. The evils of faction are best endured by restricting the damage factions might do, and this can be accomplished through balanced government, a large republic in which a multiplicity of interests—and hence of parties—will check one another, and a climate of moderation which can limit the range of contentions to those based merely on interest, and discourage those based on principle, which can tear the community apart. This argument, as has been seen, strongly permeated Madison's Federalist Number 10.[19]

And yet the actual state of things that Madison confronted in early 1792 was one to which the Humean view, and his own of *The Federalist*, were no longer wholly adequate. Madison in *The Federalist* had been far more fearful of potentially tyrannous majorities than of either obstructive or unduly influential minorities, nor had there been any place in his argument for a majority coalition through which to assert a legitimate majority will. The influence of Hamilton and his followers now presented a situation that called for a remedy, not only in fact but in theory. Madison was not likely to go as far as Edmund Burke, whose assigning of a positive function to parties found little support in America, but he certainly must have agreed at least with Burke's famous aphorism: "When bad men combine, the good must associate; else they will fall, one by one, an unpitied sacrifice in a contemptible struggle."[20]

Madison's immediate incentive was, of course, the galling frustration he and Jefferson were experiencing in the face of Hamilton's success. A less direct incentive—or perhaps more accurately, a psychological cushion against the implications of what he was about to do—was furnished by the political situation in Virginia. Virginia, having formed so much of Madison's own world-view and system of values, had always imposed herself heavily upon his conscience and spirit. Antifederalist Virginia had in the past caused him much suffering, with the obstacles she had placed in the way of ratifying the Constitution and later the Bill of Rights, to say nothing of the personal cut of having denied him a seat in the Senate and nearly done him out of one in the House. Nor had Virginia been much pleased over the bargain Madison had helped to make on assumption, and the Assembly in 1790 had actually passed a resolution pronouncing assumption unconstitutional. But Madison had been changing, and Virginia was changing toward him, though it would still be quite wrong to think of Madison's rising opposition to Hamiltonian policies throughout 1791 merely as a steady adjustment to political pressure from Virginia. It was rather that the point was being approached at which old issues were fading, and that for the first time since the Revolution a full spiritual reconciliation between James Madison and his native state—his "country," as Virginians had always called it—was at hand.

Madison might by this time, had he wished, have behaved quite differently; he might actually have accorded the Hamiltonian program at least a qualified support without incurring punitive political consequences at home. In terms of specific "interest" Virginia, as things were turning out, really had little cause for complaint. The federal contribution as a result of assumption was substantial, and would enable the state to cut taxes the following year; wheat prices rose steadily in the winter of 1790–91; even the Assembly vote on assumption, largely the work of the choleric Patrick Henry, was hardly overwhelming and represented no serious determination beyond a statement for the record; and there were even some Virginians who were prepared to concede that Hamiltonian finance had its benefits.[21]

But this was on the crass level of interest; on that of principle, Virginia was ideologically as solid as ever in its detestation of speculators and in its fear of an overly "consolidated" national government controlled by "eastern" influence. All of which meant that in their state of mind and feeling there was little that now separated the generality of Virginians—former Antifederalists and Federalists alike—from James Madison.

A significant symbolic act was performed in January 1791 by George Mason, probably the most respected Antifederalist leader in Virginia. Writing to Jefferson at that time, Mason, long at odds with Madison, made a point of asking Jefferson to present his "best Respects to our Friend Mr. Madison," and to assure him of his high esteem despite late differences "on political questions." Jefferson responded with alacrity. "I have always heard him say," he told Mason, "that tho you and he appeared to differ in your systems, yet you were in truth nearer together than most persons who were classed under the same appellation."[22] Whatever this may have meant to Madison in the way of spiritual release, it implied something even more to a man about to form a political party. He could imagine himself doing it not so much among a precariously divided public as in the bosom of a great geographical province, like-minded and organically united as an eighteenth-century community was ideally expected to be, and with which he himself was ideologically in harmony for the first time in many years. Nothing could have fortified a new feeling for the legitimacy of majorities more than being in the midst of one, nor better ratified the propriety of organizing all possible means to resist what he was fully disposed to see as an alien, perverse, unnatural, and dangerous minority.

There remained, to be sure, a powerful checking factor, in addition to the accumulated authority of anti-party doctrine, and this was the figure of George Washington. Washington, the living symbol of non-partisan politics, was an almost ideal republican embodiment of the Patriot King. In challenging Hamilton, one took the political as well as the psychological risk of challenging the President as well. This was a dilemma the Jeffersonian Republicans would never quite resolve as long as Washington remained alive.

Madison began his new course of theorizing with a series of essays in Freneau's *National Gazette,* three weeks after the paper was established. The first few were rather in the nature of a warm-up. There was one on the consolidation of government: "justly to be avoided," though another kind of consolidation should prevail "throughout the great body of the people" so that in the face of usurpation they might "interpose a common manifestation of their sentiments." In a piece on public opinion he approved, as "favorable to liberty," anything that "facilitates a general intercourse of sentiments," such as "a *circulation of newspapers through the entire body of the people,* and *Representatives going from, and returning among every part of them."* Another on government warned of the dangers of monarchy and aristocracy, and the vigilance thus required of every citizen to preserve the benefits of a republic and "the idea of popular rights." Still another declared that liberty demanded strict adherence to charters and constitutions, and that public opinion "should guarantee, with a holy zeal, these political scriptures from every attempt to add to or diminish from them." And finally, on January 23, 1792, comes Madison's first statement on "Parties."[23]

He begins with the simple declaration that in "every political society, parties are unavoidable." The "evil" of parties is perfunctorily conceded, not by saying a single word about what the evil consists of, but by proceeding directly to outline how it may be combated. First: "By establishing political equality among all." (No group should have influence out of proportion to its numbers.) Second: "By withholding *unnecessary* opportunities from a few, to increase the inequality of property, by an immoderate, and especially unmerited, accumulation of riches." (No need to guess whom he has in mind.) Third and fourth (in case we missed it the first time): "By the silent operation of laws, which, without violating the rights of property, reduce extreme wealth towards a state of mediocrity, and raise extreme indigence towards a state of comfort," and "By abstaining from measures which operate differently on different interests, and particularly such as favor one interest, at the expence of another." And finally, the key statement: "By making one party a check on the other, so far as the existence of parties cannot be prevented, nor their views accommodated. — If this is not the language of reason, it is that of republicanism." (Whatever other political theorists may say, republicanism can only be preserved by balancing one party against the other.)

Whereas in *The Federalist* Madison had assumed a multiplicity of interests and a corresponding multiplicity of parties, it now seems that the "natural" number ("one party," "the other") is two. And he hastens to add that just because checks and balances are a good thing, it does not follow that such checks need be multiplied through "artificial distinctions" such as "*kings* and *nobles,* and *plebeians,*" which would be like creating new vices to "counteract each other," whereas we can do that with the vices we already have. Parties are still a necessary evil. But in Madison's mind the emphasis is now mainly on "necessary."[24]

In another essay, "The Union: Who Are Its Real Friends?" Madison takes a step toward defining current cases. He does not use the word "party" here at all; the rubric "friends of the Union" is his device for asking how, if parties *were* to appear among us, we should discern them, and he answers himself by first characterizing the men who are *not* "friends of the Union." They are those who favor "pampering the spirit of speculation," "unnecessary accumulations of the debt," "arbitrary interpretations" of the Constitution, and "principles of monarchy and aristocracy, in opposition to . . . the republican spirit of the people." The Union's "real friends" are friends of "the authority of the people," of "liberty, the great end, for which the Union was formed," and of "limited and republican" government. They are, moreover, "enemies to every public measure that might smooth the way to hereditary government"; they regard "a public debt as injurious to the interests of the people and baneful to the virtue of government"; and they are against "every contrivance for unnecessarily increasing its amount, or protracting its duration, or extending its influence."

"In a word . . . the real friends of the Union" are "friends to republican policy throughout . . . in opposition to a spirit of usurpation and monarchy. . . ." Here, Madison comes one step short of saying, is your choice of parties.[25]

Then, in "A Candid State of Parties," he *does* take the step. He names the Union's friends and enemies as "parties," and places the entire problem in what he now sees as its proper historical setting. Not only are parties "natural"; they have actually existed since before the Revolution, first as Patriots and Tories, then as Federalists and Antifederalists (most Federalists were sincere republicans, but some were "openly or secretly attached to monarchy," while most Antifederalists, though they opposed the Constitution, were "certainly well affected to the Union and to good government"), and now the most "natural" state of all (the others having been superseded by time and events, and old issues having become irrelevant): "republicans" and "anti-republicans." The former, clearly, are the Union's "real friends."

The "real state of parties" having now been established, Madison goes on to consider "the probable conduct of each." The anti-republicans, "being the weaker in point of numbers," will of course seek "to strengthen themselves with the men of influence, particularly of moneyed, which is the most active and insinuating influence," and "to weaken their opponents by reviving exploded parties" and keeping old issues alive so that a true coalescence of general sentiment might be prevented. "The republican party," however, "conscious that the mass of people in every part of the union . . . must at bottom be with them, both in interest and sentiment, will naturally find their account in burying all antecedent questions, in banishing every other distinction than that between enemies and friends to republican government. . . ."

Which party shall prevail? Time will tell; "stratagem is often an overmatch for numbers," but on the republican side "the superiority of numbers is so great, their sentiments are so decided," that one may expect to see the time at last when the government shall "be administered in the spirit and form approved by the great body of the people."[26]

The theoretical view of parties set forth by David Hume and by Publius— Madison's own former self—has not been abrogated, but Madison's new formulation certainly represents a very important amendment to it. As to which direction, it cannot quite be said that the movement is unequivocally "forward." If Madison has taken a step toward "the idea of a party system," he has taken it in an ambiguous and even misleading way. We must deal with things, he rightly says, as they really are, recognizing that parties are with us and acting accordingly. Moreover, it is no longer overbearing majorities that are bad, but unnatural and designing minorities. With good reason he has redefined the normal state as a division between two parties rather than among several. But in so doing, he has set aside one of Hume's most important cautions. Hume saw a multiplicity of parties as corresponding to a multiplicity of interests, and assumed the advantage of such a state was that party maneuvering might *ipso facto* be limited to contentions of interest, adjustable through compromise and thereby prevented from growing into irreconcilable divisions of principle. Madison, however, is here asserting that a state of parties based on principle is precisely the state in which we should accept them, the struggle being hardly less than one between good and evil. The "evils of party" have thus been drastically relocated. They reside not in "parties" but in *one* of the parties, and the real evil—no longer figurative but palpable and visible—is even more monstrous than hitherto imagined.

So the bad party can never be seen as legitimate, and in this sense we are as far from the idea of a party system as ever. Indeed, with regard to the evolution of theory Madison has in at least one respect taken a step not toward the future but toward the past. Just as Bolingbroke envisioned a golden age, ushered in by the Patriot King, in which all parties were dissolved, so Madison's golden age was one in which "republicans" would overwhelm "anti-republicans" and render all further parties superfluous. That, to be sure, would be only after the struggle was over. Now, the struggle was just beginning.

No man, even James Madison, could have had the motive to make alterations in theory of this particular nature, and at this particular time, without being something more than simply a theoretician. In redefining the struggle of parties, and specifying the character of the evils to be combated, Madison was announcing a personal commitment. He was functioning not only as theoretician but also as a partisan.

A special and separate dimension of these essays—eighteen in all, spanning a period of about one year—is as a very full index to the ideology, the system of prejudices and beliefs, of the emerging Republican party. The attitudes, already mentioned, on speculation, the public debt, consolidation, and strict construction are spelled out in numerous combinations. Then there is an essay on husbandry that is almost a perfect echo of Jefferson's *Notes on Virginia:* "The class of citizens who provide at once their own food and their own raiment, may be viewed as the most truly independent and happy. They are more: they are the best basis of public liberty, and the strongest bulwark of public safety." They are exempt from the "distresses and vice of overgrown cities," and it follows "that the greater the proportion of this class to the whole society, the more free, the more independent, and the more happy must be the society itself." (And any form of "manufacturing and mechanical industry," Madison significantly adds, "forced or fostered by public authority," should be judged accordingly.) The strain of anglophobia, moreover, runs as deep as ever. Great Britain is the home of monarchy and aristocracy, of corruption, of Bridewell and Bedlam, of "fashion and superfluity," and of manufacturing, which of all occupations produces "the most servile dependence of one class . . . on another." And finally, in the animus against speculators (with their "unnecessary opportunities" to increase "inequality of property") and in the newly seen values of majoritarianism, Madison on behalf of his party has staked first claim upon what would in time emerge as the master symbol of an entire culture. He was making a tentative, and in certain ways accidental, first approximation to equalitarian democracy.[27]

Madison's final essay of the *National Gazette* series appeared on December 20, 1792, and the year that had elapsed between it and his first was also the critical year in which people generally first began to talk of parties. The piece is framed as a dialogue between "Republican" and "Anti-republican," and the question they debate is: "Who are the best Keepers of the People's Liberties?" They are, Republican announces, "The people themselves." "The people," retorts Anti-republican, "are stupid, suspicious, licentious. They cannot safely trust themselves. When they have established government they should think of nothing but obedience, leaving the care of their liberties to their wiser rulers." As for government, "enrich it with influence, arm it with force," and establish "two grand hereditary orders, with feelings, habits, interests, and prerogatives all inveterately hostile to the rights and interests of the people, yet by a *mysterious* operation all combining to fortify the people in both." Republican protests in horror, as well he might, and Anti-republican thereupon thunders: "You are destitute, I perceive, of every quality of a good citizen, or rather of a good *subject*. . . . I denounce you to the government as an accomplice of atheism and anarchy." "And I forbear," responds Republican with dignity (getting the last word), "to denounce you to the people, though a blasphemer of their rights and an idolater of tyranny. — Liberty disdains to persecute."[28]

This, of course, had little to do with theory; it was undiluted polemic, uttered by James Madison in his new role as partisan. The rhetoric had taken on a country-party tone not unlike the Antifederalist forensics of the previous decade. Nor was this any accident; Madison, with his words about "burying all antecedent questions," was making explicit tactical overtures for Antifederalist support. But the talk about "monarchy" and "anti-republicanism" is still intriguing. There was small likelihood of anyone's setting up a monarchy in the American republic, and no critical observer should have had much difficulty perceiving this at the time. Could Madison have been sincere? He unquestionably was, though these specters were certainly not being generated by the same part of his mind that had produced *The Federalist*.

But beyond all this, the key fact may well be that at this indistinct stage of party formation there were as yet no rules at all, and no sense of limits within which suspicion and even hate were to be graded and controlled. Parties could not yet be conceived as other than alliances for a warfare in which the stakes were no less than survival or extinction — and certainly not as alternating associative structures through which to manage the affairs of government. Even the choice of weapons was unclear, to say nothing of how effective any of them might be. ("Strategem is often an overmatch for numbers.") Under such circumstances the coolest minds may be unsettled, as is shown by the case of James Madison. The same thing, of course, would happen to Alexander Hamilton.

3

Hamilton Beleaguered

Throughout American history two classes of events in particular have always succeeded both in creating great public shock and in bringing about — at least temporarily — a solemn re-examination of first principles. One is unexpected military defeat, the other a financial panic, and in late 1791 and early 1792 Americans were subjected to both. Thus in place of the expansively receptive climate which would have been the very minimum condition for support of a broad government program of encouragement to domestic manufacturing, the public mood was possessed by something very different. The rout of St. Clair's army by the Indians, and then the money panic of March 1792 — with their consequences and the emotions they produced — probably destroyed between them any likelihood there may have been of such a program's being undertaken, or even seriously considered. The Report on Manufactures was not acted upon at all, and the Society for the Establishment of Useful Manufactures sustained reverses in the course of the year from which it would never recover. The setting, moreover, was one in which a variety of prior inhibitions against political partisanship might be, and in fact were, rudely jarred loose. "Success," wrote Fisher Ames, "is poison to party zeal."[29] Adversity had the very opposite effect.

Washington received St. Clair's first dispatches late on Friday, December 9, and communicated the melancholy details to Congress on Monday morning. A surprise attack on St. Clair's camp before dawn on November 4 had resulted in the American forces' being all but surrounded. Their ineffectual counterattacks were beaten back with fearful slaughter, and their eventual withdrawal degenerated into headlong flight, the militia flinging away their arms even after the Indians had ceased to pursue them. There were over nine hundred casualties out of a force of some fourteen hundred, and only about 580 men found their way back to Fort Washington, St. Clair's base on the Ohio River. Nothing so humiliating had occurred since Braddock's defeat more than thirty-five years before. "We are all miserable here," wrote Governor Henry Lee of Virginia to James Madison, and Lee begged his friend for "any saving circumstances" he might know of to ease his despair. "I regret," came the reply, "that I can administer no balm to the wound given by the first report of our western disaster."[30]

Soon after the first news broke a report appeared, and circulated for a few hopeful days, that fifteen hundred mounted volunteers from Kentucky were in the field and would shortly strike at the Miami settlements. But the rumor proved baseless, and the brief spell of wishful thinking gave way to lamentations and recriminations, all mixed in together and with little consistency, in letters to newspapers, speeches in Congress, and editorial outpourings.[31]

One surprisingly conspicuous argument was that Americans had done wrong by the Indians. "Is the war with the Indians a *just* one? . . . Have they not the same rights to their hunting grounds (which afford them their only means of subsistence) that we have to our houses and farms?" Yet it is not likely that such sentiments, which came principally from the Northeast, had "justice" as their primary motive. Easterners were already beginning to fret at the thought of an unregulated flow of settlement westward, and it would not be many years before fears of depopulation of the seaboard were to constitute a major theme in the utterances of political spokesmen for New England. Hostility to speculators also found its way into the criticism. "Let offensive operations cease," declared the *Connecticut Courant.* "They are calculated for land jobbers merely. . . ." Rumors of an army draft, the *Boston Gazette* jeeringly claimed, had resulted in "upwards of *Three Hundred*" speculators leaving town—men generally known "by the Name of Paper-Hunters, or Hamilton's *Rangers*."[32]

Another line of argument was to blame the British. As long as British forces were suffered to occupy posts in the Northwest Territory there would never be peace with the Indians. "Let our rulers . . . determine to break the disgraceful chain with which our northern frontiers are bound." Still another was to lament the expense of using regular troops for forest warfare. Militia and rangers would be cheaper and better; "they are, in fact, the only force that can be effectually employed in expeditions against the hostile Indians, whose mode of fighting is familiar to them."[33]

The majority feeling, however, was that the Indians had not been treated unjustly, that local militia could not adequately deal with them, that regular troops were called for, that a new and more vigorous campaign was necessary, and that it was essential to augment the present army in order to carry it out. The leadership for such views tended to come from areas that had close connections with the frontier, such as Virginia and western Pennsylvania. A long and energetic letter from Hugh Henry Brackenridge of Pittsburgh, who had no use for Indians, was made the lead article in the February 2 issue of Freneau's *National Gazette*. "All treaty with them until they are humbled and reduced," Brackenridge declared, "is absurd." "As to myself," Thomas Jefferson had written to Washington before the campaign, "I hope we shall give the Indians a thorough drubbing this summer," and he seems not to have changed his mind after St. Clair's defeat. Indeed, the Virginians gave fairly solid support in Congress—despite their grumblings about economy and their hostility to standing armies—to a substantial strengthening, at considerable cost, of the country's military force for the purpose of pacifying the Indians. The bill was passed in the House on February 1, 1792.[34]

Meanwhile there continued to be, as Timothy Pickering put it, "much murmuring on account of the manner in which the western war has been planned and conducted." Secretary of War Knox was the target of a good deal of this, though criticism of the strictly military side of the case tended to abate somewhat with the resignation of St. Clair as major-general, the appointment of Anthony Wayne in his place, and the government's clear determination to make fresh exertions. But the most sensational disclosure that emerged from a congressional investigation into the causes of the disaster—especially in view of mounting feeling against merchants and speculators generally—involved the shoddy doings of army contractors. The committee's report was a story of "fatal mismanagements and neglects" on the part of the suppliers, of insufficient rations, arms "totally unfit for use," and packsaddles and other equipment "deficient in quantity and bad in quality." The chief contractor had been none other than William Duer, the prince of speculators.[35]

William Duer, truly a symbolic figure, may be seen as the embodiment of every force, attribute, and instinct in the world of commerce most guaranteed in the year 1792 to bring that world under the darkest of clouds. Duer was the archetype, the man whose example showed better than almost anyone else's how it was that men of the marketplace—the marketplace of money in particular—could so inexorably draw down upon themselves the worst suspicions of every other element in society.

Duer's early career has about it an attractiveness reminiscent of other energetic young men who first came to public attention and made their mark in the Revolution. Born in 1747, Duer was the son of a West Indian planter who had large holdings in Antigua and Dominica. His relish for business first manifested itself at the age of twenty-one when he secured a contract—probably through family connections—for supplying masts and spars to the Royal Navy. This brought him to New York, where he met and was accepted by such personages as William Alexander ("Lord Stirling") and Philip Schuyler. He liked America, bought a large tract on the upper Hudson, built a mansion there, and erected several mills. He was made a justice of the peace and became a colonel in the local militia. All his American friends, as well as his own family in the West Indies, were Whigs, which probably meant that William Duer was never once troubled, during the onset of the Revolution, with the question of where his loyalties should lie.[36] To a man of his sanguine temperament, crises of conscience were almost unnatural.

He was ardently involved from the first. He was a delegate to the New York Provincial Congress in 1775, and in 1776 served with John Jay and Gouverneur Morris on a committee to draft a state constitution. He, Jay, and four others were named in 1777 to a secret "Committee of Correspondence" charged with "detecting and defeating all conspiracies . . . against the liberties of America." Duer seems to have been its most vigorous member, dashing here and there and popping up in dangerous areas like Westchester to assist local partisans in making life difficult for the Loyalists. He went to the Continental Congress in 1777. He was an animated talker, highly active, and served on seven different committees. He was a signer of the Articles of Confederation in 1778, and in that year helped to defeat the notorious Conway Cabal, which doubtless had something to do with the favor he found in the eyes of the commander-in-chief. According to a Tory chief justice of the New York provincial court, William Duer was "as great a rebel as ever had an existence."[37]

Duer was not unmindful, to be sure, of his own fortune during this period. Though he remained in Congress until 1779, he was asking Governor Clinton as early as 1777 to be relieved from duty so that he might attend to his private affairs. His business activities before the war had been profitable; he had a more than comfortable patrimony; and in 1779 he made an excellent marriage. His bride, "Lady Kitty" Alexander, the daughter of "Lord Stirling," was escorted to the altar by General Washington himself. The many connections Duer had now acquired brought him lucrative contracts for supplying the Continental forces, and in the course of these dealings he accumulated large amounts of state and Continental securities, warrants, and soldiers' certificates. "There is good reason to believe," says one of Duer's biographers, "that by the close of the war he was a wealthy man." In 1786 he was appointed secretary to the Board of Treasury of the Confederation government, a post he held until 1789. It was thus wholly logical that in September of that year, when the Federal Treasury was organized, he should be chosen as Hamilton's assistant. He had become, by then, the complete insider.[38]

But for all Duer's talents and energies, and for all the resemblances his early career might bear to those of other able men of his time, there were elements of his character that probably ensured all along against his being finally enrolled in the ranks of the nation-builders. One, for instance, was a rather limited span of attention. New projects, before old ones were quite rounded off, were forever drawing him on, and he always had an alarming number of things going at once. He was gregarious and affable (a portrait of him in early middle life suggests a sleek equanimity);[39] and he liked to do favors and make himself agreeable—as long as it was not too much trouble. He could outline stupendous plans, but there was always a certain carelessness about following up on details, and an appalling laziness about writing letters. Indeed, instinct as well as convenience may have persuaded him that the fewer traces in writing he left of himself and his doings the easier he would be. He lacked, one might say, a true sense of history. He lacked, at any rate, whatever sense it was that kept such men as Jefferson, Hamilton, Madison, and Washington to a certain nicety of standard with regard to duty, and of the account they might one day be rendering for their performance of it. William Duer could seldom think that far ahead. Nor was the line between public duty and private convenience one that he took quite as seriously as did some others. Nevertheless, few figures moved with greater assurance through the world of affairs in the early days of the republic, or seemed to have a better title to do so.

Making substantial profits through regular and large-scale speculation in stocks was still, in those days, a strange and rather unaccustomed business. The prices of public and semi-public securities were not regularly quoted in the newspapers before 1789, and it was not until 1792 that the New York Stock Exchange was formally established. But speculation, with the premium it placed on insidership, secrecy, and moving fast, was the medium in which William Duer's entire being found a kind of natural expression.

It was now the very high noon of Duer's heyday. There is little doubt that his most profitable activities were those involving speculation in federal securities, on his own account and in association with such fellow-spirits as Andrew Craigie and William Constable, and in other combinations the full nature of which will never be known. Duer left the Treasury after seven months, but it may be assumed that the information to which he had access during that critical period was of wonderful benefit both to his friends and to himself. Though little that he did was ever more than fractionally visible, these and various allied ventures in land and contracting (one of which, as noted above, involved the St. Clair expedition) together made up a total impression that was dazzling. It was this picture of mastery—the man of influence, resourcefulness, and almost magical acumen—that made Duer the natural choice in 1791 to be governor of the Society for the Establishment of Useful Manufactures. And the grandeur of his mode of life seemed to ratify everything. "Colonel Duer," a dinner guest once marveled, ". . . lives in the style of a nobleman. I presume he had not less than fifteen different sorts of wine at dinner, and after the cloth was removed, besides most excellent bottled cider, porter, and several other kinds of strong beer."[40]

Still, in all this picture of "success" there was a large element of the fortuitous. The basic condition, as it happened, was a quadrupling in the value of federal stocks between 1789 and 1791. Another was that Duer, with inside information, was of all men in a position to know the direction of things at times when it mattered most. His personal resources, moreover, had always been substantial. And finally, he had the connections that enabled him to organize concentrations of capital quickly for speculative purposes. In such a combination of circumstances it would have been hard *not* to succeed, at least in the short run.

The fact remains, however, that with the full record made up, many—and probably most—of William Duer's enterprises are seen to have been failures. Something, somehow, was always happening to them. It was probably not his fault that an early venture in the midst of the Revolution aborted when a contract for supplying the French navy fell through. But the complaint of Silas Deane, who was supposed to be expediting the project in France, sounded a note that was to echo in different voices throughout many a subsequent dealing: "I have been much disappointed in not receiving a line from you. . . ." While Duer was secretary to the Board of Treasury, one James Jarvis signed a contract—in which Duer demanded a share for himself—for furnishing several hundred tons of copper coins to the Confederation government. That contract also failed, for unknown reasons, but the affair produced an echoing note, also characteristic, which was Duer's telling Jarvis "that it was not proper for him to enter into written engagements."[41]

The "greatest private contract ever made in America" up to that time was Manasseh Cutler's Ohio Company scheme in 1787 for acquiring through installment purchase between five and six million acres of public lands in the Northwest Territory. It was accomplished through Duer's assistance and the use of his official position, and Duer was cut in on it through the formation of a secret group known as the Scioto Company, which would help to organize the necessary capital and promote sales. The collapse of the Scioto project between 1790 and 1792 resulted from a variety of factors. It had been conceived purely as a speculative rather than a colonizing venture, to be paid for in still-depreciated Continental securities. But the steady rise of such securities, with the promise of a stronger government, undermined the speculation from the beginning. Large holders of the debt in foreign countries proved reluctant to exchange their portfolios for tracts of Ohio land, however fertile, which meant that success would require sales in smaller parcels, reaching a vastly wider market, and the promotion of actual settlements to stimulate more settlements. The kind of attention and coordination called for by such an intricate set of variables was quite beyond men of William Duer's type. Frantic letters from agents in Europe went unanswered for months at the very time Duer and his friends were up to their chins in the excitements of funding and assumption. The Scioto scheme, which by the winter of 1791–92 was moribund, netted them nothing.[42] Nor, probably, did Duer realize anything from his contract for supplying St. Clair's army in 1791.[43] That affair was one not of corruption but of inattention and mismanagement—and it coincided in time with the frantic speculations which attended the launching of the National Bank.

The flurry of August 1791, with its gyrations of Bank scrip and public stock which so disgusted Jefferson and Madison, was largely the work of Duer and his fellow operators. Hamilton had to caution him sharply (apparently hurting his feelings), and the Treasury was compelled to enter the market in order to stabilize prices.[44] But Duer, having learned nothing, was at it again in December. Forming a secret partnership with Alexander Macomb, he began borrowing heavily from everyone in sight for the greatest speculation yet. By early 1792 William Duer, with so many things going at once that he could not possibly have kept his eyes on them all, had begun his final race to doom.

In Philadelphia, meanwhile, shadows were beginning to settle over the dreams of Alexander Hamilton. Two tests occurred in February and March of 1792—one on the principle of bounties, and the other on tariffs—which added up to a very broad hint that nothing would come in Congress of Hamilton's design for industry, and indeed that any major plans emanating from the Treasury, on any subject, would have heavy going from then on.

The first occasion concerned a bill for the encouragement of the cod fisheries which came up for debate in the House on February 3. The idea was to assist the hard-pressed fisheries through a tonnage bounty paid directly to owners of vessels in order to offset the duty on salt used in the curing of fish for export. To all intents and purposes the measure was making its appearance under the most favorable of auspices. On the one hand, Jefferson's Fisheries Report of the previous year had recommended some sort of special assistance as one aspect of his and Madison's schemes to strike at British commerce—in this case by restoring the competitive position of the American fisheries in the export market. On the other hand, such a program for the fisheries—ulterior purpose or not—was solidly in the economic interest of New England. The bill itself, which originated in the Senate, was in fact the work of George Cabot of Massachusetts.[45]

There was little disposition to deny that something ought to be done for the fisheries, but the term "bounty" touched off an uproar. William B. Giles of Virginia was "averse to bounties in almost any shape"; they were in a class with "exclusive rights, monopolies, &c."; "occupations that stand in need of bounties, instead of increasing the real wealth of a country, rather tend to lessen it"; and the authority to grant them, if admitted, "would lead to a complete system of tyranny."[46] Hugh Williamson of North Carolina warned: "Establish the doctrine of bounties, [and] . . . all manner of persons—people of every trade and occupation—may enter at the breach, until they have eaten up the bread of our children."[47] Even the members from Massachusetts—those most directly concerned to get the bill passed—found themselves squirming at the word. Gerry urged that "in reality it is no bounty,"[48] and Ames protested that "instead of asking bounties . . . we ask nothing but to give us our money back."[49] "The word "bounty"" lamented Benjamin Goodhue, "is an unfortunate expression, and I wish it were entirely out of the bill."[50]

It was at this point that James Madison stepped in. Madison would have it both ways; he would seek—successfully, as it turned out—both to save the bill and to cast the bounty principle into outer darkness. It would all be done within the framework of another pronouncement on the Constitution, a repetition in briefer scope of his previous year's performance on the occasion of the Bank bill.

"I make a material distinction in the present case," Madison said, "between an allowance as a mere continuation and modification of a drawback, and an allowance in the nature of a real and positive bounty." A bounty, he insisted, could only be granted by Congress "under a power by virtue of which they may do anything which they may think conducive to the general welfare.'" Then he expounded his newly evolved doctrine of limited government, strictly bound to its enumerated powers, and gravely cautioned that

> were the power of Congress to be established in the latitude contended for, it would subvert the very foundation, and transmute the very nature of the limited Government established by the people of America. . . .[51]

The happy solution was to substitute "allowance" every time the word "bounty" appeared, and to pass the bill. This sophistry had the effect of recognizing the fisheries as a special case, and at the same time giving the *coup de grâce* to that entire aspect of Hamilton's report which envisioned a comprehensive system of bounties on industrial products. "This is the Virginia style," wrote the long-suffering Fisher Ames to a friend back home. "It is chiefly aimed at the report of the Secretary of the Treasury on the subject of manufactures."[52]

The other test, on the principle of protective tariffs as a supplement to that of bounties, came with the problem of raising additional revenue to support the enlarged military commitments in the West. It occurred in two phases, each of considerable significance.

It began with the motion, made on March 7, "That the Secretary of the Treasury be directed to report to this House his opinion of the best mode for raising the additional supplies requisite for the ensuing year." This was a procedure that had been regularly followed in accordance with the Act of 1789 establishing the Treasury, the passage of which had been accomplished principally through the exertions of James Madison. But a former matter of routine now occasioned two days of debate over first principles. The referral was strenuously resisted on the ground that it was "a transfer of Legislative authority" to the Executive; that it was "the peculiar duty of this House, to originate money bills, and to devise ways and means"; and that "such a reference to the Secretary of the Treasury is a dereliction of our duty." Madison, who seems to have organized this opposition, was ready with more distinctions, now saying that his original intention in framing the Act of 1789 had been to distinguish between asking for facts and asking for opinions. But though Theodore Sedgwick mockingly suggested that the Secretary's opinions would not destroy "the independence and purity of the House," John Page of Virginia announced that such a motion as the present one "can be supported on no other principles, but such as may be used to subvert our Government, and to introduce a Monarchy." It passed by the barest majority. Madison "well knew," Hamilton claimed afterward, "that, if he had prevailed, a certain consequence was, my *resignation*. . . ."[53]

When Hamilton complied with the request a week later, and recommended a series of increased import duties for producing the revenue in question, the excited debate began all over again. Did "the submission of a provision to defend the frontier," demanded John Mercer of Maryland, "authorize a system for the encouragement of manufactures?" Why did the House have to consider "extensive duties operating as indirect bounties, under the pressure of providing for an Indian war?"[54] "Sir," Page declared, "it is not a bill for the protection of the frontiers, but for the encouragement of certain manufactures. . . ." The bill passed (Madison voting against), but only as a mode of raising revenue, and not to encourage manufacturing in New Jersey or anywhere else. The duties would not, in any case, prove to be of much benefit to American industry.[55]

But the warmth of congressional proceedings was as nothing compared to the excitement produced by the Panic of 1792 and disclosures of the role William Duer had played in bringing it about.

Duer and Macomb had secretly made it up between them that their partnership would be of one year's duration, and that they would "be concerned in making Speculations in the Debt of the United States, and in the Stock of the Bank . . . of the United States & Bank of New York, to the 31 Decr. 1792." They anticipated a rising market, and may even have attempted to corner it. They made extensive contracts for future delivery, and to pay for them began borrowing sums large and small, at extravagant interest, from all classes in the city. They also laid hands on most of the cash surplus of the S.U.M., of which both were leading directors. This furious activity was contagious, and by February, New York City was in a speculative frenzy. Other eastern cities were affected as well. Stocks, however, did not rise as fast as expected, and by March, Duer, his credit exhausted, was in deep trouble. On the 9th he stopped payment on a number of his obligations.[56]

Under such circumstances Duer's ruin could not have been avoided. But his condition was made manifest, and his downfall thus hastened, by a suit brought against him by the United States Treasury itself. It was for unsettled accounts dating from his service as secretary to the old Board of Treasury, amounting to some $250,000, which he had "suavely postponed" from year to year. The action was initiated by the Comptroller, Oliver Wolcott, and though Duer pleaded with his friend Hamilton to stop it, Hamilton felt that at this point the Treasury had no choice. Duer had been repeatedly pressed to settle, and had repeatedly promised to do so. But now, when to all appearances he was about to go to the wall, the reckoning could be put off no longer. He went to debtor's prison on March 23.[57]

Duer's failure led to other failures, and by early April the city was in the grip of panic. The scarcity of money, the disruption of business, the suspension of building and a variety of other activities, produced scenes of great distress. Macomb went to jail on April 12. Duer in his sanctuary was besieged by maddened creditors, who included not only every important businessman in town, and many elsewhere, but also "shopkeepers, Widows, orphans—Butchers, Cartmen, Gardners, market women, & even the noted Bawd Mrs. Macarty." Mobs threatening to drag him out and disembowel him had to be restrained by "the Mayor Sheriff &c. &c. with their Myrmidons." Duer remained in jail, hopelessly insolvent, for the rest of his days. He died in 1799.[58]

In view of the convulsions produced by the Panic—the first of its kind in our history—recovery occurred in remarkably short order. Some influence toward this end was exerted, as in the previous August, by Treasury purchases for the sinking fund. All in all the damage, though hardly inconsiderable, was not permanent, and by the fall of 1792 things were well on the mend. The atmosphere, nonetheless, had been heavily poisoned. A tendency to ascribe the most extensive evils to Treasury influence, and to see in it a steady perversion of public morals, was now very widespread. Many had come to believe—Jefferson and Madison among them—that Hamilton himself was enmeshed in corruption. There was a direct relation between such convictions and the eruption of open partisanship that occurred in the spring and summer of 1792. The last shred of likelihood, moreover, of general support for a program of encouragement to manufactures had been blown away forever.[59]

A major casualty of 1792 was the Society for the Establishment of Useful Manufactures. Though it was not until afterwards that the Society even got going, and although it continued operations until 1796, the Panic had nonetheless dealt it a mortal blow. The loss of funds through defalcations was serious enough, but even more serious was the problem of momentum and morale. The desperate distractions of those critical months—the directors either in jail or preoccupied with their creditors, sometimes without quorums for monthly meetings, and the company under a heavy cloud of hostile public opinion—meant that the exuberance and élan required at the very least for such an undertaking could never really develop.

Indeed, for more than a generation in the future no large-scale manufacturing enterprises of any sort would be successfully launched in America. Clearly something was missing from the Humean-Hamiltonian projection of a happy mercantile-industrial commonwealth which needed only the capacity to concentrate capital, under the benevolent eye of government, to set it on its way. Why should foresight and reason not have prevailed?

One obvious answer would be the failure of such indispensable elements as management and technology: problems which were not to be mastered in a day, and which in the case of the S.U.M. were being addressed under the worst possible conditions. Hamilton himself, to be sure, acted with great coolness in the crisis of 1792, dispensing much sensible advice on a surprising variety of specific and relatively technical matters. Yet he too made some real blunders, quite aside from his initial support for William Duer as the Society's governor. One of them was the appointment, upon his urging, of Pierre Charles L'Enfant to design the town and supervise the building. L'Enfant, his mind still on baroque cities and having little notion of how to plan factories, wasted much of the Society's money on ill-considered installations, including a canal for water power which if carried through according to his design would have bankrupted the company. He was dismissed in 1793. Another nightmare was Hamilton's recruiting of English artisans to initiate and supervise manufacturing operations. They proved to be an ignorant and bungling lot. There was nothing resembling day-to-day top management anywhere on the ground. Only a fraction of the manufactures originally projected—some spinning, weaving, and calico printing—were actually begun; the machinery was ill designed and ill housed; the processes were a matter of hit or miss; and the products themselves were inferior. When the directors in 1796 voted to shut down altogether to avoid "evident loss," they were putting a period to some four years of amateurishness, cross-purposes, and divided attention.[60] Not until the 1820s and '30s, with the activities of the Boston Associates, would something like what Hamilton envisioned for Paterson come into being. The foundation of Lowell, Chicopee, and Holyoke during that period would be the fruit of careful planning and two decades of prior technological experience in small mills all over New England.

And yet perhaps something deeper than deficiencies of technology and management was involved in Hamilton's imperious assumption that all this could be forced into premature existence through an act of will. At the same time, something more than country-party fundamentalism was involved in the Jeffersonian-Madisonian rage at "gambling scoundrels," and in the Virginians' hatred of Hamilton and all he stood for. Hamilton may have seen farther ahead than they, but something was to be said for their wild fears that the forces he had set loose were corrupting the morals of the people and making forever unattainable the vision *they* had of the future Good Republic.

It was all well and good to establish the public credit in such a way as to engage the resources of the community's most energetic men, thus making the public debt an instrument whereby capital might be concentrated for future development. These men's activities would result in the debt's being brought to par, and in this phase the spirit of speculation could be viewed as a benign force—as a willingness to take rational risks in the expectation of future returns, and all in the public interest. But surely some intermediate term needed to be fitted into the theory, something for which neither Hume nor Hamilton had ever quite fully provided. What is to keep the spirit of speculation from becoming an end in itself?

When the demand for immediate gratification overwhelms all impulses of sustained application and cumulative achievement, the demon is loose, and whole communities may be deeply undermined—stopping their accustomed work, entranced and hallucinated, and looking for miracles—by an epidemic of speculation. The sober prophet will warn in vain, as did Seth Johnson, writing to Andrew Craigie in 1791. "The best support & Surest resource of a nation," he said,

> is in the industry & frugality of its Citizens—whatever in any way tends to lessen or destroy those usefull habits must be considered highly prejudicial — The present rage for Speculation by producing in some, a sudden & great acquisition of wealth, allures others, of all ranks, from those regular habits of business thro' which, the acquirement of property tho slow is Certain, to engage in what, like gaming depends on chance — They feel all the anxiety & eagerness attendant on deep play — Those who gain, play in hope of more, those who lose, continue in hope of better fortune — Their industry is not only destroyed by their thus

neglecting their proper business, but many are rendered unhappy & discontented. . . .

Speculative bubbles will always burst, and gambling at any time, in which some must win and some must lose, is a destructive and divisive force. Only "a few bankruptcies," as Oliver Wolcott remarked amid the madness of 1792, will cure the "malignity of one party and the pride of the other."[61]

The demon of speculation may undoubtedly be seen as the demon of capitalism itself. The discipline for resisting it—a willingness to defer gratifications, together with the maintenance of a generally recognized relationship between work and reward—can never be more than partial. It is learned through chastening and experience, though experience seems also to show that immunity is never fully achieved. Still, evidence of some such chastening would come into view in the America of the early nineteenth century.

The demon even has a name in the language of modern theory: *"Exaggerated expectations and personalized liquidity preference."* It refers to a state frequently observed, according to Professor Hirschman, "in the psychological situation of a society which is having the first, heady taste of economic development." On the one hand, an awareness of opportunity can lead to the avoidance or abandonment of useful long-term ventures "in favor of some new 'get rich quick' activity." On the other, there is "the somewhat puzzling spectacle of so many able and wealthy persons in underdeveloped countries . . . keeping themselves and their funds uncommitted or 'liquid' so as to take advantage of the unusual opportunity whenever it comes."[62] This, in translation, may refer to an ungoverned weakness for the fast buck—a fair shorthand for what happened to the Society for the Establishment of Useful Manufactures.

In Francis Cabot Lowell and the Boston Associates would appear a breed markedly different from the men of William Duer's type. It is true that an increasing absorption with problems of technology and management—which has a way of taking on a life of its own—was part of their disciplinary process, rehearsed in many a small New England mill in the post-Embargo era, that was not accessible earlier. Moreover, the alluring spectacle of substantial profits in manufacturing, with England as the example, was easier to perceive in the years after 1815 than it was in the 1790s. But manufacturing is itself a mode of enterprise which demands not only heavy investments of money and energy but spaced-out expectations: it requires not simply a Hamiltonian vision but significant numbers of individuals willing, when they think of big money, to think of it in a framework of long-term commitments.[63]

It also requires a prepared context of cultural support, one in which the society's most conspicuous enterprisers have, among other things, made some sort of terms with the folk-suspicion against big profits reaped by somebody else. Such a carefully conceived and executed venture as, for example, the town of Lowell could exhibit clear connections not only with a range of regional interests but also with those very virtues which would make the difference in the society's willingness to ratify success: prudence, discipline, delayed gratification, and thought for the morrow. The Jeffersonian tradition, for all its occasional anti-capitalist overtones, has seldom asked for more. That tradition has taken various forms in the course of our history, but its principal function, with all the accounts in, has been as a censor only upon the demonic side, the speculative side, of capitalism.

Alexander Hamilton, in his impatience and pride, may be said to have created the conditions for the failure of his own vision. He had correctly anticipated most of the resources needed for its completion. But he had misjudged the human resources, and the Virginians saw this lapse—after their own fashion but not without reason—as monstrous. The men who were to execute his design had been only too well taught, by one side of the design, to think in terms of quick killings. Those same men were then expected, in order that the other side might be realized, somehow to restrain themselves.

Something important, then, had been unforeseen or overlooked; and it may be that with this oversight, and with its consequences, the creative phase of Hamilton's career approached its eclipse.

4

The Philadelphia Newspaper War, 1792

Another kind of demon, in addition to that of speculation, was fully loose by March 1792. This was the demon of partisanship, embodied most dramatically in Philip Freneau and the *National Gazette*. If one demon had been set at large by Alexander Hamilton, the other was most certainly released by James Madison and Thomas Jefferson, through their determination to bring down the Hamiltonian edifice and their enlistment of Freneau to aid in the work. Freneau's attack on the Treasury was systematically launched in mid-March. Hamilton would endure this for some eighteen weeks before finally striking back on his own account through the columns of John Fenno's *Gazette of the United States*. The furious newspaper war that subsequently raged in Philadelphia during the months preceding the fall elections of 1792 brought yet another new element into the process whereby political parties were taking shape in that year. Recognizable divisions had already appeared in Congress. But now those divisions were being both formalized and generalized: by being paraded before the public they were openly confirmed, and a broader sanction for them was in effect being solicited through public opinion.

The elections of 1792 in one sense greatly advanced the formation of parties, bringing accessions of strength that were very gratifying to the "republican interest," as opponents of the Treasury were now beginning to call themselves. But another factor incident to these same elections, that involving the choice of a Chief Executive, still served as an inhibiting influence upon the coalescing forces of partisanship and party formation. This was the reluctant decision of Washington not to retire as he had planned, if there should be strong sentiment in the country for his serving another term.

Given the reputation he and his paper would eventually acquire, Freneau was relatively restrained during the first few months of the *Gazette*'s existence. Though he supported Madison's position on strict construction of the "general welfare" clause, he at first wrote approvingly of the S.U.M.[64] He took an anti-British, pro-French tone from the outset, but he ran essays by a writer who thought the best remedy for undue dependence on Great Britain would be government encouragement of manufactures—to which in itself Alexander Hamilton could not have objected.[65] When Hamilton's report was issued, Freneau published it without comment, though he later opposed it.[66] He admitted material on both sides of the Indian war question, though he probably shared the hawkish views of his friend Brackenridge. Madison's articles appeared quite regularly, but his most partisan ones would not come until later.[67]

But then the speculative madness of February and the Panic of March, together with the strident debates in Congress during that same period, appear all at once to have generated immense pressures for taking sides and casting off restraints. On March 15 Freneau's "Brutus" letters began in the *National Gazette,* and in a series that ran into the following month the editor flayed the funding system with the verve of an inspired demagogue. It is "a deplorable truth," he now wrote,

> that a system of finance has issued from the Treasury of the United States and has given rise to scenes of speculation calculated to aggrandize the few and the wealthy, by oppressing the great body of the people, to transfer the best resources of the country forever into the hands of the speculators, and to fix a burthen on the people of the United States and their posterity, which time, instead of diminishing will serve to strengthen and encrease . . . with unlimited import and excise laws pledged for its support, and copied from British statute books. . . .[68]

Another series by "A Farmer" ran concurrently, attacking the S.U.M. and the principles of Hamilton's "lengthy and flimsy" Report on Manufactures. The court of Great Britain itself, the "Farmer" declared, could not have devised a better plan for our oppression and ruin "than the scheme of Duer and Hamilton to establish *national manufactories.*"[69] On April 2 appeared Madison's intensely partisan "The Union: Who Are Its Real Friends?" Nine articles by "Sidney" attacked Hamilton's excise system ("there never was in any country a more partial, oppressive, and unjust instrument of revenue") and the Secretary's recent report justifying it.[70] Front-page coverage was given to the most violent anti-Hamilton speeches in Congress, such as Baldwin's on the excise, Mercer's on ways and means for frontier defense, and William Findley's on Hamilton's proposal for an additional assumption of state debts.[71] And there were endless insinuations throughout the spring and summer that Hamilton and his followers were plotting to fasten monarchy and aristocracy upon the people of America.

> Query 1. Can those who are attached to monarchy and aristocracy, be, in their hearts, friends to . . . a republican constitution?

Query 2. Are not some amongst us avowedly, others notoriously, advocates for monarchy and aristocracy?

Query 3. Are not the principles of all such hostile to the principles of the constitution?

Query 4. Must not such naturally wish to make the constitution by stretching its powers, and aggrandizing a few, the stalking horse to hereditary government?

Query 5. Have not many public circumstances indicated such a disposition and design? . . .[72]

John Fenno, editor of the sedate *Gazette of the United States,* which he had founded in 1789 "for the purpose of disseminating favorable sentiments of the federal Constitution and the Administration," should undoubtedly have been doing something about all this. But Fenno was a large and somewhat ponderous man who deplored turmoil and was confused by it; he had little taste or talent for controversy and few resources for coping with the *National Gazette.* It pained him to see the government criticized and himself derided as the "court printer," but the most he could do was sputter and expostulate. A majority of the "abusers of government," he made the mistake of declaring on June 9, "are persons from other countries who having lately escaped from bondage, know not how to enjoy liberty." Freneau sprang upon him with shouts of glee. "Hear! Hear! hear, and attend . . . ye *foreigners,* from every country, and from every clime!" "This very morning in the *Gazette of the United States* he swears . . . that you foreigners are a set of rebellious turbulent dogs, a pack of *run-away slaves,* who are come here to overturn the government."[73]

By late July, the writhing Hamilton must have concluded that Freneau had had things his own way long enough. On the 25th he placed a venomous little paragraph, signed "T.L.," in the *Gazette of the United States:*

> The Editor of the "National Gazette" receives a salary from government. *Quere—* Whether this salary is paid him for *translations;* or for *publications,* the design of which is to vilify those to whom the voice of the people has committed the administration of our public affairs—to oppose the measures of government, and, by false insinuations, to disturb the public peace? In common life it is thought ungrateful for a man to bite the hand that puts bread in his mouth; but if the man is hired to do it, the case is altered.

Freneau, as if bitten from behind, started up at once. He called Fenno—who he assumed had written the piece—a "vile sycophant" who was trying to "poison the minds of the people." Hamilton in a second "T.L." letter pressed on, daring Freneau to tell him "what inducement our rulers can have to hire a man to abuse them." He was referring, of course, to the small stipend Freneau was being paid by the State Department as a translator, and affecting to believe he was being paid from the same source to publish the *Gazette* as well. Freneau thereupon swore out an affidavit before the mayor of Philadelphia, insisting that the *Gazette*'s editor "has consulted his own judgement alone in the conducting of it—free—

unfettered—and uninfluenced."[74] It was at this point that Hamilton finally opened fire on Thomas Jefferson.

Hamilton wanted it generally understood that Jefferson, though "the head of a principal department of the Government," was "the declared opponent of almost all the important measures which had been devised by the Government." In a stream of newspaper essays that began on August 4 and did not cease until late in December, and under a variety of pseudonyms ("American," "Catullus," "Metellus") that fooled nobody, Hamilton raised up Jefferson's iniquities for all to behold. There were three principal indictments. Jefferson had negotiated with Freneau, arranging to have him "regularly pensioned with the public money," so that Freneau might set up a newspaper which would be "an exact copy of the politics of his employer." He had revealed his questionable loyalty to the Con- stitution as early as 1788, when he "at first, went so far as to discountenance its adoption" except on a kind of contingent basis. (Although he had thought the first nine states should ratify, the other four should refuse in order to bring pressure for amendments.) And finally, Jefferson, while minister to France, had shown his "profligacy" and contempt for his country's financial honor by his willingness to cheat a company of Dutch bankers, recommending that they be allowed to assume charge, at a $16\frac{2}{3}$ percent discount, of the American debt to France—knowing, or believing, that the American government would be no more able to make payments to them than it had to the French.[75]

Jefferson remained ostensibly aloof in the face of all this, saying that he had resolved early in life "never to write in a public paper without subscribing my name," or to "engage openly an adversary who does not let himself be seen." He did not need to, since various of his friends, principally Madison, Monroe, and Randolph, rushed into print in his defense, apparently with his cooperation.[76] The public thereupon received, throughout the remainder of the year, a sustained view of political and personal warfare that was without precedent. Meanwhile Hamilton in a parallel series of papers ("Civis" and "Fact") defended the Treasury against newspaper charges that his department had wasted the public money and need- lessly augmented the public debt.[77]

Hamilton, who seems always to have required clear boundaries in order to act effectively, was very good at defending himself but exceptionally bad at attack- ing others. He could with crisp precision explain the manner in which arrears of interest were calculated, or outline the conditions under which public debts were or were not public blessings, but when it came to mounting an offensive of his own, as in the ravings of "American" and "Catullus," Hamilton ran wild.

His best case, if he had one at all, was with regard to Freneau. There was little question that Jefferson and Madison had made strenuous exertions to per- suade Freneau to establish a newspaper in Philadelphia, and that if it had not been for their persistence he would not have come. The elaborate self-justifications that Jefferson made to Washington were not very candid on this point. He pre- tended that the clerkship had had no connection in his mind with Freneau's starting a newspaper, and that when he learned of Freneau's plan (which was as much his and Madison's plan as Freneau's) he had welcomed it mainly as a way of getting foreign news from the *Leyden Gazette* translated and published in America.[78] Moreover, that part of Freneau's deposition in which he affirmed "that no negociation was ever opened with him by Thomas Jefferson, Secretary of State, for the establishment or institution of the National Gazette; that the deponent's coming to the City of Philadelphia, as the publisher of a Newspaper, was at no time urged, advised, or influenced by the above officer,"[79] was at best dubious. The actual "negociation" may have been principally carried through by Madison, but it would hardly have taken the form it did without Jefferson's close encouragement.

The interpretation that should be put upon these doings, however, is more problematical. On the one hand, a cabinet officer's abetting the establishment of an opposition newspaper could be regarded as questionable, and Jefferson's protest that in approving Freneau's political writings he "looked only to the chastisement of the aristocratical & monarchical writers, and not to any criticisms on the proceedings of the government,"[80] was one of those sophistries which Washington, to whom it was addressed, could not have found very persuasive. And whereas the horror Hamilton professed to feel over the $250 a year Jefferson paid Freneau for his translating activities was undoubtedly excessive, it was not very intelligent of Freneau to take it, and even less so in Jefferson to offer it. The very paltriness of the sum—Jefferson's willingness to push forward any plausible extra inducement—was in its way a sign of how anxious he was to bring Freneau to Philadelphia.

It could be said, on the other hand, that there was nothing immoral about the establishment of a party newspaper, and if that was what Jefferson wanted, presumably he ought to have been free to do what he could to effect it. But it is possible that Jefferson was not altogether clear in his own mind *what* he wanted. The trouble of course, was that "party" was not a respectable idea; there were as yet no rules for doing what he and Madison were in fact doing, and no neutral vocabulary for talking about it. It was this—together with his and Freneau's strained protestations—that gave Hamilton's case what color it had.

At the same time, when Freneau insisted on his complete independence in printing what he pleased, and when Jefferson swore that he himself "never did ... directly or indirectly, say a syllable, nor attempt any kind of influence" on the *Gazette*'s contents, they were both undoubtedly telling the truth.[81] Jefferson might not have been averse to some discreet coaching if Freneau had been the least bit manageable, but after discovering Freneau's touchiness he knew better than to try. Freneau during the preliminary exchanges, and while still resisting the Virginians' importunities, seems to have suspected Jefferson of wanting to circumscribe his freedom, and wrote him an insulting letter which only the protests of one of his friends persuaded him not to send. Had Jefferson tried telling Freneau what to write and print, the latter would almost certainly have had none of it.[82] But then, of course, Jefferson had no need to.

Hamilton's other charges—on the French loan and Jefferson's alleged opposition to the Constitution—cannot be taken very seriously. Hamilton may well have burned with retrospective wrath, since he and his friends in 1788 had had to labor tirelessly over every vote, at the thought of Jefferson several thousand miles away airily intimating that some states might do well to hold back their ratifications. But far from opposing the final product, Jefferson had at least some grounds for claiming, as he did, that his loyalty to the Constitution was really greater than Hamilton's.[83] On the matter of the loan, Hamilton's accusations were preposterous. The scheme Jefferson transmitted to Congress in 1786 was not an implausible one, and though the Board of Treasury eventually rejected it for sound reasons, there were respectable people in America who had thought it at least worth considering. Jefferson, as American minister to France, felt great humiliation over the arrears in pay his country owed to the French officers who had served in the Revolution, and over its failure to pay interest on the debt to the French government. He welcomed the Dutch plan as a way of doing something about both. True, he may have failed to think it all through; the Americans might continue not paying the French and still maintain their credit in Amsterdam, whereas if they renegotiated the loan and subsequently defaulted on payments to the Dutch, their credit would collapse. So it was not such a good idea. And yet not only was Hamilton, in reviving the episode a half-dozen years later, misrepresenting Jefferson by quoting his proposals out of context, but Jefferson's own concerns at that time had been—though in a different way—exactly the same as Hamilton's. Both had been preoccupied and obsessed with the desperate state of American credit.[84]

All of which raises other questions. Why this sudden assault on Jefferson, and how is one to account for the timing? In widening his efforts after the initial stabs at Freneau, might Hamilton not better have transferred them to Madison, who had taken the principal responsibility in persuading Freneau to move? Madison had hitherto been the main source of his grievances, and Hamilton's long letter to Edward Carrington in May had been a tale of distress at the way in which Madison had turned against him and his policies.[85] Why, now, should he be venting all his ferocity upon Jefferson?

Hamilton had long been suffering from a sense of persecution. He had been only too aware of Madison's opposition, manifested more or less openly in congressional debates, and was much pained by it. He also knew in a general way that Jefferson closely shared Madison's sentiments. But of Jefferson's own opposition, and the precise form it was taking, Hamilton had as yet little idea. He did not know the extent of Jefferson's efforts to undermine his standing with Washington himself, and did not learn of this until Washington in effect spelled it out to him in the summer of 1792.

Jefferson had several private conversations with Washington earlier in the year, in the course of which he seems to have put few checks on his detestation of Hamilton's Treasury and the debaucheries to which he thought its policies were leading. He believed that the Treasury "possessed already such an influence as to swallow up the whole Executive powers"; that it had contrived a system for luring the citizens into "a species of gambling, destructive of morality, & which had introduced it's poison into the government itself"; and that the Report on Manufactures, which he hoped "would be rejected," went beyond any measure yet advanced for turning the Republic into an unlimited government. He was sure the debt had been increased "beyond the possibility of paiment"; that "it had furnished the means of corrupting both branches of the legislature"; and that "there was a considerable squadron in both whose votes were devoted to the Paper & stock-jobbing interest." This meant a Congress "legislating for their own interests in opposition to those of the people," and he had no doubt that this "corrupt squadron" was plotting to change the form of government "to that of a monarchy." Jefferson wrote Washington at great length on May 23 summarizing the entire indictment.[86]

Washington, greatly disturbed, wrote an extensive letter to Hamilton on July 29 in which he listed Jefferson's criticisms. He did not bother to disguise Jefferson's language, quoting much of it verbatim and thinly paraphrasing the rest. Hamilton's thoughts as he read it may well be imagined. Here it all was, beyond any mistake, communicated to him by none other than the Chief Magistrate. To what lengths was Jefferson prepared to go to destroy him, how long had he been at it in secret, what calumnies had he been sowing, with what poisons had the President's mind been infused? Hamilton received this document on August 3. His frantic, all-out assault on Thomas Jefferson was launched in the *Gazette of the United States* the following day.[87]

The elections of 1792 were the first ones in the history of the new republic to be contested on anything resembling a partisan basis. In most of the states the congressional elections were recognized in some sense, as Clerk of the House John Beckley put it, as a "struggle between the Treasury department and the republican interest." In New York, even the gubernatorial campaign tended to be organized along such lines. The candidates were John Jay, generally sympathetic to Hamiltonian principles, and George Clinton, the longtime incumbent. Clinton and his supporters were regarded as custodians of the Republican interest in New York.[88]

Though these contests tended for the most part to be contained within the states where they occurred, there were already discernible signs, as Noble Cunningham has pointed out, of interstate cooperation. The Virginians—Madison, Monroe, Jefferson, and Beckley—were in close touch with a number of the campaigns and kept an anxious eye on them. The Virginia–New York entente, which may or may not have been implied in Jefferson's exchanges with Livingston in the previous year, was now a clear reality. When the Jay-Clinton election was run off in May and Clinton managed to keep his place only through frauds committed by his supporters in three counties, the disquieted Virginians perceived at once the implications for themselves and their allies everywhere. Jefferson thought that under the circumstances Clinton should decline taking office; otherwise, he feared, "the cause of republicanism will suffer and its votaries thrown into schism." But this did not keep them from proceeding with a plan, in concert with Republican leaders from Pennsylvania and New York, to support Clinton for the vice-presidency in order to remove Adams. Though there was some talk of putting Aaron Burr forward instead, Madison and Monroe stood adamant, and carried their point.[89]

Nevertheless, there was still in 1792 the widest range of inhibitions against out-and-out party activity, and it was this—rather than any slowness to "discover" organizational techniques—that accounts for the curious ambiguity in political behavior everywhere during that year. One area in which this could be seen was the process of nominating candidates for office. Such a process is logically one that requires some form of group action prior to the election—and when issues and sentiments that introduce divisions in a community have made their appearance, such action, by the element of informality inherent in it, verges unavoidably upon partisanship. Yet the imperatives of getting done what has to be done, on the one hand, and those of coming to terms with the negative values of factionalism and "concerting measures" outside legally sanctioned boundaries, on the other, can produce a truly divided mentality—a conscience that no longer fully knows itself. So it was in 1792.

For example, in New Hampshire the legislature had already assumed the function of nominating candidates for Congress, an arrangement that was but a step short of the subsequently developed legislative party caucus. But in 1792 the "parties," according to one member, "were so much afraid of each other that they strove only to conceal themselves and their designs."[90] Or, there was the compiling of tickets, which was in some way indispensable for the promoting of like-minded and compatible candidates. The impulse to do it was overwhelming, but who was to take the initiative, how could it be successful without the support of others, and how were such "others" to be styled? Was this not "faction"? Consequently, though there were tickets everywhere, they were offered in the newspapers by individuals, or by "a number of inhabitants," or by "respectable merchants and mechanics"—but not by any group specifically willing to call itself a party, or even an "interest." Tickets, indeed, no matter how presented, were themselves suspect. Even a good Republican like Hugh Henry Brackenridge could publish, in Philip Freneau's good Republican newspaper, a sturdy tirade against tickets, state meetings, and committees of correspondence—all instruments of faction, which invaded "the right of the citizens at large to think, judge and act for themselves."[91]

Thomas Jefferson's own mind reflected a similar ambiguity. When the results of the congressional elections were in, Jefferson had good reason to rejoice. They had produced, he wrote to Thomas Pinckney, "a decided majority in favor of the republican interest." Though party attachments were not generally announced as such, Jefferson knew enough about who was who in these various contests, and had followed them with sufficient care, to be able by now to make such a statement as a matter of course.[92]

A final set of ironies in this election year was created by the position of Washington himself, and by the significance his presence carried in the minds of all his leading associates, bitterly divided as they otherwise were.

The Father of His Country felt himself by now weighted with many cares. He was profoundly disturbed by the factionalism he had seen emerging in the spring and summer. He was especially angered at the activities of Freneau, not the least of whose many mischiefs, he thought, was stirring up the people of western Pennsylvania against the excise law. (Conditions there had already become very unsettled.) To Jefferson, he snorted at the idea that the pieces in Freneau's and other hostile papers were anything but attacks on himself, and said he "must be a fool indeed to swallow the little sugar plumbs here & there thrown out to him." He declared:

> That in condemning the admn of the govmt they condemned him, for if they thought there were measures pursued contrary to his sentiment, they must conceive him too careless to attend to them or too stupid to understand them. That tho indeed he had signed many acts which he did not approve in all their parts, yet he had never put his name to one which he did not think on the whole was eligible.[93]

And what perhaps gave Washington more pain than anything else was the unmistakable enmity he could now see emerging between his two chief cabinet officers, Jefferson and Hamilton.

At the same time, he himself was weary of office and had made up his mind to announce his retirement. This created the greatest agitation in those to whom he confided it, and all undertook the most fervent appeals that he reconsider. What this came to, in view of the values Washington represented, was that the same men who were promoting partisanship at one level were in effect resisting it at another.

Washington took up the subject of his retirement with Madison in May, saying that he "found himself . . . in the decline of life, his health becoming sensibly more infirm, & perhaps his faculties also; that the fatigues & disagreeableness of his situation were in fact scarcely tolerable to him." He wanted Madison's advice on how and when he ought to communicate his intentions to the country, and what he ought to say. Madison believed that if he were determined to do it, a direct address to the people, given to the newspapers in sufficient time before the elections, would be better than a message to Congress. Washington requested that Madison prepare him a draft of such a valedictory. Madison thereupon did so, but with a heavy heart, and in concluding his letter of transmittal he wrote:

> Having thus, Sir, complied with your wishes, by proceeding on a supposition that the idea of retiring from public life is to be carried into execution, I must now gratify my own by hoping that a reconsideration . . . will have produced an acquiescence in one more sacrifice, severe as it may be, to the desires & interests of your country.[94]

A comparable pattern emerged in Washington's communications with Hamilton and Jefferson on the same subject. But in their case an extra dimension was added by the concurrent efforts Washington was making to reconcile them in their quarrel with each other.

"How unfortunate," Washington wrote to Jefferson on August 23, ". . . whilst we are encompassed on all sides with avowed enemies and insidious friends, that internal dissensions should be harrowing and tearing our vitals." Without "more charity for the opinions and acts of one another," he feared, the parts of government could not be kept together. "My earnest wish, and my fondest hope therefore is, that instead of wounding suspicions and irritable charges, there may be liberal allowances—mutual forbearances—and temporising yieldings on *all sides.*" He addressed Hamilton in a similar spirit. He "regretted exceedingly, that subjects cannot be discussed with temper on the one hand, or decisions submitted to without having the motives which led to them, improperly implicated on the other," and he hoped "that balsam may be poured into *all* the wounds which have been given, to prevent them from gangrening; & from those fatal consequences which the community may sustain if it is withheld."[95]

Both replied on the same day. Hamilton praised Washington's efforts at reconciliation, but suggested that if they failed it would be as well for the public good that the President replace them both. Hamilton admitted that he had had "some instrumentality of late in the retaliations which have fallen upon certain public characters"—in other words that he was, in fact, responsible for the newspaper attacks on Jefferson—but that believing himself to be "the deeply injured party," he did not feel "able to recede *for the present.*" He recited his sufferings:

> I *know* that I have been an object of uniform opposition from Mr. Jefferson, from the first moment of his coming to the City of New York to enter upon his present office. I *know,* from the most authentic sources, that I have been the frequent subject of the most unkind whispers and insinuating from the same quarter. I have long seen a formed party in the Legislature, under his auspices, bent upon my subversion. I cannot doubt, from the evidence I possess, that the National Gazette was instituted by him for political purposes and that one leading object of it has been to render me and all the measures connected with my department as odious as possible.

"Nevertheless," he concluded, "I pledge my honor to you Sir, that if you shall hereafter form a plan to reunite the members of your administration, upon some steady principle of cooperation, I will faithfully concur in executing it during my continuance in office. And I will not directly or indirectly say or do a thing, that shall endanger a feud."[96]

Jefferson, in a long letter overflowing with hatred of Hamilton and justification of himself, would make no promises at all. He admitted that he disapproved of Hamilton's system ("in my private conversations"), but insisted that this was because the object of all Hamilton's plans was to create a corrupt band in Congress, "& to have that corps under the command of the Secretary of the Treasury for the purpose of subverting step by step the principles of the constitution." He too went over his grievances. Hamilton had interfered in his department, intriguing to defeat his plans for favoring French commerce and discriminating against the English, and had made charges against him in the newspapers, all of which were false. Jefferson too, like Washington, wanted soon to withdraw from public life. And, convinced that he merited the esteem of his countrymen "by an integrity that cannot be reproached," Jefferson declared: "I will not suffer my retirement to be clouded by the slanders of a man whose history, from the moment at which history can stoop to notice him, is a tissue of machinations against the liberty of the country which has not only received and given him bread, but heaped it's honors on his head."[97]

There was, however, one thing—though one thing only—upon which both agreed. This was that Washington's continuance in office was indispensable. "I am perfectly aware," wrote Jefferson,

> of the oppression under which your present office lays your mind, and of the ardor with which you pant for retirement to domestic life. But there is sometimes an eminence of character on which society have such peculiar claims as to controul the predilection of the individual for a particular walk of happiness, and restrain him to that alone arising from the present and future benedictions of mankind. This seems to be your condition. . . .

"I trust, Sir," echoed Hamilton, "and I pray God that you will determine to make a further sacrifice of your tranquility and happiness to the public good."[98]

Parties, to be sure, were now in existence. But the very men about whom they were coalescing still felt a variety of constraints that prevented them from proceeding straightforwardly to develop the logic of party. And now, in urging Washington's continuance, they were voluntarily accepting another. Neither was prepared to desist from their dispute, but each in his way was recoiling from its full implications—the division of American political forces into organized parties. Washington, like the Patriot King, still symbolized, for the country and for them, the vision of a government above party and faction. They may have moved some way toward the "idea of a party system," but they had still gone less than half the distance. Although they would not turn back, they still preferred to carry on their conflict under Washington's shadow, each still somehow hoping that it would be resolved in *his* favor and that Washington's blessing might be placed on *his* version of it. They sensed that they were approaching unknown ground, and they had apprehensions; whatever happened, they wanted it to be under an aegis that was still the most recognizable version of legitimacy in the new republic. Nevertheless, in looking to Washington in their perplexity, they were helping to prolong the very conditions—though they hardly knew it—from which they were straining to break free. Political contention would still contain a heavy element of the furtive, the pent-up, and the vicious as long as sanctioned channels for its expression were no more in evidence than in the year 1792.

Washington put off his decision from day to day, long after the time which he and Madison had agreed would be a proper one if he were to decline re-election. By fall, persons nearest him thought they detected a "relaxation" of his intentions. Weeks lengthened into months, and Washington ended by saying nothing at all, which was tantamount to his accepting. The electoral votes were counted on February 13, 1793. It was found that Adams had thwarted Clinton's try for the vice-presidency by a majority of 77 to 50. But for the presidency itself it was found, as before, that Washington had received the vote of every elector.[99]

5
Investigating Hamilton

Before the arrival of the new minister from the French Republic, two further assaults were made upon the Treasury and upon its head, one of them conducted in private and the other in public. Hamilton managed to survive them both, and even to emerge with a measure of credit, depending on whose point of view it was seen from. He could, as has been noted, act with considerable precision when he himself, and the affairs of his department, were under attack.

The first of these occasions was in consequence of whispers given out by two inmates of the Philadelphia jail, which reached the willing ears of certain members of Congress from Virginia, that Hamilton had been personally engaged in secret speculation in government securities. Nothing came of this, and the matter was settled behind closed doors to the congressmen's satisfaction.

But Hamilton, in the course of clearing himself, would unhappily find it necessary to disclose to them that at the bottom of the story was an amorous adventure in which he had got himself entangled during the previous year. His clandestine doxy, Maria Reynolds, happened to be the estranged wife of one of the indicted culprits, and would shortly emerge (though this was not known at the time) as the wife of the other. There lingered about each member of this unusual trio—Maria, James Reynolds, and Reynolds's associate Jacob Clingman—a vaguely disreputable air. The only one of them possessing qualities the least appealing was Maria, who had generous though indiscriminate emotions, and was forever wringing her hands over something. In cases of extremity, which were frequent, and with her tears and entreaties, which came easily, she could melt a heart of stone. Her loyalties, consequently, were always in a state of some confusion. Handed about as she was, and buffeted by circumstance, she led a precarious existence.[100] Reynolds and Clingman were awaiting trial in November 1792 for fraud and for suborning a person to commit perjury in order to gain administration over the effects of a deceased soldier. Reynolds had already been prosecuted several times for dealing in stolen goods; Clingman seems to have stayed off police blotters up until then, although it is not known how he came to combine his talents with those of Reynolds. As the two considered ways of getting out of this latest scrape, their thoughts turned to the Secretary of the Treasury, one of them intimating to the other that there were circumstances which might prompt Hamilton's influence on their behalf. But Hamilton, when applied to, refused to lend any such influence. Clingman, free on bail, thereupon flitted about town giving hints to Comptroller Oliver Wolcott (who had instituted the proceedings in the first place) and to Speaker Frederick A. Muhlenberg (Clingman's own former employer) that Reynolds "had it in his Power very materially to injure the Secretary of the Treasury" and that Hamilton's crime was speculation. Reynolds himself, when questioned in jail, was coy about what the "crime" really was, and the three congressmen who visited him there could get nothing explicit out of him. But whatever the claim he had on Hamilton, as events would shortly reveal, it was one which went back about a year and a half.[101]

One day in the summer of 1791 Maria Reynolds in a state of great distress had introduced herself to Hamilton saying that her husband had deserted her, and imploring his assistance that she might rejoin friends in New York. She got money from the susceptible Secretary; she also got him into her bedroom that very night. From here on, the coils of intrigue and lust fastened themselves steadily about him. The two met frequently; in time the husband returned; Reynolds, applying for a position at the Treasury, said he knew of speculative activities among the Treasury staff; Hamilton affected interest but declined to employ him; and Maria, shortly thereafter, told Hamilton that her husband had at last found them out. Hamilton had already begun to suspect the pair of collusion. The nature of the wronged husband's "outrage" was certainly equivocal; it consisted of demands for blackmail in return for keeping quiet and, when he received it, of encouragement that Hamilton continue to visit his languishing wife. Hamilton's efforts to break things off led to wild entreaties by Maria not to desert her. He relented, and money continued to flow from his pocket to that of the complaisant Reynolds. Such was the state of things when the law caught up with Reynolds and his crony Clingman in November 1792.[102]

Speaker Muhlenberg, much disturbed over the veiled accusations with which Clingman was regaling him, consulted with Representative Abraham Venable and Senator James Monroe, who had also got wind of the matter, as to what they ought to do about it. They decided to confront Hamilton himself before carrying it further, and to take with them several ambiguous notes which Hamilton had at one time or another written to Reynolds and which had been obtained from Clingman, who had in turn got them from Maria. On December 15, 1792, they called upon him and showed him the notes, which he admitted were his. He invited them to his house that evening, where he said he would show them documentary proof that he was innocent of any public wrongdoing. When they arrived he told them the real nature of his connection with the Reynoldses, and when he began reading the intimate correspondence they begged him to desist, saying they were satisfied. They abandoned their decision to lay the matter before the President.[103]

The charges against Clingman and Reynolds had meanwhile been dropped, in return for their making restitution of moneys defrauded and for giving particulars of how they came by the information upon which their frauds were committed. Reynolds, upon being released, vanished entirely and was never heard of again. Maria now consoled herself with Clingman, and these two betook themselves to Cecil County, Maryland, to begin life anew.[104]

But, thanks to Monroe, the affair as it concerned Hamilton did not quite end there, even though it was hushed up for the time being. Five years later, in 1797, the whole story would be spread before the world by a Philadelphia journalist named James T. Callender, complete with a picturesque theory that Hamilton's amour with Mrs. Reynolds had been only a fiction, invented in order to cover up speculations in which Reynolds had actually served as Hamilton's agent. This new development was not Monroe's doing, but the indirect responsibility for its occurring, in view of the passions of 1792, had probably been more his than anyone else's.[105]

Monroe, as has been seen, was furious at Hamilton's newspaper attacks upon Jefferson, and at the very time Clingman's insinuations first reached him in 1792 he was still engaged in writing his own articles in Jefferson's defense. Though Hamilton in the interview of December 15, 1792, had succeeded in exculpating himself, Monroe was by no means prepared to bury the case forever. He told Jefferson and Madison all about it, probably before the interview; more important, he made the ubiquitous John Beckley privy to the entire affair in more ways than one. Beckley, the Clerk of the House, was a man for whom gossip and inside information were the elixir of life; his gift for ferreting it out, and his willingness to serve the Virginians as a kind of general factotum, were of great assistance to them in their political activities of that year. When Hamilton requested copies of the papers Monroe had in his possession, Monroe in complying turned the job over to Beckley, who was careful to keep a set for himself. It was Beckley who gave the papers to Callender in 1797, and no doubt he was full of ideas as to the use Callender should make of them. Monroe knew all this, having himself given them to Beckley, but he kept it a secret as long as he lived.[106]

And yet the question of how sternly Monroe should be taxed for such behavior must be measured, once more, against the partisanship which was beginning everywhere to eat at the judgment of better men than he. Monroe and all the Virginians by December 1792 were utterly and absolutely convinced, in their hatred and rage, that Hamilton was in some way sunk in corruption, and if he were not guilty of one form of it he must surely be guilty of some other. It was in this spirit, early in 1793, that they had another try, on another level. They set about investigating the operations of the Treasury itself, and searching out the irregularities they were still convinced they would find there.

The man who now emerged as Hamilton's chief tormentor in the House of Representatives was William Branch Giles of Virginia. Giles was a man of tempestuous passions. But the intelligence with which he might have governed them effectively was lacking, and his normal impulse on almost any occasion was to leap before he looked. "Personal animosities," according to Dumas Malone, "frequently marred the clarity of his political judgment and rendered his career erratic and essentially destructive." Giles, as is known, received a good deal of prompting during this period from Madison and Jefferson. But this did not mean he was indefinitely tractable, nor did it give any guarantee that his legislative ventures would be undertaken judiciously. It was simply another reflection of the virtual unanimity that now prevailed within the Virginia contingent on all matters concerning the Treasury.[107]

A new train of events began with a bill being debated late in December 1792, under which authority would be granted to divert $2 million from funds already borrowed abroad for payment on the French debt, to use this money instead for repaying a loan from the new Bank of the United States which had been made for financing the government's share of Bank stock (as provided in the act of incorporation), and to negotiate a new $2 million loan in Holland. As was now regularly the case with almost any schemes originating in the Treasury, this measure aroused all manner of questions and suspicions. There was the question of why $2 million should be wanted all at once, when the servicing of the Bank loan required only $200,000 annually over a ten-year period; or why it was that large sums had already been drawn from abroad to apply to the domestic debt, whereas that money—which had been borrowed in Holland—was supposed to be used for payment on the debt to France. Giles presented a motion in the House the day before Christmas requiring the Secretary to furnish an accounting of the state of American loans: amounts, terms, uses to which put, and balances remaining unapplied.

Hamilton responded immediately, though without commentary. But Hamilton's report (which Giles claimed, doubtless truthfully, he could not understand) did nothing to set things to rest. On the contrary, it opened the way for a major inquiry into Treasury operations. The fundamental assumption of the Virginians in undertaking it (with Giles once again as their instrument) was that everything Hamilton did was for the prime purpose of making available as much capital as possible for the activities of his unholy friends, the speculators.[108] Accordingly Giles, on January 23, 1793, introduced a set of five resolutions, and at the same time explained the reasoning behind them.

The first called for copies of the specific authority (meaning an order from the President) under which loans had been negotiated in accordance with two acts of Congress (those of August 4 and 12, 1790), together with similar authority for the manner in which the proceeds had subsequently been applied. Giles asserted that Hamilton had not furnished these in his recent report (though he had not been asked to), nor had he reported the precise object of the loans as they were made. One of the Acts in question (that of August 4, 1790) provided specifically for repayment of the foreign debt, and the other (that of August 12, 1790) specifically for the domestic. For which of these purposes was each of the loans made, and when made, was each in fact applied to that purpose? Hamilton, it seems, had combined the two loans and treated them as one. Moreover, not only did he now want to divert money borrowed for payment on the debt to France and to use it instead for payment to the Bank, but he was also saying that money borrowed for the same purpose (the French debt) was "applicable to the Sinking Fund"—that is, purchases of the domestic debt. The implication, in short, was that Hamilton was doing as he pleased, shifting funds back and forth without authority, and playing fast and loose with the law.

The second resolution asked for details of how payments on the French debt had been made, by whom, and when. Here the implication was that Hamilton was not making effective use of moneys already borrowed, saying that they were not being put to their original purpose because of "the unsettled state of affairs in France." This must mean that the United States was needlessly paying extra interest—not only on the debt to France but also on the money borrowed to discharge it.

The third resolution asked for an account showing half-monthly balances between the government and the Bank of the United States to the end of 1792. From figures Giles had from the Bank and from Hamilton's report, it appeared to him that a large sum had been drawn from abroad out of moneys borrowed there, and deposited in the Bank, and also that a series of loans had been made from the Bank itself, and these too deposited there. Giles wanted to know what all this money was being used for, especially with domestic receipts more than enough to cover current expenses. He thought the United States must be paying 15 and perhaps as much as 17 percent interest on it: 5 percent on the original debt to France, 5 percent on the money borrowed to redeem it (plus "douceurs and other charges"), and 5 percent on money borrowed from the Bank.

The fourth resolution demanded an account of the operations of the sinking fund—sums that had gone into it, the source of such funds, and the sums remaining unapplied. Here was another reflection of the Virginians' suspicions of the uses to which Hamilton was putting funds drawn from Holland, and of his assertions that a substantial portion of such funds were "applicable to the purchase of the public debt." Why so, demanded Giles, at a time when the sinking fund was "already overflowing from domestic resources"? Back of this, again, was the implication that Hamilton was mobilizing Treasury resources for the benefit of speculators—preparing, that is, to do what he in fact did do in March 1792 during the Panic: support the market through the sinking fund by making large purchases of public securities at par. The Virginians saw no reason why he should make such purchases at higher than the current market price, which at that time had slipped below par.

The fifth and final resolution called for a report on all unapplied moneys, from both loans and revenues, to the end of 1792. Giles thought he had found two appalling discrepancies in the figures already available. One was a shortage of $1,554,852 in Treasury accounts; the other was that according to Hamilton's report 2.9 million florins had been drawn from abroad in 1792, whereas the Bank's account book seemed to show that it had been nearly three times that amount.

All these resolutions were adopted. Hamilton was convinced that they were inspired by pure partisanship (as of course they were), and came close to saying so. Giles and his allies, in introducing them so late in the session, assumed that Hamilton could never produce the required replies in the time remaining, which meant that Giles's indictment—the speech in which he made all his suspicions public—would hang over Hamilton and work upon the public mind at least until the new session began later in the year. On the other hand, if information were the main thing Giles wanted (and as the resolutions professed), he need not have taken up the time of the House, or a fraction of the Treasury's time, to obtain it. There was none of this that could not have been explained to him on a very brief call at the Treasury. Instead, he chose to make his charges in advance, before receiving his information rather than after.[109]

Hamilton did, however, in a furious burst of activity, produce all the materials the resolutions called for. He did it in three successive reports, the first of which was completed in eleven days and the final one two weeks later. In his first report Hamilton's immediate object was to repair the damage already done and to arrest further undermining of the public confidence by dealing with the two most sensational of Giles's charges—one being the apparent shortage of $1.5 million, and the other the apparent misreporting of an 8.6 million florin transfer from Holland to America. In both cases the answer was relatively uncomplicated, each being a matter of accounting conventions that anyone familiar with business affairs would have had little trouble grasping.

The "shortage" was the difference between taxes owed (and therefore credited to the government's account) but not yet received, and the amount of cash actually on deposit. Importers were normally permitted credit of "four, six, nine, twelve months, and in some cases, of two years" in payment of duties. (The laws alone, as Hamilton pointed out none too subtly, should have told Giles that.) Actually Giles had not figured his shortages properly anyway, even on his own terms, the real discrepancy between credits and deposits being more than twice what he thought it was.[110]

The other discrepancy was simply the result of a book transfer, a physical moving of specie having occurred only for the 2.9 million florins Hamilton reported. The remainder represented the sum required for the government's original purchase of Bank stock. Legally the government could not borrow from the Bank until it had purchased its stock, but the stock could not be purchased without a loan from the Bank—or from some other source. The dilemma was resolved by drawing bills on the government's bankers in Holland (which would then appear on the books as a fresh loan from abroad), and by selling these bills to the Bank for the amount needed to purchase the stock. Being now legally free to borrow from the Bank, the government promptly did so in the same amount, bought back its bills with the proceeds, and tore up the bills. The cumbersome process of shipping $2 million in specie from Europe had thus been entirely avoided.[111]

Hamilton dealt with the remaining questions in his two subsequent reports. He admitted that he had combined the two loans authorized by the Acts of August 4 and 12, 1790—the one for payment on the French debt and the other for purchase of the domestic debt—and treated them as a single fund, not only in floating them but also in applying the proceeds. He thereupon explained both the justification and the necessity of so proceeding. For one thing, so large a sum could not be borrowed all at once on the Antwerp and Amsterdam markets (it would have to be done in a series of loans), nor was it even prudent that it should be. The appearance of excessive need would have done our credit no good, nor was it economical that there should be larger unapplied sums drawing interest than was immediately necessary. The Dutch bankers themselves had advised that the bonds would be more readily marketable under the aspect of a single American loan. (And of its two purposes, they probably preferred to stress the French debt rather than the domestic.) Moreover, the greatest flexibility was needed for the most effective and economical application of such funds as they became available. For example, it was important in the maintenance of American credit that we begin making prompt payments of interest on the debt to France. But it was equally important to move quickly in buying up as much of the domestic debt as possible—especially that in foreign hands—while the price was still low. Not only was this a matter of simple economy, and not only would it prevent foreigners from acquiring large amounts of American property at less than its intrinsic value, but such purchases both at home and abroad would contribute powerfully to a steady appreciation of American securities everywhere. This had now in fact happened, and it could not have been done had the money been pledged in advance to separate accounts. As a result the credit of the United States government, in the infancy of its existence, was as good as any in Europe, and the cost of the loans it made had dropped in a single year from $5\frac{1}{2}$ to $4\frac{1}{2}$ percent. This drop in interest rates and the savings made possible by it was a key item, as will be seen, in the explanation of other Treasury policies.[112]

Giles had charged that great sums were wasted by making loans for applying to the French debt and then subsequently delaying payments on it. Hamilton explained the "unsettled conditions" in France that had made a temporary delay necessary, and pointed out that in view of the circumstances such delay was to the advantage of both countries. The basic difficulties had arisen from the deterioration of the French currency and from the uprising in the French colony of St. Domingue. Hamilton had agreed not to make payments in depreciated currency while French finances remained unstable (though the United States would not lose in the eventual adjustment; there would in fact be a small gain). He had also acceded to the French government's desire to convert payments into supplies (in American produce) for the relief of St. Domingue. And the residue, meanwhile, was hardly lying idle. Having been obtained at a mean interest of 5 percent, it was being used to discharge bills upon which the interest was in the neighborhood of 6 percent—effecting savings, that is, by replacing money borrowed at a higher rate with other money borrowed at a lower. (It was a similar transaction, for example, that Hamilton had in mind in recommending that the $2 million loan from the Bank of the United States be discharged with money borrowed from abroad: that loan had been made at 6 percent, whereas funds were now available for liquidating it at 5.) In setting Giles straight on the true costs of all this in the way of interest charges (Giles had wildly surmised that it could come to as much as 17 percent), Hamilton understandably made the most of the Virginians' ignorance in matters of elementary finance.[113]

As for Giles's talk of a "surplus" in the Treasury while the United States was regularly borrowing funds from the Bank for current operations, Hamilton found this equally easy to deal with. He pointed out the absolute necessity of the Treasury's maintaining on deposit a cash margin of no less than $500,000 at all times, since—as with any business operation that had the least degree of complexity—there was no close correlation between income and expenditures. Allowing for seasonal fluctuations in revenues (the bulk of which came in the spring), deferred remittances, and delays in transfers of funds from distant places, the Treasury had to be prepared not only for regular expenses (as well as unexpected emergencies), but for a range of demands the particular moment of which could never be anticipated with exactness.[114]

With his final report, and having massed together materials that would normally have taken as much as nine months to prepare, Hamilton had disposed of every one of Giles's charges. His explanations were precise, detailed, and for the most part unanswerable. He had given a full history of the Treasury's workings, and the result might seem in many ways comparable to his major expositions on public credit, the Bank, and on manufacturing. But this time both the setting and the consequences were markedly different. All he now gained—though considering the occasion it was perhaps a great deal—was the essentially negative achievement of preventing his enemies from engulfing him.

At any rate, the Virginians were not to be deterred. So far as they were concerned, Hamilton might as well not have bothered. The more famous "Giles Resolutions" of 1793 were not the ones to which Hamilton had just replied, but a new set of nine resolutions of censure introduced on February 27, with only three days in the session remaining.[115]

Two points, among others, are of special interest regarding them. One is the extent to which they appear to have been framed in disregard of Hamilton's replies to the previous ones. The other is that whereas this might be ascribed to irresponsibility on the part of Giles, such was apparently not the case. The resolutions seem to have been based on a draft prepared by Jefferson himself, and Jefferson's resolutions were in fact significantly harsher than those Giles actually presented. Conceivably it was Giles who softened them, but more likely it was the entire Virginia delegation—perhaps with Madison in the lead—that worked the resolutions into their final form. It was simply one more instance of the Virginians' essential unity on what they saw as first principles.[116]

All were defeated by large majorities, the flimsiness of the case being apparent even to many who might have preferred to think otherwise. The first two were generalities about the Secretary's duty to observe strictly the laws and the Constitution, and the final one directed that a copy of the resolutions be transmitted to the President—thus becoming in effect a call for Hamilton's dismissal. (One of Jefferson's original resolutions had made such a call explicit.) These three were thrown out with little ado. The remaining six accused Hamilton of exceeding his authority in making loans under the Acts of August 4 and 12, 1790, and in applying their proceeds, in not promptly notifying Congress of his withdrawing moneys from Europe, and in not giving official information to the commissioners of the sinking fund of sums drawn for purchase of the public debt. And finally, Hamilton in the first of his three reports replying to Giles's previous resolutions had permitted himself to cast aspersions on the motives for them, for which he was "guilty of an indecorum to this House." Hamilton's supporters were well prepared (coached in large part by Hamilton himself), while most of his attackers proved to be hopelessly out of their depth. The largest vote any of the resolutions could command was 15 out of 48; the rest were defeated by three or four to one. Only five members—among whom were Giles and Madison—voted for all of them.[117]

Did the Virginians really believe in what they were doing? They undoubtedly did, in the sense that they were convinced of Hamilton's "guilt," the only question being of what. As to what they expected to accomplish with their resolutions, the more intelligent of them probably knew the effort would fail but were nonetheless determined to cast as much suspicion on Hamilton as they could. Jefferson intimated as much to his son-in-law. "Mr. Giles & one or two others," he wrote, delicately detaching himself from the more questionable aspects of it, "were sanguine enough to believe that the palpableness of the truths rendered a negative of them impossible, & therefore forced them on." Still, they were useful in educating the people, who "will see from this the extent of their danger." And in any case the outcome was all due to "the character of the present house, one-third of which is understood to be made up of bank directors & stock jobbers who would be voting on the case of their chief; and another third of persons blindly devoted to that party, of persons not comprehending the papers, or persons comprehending them but too indulgent to pass a vote of censure. . . ."[118]

But was there not something more to the attack on Hamilton than vindictiveness and bad political judgment? Conceivably there was, and conceivably a bit too much can be made of the Virginians' "ignorance." They may indeed have been dim on particulars, and this may indeed have made a hash of fairness and sound judgment. But in a perverse sort of way they saw only too clearly the general direction in which Hamilton's policies tended, and it was this that not only rendered compromise and reconciliation unthinkable, but made it both unnecessary and superfluous that the Virginians should learn anything new about public finance.

On technical grounds of sound fiscal management that were impeccable, Hamilton had been able to justify a policy that nonetheless had broad ideological implications. The details of his financial administration coincided to the utmost nicety with his general philosophical purposes. No matter how closely his principles may have accorded with the public interest, or whatever else he may have accomplished in pursuing them, there was at least one outcome that could be trusted never to vary. Nothing he did was undertaken in a spirit basically hostile to the interests of a very special class in American society, those men in whose hands he still believed the nation's future prosperity rested. Nothing had altered for him the Humean vision of the merchant-enterpriser, the man of large affairs, as the type whose creative energies would transform the continent. True, the Virginians viewed that type through very different eyes, and the words they applied to him were not honorific ones. But otherwise they were really not wrong when they repeated in endless ways that Hamilton was using the financial power of the United States—as he had determined to do from the beginning—for the benefit of speculators.

For example, Hamilton took it as a central operating principle that in order to establish and secure the soundness of the public credit it would be necessary to commit government resources, through the operations of the sinking fund, to maintaining the debt at par. This was as unexceptionable as could be, but it could also be described as putting a solid floor under speculators. In importing specie from Europe for this purpose, and in preparing to import more, Hamilton—the Virginians could justifiably say—was pledging the credit of the United States to guaranteeing the ill-gotten gains of domestic paper-dealers. There was no way out of it. Put in another way, Hamilton as a responsible finance minister might perceive—as he did—that conditions of war in Europe might lead to a serious short-age of specie in the United States, and that he would fail in his duty if he did not take measures accordingly. But again, a natural—and indeed intended—corollary of such measures was that building up the sinking fund and augmenting the resources of the Bank of the United States was to the undoubted advantage of merchants and speculators.

And there was yet a final aspect of Hamilton's policy that had enormous ideological implications, though of a somewhat different sort. These concerned the relationship that would and should subsist between the United States govern-ment and the revolution in France, now emerging as an issue in which popular emotions were profoundly engaged. Any number of sound technical reasons might be given to justify the suspension of payments on the French debt. But among them was one which the intensely francophile Virginians had no difficulty detect-ing. Hamilton had seen it as a risk that the old regime, should it return to power, might refuse to recognize payments made to the new. That is, no matter what else he might say or do, there was no note of welcome in Hamilton's attitude toward the new revolutionary order in France, and his prudence must have sounded somewhat discordant amid the general jubilation over the turn events were taking there. France's revolution was surely a ratification of our own, and a heartening sanction for republicanism in America. But it must have been obvious that in the United States Treasury the French Revolution was being viewed with deep disapproval.

The French Revolution
in America

I
How Two Peoples Have Viewed Each Other

The two national civilizations of Western Europe with which Americans have had most to do in the course of their history are those of Great Britain and France. But between these two sets of connections there has been a vast disparity. In their character, quality, and substance the Anglo-American and the Franco-American understandings could hardly be more different.

In the case of our relations with the French, unlike those with the English, there has somehow been nothing very cumulative. One finds strikingly little in the way of interpenetration and growth, even down to the present time. Thus a modern writer can still complain of "mutual ignorance," and urge that "each society do better in educating its citizens about the other"—a sentiment no less appropriate, or no more, than at any time during the preceding two hundred years.[1]

Past experience in this respect has been full of extravagant contradictions. The most perceptive book ever written by a foreigner about America was the work of a Frenchman. But in spite of Tocqueville, it is hard to think of one major society more consistently misinformed or uninformed about another—or subject to wilder misconceptions—than France about the United States. True, our only non-American national hero has been the Marquis de Lafayette, and our most conspicuous national monument—the Statue of Liberty—was the gift of the people of France, the funds for it having been raised by popular subscription. But while there have been periods of mutual enthusiasm—indeed, of the most passionate attachment—these have been fitful and intermittent, and generally followed by disenchantment. The more normal state has been one of suspicion, even antipathy; more normal still have been long periods of unconcern and a "mutual ignorance" that had the look, at times, of being almost actively pursued.[2] In earlier times a fair number of Frenchmen were transfixed, at a distance, by the vision of America as a kind of Arcadia. The reality of what they found, in the event of an actual visit, was oftener than not appalling. "In fact," wrote a reviewer of travel books in *Blackwood's* in 1851, "no two characters can be more antagonistic than those of Frenchman and American. However strong his predetermination, the former finds it impossible to be pleased in a country where he had fondly anticipated so much gratification."[3] Considering the infinite range of dissimilarities — in language, manners, tastes, and habits of mind — between the two societies, one is hard put to find a key to this erratic cycle of attraction and repulsion. But there must be one somewhere.

A prime fact about both peoples, in the various transactions between them, has been their extraordinary self-centeredness. Neither has been intrinsically very interested in the other. In their very attachments has been a certain want of depth: for all the ardors, something curiously selective and conditional. Indeed, the closer one examines these infatuations the more apparent it is that they have originated far more out of domestic preoccupations than in particular attributes of the other society. Their fluctuations, consequently, are to be read with reference not to a pervasive mutuality so much as to the more immediate requirements of self-interest, and perhaps to something else: elements in the other society so totally lacking from one's own that they constitute as much as anything an escape from difficulty, a luxury, a kind of exotic mirage. And these things — the self-absorption and the mirage — have sometimes been very hard to separate.[4]

In this sense a pattern of some consistency does emerge — and it all began very early. First-hand knowledge in France of the British colonies before the mid-eighteenth century was almost non-existent. But this did not prevent French intellectuals from applying whatever they did know to certain philosophical and ideological concerns of their own that were animating the salons.

According to a widely credited theory that coalesced in the 1760s and persisted for years thereafter, the climate of the New World was so unfavorable that it worked a kind of massive degeneration upon all forms of animal and human life. The American wilderness produced only stunted and cowardly animals and slothful, perverted Indians; even Europeans, placed in those unfriendly zones, could only retrogress. The colonials were mean and corrupt; they lived shorter lives; their women stopped bearing children earlier; the cattle they imported became, in successive generations, smaller and smaller. This "degeneration" theory was advanced in one form or another by Cornelius DePauw, Voltaire, the Abbé Raynal, and the naturalist Buffon, none of whom had ever been to America. Their zeal actually had two objects, neither of which arose out of direct interest in the New World itself. One was to call attention to the evils of colonialism, which threatened to dissipate the true interests and energies of France; the other was to combat the alleged fancies of the outsider Rousseau (who had never been to America either) concerning the Noble Savage, clearly a menace to civilized life.[5]

But other considerations at just this very time were giving rise to another and in many ways altogether different view of America. With the humiliations of the Peace of Paris in 1763, concluding the Seven Years' War, the French were naturally disposed in the years that followed to watch with growing interest England's difficulties with her colonies and to view more benignly than they otherwise would the colonials' defense of their rights and liberties. The other preoccupation had to do with one of the ruling dogmas of the French Enlightenment. This was the famous "idea of progress," *le progrès de l'esprit humain:* the faith in people's capacity through reason to improve the conditions of their political, economic, moral, and intellectual existence, and the conviction that progress in any of these realms would be followed by progress in all the others. The *philosophes* were well aware that France's own political and economic structure had long been in need of reform, and it was beginning to occur to them that the Americans' struggle for liberty might, within reason, serve as a useful example.[6]

This of course would require some redefinition of what the Americans were really like. An almost providential precipitant arrived in the person of Benjamin Franklin in 1767, coming for the first of his visits to Paris which were to culminate in a nine-year residence there. Already known both for his scientific accomplishments and for his impressive advocacy of colonial rights in London, Franklin quickly achieved a vogue in the cultivated and aristocratic circles of Paris that took on the proportions of a mania. The Comtesse de Polignac talked so much about Franklin at court that the King gave her an elegant Sèvres chamberpot with Franklin's portrait inside, wreathed in Turgot's motto, "He snatches the lightning from Heaven and the rod from the tyrant."[7]

Franklin proved to be very adept at promoting his own popularity and—especially after Lexington and Concord, when the pro-American enthusiasm spread throughout all classes—in advancing a particular version of his country that would be agreeable both to American interests and to those of his hosts. It seemed evident that America was making great advances in political and constitutional liberty at the expense of France's ancient enemy England. America was a land of virtuous cultivators, a land of unbounded though unostentatious prosperity. (Franklin blandly told the Physiocrats that this was because they had all adopted Physiocratic doctrines.) Through stories of Quaker life and the maxims of "Bonhomme Richard" he insinuated a picture of toleration, prudence, and homely thrift. But Franklin's most remarkable feat was in persuading the *savants* that America was in addition to all this a country of immense scientific and intellectual advancement, teeming with libraries and academies. His own example charmed them, and when he judiciously passed out memberships in the Philosophical Society of Philadelphia to various of their number they were flattered as well, and ready to believe anything. "The famous Franklin has told us," one of them wrote, "that there is no working man in Pennsylvania who does not read the newspapers at lunch time and a few good works of philosophy or politics for an hour after dinner." For at least a brief historical moment, America seemed to offer tangible proof of the liberal reformers' syllogism of progress. "If Americans," as Durand Echeverria has put it, "were prosperous, free, tolerant, and virtuous, they must of necessity be enlightened."[8]

This rapturous *américanisme* would persist into the initial stages of the French Revolution, the Americans with their own Revolution having served as a great inspiration. But the inspiration was not to last very long. For all the momentary luminosity, it proved remarkably tenuous: the French, once their Revolution had taken on a life of its own, no longer needed it.[9]

The doubts and suspicions about America thereupon tended to reassert themselves, and this was to be the substratum, forever thereafter, over which any further pro-American fancies might from time to time spring up. The émigrés and exiles who found their way to America in the 1790s were mightily disenchanted. The uncouth Americans, they found, were not "enlightened" at all. They had no refinement, no manners, no leisure, and no learning. They had time for nothing but work, and they thought of nothing but money. There was something, after all, in the idea of degeneration.[10]

Actually the "degeneration" theory took a long time to die out in France, having been no more than partially eclipsed during the period of greatest enthusiasm for American "progress." To strike at that theory was Jefferson's primary object in writing his *Notes on Virginia* in the early 1780s. Indeed, in 1786 Madame Renelle, with little sense of incongruity, happily incorporated both the progressionist and degeneration versions of America in her *Nouvelle Géographie*.[11]

It might even be said that "degeneration," except for its early scientific absurdities, never did die out: that the French mind by and large has never ceased to find degeneration, as a figurative construct, the most convenient framework within which to deal with America and American ways, and that the more formidable America became as a world presence, the more serviceable such a framework would be. That is, the American environment—however one conceives it—has created a set of influences which threaten to pervade and corrupt the entire civilized world. That which governs every aspect of the American character, and every use the Americans have made of their physical and mental energies, is cupidity. Not that the Frenchman is any stranger to avarice. But whereas the greater part of his effort goes to protecting and conserving the wealth he already has, and to enjoying it, the American's whole being—with the prodigies of organization he performs and the habits of mind appropriate to devising them—is dedicated to the getting of more, more, and more, to the death of all enjoyment, refinement, or grace.

This model of perceiving and understanding America has persisted into modern times. On the hopeful side, French publicists have occasionally suggested that the Americans could teach the French something about "practical" organizing, while they themselves might still learn a thing or two from the French about the well-ordered intelligence as an end in itself. Nevertheless the dominant side is probably still the gloomy side: Georges Duhamel's fear of sixty years ago (not unlike Stendhal's a century before him) that these same feats of organization, together with the inductive method, would snuff out everything a Frenchman finds worth living for. And now degeneration, with McDonald's and the quick lunch, is more or less complete.[12]

Though Americans in general, over time, have probably tended to be better informed about France than the French about America, the difference has been mainly one of degree. They have in their way been just as distracted in their interest and attention as the French have been regarding them.

Americans' most ardent responses to France have come at times when the French were supplying their deepest needs: ministering to their self-esteem and nourishing their very uncertain sense of their own national identity. Thus it was for much more than French assistance in the Revolution that Americans poured out their gratitude to Lafayette rather than to Louis XVI. The service performed by Lafayette—dedicating himself as a soldier to republican liberty, gratefully accepting honorary citizenship, and acknowledging himself the adopted son of the Father of His Country—was immeasurable; it represented total approval of everything America wished itself to be and hoped it was. Tocqueville's *Democracy in America* was on the whole very favorably received: in direct proportion to the degree to which Tocqueville approved—or seemed to approve—of the Americans' political and social arrangements. It did not occur to them that in writing it he was more concerned with France's future than with America's, or that he would shortly lose interest in America altogether. They would never make very systematic use of Tocqueville's book anyway, even when it came back into vogue after a century of neglect. There was an enormous passion for France in 1917, Americans being moved to transports of exaltation at the thought of their own magnanimity in responding to the sacred memory of Lafayette. The safety of the British fleet may have been of greater historic value to them than the safety of French soil, but while the British mission to arrange for military cooperation was received with due cordiality, that of France was welcomed with rapture. And yet American soldiers, when they arrived, did not really cotton to the French at all. In both the First World War and the Second they seemed for some reason to get on better with the Germans.[13]

There were too many suspicions, the two peoples and their ways were too dissimilar, for it to have been much otherwise. The Americans too had their fixed habits of perception, and these too had been formed very early—as early as the French and Indian wars—and they too proved remarkably persistent. The French at their worst were treacherous (the Deerfield massacre); even as friends (in the peace negotiations at the close of the Revolution) they were at best duplicitous. In matters of religion, the French were abandoned either to Jesuitry or to freethinking. They were immoral, frivolous, and light-minded, and they allowed their women far too much influence in affairs of state, indeed in everything. And finally, they were hopelessly impractical. The French, declared James Russell Lowell, were "the most wonderful creatures for talking wisely and acting foolishly that I ever saw."[14]

The cultural impact of France upon the United States has always been erratic and essentially limited. There has been nothing like a sustained intellectual intake; any inclination young Americans may have had to study for advanced degrees at the French universities in the post–Civil War decades—at a time of vastly expanding professionalization in American life—was discouraged by the French educational system itself. They drifted to the German universities instead.[15] French importations, both literally and figuratively, tended to fall in the luxury class: cuisine, fashions, perfumery; even the literature was taken in somewhat furtively. Probably the most knowing and sympathetic American critic of French literature in the nineteenth century was Henry James, yet James had the profoundest reservations about the state of morals he saw reflected in it. Reading Musset, he recoiled at "ladies tumbling about on disordered couches, and pairs of lovers who take refuge from an exhausted vocabulary in *biting* each other." French tastes in American literature, on the other hand (when they noticed it at all), have generally left Americans somewhat bemused. The French took up Poe and Whitman for dubious motives (as an aspect of the case for Symbolism), and their infatuation for Hemingway, Steinbeck, Caldwell, and Dos Passos in the late 1940s struck American critics as being, by then, rather on the nutty side.[16]

The young Henry Adams spent a number of months in Paris in 1860. It was the first of many visits he would make there throughout his life. He went even though, as he explains in the *Education,* he "disliked the Empire and the Emperor most particularly, but . . . he disliked most the French mind." But, he continues, "the curious result followed that, being in no way responsible for the French and sincerely disapproving them he felt at liberty to enjoy to the full everything he disapproved. Stated thus crudely, the idea sounds derisive; but as a matter of fact, several thousand Americans passed much of their time there on this understanding." The qualification: "France was not serious, and he was not serious in going there."[17]

France was not serious. Neither Adams, nor his great-grandfather, nor even his great-grandfather's friend Jefferson—to say nothing of the thousands of Americans who came after them—would ever quite be rid of that suspicion.

2

First Responses to the French Revolution

For convenience in historical bookkeeping, the usual tendency is to classify the great outpouring of popular enthusiasm in America for the French Revolution— culminating in 1793 with the arrival of Citizen Edmond Charles Genet as first minister of the French Republic to the United States—as primarily an episode in foreign relations. And yet this leaves out nearly everything that is most interesting about the Genet affair and the context in which it occurred. Indeed, regarded simply as a problem in diplomacy and foreign policy, the affair makes almost no sense. Whatever the terms of the 1778 alliance with France, no aspect of the national interest nor any of the imperatives of international diplomacy would be served by tying the fortunes of the United States even in the most limited way to those of revolutionary France in the international upheaval that erupted in 1793. America's decision at that time was for neutrality, a decision that commanded more or less general agreement, even if for great numbers it was to be a neutrality in deed but hardly in thought.

The passions aroused in America by the Revolution were all out of proportion to the scant range of choices the United States actually commanded, or to the very short lengths most Americans were prepared to go in measuring them. The disproportion arose because these emotions referred only in the most indirect way to foreign interests. Primarily they reflected needs and concerns originating in America, and Genet's failure to grasp the connection may account for virtually every blunder he made during his brief mission in the United States. The extent, on the other hand, to which this was Genet's fault may be another question.

For America, the French Revolution served two broad uses. The main one, the value of which is still almost beyond calculation, lay in the nourishment it gave to Americans' own opinion of themselves. The Revolution began at the very moment at which America, having already shown the world with its own Revolution what a liberty-loving people could do, was venturing upon its career as a constitutional republic in 1789, still needing every sanction of legitimacy it could lay hold of for its past and present course, and for its very character. The other function for America, though this did not appear until the Revolution was well advanced, was as a major point of reference for domestic political partisanship, just as such partisanship was first publicly emerging. Without these two uses, the French Revolution's impact upon Americans' attention and sensibilities would probably not have been very great. There was nothing in it that they seriously considered imitating, or that required anything in the way of purposeful national action: no committees of public safety, no guillotines, no making of war upon hostile reactionary powers. On the contrary, it was the French who were imitating them, and what the French did was viewed by Americans very selectively: through American eyes and with reference to American needs only. Their enthusiasm, moreover, took its essential shape from the early phase of the Revolution, the reform phase, rather than the later one of violence, regicide, and terror. During that earlier phase, which in American eyes lasted three years or more, approval of the Revolution was all but universal. Not until it began changing character, and its utility for America became correspondingly ambiguous, would it assume the aspect of a partisan issue.

News of the meeting of the Estates-General in May 1789, the formation of the National Assembly in June, the fall of the Bastille in July, and the Declaration of the Rights of Man and Citizen in August—to be prefixed to an actual written constitution—was received with deep exultation in the United States. The very thought that a great and ancient kingdom was acting by our example was stupendous. Washington himself could not fail to be profoundly gratified upon being sent the key to the Bastille by Lafayette with the words, "It is a tribute which I owe to you, as a son to my adoptive father, as an aide-de-camp to my General, as a Missionary of Liberty to its Patriarch"; or to be told by Thomas Paine "that the principles of America opened the Bastille is not to be doubted; and therefore the key comes to the right place"; or to hear from Catharine Macaulay Graham,

> All the friends of freedom on this side the Atlantic are now rejoicing for an event which, in all probability, has been accelerated by the American Revolution. You not only possess, yourselves, the first of human blessings, but you have been the means of raising that spirit in Europe, which I sincerely hope will, in a short time, extinguish every remain of that barbarous servitude under which all the European nations, in a less or greater degree, have so long been subject.[18]

The Declaration of the Rights of Man and Citizen was clearly an imitation of our Declaration of Independence and of the Virginia Declaration of Rights.[19] The

French were engaged in the writing of a constitution, obviously inspired by our own. Many of the leading figures of the Constituent Assembly—such men as Lafayette, Condorcet, Rabaut St.-Etienne, and La Rochefoucauld—were ardent friends of America, and outspoken about saying so. Or so it all appeared in America.[20]

Every public or official gesture toward America during this period was deeply flattering. When Franklin died in April 1790, a solemn civic eulogy was pronounced in Paris and the Assembly decreed three days' mourning. In September 1791, Louis XVI addressed a royal letter to President Washington announcing his acceptance of the recently completed constitution and praying God to have France's "very dear, great friends and allies, in his just and holy keeping." In August 1792, the Assembly took the unprecedented step of conferring honorary citizenship on three Americans, George Washington, James Madison, and Alexander Hamilton.[21]

The first flush contained no hint of partisanship as Federalists and future Federalists joined their political opponents-to-be in welcoming the Revolution. The movement in France, announced Fenno's *Gazette of the United States* in October 1789, was "one of the most glorious objects that can arrest the attention of mankind," and early enthusiasts included John Jay, John Marshall, Timothy Pickering, Chauncey Goodrich, Robert Goodloe Harper, Alexander Hamilton, Noah Webster, and virtually the entire Congregational clergy of New England. Marshall later recalled, "We were all strongly attached to France—scarcely any man more strongly than myself. I sincerely believed human liberty to depend in a great measure on the success of the French Revolution."[22] The events of 1792 brought feeling in the United States to a tremendous peak. War had broken out in April between France and the monarchies of Austria and Prussia, whose forces under the Duke of Brunswick were determined to restore order within France and arrest the further progress of the Revolution. The summer campaign had gone very badly for the disorganized French armies. But when the news arrived in the United States that the French had turned back the invaders at Valmy on September 20, and that France had declared itself a republic two days later (the monarchy having already been suspended in August), all America went mad with joy. There were bells and illuminations in Philadelphia on December 14, the day the news came in, and huge civic celebrations were held in place after place throughout the succeeding six weeks. There was one in Baltimore on December 20, in New York on December 27, in Philadelphia on January 1, in Charleston on January 11, and in Savannah on January 24. The grandest of all was the one held on January 24 in Boston. It began with a parade in the morning (which included carts heaped with bread, a roasted ox, and hogsheads of punch), followed by another in the afternoon, a great banquet at Faneuil Hall, the illumination of the State House, and fireworks in the evening. At Plymouth on that same day, the Reverend Dr. Robbins took as his text the words of the prophet Daniel: "Blessed be the name of God forever and ever. . . . *He removeth Kings.*" After patriotic music and a parade through the town, according to the contemporary account, "the company retired seasonably in the afternoon, satisfied with themselves, with each other and with their country."[23]

But there was a second budget of news from France, arriving in late March and early April 1793, that served both to maintain the general excitement and at the same time to inject public and private feeling with a strain of ambiguities and afterthoughts. On January 21, 1793, King Louis XVI had been publicly executed for treason. On February 1 the French Republic had declared war on England and Holland, and now all Europe was in arms. An alternative picture of the Revolution, dark and gloomy, was forming in the background and connecting itself with certain events that had occurred in the previous year profoundly disturbing yet somehow obscured in the general rejoicing: the rioting in Paris and elsewhere, the September massacres, and above all the news that Lafayette, deserted by his troops and by his supporters in the Assembly, had fled across the border and had been taken prisoner by the Austrians. By now public men in America had begun reconsidering their views on the French Revolution, and it was becoming more and more likely that partisan divisions which had been opened with reference to other questions would shortly be widened by this one. It was at just this very time—April 8, 1793—that Citizen Genet landed at Charleston.

But Genet's adventures are not fully comprehensible without reference to still another aspect of the French Revolution. There were several Americans in public life who spent sojourns in France for one purpose or another during this period, who had extensive acquaintance with French affairs, and who gave much thought to the problems of the Revolution. Viewing matters more closely through their eyes may shed some further light on why Americans in general behaved as they did.

3
The Revolution as Seen by Certain Concerned Americans

At the beginning of the French Revolution, when the American experience stood at its highest as an ideal for emulation, a fair number of Frenchmen prided themselves with some justification on possessing a more than adequate knowledge of American affairs and American conditions. Still, there was always something rather erratic about the state of their information—shot through as it was with patches of almost charming ignorance as well as selective inattention, to say nothing of the uses to which they put it. For example, when these *américanistes,* as they were called, first began debating a constitution for France and urging one supreme and undivided legislature in opposition to the *anglomane* party's advocacy of a king-lords-commons balance, they appealed to the American example. But while it was true that the Americans had no House of Lords, the fact was that their national Congress and all their state legislatures except one were bicameral, whereas "balance"—the theoretical ground on which both the American and English constitutions rested—was the last thing the *américanistes* wanted.[24] This distractedness was evident in small things as well as large. When the French National Convention later decided to award honorary citizenship to a number of distinguished foreigners, after due study they conferred it upon "Georges Washington," "Jean Hamilton," and "N. Madisson."[25]

A good many leading figures in America, on the other hand, from the President on down, were quite well informed about France and French politics, and gave them much attention. Four of these in particular, through their having had direct experience in French affairs, are of more than ordinary interest. Vice-President John Adams had spent ten years abroad on various diplomatic missions, two of them to France, and had become acquainted there with a number of the *philosophes*. Thomas Jefferson, as previously noted, had spent four years as United States minister to France before coming home late in 1789 to assume his duties as Secretary of State. Gouverneur Morris came to Paris on private business early in 1789, was himself subsequently appointed minister there, and served in that capacity until his replacement by James Monroe, thus witnessing at first hand all phases of the Revolution through Thermidor. To these should be added Thomas Paine, an American by adoption if not by birth, whose involvement in the Revolution was in its way closer than any of the others'. It included not only an acquaintance with most of the moving spirits but also Paine's actually serving as a deputy in the French Assembly during the period of the Gironde ascendancy. Besides their having all taken part in the American Revolution, these men represented a continuity of knowledge and experience of France that spanned more than a decade. Each was in a position, moreover, being sufficiently close to the center of things, to offer important advice to the French in their novel and bewildering circumstances, and generously did so on a number of occasions.

But their advice was invariably rejected. And rightly so, even though a good deal of it might seem at first glance quite reasonable. For despite their considerable information, their sympathies, and their close connections, these men actually had little more feeling for France's requirements than the French had for America's. For all the apparent variation in their prescriptions, they could not help seeing everything with reference to American experience, hopelessly different from France's, and translating everything they saw into an American idiom. In some respects, indeed, their assessments of French affairs were most abstract at precisely the moment of their closest concern with them.

The case is clearest with regard to John Adams. Though Adams, when he first arrived in France in 1778, was somewhat irritated at being mistaken for his cousin Samuel ("ah, le fameux Adams," the author of *Common Sense*),[26] he was highly pleased and flattered by the interest the French *savants* took in the American Revolution. And yet Turgot, Condorcet, and their followers were convinced, even this early, that constitutional reform in France could be brought about only through lodging all legislative power in a supreme unicameral assembly. Adams was subsequently appalled, especially during the five years or so prior to the

French Revolution, at the extent to which this heresy, so repugnant to the soundest principles of political science (as expressed in his own *Thoughts on Government*), had gained currency in France. He himself had been the principal architect of the Massachusetts constitution of 1780, he had given much study to ancient and modern history and to innumerable works on government, and he understandably regarded himself as an authority. The publication of his own views in the three-volume *Defence of the American Constitutions* (1787–88) was undertaken in no small part to provide instruction to the French.[27]

Adams's ruling dogma was "balance." In that current of eighteenth-century English opposition thought upon which the American Revolution had itself been justified, an insistence upon balance was the central element. The miraculous equilibrium of king, lords, and commons that was presumed to have characterized the English constitution at its purest had been corrupted by the royal government, which had led in turn to a mounting climax of tyrannical abuses. The substitution of a republic in America for a constitutional monarchy did not alter the basic principle that a separation and balance of powers between an executive and an upper and a lower chamber were indispensable for checking the excesses of any one of them. And although John Adams was rather more literal-minded about it than his compatriots, some form of this conventional wisdom was taken for granted by most Americans. Adams was convinced that only within such a frame-work could reform in any government occur, and he lectured the French at great length to this effect. Then when news arrived in the United States in 1790 that the Constituent Assembly had voted to institute a weak executive and a unicameral legislature, Adams threw up his hands in disgust. This "must involve France in great and lasting calamities."[28]

There was an odd paradox in Adams's attitude about revolutions in countries other than America—though this too was widely shared by his countrymen, including Jefferson. On the one hand, America's experience was unique. No other people could be expected to duplicate it; the French were not wholly prepared for the degree of liberty which Americans had achieved. On the other hand, if they *should* make an effort in that direction (Adams was certainly not disposed to deny their right to do it), the only imaginable model was America. Whatever they did, then, would somehow be judged by the extent to which it did or did not approximate the American model.[29] Above all, there had to be balance, and the aristocracy, the Third Estate sitting separately, and the king with a veto all had an indispensable part to play in maintaining it. Adams never forgave the National Assembly for not using his *Defence* as a kind of handbook.

It was true that Adams and Edmund Burke both opposed the French Revolution from the beginning. But they did so on substantially different grounds. Adams was no Burkean (few Americans were); indeed, he thought that whatever was of value in Burke's *Reflections* had come from his own ideas. Burke's laments for the age of chivalry left him cold; he objected to Burke's "swinish multitude" phrase; and he could not imagine why Burke should have said that France before 1789 had the "elements of a constitution very nearly as good as could be wished."[30] To be sure, Adams thought the French had to begin with those elements—king and nobility—that were already there. But he never placed the massive emphasis on tradition and custom that Burke did; no American could. It was simply that if the French insisted on having a revolution, they were going about it in all the wrong ways.

The main difficulty with Adams's entire scheme of thought lay in his conception of aristocracy, and in his dogmas about division of powers. His attitudes toward both were in this context very American. Though scandalized (as most Americans were) by what he saw as the frivolity and licentiousness of the French aristocracy, he still found it difficult to think of them as being much more than persons of unusual wealth and influence, with certain advantages of birth and presumably of talent, which was all that an "aristocracy" in any society really meant to him. He saw no reason why there should not be a place for such a class in any country, even a republic. What he could not grasp—few other Americans could either, having no experience of it—was the nature and extent of entrenched privilege in French society, the determination of the bourgeoisie to strike it down, and the stark resistance of the French aristocracy to any social change that would substantially alter their position. Even the mildest of the French reformers saw that no reconstruction was possible without consolidation of state power to break this grip, and that anything short of it would mean deadlock. In America, the revolutionary spirit had arisen from *resistance* to centralized authority. Adams never realized that for France the sort of dispersal and separation of powers which he (and a majority of his countrymen) took for granted could only have reactionary implications.[31]

Thomas Jefferson's mind, whatever its imprecisions, was rather more flexible so far as France was concerned than Adams's. It was unquestionably more optimistic. But with all just allowances, it is striking how little many of their preconceptions differed, and it is doubtful whether Jefferson's appraisal of the political terrain in France was either more perceptive or less incorrigibly American than that of Adams. For example, when the Assembly of Notables in 1787 blocked the plan of Calonne, the royal Finance Minister, to reform France's antiquated tax system through a land tax from which no one would be exempt, and by establishing provincial assemblies elected by all the taxpayers, Jefferson, rather than being shocked by the Notables' crass self-interest, thought they showed a fine spirit of independence in the face of threatened royal encroachment. "I think," he wrote Adams, "that in the course of three months the royal authority has lost, and the rights of the nation gained, as much ground, by a revolution in public opinion, only, as England gained in all her civil wars under the Stuarts."[32] The aristocratic resurgence was at its peak in 1788, yet Jefferson saw the demand of the provincial assemblies for more powers for the nobility and clergy as "a liberal movement to check the crown."[33] In August of that year he was serenely assuring Monroe that "this country will within two or three years be in the enjoiment of a tolerably free constitution, and that without it's having cost them a drop of blood." (Though "the English papers," he added, "have set the whole nation to cutting throats.")[34] Not until the Parlement of Paris demanded that the Estates-General meet as separate orders did Jefferson begin to see the "cloven hoof" of the aristocracy. But like Adams, he remained essentially impervious to the critical issue of aristocratic privilege, and as late as May 1789 he was urging upon Lafayette a "compromise"—totally unacceptable to the Third Estate—providing for a two-house legislature, one for the privileged orders and the other for the Third Estate. He too thought primarily in categories of "balance," and assumed that a constitutional monarchy represented about all the liberty the French were prepared for. The "Charter of Rights" he proposed to the King on June 3, through Rabaut St.-Etienne, fell substantially short of what the principal leaders by then were willing to settle for.[35]

Not until mid-June, when the deputies constituted themselves as a single National Assembly which they declared was alone the legitimate voice of the French nation, did Jefferson begin to realize that the primary problem facing France was the unwillingness of the nobility to surrender their privileged position and the King's inability to free himself from their influence.[36] But once the Third Estate had asserted its independence, and the King appeared to have acquiesced in it, Jefferson's optimism returned with a rush. "I think," he wrote Paine as he was packing up to depart for America, "there is no possibility of any thing's hindering their final establishment of a good constitution, which will in it's principles and merit be about a middle term between that of England and the United States."[37]

Though each new stage of the Revolution took Jefferson somewhat by surprise, there is no doubt that he showed himself better prepared than Adams to adjust himself to it. This was because he wanted very much to believe that everything would turn out all right, even when the evidence before him might seem to point otherwise. One reason for this (and a factor which shaped his reception to everything that happened in France) was his hatred toward England. When Madison informed him before he left France that the United States Congress had rejected the former's proposal for tonnage discrimination against England and had placed English commerce on the same footing as France's, Jefferson aired his rage against that country which "has moved heaven, earth, and hell to exterminate us in war, has insulted us in all her councils in peace, shut her doors to us in every part where her interests would admit it, libelled us in foreign nations, [etc.] . . ." All this in contrast to France: "It is impossible to desire better dispositions towards us, than prevail in this assembly. Our proceedings have been viewed as a model for them on every occasion; and tho in the heat of debate men are generally disposed to contradict every authority urged by their opponents, ours has been treated like that of the bible, open to explanation but not to question." This was largely fancy. It was probably as true then as Pierre Adet would claim it to be seven years later, that "Mr. Jefferson loves us because he detests England. . . ."[38]

Back in the United States, Jefferson continued to receive news from France in the same spirit. By the early months of 1791 there had come to be an additional factor, arising from his domestic preoccupations and having only secondarily to do with events in France, that determined even more firmly his response to such news. This was his growing antipathy to Hamilton's Treasury system, his suspicion of Hamilton's predilections toward England, and his dawning conviction—from which nothing henceforth would shake him—that Hamilton and his followers were plotting to steer the United States government into monarchy. "I look with great anxiety," he wrote to George Mason, "for the firm establishment of the new government in France. . . . I consider the establishment and success of their government as necessary to stay up our own and to prevent it from falling back to that kind of Half-way-house, the English constitution." There were those among us, he warned, who believed the English form "to contain whatever is perfect in human institutions. . . ." In mid-June of the following year, he begins a letter to Lafayette: "Behold you, then, my dear friend, at the head of a great army establishing the liberties of your country against a foreign enemy." But from here on, the letter is all about "corruption," "stock-jobbers," and "king-jobbers" in the United States. France was really quite incidental.[39]

The news *had* to be favorable, and when it was otherwise, Jefferson could show a glint of real displeasure toward its source. Washington had some misgivings about signing a letter congratulating the King on his acceptance of the French constitution, because he suspected conditions in France were beginning to deteriorate. The vexed Jefferson was certain that this reluctance was owing not to the facts of the case but to the bad influence upon Washington of the new United States minister in Paris. "The fact is, that Gouverneur Morris, a high flying monarchy-man, shutting his eyes & his faith to every fact against his wishes, & believing everything he desires to be true, has kept the President's mind constantly poisoned with his forebodings."[40] The reports of William Short, just transferred to The Hague from Paris, where he had been chargé d'affaires since Jefferson's departure, on the events of the summer of 1792 were far less temperate than Morris's. They threw Jefferson into considerable agitation. Short in his dispatches used such phrases as "those mad and corrupted people in France who under the name of liberty have destroyed their own government," "the most mad, wicked and atrocious assembly that ever was collected in any country," "the streets literally are red with blood," "The mob and demagogues of Paris had carried their fury in this line as far as it could go," and "I should not be at all surprized to hear of the present leaders being hung by the people. Such has been the moral of this revolution from the beginning." Short was Jefferson's own protégé, and had once been his private secretary. Now here he was on his own, writing the most unpleasant things.[41]

Jefferson on January 3, 1793, addressed to him a stern reproof. "The tone of your letters had for some time given me pain, on account of the extreme warmth with which they censured the proceedings of the Jacobins of France." He then read Short a little homily along lines of having to break eggs before making omelets. "In the struggle which was necessary," he said, "many guilty persons fell without the forms of trial, and with them some innocent. These I deplore as much as any body. . . ." But, he continued, in the subsequently famous "Adam and Eve" passage,

The liberty of the whole earth was depending on the issue of the contest, and was ever such a prize won with so little innocent blood? My own affections have been deeply wounded by some of the martyrs to this cause, but rather than it should have failed, I would have seen half the earth desolated. Were there but an Adam & an Eve left in every country, & left free, it would be better than as it now is.

Jefferson was quite blunt about the reasons for his annoyance, and they had only incidentally to do with what was happening in France. One was: "I have expressed to you my sentiments, because they are really those of 99 in an hundred of our citizens. The universal feasts, and rejoicings which have lately been had on account of the successes of the French shewed the genuine effusions of their hearts. You have been ... hurried into a temper of mind which would be extremely disrelished if known to your countrymen." And the other reason: "There are in the U.S. some characters of opposite principles; ... all of them hostile to France and looking to England as the staff of their hope." These men, he said, accepted the American constitution "only as a stepping stone to monarchy." but the "successes of republicanism in France have given the coup de grace to their prospects, and I hope to their projects. I have developed to you faithfully the sentiments of your country, that you may govern yourself accordingly."[42] Four days later Jefferson was in a more equable frame of mind. Alluding to favorable news of the French armies, he exulted to his son-in-law. "The sensation it has produced here, and the indications of them in the public papers, have shown that the form our own government was to take depended much more on events in France than any body had before imagined." In other words, the French enthusiasm now appeared to be bringing great benefits to the Republican interest.[43]

Perhaps such men as Jefferson and Adams had by this time lost their capacity to judge, having been away from France too long, and were now either fitting everything they heard into preconceived abstractions that made no sense outside an American setting, or else reading all the news from abroad in the light of political requirements at home. But there were other Americans who were still on the ground, and who could still form their opinions on the basis of direct observation.

One of these was Gouverneur Morris. There are grounds for concluding that Morris was in many ways a more perceptive witness than any of the others.[44] There has also been a contrary tendency, following Jefferson, to brush him off with regard to either his reliability or his competence as hopelessly attached to the trappings of the *ancien régime*.[45] Actually Morris's case does not quite fit either judgment.

Gouverneur Morris was one of the most gifted writers of his time, though he never wrote any books and gave no thought whatever, so far as is known, to literary pursuits. Among the qualities which nourished his talent, and may in some measure account for it, were a very sharp intellect (he had a sharp tongue as well), social adroitness and an easy presence, and a connoisseur's relish for the intricate games people played with each other. He also had a wicked sense of humor, an element strikingly absent in nearly all the other founders of the American republic.

One sees all this in Morris's extraordinary diary, which was never intended for publication, and in his letters. In his perversity and differentness (Hamilton called him "a native of this country but by genius an exotic"), Morris sits somewhat uneasily in the gallery of American statesmen.[46]

He was born in 1752 at Morrisania, New York; his father, Lewis Morris, was the second lord of the manor. He was educated at King's College, read law with William Smith, and was admitted to the bar at nineteen. When the Revolution came, though his mother and one of his half-brothers remained Loyalists, Morris attached himself wholeheartedly to the American cause. He took a leading part in the New York Provincial Congress, and he, Jay, and Livingston drafted New York's first state constitution. (Morris urged religious toleration and the abolition of slavery, achieving the one but not the other.) He sat in the Continental Congress in 1778 and 1779, drafting some of Congress's most important papers, and served for four years as Assistant Superintendent of Finance under Robert Morris. He came to know Washington well, and remained devoted to him forever after. As a delegate to the Constitutional Convention he wanted a President who would be elected for life (naturally it would be Washington), and who would appoint all the senators himself. Some of the compromises—those on slavery, and on equal representation in the Senate—he did not like at all. But, as even Madison conceded, he loyally accepted them, and it was Gouverneur Morris's endowed pen that gave the Constitution the form in which we now have it. Shortly thereafter he sailed for France with various business schemes in mind, involving speculation in American lands and the American foreign debt, to be negotiated on behalf of Robert Morris, William Constable, and himself. But business would occupy only a portion of his time and attention, France being the country he most delighted in. He had little use for England.[47]

Morris, arriving with letters of introduction from Washington, Franklin, and the Comte de Moustier, found ready admission to the most influential circles of French society and was an instant success. He soon knew everyone, including Adélaïde Marie Emilie, Comtesse de Flahaut, with whom he began an enchanting love affair which would go on for the next three years. Morris's rival here was Talleyrand, the Bishop of Autun, whom he genially proceeded to unseat as the Countess's first friend. Morris heard all the inside talk of politics and court intrigues, at the same time witnessing the initial scenes of the Revolution. But he viewed it all rather sardonically. He had few illusions about what and whom he saw, and the observations he put down in his diary and letters bear many a mark of cool judgment.

He found the nobility selfish, depraved, and irresponsible. "Hugging the dear Privileges of Centuries long elapsed, they have clamored about the Court while their Adversaries have possessed themselves fully of the public Confidence everywhere."[48] He saw that the National Assembly had the loyalty of the people and of the army, and that the endless plots and maneuverings of the aristocracy were bound to fail. The moderate middle group in the Assembly ("really friends to a good free Government"), he told Washington in January 1790, were well-meaning, though they "have unfortunately acquired their ideas of Government from Books and are admirable Fellows upon Paper; . . . it is not to be wondered at if the Systems taken out of Books are fit for nothing but to be put into Books again." The third group "is composed of what are called here the *Enragés,* that is the Madmen. These are the most numerous and are of that Class which in America is known by the name of pettifogging Lawyers. . . ." He did not know what would become of the Assembly's efforts to form a constitution. ("They have all that romantic Spirit and all those romantic Ideas of Government which, happily for America, we were cured of before it was too late.") He was not impressed by the King's ministers. (Montmorin "means well, very well. But he means it feebly.") As for the King himself, Louis could probably still regain his authority if he "were not the small beer Character that he is." Undoubtedly it was candid letters like these—lucid, precise, and comprehensive—that determined Washington to appoint Morris minister to France early in 1792.[49] Morris despaired for the public finances. In the present Ministry "there is neither the Mind to conceive, the Heart to dare nor the Hand to execute such things. They will therefore continue to pile up System upon System without advancing one Inch. The dreadful primaeval Curse is repeated upon them all. Paper thou art and unto Paper thou shalt return."[50]

These were the words of an American Whig, certainly no Burke, and many of his attitudes do not seem very different from those of either Adams or Jefferson, except that his eye may have been a bit clearer and his sense of detail more picturesque. True, he was hardly optimistic about the course of events, and he saw little good in the Constitution of 1791. He continued to think that a constitutional monarchy was the best form France could expect, and he persisted in the idea that a strong executive with a veto, a popular assembly, and an upper chamber of nobles to stand between them would be the best thing—long after Jefferson had given up that idea and after the aristocracy as a separate order had itself been done away with. Nevertheless much of the advice he gave to both the aristocracy and the King—he had channels for reaching both—had a certain air of good sense.

The nobles must stop plotting. "I tell him in plain terms," Morris wrote after a conversation with the Comte de Luxembourg, "that the aristocratic party must be quiet unless they wish to be hanged."[51] He said the same thing, and more, to the King in the summer of 1791, though more respectfully. The King and Queen should forbid anyone to speak to them about the pending constitution, saying, "We do not wish in any way to influence or prejudice the question, as it is a solemn convention between the Nation and its Head."[52] The King should make a speech to the Assembly, which Morris had obligingly drafted:

> Gentlemen,
> It is no longer your King who speaks. Louis the sixteenth has become a private individual. You have just offered him the Crown and made known the conditions under which he must accept it.

After declaring that his love for the French people and his sense of duty left him no choice but to accept the constitution, the King should then proceed in manly fashion to point out the constitution's errors, propose changes, and in effect bargain for improvements which would strengthen his own position.[53]

Meanwhile a general expectation had arisen that there would be a shortage of bread by the spring of 1792, and Morris was all ready with a plan whereby the King might purchase stocks of flour in America (he, Morris, would lend his assistance without any remuneration), store them in England, and distribute them gratis to the poor in the event of famine. This would demonstrate the King's solicitude for his people and would fortify their loyalty to him.[54]

None of Morris's sage advice was taken. On September 14 the King accepted the constitution unconditionally; he made no such speech as Morris had prepared for him; nothing came of the flour plan. This conservative but humane course of action, with an eye to solid reforms—strong and responsible administration, sound finances, disciplined armies, bread for the poor, and so on—seems not to have been taken seriously for a moment. This was because such schemes, for all their ostensible hard-headedness, had almost no bearing on the state of affairs in France as they then stood, being just as abstract in their way, and just as unconnected with the realities of French politics, as the optimism of Jefferson or the pedantic dogmatism of Adams.

For one thing, the French nation in its momentum had been carried far beyond the conventional wisdom of eighteenth-century Anglo-American political science and its pieties about balanced government in which Morris was still trapped, and even the King and his leading minister Montmorin somehow understood that much. As little respect as Morris had for the French aristocracy, he could not get it out of his head that there had to be a hereditary senate to serve as a balance between a strong monarchy—which he also saw as indispensable—and a popular legislative body. He kept urging this repeatedly upon Lafayette, the King, and anyone else who would listen from the beginning of the Revolution to the very eve of the monarchy's own downfall. To be sure, he was capable of smiling at himself. "This Morning employ myself in preparing a Form of Government for this Country," Morris wrote in his diary on December 7, 1791. The next day he had a caller who told him he knew all about America even though he had never been there, that he had studied the subject of constitutions for fifty years, had concluded that the American constitution was "good for Nothing," and had written General Washington telling him so and enclosing a new one. "I get Rid of him as soon as I can but yet I cannot help being struck with the Similitude of a Frenchman who makes Constitutions for America and an American who performs the same good Office for France. Self Love tells me that there is a great Difference . . . but Self Love is a dangerous Counsellor."[55]

But the other snare, besides that of "balance," in which Morris was stuck was somewhat more subtle. Though the United States had no monarchy, and nobody seriously thought of installing one, the kind of monarchy Morris envisioned for France—for all his knowing talk of special conditions there—was one which only an American could have thought of. Morris's advice to Louis was all of a pattern. The one thing that all Americans who had been through their own Revolution took for granted, no matter how widely their opinions on other questions might vary, was that any executive person needed to devote all possible effort to obtaining the loyalty, support, and consent of the citizenry in order to function with any authority whatever. But the man Morris was saying this to was paralyzed. He no longer had the initiative, if indeed he ever did have it, and it was not simply the popular fury but also the accumulated weight, influence, and moral authority of the French aristocracy that had immobilized him. In short, the "monarch" whom Morris somehow pictured as reading his speeches and taking the measured steps he had marked out—as little faith as Morris may have had in Louis XVI—resembled nobody so much as General Washington.

Morris had been doing all these things in the capacity of a private person, and his activities had become only too well known. Even in the United States he now had the reputation of a "monarchy man," and of one who was indiscreet and who kept an insufficient check on his wit. He took up his duties as United States minister to France in June 1792. Washington wrote him gravely that there had been considerable opposition to his confirmation and told him the reasons, whereupon Morris contritely promised to observe "Circumspection of Conduct." He also told the French Foreign Minister, Dumouriez, that "being at present a public Man I consider it as my Duty not to meddle with their Affairs."[56]

Morris did not immediately live up to his promise. He was still up to his chin in inside politics, dispensing endless advice, dabbling in hypothetical constitutions, and receiving the King's money for safekeeping. With the storming of the Tuileries on August 10, 1792, and the termination of the monarchy for all practical purposes, this nonsense ceased—though a few terror-stricken aristocrats subsequently took refuge in Morris's house, and he exercised both ingenuity and courage in preventing them from being caught.

From this point on, however, Morris did no more intriguing, and the primary role he now played was that of the responsible diplomat. He played it well. He had always been a man of great industry, even when his days were filled with social calls, dinners, the opera, the Comédie, and visits to Madame. Now he no longer went out much. His reports home were detailed, detached, and unemotional, even when describing such scenes as the Paris massacres of September 1792, and when he made predictions most of them were quite accurate. Morris was the only foreign representative to remain through the period of the Terror, and he served his country's interests ably and faithfully. But to the government of the new French Republic established under the Gironde, Morris, in view of his past activities, was not a welcome personage. Its leaders had little to do with him and kept him more or less isolated. They did not bother to consult him about the new minister they were sending to America, nor did they tell him anything about the objects of his mission.

In this lies a final irony. Morris, indeed, never approved the course taken by the French Revolution. But he never associated himself with the wailings of Short, never questioned the power of the Assembly, and never doubted the right of the French or any other people to change their government in any way they chose. But more pertinently, Morris was now in a position to be of far greater use to the Girondins—instructing them as to what they might or might not expect from the Genet mission—than he ever could have been to the royal court. His very American meddling had given them to imagine a deep and sinister rapport with the Old Regime, which in fact had never existed. The truth was that for all practical purposes the court had paid no more attention to him than they themselves would.

Thomas Paine, the first clear voice to call for the independence of the American colonies, a supporter of the French Revolution from its outset, and even a participant, through a set of extraordinary circumstances, in the actual deliberations of the French Assembly, certainly deserves some special notice. But what gives his experience a particular interest is that, despite his relatively late appearance in America as an emigrant from England, Thomas Paine was in certain respects more thoroughly American than any of the Americans so far observed. In his very rootlessness, his self-promotion, his freedom from the inhibitions of class, his impatience with the claims of tradition and institutions, and in his failures as well as his successes, Paine was a modern before his time. Had he not thrown quite so much dust in his countrymen's eyes during his own lifetime—for which they took an immoderately long time to forgive him—he would surely have been recognized by the mid-nineteenth century as a type representing something basic in the American character.[57]

Paine could never be psychologically contained by the social and economic setting of eighteenth-century England, though that same milieu had the resources for ensuring that a man of his erratic sort would not be much other than a loser for the first thirty-seven years of his life. He was born in 1737 at Thetford in Norfolk; his mild and rather ineffectual father was a corsetmaker, his mother an attorney's daughter who had married beneath her station. She seems to have been something of a scold. They "distressed themselves" to send their only child to the local grammar school. Thomas was sharp enough—he liked mathematics, scientific subjects, and poetry—but he was too lazy to learn Latin, the minimum prerequisite for anyone of his class who might hope to get into the professions. He was apprenticed to his father's trade at thirteen, but though he had a natural skill with tools, he knocked about as a journeyman and then as a master staymaker for several years without success. He passed an examination for the excise service, but was discharged from his first post for stamping goods without bothering to inspect them. After being reinstated, he got involved in an episode that gave him his first taste of being generally noticed. This was a movement by the excisemen to get their salaries raised.[58] Paine wrote a petition and then a pamphlet which was distributed throughout the excise service and in government circles, and he spent a great deal of time in London frequenting coffee-houses, going to scientific lectures, and attending to the cause. He argued the excisemen's case with great eloquence. He also found the attention vastly satisfying, a thing he could never thereafter do without for very long. But nothing came of his efforts, and in fact he was discharged a second time for being away from his post in Lewes without leave, neglecting his duties, and also, probably, for having engaged in a very early version of trade-unionism. Paine was certain that it was no other than George III himself, desirous of getting his own salary raised, who was responsible for this. One may thus sympathize with his sullen conclusion, then and there, that kings in general and this one in particular were an unnecessary luxury. But one person of consequence to whose benevolent notice Paine came while in London was Benjamin Franklin, the self-made man, ever afterward the American he admired above all others.[59]

Meanwhile his second wife's tobacco shop, which he was supposedly managing on the side, was slipping into insolvency, and after his discharge from the excise service his situation was desperate. He decided to escape from his troubles by going to America. The marriage, which had never been satisfactory, was dissolved, and the settlement of £35 which he received from his wife was used to purchase a first-class passage. He landed at Philadelphia in November 1774—just after the adjournment of the First Continental Congress—armed with a letter of introduction from Franklin.[60]

Paine's first substantial success came as a journalist; he had caught on as a kind of managing editor for Robert Aitken's recently founded *Pennsylvania Magazine,* whose circulation he helped to increase more than double. He was prepared to write about anything, and began to develop a style that could hit people reading as they ran; he balanced, as he put it, "warm passions with a cool temper." He threw himself into Philadelphia life, made acquaintances high and low, embraced his new country with zest, and became more American than the Americans. By the end of 1775 the most common subject of talk everywhere was independence, and Paine, seeing how sentiment was running, saw no reason why he should not go public with it. He himself had already washed his hands of George III. *Common Sense* was published in January 1776, a little over a year after Paine's arrival, and quickly became America's first best-seller. There is no question that with this fifty-page pamphlet—with its confident call for an end to all further subservience to the trumperies of monarchy and hereditary government—Thomas Paine did more than any other individual to prepare the popular mind in America for total separation.[61]

Paine's subsequent services to the Revolution were varied and considerable, and nobody was prepared to acknowledge them more gratefully than Washington himself. Paine served in the army during the retreat across New Jersey in 1776; his *Crisis* papers ("These are the times that try men's souls") did much to hearten the troops during that winter; he was secretary to Congress's Committee on Foreign Affairs from 1777 to 1779 and Clerk of the Pennsylvania Assembly until 1781; and he accompanied John Laurens on a successful mission to France in 1781 to obtain money and supplies. When the war was over, New York recognized his services by giving him a farm in New Rochelle; Pennsylvania did so with a gift of £300; and Congress voted him $3,000. Washington had let it be known that he thought Paine deserved to be provided for.[62]

By this time Paine, honored and famous, had begun turning his mind to wholly different matters. He had invented an iron bridge, for which he had great expectations, and by 1787 he had concluded that the best way to get the bridge built and to get rich with it was to have it endorsed by the French Academy of Sciences and by the Royal Society of London. With this in mind, he set sail in April of that year for Europe. He planned on an early return, but would in fact be gone for fifteen years.[63]

Paine's subsequent reputation as a "radical" was not one which he especially sought, and it was certainly not based on his activities in the American Revolution. It was the result of his doings in Europe, and even so, he rather stumbled into it. Moreover, it would be based on one thing for the English public (his anti-monarchical and reform ideas in *The Rights of Man*), and on quite another (his deistic "blasphemies" in *The Age of Reason*) for the American. His personal characteristics—his quarrelsomeness, lack of self-discipline, slovenly habits, and addiction to drink—would then be of great assistance to those already prepared to recoil from him on other grounds. Nor did his involvement with the French Revolution endear him to the English upper classes, though prior to this he had formed quite a number of connections there which he was not at all reticent about cultivating.

In America, as Paine's most recent biographer says, he had "propagandized for no great social experiments," and "rarely risked energy or reputation on lost causes."[64] There, he was primarily an American nationalist. As early as *Common Sense* he called for a strong central government, a national navy, and a public debt. (It was not Hamilton, but Paine, who first declared, "A national debt is a national bond.")[65] He had no patience with paper-money schemes or country-party parochialism, and he, like Hamilton and Madison, favored a national impost in the 1780s. During that period he heartily agreed with Robert Morris and his allies on their policies regarding the Bank of North America and fiscal responsibility, and wrote vigorous articles in support of them. He approved of the new Constitution, and said that if he had been on hand he would have voted for it. He was, in short, a good Federalist.[66]

And he was something more: well in advance of his time, Paine was a kind of natural democrat. He believed in careers open to talent (and luck), he detested special privilege, and he was perfectly willing to associate with anybody. He was on familiar terms not only with the artisans of Philadelphia but with important persons everywhere. He was, as Americans perennially have been, an incurable name-dropper.[67] As for his ideas about government, they were admirably simple. Being ignorant of most standard treatises on the subject, he was not tied up in such abstractions as "balance." He thought there should be frequent rotation in office, and tended to favor unicameral legislatures because he assumed they would be more effective in centralizing power and in expressing the popular will—though the failure of the Federal Constitution to establish one seems not to have troubled him unduly. Most of this was in *Common Sense,* and his subsequent writings were largely variations on his original republican principles. All in all, there was no sizable sector of American opinion that could not find something in the Revolutionary writings of Thomas Paine—indeed, the greater part of them—of which it could wholeheartedly approve.

Nor would it be much of an oversimplification to say that what Paine did when he got back to England was to write *Common Sense* all over again, with a special twist for the English scene and with the topical interest of the French Revolution to spur him on. It was for this that he would ultimately be harried out of that country and indicted for seditious treason. Had he stopped there, however, his name in America would today be surrounded by few ambiguities, and would long since have simply been registered alongside those of other hallowed patriots of the War for Independence. Be all that as it may, when Paine first arrived back in the Old World he had little on his mind besides his iron bridge.

In the period from May 1787 to September 1792, Paine was back and forth between England and France so many times on behalf of his bridge that one all but loses track of him. (It was a very good bridge, entirely sound in its mechanical principles, though he never reaped the benefits of it.)[68] Thanks to certain old friends of Franklin, he managed to pry a favorable endorsement out of the Academy of Sciences, though he got nowhere—despite the promises of Jefferson and Lafayette—in his efforts to interest the French government in erecting the bridge across the Seine. Paine's interest in French politics at this period was rather perfunctory. His opinions were no sharper nor more advanced than those of Jefferson; his principal associates were the liberal nobility of Jefferson's circle; and his approval of the Revolution, once it began, proceeded along much the same mildly utopian lines as Jefferson's. During his sojourns in England, indeed, his views of events in France were wholly shaped by Jefferson's letters.[69]

Though Paine had bad luck in England with his bridge, he spent a fair portion of his time there, at least by his account, in the company of dukes and earls, which he hugely enjoyed, and he also became quite friendly with Edmund Burke. At first he and Burke talked mostly about bridges, Paine's bridge in particular, but as time went on they got more and more into politics. Paine thought it a pity that France and England were not on better terms; he believed that English society and government could do with a number of improvements, and that the efforts currently being made by the French might well serve as a salutary example. The dour Burke tended to think the opposite, on every count.[70]

Their relations seem not to have been disturbed initially by these differences of view. But by January 1791 Burke had had enough. Paine had written him enthusiastically from Paris on how well the Revolution was going, and had said that he ought to welcome it in England. Burke replied grimly that the Revolution could contaminate England irrevocably, and that he did not intend to spend the remainder of his days destroying the English constitution. "Do you not know," he grated, "that I have always opposed the things called reform . . . because I did not think them reforms." In Parliament shortly thereafter he delivered a harrowing attack on the Revolution. Paine was deeply hurt. "I am so out of humor with Mr. Burke," he reported after returning to London, ". . . that I have not called on him." Burke's *Reflections on the Revolution in France* appeared on November 1, 1790. Paine, who by now was all ready for it, brought out *The Rights of Man, Part I,* the following March.[71]

In an immediate sense, Paine's great manifesto required the stimulus of a personal falling-out even to set its ideas in order. "Had he not urged the controversy," Paine wrote of Burke, "I had most probably been a silent man," and in view of Paine's laziness, and on the other hand his touchiness and vanity, one is inclined to take him at his word. Yet the fact was that no two minds could have been less compatible. Paine's was of the New World in almost every sense, while Burke's—whatever his feeling for the American colonies at the time of the Stamp Act—was as starkly anti-American in its whole texture as that of any British thinker of the eighteenth century. Burke thought that social-contract and natural-rights theory was largely a waste of time. For him, legitimacy in government depended on a multiplicity of elements other than the mere consent of the citizens, which might be withdrawn at any moment in a gust of irresponsible agitation. The purest embodiment of legitimacy was the English constitution, which was the deposit of time, experience, wisdom, and the peculiar circumstances and character of the English people. It meant the hereditary principle in government, just as with property, and it meant an established church, all cemented in rights, duties, and affections—a totality, the subversion of one aspect of which, through thoughtless change, could bring about disintegration of the whole. The revolution in France represented an assault on all these principles, and its example could be mortally contagious. Reform societies in England rejoicing in the events in France might well succeed in compromising Englishmen's loyalty to their constitution, and they should be resisted and denounced.[72]

Paine did not fully understand Burke's argument, which, though full of venom, was subtle and intricate. He had begun his reply even before reading it; he knew very little about the actual conditions that had led up to the French Revolution, and he did not discuss these at all in *The Rights of Man*. Moreover, though some of his ideas about government had altered since 1776, his own grasp of natural-rights theory had always been shaky. But what he did know was sufficient for his purposes, which were simple and straightforward. The French had been living under the wrong kind of government and were taking steps to change it. The English ought to be doing the same, and he, Paine, intended to enlighten them. He condemned the principles of monarchy, hereditary right to rule, and a state religion as unnatural, unnecessary, inefficient, and corrupt; and he insisted that no government was legitimate that did not rest on consent, as widely and directly expressed—and as often—as possible. And the rights of man, in addition to those of self-government, indisputably included freedom of opinion, expression, and exercise of religion.[73]

Part I of *The Rights of Man* was successful enough, but Part II, which appeared in mid-February 1792, was incredibly so. The work is said to have sold 200,000 copies within a year. Part of the reason was sheer notoriety, and not all of it Paine's; Burke's own position was so extreme that it was widely deplored. Great numbers of people thus read both works, without quite approving of either. Paine's, moreover, was energetically promoted by the constitutional reform societies, furious at Burke's attack on them, even though Paine's total assault on the foundations of British government was accepted by hardly anyone. Then there was an element in Part II that greatly appealed to, and actually stimulated the growth of, the workingmen's clubs which were springing up all over England in

1792. This was the social welfare proposals Paine appended to his condemnation of kings and hereditary titles. To be sure, it was a political argument from first to last—everything, he thought, should follow from a government established on right principles—and the whole was little more than an elaborated repetition of *Common Sense.* But one corollary of Paine's "rights" theory, hazy though it may have been, was the idea of society as forming a kind of "common stock" of rights upon which the individual citizen is entitled occasionally to draw, and he saw no reason why the tax money, rather than being wasted on courts and courtiers, should not be put to such worthwhile uses as poor relief, the education of poor children, old age pensions, and (incidentally) improved salaries for excise officers. Paine did not see himself as a special spokesman for the lower orders, and he had not advocated such reforms in America because there he saw no need for them. "There the poor are not oppressed, the rich are not privileged. Industry is not mortified by the splendid extravagances of a court rioting at its expense."[74]

At any rate, doctrines which in America raised few eyebrows, being taken there as largely the common sense of the matter, proved explosive in England. On the one hand, for his sweeping attack on English institutions Paine was prosecuted and, after his leaving the country for good in September 1792, outlawed. On the other hand, *The Rights of Man* would in time become one of the sacred texts of the English working-class movement, and its contemporary success owed, among other things, to its author's being regarded not as an Englishman but as an outsider. He was an American, and Americans were lucky.[75]

Yet for all Paine's vehemence, he was never in any sense a bloodthirsty man. Violence and war had no charms for him; nor did he have any feelings of personal hostility against the King, clergy, or nobles of France. They were hardly to be blamed for having been denied up to then the benefits of a republic. Nor was he telling the English, workingmen or anyone else, that they should rise up and cut off their oppressors' heads. He simply meant to open their eyes. Americans seldom thought of social change in any other terms.

The turning point of Thomas Paine's career was his taking refuge in revolutionary France, where he was received with gratifying marks of attention. He had been voted honorary citizenship in August 1792, and in September he was elected to the National Convention as a deputy for the Pas-de-Calais. He took his seat just as the monarchy had been abolished and Dumouriez's forces had stopped the Prussians at Valmy. But though the times seemed auspicious, events from here on somehow turned into a succession of disappointments.

Paine was welcomed to the gatherings of Madame Roland and the so-called Brissotins, the most American-minded group in the Convention and still dominant there. (It was at the Rolands' that he first met Edmond Charles Genet, then being groomed as the next minister to the United States.) But he spoke no French, and could take no more than a limited part, either in informal discussion or in Convention proceedings, without the aid of an interpreter. Paine's character as an outsider was thus most sharply accented just as he was ostensibly being admitted to full participation. He was put on a committee to draft a new constitution, but had little influence there. His idea was that constitutions should be short, simple, and universally applicable (like America's), whereas the actual result, largely the work of the *américaniste* Condorcet, was eighty-five pages long and dealt in detail with an endless string of France's particular problems and requirements. His first action in open assembly was to oppose Danton's sweeping plan to remove all present judges and replace them with plain citizens elected by the people. Nobody was more committed to popular rule than Paine, except that his experience with irresponsible populism in Pennsylvania had persuaded him that educated and trained judges were essential for restraining the executive and legislature from tampering with the people's real rights. Here too, Paine's words were respectfully ignored. He had little idea of what the stagnant, reactionary, entrenched judiciary of France really was.[76]

The culminating scene in Paine's short career as a legislator, the one that shows him at his most attractive and at the same time most American, was his supreme effort to save the King's life. The speech Paine made before the Convention at Louis's trial in January 1793, translated and read by another deputy, laid out an altogether logical case. He declared that he had opposed monarchy on principle all his public life, that he had helped to form a republican club in Paris well before such sentiments were popular, and that he had believed the Constituent Assembly should have grasped the chance to get rid of monarchy at the time of the King's flight to Varennes in June 1791 instead of welcoming him back. He had voted, moreover, to bring Louis to trial in order to demonstrate the corrupting force, on any man, of monarchy. But this had now been proven. Why, then, take vengeance upon Louis Capet, the man? The Convention ought to consider the disadvantages of his upbringing, and how he might have turned out if he had been raised in more virtuous circumstances. Why not, Paine urged, rehabilitate Louis by banishing him to the United States? "There, hereafter, far removed from the miseries and crimes of royalty, he may learn, from the constant aspect of public prosperity, that the true system of government consists not in kings, but in fair, equal, and honorable representation."

After the verdict of death was voted by the narrowest of margins, Paine made a final plea for reprieve. He pointed out that in America Louis's execution would cause "universal sorrow," and urged the Convention "not thus to wound the feelings of your ally." But whatever likelihood there may have been of Paine's tipping the balance was in effect shattered by the murderous Marat, who threw all into disorder by screaming that Thomas Paine, being a Quaker and against all capital punishment on principle, was not qualified to vote on the case.[77]

And yet the vote, being as narrow as it was, gives no true measure of Paine's actual isolation—either from the feelings that led up to the sentence or from the needs that gave a kind of inevitability to its being carried out. Thomas Paine was probably more totally alienated from monarchy, and from the very idea of monarchy, than any man in the National Convention. But that was just the trouble. For him, the entire question had been settled eighteen years before; for them, as yet nothing was settled. It is quite likely that in order for the Revolution to continue, having reached the point where it now was, the execution of Louis XVI was the only course possible. For generations of Frenchmen it was not simply government that had been embodied in the sovereign, but France herself, and although the authority of Louis XVI had fearfully eroded by 1793, the mystical essence of kingship lingered in the very air. If monarchy were to be truly done away with, the point of no return having now passed, a total gesture was imperative. It had to be shown that Louis had committed treason against France—he had plotted with the émigrés and foreign princes to overturn the Revolution—and after that, there was no way to justify *not* punishing him. The most logical way now to nullify the divinity of kings was by judicial execution.[78]

The emotions in the Convention on both sides of the question—the fear, the ferocity, the inhibitions, the horror—all betrayed one or another aspect of this knowledge. Paine's was the only vote given in true detachment; the magic of kingship had never touched him. Back in 1776 Thomas Paine had taken part, as one writer has suggested, in the symbolic "killing" of George III.[79] Perhaps true, but no more than symbolic. For him, and for most other Americans, no other kind of killing was needed or desired. Nor was it now. (Paine was quite right about the effect Louis's execution would have in America.) Still, this was a profoundly un-French view of the case. Thomas Paine as a legislator may have had more of a technical right than John Adams, Thomas Jefferson, or Gouverneur Morris to advise the French on how to manage their revolution. Whether he was any better qualified to do so is another question. He saw himself as a "citizen of the world," but all that this came to in practice was universalizing the Spirit of 1776.

With the triumph of the Jacobins, most of Paine's Girondin friends would go to the guillotine before the year 1793 was out, and Paine himself would be thrown into prison. While there, he completed *The Age of Reason,* an attack on all organized religion and orthodox scriptural doctrine. Paine certainly believed in a Creator, though the ambiguous spiritual life of his childhood—his father a Quaker, his mother an Anglican—could not otherwise have left him with strongly settled convictions. Nor was the work at all inconsistent with his political writings. He had always been against establishments; the Creator himself, moreover, had been invested with too many kingly pomps and fictions, and reason demanded that these be pulled away. A further occasion for writing it was the rising tide of atheism in France, which he deplored. But now, whether he understood it or not, Paine was at last cutting his ties with America. He was making a direct assault on the forms in which most Americans worshiped, and with this he had gone too far. They drew away, and Samuel Adams and Patrick Henry were among the patriots of the Revolution who now denounced him.[80] The subsequent legend in America of Tom Paine the "radical"—insofar as radicalism meant something extreme and dangerous—was based not on his political and social doctrines, but on his alleged "infidelity."

After the execution of the King and with the onset of the Terror, Thomas Paine became more and more disillusioned and cynical, and would continue so even after his own release. Not about revolutions in general, which he still thought of in universal—that is, American—terms, but about this revolution in particular. This one was French, and France, alas, was not serious.

4
Citizen Genet and His Mission

The new minister from the French Republic—young, gallant, and dashing—who arrived in the United States early in April 1793 was welcomed with tremendous enthusiasm. Scarcely three months later, Washington's cabinet would agree unanimously that he had to be recalled, the Minister having by then done one foolish thing after another to muddle the relations of the two countries. The idiosyncrasies of his personality undoubtedly had much to do with this. But how much? The times and circumstances were in themselves extraordinary, and there can be elements in any revolutionary situation that will unsettle the judgment of almost anyone. But with Genet there was an extra something, quite outside himself, that made his case a special one. It was this something, not in the hectic storms of revolutionary France but in the seemingly untroubled air of post-Revolutionary America, that would drive him all but out of his wits.

The family of Edmond Charles Genet, who was born at Versailles on January 8, 1763, was of Burgundian origins, once landholding though apparently not titled, and had somewhere in the past fallen on bad days. They had been sustained through his grandfather's and father's time, and into his own, by noble and royal patronage. Edmond's father, Edmé Jacques Genet, had been installed in the Foreign Office by the Duc de Choiseul, and eventually became Chief of the Bureau of Interpretaton. As an expert in Anglo-American affairs, Edmé was strategically situated. His bureau was very helpful to the Ministry after the outbreak of the American Revolution in supplying information favorable to the American cause, as well as to American agents in France who found him highly genial and sociable. (It was Edmé Genet who arranged for the French edition of *Common Sense*, though he got the author's name wrong.)[81] His four daughters—Edmond's older sisters—all entered the queen's service and became great favorites of Marie Antoinette.[82]

Edmond as the only son, indulged by his parents and sisters and a familiar at court, was consequently somewhat spoiled. But he was also very bright, and was in fact something of a prodigy. He was exceptional at picking up languages (at thirteen he translated Celsius' *History of Eric XIV* from the Swedish, for which he was given a gold medal by King Gustavus III); he was also a good musician and sang delightfully. He was destined for the diplomatic service, a career normally restricted to the nobility but made possible in this case by his family's influence at court, and his apprenticeship included temporary assignments in several European capitals. When his father died in 1781, Edmond was named as his successor, though only eighteen, as Chief of the Bureau of Interpretation. The young man was handsome, somewhat above middle height with reddish hair, and with his energy, enthusiasm, and charming manners he cut a fine figure. He could also, at times, be over-impulsive.

When Edmond Charles Genet arrived in America in 1793 at the age of thirty he was full of revolutionary ardor, and one might well wonder how, in view of his background of royal favor and advancement, he came by these extravagant republican sentiments. Opportunism would be too strong a word, and probably unfair, for he undoubtedly believed them; nor was Genet the only civil servant during those violently changing times for whom considerations of staying afloat demanded some emotional mobility. Actually a degree of republican chic had always been permissible within the family, on account of his father's work. Then his misadventures at the court of Catherine II between 1787 and 1792, first as secretary of legation and then as chargé d'affaires, not only served rather dramatically to settle his outlook but also brought him to the notice of the Gironde, the faction that happened to be in control of the French government at the time of his return. The Empress had taken rather a fancy to him personally, but she was suspicious of constitutions on principle, and when she learned that the King had agreed to one, and that he was being held as a virtual prisoner in the Tuileries following his arrest at Varennes in mid-1791, she broke off relations with France and would receive no more communications from Genet. He seems to have made some spirited pronouncements about constitutional liberty and other matters before being finally ordered out of Russia in July 1792.

Back in Paris, Genet was received cordially by the Girondins Brissot, Lebrun, Dumouriez, and Roland and welcomed into their social circle. These were the very sort who, with their grand visions of spreading universal liberty, would have been most congenial to him, as he was to them.

Sometime in November he was designated as minister to the United States to succeed Jean-Baptiste Ternant, probably at the suggestion of the *américaniste* Brissot. The King by then was awaiting trial, and one of the things the Brissotins, under the encouragement of Paine, wanted Genet to do was to escort the royal family to America. This plan was overtaken by the King's execution on January 21, 1793, and Genet set sail for the United States the following month in the frigate *Embuscade*.[83]

The irresponsibility of the Gironde in matters of foreign affairs, about which they knew virtually nothing, has been generally conceded. They had come to the fore as the largest single group with any kind of identity during the period of the Legislative Assembly, which sat from October 1791 to August 1792; they captured the ministry in March 1792, and would maintain their predominance in the succeeding National Convention until June 1793. All the deputies who entered the Legislative Assembly had been novices, the preceding Constituent Assembly having disqualified its members for re-election. Their guide and counselor in foreign relations was Jacques Pierre Brissot de Warville, whose preeminence seems to have depended largely on their ignorance.

Brissot was a man of obscure origins who had made his way into public notice through the nether world of hack journalism. Though he had few practical talents, his energy was overflowing. He had a somewhat universalist turn of mind, being full of plans for universal philosophical dictionaries, a universal language, and societies of universal brotherhood. At some point he had been touched with the vision of America, the seat of universal liberty. His rampant optimism was impatient of arbitrary obstacles.[84]

Brissot's zeal was such that he saw no reason why the Revolution's principles should not be spread across the world, if necessary by force. He was enraged that German princes should be harboring and encouraging the counter-revolutionary émigrés across France's eastern frontiers, and began calling for war against Austria. He had become the leading member of the Diplomatic Committee, though having little use for "diplomacy" as traditionally practiced; he was convinced that the old forms were corrupt and should be done away with. Peoples spoke to peoples; when war was waged not against peoples but against the governments of despots, the populations under them would be inspired to throw off their chains.[85] But the Jacobins of the so-called Mountain bitterly opposed the movement toward war, on the ground that it would exhaust the country. "America's example, as an argument for our success," warned Robespierre,

> is worthless, because the circumstances are different; and as for the statement that we will find a ready response among the countries against which we fight, it is well to remember . . . that no one loves armed missionaries. The thing for us to do is to set our own affairs in order and to acquire liberty for ourselves before offering it to others.[86]

When war was declared in April 1792, Brissot's efforts had had a great deal to do with it. To France's enemies would then be added Prussia, and in time England, Holland, and Spain. "It is this wretch," wrote the bilious Hippolyte Taine, ". . . who, with the half-information of a nomad, scraps of newspaper ideas and reading-room lore, added to his scribblings as a writer and his club declamation, directs the destinies of France and starts a war in Europe which is to destroy six millions of lives."[87] And it was the mentality represented by Brissot that gave the tone to the Genet mission, and that shaped Genet's instructions.

What sort of place America occupied in French policy, however, or even whether it had much of a place at all, is another question. "Policy" itself was problematical at the opening of the year 1793, a time of enormous confusion in France's affairs, and most of the distracted public servants who had anything to say about making it would in a few months be fleeing for their lives. Moreover, the sessions of the Provisory Executive Council at which Genet's instructions were approved took place during the very time Louis XVI was on trial for his own life. (Brissot himself, palsied with fear, reversed his position of a few weeks earlier and cast his vote for death.) How sharply America could have figured in anyone's mind under such circumstances may well be doubted.

In view of the background of France's preoccupations at home and in Europe, it should be no wonder that the set of instructions Genet took with him to America reflected little sense of conditions there, or of what might be expected of the Americans themselves. There was much in them about mutual fraternal interests. But probably few Americans reading them would have recognized anything very appealing or pertinent to *their* interests. The outline of policy revealed in these instructions—to the rhetoric of which Genet himself had apparently been allowed to add some flourishes[88]—had about it a certain grand audacity, especially in its language and sentiments. But the structure, insofar as there was one, was rather

Rube Goldberg-like in its intended workings, in that every assumption depended in a peculiar way on every other, and if something went wrong with any part of it the entire framework would come clattering down. At the same time, the instructions were riddled with contradictions.[89]

The most sweeping of the objectives Genet was to pursue involved rousing up the peoples of Louisiana, Florida, and Canada by spreading among them the principles of the French Revolution. They would then cast off the yoke of their oppressors, and this would benefit France in the forthcoming war by striking at Spanish and British power in the New World. He was to employ a variety of techniques: propaganda, secret agents, and American adventurers in the border areas—Kentucky in particular—whose desire to obtain the opening of the Mississippi would inspire them to assist in organizing expeditions against the Spanish possessions. He would also encourage privateering against British shipping by French and American seamen operating from New World bases. He was accordingly given a supply of blank letters of marque and military commissions to distribute where they would be most effective. None of this was very specific. On the one hand, it was "a vast project," requiring "the greatest activity"; on the other hand, "it will be easy to execute if the Americans are willing,"[90] willing, that is, to play the parts assigned to them. But in another passage, the possibility was recognized "that at least for some time the Americans will observe an absolute neutrality"[91]—whereas if they did, they would set their faces against the entire demoniac script. Moreover, if the French expected to obtain the American supplies referred to in another part of the instructions, such neutrality would be flatly indispensable.

A second great objective was the negotiation of a new treaty, one that would go beyond those that had been concluded in 1778 and were still in force. It would begin with the idea of "renewing and consolidating our commercial ties and establishing them upon principles of eternal truth"; such a treaty would then be given "a wider latitude by turning it into a national pact in which the two peoples would mingle their commercial and political interests and establish an intimate accord to assist in every way the extension of the empire of liberty, guarantee the sovereignty of peoples, and punish the powers that still hold to an exclusive colonial and commercial system, by declaring that the vessels of those powers shall not be admitted to the ports of the two contracting nations."[92] The Girondins conceded that there might be some hesitation on the Americans' part. Consequently Genet, while pressing for a new pact, was to insist on strict observance of the treaties already existing, especially those articles having to do with privileges mutually accorded to privateers of the two countries. At the same time he would show them a new decree, passed by the National Convention on February 19, which fully threw open the ports of France and her colonies to American commerce, as encouragement and as further evidence of France's good will.

But here too the logic was somewhat unreal. The decree opening France's home and colonial ports was a matter not of generosity but of wartime necessity, and so far as the Americans were concerned it made a new treaty superfluous, at least for the time being, since it gave them most of what they had been asking for throughout the previous decade. The only political aspect of the new pact that the French were at all specific about was a reaffirmation of the reciprocal guarantee, provided for in the 1778 Treaty of Alliance, of each others' possessions. On the one hand, they said they would not invoke the guarantee for some time to come; on the other, they instructed Genet to make it a *sine qua non* for free entry into French colonial ports, which they had already just granted. They added that whereas for the Americans the guarantee would be merely nominal, for France it would be "very real," because in the event of danger French forces would be sent to American ports to "shield them from every insult."[93] (How "real" would depend on whether the entire British fleet were swallowed up in a tropical hurricane.)

As for the instruction to insist rigorously on observance of existing treaties, this meant Genet was to press for a French reading, significantly at variance with the Americans' understanding of them. Such a reading would allow French privateers not simply to bring their prizes into American ports while denying the same privilege to the British (that much the treaties did permit), but actually the arming and equipping of such privateers as well, not to mention adjudicating their own prizes on American territory. Another thing the French thought the 1778 treaties called for was discriminatory tonnage duties in their favor, the merest possibility of which, back in 1789, had brought Major Beckwith hurrying to New York with veiled warnings.[94] In short, if the Americans were to accept the French interpretation of the existing treaties, the French would then have got all they were asking for in a new one, and this—with or without a new treaty—would be tantamount to an American declaration of war against Great Britain, and would bring immediate reprisals.

And finally, the least flamboyant and least prominent but perhaps the most vital of Genet's objectives was to obtain the total liquidation of America's Revolutionary debt to France, which then stood at about $5.6 million. The Americans had already begun making regular payments in 1790, prior to all expectations; in addition, they had granted emergency advances to Ternant for the relief of the French colony of St. Domingue; all of this now inspired the Girondins with the idea of massive advances for the greatest emergency of all, France's struggle for universal liberty. Genet's entire mission was to be financed out of these anticipated funds: the provisions he was expected to obtain for France's armies and colonies, the maintenance of the French diplomatic and consular establishments in America, and the expenses of any activities he might undertake in Canada, the Floridas, or Louisiana.[95]

What all this in effect came to was that neither of the first two broad objectives—action against France's enemies in the New World, or an enlarged treaty with the United States—could have any meaning apart from the third. And yet to have the least chance of achieving the third—the funds with which it was all to be paid for—Genet should logically have had to renounce the first two. That is, the only way France could continue to receive American supplies was for the United States to remain in all other respects neutral, since a belligerent America would have its shipping swept from the seas, whereas American neutrality would be destroyed by any connivance in the kind of activities entailed in the Louisiana and Florida schemes, or by the kind of treaty Genet was instructed to negotiate. It would almost seem that the Girondist council, to the extent that they were able to keep their minds on America at all, wanted only to use the Americans in every way they could think of for their own struggle against England and Spain, somehow hoping for the advantages of American neutrality on the one hand and American co-belligerency on the other, and expecting that with proper management by their energetic minister, the Americans would happily agree to both.

With the burden of such a commission weighing upon him, even so sanguine an enthusiast as Genet might have experienced a misgiving or two as his ship drew near its destination in America. Moreover, with his personal success, his very career, balanced upon his carrying it out, he *had* to believe in the grand sentiments he was instructed to proclaim, and there is every likelihood that he did. But then the circumstances of his arrival and reception at Charleston on April 8, 1793 — contrary winds having brought the *Embuscade* to land there instead of at Philadelphia[96] — seem to have blown away all his doubts in an enormous gust of euphoria from which he never quite recovered. And it was the Americans themselves who did it.

Genet was met at the pier by a huge crowd, wild with enthusiasm; he was welcomed by the local dignitaries and by members of the South Carolina legislature; and in no time at all he had had a long talk with Governor William Moultrie. Moultrie was a jovial fountainhead of reassurance and bounty. That "venerable veteran, a sincere friend of our revolution," Genet wrote home in jubilation, "gave me all the assistance within his power." He did indeed. Moultrie listened with delight as Genet unfolded his entire plan to him. He saw no reason why Genet should not begin arming and commissioning privateers immediately, and gave him permission to start doing so at Charleston. He saw no breach of neutrality in the organizing of expeditions against the Spanish colonies. He even recommended men who he thought might take part, and gave Genet letters of introduction to them. He gave orders for strengthening the harbor defenses. He assured Genet that he knew of no law forbidding any of these activities.[97]

Genet thereupon went to work at once. He used four of his blank letters of marque to commission four French privateers (*Républicain, Sans culotte, Anti-George,* and *Patriote Genet*), manned largely by American sailors, and set up courts under the local French consul, Michel-Ange de Mangourit, for condemning the British prizes they brought in. All this of course was before he had had any official consultation with the United States government, and before he was even officially received. He also set afoot then and there the scheme for expeditions into Spanish Florida, arrangements for which were placed in the hands of the zealous Mangourit.[98]

On April 18 Genet left Charleston for Philadelphia, a journey which took him twenty-eight days, twice as long as he had estimated. He had decided to send the *Embuscade* on by sea and make the trip himself by land, now having reason to believe that the sort of reception he had had at Charleston would be repeated elsewhere, and if the citizens of America wished to honor him—or rather, France—he thought they ought to be given the widest possible opportunity to do it. He was escorted out of town by Governor Moultrie and Senator Ralph Izard. The entire trip was most gratifying. There were thundering welcomes all along the way—banquets, addresses, bells, cannon—and when he arrived at Philadelphia on May 16, the city gave itself over to transports of joy.[99]

5

Defining American Neutrality

Many authorities have remarked upon the durability and soundness of the neutrality policy which was adopted by the United States government toward the warring powers of Europe in the spring of 1793 and worked out in detail during the remainder of that year. Not only would the policy stand the test of a subsequent century and a half of usefulness, but it was originally arrived at with no clear body of precedent or experience to draw upon.[100] It all occurred, moreover, in the face of what appeared to be two violently conflicting versions of foreign policy as advocated by the Secretary of the Treasury and the Secretary of State respectively, the one partial to England, the other to France. Thus an accounting for the policy's success does not quite come automatically. It is undoubtedly true that good judgment on Washington's part in steering a sensible course between his two chief cabinet officers had a great deal to do with it. But what else?

Actually these divisions, bitter though they may have been, were hardly as wide as they seemed. Indeed, simply as a question of foreign policy, a division scarcely existed at all. Every member of the cabinet was convinced of the indispensability of the United States' staying out of war, and there was little question in anyone's mind that a determination to remain at peace with all the powers of Europe should in some way be made clear. This end was sufficiently urgent that any differences as to implementing it were relatively minor.

In another sense, to be sure, the differences were not minor. And yet their significance derives not from principles of international relations but from considerations of domestic partisanship and ideology, and the determination of both sides to extract maximum partisan advantage from the questions before them. There was thus an inordinate amount of quibbling and hair-splitting. But at any point of clear choice between the national interest and something else, despite private grumblings nobody really hesitated; there were few doubts as to what the national interest was.

Washington's role was thus strategically critical, since in each case the final decisions on policy were in effect made by him. Washington was the only one present whose viewpoint was in no way complicated by partisan concerns. He was confronted with two distinct lines of argument, each advocated with ingenuity and intelligence. The distance between them, however, was sufficiently close as to enable his own judgment to operate at a level of selective precision, and the end-product reflected it. Thus the circumstances under which Washington made his choices were really little short of ideal, though he himself could hardly have thought so at the time.

France declared war on Great Britain and Holland on February 1, 1793, and as soon as the news was confirmed in the United States early in April, Washington cut short his visit to Mount Vernon and hastened back to Philadelphia. He arrived on April 17. The following day he sent his four cabinet officers a list of thirteen questions on the conduct to be followed by the Executive in the light of the European war, and asked for a meeting on the 19th to consider them. Jefferson was rather irritated. He suspected (rightly) that the questions had been for the most part prepared by Hamilton. They were in the President's handwriting, he noted, "yet it was palpable from the style, their ingenious tissu & suite that they were not the President's, that they were raised upon a prepared chain of argument, in short that the language was Hamilton's, and the doubts his alone." The questions in themselves do not altogether account for Jefferson's edginess. (They could, after all, be taken up singly on their merits, and in fact were.) But Hamilton had taken the initiative, and Jefferson by now was grimly suspicious of his every move. Jefferson was certainly aware that a policy had to be formulated. But he was also aware that it could hardly be done without some conflict with the advantages which the Republican interest was currently deriving from the popular enthusiasm for France. He would thus have liked, if possible, to temporize. Actually he too had been invited to prepare something in the way of an agenda, and had avoided doing so.[101]

Of the thirteen questions, only the first two and the thirteenth were settled at the April 19 meeting. The first, and most pressing, was: "Shall a proclamation issue for the purpose of preventing interferences of the citizens of the United States in the war between France and Great Britain, &c.? Shall it contain a declaration of neutrality or not? What shall it contain?" This put Jefferson in a position of much discomfort. Something had to be said, since the citizens must both be reminded that the country was at peace and be warned against acts which would either assist or injure the belligerents, and the world should know that such warnings had been issued. But Jefferson did not want it to be a formal declaration of neutrality, and he was reluctant to issue anything immediately. The two reasons he gave were somewhat ambiguous. He said that a specific proclamation of neutrality was not constitutionally within the Executive's power, since it would be a declaration that "there should be no war," a matter only Congress could decide. Hamilton's reply was that the question of whether or not to make war did indeed rest with Congress, but that this was not such a question. Whatever Congress might eventually do, it was the Executive's function in the meantime to enforce the laws, and if the laws incident to a state of neutrality were to be administered, he had to determine that such a state existed, and to say so forthwith. (Question 13, whether Congress should be called into special session to consider the European war, had already been decided in the negative.) Jefferson's other objection was that any statement on neutrality were better held back "as a thing worth something to the powers at war, that they should bid for it, & we might reasonably ask a price, the *broadest privileges* of neutral nations." Hamilton's answer to this was that the nation's neutrality was not in any way a negotiable commodity, that it was both contemptible and absurd to pretend that it could be, and that the longer the delay in announcing it the greater the danger of being dragged into war. He knew, and all Europe knew, that the United States was in no position to be *other* than neutral, and if we invited any "bidding," the sole effect would be to show the world that we overrated our own consequence while putting our principles up for auction.[102]

Jefferson seems to have made no rebuttal; he agreed to the immediate issuance of a proclamation; and it may even be wondered how strongly, or with what degree of conviction, he could have made his argument in the first place. The only evidence that he made it at all is found not in his private memoranda, which say nothing, but in his subsequent letters to Madison and Monroe, which contain overtones of both evasiveness and self-justification. Jefferson was a good enough diplomat and foreign minister, and was solicitous enough of his country's best interests, to perceive that there was no real choice. Nor did he seriously advocate—as some writers have carelessly claimed—a "benevolent"[103] neutrality toward France, being fully aware of the dangers such a course would invite. But in his other capacity, as the emergent head of the Republican interest, he was prey to other and conflicting impulses. He was consumed with hatred for England; moreover, neither Washington nor anyone else could drive from his head the obsession that monarchy was just around the corner, that Hamilton and his "fiscalist," "anglocrat" followers were plotting to make an end to republican government in America. The best bulwark against these designs was the success of the French Revolution—more specifically, the continued enthusiasm for it in America. Keeping this alive would strengthen the people in the cause of "human liberty," a term Jefferson habitually used in his references to French and American affairs. Jefferson also knew that there were some illusions afoot among his own friends and followers as to how far the United States might go, without paying any price for it, in abetting the French in their struggle against England. It was undoubtedly with this in mind that he cautioned Madison, "I fear that a fair neutrality will prove a disagreeable pill to our friends, tho' necessary to keep out of the calamities of a war."[104] The Jefferson one sees in this and similar letters of the time is a man who somehow knows, though reluctant to admit it, that he cannot have it both ways.

It was "agreed by all," according to Jefferson's own memorandum,

> that a Proclamation shall issue, forbidding our citizens to take part in any hostilities on the seas with or against any of the belligerent powers, and warning them against carrying to any such powers any of those articles deemed contraband according to the modern usage of nations, and enjoining them from all acts and proceedings inconsistent with the duties of a friendly nation towards those at war.[105]

Jefferson's discontent, however, was eased in two particulars. One was the omission of the word "neutrality," though how great a concession this was, or whether anyone present really argued for the word, is doubtful. Actually all of them, Jefferson included, used it in referring to the policy both before and afterward, there being no real synonym. The other was the designation of Randolph to draft the document. This dispensed Jefferson, who would normally have been the one to draw up such a paper, from having to take direct responsibility for it. To Madison, he later professed to find the proclamation "badly drawn," "pusillanimous," and of "milk and water views." But when Randolph's draft was shown to him he made no objections and suggested no changes. The Neutrality Proclamation was issued on April 22.[106]

The second of the thirteen questions was likewise decided at the April 19 meeting. "Shall a Minister from the Republic of France be received?" On this there was no dispute at all, Washington, Hamilton, Knox, Randolph, and Jefferson all agreeing that one should be. Washington had in fact already written Morris to this effect, and Hamilton and John Jay had come to the same conclusion weeks before. It was the third question, however—whether the minister should be received with or without qualifications—that caused the most trouble, and was accordingly postponed. "Without qualifications" meant that the United States still considered itself bound by the treaties of 1778; "with qualifications" implied either a repudiation or temporary suspension of the treaties. On this and the remaining questions—all of which concerned the treaties and America's obligations under them—it was decided that written opinions should be submitted. Washington had them in hand by May 6, and made his decision that same day. This time it was not Hamilton's view but Jefferson's—that the minister should be received without qualifications, and that the treaties were still in full effect—that was much the sounder.

Hamilton held that in the current state of France's internal and external affairs the treaties between that country and the United States should be regarded as "temporarily and provisionally suspended." Out of his long and rather tortured argument emerged four principal reasons for this contention. The first was that they had been made with Louis XVI and his heirs and successors, and although they were real treaties, made between nations and not merely between governments, and although a nation had the right to change its government in any way it chose, the present case involved a civil war whose outcome was still unclear, and in the meantime such treaties did not require one nation to assist another against its own sovereign any more than to assist the sovereign against his subjects. A second reason was that the external war, having been begun by France, was offensive, whereas the Treaty of Alliance was defensive. Still a further one was that according to authorities on international law any alliance which circumstances had rendered "useless, dangerous, or disagreeable" might be renounced, and the United States should hold itself free to determine whether in the present case such circumstances indeed existed. And finally, Hamilton demanded, suppose the United States should reaffirm itself as France's ally, through an unqualified reception of the new minister, and then "suppose the contest unsuccessfull on the part of the present governing Powers of France. What would be our situation with the future Government of that Country?"[107]

Jefferson made short work of this argument, and in so doing added another increment of clarity to the outline of policy now in the process of emerging. He thought it fully possible to postpone decisions on how specific articles of the treaties applied, without having to suspend the treaties as a whole in anticipation of dangers and inconveniences which might never occur. Not only was such suspension morally unjustified but it was a direct act of hostility, far more risky than doing nothing until an immediate danger presented itself. Treaties were made with nations, not with governments—Hamilton had admitted that much—but then it followed that there could be nothing in international law that justified either annulling or suspending a treaty because of changes in forms of government. In any case it could hardly be maintained that Americans would have preferred to make their alliance with a monarchy rather than with a republic.

Jefferson took up those articles of the treaties that might in any way cause difficulty. Article XI of the Treaty of Alliance provided for a mutual guarantee of each nation's possessions. But there was very little likelihood that the United States would be called upon to defend the French West Indies. This would be so manifestly dangerous that a refusal to comply would be fully justified under international law, but since France would most probably not demand it anyway there was no point in insulting her unnecessarily by anticipation. Article XVII of the Treaty of Amity and Commerce specified that French warships and privateers were to be admitted to American ports with their prizes, while denying the same privileges to France's enemies. But there were similar provisions in other treaties made by all the powers presently concerned, and none of them could have any right to complain of this one. (As it turned out, none did.) And finally, there was Article XXII of the same treaty, which denied France's enemies the right to equip privateers in American ports or to sell their prizes there. "But we are free to refuse the same thing to France," Jefferson asserted, "there being no stipulation to the contrary, and we ought to refuse it on principles of fair neutrality."

As for the reception of a minister, Hamilton had seemed to think that if the United States were not to couple such reception with an explicit qualification that the treaties were "provisionally suspended," it would be telling Europe in effect that America regarded herself as France's ally in the present conflict, and would not only acknowledge the full operation of the treaties but preclude any future renunciation of them. "But," insisted Jefferson, "I deny that the reception of a Minister has any thing to do with the treaties. There is not a word, in either of them, about sending ministers. This has been done between us under the common usage of nations, & can have no effect either to continue or annul the treaties." On the one hand, to receive a nation's minister was to recognize the legitimacy of his government, but on the other, to qualify the precaution by saying that treaties with his nation were suspended was to deny that same legitimacy. On general principles Jefferson wanted to place as little significance as possible on the act of recognition. It did no more than acknowledge a *de facto* situation, it did not preclude an equally ready recognition of a successor government that might conceivably be in control the following month, and it placed no impediments whatever against future modification of existing treaties.[108]

Actually Washington had never doubted the validity of the treaties, and told Jefferson as much on May 6. He had also decided to receive Genet without qualification—though "not with too much warmth or cordiality, so only as to be satisfactory to him."[109] The thirteen questions—though it was only a beginning—were in effect settled.

On these final points the divergence between Jefferson and Hamilton had been substantial. But here too, it was domestic partisanship, rather than their views on America's treaty obligations to France, that made the main difference. Hamilton detested the French Revolution as much as Jefferson detested England, and he was determined to block Republican attacks on his Treasury system—whose success, as he saw it, depended on the absence of any friction with England—in every way he could. As for the treaties, however, Jefferson was no more prepared than Hamilton to be bound by them in any way that might endanger the external security of the United States.

Events throughout the remainder of the year 1793 were to show, on the one hand, how the principles of American neutrality would be elaborated step by step, and how, on the other, Citizen Genet would rush headlong to his doom.

6
Collapse of the Genet Mission

Any full survey of the Genet affair—and none has been made except through American eyes—generally concludes with a kind of wonder at the completeness of the man's ruin and the totality of his mission's failure. Genet had time for observation; how could he not have seen, during the spring and summer of 1793, at least some of the ways in which both the objects of his mission and the methods he was using to pursue them had to be modified, if he were to expect any success at all in attaining even a portion of them? The tendency has been to write the man himself off as hopeless. But looking at the episode from some other viewpoint— say, Genet's own—might prompt other thoughts and raise further questions. For instance, how many other Frenchmen, however experienced in diplomacy, would have responded to this particular situation very much differently? Conceivably Genet, in ways he had no means of comprehending, was profoundly deceived as to the Americans' intentions—and although neither the Girondist mentality nor Genet's own temper could have functioned as very great assets, nevertheless the logic of the picture America presented to his eye was put there, and to all intents and purposes completed by the Americans' own behavior. The chronology, moreover, strongly suggests that Genet did *not* have time to adjust his perceptions until it was too late. The critical period, which came in mid-June, was really painfully short. The first full exposition of American policy came to him at that time, and he was so unprepared for it by anything that had happened to him up until then that he simply could not believe it. In a matter of days he proceeded to commit French diplomacy so absolutely that there was no turning back.

Genet arrived at Philadelphia on May 16, and was received by the President on the afternoon of the 18th, at which time he presented his letter of credence and a copy of his powers to negotiate a new treaty. He made a little speech, and the Secretary of State, who was present, seems to have been immensely gratified. "We know," Genet announced,

> that under present circumstances we have a right to call upon you for the guarantee of our islands. But we do not desire it. We wish you to do nothing but what is for your own good, and we will do all in our power to promote it. . . . We see in you the only person on earth who can love us sincerely & merit to be so loved.

"It is impossible," Jefferson delightedly told Madison, "for anything to be more affectionate, more magnanimous than the purport of his mission. . . . In short he offers everything & asks nothing."[110]

Genet did not describe the President's demeanor in his report home. Washington's welcome could not have been other than gravely courteous, but whatever the degree of either cordiality or reserve, Genet seems not to have noticed.[111] The leading figure in the city, which at that very moment was humming with excitement, was himself. The previous day a vast concourse of people, filling the surrounding streets, had marched to his quarters bearing a congratulatory address from the citizens of Philadelphia, to which he responded extempore. There were other addresses from Philadelphia's French Benevolent, German Republican, and Ciceronian Societies. There was a dinner that evening given by the French residents of the city at which the hall rang with fraternal sentiments and ardent affirmations of Franco-American friendship. (In the course of it, Genet himself got up and sang a patriotic air.) The Democratic Society of Philadelphia, the most recent of those that had been springing up everywhere since the beginning of the year, was currently being organized, and Genet was asked to propose a name for it, which he obligingly did.[112]

Four days after presenting his credentials the new minister, overflowing with confidence and well-being, addressed his first official letter to the Secretary of State, on whom he already rested the most extensive hopes.[113] In it he proposed that the United States discharge by advance payments the remainder of its debt to France. He represented this, with some logic, as a great favor to the Americans. It would give a tremendous stimulus to the commerce of the two countries, because the money would be used "in drawing henceforth from the United States the greatest part of the subsistence and stores necessary for the armies, fleets, and colonies of the French republic." "Now, what advantage more sensible can we offer to you," he demanded with a fine flourish, "than that of discharging your debt to us with your own productions, without exporting your cash, without recurring to . . . the burdensome operations of bankers? It is furnishing you, at the same time, with the means of paying your debts, and enriching your citizens. . . ."[114]

With a second letter the following day, May 23, Genet made a second magniloquent gesture. He enclosed a copy of the February 19 decree by which France ("that generous nation — that faithful friend") had thrown open her ports to American trade. The French Republic, he said, wishing only to treat the Americans as brothers, "has granted them all the favors which her own citizens enjoy in her vast possessions; has invited them to participate in the benefits of her navigation, in granting to their vessels the same rights as to her own; and has charged me to propose to your government to establish, in a true family compact, that is, in a national compact, the liberal and fraternal basis, on which she wishes to see raised the commercial and political system of [the] two Peoples. . . ."[115]

Before receiving any replies—upon which would hang two of the three great objects of his mission—he wrote a third letter and made still another *beau geste.* Just before Genet's arrival Jefferson had written Ternant, upon receiving strong complaints from the British minister, George Hammond, about the activities of French armed vessels operating from American bases (and whose work had been largely set afoot by Genet), and the retiring Ternant had turned the letter over to his successor for reply. In it, Jefferson had pointed out that the French consul had assumed unwarranted powers in condemning a British ship taken prize by a French frigate; that French vessels had been illegally outfitted and commissioned at Charleston, and manned partly by citizens of the United States "to cruise against nations at peace with us"; and that the British ship *Grange,* having been captured by the *Embuscade* within United States territorial waters, must be restored to its owners. Genet's response was to restore the *Grange,* grandly representing this as a free gift "to convince the American government of our deference and friendship," without admitting that the other actions complained of were in any way contrary either to American law or to the Treaty of 1778. He appeared to be certain that with more discussion and a closer examination, the full meaning of the treaty would be seen in its true and proper light.[116]

A few days later, June 1, Genet was the guest of honor at another public dinner, the grandest so far ("I live here in the midst of perpetual fetes, I receive addresses from all parts of the Continent"), sponsored by many of the leading citizens of Philadelphia. There were songs and toasts and, from a battery located outside, even bursts of artillery. Jefferson was not present, but Genet had reason to believe—or thought he had—that it was no other than the Secretary of State who had prepared the toasts. That same day in Freneau's *National Gazette* appeared the first of a series of essays signed "Veritas." The series constituted a direct attack on the President himself for having presumed, without consulting the nation's will, to issue a proclamation of neutrality which made no distinction between the duties America owed to the respective belligerents, and which was thus in effect a repudiation of America's friendship with France. It was an announcement that "those treaties, from which we have long enjoyed important advantages, are now to be considered as of no obligation. . . ." Here too, Genet assumed that the author was Jefferson.[117]

It is certain that Jefferson could not have had anything to do with the notorious "Veritas" letters, nor was he likely to have occupied his time writing out toasts for public dinners in honor of the French minister. But how could Genet have supposed that he had? And how is Genet's particular view of Jefferson, and of what he might hope for at Jefferson's hands, to be accounted for?

Genet's first meetings with Jefferson provide a critical element for reconstructing his state of mind during this period. It was here that he received his most authoritative cues on how to interpret his relations with the federal government, possible divisions within it, the formation of his attitude toward Washington, the influence of public opinion, and even the nature of the federal system itself. His impressions on these matters seem to have been fairly well set by about June 1.

About two aspects of these early meetings there appears little doubt. One is that Jefferson took Genet into his confidence as to the state of opinion within the cabinet. "Jefferson . . . gave me useful notions on men in office, and did not at all conceal from me that Senator Morris and Secretary of the Treasury Hamilton, attached to the interests of England, had the greatest influence over the President's mind, and that it was only with difficulty that he [Jefferson] counterbalanced their efforts. . . ." There was also talk, if Genet's later recriminations to Jefferson are to be given any credit, "that the people, however, was for us, that your friends would have a majority in the next Congress but that the convening of that legislative body must not be hurried because all the idle speculators and brokers of the towns would come crowding while the cultivators occupied with their labors would be slow to respond and would leave time for the former to take contrary measures."[118]

The other thing Jefferson did was to dispose orally, for the time being, of Genet's proposal for a new treaty in a manner which Genet seems to have found satisfactory. He told Genet that according to the Constitution control over treaties was vested in the Senate, and that the subject could not be taken up until the Senate met. Genet accepted this explanation—which was really an evasion, but which happened to accord with other misconceptions—with equanimity, and the matter was left in suspension.

Taken altogether, these early conversations gave Genet grounds for certain conclusions, however overdrawn they might later prove to have been. One was that there was a clear distinction, which Jefferson deplored, between the Secretary of State's own views and those of his colleagues and President Washington, and that Jefferson's real sentiments, if openly avowed, would most closely resemble those of "Veritas." Another was that the matter of the privateers and how the treaties were to be interpreted was still an open question. "I told him I had no doubt," Jefferson himself noted, "but that the President, out of respect to him & his country, would receive whatever he should have to urge on the subject, and would reconsider it with candour." And then there was Genet's conception of Congress as the final arbiter, the supreme power, the ultimate expression of the people's will, however the Executive might think or act. This had now become immutably fixed in his mind. He was obviously not told that no member of the executive establishment had the least wish to begin negotiations for a new treaty then, since it would entail no end of complications; on the contrary, Jefferson's excuse that they had to wait to consult the Senate seemed perfectly reasonable, especially with Jefferson's telling him that the new Congress would be better disposed than the Executive to "second our views." Jefferson at this period was certainly neither precise nor candid with regard to any of those points upon which Genet most required instruction. On Jefferson's behalf, however, it might be observed that this was the very period at which he himself was most tense, even confused, over the policy he somehow knew he had to administer.[119]

As for the voice of the people, to which Genet was listening every day, and to the people's representatives, the French minister was superbly free of doubts. But the people's representatives would not meet until December, and meanwhile he would be dealing with an Executive that might not fully meet the popular will. He would do this, keeping to the forms with what forbearance he could muster, though there was always that disdainful phrase in his instructions about the "crooked paths" of "the old diplomacy."[120] But should he overstep himself a time or two, it surely need not be fatal, since he had a clear margin within which to function. Back of him stood the mass of the people, and Jefferson's own demeanor appeared to encourage this conviction. The Secretary of State could serve him as a kind of buffer.

On June 1 (the day of the grand dinner, and the day the first "Veritas" letter appeared), Genet wrote another letter to Jefferson. It was about two Americans, Gideon Henfield and John Singletary, who had enlisted aboard a French privateer and who—he had just "this moment been informed"—had been arrested and imprisoned by federal authorities. "The crime laid to their charge, the crime which my mind cannot conceive, and which my pen almost refuses to state, is the serving of France, and defending with her children the common and glorious cause of liberty." Knowing no law or treaty forbidding what they had done, Genet called upon the Secretary's and the President's "intervention" for their immediate release. Jefferson's reply was conciliatory. (His original draft had been even more so, until his colleagues insisted on its being toned down.) Henfield and Singletary, he said, were in custody of the civil magistrates, over whose proceedings the Executive had no control; they would have a jury trial before respectable judges; "and if it is not contrary to the laws of the land, no doubt need be entertained that [their] case will issue accordingly."[121]

On June 5 came the first really unambiguous indication of trouble. On that day Jefferson informed Genet that the President had duly reconsidered the Minister's arguments on the subject of the privateers (as expressed in his letter of May 27), but remained fully persuaded that it was "the *right* of every nation to prohibit acts of sovereignty [i.e., the arming of privateers or the recruiting of its citizens] from being exercised by any other within its limits, and the *duty* of a neutral nation to prohibit such as would injure one of the warring powers," and that any vessels so armed must depart from American ports. This meant that the American attitude—or rather, the Executive's attitude—and that of France as to how the treaties of 1778 should be construed on these questions were, had been, and would continue to be flatly at odds. Until, that is, the Executive could be touched by the popular will, or the people's representatives called the Executive to account.[122]

An even more serious blow fell on June 11. Jefferson wrote Genet that although the United States would fulfill its agreement to make regular payments on the debt as they fell due, ordinary resources were greatly strained in doing even this, and that a liquidation of the debt through advance payments for the purchase of supplies was out of the question. This was accompanied by a very terse memorandum on Genet's proposition from the Secretary of the Treasury. Hamilton said that the state of American credit would not allow it, and that in view of the current demand elsewhere for American products, the supposed inducement of the money's being spent within the country would amount to no great advantage anyway. This meant, supposing it should prove to be the American government's final word, that Genet would have funds for no more than a fraction of the objects he had been instructed to achieve.[123]

Genet, upon taking in some of this, flung himself down at his writing desk in the awareness that he was no longer in a position of negotiation, that in both cases—the rights of privateers under the Treaty of 1778, and funds to finance his mission—negotiations in the ordinary sense were closed. The margin he could expect to gain from continued dealings with the executive branch of the United States government was henceforth minimal. But if he accepted this, his mission was in effect finished. He was checked, but unnaturally checked. As he saw it, he had proceeded according to the Revolutionary philosophy of the new diplomacy, freely laying his plans upon the table and hiding nothing, in the confidence that the inclinations of the Executive and the will of the nation would prove to be one. And what had he got from it? The ungrateful obstinacy of Washington, for one thing, blind to the sacred obligations of treaties. The Minister did have something of a case. He had as example the eighteenth-century concept of a benevolent neutrality; there was nothing in the 1778 treaties that prohibited what he was doing (Jefferson himself seems to have toyed at least briefly with that idea), nor in any law of the United States; and France had allowed the Americans to equip privateers in her own ports during the Revolution. The popular enthusiasm in America for France, moreover, was unquestionable.[124]

For another thing, there was the self-interested, even dishonest refusal to consider the needs of France in the one way the United States could help the Republic most. Genet could not believe that in view of France's desperate situation, and especially if business were as flourishing as Hamilton himself said it was, paying the remainder of the French debt was not well within America's capacities. Here too, he had a case. The United States government would in fact change its mind within two years and do just that.[125] But in the present situation Hamilton had privately assured the British minister before Genet's arrival that the United States would pay no extraordinary advances, Hammond having told him that Great Britain on the high seas would regard goods purchased with such funds, even if carried in American ships and not yet paid for, as French, and treat them accordingly.[126]

The emotional state Genet was in, or rather the several states, were only too apparent in the three letters he proceeded to write to Jefferson, all of which were delivered on the same day. He seethed with frustration at finding "that the President of the United States persists in thinking, that a nation at war had not the right of giving commissions of war to those of its vessels which may be in the ports of a neutral nation; this being, in his opinion, an act of sovereignty." He could see no ground in natural law, the usages of nations, or even in the President's proclamation, for denying the right of vessels to arm for their own defense or for declaring that to do so was an act of "sovereignty." This "is certainly not the intention of the people of America. Their fraternal voice has resounded from every quarter around me, and their accents are not equivocal. . . ." He concluded with the wish "that the Federal government should observe, as far as in their power, the public engagements contracted by both nations; and that by this generous and prudent conduct, they will give at least to the world the example of a true neutrality, which does not consist in the cowardly abandonment of their friends in the moment when danger menaces them, but in adhering strictly, if they can do no better, to the obligations they have contracted with them." He did make one "concession." He had instructed the consuls, he said, to grant commissions only to those captains who engaged themselves by oath to respect the territory of the United States "and the political opinions of their President, until the representatives of the sovereign shall have confirmed or rejected them." Genet may have been little aware that this language was pushing the outer limits of acceptability, or that he was evading the real issue—that he was arming privateers to prey on British commerce, not merchant ships to defend themselves.[127]

In taking up the question of supplies and the debt, his tone was one of lofty injury, tinged with disdain. "It is the character of elevated minds, of freemen, not to expose themselves twice to a refusal." He now had no alternative but to give American merchants and farmers "assignments" on future installments of the French debt. "The expedient to which I am about to have recourse, will, probably, be onerous to the French nation; but as the Federal Government thinks it may take on itself to place us under the necessity of employing it, without consulting Congress upon so important a matter, I am obliged to follow my instructions."[128]

Finally, the civil authorities of Philadelphia ("in contempt of treaties" and "in contempt of the law of nations") had stopped the sale of prizes taken by a French privateer, and in New York another privateer had been detained on the point of sailing. The tone now was one of contained fury, and cuttingly peremptory. He demanded immediate restitution, "with damages and interest"; he expected support in his efforts to defend "the interests, the rights, and the dignity of the French nation" against those persons "laboring secretly to misrepresent" them; and he wanted the President to use "all the authority which the people have confided to him to enforce the execution of the laws and treaties."[129]

On June 17 Jefferson sent Genet what amounted to a comprehensive treatise on neutrality, international law, the nature of the 1778 treaties, and the position of the United States government on all these matters. He pointed out that the issue was one of arming not for self-defense but "for the purpose of committing hostilities on nations at peace with the United States." He made it very explicit that the United States did not intend to allow French agents to arm and equip any more privateers in its ports. He denied that any article in the Treaty of 1778 granted that right, and declared that there was "not a syllable" in the President's proclamation that even so hinted. "You think, sir," he continued, "that this opinion is also contrary to the law of nature, and usage of nations." Yet it was that very law and usage upon which American policy was based, and he quoted exten-sively from the jurist Vattel on such questions as strict impartiality and the recruit-ment of forces on foreign territory without the sovereign's permission. Then, in the strongest language: "For our citizens then to commit murders and depreda-tions on the members of nations at peace with us, or to combine to do it, appeared to the Executive, and to those whom they consulted, as much against the laws of the land, as to murder or rob, or combine to murder and rob, its own citizens; and as much to require punishment, if done within their limits. . . ." The United States therefore intended to prosecute any violators, and from now on this would include foreigners within its jurisdiction as well as its own citizens.[130]

This letter was accompanied by another pointing out that it was not within the Executive's competence to interfere in cases where private individuals were suing for control of a prize. These were in the hands of the judicial authority, and would be determined upon legal principles "admitted and practised in all civilized countries" including the Republic of France.[131]

Then on June 19, two days later, Jefferson took up Genet's threat to issue "assignments" on the debt in payment for supplies. He thought Genet would find upon reflection that such a measure was "too questionable, both in principle and practicality, too deeply interesting to the credit of the United States, and too unpromising in its result to France, to be found eligible to yourself," and trusted that nothing of such "mutual concern" would be done without "mutual con-cert."[132]

All this, from the author of "Veritas"! The stage was thus set for Genet's great explosion of June 22, to which Alexander Hamilton would later solemnly refer as "the most offensive paper, perhaps, that ever was offered by a foreign Minister to a friendly power, with which he resided."[133]

Genet began with a hiss of scorn for the old diplomacy, to which the official servants of the United States—of all nations—was resorting. "Discussions are short, when matters are taken upon their true principles. Let us explain ourselves as republicans. Let us not lower ourselves to the level of ancient politics by diplomatic subtleties." The Secretary's reasonings, though "extremely ingenious," were inadmissible. The Minister's just protestations had been met with the Pres-ident's "opinions," and these not being sufficient, "you bring forward aphorisms of Vattel, to justify or excuse infractions committed on positive treaties. Sir, this conduct is not like ours."[134]

Rather than press the American government to fulfill all its treaty obligations, he had instead brought proofs, he insisted, of the French Republic's solicitude in the form of new favors to American commerce. And for this, instead of waiting for Congress to meet, it had put nothing but obstacles in his way. "It is not thus that the American people wish we should be treated." Jurisdiction over prizes, he insisted, belonged exclusively to France's consular tribunals, and he expected immediate redress for irregularities on the part of civil authorities at both New York and Philadelphia. The treaty *did* allow France to arm in the ports of the United States, and if the federal government could not protect France's commerce or her islands, it should at least not immobilize the patriotism of her citizens, or oblige them "to go out of your ports unarmed," or punish those of its own citizens "who array themselves under our banners, knowing perfectly well, that no law of the United States gives to the Government the sad power of arresting their zeal by acts of rigor." As for the judges to whom the government planned to submit these questions, he was ignorant of them. The only true arbiters, he intoned, should be "good faith and reason."[135]

So far as ordinary diplomacy was concerned, this was a burning of bridges. The President had meanwhile departed for Mount Vernon and would not be back until July 11, so there could be no reply before then. (In fact there never would be one.) It might be supposed that meanwhile, considering the language Genet had just addressed to Jefferson, the Secretary of State would not henceforth have permitted any but the most narrowly correct official business between them. But this seems not to have been the case. Personal relations remained unimpaired, and Genet, for his part, continued to describe Jefferson as "a man endowed with good qualities, but weak enough to sign what he does not believe and to defend officially threats which he condemns in his conversations and anonymous writings."[136]

There was a final aspect of Genet's mission—his plans for an expedition against Spanish possessions in the Southwest—that remained to be taken up in some form. On July 5 Jefferson allowed Genet to call and to discuss with him, "not as Secretary of State but as Mr. Jefferson," what he had in mind. There are two versions of this interview, one Jefferson's and the other Genet's. They are not contradictory, though each includes some interesting details missing from the other.

According to Jefferson, Genet read to him "very rapidly" instructions he had prepared for André Michaux, a French botanist whom he had engaged to go to Kentucky as an agent. Michaux was to disseminate propaganda encouraging the people of Louisiana to insurrection (there would be a similar call to the people of Canada); he was also to make contact with Americans in Kentucky who proposed to raise a force, supplemented by any Indians they might get to go along, to march upon New Orleans. (One of the Americans was General George Rogers Clark, currently down on his luck and restless.) About two weeks previously Genet, wishing to appoint Michaux as a consul in Kentucky, had asked Jefferson for an exequatur for him, but Jefferson had replied that foreign governments were not entitled to consuls in the interior. He did, however, send Genet a letter of introduction for Michaux to Isaac Shelby, the Governor of Kentucky.

As for the expedition Genet planned to raise, "I told him," Jefferson recorded, "that his enticing officers & souldiers from Kentucky to go against Spain, was really putting a halter about their necks, for that they would assuredly be hung, if they commd. hostilities agt. a nation at peace with the U.S. That leaving out that article I did not care what insurrections should be excited in Louisiana." Genet then produced the letter Jefferson had written for Michaux, saying, according to Jefferson, "that in that letter I speak of him only as a person of botanical & natural pursuits, but that he wished the Govr. to view him as something more, as a French citizen possessing his confidence. I took back the letter, & wrote another."[137]

Genet's account, written in one of his dispatches home, was more extended. The heart of it, however, was that

> Mr. Jefferson seemed to have a lively awareness of the utility of this plan, but he told me that the United States had begun negotiations with Spain on the subject of an outlet for the Americans below New Orleans, and so long as that negotiation were not broken off, the delicacy of the United States did not permit them to take part in our operations; nevertheless he gave me to understand that he thought a little spontaneous irruption of the inhabitants of Kentucky into New Orleans could advance matters; he put me in touch with several deputies [congressmen] of Kentucky, notably with Mr. Brown, who, convinced that his region would never flourish as long as the navigation of the Mississippi were not free, adopted our plans with as much enthusiasm as an American can manifest. He showed me ways of acting with success, gave me the addresses of many dependable men, and promised he would apply all his influence to the success of our plans.[138]

There were no visible diplomatic consequences of this interview, inasmuch as Jefferson did not tell the President about it, and plans for the expedition proceeded.[139] But meanwhile another incident—the one which would persuade the entire cabinet that they had had enough and that Genet would have to go—was already in motion. This was the case of the *Little Sarah.*

Early in July, rumors reached the cabinet concerning a British merchant ship, the *Little Sarah,* which had been taken prize by the *Embuscade* early in May and held by the French since then at the port of Philadelphia. The story was that this ship, renamed the *Little Democrat,* was increasing her armament and fitting out as a privateer, contrary to the President's orders. Governor Thomas Mifflin of Pennsylvania, being asked for further information, reported on the 6th that the *Little Democrat,* carrying four guns upon entering port, now had fourteen, and appeared ready to sail. On the 7th Mifflin further reported that he had sent Alexander J. Dallas, the Pennsylvania Secretary of State, to see Genet the previous evening and request that he not allow the *Little Democrat* to put to sea. Genet had flown into a great rage, refused to detain the ship, giving the impression she would sail the next day, and had threatened in high passion to make a direct appeal to the people over the President's head.[140]

Jefferson thereupon undertook to call on Genet himself. When he urged that the *Little Democrat* be detained until the President's return, Genet flew into another rage, repeating most of the arguments of his June 22 letter about France's right to arm in American ports. In the course of it the Minister calmed down, and although he still refused to give an exact promise, he conveyed, by "look and gesture," according to Jefferson, "that she would not be gone before that time." (Jefferson afterwards told Mifflin, "I was satisfied, that, though the vessel was to fall somewhere down the river, she would not sail.") It seems, moreover, that it was in this same conversation that Genet's notion of Congress as the sovereign power was for the first time clearly contradicted by Jefferson, and Genet thereupon "expressed the utmost astonishment." Jefferson, who had become increasingly uneasy about the French minister, wrote Madison that night in great distress. "Never in my opinion, was so calamitous an appointment made[;] . . . hot headed, all imagination, no judgment, passionate, disrespectful & even indecent towards the P. in his written as well as verbal communications, talking of appeals from him to Congress, from them to the people, urging the most unreasonable and groundless propositions, & in the most dictatorial style &c. &c. &c. . . . He renders my position immensely difficult. He does me justice personally, and, giving him time to vent himself & then cool, I am on a footing to advise him freely, & he respects it, but he breaks out again on the very first occasion. . . ." Jefferson may indeed have been "on a footing to advise him freely." But the one thing he seems not to have done was to tell Genet in plain words that if he insisted on letting the *Little Democrat* sail, the certain result would be a demand for his recall—as in fact it was.[141]

When Washington got back to Philadelphia on July 11, he found a sheaf of papers from the Secretary of State marked "Instant attention." It consisted of three documents, all of which concerned the *Little Democrat.*[142]

The first was a memorandum describing Jefferson's interview with Genet and Genet's threats to Dallas about going to the people.[143]

The second described a meeting of Jefferson, Hamilton, and Knox with Governor Mifflin on July 8 (the day after the meeting with Genet), the occasion for which was Mifflin's perplexity over what steps, if any, he ought to take next. Hamilton and Knox wanted to set up a battery on Mud Island in the Delaware, supported by militia, to stop the *Little Democrat* if she tried to depart before the President ruled on the matter. (Hamilton was noticeably less concerned about French reaction than British.) Jefferson vigorously dissented. He said he was certain the vessel would not go before the President's return, and that an attempt to stop her by force would almost certainly lead to bloodshed, especially since the arrival of a French fleet was momentarily expected, and thus possibly even war. He did not see why the United States government needed to be so tender about the reactions of the British; they had no reason to complain, having taken more American citizens by impressment than the French had by enlistment. All of this was probably true. Meanwhile, however, the *Little Democrat* had dropped downriver to Chester, below Mud Island (as Genet had said she would, though he had not said where), so it was too late to take action anyway.[144]

The third paper was a letter dated July 9 in which Genet informed Jefferson that the *Little Democrat* would sail when ready. This, he asserted, requires "no discussion on my part, and . . . cannot create any difficulty on that of your government. When treaties speak, the agents of nations have but to obey."[145]

Washington was exceedingly angry. "Is the Minister of the French Republic to set the Acts of this Government at defiance, *with impunity?* and then threaten the Executive with an appeal to the People[?] What must the world think of such conduct, and of the Governmt. of the U. States in submitting to it?" He called a meeting for the next day, and it was at that meeting, July 12, that Genet's fate was to all intents and purposes determined. True, it would be another five weeks before all details of the request for his recall were finally settled. The cabinet meanwhile considered a variety of modes, including suspending the Minister from his functions, making his correspondence public, and expressing its desire for his recall in the form of a peremptory demand. None of these was taken. But the decision they did eventually reach was agreed to unanimously. There would be a letter drafted by the Secretary of State, to be transmitted to the French government by the American minister in Paris, giving an account of Genet's actions accompanied by quotations from his correspondence. These would simply speak for themselves. A distinction would be made between these actions and the intentions of his own government; there would be renewed expressions of friendship, and of confidence that the same friendship which urged the United States to bear with that minister would cause his government to replace him.[146]

There was a more general, and in many ways even more urgent, problem upon which the cabinet set to work at the meeting of July 12. This was the need for a comprehensive set of rules to govern the conduct of belligerents in American ports and on American territory. The process of defining the conditions of American neutrality had begun with the Proclamation. The President and his advisors had since then been furnished with a series of specific cases, virtually all arising from Genet's activities, which they might—indeed, must—combine with more general principles and bring that process to completion. As the cases multiplied, it could wait no longer; neutrality had to be made into a system.

They hoped at first for assistance from the justices of the Supreme Court. Their first effort was accordingly to devise a series of questions addressed to the Court regarding procedures that might or might not be justified under existing laws and treaties. The ministers of France and Great Britain were meanwhile notified that any privateers in American ports would be expected to remain there pending further orders from the President. (Ignoring this directive, Genet two or three days later sent the *Little Democrat* to sea.) The justices, however, were reluctant to assume extra-judicial functions in passing upon these questions, and on constitutional grounds politely declined to do so. The cabinet, not unprepared for this, thereupon proceeded to formulate the rules on its own. They were completed, with a remarkable minimum of disagreement, by July 29 and signed by all on August 3, 1793.[147]

The rules—and subsequent amplifications of them—fell under several main categories, by far the most important of which concerned the arming and equipping of foreign vessels in American ports. The original equipping of such vessels for military purposes was prohibited, and this settled once and for all the United States' interpretation of the French treaties of 1778. (Although the treaties had not permitted such armaments, neither had they forbidden them; now they were forbidden.) This also included the arming of merchant vessels, even for their own defense. Upon the general principle would be certain qualifications, designed to avoid contravening the Treaty of 1778 and to avoid unnecessary litigation.[148]

Recruitment of United States citizens by foreign belligerents on American territory was a question dealt with only indirectly by the cabinet rules themselves.

But the outcome of the Henfield trial (Henfield was acquitted on July 29 by a pro-French jury) made it important that the illegality of such enlistments be established as an unquestioned principle. The position of the federal prosecution and of the district court had been that Henfield was punishable as a disturber of the peace (quite literally) under the common law, the law of nations, and the treaties of the United States. But the legal profession itself being far from clear on these points, the ambiguity was in a few months resolved by federal statute. Meanwhile the same principle was maintained for soldiers as for seamen. For example, when the cabinet as a whole finally received clear information late in August 1793 about Genet's plan to raise men in Kentucky for an attack on New Orleans, Governor Shelby was immediately asked to take steps to prevent it.[149]

The limit of United States territorial waters had first become an issue when French privateers began taking prizes close to American shores. Washington in November 1793 decided to fix the limit at the minimum distance from shore that any other nation was known to claim, one sea league, or three miles. This was one rule that proved highly acceptable to both the British and French governments.[150]

As for consular jurisdiction over prizes, the American position all along had been that for foreign consuls to set up admiralty courts on United States territory for condemning prizes brought in by their nation's armed private vessels was a violation of this country's sovereignty under the law of nations. This principle was decisively established when in September 1793, after repeated warnings to the Minister that his consuls must not arrogate such jurisdiction to themselves, the exequatur of the French consul at Boston was revoked for defying a district marshal and holding a prize by force. Regarding the sale in the United States of prizes legally condemned elsewhere, this would be more or less tacitly permitted until the Jay Treaty of 1794 prohibited that practice as well.[151] And finally, there was the question of contraband, one upon which the United States had announced its position in the spring of 1793 in response to a complaint by the British minister. The United States would not forbid its citizens to sell goods which in wartime fell under internationally recognized categories of contraband, though if the goods were sold to one belligerent and confiscated by another, those who purveyed them would not—as had been clearly stated in the President's proclamation—receive any protection from their government. (The United States subsequently refused, however, to recognize a British Order in Council of June 8, 1793, which extended the definition of contraband to foodstuffs.) A related question involving neutral rights was the "free ships, free goods" principle embodied in the Franco-American Treaty of Commerce of 1778, according to which non-contraband goods—no matter who owned them—carried in a neutral vessel were not subject to seizure by ships of a belligerent power. This was a principle to which the United States could and did subscribe in theory, but could hardly insist on in practice as long as the most formidable naval power in the world refused to accept it. Jefferson flatly told Genet as much on July 24, 1793. Indeed, impotence to bring about any alteration in this particular aspect of neutral rights would hang as a cloud over Americans' external relations for the next quarter-century.[152]

These principles would be for the most part embodied in the Neutrality Act of 1794, passed in the spring of the following year. They thus formed the basis of a system of such precision, anticipating as it did the widest range of contingencies, that it would prove dependably sufficient well into the twentieth century. This was probably the greatest service Edmond Charles Genet could have rendered to the United States, though by the nature of the case he would get no credit for it. "If I wished for a guide in a system of neutrality," George Canning declared to the House of Commons in 1823, "I should take that laid down by America in the days of the presidency of Washington and the secretaryship of Jefferson, in 1793."[153]

Unknown to Genet, or to anyone in the United States before mid-August, the Gironde ministry had fallen during the first week of June. Thus began the rule of the extreme Jacobins and of the Committee of Public Safety, dominated by Maximilien Robespierre. Most of the leading Girondins would go to the guillotine by the end of the year, and under the circumstances there were few compunctions about sacrificing Genet when Morris turned over Jefferson's report to Deforgues, the new Foreign Minister, on October 8.

7

The French Revolution and Partisan Politics in America

Popular sentiment for France, as has been noted, was both widespread and generous. But there had all along been a nice distinction, an underlying qualification which few Europeans could be expected to grasp, least of all an agent of the French Republic. It was based not on mutual considerations of international political or economic interest (though there was certainly some wishful thinking that such "interests" might be coaxed into being), but rather on something of incalculable symbolic importance in America itself that had remarkably little, if anything, to do with the struggles of the French Revolution or the international politics of Europe. This was the Americans' own self-estimation, their own picture of themselves, their conception of the moral essence of their own newly created Republic. A deeply lodged component of this picture was the urge to dissociate the national character, as generally as might be, from the shadow of England, and from all that seemed to savor of English influence. France represented a metaphorical alternative full of promise. The efforts of the French people to establish republican liberty, France's challenge to the menace of England, her struggle against the ancient forces of monarchy, aristocracy, and European despotism: all this worked powerfully on the American imagination. But there was nothing in this inspiration that in any serious way contemplated American involvement in the affairs of Europe. Few Americans could conceive of engaging in actual hostilities of any kind on behalf of this; sympathy for France could be maintained in the most wholehearted way without its occurring to them that they needed to pay any tangible price for it.

It was this sentiment that leaders of the Republican interest had made every effort to preempt, according as it did with their determination to expel the pernicious influences which Hamilton's Treasury was exerting upon the character of the United States government and upon the very character of the republic itself. This, for them, was the real war—against "English" principles and the advancing threat of monarchy—a bloodless war, as it were, to the death. The sentiment for France was a major means to this end, anything but an end in itself, and a basic concern was to maintain it in as much of its original simplicity and generality as they could. Events which introduced complexity and required specificity of response would in all likelihood bring nothing but trouble.

There was little question, with the approach of war, that American neutrality was imperative. But for the Republican interest, that made rather a difficulty just in itself. The Republicans wanted neutrality and they wanted the sentiment, hoping in a general way that neither need compromise the other. Thus the key to these men's activities throughout the spring, summer, and fall of 1793 was their effort to keep not one but both, and to ward off complications. Something more, moreover, was beginning in a rudimentary sort of way to transcend the importance of any given issue; this was the well-being of the Republican interest itself. Thus the real drama of the French Revolution in America in 1793 was one not of foreign policy but of domestic partisanship, the principal victim of which would be Edmond Genet.

Appearing here was an element of real innovation. Historians have always correctly perceived that American politics after the coming of the French Revolution were not the same as before, because another step had been taken toward the fashioning of parties. But what kind of step? It seems to have consisted of efforts to manage public opinion not so much with reference either to personalities, on the one hand, or, on the other, to particular issues—that had been done before—but on a broad question of sentiment, back of which lurked the question of who should be the custodians of that sentiment. In the course of it, the sentiment itself became paradoxically blurred, while the contenders, and the divisions between them, became publicly sharper. The need for cohesion among the contenders was apparently becoming as important as the sentiment, possibly more so.

The principal actors for the Republican interest were Jefferson, Madison, and Monroe; for the "friends of government"—the incipient Federalists—they were Hamilton, Jay, and Rufus King. The Federalist effort, which was not very subtle, presents few paradoxes. Hamilton and his allies set about to make the neutrality principle a test not only of right reason but of loyalty to the United States government, to expose the enormity of Genet's activities in as much detail as possible, and, in placing as great a share of the onus on the Republicans as they could, to exhibit them as enemies of peace and order. The Republican effort, on the other hand, called for a considerable degree of agility. Things were not going their way;

the best arguments were all on the other side; and it was important that they prevent the problem of France from taking on any more specificity than they could help. That they could in the end manage a stand-off was the real measure of their success.

With regard to public opinion, perplexities were created at the very outset by two events the specificity of which was hard to circumvent. One was the Neutrality Proclamation; the other, the execution of Louis XVI.

The Proclamation was by and large favorably received,[154] for two fairly obvious reasons. One was that the desire for peace was all but universal. Jefferson himself was very explicit about this. "No country perhaps was ever so thoroughly against war as ours," he wrote to Morris on April 20. "These dispositions pervade every description of its citizens." The other reason was the tremendous prestige of Washington. This did not mean, however, that the Proclamation failed to arouse criticism, or that it did not provoke sensations of acute discomfort among the Republican interest. Of this, too, Jefferson was aware when he warned Madison that a fair neutrality would "prove a disagreeable pill to our friends."[155] This was because of the feeling that neutrality ought not to require that one be absolutely impartial, and that declaring the nation's neutrality too explicitly tended to minimize the people's affection for France. There was thus an understandable tendency to seek out objections, and, since this was the first time such a major responsibility had been assumed by the Executive while Congress was out of session, these were not hard to find.[156] The Executive, it was said, had here assumed functions more properly belonging to the legislative branch. A number of Republican ideologues took this line, Madison and Monroe among them.

And yet the inherent fragility of such a position was exposed only too baldly by the length to which it was carried early in June by "Veritas" in the *National Gazette*. "Veritas" argued, with some logic, that impartial neutrality meant deserting France, whereas an ally's obligations had to include a willingness to take up arms, and he attacked Washington for presuming to disregard that obligation. Jefferson, when he saw the articles, was appalled. He thought them a caricature of the Republican position, fabricated by "anglomen" and "monocrats" in the Treasury Office to discredit the Republican interest. Whereas Genet, when he saw them, assumed they were the work of Jefferson. Here was another measure of the actual distance between these two minds.[157]

As for the execution of the French king, the first news of which reached the United States in late March, Jefferson could only report—perhaps wishfully— that it had "not produced as open condemnations from the Monocrats as I expected." George Hammond, on the other hand, declared that the same event had "excited a much more universal and considerable degree of abhorrence in this country than I could have hoped or expected." The least that can be said, probably, is that the news was generally received with no enthusiasm, and that the few exceptions—such as the *Gazette*'s raucous "Louis Capet has lost his Caput"—could not have been regarded by most Republicans without a twinge of discomfort.[158] The execution served as the clearest dividing principle so far whereby Republicans and Federalists would go separate ways in their attitudes on the French Revolution. It was a hard test for Republicans, and many were deeply downcast by it, though it would probably be wrong to conclude that Republican support for the Revolution was thereby substantially cut away.[159] Nevertheless it was a difficulty, and the response was invariably defensive. People said strident things they did not altogether mean, such as Madison's that if Louis "was a Traytor, he ought to be punished as well as another man," or Jefferson's about monarchs being "amenable to punishment like other criminals."[160] In any case the event probably accentuated rather than diminished the general inclination to neutrality. The most logical solvent for perplexities of all kinds, however sympathies might lie in other respects, was the conviction that the soundest policy for America was peace.

The fairest viewpoint from which to observe the political implications of what followed is probably that of Jefferson himself. Not in his role as Secretary of State, which was relatively straightforward, but as senior aegis of an emerging political party. It is in Jefferson's handling of this role that one sees most clearly the partisan objectives of the Republican interest, which were to maintain the benefits both of pro-French sentiment and of neutrality, and to keep the sentiment as broadly non-specific as possible. A pattern thus emerges, taking its shape from Jefferson's dealings with Madison and Monroe, on the one hand, and their adversary relations with the Hamilton group, on the other.

Much of the strain on Jefferson during this period arose from the necessity of justifying his conduct not to his enemies but to his two friends, whose minds were significantly less complicated than they would have been if either had had to carry *his* responsibilities. Jefferson at the outset entertained no doubt about the absolute necessity of neutrality, and said as much to Madison, just as he had to Morris, even while recognizing that the effect on "our friends" might be "disagreeable." On the latter point, he had provided some insurance by keeping the word "neutrality" out of the Proclamation, and by contriving to have the document drafted by someone other than himself. At the same time, he was positively euphoric over the great public scene on May 2 (still before Genet's arrival) when the *Embuscade* captured a British prize and sent the ship up the Delaware to the port of Philadelphia. "Upon her coming into sight," he wrote jubilantly to Monroe, "thousands & thousands . . . crowded & covered the wharves. Never before was such a crowd seen there, and when the British colours were seen *reversed*, & the French flag flying above them they burst into peals of exultation." He was similarly elated at the obvious enthusiasm of preparations to welcome Genet. "It seems as if his arrival would furnish occasion for the *people* to testify their affections without respect to the cold caution of their government." And yet that very enthusiasm, the very intensity of the sentiment, might itself create embarrassments. It might put official government policy under greater popular pressure than was convenient, and thus endanger the other side of the balance. "I wish we may be able to repress the spirit of the people within the limits of a fair neutrality."[161]

The real villains, in any case, were the "monocrats" and "paper dealers," and

Jefferson's letters sweat with this. Those who welcomed the French prize were the "yeomanry," and "not the fashionable people nor paper men." "We, too," he assures Brissot, "have our aristocrats and monocrats." He hopes the Revolution will result in a government capable of maintaining liberty. "If it does not, I feel that the zealous apostles of English despotism here, will increase the number of its disciples." "The old tories," he tells Monroe, "joined by our merchants who trade on British capital, paper dealers, and the idle rich of the great commercial towns, are with the kings. All other descriptions with the French. The war has kindled & brought forward the two parties which our own interests merely, could never excite." Hamilton, he claimed, was "panic-struck if we refuse our breach to every kick which Gr. Brit. may chuse to give it." It was all very simple, very general, and very non-specific.[162]

Then came Genet, who "offers everything & asks nothing." Perhaps the French themselves would cooperate in letting us keep both the sentiment and our neutrality. As a diplomat Jefferson may not really have believed this, but as a partisan he obviously wanted to. It was as important in any case to convince Madison as himself, because Madison, back in Virginia, has begun to give him trouble. Madison was in fact very angry about the Proclamation, which he regarded as "a most unfortunate error." "It wounds the National honor, by seeming to disregard the stipulated duties to France. It wounds the popular feelings by a seeming indifference to the cause of liberty. And it seems to violate the forms & spirit of the Constitution, by making the executive Magistrate the organ . . . of the Nation in relation to war & peace, subjects appropriated to other departments of the Government."[163]

Jefferson's response was to dissociate himself from the Proclamation still further. "A manly neutrality, claiming the liberal rights ascribed to that condition by the very powers at war, was the part we should have taken, & would I believe have given satisfaction to our allies." It was not *his* proclamation, but Randolph's. "I dare say you will have judged from the pusillanimity of the proclamation, from whose pen it came." The Randolph theme in Jefferson's correspondence — the venom Jefferson shows throughout this period toward the hapless Attorney-General — is intriguing. Randolph was more or less pro-French and reasonably Republican in his leanings, and, though not a strong personality, he tried in cabinet meetings to examine things on their merits and to act as something of a moderating influence. Knox, on the other hand, nearly always supported Hamilton. Randolph, then, was the only one — besides Washington — who tried to be non-partisan. But that was just the trouble. Jefferson pictured himself to Madison and Monroe as battling alone, never knowing whether he could count on Randolph or not (with "his half-way system between wrong & right"), and privately heaped abuse on him at every show of independence. "And indeed," he told Monroe, "every inch of the ground must be fought in our councils in desperation in order to hold up the face of even a sneaking neutrality, for our votes are generally $2\frac{1}{2}$ against $1\frac{1}{2}$." And to Madison: "E.R. found out a hair to split, which, as always happens, became the decision. . . . Everything, my dear sir, now hangs on the opinion of a single person, and that the most indecisive one I ever had to do business with." "He is the poorest Cameleon I ever saw having no colour of his own, & reflecting that nearest him." Jefferson was irked at Hamilton's having Knox in his pocket ("fool that he is"), and seems to have been equally irked at not having Randolph in his.[164]

Another question on which Jefferson tried to cover himself, knowing on the one hand that action was out of the question, and aware, on the other, of Madison's own special concern about commerce, was that of Genet's proposed commercial treaty. He intimated that he himself was in favor of it, which he probably was in theory, though he could not have been much so in fact. "Yet I know the offers will be opposed, & suspect they will not be accepted." On May 27 he could announce that he had been right. "He [Randolph] whose vote for the most part, or say always, is casting, has . . . shewn his opinion to be against doing what would be a mark of predilection to one of the parties, tho' not a breach of neutrality in form."[165]

Jefferson's woes—with Genet beginning to make complications by his refusal to accept the American view of neutrality, the "Veritas" letters and the hostile public reaction to them, and Freneau's insolence toward Washington—were mounting. He was now looking with greater and greater longing to the prospect of ridding himself forever of all his troubles by retiring to Monticello. But Madison gave him no peace, undertaking to lecture him about his public duty and admonishing him not to leave until he could do so under "circumstances which all good citizens will respect." This was a cut, and Jefferson erupted with anguish and self-pity. His debt of service, he lamented on June 9, had been "fully & faithfully paid," nobody had any further claims on him, he was "worn down with labours from morning to night," "& so never let there be more between you & me, on this subject."[166]

The picture was, however, changing. By the last week in June it had become hideously clear, following Genet's outrageous letter of the 22nd, that Jefferson's chief nemesis—a standing reproach to his hopes of balance, simplicity, and generality of sentiment—was the French minister himself. He began cautiously to reveal this to Madison and Monroe, and in so doing was already tentatively preparing a new position for the Republican interest. Then, with the *Little Sarah* affair, came a real break in the weather.

Hamilton in cabinet on July 12 moved the recall of Genet.[167] Not only did Jefferson not oppose it; he undoubtedly saw, coming as it did from the enemy, a providential solution for all his problems. True, there were still risks. But it now becomes apparent, Genet having now been marked for the block, that Jefferson has begun to recover his nerve. His mind begins to clear; he now emerges as the partisan tactician. Now, instead of distressed immobility, instead of wincing at the sight of each new letter from Monroe or Madison, he begins to take the initiative and issue directions.

As for the other side of the picture, it is obvious that Hamilton's efforts were every bit as partisan as those of Jefferson, Madison, and Monroe. But for Hamilton, partisan requirements and requirements of the public interest—at least as he saw them—fit together with far less ambiguity than was the case with the

Republicans. He could pursue them, in the opening stages at least, with a specificity and singleness of purpose not possible for his adversaries.

Hamilton, unlike Jefferson, never had any second thoughts about the policy to be followed regarding France and the French minister; his commitment to a strict neutrality was absolute, unqualified, and uncompromising. On the one hand, he had no sympathy whatever for the French Revolution in the state it had now reached; the present ruling elements in France had "sullied a cause once glorious and that might have been triumphant." On the other, his entire financial system depended on peaceful relations with Great Britain. At the first hint of war, he had hastened to assure Hammond of "his determination whenever that event may occur, of employing every exertion in his power to incline this country to adopt as strict a neutrality as may not be directly contrary to its public engagements. . . ."[168] This he proceeded to do in the most aggressive way in the cabinet discussions on the Proclamation, on obligations under the treaties, on the reception of a minister, on making a new treaty, and with regard to advance payments on the French debt. Righteously convinced as he was of the identity between his own views and the true voice of the United States government, Hamilton had little idea of where in his own behavior public policy left off and partisanship began, or even whether partisanship had anything to do with it.

The warmth of Genet's public welcome gave him no pleasure, and he did what he could to minimize or counteract it. The address to Washington of the Philadelphia merchants on May 17 in support of the Proclamation was undoubtedly encouraged by him, though it was overshadowed by the popular address to Genet that same evening. Replying, however, to an inquiry about the numbers of citizens involved, Hamilton wrote, "Comparatively speaking, but a small proportion of them have had an agency in the business." What pushed Hamilton's writings and sayings directly into partisanship was the theme of subversion. As for those who organized the welcome, "with *very few exceptions,* they were the same men who have been uniformly the enemies and the disturbers of the Government of the U States. . . . We too have our disorganizers." The zeal for France was "intended by every art of misrepresentation and deception to be made the instrument first of controuling[,] finally of overturning the Government of the Union." The shadow of conspiracy and subversion that so obsessed Jefferson had its exact counterpart in Hamilton.[169]

The jingoism of Freneau and the excesses of "Veritas" (the two may well have been one and the same) provided the ideal occasion for Hamilton to leap into print and seize the offensive. "Veritas" had insinuated that the Proclamation, issued under "the opiate of sycophancy" and without consulting the will of the people, savored of "double dealing," "monarchical mystery," and "court intrigue." This line could not have been of much help to the Republican interest, and it was against this background that Hamilton on June 29 descended upon the public with "Pacificus."[170]

In these seven essays, appearing at intervals throughout July in the *Gazette of the United States,* Hamilton took up the questions of executive authority to proclaim neutrality, commitments to France under the treaties of 1778, the requirements of gratitude for French assistance during the Revolution, and of the

Proclamation's appropriateness and timing. With the ruthlessness of a trial lawyer, he proceeded to show that the President had both the authority and the responsibility to notify foreign powers as well as the United States' own citizens that the country was in a state of peace, and that it regarded itself as legally bound to abide by the duties of a neutral. (Those who objected must either want to get us into war or were looking for a pretext to attack the President.) The United States was not thereby prevented from fulfilling its treaty obligations—those not requiring war—though these could not include defending the French West Indies. (Such a guarantee must assume the means for carrying it out without peril to the nation's basic safety, which the United States obviously did not have, and it applied only to a defensive war.) As for obligations of gratitude, this had to be judged with reference to France's particular interest at the time the treaties were made, which was to cut down the power of England, and also in view of the royal court's desire to limit America's own power afterward. The National Convention itself had taken great satisfaction in pointing this out to us, as well as in revealing that the perfidious Bourbon court had not wanted the Americans to form a stronger government in 1787. This was something we already knew, and we also knew (Hamilton maliciously added) that France's most zealous partisans in America (the Antifederalists) had not wanted it either. And finally, critics had asked why the government could not have delayed the announcement of neutrality in order to see what might be gained from the belligerents in return for it. But the whole point of such a declaration, Hamilton insisted, was that it should be a spontaneous act in keeping with the occasion, done before anyone asked for it, and that in order to remove all ambiguities, temptations, and dangers it had to be issued as promptly as possible. "Pacificus" was a strong performance, and seems to have been generally so recognized.[171]

Hamilton by the second week in July had acquired another powerful weapon—besides the general desire for peace and the prestige of Washington—which was the behavior of Genet and his threat to make a popular appeal. With this advantage he pounded away in cabinet meetings, declaring that Genet's proceedings ought to be spread before the public. His arguments carried a good deal of weight with Washington, who was exceedingly harassed and tired, while the sessions were punctuated by clumsy goadings from Knox in the form of gossip about the President's tormentors. At one point, according to Jefferson, Washington lost control of himself, exclaiming "that *by god* he had rather be in his grave than in his present situation," and that

> he had rather be on his farm than to be made *emperor of the world*, and yet that they were charging him with wanting to be a king. That that *rascal Freneau* sent him 3 of his papers every day, as if he thought he would become the distributor of his papers, that he could see in this nothing but an impudent design to insult him.[172]

It is rather an irony that during this same period Hamilton and Jefferson, on another level, were collaborating with great effectiveness to formulate a set of rules on neutrality.

Hamilton was tireless. By late July his friends, with his active encouragement, were organizing public meetings everywhere, even in Virginia, to express popular support for the President and approval of the Proclamation. They seem to have been greatly successful. And while laboring to bring about an official disclosure of Genet's conduct, Hamilton let it out unofficially in the first of his "No Jacobin" letters on July 31. "It is publicly rumoured in this City," he declared, "that the Minister of the French Republic has *threatened to appeal from The President of the United States to the People*." All of this gave rise to a further series of meetings denouncing appeals to the people by foreign agents. Partisanship now permeated all levels, private and public, and the Hamiltonians to all appearances had the francophiles in full retreat. One of Hamilton's correspondents in Maryland who had been hectoring him for copies of "Pacificus" to distribute now assured him that they were no longer necessary. The object, he wrote,

> is done away by the Sentiment becoming so very general here in support of the measures of Government.... Mr Genet's conduct is considered a very lucky circumstance as it has been the means of proving so great a confidence of the People, in, and a desire to support the Dignity, of, their own Government exceeding the expectations of its warmest friends.[173]

And yet appearances were deceptive, and in the end, real victory somehow eluded them. Exactly how this happened is not wholly clear, but in some way the dexterity of Jefferson had a great deal to do with it. Jefferson's hand was visibly and invisibly at work, his touch directly and indirectly felt, in minimizing the damage, quarantining and then disposing of Genet, resisting full disclosure, salvaging the considerable remnants of pro-French sentiment, and finally, in neutralizing the Federalists' best arguments simply by absorbing them.

One of Jefferson's first moves was to give Madison something with which to occupy himself by egging him on against "Pacificus." "Nobody answers him," he wrote exasperatedly on July 7, "& his doctrines will therefore be taken for confessed. For God's sake, my dear Sir, take up your pen, select the most striking heresies and cut him to pieces in the face of the public. There is nobody else who can & will enter the lists with him." (Jefferson had complained the week before that "none but mere brawlers & bunglers have for some time past taken the trouble to answer any thing.") Madison accepted the commission with leaden heart, knowing there was not a great deal he could do. ("I am in hopes of finding that some one else has undertaken it.") The task was, he confessed, "the most grating one I ever experienced," and the subsequent "Helvidius" letters showed it. They were rather melancholy discourses on the constitutional limitations of executive power in foreign as well as domestic affairs, to counteract doctrines which he accused "Pacificus" of having borrowed from "*royal prerogatives in the British government*." Still, it seems not to have mattered. "Helvidius" may not have been very persuasive, but it was only a rear-guard action, and meanwhile other movements were having their effect, on other grounds.[174]

A factor of great importance was Jefferson's stubborn campaign in cabinet to get the management of Genet's recall entirely into his own hands, without suspending the Minister's functions and without official public disclosure of his correspondence and activities. The odds were against him, inclinations being generally the other way, but the effort at length succeeded. The matter was not fully settled until August, when Jefferson brought the President around in two stages. The first was Jefferson's evidently effective answer to Hamilton's long "jury speeches," in which Hamilton had argued that the best way to counteract the pernicious influence of the Democratic Societies was to lay the Genet affair fully before the public. Jefferson retorted that this would make multitudes join the Societies "merely to assert the right of voluntary associations," and would turn it into a contest between the President and Genet, which was beneath the former's dignity; it would air internal differences, and to make the President "declare war against the Republican party" would "dismount him from being the head of the nation, & make him the head of a party."[175]

The other stage was Jefferson's notifying Washington of his intention to resign at the end of September, the effect of which was decisive. Washington rode out to see him on August 6, and a tacit bargain was apparently struck whereby Washington would not make a public issue of the Genet affair, and Jefferson would remain in office a few months longer. Other assurances were exchanged as well. "Without knowing the views of what is called the Republican party here," Jefferson said piously, "or have any communication with them," he gave the President to understand that they "were firm in the dispositions to support the government." Washington in turn said he thought "the views of the Republican party were perfectly pure," and that if anyone wanted to change the government into a monarchy "there was not a man in the U.S. who would set his face more decidedly against it than himself." Jefferson thereupon declared that "no rational man in the U.S. suspects you of any other disposn"—though he could not resist adding that there were nonetheless those who believed "that our government is good for nothing," and that "we must knock it down & set up something of more energy." They then vigorously agreed on "the republican spirit of the Union." Jefferson wrote a few days later that he would remain until the end of the year, and he got his way on the handling of Genet.[176]

At the same time, aware of plans by Madison and Monroe to present strong pro-French resolutions at forthcoming meetings in Virginia, and knowing that Monroe in particular was still partial to the French minister, Jefferson sent off a crisp warning. "We have decided unanimously to require the recall of Genet. He will sink the republican interest if they do not abandon him."[177]

Jefferson's long and masterful communication to the American minister in Paris, laying before the French government those actions and utterances which had made their emissary an embarrassment to the United States, was completed by mid-August. It was not a peremptory demand for recall but an appeal to the friendship between the two peoples, which was as warm as ever, in the confidence that the French government when made aware of the circumstances would not fail to do the right thing. "In the course of these transactions," Jefferson blandly wrote, "it has been a great comfort to us to believe, that none of them were within the intentions and expectations of his employers." A choice selection of Genet's own letters was then permitted to tell the rest. Jefferson's draft was unanimously approved on August 20, with only a few trifling changes.[178]

The way in which the Republicans managed to get back in tune with public opinion in their subsequent meetings and resolutions (Madison had been given a confidential copy of the letter on Genet) shows the political instincts of Thomas Jefferson at their surest. On August 11 Jefferson dispatched to Madison a sharp analysis both of present possibilities and of what might be accomplished in the forthcoming session of Congress, together with what amounted to a set of blunt party instructions. The republicans should resume their attacks on the Treasury, as begun with the Giles Resolutions of the previous session. (The House may have vindicated Hamilton, but pay no attention; Jefferson was not for giving an inch.) On the other hand, everyone must stop quibbling over the Proclamation. The desire for neutrality was overwhelming, and so was support for the President; the towns everywhere were declaring as much, and under the circumstances the Republicans would show in a very bad light splitting hairs "about small points of propriety." Genet's conduct was arousing universal indignation. "The towns are beginning generally to make known their disapprobation to any such opposition to their govmt by a foreigner, are declaring their firm adherence to their President, & the Proclamation is made the groundwork of these declarations." Jefferson himself had come to see "the necessity of quitting a wreck which could not but sink all who should cling to it." So, he briskly summed up, "I believe that it will be true wisdom in the Republican party to approve unequivocally of a state of neutrality, to avoid little cavils about who should declare it, to abandon G. entirely, with expressions of strong friendship & adherence to his nation & confidence that he has acted against their sense. In this way we shall keep the people on our side by keeping ourselves in the right."[179]

The Republican meetings in effect did just that. The resolutions invariably began with expressions of strong support for the Constitution against any efforts "to subvert or violate the same," in words to which no Federalist could object; this would be followed by approval of all "just and honorable means" for preserving peace, and of the Executive's authority in the exercise of its powers to do so. This circumlocution was the work of the still-stubborn Madison, but most of the meetings made a point of including the Proclamation among such powers, just as the Federalists did. Then would come words of praise and gratitude for the "eminent services" and "patriotic virtues" of Washington which were just as fulsome ("our beloved president") as those of any Federalist. There was gratitude for France's aid to America in the Revolution, and praise for the French people's own struggle for liberty (similar sentiments appeared in Federalist resolutions as well), together with disapproval of any effort to alienate the two peoples. Meetings dominated by the model resolutions of Madison and Monroe extended this thought by adding that a weakening of ties with France automatically meant a step toward the British system and thus toward monarchy, but most of them were reluctant to go that far or be that specific. And finally, it was declared that all foreign agents should deal only with the Executive, and that any appeals to the people ("who act with foreign nations only by their representatives in the different departments") were "highly improper." Except for matters of shading and emphasis—on the Proclamation and on friendship for the French people—there was now little in substance to choose between Republican resolutions and Federalist resolutions, and Washington benignly welcomed them all.[180]

There was, however, an additional point which Jefferson had implanted in his various instructions, the partisan urgency of which was on no account to be blunted. News had just arrived of a British Order in Council of June 8, 1793, directing that all ships carrying grain or flour to French home or colonial ports for the use of the French armies be stopped, and their cargos seized. Jefferson was "for laying the whole business . . . before Congress." He was already planning to submit, as his farewell to office, the weighty report he had withheld so long on the state of American commerce and on the restrictions to which it was subjected by Great Britain. This was to be the basis for a resumption of his and Madison's unremitting campaign, annually renewed in some form since 1789, for a system of commercial retaliation against the British, and the new Order in Council was one more item in support of it. Most specifically, drawing attention to it now would go far to neutralize the harm done by the conduct of Genet.[181]

The epidemic of yellow fever in Philadelphia which took some four thousand lives during the months of September and October had as one of its effects that of bringing politics to a temporary standstill. Some twenty thousand inhabitants, including all the high officers of government, simply fled from the city. The Philadelphia newspapers, which acted as a kind of news service for papers throughout the country, all suspended publication except for Freneau's *National Gazette,* and even Freneau gave up at last on October 26, never to resume. It is not certain to whose advantage this paralysis of activity and communication worked. But in all likelihood it did the Republicans little harm, despite their loss of Freneau and two of their most energetic local leaders, while it did the Federalists—whose momentum of August and early September was considerably slowed—little good. Indeed, Philip Freneau, not unlike Edmond Charles Genet, had largely lived out his usefulness.[182]

By the time Congress reassembled in the first week of December 1793, a kind of partisan equilibrium had been reached, and the Republicans had survived with a minimum of damage. Washington in his message said good things about France and bad things about England, and in a matter-of-fact way—it being no longer a live issue—transmitted most of the Jefferson-Genet correspondence to Congress. Both houses, each now with Republican majorities, thereupon assured the President of their full and hearty support. For Genet this meant the game was finally up: he was ruined. And with Jefferson's report on commerce and the resumption of his and Madison's old schemes against British shipping, the Republicans were once more taking the offensive.[183]

8

Afterthought: The View from Paris

Genet was promptly recalled, though he would never again set foot on French soil, which was just as well for him. One or two questions remain as to what consequences, if any, the Genet mission may have had for French policy toward the United States.

One answer, probably the best one, would be that it did not make much difference one way or the other. Still, the manner in which Genet's case was disposed of makes for some interesting qualifications. The French government was perfectly willing to repudiate all the most flamboyant of Genet's efforts to implement his mission—his privateering, his efforts to recruit American citizens for military purposes, the schemes for expeditions against Florida and Louisiana, and most of his official utterances. From this it might be concluded that French policy was really quite flexible, even frighteningly so. But that would depend on how highly articulated it was in the first place, and on what role, if any, America played in the new French government's view of its own external relations, con-sidering that French ministries since the beginning had not bothered most of the time to write to their representatives in America at all.[184] France certainly had a policy of sorts toward America, but it was a very stark and simple one. When all was said and done, France—the new Jacobin regime in particular—wanted one thing from America and one thing only, which was provisions for her armies. All else—all the airy Girondin fancies—was of so little consequence that the Jacobins could take it or leave it with hardly a second thought.

Therein lies one of the keys to the Jacobins' handling of the Genet mission. For them the measure of Genet's success, or lack of it, must lie not in his *beaux gestes,* his revolutionary ardor, the prizes captured by his privateers, or the military movements he projected in the South and Southwest, but in whether or not he kept those supplies moving. And when he fell out of favor with the American government, he would cease to be of any use to his own. But there is another key as well, one that hardly concerned America at all. This was the exigencies of France's own domestic politics, a curious counterpart of what was happening in American politics vis-à-vis France. Genet and his activities could constitute one more piece of evidence, convenient if not highly important, in the case against Brissot and the other Girondins, all of whom were headed for the guillotine.

The Gironde, with little power in the Ministry since mid-April, was expelled from the Convention on June 2 amid popular uprisings in Paris and displaced by the Jacobins as the dominant group there. The leading Girondins either took flight or were immediately arrested. On June 14, Deforgues replaced Lebrun as Foreign Minister. For some months the French military position had been dete-riorating; the armies were in disarray; and Dumouriez had defected to the enemy. There were murderous outbreaks of rebellion in the Vendée and other provinces. All France's troubles were of course blamed on the Gironde. The Committee of Public Safety was reorganized on July 10, and Robespierre became a member on July 27. The Committee, which sat every day, often well into the night, thereupon began to emerge as the tireless executive council that was to rally a demoralized and near-defeated France, and bring order and victory out of anarchy.

Genet's first dispatches following his official reception—those up through June 19—arrived at the Ministry of Foreign Affairs late in July. They were full of glowing stories of his popular successes, his outfitting of privateers, and his Florida and Louisiana plans; they were, however, somewhat overcast by complaints of how "the old Washington" was obstructing his activities. The harassed Deforgues, who was not the least interested in any of this, replied in a gesture of impatience. All he saw in it was the likelihood of exasperating the United States government, which "has not ceased to make very considerable advances to furnish us with provisions."[185]

Being unduly flattered by friendly demonstrations, Deforgues told Genet, "you have taken upon yourself to arm privateers, to order recruiting in the city of Charleston; to condemn prizes even before you are recognized by the American government and before receiving its consent to so important a measure, nay, with the certainty of its disapproval; because you have before your eyes the proclamation of the President of the United States." What would happen if a foreign agent did such things in France? Deforgues was decidedly skeptical about Genet's measures "for arming the Kentuckians and Canadians 200 leagues away from your residence, where you have sojourned but four weeks. I cannot imagine, moreover, how you could have prepared a naval expedition against New Orleans." Nor could Genet do any of these things "without compromising the neutrality of the United States," and the very least of the consequences would be that of "rendering you odious to the heads of their government." He concluded by admonishing Genet to stop all this nonsense, to have no further illusions about his "false popularity," and to concentrate upon "gaining the confidence of the President and Congress." Genet would of course not receive this advice until it was too late.[186]

The months of August and September were a period of maximum crisis for France and the Committee of Public Safety. The allied armies were concentrated along the Belgian frontier. On August 29 Toulon was surrendered to the British, together with France's entire Mediterranean fleet. Food shortages, aggravated by the British blockade, led to rioting in Paris on September 5. The Convention on August 27 voted the *levée en masse* and total mobilization, and throughout September and October, Lazare Carnot would be immersed in the stupendous task of organizing and equipping a national army. The Law of Suspects (the basis for the Terror) was passed on September 17, and the Law of Maximum (price controls) on September 29.

A memorandum on American affairs was submitted to the Committee of Public Safety on September 13 by Bertrand Barère, one of the Committee's leading members. Much of the work on it had been done by Thomas Paine, as a result of a chance encounter with Barère on the street about a week previously, and many if not most of the recommendations came from Paine's ideas. The memorandum was somewhat reminiscent of the Girondist schemes for America (in which Paine the previous year had taken some part); and in it there was a little of everything. There had been a recent rumor (unfounded, as it turned out) that the United States had closed its ports to all English vessels because of seizures made under the Order in Council of June 8, and was preparing to break off relations. The paper accordingly indicated some of the advantages that might accrue to France from this situation, and some of the steps she might take to exploit it. A "perpetual alliance" should be formed, together with a treaty containing unrestricted commercial privileges. The Americans themselves might take Canada, not to mention Louisiana, and should be encouraged to do so. The Americans were "the best privateers in the world," and could be very useful against France's enemies at sea. But the foremost thing, the very first item on the list and subordinate to all else was supplies. "She will furnish us at least 200 cargoes of grain, which we can convoy with our warships." A special commission should be sent to "treat with Congress." The Foreign Ministry already had doubts about Citizen Genet, not because of any complaints from the American government (these would not be received for another month), but judging from Genet's own despatches. Barère's advice, however (or more likely that of Paine or Louis Otto), was to leave him in place for the time being on account of his popular following in the United States.[187]

This paper was part of the general effort currently being made by the Committee of Public Safety to explore every conceivable source of supply for France's armies during the year to come, of which America was but one of several. On September 13 the Committee issued a general order "that the Provisory Executive Council shall immediately undertake to send informed agents of clear patriotism, or take such other measures as they shall judge suitable, for the purpose of purchasing grain in Turkish Dalmatia, the Barbary States, Italy, Sweden, Denmark, and North America. . . ."[188]

Later that month Deforgues again wrote Genet, having one thing only on his mind. The lack of news, he said (he had still heard nothing since June 19), "is the more acutely felt in that the considerable purchases of subsistence for the various administrations which you are charged with do not admit of the least delay, and we are absolutely ignorant of the steps you have taken in this regard." He insisted "that you inform us without delay of the names and destinations of the American ships that have been sent on the Republic's account," together with "an exact and detailed report of the products making up the shipments, and the cost of the purchases, freight, and insurance."[189]

Genet had in fact been occupied with all manner of other problems. His proposal for full liquidation of the American debt had been flatly turned down, and although he would eventually be given payments of amounts due through the year 1793, he was obliged to meet all the expenses of his mission out of this, and would actually run out of money early in November. These expenses included support of the entire consular and ministerial establishments in America, the large sums required for refitting and provisioning the French fleet that had arrived in mid-July from strife-torn St. Domingue, relief for the thousands of refugees it had brought in, and any supplies he was able to purchase for St. Domingue and the other colonies of the Antilles. Whatever provision ships reached France itself in the summer of 1793 were either those already arranged for by Genet's predecessor Ternant, or that had come on private account. It is doubtful whether he himself sent a single one. Genet wrote home on July 22 and said somewhat lamely, amid a recital of his many difficulties, that "the season does not permit shipments of flour, which run a great risk of arriving spoiled," and in any case he was "convinced that the Council has never considered the supplies of grain France could draw from the United States as a real and sufficient resource," and that such shipments could "never do more than restore her confidence and reestablish competition in the various markets of the Republic." "I now think," he added hopefully, "that the consignments ordered by my predecessor have completely fulfilled that purpose."[190]

Well before this dispatch arrived, the Committee of Public Safety was scrutinizing the loyalty and performance of their foreign representatives everywhere.[191] The report prepared sometime in September on the United States, probably by Otto, tried to take a temperate view of Genet's conduct (some details of which had by now filtered into France), but recognized that something needed to be done about it. "The giddiness of this minister is the more surprising in that he should have known that only the government, and not the portion of the people that played on his vanity, could procure him the advantages he was charged to solicit. . . ." It was "to be feared that we can no longer draw as many supplies from that country as formerly." Citizen Genet's intentions, the report concluded, "are very patriotic," and it "would thus be impolitic" to recall him. Nevertheless it was "urgently necessary to curb his impetuous character, to prescribe the most circumspect behavior toward the government, and to put him back on the road to winning its confidence."[192]

Any reasons for retaining Genet were already, it seems, sufficiently attenuated that when Gouverneur Morris showed Deforgues Jefferson's long memorandum on October 8, Deforgues could tell Morris without even consulting the Committee that Genet would be recalled. He repeated the assurance in writing on October 10, saying that they would regard the Minister's conduct "with the liveliest indignation." The Committee dealt with the matter the following day, and had little difficulty disposing of it. The members had before them a very brief memorandum by Otto, still recommending that Genet not be recalled outright, since it was believed that "his operations in finance and other matters are very advanced," and that he still "enjoyed great popularity." Since there were now "some doubts about the sincerity of his patriotism," and since he had become "disagreeable to the American government," he should at once be given "two adjuncts under the title of commissioners" and ordered "to work only in concert with them." But the Committee was not so inclined. The idea of a commission was retained, but opposite Genet's own name in Otto's memorandum, "recall" was written in the margin. "To be placed under arrest, in accordance with a report, and taking the necessary measures." An order was thereupon drawn up to this effect. There was to be a four-man commission which would "finally disavow the criminal conduct of Genet and his accomplices," "ask authority to put them on board a frigate to be taken to France," "disarm all privateers despatched by Genet, and . . . forbid all Frenchmen to violate the neutrality of the United States."[193]

As this commission, headed by Joseph Fauchet, prepared to depart, Genet's name received two more very brief flickers of notoriety before disappearing forever from view. In both cases this was a somewhat incidental by-product of the general damnation being invoked by the Jacobins upon the Girondin leaders, particularly Brissot, Lebrun, and the former Finance Minister Etienne Clavière. The first was a pamphlet by one G. J. A. Ducher, who wrote regularly on questions of trade and finance, and who had recently found some favor with Robespierre. Ducher had long advocated a policy of economic nationalism for France, and had abominated such free-trade schemes as those promoted by Jefferson, which the Gironde ministry had instructed their representative in the United States to press for. It was all in reality a foul conspiracy hatched by Pitt, which Pitt's paid agents, headed by Clavière, had tried to carry out. Had they been successful, they would have divested France of her colonies (or at any rate of their commerce), raised the standard of counter-revolution in all centers of French manufacturing and trade, and then destroyed all the benefits to France of American neutrality by embroiling the United States in war with Great Britain. This pamphlet, for the preparation of which Ducher had been given access to the Foreign Office files, appeared on October 28, printed by order of the National Convention. The trial of the Girondins had just begun; twenty-one of them, including Brissot, were guillotined on October 31. Clavière committed suicide in prison; Lebrun, in hiding, would be caught and executed late in December.[194]

The other mention of Genet was made in the course of a long speech delivered by Robespierre before the Convention on November 17. The ostensible subject was the foreign relations of the French Republic, and the discourse may be read on several levels. Containing little of actual substance, it was an ideological harangue intended to give heart and inspiration to the French people, and at the same time to redefine to the world the principles of the Revolution. The existence of the French Republic was indispensable to the rest of mankind as the bulwark and defender of reason and liberty. Part of the argument was designed to exhibit France as the friend of small and powerless nations, among which were the Swiss cantons and the United States, and another part to prove that any setbacks either to this intention or to the larger purposes of the Revolution were owing to the machinations of Pitt and the perfidy of the Girondist traitors. The theater of the struggle, however, was the land mass of Europe. In this declamation of thirty pages there was only one paragraph devoted to American affairs, largely lifted from Ducher's pamphlet. The point of it simply was that "a man named Genest,"

> sent by Lebrun and Brissot to Philadelphia in the capacity of agent plenipotentiary, has faithfully carried out the views and instructions of the faction that appointed him. He has used the most extraordinary means to irritate the American government against us. He has affected, without the least pretext, to address them in a menacing tone, and to make proposals to them equally contrary to the interests of both nations; he has exerted himself to render our principles suspect or fearsome in going beyond them by ridiculous applications.[195]

The various papers and memoranda that had figured in some way in the disposition of the Genet case contained a wide variety of recommendations which taken as a whole show very little consistency, either within themselves or with the decisions finally made by the Committee of Public Safety. This disparity is probably best explained by the fact that they were largely prepared by "America hands"—men with some acquaintance or concern with American affairs, such as Otto, Paine, and Ducher, though of limited influence otherwise—whereas the Committee, whose minds were not thus burdened, acted very selectively with reference only to what concerned France's internal affairs and her position in Europe. One sees Genet himself being defined on the one hand as a man of unquestioned patriotism, and on the other as a counter-revolutionary traitor. One also sees recommendations of sweeping commercial privileges to the United States, and, on the other hand, a tight resistance to any system which—in opening French markets permanently to the Americans—would reduce or otherwise injure French navigation, commerce, or manufacturing. All recognized the urgent need for wartime supplies. The Committee, however, saw with stark clarity that this need was far more important than anything else.

All the difficulties that had been encountered could most expediently be laid to the Girondist account, and the most logical way to deal with Genet was to eliminate him along with the rest. For this, Ducher's pamphlet provided the most convenient formula: they were all working in the interests of Pitt. An equally useful formula, though a less obvious one, was Ducher's argument about the damage to French business interests that would result from the Girondist free-trade plans. True, the instructions to Genet's successor Fauchet would contain a clause at the very end about negotiating a new commercial treaty with the United States containing broad mutual privileges. But it does not appear that the French were very serious about this. For one thing, Fauchet and the commissioners were not given actual powers, as Genet had been, to conclude such a treaty; they would simply discuss it, and refer any proposals back to Paris. It was undoubtedly politic to profess continued interest, as long as any similar interest on America's part remained, but it must have been obvious that the Americans' own desire, expressed in time of peace, was at present not very intense. In any case it was Ducher's position, not this, that most accorded with the sentiment of France's commercial classes, whose political support in the current national crisis the Jacobins were not disposed to do without.[196]

All these same considerations applied to the Girondins' visions of conquest or of fomenting insurrection in North America. These were entirely marginal, and there is little evidence, even in the long history of apparent French interest in Louisiana, that they ever occupied much of a place in French national policy. Again, it was only the "America hands," and, more especially, adventurers on the American frontier, who paid any attention, or took any real part in them.

The most ephemeral of all concerned Canada. It never was clear, nor did it seem to matter, whether "the bright star of Canada," with its French population, should be "restored to the American constellation" (as Genet's instructions had put it), or whether the Americans should be encouraged to seize that province (in accordance with the Barère-Paine paper), or whether the Canadians (as per Otto's memorandum) should simply throw off the British yoke themselves. The Canadians' own dispositions had been pretty well revealed to Genet's agent Henri Mézières, who found them so hostile that he did not even dare to publish Genet's revolutionary manifesto. "It is not suitable," Mézières reported gloomily in September 1793, "suddenly to shine the meridian sun of liberty before a people entirely plunged in the thick shadows of ignorance and slavery."[197]

As for the projected movements against Florida and Louisiana, neither got very close to the sticking point, though the Florida expedition was more advanced than the other. (Sufficiently so, indeed, that Fauchet was rather reluctant to give it up.) The new commission was nonetheless summarily instructed to cancel both. They were not worth the trouble, and not worth irritating the American government by compromising its neutrality.[198]

The case of Louisiana is the most interesting, in view of Frederick Jackson Turner's long-famous conviction that French statesmen, royalist and revolutionary alike, had never ceased to dream of Louisiana and the restoration of a vast imperial domain in the Mississippi Valley, the heartland of the New World. Turner's picture was almost certainly far-fetched, much depending on which "statesmen" were meant, how much influence they had, and how central their advice was to French policy at any time. "France had given Louisiana to Spain in 1763 without reluctance," as Mildred Fletcher has written, "and Spain had received it without enthusiasm. As a French colony it had not paid the expenses of administration nor was it destined to do so under Spanish rule." Vergennes made no effort to get it back. Elie de Moustier, the French minister to the United States from 1787 to 1789, was greatly taken by Louisiana and wrote a 330-page memorandum urging its recovery, but nobody in Paris seems to have been much interested. Brissot and the *américanistes,* as we have seen, were similarly intrigued. The subject would come up occasionally in the middle and late 1790s, but mostly for purposes of diplomatic trading. The only figure of continuing importance who strongly promoted the Louisiana idea was Talleyrand, who did succeed in persuading Bonaparte to recover it through the channels of secret diplomacy. This novel arrangement lasted less than three years, in the face of the First Consul's primary concern with Europe. But then Talleyrand too—like Moustier, Brissot, Paine, Otto, and Genet—was himself something of an "America hand."[199]

Edmond Charles Genet lived out the remainder of his days in the Empire State of New York. Fauchet upon his arrival in February 1794 requested permission of the American government, in accordance with his orders, to put his predecessor under arrest. Washington had a conversation with Rufus King on this subject on the very day of Fauchet's first appearance. "I . . . intimated my concern," King noted shortly thereafter, "relative to the Fate of Genet; as long as we were in danger from his Intrigues, we wished him ill—that no longer existing we felt compassion and were anxious he should not be sacrificed." Washington had already made up his mind to the same effect. He politely declined the new minister's request, which had been politely presented, and the matter passed with scarcely a murmur. In the meantime Edmond and Cornelia Clinton of New York, the Governor's daughter, had fallen blissfully in love. They were married on November 6, 1794, and were romantically happy for more than fifteen years until Cornelia's untimely death in 1810. They had six children. His remarriage to Martha Osgood in 1814, also happy, produced five more. He took no part in public life, though he became an American citizen in 1804; he was, however, reasonably active otherwise. He could have gone back to France after the accession of Bonaparte, and considered it, then put the thought behind him. He busied himself with agriculture and schemes for public improvement, such as canals and the prevention of epidemics; his business ventures were not very successful, but he moved agreeably in society and seems to have been generally liked. He died in 1834, and at the present day there are Genet descendants sprinkled throughout the Hudson Valley and many other places. As for Edmond himself, Martha Genet always "grieved that his splendid talents should be buried in obscurity." Edmond Genet never quite understood what had happened to him in 1793, though he devoted some reflection to whom he should blame for it. Eventually he concluded that the evil genius of his downfall was not, after all, the glacial "old Washington," nor yet the Anglocrat Hamilton, but his pretended friend, Jefferson.[200]

In the twilight of his age, Farmer Genet was visited one Sunday in August 1831 at his country seat near Albany by two young Frenchmen, Gustave de Beaumont and Alexis de Tocqueville. The latter especially was eager to discover all that he could about the Americans and their ways, and he undoubtedly supposed that this venerable gentleman was ripe in knowledge on that subject. As Genet's son remembers it, they talked on that summer day until nearly sunset, and then the young men rode away. Tocqueville's great *Democracy in America* duly made its appearance. But of that visit, and that long and earnest conversation—either in the book or in the author's private journals—there was never a word.[201]

CHAPTER IX

America and Great Britain

I
Politics and Commerce

As a general rule treaties between governments are transactions which seldom attract more than mild public attention. Thus it may well be wondered why the Jay Treaty, concluded with Great Britain in the fall of 1794 and made public in the United States the following year, should have made so violent an impression on the public consciousness, and left so deep a trace in the nation's historical memory. No international treaty was ever more passionately denounced in the United States, though the benefits which followed from it were actually considerable. Why this transaction was so overwhelming an event in the life of the early American republic is a question about which the more obvious categories of national interest are not very helpful.

Like the Genet affair, upon which it followed so closely, the Jay negotiations and their aftermath make little sense simply as a problem in foreign relations. But here too, as in the case of American's dealings with France, the matter takes on a deep significance when viewed on the level of domestic politics and ideology. By the spring of 1794 a settlement of some sort with Great Britain was imperative, if armed hostilities were to be avoided. Enormous tensions, over both the border situation in the Northwest and the harassment of American shipping in the Caribbean, had made it so. The treaty which John Jay brought back in 1795 was by and large successful in stabilizing this situation, and might thus be said to have achieved its primary intention. At the same time, a basic feature of Americans' ideal picture of themselves was defaced by the idea of *any* dealings with England which might expose a disparity in power between them, or of accepting anything less than a total acknowledgment of what they saw as their due rights on sea and land. American citizens carried on their commerce in a world whose rules and conditions were largely laid down not by themselves but by Great Britain. Those conditions were not greatly altered by the Jay Treaty, at least not formally. True, once the treaty went into effect, American economic life would flourish as never before, and that aspect of it that flourished most—maritime commerce—was precisely the one widely claimed to have been most slighted by the treaty. But in a way that was just the trouble. American commerce in its very prosperity was as closely tied to England as ever, and consequently Americans everywhere were still unable to see themselves as truly liberated from the former mother country. The Jay Treaty was in large part concerned with commercial matters, but what Americans most hoped for from it had little to do with commerce. If they accepted Jay's work, they sacrificed a measure of their own national self-esteem; if they rejected it, they sacrificed their own material prosperity. They chose in the end to take it, but they underwent a deep crisis of spirit before doing so.

The external provocations which gave the immediate occasion for the war crisis were to some extent a case of coincidence. Things were headed for a showdown already, owing to the initiatives taken by Madison and Jefferson months before to bring it on, though as they hoped, without violence and short of war. It all began in December 1793 with Madison's and Jefferson's ultimate effort to rid America of her commercial dependence on Great Britain.

Madison would carry on the effort largely alone after Jefferson's withdrawal to Monticello. This involved the tireless promotion of a series of restrictions on British shipping and trade—sweeping duties on tonnage and imports, and various retaliatory penalties—which he insisted would compel the English to withdraw their restrictions on ours if we held firm. Madison's case was not without its ambiguities. The purely economic side of it did not hold up at all: his figures were either wrong or obsolete, his reasoning was dotted with fallacies, and his knowledge of the state of trade and shipping was very shaky. But then nobody whose primary concern was material well-being would have made such an argument anyway. Madison's was not an economic case but a moral one. On the one hand, he claimed that the British in the face of his program would give in and abandon their restrictive navigation system, because they needed America's trade more than America needed theirs. That is, American raw materials and markets were necessary to sustain British industry, whereas British manufactured goods— according to him—were largely luxuries which America could do without. But on the other hand, it could well be suspected that he would rather they did not give in, and that his program was actually designed to discourage their doing so. It was this side of the argument—what would happen should Anglo-American commerce, as a consequence of British recalcitrance, be cut back—that seems to have set his imagination racing.

If such a thing occurred (though he insisted it would not, at least not for long), there would be temporary sacrifices. But they would be easily bearable. There was an echo here of the heroic days of Non-Importation prior to the Revolution. Domestic manufactures would be encouraged. (Here was Madison's and Jefferson's vision not so much of factories as of wholesome cottage industry.) A major share of United States trade would be diverted from England to France, an end much to be desired. The failure of this to happen so far was due largely to unnatural conditions. Remove those conditions, and there would be a great increase in American shipbuilding that would benefit all regions of the country. This raised something of a difficulty, inasmuch as Americans were already building ships as fast as they could without such a program, and protesting that this one, if enacted, would deal them nothing but injury. But Madison's patience with the entire shipping and mercantile community was very short. When challenged by such men he could take lofty ground, implying that they were not wholly trustworthy as spokesmen for America's true national welfare, being unduly bound by British interests and under British influence. On Madison's terms, this was largely true. And his case had certainly been strengthened by the attitude of British ministries ever since the conclusion of peace in 1783: their sublime persuasion that no essential change was to be thought of in the hallowed Navigation Act or in the system based on it.

And yet Madison's own system embodied a dilemma. On the one hand, he would never quite face the superior efficiency of the British mercantile system or the inadequacy of France as even a potential, let alone present, supplier of essential manufactures. On the other, if the British *should* yield, and do away with their commercial restrictions, America's trade would be more closely involved with Britain's than ever—and for those same reasons.

So the dilemma remained. It is true that Madison's program was not very coherent on economic grounds, and he was never quite able to persuade his fellow-citizens to accept it. But on other grounds it was not contemptible, and they did not reject it lightly. As a patriotic appeal it called to something deep in the American spirit; men turned away only with the greatest reluctance, and not without inner conflict.

The opening stroke of the campaign was Washington's message of December 5, 1793, on foreign relations, in the shaping of which Jefferson's influence was significant. Jefferson had persuaded Washington, in the face of opposition from Hamilton, Knox, and Randolph, to include a strong passage on the behavior of the British government, accompanied by selections from the correspondence between himself and George Hammond, together with various other papers, going back to the time of Hammond's arrival in 1791. (This was the counter-balance to the material on the Genet mission, which was treated as having been satisfactorily settled and done with.) These documents were offered as evidence in three major areas of complaint. One was the British failure to carry out their side of the 1783 Peace Treaty, the most notorious aspect of which was their continued occupation of the Northwest posts. The second was Great Britain's having unilaterally widened the understood meaning of wartime contraband, in an effort to prevent France from receiving American provisions. This was embodied in the Order in Council of June 8, 1793, which declared it "lawful to stop and detain all vessels loaded wholly or in part with corn, flour, or meal, bound to any port in France, or any port occupied by the armies of France. . . ." A third complaint, not specifically mentioned in the message but strongly implied in the correspondence Jefferson submitted to go with it, was Great Britain's persistent refusal to alter her established system of restrictions on America's regular maritime commerce in British ports. Jefferson had so arranged the papers as to give this point a particular emphasis, and to make it appear that the British would under no circumstances negotiate a commercial treaty with the United States. Hammond was furious when he saw what Jefferson had done. He had no doubt—since the Secretary of State had, as he thought, deliberately omitted letters which might serve to extenuate the British position or to cast doubts on his own—as to Jefferson's real object. It was "to encrease the popular resentment" against the British government "by collecting under one point of view the different aggressions attributed to it—and thereby to influence the debates, which he *foresaw* would arise in the commencement of this session. . . ."[1]

Consequently the implication of the President's message and its accompanying documents was that while France remained friendly, Great Britain was as hostile as ever, if not more so. A further push to the emerging Jefferson-Madison effort was the news, which arrived on December 11, 1793, that Great Britain had helped to arrange a truce between Portugal and Algiers. Though the object had been to gain the assistance of the Portuguese navy in the current war, many Americans suspected the British of an ulterior purpose. That navy had heretofore been used to bottle up the Algerian pirates in the Mediterranean, and thus to prevent their preying on Atlantic commerce, whereas with the fleet's removal they were now free to go in and out as they pleased. It was thus plausible for Americans to think that the truce was simply one more stroke of British ill will directed at them.[2]

The next step was taken on December 16, when Jefferson transmitted to Congress his long-withheld Report on the Privileges and Restrictions on the Commerce of the United States in Foreign Countries. The report had been ready for two years, though circumstances had not until then provided an appropriate occasion for presenting it. But now, with Jefferson about to retire, and with a clear Republican majority in Congress at last, the opportune moment had arrived. This was the document upon which Madison would base his campaign in Congress in the months to come.[3]

It was replete with figures, but the most substantial part was not so much a "report" as a political and ideological polemic, designed as a counter-force to two other documents, equally polemical and equally ideological, that had originated in Great Britain. One was the now-classic *Observations on the Commerce of the American States,* by Lord Sheffield; the other, a lengthy paper by Lord Hawkesbury which in effect brought Sheffield up to date and reaffirmed all his principles. Jefferson's argument, to have any real effect, depended on that of Sheffield and Hawkesbury and required that their leading assertions be in some sense "true," though it is quite probable that by then neither his nor theirs any longer reflected with accuracy the economic realities of the time. In any case, the Sheffield and Hawkesbury statements are indispensable for making full sense of Jefferson's.

Sheffield's *Observations,* first published in 1783, had for a decade served Madison and Jefferson as a kind of negative model, an unholy text which stood as proof of the malevolence of the British mind and of the sort of treatment Americans might expect from Great Britain long into the future should they fail to bestir themselves. Sheffield's pamphlet had been designed to forestall Shelburne's proposal for a liberal trade treaty which would have accorded the Americans most of the privileges they had enjoyed while still within the Empire, and would thus— so Shelburne had argued—retain the American market for British manufactures.

Sheffield violently objected that not only was such a liberal policy unnecessary, it would actually be destructive to Great Britain's most vital interests. Britain, owing to superior products, greater efficiency and lower prices, intimate knowledge of the market, and extensive credit facilities, would keep the lion's share of the market anyway. The Americans, on the other hand, even while still in a colonial status, had already come to monopolize the supplying of the West Indies; they were, moreover, "rapidly robbing us of the shipbuilding business" and "engross-ing the carrying trade."[4] Now that the colonies were independent, all this ought to be stopped. American shipping and American products should be systemati-cally excluded whenever it was in Great Britain's interest to do it. Specifically this should mean requiring all British ships to be built in British shipyards; shutting out American vessels from the British West Indies and the remaining North American colonies; excluding American fish, even if carried in British vessels, from the West Indies; and encouraging Canada and Nova Scotia to increase their production of timber and provisions, so that with these products (as well as with their fish), British subjects could in time displace the Americans altogether as suppliers to the West Indies. If the Americans insisted on political independence, they should have to pay for it. When the Shelburne ministry fell in 1783, these principles became England's official trade policy, and in July of that year they were embodied in an Order in Council.

Shortly after the institution of the federal government in 1789, a new study of British policy was begun by Lord Hawkesbury, the president of the Privy Coun-cil's Committee on Trade and one of Sheffield's most devoted followers. The product of his efforts was the Committee's *Report . . . on the Commerce and Navigation between his Majesty's Dominions, and . . . the United States of America,* submitted to the King on January 28, 1791. From the British point of view it might better have been kept secret, but abstracts reached Jefferson and others in the summer of 1791 by way of an inside person who had access to the original.[5] The principal argument of the Hawkesbury Report, based on considerable research, was that Sheffield had been right on every count. British policy had been an unqualified success, and there was no need whatever to change it. The report proceeded, moreover, on the charming assumption that any American losses in trade and tonnage subsequent to the Revolution were automatic gains for Great Britain.

It opened with the assertion that America's trade was treated more favorably than that of any other nation, many of its exports receiving special preference, and that the United States had no reason to complain of being excluded from the British West Indies. All nations customarily regulated their own colonies' trade as might be most conducive to their interests. The heart of the report was a comparison of British and American gains and losses in trade and shipping between the years 1772–74 and 1787–89. There had been some drop in exports to the United States, but these had been more than offset by an increase of exports to Canada, Nova Scotia, and the West Indies. The decrease, moreover, had been all in raw materials, while there had actually been a net increase in the export of manufactured goods. As for imports from the United States, these too had dropped. All of this meant that the balance of trade had altered sharply in Great Britain's favor. Tonnage statistics followed a similar pattern. The annual total of shipping engaged in trade between Great Britain and the United States had fallen, but this had been all to Britain's advantage. Merchants resident in Great Britain had formerly controlled slightly over half of it, but now they had about two-thirds; any decrease had been offset by a great increase in Great Britain's direct trade with the West Indies; and whereas before the Revolution five-eighths of the tonnage in the trade in West Indies products to the United States had been American, now it was all British. In short, Great Britain had gained and the United States had lost, and that was a good thing.

Nor was there any reason why it should not so continue. The Americans were dependent on Great Britain for their manufactured goods and were not likely to develop any significant industry of their own for some time to come. American discrimination against foreign shipping was not presently serious, but if particular discriminatory duties should be laid on British tonnage or on British goods, then Great Britain ought to retaliate in kind. Americans must not under any conditions be allowed to trade in their own ships with the West Indies or with British North America, nor should such an idea even be discussed. And finally, the provisions and lumber still being brought into the West Indies from the United States (though in British ships) should themselves be displaced in time by those same articles produced in Canada. In other words, the Americans really ought to be cut out of all West Indies commerce, the export as well as the carrying trade.

The report was mean-minded and backward-looking, a particularly reactionary form of mercantilism, even assuming its main statistics to be correct. With its implicit principle of "beggar thy neighbor," and oriented as it was so narrowly to shipping, it fell substantially short of reflecting the interests of the British economic community as a whole. It effectually ignored the implications of British manufacturing and of the expanding American market for it, or of the balances required by American buyers in order that such a market might be sustained. Moreover, the report cemented an ironic transatlantic alliance between Jefferson and Madison on the one side and Sheffield and Hawkesbury on the other. Each had an equal stake in the accuracy of its statistics. But in fact the statistics never had been accurate. There was no place in them for the actual state of American trade with the British West Indies, which was not really much altered after the Revolution from what it had been before. But more significantly, since the report had been issued, and following the outbreak of war in 1792, the entire picture had altered. By the time Jefferson presented his own report, and Madison his set of proposals based on it, the advantage in shipping claimed for Great Britain in the Anglo-American trade had actually been reversed in the Americans' favor.

Nevertheless Jefferson, taking the Hawkesbury Report as his point of reference, argued that the British with their Navigation Law had robbed Americans of a commerce rightfully theirs, and that since Great Britain had no incentive to change a system which worked so obviously to her advantage, the only way to effect an alteration of it would be the threat of retaliation. The formula was "reciprocity": do the same things to them, all up and down the line, as they were doing to us.[6]

In the House of Representatives on January 3, 1794, James Madison, using all of Jefferson's arguments, offered a series of resolutions which would in effect have enacted all of Jefferson's proposed remedies into law. "Reciprocity" would be relentlessly applied to all nations with which the United States did not have commercial treaties — the only one of consequence, as everyone understood, being Great Britain. There would be increased duties on a wide range of manufactured goods, which Madison listed, virtually all of which happened to be British. There would also be increased tonnage duties on ships of nations having no commercial treaty with the United States, and reduced duties on those that did. (This was a revival of his discrimination plan of 1789.) If a nation refused to admit the produce or manufactures of the United States unless brought in American vessels, or if it excluded goods carried in American vessels but not produced in the United States, similar restrictions should be placed on goods exported by that nation. And if a nation should exclude American produce carried in American vessels, a reciprocal exclusion should be applied to her produce. (This would amount to an embargo on the West Indian trade in British vessels.) And finally, mostly in reference to the British principle of food as contraband, these additional duties should be used to compensate American shippers suffering losses "contrary to the Law of Nations."[7]

Madison's language had the ring of both reason and patriotism. But "reciprocity," for all its ostensible justice, was something of a trap. On the one hand its logic, to which Madison doggedly hewed, required that it be extended to a range of matters that were not very consequential, beyond petty annoyance, to either side. But on the other hand, that same logic demanded that Great Britain do away with the two central supports of her national economic policy, the Navigation Act and the Corn Laws. Whether Madison really believed the United States had the resources to make England do this can only be guessed. But he certainly knew that *something* would happen as a consequence of his program, which was just as mercantilist in its thinking as was that of Sheffield and Hawkesbury, and which American businessmen could not have found encouraging.

The most serious difficulties, however, lay elsewhere. Jefferson's report and Madison's resolutions were designed to confront the kind of world depicted in the Hawkesbury Report, one in which American trade and shipping were limited at every point. It was a world of reduced exports, reduced shipping, a virtual collapse of shipbuilding, an inordinate share of America's trade preempted by the British, and a projected future that included a further decline in American exports and an indefinite dependence on British manufactures. But such a picture never had really been a true one, and the American merchant community, probably the British as well, could not have helped knowing this.

For one thing, American exports had already begun to pick up by 1787–88, and would continue to rise through 1792. (The Hawkesbury Report was concerned not with American trade as a whole, only with the Anglo-American trade.) For

Tonnage and Shipping, 1790–96

Year	Tonnage, U.S. vessels in foreign trade entering U.S. ports[a]	Tonnage, British vessels entering U.S. ports[a]	U.S. shipping earnings (Millions)[b]		Percentage U.S. trade carried in U.S. ships[c]
			Gross	Net	
1790	354,767	216,914	$7.4	$5.9	58.6
1791	363,662	210,618	7.8	6.2	60.2
1792	414,679	206,065	9.2	7.4	63.0
1793	447,754	100,180	14.9	11.9	73.2
1794	525,649	37,658	19.4	15.5	86.2
1795	580,277	27,079	23.9	19.0	91.3
1796	675,046	19,669	27.0	21.6	93.1

a. *ASP:CN,* I, 389.

b. Douglass C. North, "The United States Balance of Payments, 1790–1860," William Parker, ed., *Trends in the American Economy in the Nineteenth Century* (Princeton, N.J., 1960), p. 595.

c. Derived from Adam Seybert, *Statistical Annals* . . . (Philadelphia, 1818), pp. 318–319. It is this column of the table that shows most dramatically the American advantage in shipping in the Anglo-American trade, though statistics for British ships in that trade are not available. Note, however, that even if the differences in percentage were assigned as *all* British instead of just mostly (as was certainly the case), the point would still be obvious. For instance, Herbert Heaton notes that in 1796–97, "$25,000,000 of British goods paying *ad valorem* duties entered the United States in American vessels, but only $600,000 in foreign [read British] ships." "The American Trade," C. Northcote Parkinson, ed., *The Trade Winds: A Study of British Overseas Trade during the French Wars, 1793–1815* (London, 1948), p. 204n.

another, American tonnage had increased slowly but steadily from 1789 through the latest available statistics, which included 1792. These were not reflected in the Hawkesbury Report at all. As for the West Indies, the regular trade had of course been legally cut off, and so far as Hawkesbury was concerned that was the end of it. But the shadow trade—not simply smuggling but the repeated opening of the ports to American ships by dispensation of the island governors—had become so dependable that it was no longer even seen as very risky, and was flourishing. Here the Hawkesbury Report gave no statistics whatever: that trade, it assumed, simply did not exist.[8]

In fact the Hawkesbury universe had begun dissolving altogether during 1793. Although the evidence for this had not yet shown up in the official trade figures (which ran a full year behind) at the time Madison presented his program, to any man engaged in commerce the evidence was everywhere around him. Great Britain's share of the carrying trade dropped sharply in 1793 and would so continue; the profits of American shippers had risen dramatically in that year and would soar for the next several to come. And despite the absence of good shipbuilding statistics before 1797, there is every indication that a shipbuilding boom—inspired, logically enough, by a shortage on the one hand and rapidly rising profits in ocean freight on the other—began in 1793 and rose to a peak of some 100,000 tons of new shipping annually by 1795 and 1796.[9] In short, things had never been better, and it was against this background, rather than one of economic strangulation, that debate on Madison's resolutions began.

Madison's two ablest opponents were William Loughton Smith of South Carolina and Fisher Ames of Massachusetts. Smith's effectiveness derived from his close connections with Hamilton, who provided him with all his best arguments and probably took a hand in the writing of his principal speech on commerce.[10]

Smith opened by proposing that the debate be limited to purely commercial matters, and that these not be confused with political questions such as the Northwest posts or the Algerian pirates. Smith knew that Madison's case, based as it was on Jefferson's report as well as on the documents transmitted with Washington's message, depended on lumping them all together, whereas if the argument were restricted to commerce, Madison would probably lose it. He then struck at the report's underlying assumption, that France favored American commerce while England discriminated against it in every way possible. He recited a long and rather tedious list of products to show that on balance American exports had more favorable treatment from England than from France, but the most striking thing about this part of the argument was the comparison of actual volume. From 1790 through 1792 Great Britain had taken $8.5 million worth of American exports, France only $4.9 million; as for imports, the United States had received $15.28 million from Great Britain and only $2.06 million from France. The reasons, he thought, were obvious:

> 1st. Because Great Britain is unquestionably the first manufacturing country in the world, and can supply us with the greatest number of articles we want, on the best terms.
>
> 2d. Because her merchants have large capitals, and can afford to give us extensive credit. Our merchants . . . have small capitals, and want credit.[11]

Smith patiently pointed out the economic benefits of buying from the most efficient supplier and of taking advantage of someone else's capital in the form of credit, and although he admitted that it would be better not to have to depend on a single country for manufactures, he saw no point in placing high duties on England's in order to encourage France's, because "the people of the United States would have to pay higher prices . . . not for their own advantage, but for that of foreigners."[12]

Would anyone believe, Smith wanted to know, "that all this [Madison's program] proceeds from a pure zeal for the advancement of commerce and navigation?" The Secretary of State has said of Great Britain "that she alone has declined friendly arrangements by treaty," whereas it was obviously he and not the British minister who "declined," on the ground that Mr. Hammond did not have the proper powers.[13] And now, Smith wondered, how was Great Britain likely to respond to these new measures? There might well be war, on the ground that they represented a hostile act on behalf of France; there would, at the very least, be counter-measures. The likelihood of America's winning this battle of commercial regulations did not seem very promising. American trade involved only about a sixth of Britain's entire foreign commerce, whereas hers was involved in half of ours, which meant that half of America's trade would be disrupted compared to a sixth of hers. Great Britain, moreover, with her superior capital, could mobilize her resources far more readily. The West Indies, claimed to be unable to survive without American supplies, certainly had other sources on which to draw. And finally, since Great Britain was the only source for many articles vital to American prosperity, these regulations would force their being supplied through third parties, the charge falling on Americans without essentially injuring British industry. Conditions as they stood—American tonnage rising, foreign tonnage declining, exports at last returns far outdistancing those of the previous two years, and revenues from imports in excess of $4.6 million—ought to speak for themselves. "This," Smith declared, "certainly is not a state of things that invites to hazardous experiments."[14]

Predictably, Madison refused to confine the debate to purely commercial questions. He wanted it kept on high nationalist ground. He too, he said, favored friendly negotiations as the best way to settle commercial and other differences, and he recalled that in 1789 it had been urged that time be allowed for such negotiations. But after four years the Peace Treaty remained unexecuted, there was no treaty of commerce "either in train, or in prospect," and "we suffer new and aggravated violations of our rights."[15]

The most unreasonable aspect of British policy, he thought, was that of navigation. The only products Americans could themselves carry to British ports were their own; to the West Indies, even Americans' own products had to go in British ships; American ships were thus deprived of a commerce in which America would otherwise have a natural advantage. The result, he asserted, was a British advantage of three to one in the Anglo-American trade, which by right should be exactly reversed. (Madison did not know that by the end of the previous year the advantage had already shifted in the Americans' favor, and that by the end of the current year it would be about six to one, double what he himself thought it should be.)[16] As for manufactured goods, Madison believed it unjust that Americans should admit everything the British sent them while America's own best products (wheat, flour, fish, and salted provisions) were restricted or refused. Moreover, it was dangerous to depend on a single source, not only because that country was subject to continued wars and impending bankruptcy, but most especially because of

> the influence that may be conveyed into the public councils by a nation directing the course of our trade by her capital, and holding so great a share in our pecuniary institutions, and the effect that may finally ensue on our taste, our manners, and our form of Government itself.[17]

There it was, and the intricacy of Madison's reasoning needs to be appreciated. He professed to seek a world, like that of Adam Smith, free from artificial and unnatural hindrances on commerce, but such a world would hardly have been to his purpose. Not while the manners and morals of the Republic needed protection—protection against British money, British consumer goods, and British ideas: that was what Madison really meant by "commerce." The real menace was corruption.

The debate surged back and forth for some two weeks, and Madison's proposals, despite a great deal of patriotic animus against Great Britain, did not have an easy time of it. Madison's fellow-Virginian, Richard Bland Lee, thought it insulting to be told that Great Britain, merely through trade, "would acquire a predominant influence over our public councils." (Such influence, far greater in 1776, had not prevented the colonies from asserting themselves then.) Nor did Lee believe the government had any business interfering in the pecuniary affairs of its citizens. Credit might contain many mischiefs, but "I do not think they will be prevented by sumptuary laws, or laws which may be calculated to operate that way, and I doubt the consistency of such laws with civil liberty."[18] Samuel Smith of Maryland scoffed at the idea of "excluding British luxuries for French manufactures," when the British supplied such useful articles as textiles, leather goods, and tools, while most French cargoes contained such fripperies as fans, lutestrings, silk stockings, slippers, walking canes, combs, perfumes, and umbrellas. France could never supply the things "which the gentleman wished to exclude by the duties contemplated in his propositions." And if an embargo on British manufactures could throw 250,000 British subjects out of employment, as the gentleman claimed, what would it do to an equivalent number of American farmers, cut off from their markets and "compelled to pay twenty-five per cent. more for their necessary supplies"?[19]

But the real heart-breaker was Fisher Ames, who read Madison a merciless lecture which might well have come directly out of Adam Smith. If there were any proper measure which would "put our trade and navigation on a better footing," Ames began, "it is our undoubted right to adopt it." But "better" meant "more profitable," and that in turn meant "to sell dearer and buy cheaper than we do at present." If these resolutions were to have the opposite effect, American trade would suffer, and the money lost would be even greater than appeared in the balance, since it would reduce the profits that encouraged greater production. Ames's key precept was to examine the market as it now existed—what it was rather than what it ought to be—on the theory that "the merchants will find out the best market sooner than we shall."[20]

The market everywhere, he said, was more or less characterized by restrictions by England, by France, by the United States, and by all others—and the proper question was whether this "restricted" market for American exports was a good one or a bad one. He found, just as Smith had, that the state of trade with England and the English possessions was excellent, while the French market was "very trivial." Even the case of grain, which the English restricted by high duties and the French admitted free, was misleading. The key, again, was the actual market: in normal years American grain was excluded from France by more cheaply produced French grain, and from England by tariffs, but in years of scarcity— which in England occurred with fair frequency, and prices rose higher than duties—the English market was actually better. (Over $1 million worth of American breadstuffs were sold there in 1790.) As for British imports, Ames twitted Madison for having reversed his standards: now it was not that the market was too restricted but that the goods were too cheap, and that Americans consumed too many of them, "not only as much as we can pay for, but to the extent of our credit also."[21] What it came down to, again, was that Americans, like everyone else, bought in the best market available.

Turning to navigation, Ames applied the same measure: leave aside the question of regulation and consider its actual condition. "Trade flourishes on our wharves, though it droops in speeches." Shipping had been "augmented beyond the most sanguine expectation," the excess of American over all foreign tonnage in American commerce between 1789 and 1792 having gone from 32,352 to 171,067. "Is not this increase . . . rapid enough?" And to retaliate against the West Indies for excluding our shipping would simply be to deprive ourselves of our own market. "I hope we shall show . . . that we deem it better policy to feed nations than to starve them, and that we shall never be so unwise as to put our good customers into a situation to be forced to make every exertion to do without us."[22] There was little in the proposals being offered that accorded with modern economic doctrine; "the whole theory of balances of trade," and "systems of prohibition and restriction," Ames asserted, were "exploded dogmas." Support for Madison's system was least forthcoming from those most concerned. "Not one merchant has spoken in favor of it in this body; not one navigating or commercial State has patronized it." Great Britain, it was being claimed, would subordinate her passions to her interests, while Americans were expected to do the opposite. We are being invited, he said, "to engage in a contest of self-denial. For what?"[23]

By the end of January Madison seems to have been aware that his support, at first considerable, was now slipping, and on the 29th he tried to shore up his position with another speech. It consisted largely of debaters' points to cast doubts on the arguments of Smith and Ames, and lacked the unity of his previous efforts. Madison was petulant and angry; it was now apparent that he was on the defensive. Probably his best point was that discrimination against foreign fish in the West Indies cut Americans out of a valuable market, and another good one—though it was rather a negative point—was that favorable discriminatory duties in Great Britain, such as that accorded American lumber, were of no particular consequence.[24]

But the rest of it could not have done his case much good. He quibbled over statistics, which he might better have left alone. He claimed that the Treasury's figures on increased tonnage were misleading, which indeed they were, since they went no further than 1792, but the shipbuilding boom then in full tilt had effected an increase greater even than Hamilton had said it was. He launched into a series of political grievances that included the broadening of contraband, the stirring up of the Indians, and the letting loose of the Algerian pirates. He assigned a kind of price tag to each of the "losses," and insisted that no matter how prosperous in some respects the country might be, these violations demanded "the serious attention of the legislature." (Even if such "serious attention" should bring further serious losses.) He heatedly denied that this would lead to war; he also denied that it was Jefferson rather than Hammond who was responsible for the failure to begin negotiations on a commercial treaty. Hammond may have had the authority to negotiate a treaty but not to conclude one, and no European power, Madison insisted, would have undertaken negotiations under such conditions. (Though in fact Genet's successor as minister from France was under precisely the same restriction.)[25] He argued that a temporary sacrifice was justified should it enable the United States to find an alternative source of manufactured goods—though, as his opponents had pointed out, Madison was asking for a tariff to protect French industry. He minimized fears for the public credit by denying that his measures would endanger it, at the same time blurting out that the public debt should not be a "hostage to foreign countries for our unqualified acquiescence in their unequal laws, and to be worn, as long as the debt should continue, as a badge of national humiliation."[26]

Madison struck the depths of desperation when he questioned the competence of the mercantile community to judge properly what was in the general interest, even when this involved matters directly concerning commerce. "If in any country," he declared,

> the mercantile opinion ought not to be implicitly followed, there were the strongest reasons why it ought not in this. The body of merchants who carry on the American commerce is well known to be composed of so great a proportion of individuals who are either British subjects, or trading on British capital, or enjoying the profits of British consignments, that the mercantile opinion here, might not be an American opinion; nay, it might be the opinion of the very country of which, in the present instance at least, we ought not to take counsel.[27]

Madison, it seems, was by this time blind to the virtual certainty that if any substantial portion of that community were alienated, his measures were lost.

Indeed, in all likelihood they were lost already. "The ground is avowedly changed," wrote Fisher Ames to his friend Christopher Gore; "Madison & Co. now avow that the political wrongs are *the* wrongs to be cured by commercial restrictions, which, in plain English is, we set out with a tale of restrictions and injuries on our commerce, that has been refuted solidly; pressed for a pretext, we avow that we will make war, not for our commerce, but with it; not to make our commerce better, but to make it nothing, in order to reach the tender sides of our enemy, which are not to be wounded in any other way." The first vote, Ames thought, might be "rather doubtful, yet we think the chance in our favor."[28] Ames's optimism was substantially justified by the events of the next several weeks. Madison's first resolution did pass by a narrow vote on February 3, but this was no more than a general affirmation of principle, which would have no force until specifically implemented by the succeeding ones.[29] Such implementation never came. Two days later a Republican motion for delay until March 3 was carried by an even narrower vote. Ames and his friends had pressed for an immediate decision, confident that they would win it, while Madison hoped that in the interim the British might commit new outrages that would gain his case a few more votes. One of the motives for postponement, he admitted to Jefferson, "was the chance of hearing from England, and the probability that the intelligence would strengthen the arguments for retaliation."[30]

During this interval, however, efforts at various public meetings to organize support for the resolutions indicated that the outlook for them was fairly bleak. In Boston a group of local Republicans tried to persuade an open town meeting to endorse a declaration favoring them, but it was voted down by a two-thirds majority. An opposition statement was read at the same meeting and greeted with approval.[31] The story in New York was similar. The Democratic Society there called a meeting in the last days of February and appointed a committee to draw up resolutions to be presented to another meeting the following week. But the committee itself seems to have been paralyzed. The result was a set of very moderate resolutions which condemned England for keeping the Northwest posts but condemned both the English and French for stopping American ships, and said not a word about Madison's proposals. "Since the Resolutions have *passed,*" wrote John Laurance to Rufus King, "we have been tranquil & I suppose that we shall remain so."[32]

A further delay of one week—though the Madisonians had wanted two—was voted on March 3.[33] Before the day came for resuming, however, the news of British provocations that Madison had been hoping for finally did arrive. The effect of it turned out to be quite other than what he had counted on. The news was so bad that *his* remedies became obsolete overnight, and it now looked as though the only adequate remedy might be war.

2

Washington and the War Crisis, 1794

An extraordinary sequence of events between early March and mid-April 1794 began with news of provocations by the British government which were generally seen in the United States as warlike, and culminated with a decision on the part of the American government as to what ought to be done about them. The decision was to send John Jay to London as a special envoy to negotiate a general settlement of outstanding differences between the two countries.

One way of reading these events would be to see Washington as acceding to strong pressures from a contingent of leading Federalists to appoint such an envoy; that is, to handle the crisis in this manner rather than in some other.[34] But that would be quite misleading, and would take for granted things that were not at all taken for granted at the time. With an issue in foreign affairs which might involve war, and especially with Congress in actual session, the question of where the initiative should come from was one about which there was anything but a settled understanding. The case was arising for the first time, and the significance of this six-week period lies in the process whereby such an understanding emerged. By the end of it Washington had convinced himself—in the face of divided councils in Congress, of measures both actual and contemplated that might inhibit his own range of choice, and of divergent advice within his own cabinet—that it was *his* responsibility, with no more than the consent of the Senate, to assume full charge of the crisis. Largely through the weight of his own prestige, Washington was able to establish a precedent which did not yet exist, and the result was another major step whereby content was added to the American presidency.

But the step was not taken without considerable resistance, and it carried from the outset all manner of potential embarrassments. The man Washington appointed, John Jay, was not the most sensitive to the domestic implications of the case, or to its political context. But the main trouble was that any treaty with Great Britain, negotiated by any American, would be encumbered in advance by the heaviest liabilities. Leading Republicans knew better than to offer themselves for such a mission at all, if only because they had already defined the situation as one in which negotiations were fruitless. If the Federalists had had *their* way, on the other hand, the appointee would have been Hamilton, and it has subsequently been suggested that Hamilton would have driven a significantly harder bargain with the British than did Jay. Conceivably so, and yet the mere fact of his being Alexander Hamilton, as Washington himself knew, was a greater liability than any carried by John Jay. Any treaty *he* brought back might not even have got through the Senate.

On March 7, 1794, came news of a British Order in Council, issued on November 6, 1793, but not made public until late in December, which was much more sweeping in its effect than anything previous. Whereas the "Provision Order" of June 8, 1793, had applied primarily to grain ships bound for France, the cargoes of which would be paid for, this one amounted to a total blockade of the French West Indies. Anything bound to or from there was subject to confiscation. Though there was as yet no clear news of how the Order was being executed, rumors were already filtering in of widespread depredations on American commerce in the Caribbean.[35]

Alexander Hamilton was one of the first to perceive the crisis implications of this, and he wrote a brief memorandum to Washington the next day with a few notions of his own. He thought that defense measures, including fortification of the principal ports and the raising of an auxiliary army of twenty thousand men, should be considered, and that Congress ought to give the President authority to lay a full or partial embargo. And if such a plan were in fact deemed advisable, he wondered "whether there ought not to be some executive impulse" for it. "Many persons," he added, "look to the President for the suggestion of measures corresponding with the exigency of Affairs."[36] But Washington kept his own counsel and, so far as is known, made no response.

Two days later, on March 10, there was a private meeting of Senators Rufus King, Oliver Ellsworth, George Cabot, and Caleb Strong in King's room. They decided that Ellsworth should seek an interview with Washington and urge upon him a course of action similar to the one that had already been outlined by Hamilton. But it would include something more than simple defense preparations. Not only should an agent be sent to the West Indies "for the purpose of ascertaining the true situation," but—far more important—an envoy extraordinary should be "sent to England to require satisfaction for the loss of our Property and to adjust those points which menaced a war between the two Countries. . . ."

Ellsworth was to "insinuate," moreover, that the best-qualified choice for that mission would be Hamilton himself. Ellsworth had his meeting with the President on March 12, but the latter would make no commitment on any of it.[37]

The Federalists, meanwhile, were busy also in the House of Representatives. Theodore Sedgwick on March 10 announced his intention to offer a program for "national defense." (This came immediately after a bill had passed, following some weeks of debate on the subject of the Algerian pirates, for the construction of six frigates.) When Sedgwick presented his plan two days later, it was exactly the one Hamilton had proposed to Washington: military preparations and authorization for the President to declare an embargo. The initiative had thereby passed to the Federalists, and James Madison was only too well aware of this. "The partizans of England," he wrote grimly to Jefferson, "considering a war as now probable, are endeavoring to take the lead in defensive preparations, and to acquire merit with the people by anticipating their wishes."[38]

Madison was in a quandary over what might now become of his cherished commercial restrictions, which had been before the House more than two months. On the one hand, some of the resolutions' own supporters were beginning to chafe, saying "that more vigorous measures are rendered necessary by the progress of British outrages." But on the other, Madison himself was dead set against armaments. He had vehemently opposed the frigates bill, arguing that building ships of war would begin an endless cycle of expense, entanglement, and risk, and he was equally hostile to the idea of an army. Writing to Jefferson, he made it clear why. "You will understand the game behind the curtain too well not to perceive the old trick of turning every contingency into a resource for accumulating force in the Government."[39] Accordingly he undertook another push for the adoption of his own resolutions. But the House was now more reluctant than ever. "In a moment of danger," declared Fisher Ames, "when our commerce is nearly annihilated, it is trifling to talk of regulating it, when we should attend to our defence only." The House set the question aside indefinitely, and at this point—March 14—Madison turned his attention to a more immediate measure. It was one that he had been considering some four or five days, a general embargo.[40]

Hamilton and his friends, however, were by no means so fully in control of events as Madison imagined. A key variable in their plan to combine armament with a final effort to negotiate a settlement with England was the President himself, and Washington's inclinations were running in a direction significantly divergent from theirs. For one thing, Washington's own suspicions of British intentions had been steadily mounting. He had received a dispatch from the American minister in London more than three weeks before, itself sufficiently alarming that he had kept it to himself rather than create excitement prematurely,[41] and the most recent news only raised his suspicions further. Under the circumstances, sending an envoy extraordinary would be to invite humiliation. Thus when Ellsworth presented the senators' plan to him on March 12, he was not very receptive. And he made it clear that in any case the choice of Hamilton was out of the question.

"Col. H.," he told Ellsworth, "did not possess the confidence of the country. . . ."[42]

For the next two weeks the initiative remained where it had been, in Congress. But the congressmen, it seems, were not able to do very much with it one way or the other. For five days beginning March 17, they debated behind closed doors the one action short of war that might have an immediate impact on American relations with Great Britain, a general embargo that would cut off all supplies to the West Indies. In the end, it was defeated by a margin of two votes.[43] While the debate continued, it was not likely that Washington would take any step that might be construed as interference. He was sensitive about his own prerogatives, but was equally so to those of Congress. But as unofficial scraps of news from the West Indies became ever gloomier, and voices everywhere were calling for action, it was apparent that this impasse could not go on much longer.[44] Eventually it was Washington, and not Congress, who would take the first decisive step. And from that point forward, until the crisis was finally set to rest nearly two years later, each of the critical decisions would be made by him.

Any doubts Washington may have had were whisked away by two sets of messages that reached him almost simultaneously, probably by the weekend of March 22–23 and certainly by Monday morning, March 24. The first was from Fulwar Skipwith, the American consul at St. Eustatius in the Dutch West Indies. Skipwith's letters provided the first official account of British depredations on American shipping under the Order in Council of November 6, and of the ruthless treatment of American seamen and property by British naval commanders and admiralty courts in the West Indies. Over 250 ships had been seized, and 150 already confiscated. Many of these, though cleared for neutral—and even British—ports, were stripped of their sails and condemned, on the mere suspicion of intending to trade with the French. Sailors, all their possessions taken from them, were in considerable distress. It had been necessary for the American consul to lay out all his resources to assist them, and to prevent their being obliged to take foreign service.[45]

This was not the sort of information the former military commander was likely to receive without a strong flush of anger. The other piece of news was from Canada, by way of Governor George Clinton of New York. The background of it was the Indian situation in the Northwest, which had been an intermittent vexation for Washington virtually from the time he first assumed office.

By the spring of 1794, after periodic outbreaks of hostilities that had gone on for years, and after the final failure of boundary negotiations, Washington had come to the conclusion that the situation was only to be resolved by force. He was anticipating a decisive campaign by Wayne's army in the coming summer. But the unpredictable factor, as it had been all along, was the extent to which the Indians might receive encouragement and assistance from the British. The authorities in Canada had always had to tread a very precarious line. On one side of it was an official policy of peace with the United States, and of self-restraint with regard to stirring up the Indians against American incursions; on the other were the realities of their own defense situation and the requirements of border security. With a very small military presence and a vastly extended frontier, everything depended on relations with the Indians, and it was vital above all that the tribes not be actively hostile. Now, with an American army moving north, all these considerations were drawing to the crisis point for Governor Lord Dorchester and Lieutenant-Governor John Graves Simcoe. Dorchester, it now appeared from Clinton's dispatch, had dropped all restraints and was openly inciting the Indians to bloody acts.

On February 10, Dorchester had made a vigorous speech at Quebec to a deputation of "the Seven Villages of Lower Canada" and "the Nations of the Upper Country," in response to "the grievances they had complained of, on the part of the United States." He declared to the Indians that since the treaty line of 1783 separating Canada from the United States had been disregarded by the Americans, he fully expected war within the year, in which case the new line must be drawn by the Indians themselves. And however it might be drawn, the Americans "must lose all their improvements and houses on our side of it; the people must all be gone, who do not obtain leave to become the King's subjects; what belongs to the Indians will of course be confirmed and secured to them."[46]

Washington was now prepared to act. On Tuesday, March 25, he transmitted Skipwith's letters describing the West Indies seizures to Congress. He said they contained "information which will probably be thought to require some pecuniary provision," though beneath this indirect formula (aid to the distressed seamen) it was perfectly clear what the President wanted. The House immediately passed a general thirty-day embargo, which was accepted by the Senate the following day. As for Dorchester's speech, Washington concluded that it would be superfluous to transmit this document now, since it had already reached the newspapers.[47]

Washington was clearly convinced that the British intended war, and by Thursday the 27th it was also obvious that his effort to get the congressmen into motion had been all too successful. So much so, indeed, that it was becoming anyone's guess as to what they might do next. After passing the embargo, the House took up a proposition from the Federalist Jonathan Dayton of New Jersey "for the sequestration of all the debts due from the citizens of the United States to the subjects of Great Britain"—and although there were other Federalist efforts to modify this very serious step toward war, there seemed for a time every indication that Dayton's bill would pass.[48] War appeared inevitable, even to those most desperately anxious to avoid it. But then came further news, the tendency of which was to arrest somewhat the gathering momentum of war preparations.

On Friday, March 28, a special express from New York brought information that the Order in Council of November 6, under which the recent seizures had been made, was revoked. A new one, dated January 8, now replaced it. Whereas the previous Order had instructed commanders to seize all ships going to or from the French islands, or even suspected of intentions thereof, the new Order in effect permitted the resumption of such trade—unless in contraband, and excepting any direct trade between the islands and the ports of France. Shortly thereafter, information from London reached Rufus King through a private source "that a

Committee of Merchants interested in the American trade waited upon Mr. Pitt to know the cause of the condemnation of so many American vessels in the W. Indies; to whh. he replied that it was contrary to instructions given, and that the most ample compensation to the sufferers would be given."[49]

Doubts also, meanwhile, were being cast on the authenticity of Dorchester's speech. Washington, though emphatically refusing to share them, thought he would do well to inquire into it further. He was still certain that the speech had been made in accordance with instructions from London, and that the Ministry there had meant war at least as late as December. Perhaps, on the other hand, reverses in Europe—the French had recaptured Toulon on December 18—"may have wrought a change in the political conduct of G. Britain toward this Country. . . ." Then on April 3 a dispatch arrived from Thomas Pinckney, the American minister in London, with official confirmation of the new Order in Council, together with the conciliatory explanations Grenville had given to the American minister when he made his protests. Grenville assured Pinckney that Great Britain wished "to maintain the best understanding and harmony with the United States," that the Order of November 6 had been temporary, and that it had been designed to deal with a special situation. He explained that since the entire French fleet of St. Domingue had sailed to the United States the previous summer loaded with West Indies produce, the Ministry had resolved to prevent subsequent "abuses"; that in preparation for a forthcoming British attack on the French islands the intention was to prevent their receiving supplies, "but that it was now no longer necessary to continue that regulation for those purposes"; and that no vessel seized under it would be condemned unless already liable to condemnation under previous Orders. This was confusing and not altogether satisfactory, and it certainly did not explain the sweeping condemnations described in Skipwith's letters. Still, it must have created a whole new area of doubt in Washington's mind. What was the present state of British intentions?[50] Washington now was in rather a dilemma. If he sent a special envoy to London, as the King-Ellsworth group had urged, he might be open to the charge of foreclosing more direct steps to defend American lives and property. On the other hand, if he took any aggressive action—or even simply did nothing—Congress on its present path might enact measures which would greatly narrow the likelihood of any successful negotiation, and which might make war the only possible outcome. He sent Pinckney's dispatches to Congress the day after he received them, and rumors began spreading about town that he was considering a special mission, and that Alexander Hamilton was the leading candidate for it.[51]

But if these rumors reflected in some way the logic of things as they stood in the first week of April, they did so only partially, and they in no way reflected the process whereby Washington was making up his mind, or how he was reacting to the various kinds of advice he was getting.

For instance, Edmund Randolph, Jefferson's successor as Secretary of State, now told Washington that he favored sending a special envoy, and, knowing Washington's reluctance to give offense to Pinckney by thus displacing him, reassured the President that the special circumstances called for special steps, and that Pinckney would undoubtedly so see it. But he also urged Washington to delay making his final choice of a nominee, partly to allow Congress to enact threatening weapons to put in the envoy's hands (such as the pending sequestration bill), and partly—though he did not come out and say so—to discourage an over-hasty nomination of Hamilton. Two Virginians, James Monroe and Randolph's brother-in-law John Nicholas, then wrote Washington in suspiciously close succession, each with dire warnings against Hamilton. Washington manifested his displeasure. He let Randolph know that he was not deceived as to who had inspired them, and he told Monroe that Hamilton was, to be sure, one of those being considered in case a mission were sent, but that

> no one (if the measure should be adopted) is yet absolutely decided in my mind
> . . . and as I *alone* am responsible for a proper nomination, it certainly behoves
> me to name such an one as in my judgment combines the requisites for a mission
> so peculiarly interesting to the *peace* and happiness of this country.

To Nicholas, whose letter bordered on insolence, he did not reply at all.[52] Actually he had no intention of nominating Hamilton. In a talk with his old friend Robert Morris on April 8, he named several possible persons—Adams, Hamilton, Jay, and Jefferson—and asked Morris what he thought. Morris, according to King, "decidedly supports the appointment of Hamilton." That evening Washington invited John Jay to dinner. They discussed the crisis and how the country might avoid war, though Washington—so far as is known—still did not offer the mission to Jay.[53]

The momentum of the House of Representatives, meanwhile, though slowing, remained well up. Attention had shifted from a sequestration bill to a resolution offered on April 7 by Abraham Clark of New Jersey, ending all commercial intercourse with Great Britain until restitution was made for spoliations and until the Northwest posts were surrendered. It was debated for ten days. On April 18 an amendment was proposed by Madison which would suspend trade as of November 1, rather than at once. This was more moderate, in that it did not require immediate sacrifices, and it allowed the British six months to make restitution and evacuate the posts before being subject to retaliation. But it certainly complicated the problem of conducting a successful negotiation, there being no way of knowing whether it would inspire greater concessions or whether the British would refuse under such a threat to negotiate at all. Madison's measure passed the House on April 21, 58 to 38.[54]

Washington had meanwhile made up his mind at last to nominate Jay, and had actually done it nearly a week before. Moreover he had, in so doing, made known what he thought about the drift things had taken in Congress. Hamilton removed himself from consideration on the 14th; Washington offered the mission to Jay on the 15th, at which time Jay told him that the resolutions being debated in Congress were "in the nature of a menace and that G. Britain would, and ought to, refuse to treat with us if they were adopted." If Washington had not already been acquainted with these views, and if he had not come to share them himself, he would hardly have made the offer. That afternoon Hamilton, Strong,

Cabot, Ellsworth, and King called on Jay and urged him to accept. He did so on the following day, repeating his opposition to both the sequestration and non-intercourse resolutions. The nomination was confirmed in the Senate 20–8 on April 19. Madison's amended non-intercourse bill reached the Senate on the 25th, and on the 28th was defeated by the casting vote of Vice-President Adams. No further measures either for retaliation or even for defense made any progress thereafter. On May 12 the thirty-day embargo, which had already been renewed once, was discontinued by general agreement, though subsequently the President was authorized to reimpose it if he thought conditions required doing so. That same day, John Jay sailed for Great Britain.[55]

But Washington had not taken matters into his own hands without paying a price for it. There was scarcely an objection the Republican press did not think of, and vigorously express, as soon as the mission became generally known. If America had got nothing in the way of redress for her many grievances in the past ten years, there was little reason to imagine that anything would come from negotiating, now that the outrages were greater than ever. On the other hand, compensation for injuries to commerce, if secured, would only serve England as an admirable pretext for ignoring everything else. The recovery of "mercantile wealth," so that the "English faction" might continue its rule, was really "the secret object of the mission" anyway, and "every thing we fail in getting will be justly chargeable on the treachery of the agent." The Executive, moreover, had grossly overstepped its authority. Those who had "usurped the ear and confidence of the President" had induced him not only to arrest the proper course of legislative deliberations but actually to violate the Constitution, to breach the separation of powers by appointing the nation's highest judicial officer to make a treaty that was to become the law of the land.[56] "If a Chief Justice is to sit in judgment upon his own acts, if he is to be the expositor of a law of his own making, our boasted constitution has become a dead letter, contrived to entrap an unsuspecting people."[57] John Jay himself, moreover, was the acknowledged servant of the English interest in America, being known to have asserted at one time or another that the American states had violated the Peace Treaty as regularly as had the British, and that the confiscation of British debts was illegal. One might well have concluded that if the mission were not doomed to shame for one reason, it was bound to be so for some other. James Madison, though perhaps not the most dependable witness, declared to Jefferson that "as involving the appointment of Jay," it was "the most powerful blow ever suffered by the popularity of the President." Nor did Madison intend to let matters lie. "If animadversions are undertaken by skilful hands," he suggested, "there is no measure of the Ex[ecutive] administration perhaps that will be found more severely vulnerable."[58]

Nor, indeed, had the country yet seen the last of British provocations. George Hammond had already indicated his belief that Lord Dorchester's speech to the Indians, though genuine, was not authorized; yet on May 20 came news of a move on Dorchester's part that was in every way as serious. Believing that Wayne's objective in the Northwest was in reality British-occupied Detroit, Dorchester had ordered Lieutenant-Governor Simcoe to reoccupy and fortify an abandoned post at the Rapids of the Maumee, a place well within acknowledged American territory. Had this been known in Philadelphia a few weeks earlier, it might well have scuttled the entire Jay mission.[59]

3
A Vision of the Commercial Future

The way one thinks about the treaty Jay brought back depends in very large part on how one views the instructions he took with him, and whether the view is a broad or a narrow one. The instructions might simply be seen as the agenda for a course of adversary bargaining, which most treaty-making diplomacy normally amounts to, the evaluation of which depends on how much each side "wins." These instructions in particular could be judged, as they largely have been, as having a defeatist, defensive, and negative quality. Such was the suspicion many had of them at the time, and the tendency then was to conclude that Jay got much the worst of the "bargain." Such a view has to a great degree persisted ever since.

Yet those are not the only grounds for viewing the instructions and the spirit in which they were devised. They may well have represented not a cramped holding action on the part of a weak power but a bold initiative, a grand imaginative projection, simply the first step of a comprehensive policy that would not merely settle outstanding past differences and recent grievances but usher in a new era of prosperity in Anglo-American trade. With the objectives so seen, the results might look somewhat different. Jay might then reappear as having made very few errors, and having conducted his mission with a good measure of skill. And the evidence, thus re-examined, would give surprisingly little warrant for the traditional assumption that Jay was "outwitted" and "outmaneuvered."

A more positive view such as this would not be wrong, except that it carries one big difficulty. It would require that Jay's conception and that of his British counterparts as to the overall objectives of the negotiation be essentially similar, whereas there is little indication that they were. True, the negotiators got on very well, and neither seems to have behaved in a mean and haggling way. Yet the American had a sweeping view of the future, while that of the British was distinctly limited, their minds being essentially elsewhere. They may have been more accommodating than usual, and even more enlightened; they may actually have altered some of their fixed prejudices for the occasion, in order to placate the Americans. But that was about the limit of their concern, which was not really for the future at all. It was simply for reverting once again to a state of things in which America did not constitute a problem.

The leading role in the devising of Jay's instructions, as has always been known, was played by Alexander Hamilton.

The main principles were initially blocked out at a meeting on April 21, 1794, two days after Jay's nomination had been confirmed by the Senate. Hamilton, King, Cabot, Ellsworth, and Jay himself were present. They agreed that Jay's instructions should be issued to him by the President without prior consultation with the Senate as to what they should contain, though any treaty he might make would of course require Senate approval. (This was in accordance with the precedent established in 1789: "consent," not "advice," was the operative term for the Senate's role in the making of treaties. Otherwise Jay might be loaded with impossible *sine qua nons.*) Jay would make the most "strenuous efforts" to obtain satisfaction for spoliations on American commerce and to establish rules that would preclude such depredations in the future. (The implication was that without such an understanding war would be likely, if not unavoidable.) He should insist on fulfillment of the Peace Treaty of 1783, which meant principally the evacuation of the Northwest posts. If the British acceded to this, and if they agreed to pay damages for the spoliations, then "we might agree" to assume responsibility for the prewar debts owed by Americans to British creditors, up to the amount of £500,000 sterling. Various other matters, such as navigation on the Great Lakes, Indian trade, and admission of American ships into the British West Indies, were also discussed.[60]

The next day (April 22) Hamilton had a long talk with Jay, and the day after that he sent Washington, at the latter's request, a memorandum on what he thought Jay's instructions should consist of. In it he developed in detail the points established in outline by the meetings of the previous two days.[61] First in importance were indemnification for damages to American commerce and rules regarding interception and seizure. Ideally, only instruments of war should be treated as contraband. But if necessary (and obviously it would be necessary), the United States should be prepared to accept qualifications. Food might have to be regarded as conditional contraband; that is, cargoes of provisions might under certain circumstances be preempted, though they would have to be paid for. The British "Rule of 1756" (that a trade ordinarily closed in peacetime was not to be reopened to neutrals in time of war) might be acceptable as a "last resort," if construed as containing a loophole for the "broken voyage."[62] The United States might also agree to pay indemnities for prizes taken by French privateers illegally fitted out in American ports, in accordance with assurances previously given by the President. Among other rules desirable for the future were that a port should be actually blockaded for the blockade to be legal, and that no additional supplies should be sold to Indian tribes in case either nation were at war with them. Nor should the sale of prizes be permitted in American ports.

As for issues remaining from the Peace Treaty of 1783, Great Britain should surrender the posts and make indemnification for slaves carried away, and the United States would pay an indemnity for obstructions to the recovery of debts owed to British creditors. It would be desirable in addition that the Great Lakes be kept clear of armed vessels and fortifications, and that both nations be free to trade with the Indians on either side of the border.

If a commercial treaty were made, it should stipulate that the British West Indies be opened to American vessels of sixty to eighty tons burden, and also that American manufactures going to Great Britain and Ireland should be received there on a most-favored-nation basis. In return, British and Irish manufactures would be given the same status in America—that is, they would not be discriminated against — and the United States would guarantee not to raise above 10 percent the duties on any British goods currently taxed below that figure. Duties that already stood at 10 percent or more would not be raised at all.[63] Hamilton's memorandum provided the basis on which Jay's instructions were drawn up by Secretary of State Randolph. The first aim was compensation for spoliations; equally important was to settle differences arising from the Peace Treaty (the posts and the debts); and if these should be satisfactorily settled, Jay might consider a treaty of commerce. A number of possible provisions were listed as "desirable": the "free ships, free goods" principle, no assistance to Indians in time of war, and a narrow definition of contraband. But these were not absolutely indispensable. The only *sine qua non* for a commercial treaty was the admission of American ships "of certain defined burthens" to the West Indies. Randolph also put in something of his own. Jay might sound the ministers of Russia, Denmark, and Sweden — since there had been talk of reviving the League of Armed Neutrality of 1780 — on joining in an alliance to support America's neutral rights, if in his judgment the situation appeared to warrant such a step. And no treaty was to be signed that would "derogate from our treaties and engagements with France."[64]

The instructions were dated May 6. On that same day Hamilton sent a letter to Jay which was evidently a kind of recapitulation of principles they had already agreed upon in private. ("Our conversations," Hamilton wrote in his draft, though he omitted the sentence from his final copy, "have anticipated so much that I could say little here which would not be repetitive.") Some things, to be sure, were repetitive. But taken as a whole this fascinating letter, which was rather lengthy, offers a special glimpse at the scope of Hamilton's purposes, and sheds much light on Jay's subsequent negotiating strategy. "We are both impressed equally strongly," he began,

> with the great importance of a right adjustment of all matters of past controversy and future good understanding with G Britain. Yet important as this object is, it will be better to do nothing than to do any thing which will not stand the test of the severest scrutiny and especially which may be construed into the relinquishment of a substantial right or interest.[65]

Whatever was done, that is, it should rest on a solid base, and "the relinquishment of a substantial right or interest" would make such a base very difficult to establish. Indemnification for illegal seizures under the November 6 Order in Council (the "proceeding was an atrocious one") was of the utmost importance. The "mere appearance" of indemnification would not do, though this might be managed with "less rigor" if a good arrangement on the unsettled issues of the Peace Treaty were reached, and especially if "a truly beneficial treaty of Commerce" could be made.[66] Hamilton further implied, as he had in his memorandum to Washington, that the Rule of 1756 might if necessary be acceptable inasmuch as France had already opened portions of her West Indies trade to American shipping while still at peace with England.

Hamilton then pointed out the increasing dependence of the British West Indies on the United States for supplies, and he dwelt on the paramount importance of American trade to British prosperity. This, together with an agreement by the United States not to resort to the sequestration of British debts as a mode of reprisal, should suffice to make the British see the wisdom of making a good treaty in order to stabilize these commercial relations. He also discussed the further mutual benefits that could ensue from British assistance in American efforts to acquire full navigation of the Mississippi.

Some reference should here be made to the assertion by the late Professor Bemis, whose work has greatly influenced most modern thinking on the Jay Treaty, that Hamilton and those who followed his views

> were prepared to admit the Rule of the War of 1756, to allow provisions to be so dangerously near the definition of contraband as to be susceptible of preemption, to let enemy property be taken from neutral decks. In the last resort, to preserve peace and national credit, which depended for its revenues on commerce, they were willing, in the face of British sea power, to acquiesce in a complete reversion or suspension of the liberal principles incorporated in the American treaties with France, Sweden, Holland, and Prussia.[67]

This is, of course, technically correct. But it gives few clues to the full workings of Hamilton's mind. From it, one might suppose that Hamilton's willingness to overlook the "liberal principles" embodied in the treaty with France, and written into those with Sweden, Holland, and Prussia by Jefferson, represented a craven and perhaps even treacherous retreat. But the nations that had accepted these principles had done so at no particular cost to themselves, whereas the only mode of enforcing them that Jefferson or Madison had ever been able to think of was a war of commercial reprisals that could only strike Hamilton as a form of madness.

A more basic misunderstanding is to see Hamilton's plan as something merely defensive, as simply a way of protecting his financial system. It was obviously that; it was also much more. Alexander Hamilton was acting fully in character, and for better or worse there was nothing very timid or halfway about what he had in mind. Once again, Hamilton was prepared to take advantage of a crisis—as at Annapolis in 1786, or New York in 1789—to press for a bold new initiative and to make a sweeping projection. Then, it was a new constitution of government, a new system of public credit; now, it was a newly stabilized system of international trade, the governing element of which would be a plenary understanding with Great Britain.

The projection was founded on a series of premises. The British would recognize that their treatment of American shipping in the Caribbean was both unacceptable and irrational, that it would have to cease, and that compensation for the damage so far done by it was essential. They would also see that the time had come to settle once and for all the question of the Northwest posts, in conjunction with that of the prewar debts. This satisfactorily accomplished, a state of mind conducive to imaginative negotiation would thereby have been established in which the British would perceive the logic of making a departure from past policy on their West Indies trade. They would open the islands to American ships of seventy tons or less, and the Americans would reciprocate by engaging not to lay further taxes on British manufactured goods—or at least not to discriminate against them—and not to sequester debts owed to British creditors. Actually neither of these concessions, on the British or on the American side, would cost very much, and they could thus be regarded as largely symbolic. That is, since the governors had out of necessity been regularly opening the islands to American supplies, the seventy-ton provision would simply be a limited official recognition of circumstances that had been present for some time. As for sequestration of debts, any American engaged in overseas trade knew already that such a policy would be an automatic calamity for all commerce, so that this "concession" would be mainly symbolic in nature. "Yet the point of right," as Hamilton told Jay, "cannot be so absolutely settled as not to make it interesting to fix it by Treaty."[68]

In any case, these would be very critical first steps toward a recognition, on both sides, of the mutual advantages which still further steps might procure in the future. From here, it was sooner or later bound to dawn on the British mind that there was a simple logic in permitting the Americans to supply the West Indies more or less unconditionally, since the profits would inevitably be spent on British manufactured goods. The Americans would in turn abandon the mirage of a vastly expanded trade with France, it being reasonably certain by now that nothing would come of it, and would concentrate their energies on developing the profitable commercial relations that existed already with their best customers and natural suppliers, the British. An even more inspiring prospect was the opening of the entire Northwest to American farmers, once the issues of the posts and Indians were laid to rest. The British, perceiving a vast new market to be supplied by way of the St. Lawrence and the Great Lakes, and the prospect of cheap food for the West Indies shipped down the Mississippi and across the Gulf, would find it entirely to their interest to assist us in getting the Mississippi opened, and to help protect our trade once it had been established there. Inevitably they would come to realize that the "beggar thy neighbor" philosophy that had so permeated the Privy Council Report of 1791 was hopelessly outmoded, and indeed quite subversive of their own best interests. It was wholly to their advantage to foster American trade, American growth, and even American territorial expansion: it all added up to ever-greater markets for British goods. Undoubtedly, America would some day acquire the population, the skills, and the wealth to do her own manufacturing. But such a day was still far off, and even this would occur within the framework of an immensely expanded and far-flung Anglo-American economy.

A dazzling vision indeed, and an opportunity for which Hamilton had been waiting ever since his first talks with George Beckwith back in 1789. If he could succeed in getting the broad principles of it implanted, a few concessions would be well worth the price. The Rule of 1756 would in any case have to be one of them, and the price here would be more than tolerable. There was every likelihood that both this and the principles of the Navigation Act could be construed with some latitude, given the current state of the West Indies trade, without insisting— at least for the moment—on their being literally and explicitly abandoned.

Herein was implied a distinct strategy and style of negotiation, both of which

Jay would in fact maintain with steadiness and consistency throughout his mission. There could be no essential compromises on territorial questions or on stirring up the Indians. Jay would make a firm statement on spoliation claims. He would not, however, let himself be hamstrung over "prior infractions" of the Peace Treaty, an issue which in Jefferson's hands had ended in paralysis. He would move to an agreement which would both give satisfaction to British creditors and deliver the Northwest posts into American hands. Nor would he let the negotiations be stalled over the issue of slaves carried off. That there was not a word about this in Hamilton's letter of May 6 to Jay is some indication of what they must have said about it in private. (It was not likely, on the other hand, that anything would be done about the Loyalists either.) Jay would, moreover, place the utmost stress on a concession from the British—a symbolic first step—on the West Indies trade.

For the rest, Jay's demeanor would be courteous, dignified, and accommodating. There would be no belligerent threats or confrontations: if the object was to initiate a future era of cooperation, this would obviously be the least promising way to go about it. Every effort should be made to show the British that their interests and those of the United States were not antagonistic, and that mutual concessions would lead to mutual advantages. Above all, this should not be the sort of encounter in which one side wins and the other loses, one's gain automatically the other's loss. A successful negotiation would mean more for all.

There is much reason to think that this was in principle the most effective strategy Jay could have adopted, and little for supposing that a more pugnacious one would have been nearly as successful. And yet it did have a fundamental weakness. It assumed—indeed, required—that the British would in fact see the overall aims in the same light in which the Americans saw them, and that if the negotiation did turn out to be generally successful, this would signify their acceptance of the Americans' vision of the future. That is, if Grenville were to concede things which Jay knew might not be politically easy for him, such as accepting in principle the admission of American ships into the West Indies, then Jay would find it very difficult not to conclude that Grenville and Pitt had been truly converted, that they had indeed come to grasp the advantages of a whole new Anglo-American system. Thus the precise details of any agreement would appear less important than the general direction, a willingness to loosen restrictions, and temporary difficulties should not be allowed to obstruct overall intentions. In that setting, to make obstructions would in effect be a sign of bad faith, and Jay was probably right in having discerned no such signs. And yet bad faith need not have been the only influence for impediments. They could arise from sheer preoccupation, and even from carelessness.

Still, the atmosphere in which Jay began his efforts, and which he himself helped to make, was an accommodating one. It did not dispose him to haggle over every little item, and thereby risk the good will and conciliatory temper he met in Pitt and Grenville.

What, then, was the British view of the case? We have surprisingly little direct evidence to go on, which may in itself be a clue of sorts. No British writer has taken up the matter at all, and the two leading American authorities have advanced sharply differing versions of how the British responded to Jay and to the proposals he made to them. According to Samuel Bemis, Grenville saw the American demands as a kind of threat which he managed to neutralize by outmaneuvering the unwary Jay. A more recent writer, Charles R. Ritcheson, has made great efforts to counteract the anglophobic strain that has affected even the most judicious work on the Anglo-American diplomacy of this period. Ritcheson insists that Grenville and Pitt, in agreeing to open the West Indies, *were* in fact converted; they were persuaded by Jay over the bitter opposition of Hawkesbury and Sheffield to reverse the established commercial policy of Great Britain, thus offsetting a belated but real victory for the liberal principles of Shelburne.[69]

Both these versions, however, opposite though they are, take for granted an allocation of British attention and a definition of the diplomatic situation that is curiously solipsistic and very American-centered. The assumption in each case is somehow that of America as constituting for the British a central and pressing concern which would in turn absorb a significant increment of their time and effort. Accordingly the Americans (depending on which view one took) would either let themselves be shrewdly outguessed and accorded a minimum of concessions, or else they would succeed in bringing the British round and persuading them to accept a major break in their own Navigation System. There is the further explicit premise of a rough comparability in weight between the two negotiating parties, and on each side a more or less equal awareness of the other's interests, requirements, and bargaining power.[70]

This set of assumptions almost certainly amounts to a distortion. America was only one of innumerable difficulties Pitt and Grenville were facing in 1794, and by no means the most urgent one. Moreover, the minimum terms that would have been necessary to avoid war with the United States—satisfaction for the spoliations and evacuation of the posts—were concessions that Grenville, and even Hawkesbury, were prepared to make from the first.[71] It was not the sort of negotiation likely to engage on their part a very high degree of concentration or imagination. Indeed, they were not even aware, until Jay actually appeared, that a negotiation on this level was to be entered upon at all.

Normally, the Americans required no particular attention, and the British would have been just as glad to keep it that way. The posts and the debts had always been irritants, but they hardly made for a matter of overriding concern. All reports from Hammond prior to Jay's arrival had seemed to indicate that the Americans, their government at least, were maintaining a strict neutrality in the European war, and that Genet's efforts to engage their assistance for France had all come to nothing. As for the decision that had produced the current difficulties with America (the Order in Council of November 6, 1793), that decision had been made eight months earlier, and it was generally assumed—until the simultaneous arrival of Jay and a great backlog of Hammond's delayed dispatches—that the Order's irritating effects had been suitably counteracted by the subsequent one revoking it. It was thus not until the last minute that Pitt and Grenville had conclusive evidence that anything had gone seriously wrong.

Back in the previous fall, Pitt was still seeing the European conflict in the relatively measured and limited categories of mid-eighteenth-century warfare. But by the time of Jay's arrival in June 1794, the entire diplomatic and political world in which Great Britain functioned had drastically altered, and the Ministry was laboring under a thousand cares and preoccupations. Pitt's choice in 1793, rather than reinforcing Toulon or supporting an émigré attack on the Continent, had been to send British troops to the West Indies in the hope of snatching the rich prize of St. Domingue, and it was in this context that the Order of November 6 had been issued. It was intended to accomplish a specific, immediate, and temporary purpose, to prevent the French West Indies from using American ships either to procure needed supplies or to evacuate valuable crops; and once that was effected by a swift descent on American shipping, the Order would be revoked forthwith. It was a careless plan, and was carried out by the British naval officers with even more than their usual callous brutality. It went wrong, moreover, in two particulars. The revoking Order, intended to reach the United States simultaneously with the original one, was delayed several weeks by the vicissitudes of Atlantic weather. But delay or no delay, the scheme as a whole took no account of American interests or sensibilities, and succeeded only in enraging every sector of the American public.[72] (Indeed, the St. Domingue invasion itself, despite some initial successes, would prove within a year to have been largely a fruitless undertaking.)[73] In any case, once it became apparent to Grenville that the Orders had been bungled, the sensible thing was obviously to do something to mollify the Americans. But the mollifying impulse would still have to compete with a variety of far more pressing claims on the Ministry's attention. A note or two on the main ones might help to reconstruct something of the state of mind in which Jay was received.

The very character of the war had been transformed in unprecedented ways, and psychologically the entire British nation, at all levels, was in the process of readjustment. France's military position, which had seemed so bad in the late summer of 1793—Toulon in English hands, the Vendée in open rebellion, and the Prussians threatening to move directly on Paris—had been dramatically reversed. The French had now retaken Toulon, the uprising was suppressed, and the French armies, reorganized and directed by Carnot, were advancing on all fronts. By mid-May, with the defeat of the British at Turcoing in Flanders, it was becoming increasingly doubtful whether the Allies could even stabilize their lines. The French advances in the Netherlands would culminate in victory over the Anglo-Austrian forces at Fleurus in June. Although a growing sense of panic in England was eased by the naval victory of Admiral Lord Howe in the Atlantic on June 1, and by news of initial successes in the West Indies, it was now fully apparent that the war would be long and arduous.[74]

More significantly, it had been a war which could no longer be defined through such familiar and limited objectives as improved boundaries or colonial spoils. Great Britain was now facing a revolutionary and ideological contest the outcome of which might well determine the entire future character of European society, including that of Britain herself. Though Pitt had been decidedly unimpressed by

Burke's *Reflections on the Revolution in France* when that work first appeared four years before, patriotic and ideological solidarity had by now become almost an obsession with him. The growth of reform societies sympathetic to the Revolution and the popularity of Paine's *Rights of Man* among the working classes had come to seem more and more ominous with the onset of the Terror, and by the spring of 1794 public opinion was prepared to support draconian measures to wipe out Jacobinism and any trace of French influence in Great Britain. In May, Pitt launched a sweeping campaign against subversion. It entailed suspension of habeas corpus, action against seditious utterances, and the arrest of leading radicals. The Prime Minister made emotional speeches in Parliament and took a personal part in the examination of witnesses, all of which absorbed enormous amounts of his time and energy.[75]

Still a further claim on the attention of Pitt and his Foreign Minister was the changing political situation and the complicated negotiations they were undertaking to enlist the Portland Whigs in a wartime cabinet coalition. (Grenville at one point was not certain how long he himself would remain in office.) The conservative Whigs had long been restive over the sympathy shown by their colleague Charles James Fox toward the French Revolution, but had been reluctant to risk splitting the party by an open break with Fox. The point had now been reached, however, where the great majority of the Whigs under the leadership of the Duke of Portland were at last prepared to make such a break, and to join Pitt in a coalition goverment, even though it might well mean the end of the Whig party. To make this possible, the Pitt ministry for their part were prepared both to offer their longtime opponents a substantial share of the cabinet posts and to declare as their war aims the restoration of the French monarchy and the re-establishment in France of a government based on property. (This was the only basis the aristocratic Whigs could imagine for stable and responsible government anywhere.) There followed five weeks of tortuous inside diplomacy, which threatened to break down any number of times, all through June and July. Grenville was ready to give up the Foreign Office to make way for Portland, but the Duke eventually settled for the Home Office, and when the new arrangements were finally complete, five Portland Whigs had been established in high office. This was probably the most important political act of Pitt's career, and with it his ministry had undertaken a vastly enlarged commitment as to the nation's aims in the European war.[76]

Such was the setting—with the French campaign in the Netherlands, the drive against subversion in Britain, and negotiations for reorganizing the British goverment all moving toward their climax—that John Jay stepped into when he arrived in England on June 8, 1794.

As for American affairs, there is little or no evidence that up to this point they had occupied much of a place in either Pitt's or Grenville's thinking. Rumors began reaching London in late April that there was trouble in America on account of the November 6 Order in Council; the opposition newspaper subsequently made a point of describing the angry reaction in Congress to news of the spoliations, and in May it reported the passage of the American embargo. The Ministry dismissed all such reports as having originated before news of the revoking order had reached the United States. But when Shelburne read an account of Dorchester's speech to the Indians to the House of Lords, and when fresh news arrived about the state of feeling in America, it was at last obvious to Grenville that things in that quarter had taken a nasty turn. On June 5 he got off a somewhat fretful letter to Hammond complaining of the lack of authoritative information and urging that Hammond bring him up to date on the steps the Americans appeared to be taking.[77]

But within a week, as it happened, Grenville would have all the information he needed. Between the time of Jay's landing at Falmouth on June 8 and his appearance in London on the 15th, all of Hammond's correspondence from late February to mid-May, together with the American newspapers from that period and reports from the officials in Canada, arrived at the Foreign Office in one batch.[78] Grenville could thus at a sitting take in the entire picture.

It was apparent from Hammond's reports that well before the news of the Order in Council and its results, the build-up of feeling in America against Great Britain had already begun. The selective publication of Hammond's correspondence with Jefferson and the issuance of Jefferson's report on commerce had been followed by Madison's efforts to establish "a direct system of commercial hostility with Great Britain."[79] The American public was then raised to a pitch of fury over the news of the spoliations and of Dorchester's speech to the Indians. The people would be angrier still when they heard of Simcoe's occupation of a fort well within their national territory. There was information on this too in the materials accompanying Hammond's dispatches, and there would be still more within the next two weeks. The Americans had been prepared to go to desperate lengths. They were making military and naval preparations, strengthening their harbor defenses, and there was even talk of sequestering British debts. They had already declared an embargo, and a non-intercourse measure was barely defeated in the Senate by the casting vote of the Vice-President. Moreover, it was evident that Hammond found his own position heavily embarrassing. For all his industry and zeal, circumstances over which he had little control had combined to inflame his relations with the new Secretary of State and to reduce his effectiveness in America to a discouraging minimum.

Even those in America most favorably disposed toward Great Britain had come to the end of their patience. Hammond must have still been smarting from the roasting he had got from Alexander Hamilton in mid-April. Having just received the official explanations regarding the November 6 Order in Council and the revoking Order of January 8, Hammond had supposed that this might make the occasion for a soothing confidential chat with the Secretary of the Treasury about matters in general, but was "much surprized at perceiving that he did not receive those explanations with the cordiality I expected." Instead, the angry Hamilton "entered into a pretty copious recital of the injuries which the commerce of this country had suffered," and when the discomposed minister tried to put in something about neutrals having to expect inconveniences while trying to cover enemy property with their own flags in the midst of a "just war," Hamilton simply cut him off. He declared that it was all well and good for the

British people to be united in their exertions against France, but their government would find that when such outrages as these were known, there would be powerful opposition within Great Britain itself. In short, if even Alexander Hamilton, hitherto "the most moderate of the American Ministers," was "so much excited," it would be well to take the situation seriously.[80]

Grenville undoubtedly found all this rather disconcerting. There was, nevertheless, another side to it. There was still a strong disposition in America to settle all these questions through peaceful negotiations, which was evident from the full account Hammond gave him of the Jay appointment and of Jay's own views.[81] Jay himself was apparently a reasonable man, an impression which would be confirmed when they first met face to face on June 18. To be sure, the news from America added one more to His Lordship's many burdens. But with the military situation on the Continent deteriorating, the Spanish beginning to signal that they might want to make peace, the campaign against domestic subversion in full tilt, and negotiations with the Portland Whigs in their final and most difficult stage, the materialization of John Jay may well have been seen as rather a relief. Here, at least, was one difficulty that was more or less manageable. If the American envoy were disposed to be reasonable, why not meet him on his own ground and do it up decently? From what was now before him, Grenville could see at a glance what the two really critical issues were: the spoliations and the posts. A decision to satisfy the Americans on both these points made sense; he and Pitt appear to have reached it virtually at once, and with a minimum of strain.[82]

4

Negotiating Jay's Treaty

John Jay, in reporting home about his doings, was inclined in both his official and private letters to be reserved and circumspect. But he did come away from his first meeting with Grenville with an impression "favorable to his character and manners." "From some light circumstances," he told Washington, "I incline to believe that our mercantile injuries will be redressed," though he would not conjecture "how or how far." At their next meeting on June 27, Grenville conceded "very frankly" that in the matter of captures some sort of government intervention might be called for, and requested any details the American could furnish him. Jay saw no disposition anywhere to defend the actions of Dorchester and Simcoe. In fact the Home Secretary, Henry Dundas, sent off a sharp reprimand to Dorchester, and wrote Simcoe confidentially that the Northwest posts should "only be considered as temporary objects; a final arrangement with the United States of America, in all probability, leading to their evacuation."[83]

Meanwhile efforts were made to see that Jay was fittingly entertained. He was presented to the King on July 2, and to the Queen the following day. The King, it appeared, had been suitably briefed, expressing "many general sentiments that were liberal and proper." As to "how far these appearances will correspond with future facts," Jay cautiously observed, "time only can decide. . . ." Shortly after his arrival he was invited to dine with the Foreign Secretary and other cabinet ministers, and in the early weeks of July he dined with the Prime Minister and the Lord Chancellor on separate occasions. Appearances, he thought, "continue to be singularly favorable; but appearances merit only a certain degree of circumspect Reliance." But while forbearing from undue optimism on his own part, Jay could not fail to observe it in others. "The merchants here, it seems, entertain sanguine expectations that all difficulties will be amicably settled, and I believe that the ministry has encouraged and countenanced these expectations, though not in a manner so explicit and decided as to have committed themselves."[84]

On July 11, with the new cabinet installed and Grenville's own position assured, he and Jay had another conference. Grenville explained that it would take some time for the new ministers to be informed and consulted, but promised "that no unnecessary delays should retard a full discussion of the points in question." They agreed that for the time being the situation on the Canadian frontier should be "preserved in *statu quo*," that encroachments and hostile acts on either side should cease, and that prisoners or property, if taken, should be returned. The preparatory stage of the negotiation was thus completed, and both parties had grounds for satisfaction with prospects as they then stood.[85]

It would actually be four more months before the negotiations were completed, interspersed as they had to be by extended intervals during which Grenville was absorbed with urgent business elsewhere. Nor do we know very much of what went on during these discussions, the respective secretaries being excluded and no minutes kept. But this was undoubtedly just as well. Back in 1791 and 1792 the negotiations, if such they could be called, between Jefferson and Hammond had been carried on through formal notes intended, as it were, for posterity, and were thus condemned to stalemate before they began. The present procedure was to range over the entire ground in "free conversations, neither of us considering the other as being committed by anything that was said or proposed." This arrangement may well have been Jay's own idea. "Formal discussion of disputed points," he had earlier observed, "should, in my judgment, be postponed until the case becomes desperate. My present object is to accommodate, rather than to convict or convince. Men who sign their names to arguments seldom retract."[86]

One major obstacle was the issue of prior infractions of the Peace Treaty, and another was that of slaves carried off by the British at the close of the war. Jay duly made the American case on both these questions, but when it became apparent that no accord was possible on either one, it was agreed "to quit those topics, and to try to agree on such a set of reciprocal concessions as (balancing each other) might afford articles for a treaty, so beneficial to all parties, as to induce them to bury in it, all former questions and disputes."[87] Herein was a fair glimpse of Jay's entire negotiating strategy, that of applying to diplomacy the same device—the projection—that Hamilton had used so effectively in finance. He would try to project an end result sufficiently attractive to all concerned as might justify certain short-term concessions in order to attain it. He assumed, of course, that Grenville and Pitt would be as interested in this particular end result as he and Hamilton were.

With the way open for taking up the more serious issues, Jay was prepared on July 30 to present a strong memorandum in support of the merchants' claims for reparation in the West Indies spoliation cases. He did so on the 31st, and Grenville replied the following day, clearly by prior arrangement, assuring Jay of "His Majesty's wish that the most *complete and impartial justice* should be done to all citizens of America who may, in fact, have been injured by any of the proceedings above mentioned." Instances of personal severity to American seamen would be punished, any Americans impressed into the Royal Navy would be released, and on August 6 an Order in Council was issued enabling merchants to appeal their cases notwithstanding the lapse of the normal time limit. Another Order was issued the same day, significantly modifying that of June 8, 1793, which applied to provisions.[88]

Jay had reason to be gratified. The time had come for spelling out in detail what he thought should be the principal terms for a general understanding between the two countries. On August 6 he submitted a draft proposal to Grenville, and two days later wrote Randolph with his customary restraint. "My present prospects are not discouraging. I expect to be able, in about a fortnight, to give you some interesting details; and I *hope* some of them will be *agreeable,* but of this I cannot be *certain.*" For all their caution, these were the words of a man who expected to bring home something fairly good.[89]

Jay's draft was a partial outline; it did not include certain matters that still required further discussion. Among the items in it were proposals for a series of mixed arbitral commissions. One would examine and settle questions which remained in doubt from the Peace Treaty of 1783 as to the proper northern boundary of the United States; another commission would determine compensation to American merchants for illegal seizures, satisfaction for which had not been obtained "in the ordinary course of judicial proceedings"; still another would settle the claims of British creditors for unpaid debts contracted before the peace. The Northwest posts would be evacuated by June 1, 1795. Ports of the British West Indies would be opened to American ships of a hundred tons or less on the same basis as British ships, provided that produce from the islands be carried only to the United States and not re-exported from there in American vessels. The products, merchants, and ships of both countries would be given the same treatment in each other's ports, "tonnage only excepted." Neither country would permit the sale in its own ports of prizes taken from the other, and in the event of "war or national differences" there would be no sequestration or confiscation by either government of debts owed to individual citizens or subjects of the other.[90]

Jay's draft, while recognizing the need for a definitive adjustment of outstanding differences, showed that he was intent on doing this in a way that would go beyond these immediate issues and lay the foundation for future peace and cooperation. The plan for mixed commissions, for instance, was a real innovation, a device of great potential usefulness. On the other hand, the concessions he was willing to make on the re-export trade in order to get an article on admission to the British West Indies may have smoothed the path of negotiation, but they would get Jay into considerable trouble at home later on.

Grenville, amid his preoccupations, did not get around to responding until the end of August, at which time he presented a set of counter-proposals. In them, he accepted the substance of most of Jay's outline, but inserted some alterations and added certain provisions of his own. The posts would be evacuated, but a year later than Jay had proposed, and British traders would be free to trade with the Indians south of the border. American ships would be admitted to the West Indies, but with a limit of seventy rather than a hundred tons burden. There would be compensation for British vessels captured within American territorial jurisdiction or by privateers outfitted in American ports. (The Americans had in fact accepted this principle before Jay's departure for England.)[91] The *consolato del mare,* the rule that enemy property was not protected by neutral ships, was reaffirmed, though not directly; and contraband was referred to, though not specifically defined. There should be an immediate rectification of the northern boundary to permit British access to the Mississippi without having to pass through foreign territory, as had been intended—or so the British alleged—by the Treaty of 1783. British ships and products would receive most-favored-nation treatment, which meant in effect no discriminatory tariff or tonnage duties.[92]

Jay's immediate response was directed at the proposed boundary change. He declared that the new line Grenville wanted to draw would involve an outright cession of "more than thirty thousand square *miles,*" that it was outside his authority to agree to it, and that "many circumstances and considerations . . . will restrain the United States from such a cession."[93] Within a few days he also expressed some minor reservations to other parts of Grenville's project. He thought, for instance, that if British subjects could trade with the Indians south of the border, Americans should have similar privileges in Canadian territory. Though Grenville continued to argue that his boundary proposal would not involve a "cession" but would simply be a rectification in accord with the intentions of the Peace Treaty regarding navigation of the Mississippi, he eventually dropped his effort to obtain it. He also conceded Jay's claim for trading privileges in each other's territory, excluding that under the jurisdiction of the Hudson's Bay Company.[94] With these exceptions, together with an article on the East India trade, the balance of Grenville's proposals would substantially find their way into the completed treaty.

By September, Jay was becoming increasingly impatient to conclude his mission. He had been much annoyed by the doings of James Monroe, the newly arrived American minister to France. In a florid scene enacted before the National Convention the previous month, Monroe had received the fraternal embrace from the President of the Assembly and had delivered an effusive speech about the union of spirit between the two republics and the "heroic valor" of French troops. Here was Jay, as he saw himself, laboring to convince Britain of the advantages of American friendship, while Monroe was praising France's military successes and swearing America's undying attachment to the French people and their cause.

The proceedings were published in the English newspapers; Grenville was naturally irked, and mentioned the matter to Jay in a tone of some irony. Jay complained to Washington, Hamilton, and Randolph that such things were not very helpful to his mission. "If I should be able to conclude the Business on admissible terms," he told Hamilton, "I shall do it, and risque Consequences; rather than . . . hazard a Change in the Disposition of this Court. . . ."[95]

On September 30 he sent Grenville a new proposed draft, incorporating what had already been agreed on and adding a number of items that had not yet been settled. There was probably a good reason for their having been postponed to the end. They were the last things any British negotiator was likely to agree to, and it may be doubted whether Jay himself expected to get very far with them. They included those points which his instructions and Hamilton's private communications had defined as "desirable," though not indispensable.

Jay proposed that in case of war neither party should make alliances with Indians living within the other's boundaries, or accept assistance from any of them. Both parties would "endeavour to restrain their respective Indians from war," to the point of prohibiting "any supplies of ammunition or arms" to belligerent tribes. No armed vessels should be kept on the Great Lakes; military forces on the borders should be reduced and eventually done away with. Jay also advanced some rules for the treatment of neutrals in wartime. Free ships should make free goods, and contraband should be defined strictly so as to include only materials of war. Foodstuffs were admitted to be contraband only if there was a clear likelihood "of reducing the enemy by the want thereof," in which case they would be preempted and paid for rather than confiscated. There would be strict limits on search procedures and on the size of boarding parties.[96]

After a week, Grenville wrote Jay that there was so much new material in his draft that a great deal more time might be required to complete a treaty than had been expected, and that there were now points "which must if insisted upon on your part create as I fear insurmountable obstacles." Jay was not prepared to insist, and in the ensuing weeks a final treaty, fairly close to Grenville's project of August 30, was agreed upon and signed on November 19, 1794. Matters appear to have been concluded in a climate of general satisfaction, and Jay and Grenville parted with mutual opinions of respect and esteem.[97]

Was this the best treaty Jay could have obtained? It probably was; it is even likely that no other American could have got anything nearly as good. But "good" in relation to what, and "best" for whose purposes? There could be several answers.

The question of neutral rights was for practical purposes not negotiable at all. In the desperate wartime conditions then existing, Great Britain was not prepared to accept any substantial limitations on the use of her fleet. A reversal of the *consolato del mare* to make "free ships, free goods" was never at any time a possibility. Even Jefferson, in his published correspondence of the previous year with Genet, had in effect recognized this; seven years later he would still say of neutral rights that "in the present state of things they are not worth a war."[98] Nor was there ever a likelihood that contraband would be so defined as to exclude food, though seizure of food cargoes would be made only under special circumstances, and such cargoes would be preempted rather than confiscated. (Merchants and farmers were not likely to lose much under such an arrangement.) In any event, Article XII provided that both these principles—contraband and the status of enemy property aboard neutral vessels—were to be reopened for negotiation at the close of the present hostilities. Nothing at all was said about the Rule of 1756, or about the impressment of American seamen.

It was also unlikely that Jay could have persuaded Great Britain to remove naval vessels from the Lakes or to forgo assistance from the Indians in case of war, both being regarded as critical for the defense of Canada. Not until the return of world peace twenty years thence would the British think of abandoning either of these principles. Jay might have refused them the right to trade south of the border (that right would eventually be withdrawn by the Treaty of Ghent in 1815), but this would have been directly contrary to his own policy of accommodation, and it might well have made Grenville much more stubborn about "rectifying" the boundary. Jay did, on the other hand, successfully resist Grenville's effort to open a back-door free-trade entry from Canada into the American Northwest; he also refused to admit the British contention that their ships should pay no higher tonnage duties in American ports than those charged there on American ships.[99]

Jay was unable to get compensation for slaves carried off at the close of the Revolution; nor, apparently, did he make great exertions to do so. For this there were several reasons: sheer lack of evidence, the confused circumstances under which great numbers of slaves had been separated from their masters (and the question of who was responsible for it, and when), and the humanitarian dilemma of how a person once freed could be forcibly re-enslaved. These considerations, to which Jay with his own antislavery views was evidently susceptible, induced him to abandon the issue. Jefferson, too, had called it a "bagatelle."[100]

Professor Bemis, mired in his labors amid the comparatively primitive research conditions of seventy years ago, was understandably exhilarated at the discovery of George Hammond's dispatch informing Grenville, after a private talk with Hamilton early in July 1794, that the United States government had no intention of joining the League of Armed Neutrality. Bemis could not resist ascribing the greatest significance to this "amazing revelation," which reached Grenville on September 20 while negotiations were still going on. He declared that Jay was thereby deprived of one of his strongest bargaining points, since Grenville "now knew every one of the cards"; he "now knew that there was no danger of what he most feared."[101] No single assertion has done more to shape the way in which the entire Jay mission has fared in American historical thought for the past half-century. It is, however, a dubious one.

Efforts by Denmark and Sweden to concert measures for protecting their commerce in the Baltic had been afoot for some time, and a convention looking to this end had been signed and made known to the world in April 1794. The Swedish minister in London had given a copy of it to Thomas Pinckney with the suggestion that the United States might be interested in joining, which Pinckney duly referred home. All of this was known to the British Foreign Office. But it soon became obvious that little was likely to come of the projected League, especially against the opposition of Russia, currently an ally of Great Britain. (In fact nothing would.) It was also obvious that the United States, having no navy, had little to gain from such a connection and nothing to contribute. For this reason Denmark, despite the zeal of the Swedish minister, was not at all disposed to see the United States join anyway. This too was known to Grenville. Moreover, Randolph's instruction to Jay on the matter—that agents of the governments concerned might be sounded if "the situation of things with respect to Great Britain should dictate the necessity"—was so hedged with contingencies that even Hamilton had made no objection to it. The disinclination of Jay to resort to any such maneuver, in view of the larger objects of his mission, was obvious from the first, and had become more and more so as the negotiations proceeded. So Hammond's "amazing revelation" could have told Grenville nothing of consequence that he did not already know. And the points still remaining to be settled at the time he received it—those the British government saw as affecting its capacity to make war—were such that no form of pressure, and certainly not this one, could have altered its position on them. To have brought it up at this stage would have been in effect an announcement that negotiations were at an end, a likelihood that even Randolph's instructions had implicitly recognized. In short, it need not have taken much astuteness on Jay's part to guess that the use of the Armed Neutrality as a "bargaining" point would gain him not more but substantially less than he actually got.[102]

But although Jay could get nowhere on the question of neutral rights, as no American would for many years to come, he did get all his *sine qua nons:* the posts, compensation for seizures, and limited access to the British West Indies, together with some very favorable arrangements on the East India trade.[103] True, there would be tremendous criticism in America—mixed in as it was with sentiments about France—of nearly every article in the treaty. But most of this will need to be considered (as it shortly will be) on a very different plane from that of the actual substantive benefits the United States derived from the treaty. Richard Hofstadter, writing about the Populists of the 1890s, ascribed a "soft" side and a "hard" side to their program, the one having primarily a symbolic importance and the other concerning matters of immediate material consequence. Something similar might be said of Jay's program and the treaty that resulted from it. Jay's record on the "soft" side was subject to many objections; on the "hard" side it was a substantial success, which included the prevention of war with Great Britain.

But there was one great lapse, and it happened to be on the "hard" side. This was the concession Jay made in renouncing the re-export of certain enumerated tropical products, including cotton (any cotton), to obtain an article formally opening the British West Indies. (Here he actually traded a "hard" item for a "soft" one.) It was commercial-minded Federalists, rather than Republican anglophobes and agrarian ideologues, who would be the first to see the implications. When the treaty came before the Senate it was they, and not the anti-treaty forces, who took the lead in getting that article struck out altogether. The treaty was eventually ratified without it.

The question of why Jay should have agreed to such a concession—that as long as that article remained in force no molasses, sugar, coffee, cocoa, or cotton could leave the United States in American ships—remains one of the great imponderables of his entire mission. Nor is this the only difficulty. As to why the British should have agreed to their side of the arrangement—Lord Hawkesbury and the hard-line mercantilists having throughout the negotiations strenuously opposed any opening, however limited, of the West Indian ports—that too presents its ambiguities.

Jay had left the United States in May 1794, at a time when the full implications of the boom in shipbuilding and the export trade were only beginning to sink in. Moreover, the vast potentialities of the cotton gin for American plantation agriculture were still but barely visible. In removing himself from the scene when he did, Jay undoubtedly missed a good many of the reverberations; what may have looked reasonable to him with the impressions of 1794 and the figures of 1793 was not so at all to profit-happy American shipowners and exporters amid the soaring expectations of 1795. But for Jay there was something even more fundamental that blocked his sensitivity to day-to-day changes in the American economy, and that was the grand projection, which had become rather an obsession. Once the British were persuaded to open their islands even in the most limited way, that would be enough for his immediate purposes. The rest would be inevitable, as they came more and more to perceive the unfolding mutual advantages. As Jay insisted to Washington, "it breaks the ice—that is, it breaks in upon the navigation act. The least stream from a mass of water passing through a bank will enlarge its passage." With regard to limitations on the re-export trade, his countrymen should perceive that these were hardly total, and certainly should be bearable. Jay may even have had informal assurances from Grenville on this. But the Americans, who already had the lion's share of the carrying trade, saw no reason why they should be subject to any restrictions.[104]

The British, for their part, seem to have taken the West Indies article decidedly less seriously than did Jay. The exception was Hawkesbury, who was opposed to any concessions, and from this it has been inferred by some that there must have been a bitter struggle within the cabinet over the entire question.[105] But this "struggle" was over a very small point indeed. Nobody in the British cabinet had any intention of doing away with the navigation system—they were not thinking ahead that far—and on basic principles there could have been no very great differences among them. It was just that Hawkesbury's zealotry had become a bit awkward under these particular circumstances, and might better be blandly ignored. As Pitt and Grenville saw it, if Jay and the Americans were so intent on a formal access to the West Indies that was no more extensive than that, there was no harm in giving it to them. It was certainly not a permanent arrangement, being limited to two years after a preliminary peace treaty ending the current war. Besides, as Grenville pointed out, there was something to be said for giving America "an Interest in our retaining the newly acquired Colonies." But most of

all, under present wartime conditions the Americans could not be kept out anyway. They "would conceive it a very great boon" to have this put into a treaty,
wrote the Marquis of Buckingham to Grenville, "but either the direct or the
indirect boon seems unavoidable, for they will trade by exchanging provisions
and lumber for molasses and sugar, in spite of you."[106]

The equivalent which Grenville exacted from Jay—that the United States
should agree to export no West Indies products—was probably less a defense of
vital British interests than an effort to mollify Hawkesbury and those who shared
his intransigent views. Why cotton was added to the list remains unclear. Jay
seems not to have been aware of how important American cotton would shortly
become as an item of export, but Grenville was probably not aware of it either.
In any case, Pitt, Grenville, and the rest of the cabinet were quite willing to sweep
the entire West Indies question under the rug for the time being in order to
accommodate the Americans, without conceiving that it involved them in any
permanent commitments. The only ones on hand who seem to have imagined
otherwise were John Jay and Lord Hawkesbury. And when the Americans later
decided that they did not want Article XII after all, the British made no objection.
It hardly mattered to them one way or the other.

Jay could, of course, have avoided a commercial agreement altogether, limiting
his treaty to the settling of outstanding prior differences. This would have been
quite acceptable to the British, and he would not have needed to make the
concessions renouncing such potential weapons as discriminatory tariffs or tonnage duties, or the sequestration of British debts. Not that these cost the United
States anything, now that peace was assured; it was rather that they would all
shortly prove irrelevant. As prosperity mounted and the extent of United States
control of the Anglo-American carrying trade became ever greater—it would
reach 93 percent by 1796—the idea of coercive or discriminatory legislation of
any kind, designed to increase the American monopoly still further, would have
been ridiculous.[107]

And yet it would have been exceedingly difficult psychologically for John Jay
to stop short of what he did do. He saw himself as building for the long future,
and to do anything less would have involved a recognition of something that all
appearances belied, at least to him: that his hosts did not share his vision at all,
that they were not really interested. What they mainly wanted was to simplify
their current difficulties. Jay had put his whole mind to the effort; they had put
barely half of theirs. True, they were not at all ill disposed. On the whole they
had come around quite decently; they had even extended themselves, at least as
they saw it, and Jay could thank himself for having done something to create the
atmosphere in which they did so.

All of which made it the more inconceivable. How could John Jay, or any
other American of whatever political persuasion in only the sixth year of the
Republic's existence, bear to face the real truth about Great Britain? Here were
the British at the very center of our universe, and they did not really care about
us, not half enough! How could any American imagine that his country, friendly
or unfriendly, could be of such small consequence, could occupy the British mind
so little?

5

Ratifying the Treaty

The outpouring of popular feeling over the Jay Treaty, as has long been understood, was more directly responsible than anything else for the full emergence of political parties in America, and of clearly recognized Federalist and Republican points of view on all political questions. Opposition to the treaty was at first overwhelming. And yet within a year of the treaty's terms' first becoming known, public opinion had reversed itself, and by the spring of 1796 would be running decidedly in the other direction.

This reversal created many embarrassments for the Republican opposition at the time, and has left many impediments to a proper historical comprehension of the entire affair. There has been a tendency to assume that the turnabout must somehow have been "artificially" produced by means of inordinate Federalist exertions. That the Federalists made their exertions is, of course, sweepingly evident. But the public sentiment which by 1796 was insisting that the treaty be carried into effect was fully as authentic—in certain ways perhaps even more so—as that which in 1795 had invoked the entire wrath of Heaven against it. Perhaps one may venture a distinction. The initial impulse was based on national pride and patriotic feeling; the subsequent one, no less widespread and no less genuine, was based on unexalted (and perhaps even crass) considerations of national, regional, group, and individual self-interest.

To this should be added something else. The opposition, when it first took form, was in no way a response to the actual terms of the treaty. Such opposition was fully in being before anyone had the least idea how Jay's efforts would turn out, and it had two principal components. One was the well-founded fear that an understanding with Great Britain, no matter what its terms and no matter how good, would somehow contaminate the fraternal attachment between Americans and the people of France—or, more fundamentally, that any arrangement whatever implying a friendly connection with the British was odious by its very nature. The other, which went right along with it, was solicitude for the ideological, and in a sense even the organizational, cohesion of the Republican party.

One sees these various anxieties reflected in their purest form in the guileless mind of James Monroe. Rumors, hopelessly garbled, reached Monroe in Paris in December 1794 to the effect that Jay had just completed a brilliant negotiation in which the British had yielded everything—including the entire territory of Canada—that Jay could possibly have desired. Monroe got off an anguished letter to Madison. "If any thing of this kind should have taken place," he wrote, "I know the dilemma into which you will be all thrown."

> The western posts are offered you — compensation for losses — free trade to the Islands under the protection of the all powerful British flag — Canada is or will be given up, whereby the fisheries become more accessible — England will no longer support Spain in favor of the Mississippi &c. This will be resounded in the publick papers, and the impudence of the British faction become intolerable. But will it not be perceived that whatever is offered cannot be deemed the amicable

concession of England but is already your own, attained by the illustrious achievements and prosperous fortunes of your ally, & the decision of your own councils? Will you take therefore in breach of plighted faith, and expence of our national character, and as an amicable concession of England what may be obtained without loss, and is in truth due to the merits of our ally?[108]

It is not likely that Madison or Jefferson, for their part, would have committed any such thoughts so innocently to paper. But that they, and other Republican notables, failed at least to think them may be less certain. It might even be said that the better the treaty, the more of a menace it was to Madison's party.

Jay in England made particular efforts with Randolph and his other correspondents to ensure that no accounts of his activities there, especially those of a social nature, should get into the American newspapers. Such things, he told Hamilton, "may be misinterpreted, tho' not by you."[109] But scraps of gossip about the dinners and receptions made their way across, despite all Jay's precautions, and were greeted with hoots and jeers. When it was reported that Jay had been received by the Queen and had kissed the Queen's hand, the cry went up that for this he deserved to have "his lips blistered to the bone [*sic.*]"[110] One document which Jay did think should be published was his forthright representation to Grenville regarding damages done to American shipping, along with Grenville's conciliatory reply. It was, accordingly, published; but he might as well not have bothered. Jay's restrained language, with its diplomatic euphemisms, was denounced in Republican newspapers as "pusillanimous" and "courtier-like," and for having contained no threats or recriminations. On behalf of "Americans who had their property pirated," Jay had merely represented "to his Majesty, in the most humiliating manner, that the vessels . . . were *'irregularly captured.'*" The spirited American, according to "A" in the *New York Journal,* looked in vain "for those just and animated complaints which years of provocations and insults so forcibly demanded," or for "those firm but temperate menaces which the United States had a right to hold out in case of a refusal to render complete justice." The only really satisfactory concessions would be those extorted by fear.[111] Thus among the liabilities John Jay had to contend with, in addition to everything else, was the shaky psychology of an infant nation.

The first extended attack on the treaty came with the so-called "Letters of Franklin." This passionate series of fourteen essays began appearing in the *Philadelphia Independent Gazetteer* early in March 1795; they were widely reprinted elsewhere and when finished were immediately republished as a pamphlet. The identity of "Franklin" has never been discovered, but the particular interest of his "Letters" lies in their having all been written without any knowledge, beyond a few rumors, of the treaty's actual contents. What little he did know of the terms was scarcely discussed at all. It was enough for "Franklin" that "there is not a nation upon earth so truly and justly abhorred by *the People* of the United States as Great Britain; and if *their* temper and sensibility were consulted, no Treaty whatever would have been formed, especially at the expence of the *French Republic.*" In courting England we had treated France, our only natural friend and ally, with indifference. "That gallant nation, whose proffers we have neglected, is the sheet anchor which sustains our hopes"; France, "Franklin" declared, "is struggling in the same cause in which we struggled—she is combatting for the liberties of mankind. . . ." What it came down to, quite aside from any and all particulars, was no less than a threat to the national character. "Is it advantageous to a Republic to have a connection with a Monarch? What has accelerated the destruction of all Republics? The corruption of principles which has resulted from the introduction of the fashions, the forms and the precedents of Monarchical Government."[112]

Through a variety of obstacles and accidents, the text of the treaty and Jay's dispatches accompanying and explaining it did not arrive at Philadelphia until March 7, 1795. Washington determined at once, if he had not done so already, that he and the Secretary of State would be the only ones to know the treaty's contents prior to its being laid before the Senate on June 8, which was the date he had fixed for a special session to consider it.[113] The Senate, in turn, would continue for a while longer to keep the text a secret. There was thus a period of five months—from the end of January 1795, when it was first reported in the newspapers from informal sources that a treaty had actually been signed, to the beginning of July, when the text was at last revealed to the world—in which the American public knew there was a treaty but did not know what was in it.

This period seems to have gone through roughly three phases, to each of which the Republicans gave a special response. The first began with impressions that had accumulated from late December and into January of the new year, to the effect that the results of the negotiation would be generally favorable. But if they were favorable, it would be no thanks to Jay. It would be due rather to the successes of France and to the reprisals threatened in 1794 by the American Congress, which ought to make things simple for any negotiator. So if they were not favorable, it would be all Jay's fault.[114] Fisher Ames thought he knew how all this would turn out. "The success of Mr. Jay," he wrote to Thomas Dwight on February 3, "will secure peace abroad, and kindle war at home. Faction will sound the tocsin against the treaty. I see a little cloud, as big as a man's hand, in Bache's paper, that indicates a storm. Two things will be attempted. First, before the event is known, to raise the expectation of the public, that we have every thing granted, and nothing given in return; and secondly, that the treaty, when published, has surrendered every thing."[115]

The second phase took its character from disjointed reports of the treaty's main provisions, roughly accurate though not invariably so, which began reaching the United States early in February. For anyone disposed in advance to attack the treaty, anything short of Ames's "every thing granted, and nothing given in return" would be a clear signal. The first news was that although Jay had in some sense achieved his main objects (return of the posts, redress for the spoliations, and admission to the British West Indies trade), each was subject to conditions and qualifications. The "free ships, free goods" principle, moreover, would receive consideration only after the conclusion of the war.[116] Madison, for one, was at first cautious. He told his correspondents that "scraps from private letters afford too imperfect as well as too inauthentic an account of it to justify an opinion on its merits."[117] But his mind was working rapidly. Robert R. Livingston was all for passing a law to prevent "the exportation or importation of articles to or from Canada into our western territories" as a way of forestalling any trading concessions Jay might have agreed to in that quarter, whereupon Madison warned him that this might have "the appearance of an *anticipated attack,* on the Treaty," and that "it could be said with so much plausibility that the Treaty ought to be seen and understood in the whole, before it be prejudged in any of its parts." Madison was, of course, rehearsing his own perplexity. "I shall however," he added, "reflect attentively on the idea you have suggested. . . ." A week later he was writing to Jefferson, "It is inferred that the bargain is much less in our favor than might be expected from the circumstances [French victories, British distresses, American menaces] which co-operated with the justice of our demands."[118]

Actually the campaign of opposition was already gathering its forces, and Madison, for all his caution, was fully prepared to join it. "It is apparent," he told Jefferson significantly, "that those most likely to be in the secret of the affair, do not assume an air of triumph."[119] In short, the Republicans could now be reasonably certain that no subsequent news need be anticipated which would dramatically reverse what they already knew, particularly after March 7, when it was learned that the treaty had actually arrived and that the Administration was still keeping its contents secret. If it were otherwise, then "those most likely to be in the secret" would find some way of saying so. Consequently every fresh detail that might be revealed would turn out to be one more qualification agreed to by Jay, another concession he had yielded, and would make the treaty by definition that much more shameful. It was in this confidence, which was of course entirely justified, that "Franklin" let loose his first blast on March 11. He was still at it, along with a rising chorus of others, when the Senate met on June 8 to consider the treaty.[120]

In the third and final phase of public non-knowledge, which lasted through the month of June, another great issue would assume a menacing predominance. This was the issue of secrecy itself. "How does *the secrecy* of the Senate," demanded a polemicist in the *Aurora,* "in relation to the Treaty, comport with THE SOVEREIGNTY of the people?" "The Constitution of the United States," he continued, "gives to the President and Senate the power of making Treaties; but it communicates no power to hatch those things *in darkness.* This practice is borrowed *from Kings and their Ministers,* and seems to imply a disposition to assimilate our Government, if not in theory, at least *in practice,* to Monarchy."[121]

The Senate sat from June 8 to June 26. When all had taken their seats there were thirty members present, twenty Federalists and ten Republicans, and they maintained their party character from first to last. The most objectionable feature of the treaty was Article XII, the one on the British West Indies trade which limited American ships to those of seventy tons and specified those items of tropical produce which were not to be re-exported from the United States. To meet this embarrassment the Federalists themselves took the initiative with a resolution, probably offered by Rufus King, that the treaty be approved except for that article. This was the motion that set the terms for the entire debate, and when it was carried 20–10 on June 24, the treaty had in effect been accepted.[122]

The margin, to be sure, was the bare minimum, just enough for approval, and the opposition was very intense. But the votes were there from the beginning, everyone knew it, and not a man changed his mind throughout. There had been only two serious distractions. One was a motion by Aaron Burr to postpone consideration of the treaty, and recommending that negotiations be reopened "in order to effect alterations" in it. Seven such alterations were proposed, of such a sweeping nature that "the President," as one authority has put it, "might as well have been advised to secure the cession of Canada. . . ." It was defeated, 20 to 10. The other was a motion to amend the resolution of acceptance by adding a demand for "adequate compensation for the negroes, or other property" carried off in violation of the Peace Treaty. This inducement to southern Federalists to break ranks, though temporarily disruptive, likewise failed. In adjourning, the Senate by resolution rescinded the injunction of secrecy it had imposed on itself at the beginning, but with a proviso "not to authorize or allow any copy [to be made] of the said [treaty], or any article thereof." The senators, presumably, could talk about it but not publish it.[123]

The Senate had accepted the treaty, subject to the suspension or renegotiation of the West Indies article, and now it was all up to Washington. It was at this point that Washington's supreme hour of trial began. It was to last through the next seven weeks, and amounted to the severest crisis he had yet undergone since assuming the presidency in 1789. He knew he did not have a wide range of choice, and he seems never to have thought seriously of rejecting the treaty, but the choices he did have gave him no end of torment.

There was first the question of what exactly the Senate had done, and just what it expected him to do, and when, as a result of it. Should he respond in any way before the Senate adjourned? Their resolution had read:

> That they do consent to, and advise the President of the United States to ratify the Treaty . . . on condition that there be added to the said Treaty an article, whereby it shall be agreed to suspend the operation of so much of the 12th article, as respects the trade which his said Majesty thereby consents may be carried on, between the United States and his islands in the West Indies, in the manner, and on the terms and conditions therein specified.
>
> And the Senate recommend to the PRESIDENT to proceed, without delay, to further friendly negotiations with His Majesty, on the subject of the said trade, and of the terms and conditions in question.[124]

If Washington were to draft a revised article at once and submit it to the Senate for approval, this would signify then and there his own approval of the treaty; it would also imply a particular version of the Executive's treaty-making powers, about which there was certainly more than one opinion. According to this one, every modification of any given treaty, subsequent to its initial conclusion, would have to be submitted to the Senate for its advice and consent. Indeed, any response to the Senate's "recommendation" to him would involve a commitment of some sort as to his intentions. He decided to remain silent for the time being and let the Senate adjourn without any word from him at all. But the other question remained. If he were now to sign the treaty, as modified by the Senate's non-approval of Article XII, what would be put in the place of that article, and who would put it there? Would it consist simply of a suspending clause, or would there be something more, as a result of "further friendly negotiations with His Majesty, on the subject of the said trade"? And would he then resubmit that result to a future session of the Senate for its approval?[125]

Whatever he did would require further reflection upon the entire treaty, about which he was certainly not enthusiastic, having a variety of reservations in his own mind about several parts of it.[126] He needed more counsel, and a little leisure to collect his own thoughts, which a brief sojourn at Mount Vernon would assist him to do. Meanwhile he would receive a fair amount of advice, some of it from Randolph and some from Hamilton, who by this time had left the Treasury and returned to private life in New York.[127] Hamilton's advice—whether Washington took all of it or not—would be quite helpful in assisting him to concentrate the alternatives and simplify the total problem. Randolph's, on the other hand, though by no means lacking in value, somehow had the effect, each time, of making things that much more complicated.

Then there was the question of continued secrecy, a matter which was to be taken out of Washington's hands by events, and in the worst possible way. Hamilton and King both believed "that all further mystery," as the former put it, was "unnecessary & ought to be waved for the satisfaction of the public mind." It would all soon be out anyway, and the Administration might better take the initiative itself and have the treaty published before someone else did it. Washington agreed, and authorized publication for July 1.[128] But the editor of the *Aurora*, Benjamin F. Bache, a hot Republican noted neither for moderation nor scruple, got in ahead of him. Senator Stevens T. Mason of Virginia appears to have sold his copy of the treaty to Pierre Adet, the newly arrived minister from France, who thereupon turned it over to Bache. An extended abstract appeared in the *Aurora* on June 29, and by July 1 Bache had ready a large printing of the entire treaty in pamphlet form which he proceeded personally to hawk all up and down the seaboard. It was a sensation, and the effect was exactly what he had hoped. One reason for this had to do with the psychology of exposure itself, following a long interval of secrecy: anything kept hidden must by definition be disreputable. The other was the exposure's timing, coming as it did on the eve of Independence Day civic gatherings in every town and hamlet in the land. The treaty was denounced in place after place, and the proceedings exultantly reported in the *Aurora* and in Republican newspapers everywhere.[129]

But this was only the beginning. From the second week in July until the end of August, there was hardly a day upon which a large public meeting organized to protest the treaty did not take place somewhere. Memorials, petitions. addresses, resolutions, and remonstrances began pouring in upon the President from all the states of the Union, imploring and even demanding that he refuse his signature to it. There were scenes of tumult and rage in all the leading cities. John Jay was burned in effigy in Philadelphia, New York, and Boston; the British flag was dragged in the dirt through the streets of Charleston, and copies of the treaty were burned there by the public hangman; in New York Alexander Hamilton, trying to speak in defense of the treaty, was hit by a stone; rioters in Philadelphia broke windows in the houses of the British minister, the British consul, and the Federalist senator.[130] For hostility of feeling against a measure of government, and for violence of language, nothing comparable had been seen on so wide a scale since the founding of the Republic. But by the same token, who could say that this was not an expression, as spontaneous as any such thing could be, of the popular will? To Washington it was heavily unsettling. What was now required of him?

Then there was another affliction. Washington received news early in July that the British were again seizing American grain ships bound for France, apparently on the authority of a new Order in Council the text of which nobody had yet seen, and in fact never would.[131] Did this mean bad faith, and were the British now renewing a policy they had merely suspended during the period of Jay's negotiations? On what ground were they doing it, and how might this affect Washington's procedure in the matter of ratification?

Some details of the episode were not to be discovered for another 140 years. A new secret Order had in fact been issued on April 25, 1795, the result of a conjunction of two separate and only casually related circumstances. One was that the final payments had just been made on the American debt to France, and with the proceeds French agents were arranging enormous purchases of grain and other provisions to be shipped to France, all of this being fully known to the British government. The other circumstance was a calamitous grain shortage that was leading to bread riots all over England. Thus the British ministry had determined that however the thing were done, those provisions should be stopped. Upon orders from the Admiralty not to be "over nice or scrupulous respecting the nature of the papers of those ships," British cruisers began bringing them in; the cargoes were seized as though they were contraband—and paid for, as the British had agreed to do whenever they did take food as contraband—and promptly sent to places in the Kingdom where the need was most acute.[132]

But in order to accomplish what they wanted to accomplish with the greatest possible despatch and yet remain within the letter of their recent undertakings with regard to neutral trade, the British had to resort to certain slurrings and sophistries. The ground they subsequently took when challenged was that these provisions were being seized not as contraband but as suspected enemy property on board neutral vessels, in accordance with the principle of *consolato del mare* (which the Jay Treaty had tacitly reaffirmed), and that the reason they were being paid for was simply that pending adjudication they might spoil and be of no use to anyone.[133] As it happened, the worst of the food crisis would be over by September, and by then the Order would be quietly withdrawn.[134] Thus by the time ratifications were exchanged in London in October, the matter was no longer a serious problem. But of course none of this was known to Washington at the beginning of July, or would be for several months to come. All that he or any other American could perceive for the time being were new and unexplained outrages on the part of Great Britain.[135]

Such, then, were the various perplexities amid which Washington began the process of making up his mind on how he would act as to the treaty. Part of that period was spent at Mount Vernon, the remainder at Philadelphia. A major consideration affecting the entire process—which did not terminate until August 12, when he made known his final decision—was the words and behavior of his Secretary of State, Edmund Randolph. Washington wanted to act as quickly as possible if he could persuade himself that conditions warranted it, and he had already told Randolph even before the Senate met that he would ratify the treaty if the Senate should approve it.[136] On the other hand, every piece of advice Randolph offered him—though some of it was sound in principle, and all of it plausible—from whatever premise it began, seemed to point in one direction only, which was delay.

Indeed, Randolph had been doing this in one way or another ever since the mission had first been proposed, more than a year before. He had tried to get Washington to put off making his nomination of a special envoy, though he supported the mission loyally enough after Washington pointedly overlooked his little strategems.[137] Then in his correspondence with Jay, Randolph had raised any number of objections to the various points of the treaty project Jay had sent him, though these criticisms did not reach Jay until the treaty itself was concluded and signed. Jay appears to have been deeply exasperated at what he probably saw as obstructive carping, especially after having to mollify Grenville over the effusive communications Randolph had sent to the French Assembly through Monroe. Jay's own official letters home from that point on became bafflingly non-committal, and breathed an air of patient suffering.[138]

This clogging pattern of delay was resumed upon the Senate's approval of the treaty, and continued all through July and into August. Not that there was anything very Machiavellian about it. Some of it, indeed, was diffuse and rather dithering, and Randolph himself may not always have been aware of exactly the part he was playing. His personal loyalty to Washington was dog-like, whatever doubts may later have been cast upon it, and Washington clearly valued it. But Edmund Randolph (as Jefferson had not tired of complaining all through the summer of 1793) was not a man of the strongest character, and he could hardly help being oppressed by a whole set of other loyalties as well, those represented by the network of his Virginia connections, overwhelmingly Republican, anglophobe and francophile to the point of fanaticism, and hating every word of Jay's infernal treaty. No doubt he wanted to tread a straight and honorable path, beset as he was and wishing to give no offense to anyone, but he did so with dragging feet. Besides, he always talked a little too much, and only, somehow, at about sixty percent efficiency.

Actually Randolph's first counsel to Washington—as to the risks of committing himself on the treaty until after the Senate adjourned—was in itself quite sensible, and Washington followed it. But he warned of other risks as well in the various unsolicited memoranda with which he favored the President, such as that of public disapproval if the revised Article XII were not resubmitted to a future Senate for its advice and consent.[139] (Such a step could not have been taken for another six months.) When Washington asked the cabinet members for their written opinions on this point ("as soon as possible," in order "that I may without delay take some definitive step upon the Treaty"), they all replied immediately, each believing that the President did not need to resubmit such an article.[140] Randolph delayed his opinion for some two weeks. (Apparently Hamilton too had originally thought the Senate should again be consulted, but had changed his mind, which rather annoyed Randolph.)[141] While Washington awaited Randolph's reply, he received from him instead an obscure and rather fatuous letter angling for the next vacancy on the Supreme Court. Washington thought it as well to take no notice.[142]

Randolph's opinion was finally delivered on July 12, and he had now shifted his ground. He had previously said that the Senate majority expected "that the President will send to the Senate" a new article "and ask them whether they do assent" to it; but now he asserted that "they intended their resolution of the 24 of June 1795, to be a final act," that "they do not expect the proposed article to be submitted to them," and that this was "the plain signification of their words." On that point Randolph was now in line with the other cabinet officers. But meanwhile the news of the British provision order had been confirmed, and Randolph saw this as placing a whole new set of difficulties in the way of ratification.[143]

He now proposed to tell the British minister that the President was prepared to sign the treaty but that he could not "persuade himself, that he ought to ratify, during the existence of that order." As soon as the Order was removed, however, he would "ratify without delay or further scruple."[144] This would mean that three or four more months would have to go by before the treaty could be ratified, depending on whether the British government accepted what would be a kind of ultimatum, and how soon the news of it could be brought back to America. Washington authorized Randolph to discuss this with Hammond, and the resulting conversation appears to have been somewhat at cross-purposes. Hammond wanted to know whether "the President was irrevocably determined not to ratify if the provision-order was not removed"; Randolph said he was "not instructed upon that point." Washington, according to Randolph's later account, asserted that Randolph "might have informed Mr. Hammond, that he would never ratify, if the provision-order was not removed out of the way." But Hammond asked Randolph the same question the next day, and Randolph gave him the same answer. Washington, it seems, was not yet prepared to say, nor did his Secretary of State quite dare to say it for him, that his determination was "irrevocable." Randolph then began work on a memorial which, subject to the President's approval, would be handed to Hammond to transmit to his government. The next morning, July 15, Washington set off for Mount Vernon.[145]

Though "one great object" of his visit, as he told Hamilton, was "relaxation," he did not get very much of it. He was preoccupied most of the time with questions relating to the treaty; his plans for an extended rest were in effect destroyed by the detailed accounts Randolph began sending him of the tumultuous public meetings and of the general outcry against the treaty, and by the lengthy petitions addressed to himself, to which he thought himself obliged to reply. He asked Randolph to prepare drafts of replies, in consultation with his colleagues, and in the one which he approved he referred to having "resolved on the manner of executing the duty now before me . . . without passion" and only after "a temperate and well-informed investigation."[146] Naturally he still did not say just what it was he had "resolved on." He was not entirely sure himself, though he did know, or thought he knew, that it was "better to ratify it in the manner the Senate have advised . . . , than to suffer matters to remain as they are, unsettled."[147]

Washington was greatly disturbed by the popular agitation, and this gave a heightened importance to the materials Randolph was preparing—the memorial, the form of ratification, and the instructions for further negotiations with Great Britain—about which he was growing both more uneasy and more impatient. Randolph thought he might "run down to Mount Vernon" and go over them with him. But the last thing Washington needed now was further talk with Randolph; he had at least made up his mind that the decision could not be made satisfactorily in that manner. If there were to be any conferences, they had better be held in Philadelphia, where the pertinent documents, information, and other consultants were, and Washington would if necessary cut short his vacation and go back there himself.[148]

In fact he had been at Mount Vernon hardly more than a week before he determined to do that very thing, and to get matters settled once and for all, even though the members of his cabinet had at first assured him it would not be necessary. There seem to have been several reasons for this change of plans. "I am excited to this resolution," he wrote, "by the violent and extraordinary proceedings" taking place, which he viewed "in a very serious light."[149] Much of this agitation he believed to be irresponsible, and the sooner it was quieted the better. More specifically, he had become highly apprehensive over what the French might take it into their heads to do as a result of it. They were almost certain to exploit it in some way; this, he believed, was the paramount thing to be avoided, and "too much pains cannot be taken by those who speak, or write, in favor of the treaty, to place this matter in its true light."[150] A final consideration was the news that Hammond had received his letter of recall, to which the Minister had been looking forward for some time, and was planning to leave the country in about a fortnight.[151] This made it essential that the appropriate materials, whatever they might be, should be ready to place in his hands before his departure.

In view of the dramatic scenes that occurred behind closed doors during the week that followed Washington's return to Philadelphia, culminating with the disgrace of Edmund Randolph, one is naturally led to further surmises about the state of Washington's mind before that time, and about the apparent abruptness of his decision to ratify after he got there, in the face of prior inclinations to the contrary. Beyond doubt Washington had intended, in principle, to withhold ratification until the question of the Order in Council was cleared up. But Randolph's memorial to this effect — a draft of which Washington now had, and was considering — made for one side of a balance that was becoming more and more precarious, and there is evidence that Washington was uncomfortably aware of this.[152] There may have been disadvantages in an immediate ratification. But on the other side of the scale were the disadvantages, now multiplying, of continued uncertainty and delay, and it was this that decided him to go back to Philadelphia instead of doing things by mail or letting Randolph come down to wind it up informally. He wanted to act, he wanted his entire cabinet taking part, and he wanted the conclusion to be the product of everyone's efforts. The questions were of "such vast magnitude as not only to require great individual consideration, but a solemn conjunct revision."[153] It was a major occasion, and Washington wanted it done right.

Besides, the cabinet members had now changed *their* minds, and decided that his presence was required after all. And while he had already come to the same conclusion, he was now moved to go back a week sooner than he intended, especially after an urgent private letter which Secretary of War Timothy Pickering sent him on his own. In it, Pickering told the President that his return was necessary "for a *special reason* which can be communicated to you only in person," and prayed him in the meantime "to decide on no important political measure in whatever form it may be presented to you."[154]

The *"special reason"* became apparent the very day Washington arrived back in Philadelphia. Pickering came to Washington's house while the President was closeted with Randolph, and Washington took Pickering out of the room to ask why he had written him such a letter. Pickering pointed a baleful finger and replied, "That man is a traitor." Later in the evening, Secretary of the Treasury Oliver Wolcott brought him a paper that was represented as proving it.[155]

The paper was a dispatch intended for France, dated October 31, 1794, written by Joseph Fauchet, the French minister who had recently been succeeded by Pierre Adet and was now on the point of returning home. The dispatch had been intercepted at sea by a British cruiser and taken to the Foreign Office; Grenville had transmitted it to George Hammond, and Hammond had turned it over to Wolcott on July 28.[156] The letter appeared to show — it also referred mysteriously to two previous letters which were not at hand — that Randolph had made improper disclosures about the affairs of the American government to the French minister, and had actually asked the Minister for a bribe which was to influence in some unexplained way the course of the Whiskey Insurrection that had been going on in western Pennsylvania.

There was much in the paper that was impenetrable, and no final judgment on it could be made without some explanations from Randolph. Whether Washington ever took Pickering's lurid word "traitor" in its extreme literal meaning may be doubted. But one thing was obvious: the paper breathed malevolence and contempt for the United States government on the part of the resident French minister, and the confidences of Edmund Randolph had had a great deal to do with the way he had arrived at those sentiments. At the very least, there was something here profoundly disreputable to the government's good faith and character. Washington made two decisions that night. He would set this entire matter to one side for a few days, saying nothing about it for now to Randolph. The other was to call a cabinet meeting the next morning, August 12, and dispose of the treaty. He would ask for advice and discussion, as usual, but in all likelihood he knew in advance what he was going to do.

They met; Washington called for opinions on immediate ratification. Pickering, Wolcott and Attorney-General Bradford argued strongly for it. Randolph of course argued for delay, which he still assumed the President favored. Washington rose and ended the meeting by announcing, to Randolph's astonishment, "I will ratify the treaty."[157] Randolph's memorial would thus have to be discarded and a new one drafted in its place. It was duly done, and the papers were delivered to Hammond on August 14, the day before his departure. Randolph, as Hammond reported to Grenville, "did not attempt to conceal his chagrin," and "voluntarily confessed that his opinion had been overruled in the President's Cabinet." The new memorial still protested the Provision Order, but simply stated that the ratification "must not be construed into an admission of the legality of the said order."[158]

Even to Hammond, "the declining influence of that gentleman" in the inner councils was obvious, and Randolph's final downfall came on the following Wednesday, four days after Hammond had gone. On the morning of August 19, Washington in the presence of the entire cabinet put Fauchet's letter in his hand and peremptorily asked him to explain it. Randolph made an attempt, but soon realized that he could not remember all the details to which it referred, and asked for time in which he might make a full explanation in writing. But before the scene was over, the humiliated Randolph also realized that he had no choice but to resign, and he did so that same day.[159]

The Randolph affair has been the subject of intermittent discussion from that day to this. It seems generally established that Randolph's relations with the French minister were in no remote sense "treasonable," nor was he guilty of having solicited money for himself, though his own chronically straitened affairs and the shortages later found in his department's accounts made for suspicions that were not wholly dispelled for many years. But that is about all that has been established, for all the attention that has been paid to the case, and there is much in the tangled tale that will never be fully cleared up. That Randolph was rather a pitiable figure, possessed of some talents and surprisingly little malice, but subject to self-absorbed silliness and lapses of good sense, is the dominant impression that has come down to us. Whether that portrait will ever undergo major revisions is by now somewhat doubtful.[160]

A question which is still of some interest, however, concerns the way in which all this affected the behavior of George Washington. What was it that made his decision on the treaty so abrupt, and what was there in Fauchet's intercepted dispatch that filled him with such a cold fury, a fury that did not lessen but grew more brutally implacable with every subsequent effort Randolph made to exculpate himself? How, in short, did *he* see it? Obviously we cannot know for certain, but the surrounding context, which is visible enough, contains several striking elements.

The most immediate one was Washington's misgivings about France, of which his mind had already been full as he made his way back to Philadelphia. Almost the first thing that had struck him while at Mount Vernon reading the accounts of the popular demonstrations was that "the string . . . most played upon, because it strikes with most force the popular ear, is the violation, as they term it, of our engagements with France," and that this was more to be feared than any other consequence. He was certain, he wrote to Hamilton, that "it is the interest of the French . . . to avail themselves of such a spirit to keep *us & Great Britain* at variance; and they will, in my opinion, accordingly do it. To what *length* their policy may induce them to carry matters, is too much in embryo at this moment to decide: but I predict much embarrassment to the government therefrom. . . ."[161] Such fears, as subsequent events would show, were well founded.

Also at work were Washington's powerful feelings about parties and partisanship, to which he would never be reconciled, especially with regard to the way these affected America's dealings with foreign governments—a preoccupation which was to suffuse the whole of his Farewell Address in the following year. And finally, there was the burden of his own altogether unique position as the first Chief Magistrate of a new and still fragile republican state, and his painful sensitivity to all the shades of character that this state and its people would exhibit to the world at large. The weight of it, as he had already confessed more than once in his self-doubt, was almost unbearable.

All these considerations most certainly hovered in the very air as Washington sat down on the night of August 11, 1795, to read Dispatch Number 10 of Joseph Fauchet. We might read it with him.[162]

Fauchet begins by saying that in his efforts to keep his government informed about the crisis occasioned by the recent Whiskey Insurrection in the United States, and to discover the "secret views" of the American government, he had not considered it wise to confide in his own colleagues (the commissioners who had accompanied him), or in anyone "whose known partiality to that government, and similitude of passions and interests with its chiefs" might lead to imprudent disclosures. "Besides, the precious confessions of Mr. Randolph alone throw a satisfactory light on every thing that comes to pass." (Fauchet is presumably telling his superiors that no one can accuse *him* of "partiality to that government," and that the version he is about to give them of its policies and "secret views" has been based on things obligingly revealed to him by Mr. Randolph.)

He then goes on to picture the country as rent by party divisions, a popular majority having risen in opposition to the government's Treasury system—a system which had "created a financiering class" bent on converting the nation to monarchy "by insensible gradations." The "patriotic party" gains strength through the widespread indignation at "the abasement of commerce, the slavery of navigation, and the audacity of England," and casts censures upon the government "at which the latter is even itself astonished." Thus by the beginning of 1794 there existed a general state of discontent over "the imbecility of the government towards Great Britain, the defenceless state of the country against possible invasions, the coldness towards the French Republic," the financial system so complicated as to protect it "from general inspection," the "immoral and impolitic modes of taxation" which the Treasurer "first presents as expedients, and afterwards raises to permanency." (Washington was here reading a "history" of his administration, upon which a foreign government was presumably to base its policy, that might as well have been written by Benjamin Bache or Philip Freneau.)

Fauchet now comes to the connection between all this background and the uprising of 1794 in western Pennsylvania. "Republicans by principle, independent by character and situation," the western people, oppressed by the government's excise tax, have naturally adopted the opposition viewpoint. They are further embittered by the knowledge that no serious efforts are being made to open the Mississippi to their products (the commerce of the "barren coast," which controls official policy, "dreads having rivals in those interior parts"), and that the government refuses to open land offices for general sale, reserving the western lands instead for its special favorites: "capitalists," "flatterers," and "courtiers." (Disgraceful that the President should be handing out public property to his courtiers.)

Such a system, and the discontents created by it, were bound sooner or later to bring on "either a revolution or a civil war." Indeed, the government may well have provoked the western insurrection deliberately, "in order to make an advantageous diversion, and to lay the more general storm which it saw gathering." ("Am I not authorized in forming this conjecture from the conversation which the Secretary of State had with me. . . ?") An unusually severe law for collecting the excise was asked for and passed at the very close of the previous session, and when the expected resistance arose, the government was all ready with "the means of repression." And "this was undoubtedly what Mr. Randolph meant in telling me *that under the pretext of giving energy to the government it was intended to introduce absolute power and to mislead the President in paths which would conduct him to unpopularity.*" ("Precious confessions" indeed, if this were anything like a direct quotation. Randolph had made charges against his own colleagues, not to the President of the United States but to the minister of the French Republic.)

Then, in order to "justify the raising of so great a force as 15,000 men," it was necessary "to magnify the danger," to distort the pacific intentions of the western people, "to attribute to them the design of uniting themselves with England, to alarm the citizens for the fate of the constitution, whilst in reality the revolution threatened only the ministers." The step succeeded, and the army was raised. But whereas this military part of the suppression is doubtless Mr. Hamilton's, the "pacific part" was "due to the influence of Mr. Randolph over the mind of the President. . . ." Fauchet concludes this passage with the assertion, both pious and patronizing, that the President himself is nonetheless "truly virtuous, and the friend of his fellow-citizens and [their] principles." (In that case things have certainly got away from him: it seems that the President's virtue, being inert, requires the constant surveillance of Edmund Randolph.)

The climax of Fauchet's dispatch is his tantalizing story of Randolph's soliciting money from him to influence somehow or other the course of the rebellion. The government had its army but was not assured of the full support of various state officials; these men, "all having without doubt Randolph at their head," were "balancing to decide" what part they would take. It was at this point that "Mr. Randolph called upon me with a countenance expressive of much anxiety and made the overtures of which I have given you a detail in my No. 6." (This was awkward; nobody knew what was in Dispatch Number 6.) The narrative resumes: "Thus with some thousands of dollars the [French] Republic would have decided on civil war or in favor of peace. Thus the consciences of the pretended patriots in America have already a price." (This at the very least was a matter that needed looking into.)

Now comes a separation of the good men from the scoundrels. The source of all corruption is obviously Hamilton, who "has made of a whole nation a stock-jobbing, speculating, selfish people." But there are still patriots, such as Madison, "an honest man," and Jefferson, who has "prudently retired" to avoid taking part in such scenes as just described. "Consult Monroe, he is of their number; he had apprised me of the men whom the current of events had dragged along as bodies devoid of weight." (Monroe, who had just made such a booby of himself before the French Assembly, was apparently another of the Minister's confidants.)

The paper closes with a not very flattering account of Washington's role as commander of the militia force that marched westward (ever "virtuous," but controlled by others), together with some concluding insights as to the true objects of the campaign. One such object was to spend enough money on it that the taxpayers would vent all their wrath on "the insurgent principles of the patriots" rather than on those who really deserved it. The other was to divert public attention from the continued aggressions of the British, and from the "ridiculous negotiations lingering at London."

Washington at this point could well have wished he might lay hold of the treaty, sign it, and send it on its way that very night instead of waiting, as he did, to do it the first thing next morning. And now that he thought of it, there was no one person whose advice he had regularly listened to who from the very first had managed to discover more obstacles in the way of winding all this up—all the while professing to wish for its success—than Edmund Randolph. He would listen no longer, now that it seemed clear that Randolph's advice was not disinterested, being the product of a mind unaware that it was not its own master, and which had at worst been corrupted. He was now determined to be rid of Randolph once and for all, and he did not much care how he did it.[163] All the explaining in the world, no matter what it revealed or failed to reveal, could not re-establish this man's dependability, or greatly rearrange the web of liabilities Washington now saw in keeping such a fool in his councils.

Washington's resolve was probably further stiffened by certain papers of Randolph's authorship which came under his eye during the next few days, prior to the great showdown of August 19. One was a circular letter Randolph had sent out on July 21 to all American representatives abroad, in which he undertook to tell them what he thought the President should do about the treaty: "he should not sign it, until it should return from England, with the addition of the suspending article; and probably not even then, if a late British order for the capture of provisions, going to France should have been issued as we suppose, and increase the objections which have been lavished upon it." The other was a letter to Monroe, also already sent, about the recent behavior of Fauchet. Randolph's relations with the French minister had deteriorated over the past year for a variety of reasons, and he was now telling Monroe that Fauchet had engaged in all manner of plots and machinations, and "has endeavoured to procure some information from some members of the executive to whom he has resorted. I was not one of them."[164] This could only be read as the clumsy effort, by a man who knows he has talked too freely, to cover his tracks. The idea of Fauchet trying to pump information not from himself, who had been pouring it out all along, but by "resorting" to Hamilton, Knox, Bradford, Wolcott, or Pickering, was not very convincing.

Randolph's promised "vindication," when it came out a few months later in the form of a pamphlet, was a sad effort. Fauchet had in the meantime given him an affidavit, hastily composed on the day of his embarkation for France, declaring Randolph innocent of corruption (as he undoubtedly was), and Fauchet's successor Adet provided extracts from Dispatches 3 and 6 which gave more information about matters referred to in Number 10. Randolph published all these documents, and a good many more, in his pamphlet. But the story of the money, and exactly how Randolph wanted it used, remained vague and implausible, and still does. According to Fauchet, Randolph believed that British influence was being used in Pennsylvania to incite the people to rebellion and to detach the western country from the United States; this same influence was being used to discredit France and defame leading Republicans in America. Randolph's idea was that certain American flour merchants, who had supply contracts with French agents, might be induced to uncover these British intrigues and denounce them if offered a proper incentive to do so. It would take the form of advances on their French contracts so they might satisfy their British creditors and thereby avoid harassment. Just who these men were, and which ones in particular Randolph had in mind, remained forever a mystery. But Fauchet had no such funds at his disposal, and obviously regarded the whole idea as somewhat preposterous. Making this harebrained scheme public was the price Randolph paid to exhibit his "innocence."

The more he "explained" in this pamphlet of over a hundred pages, the more he seemed to entangle himself. The extracts he included from Fauchet's other dispatches did him little good. Washington had been aware in advance that Randolph wanted to spread before the public a number of his and Randolph's private communications, and had written in icy contempt that "you are at full liberty to publish, without reserve, *any,* and every private and confidential letter I ever wrote you; nay more, every word I ever uttered to, or in your presence, from whence you can derive any advantage in your vindication." The "public will judge," he added, "how far, and how proper it has been for you to publish [such] communications. . . ."[165] In length and detail, Randolph's subsequent disclosures of confidential business went much beyond what the public of the time was used to, and the proportions of his indiscretion seemed to bear a direct relation to the number of words he used to deny it. Moreover, the very effort to exculpate himself required, as he saw it, a debate over the wisdom of Washington's action on the treaty, and worse, one long indictment of the Chief Executive for being unable to resist evil influences, for having become a partisan tool in the hands of an unscrupulous, unrepublican, "British" faction. And it was done in language that could only come from a partisan of the opposite side, all the while professing to have acted "above party."

The defense was hardly a success, and to the Republicans it was a decided embarrassment. The impression it made was most succinctly summarized by James Madison. "His greatest enemies will not easily persuade themselves that he was under a corrupt influence of France[,] and his best friends can't save him from the self-condemnation of his political career as explained by himself."[166]

A little scene is said to have occurred—depending on the recollections of a very old man—at the time Washington received Randolph's panphlet. When the President had finished reading it, he called in Timothy Pickering, whom he had appointed (with misgivings on both sides) to be Randolph's successor as Secretary of State. He told Pickering, with rising voice, of all the woes he had let himself in for in keeping this man Randolph as a trusted member of his cabinet. And now, said the outraged President, "he has written and published this." With that, he threw the pamphlet on the floor in a great burst of violent language. "He then calmly resumed his seat. The storm was over."[167]

5

The "Golden Shower"

The final acceptance of the Jay Treaty by the American public in the spring of 1796 probably represented the most dramatic step taken so far toward popular politics, though at first glance the circumstances appear logically all wrong, and full of ideological contradictions. Popular sentiment in the spring and summer of 1795 had been overwhelmingly against the treaty, and the Republicans—the "popular" party—both took the lead in organizing this opposition and benefited politically from having done so. Thus when the Republican effort in the House of Representatives to prevent the treaty's going into effect was thwarted by popular protest the following spring—an extraordinary turnabout in public opinion—the discomfited Republicans appeared to be the losers. And so they were, at least in the short run. But in the long run it would not be the Federalists who were the beneficiaries. Every new instance of popular agitation and popular participation, whatever the issue and no matter what the outcome, would be another stage in the Federalists' eventual decline. It was the very process itself, and the political habits being formed by it, that would undermine their influence. Besides, the liquidation of the Jay Treaty episode would relieve the Republicans for a period of years, however unwilling they may have been to see it that way, of a growing ideological liability, that of Madison's stubborn commitment to a system of coercive legislation against the commerce of Great Britain.

But why *did* the people on this occasion turn against their Republican spokesmen, who had a substantial majority in the House of Representatives, and insist that they make no further obstacles to putting the treaty into effect? Certainly not because they had thought the better of their habitual anglophobia, or abandoned their chronic suspicion of all things British. It was rather that events and possibilities had begun to spell out very plainly that for purposes of their own current interests an overly literal ideological purity was no longer worth it. One such consideration was that thanks to Wayne's military and diplomatic success against the Indians, and with the imminent delivery of the posts, the opening of the Northwest for settlement and exploitation could be seen as a reality for the first time since the end of the Revolution. Another was that Spain, confronted by an Anglo-American settlement, was at last ready to concede the Americans full freedom to navigate the Mississippi, which meant for the first time ever an unrestricted outlet for the produce of the interior. But underlying everything else was the noonday blaze of prosperity, the primary source of which was the overseas carrying trade, and to whose happy promise—coupled with new opportunities erupting everywhere—there now appeared to be few limits. Whether or not the keepers of the Republican conscience had quite caught up with the implications, these things were all tied in together, and a failure now to put the British treaty into operation would shatter the whole bright picture. From the moment Washington signed the treaty on August 14, 1795, to the point at which the House on April 30, 1796, at last voted the funds to give it force, the case for holding out grew steadily weaker. This period of eight and a half months has an interest all its own.

One consequence of the President's ratification, logically enough, was that the stream of petitions to him, and the public meetings organized for inspiring them, abruptly stopped. At about the same time, moreover, public discussion of the treaty moved to a level markedly less agitated than had been the case before. From meetings, open-air harangues, and heated editorials came a shift of emphasis to the more deliberate and measured media of pamphlet and serial essay. And on this ground it would shortly be apparent that the Federalists had all the better of it. Though Robert R. Livingston, Alexander J. Dallas, and Brockholst Livingston were certainly men of respectable talents, they were no match for such as Noah Webster, James Kent, Rufus King, and Alexander Hamilton.[168] Hamilton, whose energies could be brought to a peculiar pitch of efficiency by a challenge like this, soon dominated the debate and in the end outstayed all the others.

The initial outburst against the treaty, as has been seen, was wildly emotional, the treaty's faults being taken as so self-evident that a serious debate was hardly warranted. Such an attitude reached a kind of rollicking epitome in Blair McClenachan, a leading demagogue of Philadelphia: *"Kick this damned treaty to hell!"*[169] But although this first torrent of abuse was exceedingly difficult to resist, it also tended to generate its own reaction. Assuming as it did that only knaves and skulking Tories could see matters otherwise, and that counter-argument was empty sophistry, it stirred currents of unease among doubters who wanted more enlightenment. By the same token, a good many moderates swept up in the first whirlwind were left open to dismayed second thoughts should it begin to appear (as it shortly would) that things were not as simple as they seemed. And finally, the very atmosphere of uncontradicted hyperbole was one which inspired the treaty's enemies to overreach themselves. The assertions they made were so extravagant as to open them to a fresh round of critical scrutiny with the approach of cooler weather.

Such was what happened even to the most judicious of the treaty's attackers, foremost among whom was Chancellor Robert R. Livingston of New York. Livingston, as "Cato," began a series of essays in the *New York Argus* by declaring that Great Britain had been on the verge of collapse in 1794, and that Jay might have exacted any terms he chose. ("Cato" even claimed that the naval forces of England and France were "nearly balanced," and that if America had entered the war she could have "completed the ruin" of British commerce.) The British had broken the treaty first; America was the injured party, and so instead of negotiating, Jay should have demanded "*delivery* of the posts—*reparation* for the loss of trade—a *compensation* for the expence of the war the British had excited with the Indians—a *public* punishment of the British subjects who had personally appeared in arms against us, with the removal from office of Lord Dorchester, who had, in his address to the Indians, encouraged them to violate the treaty of peace." We were entitled to at least $10 million in damages, and might in any case await "the magnanimity of France," which would not permit her to make peace with England "without procuring us the satisfaction which her guarantee of our territories entitled us to ask."[170] "Cato" in subsequent numbers went on to claim that Jay ought to have insisted on additional compensation for slaves carried off and for seamen impressed, and national as well as individual compensation (because of insults to the national honor) for spoliations upon American commerce. He also charged that Jay, in agreeing to allow the British to trade with the Indians south of the Canadian boundary, was in effect turning over the entire fur trade to them, and that he had permitted Article III to be so drafted as to eliminate—contrary to law—the 10 percent duty previously collected on goods imported in foreign ships.[171]

With these assertions, most of which were in print before Hamilton entered the debate, Cato-Livingston left himself widely exposed, and helped to determine Hamilton's own polemical strategy. Hamilton, writing as "Camillus," could present himself as meeting irresponsible charges and uninformed half-truths with reason and facts.

In the first number of a series titled "The Defence," "Camillus" observed that the outcry against the treaty had been abruptly precipitated, and that those who fomented it, knowing that "time, examination and reflection would be requisite to fix the public opinion on a true basis," had "resisted all discussion" and done everything they could to "render the treaty odious." He, on the other hand, promised to take it up article by article and show that it adjusted "in a reasonable manner the points in controversy," that it made "no improper concessions" nor imposed any restrictions incompatible with American honor or interest, that the United States gained equivalents for everything given, that no treaty with any other power had been violated, that advantages had been conceded by Great Britain "which no other nation has obtained from the same power," that "interests of primary importance to our general welfare" were promoted by the treaty, and that the "too probable result" of non-ratification would be war.[172]

In his next paper, "Camillus" reminded his readers once more of the crisis that had preceded Jay's mission: provocations and violations of rights "too injurious to be submitted to," leading to a general fear "that War was inevitable." Two courses had appeared to be open. One was reprisals intended for coercive effect (sequestration of British debts and the cutting off of trade); the other, "*vigorous preparation* for war and *one more effort* of negotiation by a solemn mission to avert it." But no sensible person could imagine that reprisals *prior* to negotiation would coerce anyone; they could only bring war a step closer. "To begin with reprisals is to meet on the ground of war and puts the other party in a condition not to be able to recede without humiliation." These "alternatives," then, were illusory; the real alternative was war or negotiation. Nor was America in any proper condition to make war, though critics of the mission seemed "to consider the U States as among the first rate powers of the world." War at the present time would destroy our trade and navigation, ravage our frontiers, impoverish our industry and agriculture, and render the public debt insupportable. Time, however, was on America's side. If we could honorably avoid war while steadily growing in strength and prosperity, the chances were that much greater of postponing it indefinitely. And meanwhile, "Camillus" added in what was to prove a canny afterthought, peace with England would significantly help America's chances of a favorable settlement with Spain.[173]

Hamilton-Camillus then turned to the treaty's preamble, wherein the parties had agreed to settle their differences "without reference to the Merits of their respective Complaints and Pretensions"—that is, without further debate over the rightness or wrongness of the various infractions of the Peace Treaty. Jay's attackers had insisted that the American position on these questions had been incontestably right all along, that the British were obviously the first violators, and that Jay ought to have maintained this ground and demanded fullest satisfaction on both the carrying off of slaves and detention of the posts. "Camillus" pointed out in much circumstantial detail why these things were not obvious. He showed the lengths to which the state governments—especially that of Virginia—had gone to obstruct British creditors in collecting their debts, which was the British justification for continuing to occupy the posts; he also showed how far apart the American and British positions were on Article VII of the Peace Treaty, the one on carrying away "Negroes or other Property of the American Inhabitants." One point of difference was whether this applied to slaves freed or abducted before the conclusion of peace, as the Americans claimed, or only afterward, as the British claimed, and another was whether compensation for lost property could be demanded with reference to persons who could neither morally nor legally be returned to a state of slavery. As to which side had violated the treaty first, this was endlessly debatable ("Camillus" pointed out a series of state enactments on confiscation and debt recovery which might well be seen as first infractions), and it was very difficult to prove that the American position on this entire question was inherently better than the British. If we had a plausible case, so did they, and if each negotiator were to hold his ground here, no negotiations could occur at all. Hence the formula agreed upon in the preamble.[174]

From this it followed, since the British did not feel themselves bound to evacuate the posts until the Americans at least did something about the debts, that any idea of successfully pressing claims of indemnification for detention of the posts was quixotic. There was no known precedent for such a demand anyway, except in cases of terms imposed by a conqueror in war; nor was there any mode of computing the degree to which the expenses of Indian hostilities were attributable to British connivance. (We might as logically claim indemnity for the expenses of the Revolution.) As for losses in the fur trade, "Camillus" took a cut at "Cato's" assertions on that point by showing, with figures, that the American share of the trade was in fact about one-fortieth of what "Cato" claimed it was. No British minister would dare go to Parliament and ask for any such thing as an indemnity to the United States, on any of these grounds. "Camillus" had some further sport with "Cato's" picture of Britain on the point of collapse, and with his notion that if we were not in a state to enforce our claims we could wait and rely on the "magnanimity of France" to do it for us. He called this merely "silly," and asked how it happened "that France, with all her victories, has not yet been able, even to extort Peace?"[175]

By the first or second week in August, when he began his examination of the separate articles, Hamilton had largely taken charge of the argument. "Cato" dropped out at the end of September, most of the others having left well before then. Hamilton went on until January 9, 1796. "The Defence" consisted of thirty-eight assays in all (ten of them written by Rufus King), and even Hamilton's enemies conceded their effectiveness. "Hamilton is really a colossus to the antirepublican party," wrote Jefferson to Madison. "Without numbers, he is an host within himself. . . . We have only had middling performances to oppose to him. In truth, when he comes forward, there is nobody but yourself who can meet him. . . . For god's sake take up your pen, and give a fundamental reply. . . ." But Madison, who had answered a similar call two years before and had not come off well in the "Pacificus-Helvidius" exchange that followed, was not disposed to do it again.[176]

In the remaining numbers of "The Defence" Hamilton went over the entire treaty, dealing with every criticism that had been directed at it, making the most of its advantages, and naturally minimizing its real or alleged shortcomings. He showed that Article III on the inland trade had surrendered no privilege in maritime trade or navigation (as "Cato" had claimed), since it had nothing to do with those subjects. He argued that a general article on impressment was impossible to obtain, and that the best way to limit abuses was by making regular representations and taking up particular cases as they arose. Nor could the British be made to accept the American version of neutral rights (free ships, free goods) in place of their own, and the United States had long since admitted as much. Defining food as contraband, as the British insisted on doing under special circumstances, was at least a tolerable compromise when cargoes so seized were paid for. He could defend the arbitration commissions on very strong grounds, especially the one on the pre-Revolutionary debts, having shown in much detail that this was the only reasonable way that remained for creditors to get satisfaction, though few Virginians were likely to thank him for pointing this out. And whereas the principal restrictions of Great Britain's navigation system remained, American trade was clearly on a better footing now than it had been before.[177]

Thus in what amounted to a book-length treatise of nearly 100,000 words, Hamilton had put the best possible face on the treaty and had made a persuasive case that it was as favorable a settlement as could be had. But his effort was more than merely a negative defense. He argued that the treaty brought the United States substantial advantages, and he showed with a wealth of particulars what it was that made them so. Moreover, he repeated at every turn the point that to block the treaty now would be to take the question back to where it had been in the spring of 1794, when it had been apparent to all that the country was on the brink of war. His ding-dong insistence that the alternative was negotiation or war was the one thing that most maddened the opposition, the one they protested most loudly and were least plausibly able to deny. His extended appeal that the treaty be judged not in passion but on its merits at least insured that if the people should still reject it they would do so much less lightly now than they would have done six months earlier.

By the time "Camillus" reached the final stage of his case, that of demonstrating that the treaty was in no way contrary to the Federal Constitution, even the treaty's friends had had enough. Fisher Ames thought "so much answer to so little weight of objection is [at] odds. . . . Jove's eagle holds his bolts in his talons, and hurls them, not at the Titans, but at sparrows and mice."[178]

By early September 1795, two critical pieces of news had reached the frontier settlements of western Pennsylvania, upper New York, Ohio, and Kentucky. One was that Washington on August 14 had signed Jay's treaty, which promised British evacuation of the Northwest posts; the other, that General Anthony Wayne on August 3 had concluded the Treaty of Greenville with the Northwest Indians, and that the Indians had thereby ceded to the United States about three-fourths of the present state of Ohio and a wedge of southeastern Indiana. In the minds of the frontier population these two facts were inseparable. If the posts were *not* occupied by Americans, Wayne's treaty would be just as meaningless as the four previous treaties—Fort Stanwix (1785), Fort McIntosh (1786), Fort Finney (1786), and Fort Harmar (1789)—in which the Indians under duress had ceded substantially the same territory but had felt free, under British patronage, to repudiate the cessions as soon as they had made them. The settlers knew, in other words, from a decade and more under the shadow of dread, anxiety, and chronic warfare, that the posts were the key to peace in the Northwest. With the posts in American hands, with the Americans thus able to cut off British supplies to the Indians, with the Indians becoming regularly dependent for their supplies on American rather than British traders, British influence over them would be vastly reduced. The men of the frontier, unlike the Robert Livingstons, tended to view the fur trade less in economic than in military and strategic terms; to control that trade, whatever its monetary value, was to control the Indians—or, at the very least, to effect a drastic shift in the balance of influence.[179]

Nor, so far as the frontier was concerned, had the Indian policy of the federal government up to then given very consistent grounds for confidence. The initial line of the Washington administration had been laid down in 1789 with the report on Indian affairs submitted to the President in June of that year by Secretary of War Henry Knox. A basic theme in it was that the Continental Congress had stirred up unnecessary turmoil among the Indians following the Revolution by insisting on American ownership in fee simple of all territory east of the Mississippi in accordance with the Treaty of Paris, and by taking the position that the Indians, in siding with the British in the war, had forfeited all claim to it. Knox now recommended that the new federal government calm this unrest by recognizing the legitimacy of the Indians' claims, restraining the settlers, and permitting occupation only of those lands the Indians were prepared to sell voluntarily. Not that the whites would fail to get their hands on them in the end. "As the settlements of the whites shall approach near to the Indian boundaries established by treaties," Knox reasoned, "the game will be diminished, and the lands being valuable to the Indians only as hunting grounds, they will be willing to sell further tracts for small considerations." The whites—at least those in charge of policy-making—could thus have it both ways. A conciliatory system would permit the Indians to be "managed" at small expense, whereas a coercive one would require the maintenance of a greatly expanded military force in the Northwest, at proportionately expanded cost. The argument was both persuasive and convenient, and very easy to accept. The expense of a major military campaign against the Indians could become a heavy charge on the federal treasury, and there were deep prejudices in Congress against the establishment of a large regular army.[180]

But behind this hopeful policy lay two critical premises, in which the frontiersmen could put no faith whatever. One was that the Indians could be persuaded in equanimity to give up their entire tribal warrior-hunter culture and be absorbed as peaceful American farmers. The other was that they would allow the cutting edge of the frontier to approach, in full knowledge that this meant the destruction of the game on which they depended, without any effort to strike back and preserve their ancestral hunting grounds. The Westerners knew better. If the white man were to have his way, as both they and the authorities back East intended, then it would require force, and force was exactly what those authorities were most reluctant to provide.[181]

Nevertheless the federal government soon slipped into a policy of force anyway, more or less in spite of itself. After hearing reports of Indian depredations all through the summer of 1789, desperate cries from the Ohio Valley for protection, and threats of retaliatory raids by Kentucky rangers, Washington and Knox were persuaded that United States military strength in the Northwest had to be increased (chiefly through levies of militia), even while encouraging the tribes to negotiate for peace. In June 1790 Washington under great pressure agreed to allow Generals Josiah Harmar and Arthur St. Clair to organize a limited punitive expedition. Under Harmar's command this force penetrated some 170 miles into Indian territory in October, but was obliged to withdraw when one of Harmar's picked units was ambushed, beaten, and scattered on the Maumee in northwestern Ohio. Plans were thereupon laid for a fresh expedition in 1791 under St. Clair. Washington and Knox blamed Harmar's defeat on ill-trained and unruly militia, and Jefferson was optimistic that a short and successful campaign now would enable the government to shift once more from a war policy to one of bribery. The St. Clair expedition, as has already been seen, ended in disaster and humiliation. The Indian tribes, moreover, were now largely united in their determination that the whites, if they wanted peace, would have to give up all lands north of the Ohio.[182]

Washington gloomily concluded that the restoration of peace in the Northwest Territory would require a paramount military effort. Congress agreed with the greatest reluctance to authorize a five-thousand-man regular army, and Anthony Wayne was appointed to take command of the force in Ohio. In mid-1792 Wayne began systematically organizing and training the army that would eventually defeat the Indians at Fallen Timbers.[183]

But military success was not to occur for another two years, nor a peace settlement for another year after that. The Administration still deemed it expedient to continue its efforts at negotiation, and such efforts—which proved utterly fruitless—consumed most of the summer of 1793. A three-man commission consisting of Timothy Pickering, Benjamin Lincoln, and Beverley Randolph journeyed west for that purpose, but the British prevented them from meeting with a full Indian council at Detroit—a practical demonstration of what continued British occupation meant—and the most hostile tribes still insisted on an Ohio River boundary. This delay probably made sense politically, and it gave Wayne further time for his preparations. But to the West it appeared as simply another proof of the federal government's muddle-headedness and lack of zeal for the safety of the frontier.[184]

By the spring of 1794 the government to all intents and purposes was at last ready for action. Dorchester's violent speech was viewed as an invitation to the Indians for a general attack, and when Simcoe undertook the rebuilding of Fort Miami, war seemed very close. Wayne moved out from Fort Greenville in July and pushed deep into Indian country, though British Indian agents Alexander McKee and Matthew Elliott meanwhile made great efforts to keep the Indians supplied and encouraged them to maintain their forces intact. The engagement of August 20, 1794, at Fallen Timbers on the Maumee (a few miles south of present-day Toledo) was a major victory for the Americans. What made it decisive was the refusal of the British commander at nearby Fort Miami to give the fleeing warriors shelter inside his stockade. Considerations of international diplomacy (John Jay and Lord Grenville were at that moment in the midst of their negotiations), together with the presence of a menacing army outside his walls, made the preservation of neutrality a matter of highest importance. Indeed, had not both sides determined to use restraint, the spark of war might have been struck then and there.[185]

But the British did keep the Indians from starving that winter, and covertly continued to discourage them from negotiating with the Americans. So it was not until late the following summer that Wayne could get the dispersed chiefs together at Fort Greenville to receive and acquiesce in his peace terms. From the viewpoint of the frontier, then, it still had to be assumed that so long as the British retained the posts, and so long as they exerted any substantial influence over the Indians, no settlement could be seen as final.[186]

The news, however, that the British were at last to evacuate the posts on the first of June, 1796, now altered everything, and a great swell of optimism after long years of frustration erupted all across the Northwest. Plans were immediately laid for new settlements—the towns of Cleveland, Dayton, Youngstown, Chillicothe, and Conneaut would spring into existence in a matter of months—and thus began the surge of migration which would bring Ohio a population of over 45,000 within four years, and admission to statehood within seven.[187] The price of grain and provisions had meanwhile reached a new high in eastern markets, and farmers, merchants, politicians, and land speculators were jubilantly united in visions of a tremendous future.

The one thing that might conceivably stop all this now would be a refusal by the British—for whatever reason—to get out of the posts after all. This could well be followed by a new round of Indian hostilities, with the old nightmares beginning all over again.

A further piece of news that brought great rejoicing reached the United States in late February 1796. After a dozen years of fruitless exertions by previous American representatives, Thomas Pinckney in October had at last concluded a settlement with Spain which delivered into American hands everything they had been vainly demanding since the end of the Revolution: free navigation of the Mississippi, the right of deposit at New Orleans (of storing goods duty-free while awaiting trans-shipment in ocean vessels), with the option of renewal or an alternate site at the end of three years, and the boundary between the United States and West Florida fixed at the 31st parallel. The Treaty of San Lorenzo marked the final abandonment of Spain's long-standing policy of keeping the Americans as far away from Louisiana as possible.[188]

Certain external pressures within the past two or three years had already weakened Spain's determination, though the ways of the Spanish court, muffled in mystery as they were, prevented the Americans most of the time from seeing very clearly where they stood. One of these pressures came through the wars of the French Revolution, which created a shortage of European shipping for the trade of Louisiana and the other Spanish colonies, together with a great demand there for grain, flour, and other products. The governor at New Orleans, Hector de Carondelet, was forced to sanction an increasing volume of trade with the Americans, much of it illicit, being afraid of what both the Kentuckians and his own colonists might do if he tried to prevent it.[189] The other pressure was that created by the alarming growth of the American population south of the Ohio River. The population of Kentucky had increased from 12,000 souls in 1783 to about 160,000 in 1795, and the combined population of Kentucky and Tennessee in that year must have approached 240,000.[190] The military force available to the Spanish governor for containing this burgeoning menace consisted of one demoralized and undermanned regiment and a string of decaying forts. In the nature of things it was bound to penetrate, even to the Council of State at Madrid, that an accommodation with the Americans would sooner or later be the only prudent course left.[191]

The immediate stimulus for such an accommodation, however, came not from the American frontier but from developments in the international politics of Europe. French successes, and Spanish participation in the war in unnatural alliance with Great Britain, were steadily bringing Spain to the point of ruin and causing her to look for a way of making peace with France. Then came the news that the United States was sending an emissary to negotiate a treaty with Great Britain. The chief minister, Manuel de Godoy, perceiving that the power from which Spain had most to fear was now England, especially if the English were to reach an understanding with the Americans in regard to Spain's North American colonies, determined at last to negotiate with the Americans in earnest. He had not done so up to then, though William Short and William Carmichael had been on hand since early in 1793 as plenipotentiaries, vainly seeking a settlement and being put off from month to month. Godoy now asked the American government to send a more eminent gentleman in their place, and Washington sent Thomas Pinckney, the eminent gentleman from South Carolina, then serving as United States minister to Great Britain. Pinckney arrived at the end of June 1795, just as Spain was concluding a separate peace with France in the Treaty of Basel—from which the full wrath of Great Britain was expected to result—and just as Jay's treaty was being approved by the United States Senate. He did not have to wait long for a settlement. He was told initially that Spain was prepared to grant the United States a favorable boundary and the right of navigating the Mississippi in return for an alliance with Spain—or a triple alliance which included France—mutually guaranteeing Spanish and American territory. Pinckney declined either alliance. Godoy then informed him, after consultation with the Council of State, that Spain would concede navigation of the Mississippi and the 31st parallel without the alliance, but could not agree to the right of deposit at New Orleans. Pinckney made the deposit a *sine qua non* and asked for his passports. Godoy thereupon conceded that point as well. Hopes which up to that moment had been repeatedly baffled were all brought to a pleasing fruition in the treaty signed at San Lorenzo on October 27, 1795.[192]

The glowing possibilities, then, inherent in the opening up of the great West were there to be laid hold of in the very near future, the only limit being—other things being equal—how quickly people could get there. But for the rest of the country there was not simply the future but a very immediate present as well, one that vibrated with the sights, sounds, and emotions of a general and accelerating prosperity.

The basic explanation for it was the turmoil in Europe, with the demand thereby generated for American products, especially food, and the vast opportunities the war opened up for American shipping, which now constituted the only large body of neutral tonnage available in the world. With shipbuilding and shipping profits having risen rapidly since 1792, and with export prices mounting, it was apparent by the spring of 1794 that the United States was on the verge of a major expansion in the export and carrying trade. Enthusiasm was naturally dampened by the crisis with Great Britain, but only temporarily. With the lifting of the embargo in May, the dispatch of the grain fleet to France, and substantial British shipments of merchandise to America in the fall—a clear sign that Britain neither expected nor intended war with the United States—optimism returned with a rush. Thereupon began one of the most exhilarating boom periods in all of American history. "The affairs of Europe," wrote a delirious correspondent to the *Columbian Centinel* in May 1795, ". . . rain riches upon us; and it is as much as we can do to find dishes to catch the golden shower."[193]

And the "golden shower" fell everywhere. For the shippers themselves it brought a three-fold rise in profits between 1792 and 1796, which in turn nourished a great upsurge in shipbuilding, reaching an annual level of 100,000 tons in 1795 and 1796. Accompanying it were demands for more lumber, more ship stores, canvas, rope, and tar—and for more and more men, skilled and unskilled. Daily wages in Philadelphia for ship carpenters and laborers alike doubled between 1790 and 1796. It was a full-employment economy; there was work for all available hands.[194]

The value of domestic exports began to rise in 1793 with an increase in their price. The increase in 1796—50 percent in both categories—was striking. And of course the rise in export commodities brought much satisfaction both to those who shipped them and to those who grew them. The price of exports, moreover, rose much faster in both 1795 and 1796 than did the price of imports, so that the terms of trade shifted spectacularly. Americans were selling dearer and buying cheaper, a situation which has always generated its own dynamic, people being tempted not only to buy cheaper but to buy more and more, which is what they did with great abandon in 1795. The most dramatic index of flush times was the rise of that year in the value of imports for domestic consumption, which more than doubled over the year previous. The American people were now relishing the fruits of a long-delayed prosperity.[195]

Amid all this, and with public feeling over the Jay Treaty having rapidly calmed down in the months following the President's ratification, the whole treaty question should logically have been all but laid to rest by the time the Fourth Congress met for its first session in December 1795. But such was not to be the case. By this time the treaty issue had one form of existence in the realm of public opinion and quite another in the councils of the now fully emergent Republican party. Opposition to the treaty had become a party commitment and had taken on a life of its own, in some degree independent of the ebb and flow of popular sentiment, even though a great billow of popular sentiment was what had ratified the commitment in the first place. Nothing up to then had brought such a unifying surge; public feeling and the partisan impulse had seemed in total harmony in the summer of 1795. And for the spokesmen of Republicanism it was pure principle, as pure as such things could be. It was principle that created partisanship, not "interest," and even if partisanship was itself becoming a form of interest, conscience truly forbade a trimming of sails. No wonder, then, that the thought of blocking the treaty in the House of Representatives by refusing to appropriate the funds for putting it into effect should appear so plainly the path of duty. There was good reason to expect a Republican majority. With their newfound unity and vastly extended support, how many other commitments, principles, and sentiments might they not consolidate and simplify, were they now to push forward with the effort and make it succeed? And there was something else, something few quite knew how to manage even in their own minds, so novel and hitherto so remote an idea had it been: the possibility of taking actual control of the national government. The Federalists, for all their raving about the menace of jacobinism and anarchy, were not really wrong in claiming that the real issue taking shape in the House of Representatives was whether the Republican party, without "the vital nourishment it derived from a deadly, implacable, and everlasting enmity to that accursed island [Britain] would be able to sustain itself,"[196] or in hinting, as Alexander Hamilton did in the first number of "The Defence," that the Republicans' not-too-distant object was to bring Thomas Jefferson to the presidency.[197]

Madison, so much of whose effort ever since 1789 had been devoted to protecting the American republic from the corruptions of British commerce, and who could now see his entire projected system being wrecked by the treaty, was irreconcilable. "A Treaty thus unequal in its conditions," he wrote late in August 1795, "thus derogating from our national rights, thus insidious in some of its objects, and thus alarming in its operation to the dearest interests of the U.S. in their commerce and navigation, is, in the present form, unworthy the voluntary acceptance of an Independent people...."[198] Jefferson in his retirement took for granted that notwithstanding the President's having signed the treaty, "the H. of representatives will oppose it as constitutionally void," and at the end of November was saying to Edward Rutledge: "I trust the popular branch of our legislature will disapprove of it, and thus rid us of this infamous act, which is really nothing more than a treaty of alliance between England & the Anglomen of this country against the legislature & people of the United States."[199]

Although most Republican congressmen could probably be counted on to close ranks in opposition to the treaty, it seemed desirable that their resolve be stiffened by renewed expressions of popular disapproval. Accordingly a petition campaign was mounted from Philadelphia by the zealous John Beckley. DeWitt Clinton agreed to take charge of it in New York, and Benjamin Bache and Michael Leib assisted Beckley in Pennsylvania.[200] In Virginia—to whose entire outlook, way of life, and past conduct Jay's work stood as a baleful reproach—the campaign to stop the treaty in the House took another form. By a sizable majority the Virginia Assembly in November approved the opposition votes that had been given the previous June by Senators Tazewell and Mason, and instructed Virginia's congressmen to offer a series of constitutional amendments. These proposed amendments would guarantee a vote by the House of Representatives on any aspect of a treaty that would limit the House's power to legislate, and would establish a body other than the Senate to try impeachments. The submission of such amendments to the House would, at the very least, provide an occasion for debating the Jay Treaty.[201]

But there were growing indications that things might be anything but easy, and the more perceptive of the Republicans sensed this. For one thing, Beckley's petition campaign seems not to have made much progress. Robert R. Livingston warned his nephew Edward, a member of the New York congressional delegation, that the petitions would "not be so respectable as to give much weight to your measures."[202] The Republicans in Pennsylvania were divided when Alexander J. Dallas refused to take part in the campaign at all.[203] At the same time, the state legislatures one after another declined to endorse the Virginia amendments, being very reluctant to appear to be challenging Washington. "The writers in opposition are too violent in their attacks on the P.," Joseph Jones (himself a Virginian) wrote nervously of the extreme fringe. "Such licentious charges will injure rather than promote the Republican interest."[204]

And then there was prosperity. Federalists noted with satisfaction that the people's only complaint was "getting Rich too fast"; that they went about with "pockets full of money, prosperity shining"; and that "the farmers are so intent on improving the means of getting rich, that they can hardly be got to lend an ear to any political subject, however interesting." Washington in his annual message benignly announced what everyone already knew. "Our agriculture, commerce and manufactures," he said, "prosper beyond former example. . . ."[205] Madison, assessing matters in December, was inclined to be moody. "There is a clear majority who disapprove of the Treaty," he wrote to Monroe, "but it will dwindle under the influence of causes well known to you; more especially as the States, instead of backing the wavering, are themselves rather giving way." He thought the supporters of the treaty would delay a debate on its merits in the hope of meanwhile persuading the public that on the whole it was better to take it than to reject it. "The means employed," he told Jefferson, "are to blazon the public prosperity, to confound the Treaty with the President, & to mouth over the stale topics of war and confusion."[206] Another Republican, Dr. Benjamin Rush of Philadelphia, appears to have been among those so persuaded. "General Washington," he wrote in mid-January, "is still esteemed by a great majority of our citizens[,] and his treaty with Great Britain becomes less unpopular in proportion as it is understood."[207]

The Republicans fretted increasingly at the lack of a suitable occasion to open their attack. Washington had mentioned the treaty in his annual message, but, still awaiting the British ratification, he had not yet transmitted it to the House. So the Republicans, if they were to avoid the appearance of a direct challenge, could do nothing but wait. "The situation is truly perplexing," wrote Madison to Jefferson. He was certain of a majority. "But as the Treaty is not regularly before the House, & an application to the P. brings him personally into the question . . . there is great danger that eno' will fly off to leave the opponents of the Treaty in a minority."[208] They became ever more impatient as the delay stretched through the month of February. Meanwhile three other treaties, all highly satisfactory, awaited final disposition. Wayne's Treaty of Greenville, a treaty with Algiers for the release of American prisoners, and Pinckney's treaty with Spain were all approved by the Senate, and all unanimously. At last on March 1 Washington sent Jay's treaty to the House of Representatives, having declared it to be in effect by proclamation the previous day.[209] That treaty, Benjamin Rush conceded, "once reprobated by $\frac{19}{20}$ of our citizens, is now approved of, or peaceably acquiesced in, by the same proportion of the people."[210]

But not by the House of Representatives. On March 2 Edward Livingston, somewhat to Madison's dismay, moved a resolution calling upon the President to lay before the House copies of Jay's instructions, together with all correspondence and other documents pertaining to the treaty.[211] The resolution bore with it the implication that the House, which would have to appropriate the necessary funds before a treaty could be in full operation, had the constitutional right, just as the Senate had, to pass on the treaty's merits. It was on this constitutional ground, and on the propriety of the resolution, that the debate opened. Madison thought the question had been prematurely forced, and would have preferred it done less directly, but now that the issue was joined he had no choice but to plunge in with the rest.[212] The leading Federalist spokesman for the treaty, William L. Smith of South Carolina, declared that the Constitution gave the House no such right as was now being claimed for it. The treaty-making power rested with the President and Senate, and the House's duty, once a treaty was proclaimed as the law of the land, extended no farther than voting the appropriations needed for executing it—unless it was clearly unconstitutional on its face (which was not being claimed), and no additional papers were needed to determine that.[213]

The Republican case was made most ably by Albert Gallatin, the Swiss-French émigré from Geneva who had been elected to the House in 1794 from western Pennsylvania and who was rapidly emerging as a figure of prominence. Gallatin said he did not deny the power of the President and Senate to make treaties, but that such power was not limitless. It did not override the House's power to make appropriations, nor could it automatically repeal existing legislation. Otherwise the President and two-thirds of the Senate might themselves appropriate money or set aside existing laws under the guise of making treaties. Nor did he claim such power for the House, only the right of checking it when it encroached on the House's own functions.[214] Madison added that "the Congressional power may be viewed as co-operative with the Treaty power, on the Legislative subjects submitted to Congress by the Constitution," and that in exercising it the House had to deliberate, giving "due weight to the reasons which led to the Treaty, and to the circumstances of the existence of the Treaty."[215]

Smith replied that there was not the least evidence, from the time of the

Constitutional Convention to the moment the present issue had come up, that such a role belonged to the House. He mentioned a meeting at Harrisburg at which Gallatin had been present, where a constitutional amendment was proposed requiring the House's assent to treaties, which meant that such power was understood not to exist otherwise. He also called attention to the language of the petitions addressed to Washington the previous summer: "We look up to the PRESIDENT alone for preservation from the fatal instrument; if he signs it, nothing can save us from it but war. . . ." Applying to the House now was "an after-thought"; that the Constitution contained any such remedy was an "*ex post facto* construction."[216] A former Antifederalist from western New York, John Williams, said he himself had opposed the treaty-making power of the President and Senate at his state ratifying convention, but had never doubted that the Constitution gave it to them, nor understood that the House of Representatives had been given the power to interfere in treaties. It seems that among the things Williams now had most on his mind was: "On the first of June, the British were to give up the Western posts; if money was not appropriated, would they not be deceived?"[217]

After two weeks of debate, Livingston's resolution was carried, 62–37, and on March 25 the call for papers was conveyed to the President.[218] Washington in a message to the House five days later politely declined to comply. He said he had never been disposed to withhold information to which either house had a right, but that negotiations with foreign powers required caution and often secrecy, which was one of the reasons why the Constitution had vested "the power of making Treaties in the President with the advice and consent of the Senate." To admit now the right of the House of Representatives to demand all the papers regarding such a negotiation "would be to establish a dangerous precedent." He saw no proper purpose for it in the present case "except that of an impeachment; which the resolution has not expressed." Moreover, having himself been a member of the Philadelphia Convention, he could report his clear understanding of the Constitution's intent that when treaties are "ratified by the President, with the advice and consent of the Senate," and promulgated, "they become obligatory." Foreign nations, he said, have so understood our procedures; in previous negotiations it is what "*we* have declared, and *they* have believed," and this had been the construction to which "every House of Representatives has heretofore acquiesced. . . ." And finally, he referred the House to the Convention Journal, which showed that a provision requiring a treaty to be ratified by legislation had been "explicitly rejected."[219]

The Republicans, though taken aback, voted on April 7 to reassert what they saw as the House's constitutional right to deliberate on any aspect of a treaty needing House action before being executed, and thus the final and critical stage of debate—on the treaty's merits—began.[220] Their majority, after five weeks, had remained substantially intact. But they now had to face the question directly of whether they could and would use the power they were asserting in order to set aside the treaty.

Indications that they would actually succeed in doing it were now qualified by danger signals coming in from every side. A Republican caucus on April 2 was apparently far from unanimous.[221] John Beckley reported on April 11 that three Republican members from the lower counties of New York, who had been very narrowly elected, were wavering.[222] On April 18, Madison was still bravely predicting defeat of the treaty by some twenty votes, provided "no defections take place." "But vast exertions are on foot," he added, "without & within doors." He trusted, "without being sure," that the House would remain steady. "If so, the public mind will rally, under their auspices." (The former emphasis was somehow altering: from the House as reflecting and representing the public mind, to a new role, that of instructing the public mind and perhaps even changing it.) By the 23rd, Madison's assurance was sinking. "The majority," he wrote Jefferson, "has melted by changes and absence, to 8 or 9 votes. Whether these will continue firm is more than I can decide."[223]

This "melting" was being induced by a vast new swell of public opinion in support of the treaty, and those who melted eventually admitted as much.[224] It was expressed through newspaper pieces, letters, and most conspicuously through public meetings and petitions, all in response to what was coming more and more generally to be seen as a crisis, produced by the House's apparent determination to kill the treaty by refusing appropriations. Petitions came in from all parts of the country, even Virginia.[225] Sentiment in New York had so turned about that the Republicans did not even dare risk a counter-petition there.[226] New England was virtually solid, "ready to rise in mass agst. the H. of Reps.," according to Madison, and Federalist leaders in the large mercantile centers were furiously active. The new sentiment, Madison charged, was due to "the exertions and influence of Aristocracy, Anglicism, & mercantilism."[227] All of which was in a sense true, except that those same influences had been impotent to prevent the enormous wave of sentiment on the opposite side the year before. "A great and general alarm appears to have been given to the citizens of Philadelphia and New York," reported the *American Daily Advertiser* of Philadelphia, "by the proceedings of the House of Representatives, on the British Treaty. Business is almost suspended. Apprehending a war with England, should the Treaty not be put into operation, the several insurance companies have stopped underwriting; the banks have ceased discounting; and American produce has become almost stagnant in market." The *Columbian Centinel* issued a special supplement entitled "THE CRISIS," which described meetings in Boston, Salem, Marblehead, Newburyport, Newbury, Lynn, Hingham, and Gloucester, and declared that if the representatives should withhold the appropriations, "and involve their country in a war, they will find, to their confusion, that they have not acted in conformity with the sentiments of their constituents, and will draw upon themselves almost universal execration."[228]

From the West, petitions and protests had been coming in since early in March. A memorial from Otsego County, New York bore over five thousand signatures, with no more than ten freeholders opposed.[229] In Gallatin's district in the Pittsburgh area, Republicans and Federalists alike united in support of the treaty.[230] Gallatin had tried to argue that what the Westerners most wanted was really the Spanish treaty, and that their reason for demanding the British treaty was simply that they believed they could not get the one without the other. One of his correspondents hastened to set him straight, pointing out that petitions for the British treaty had begun circulating before anyone knew about the other. "But in which treaty," demanded a writer in the *Pittsburgh Gazette,* "has the western country the *most interest?* I think *in the British;* at least the most immediate interest."

> I would rather have the posts, and command of the Indians, and peace, until we get our country settled, than have the privilege of selling flour *without duty,* for a while. If we cannot get the command of the Indians, and keep them in peace, the descent of the river will be disturbed; and though the Spaniards make it open, the Indians will make it shut; and come upon our settlements, and hinder our making flour; so that we shall not have much to take to market. . . . I do not know that war will be the consequence generally: But it will to the western country. I mean an *Indian war.* In the course of twelve months at the farthest, we shall be where we were. . . .[231]

It was against this background that the climactic stage of the debate took place during the last two and a half weeks of April. A Federalist move by Theodore Sedgwick to combine all four of the treaties—Indian, Spanish, Algerine, and British—in one appropriation bill was blocked by deft management on Gallatin's part, and the first three were passed separately on April 14.[232] All the familiar arguments on the British treaty, for and against, thereupon began pouring forth. The treaty's supporters warned that war and even disunion might follow a failure to execute it; opponents declared these empty threats. The spokesmen for the frontier interest, John Williams and William Cooper, both insisted that the peace and prosperity of the West depended on repossessing the posts; the alternative, as Cooper put it, was to be "destroyed by an Indian war, supported by Canada."[233]

By April 22 it was evident that the anti-treaty majority was slipping, as Samuel Smith of Maryland openly defected, announcing "that notwithstanding the many objections he had to the Treaty, yet he would give his consent to carry it into effect in a Constitutional manner," because, among other things, it now appeared "to be the opinion of the great majority of the people of Maryland, whom he had the honor to represent," that fewer evils would come from adopting than from rejecting it.[234] Gallatin on April 26 (though he too was under great pressure from his constituents) made the most comprehensive of all the attacks on the treaty. He questioned it article by article, denying "that a single commercial advantage had been obtained," and insisted that the British right to trade with the Indians would eliminate the advantage of the Americans' occupying the posts. He especially resented the treaty's having removed such weapons of coercion as sequestration of debts and commercial discrimination, "for fear they might be abused by ourselves." The alarm of war, moreover, came only from men who had formed "such a habit of carrying every measure of Government as they pleased, that they really thought that everything must be thrown into confusion the moment they were thwarted in a matter of importance."[235]

Two days later, word began to spread that Fisher Ames of Massachusetts, racked by illness throughout the session and heretofore silent, was at last about to say something in defense of the treaty. The galleries were full as the ashen-faced Ames rose, dressed all in black. "I entertain the hope, perhaps a rash one," he faltered, "that my strength will hold me out to speak a few minutes." Then for an hour and a half he proceeded to show that he could still perform the part, without notes to prompt him, of the wiliest demagogue in the House.

He played upon the two solemn themes of violated faith and war, the two dire consequences of the House's refusal to carry out its duty. The House, he said, was about to break a treaty, constitutionally made and ratified, even with the voice of the people unmistakably raised against "the non-performance of our engagements." In so doing, we say to the victims of $5 million in spoliations that they shall have no remedies; in refusing the posts, we tell frontiersmen that their safety is denied and their settlements not to be extended. Even if Great Britain had granted everything, the treaty's enemies would still be unsatisfied. Any treaty would offend them, even one that merely "left King George his island," and even "if he stipulated to pay rent for it." Who can believe that with no posts and no treaty, the frontier could possibly remain secure? "In the day time, your path through the woods is ambushed; the darkness of midnight will glitter with the blaze of your dwellings. You are a father: the blood of your sons shall fatten your corn-field! You are a mother: the war-whoop shall wake the sleep of the cradle!" Today "we render account to the widows and orphans whom our decision will make; to the wretches that will be roasted at the stake"; already (the speaker sepulchrally warned), "I can fancy that I listen to the yells of savage vengeance, and the shrieks of torture." Is this the kind of peace they mean to give us? And now, Ames gasped in conclusion, should the House refuse this appropriation, "even I, slender and almost broken as my hold on life is, may outlive the Government and Constitution of my country."[236]

It was quite an effort, bringing tears, John Adams reported, to many of those present. As the orator dropped to his seat amid the din and babble, there were Federalist shouts of "the Question!" But the Republicans rallied to stave it off, and the House adjourned to the following day.[237]

On the 29th Speaker Jonathan Dayton of New Jersey told the House that although he had never liked the treaty he now believed the public good would be best served by allowing it to go into operation. "The effects of a rejection," he counseled, "would operate like a subtle poison, which . . . would quickly insinuate itself into the system, and affect the whole mass." Commerce, shipbuilding, navigation, agriculture, the frontier, "public faith and private credit," all would be touched by it. (He might also have mentioned his lately receiving word from home that the people of New Jersey "would tear any of their representatives to pieces who should vote against the treaty.")[238] Finally a Republican from Maryland, Gabriel Christie, who had opposed the treaty all along, rose and said that "though he thought the Treaty a bad one, his constituents were desirous it should be carried into effect, and he found himself bound to lay aside his own opinion, and act according to their will."[239]

The question was then put, and the House divided, 49–49. The Chairman of the Committee of the Whole, Frederick A. Muhlenberg, a Republican from Pennsylvania, broke the tie to carry the question to the House in open session. It was now evident that the funds would be voted. The next day, April 30, there was a final Republican attempt, through a motion offered by Henry Dearborn, to declare the treaty "highly objectionable" even while agreeing to the appropriation. It failed by the casting vote of Speaker Dayton. Then to the great joy and relief of the Federalists, the appropriation finally passed, 51–48, and the treaty was at last safe.[240]

James Madison had been greatly shaken. He had sat mute during the last two weeks of debate ("wrapt in his mantle of doubts and problems," as one member put it), while leadership of the Republican forces passed, for the time being at least, from his hands to those of Albert Gallatin. "The Banks," he bitterly told Jefferson, "have been powerfully felt in the progress of the petitions in the Cities for the Treaty."[241] Other irreconcilables accounted for the result in much the same way. The Federalists, according to Bache's *Aurora,* had been "armed with all the terrors of Banks and Discounts and with all the influence which wealth can give."[242] And yet it may be doubted whether it was really big money in the cities that had killed Madison's majority. It was small money circulating everywhere and shared by all, which a revived Spirit of 1776 had threatened to dry up at its sources.

Still, amid the general jubilation there was one faint note of Federalist foreboding. "The appeal to the people by the disorganizers the last summer," ruminated John Fenno in his editorial chair, "was a gross violation offered to Freedom of Deliberation, in the constituted authorities." The more recent appeal by "the friends of the Constitution" was of course less so, being in support of the law of the land. Yet that too was improper. It was unknown to the regular proceedings of government, and liable to be "misused and perverted to dangerous purposes."[243] Who could tell where it all might lead?

The Populist Impulse

"Democracy" was not to emerge as a fully legitimate cultural value in America, commanding more or less universal approval, until the 1830s, with the appearance of a national system of mass political parties. Yet as early as the mid-1790s with the agitation stirred by the French Revolution and the Jay Treaty, one already sees a clear turn in the direction of popular politics. Beyond doubt popular attitudes and popular participation took on qualities and proportions—a "populist impulse" became discernible—which had not quite been there before. But a "populist impulse" is not the same thing as functional democracy. Due account must be taken of the limits and inhibitions within which popular politics in the 1790s still operated.

I

The Democratic Societies

The fate of the Democratic Societies, between the first enthusiastic emergence of so many of these groups in 1793–94 and their utter disappearance within the following year or so, invites questions about the whole subject of voluntary associations in America. Voluntary associations are mentioned from time to time throughout our historical literature, though for the most part rather casually. This lack of attention is curious, inasmuch as few features of American society struck Tocqueville more forcibly in the 1830s than the proliferation of its associational life. Whatever the reasons, these associations still tend to be taken largely for granted; some have been examined piecemeal, but they have not been studied systematically; and there is surprisingly little in the way of a general theory on that subject.[1]

It has of course been pointed out that by means of voluntary associations in America a variety of religious, economic, fraternal, humanitarian, and political ends have been achieved, without coercion and under no official auspices of the state, to an extent unparalleled in any other national civilization. The device is one peculiarly characteristic of American society. It has been said that Americans have historically been a "nation of joiners," a term which is a kind of shorthand for the wide and complex variety of functions these associations have fulfilled in the ongoing current of American life. That is, they have had not only a very stark instrumental character, having in so many cases been brought into being to effect specific and immediate objects; they have in addition provided a diffuse but impressive range of non-specific, non-immediate satisfactions for the individuals who organized or joined them.[2]

All this has been true for at least 150 years, and quite possibly for more. But what is less apparent is that there may have been a time when it was not true. There may have been an era in the American past when such associations did not generally exist, when they were not regarded as obvious or logical responses to public, private, or individual needs, when social values had little place for them, and when social habits may actually have discouraged and even resisted them. It would seem that useful generalizations about an emerging social process would need to take account not only of the forces impelling it but also of those obstructing it.

We do not have much information on these questions, and an initial test would probably require casting a fairly wide net. One revealing point at which to do it might be the society of mid-eighteenth-century New England.

The representative community of that age, according to Michael Zuckerman, was the hamlet or village, an entity so small and self-contained that it could not afford any appreciable degree of conflict or contention. All its social values emphasized peace, and its rudimentary institutional structure—the church and town meeting in particular—was organized not so much to "manage" conflict as simply to absorb and perhaps even to evade it. The urge was toward settling potentially divisive issues informally before they became matters of open contention; the town meeting was seen not primarily as a forum for debating issues but rather as a device for exacting consent. Nor was majority consent enough. The ideal was unanimity; the town could not afford disaffected minorities. The suffrage, moreover, was very broad, not out of any great attachment to "democratic" principles but because of its usefulness in "consolidating a consensus." Even the practice of open confession in church of one's misdoings (among the worst of which were threats to the peace) was part of the same process, involving as it did "a curbing of . . . pride, a denial of the individual will, and an affirmation of the primacy of public values over any possible private ones." And the most infamous form which conflict in a community could take was faction and party, a kind of iniquity which, according to Jonathan Edwards, left men's souls "destitute."[3]

If a community could not afford conflict, by the same token it could not afford much diversity either. Anything in the way of particular combinations or interest groups within the community would be regarded with apprehension. They subtracted something from its homogeneity, from the sense of its own harmony; communities could not as a rule support a wide range of social roles or differentiation of labor. (For example, the appearance of a substantial commercial element in a town of farmers could lead the town to seek its own partition, as in the case of Newbury and Newburyport.)[4] A society whose collective decisions are governed by a value-system of this nature seems not to provide a very receptive soil for a variety of associational activities, reflecting as they would corresponding divisions of interest within the community. Such associations and such diversity were on the whole neither needed nor desired in the communal life of pre-Revolutionary Massachusetts. When they did appear, they appeared first in Boston and at places in the coastal area most susceptible to cosmopolitan influences.[5] But it is unlikely that their appearance anywhere went unresisted, which is to say that the urge for homogeneity and unanimity was not abandoned lightly.

Though their first real cycle of growth did not occur until after the Revolution, voluntary associations certainly were not unknown before that time. The first ones throughout the colonies in general were in the realm of religion, where the will to impose conformity could not be maintained in the face of numerous contrary tendencies and interests. In a province where there was an established church—one receiving official public support, which was the case in all but two of them—and if a dissenting church should also be admitted to exist (not on principle but out of necessity and experience), then that church could exist on one basis only. It must make its way as a voluntary association of like-minded individuals, supported solely by their private resources and exertions. But that is hardly to say, as the Anglicans found in New England and the Baptists in Virginia, that they ever received a wholehearted welcome from the rest of the community.[6]

Just as with religion, there were at first no familiar categories in which organized business enterprises might readily be conceived apart from the enveloping aegis of the state. The chartered company in Tudor and Stuart England had received privileges, protection, and monopolies from the Crown in return for which it became an adjunct to state power and a promoter of state interests. Translated to the colonies, the habits of mind which had accompanied this tradition underwent many modifications, but they persisted in some form, however attenuated, well after independence. The interests and well-being of the Crown had been replaced by a generalized conception of the public good, and it was with reference to this—so the assumption went—that charters of incorporation would henceforth be granted. And yet this "commonwealth" ideal, as Oscar and Mary Handlin have called it, was beset by anomalies. The Revolutionary heritage had sharpened certain public values that included an abhorrence of special privileges and monopolies; at the same time, it was found less and less easy to determine for any given purpose what the public good was. This meant a corresponding difficulty in deciding that the advantages of incorporation should be extended to some groups and denied to others.

Entrepreneurs seeking special charters naturally looked more to the benefits than to the restraints, but with competition everywhere around them they found most of the traditional benefits to be illusory, except for the legal one of limited liability, and they learned to do without them. The enactment of general incorporation laws in the nineteenth century was the ultimate recognition that a government charter no longer brought with it any exclusiveness. With government making no discriminations among them, business enterprises had in effect become private voluntary associations, making their own decisions and dependent on their own unaided efforts. The "commonwealth" ideal had thus faded, but it had taken a long time to do so. Though the usefulness of the private corporation in the country's development had become apparent very early, there remained a characteristic suspicion of privately organized power functioning outside the control of the community at large. There was thus a residue of resistance to the full meaning of this kind of voluntary association and to the idea that if the government did not help, neither should it hinder.[7]

We have sufficient evidence, in the period following the Revolution, of a variety of voluntary associations, for philanthropic and benevolent as well as social and fraternal objects, for concluding that it was not until then that such associations generally began to appear in appreciable numbers. Richard D. Brown finds this to be the case with Massachusetts, and adds that Tocqueville's observations about the extent and prevalence of voluntary associations in the 1830s "would have been drastically out of place in the decade preceding the Revolution." More specifically, according to a study of late eighteenth-century Concord, it was in the 1790s that the associational life of the town became noticeably more lively, and something similar evidently occurred in Salem at about the same time. This seems to have been the decade in which the associational impulse was first generally felt.[8]

Some efforts have been made to correlate the growth of voluntary associations with the process variously described as "modernization," or "the rise of a market society," or "the advent of a capitalist order," a process which involved the intensification, over time, of technological development, social and economic complexity, and specialization of function. Various theorists have described it in various ways. It is usually seen as a series of transformations, each with reference to some sort of dichotomy: from stability to movement and change, from localism to cosmopolitanism, from local to supra-local systems of marketing and communication, and so on. There are changes in individual relationships, personality structure, and social behavior. They go from "status" to "contract"; from "natural relationships" to "money relationships"; from *Gemeinschaft* (communal and organic units) to *Gesellschaft* (abstract, impersonal, limited social aggregations); and from behavioral responses which are qualitative and "affective" to those which are instrumental and neutral. There is both a widening of horizons and a diversification — or fragmentation — of social objects.[9]

Thus it may be supposed that when communities no longer moved as a unit to achieve their purposes, and supra-local claims began competing with local ones, individuals reallocated their energies in certain very striking ways. As Tocqueville put it, in such a society as America's "all the citizens are independent and feeble; they can do hardly anything by themselves, and none of them can oblige his fellow men to lend him their assistance. They all, therefore, become powerless if they do not learn voluntarily to help one another." As a result, they form associations for every imaginable purpose. This tendency was new enough that William Ellery

Channing in 1829—two years before Tocqueville's visit—could still write with some astonishment that "one of the most remarkable circumstances or features of our age is the energy with which the principle of combination, or of action by joint forces, by associated numbers, is manifesting itself."

> You can scarcely name an object for which some institution has not been formed. Would men spread one set of opinions or crush another? They make a society. Would they improve the penal codes or relieve poor debtors? They make societies. Would one class encourage horse-racing, and another discourage travelling on Sunday? They form societies.[10]

Channing placed his primary emphasis, as would Tocqueville shortly thereafter, on associations formed for specific purposes and for accomplishing specific objects. But there was another kind, as Thomas Handasyd Perkins noted in 1838, formed not for any particular object but intended simply "to unite men by acquaintance, common interests, and brotherly sympathy. . . ." It seems to have been this kind of association—the principal function of which was that of individual gratification, of providing a mode whereby individuals might locate themselves in an ever-shifting society—that Page Smith had in mind in asserting that the most dramatic phase of associational activity really did not begin until after the Civil War.[11]

But the time was, coming back to the early days of the American republic, when the forming of associations was still a novel form of social action. The Framers did not think to put "freedom of association" anywhere in the Constitution, nor did it appear in the Bill of Rights, nor did anyone even propose that it should. Such a guarantee has since been construed to have been there implicitly all along, but this point is at least debatable. There was no such thing as a general rule of law that applied directly to the forming of associations, since the problem was still too new for people to have given any appreciable thought to it.[12] At any rate, the climate was by no means unequivocally hospitable, as it largely would be by Channing's and Tocqueville's time, and there was certainly one kind of association to which there was still great resistance. This was the society, or combination, or club, formed for political purposes. Such a combination bespoke faction; it seemed to stand as a challenge to the constituted agencies, authorities, and procedures of government; and it remained, in some elusive sense, outside the community's control.

Perhaps the most striking form taken by the various associational activities of the 1790s was the phenomenon of the Democratic-Republican Societies. Though the principle of "modernization," or something like it, might be very useful in considering the growth of voluntary associations in America over the long cycle, it will not quite cover the case here. Something more circumstantial and more immediate was at work; these societies, and perhaps other kinds as well, might simply be thought of as being among the unanticipated first fruits of nationhood.

Hundreds of thousands of people were now seeing each other, addressing each other, and questioning each other in a new social role, newly assumed, that of citizen-members of a newly constituted federal republic. Judging, for example, from the enormous growth in the number of post offices and newspapers during the decade of the 1790s, the urge to talk to each other, write to each other, and harangue each other was more than a casual impulse.[13] They were testing in any number of ways what this new role meant and what it ought to mean: how they should talk and think as republican citizens, "republic" itself being a novel fact in the civic universe. Precisely where, with their visions and aspirations, did they, or any particular person, fit in it? The sovereignty of the people was now officially established doctrine. What did it mean in practice, and how was it to be expressed?

As we have already seen, no influence in the entire contemporary world could have been more critical in elevating the national self-esteem, or in giving a special sharpness to the question of national self-definition, than the events of the French Revolution. The utmost pitch of popular emotion was reached in the early months of 1793 with the news of France's having at last emulated the American example and become a republic, of the initial successes of the French armies against their continental enemies, of France's entering upon war with America's own ancient oppressor England, and of the arrival of Citizen Genet, the Republic's first minister to the United States. But along with the jubilation went a piercing anxiety: republican liberty was on trial and under siege. It was in this excited setting that the Democratic Societies began making their appearance. The most prominent of them, as well as one of the very earliest, was the Democratic Society of Pennsylvania, organized at Philadelphia in May 1793.

It has been asserted that these societies were erected more on native American than on foreign precedents, the Sons of Liberty of the 1770s being cited as the primary example. But if the strength of the Revolutionary organizations derived from their reflecting the sense of a united community, as in so many cases they did, then the example could be misleading, since no such claims could be made for the Democratic Societies.[14] Most of the societies' immediate inspiration actually came from France, and in deference to the fraternal sentiments believed to subsist between the two peoples a general effort was understandably made to impart to their doings a certain French accent. The Jacobin clubs of France, with which they were widely compared at the time, had not yet acquired the full odium that would befall them in later stages of the Revolution. "Citizen," as a title of address, was universally adopted by the clubs' members, just as the French themselves had already done.[15] The term "democratic," already entrenched in France's revolutionary vocabulary, was suggested to the Philadelphia group by Citizen Genet as a name for their society, though this was not the one they had originally intended to use.[16] Indeed, the word "democratic" was still somewhat premature in America. It was no more than partially domesticated; it still served as something of a taunting reproach; the better part of a generation would have to pass before it could assume an undisputedly honorific status in the public language.

A principal theme in their statements of purpose was simply the importance of discussion, the exchange of views, the spread of information. Ignorance, they asserted, was "the irreconcilable enemy of Liberty." "Thus it is, that from want of information, the moral features of a state become distorted. . . ."[17] Another theme, repeatedly stressed, was patriotism: "the love of their country, and a respect for its Laws and Constitution." The societies believed it necessary, if republican principles were to be upheld, "not only to discuss the proceedings of Government, but to examine into the conduct of its officers in every department."[18] And the most pervasive sentiment of all: "we view with inexpressible horror the cruel and unjust war carried on by the combined powers of Europe" against France—and this "spirit of domination" (according to the constitution of the Baltimore society) "excites a well grounded apprehension, that America is implicated in the fate of the French republic." The despots of Europe, determined to extinguish republicanism in France, would not be satisfied until they had stifled it everywhere, and there were men in our very midst lying in wait to give them assistance. They "are secretly endeavouring to destroy those fundamental principles of liberty and equality, on which are founded the happiness and security of mankind." All of this demanded ceaseless vigilance. "The eyes of the republican patriot must ever be watchful; and as many characters have crept in among us, who are not *with us,* their steps should be carefully watched. . . ."[19] About ten of the societies were formed in 1793, and more than twice that many (further inspired by the British outrages which led eventually to the Jay mission) made their appearance the following year. There were some thirty-five in all, with one or more in every state except Rhode Island and Georgia.[20]

Did the societies see themselves as appendages to the newly emerging Republican party? One would certainly not suppose so from their announced principles, or even assume that they approved of parties at all. They professed to be "unbiased by any party views, and actuated solely by patriotic motives." Indeed, they spoke the language of the past when they declared that any attempt "to influence the vote of a freeman, either by the wily arts of promised favor, or by base calumniation," should be spurned "with contempt and abhorrence."[21] They piously insisted, moreover, that harmony should prevail, that there should be no divisions, that the people formed "one joint, equal community," and that "the political errors or misapprehensions of a part, must, consequently, injure the whole." It was therefore the duty of every member "not only to remove prejudices, to conciliate the affections, to inform the understanding, and to promote the happiness of all our Fellow Citizens;—but to *detect* and *publish* to the world, every violation of our Constitutions, or instance of Mal-Administration."[22] This last sentiment, which appeared in some form in the resolutions of each of the societies, of course meant that for all their protestations about being free from the prejudice of party, they had by definition cast themselves in an opposition role from the first. To put it in another way, there were very few Federalists in the Democratic Societies.

As to just what sorts of people joined them, it seems there was quite a variety—up to a point. Eugene Link's inclination, in his study of fifty years ago, to accord a major representation to the humbler orders has been shown by more recent scrutiny to have been exaggerated. There were a great many more persons of wealth and power than was formerly supposed, even if most Federalists thought of them all as rabble. The officers of the societies—as has always been known—

were a fairly tight group, virtually without exception men of considerable substance. In the West they consisted of large landholders, with speculator types being especially prominent. The large "craftsman" category was exceedingly fluid, the Philadelphia group, for example, containing many such who were well on their way to becoming "manufacturers," held turnpike shares, invested in city lots, and owned the houses they lived in. There was nothing comparable to a "lower orders" mentality in the ranks of the societies (out of 207 members of the Philadelphia society whose occupations are known, only 2 are listed as "laborers"); the mechanics and manufacturers alike, according to Roland Baumann, "were very mobile, commercial minded, and status conscious."[23] It is probably safe to assume that the membership from top to bottom was characterized by energy, restlessness, and ambition, and that they were a determined, self-assertive, upward-moving lot. What they wanted for themselves was less a matter of justice and a helping hand than of notice and recognition.

As for the officers and other more conspicuous members, there seems to have hovered over a number of these men, however affluent or influential they may have been or later became, a touch of social outsidership. Though cause and consequence are not always easy to discriminate, the Philadelphia Democratic Society offers some intriguing cases. Alexander James Dallas, still a British subject at the close of the Revolution, came to Philadelphia in the early 1780s to establish himself through the practice of law. He went at it very purposefully, but since business did not come flooding to him right away, he had to support himself and his young bride for a time by writing and editing on the side. Nor were his ingratiating manners quite enough to get him into the best social circles, hard as he tried. (He and the charming Maria gave extravagant parties which they could not afford.) His great opportunity arrived in 1791 when his not inconsiderable talents came to the notice of the Governor, the popular Thomas Mifflin, who was seeking a suitable person to appoint as Secretary of the Commonwealth, a position which, properly managed, potentially carried with it a good deal of influence. The appointment was made in order — among other reasons — to avoid factionalism, Dallas having up to then shown little interest in politics. This stroke of luck did indeed set the young climber on his way, but it did not in the fullest sense make him an insider. He was still being referred to eight years later as one of the "leaches of society."[24]

Benjamin F. Bache, eventually the journalistic scourge of the Federalists though originally a strong supporter of the Constitution, would have loved to be taken into the federal establishment when the seat of government moved to Philadelphia in 1790. But the Bache family was unlucky. Benjamin's father, Richard Bache, had been dismissed as Postmaster of Pennsylvania in 1781 and had pleaded, without success, to be appointed Postmaster-General in the federal government in 1789. Benjamin's great patron was his grandfather, the honored Franklin — honored, that is, everywhere but among the elite of Philadelphia. Franklin's death in 1790 left the young man inconsolable. But his grandfather had established him in the printing business with the best equipment available, and his newspaper, the *General Advertiser* — later the notorious *Aurora* — made a good appearance.

He applied for the government's printing but was turned down. As a youth Benjamin Bache (later to be known as "Lightning Rod Junior") had been well behaved and anxious to please; as a beginning newspaper editor he had taken a generally moderate line in politics. But he never quite found the right formula for success, and in 1793 something quite evidently snapped.[25]

Doctor Benjamin Rush had been known all over town for years. Rush had a huge practice, and he has been called "the most influential physician in the history of American medicine down to the Civil War." Yet his self-pity was boundless. ("*Expect* to be persecuted for doing good," he told Noah Webster with gloomy pleasure, "and *learn* to rejoice in persecution.") The rich and powerful had done what they could to keep him from getting ahead. He lacked the "patronage of a great man"; he had no "extensive and powerful family connections"; and he "found it difficult to forget," according to his biographer, "that he was the son of a gunsmith, that his mother ran a grocery store, that he was a Presbyterian in a city whose elite were Quakers and Anglicans."[26] Stephen Girard, Blair McClenachan, and John Swanwick were among the richest men in North America. Girard (who may have been *the* richest) was probably an exile from society by his own choice. He was wall-eyed, spoke with a thick French accent, and shrank from ridicule. He regarded the elite with a furtive sourness, and even his fellow-merchants gossiped about the miserly single-mindedness with which he pursued money. He would leave his wealth to public causes rather than allow any particular persons to get near it.[27] Blair McClenachan had come from Ireland as a young man and had made stupendous profits in privateering during the Revolution, becoming the city's leading investor in that specialty. He was a partner of Robert Morris during the 1780s; he bought Cliveden, the great country seat of former Attorney-General Benjamin Chew, then somewhat down on his luck, and occupied it in baronial opulence for eighteen years. But McClenachan was congenitally uncouth, and never established himself in Philadelphia's most refined precincts. When Robert Morris went to debtor's prison in 1798, the sheriff's writ was issued in the name of a vengeful Blair McClenachan.[28] John Swanwick was very rich and very small. He was forever having to overcome obstacles, which with certain important exceptions he usually managed to do. His father gained notoriety during the Revolution as a Tory wagonmaster, which placed the youth John under frequent suspicion as he made his way up through Robert Morris's counting house. But he became a Morris partner in 1783, then a leading import-export merchant, and a director and leading shareholder in the Bank of North America. He was dandified, wore big cravats, and was "duck-legged"; he gave discourses to ladies' academies and was highly active in the City Dancing Assembly. He was not, however, successful in obtaining appointive office in 1789 or 1790 despite having been a strong Federalist. Nor could he buy his way into Philadelphia's highest society, "because he was an arriviste who lacked breeding and family."[29]

These men, all of whom joined the Democratic Society, had one thing in common if nothing else. They were all self-made, and their achievements were not fully appreciated by those who had got in a little ahead of them.[30] Finally, it is undoubtedly true that few if any Federalists joined the Democratic Societies, and that almost all the members turn out to have been Republicans. But not, it seems, very important Republicans. With certain notable exceptions, surprisingly few members of the Democratic Societies ever reached positions of prominence in public office or in Republican politics. And conversely, the leading Republicans in all the states tended to stay well clear of the Democratic Societies. Jefferson, Madison, Monroe, Giles, and the other Virginians would have nothing to do with them; in Maryland there were no Smith brothers, in New York no Burrs, Clintons, or Livingstons, in the societies' ranks.[31]

And there was at least one good reason for this. There seem to have been strong underlying doubts everywhere—the members themselves were not untouched by them—as to just how legitimate the societies actually were. They were questioned from the first, and Washington's subsequent expletive phrase "self-created societies" did not originate with him at all, being part of the common currency. Judge Jonathan Sayward of York, Maine, was impressed when he read the circular of the Pennsylvania Society early in 1794, but he was opposed to any "self-created clubb."[32] "Self-created" implied a real threat to the sovereignty of the people, and the charged quality of the phrase was exactly caught in a letter to the *New York Daily Gazette* in February 1794. "Do the people require intermediary guides betwixt them and the constituted authorities?" the writer demanded. "Do they associate to electioneer . . . or to prevent others from doing it? Above all, Mr. Printer, I ask, Are they chosen by the people? If not, as I know no other authority, I shall hereafter regard them as self-creators, as a branch, perhaps, of the Jacobin Society of Paris."[33] Another correspondent insisted that he was

> no tory, no British agent, no speculator. He is a native American, an old whig of 1775, a plebean, educated in the country on a farm, where his friends follow the plough for a living; he is not connected with an Englishman nor Frenchman on earth, and hopes he never shall be. He never owned a shilling in the funds and is under no influence but that of truth and integrity; a real lover to his country and its republican government. He knows the general opinion of the middling class of people about the country, and he knows that they generally reprobate Democratic Societies; considering them merely as Genet's scouting parties.[34]

Even if most of the societies' attackers had been Federalists, or if all of them had been enemies of liberty as the societies themselves claimed, the fact remains that the tone taken by the societies in referring to such attacks was not exactly a tone of confidence. They kept saying that their association needed no excuses. There "can be no necessity of an apology to the public," said one. "We make no apology," said another, "for thus associating ourselves. . . ." "It is unnecessary," protested the Democratic Society of Chittenden County, Vermont, "for us to demonstrate our undoubted right to form this association"—but since there might be "some few really virtuous Republicans, who while they fully acknowledged the right, seem to doubt the propriety of such Associations at present," the Society thought it as well to go ahead and argue the case anyway, and did so at some length.[35]

Any attempt to assess the societies' actual functions raises puzzles. They are sometimes referred to as "pressure groups," which in one or two limited instances they may have been.[36] But the closer one looks at the records that have survived of their activities and resolutions as organized bodies, the less one is impressed by evidence of sustained group purpose. There were, of course, strong affirmations of sympathy with the struggles of the French Republic, with a few expressions of disapproval of Washington's Neutrality Proclamation of 1793.[37] There were resolutions of indignation at British maritime outrages, their stirring up of the Indians, and their allowing the Algerian pirates to prey on American shipping in the Atlantic.[38] They condemned the appointment of John Jay as special envoy to London, and those societies still active in mid-1795 passed resolutions of protest against the treaty Jay sent back.[39] Two of them went on record in support of public schools; two others favored reform of the courts and criminal codes.[40] Several disapproved of the federal whiskey excise, but explicitly opposed any use of force in resisting it.[41] The Pennsylvania Society endorsed a popular local demand, that of protection for native manufactures.[42] The Charleston Society seems to have made promises to aid in Genet's Florida schemes; this was all talk and no action.[43] The closest any of them came to concentrated and purposeful effort was the memorials and addresses a number of the western societies prepared with the object of securing the navigation of the Mississippi.[44]

But again, by the end of 1795 most of the societies that had been begun in 1793 and 1794 had either gone out of existence or become inactive: how is their disappearance to be accounted for? The best-known explanation is that they simply withered under the wrath of Washington, as vented in the latter's message to Congress of November 1794 at the conclusion of the Whiskey Insurrection in western Pennsylvania. This formula actually has much to be said for it—though not quite everything. The societies' position in the communities where they existed seems never to have been very substantial in the first place.[45] They came into being in a burst of enthusiasm for France and of hatred for England; but once past that, the claims they were able to make on community loyalty were actually rather tenuous. It seems that these "popular" societies never did have a great degree of popular support. For a further test of this, and of other aspects of popular politics, we might now turn to events in western Pennsylvania in the year 1794.

2

The Whiskey Insurrection

There was nothing spurious about the state of feeling in the four westernmost counties of Pennsylvania—Allegheny, Westmoreland, Fayette, and Washington— against the federal government in the summer of 1794. Sentiment in that area had in fact been building up for the previous three years, taking the form of a bitter and widespread hostility to the federal excise on whiskey. In view of the numbers involved, and inasmuch as the entire region appeared on the verge of armed rebellion by midsummer, one can only conclude that this feeling had struck deep in every community, and may thus be regarded as an authentic popular manifestation. One question, then, is that of how things could have come to such a pass. The other: once the federal government decided at length to act, how was it that reconciliation and resolution could have been effected so swiftly?

On the face of it, the leading facts are fairly straightforward. They begin with the passage in Congress of the excise law of March 3, 1791, with bipartisan support, the excise being intended as part of the revenue structure which was to sustain the Treasury's funding system. The law was denounced in the Pennsylvania legislature, and resolutions condemning it were carried in the lower house by a large majority. Meetings of protest were held in several places during the summer of 1791, and the resolutions passed at the one in Washington County laid down a principle of action that was to prove significant. The citizens were called upon to treat all excisemen "with contempt, and absolutely refuse all kind of communication or intercourse" with the officers, and to withhold from them "all aid, support, or comfort."[46] There were several cases of violence, in which collectors and those who cooperated with them were tarred and feathered. These began in the fall of 1791 and resumed in the summer of 1792. A large public meeting at Pittsburgh in August 1792 produced a strong resolution against excise officers similar to that of the Washington County meeting of the year before. Albert Gallatin, who was secretary of the meeting, later repented having signed it, saying it had been his "only political sin."[47] Yet a fair number of other respectable persons were present who had done the same thing. Secretary of the Treasury Hamilton by this time was all for a show of federal force, but the President chose to limit himself to a proclamation calling upon the malcontents to desist from further obstructing the operation of the laws. The Supervisor of the Pennsylvania district, George Clymer, was sent out to report on conditions in the Fourth Survey (which embraced the western counties), to encourage the excise officers in their duty, and to exert persuasion upon the citizens to obey the law. Clymer's mission was not very successful. He reported that nearly the whole Survey was disaffected, and cited the influence of Albert Gallatin, John Smilie, and William Findley—together with others more violent, such as David Bradford and James Marshall of Washington County—in arousing local feeling.[48] 1793 was quieter than the preceding year, though there were several outbreaks in Fayette County, the collector there being an especially obnoxious person.

The year of climax was 1794. Two Democratic Societies had meanwhile been formed in the area, one at Washington Town and the other at Mingo Creek—the latter, according to Hugh Henry Brackenridge, being the "cradle of the insurrection." Violence was now being widened to reach not only excise officers but those distillers inclined, or suspected of being inclined, to comply with the law. They were visited with tar and feathers or barn-burning, and some had their stills shot full of holes, a technique drolly referred to as the still's having been "mended" by "Tom the Tinker." Handbills of warning from Tom the Tinker began appearing everywhere. Tom's object was to force the excise offices to close, and meanwhile to prevent any distillers from coming in to enter their stills as the law required to be done in June of each year.

The final provocation for a general outbreak was the serving of processes on a number who had failed to register their stills in June of 1793. One of the most irritating features of the 1791 law was the provision that cases of violation be tried at the United States District Court in Philadelphia, an excessive distance for anyone in the Fourth Survey. To remove this hardship the law had recently been amended, effective June 5, 1794, to enable cases arising in places fifty miles or more from the district court to be cognizable in the state courts. The amended law was not, however, made retroactive, so that these particular processes were served under the old law.

Major violence erupted after the United States Marshal, David Lenox, and the Inspector of Excise for the Fourth Survey, General John Neville, had served the last of the writs in Allegheny County, where Neville's house was located. On July 16, 1794, about five hundred men, members of the Mingo Creek and other militia units who happened to be assembling for a muster, converged on Neville's house at Bower Hill with the object of forcing the Inspector to resign his commission. The place was defended by Neville and members of his household, assisted by a handful of soldiers from the nearby military post, in the course of which two of the besiegers were killed, including their commander, and six others wounded. After the defenders made their escape, the cellar was looted and the house burned. Marshal Lenox was taken captive in order to prevent his serving any more processes. The culminating event was the great gathering of militia companies called by insurgent leaders for August 1 at Braddock's Field, a few miles outside Pittsburgh. Some six thousand men converged there; they held a grand review and put on a menacing display of massed force. Some wanted to wreak destruction on the town of Pittsburgh, where Neville's headquarters was situated, though the dispersal on the second day was effected without any such extreme action. Nevertheless the month of August was taken up with meetings and consultations, and the air was full of rumors, extending as far as secession and civil war.

Meanwhile the federal government had determined to act. In a new proclamation of August 7, Washington announced his intention to call out the militia in order to suppress disorder and enforce the law. At the same time he undertook a final effort short of force, which was to send out commissioners with power to offer amnesty in return for an oath of submission. Upon reaching the scene, the commissioners were not satisfied that the rebellious communities were fully prepared to submit, whereupon the large force of militia from eastern Pennsylvania, Maryland, Virginia, and New Jersey which had meanwhile been mobilizing was now, September 25, ordered to march. But by the time the first of these units arrived in the Pittsburgh area in late October, all signs of rebellion had vanished.

Such were the principal events of the so-called Whiskey Insurrection. But as to how those events ought to be interpreted and accounted for, the available versions of them show a number of sharp discrepancies. We have for practical purposes two contemporary versions, both based on bodies of reasonably sound evidence. One is the work of the tireless Secretary of the Treasury, Alexander Hamilton; the other is by William Findley, the congressman from western Pennsylvania who took a part, though on the whole a moderate one, in that region's opposition to the federal excise. Hamilton's version is the one which public opinion accepted at the time. But Findley's is the one that has since been preferred by historians; that is, until fairly recently. Scholars in our own time have added touches to the picture that make it look more complicated now than it did then.

Hamilton's account is contained in an extended letter to George Washington, written early in August 1794 and published in the newspapers later that month. Its purpose, in addition to organizing the main facts for the President's convenience, was to justify to public opinion the steps which the government was about to take. He described the principal acts of violence in sufficient detail to show that the law could not be enforced in the ordinary course of judicial proceedings, and that it was necessary for the Executive to come to the aid of the judiciary. He went further, giving particular attention to the meetings that had preceded so many of these acts, to the men who organized them ("malcontent persons"), and especially to the resolutions they had passed. These were "calculated at once to confirm inflame and systematize the spirit of opposition." The real force behind the rebellion was not a burdensome tax (he showed, with his customary precision, how much less onerous and more reasonable the excise was for the government's purposes than was a tax of any other kind); rather, it was a group of organized conspirators determined to undermine the authority and influence of the government.[49]

Nor did their public resolutions have simply a passive character. These men had determined not merely to "forbear" compliance with the law; more significantly, "the anathema pronounced against the Officers of the Revenue placed them in a state of virtual outlawry"; it gave the signal for violence against their persons and property; and more significantly still, by widening the scope of the resolutions to include a whole series of questions "foreign to the object which had brought them together"—the salaries of public officials, the interest on the public debt, the establishment of a national bank, and so on—they were clearly aiming "to render the Government itself unpopular and odious." In short, these meetings had been organized by a small number of "active and designing leaders" in order to inflame the people "not against the particular laws in question, only, but . . . against the Government of the U States itself." Hamilton, it seems, was defining opposition to government policies—they also happened to be his policies—as subversion, as a threat to "the Government of the U States itself."[50]

But there is another dimension of Hamilton's report, one which probably struck a clearer echo in the public sensibility of the eighteenth century than it does in our own. This is the detailed emphasis the writer puts upon the government's restraint, its measured response to popular defiance of its authority, its avoidance of "the ultimate resort, till all the milder means had been tried without success." He proceeds with much care to describe the amending act of May 1792 which reduced duties and adjusted payments to the period of the year in which the still was in actual use; the President's proclamation of September 15, 1792, "earnestly admonishing and exhorting" to compliance with the law; the fruitless mission of Supervisor Clymer; and the government's decision to undertake no prosecutions in connection with the inflammatory Pittsburgh meeting of August 22, 1792. He outlined the comprehensive new plan devised for encouraging compliance without the use of force: the systematic prosecution of all who were clearly delinquent, the seizing of spirits being brought to market by non-complying distillers, and the purchase of whiskey for the army only from distillers who had paid the tax, all of which would presumably give them a strong interest in complying. But all to no avail. The very spirit of compliance which these measures might have encouraged inspired a contrary determination to impede the law at all costs, and thus the final sequence of violence that produced a state of open rebellion by 1794.[51]

The striking thing about this aspect of Hamilton's report (measures of government short of force) is the way in which it accepts the standard eighteenth-century Whig assumptions about mob action and the ways in which public author-ity—the restraints as well as the sanctions—is obliged to handle such action. Equally striking is that William Findley's narrative, intended as a direct challenge to Hamilton's version, proceeds on all the same assumptions. The argument is thus carried on from opposite sides within the same rules, the difference being not in the standards themselves but in how they should apply.

Americans of the late eighteenth century, in the light of their own historical experience, were not as frightened of mobs as they tended to become later on. Violence, when it occurred, was seldom indiscriminate; it was the exception rather than otherwise; and when it occurred at all it did so largely within limits. The presumption was that a normally law-abiding people did not take mob action without good cause, that if they did there must be injustice somewhere, and that within reason it behooved the authorities to do what they could to correct it. The idea was summed up in the late 1760s by Lieutenant-Governor Hutchinson of Massachusetts when he said that the people of his province "seldom, if ever, have assembled in a tumultuous manner unless they have been oppressed," and that "Mobs, a sort of them at least, are constitutional." But there, of course, was the rub. "A sort of them at least": it all depended. The emphasis was on prudence and respect for the law; and there was always the common-law prohibition of riot, defined by Blackstone as three or more persons combining to perform an unlawful act of violence for a private purpose. If the act were spontaneous and involved large numbers, the tendency was to excuse or extenuate it; but if it showed signs of deliberate organization, then it was faction and conspiracy. (This was where Hamilton rested his case.) A final implication in this line of thought was that whatever a man did, with or without provocation, he was answerable for it. If he were a leader in stirring up tumult, and if in the course of it he broke the law, he must be prepared to take the consequences. And if he were spared the consequences, it would be not through strict justice but through pardon and mercy.[52]

The precision of such "rules" was not their most prominent characteristic. William Findley, himself a participant, understandably had a very different version from Hamilton's of how the "insurrection" had come about and of how, consequently, the rules pertained to what had been done in the course of it. "Perhaps no part of the American character," Findley declared, "is more prominent than that of mildness of temper; even their mobs and riots are accompanied with less ferocity, and marked with fewer instances of bloodshed, than those of any other nation." And the western counties of Pennsylvania were no exception, considering the provocations to which the people there had been subjected. The initial one was an unreasonable and burdensome tax on whiskey on top of the low price per gallon already received by those who made it. (Findley did not repeat the whole argument, because everybody at the time had already heard it over and over: the farmers of western Pennsylvania had no choice but to distill much of their grain crop into whiskey because of the expense of hauling it over the mountains to the best markets, which were in the East; then, with the excise, they paid an additional penalty for having so converted it; the whiskey not transported to distant markets these people either consumed themselves or used for barter; and in any case the tax, which of course could not be paid in kind, had the effect of draining the region of badly needed cash, and fell indiscriminately on rich and poor.) And naturally they protested.[53]

The meetings held in 1791, however, were not conspiracies to circumvent the law. Indeed, one of them, Findley argued (with some sophistry), was even "intended to promote submission, and not opposition, to the law." Rather they represented an exercise of the people's right at any time to remonstrate against acts of government — excises, funding systems, or anything else — which they found obnoxious. He admitted that the language was at times intemperate, and that leaders ought in general to avoid unduly agitating the public mind. He even conceded that resolving to shun excise officers and to refuse them assistance was "morally wrong." But it was not illegal, and the people were much provoked.[54]

Yet Findley did draw the line at organized opposition, as in his references to Mingo Creek, where one of the Democratic Societies of the region had been formed. He would not defend any group that "imitated the language, and assumed the forms of regularly constituted authority"; and he made a distinction between "occasional societies," which were acceptable, and "permanent associations," which were dangerous. Here Findley was fully in line with the values of the time. Washington had made the same distinction, insisting that "no one denies the right of the people to meet occasionally" for petitioning or remonstrance, but that "a self created, *permanent* body" was another matter.[55]

Findley did not rest his final case on the injustice of the whiskey tax. The tax may have been odious but it was law, and law must in the last analysis be obeyed. Nor, indeed, did he claim that the law had been enforced harshly. It was rather that the government failed to administer the law with energy and decision. The law was enforced either not at all or else sporadically, or in a cowardly, or stupid, or provocative way. And the people's response was not the result of preconcerted and organized planning. It was spontaneous; they were goaded into it.

He described a whole series of incidents that served to arouse the popular wrath. There was the case of John Neville, a man of great weight and influence in the Pittsburgh area, who had been as vocal against the excise as anyone, had voted for the resolutions condemning it in the state legislature, and had then shocked the entire population by accepting the office of inspector and thereby "giving up his principles for a bribe, and bartering the confidence they had in him for money." This, together with the unpopularity of most of the collectors, confirmed the people in their tendency to see all excise officers as hateful in the nature of things. Then there was the cowardice of Supervisor George Clymer, who scarcely showed himself during his visit, who refused to go to those places where evidence of lawbreaking was most to be found, who stayed "but a few days at Pittsburgh" and "returned to Philadelphia with the rapidity of a post rider," and whose journey, described in all the newspapers, was the subject of both contempt and ridicule. The serving of the processes by the Marshal and Inspector Neville under the old law rather than the new, which led to the attack on Neville's house, was clear evidence that Secretary Hamilton had intended all along to create a situation which could justify the government in asserting itself with military force—beginning with the law itself, then the irregular enforcement, and then this final provocation. Even the burning of the house was the fault not of the rioters but of those inside who had opened fire on them. It was only at this point, July and early August 1794, that the opposition movement fell into the hands of such irresponsible demagogues as David Bradford, Benjamin Parkinson, and James Marshall.[56]

Nevertheless the government's response in sending the army was premature, even unnecessary. The spirit of submission was already gaining ground by the time the commissioners left; if the issues had been explained to the people a little more clearly and if they had been given a week's more time, it would have been complete.[57]

It was the Hamilton version, accepted and extended by Washington in his annual message of 1794 to Congress, that proved the more persuasive, for reasons which will emerge later on. Historians, on the other hand, particularly those writing in the early and middle years of the twentieth century, have tended to be more receptive to the Findley version, supplemented as it was by accounts similar in viewpoint from Gallatin, Hugh Henry Brackenridge, and one or two others who used similar arguments. This may be ascribed partly to a heightened interest in popular politics that arose early in the present century, and especially to an awakening concern with the economic factors thought to influence social and political events.[58] But now in more recent years, the wheel has taken some further turns.

For instance, some writers have turned a skeptical eye on several of the key assumptions of the Findley-Gallatin-Brackenridge view of the Whiskey Insurrection. The whiskey tax in itself, they argue, was in no sense an economic burden. Whether the whiskey was sent to distant markets or consumed locally, it was the consumer, not the distiller, who ultimately paid the tax. Moreover, the claim that western Pennsylvania was dependent on the transmontane markets of the East seems to have been much exaggerated. In addition to an extensive local and regional market, there were by this time large amounts not only of whiskey but also of flour and other provisions being shipped down the Mississippi and received by Spanish merchants, whether the river was officially open or not, all of which brought good prices in hard cash. Relatively small amounts, it seems, were actually carted over the mountains. And consumers of whiskey in western Pennsylvania were hardly oppressed by the tax, unless their sufferings be measured by their lamentations. If each of them drank no less than two gallons a month, the increased cost per capita (if they had actually paid it) would have been no more than $1.68 a year. As for scarce specie being drained away by the Federal Treasury, the sums spent by the government in that same region for whiskey and provisions for the army amounted to as much in one year as it could hope to collect in excises for five or six.[59]

The charge that Hamilton was deliberately goading the people of western Pennsylvania to defiance so that there might be a pretext to use military force—by first promoting an unnecessary tax, and later causing writs to be served under a superseded law rather than the amended one—has been held up as equally dubious. Madison himself had recognized that once assumption of the state debts was agreed to, an additional source of income beyond import duties was absolutely necessary to support the funding system, and he also thought that the most rational one by far was an excise on whiskey. A direct tax, he said, "wd. be still more generally obnoxious, and as imports are already loaded as far as they will bear, an excise is the only resource, and of all articles, distilled spirits are the least objectionable."[60] As for the indictments, the amended law applied to future violations, whereas those in question had occurred over a year before; and there is no evidence that Hamilton had anything to do with the writs.[61]

There might be, then, more evidence for the Hamiltonian version of the Whiskey Insurrection than was once thought. But suppose there were: would we then be obliged to accept the remainder of the Hamiltonian argument, that side of it having to do with the causes of the uprising? Logic could well point that way. That is, if the tax itself was an "artificial" cause, not onerous enough to have been the "real" one, then the whole crisis must in some way have been artificially concocted. Was it, as Hamilton insisted, the work of designing men, stirring up the people and inflaming popular passions against the government? Some recent writers have made plausible cases on just such grounds. One has placed the primary responsibility on the political followers of John Neville. Neville, after his loud condemnations of the excise, had then isolated himself and cut his supporters adrift by accepting the inspectorship, forcing them to promote the anti-excise movement with abnormal zeal simply to retain their claim on local loyalties.[62] Another version emphasizes the role played by such state leaders of the emerging Republican interest as Gallatin and Findley, just as Hamilton had done, arguing that prior to their activities in opposition to the excise there had been little evidence of what could be called a true popular movement in western Pennsylvania.[63] Something could be said for each of these variations. The public meetings at which regional leaders in effect invited their constituents to withdraw all aid from excise officers, and thus implicitly indicated to the entire community that these wretches were fair game for vigilante action, were potentially explosive in their consequences. And yet this still does not quite account for the passion that suffused the entire region by 1794, nor for the numbers that turned out at Braddock's Field in August of that year. Bringing a substantial portion of the citizens to the verge of armed rebellion was more than a few "designing men," acting for whatever special motives, could have effected.

All things added up, there were probably more grounds for disaffection and hostility to the federal government in western Pennsylvania as a geographic entity in the period between 1791 and 1794 than was the case with any other single region of the country. The political leaders of the region—Findley, Gallatin, Smilie, Brackenridge, and the others—may have said and done things in the early stages that could retrospectively be seen as irresponsible. But only retrospectively; and the fact remains that these men, though associated with the opposition, were not normally self-seeking demagogues. And they did eventually come to play a role in dampening passions the intensity of which neither they nor anyone else could have foreseen.

To begin with, the excise itself, even if perfectly just, was no trifling matter. The very idea of excises had inflammatory implications everywhere in post-Revolutionary America, though in some places much more so than in others. The excise collector, already a figure of legend in the old country, was deep in the lore of the Scotch-Irish population of western Pennsylvania. The state excise laws of the 1780s had been virtually a dead letter in the West all along; at the same time, it had been all but impossible to find respectable men to serve there as collectors. During that period a series of episodes involving rough handling had ratified certain patterns of mind; excisemen, not of very high character anyway, had come to serve as acceptable objects for social aggression.[64] Moreover, by the time the federal excise of 1791 was enacted, there were in western Pennsylvania more stills, making more whiskey per capita from the grain crops of the area, than in any other part of the country.[65] Thus the opposition in the Pennsylvania legislature to the pending bill was natural, logical, and predictable; it came from a broad social base; and it was hardly a coincidence that the author of the resolutions against it—Albert Gallatin—should have been an assemblyman from that part of the state most affected. The legislatures of three other states (Virginia, North Carolina, and Maryland) also passed such resolutions, but western Pennsylvania had a serious alternative to propose—a land tax to get at absentee speculators who held large tracts in the West—which none of these other states was willing to support, or even listen to. At any rate the later efforts of such men to mobilize sentiment for repealing the law in the meetings of 1791 and 1792—sentiment which was already there—were a natural extension of what they had been doing since the law was first proposed. And the shunning of excise officers, though a procedure of very serious implications, was one with which the people of western Pennsylvania were well acquainted already.

For that matter, even the bare economics of the excise, in view of the particular conditions of the distilling business, were hardly as straightforward as Hamilton pictured them. His argument as to the tax's being paid in the last analysis by the consumer may appear sophisticated enough as microeconomic theory.[66] But there was more to it. The excise widened a competitive disparity between large distillers and small family distillers that was already there but was now made potentially worse. As Dorothy Fennell has ably shown, the workings of the tax if allowed to go fully into effect would have driven a fair number of backyard stills out of business. The tax was levied on the capacity of the still rather than on the number of gallons of whiskey produced, which meant that the large operator with advanced equipment who ran his still twelve months in the year would in effect be paying a significantly lower tax per gallon than the smaller, seasonal, and less efficient one, and could thus sell his product cheaper.[67] The federal government was among other things giving clear encouragement to the development of pro-ductive efficiency and improved technology. It cannot be said that Alexander Hamilton's heart was very responsive to the pathos of the family still.

Actual enforcement, however, was another matter. By 1792 this problem, from the government's viewpoint, was turning into a nightmare of proportions unfore-seen at the time the law was passed. Though compliance would be largely achieved in the country east of the Appalachians and along the seaboard, the frontier regions—of which western Pennsylvania was but one among several—were prov-ing all but impenetrable to the reach of the law.[68] No vigorous steps were taken at first in any of these places. Hamilton meanwhile experimented with efforts at persuasion—such as a series of amendments passed in 1792 on his recommen-dation whereby the tax was both lowered and adjusted for seasonal activity, as well as placing substantial orders of whiskey for the western army with distillers complying with the law—but all to little effect.[69]

At the same time, western Pennsylvania presented both a danger and a pos-sibility. The Pittsburgh area was closer than any other frontier settlement to the seat of the national government, and was in fact far enough along in its devel-opment that it would shortly cease to be classifiable as a "frontier" at all. This meant that defiance of the law here would be an especially dangerous example if allowed to continue in full view of the rest of the country. On the other hand, the place was at least within reach if something decisive needed to be done there. And as it happened, the officer who had been appointed as inspector in western Pennsylvania—John Neville—was from Hamilton's viewpoint the very sort who might best be counted on, if anyone could be, to lead the way to some kind of order in that region, and perhaps by example elsewhere as well. The man's qual-ifications could hardly be improved on. Neville was a Virginian, a contemporary and longtime comrade-in-arms of Washington, with an excellent record of service both in the French and Indian war and in the Revolution; he had subsequently been a leading figure in the founding and early growth of the Pittsburgh settle-ment; he had a powerful network of family connections, had served in several high public offices there, and had acquired both influence and respect in that part of the state. He was a man of considerable personal courage, as well as being proud and stubborn. With his wealth, he had certainly had no need of the derisory salary attached to the inspectorship when he was asked to take it, but had not hesitated to answer the call from his Commander-in-Chief.[70] Moreover—again as Hamilton saw it—Neville's blunt and forthright reports upon undertaking his work seemed to contain the only practical advice worth listening to in the matter of bringing about compliance with the law. It could be done, Neville asserted—but only if backed up by visible force.[71]

But as seen from western Pennsylvania, the picture of John Neville had understandably turned into something quite different from what it had once been. He had betrayed them all, and henceforth his willful arrogance seemed to know no bounds. He referred to "the rabble" in his letters, may well have done the same in his talk, and certainly did so in his demeanor. Besides, in the new order of things—if it could be brought about—the extended "Neville connection" would have plenty to gain. This network of family and in-laws may have been a force for "progress," but what they looked most like now was a gang of insiders who were fastening their grip on everything. They owned the biggest stills, they had a large hand in the local mercantile business—which together meant that if they cooperated with federal authority the lion's share of supplying Wayne's army would go to them—and some of the most extensive speculative landholdings in the region were in their hands.[72] John Neville himself may never have done anything corrupt. Nor was he afraid of anyone; he would not run away from his duty; the law, after all, was the law. Well and good, but when John Neville set off in company with Marshal Lenox on that July morning in 1794 to serve those writs, the least speck of prudence should have told him he was heading for trouble.

But the whiskey tax was by no means the only inducement to believe the worst of the federal government. It was all too easy in 1791–92 to imagine that callousness, bungling, and the predominance of eastern interests were combining to stifle the very growth and prosperity of western Pennsylvania. There was a deepening frustration over the Indian situation in the neighboring Ohio country, culminating in the bitterness of St. Clair's defeat in the fall of 1791 and rumors of incompetence, perhaps even corruption, in the army supply system. The most luridly hawkish sentiments in the entire country with regard to dealing summarily with the Indians were coming from the Pittsburgh area. This was closely related, as we have already noted, to the continued occupation by the British of the Northwest posts, about which none were more sensitive or more vocal than the people of western Pennsylvania. Then there was the Mississippi River. The Allegheny Mountains were a natural barrier to the markets of the East, while the Mississippi was a natural highway to the rest of the world. From Pittsburgh, situated at the forks of the Ohio, there was a great deal of traffic already. But the Mississippi remained officially closed by the Spanish, and to all intents and purposes the federal government had still done nothing to get them to open it.

And the whiskey tax? But there it was, all part of the pattern. The speculative mania of 1791, the financial panic of 1792, the congressional investigation of Hamilton's management of the Treasury in the spring of 1793: all this showed what part the excise really played in support of a corrupt funding and revenue system that enriched eastern speculators while both neglecting western interests and siphoning off the West's cash resources.

So the situation was politically much inflamed; western Pennsylvania was becoming an especially strong salient of opposition sentiment, even though there had been a heavy proportion of support for the new federal constitution in that same area only a few years before. But in addition to all this (western Pennsylvania was not, after all, the only place in the country opposed to the excise) there were changes occurring in the economic and social environment of the region that generated strains of a very particular sort.

Western Pennsylvania in this period is commonly pictured as a society of frontier farmers, perhaps pinched for cash but sturdily independent, with high hopes for the future in a region of rapid population growth and an open, fluid social structure. At the very minimum, it was a setting in which a man might expect to own his own land and acquire a decent competence for himself and his family, given a little time and hard work. This, however, is not an accurate description of western Pennsylvania by the mid-1790s. The region was no longer experiencing—in marked contrast to, say, Kentucky and Tennessee—the soaring growth in population it had seen in the mid-1780s; western Pennsylvania, moreover, had reached a point in its economic development, with a degree of social stratification and differentiation of economic function, that would not be attained in those places for many years to come.

For instance, 40 percent of the taxable property was owned by the upper decile of taxpayers (about the proportion reached in Boston by 1771); more significantly, 40 percent of the names on the tax rolls were listed as "dependents." What this came to specifically was 20 percent tenant farmers, 6 percent farm laborers, 10 percent general laborers, and 4 percent unemployed poor. One-third of the rural population—about 70 percent of the total—were thus farmers without land.[73] Given the high cost of land, there was not a great likelihood of many of this class acquiring substantial amounts of it in western Pennsylvania. The rich lands of Ohio were tantalizingly near. But they were full of unpacified Indians; for the time being, and as far as anyone could tell for an indefinite time to come, there was no going into them. Even in Pennsylvania itself, a projected new settlement at Presqu'Isle had just been suspended by the federal government on the ground that it might stir up the Six Nations.[74]

Meanwhile that proportion of the adult male population listed as "artisans" was 16 percent, as high as in the settled areas of eastern Pennsylvania, which is another way of saying that the region was well on its way to industrialization. Moreover, the sizable exports of flour and whiskey to New Orleans meant that a fair proportion of the farmers were engaged in all-out commercial agriculture.[75]

Here, then, was a developing regional economy that felt itself being arbitrarily contained, hemmed in, and sat upon. The mountains to the east were both a natural and a psychological barrier that nobody could do much about. But the great river to the west, and the expanses of fertile land beyond it, need remain shut off only so long as the federal government failed to bestir itself; meanwhile expectations were being blocked all up and down the scale. River traffic was certainly not closed. But it was not officially open either, and thus the markets of every sort that it potentially represented remained tenuous, uncertain, precarious.

The social and economic structure of western Pennsylvania, then, was not exactly fluid or homogeneous. And yet if there was ever a universal bond of brotherhood there, or something very close to it, it was whiskey. There was scarcely a family that did not use it, scarcely a neighborhood in which someone was not engaged in making it, scarcely a soul in all of western Pennsylvania who did not have something to do with the making, or buying, or selling, or imbibing of whiskey. There were big traffickers and small. The fiery fluid brought in goodly amounts of cash; at the same time, it was widely used as an article of barter. Even ministers' salaries were often paid in it. Meanwhile the federal government, rather than suppressing Indians or seeing to the opening of the Mississippi, had chosen in its perversity to lay a tax on this most necessary and indispensable article, a tax mainly intended, as everyone in the region was convinced, to support windfall gains for speculators and swollen salaries for officeholders.

Arguments for an excise may have been rational enough. But a new tax that has not been generally paid before, especially a tax as widely applied as this one, is invariably disruptive. More important, in this case the tax and the article taxed at once afforded the citizens a stimulant and a vocabulary, a shared body of reference; and whatever its logic, there could have been no more common a denominator for a catalogue of heaped-up disgruntlement. The excise was undeniably regressive, a person being taxed on need rather than ability to pay. But the distiller too had his complaints. True, he could pass it on to the consumer even though it was levied on his own still, but in practice it did not work quite so neatly. The smaller distiller who did this, especially in a barter situation, was putting a real strain on his neighbors, and risking a loss of customers to distillers who evaded the tax. The end result was a process, whatever else might be said for it, that was socially integrative: a ritual of complaint and aggression, with the intoxicating bravado of non-compliance, that united all classes.

The whiskey excise was the most visible and audible complaint; it may also have been the simplest. But it was most certainly not the only one. When the federal commissioners came through in their effort to reach a settlement, they were much taken aback to find that in addition to the excise—which was the only thing they had authority to discuss—every one of the aforementioned items was being thrown in their faces. The people were full of protests about "the war which had so long vexed the frontiers" and "the manner in which the war had been conducted"; they declared that "the General Government had been inattentive to the execution of the treaty of peace respecting the western posts" and had been "remiss in asserting the claim to the navigation of the Mississippi"; they complained of the government's having allowed speculators to engross "large quantities of land," of court decisions which discountenanced squatting, and of the "suspension of the settlement at Presqu'isle." The commissioners reported having "expressed their surprise at the extent of these complaints, and intimated that if all these matters were really causes of uneasiness and disaffection in the minds of the people, it would be impossible for any Government to satisfy them."[76]

In short, it *was* a popular movement, beyond much doubt; it was not artificially

THE AGE OF FEDERALISM

concocted; it did authentically reflect sentiment throughout the region; and its ramifications were spread very wide. But how deep? Judging from the tests available, perhaps less than it might seem. One test was the region's willingness to make its submission in September and October, as compared to the ferocity of July and early August. The other is the overwhelming, all but unequivocal approval given by public opinion to Washington's use of force in bringing the rebellion to an end. These two questions may not appear related; they are in fact closely so.

3

Popular Sovereignty and the End of the Rebellion

Another account we have, generally following the Findley line but rather more lurid in its colors—indeed, it preceded Findley's in point of time and in some respects actually influenced it—is that of Hugh Henry Brackenridge. The picture this writer paints is that of an enraged populace, all but out of control by the summer of 1794, and on the very brink of revolutionary action. Its verisimilitude need not be questioned—an aroused popular temper is attested to by all the accounts—but there were good reasons why Hugh Henry Brackenridge should want to do full justice to the more hair-raising aspects of the summer's doings. Brackenridge, who had come out to Pittsburgh a few years earlier to practice law and grow up with the country, was something of an eccentric (he would sometimes rise up and drive a prospective client out of his office if the man happened to irritate him) who saw himself as an unappreciated literary genius. He had been a schoolmate of Madison, Freneau, and Burr at Princeton, and he was the author of *Modern Chivalry,* still generally referred to as the first American "novel." Everything he said and did was replete with literary flourishes. Moreover, Brackenridge—like Findley, Gallatin, Smilie, and most of the other public characters of the region, even John Neville—in his pronouncements against federal policy had played a very equivocal role in the earlier stages. (He had, incidentally, been a hardy contributor to Freneau's *National Gazette* in its heyday; the notorious "Louis Capet has lost his Caput" piece in 1793 was his handiwork.) Like the others, he had come to have second thoughts as popular passions over the excise mounted, and by the time he wrote *Incidents of the Insurrection* he was very much concerned to exhibit himself as one of those who had courageously labored, though at times forced to dissemble, to dampen an incipient revolutionary rampage. To be sure, he may have tried a bit too hard. He had always been rather too clever in his efforts to stay right with the malcontents and then to exculpate himself to the world at large, with the result that none of the parties quite trusted him afterwards. And yet his narrative, in its very movement and color, does have its compelling side. Considering what was at stake, this, rather than *Modern Chivalry,* may have been Brackenridge's masterpiece.[77]

In his pages we see the "revolutionary" phase as beginning with the attack on Inspector Neville's house on July 16 and 17. With this act of terror, and with such numbers involved, there was no turning back. Brackenridge describes the Mingo

Creek meeting of July 23 at which the mercurial David Bradford, swept along in the popular fury, emerged as an advocate of forcible resistance both to the excise and to the federal government itself. Brackenridge, meanwhile, tried to persuade the meeting that it would be best to sue for a general amnesty. But Bradford and his coterie pushed blindly on. They caused the Pittsburgh-Philadelphia mail to be robbed on July 26 in order to discover the true views of the Pittsburgh citizenry with regard to the rising movement. A number of the intercepted letters voiced disapproval, and it was this that determined them to call the great muster of August 1–2 at Braddock's Field. It would be the occasion for imprisoning or exiling all obnoxious persons, possibly seizing the magazine of Fort Fayette, and in any case affording an awesome spectacle of force. The town of Pittsburgh trembled that it might be sacked or burned. It was only the efforts of a local committee (Brackenridge again playing a mediating part) to persuade these objectionable persons (generally members of the "Neville Connection") to absent themselves that permitted the march through town and subsequent dispersal of the militia, full of Brackenridge's whiskey, to be effected without incident. But things still looked very ominous. On August 8, Brackenridge sent a dispatch to Tench Coxe in Philadelphia that he would later somewhat regret. "Should an attempt be made to suppress these people," he warned,

> I am afraid the question will not be, whether you will march to Pittsburgh, but whether they will march to Philadelphia, accumulating in their course, and swelling over the banks of the Susquehanna like a torrent, irresistible, and devouring in its progress. There can be no equality of contest, between the rage of a forest, and the abundance, indolence, and opulence of a city.[78]

Brackenridge goes on to describe the meeting of 226 elected delegates from the entire region at Parkinson's Ferry on August 14. Bradford and Marshall were all for setting up a "committee of public safety" with powers to govern the region on the basis of unyielding opposition to the excise law, and to prepare if necessary for war. (They had all been reading about the French Revolution in the *Pittsburgh Gazette*.) News of the approach of Washington's commissioners which arrived in the course of the meeting, together with the proclamation which announced the President's intention to call out the militia, was angrily received. Only through the painstaking finesse of Brackenridge, Gallatin, and other moderate spirits was the proposed committee of public safety renamed the "standing committee" and a special conference committee appointed to meet the commissioners and hear their proposals. These conferences took place between August 20 and 23, and largely through the efforts of Brackenridge and Gallatin, who were members of it, the conference committee agreed to recommend to the standing committee of sixty that the people of the region should make their submission.[79]

But Brackenridge was darkly pessimistic, and when the committee of sixty met at Brownsville on August 28 to hear the conference committee's report, everything trembled in the balance. There was fiery talk; the would-be Robespierre, Bradford, warned of setting up guillotines (none of them yet knew that Robespierre himself had just been guillotined), and declared, "We will defeat the first army that comes over the mountains and take their arms and baggage."[80] By now, however, the moderates felt able to drop the mask and make earnest speeches for submission. The drift seemed to be changing, though the delegates, with a large gallery of onlookers, were still afraid to have an open vote. Whereupon they took a secret one, and it was 34–23 for submission.

For the commissioners this was still short of satisfactory, and they did not believe they could conscientiously report to the President on the basis of it that the western country was suitably pacified. But the "revolutionary" phase was over; there was not going to be any revolution. Nor had it at any time been very likely, as we may now see by hindsight, that there ever would be one.

Why not? To be sure, Brackenridge was there, more so than any of the other narrators, and one must not take too lightly the personal danger he was in, or thought he was in, throughout most of the proceedings he describes. But what is exceedingly muted in his perception of events is a sense of the counter-forces (whether he himself were a part of them or not), the sheer magnitude of the inhibitions against the mounting of anything like an organized rebellion. Organizing was wicked; deep down they all believed this, even the would-be organizers.

The "radicals," if such they may be called, who rose to prominence in the climactic stages were both distractedly erratic and desperately unsure of themselves, and this was not simply a matter of individual character. It was inherent in the very circumstances. The basis on which the rebellion at its most dramatic point had come to rest was no longer primarily disaffection to the federal government, widespread as that was; it was simply the attack on Neville's house at Bower Hill and the dilemma it posed for all who had had anything to do with it. Bradford's behavior is revealing. He was visited before the Mingo Creek meeting by a party of men who had been at Bower Hill; they urged him to make common cause, he having previously encouraged them to do what they had done. "I encourage?" Bradford protested. "Good God! I never thought of such a thing." Oh yes you did, they replied, "and if you do not come forward now, and support us, you shall be treated in the same, or a worse manner, [as] the excise officer." From that time on, observes Brackenridge, Bradford "adopted the most violent counsels." Others were put under the same pressure. Having broken the law, they felt they all had to stand together.[81]

That much is understandable, but more than a scrape with the law is needed to build a revolutionary movement, and in this case nobody had much idea what the next step should be. Proposals for meeting federal force, should it appear, were vague and unconvincing even to those present;[82] plans for what might follow a victory over federal force (unlikely as that was) were even more vague and less convincing. The citizens of western Pennsylvania, for all their discontent, were not really prepared to challenge the ultimate sovereign power in post-Revolutionary America, the people at large. Were it to be otherwise, they would have had to persuade themselves that a majority beyond the mountains and elsewhere would refuse to support the government in the use of force against them — that the militia, one of the salient symbols of both local autonomy and popular sovereignty, would not turn out. If any did believe this, the time was close at hand when they could do so no longer.

Bradford's nerve all but failed him again when a number of persons intimated to him, probably in private, that the orders for the Braddock's Field muster might have been somewhat rash after all, whereupon he and Marshall countermanded them. But an angry meeting in Washington County, where most of the culprits were from, moved him to un-countermand them. "David Bradford, seeing the violence of the multitude by which he was always governed, became more inflammatory than he had ever been, denied that he had consented to a countermand and asked with confidence, who was the scoundrel who would say he had consented?" Marshall too was persuaded to go to Braddock's Field, especially upon finding his door one morning daubed with tar and feathers.[83]

With the arrival of the commissioners and Washington's proclamation, at least two things became newly clear. One was that the federal government would under no circumstances back down on the excise, at least not now. The other was that the offer of amnesty provided "a standard [which had not been there before] around which those opposed to the insurrection could rally."[84] It was a specific choice, indeed a way out, for all who may have thought it best to stop short of going the whole way, and this for practical purposes included just about everyone. It most certainly included David Bradford, who by September was advocating submission in Washington County.[85] We hear from Bradford once more in a pathetic letter to Governor Mifflin written on October 4, when he may already have been preparing to flee the country forever, as he eventually did. His words and actions, he lamented, had been either "misrepresented or entirely misunderstood." It was true that he had never liked the excise law, "but it was never in my mind to go farther than the Committees who met at Pittsburgh . . . to wit: a negative opposition." (The mere tarring and feathering of collectors?) He could not immediately agree to the commissioners' terms, because the people "would have believed I had been bribed." Such conduct, he said, "would have defeated my Design, to wit: to bring about a submission to the Laws." And yet since then he had done as much as anybody, he insisted, "towards Reconciliation & Submission."[86]

He protests too much, one may think, but perhaps poor Bradford was not *that* far off. It was the same process they had all undergone, the differences in a way being largely those of degree. It was just that Gallatin, Brackenridge, and their like had seen the limits of the situation earlier on, and had pulled out a little sooner. Even Brackenridge, tossing sleeplessly one night in August between meetings, wondered whether in order to save his own skin from the unpredictable caprice and ire of his neighbors he might, after all, be better advised to become a rebel.[87] But not after discovering, as he shortly did, that more and more of them had been having the same reveries as himself.

True, a 34–23 vote of the standing committee on August 29 was not good enough for the commissioners. It may have been a majority, but it was not yet submission. But it is also true, or would seem to be, that in a committee of public safety a vote for continued resistance that is no more than a minority is worse than useless. While not exactly a surrender, it was not a revolution either.

The principal reason for noting in any detail the steps whereby Washington fashioned the policy of his administration toward the whiskey rebels in August and September 1794 is to show him once more in a setting which has by now become familiar. It was one in which he was receiving advice, and being subjected to pressures, from several directions at once—a setting which had in the past called forth from him a certain precision of judgment.

The first news of the assault on Bower Hill, which had been led by a former officer of the Pennsylvania line, reached Philadelphia on July 25. It was one more billow in a sea of uncertainty in the national affairs. For weeks there had been no news from Wayne, now operating deep in Indian territory; it was still not clear what Lord Dorchester's intentions had been in ordering the reoccupation of Fort Miami; no word had yet arrived from Jay concerning his first meetings with Grenville; and there were depressing reports from Kentucky, the people there complaining more loudly than ever about the government's failure to open the Mississippi.[88]

Washington's first inclination with regard to western Pennsylvania was probably to use military force at once, especially with Hamilton egging him on. He had refrained from doing it two years earlier, and things had obviously got worse. But owing to a variety of circumstances he again refrained from moving precipitously, and nearly two more months went by before he took his final step. He reached it through a series of tentatively graded approaches with the entire country looking on, at the end of which his support by public opinion had grown to immense proportions.

The Militia Act of 1792 required a federal judge to certify that law and order could no longer be maintained, that there were "combinations too powerful to be suppressed by the ordinary course of judicial proceedings," before the Executive could call out troops. Justice James Wilson of the Supreme Court was furnished with the pertinent facts so that he might do this if he saw proper. But Wilson was not disposed to move hastily; he wanted the reports authenticated and their handwriting verified.[89] Here was one delaying influence. Another, more formidable, came from officials of the state of Pennsylvania. Washington and his cabinet met with Governor Mifflin, Secretary Dallas, Attorney-General Jared Ingersoll, and Chief Justice Thomas McKean on August 2 to determine whether the Pennsylvanians might be disposed to issue the first call for militia on their own. They proved to be not very cooperative. McKean denied that the state judiciary was unequal to the emergency, and the use of force by Pennsylvania would thus be illegal; Mifflin flatly refused to issue an immediate call, arguing (rather unhelpfully) that such was the general opposition to the excise that the militia might well refuse to respond.[90] Washington was undoubtedly irritated. But he perceived that even if Justice Wilson should certify that judicial process had broken down (as in fact two days later, on August 4, he did),[91] it would be very unwise to proceed, though he was legally free to do so, without the bona fide support of Pennsylvania. He thereupon struck a kind of provisional bargain with Mifflin. Should the federal government take matters into its own hands, the Governor would still see himself as free to take certain steps separately—to convene the state legislature and send state commissioners to the western counties—while the President would publish a proclamation outlining the "views" of the federal government.

Washington was thus tolerating, for the time being, Mifflin's impulse to dissociate himself from federal policy. He then requested opinions in writing from his cabinet as to how the Administration should proceed.[92] Hamilton's reply was immediate and straightforward: call out the militia. "It appears to me that the very existence of Government demands this course and that a duty of the highest nature urges the Chief Magistrate to pursue it." Hamilton was appealing both to Washington's sense of duty and to his dread of a government which might through impotence forfeit the respect of the citizenry.[93] Secretary of War Knox recommended "a super abundant force." He figured that 12,400 men from Pennsylvania, New Jersey, Maryland, and Virginia would be about right, and that there should be a proclamation giving "a short but comprehensive recital" of the "mild measures which heretofore have been taken . . . and of the objects intended to be attained thereby."[94] Attorney-General William Bradford was convinced from the evidence that the insurgents' efforts to obstruct the law through intimidation constituted high treason, and he agreed with Hamilton and Knox that only a call of militia could restore order. Moreover, "the force ought to be such as by suppressing the hope of successful resistance may induce an early submission to the Laws & prevent the unhappy consequences that further opposition may produce." But Bradford also thought that some delay was all-important for the preparation of public opinion. There might be resistance to militia service, "unless the public mind be satisfied that all other means in the power of the Executive have failed and that military coercion is absolutely necessary to support the Laws."[95]

The paper submitted by Secretary of State Randolph appears to have been the product of considerable agitation. It was a long and rather disconnected plea for delay—delay, it might almost be supposed, no matter what—ending with a series of proposals which would in effect have ruled out any military action until the following spring, if not indefinitely. He questioned the validity of Justice Wilson's certificate on the ground that "it specifies no particular law which has been opposed" (as if everyone did not know very well which law it was); he insisted that "dissatisfaction with the excise" west of the mountains was "radical and universal"; he thought the militia of Pennsylvania were not to be depended on, and that those from other states might also refuse service; and he argued that the expense would in any case be "very great." Parties were already inflamed, and with the sword once drawn, "nothing will be able to restrain them." Moreover, he was obsessed with the idea that the British were somehow mixed up in the insurrection too, and that we would find ourselves in a war with them before we knew it. (The very day he wrote all this, Randolph was having his subsequently famous interview with the French minister, Fauchet, and making his "précieuses confessions.")[96]

Randolph's remedy was to attempt conciliation through an Executive-appointed commission, and to refrain from sending troops or even from making them ready, because if "reconciliation is offered with one hand" and "terror borne in the other," the "overtures of peace will be considered delusive by the insurgents and the rest of the world." The President should issue a proclamation explaining the Executive's powers but declaring that they were being "withheld from motives of humanity and a wish for conciliation." If the commission failed, the insurgents should be prosecuted. If justice could not be had in the courts, "then let the militia be called." Randolph, whatever his fatuities, was appealing throughout to Washington's other great preoccupation, government not by coercion but by consent.

Meanwhile Governor Mifflin put in his oar with a long letter setting forth in a particularly lofty tone the arguments he had already made verbally three days before. State agencies of law enforcement in Pennsylvania, he said, were not yet shown to be incompetent; he reiterated his plans to send state commissioners; if that failed, he intended to convene the legislature so that means of restoring order "may be prescribed by their wisdom and authority." He would fulfill "any duty you may impose, in pursuance of your constitutional and legal powers," though the broad hint was that any move Washington made must be on his own responsibility, and that he ought not to make it without prudent deliberation and delay, as the Governor himself was doing.[97]

Washington now had a range of choices before him, and he proceeded to balance them. He would delay sending any force for the time being, but would see that one was ready when and if it should be wanted. He would issue a proclamation, not to make the overtures Randolph wanted him to make but rather to announce Justice Wilson's finding that law and order had broken down, and that he intended "calling forth the militia in order to suppress the combinations aforesaid, and to cause the laws to be duly executed." Concurrently, however, he would appoint a set of federal commissioners, as Randolph had urged, with authority to offer "an amnesty and perpetual oblivion for every thing that has past" and forgiveness of excise duties from previous years, on condition of compliance for the present and satisfactory assurances that execution of the laws would no longer be obstructed.[98] Mifflin would be told off smartly that his and the President's findings on the state of order in western Pennsylvania did not coincide, and that the President could not allow his measures to depend on the Governor's. He would, however, observe delay while he sent his own commissioners; and he was glad to know that Mifflin did not intend to withhold his cooperation, because the time might shortly be at hand when he would need it.[99] Washington asked Knox to inform the governors of the numbers of troops he required, using Knox's own estimates; he asked Randolph to draft instructions to the commissioners; he asked Hamilton to prepare a comprehensive account of the entire insurrection up to then (Hamilton also drafted the reply to Mifflin, though it was sent out over Randolph's signature); and he asked Bradford to serve as one of the commissioners. Bradford set off at once, August 7, the moment his instructions were ready.[100]

The timing and the full unfolding of federal policy were henceforth determined by the reports received from the commissioners. But the policy itself had probably been all but settled by August 7 and remained essentially the same from then on. Hamilton and Knox had advocated force; Randolph had advocated conciliation. But these were not the only available categories of action. There was a third, conciliation *and* a display of force, sufficiently formidable that its purposes could be achieved without actually using it, accompanied by both the expressed hope that it need not be used and the implicit confidence that it probably would not be. This might be called, in Randolph's words, offering reconciliation with one hand and brandishing terror with the other, but what it amounted to was that the spectacle of available force was itself a part of the reconciliation process, a process to be enacted in the sight of the world. This at any rate was the category Washington chose, and William Bradford put it succinctly when he told his father-in-law just before starting westward that "the Presdt. means to convince these people & the World at once of the *moderation & the firmness* of the Gov."[101]

And it was successful beyond anyone's expectations. The commissioners concluded very early that although a majority would probably take the oath of submission, and a general armed rebellion in the West was no longer very likely, the state of mind there was so disturbed, with so many pockets of intransigence remaining, that normality would not be restored until after visible force had entered their midst. The commissioners' first report of substance was written on the evening of August 17. They were discouraged by the accounts of the Parkinson's Ferry meeting on the 14th when the committee of sixty had been set up, and by the things they were hearing in Pittsburgh. The report reached Philadelphia on August 23.[102] The cabinet met on the 24th, and took another step. Orders were to be issued for the assembling of militia units, now raised to fifteen thousand in number, but the orders would not be made public until September 1.[103]

Things looked somewhat better to the commissioners after the meetings of August 21–23 with the conference committee, which agreed to recommend submission to the committee of sixty, but their hopes dropped once more with the violence of the speeches and the closeness of the vote at Brownsville on the 28th. The state commissioners were just as discouraged as the federal ones. This news arrived in Philadelphia on September 8, and on the 9th Washington ordered all units to their designated rendezvous.[104]

The Philadelphia militia turned out with great enthusiasm on the 10th, and there was a great surge of public opinion, kept well informed since the beginning of the month, in support of the Administration. It was entirely bipartisan; even the scurrilous Bache denounced the insurrection and declared that it had to be suppressed; even the Democratic Societies rose up in dismay at what their western brethren were doing.[105] The Baltimore society, to take but one example, resolved "that the conduct of the President of the United States, as well in calling forth the militia to suppress so dangerous a spirit, as also first attempting an amicable termination by negociation, was wise, prudent, and constitutional, and therefore deserving of the approbation and support of this society."[106]

Final action was withheld until after the oath-taking, which was to occur in the various polling places on September 11. The commissioners arrived in Philadelphia on the 24th, and reported to the President their belief

> that there is a considerable majority of the inhabitants of the fourth survey who are now disposed to submit to the execution of the laws; at the same time, they conceive it their duty explicitly to declare their opinion that such is the state of things in that survey, that there is no probability that the act for raising a revenue on distilled spirits and stills can at present be enforced by the usual course of civil authority; and that some more competent force is necessary to cause the laws to be duly executed, and to ensure to the officers and well-disposed citizens that protection which it is the duty of Government to afford.[107]

The next day, September 25, Washington issued orders for the troops to begin the westward march. He and Hamilton set off to Carlisle on September 30 to join them. From thence the Commander-in-Chief rode serenely at their head, accompanied by governors and other dignitaries of the states concerned, conspicuous among whom was Thomas Mifflin of Pennsylvania. The army met no resistance whatever. The most violent leaders had meanwhile disappeared from the region; a few men were arrested and brought back to Philadelphia for trial; all were acquitted except two, and these were eventually pardoned.[108]

The master key, not so much to the Whiskey Rebellion itself but to its collapse, was an abstraction, perhaps the most formidable abstraction of the Revolutionary era: the sovereignty of the people. An outpouring of popular protest, a forthright expression of the republican spirit, was itself stifled by the popular will and the force of republican principles. Another name would be given to that force a generation or so later, and by no means in full approval: the tyranny of the majority. Such "tyranny" exerts its coercions not through naked power; it overcomes all but the hardiest resistance by working from within.

The rebels of western Pennsylvania may at one time have imagined themselves as re-enacting the scenes of the Revolution and resisting an alien sovereign; a number of them did, indeed, define their doings in just such a way. The rest of the country might have so defined them too, but refused to do it. One of the many public resolutions that poured forth in September 1794 declared it to be "an essential ingredient in . . . Republican government, that the voice of the majority govern; that a deviation from this rule unhinges every principle of freedom, by setting up the will of the few against that of the many. That the conduct of our fellow-citizens in several counties of a neighboring state, is a flagrant violation of this important principle—the law which they have refused obedience to, having been constitutionally enacted by a majority of the representatives of the people." This came not from any merchants' coffee-house or chamber of commerce, but from the Democratic Society of the town of Newark.[109] And thus it began to penetrate these people, isolated as they may have been; it was under such coercions as this, as more and more of them signed up, that the earlier sense of the righteousness of their cause simply ebbed away. Military force obviously had something to do with it. But perhaps misleadingly so; it was force approved by the country at large. Force in the form of a citizen militia was the visible measure of public support for the President's course. On October 18 the *Pittsburgh Gazette* carried a notice in large print. The post-rider had just reported having seen the Jersey and Pennsylvania troops between Carlisle and Bedford, shortly to be joined by those of Maryland and Virginia. *"The number exceeds the requisition demanded by the President of the U. States."*

Moreover, the most extensive narratives we have of the insurrection were the work of men whose motive was not primarily to square themselves with the federal government. (They were, after all, opposition Republicans, and so remained.) What they wanted above all else was to set themselves right with public opinion. Then there was the spectacle of what Washington himself had just done, in his acts and in his person, to reaffirm the legitimacy of republican government. At no time had he stood in greater eminence as the republican counterpart of the mythical Patriot King, above party and faction, in a society that still deplored its own factious impulses but could no longer function without them. He thus embodied the values of past and present; his rectitude was that of the head of a great state; he was at the same time the very personification of popular sovereignty, the man who had been placed where he was through the free suffrages of his fellow-citizens but who could still burst forth that *"by god . . . he had rather be on his farm than to be made emperor of the world."*[110] He had handled the mob in the way the good sovereign, popular or otherwise, was expected to do. This was praised more consistently than any other aspect of his policy toward the rebels, even by the opposition. "He was anxious to prevent bloodshed," conceded William Findley, "and at the same time to enforce due submission to the laws. . . ."[111] With Washington, the people did not yet feel obliged to separate the President from the abstraction over which he presided, though they would do it to a greater or lesser degree with all his successors. And when he gave voice to the common values, they saw little reason not to believe what he told them. Or rather, as we shall see, *most* of what he told them.

As for the grievances of western Pennsylvania, it should probably be noted that the forces of popular sovereignty were not the only ones at work to spread reconciliation in that region. The events closely following would do wonders to liberate the exuberant forces of petty and not-so-petty capitalism as well. During the first week in October 1794, the first news of Wayne's victory at Fallen Timbers reached Pittsburgh. The following summer the people learned of the Jay Treaty, which returned the Northwest posts to American hands; shortly thereafter they heard of Wayne's Treaty of Greenville with the Indians; and not long after that, Pinckney's treaty, which opened up the Mississippi. They also heard at some point that a number of Republican congressmen, including their own representatives Gallatin and Findley, were making a great deal of trouble over the Jay Treaty. Whereupon they rose up in their character as the sovereign people to demand that such obstructions cease, the treaty having been duly and constitutionally made and being now entitled to compliance as the law of the land.[112] Scarcely a year after the rebellion was over, things were really buzzing in western Pennsylvania. Thousands were moving out, and thousands were coming in. "The emigration to this country this fall," announced the *Pittsburgh Gazette,* surpasses that of any other season—and we are informed, that the banks of the Monongahela, from M'Kees Port to Redstone, are lined with people intending for the settlement on the Ohio, and Kentucky.

As an instance of the increasing prosperity of this part of the state, land that two or three years since was sold for ten shillings per acre, will now bring upwards of three pounds.[113]

A final question remains. If public approval of Washington's policy was so overwhelming, and if Washington's views about "self-created societies" were so generally shared, why should a passing reference to these societies have occasioned so wordy a debate? James Madison, who was probably the most responsible for setting it off, had no sympathy whatever for the rebellion and no connection with any Democratic Society. He could not but approve the President's recent conduct. Yet it was precisely Washington's current prestige and popular support, at least as he saw it, that gave promise of trouble. The very power of popular sovereignty might well be wielded in ways that would not be advantageous to the emergent Republican interest, a possibility Madison saw as connected not with the insurrection but with some more extended principle. The period between 1792 and 1796 was the one which saw the growth of Madison's conviction that something in the way of an organized opposition—for all the inhibitions against such organizing, many if not most of which were shared by himself—was somehow both inevitable and indispensable. We see him in November 1794 acting on this conviction, without feeling altogether free to say so.

If Washington ever had a fixed obsession, it was these societies, "self-created" in the sense of having no sanction in popular authority, societies which had been up to nothing but mischief since the first ones were formed. First they had tried without success to embroil us in war on behalf of France, and now here was this insurrection, "the first *ripe fruit* of the Democratic Societies." He had felt very early that if they were not counteracted they would "shake the government to its foundations"; and now if this uprising were not subdued, we could "bid adieu to all government in this Country, except Mob and Club Govt. . . ."[114]

By October 11 Randolph, who earlier had not favored attacking the societies, changed his mind. "As I remarked to you in conversation," he wrote to Washington, "I never did see an opportunity of destroying these self-constituted bodies until the fruit of their operations was declared in the insurrection at Pittsburg. . . . They may now I believe be crushed. The prospect ought not to be lost."[115]

Washington did not intend to "crush" them exactly, and what he said was measured, but he did want to say something. Hence the reference in his message to "certain self-created societies," and to the insurrection's having been "fomented by combinations of men, who, careless of consequences . . . have disseminated . . . suspicions, jealousies, and accusations, of the whole Government."[116] The Senate in its reply not only agreed resoundingly but rephrased the point so that there would be no mistaking it.

Our anxiety arising from the licentious and open resistance to the laws in the

Western counties of Pennsylvania, has been increased by the proceedings of certain self-created societies ... proceedings, in our apprehension, founded in political error, calculated, if not intended, to disorganize our Government, and which ... have been influential in misleading our fellow citizens in the scene of insurrection.[117]

As to whether the imputation was justified, and how much the societies did have to do with the insurrection, it all depended on how the question was framed, and Washington had not done it with much precision. In one sense he was right; there was plenty of connection. Neither Findley nor Brackenridge had any doubt of it, and Congressman Thomas Scott, who came from Washington County, declared "that there were self-created societies in that part of the country, and he likewise knew that they had inflamed the insurrection; for some of the leaders of those societies had likewise been the leaders of the riots."[118] It was true that of the three most violent insurgent leaders, Benjamin Parkinson was president of the Mingo Creek society, and James Marshall and David Bradford were president and vice-president respectively of the one in Washington Town.[119] And if a majority of the five hundred men at Bower Hill were from the Mingo Creek militia, and if most of the militia at that place were members of the Democratic Society, and if the society's meetings were "frequently attended by three hundred persons," then it would seem that just about the entire membership had to have been out there storming Neville's house.[120] Moreover, western Pennsylvania was the only part of the country where the societies seem to have had strong local support. On the other hand, the fact remains that the insurrection was the product primarily of the region rather than its societies. The ones outside the region invariably tried to discourage them; conversely, it is fairly certain that even if there had been no societies there would still have been an insurrection.

James Madison, who was chairman of the House committee to draft a reply to the message, a process which normally consisted of echoing the President's sentiments back to him in ceremonial approval, had not intended to precipitate any major debate. Nor was he himself planning to contest or defend any great principle. It was just that he felt, by a kind of instinct, that it might be as well simply to omit that particular expression, "self-created societies." He wished, as he put it in a private letter, "that it might be passed over in silence by the H. of Reps.," and his committee "so reported."[121] But it was not to get by so easily. When the report reached the floor, Thomas FitzSimons of Pennsylvania did not see why the phrase should be left out, because such societies, "though not strictly unlawful," were "yet not less fatal to good order and true liberty"; and the debate was on.[122] Actually much of it, for and against, took the ground that the societies were not really so important and did not make that much difference. Why mention them, said one side; why *not* mention them, said the other; why rebuke the President on such a trifling point? Nobody cared much about the societies; nobody was much disposed to embarrass the President at the crest of his popularity; most of them rather wished the matter had not come up. But now that it had, for some reason they were not disposed to let go of it.

Fisher Ames insisted on making it a matter of principle and on making the principle explicit. The right to form political clubs was not being denied, nor their right to meet; "it is the abuse of the right after they have met that is charged upon them." Do the people need clubs to come between them and their representatives? If they have grievances, "are they to be brought to a knowledge of them only by clubs?" Are "the most inflamed party men, who usually lead the clubs . . . the best organs of authentic information? . . . They affect to feel more zeal for a popular Government, and to enforce more respect for Republican principles, than the real Representatives. . . ." But they represent only themselves. The clubs draw "the ambitious and desperate," "the credulous, the ignorant, the rash, and violent"; they acquire power through calumny, "by rumors and falsehoods"; and if they prevail, "they will be the Government." (Ames read resolutions from a number of their meetings, including one that would have liked to set up a guillotine in order to punish stockholders.) Do we intend to punish the clubs? "Censure is not punishment, unless it is merited, for we merely allude to certain self-created societies, which have disregarded the truth, and fomented the outrages against the laws."[123]

Madison replied the following day. He deplored the discussion's having occurred at all, but now it would have to be finished. It was a short and modest speech, and hardly more specific in its application than the principles of Milton's *Areopagitica*. He did not defend Democratic Societies; indeed, he almost succeeded in not even mentioning them. Nor would we be abandoning the President, he said, "should we pass over the whole business." It was just that the mode of procedure being proposed—censure—was an "innovation" which he was inclined to question. He did so on grounds of strict construction, with a bit of popular sovereignty thrown in. "When the people have formed a Constitution, they retain those rights which they have not expressly delegated," and Congress was not competent to censure that which was not cognizable by law, in this case, opinions. Such censure *is* punishment; it might well extend to freedom of speech and press. The power of censure "is in the people over the Government, and not in the Government over the people." Any writings must "stand or fall by the public opinion"; the press cannot shake the people's confidence in their government. "In a Republic, light will prevail over darkness, truth over error. . . ."[124]

After two tie votes, they left the phrase out. They compromised on "combinations of men," each construing it as he wanted, and under the circumstances this was fully good enough for James Madison.[125]

But Madison did have something rather more specific in mind than what he had actually said. He thought he knew what FitzSimons, Ames, and the others on their side of the question were up to, and he told Monroe what it was. The President himself was not to blame; he may have just made "the greatest error of his political life," but he, Madison, had simply wanted to rescue him from it. Yet the "moderate course" his committee had proposed, he said, "would not satisfy those who hoped to draw a party advantage out of the P's popularity. The game was, to connect the democratic Societies with the odium of the insurrection—to connect the Republicans in Congs. with those Societies—to put the P. ostensibly at the head of the other party, in opposition to both. . . ."[126]

So there it was: Madison seems to have been saying something, privately at least, about parties, in addition to making some effort to deflect the full ire of Washington from the hapless self-created societies. But how clearly was he saying it, or even thinking it?

The societies themselves did not survive this public ordeal—at least not these societies. Most of them recoiled in pained protest, as well they might, having disapproved of the insurrection as much as the rest of the public. Nevertheless they seem to have been fatally affected by what their embodied sovereign had just told them. A little later one of their prominent members in western Pennsylvania publicly advised them to dissolve, and he cannot have been the only one. Few are known to have carried on much longer.[127] It has been claimed that Madison, in defense of his committee's report, was making a statement on behalf of freedom of association, as perhaps in some sense he was. But it may be doubted whether he himself would have put it with that kind of clarity; his solicitude for the societies was, to say the least, muted. The "right" of legislative censure was the only principle he claimed to be discussing. Others, with the assurance of hindsight, have assumed that a further step was taken here in defining the legitimacy of political parties.[128] There is undoubtedly something in this too, though no steps of this nature, taken in these years, were very long ones. There was not a word about parties in the speech itself. Still, there was *some* kind of issue here over what popular sovereignty meant; Madison did sense that much, and probably more.

Fisher Ames's view was not on its face a perverse one, nor was Washington's, which it echoed; it was the common wisdom of the time. Ames wanted all intermediate bodies that tried to interpose between the people and their representatives to be defined not as illegal, but certainly as something less than legitimate. The government—the President and the legislative authority—having been chosen by the people, were answerable, Ames insisted, only to the people and not to any intervening factions.

Yet Madison was convinced that the government, a significant portion of it at least, was already in the hands of a faction. It might capture the President himself; it was obviously seeking "to draw a party advantage out of the P.'s popularity." He had just seen the President combine his own authority with that of the people to put down a rebellion; popular sovereignty could not have manifested itself with greater power, and it was *that* power which he did not want turned against the Republican interest. That was the "game," and he was reaching for the principle of censure to hold it off.

As for his own "game," and why it was played on such narrow ground, it is worth noting that even in his private letters to such Republican intimates as Monroe and Jefferson, Madison is full of inhibitions; he too is still very much limited by the conventional wisdom. He refers to the *other* side, with their dark designs and their "game," as a party; how can he use the same words, with all that they would denote and imply, for his own company, whose purity of intention and principle was its only claim to being? Nor is this the only fiction, echoing traditional habits of mind, that he resorts to. He must have known that the "self-created societies" reference was Washington's own notion, one that he had brooded about for months. (Not even Hamilton was nearly so obsessed with them.) Yet Madison pretends that it was not Washington's thought, but one that had somehow been implanted by the party schemers who surrounded him — that it was not the Patriot King who was doing wrong; it was all the fault of his wicked councillors.[129]

So it is still at best an asymmetrical view of parties: theirs is bad, and ours is better than a *mere* party. Madison is still not at the point of defining parties as a good thing — not openly, and not even privately. But again, the Republican interest to James Madison was a kind of opposition force that needed protecting, because it was the only force capable of thwarting *them*. An intermediate entity did have to be there, Fisher Ames to the contrary notwithstanding. It had to be kept in being; it must in some sense be organized.

If a theoretical advance, then, is to be discerned here, James Madison's words will require a great deal of construing. He was not arguing for parties, but against a principle that might prevent parties. And yet it might also be said that if he was not offering a comprehensive statement on that subject, he was at least reserving the ground for those who would.

Nor can we be certain he would have liked the rest of the logic had he chosen to draw it out. The time would come when the difference between "them" and "us" must be theoretically neutral, when parties would capture the government, the presidency, every form of opposition "interest," and be a permanent intermediate entity between the people and their representatives. All sorts would be found in them, not excluding the very types Fisher Ames perceived in the self-created clubs: "the ambitious and desperate," "the credulous, the ignorant, the rash, and violent." They would not be above resorting, from time to time, to "rumors and falsehoods." Nevertheless such entities would in time prove to be a more logical and serviceable vehicle than any other for the functioning of popular sovereignty in America.

CHAPTER XI

The Retirement of Washington

George Washington's Farewell Address, which was never delivered in person before any assembly, was first given to the public through the newspapers in September 1796, prior to that year's presidential election. Few American state papers have been more extensively written about, and the aggregate of ideas contained in the Address shows a sufficient complexity of intent that there is still no telling when or where the commentary ought to stop. The greater portion of this writing has been a product of the present century, though the Address excited a variety of responses from the very first, not all of them favorable.[1]

Nor has the Olympian tone of the Farewell Address or the monumentality it has acquired over the years, for better or worse, always been helpful in the effort to penetrate the various levels of its logic and design. Perhaps too much attention has been given to the explicit principles which Washington was affirming, or seemed to be affirming, for the guidance of his fellow-citizens and their posterity. The validity of those principles — or even their exact nature — is not a matter about which there has been anything like agreement. Nor can there be, unless the sentiments of the Address are directly and circumstantially correlated with the experience of Washington's final three years in office. Though the text is impressive enough to merit close study, it does not entirely speak for itself. But considered with reference to the circumstances in which it was composed, it speaks volumes.

I

Logic of the Farewell Address

Most interpretations of the Address have depended in some way on the question of which of the two principal subjects it deals with — foreign affairs or domestic politics — should be given the greater weight. Much the largest share of attention and analysis has been devoted to its implications for American foreign policy, and since questions of foreign involvement constitute the culminating section of the Address, there is clearly a strong case for assuming that this was the emphasis Washington wished to leave in his readers' minds. But more recently, increased attention has been called to the other main section, the one in which Washington deplores the spirit of faction and party in the nation's politics. Some have concluded that Washington's primary intention was to denounce and discredit the Republican opposition to his administration, and that in so doing Washington had in effect become a partisan himself. He had, to all intents and purposes, become a Federalist without openly acknowledging it. This too can be argued with a good deal of plausibility. But before considering these and related claims, we should take note of the immediate occasion, and examine what Washington actually said.

By the year 1796, Washington had had enough, in every sense of the word. Worn down by the cares of public service, he was determined to withdraw to the pleasures of private life, and was looking for a suitable way of letting this be known. And characteristically, he sought advice and assistance on how he ought to proceed. A similar situation had arisen once before. He had wanted to retire in 1792, and at that time had consulted James Madison; this time, for a variety of reasons, he thought the ideas of Hamilton would be those most likely to suit his purposes. But his general procedure would be more or less the same: to prepare a leave-taking statement in rough draft himself, and then ask that it be refined into finished form. Moreover, he wanted the version of four years before, which had been prepared with Madison's assistance, combined with his more recent thoughts, so that the final rendering would in a way be the product of both occasions.

The problem was not altogether a straightforward one; it contained potential embarrassments. At this early stage in the evolution of modern politics it was still not regarded as seemly for a man to announce himself as a candidate for public office, it being assumed that the call came from his fellow-citizens. By the same token, it could be presumptuous to announce that he would *not* be a candidate: how was he to know whether his fellow-citizens would ask him? And how, in this particular case, were *they* to know that he was not doing it simply out of fear of having become too unpopular to be re-elected? Besides, Washington rather wanted—if it could be done with propriety—to make some justification of his executive policies. His solution was to combine a brief expression of his immediate intentions with a set of what he took to be broader and more enduring maxims into a general valedictory message. He prepared a draft during the early months of 1796 and sent it to Hamilton for suggestions and revisions. Hamilton thereupon wrote out two amplified drafts based upon it, one in July and the other in August, of which Washington preferred the first. The completed version, with a final re-editing by Washington, was given to the press and published on September 19, 1796.[2]

The Address begins in a tone of deferential modesty by Washington's observing that with the time for a new election approaching, he has thought it proper to make known his resolution "to decline being considered among the number of those out of whom a choice is to be made." He had hoped, he says, to withdraw four years earlier, and had actually prepared a paper declaring his intention to do so. But the "critical posture" of the country's foreign relations and the "unanimous advice of persons entitled to my confidence" had impelled him to abandon that idea. Now, however, the nation's affairs no longer require his services. Indeed, he has always felt the "inferiority" of his qualifications, and "every day the increasing weight of years" admonishes him that "the shade of retirement" is both welcome and necessary. He expresses his gratitude for the many honors accorded him, and hopes that the blessings of America's free Constitution may inspire "every nation which is yet a stranger to it."[3]

"Here, perhaps, I ought to stop." But of course he does not; he is just getting started. He has a number of things on his mind, "sentiments which are the result of much reflection," and which he sees as "all important to the permanency of your felicity as a people." He thereupon proceeds to discuss the Union, and to stress the urgency of preserving it. North, South, East, and West are united not only by "common dangers, sufferings, and successes," but also by interest. He points out the ways in which the diverse economic activities of the several regions complement each other, and indicates the "greater strength" and "greater security from external danger" afforded by their being bound together under one government. "Is there a doubt whether a common government can embrace so large a sphere? Let experience solve it." From here he moves to a warning against divisions and factions based on alleged differences of interest between geographic sections. Most of this, together with the introductory portion of the Address, he had already planned to say in 1792. But the parts that follow are those conceived subsequent to that time, and are the ones for which the Address is most remembered.[4]

Washington has already sounded a caution against parties based on geography. "Let me now," he continues, "take a more comprehensive view, and warn you in the most solemn manner against the baneful effects of the spirit of party generally." Such a spirit exists in all governments, "but in those of the popular form it is seen in its greatest rankness and is truly their worst enemy."

> The alternate domination of one faction over another, sharpened by the spirit of revenge natural to party dissension, which in different ages and countries has perpetrated the most horrid enormities, is itself a frightful despotism. But this leads at length to a more formal and permanent despotism. The disorders and miseries which result gradually incline the minds of men to seek security and repose in the absolute power of an individual, and sooner or later the chief of some prevailing faction, more able or more fortunate than his competitors, turns this disposition to the purposes of his own elevation on the ruins of public liberty.[5]

He is aware of its being sometimes said that parties can be useful in maintaining a check on the government and keeping alive the spirit of liberty. This may be true in monarchical governments. But in popular ones, he bluntly asserts, "it is a spirit not to be encouraged." In the nature of the case "there will always be enough of that spirit for every salutary purpose," and it is like a fire which instead of giving warmth, consumes.[6]

Then, following a transitional passage on the importance of religion, public morality, maintenance of the public credit, and the cheerful payment of taxes, Washington moves to the final section of his message, the one on foreign affairs.

"Observe good faith and justice toward all nations. Cultivate peace and harmony with all." This is only possible through avoiding both "inveterate antipathies" and "passionate attachments" to any foreign country; a nation may be enslaved either by its "animosity" or by its "affection." Ill will and resentment may impel a government to war "contrary to the best calculations of policy"; habitual fondness, creating the illusion of common interests where none exist, may lead to the same result. (There is of course no question about which two foreign countries he has in mind.) Such a drift will be advanced by unscrupulous demagogues who, under the guise of "a virtuous sense of obligation," may "mislead public opinion" and "awe the public councils."[7]

We may extend our commercial relations with all, but we should "have with them as little *political* connection as possible." "It is our true policy," Washington insists, in the phrase that would subsequently draw more discussion and commentary than any other, "to steer clear of permanent alliances with any portion of the foreign world. . . ." Keeping a respectable posture of defense, "we may safely trust to temporary alliances for extraordinary emergencies." Even our commercial relations should be impartial. While seeking the best terms available, we should remain free to change our policy "as experience and circumstances shall dictate," neither seeking nor granting exclusive preferences, nor trying to force trade out of its natural channels. It is "folly in one nation to look for disinterested favors from another," and the nation that does so "must pay with a portion of its independence for whatever it may accept under that character."[8]

Washington indicates how he himself has tried to follow these rules, the basis for his policy having been the Neutrality Proclamation of April 1793. Has he truly been guided by such principles? "To myself, the assurance of my own conscience is that I have at least believed myself to have been guided by them." He closes with the hope that the Almighty may mitigate the many errors which he—though not intentionally—has probably made, and meanwhile:

> I anticipate with pleasing expectation that retreat in which I promise myself to realize without alloy the sweet enjoyment of partaking in the midst of my fellow-citizens the benign influence of good laws under a free government—the ever-favorite object of my heart, and the happy reward, as I trust, of our mutual cares, labors, and dangers.[9]

Earlier in the present century, Washington's Farewell Address was widely invoked in support of a foreign policy of strict isolation. A kind of climax in this respect was reached in the period between the two World Wars, the Address having figured in the debates after Versailles over joining the League of Nations and later the World Court, and then in the contentions surrounding the Neutrality Act and related questions amid the worsening international conditions of the 1930s. But however incessantly this isolationist note may have been sounded in political speeches and the popular press, and whatever echoes it may have aroused in the general temper of the times, probably few serious students either of foreign affairs or of the Address itself have ever taken Washington's words as a warrant for unconditional non-involvement in the political or even military concerns of the foreign world. Washington himself made too many hedges and qualifications to permit any such reading, and these have been pointed out many times. He had said, "steer clear of *permanent* alliances," qualified by "so far, I mean, as we are now at liberty to do it," and further qualified by the phrase about "temporary alliances for extraordinary emergencies." He had also said that "a predominant motive" with him in the formulation of his own current policy was "to gain time," so that the country might mature its institutions and acquire the strength to command its own fortunes. The period "is not far off ... when we may choose peace or war, as our interest, guided by justice, shall counsel."[10] So the Farewell Address cannot be construed, except in the most tortured sense, as an "isolationist" document.

But it can be, and has been, construed in other ways, and to exhibit other principles. One authority has said that it should be read primarily as a declaration of sovereignty, of "vigilant defense and maintenance of sovereign national independence against foreign meddling."[11] Another sees it as a combining, under Hamilton's hand, of disparate eighteenth-century European and American conceptions of foreign policy — the doctrine of "the interest of the state" and the idea of America's moral uniqueness — such that the Address embodies a basic tension which has characterized American attitudes about foreign affairs ever since, the tension "between Idealism and Realism."[12] Still another has gone so far as to call the Address a "statement of empire." Washington's real preoccupation, he says, was with westward expansion and with the maintenance of peace and union until such time as the United States might "become one of the great powers of the world," and thus the Farewell Address "can be properly understood only in relation to Washington's concept of his country's imperial future."[13] There is much to be said for each of these views, even with a reservation or two on the "imperial future" argument. (Whether that aim would in itself have impelled Washington to produce such a document as the Farewell Address is a nice question, since it was one about which few Americans disagreed, and on which they needed little advice.) But in any case, what each has in common is the taking for granted that in one way or another the Address's basic concern is with foreign affairs.

Other writers in recent years, however, have placed the emphasis quite differently, insisting that the Address deals "much more with domestic than foreign policy," and that the key section is the one on political parties. They argue, moreover, that Washington was doing two quite contradictory things. In repeating traditional dogmas against party and faction, he was striking at the Republican opposition, thus in effect making a partisan statement himself, and this reflected "his intellectual confusion" (as Richard Hofstadter has put it) "about the problem of government and opposition."[14] He was "allying himself with a party . . . not knowing that he had done so," having just issued a "campaign document" against the other party.[15]

He certainly was striking at the Republican opposition—the more one examines the Address as a whole with this in mind, the more apparent it becomes—and indeed against any form of organized opposition. Basic to the right of the people to establish government, he declares, is "the duty of every individual to obey the established government." Therefore "all combinations and associations, under whatever plausible character, with the real design to direct, controul, counteract, or awe the regular deliberation and action of the constituted authorities, are destructive of this fundamental principle. . . ."

> They serve to organize faction; to give it an artificial and extraordinary force; to put in the place of the delegated will of the nation the will of a party, often a small but artful and enterprising minority of the community, and, according to the alternate triumphs of different parties, to make the public administration the mirror of ill-concerted and incongruous projects of faction rather than the organ of consistent and wholesome plans, digested by common counsels and modified by mutual interests.[16]

Nor was this simply a theoretical abstraction and no more; Washington had specific men in mind who, as he saw it, had been doing these things, and he thought his fellow-citizens should be warned against them. There is thus good ground for viewing his valedictory, in some of its aspects at least, as a kind of party "campaign document." A fair number at the time did in fact so view it.[17]

All of this raises a bewildering series of issues, beginning with that of which, after all, of the two main sections of the Address—the one on parties or the one on foreign affairs—should be seen as the more important. But the answer may well be, neither one. Or rather, both—because the two sections are not separate at all, nor were they intended to be. They are organically connected; each is part of the same argument; both are aimed at a common evil. For Washington the transition from parties to foreign affairs was altogether a logical one; foreign affairs as he saw it constituted by all odds the predominant area of partisanship, the prime example of the curse of party. His experience was one long proof of it.

Washington was saying in effect that if foreign affairs should serve as the basis for domestic partisanship—especially if the fortunes of domestic parties are tied to the fortunes of contending foreign powers—conditions are thereby created which have the capacity to tear a society apart. Foreign influence finds its way into the government itself "through the channels of party passion," and "the policy and will of one country are subjected to the policy and will of another."[18] As for Washington's "intellectual confusion," it can probably be said that in warning against "the baneful effects of the spirit of party generally," he was, from the perspective of a long future, resisting a trend of modernization in politics, one that would in time become benign and constructive. To that extent he may have been "confused," but it can only be added that in this respect few men of his time were any less so. Moreover, if the events of his second administration were any kind of guide, politics *had* come to be based on foreign issues, and the more it became so the more destructive it was. If that was what "party" amounted to, he wanted no more of it. And to the degree that the first party "system," such as it was, did function on such a basis—divisions on foreign policy, and rival attachments to rival foreign powers (as in some sense it would continue to do through most of the next two decades to come)—to that degree it would work more or less the way Washington said it would. Indeed, domestic divisions on such matters, partisan or otherwise, have always meant the deepest kind of trouble, down to the present day.

But there is still the question of whether Washington, in striking at the Republican party and in apparently denying the legitimacy of any partisan opposition, had thereby himself become a partisan on the Federalist side. "No one can doubt," says one eminent critic, "that by the end of his administration Washington's role had become that of a committed partisan. . . ."[19] The assertion is in a sense plausible; still, it *can* be doubted. Behind it are assumptions about party politics developed only in the nineteenth century (a game with understood rules, and nothing personal intended), for which in Washington's time there was no precedent whatever, and of which Washington himself could have no conception. Nor, for that matter, could the opposition. Better to say that the role Washington had marked out for himself—that of a chief magistrate resolutely above all party and faction—was one which by the end of his administration he saw himself less and less able to protect. The unity which he, as the first head of a fragile republic exposed to all the broils of world conflict, had worked so painfully to construct was being threatened by irresponsible partisans in the nation's midst. And despite all such labors, here they were—these demagogues and vicious journalists—attacking *him*. Why?

Thus uniquely situated, whether he wanted to be there or not, he could hardly have seen things otherwise. The decisions he had made at every point of crisis during the previous twenty-four months—indeed, going back to the Neutrality Proclamation of 1793—had been unmistakably approved by the country at large. Less than ever, then, could he comprehend this mad attachment to France, this blind hatred of England, on the part of otherwise sensible men including many of his fellow-Virginians. They had been willing in 1794 to risk a disastrous war, one that would certainly have meant the destruction of America's merchant fleet, collapse of the finances, perhaps even dismemberment of the country itself. Some had even hinted that he himself had become a dupe and partisan of England. He, whose view of England had always been one of suspicion; he, who if necessary (though only if he saw no honorable alternative) would go to war with England or any other power in defense of his country's independence. And now (or so he could hardly help supposing) he had been fully vindicated by events. In the fall of 1794 the country had repudiated the Whiskey Rebels and overwhelmingly applauded his handling of the insurrection. The violent feeling over the Jay Treaty in the summer of 1795 had ebbed away, and by the end of the year it was obvious that Washington's ratification had met with general approval. Meanwhile Wayne's and Pinckney's treaties had given the West everything it had been clamoring for since 1789 and before: peace, land, and the free navigation of the Mississippi. Thus Washington's restraint in the face of repeated provocations—the spoliations, Dorchester's harangue to the Indians, Simcoe's activities on the Miami, and so on, had been totally justified. And finally, the country's prosperity by the end of 1795 had reached a splendid pinnacle, with large profits in shipping, high prices for exports, and a near doubling of imports. He was surely warranted (as he saw it) in telling his fellow-citizens, as he did in his annual message, that "the situation of our public affairs" had never given better cause for "mutual congratulation," and inviting them "to join with me, in profound gratitude to the Author of all good, for the numerous, and extraordinary blessings we enjoy."[20]

And yet it scarcely seemed to matter. They—the factious partisans—were bent on destruction. For all his efforts to keep the country safely neutral in the struggle between France and England, these men in the spring of 1796 were still prepared to risk everything—peace, prosperity, and domestic felicity—in a blind, even unconstitutional effort to wreck the very settlement by which all this had been preserved. It was accompanied, moreover, by vicious attacks on his own honor and patriotism, to say nothing of his judgment. Republican journalists were accusing him of treachery to France and to the French alliance, and this at the very moment when French privateers were defying the alliance and beginning to prey on American ships, and while French agents in America were intriguing to influence the forthcoming election.[21] They even spread stories that he had overdrawn his salary. Unavoidably he had, but they were throwing this up at the man who had served without pay throughout the Revolution.[22] Bache's paper in particular seemed devoid of all scruple, and the bitterness of Washington's feelings deepened month by month. He wrote in a private letter that until the previous year or so, "I had no conception that Parties would, or even could go, the length I have been witness to";

> nor did I believe until lately, that it was within the bonds of probability; hardly within those of possibility, that, while I was using my utmost exertions to establish a national character of our own, independent, as far as our obligations, and justice would permit, of every nation of the earth; and wished, by steering a steady course, to preserve this Country from the horrors of a desolating war, that I should be accused of being the enemy of one Nation, and subject to the influence of another; and to prove it, that every act of my administration would be tortured, and the grossest, and most insidious mis-representations of them be made (by giving one side *only* of a subject, and that too in such exaggerated and indecent terms as could scarcely be applied to a Nero; a notorious defaulter, or even to a common pickpocket).[23]

Such, then, was the context in which Washington arranged his thoughts for his valedictory address. Indeed, he was simmering when he composed his initial draft. As for his being unduly under Hamilton's influence (as is sometimes hinted), it might be well to note that one of Hamilton's friendly offices was that of toning down his language. He had originally wanted to say that as some of the Gazettes of the United States have teemed with all the Invective that disappointment, ignorance of facts, and malicious falsehoods could invent, to misrepresent my politics & affections; — to wound my reputation and feelings; — and to weaken, if not entirely to destroy the confidence you had been pleased to repose in me; it might be expected at the parting scene of my public life that I should take some notice of such virulent abuse.

He came close to telling them, in a self-pitying passage which Hamilton tactfully persuaded him to omit, that they would not have George Washington to kick around any more.[24]

So the first President of the United States could be very testy about his honor and reputation. But this was part of the larger pattern in which he had conceived his public duty and function from the first, and he was under no "intellectual confusion" as to what it was. His every care must be to preserve the safety of the country and of the government over which he had been summoned to preside, and this required, at the very least, the country's presenting a united face to an outside world only too happy to divide it. The principal menace here was party, and to charge *him* with partisanship was in effect to ignore the great obsession of his days and nights. There were "abundant proofs" in all his past public career, he insisted in the letter cited above, "that I was no party man myself, and the first wish of my heart was, if parties did exist, to reconcile them."[25] To be sure, it would be difficult to find an instance anywhere, from Washington's time to our own, of a new head of a revolutionary state who had much tolerance for opposition. Washington himself was no exception, and by the same token he could not but welcome the support of men who called themselves "the friends of government"; this may have made him a "partisan" of his own regime, but that is about as far as the logic can be carried. Prominent among such men was, of course, Alexander Hamilton. Nevertheless, as he pointedly reminded Jefferson, "there were as many instances within [your] own knowledge of my having decided *against,* as in *favor of* the opinions of the person evidently alluded to [Hamilton]; and moreover, that I was no believer in the infallibility of the politics, or measures of *any man living.*"[26] The first wish of his heart, he had said with regard to parties, was "to reconcile them." And in the light of his efforts to draw upon the best talents of such men as Jefferson, Madison, Randolph, and Monroe — each of whom had been heavily involved in the country's foreign relations — he thought it should be evident that he had done what reconciling he could. Yet the "spirit of party" had done something to them all. This in effect was the extended lament of the Farewell Address.

As it happened, the principles of the Farewell Address were in no single case exemplified more fully and at the same time more gloomily than in the current doings of James Monroe, charged with the affairs and interests of the United States as minister to the French Republic. The Monroe mission had done much to cast a cloud upon Washington's retirement, with consequences that were to occupy the whole term of Washington's successor.

2
Monroe in Paris

The nomination of James Monroe in May 1794 to succeed Gouverneur Morris as minister to France, immediately after Jay had departed on his mission to London, had been Randolph's idea. Washington may have had a misgiving or two about doing it, in view of the rather immoderate efforts Monroe had just made to obstruct the Jay mission, and in fact there were three others upon whom he had already tried without success to confer the appointment before finally offering it, under Randolph's urging, to Monroe. Still, the logic of it seemed by no means unreasonable at the time. At the outset of a major effort to achieve a settlement with Great Britain, and with both the previous French and American ministers— Genet and Morris—having so recently been recalled by their respective governments, each at the pointed request of the other, it was important to prevent relations with France from getting any worse. It was desirable to reassure her of America's continuing good will, and there should be no better way of doing this than through a representative known, as Monroe was, to be warmly disposed toward France and an ardent advocate of Franco-American friendship. And how better protect the national interest, and preserve a constantly menaced neutrality, than by keeping in the best possible repair our relations with both of the two great warring powers of Europe?

True, James Monroe was a partisan Republican. But in 1794 the spirit of party did not appear quite so baneful to Washington as it would two years later.

Washington's own freedom from partisanship had not yet been seriously challenged; the role he played from this detached eminence—that of reconciling, resolving, and balancing the counsels of men of sometimes violently clashing views—was more than aptly suited, as we have seen, to his particular gifts. He himself must have known, for all his doubts about the general adequacy of his talents, that he performed it with some astuteness. (Hamilton and Jefferson, agreeing in nothing else, had been at one in imploring him to serve a second term.) And if anything required a balancing now, it was the country's relations with England on the one side and France on the other. With John Jay, a man widely thought to be predisposed to an "English" viewpoint, bound for London in the hope of reaching an agreement there, it was wholly logical that a man of pro-French sentiments should proceed to Paris for similar purposes—if not to make a formal settlement, none being required, at least to repair and strengthen a good understanding which was in need of attention. And there was no reason to suppose that James Monroe or any other patriot representing America in a foreign capital would not do so with a primary zeal for his country's highest interests. The nomination was confirmed by the Senate on May 27, 1794, and Monroe set sail from Baltimore on June 18.[27]

Monroe's instructions required him to strive for two main objects. One was to reassure France, to "strengthen our friendship with that country," and to "show our confidence in the French Republic." The other was to persuade the French to lift the restrictions they had placed upon American commerce at the outbreak of hostilities in 1793, and to "insist upon compensation for the capture and spo-liations of our property, and injuries to the persons of our citizens, by French cruisers."[28] Yet from the moment he arrived in France, Monroe to all intents and purposes had redefined the scope of his mission to include a vastly broader aim, that of committing the United States unreservedly to the French cause, even to the point of war with Great Britain.

Viewed from Philadelphia, the succeeding two years—from the summer of 1794 to the summer of 1796, when Washington was considering his Farewell Address—seemed to embrace one continuous train of blunders, indiscretions, and bad judgment on Monroe's part, and cynicism, manipulation, and duplicity on that of the French. It all terminated in Monroe's being peremptorily recalled, in sufficient disgrace that his career came close to being ruined then and there, and with relations between America and France in a worse state than ever. The prin-cipal items in this extraordinary sequence merit some examination.

The first, of course, was the reception of Monroe by the National Convention on August 14, 1794, and Monroe's own performance there. Just in itself, this scene of enthusiasm for Monroe and America would have been all to the good—or, at the very least, harmless—had Monroe not been carried away to the point of raptures over "the fortitude, magnanimity, and heroic valor" of the French forces warring against England, the very country with which his fellow-diplomat Jay was then laboring to reach a peaceable settlement, or if he had not so happily received the kiss from Merlin de Douai, president of the Convention, sealing the fraternal union which was to "complete the annihilation of an impious coalition of tyrants." Washington felt obliged to get off a brisk reprimand. We all supposed, he had Randolph tell Monroe, that "your audience . . . would take place in the private chamber of some committee." Moreover,

> if private affection and opinions had been the only points to be consulted, it would have been immaterial where or how they were delivered. But the range of a public minister's mind will go to all the relations of our country with the whole world. We do not perceive that your instructions have imposed upon you the extreme glow of some parts of your address. . . .

Nevertheless Washington was still disposed to be forbearing, and even to conjec-ture privately that the incident might have a not unwholesome effect upon the negotiations in London.[29]

But Monroe's succeeding reports gave cause for some real apprehension. In his first attempt to get the French to withdraw their decree of May 9, 1793, authorizing seizure of American grain cargoes bound for enemy ports—illegal under the Treaty of 1778—he had gratuitously volunteered that if, on the contrary, the French government should find that such restrictions produced "any solid benefits," then "the American Government, and my countrymen in general, will not only bear the departure with patience, but with pleasure." He also told the Committee of Public Safety that he was not instructed to base his appeal on the Treaty of 1778 but only on France's own interest, which was identical with that of the United States, and on the "happiest effect" a repeal would have in "conciliating the affections of the citizens of both republics, and thereby cementing more closely their union. . . ." Randolph could only expostulate that Monroe's instructions gave no ground for his representing the American case in any such way. If repeal of the decree and compensation for the damages incurred under it were not based on the Treaty of 1778, America could have no other real "cause or pretext for asking relief," and the President was not disposed to promise that the American people would bear with either patience or pleasure "a departure from stipulations which are generally believed to be important to us." The French paid little attention to Monroe's appeal, and for the time being did nothing about the decree. Eventually they did revoke it, but only after the British had withdrawn their Provision Order of June 1793, and then not for long.[30]

By late November 1794, Monroe was jubilant over France's military successes. "The fortune of France," he exulted in his dispatch of the 20th, "has risen to the utmost height of splendor, whilst that of her enemies has declined to the lowest state of depression. Her armies are every where triumphant, whilst theirs are every where routed and broken." France's movements in the Netherlands were certain to produce such an effect upon England "that, if America strikes the blow her own interest dictates, and which every other consideration prompts, it must be decisive, and, if not ruinous to the fortunes of that proud and insolent nation, will certainly secure us the objects we have in view."[31] What "blow"? The "objects" were those John Jay was trying to achieve through amicable negotiation.

Two weeks later, Monroe was inspired with another idea. During one of his appearances before the Committee of Public Safety he had been asked whether, France being distressed for funds, any aid might be obtained from the United States. Monroe replied that although he had no instructions on that point, he was "satisfied" that such aid would be rendered if it were in his country's power to do it. And now, he proposed to his superiors, why should we not make a loan of $5 million to France, under the guarantee of the United States and with a mortgage on a portion of France's national domain to secure it? He was persuaded, he said, "that the [American] people would cheerfully bear a tax, the product of which was to be applied in aid of the French Republic." There was a chilly non-response from Philadelphia. Washington might well have wondered whether the American minister to France would have liked to try laying an additional tax on whiskey.[32]

Monroe then proceeded to repeat his case for military action against Great Britain. "And I am likewise persuaded, if we do embark in the war, that [the French] will see us through it; and . . . [even] if we do not, and especially if we aid them in the article of money, that they will support, as far as they are able, our demands upon Spain and England." (The demand upon Spain was for the opening of the Mississippi, which Pinckney was to secure the following year with no help from France.) Now, he thought, was the moment to seize what was rightfully ours. "Britain is certainly not in a condition to embark in a war against us, though we should dispossess her of Canada; she would of course be less apt to do it, if we only placed her troops beyond the lakes."[33]

But there was still the troublesome matter of the Jay negotiations, which did not fit anywhere in Monroe's expanding vision. By mid-December, Monroe, temporarily deceived by premature newspaper reports, was wild with anxiety that Jay's mission might actually succeed. What if it should? Suppose England were to grant everything we asked? "If any thing of this kind should have taken place," he wrote agitatedly to Randolph, "I know the dilemma in which you will be all thrown." Randolph had the good sense not to show this to Washington, while he himself was becoming more and more apprehensive over Monroe's warlike recommendations.[34]

By this time, of course, Jay had actually concluded his treaty, though nobody as yet, including Monroe, had any idea of its contents, which would not be generally known until the following July. This was a problem that involved Monroe in a growing round of difficulties as the French, prompted by their minister in America, began pressing him for details which he was unable to furnish them. In his original instructions he had been told that "to remove all jealousy with respect to Mr. Jay's mission to London, you may say, that he is positively forbidden to weaken the engagements between this country and France." Monroe certainly sounded this note in all his communications on the subject to the French government. But he went much farther, telling them that Jay had authority only to demand return of the posts and compensation for losses of property, and that he had no powers to conclude a treaty of commerce. The harassed Randolph, who of course knew otherwise, and in fact now had the text of the treaty before him, sent off another reprimand. "You intimate," he wrote,

> that *your* instructions amount to an exclusion from Mr. Jay's mission of every object, except compensation for plundered property, and restitution of the posts. For a moment, let me entreat you to call to mind the different topics for negotiation, which were actually before the Senate at the time of Mr. Jay's nomination, and which were not included in either of those points. Were not Mr. Jefferson's animadversions upon the refusal of Great Britain to enter into a commercial treaty, and his plan for commercial reprisals, before you? Would it not have been extraordinary to pass by so fair an opportunity of bringing forward *all* our discontents? Was it not urged as an objection ... that the terms of the nomination were sufficiently broad for any purpose of negotiation?[35]

Long before he received this, Monroe had actually promised to show the French a copy of the treaty as soon as he could obtain one, and before its contents should become public. He was prevented from doing so by Jay's own refusal to communicate it to him except on condition of confidentiality. "Solicitous always to get hold of the Treaty prematurely, for the use of the French government," Washington later commented, "he . . . would have wished to see the Executive of the U. States as indiscreetly forward as himself in promulgating it, before it had been submitted to the Senate." When had the French ever shown us one of their treaties before it was ratified? "None but a party man, lost to all sense of propriety would have asked such a thing; and, no other wd. have brot. himself into such a predicament."[36]But Monroe could not let well enough alone, and by September 1795 he was back at his bellicose schemes of the year before. In a dispatch which Washington received at about the time he was preparing his annual message for that year—the one in which he gave thanks for the blessings of peace and prosperity, and for the country's having escaped the horrors of war through the negotiated settlement of all outstanding causes of discord—Monroe was once more breathing fire and proposing to cow England by the combined might of France and America. The Jay Treaty, whose contents were now known, had given great offense to France; it had procured for the United States, as Monroe saw it, only dishonor and no benefits. Assuming that it would never be ratified, he now urged that there should be a fresh negotiation, to be held either in France or perhaps in Switzerland (he himself would be the logical man to conduct it); it would be carried on in conjunction with France; and it would be supported not only by a show of force but by the actual use of it. In order to "secure success," he raved, "by our embarking this Government with full zeal in our behalf, and striking terror into England, it will be necessary to lay hold of her property within the United States, take the posts, and then invade Canada. This would not only secure to us completely our claims upon Britain, and especially if we likewise cut up her trade by privateers; but, by making a decisive and powerful diversion in favor of France, promote, and very essentially, a general peace."[37]

It is likely that about the time Washington was contemplating this hymn to the invincibility of France and prophecy of England's impending destruction, a report from another American diplomat in Europe was also brought to his attention.

"The force of Great Britain is so far from being exhausted," wrote John Quincy Adams from The Hague,

> that her maritime power was never at any period so great as it is at present. Her naval superiority is everywhere so indisputably established that in the Mediterranean, on the ocean, in the channel, or in the North sea, a French or a Dutch armed vessel can scarce venture out of an harbor without being intercepted. . . . The French frigates which during the last season were very successful against their British commerce have all been taken, or dare not keep the sea, and for several months past there has been scarce a single capture made by them. . . .[38]

How could Monroe have been ignorant of, or refused to take account of, or failed to report, such important information?

By the spring of 1796 there had come to be a general feeling in the Administration that the Monroe mission was producing nothing but mischief. Monroe was certainly not defending the Jay Treaty to the French with anything like the conviction and vigor his official position required of him. Timothy Pickering, who had become Secretary of State after the disgrace of Randolph in the summer of 1795, reminded him more than once of the many opportunities he had had in this regard and failed to take advantage of.[39] Meanwhile the French were sending Monroe denunciations of the treaty and warning him of the steps they would have to take to show their displeasure. An envoy extraordinary would soon be sent to the United States to declare France's view that the alliance was at an end, and Minister Adet, who had asked for his own recall, might not be replaced. As for

Monroe, being violently opposed to the treaty himself, he found it very difficult to conceal his conviction that the French were justified in their outrage over it. His views, circulated to his Republican friends in private letters, were becoming a matter of common knowledge.[40] But most of all, and to an even greater degree than anyone in America suspected, he was taking part with the French against his own government, first giving them to expect that the Republican majority in the House of Representatives would refuse to implement the treaty, then making excuses for their not having done it, and finally counseling the French Foreign Minister that all would come right if the French government would only wait until the Republicans should have overthrown the current administration in the forthcoming election of 1796. Hostilities with France, Monroe told them, "will force the American government to throw itself into the arms of the English and hand it over to their influence; aristocracy will predominate in the United States and liberty will be betrayed. On the other hand, by patiently enduring the wrongs of the present president, you will leave it no excuse; you will enlighten the Americans and influence a contrary choice in the next election. Every grievance of which France can complain will then be redressed."[41]

Washington never knew that Monroe had gone quite this far. But by now he had good reason to suspect him of activities almost as questionable. The last straw was a letter Monroe had written to George Logan a year before, which had just fallen into the hands of Wolcott and Pickering (by what means has never been quite certain) early in July 1796. In his covering note, Monroe offered to provide Logan with a regular series of letters, this one being a starter, about affairs in France from "a gentleman in Paris to his friend in Philadelphia," which might be given to the public through Bache's newspaper. The letter was full of praise for the achievements of French arms, and of warning, with regard to England, as to "how little confidence we ought to place in treaties with that power." The busy John Beckley also received a copy, as had Jefferson, Burr, and Robert R. Livingston. "You will," Monroe told Logan, "arrange matters confidentially with Mr. B[ache] himself, who likewise possesses mine."[42]

Washington and the entire cabinet were now agreed that Monroe would have to be recalled. The American minister to France had communicated "less confidentially," according to the Attorney-General, Charles Lee, "with the executive of the United States than with the opposers and libellers of his administration, and . . . there is too much reason to believe he is furthering the views of a faction in America, more than the peace and happiness of the United States."[43]

Meanwhile, still another sequence of revelations had been coming into Philadelphia shedding light upon the depth of France's devotion to the United States. They concerned French designs upon Spanish Louisiana, and must have made something of a contrast to the innocence of James Monroe on that same subject. Almost from the beginning of his mission Monroe had repeatedly written of France's willingness and desire to assist the United States in the opening of the Mississippi to American navigation. In May 1795 he was saying that the French minister then about to negotiate peace terms with Spain at Basel had been instructed "to secure in their treaty the points insisted on by us," and that Spain would find "that a good understanding with France is not to be expected or preserved without a good understanding with us." Actually the French negotiator never had any such instructions, whatever Monroe may have been told in Paris to jolly him along. Quite the contrary; he was doing everything he could to persuade Spain to cede Louisiana to France, promising that the French would close the Mississippi to American trade and prevent American expansion westward.[44] And in America the French minister, Pierre Adet, had commissioned an agent, General Victor Collot, to reconnoiter the Mississippi basin from Pittsburgh to New Orleans; in March 1796, Washington began to receive from various sources a running account of Collot's flamboyant doings.[45]

Collot, who was not a very good general but had some talents as a cartographer and military engineer, proceeded, with copious notes and commentary, to map every settlement, outpost, and fortification along his way that he deemed to be of any military significance. Since he was incapable of holding his tongue, rumors of the grandiose plans concocted by him and his employers quickly drifted back to Philadelphia. France would soon reoccupy Louisiana, and Collot would meanwhile test the likelihood of inducing the western inhabitants to separate from the United States and join France's new western salient. The idea was that since the eastern states would probably fall under British influence, the best way to counteract such influence was for France to regain control of the Mississippi, which in turn meant control of the whole western country, which in turn could be made militarily impregnable through the mountains, bluffs, and other natural barriers; and of course the benefit for France's new friend, Spain, would be an end to American expansion. Collot openly boasted to various Americans he talked to that "you will be reduced to the necessity of throwing yourselves into the arms of France, and abandon the Union which cannot give you a market, &c., &c., &c." One of Washington's informants, to whom Collot had unfolded this project, was Hugh Henry Brackenridge, the onetime peacemaker of Pittsburgh. Brackenridge since the days of the Whiskey Rebellion seems to have had no further stomach for grand talk about defending mountain passes against federal armies.[46]

Probably one of the last Americans to get wind of these schemes was James Monroe, who picked up a "whisper" of them in Paris in August 1796 and passed it on in one of his dispatches. By that time, however, Spain had already decided she was not interested. And Monroe's own letters of recall were already on their way.[47]

As for an explanation of James Monroe and his behavior in Paris—the fatuities, the self-deception, and all the rest: this makes for rather a large question. Here, neither Monroe's subsequent career nor even his basic character can tell us much. He was to have a decent and honorable record of public service stretching thirty years into the future. It would even include two quite creditable stints of diplomacy, one involving the purchase of Louisiana and the other the making of a treaty with Great Britain in 1806 not so very different from the one made by John Jay in 1794. True, the scope of his mind cannot justly be compared with that of his foremost contemporaries. Yet for honest patriotism and devotion to duty,

James Monroe must certainly have his place among the worthies of the early republic, and Jefferson was probably right when he said of Monroe, "Turn his soul wrong side outwards and there is not a speck on it."[48] The fact remains, though, that few Americans of the time could have been more thoroughly victimized by the delirium of the French Revolution. Why? And how could he, when asked to represent his country's interests in Paris—a mission he embraced with alacrity—have made such a botch of it?

There is no knowing, of course, whether any other American in the international circumstances of the 1790s, with or without Monroe's particular predispositions, could have done much better. In any case, Monroe operated under some heavy liabilities, not all of which were of his own making.

One of them was the American Secretary of State, the ill-starred Edmund Randolph. Randolph is a whole problem in himself, and the more we see of his furtive dithering the more we can appreciate Washington's flinging aside all compunction in the summer of 1795 in his ferocious urge to be rid of the man once and for all. Randolph in his own murky way shared many of Monroe's francophile sentiments, which had been the main reason for his pressing Monroe forward for the Paris mission after the President's "several attempts" (as Washington himself drily put it) "had failed to obtain a more eligible character." Randolph and Monroe had both done what they could—and there is evidence that they did it more or less in concert—to clog up the special mission to England while plans for it were being completed in the spring of 1794. Randolph himself never had any faith in Jay's mission, and he let Monroe know it. He told him in an official dispatch that "notwithstanding all the pompous expectations announced in the gazettes, of compensation to the merchants, the prospect of it is, in my judgment, illusory; and I do not entertain the most distant hope of the surrender of the western posts." It is likely that in their private talks before Monroe's departure he expressed himself with even less restraint. Moreover, he never showed Monroe a copy of Jay's instructions, and seems actually to have deceived him as to their full scope. By innuendo and omission, he gave Monroe to understand that Jay had powers only to demand satisfaction for injuries done, not to conclude a treaty of commerce. Randolph later denied it, but apparently he gave Joseph Fauchet, then France's minister to the United States, the same impression, and felt called upon to issue a denial of that too.[49]

Why should Randolph, sharing so many of Monroe's pro-French views, so mislead him? Randolph's mind was so bemused most of the time, what with his urge to stay right with both Washington and his Republican friends in Virginia, that he may not have known himself. But his private expectations, or hopes, or whatever, that the Jay mission would fail, together with his own part in promoting Monroe for the mission to France, probably had a great deal to do with it. He may have sensed that if he had given Monroe a full outline of the Administration's desires and aspirations, as set forth in Jay's instructions, Monroe might have made inconvenient difficulties. Either he might have refused to go, or would have gone without the requisite energy and zeal to conciliate the French or to seize the opportunities which might be afforded by a breakdown of American relations with England. In any case, there was some ground for Monroe's subsequent complaints that he was not fully informed of the Administration's intentions, though it probably has to be added that since they were so at odds with his own he was only too disposed to be misled.[50]

But Monroe had another and far greater liability than Randolph, something entirely beyond his capacity to influence or even to understand. This was the French themselves, and the urgencies they were under in the all-absorbing European conflict, to say nothing of their own anything-but-settled internal conditions. One may take it as a guiding principle that no review of Franco-American diplomacy during this entire period, no matter how extensive, can make much sense if it does not take into account the minimal importance, the superlative inconsequentiality, of the United States to any aspect of French policy. Given France's national and international situation, there was hardly a reason for it to be otherwise. Their preoccupied inattention with regard to American affairs, their garbled ignorance, their unconcern—which has so seldom fully penetrated American minds, then or later—must be taken as the starting point for every observation made and every conclusion drawn respecting France and America throughout the wars of the French Revolution. In France, histories continue to be written of the Revolution in its various phases and aspects, in which America is not so much as mentioned. We, on the other hand, write whole books on Franco-American affairs during that same era which even the most learned of French authorities on French diplomacy would find all but unintelligible, for reasons having nothing to do with their accuracy or minuteness of detail, only with their pertinence to the course of French history.[51]

To be sure, the *idea* of America—the idea of a free republic given birth by a victorious revolutionary struggle against the monarchical oppressions of Great Britain and gallantly assisted by France herself—was of no small ideological usefulness to the French in the turmoil of their own revolution. A perfect instance of this was the reception of James Monroe, and it was no accident that it occurred as it did. Monroe arrived in Paris on August 2, 1794, just five days after the execution of Robespierre, and was kept waiting nearly two weeks to be received. The Committee of Public Safety was intensely preoccupied with more important matters; nobody was much inclined to bestir himself on this one. The period of executions had more or less ended, but no one as yet could be certain of it; meanwhile a wrong step on anything, no matter how trivial, might (who could tell?) cost any individual official his head. But meanwhile the National Convention of some seven hundred members was beginning to reassert its authority, and it occurred to a functionary in one of the diplomatic bureaus that the Convention might itself wish to receive the new American minister. This struck everyone as a capital idea, as well it might. France had just passed through one of the most fearful and divisive periods of the entire Revolution, one in which, especially in the final weeks preceding Robespierre's downfall, few could have had much idea what the next day might bring. Here, now, was the opportunity to stage a tremendous ritual of reintegration. After all that the Jacobins had done, in their obsession with internal treason, to separate Frenchmen from each other, this could be a ceremonial reinvocation of revolutionary unity, of the original generosity and élan of 1789, on wholly safe and non-controversial ground. And it was the abstraction of America, the mythical republic of the West, that provided the perfect occasion.[52]

But the ideological abstraction was one thing; what would happen when the scene was over? What about America as a fact, as an entity that had separate interests of its own? That was really another matter, and to no Frenchman was it a very pressing one. For instance, there were the representations Monroe was instructed to make about damages to American shipping and about France's general commercial policy toward the United States—which was currently about the same as England's, and which included the vexatious decree of May 1793 authorizing the seizures. The Committee gave Monroe fair words, but did nothing about the decree for the time being, and never would make compensation for the damages. But then when the British revoked their Order in Council of June 1793 (the obnoxious "provision order"), the case was different. France could have no pretext for treating neutral commerce more severely than England did, and in January 1795 the decree (with more high-flown words for Monroe's benefit) was withdrawn.[53]

The Americans, as we have said, carried a certain ideological usefulness for France. But what other kinds of usefulness? It might be supposed that, revolutionary fervor or not, the worldly French must have known exactly what they wanted from America and exactly how America suited their interests. But whether many of them ever devoted much thought to that question is dubious. For instance, there were two broad, more or less obvious ways of viewing America— as a source of food or as an ally in war—and few Frenchmen seem to have had a very clear idea which was the better one.

Of these alternatives, America as a supplier of provisions was certainly the more logical, and one for which American neutrality was essential. And in fact the Jacobin regime which overthrew the Gironde in 1793 had told Genet in no uncertain words that he should regard the movement of supplies as his most important object. It is also true that large shipments of American grain and flour had been exceedingly helpful to France in the summer of 1794. But the need for such provisions was not a stable factor in French policy. For one thing, it became pressing only in periods of poor harvests in France, and for another, America was not the only source, nor even the most important one. Then, after Howe's naval victory in the Channel on June 1, 1794, France's capacity to provide armed convoys was sharply reduced, and would in the following year be still more so. France's claims upon America for money, moreover, would be removed when the last of America's Revolutionary debt was liquidated in the summer of 1795.[54]

Did France, on the other hand, seriously want the United States to go to war with England? John Quincy Adams certainly thought so, and George Washington had no doubt that if France could find a way of pushing us into the war she would do it. Monroe himself, though not seeing the case in any such sinister light, in effect thought so too. He believed that the French would find it highly useful for America to engage in some form of hostilities with Great Britain, and, as we have seen, he actually hoped to bring it on. Yet here too it is difficult to perceive any clear line of consistency in French policy. Monroe would have been greatly dashed if he could have seen the instructions drawn up in October 1794 for Citizen Oudart, the man who was scheduled (before the French changed their minds and sent Pierre Adet instead) to replace Fauchet as minister to the United States. Oudart was told that the Americans should be discouraged from joining "in this war of liberty against despotism," and that if they were determined upon reprisals against Great Britain they should not count on French assistance.[55] But then it seems that when the new French government, the Directory, was set up in October 1795, the new Foreign Minister, Charles Delacroix, had different ideas. Delacroix in January 1796 produced a remarkable plan for America, largely pieced together from the dispatches of Adet, whereby France would "take advantage of the ferment that agitates the United States, to make them declare that power against England." This would be done by arousing the people ("while adroitly concealing the arouser," namely the French minister) to regain their liberty by unseating Washington and electing Jefferson, which would then "give the French Republic the influence she ought to have in America." America would thereupon break the Jay Treaty and enter the war; she would regain Canada for France; French naval forces would convoy American supplies to France and her colonies (he did not say where the ships would come from); the Americans, deprived of British manufactures, "will favor our industry and new channels will open for our commerce which from then on will be without competition." Every part of the scheme was the idlest fantasy. The Directory seems not to have taken it very seriously, though they saw no harm in letting Adet stir up whatever mischief he could in the coming American elections.[56]

America, then, was not enough of a factor in French calculations to require a particularly thought-out policy. Was there anything, then, that did pass for "policy"? The Louisiana plan was something that seemed to have a certain specificity, at least to the extent that the French negotiator at Basel was instructed to persuade Spain to retrocede the province to France, with promises to contain the Americans east of the mountains. But how coherent a plan was it, and what would have been its consequences, especially if France had closed the river? Even Jefferson would have an answer to that, when he said in a similar situation a few years later: "The day that France takes possession of New Orleans, fixes the sentence which is to restrain her forever within her low-water mark. . . . From that moment, we must marry ourselves to the British fleet and nation."[57] The French had neither the ships nor the troops which would have had to be committed to an enterprise of this scale, whereas the ships the British might require for a blockade of New Orleans would have cost the Royal Navy nothing. (Or the Americans, with the force they had at sea by mid-1798, could have done that themselves.) Meanwhile American militia could have occupied the entire Mississippi Valley in a matter of months. True, Napoleon Bonaparte's daydream on Louisiana in 1800 was no more real than this one. But at least Bonaparte had an army, or thought he had. As it happened, of course, Spain in 1796 was not yet prepared to let go of Louisiana, so nothing came of it. In any case, the French were diverting themselves with whimsies that had little substance. Once they turned to examine them systematically, as Bonaparte would eventually have to do, this became only too obvious.

The other question concerns France's reaction to the Jay Treaty as such, and how much of a determinant this was in France's subsequent attitude toward the United States. One answer might be that "France" had no reaction at all. Even that of the French government, judging from its official newspaper, was sluggish at best. The *Moniteur* carried a brief notice in December 1794 that a treaty of commerce and navigation had been concluded in London between Great Britain and the United States, but without any comment. Nine months later an outline of the treaty, again brief, appeared in the same paper, still without comment. By that time the Republican press in America was in effect telling the French how they *ought* to react, by means of voluminous reports of criticism forwarded by Pierre Adet, the French minister there, to his home government. Adet implored the Committee of Public Safety to bestir itself. "In the six months since the treaty was known in Europe, what have you done? Does anyone know what you think of that treaty? Whether it displeases or offends you? Must not your silence be seen as a mark of approval? Or rather, must it not appear that you take no interest whatsoever in the affairs of this country?"[58]

The fact was that when the French in 1796 did inaugurate the system of commerce-raiding that would prove so destructive to American shipping, it was only in the most strained sense a reaction to the Jay Treaty. It was rather in response to the exigencies of war with Great Britain. In the circumstances which governed the conflict between these two powers that had begun in 1793 and would go on for nearly a quarter-century, the urge to take bites out of neutral commerce from time to time, especially cargoes likely to end up in enemy ports, was overwhelming. Both powers did it; each had in fact done it off and on since the very beginning of the war, regardless of their official relations with the governments concerned. Nor did either of them, in the face of what they saw as necessity, require very substantial pretexts. And for the French there was an additional necessity, especially in the period following the installation of the Directory in October 1795, which was simply that of money. The sheer stringencies of the French treasury had more to do with the policies of the Directory, from then until the time of its downfall four years later, than did any action taken either by the United States or by any of the lesser states of Europe.

As for pretexts based on the Jay Treaty, the French were getting whatever prompting they may have needed from the Americans themselves. A steady series of cues as to how they ought to respond if such a treaty were made came from Monroe, months before it was known what kind of treaty it would be. His own feelings were apparent all along; afterwards, his mortification was obvious. Even more obvious were the cues coming from Republican partisans in America, to say nothing of the American colony in Paris. Indeed, when the Directory eventually decreed that France would henceforth "treat neutral vessels . . . in the same manner as they shall suffer the English to treat them," they hardly needed a Jay Treaty to provide the occasion. They could refer to a string of other complaints as well, and did so. French ministers in America, beginning with Genet, had been construing the Franco-American treaty of 1778, with reference to the treatment of privateers and other matters, in their own special way, and had thereby accumulated a weighty catalogue of grievances against the American government. The authorities in Paris had not paid a great deal of attention. But it was all there in the files, for whenever it might prove useful.[59]

Even so, the steps they did take were erratic, ill-considered, even mindless. The decree of July 2, 1796, on the treatment of commerce was so sweepingly and carelessly drawn as to give warrant for almost anything, as in fact it did. Then there was their treatment of Monroe's successor, Charles Cotesworth Pinckney, who arrived in Paris to take up his post in December 1796. Pinckney was a Federalist, though hardly of an obnoxious sort; he had been selected precisely for the friendliness of his feelings toward France, and in the hope that matters might somehow be patched up. But in a fit of pique at Monroe's recall—the Directory found it convenient to have Monroe on hand, though they had paid little attention to him for months—the French government not only refused to receive Pinckney but in fact ordered him out of the country, contrary to all known diplomatic usage. (Thomas Paine, back in his former role as a sort of free-lance consultant on American affairs, had told someone in the Directory that Pinckney's appointment was unconstitutional.)[60] And meanwhile, on the question of what to do with their own diplomatic establishment in America, the Directory had pitched upon, and then altered or abandoned, one irritably absent-minded scheme after another.

First they thought they might replace Adet, who did not like America and wanted to come home, with an envoy extraordinary. This was to be a Citizen Vincent, who was instructed to demand reparations for the treaty violations Adet had been complaining of, to work for the annulment of the Jay Treaty, and to propose a new treaty of alliance. If the Americans did not properly respond, he would leave. Vincent was to have embarked in March 1796, but for some reason the Directory changed their minds about sending him. Then they decided to leave Adet where he was for the time being. Then, against the day when Adet should eventually depart, they appointed not a new minister but simply a chargé d'affaires who would take over the legation. The man they appointed was the violent Michel-Ange Mangourit, formerly consul at Charleston and later attached to the French legation at Madrid, who had already made himself *persona non grata* to both the American and Spanish governments. Monroe managed to talk them out of this one. But then they decided to recall Adet without appointing any successor at all. Adet would suspend his ministerial functions, remaining for a time as a private French citizen and doing what he could to be useful. This, so the announcement went, was not intended as a total rupture but "as a mark of discontent, which is to last until the Government of the United States returns to sentiments, and to measures, more conformable to the interests of the alliance, and the sworn friendship between the two nations."[61] Adet, with high hopes for Jefferson, proceeded to intrigue vigorously for Republican victory in the elections. Even many Republicans, including James Madison, were dismayed; this was the very sort of "foreign interference" which Washington had been so explicit about in his recent address.

Adet at length had to give up on Jefferson, who, he concluded regretfully, was no more dependable than the others. "Jefferson, I say, is an American and, on this account, he cannot sincerely be our friend. An American is the born enemy of all European peoples."[62]

One looks in vain for any of this in books of French history, and understandably so, for two main reasons. One is that if the United States were to make more than the most marginal difference, or be taken with the least seriousness, it would have required an America with both the power and the willingness to give France active assistance in her struggle with the allied monarchs of Europe. Any Frenchman who thought twice about it must have known, if he knew nothing else, that such a condition did not exist. The logical "policy," then, toward the Americans, so far as it suited France's requirements to have one, was simply to toy with them.

The other reason for America's obscurity in French memory for the period under review is that during this very time events were afoot, with which America had not the remotest connection, which would transform the course of the Revolution and alter the face of Europe. The Directory, though it would survive in some form until November 1799, was never a popular government. Resting on a narrow political base, it was under a chronic menace from both right and left. It began its career with the suppression of the royalist uprising of Vendémiaire (October 1795); then in May of the following year a radical plot to overthrow the Directory, the so-called "Babeuf conspiracy," was likewise crushed and its leaders executed. Some two months previous the Corsican artillery officer Bonaparte, then twenty-seven and already a brigadier-general, had enforced the closing of the Panthéon Club, where the Babouvists had been meeting before they went underground. He had also, with his celebrated "whiff of grapeshot," helped to put down the Vendémiaire insurrection. And now this same Bonaparte, in command of a small army, was beginning his unbelievable exploits in Italy. Knowing in reality no authority but his own, dictating his terms as province after province fell before him, he sent back news which filled the Directors with mixed tremors of joy and dread. He completed the conquest of Piedmont in April and then pushed into Lombardy, brought off his miracle against the Austrians at Lodi, then to Pavia, then Cremona, and made his triumphal entry into Milan on May 15. "He had become," says Louis Madelin, "the arbiter of the whole country." In three more years he would be the arbiter of France as well.[63]

As for the Monroe mission, the final liability under which it labored was James Monroe himself. It was not a question of ability, or character, or patriotism, and certainly not of good will. It was rather that the man was bound to an ideological stake from which he was able to view events, and his own part in them, in one way only—and to do, say, and believe things that he would not otherwise have imagined. If, however, Monroe's conception of America and the French Revolution were simply taken as a kind of given, then the manner in which he responded to what he saw and heard makes a certain amount of sense. It even merits a certain sympathy.

The basic conviction Monroe was under when he arrived, which would be echoed in all his reports and reflected in all his acts, was that Great Britain was fundamentally corrupt, inherently weak, and in all likelihood on the point of collapse. The interests of the sister republics, France and America, in the humbling of British power were identical. It was only such men as Gouverneur Morris, with their starkly anti-republican prejudices, that had prevented the French all along from seeing where America's real sympathies lay. But now America had a true and undoubted republican representing her. He, Monroe, would open their eyes, re-establish the fraternal bonds, and at the same time rescue America from the worst of evils, that of slipping back into the orbit of England, of monarchy, of re-enslavement.

And it all started off so well. The scene before the Convention, in which he was the central figure, was undoubtedly one of the profoundest experiences of his life. Then, in his representations on American commerce, he amazed the French (as he must have thought) with his frankness and magnanimity in assuring them that he was grounding his case not on the rights to which America was entitled under their mutual treaty, but simply on France's own interests, the same in all ways as America's, from which it followed that if France saw it otherwise, America would bear her restrictions not only "with patience, but with pleasure." By November he had indications that his efforts were bearing fruit, and by the beginning of the year 1795, with the repeal of the decree of May 1793 on provisions, he was overjoyed to think that his view of things and his handling of them had been entirely vindicated. Moreover, French victories all through 1794—and more were forthcoming—filled him with euphoria. These successes, which served America's interest as fully as France's, were overwhelming proof that France was master of the future, and that he and all his Republican friends in America had been right all along in perceiving America's fortunes and those of France as being naturally and inevitably bound together. The moment was surely at hand, he pleaded, as he piled up the breathtaking possibilities in his reports home, for America to throw in her financial and even military resources with those of France to complete the ruin of England and inaugurate for America and Europe a new republican age.

But the shadow that hung over everything was the mission of John Jay in London, and the menace of what Jay might be doing there. What, really, was the point of it? Uneasy premonitions came to be transformed, as the months passed, into a nightmare. And for Monroe, the nightmare would never end. What opportunities, what prizes, had been within his grasp only to slide away: with this infamous bargain, all his labors had come to nothing. Everything that happened to him in his final year—the neglect by his hosts; their injured reproaches; the withdrawal of French aid in opening the Mississippi; the brutal repudiation by his own government; the wrecking of his mission, perhaps of his very career—all had but a single explanation. Small wonder that he should clutch at straws, send frantic warnings to his friends, write indiscreet letters, even plead with the French to be patient until the Republicans could set things right in the coming elections. The great alliance was in ruins. Was it France's fault? How could it be? It was England, and her dupes in America, that had brought all this to pass. Monroe did, to be sure, make a belated effort in July 1796 to defend the treaty. But by then it was too late. "I have detained them seven months," he exclaimed from the bitterness of his heart, "from doing what they ought to have done at once."[64]

Upon reading Washington's Farewell Address, though it mentioned no person or no country by name, James Monroe perceived only too well what the President was driving at. Understandably enough, he burst forth once more in lamentation:

> Most of the monarchs of the earth practice ingratitude in their transactions with other powers . . . but Mr. Washington has the merit of transcending, not the great men of the antient republicks, but the little monarchs of the present day in preaching it as a publick virtue.[65]

3

The State of Politics in 1796

Few who have written about the retirement of Washington have been able to resist Fisher Ames's remark that the publication of the Farewell Address would "serve as a signal, like dropping a hat, for party racers to start."[66] A savory quip, and not altogether wrong—but misleading to any extent that it suggests a modern election with national parties, national party candidates, and concerted party strategies. The election of 1796 was very little like that; the variables one might refer to with some confidence in analyzing a typical election, say, of the mid-nineteenth century are almost all missing here. But Ames was at least right so far as perceiving that a main key to the election of 1796—one which could never be applied to another—was George Washington and the political habits of mind implanted by Washington's example. Yet even with these considered, the political year 1796 still presents a baffling series of anomalies.

For one thing, the state of parties in 1796, if this can in any way be judged from the complexion of Congress and the state legislatures, gives very few signs of what might be expected for even the immediate future. That is, if one wished to make predictions about the relative strength and stability of Federalism and Republicanism as party ideologies, or to detect signs that within a few years a "Republican" outlook would assert itself as the dominant political persuasion of a vast majority of the American people, and would govern their party behavior for a generation to come, then the election results of 1796 would not be very helpful. If anything, they brought in more Federalists than before. The most precise calculations available show that in the Fourth Congress, the one elected in 1794, there had been 57 Federalists and 58 Republicans, whereas in the new one there would be 64 Federalists and 53 Republicans. And since candidates did not as a rule make a point of their party connections when standing for office (as often as not they had none anyway), we must base our judgments on how they behaved after they got there.

The state legislatures present an even hazier pattern. In places where issues of state and national politics came closest to being merged—New York, Pennsylvania, Massachusetts, and Georgia—the first three had strong Federalist majorities and the fourth was solidly Republican. Virginia could also be counted as Republican. But elsewhere, as in the Carolinas and the rest of New England, the connections were rather tenuous. South Carolina was "Federalist," though peculiarly so, as we shall see, and something similar might be said of North Carolina's Republicanism. State legislatures are not the best places to look for emerging patterns of party. There and in Congress alike, the signs must at best be read as indeterminate.[67]

As for the presidential question, there are certain structural elements in the situation of 1796 which protect it from the logic of modern politics. There was a constitutional anomaly, to be removed within a decade, as well as incongruities in state electoral laws, likewise to be modified with time and experience, which simply in themselves make it difficult to apply later standards to the "party racers" of 1796, and which served at the time to discourage the formation of widely-inclusive party alliances. The as-yet-unamended Section 2 of Article II specified that no distinction be made between electoral votes cast for President and Vice-President, which prevented a presidential election from being a fully national effort and serving a truly nationalizing function. That is, the fashioning of a "balanced" ticket, the appeal of which required extensive state and regional—indeed, national—coalitions to legitimize the choices and make them stick, was an instrument not available in 1796. Instead, an elector's freedom of choice permitted him to pick any two candidates that suited him, even if they happened to be from opposing parties. Thus whatever rudimentary efforts that might be made in advance to designate a suitable pair of candidates—by a congressional party caucus, say, or informal correspondence among party eminents—could carry no very heavy sanctions. State figures who might not happen to like one or both of such choices might simply refuse to support them, as when the Virginia Republicans determined to have nothing to do with Aaron Burr for Vice-President in 1796. That such behavior could result in an opposition candidate's being elected to the vice-presidency was still a secondary consideration.

The diversity of state electoral laws permitted a similar fragmentation of incentive to concerted effort. Electors might be chosen by the state legislature, or elected by congressional districts, or even both at once; a general ticket of electors chosen by popular vote in a statewide election was not yet the norm. Doing it by district put a premium on local loyalties and the influence of local magnates, rather than encouraging the development of statewide party organizations. The choice of electors by state legislatures, on the other hand, sharply reduced popular concern with the presidential contest and made it something less than a general "campaign." (The word was not even used then.) Perhaps the Electoral College could be said to have functioned in 1796 more or less the way the Founders intended, with the people or their representatives choosing their most prominent citizens to serve as electors, and the electors in turn meeting and choosing without coercion the two worthiest of the candidates for the nation's two highest offices. A presidential contest organized by competing parties and designed to draw in as many voters as possible was a thing the Fathers neither planned nor wanted.[68]

Yes and no: 1796 does not quite fit that picture either. By this time there *were* party divisions, if much less clear than one would like for analytical purposes; there were statewide organizations, if not very cohesive or disciplined; there were national candidates, even if not so acknowledged in all parts of the nation. All of this presents us with a political system still in the process of defining itself and an election "campaign" full of the most illogical features.

One was the behavior of the candidates, another the manner in which they were chosen. The Republican caucus in Congress proposed Jefferson's name for the presidency, a choice which to most Republicans everywhere seemed more or less obvious. But Aaron Burr for Vice-President was another matter. Burr would run far behind Jefferson in the final balloting; he would get only one vote in Virginia; the main body of Jefferson men felt in no way obliged to support Burr, and Burr would not forget this in 1800.[69] But then the conduct of Jefferson, by any modern measure, was decidedly odd. He did not stir out of Monticello the whole time, and avoided making any commitments whatever, beyond observing that he rather thought the best available candidate was James Madison. One infers that he was not very eager to be the successor of Washington. Meanwhile the great fear of Madison himself was that Jefferson would spoil the whole Republican effort by declaring publicly that his name was not to be used at all. The resulting picture—again to the modern eye—has a certain bygone charm: James Madison, the candidate's chief friend and promoter, staying away from Monticello all summer long so that the candidate might have no chance to tell him he was *not* a candidate.[70]

The official Federalist candidates, so far as "official" had any meaning then, were John Adams of Massachusetts, the incumbent Vice-President, and Thomas Pinckney of South Carolina. On the face of it, this was an admirably "balanced" ticket, and Adams, unlike Jefferson, clearly wanted to be President. But Adams did not see the presidency as a party matter at all. It was simply the recognition to which he was entitled for nearly thirty years of meritorious public service. When Adams later discovered that there had been a plot to slip Pinckney into the presidency ahead of him, what annoyed him most was not party treachery but that Pinckney, whose service and experience in no way compared with his own, should even be thought of. (Thomas Jefferson's politics might be open to question, but at least Jefferson's claim to high office on the basis of prior service was beyond dispute.) Meanwhile Pinckney, whose name had been proposed by northern Federalists, was in the middle of the Atlantic on his way home from Europe, and knew nothing of any plans to make him Vice-President, much less President. So of course nobody had any idea what Pinckney's thoughts might have been about serving in either office. Thomas Pinckney is sometimes said to have been the first "dark horse" in the history of the American presidency. But that is to distort a concept that could have no meaning for another fifty years. A "dark horse"—such as James K. Polk—represents a negotiated choice, unanticipated at the outset, by a national party concourse that has been unable to join forces behind one or more of the original contenders. In the case of Thomas Pinckney, the only ones who advanced his presidential candidacy with any seriousness were a few men who were working more or less under cover, and never did come out in the open. They included adherents of the Pinckney-Rutledge interest in South Carolina and a few northern Federalists around Alexander Hamilton.[71]

But the most weighty factor of all in 1796 was George Washington, and to the extent that any one man may at any time be transformed into a kind of explanatory historical principle, without which anomalies remain impenetrable, it would have to be precisely here. Hardly a step in the process of nation-building nine years before at Philadelphia would have been what it was were it not for the expectation, universal in every sense, that George Washington would be the republic's first Chief Magistrate. What, then, would happen when Washington made his departure? Scarcely a citizen in all the Republic had more than the remotest idea: it was, in a way, like beginning all over.

So long as there could be any likelihood, however distant, that Washington might be disposed to serve another term, no serious party competition for the presidency was possible, and this much was fully recognized by Federalists and Republicans alike. True, there had been attacks of late upon the President's judgment and conduct. But Washington himself had been the first to magnify them out of all proportion, so it is perhaps no wonder that succeeding generations as well as his own, looking back upon that time, should have tended to follow Washington's prompting and done the same thing. What public figure of today, on the other hand, would not gratefully settle for a budget of abuse no greater than that bestowed upon Washington? The greater proportion of it is probably traceable to a single source. Aside from the frenzied Bache, and the handful of those Republican editors who picked up Bache's words and reprinted them (with perhaps a pleasurable shiver at having done the unthinkable), even Washington would have had little to complain of. Naturally it was shocking, and certainly to him. But the very shock depended on its being so rare and so little expected, and—as most people at the time seem to have thought—so little called for.[72]

The presidency of George Washington was more like a "reign" than anything we have had since. This is not simply a figure of speech; it should be taken as a functional item in the as-yet-unoriented state of politics in 1796. Prior to the American and French Revolutions the peoples of Europe and America alike had been accustomed to picturing ultimate authority—from whatever source the legitimacy of it might be supposed to derive—as embodied in a crowned sovereign. So deep, apparently, was this need that the French themselves would shortly clutch at it once again, and retain a royal or imperial person at their head for another sixty-five years. Not so the Americans. One of the things that permitted so easy a transition to a republic, and emboldened the Americans to have done with kings forever, was the confident realization that with Washington they needed no king. They had a republican counterpart, with all the attributes of a legendary deliverer materialized out of the golden mists of antiquity, and meeting all the requirements, past and present, of royal majesty and republican virtue. He had led them to victory and freedom, had withdrawn becomingly to his Sabine farm, and been summoned forth once more to wear a republican crown. He had been anointed without a dissenting voice. He had fulfilled in all believability the part of the wise and austere patriarch who could be trusted to desire nothing for himself and all for his people. He had met every crisis with fortitude, suppressing a rebellion with both justice and mildness, persuading the people by his own example to accept what they had at first supposed to be an odious treaty with their ancient oppressors, and had brought them peace, happiness, and well-being. Hence it was that a people loudly professing to have repudiated all traces of monarchy could present to the world the greatest of historical ironies. It was America, the Republic of the new age, that had produced what without any question came closest to Bolingbroke's vision of the Patriot King, the ideal ruler who governed through disinterested statecraft and stood above all intrigue, untouched by the claims of faction and party.

To be sure, parties had appeared in spite of him; even Washington could do little to stop them. Parties were there to stay, which was why there could be no more "reigns" in America, and for that matter no more Washingtons. Nevertheless, it was the very kingly aspects of the case, combined with the anomaly of parties, that made the problem of succession so choked with perplexities.

The Republicans in particular were only too aware of this. Jefferson was obsessed with Washington's hold upon the people's affections, and with how the "monocrats," "anglomen," and enemies of true republicanism had huddled themselves under Washington's protecting mantle. (It was the story all over again of the wicked councillors poisoning the ear of the sovereign.) Deeply mortified in June 1796 at the House's failure to hold up the Jay Treaty, Jefferson wrote to Monroe: "Congress has risen. You will have seen ... that one man outweighs them all in influence over the people, who have supported his judgement over their own and that of their representatives. Republicanism must lie on its oars, resign the vessel to its pilot, and themselves to the course he thinks best for them." And to Madison: "Curse on his virtues, they've undone his country."[73] Nevertheless it was not the Republicans, but the Federalists, who would be undone by the virtues of Washington.

It might be supposed on the face of things that the Federalists in 1796 could look forward with confidence to a splendid victory. They had not only established a government but had disposed of every outstanding problem that had afflicted the Confederation: pacifying the Indians, opening the Mississippi, and achieving a stable national credit. Whatever the difficulties with England and France, the country had preserved an honorable neutrality, was at peace with the world, and enjoyed a material prosperity the extent of which could scarcely have been imagined in 1789. The Federalists might look upon the past eight years with the greatest satisfaction. Yet the public's gratitude for these blessings somehow fell not upon *their* wisdom and statesmanship, but on that of Washington.

There was a peculiar sense, moreover, in which the Federalists—however experienced in public life they may have been as individuals—were even less prepared as a group than the Republicans to assume the responsibilities of power. Having never had to function in a situation requiring broad public support without the protection of Washington's moral authority, the Federalists were rather less cohesive than the Republicans as an independent entity that had an independent claim on public loyalty. Even their most striking victory, the turnabout in public opinion that arrested the House's attempt to withhold funds for the Jay Treaty, had been fought for ostensibly on the President's behalf. They saw themselves not really as a party at all, but as the "friends of government." They were the king's men, and now they were about to lose their king—somehow sensing, as did the Republican opposition, that they would never have another. Indeed, the model of leadership which Washington represented, and to which they themselves were of necessity bound—that of the stern patriot, aloof from party cabals and unruffled by the winds of popular passion—would be more and more of a burden in a world of ambitious men anxious for social and political recognition and increasingly less willing to have their public affairs managed by inside elites, stern patriots or otherwise. The values that Washington exemplified, those of duty and public service, were precisely the ones that justified exclusivist rule, and the Federalists found it hard to imagine governing under any other. Nor did they have much taste for pandering to the multitude, and they frequently said so.

The Republicans on the other hand, despite a recent string of electoral defeats over the treaty question, were decidedly less bound by such prescriptions. As outsiders, they had no choice but to appeal to the widest public possible, and it followed that any and all who might support them in expelling the monocrats and anglomen were by definition worthy of being consulted, and indeed included, in the process of governing the republic. Besides, if the Federalists could claim the mantle of Washington, the Republicans could claim something even more enveloping. They had succeeded in preempting the main elements of the American idea. It was the core of a world-view born of the Revolution, a parochial but far-flung anglophobia, a rural suspicion of taxes, of manipulators of money, of great military and naval establishments, and of "energetic" government. It was a popular temper, in the long run better matched in season and out to the ordinary pursuits of the spreading Republic than were the more demanding and exclusive standards of Federalism even at its best. The ideological contest had always been unequal, and the Republicans, whether they knew it or not, had probably won it already. And, ideology apart, the Republicans, unlike the Federalists, were fully prepared to absorb the growing numbers of new men, some of them already rich, who were coming to the fore in the expanding world of business.[74]

This compound of incongruities, this mingling of old standards and new, imparted to the presidential contentions of 1796—which could not begin at all until Washington announced his retirement—a certain formlessness. The "party racers" did no racing; no candidate on either side made any speeches or issued any addresses. In the respective newspaper campaigns, however, there was a difference perhaps worth noting. Such Republican editors as Benjamin Bache and others were in regular touch with leading party figures, whereas the foremost editorial spokesmen for the "friends of government," such as William Cobbett and John Fenno, were never on terms of intimacy or equality with leading Federalists.[75] The proceedings in general varied widely from state to state, depending on how the electors were chosen.

In New York—one of the two states, with Pennsylvania, where state party divisions corresponded most closely with national ones—the legislature chose all the electors, and the whole presidential question was in effect settled in the spring when the Federalists won majorities in both houses. Adams and Pinckney would each receive twelve votes there. In Massachusetts, where some electors were chosen by the legislature and the rest by district elections, Adams captured them all despite a vigorous effort by the Republican opposition. (Even the popular Samuel Adams, just re-elected governor by a heavy majority, was defeated by an unknown when he ran as a Republican elector in the First District.) All the second votes were cast for Pinckney. The rest of New England, despite strong Republican exertions in Vermont and Rhode Island, went for John Adams, while a number of electors in New Hampshire, fearing that Pinckney might get more votes in the South than Adams, threw away their second votes on Oliver Ellsworth, the new Chief Justice. The Federalists likewise carried Delaware and New Jersey, and divided the Maryland votes with Jefferson. Virginia went overwhelmingly for Jefferson, Adams getting the vote of only one elector from the western part of the state, with another large block of Jefferson votes coming from Pennsylvania. Burr, as mentioned, received but one vote in Virginia, the Republican electors throwing away their second votes on Samuel Adams. Elsewhere in the South, despite predictions that John Adams would be given a scattering of first votes in Georgia and the Carolinas, and that Pinckney would get all the second votes, only one in North Carolina went to Adams, and outside South Carolina no Republican elector cast a vote for Pinckney. The result: Adams 71, Jefferson 68, Pinckney 59, Burr 30, with the remaining votes divided among nine others. The country had a Federalist President, by an exceedingly narrow margin, and a Republican Vice-President.[76]

The two most interesting state efforts were those of Pennsylvania and South Carolina. Pennsylvania's shows the closest resemblance to a campaign of modern times, while South Carolina's was one that the twentieth century, or even the nineteenth, would find hard to penetrate. But each had its share of oddities, and each merits some attention.

By 1796 Pennsylvania, like New York, had developed something that approximated a "system" of two-party politics. Thomas Mifflin, the perennial governor, was still nominally a non-party figure. But Mifflin had made occasional difficulties for the Washington administration, and was being systematically corrupted, so the Federalists thought, by his Secretary of State and coadjutor Alexander J. Dallas, who was doing an increasing share of the bibulous governor's work for him and giving his office more and more of a Republican tone. At the same time, Pennsylvania's Congressional delegation was divided between two factions which voted more or less consistently with Republicans and Federalists in the House.

The Federalists, however, retained a firm hold on the state legislature, and in the city of Philadelphia they appeared all but unbeatable. This group, known as the "Junto," had managed to elect their candidates to the city council and to Philadelphia's Assembly seats by heavy majorities since 1789. The Republicans led the reaction against the Jay Treaty in the summer of 1795, but when they tried to convert it into votes for Republican Assembly candidates in the fall, they were badly beaten. Though their efforts had helped to bring an unheard-of 39 percent of the qualified voters to the polls, 60 percent of them voted for Federalists.[77]

It was probably on the strength of these victories, and of the Republicans' failure in the spring of 1796 to hold up the Jay Treaty in Congress, that the Pennsylvania Federalists made what was to be a most critical decision to change the electoral law. They forced a measure through the Assembly which provided that presidential electors be chosen on a statewide basis, rather than by districts as formerly, with the voters now being given a choice of two general tickets. It was a winner-take-all strategy, the Federalists being convinced that they could carry a majority in the state at large for their own slate of electors. The Republicans greatly feared that they were right. They vainly fought the change, complaining that the Federalists had designed it to give "full scope to their talent for intrigue and combination."[78]

But once the matter had been settled the Republicans determined to make the most of it, and did so with remarkable success. It was they, rather than the Federalists, who showed the superior aptness for "intrigue & combination," and their blithe spirit was John Beckley, the Clerk of the House of Representatives, who now spent most of his time on the back stairs. Both Republican and Federalist assemblymen held meetings on the last day of the 1796 spring session to nominate their respective slates of fifteen electors each. But the Republicans, alert to every possible tactical advantage, chose a list of men—including Chief Justice Thomas McKean, Peter Muhlenberg, William Maclay, John Smilie, and William Irvine— whose names would be recognized not simply in their home districts but throughout the state. Then, under instructions from Beckley, they kept the list a secret to prevent the Federalists, if they failed to think of such a thing themselves, from adopting the same idea. The Federalist slate, consisting in large part of men with only district reputations, was notably less distinguished.[79]

Under the general supervision of Beckley, Michael Leib, and Benjamin Bache, a statewide effort was thereupon set in motion. Handbills were sent out for posting in all the districts; such leading Republican figures as Albert Gallatin, William Findley, and General Irvine were exhorted with predictions that a Republican majority would be sure to make Jefferson President, and were promised an ample supply of ballots with the names of all fifteen electoral candidates written out by hand as the law required. A staff of clerks, assisted by volunteers, then produced fifty thousand hand-written tickets, and arrangements were made to have them in the hands of local leaders a week before election time. Meanwhile a stream of propaganda in the form of broadsides and of political "letters" in Bache's *Aurora* poured forth from Philadelphia. Then at the last minute, on November 2, the French minister, Pierre Adet, published an official diplomatic note in the

Aurora—before Washington himself had received the original—breathing France's resentment against the Administration and revealing the secret French decree of the previous July that henceforth American vessels would be treated "in the same manner as they shall suffer the English to treat them." There is no doubt that whatever dismay this maneuver may have caused among Republicans elsewhere, it was done with the full connivance of the Philadelphia committee.[80]

The result was a victory, though a very narrow one, for the Republican ticket. The margin was no more than one or two hundred votes, but it gave fourteen of the fifteen electors to Jefferson, who but for a technicality would have got them all.[81] The true dynamics of this victory, before we quit the subject, can do something to prefigure the coming state of politics in America.

The total vote of 24,420 accounted for only 25 percent of those qualified, and was well short, even, of the 31–33 percent turnouts for the virtually uncontested gubernatorial elections of 1790 and 1796, to say nothing of the 51 percent who would vote in that of 1799. So it was in no sense a popular sweep, but rather a case of concentrated planning and of steady assaults upon a more or less unaroused electorate in the state at large. Within Philadelphia and Philadelphia County, on the other hand, where they carried their effort to saturation, the Republicans gathered a remarkable harvest. Their electoral slate carried the city, up to now a Federalist stronghold, by 61.1 percent of the vote with a 41 percent turnout, which was almost exactly the margin whereby the Federalists had won the Assembly elections there only two weeks before. A good part of the explanation, to be sure, was the appearance of Adet's manifesto. The sensation this caused among the Quaker element, with the vague threat of war and disruption of business which it portended, apparently had much to do with turning the election for the Republicans.[82] But perhaps fundamentally more important was the emergence of a Republican organization fast learning how to intertwine national, state, and local issues into a coherent set of party symbols, something that enabled Republican candidates to present themselves on behalf of everything that was most desirable: as defenders of peace, enemies of privilege, and ardent friends of the city's artisans, small tradesmen, and rising merchants. This was more or less the formula that had captured a congressional seat for them in 1794 and allowed them to retain it in 1796. And this, combined with the flurry over possible trouble with France for which the promised solvent would be Jefferson, made possible a two-thousand-vote margin for Jefferson electors in Philadelphia and Philadelphia County.

Nor had this happy intersection of desires, interests, and energy been just conjured out of nothing. The groundwork for it had been laid a few years before when a formidable coterie of outsiders—John Swanwick, Alexander J. Dallas, Israel Israel, Michael Leib, Benjamin Rush, Stephen Girard, and John Beckley, some of whom we have met already—resolved to challenge the virtual monopoly held by the Junto upon local government. Some of their adherents were remnants of the old "Constitutionalists," the quasi-populist coalition that had controlled Pennsylvania politics from 1776 until the late 1780s, but the dynamic element consisted of newcomers who had made their mark in business but had been excluded from the recognition in society and politics to which they felt themselves entitled. The Junto, on the other hand, included such established figures as Robert Morris, Thomas FitzSimons, and George Latimer who had served in the Continental army or the Continental government, together with a few former Tories such as Samuel Powell, Benjamin Chew, and Henry Drinker; most of them had family and business connections easily convertible to political uses. In 1786 the Junto had won control of the city government after a protracted battle with the Constitutionalists; in 1787 they brought over most of Philadelphia's voters to support the Federal Constitution; and in 1790 they successfully led the fight to replace the state constitution of 1776, under which Pennsylvania had been governed by a unicameral legislature without an independent executive, with a new one closely patterned after that of the Federal Union. By now the Junto elite was in solid control of the city, and most of the citizens seemed content to leave it that way.[83]

The outsiders' first point of attack was on Hamilton's Treasury system. But this line did not take them very far, the Hamiltonian program seeming well suited to most of the requirements of a large commercial city. But gradually they evolved an appeal which stressed a callousness on the part of the entrenched magnates toward the world of artisans, petty merchants, and shopkeepers with their varied aspirations and interests. The excitements raised by the French Revolution and by the local Democratic Society (which a number of them had joined) gave them their first taste of what popular politics might accomplish, and in 1794, now functioning as "Republicans," they managed to elect Swanwick to Congress after a hard fight against the Hamiltonian incumbent FitzSimons. The issues were the unpopular federal excise, which FitzSimons had strongly supported, and the charge that FitzSimons had taken advantage of inside information about the pending embargo in the spring of 1794 to hurry his ships out of harbor before the law was passed.

From here on, the Federalist Junto would find itself persistently harassed by opposition scouts probing for the soft spot and watching for the lucky issue. They thought they had found it with the popular uproar over the Jay Treaty in the summer of 1795. But by the time they could put up an anti-treaty ticket for Philadelphia's six Assembly seats in the fall, public opinion had greatly changed, and they were overwhelmed by the pro-treaty forces of the Federalists. They tried again in 1796 and were again beaten. Swanwick retained his congressional seat, but only by the tiniest of margins. It was in the vote for presidential electors, already described, that the Republicans finally broke through. To be sure, there would be setbacks, but in 1801 they were to come into their own. By then, at every level—local, state, and national—the outsiders would at last be insiders.

In 1796, then, the politics of Pennsylvania had already taken on many of the aspects of a bipartisan future. But by no means all. The Republicans may have been functioning "as" a party, but were they yet fully prepared to say so, and were they yet altogether comfortable about doing it? In elevating the name of Jefferson, they had announced:

Of no party but the great party of human benefactors, he will allay the heats of our country, heal its divisions, and calm the boisterous elements of political controversy—Under the administration of a man, untinctured with party spirit, citizens may smoke the calumet of peace with citizen, and every man may sit down in quiet under his own vine and his own fig-tree.[84]

They also rather brazenly declared: "President Washington loves a republican and hates a monarchist. He therefore wishes that the republican Jefferson may be his successor."[85]

If partisanship in its most rationally "modern" aspects, however embryonic, is to be discerned in the political affairs of Pennsylvania, it was surely least so in the case of South Carolina. Of all places, South Carolina best exemplifies what Richard Hofstadter had in mind when he referred to a generation to which party standards as later understood were still largely unknown, a generation that "waged its politics in the code of proud and jealous notables."[86] South Carolina in the 1790s was the only southern state which might in some way be called substantially Federalist. But its "Federalism"—or rather that of its notables—was exceedingly fluid, and the principle of "party" as we know it is no more than marginally helpful in understanding how Federalism in South Carolina could dissolve aimlessly into Republicanism in 1800.

Be that as it may, South Carolina in 1796 was the one state in the South, Maryland perhaps excepted, where a Federalist candidate for the presidency might logically expect a decisive measure of support. The state's political life was controlled by a Low Country planter elite that had been prominent in the Revolution, taken an active part in the Philadelphia Convention, and led the state in the movement for ratification. South Carolina had on the whole supported Hamilton's program and, with its heavy war debt, benefited substantially from the assumption of state debts by the federal government. Some of South Carolina's leading figures had not liked the Jay Treaty very much. But by the spring of 1796 the urgency of that issue had receded and South Carolina was in the midst of an agricultural boom, the price of its prime crop, rice, having nearly tripled in the previous year.[87]

So one might imagine that an elite fortified by this kind of authority and experience would be both disposed and able to deliver a good portion of the state's electoral votes to John Adams, especially with northern Adams men fully supporting a South Carolinian, Thomas Pinckney, for the vice-presidency. Indeed, the South Carolina Congressman William Loughton Smith, acting as intermediary, made great efforts to bring about this very result. The Pinckney interest, meanwhile, was much gratified at Washington's having invited Pinckney's brother, Charles Cotesworth Pinckney, to serve as Monroe's successor in Paris. Thomas Pinckney himself, a former Governor of South Carolina, minister to Great Britain, and special envoy to Spain, had loyally supported the Jay Treaty and helped persuade his state to accept it, and his own treaty with Spain in 1795 was immensely popular.[88] Thus an Adams-Pinckney ticket in 1796 not only seemed a real possibility, but as a party ticket, in the best rather than the worst sense, it would have been hard to improve on. As a balancing device it was all but ideal, and might be seen as a salutary instance of a national party acting constructively to bridge the sentiments and loyalties of North and South for national ends. But such was not to be. The Pinckney candidacy would in fact serve as the occasion for the most irresponsible intrigues, and for jockeyings that ignored the simplest premises of party loyalty, party organization, and party purpose.

At the very moment when William Smith, at the instance of Oliver Wolcott and other New Englanders, was taking his soundings in South Carolina with regard to an Adams-Pinckney ticket, Alexander Hamilton in New York was showing the first signs of what would happen to his judgment—indeed, to his entire sense of proportion respecting the civic universe—once the steadying aegis of Washington was removed. He and Rufus King began murmuring to each other about the presidential question in April, and their first thought was whether Patrick Henry, now disaffected from the leading Republicans of Virginia, might let himself be mentioned for the presidency. What they had in mind for the aging Henry is unclear. It may actually have been to bring him in as Vice-President, or simply to flatter him, in either case drawing away some support from Jefferson in Virginia. But Hamilton shortly concluded that he would just as soon "be rid of P.H. that we may be at full liberty to take up Pinckney."[89]

For what purpose? Hamilton would later profess that his only intention had been to have a candidate in reserve should Adams's strength in the North prove less solid than had been hoped. But Adams's northern support was not then generally seen as a difficulty, and there is little doubt that what Hamilton really wanted was to get Adams out of the way altogether (Adams's views on finance, on England, and on Hamilton himself were not entirely sound), and ease in the more tractable Pinckney as President. If so, the strategy for doing it would be self-evident, and was in fact the one he pursued: to exhort northern Federalists to vote a straight Adams-Pinckney ticket and not waste votes on a third candidate lest it bring Jefferson in as President, trusting in the meantime that Pinckney would get more votes in the South than Adams, certainly in South Carolina, which would thereby make Pinckney President.[90]

The state of the Federalist party in South Carolina, or of what might in some way pass for a "party," lent itself only too well to thimble-rigging of this kind. For purposes of the 1796 election, the South Carolina Federalists might be divided into three more or less discernible factions or interests. One was associated with William L. Smith and Ralph Izard; the second, with Robert Goodloe Harper; and the third might be called the Pinckney-Rutledge connection.

The main strength of the Smith-Izard group, for whom Smith spoke in Congress, was drawn from Low Country planters and Charleston merchants, especially those with substantial British connections. Smith had been in Congress since 1789, and had emerged very early as Hamilton's chief spokesman in the South. He had strongly opposed Madison's repeated schemes for striking at British commerce, as well as Madison's efforts to scuttle the Jay Treaty. His family and friends had profited nicely from the assumption of state debts. He was on the best of terms with the merchants, both native and British, who resided in Charleston. It was logical enough that Smith should be the one to whom the northern Adams men confided the fortunes of an Adams-Pinckney ticket in South Carolina—though less logical that Smith's New York preceptor, Hamilton, should be hatching contrary schemes of which he knew nothing. Smith at least had the merit of loyalty to his New England party friends, and would do his best for Adams even after it became evident that Adams had little support in South Carolina.

The case of Robert Goodloe Harper was less that of a "faction" than of a single rising career. Harper had been elected to Congress in 1794 as an Up Country representative committed to challenging the Low Country's domination of the state. He arrived with Republican and pro-French leanings but was rapidly converted to sound Federalism, and he wrote the most powerful tract in defense of the Jay Treaty to appear in the South. Harper's contribution to the presidential election of 1796 was to do Hamilton's dirty work in South Carolina. Something of Harper's movements may be seen in what he wrote to Ralph Izard, William Smith's father-in-law and an Adams supporter, early in November. He told Izard that if Adams should carry Pennsylvania all would be well, but that Adams was not likely to get more than a handful of votes in South Carolina, and if he lost Pennsylvania, then the Federalists' only hope was Pinckney. Harper's great anxiety was that Pinckney's powerful friend Edward Rutledge might persuade Pinckney to withdraw on the ground that he was merely being used by Northerners to split the southern vote. So he wanted Izard to urge Rutledge to urge Pinckney to remain in the contest because the northern ("eastern") men were not only serious about making him Vice-President but really wanted to make him President.

> . . . Major Pinckney may be assured, I speak from the most certain knowledge, that the intention of bringing him forward was to make him President, and that he will be supported with that view. I do not say that the eastern people would prefer him to Mr. Adams, but they infinitely prefer him to Jefferson, and they support him because it gives them an additional chance to exclude Jefferson, and to get a man whom they can trust.[91]

Izard may well have asked himself upon reading this, *which* "eastern people"? How many of these men would be prepared to see Thomas Pinckney elected President by second votes, the great majority of which would have come from Adams supporters in the North, with the margin of victory supplied by Jefferson men in places like South Carolina (where there were in fact quite a few) who were willing to accept Pinckney as their second candidate? What kind of party unity could that bring, and what kind of mandate could such a result give Thomas Pinckney as the successor of Washington? Had any such thoughts occurred to Harper or to the "eastern people" he claimed to be speaking for?

As it happened, Edward Rutledge, the only member of the Pinckney-Rutledge interest who was both resident in South Carolina at the moment and in a position to act, needed no advice from Harper or Izard or anyone else. He had plans of his own. Edward Rutledge was not in the least troubled at the possibility of Thomas Jefferson's becoming President of the United States. Jefferson was an old friend, many of whose views he shared, and Rutledge would in fact shortly serve as a Jefferson elector in South Carolina. But what he really wanted, as he confided to his son in October, was to see the votes Pinckney would get in the North as Adams's vice-presidential candidate combined with those he would get in the South as a second choice to Jefferson, thus making Pinckney President. With luck, Jefferson would be given enough votes to be Vice-President. This would have the gratifying result of excluding both the northern Republican George Clinton (true, Clinton was not a candidate; Rutledge was still thinking of 1792) and the northern Federalist Adams.[92]

The key to these airy fancies, if there is one, had best be looked for in the "code of proud and jealous notables" of South Carolina. Edward Rutledge, John Rutledge, Thomas Pinckney, Charles Cotesworth Pinckney, and Ralph Izard were all Low Country grandees who had served with distinction in the Revolution as military officers or elected officials, in some cases suffering heavy property losses during the fighting and the British occupation. After the war their political power had been briefly challenged by Up Country elements and a "radical" group in Charleston, but the movement for a Federal Constitution, in which they played a leading part, enabled them to reassert their predominance. It was confirmed by the new state constitution of 1790, which continued the gross over-representation of the Low Country in the legislature. In that same year they were successful in their agitation for the assumption of state debts, and meanwhile the state's repressed economic life began to show signs of reviving. So South Carolina could look with favor on the new federal government, and the state could be regarded, in a manner of speaking, as "Federalist."[93]

Nevertheless there were growing differences within the ruling company of Low Country potentates. The Pinckneys and Rutledges, unlike Izard and Smith, had benefited only minimally from assumption (Smith had made a mighty killing from buying up state paper), and were beginning to grumble about the coterie of British merchants and anglophile planters who were promoting the career of William L. Smith. Edward Rutledge could bristle with upright ire when Jefferson goaded him in 1791 with descriptions of the speculators' "scramble" for federal booty, one which he and his brother had somehow failed to get in on. As for South Carolina, Rutledge could now see former Tories, lukewarm patriots (Smith had spent the Revolutionary years as a student in London), and naturalized British merchants preempting the state's wealth while honest men who had shed their blood for freedom were modestly scraping by. By early 1792, Rutledge was a potential recruit to the Republican interest. In 1793 he joined in welcoming Genet to Charleston and rejoiced in the news that France had become a republic, though not approving of Genet's plans for Louisiana. Nor did he much care for the Charleston radicals and their Democratic Society.[94]

But the Rutledges and Pinckneys were sufficiently cross with the Administration, especially for not taking a stronger line with the British, that they put up John Rutledge, Jr., against William L. Smith in the congressional election of 1794, only to see him beaten. The Jay Treaty enraged them. Not only had Jay made no effort to get an indemnity for slaves carried off by the British, Carolinians were henceforth not allowed to export their own Sea Island cotton in American ships. Edward Rutledge joined in the movements of 1795 to rally the state against the treaty, and Edward's brother John—whose nomination as Chief Justice was then pending—made so wild and disjointed an attack on it that northern Federalists concluded he was in no fit state to be confirmed.[95]

Members of the Rutledge-Pinckney interest were nevertheless under painfully conflicting pressures. Charles Cotesworth Pinckney for one, knowing that his brother Thomas supported the treaty, refused to join the assault. Then, with Washington's decision to sign, concurrent with the excitement over soaring rice and cotton prices and the wide praise for Thomas Pinckney's treaty with Spain, Edward Rutledge began to change his mind. He did not want to endanger his relations with Pinckney; moreover, it was clear that Washington appreciated the value of Pinckneys and Rutledges, having offered Randolph's vacant place to Charles Cotesworth Pinckney and nominated Edward's own brother to the Supreme Court. Rutledge accordingly rose to the occasion when a resolution hostile to the Administration was brought before the South Carolina legislature, and helped to suppress it. He would not tolerate an attack on the First Citizen. Once more, in the summer of 1796, Washington called upon Charles Cotesworth Pinckney to serve his country, this time abroad, and this time he accepted. And by now there was beginning to be talk about putting Thomas Pinckney on the presidential ticket with John Adams.[96]

Here, then, was Edward Rutledge's golden hour. The virtuous sensations which stirred in his breast were splendidly mingled. There was loyalty to Washington (the President understood who was who in South Carolina), affection for Jefferson (a gentleman planter who had no use for the British), disdain for Hamilton and his tools in South Carolina (anglomen, Tories, and speculators), vexation at those who were stirring the waters at home (Charleston radicals and Up Country malcontents), and outrage over Northerners who had kept his brother John off the High Court (even if all by then could see that John was too addled to serve). The presidency! He, Edward Rutledge, would settle it all himself in a nobly nonpartisan way, and all for the good of the country, by making his old friend Thomas Pinckney President and his old friend Thomas Jefferson Vice-President. The electors of South Carolina were chosen by the legislature, which was as it should be. Rutledge headed a Jefferson-Pinckney electoral ticket which swept the legislature in December by nearly three to one. William L. Smith, who had at least some idea of what it meant to be an honest Federalist partisan, knew in advance exactly what would come of this. "If Major Pinckney is thrown out," he wrote to his brother-in-law Gabriel Manigault, "it will be owing entirely to the ridiculous & wicked conduct of his own state & particular friends. It will be a very mortifying thing, when to have been held up even as President, to be handsomely supported by the Eastern people & yet to lose his Election even as V.P. by the folly & mismanagement of his friend, E.R.!!"[97]

Party politics, to such as Edward Rutledge, was a low and trifling business. But Rutledge was not in much of a position to judge, having not the least understanding of what party politics amounted to or how it should work. And Pinckney, still on the high seas and not to arrive home until mid-December, had no clue of what a future was being conjured up for him. John Adams, as it happened, would himself have a shaky enough hold on the Federalist party, such as it was. How, then, could Thomas Pinckney have faced the northern Federalists who, if the Rutledge maneuver had gone according to plan, would have loyally supported him as their second candidate while his great friend in South Carolina was easing him into the presidency with Jefferson votes? It was as well for Major Pinckney that he *was* "thrown out."

Nor was it really so strange that Edward Rutledge, two years hence, should turn out to be the successful Federalist candidate for Governor of South Carolina, and emerge as a strong supporter of the Adams administration. By then the perfidious French had insulted Charles Cotesworth Pinckney by ordering him out of the country, and then demanded a bribe from the American commission of which Pinckney was a member. Rutledge had flirted with Republicanism and was now returning to Federalism, at least for the time being.[98] But what other course was open to a gentleman of South Carolina? What, after all, were party principles when it was a question of his country's honor, and especially the honor of his friends?

John Adams, the only real "heir" to Washington, was President of the United States by a margin of three votes. But on inauguration day the lion of the hour was not John Adams but George Washington. "He seemed to me," wrote Adams the following morning, "to enjoy a triumph over me. Methought I heard him say, 'Ay! I am fairly out and you fairly in! See which of us will be the happiest!'"[99]

Washington and the new Vice-President, Thomas Jefferson, never saw each other again. Both of them were probably just as glad of it. But seventeen years later it was Jefferson who would say of Washington, on no public occasion but in a private letter:

> His integrity was most pure, his justice the most inflexible I have ever known, no motives of interest or consanguinity, of friendship or hatred, being able to bias his decision. He was indeed, in every sense of the words, a wise, a good and a great man. . . . On the whole, his character was, in its mass, perfect, in nothing bad, in few points indifferent; and it may truly be said, that never did nature and fortune combine more perfectly to make a man great. . . .[100]

CHAPTER XII

John Adams and
The Dogma of "Balance"

Few commentators on the American past have ever been altogether certain what to do with John Adams or just where to place him—least of all with regard to his presidency. The whole of Adams's single term was absorbed, to a degree unequaled in any other American presidency, with a single problem, a crisis in foreign relations. The crisis had arisen out of hostile actions by the French Republic, ostensibly in retaliation for America's having reached an accommodation by treaty with France's enemy England. American representatives seeking a peaceful resolution with the French government had been accorded insulting treatment, while increasing depredations were being made upon American commerce by French cruisers and privateers, all of which threatened to involve the two former allies in war. The manner in which Adams handled the crisis has been seen in strikingly opposite ways.

One view has Adams in the role of intrepid pacificator, putting country above party, defying Federalist warmongers by dispatching a new and eventually successful mission to France. He thus achieved both peace and an end to rebellious sentiment at home over rising taxes and the fear of an overbearing military establishment, all at the foregone risk of dividing his own party and ruining his own chances of re-election. It is a view widely held today, and one with which Adams himself would certainly have concurred. It was precisely the one *he* held, and in later life he was not at all backward about saying so.[1] Nevertheless, such a view does not command anything like general agreement. Indeed, writers in recent years, calling attention to Adams's erratic executive behavior—his touchiness, vanity, impulsiveness, and failure to consult adequately with his cabinet and other leading advisors—have contended that what Adams did accomplish he accomplished in spite of himself, and at unnecessary cost to both his own political fortunes and those of the Federalist party. He had the amplest opportunity to strike for control of the entire party in preparation for the election of 1800. He might still have pursued his policy of making peace with France, but in a far more deliberate and measured way than the one he took, without catching party leaders by surprise with impetuous executive decisions and without alienating sentiment for a resolute footing of military preparedness. But it was an opportunity he refused to take. Nor, they argue, did Adams even achieve the sort of settlement with France that he ought to have had. His agents failed to extract any indemnities for damages to American shipping, and at best the settlement would be an unstable and temporary one.[2]

Still another difficulty with Adams's historical reputation has had to do with the role he fancied for himself as a political scientist. Adams insisted, having read far more widely and being a more prolific writer himself than any public man of his time, that no statesman could act wisely without a right understanding of the principles of government and the nature of man. But how did his own behavior square with his theories? There is little agreement on this question either. There are not even any generally accepted conclusions on what a comprehensive statement of Adams's theories in summary form would really look like. Some have declared his writings downright reactionary; others have seen in them the basis for a judicious and responsible conservatism; still others conclude that Adams's philosophy, for all its convolutions, simply comes down to a stout libertarian republicanism that was no more than a variation upon the general beliefs of his time.[3] Some have discerned significant changes, or phases, in the evolution of Adams's political thought, though they differ as to how, or when, or even what. Others see few basic alterations from first to last.[4] It has also been said that there never was anything very systematic about his writings; that their most pervasive feature is a maddening state of disorganization, much of them simply consisting of whole blocks of quotations from other authors endlessly strung together; and that his thought cannot be periodized at all, having fluctuated and oscillated most of the time in response to events and to his moods of the hour. It has, on the other hand, been suggested that the key to the tossings and turnings of Adams's own behavior is itself to be found in his political theorizing.[5] Despite their many incompatibilities, most of these assertions seem to have a degree of truth in them.

But however all this is settled, one might at least conjecture that the outcome of Adams's presidency did have *something* to do with his political science—that this in turn is not unconnected with his own character, with the formative experiences of his life, and with the manner in which he negotiated them. Beyond these elements, however, is something else that needs to be fitted into the picture, but seldom is. There were two gross conditions intruding upon Adams's presidency for which neither theory nor experience had given him much preparation, and to which he could apply little insight or control. One was the sheer illogic of French policy toward the United States; the other, the bafflingly indeterminate and transitional state of political parties in America. Since Adams had little use for either party, or for parties in general, and since France's concern with America continued to be as intermittent and fitful as ever, one may well wonder how he managed to scrape through at all.

I

The Trouble with Adams

Many of Adams's contemporaries, including his off-again, on-again friend Jefferson, came to suspect him of leanings toward monarchy and aristocracy. There was certainly ground for construing this from his writings (though Adams himself always denied it), but there is little in Adams's own life from beginning to end that suggests a hankering for anything resembling an aristocratic style. His origins were of the most middling sort; he never acquired wealth, nor ever much coveted it; he quite obviously did not know how to put on airs; and his manner of living was always unaffectedly frugal—vastly more so than Jefferson's. He was born in 1735 and grew up in the country town of Braintree, later called Quincy, some twelve miles from Boston. As a youth he wanted to be a farmer as his forbears had been, but his father wanted him to be educated and become a minister. To the education he grudgingly agreed, but he formed a private determination not to enter the ministry no matter what. He would go into the law instead, though lawyers and their profession at that period hardly enjoyed the high repute they would acquire later on. This contest of wills between Adams and his father, though in itself waged amiably enough, pointed to what would be a governing theme in Adams's life, his almost rabid insistence upon independence—usually in opposition to somebody, and sometimes to everybody. It was better if there were costs and obstacles.[6]

In the course of his studies Adams developed an enormous appetite for reading. Harvard students in those days were listed in order not of performance but of their families' social rank; in the class of 1755 John Adams stood fourteenth of twenty-five.[7] Adams spent the three years following his graduation as a schoolmaster in Worcester, during which time he applied himself to the study of law, mastering more than enough of it to be admitted to the Suffolk bar in 1758. His talents and assiduity were recognized very early, though for the first few years he had to scour for business. Upon his father's death in 1761 he inherited the family farm in Braintree, and when he married Abigail Smith in 1764 it was this, together with a practice that had finally begun to grow, that constituted the capital upon which he started his own family.

Adams threw himself into resistance to the Crown from the very beginning of the imperial crisis. As early as 1760 he had been set afire by James Otis's rousing speech against the Writs of Assistance in the Superior Court at Boston. On behalf of the Braintree town meeting he drew up instructions for the town's delegate to the General Court on opposition to the Stamp Act in 1765; Adams's paper was widely reprinted, serving as a model for other towns, and it brought him attention throughout the province. That same year he wrote *A Dissertation on the Feudal and Canon Law,* first published in newspaper installments, on the ways in which liberty had been menaced by power throughout history—a tract which, despite its learned citations and examples, was pure Whig propaganda. By 1769 Governor Francis Bernard was moved to offer Adams the post of Advocate-General in the

Court of Admiralty, hoping to buy him off from his opposition activities. Adams loftily refused. He accepted the case of the British soldiers accused of murder in the Boston Massacre of 1770 and got them acquitted, fully expecting it would make a martyr of him. Instead he was elected by a large majority to the General Court, where he and his cousin Samuel became thorns in the side of Acting Governor Thomas Hutchinson. In 1773 Hutchinson vetoed his election to the Council because of "the very conspicuous part" he had taken in the opposition.[8] Adams was chosen as one of Massachusetts's five delegates to the First Continental Congress in 1774.

From that point on, Adams was never out of public life until the day he left the presidency. Despite endless physical complaints, his industry was tremendous. He served on innumerable committees over the next four years; he was chairman of the Board of War; he took the lead in promoting the establishment of a Continental navy; he was one of the strongest advocates of independence after the outbreak of fighting at Lexington and Concord; and he served with Jefferson, Franklin, Livingston, and Sherman on the committee to draft the Declaration in 1776. He somehow found time to dash off *Thoughts on Government,* which was used as a kind of handbook in several states for the drafting of new constitutions. He was appointed in 1778 to join the American commission in Paris to negotiate a treaty of alliance with the French, and was abroad continuously for the next ten years, except for a very brief homecoming in 1779. During that interval he was elected as a delegate to the Massachusetts constitutional convention, and the resulting constitution was almost wholly Adams's work. Returning to Europe, he served as Congress's first minister plenipotentiary to the Dutch Republic and successfully arranged the first American loans with Amsterdam bankers. He was on the peace commission with Franklin and Jay, and on another commission with Jefferson to negotiate commercial treaties. He was appointed by Congress in 1785 to be the first American minister to Great Britain, where he remained for three years in a vain effort to get the British to carry out their part of the Peace Treaty. While there, he wrote his *Defence of the Constitutions of Government of the United States of America,* the first volume of which may have had some influence on the delegates at Philadelphia in 1787.[9] Just as the last of the required number of states were ratifying the new Constitution, Adams returned home in 1788, in time to be elected Vice-President of the United States.

Adams always thirsted for fame, but it had to be on his terms, and his terms seldom fitted anyone else's. He could never put himself out to flatter others or to court popularity, these things being in any case a matter of instinct, and Adams had no such instinct. He talked too much, was too opinionated and too censorious, too often he said what he thought (though he often fretted about it afterward); he was too irritable and irritated too many others. He rather expected to be unpopular; indeed, he was all but determined to be so, and in large part he was. What renown he acquired was certainly not for commanding qualities of manner or person (being short and stout, he had to admit he was "but an ordinary Man" and "not like the Lion"), but rather for the fruits of his pertinacious industry. He could not be quite settled in his mind about the worth of any choice to be made or any end to be pursued unless it somehow held out personal disadvantage, difficulty, and even a strong prospect of failure. He would eventually be vindicated, no doubt, but only eventually. Desperately as he wanted to be America's first ambassador to the Court of St. James's at the close of the Revolution, he could fall into great sweats over what might happen if he were actually chosen. "How will the King & the Courtiers the City and the Country look at me? What Prospect can I have of a tolerable Life there? I shall be Slandered and plagued there more than in France—it is a sad Thing that Simple Integrity should have so many Enemies in this world, without deserving one." The Adams pride typically expressed itself, as Peter Shaw has said, "in acts of self-denial," and pride and self-denial prevented him from ever actively soliciting any advancement or campaigning for any office. He was determined above all, he insisted, "to preserve my Independence, at the Expense of my Ambition."[10]

But Adams could never be easy about his own motives for anything until after great self-scrutiny and self-criticism. Though he contended with everyone, his grimmest contentions were with himself. "Oh! that I could wear out of my mind every mean and base affectation, conquer my natural Pride and Self Conceit, expect no more defference from my fellows than I deserve, acquire that meekness, and humility, which are the sure marks and Characters of a great and generous Soul. . . ." If only he could curb his passions, hold his tongue, and spend less time in disputation: "I am constantly forming, but never executing good resolutions." Once after an especially heavy bout of overwork, Abigail packed him off to Stafford Springs for a few days of rest and to take the waters there; he was greatly refreshed, but before his return he fell to brooding. "I feel guilty—I feel as if I ought not to saunter and loyter and trifle away this Time—I feel as if I ought to be employed, for the Benefit of my fellow Men, in some Way or other." On the very eve of his election to the presidency he was still examining himself, wondering whether he really wanted it, and preparing himself for defeat. "It really seems to me as if I wished to be left out. Let me See! do I know my own heart? I am not sure." One consequence of Adams's incessant self-criticism was that he was not very patient with criticism from any other source. Another was that, for all his inner torments, it was an easy step from self-censure to censure of others. So much for his resolutions.[11]

The great thing, in any case, was his independence, in politics as in everything else. All Adams's contemporaries deplored, at least in theory, the evils of party and faction. But Adams took the evils literally; with him it amounted to an obsession. All parties, he declared late in life, were "violent Friends of Order, Law, Government, and Religion, when in Power; and all Parties libellous, Seditious, and rebellious, when out of Power." Throughout the revolutionary crisis, whatever his ardor in the Patriot cause, he would not associate himself with any of the factions in Massachusetts politics. He would "quarrel with both parties and every Individual in each, before I would subjugate my understanding, or prostitute my tongue or pen to either." Arriving in Europe in 1778 and finding the American agents there rent in two factions, he refused to join either one and ended by alienating both.[12] Politics, as a matter of parties or simply of managing other men and groups, was something for which Adams had surprisingly little feeling. Few men of his time could claim as long, as extensive, or as tireless a record of public service as he could. But for all this, and for all his theories about the true basis of political society, few men could have approached the presidency with less practical political experience than John Adams.

Still, for Adams there had to be a *right* way of confronting the problems of political order, and it could not be done without a full comprehension of correct principles. Preparing to set off for the First Continental Congress in 1774, he resolved to make himself "a scholar" of statesmanship: "I feel my own insufficiency for this important Business."[13] (In his youth he had undertaken the study of law in much the same spirit.) From his "Novanglus" papers and *Thoughts on Government* in the 1770s to his *Defence of the Constitutions* in the 1780s and *Discourses on Davila* in 1790 and 1791—and the many newspaper essays and letters in between—everything Adams wrote testified to his determination to piece out a proper science of politics. "If only because of these significant contributions to American constitutionalism," concedes one writer, "Adams deserves to be singled out for consideration." In the realm of political theory, says another, Adams "was perhaps the leading man of his generation."[14] What, then, do all these theoretical outpourings amount to?

It is at least convenient—if perhaps not strictly accurate—to view Adams's thought as falling into two rough phases, the earlier one characterized by a certain guarded optimism and the later one by a downright pessimism, about men's capacity for governing themselves. In his more sanguine period, coinciding with the years of the revolutionary struggle, Adams in his reflections upon the experiment of republicanism in America was disposed to emphasize its possibilities and promise; subsequently, by the middle and late 1780s, he had become more and more preoccupied with its fragility and with the corrosive forces that threatened to dissolve it.[15]

It may be unfair, but not extravagantly so, to say that what Adams came out with after all his theorizing was one idea, and that was the idea of "balance." The same term, of course, was used by many others to specify what a suitable constitution of government ought to be and do, but with Adams it took a form that was rather idiosyncratic. He strongly approved of the Federal Constitution when a copy of it reached him in England, but he did so on grounds quite different from what most of the Framers had intended, or said they intended. *His* model of "balance" was the classical mixed government of king, lords, and commons as embodied in the English constitution—the constitution, that is, as it had been before being corrupted in the course of the eighteenth century—and adapted to republican conditions. He thought the American Constitution did in fact reproduce this same balance, and the terminology he frequently insisted on using to describe it—the "monarchical" branch in referring to the Executive, "aristocratical" and "democratical" with regard to the upper and lower houses of the legislature—led many, Jefferson and Madison among them, to the conclusion that Adams had by then ceased to be a republican at all.[16] This was both unjust and untrue, though Adams had not always used words in quite so perverse a way.

The dogma of "balance," nevertheless, had always been there in some form, from the very beginning to the very end.[17]

Adams had always believed that man was a creature of intractable passions, and that the central drama both of man within himself and of man in society was the ceaseless contest between his reason and his passions, paralleling that in the realm of government between liberty and power. The passions were varied and numerous — "Malice, Hatred, Envy, Pride, fear, Rage, Despair," indolence, avarice, not to mention "Love, fear, Hope &c." — but among the worst were the lust for power and "that fiend the Spirit of Party." Still, Adams in his earlier, optimistic period thought there was ground for hope that the Americans as a people might find the means for rising above their individual and collective frailties even if no other nation in history had ever quite succeeded in doing it. This was because the Americans, in their resistance first to religious and now to political tyranny, seemed to have discovered a special capacity for virtue. To Adams, as to the eighteenth-century understanding in general, virtue was "a positive Passion for the public good," but unlike the natural, private passions, virtue had to be inculcated through experience, instruction, discipline, and reason. Virtue enabled men to put the good of the whole above selfish private advantage, and to dedicate themselves to the extension and preservation of liberty. Virtue, moreover, was "the only Foundation of Republics."[18]

And so it followed that government must be constructed in such a way as to control the passions and encourage virtue. This could only be accomplished through balancing each of the powers of government against the others, and basing government itself on the impartial rule of law. No individual, no single part of government, could be trusted with unlimited power. Balance required a separation of the three branches; it was especially important that there be a balance within the legislative power — the power most liable to abuse — and between the legislature and the Executive. The hand of the Executive was in effect the hand that held the scales, which meant that the Executive should be both strong and independent. Single-house legislatures, moreover, ought to be avoided. This was where Pennsylvania's constitution of 1776 went wrong: it had no balance.[19]

But by the late 1780s Adams had become decidedly less hopeful. Whatever the continuities that persisted in his political thought, there were certainly some striking reallocations of emphasis. This was because by then he saw in his countrymen, or thought he saw, an extreme falling-off of virtue. Their independence achieved, they had with appalling suddenness lapsed into sloth, luxury, and absorption with private gain; they were not meeting their public obligations nor exerting themselves to arrest the decline of public order. Now, when Adams wrote about government, he was moved to put the stress not on the people's virtue but on their selfishness. It was in this temper of pessimism that he gave more attention than ever before to distinctions between the "aristocratic" and "democratic" elements in society and government.[20]

He had always thought there was something resembling natural "orders" in any society, including his own, and although no aristocracy existed officially in

America there had always been one in fact. By "aristocrats" Adams simply meant men of "influence," however they may have acquired it: through "Education, Wealth, Strength, Beauty, Stature, Birth, Marriage, graceful Attributes and Motions, Gait, Air, Complexion, Physiognomy." An aristocrat, he insisted, was anyone who could "command *two votes; one besides his own.*" By the mid-1780s the original simplicity and frugality of American society were disappearing; distinctions between the aristocracy and democracy, the few and the many, the rich and the poor, were becoming more and more pronounced; and they had now developed opposing interests and opposing sets of passions. At one point Adams had assumed, as in the first two volumes of the *Defence,* that in government it was the aristocracy that was most in need of checking and balancing ("ostracized" in an upper house); but by the time he got to the third volume—and especially in writing *Discourses on Davila* in response to what was happening in France—he had come to see the greater danger in an unbalanced democracy. The importance, moreover, of a strong and independent Executive seemed more obvious than ever.[21]

One consequence of the altered emphasis in Adams's thinking was of course the squabble over titles in 1789, set off by Adams's opinion that Washington ought to be called "His Majesty the President" or something of the sort, and that the other high officials of government should have titles as well. This was no whim; there was a theoretical argument for it. One of the passions that ought to be harnessed was the passion for "distinction" or "emulation," and titles would compel respect for a national government which needed all the respect it could muster.[22] Another consequence was the gloomy but imprudent assertions Adams began making that the time would come when the American people, weary of corrupt presidential elections, would demand a hereditary Executive. (What he meant by "corrupt" was contamination by the spirit of party.) Accused of favoring monarchy, he repeatedly protested that he favored no such thing. He was only judging from the signs he saw with regret everywhere around him; he was, in effect, only making a prediction.[23] And finally, in supporting the Federal Constitution on the ground not of popular sovereignty but of its resemblance to the "mixed" government of the English constitution, Adams was refusing—as Gordon Wood has argued—to take account of the innovations in political theory that had been effected at Philadelphia while he was away.[24]

All these aspects of Adams's thought, as we have said, have been endlessly discussed and debated. But the theme of "balance" might still call for a note or two further. That principle—balance—was not only a device of thought, a guide to action, an axiom of government; it represented the deepest requirement of Adams's very being. It was the principle he invoked in his earliest struggles with his own passionate nature, and in the desperate hope, never quite achieved, of bringing a kind of order to an inner anarchy. "Balance" for him was not a way of prudent moderation, not a matter of fine calibrations and adjustments; it was not the calm equilibrium we ordinarily associate with balances and balancing. It was rather a case of something that needed to be redressed, usually drastically and often belatedly. Things were always going wrong, behind his back or when his guard was down; forces were forever being set loose, both within himself and in the world around him, that called for some great exertion of rescue. Repairs were always being needed for something—for mistakes made, damage done, resolutions broken, all the way from his personal affairs to the affairs of a whole society. Appalled at having spoken his mind too freely, he would vow "never to shew my own Importance or Superiority, by remarking the Foibles, Vices, or Inferiority of others."[25] Immersed in the Patriot cause, he would nevertheless challenge Patriot juries when he saw justice endangered, or denounce a town meeting for howling down an unpopular speaker.[26] Responding with all his sensuous nature to France—to the women, the ballet, the gardens, the Roman church—he must then turn about and condemn all France as a sink of folly and depravity.[27] In the systems he constructed, he would check aristocracy with democracy, then rush to check democracy with aristocracy. Seeing his great principle of "balance" itself coming under attack, he would launch three ponderous volumes in defense of it, with examples of balance, ancient and modern, erupting on every page. And throughout his life, there could be mystifying alternations in behavior between the warlike and the conciliatory. Balance, for Adams, seldom corresponded to anything that was at rest. It was a case of challenge and response, tug and heave, something better compared to a see-saw. "Power," he declared, "must be opposed to power, force to force, strength to strength, interest to interest, as well as reason to reason, eloquence to eloquence, and passion to passion." The whole "mystery of a commonwealth"—as well as of life itself—consisted of "dividing and equalizing forces."[28]

What Adams brought to his presidency in 1797, then, was a passion for independence, a long career in public life oddly devoid of political experience, a detestation of political parties—Federalist and Republican alike—and a deep suspicion of both of the great powers of Europe. It was, indeed, a "balance" of sorts, at least for the time being: the balance of a plague on both your houses. Such was the spirit in which he faced the crisis that now loomed before him.

2

Preparing for Crisis

Ever since late in the year 1796 it had been evident that relations with France were falling into a bad state. But though matters became steadily more serious from then on, their evil magnitude did not reach full term until after John Adams had taken office in March 1797. The French had been rumbling in fitful ill humor against the United States since learning of the Jay Treaty, and especially after news came that the Republicans had failed in the spring of 1796 to prevent the treaty's going into effect. But nobody knew exactly what form their displeasure would take, or how far they would go with it. It is more than probable they did not altogether know themselves. The Directory had issued a decree on July 2, 1796, saying that the French Republic would "treat neutral vessels, either as to confiscation, as to searches, or capture, in the same manner as they shall suffer the English to treat them." Monroe, who was still in Paris, could not get anyone to tell him what this meant, because although he knew of the decree's existence it had neither been officially communicated to him nor publicly announced. The first knowledge Washington had of it was when Minister Adet published it in the Philadelphia newspapers on October 31, 1796, together with a letter of complaint about America's conduct toward her faithful ally.[29] The decree was ostensibly in retaliation for British depredations on neutral commerce. But in fact the British had issued no recent orders concerning such commerce, nor had they for some months interfered with neutral shipping bound for France or the Netherlands. Meanwhile the French, whatever their intentions, were misleading Monroe as to what they might be.[30]

Actually France's treatment of neutral shipping, despite the Treaty of 1778, had much of the time been very little different from England's. The French had been ignoring the treaty's "free ships, free goods" stipulations off and on ever since the outbreak of hostilities in 1793. It began with the law of May 9, 1793, authorizing French privateers to confiscate neutral ships loaded with provisions bound for enemy ports; this law was rescinded on May 23, restored on May 28, rescinded again on July 1, and again restored on July 27. It was rescinded again March 24, 1794, and then restored, with modifications, on November 18, 1794. The restrictions of May 9, 1793, were once more rescinded on January 2, 1795, and so remained until July 2, 1796.[31] Throughout this entire time French actions had been arbitrary, erratic, and unpredictable, depending less upon treaty provisions or the current policy of England than upon food shortages or the pressure of local merchants for regular trade, on the one hand, or the attractions of rich American cargoes and the exigencies of a depleted treasury on the other.[32]

So the American government, understandably, could not be certain exactly how the decree of July 2, 1796, was to be put into effect when Adet announced it at the end of October. Had orders "been actually given to the ships of war and privateers of the French republic," inquired Secretary of State Pickering in his note to Adet of November 1, "to capture the vessels of the United States? And what, if they exist, are the precise terms of these orders?"[33]

But there were no "precise terms." The decree was so loosely formulated that French agents and ship captains in the West Indies and elsewhere could use it as a virtual hunting license to prey on American shipping, and did so. Moreover, the very circumstances of Adet's announcement—a public letter to the Secretary of State, followed two weeks later by an extended justification of France's dissatisfaction with the United States, together with Adet's suspension of his own functions as minister—gave ground for suspicion that punishing the Americans for having made a treaty with France's enemy England was simply the latest pretext for doing what it suited France's current convenience for doing anyway, and which was being done to Denmark and Sweden on other pretexts.[34] The air was further charged by Pickering's snarling replies, also published, to Adet's two communications. Meanwhile news of sharp increases in French spoliations began reaching the United States; there were rumors that the French did not intend to receive Monroe's successor, Charles Cotesworth Pinckney; and it appeared more and more likely that the incoming President would have to deal with a crisis not unlike the one Washington had faced with Great Britain in the spring of 1794.[35]

And Adams, it seems, already had it worked out in his mind what he would do. A fresh effort to negotiate differences with France was much preferable to embargo or war, and he thought it should be done by sending a specially appointed three-man commission to Paris. The commission should consist of James Madison of Virginia, Elbridge Gerry of Massachusetts, and Pinckney.[36] The idea itself, and the spirit in which Adams prepared to carry it out, were fully in accord with Adams's character, his experience, and most of his notions about government. He would do it all himself, this being entirely an executive function; there would be no systematic building up of support for his policy, no fashioning of party alliances; he had never done that sort of thing in his life. Indeed, there is no evidence of his having consulted with anyone about the French situation until the day before his inauguration. And when he did, it was to reach *across* party lines, in response to the conciliatory overtures which his old friend Jefferson was reported to be making toward him. As it turned out, those overtures were more qualified than they appeared.

Nor did it occur to Adams that the cabinet he had inherited from Washington need be a source of any particular difficulty. He saw little reason to view the Secretaries as a liability, or to doubt their loyalty, and he was certainly not inclined to go to the trouble of replacing them.[37] He was simply not disposed to see this as a problem. Foreign affairs were ultimately matters for executive decision, and he had already decided that he would deal with France more or less as Washington had done with Great Britain three years before.

Yet there *was* a difficulty. Though Adams had a good deal of experience in European diplomacy, he had none whatever as an executive, or in any public function requiring a degree of political management. He had never served as a state governor, or as a cabinet officer, or as a military commander; he had not been present at the Constitutional Convention or at his state's ratifying convention; as Vice-President he had been excluded from both the discussions and the decisions of the preceding administration. Still, he appears not to have seen this as a problem either. His picture of the Executive was not that of a political person, and it was certainly not that of a partisan. It was simply that the Executive's was the hand that held the scales: it was all a matter of balance. Indeed, it was less a powerful Executive that Adams insisted on than an independent one, beholden to nobody.[38]

The story of the rapprochement with Jefferson, initially promising but ultimately abortive, is fairly familiar, though the conditions which hemmed it about may be somewhat less so. The two had been very cool since their brush over Paine's *Rights of Man* in 1791, and they had not seen each other at all since Jefferson's withdrawal to Virginia at the end of 1793. In the recent election they had in effect competed for the presidency—though neither, as we have seen, had actually made any efforts in his own behalf. Then in December, before the outcome was known for certain, various signals began going out from Monticello. If a tie vote should force the election into the House of Representatives, Jefferson told Madison on the 17th, "I pray you and authorize you fully to sollicit on my behalf that mr. Adams may be preferred. He has always been my senior from the commencement of our public life, and the expression of the public will being equal, this circumstance ought to give him the preference."[39]

Jefferson's letter was shown about as soon as it was received (though the final result of the election had meanwhile become known); Adams was told of it immediately, and was much gratified. "It is considered as Evidence of his determination to accept [the vice-presidency]," he wrote to Abigail, "of his Friendship for me — And of his Modesty and Moderation." Jefferson revealed his generous sentiments in other letters as well, in order that there should be no doubt of Adams's hearing about them, which he did. Adams for his part, though a little less fulsome, said sufficiently complimentary things about Jefferson that Benjamin Rush could report with great satisfaction that Mr. Adams "does you justice on all occasions, and it is currently said, views the attempt which originated in New York [by Hamilton] to prefer Mr. Pinckney to him, in its proper light." It was all logical enough, Jefferson and Adams being in most ways far more congenial than Adams and Hamilton could be, especially after Adams found out what Hamilton had been up to in the recent election.[40]

But how far were they to go in their reconciliation and rapprochement? One test was Jefferson's subsequently famous letter of congratulation, written at the beginning of the year, which Adams never received — the letter Jefferson first sent to Madison, unsealed for the latter's inspection and judgment, and which Madison decided not to send on.

This is how he instructed Madison:

> I had intended [writing] it some time, but had deferred it under the despair of making him believe I could be sincere in it. . . . I inclose it open for your perusal, not only that you may possess the actual state of dispositions between us, but that if any thing should render the delivery of it ineligible in your opinion, you may return it to me. If mr. Adams can be induced to administer the government on it's true principles, and to relinquish his bias to an English constitution, it is to be considered whether it Would not be on the whole for the Public good to come to a good understanding with him. . . . He is perhaps the only sure barrier against Hamilton's getting in.[41]

And here, in part, is what he intended to say to Adams:

> The public & the papers have been much occupied lately in placing us in a point of opposition to each other. I trust with confidence that less of it has been felt by ourselves personally. . . . I have never one single moment expected [that the election would turn out otherwise than it has]; & tho I know I shall not be believed, yet it is not the less true that I have never wished it. . . . Indeed it is [not] impossible that you may be cheated of your succession by a trick worthy the subtlety of your arch-friend of New York who has been able to make of your real friends tools to defeat their and your just wishes. Most probably he will be disappointed

as to you; and my inclinations place me out of his reach. I leave to others the sublime delights of riding in the storm, better pleased with sound sleep and a warm berth below, with the society of neighbors, friends & fellow-laborers of the earth, than of spies & sycophants. No one then will congratulate you with purer disinterestedness than myself. [I retain] still for you the solid esteem of the moments when we were working for our independence, and sentiments of respect & affectionate attachment.[42]

But Madison did not like the letter, and his instincts warned him against sending it on. He withheld it, explaining himself as follows:

1. It is certain that Mr. Adams, on his coming to this place, expressed to different persons a respectful cordiality towards you. . . . And it is equally known that your sentiments towards him personally have found their way to him in the most conciliating form. This being the state of things between you, it deserves to be considered whether the idea of bettering it is not outweighed by the possibility of changing it for the worse. 2. There is perhaps a general air on the letter which betrays the difficulty of your situation in writing it, and it is uncertain what the impression might be. . . . 3. It is certain that Mr. A. is fully apprized of the trick aimed at by his pseudo-friends of N.Y. and there may be danger of his suspecting in memento's on that subject, a wish to make this resentment an instrument for avenging that of others. . . . 4. May not what is said of "the sublime delights of riding in the storm &c." be misconstrued into a reflexion on those who have no distaste to the helm at the present crisis? . . . 5. The tenderness due to the zealous & active promoters of your election, makes it doubtful whether their anxieties & exertions ought to be depreciated. . . . 6. Considering the probability that Mr. A.s course of administration may force an opposition to it from the Republican quarter, & the general uncertainty of the posture which our affairs may take, there may be real embarrassments from giving written possession to him, of the degree of compliment & confidence which your personal delicacy & friendship have suggested.[43]

Jefferson was not at all irritated at this exercise by Madison of his own discretion; in fact he was relieved and "very thankful" for it. He agreed that he had not got it right,

& I would not have hazarded the attempt if you had not been in place to decide upon it's expediency. It is now become necessary to repeat it, by a letter I have had occasion to write to Langdon in answer to one from him, in which I have said exactly the things which will be grateful to mr. A. & no more. This I imagine will be shewn to him.[44]

But why "no more"?

We shall return to this point, but meanwhile the thing was kept going, and thus retained its many possibilities. The Republicans in general, perhaps largely on cue from Jefferson himself, awaited Adams's accession with a certain optimism. The final episode, the test which the incipient understanding proved *not* able to pass, came just before, and just after, Adams's inauguration.

Jefferson arrived in Philadelphia on March 2, and promptly paid a call on

Adams. There is no record of what they talked about, perhaps mostly reminiscences of the past, but Adams returned the call next day. He had one purpose above all in mind for doing so. He unfolded to Jefferson his entire scheme for making peace with France, his idea of a three-man commission consisting of Madison, Gerry, and Pinckney — one "which, by its dignity, should satisfy France, and by its selection from the three great divisions of the continent, should satisfy all parts of the United States" — and he wanted Jefferson's assistance. He would most have liked Jefferson himself to go, he explained, but he supposed it improper to send away the Vice-President, and he therefore hoped Jefferson would use his influence with Madison.[45]

Jefferson, as Adams's grandson wrote many years later, "appears to have met this proposition with less cordiality than it merited at his hands." As for himself, he flatly declined to go, saying that "without considering whether the Constitution will allow it or not, I am so sick of residing in Europe, that I believe I shall never go there again." As for Madison, Jefferson did not think he would be willing to go either, giving as his reason Madison's having declined the post of minister to France when Washington offered it to him eight years before, but said he would consult him. Adams was rather crestfallen, murmuring that if Madison refused he would appoint him anyway "and leave the responsibility on him."[46]

The next day, March 4, was the inauguration, and Adams's message, which was rather short, was generally welcomed, especially by Republicans. Much of it was devoted to praising the Constitution, to which he had "acquired an habitual attachment" and "veneration." He saw no reason to change it; he had never objected "that the Executive and Senate were not more permanent"; there was no spectacle, he said, "more pleasing, more noble, majestic, or august" than of an executive and legislature composed of citizens "selected at regular periods by their neighbors." "Can any thing essential . . . be added to this by robes and diamonds?" (He had no thought of turning the government into a monarchy.) Among the greatest menaces to "our free, fair, virtuous, and independent elections" was "the spirit of party." (Everyone agreed to that too, at least in theory.) And most especially, he asserted his "personal esteem for the French nation," his "sincere desire to preserve the friendship which has been so much for the honor and interest of both nations," and his intention, "by amicable negotiation," both to "investigate every just cause . . . of complaint" and to pursue "reparation for the injuries that have been committed on the commerce of our fellow-citizens." Benjamin Bache was overjoyed. Mr. Adams, he declared in the *Aurora,* was "a man of incorruptible integrity," "the friend of France and of peace, the admirer of republicanism, the enemy of party. . . . How honorable are these sentiments; how characteristic of a patriot!"[47]

But the Federalists were already on their guard. The day after the inauguration, March 5, the unsuspecting Adams had a talk with the Secretary of the Treasury, Oliver Wolcott, about his plans for a mission to France, with Madison as a special envoy. He was much taken aback at Wolcott's dour opposition.

"Is it determined [Wolcott demanded] to send Mr. Madison?" "No; but it deserves consideration." "Sending Mr. Madison will make dire work among the passions of our parties in Congress, and out of doors, through the States!" "Are we forever to be overawed and directed by party passions?" All this conversation on my part was with the most perfect civility, good humor, and indeed familiarity; but I found it excited a profound gloom and solemn countenance in my companion, which after some time broke out in, "Mr. President, we are willing to resign." Nothing could have been more unexpected to me . . . nothing was farther from my thoughts than to give any pain or uneasiness. I had said nothing that could possibly displease, except pronouncing the name of Madison. I restrained my surprise, however, and only said, I hope nobody will resign; I am satisfied with all the public officers.[48]

Then the day after that, March 6, both Adams and Jefferson were guests at a farewell dinner given by Washington, and afterward they walked homeward a short way together. Jefferson told Adams that Madison ("as I expected") would not consider going on such a mission; Adams replied in effect that it was just as well, since "some objections to that nomination had been raised" which he had not counted on; they parted, and never discussed the subject again. According to Adams, they "consulted very little together afterwards" about anything, and as Jefferson recalled it, on "measures of government" they never consulted again at all.[49]

So Adams's plan, from the time of his broaching it, lasted at most a period of four days before crashing in ruins, and in all likelihood less than that. There may not have been at any time much chance of its being carried into effect. But why not?

There is no doubt that a major force for obstruction lay in Adams's own cabinet. The opposition of Pickering, Wolcott, and McHenry, singly and collectively, to sending any Republican to France was baleful and unrelenting, and thus one very logical way of assessing the matter is to place much of the responsibility on them.[50] Yet Oliver Wolcott's grandson and self-appointed vindicator, George Gibbs, could still feel some outrage a half-century later to think that Adams in consulting on so bitterly disputed a question should have gone first not to a member of the party that elected him, but of all people to his defeated rival Jefferson. Gibbs put much stress on Adams's "restless and irritable temperament," "obstinate and yet fickle," his impulsiveness and inconsistency on matters "demanding cool deliberation, and . . . the opinions at least of his constitutional advisers" — and perhaps not without some justice.[51]

So although the cabinet's view of the crisis need not be seen as the correct one, it may at least be suspected that Adams did to some extent have himself to blame for his initial difficulties. One may imagine that if he had prepared his ground more carefully and much earlier as President-elect, he might have been able to secure the sort of commission that could achieve his purposes in a matter of months, instead of their requiring two commissions and his entire term of office. He might indeed, in devising his commission, have gone even a notch better than with the one he did think of. He might have appointed James Madison and two others who were already in Europe, Pinckney and his own son John Quincy Adams. The logic of Madison he had of course already recognized, as he had that of Pinckney. In Madison the French would have had before them the embodied authority of the pro-French party in America, and thus as strong an inducement as the United States government could give them to take its representatives seriously. In Pinckney's case, the country's honor required that France's arbitrary treatment of him could in no way be condoned, as it would be if he were left off the commission; moreover, despite Pinckney's moderate Federalism he had strong sympathies with France, and his merits were recognized by Republicans and Federalists alike.[52] As for John Quincy Adams, the President's son was the most astute and best-informed American on the European scene, with few illusions about either France or England, but convinced like his father that the right approach to the French was to be firm but friendly and reasonable. That John Adams's scruples about special preferment to his own family should extend to this case was rather a pity, and it seems that more than one important person told him so. It is quite probable that had Washington remained to deal with the crisis, young Adams would have played a leading role in his effort to settle it, and when Adams's cabinet finally did acquiesce in the idea of a commission late in the spring, they all wanted John Quincy Adams to be a member of it.[53]

For an ally, Adams might have had Alexander Hamilton himself. Much has been made of the subservience of the cabinet to Hamilton's opinions, and there is certainly no doubt that Hamilton exerted much influence there, but the fact is that on the greatest single issue facing the incoming administration, Hamilton and the trio of Pickering, Wolcott, and McHenry were profoundly at odds. Hamilton's view was much closer to that of Adams than to theirs; indeed they were virtually identical. Hamilton saw, as Adams did, that the state of relations with France was closely analogous to what the United States had faced with regard to Great Britain in 1794 and should be handled in the same way: that every effort should be made to avoid war; differences should be settled through amicable negotiation, and a special mission should be appointed for that purpose. He also believed, as did Adams, that for such a mission to be successful the key man, the indispensable member, would have to be James Madison. Through no less a person than Madison could the French be persuaded of America's good faith and seriousness of purpose, and however misguided Hamilton may have thought Madison's political views, like Adams (but very much unlike Adams's cabinet secretaries), he had no doubt of Madison's patriotism or of his care for the national interest.

Hamilton, with many an inward groan over the crude bellicosity of Pickering, had in fact begun pressing such views back in January, while the Washington administration was still in office. Hamilton saw trouble as early as November 1796, with the publication of Adet's note of October 27. Too late, he urged that the American reply not be published ("I should be afraid of Mr. Pickerings *warmth*"); when it was, he deplored it ("It is all important . . . to avoid rupture with France"); and although it could no longer be undone, "the more I have considered that paper the less I like it."[54] On January 19 he broached, and on the 22nd fully outlined, his own plan in letters to Washington. "We seem to be where we were with G Britain when Mr. Jay was sent there—and I cannot discern but that the Spirit of the Policy then pursued with regard to England will be the proper one now in respect to France (viz) a solemn and final appeal to the Justice and interest of France & if this will not do, measures of self defence." The best form, he urged, would be through a commission of three persons, "plenipotentiary & extraordinary," two of whom "should be Mr. Madison and Mr. Pinckney." Moreover, "Unless Mr. *Madison* will go there is scarcely another character that will afford advantage." But Washington, not disposed to commit his successor, and doubtless counting the days until his own release, was understandably fretful. "But is not General Pinckney gone there already for the express purpose of explaining matters, and removing inquietudes? With what more could another be charged?"[55]

Hamilton made no further effort to persuade Washington, but the thing was constantly on his mind, and its urgency mounted with news of spoliations, publication of another of Pickering's inflammatory letters, and the increasing likelihood that Pinckney had not been received. From January until mid-May he wrote letters to all those of his friends who he thought might have some influence in or with the new administration: Wolcott, Sedgwick, Tracy, Pickering, Ames, McHenry, William L. Smith—everybody, that is, except John Adams himself. All except Ames and Sedgwick rejected his ideas—decisively, even peremptorily, and none more so than the members of Adams's cabinet. "We more than doubt the propriety of this step," Pickering replied bluntly. "This new mission is what the enemies of our government wish for. . . ." (All the more reason, Hamilton protested, for sending it.) "The idea of a Commission consisting of Mr. M. or any man like him," said Wolcott, "I must own to you is one which I can never adopt without the utmost reluctance." "For my own part," wrote McHenry, "I have not been able to discover any advantage attending a trio. It will please nobody . . . and will not ensure the United States against a single possible evil, nor create to government one additional friend."[56]

It is difficult to gauge more than approximately the way Adams responded to the pressures of Federalist feeling to which he was exposed during this period. The evidence suggests that he did give ground in the face of strong Federalist antagonism to a Republican appointment.[57] But equally significant is evidence that he bridled at any attempt by Hamilton to influence the policy of his administration. The two may have been thinking along parallel lines, as Adams at some point discovered, but he had meanwhile also discovered the part Hamilton had taken in the election.[58] Had they overtly joined forces on a matter of policy, they would have been hard to resist. As it was, nothing Hamilton might say, or think, or do from then on would gain him much credit with John Adams.

But such conjectures must here be brought to an end, since it was not primarily the Federalists, or John Adams, who scuttled this promising idea. It never had a chance in the first place, and this was because there was no point at which Jefferson and Madison would for a moment have entertained such a plan, or have been the least willing to take any part in it. (It might be added—though that is a later story—that the French had nothing to gain at that particular time by negotiating with any American commission, no matter who was on it.)

Many a commentator has been impressed by the graciousness of Jefferson's urging, back in December when the election was still in doubt, that Adams be "preferred" (he having "always been my senior" and so on), and there has always been something wistfully attractive about the vision of a genuine working arrangement between the two old friends of Revolutionary times. Yet paradoxically, there was a clear connection between this incipient rapprochement and a determination in the top Republican councils to have nothing to do with a bipartisan diplomatic effort. Jefferson by December genuinely did not want to be President, because by then the mounting evils with regard to France were becoming such that he did not want the responsibility of handling them himself. "I wish any body rather than myself," he wrote, "and there is nothing I so anxiously hope, as that my name may come out either second or third." As for foreign affairs, "I think they never wore so gloomy an aspect since the year 83. Let those come to the helm who think they can steer clear of the difficulties." He could be at home planting his corn and peas, he told Edward Rutledge, "while our Eastern friend [Adams] will be struggling with the storm which is gathering over us; perhaps be shipwrecked in it." Washington, he told Madison, was "fortunate to get off just as the bubble is bursting leaving others to hold the bag."[59] Jefferson was eager that it be known he did not in the least mind serving under Adams, and he was glad to hear that Adams was speaking of him with friendship and "with satisfaction in the prospect of administering the government in concurrence with me." But, he cautioned, "if by that he meant the executive cabinet, both duty & inclination will shut that door to me."

> I cannot have a wish to . . . descend daily into the arena like a gladiator, to suffer martyrdom in every conflict. As to duty, the constitution will know me only as the member of a legislative body; and it's principle is, that of a separation of legislative, executive & judiciary functions, except in cases specified.[60]

In short, renewed friendship with Adams was a fine bargain for getting out of the main responsibility, and in washing his hands of the presidency he was also washing his hands of the French crisis.

But it was more than a matter simply of Jefferson's personal distaste for trouble. Though most Republicans dreaded the prospect of war with France, and would have given much to avoid it, it was not at all to the interest of any Republican of consequence to let himself be involved in bipartisan efforts at peacemaking. Nobody understood this more starkly all along than Jefferson and Madison, and most especially Madison. Thus Republican sentiment in response to the gathering crisis had a certain element of ambiguity.

Adet's announcement of the French decree on neutral commerce was certainly shocking, but the principal tendency at first was to say that this action was a perfectly understandable response to the Jay Treaty—the hope meanwhile being that Jefferson would be the next President, and then all would be set to rights.

But by January it was clear that Adams and not Jefferson would be Washington's successor; there was the news of extensive spoliations, and then the publication of Pickering's latest blast at the French, couched in the form of a dispatch to Pinckney. It was a time of considerable agitation, with a real possibility of war, and fears that "the British party" actually wanted such a war and were trying to push Washington into it before he left office. During this period there was talk among Republicans about the urgency of another effort at peacemaking; Bache's newspaper pressed several times for a fresh mission to France with Madison as a minister with plenipotentiary powers, and the rumor actually got around that such a mission had been appointed.[61] The tendency of the Federalists, on the other hand, was to resist such a solution, especially after the Monroe experience. Republican participation might well mean paying too high a price for any new understanding that might be reached—repudiating the Jay Treaty and perhaps tying America even more closely to France instead of freeing us, as had now come to seem desirable, from the worst constraints of the 1778 alliance.[62]

Then another tendency began to appear in Republican circles during this same period. They were inclined to look on the brighter side of Adams's victory and to picture him as preferable, if not to Jefferson at least to a Washington administration dominated by Hamiltonian and British influence. That there was no love lost between Adams and Hamilton was common knowledge, and it was to the Republicans' interest—since this was sure to function as a divisive force—to keep it that way. It was in this context that an Adams-Jefferson rapprochement was welcomed among Republicans but not among Federalists.[63] All of this was certain to create powerful cross-currents of feeling and purpose, and the greatest single loser was pretty much bound to be Adams himself.

Meanwhile a key figure in each party (Hamilton, Madison) was laying down a line of strategy which in each case ran counter to what was being supported by most of his friends and coadjutors. While Hamilton was trying to persuade other Federalists of the wisdom of a new mission under Madison, Madison himself was carefully seeing to it that he and Jefferson (whatever benign expressions about Adams their friends might indulge in) kept their distance from Adams, that any dealings with him would be within the narrowest limits, and that under no circumstances would either be a party to any transactions with France undertaken by an Adams administration, no matter how pacific Adams's own inclinations might be.

The workings of Madison's mind can be followed through his letters to Jefferson during the winter of 1796–97. In December, still apprehensive whether Jefferson was willing to serve as Vice-President, Madison was quite prepared to urge the importance of friendly relations with Adams as part of the argument for his accepting:

> There is reason to believe also that your neighbourhood to Adams may have a valuable effect on his councils particularly in relation to our external system. You know that his feelings will not enslave him to the example of his predecessor. It is certain that his censures of our paper system & the intrigues at New York for setting P above him have fixed an enmity with the British faction.

But with all doubts about Jefferson's acceptance removed, we hear no more of that argument, and nothing further in the way of kind things about John Adams. He remarks on January 29: "No further discovery has been made of the mind of the P. elect. I can not prevail on myself to augur much that is consoling from him." A week later, he says he will reserve for a confidential talk a consideration of the prospects "from the accession of Mr. A. to the Helm. They are not, I conceive, very flattering." And when he gives his reasons for withholding Jefferson's letter to Adams, it is not for the purpose of pulling Jefferson back from a contemplated alliance, it being in no way likely that Jefferson had such a thing in mind anyway. It is simply to prevent him from striking the wrong note on a policy they were more or less implicitly agreed on already. You squirm too much, he tells Jefferson in effect, and your discomfort is much too obvious. Goad him about Hamilton, and he will suspect you of doing it for your own ends. The more you profess having no wish for power, the more you reflect on Adams, who has no distaste for it. Nor should you be *too* airy about the efforts of those who worked for your election. And, above all:

> Considering the *probability* that Mr. A.s course of administration may force an opposition from the Republican quarter . . . there may be real embarrassments from giving written possession to him, of the degree of compliment . . . [etc., etc.][64]

Among the things that may be read into this last was that he, Madison, would have nothing to do with any move to send him to France. He knew he was being talked about for such a purpose; the report, he assured Jefferson, was "pure fiction."[65] Not only was the story not true, he had no intention of making it so, and Jefferson knew this when Adams later asked Jefferson if he thought Madison would go. Why, indeed, should he go? After his bitter resistance to the Jay Treaty down to the end—a major commitment of principle—to accept such a mission as this would be to stultify himself. It would in effect be to reverse his principles and accept the treaty after all, since any instructions he took with him would be sure to stipulate that the Jay Treaty, now enacted into law, was not a subject for discussion. James Madison may not have been against a fresh negotiation, and he certainly hoped the country might avoid war. But he would not hear of his or Jefferson's having any responsibility for such a negotiation.

Jefferson concurred in this, and in effect told Adams as much when Adams asked him. He knew, and Adams by then knew, that "consulting" Madison was purely *pro forma*—but he duly reported the result, and they "consulted very little together" from that time on.

Such, then, were the limiting conditions—from the string of French decrees that began back in 1793 to the domestic political currents of early 1797—within which John Adams would have to function in anything he did about the state of American relations with France. Further news from abroad in March made things even worse, and it now became necessary to act. The course he took may henceforth be seen in three main phases, the last of which would not be consummated until his term was almost over. The first phase extended from March 1797 to March 1798 with the reception of the XYZ dispatches; the second, through the remainder of 1798 until the nomination of the Murray mission in February 1799; and the third terminated with the Convention of Môrtefontaine in October 1800.

3
First Phase: The XYZ Mission

The limits being imposed upon Adams from every side—by the Federalists, by the Republicans, and, of course, by the French themselves—constricted Adams's cherished "independence" to the vanishing point and made the first phase of his great effort a failure. The spirit of "balance" he had conceived for the Executive could not, somehow, function that way at all; every step was curiously *off* balance, strain as he might to make it otherwise. The case he presented to Congress in May was intended to achieve unity; it resulted instead in a great polarization of party feeling—and nothing, or almost nothing, in the way of defense preparations. Adams succeeded in appointing his three-man commission, but not composed in the way he originally had in mind, with a leading Republican representative, while the one member he particularly insisted on, Elbridge Gerry, turned out to be a compulsive expedient on his part, the very one who made the greatest trouble for him. As for his old friend Jefferson, far from being his well-wisher and perhaps even collaborator, it was as though the man had been dissembling all along only to emerge as a great force for obstruction. "The constitution will know me only as the member of a legislative body," Jefferson had piously said in January, and the Constitution, to be sure, had nothing to do with the role Madison had already marked out for him, now that Madison himself was retiring from Congress and going back to Virginia, the role of leader of the Republican opposition. But of course there was bound to be opposition, at the very climax of a time when party feeling was so predominantly based on foreign attachments and foreign antipathies. And as in 1794, when to the opposition anything the Federalists did with regard to England was bound to be bad, so now nothing they might do concerning France had much chance of being good. Everything for Adams, in short, seemed to be occurring under the worst possible circumstances when it was a question of taking purposeful action, and all without the magisterial sanction of Washington to compel at least a rough and provisional unity. "Jealousies and rivalries have been my theme, and checks and balances as their antidotes," Adams was already lamenting after only two weeks in office, "till I am ashamed to repeat the words; but they never stared me in the face in such horrid forms as at present."[66]

As for the misadventures about to befall the American commissioners in France, Pinckney, Gerry, and John Marshall—and which were to give so drastic a turn to the entire domestic situation in the United States—the very luridness of the famous XYZ affair presents us with what almost amounts to a problem of attitude. Even at the time, there could be more than one possible response to it, and something of this ambiguity has persisted ever since. The dominant one, of course, was outrage. This was the fuel for the great explosion of national feeling which occurred in 1798: that the government of one sovereign nation should refuse to negotiate with the accredited representatives of another, or even to receive them, without bribes for its leading members and a loan for that nation's military incursions in Europe, seemed to touch the utmost limits of insult. Another response was incredulity. The first thing that struck James Madison, for example, on hearing the news was not so much the venality of the French Foreign Minister, Talleyrand, but rather how the Minister, acquainted as he was with America and the Americans, could have behaved so stupidly. Still another was a kind of pervasive skepticism, an attitude that has tended to entrench itself with the passage of time. Here the cue comes from Jefferson, with his remark about "the X.Y.Z. dish cooked up by Marshall, where the swindlers are made to appear as the French government." The story told by the dispatches, which were all written by Marshall, seemed entirely too bad to be true.[67]

And it may well be that such skepticism, even allowing for the partisanship in Jefferson's case and his evident wish that the whole thing *not* be true, should have some place in the fashioning of a historical viewpoint. Was it simply the paying of a bribe, for all that was made of it, that the Americans most objected to, or was it their uncertainty of what they might get for it? In the picture that emerges from the dispatches, do not the upright American republicans contrast a little *too* sharply with the classically corrupt and cynical French? The Americans were there for six months, and they could hardly have spent all their time working; were they altogether untouched by the blandishments and pleasures of Paris under the Directory?[68] There is a beguiling plainspokenness, a kind of dramatic simplicity, about the dispatches that were sent home. Nonetheless there is reason to suspect—as there was at the time—that Marshall did not make his case artlessly, that he well knew what he was doing, that he already understood the best ways of persuading a jury. And finally, the subsequent behavior of Talleyrand, together with evidence turned up many years later in the French archives, suggests that he never intended to drive the Americans to the point of war, and that from the very first he expected in the final reckoning—when it finally suited France's convenience—to make a satisfactory settlement.[69]

Consequently the picture we have of the famous episode tends always to blur somewhat around the edges; we do not approach it with confidence. And yet there are further twists: Marshall, so far as is known, did not write anything that was not true. Even Gerry, who disagreed sharply with him and Pinckney over the meaning of what was happening to them, had no quarrel with the information itself, and signed the dispatches with the others.

Adams had been in office less than three weeks when he decided he would have to call a special session of Congress, and on March 25, 1797, he issued a proclamation to that effect, the session to convene on May 15. The long-awaited news from France had finally arrived, with full particulars of how the French had treated Pinckney. Their procedure, as usual, had been a mixture of improvisation and absent-mindedness. Monroe, though greatly upset at being recalled, gave his successor a courteous welcome and made arrangements for his reception. He presented Pinckney to Charles Delacroix, the then Foreign Minister, on December 9, 1796; Delacroix accepted his letters of credence and promised cards of hospitality for him and his family immediately. But the cards failed to materialize, which meant that the Pinckneys could be picked up by the police at any time the latter chose, and then word arrived that the Directory had decided it would "no longer recognize or receive a minister plenipotentiary from the United States" until a full reparation was made for France's grievances. Pinckney did not see how this or anything else in the way of an amicable resolution could occur if the two governments were not allowed to communicate with each other, and he wondered whether this meant he would have to leave. He was told through an intermediary that it did. Did that mean Paris, or the entire territory of France? The intermediary was not sure; he came back later to say it meant France, not just Paris. Would he have to go immediately? The man was not sure about that either, but told Pinckney the authorities would let him know. Pinckney said he wanted it in writing; he did not intend to leave and report to his government that he had been ordered out without something he could show that indicated as much. There was no reply. Finally, six and a half weeks after his first and only interview, he received a written order to quit the country, and he did so forthwith, taking his family to Amsterdam.[70]

There had been a further affront to the United States in connection with the departure of Monroe. The Directory and Ministers had for some time been treating Monroe, as he himself admitted, "with great coolness; but as soon as they heard of his recall, their attentions to him were renewed." His audience of leave-taking occurred on December 30. The president of the Directory, Paul F. N. Barras, read an insolent little speech in which he said that Monroe in presenting his letters of recall was giving Europe "a very strange spectacle"; that the American government was still under the influence "of its ancient tyrants"; that Americans should be "proud of their liberty" and "never forget that they owe it to France." He intimated that they were being divided, and must beware "the crafty caresses of perfidious men, who meditate to bring them again under their former yoke." "As for you, Mr. minister plenipotentiary," he concluded,

> you have combated for principles; you have known the true interests of your country—depart with our regret. We restore, in you, a representative to America; and we preserve the remembrance of a citizen whose personal qualities did honor to that title.[71]

"I cannot fully account for this Step," wrote Rufus King from London when he heard of Pinckney's dismissal, "after the irresolution that for some time has existed. . . ." Washington in his retirement was equally mystified. "The conduct of the French government is so much beyond calculation," he wrote to McHenry, "and so unaccountable upon any principle of justice or even of that sort of policy wch. is familiar to plain understanding that I shall not now puzzle my brains in attempting to develop their motives to it."[72]

Still another piece of news, and a very serious one, concerned the most recent decree against American maritime commerce. Though it could be represented as yet another expression of the Directory's ire, more fundamentally it reflected the demands of the European war and the French government's desperate need of money; it was part of the mounting system of tribute now being practiced, with variations, upon every state in Europe. This new decree, dated March 2, 1797, specified that the "free ships, free goods" provision of the Treaty of 1778 was formally abrogated, which meant that any English goods found aboard American ships could be confiscated; that any American found serving under an enemy flag, whether forced to do so or not, would be treated as a pirate; and that any American ship without a list of the crew and passengers in proper form (*rôle d'équipage*) was to be regarded as good prize. The pretext for this last provision was that a model for the *rôle d'équipage* had been attached to the Treaty of 1778, which was in fact not true. American vessels had never carried such a paper, and it had never heretofore been insisted on.[73]

Adams had two purposes in mind in calling the special session, for which all this new information served as both provocation and background. One was his intention, despite the aggressions and insults, to seek a reconciliation by sending a fresh mission to France. The other was to recommend and solicit support for measures of armament, primarily naval, for the protection of American commerce in case the projected negotiations should end in failure.

On May 16 Adams delivered his message to Congress. The language was forthright and was approved by most Federalists, but it was denounced more or less generally by Republicans as being essentially a war speech. Bache's praise for Adams was heard no more; the President, he said, had "completely deceived the people," led as they were by his inaugural discourse "to believe that he was under no *extraneous influence.*" Giles, who a few months earlier had said that "the old man will make a good President," now professed himself mistaken. Jefferson, claiming that "nothing new" had really happened since the regular session adjourned, was now convinced that "war was the object for which we were called," and would repeatedly say as much to his correspondents as long as the special session lasted. Bache declared it was obvious from the President's speech "that his men TIMOTHY and OLIVER have fed him upon pepperpot these three weeks in order to bring his nerves to a proper anti-gallic tone."[74]

So there is the question of exactly how Adams *was* being advised in the period immediately prior to the special session, of how he responded to the advice he received, and how it all came out in his message. The record on this is actually fairly complete. Having already determined on a special session, he asked for opinions in writing from all the members of his cabinet on how he ought to proceed and what he should say. The responses have all been preserved. Circumstances by now had brought each of the Secretaries around to advising roughly the same course of action: another effort at negotiation through the dispatch of a new mission to France; coupled with measures of defense. But there were some wide and rather interesting variations in tone. Pickering and Wolcott had indeed served up helpings of "pepperpot," as Bache had said, each being highly exercised over France's actions. McHenry's memoranda, on the other hand (following closely as they did the suggestions of Hamilton), were restrained and sophisticated. Those of Charles Lee, the Attorney-General, were also moderate and without animus.[75] Adams took a little from each, though in no instance more than phrases, and the style, proportion, and emphasis were peculiarly his own. If there were one or two missteps, these too were largely his own doing.

The most he drew from anyone was in his report of Pinckney's treatment by the French government, the outlines of which came from Pickering, though Adams's recital was shorter, more straightforward, and less indignant than Pickering's. As for the spoliations, extensive as they were, he did not discuss these at all (as Pickering had done at great length); he simply referred to them as though their existence were well known, as indeed it was. In his recommendations for defensive steps, Adams's entire emphasis was on maritime measures for the protection of American commerce (permitting merchant vessels to arm for their own defense, completing the three frigates begun in 1794 and building some sloops of war, and strengthening harbor fortifications); whereas it was only in two sentences at the end of six paragraphs that he added, rather perfunctorily, that Congress might consider additions to the regular artillery and cavalry, arrangements for forming a provisional army, and revision of the militia laws. Pickering and Lee had urged a program of direct taxes; Adams slid over the whole revenue question by referring it to the House of Representatives. McHenry proposed an embargo; Adams did not mention such a step. Pickering wanted an alien law; Adams did not take that up either.

A few of the documents Adams submitted to accompany his message—dispatches from John Quincy Adams describing France's brutal exploitation of her ally the Dutch Republic—were unnecessarily provocative and served no direct purpose. Then there were two passages in the address itself, neither of them proposed by any of the Secretaries, which in the end probably caused more trouble than anything else in it. One referred to "endeavors ... to foster and establish a division between the government and people of the United States"; the other, to Barras's speech to Monroe as a notorious example of such endeavors. The French, as might have been expected, would throw this back at the American commissioners later on, and these same charges (the danger of Americans "surrendering themselves to the direction of foreign and domestic factions, in opposition to their own government") would enrage Republicans at home. According to Jefferson, men who desired only peace were "overwhelmed" by a cry "of being under French influence, & this raised by a faction composed of English subjects residing among us, or such as are English in all their relations & sentiments."[76]

It was such thoughts as these that marked Jefferson's full re-emergence on the stage of public life—"backstage" might be the better word—and it may be worth turning aside to take some account of the current state of Jefferson's mind. It is generally said, correctly, that this was the period which saw Jefferson assuming full charge of the Republican opposition. How rational was the spirit in which he did it, at a time when party passions were moving to a level never again quite equaled in American history, is a question of much interest. His most distinguished biographer has found the things Jefferson repeatedly said during this period ("unprovable assertions" and "unwarranted suspicions") painfully disturbing, and some of them merit examination for the light they may cast on the extreme difficulty of forming a national policy toward France. His hatred of Great Britain, and the extent to which he imagined the corruptions of British influence penetrating to every corner of American life, now formed the themes of virtually all he said and thought.[77] A kind of epitome was reached in a letter he wrote to Elbridge Gerry in May 1797. The British, he declared,

> have wished a monopoly of commerce & influence with us; and they have in fact obtained it. When we take notice that theirs is the workshop to which we go for all we want; that with them centre either immediately or ultimately all the labors of our hands and lands; that to them belongs either openly or secretly the great mass of our navigation; that even the factorage of their affairs here, is kept to themselves by factitious citizenships; that these foreign & false citizens now constitute the great body of what are called our merchants, fill our sea ports, are planted in every little town & district in the interior country, sway everything in the former places by their own votes, & those of their dependants, in the latter, by their insinuations & the influence of their ledgers; that they are advancing fast to a monopoly of our banks & public funds, and thereby placing our public finances under their control; that they have in their alliance the most influential characters in & out of office; when they have shewn that by all these bearings on the different branches of the government, they can force it to proceed in whatever direction they dictate, and bend the interests of this country entirely to the will of another; when all this, I say, is attended to, it is impossible for us to say we stand on independent ground, impossible for a free mind not to see & to groan under the bondage in which it is bound.[78]

There was very little in this outburst that corresponded with the actual state of American economic life in the late 1790s. The "great mass of our navigation" did not belong to the British at all, either "openly or secretly"; 90 percent of it in fact belonged to Americans. Englishmen ("factitious," "false," or otherwise) did not constitute the "great body" of our merchants either, even in the Chesapeake region where many English and Scottish factors had once made their headquarters. In banking and finance, foreign influence, British or other, was altogether marginal. One item in Jefferson's catalogue was correct enough: the vast bulk of American imports came from Great Britain, and most of our exports went there as well. A moral case on that ground was certainly arguable—analogous, for example, to the many complaints by Europeans after the Second World War that American consumer goods were debasing their character and culture. But amid the flourishing state of American business, with the terms of trade having by the mid-1790s altered sharply in the Americans' favor, and with Americans having displaced extraterritorial British subjects in economic functions everywhere, for economic exploitation there was no case whatever.[79]

Jefferson's many assertions about British political influence—an "English faction" in America seeking to maneuver the country into an alliance with Great Britain and a war with France — were equally questionable when it came down to details. No leading Federalist in 1797 wanted either one, or saw the least point in going to war. The only journalist who did, or appeared to, was William Cobbett, the perfect caricature of a British subject bent on luring Americans into a monarchical, anti-jacobinical crusade. Fastidious American Federalists squirmed with discomfort, and tried to keep Cobbett at a distance.[80] Jefferson's fear of war was nothing if not genuine. Indeed, it was so profound that he was not only unwilling but quite unable to grasp the prudential side of Adams's policy; to him, negotiation could not be coupled with measures of defense; the two were simply incompatible. What he wanted was inaction and delay, and he let all his friends know it, hoping for an eventual military culmination in Europe which would see England "sunk" by France. He accused Adams of warmongering in nearly every letter he wrote, and he had regular talks with the French consul-general in Philadelphia, telling him of Adams's "vanity" and "stubbornness."[81] These things were sooner or later bound to get back to Adams himself. When some of them did, Adams sardonically wrote: "It is evidence of a mind, soured, yet seeking for popularity, and eaten to a honeycomb with ambition, yet weak, confused, uninformed, and ignorant."[82]

All this was what was involved in Jefferson's emerging as the Republican party leader. Jefferson was postulating a radically different policy from the one being pursued by the government, and he was using this projection to justify a wide-ranging effort to place a warlike construction on the government's program and to block it at every turn. Jefferson's influence as the foremost Republican was certainly connected with the course of legislative events in the spring and early summer of 1797. The Republicans during the special session succeeded in thwarting most of the measures Adams asked for; except for completion of the three frigates already under construction and the strengthening of harbor defenses, little else was done. The disgraced Monroe arrived home near the end of June and was given a grand public dinner on July 1. More than fifty Republican dignitaries were present, headed by Vice-President Jefferson.[83] The impressions that the American people were in fact divided, that the pro-French party in America had prevented the enactment of the President's program, and that there was thus no immediate need to fear the Americans' going to war were all duly reported to the French government before the arrival of the American commissioners.[84]

The process of appointing members to the new mission and having them approved was at last completed by early summer. Earlier resistance in the cabinet to a three-man commission, rather than simply the reappointment of Pinckney as envoy extraordinary, had weakened by late May, though it is doubtful whether Hamilton was the main influence there. For the most part the obstinate ones seem to have been worn down by Adams himself — and by news of fresh victories by Bonaparte and financial distress in England — but they were as dead set as ever against including any leading Republican, desperately as Hamilton kept urging this almost to the end. There was no disagreement on John Marshall of Virginia, but when Adams brought up the name of Elbridge Gerry — whose qualifications were that Adams had known him since Revolutionary days and that Gerry had remained personally loyal all that time, also that Adams saw Gerry as not strongly attached to any party, which was more or less true—the cabinet put up great objections. Adams backed off, and Francis Dana, Chief Justice of the Massachusetts Supreme Judicial Court, was agreed on instead. The nominations of Marshall, Dana, and Pinckney were sent to the Senate on May 31 and approved on June 5. Dana declined, as Adams seems to have expected he would, and Adams sent Gerry's name in on June 24, objections notwithstanding. The nomination was approved June 22, though again not without opposition. Gerry sailed August 9, Marshall having already departed three weeks earlier to join Pinckney in Amsterdam. It had been rather an erratic and willful choice. It was not that Gerry had any special leanings toward France, nor that he was known as a Republican; despite his Antifederalist past he had supported many Federalist measures, including Hamilton's entire financial system. It was just that nobody ever quite knew what he would say or do next. When Adams presented Gerry's name to the cabinet, McHenry after a long pause ventured, "If, sir, it was a desirable thing to distract the mission, a fitter person could not perhaps be found. It is ten to one against his agreeing with his colleagues."[85]

Why it should be that Elbridge Gerry's public career—which already included service as a signer of the Declaration of Independence and of the Articles of Confederation, member of the Continental Congress, delegate to the Constitutional Convention, and member of the House of Representatives, and would in time include two terms as Governor of Massachusetts and, at the end of his life, the vice-presidency of the United States—should so regularly misfire, that every other step should somehow be in the wrong direction, that in the course of it he would exhaust the patience of colleagues and lose most of his friends (about the only ones who remained with him throughout were John Adams and Thomas Jefferson), has challenged the wits of more than one able historian. The key to all Gerry's quirks, dottiness, and apparent inconsistencies, according to his most recent biographer, was his ferocious attachment to the republican idea, to the abstraction of the classical republican commonwealth.[86] This is a very serviceable formula, for which there is much to be said. Provided, that is—since there were many others attached to the same idea—one adds that Gerry was the sort of person who seemed to think his "conscience" had an existence separate from himself, that he showed an uncanny preference for making a point of small issues at the expense of large ones, and that with Gerry (as with a younger contemporary of his, John Randolph of Roanoke), the disharmony between his republican ideal and the world that unfolded before him hovered always on the verge of dislocating his mind. "Poor Gerry," exclaimed Abigail Adams, who knew him as well as anyone did, "always had a wrong kink in his head."[87]

He was born in Marblehead in 1744. His father, a merchant-shipowner, had become wealthy by his own exertions and energy, and was one of the leading men in town. But Thomas Gerry was against luxury and frivolity, and the family did not live ostentatiously. Elbridge was the only one of the large family who went to college, entering Harvard at fourteen. There he seems to have caught the vision of the golden age: of statesmanship, public service, and Roman virtue. He learned enough Latin to keep him in maxims for the rest of his life, and was fond of citing the fall of the Roman Republic as a warning of what vice and corruption might do to America. His private library came to include Virgil, Pliny, Cicero, Locke, Montesquieu, Gibbon, and the great authorities on the law of nations. By the time of the Revolution, in which he took an immediate part, the whole thing was in place: the world-view of classical republicanism, of civic humanism, the entire set of Country opposition attitudes of eighteenth-century England. With Gerry it was "classical" in both senses, and he took it as literally as any man of his time. The central fact of political existence was the unceasing struggle between liberty and power, appropriate to which should be a horror of corruption, pensioners, and placemen, of standing armies, of centralized authority and executive usurpation. The fittest governors were those with the most virtue, those who, like himself, had the greatest passion for the public good. Indeed, in this sense few showed more of it than Gerry, having both the means and inclination for public service and not distracted by family cares until he had been in public life for over fifteen years. The "genius of the people" should be trusted, though not too far: "it requires great skill in gradually checking them, to such a subordination as is necessary to good Government."[88] All in all it was suspicion, according to Gerry's otherwise respectful son-in-law, that "was the weakest trait of his mind."[89] He was suspicious of power of any sort, and military power above all else.

Gerry first entered public affairs during the agitation over the Townshend Acts. He was elected to the Marblehead committee of correspondence in 1770, to the General Court in 1772, and in 1774 to the Massachusetts Provincial Congress. His election to the Continental Congress in 1775 in effect gave Massachusetts a majority for independence. Independence, he thought, was inevitable, because the royal government by then had become "corrupt and totally destitute of Virtue."[90] Except for an absence of three years after resigning in a huff over a point of parliamentary privilege, he remained in Congress, serving on innumerable committees, until 1785 when his term expired. He maintained his mercantile activities all through the war and did sufficiently well to retire from business and get married in 1786, though he never engaged, as a fair number did, in any profiteering.

For all Gerry's diligent wartime service, his work in Congress was remembered most for its caprices and contrariness. His phobias against sword, purse, and centralized power drove him to oppose any kind of peacetime army and any taxing scheme to raise revenue for the central government. His plan for having two permanent seats of government and an itinerant legislature caused the Secretary of Congress to grumble that Gerry was "of so peculiar a cast of mind that his pleasure seems proportioned to the absurdity of his schemes and [he] is only mortified when reason and common sense prevail."[91] He reached a certain peak of notoriety at the Constitutional Convention, despite being one of the most active delegates there (on a single day he made seven speeches against one or another aspect of military power), by being the only one remaining to the end who refused to sign. "He was of service," observed a colleague, "by objecting to every thing he did not propose."[92] Gerry served in the new Federal Congress until 1793, when he retired because of disillusionment over the rising spirit of faction. He re-emerged as a presidential elector in 1796 pledged to Adams, and on anti-party principles. The perfect ticket, he thought, was Adams and Jefferson, and he was delighted to see it turn out just so.

Adams appointed Gerry to the French mission in 1797 out of a mutual personal loyalty (they had been men of '76 together), in approval of Gerry's feelings about party, and, perhaps, out of a certain perversity not unrelated to Gerry's own. But as it happened they did not see eye to eye on the main thing, which was what to do about France, and they never did get together to talk about it before Gerry sailed. Gerry was certainly not pro-French, but he did imagine himself—perhaps prompted by Jefferson[93]—as a counterweight to any undue "English" influence on the commission. His great obsession was war, and he was prepared to go to all lengths to avoid it. France was far too powerful, he thought, but even if America should somehow prevail she would have a standing army at the end of it.

"My entrance into office is marked by a misunderstanding with France, which I shall endeavor to reconcile," John Adams had written to his son in March. But not at the cost of "too much humiliation." And, he added: "America is not SCARED."[94] Yet the man he sent to France in August was very "scared," and all too ready to act on his fears.

John Marshall, the second member of the commission, could not have been more unlike Gerry in temperament or background. Even in appearance they made quite a contrast. Marshall was tall, rangy, and relaxed, Gerry small, nervous, and bird-like; Marshall had rather a small head, Gerry's was proportionally oversized. Both were men of the Revolution, and both republican to the core. But their experience of the Revolution and the lessons they drew from it were almost opposite in quality. Marshall became a resolute nationalist, in contrast with Gerry's state-sovereignty particularism. But above all, their minds functioned in strikingly divergent ways. Marshall was a loose constructionist in temper as well as legal philosophy. He was a powerful debater, but interested less in creating difficulties than in removing them. He was not normally given to suspicion, inclining rather to cheerfulness and a certain equanimity, with a simple confidence in the laws of reason and nature.[95]

He was born in 1755 in Prince William County, then on the Virginia frontier, and was the oldest of a very large family. His father was of humble origins, though he became a man of some consequence while John was growing up, and his mother was a Randolph, which made him a distant cousin of Thomas Jefferson. He and Jefferson never much liked each other. He was educated by tutors and did not go to college, though he did briefly attend a course of law lectures at William and Mary. The breadth of his reading was comparatively limited, but what he did read he tended to subdue by sheer force of mind. At the age of twelve he committed to memory large sections of Pope's *Essay on Man,* and he went through Horace and Livy "with no other aid than my Dictionary."[96] In the crisis of the

1770s he and his father followed the political principles of Patrick Henry. He entered military service a few months after Lexington and Concord at the age of twenty and served as an officer in the Continental line until 1781, seeing action at Brandywine, Germantown, Monmouth, Valley Forge, and Stony Point. It was an experience that made him a fully committed Continentalist and later a Federalist, as would happen with most others who underwent a similar one. He was thus "confirmed in the habit of considering America as my country, and congress as my government."[97] He prepared himself for the bar, to which he was admitted in 1780, and in 1783 he married Mary Ambler, the daughter of the state treasurer. He opened a practice in Richmond which was very successful, one reason being that the conditions of the time were exactly suited to his type of self-regulated mind. English precedents were out of favor, American ones hardly existed, and Marshall had an unusual capacity in the courtroom for trapping adversaries with arguments constructed out of logic, natural law, and whatever information they themselves might furnish in the course of making theirs. He cited few authorities, making his own as he went along, a practice he would continue many years later on the Supreme Court. He was easy and genial, a natural mixer; he put on no airs, and was rather slovenly in dress. He loved to pitch horseshoes, and in his army days he was nicknamed "Silver Heels" because he could jump higher and run faster than anyone in his regiment. His "lax, lounging manners" for some reason infuriated Thomas Jefferson.[98]

He was elected to the Virginia Assembly in 1782 and quickly came to prominence there, serving several terms. He despised what he saw as the parochial irresponsibility of many state legislatures, including his own, during the Confederation period. He was a strong advocate of the Federal Constitution at the Virginia ratifying convention. In the 1790s he supported the Washington administration by, among other things, a vigorous defense of the Jay Treaty, and became, as Edward Corwin put it, "the recognized leader of the Federalist interest in Virginia."[99] Washington twice tried without success to appoint him to office. Rufus King, who was present when Marshall argued the case of *Ware* v. *Hylton* in 1796, said that "his head is one of the best organized of any one that I have known."[100] Marshall did, of course, accept Adams's appointment as a member of the mission to France. "Balance," for Adams, by then no longer meant a balance of parties but rather one of geography. Massachusetts, then, would be balanced by Virginia.

The third member, Charles Cotesworth Pinckney, was a man who, given a few key facts about his character and position in society, is—unlike Elbridge Gerry—almost a hundred percent predictable. Pinckney was moderate in intelligence, but also moderate in everything else. He was dependable, a man of generosity and good sense, and reasonable. He could probably not have imagined what it was like to be connected with other than the topmost families of South Carolina. He was honor and duty personified, which was not really so odd; it was just that he could not help it. He was naturally responsible, so much so that his mother once marveled, a bit bemusedly, that he had "lived to near twenty-three years of age without once offending me."[101] He was fully orthodox in all he did and thought, which included both the interests of his class and his unquestioning republicanism.

He was born in 1746 of a family whose founder had arrived in the province in 1692 and prospered from the outset. Charles Cotesworth and his brother Thomas were taken to England in 1753 for their education, which included Westminster School, Christ Church, Oxford, and legal training in the Middle Temple. Charles Cotesworth then went to France for a time to study military science, attending the Royal Military Academy at Caen in Normandy. Returning in 1769, he was immediately elected to the South Carolina Assembly, and would be in public life continually for the next thirty-five years. He had received substantial property on his father's death nine years before; in 1773 he married Sally Middleton, whose father owned twenty plantations and eight-hundred slaves. With such assets and a flourishing law practice Charles Cotesworth Pinckney, while still in his twenties, was one of the wealthiest and most influential men in South Carolina.

Pinckney was an ideal example of why it should so often happen that ruling aristocracies in the American colonies became such natural republicans, almost in direct proportion to how solidly entrenched they were, and especially if they had spent time in England. There, they were provincial outsiders, and the more consequential they were at home the more they felt it. But more pertinently, when Parliament started chipping away at their oligarchic prerogatives and privileges, their response was almost instinctive. (Pinckney's father was done out of the chief-justiceship of the province by an English placeman of dubious record and merit; Charles Cotesworth at nineteen commissioned a portrait of himself declaiming against the Stamp Act.) Just about everyone, according to Pinckney's biographer, "was a Whig of one stripe or another," and Pinckney, though temperate in speech, was generally associated with the most advanced of them.[102] He was very active in legislative affairs, rose rapidly, and became chairman of the committee to draft a state constitution in 1776. He entered military service at the beginning of the war, though his deeds were hardly brilliant. He was in no important engagements; a fall from his horse accounted for the only injury he received; and he spent the last two years as a prisoner. But his discipline and devotion to duty impressed his superiors, and he ended the war as a brigadier general.

By the mid-1780s Pinckney thought the welfare of his state required a stronger central government. He was a delegate to the Constitutional Convention, where he said little that was either idiosyncratic or original. He was not sure at first whether the Convention had the authority to do more than revise the Articles of Confederation; he wanted slaves fully counted for apportionment, and he was not satisfied with the clause on slave importation. But when such matters were settled otherwise than he wished, he cheerfully accepted the result and believed the compromises to be on the whole reasonable. When Elbridge Gerry made his dramatic announcement that he could not sign the completed document, Pinckney declared he would not only sign but "support it with all his influence." He did so, and it was ratified in South Carolina with relative ease. The doctrine of state sovereignty, he said, was a kind of heresy "which can never benefit us, but may bring on us the most serious distresses."[103]

Though he supported the Washington administration and was thus nominally a Federalist, he was not an outspoken one and not really a partisan at all. He declined federal office despite several efforts by Washington to appoint him to one. He enthusiastically welcomed the French Revolution, and he wrote in 1793 that he was glad his nephew had "been so long in France, as I trust he shall return a good Republican. . . ."[104] He joined in the welcoming of Genet at Charleston, though later he greatly disapproved Genet's not paying the proper respect to Washington. Nor would he join the outcry against the Jay Treaty in South Carolina, especially with his brother Thomas supporting it. When Washington made a special appeal to his sense of duty in urging him to accept appointment to succeed Monroe as minister to France, he yielded at last.

The disregard of all propriety that met him when he got there was quite beyond his understanding. Then in the fall of 1797, when he went back to France from his temporary exile in Holland with his new colleagues on President Adams's mission, he would be in for fresh perplexities. By then the French had a new Foreign Minister, Talleyrand, a type for whom none of them was quite prepared, least of all Charles Cotesworth Pinckney. Pinckney knew what an aristocrat was, or thought he did; he also believed he knew a republican when he saw one. Talleyrand had pretensions to both. It was hard for Pinckney to see him as either, or indeed as anything more than an adventurer—one who, in South Carolina, could not quite be taken as a gentleman.

Charles-Maurice de Talleyrand-Périgord was in fact descended from one of the oldest noble families of France. (One of his ancestors back in the tenth century had reportedly demanded of Hugh Capet, "Who made you king?") In infancy Charles-Maurice was dropped on the floor by a careless nurse; his foot was deformed and he was lamed for life. Thus incapacitated for a military career, he was forced by his parents, who never wasted much affection on him anyway, to renounce the rights of the eldest son in favor of a younger brother and be trained for the Church. He studied at Saint-Sulpice and took orders, but without in any way renouncing the passion he had acquired for luxury, women, and intrigue. "They forced me to be a priest," he told one of his friends, "and they'll repent it." His pious mother certainly did. Though the King granted his father's deathbed wish that Charles-Maurice be made a bishop, he did so despite his own misgivings and despite the Countess's anguished entreaties to desist. By now she had reason to fear that the higher her son rose, the wider would be the circle of his depravities. He was consecrated, if that is the word, as Bishop of Autun in January 1789.[105]

Talleyrand correctly saw the Revolution as charged with irresistible force, and contrived to be on the right side of it when the Estates-General were called by the King in 1789 to deal with the financial collapse which threatened the royal government. As a privileged deputy of the First Estate he became prominent at once by his willingness to sacrifice the interests of the Church through the nationalization of ecclesiastical property and elimination of other privileges. He took a leading part in this work before washing his hands of the Church and leaving it altogether, amid the curses of most of the nobility and excommunication from Rome. His hopes of going into the royal ministry were frustrated by the National Assembly's decision not to let the King choose his ministers from its membership, and then an alliance with Mirabeau for seizing control of the Assembly was aborted by Mirabeau's death in 1791. He saw by 1792 that it would be unwise, all things considered, to remain in France, and he was absent for four years, two of them in England and two in America. He had gone to England on a somewhat contrived informal diplomatic mission, which ended with his being ordered out under the terms of Pitt's Alien Act. He was offended—he rather liked England and the English—but they seem to have thought it as well to risk no double dealing from an unfrocked bishop in their midst. The Jacobins had meanwhile placed him on the list of proscribed émigrés. He regarded the Americans with some disdain for their uncouth and mercenary ways, though most of his own time in America was occupied with speculation and schemes for making money. He was astonished that a man of such talent as Alexander Hamilton, who otherwise greatly impressed him, should have felt obliged to resign as finance minister merely because the salary was inadequate.[106] With the Thermidorean Reaction his name was stricken from the proscribed list through the influence of his friend Madame de Staël, and he returned to France in July 1796. A year later, largely through the same influence, he became the Directory's Minister of Exterior Relations. He would somehow make himself *disponible* for serving every subsequent French government—Consulate, Empire, Restoration, July Monarchy—whatever upheavals and *coups d'état* might come in between, for more than thirty years in the future.

When after months of intrigue to displace Delacroix and get the Foreign Ministry for himself, the news of his appointment came at last on July 18, 1797, Talleyrand was delirious with joy. "I'll hold the job," he exulted over and over; "I have to make an immense fortune out of it, a really immense fortune."[107]

Theoretically and on paper—judging, that is, from the aggregate of documents prepared by and for both governments in anticipation of the forthcoming negotiations—there was ground for hope that all points at issue would be settled with a minimum of difficulty. On the American side, the instructions given to the commissioners by the Secretary of State represented the utmost in circumspection and moderation. Indeed, in both tone and content they rather resembled those given to Jay in 1794, which has suggested to some that Hamilton may have had a hand in drawing them up.[108] For instance, however intense American grievances might be, "however exceptionable . . . may have been the conduct of France," the envoys should neither allow their own government to be blamed nor insist on imputing any to France, but simply "adopt . . . the principle of the British Treaty; and 'terminate our differences in such manner, as without referring to the merits of our respective complaints and pretensions, may be the best calculated to produce mutual satisfaction and good understanding.'"[109] The commissioners were to make every effort to procure compensation to American citizens for irregular depredations on American commerce and for unpaid claims on contracts for supplies made with agents of the French government. But the commissioners could be very flexible as to terms and conditions of payment. Much would depend on what was "practicable in relation to the French finances" (public securities might be acceptable), all of which could be determined by joint commissions as with the Jay and Pinckney treaties. And however important such reparation might be, "yet it is not to be insisted on as an indispensable condition of the proposed treaty." The American government, in short, rather than allow the negotiations to fail, was prepared in the last resort to forego compensation altogether. John Jay had not been given this kind of leeway.

The "proposed treaty" should be a revision and clarification of those currently existing, since among other reasons these had been subject to so wide a range of "erroneous constructions." The United States was prepared to place France on the same maritime footing as Great Britain, which would mean giving up the "free ships, free goods" principle of the 1778 treaties. The kind of documents prerequisite to a given ship's papers being regarded as above suspicion, and thus the ship's not being subject to confiscation, should be very precisely specified. (This was a reference to the *rôle d'équipage*.) The same precision should be applied to the way in which the naval vessels and prizes of belligerent powers were in the future to be treated in neutral ports. (This had been an incessant subject of dispute since Genet's time.) It was also desirable to terminate the mutual guarantee clause of the 1778 alliance pertaining to a defensive war (America had no further need of a guarantee of her "Liberty, Sovereignty and Independence," whereas guaranteeing France's possessions in the Western Hemisphere could be very dangerous), or at least to restrict it to supplies and money rather than troops.

Finally, there were certain limits imposed on the commissioners. They were to make "no engagement inconsistent with the obligations of any prior treaty" (a reference to the Jay Treaty similar to the instructions Jay was given regarding the French treaty); they should agree to no restrictions on American trade to which that trade was legally entitled under the law of nations (precision again: there should be no more free and easy decrees); and they should agree to no loans to France during the course of the present war.

The Americans' instructions, then, were on the whole straightforward and unprovocative. At the same time there were a number of indications, from advice coming to the Foreign Ministry from various sources as well as from Talleyrand's own views on the question, that France, when all was said and done, really had no wish or intention to bring matters to the point of war, and had in fact reached the conclusion that in principle the time had come to reach a general settlement with the United States.

The first sign came from an opposition spokesman, Claude E. J. P. Pastoret, who made a very strong speech in the Council of Five Hundred in June. Pastoret attacked the Executive Directory for having usurped numerous functions which constitutionally belonged to the legislative body, including that of making war, and the example he used was the Directory's high-handed treatment of the United

States. He held up to scorn the pretexts used—the Jay Treaty, the *rôle d'équipage,* and the appointment of Pinckney, "a firm and decided friend of peace and of France" and "a man whom we can hardly suspect of predilection or favor for Great Britain"—for France's continuing aggressions. The actions of the French commissaries in the West Indies were derided as pure piracy:

> They announce that having no financial resources and knowing the unfriendly dispositions of the Americans, to keep from perishing miserably they have fitted out privateers and that 87 are already at sea, and that for the past three months the administration there has supported itself, and private individuals have enriched themselves, from the proceeds of the prizes. . . .[110]

The case was put more moderately but with equal effect by a long memorandum from Louis-Guillaume Otto at about the same time. Otto, who had served for more than a dozen years with various French missions in America, went over the entire course of relations between the two countries since 1789 analyzing the clumsiness of successive French ministers, which consisted in each case, except that of Ternant, in imagining that the American people could be divided from their government by being induced to take sides with a "French" or "Antifederalist" party. He explained that Americans saw no inconsistency between their own good wishes for the French Republic and "the neutrality they wanted at all costs to maintain." But French agents, he said, had persisted in seeing only two parties in America, a French and an English party, whereas there was a far more numerous "American party, which loves its country above all and for whom prejudices either for France or for England are only accessory and often passing affections." Yet the Americans had given innumerable proofs of their good will: they had kept St. Domingue from starving, succored the French refugees, supplied the French armies, paid the last of the debt which was not scheduled for extinction until 1802, rejoiced in the successes of the Revolution, and been the first to felicitate the National Convention and recognize the French Republic. For this, French agents "for five years heaped insults and contempt upon the First Magistrate of the United States," and were now preying on American commerce in a system of robbery. France, he hoped, would awaken before it was too late to the consequences of pushing Americans into "leaguing themselves with England."[111]

There were also papers from both Joseph Fauchet and Pierre Adet, the two most recent French ministers to the United States. Though Otto had roundly criticized them both, they too believed things had gone too far and that it was time to settle. Fauchet thought that "great as the animosity may be," there was nonetheless "a common interest, which reprobates a rupture." It was true that America's treaty with England was "derogatory to that of 1778" and contained "clauses hostile to us," but the decree of reprisal, that of November 2, 1796, was excessive, becoming "the source of a crowd of vexatory proceedings which are only detrimental to the end, and throw much embarrassment in the negociation which is about being opened." France, he believed, had "a strong interest to pursue a good understanding with America," and whatever might be said of President Adams, "we have every thing to hope from the rectitude of his judgment. . . ."[112] Adet put it more succinctly. "The reception of the comissioners," he wrote, "and a frank negotiation: these I believe are the means of settling differences which it is not in our interest to prolong. I have nothing further to say."[113]

As for Talleyrand himself, there are memoranda, diplomatic dispatches, and other papers of this period from which it may certainly be inferred that he expected not only to receive the American envoys but that a mutually acceptable arrangement with them would be reached. He told the French consul-general at Philadelphia, Joseph Philippe Létombe, that if the commissioners came "with powers permitting them to negotiate on a basis compatible with the dignity of the Republic and her interests, the differences will soon be terminated." He allowed that the rejection of Pinckney and its consequences were "regrettable," that they "involved nothing personal against Mr. Pinckney" and could be "repaired," and that "we shall do everything necessary when the commissioners arrive to exhibit fully our peaceful intentions."[114]

Well before this time, moreover, Talleyrand had indicated privately and not so privately that he could not take the Jay Treaty seriously as a cause of umbrage on France's part, since it was so obviously to America's advantage.[115] He was not even inclined, except for tactical purposes, to claim that it did France any really deep injury, and he certainly did not intend to propose that it be renounced. "In examining that question," he wrote in a memorandum prepared just prior to the Americans' arrival, "one should not lose sight, on the one hand, of the obstacles which so great a sacrifice of national dignity on the part of the American commissioners would encounter, nor, on the other, what interest we might have in demanding it." France, he continued, "never disputed the right of the United States to make even a shameful commercial treaty with Great Britain provided it does not violate their stipulations to us," and he thought that on the whole "we do not have a great interest in literally requiring the breaking of the treaty of London." Any clauses in it injurious to France could simply be matched by stipulations in the new treaty which would have the effect of canceling them.[116] In this and in another memorandum of the same period, Talleyrand outlined the background of the current differences, and established the principle "that we have major reasons favoring a reconciliation" (the harm that might be done to French and Spanish possessions should the Americans be "in league with England") and that the "time has come to remove the despotic actions and violence which are carried out against the Americans in our Antilles." He also sketched out tactics for dealing with American claims for damage, which were bound to be considerable.[117]

But in fact these negotiations never took place, and the Americans were not even received. Why?

It was true that most of those who gave any attention to the case seem to have understood that it was desirable in principle to settle with the Americans, and that sooner or later this would have to be done. But "in principle" was one thing; any particular urgency about doing it now, in an orderly and businesslike way, was quite another. Except for Otto and Pastoret (whose opinions, for political reasons, did not then count for much), no voice Talleyrand listened to, including his own, really advocated such a course without qualification; all their views were far too clogged with counter-purposes for that. The letters of Fauchet and Adet were not so much dossiers for the guidance of the Foreign Minister on his future policy toward the United States—that aspect constituted no more than a fraction of either paper—as rambling and rather plaintive justifications of their own past conduct in America. Adet in particular went on at great length about his Louisiana schemes and dealings with General Collot, and how he might have got more Republican congressmen to support France's interests if he had had more money with which to influence them. The former French consul at New York, Alexandre Hauterive, favored Adet and then Talleyrand with letters containing innumerable theories and prophecies about the Americans' character and future development, few of which could have been very useful for purposes at hand. But on the specific question of negotiations with the United States, Hauterive saw no danger in delaying them indefinitely. America was a "far from warlike country." The French government need not be hurried by "arrogant pretensions" or by the "impatience" of the American envoys, "for, in truth, I see nothing pressing to be concluded." Let them fret: "I am sure that nothing will disconcert or try them more than a cold and polite reception, rare, vague, and private discussions, and a far-distant prospect of results."[118]

It appeared, moreover, that the Republicans in America, "the friends of France and of liberty," were actually encouraging the same policy. Hauterive and Consul-General Létombe made a repeated point of this in their reports, Létombe on the basis of long talks with Jefferson himself. By May 1797 Jefferson had begun giving the Consul-General much advice on how France should deal with the designs of President Adams. "Mr. Adams," he confided, "is vain, suspicious, and stubborn, of an excessive self-regard, taking counsel with nobody. . . . But his presidency will only last five years [sic]; he is only President by three votes, and the system of the United States will change with him." Jefferson believed that the agitation over injuries done to American navigation by French privateers "will be of short duration. It is for France, great, generous, at the summit of her glory, to pretend to take no notice, to be patient, to precipitate nothing, and all will return to order." As for the American commissioners about to depart, the Directory "should receive them and hear them, drag out the negotiations at length, and mollify them by the urbanity of the proceedings."[119]

Jefferson, as we have seen, had persuaded himself that the course Adams was pursuing, even with the new mission to France, would lead to war. But equally to be dreaded, if not more, was a rapprochement with Great Britain, and the best way to prevent both was delay. His grand solution, meanwhile was a French invasion of England ("Jefferson never ceases to repeat that the thing is practicable"), so that the Directory might then "dictate in London the conditions of a peace which in assuring the repose and happiness of the world, shall be based on the freedom of the seas, the reciprocity of commerce, and the liberation of all colonies under the guarantee of their metropoles." Létombe had his own solution, which resembled Jefferson's but was hardly the same, and it may be doubted whether he confided it all to Jefferson. One side of it, to be sure, was a descent upon England (which the French were in fact already planning), but the other was for France to "possess herself of the Floridas, Louisiana, and Canada," and thus to contain not only the English but the Americans as well. The Americans were best kept at arm's length. "May the French, then," Létombe wrote home to Paris, "know how to temporize; it is up to the Directory, Citizen Minister, whether it is suitable to imitate the wisdom of Fabius. . . ." In this he and Jefferson were at one. "The Vice-President still argues," he wrote Talleyrand a number of months later, "that the Directory has everything to gain here by temporizing, and he repeats to me incessantly that Machiavelli's maxim 'Nil repentè' is the soul of great affairs."[120]

Talleyrand needed little instruction in ways of temporizing, especially since almost nobody concerned saw any need of doing otherwise. In his own papers on the subject Talleyrand struck a nice balance between the picture, on the one hand, of France as the injured party at every turn in the two countries' relations since 1793, and, on the other, of a France both magnanimous and reasonable, prepared to terminate differences which it was not in either country's interest to prolong—but not too hastily. For one thing, the American commissioners should be made to tender an official apology for the passages in President Adams's speech of May 16 to the special session of Congress which imputed to France the design of dividing the American people from their government, and this should take place before negotiations even began.[121] Then with regard to American claims for damages to their trade and shipping, Talleyrand outlined a whole series of contingencies under which France was dispensed from any obligations, and whereby even those claims admitted as legitimate could still be conceded "without untying any purse-strings" until the distant future, if then, and probably not at all.[122] And in any case, no matter how rationally Talleyrand may have been inclined to regard American affairs, no matter how disposed he was "in principle" to settle them, the Directory cared little about his views anyway, on this or on anything else. His own position in the French government was in fact precarious beyond measure, and he had no intention of risking it further on a matter of principle, having seldom done anything on principle in his life.

The logic of Talleyrand's appointment as Foreign Minister, in which there was a certain element of accident, has never been more than approximately explained. Only three of the five Directors voted for it, and even Talleyrand's sponsor, Paul Barras, had only been brought over after merciless pressure from Germaine de Staël, one of Talleyrand's former mistresses, who persuaded him that in Talleyrand he would have an ideal retainer. Even so, Barras never much trusted Talleyrand, and for good reason. The others, even the two who for the sake of Barras's support in other matters had supported him in this, despised him.[123] "To enter a government in which nobody wants you," commented Hippolyte Carnot, "is no mean trick." Talleyrand was actually Foreign Minister in name only, as he himself admitted, his duties being confined "to signing passports and other administrative documents, and to forwarding to the proper authorities the despatches or communications already drafted by the executive. . . ." The Prussian minister Sandoz-Rollin, writing home to Berlin in the fall of 1797, declared that it would be "a phenomenon of wit and management" if Talleyrand succeeded in hanging on at all. Except for Barras, "the other Directors, I am told, scarcely speak to him."[124] That was not exactly true in the case of Jean-François Reubell, the Director in whose hands rested all the important decisions in foreign affairs, whose abusive contempt for Talleyrand knew no bounds, and who cuffed him about like a lackey. Reubell's manners were oafish, and he and the other Directors had little use for the formulas and ceremonies of traditional European diplomacy. Under the Directory France's dealings with other European governments, frequently carried on by appointees of no professional experience, had generally become those of an international bully, not to say brigand. That which the Directory most lacked, and which was thus the keynote of all its treaties and other transactions, was money.[125]

To all of this Talleyrand adjusted with great suppleness, as well he might, being determined above all to keep his place. His primary passion was to enrich himself, and he made no secret of it; his other object was a world in which the realm of his own power, influence, and pleasures might be consolidated and stabilized. That realm was no less than France herself; France too must be stabilized, and one day brought back peaceably to rejoin the society of European nations. It was no small stage that Talleyrand envisioned for his movements, and he could accordingly postulate a "foreign policy" for himself before he was permitted to have one. It certainly had its logic; it was even to have, from time to time, some positive consequences. But not yet. For now he must lie in wait, endure the abuse of such brutes as Reubell and Merlin de Douai, conceal his hatred for his masters, change his mind when they ordered him to, praise their "courage" and "the breadth of their vision,"[126] swear eternal devotion to Barras, enter into covert relations with the rising Bonaparte, and await the day when he might betray them all, as eventually he would.

But the interim was amply endurable, for by the nature of the case the Ministry of Exterior Relations, if it had few other powers, had been placed by circumstances at the focal point of a vast network of international plunder, imposed by the Directory and upon which the Directory subsisted. It was "a system of contributions of war, of subsidies and pillage, everywhere applied to friendly, neutral, and enemy Powers, and of which the minister of external relations was the hand most active."[127] It was widely understood that anything of value had to be bought, and in this respect, according to Sandoz-Rollin, the Directors had their business done for them by "the ministers who are their subordinates." It had "become the custom under the Directory that every large transaction should be preceded by a *douceur.*"[128] Talleyrand's own profits from the system were stupendous. His personal receipts during the first two years or so of his ministry—in payment for such diverse items as the expediting of secret treaties, guarantees of immunity for neutral territory, and shares from the spoliations upon neutral shipping—has been estimated at between thirteen and fourteen million francs.[129]

The Executive Directory itself represented the Revolution come to its sorriest pass, its vices heaped up and multiplied, its virtues all but vanished, and bankrupt in nearly every sense. It was a government divided within itself, detested by its own legislative adjunct, the Councils of the Five Hundred and of the Ancients, and held in contempt by the people. The elections of the Year V in March 1797, in which one-third of the Councils were to be replaced, brought a large influx of deputies disposed to some form of royalist restoration, which greatly strengthened a determination in the Councils to recapture legislative functions usurped by the Executive Directory, to restore peace in Europe, and to deprive the executive of the power of the purse. The Directory's response was the *coup d'état* of 18 Fructidor (September 4, 1797), carried out with the assistance of troops under Pierre Augereau, one of Bonaparte's generals from the army of Italy. The elections were nullified; 177 deputies were eliminated and 65 persons sentenced to transportation to Guiana; and the Directory's two dissident members, Lazare Carnot and François Barthélemy, were purged. The Directory thus gave itself a reprieve, but its fortunes were now more than ever tied to the army and its territorial conquests. The survivors of the purge, the original triumvirate of Barras, Reubell, and Larevellière-Lépeaux, together with the new members Merlin de Douai and François de Neufchâteau — no two of whom trusted each other — were united only in adversity, and were scarcely an attractive lot. Their leading spirit, Barras, was as debauched a type in both his public and private morals as any the Revolution produced, and the portraits he has left of the others in his memoirs are hardly less fly-blown than the one we have of him.[130] For Talleyrand, the only room for maneuver in such a setting had to be made by obeying their whims, fawning on them, and sharing out the booty.

The Americans by this time were on their way to Paris. Under the circumstances their chances of obtaining any kind of straightforward settlement in that catacomb of traffickers, warlords, and bravoes — even had there been an incorruptible Talleyrand waiting to accommodate them — were fairly close to zero. Talleyrand could imagine only one way to get the question so much as opened, and kept open even provisionally, which was to impose a welter of prior conditions. The honor of his patron Barras should be sedulously vindicated. It was Barras's sneering speech at the farewell audience of Monroe that President Adams had so much objected to in his message of May 16, so the Americans must be required in some way to eat Adams's words, which was sure to take a good bit of doing. In addition the Americans should be made to pay, and pay well. Every other petitioner did; why not they? There should first be a "gratification," followed by a subsidy of some sort for the government, in this case — as in a number of other such cases — disguised as a loan. The very least consequence would be delay, and against such an outcome there were no counter-sanctions whatever, even in the view of France's friends in America, who for their own reasons were hoping for the same result. So again, why not? Talleyrand seems to have understood, moreover, that otherwise the Directory would allow him to take no steps at all.

Still, it should probably be added that the underlying reason why things were all but certain to take this sort of course for the Americans, for all the special circumstances, was really the same one it had been all along: the perfectly bound-less insignificance of the United States. The *coup d'état* of Fructidor had set off a widening circle of tremors with which America, as usual, had little or nothing to do. The Directory was thus committed by yet another step to the vast ambitions, military and ultimately political, of Bonaparte, who was already making his own foreign policy. It was Bonaparte and not his government that made the Treaty of Campo Formio with Austria in October 1797 — a callous bartering of territory that created consternation everywhere in Europe and in France itself. It brought Europe both a momentary peace and greater instability than ever. France was meanwhile preparing to deal with, and hoping to destroy, her ancient enemy England. This would require a major heave to shore up French finances, which could only be done by extracting huge sums from France's client states and "sister republics." Meanwhile the Directors, if and when they thought of America at all—with a hundred more important things on their minds—did so, taking their cue from Reubell and Barras, with impatience and contempt. The proceedings of the Directory, which sat every day, contain only three references to the United States for the first three months the Americans were there.[131] Talleyrand himself was known to have remarked that America was "not of greater consequence . . . nor ought to be treated with greater respect, than Geneva or Genoa."[132] One might almost suspect, therefore, that the only way the Americans could conceiv-ably effect any change in such a ranking would be by somehow managing, inten-tionally or otherwise, to create a colossal scandal, the uproar of which would echo across two continents. Short of this, it is hard to imagine them receiving much notice at all, either at the time or in the subsequent annals of French history.

Such at any rate was the setting in which the American envoys arrived the first week in October 1797 to do business with the French government. And yet despite the confusion everywhere, and the obstacles and discouragements that were thrown in their way almost at once, it is at this point that one discerns an astonishingly steady hand, guided by a brutally strong intelligence, beginning in an unmistakable way to lay hold of events. John Marshall, being the junior member of the commission, seems to have appointed himself as the recorder of its pro-ceedings, and he subsequently assumed the duty of composing its dispatches. Whether he did this simply as a gesture of deference to the others or for more complicated reasons, the result was that since Marshall's words are the only ver-sion we have of the whole episode, Marshall could impose *his* definition of what each succeeding phase of the commission's dealings meant, and in effect decide just how each turn was to be described to the world at large. But in addition to the power this role gave him, the authority of Marshall's own personality more often than not defined the occasion for the others as soon as it arose, and before it was put down on paper. This was the more remarkable in that Gerry made obstructions all along, and Talleyrand did all he could to demoralize the com-mission through threats and intrigue, as had been successfully practiced upon every country in Europe. The Americans might thus have been tossed like chips on an angry ocean throughout the six months—longer in Gerry's case—in which they were there, but this most certainly did not happen. It took a special balance of judgment and will on Marshall's part to maintain his conviction throughout that however stubbornly the Americans might dig in, and whatever the French might say or do, France did not intend to make war on the United States. Thus in a peculiar way he trusted the French more than Gerry did, and it is significant that when he got home to an America by then ringing with patriotic bellicosity, he himself refrained from making any warlike utterances.[133]

The envoys had a fifteen-minute audience with Talleyrand on October 8, presented their credentials, and were told that the Directory had asked for a report on relations with the United States which he expected to have finished in two or three days, "after which its further intentions with respect to us would be known." Cards of hospitality were delivered to them the following day. On the 14th an intermediary (Talleyrand's secretary) told them he had heard that the Directory were much incensed by certain passages in Adams's speech of May 16 and would not receive them until they gave a satisfactory explanation of it. But nothing official was communicated to them, and they decided—cued by Marshall—to make no response. Four days later they received a visit from a Jean Conrad Hottinguer (later referred to as "X" in the dispatches published in America), who said he had Talleyrand's confidence and who proceeded to outline the conditions he believed would have to be met before the Directory would permit any negotiations to begin, or would even consider it. The President's speech must in effect be "disavowed." ("It is feared that in not satisfying certain individuals in this respect they may give way to all their resentment.") All unpaid debts contracted by France with American suppliers should be assumed by the United States government. Indemnities for spoliations committed on American commerce which any future claims commission might find France liable for should also be paid by the American government. The United States must make a "considerable loan" to France, and finally, there must be "something for the pocket": a large sum of money for the "private use" of the Directory and Foreign Minister "under the form of satisfying claims which did not in fact exist"; that is, a substantial bribe.[134]

Marshall was "decidedly of opinion" that such propositions could not be considered as a basis for negotiation, and Pinckney (though "without expressing himself so fully") agreed with him. But Gerry protested that everything would be broken off if they gave such an answer, and then there would be war. They agreed to try to obtain fuller details. Hottinguer put them in writing on the 19th, and on the 20th Pierre Bellamy, represented as "the confidential friend" of Talleyrand and later designated as "Y," called to amplify these propositions. The disavowal had to be formal and in writing; they must say "that the speech of the citizen President Barras did not contain any thing offensive to the government of the United States, nor any thing which deserved the epithets contained in the whole paragraph." They would also have to take back Adams's complaint of the Directory's decree of March 2, 1797, saying that there was nothing in it "contrary to the treaty of 1778," and that it "had none of those fatal consequences that the paragraph reproaches to it." With regard to the President's remark about efforts to create "a division between the government and people of the United States," there must be a declaration that it was "not the government of France, nor its agents that this paragraph meant to designate."[135]

But this was only a preliminary to the really essential thing. "You must pay money—you must pay a great deal of money." The loan would be to the amount of 32 million Dutch florins, and the bribe, 50,000 pounds sterling. Then if the Directory were satisfied, a letter would be sent to the American commissioners to ascertain whether their powers extended to making a treaty which would put France on an equal footing with Great Britain, and if the answer were satisfactory, then the Minister would use his influence with the Directors to persuade them to receive the commissioners. But there could be no guarantee, because "M. Talleyrand himself was not authorized to speak to us of the will of the Directory," and in any case the Directory were not inclined to relinquish the principle of the *rôle d'équipage,* because Merlin de Douai, while Minister of Justice, had "written a treatise" on that subject.[136]

Marshall thought all such conditions preposterous, and again Pinckney agreed with him. But even if they *had* thought them admissible, he argued, what means did they have of saying so, and to whom? They themselves were unreceived and unacknowledged, and these agents had no official capacity either. Marshall did not see how he and his colleagues could allow themselves, consistent with the interests of their government, "to carry on this clandestine negotiation" with persons who had no authority to speak for the Directory, or even for the Foreign Minister. The longer it continued the more they bound themselves, while nobody on the French side was committed to anything. Yet Gerry wanted more delay. He wanted to tell the agents that the commissioners "would take their propositions into consideration." Marshall thought the ground had been gone over enough already, but after much discussion among themselves, Marshall in an effort to preserve unanimity offered to return at once to the United States for fresh instructions provided the French would agree to suspend immediately their depredations on American shipping, a proposal to which Gerry consented.[137]

So when Bellamy and Hottinguer called on October 21, the Americans gave them their answer. They declared that their powers were ample to make a treaty which should comport with the interests of both parties and "place France on an equal ground with England, in any respects in which an inequality might be supposed to exist at present, to the disadvantage of France." They said that the proposal of a loan in any form was beyond their instructions, but that one of the American ministers would depart forthwith to consult his government, provided the Directory would "suspend all further captures on American vessels, and will suspend proceedings on those already captured. . . ." As for any apology or disavowal of the President's speech, they explained that

> the constitution of the United States authorised and required our President to communicate his ideas on the affairs of the nation; that in obedience to the constitution he had done so; that we had not power to confirm or invalidate any part

of the President's speech; that such an attempt could produce no other effect than to make us ridiculous to the government and to the citizens at large of the United States; and to produce, on the part of the President, an immediate disavowal and recall of us as his agents; that independent of this, all America was acquainted with the facts stated by the President; and our disavowing them would not change the public sentiment concerning them.[138]

Bellamy, in rising frustration at seeing the only item in the picture that had the least interest for him — money — slipping out of reach, declared that he "could not take charge of such propositions," and that in view of "the resentment of France" and "the respect which the Directory required," the Americans were in no position to make them. The next day Marshall prepared the first of the two lengthy dispatches, to which all three of the envoys put their signatures, constituting the information to which the American government and public would respond the following spring.[139]

But the agents would give the Americans no rest. Now joined by Lucien Hauteval ("Z"), a former planter who had fled from St. Domingue during the disturbances of 1793, they seized upon the news of Campo Formio to begin threatening the envoys more or less openly. The Directory, they said, was now taking a higher tone than ever toward neutrals; now *all* nations must aid France or be treated as enemies. As Pinckney and Gerry were trying to explain that if there should be war it would not be America's doing, Hottinguer said, "Gentlemen, you do not speak to the point. It is money — it is expected that you will offer money." Pinckney replied that they had already "spoken to that point very explicitly." "No," said Hottinguer, "you have not, what is your answer?" Then came Pinckney's famous explosion: "No! No! Not a sixpence!" But did the American government not know, the agent persisted, "that nothing was to be obtained here without money?" Why no, said the virtuous Pinckney, our government "had not even suspected" such a thing; the letters of our previous minister (Monroe) had given us a very different picture of the French government. He had "represented it as acting entirely upon principle & as feeling a very pure and disinterested affection for America." The agent, Marshall ingenuously noted, "looked somewhat surprised."[140]

On October 28, Gerry and Hauteval paid a private call on Talleyrand, who informed them that a loan "was an absolute sine qua non." When Gerry told him their powers precluded a loan, but that if they could begin the negotiations one of them "would return to the United States to obtain instructions on that subject," Talleyrand said the Directory could not wait. If their powers did not extend to a loan, they could assume such powers. Again the answer was no, whereupon Hottinguer turned up next day with a new proposition. If the Americans were to pay the bribe, one of them might then be allowed to go home for new instructions. They pressed him as to exactly what this meant. Would the Directory then receive them? No, but they would be allowed in the meantime to remain in Paris; otherwise they would be ordered to leave. Would the Directory order the restoration of American property not yet awarded to captors? No. Would it suspend further depredations? No, but with winter coming on, there should not be so many of them. They thereupon gave Hottinguer to understand that if they could perceive in France "a temper sincerely disposed to do us justice," then they "might not so much regard a little money" of this sort, but that they saw no evidence of it. All that such a payment could gain them was "the benefit of seeing the plays & operas of Paris for the winter that we might have time to ask from our country to exhaust her resources for France whose depredations on us would be continued."[141]

On October 30 the invariable Bellamy reappeared, maddened by the receding mirage of money, and abandoned the last pretense of circumspection. The fate of Venice, delivered over in captivity to Austria by the Treaty of Campo Formio, might well befall the United States. And if America had any thought of calling on England for assistance it was a vain hope, because an army of 150,000 men under Bonaparte was preparing to descend upon England and overturn her government. Bellamy brought in another twist; France *might* suspend hostilities against the United States for a six-month period while one of the envoys went home for instructions (this was his own idea, he said, not authorized by the Foreign Minister), *if* in addition to a loan (and of course the bribe) the Americans should make an "advance" to the French government to the amount of the sums owed by it to American citizens, together with what might be adjudged due for vessels improperly seized. "Perhaps," he hastened to add, "you believe that in returning & exposing to your country men the unreasonableness of the demands of this government you will unite them in their resistance to those demands. You are mistaken. You ought to know that the diplomatic skill of France & the means she possesses in your country are sufficient to enable her with the French party in America to throw the blame which will attend the rupture of the negotiations on the federalists as you term yourselves & on the British Party as France terms you: And you may assure yourselves this will be done."[142]

The Americans proceeded to spell out why all these demands were out of the question. They said that "America was the only nation upon earth which felt & had exhibited a real friendship for France," and that if America had given "just cause for umbrage" they wished it pointed out to them. As for France's "conduct & language," she takes our property from us, "determines to treat us as enemies," "abuses & insults our government," "recalls her own minister, refuses to receive ours[;] & when extraordinary means [the present commission] are taken to . . . do away misunderstandings," the envoys are not received but are instead haughtily told "that unless they will pay a sum to which their resources scarcely extend they may expect the vengeance of France & like Venice be erazed from the list of nations." "What impression must this make on the mind of America? If with out provocation, France was determined to make war on us unless we purchased peace[,] we could not easily believe that even our money would save us."[143]

Bellamy, hopping with impatient rage, interrupted them to say that "this eloquent dissertation might be true," but that he had "not come to listen to those complaints." Actually they had been trying to tell him all along, as tactfully as they could, that he need not have come at all, and the next day they did. When he still wanted to come again, they sent word that they would "at any time be glad to see him as a private gentleman," but that if he only wanted to "repeat his propositions for money" he might as well save himself the trouble.[144] This did not prevent further visits, but the exchange concluded what would prove to be the critical phase of the commission's dealings with Talleyrand's agents. The second of the two dispatches was prepared under the date of November 8, again by Marshall and again signed by all. It was the material in these two dispatches— this and the previous letter of October 22—that would be made public in the spring of 1798, first in America and later in France. The resolution of the affair, if not exactly in sight, was at least in the making.

Matters now entered a stage whose key feature was the growing apprehension of Gerry, with his dread of war, as to how seriously French threats ought to be taken, and Gerry's increasing disposition to make delays both large and small in the way of discharging the commission's business. Despite great efforts on Pinckney's and Marshall's part to preserve unanimity in the commission, and frequent yieldings of view on matters of procedure in order to accommodate Gerry, there arose tensions and at length a state of personal relations in which Gerry had used up the patience of both his younger colleagues. It was a situation which Talleyrand did all he could to exploit. On November 11 the envoys wrote a very respectful letter to Talleyrand soliciting the Minister's attention to their presence, first made known to him five weeks before, and hoping that their negotiations for a reconciliation might soon begin. The letter was never answered. On December 18 they agreed to prepare an extended memorandum to the Minister, "stating the objects of our mission and discussing the subjects of difference between the two nations in like manner as if we had been actually received and to close the letter with requesting the Government to open the negotiation with us or to grant us our passports." Gerry found so many reasons for procrastination that the letter was not completed and sent until January 31.[145]

On February 4, Gerry came home from another private visit with Talleyrand, and told Marshall that the Minister had made some propositions to him different from the previous ones, propositions Gerry said "he was not at liberty to impart to Genl. Pinckney or myself." This, Marshall noted in his journal, "necessarily gives birth to some very serious reflections." Actually Marshall guessed at once what it was Talleyrand was up to, and it was on this basis that he and Pinckney shaped their movements from here on. Talleyrand had been trying from the first to play upon the Americans' fears, especially Gerry's, and to divide the commission by threats of their being ordered out of France. But the threat had not been carried out, and Marshall did not believe that it would be. Talleyrand, he thought, would not want to send all three away while the outcome of the war with England remained in suspense, because for one thing it would antagonize the "French" party in America (Marshall knew that dispatches from Létombe had just arrived in Paris), and for another, it stood to reason that Talleyrand would see no point in forcing America to make common cause with England. But if he could get Marshall and Pinckney to ask for their passports and keep Gerry there and deal with him alone, the blame could be cast on them if negotiations were broken off, and the credit withheld from them if they were not. Talleyrand would be "well pleased," Marshall thought, "to retain only one Minister and to chuse that one."[146]

Subsequent events, together with the evidence of Talleyrand's own papers,[147] show Marshall's guesses to have been correct in every essential. Marshall also knew that the magnificent crassness of French behavior, judiciously exhibited, would simply speak for itself. But then there was something more which was to carry them all through, something they may never have thought much about but upon which none of them really needed any prompting. They were all republicans, and they all acted the role, each in his own special way but each quite unaffectedly, of New World provincials confronted by the corruptions of wicked old Europe. Their incredulity, and scarcely disguised contempt, at the idea that representatives of one sovereign nation could actually be badgering those of another for money, like footmen and barbers, gave them a peculiar kind of immunity that neither Talleyrand nor his stipendiaries could ever quite penetrate—and baffled old Europe would eventually throw up her hands.

Gerry did subsequently have several private talks with Talleyrand, and he finally admitted, upon direct challenge from Pinckney, that Talleyrand wanted to send Marshall and Pinckney away and keep him there. In the course of the talks, moreover, a new proposition emerged, and it proved to be the precipitant for the manner in which the mission was to wind up its business in Paris. This was the idea of a loan payable not at present but at the end of the war. Both Pinckney and Marshall promptly declared that this was in fact no different from the previous proposal, because there would be nothing to prevent the French from using the stipulation in hand and raising money on it immediately. Gerry, however, was strongly in favor of it. He did not think their instructions forbade an arrangement of this sort, and he insisted that it was the only formula left whereby a war between France and the United States might be prevented.[148] Marshall thereupon went over all the previous ground with Gerry, and added one or two finishing touches. Since it was not to either the interest or inclination of the United States to make a loan to either belligerent (it would be furnishing aid to the other, and thus taking part in the war, the only part America had the capacity to take), if, consequently, America did make a loan to France, it would be made under threat. Henceforth "we no longer acted for ourselves according to our own will but according to the will of France." Nor would the French, if they had not intended to use this loan for war, threaten us with war if we refused to make it. And being forbidden by instructions it was sure to be repudiated at home, which would irritate the French more than refusing it now. Marshall did not believe the proposal was designed as a basis for reconciliation, but neither did he believe peace or war depended on it. The French had threatened "that in case of refusal we should be ordered out of France"; the threat "had been repeated three times but had never been executed." They were reluctant "to part with us during the uncertain state of the war with England," and were only "amusing us" in the meantime. And in any case, he insisted, if any thing could preserve us from that calamity [war] it was a firm and moderate conduct on our part. That if we should leave France because we could not effect the object of our mission and because we would not lend her money, and a failure of the expedition against England or any future state of war should render her desirous of accommodating with the United States we should have the advantage of having impressed her with the conviction that the accommodation could only be made on terms compatible with the liberty of our Country.[149]

They debated all this back and forth for about a week. They finally agreed, again for the sake of unanimity, to seek an informal interview with Talleyrand. If the Minister should repeat the proposal of a loan payable after the war, then Marshall and Gerry would return to the United States for new instructions while Pinckney remained behind. To this idea, broached during the subsequent visit, Talleyrand avoided any comment.[150] But by the end of the third week in March his own purposes had revealed themselves. If anyone was to go or stay, the question of who it should be would be decided not by them but by him. Thus began the final contest of nerves in which Marshall, by now the mission's leader in fact if not in name, would see to it that the going and the staying should occur not on Talleyrand's terms but on his and Pinckney's.

Talleyrand at last came out in the open with his intentions and those of the Directory in a lengthy reply, dated March 18 and received the next day, to the envoys' memorial of January 17. Talleyrand's paper consisted of a recital of all France's grievances against the United States, most prominent of which were the Jay Treaty, the President's speech of May 16, and the disinclination of the commission itself to be "sincerely conciliatory," but culminating with the announcement that

notwithstanding the kind of prejudice which has been entertained with respect to them, the Executive Directory is disposed to treat with that one of the three, whose opinions, presumed to be more impartial, promise, in the course of the explanations, more of that reciprocal confidence which is indispensable.[151]

His intention was, though without having to name names, to make it plain that he would henceforth deal with Gerry but not with the other two. He was counting on the idea that Marshall and Pinckney were determined to leave anyway,[152] and that this would offer them a way of doing it without his having to order them out. By maneuvering them into asking for their passports he could make them acquiesce in their own division, and thus accept both France's definition of where things stood as well as France's decision on which of the three should withdraw and which remain. It was a neat tactic, but it did not work, at least not the way he intended. The reaction of Marshall and Pinckney, and initially of Gerry as well, was that the commission would not allow itself to be thus divided. Gerry had been saying all along that he would not remain alone, that "he would sooner be thrown into the Seine than consent to stay under the actual circumstances," and Pinckney had been rather grimly assuring him that he had better not. They agreed to prepare a reply to the effect that "no one of the Ministers could consent to remain on a business committed to all three, and that none of us felt ourselves at liberty to withdraw, but by the direction of our own government, from a service which had been entrusted to us, and that at a time when there existed a prospect of performing it."[153] In other words they still very much wanted to negotiate, but they would do it together or not at all.

But then the crack appeared. Talleyrand's secretary called to give the screw another turn, intimating that the Directors were now exceedingly angry with them but that their wrath might be softened if Marshall should agree "to an application to the French government to permit Genl. Pinckney and myself to return to enlighten the minds of our government and fellow citizens on the politics of Europe, while Mr. Gerry should remain until such powers should be received, as would enable him to take those measures, which would preserve peace with France." Moreover, if they did not do it within three days, "we should be all three ordered off." This was too much for Gerry, who now reversed himself and urged that such a letter be sent at once. Marshall flatly refused. Gerry "then said that to prevent a war he would stay."[154]

Marshall had stood his ground because he was certain this latest threat was a bluff like all the others. Talleyrand was not willing to risk ordering away all three, or even the two of them if he could avoid doing it explicitly, though he very much wanted to be rid of Marshall and Pinckney if he could get them to take the initiative. Marshall also knew, and made sure Talleyrand knew it too, that there were ships at Bordeaux and Nantes about to sail for the United States, no others being expected for the time being, and that if Talleyrand wanted him and Pinckney gone despite their professed desire to remain and negotiate, he would have to say so, and soon. Talleyrand was furious. He knew this would transfer the blame to France, but he realized, with the approach of sailing time, that he had been outmaneuvered and had no choice. Since he now knew that Gerry had capitulated and was ready to stay, he would have to take the initiative himself, issue passports and safe-conducts to the others, and bid them good riddance. Marshall sailed from Bordeaux on April 23, 1798, while Pinckney and his family remained for a sojourn of several weeks in the south of France.[155]

There had been a bitter final scene with Gerry, with Pinckney doing most of the talking, which left Gerry much shaken. For having broken ranks, Gerry would come in for a good deal more abuse before the affair was over, traces of which have remained in historians' writings to the present day. But much of this may be seen in the long view as rather unjust, for all the ambiguity of Gerry's own grasp of the case, and one should probably agree with Gerry's biographer that he did the right thing for the wrong reasons.[156] The fact was, Marshall had gained his point already. He had not only put the responsibility on France for the failure of the mission, but in addition he and Pinckney had so thoroughly impressed Gerry with the difficulty of his position that the one thing Gerry would not do—for all his fears of war, and mercilessly as Talleyrand would press him after the others had left—was to assume negotiating powers for his government.[157]

So in the end it was as well that Gerry did stay, for while remaining on hand to keep an eye on things he could, at the same time, be as much of a hair-splitter with Talleyrand as he had been with Pinckney and Marshall. He would drive the Minister to distraction, and eventually wear him down, by not budging an inch. And what he *was* able to do, when he himself finally arrived home five months later, was to bring President Adams some gratifying news. For one thing the XYZ story, having drifted back to France from America, had made quite a sensation in the Paris newspapers. The Foreign Minister was being put to some trouble explaining his way out of it. And for another, Talleyrand was by then ready to negotiate a settlement without any further demands for bribes, loans, or even apologies.

What the Directory itself was ready to do, then or later, would remain inscrutable, and still does.

CHAPTER XIII

Adams and Hamilton

The year 1798 was for John Adams both the highest and lowest, the best and the worst, of his entire presidency. That year encompassed a cycle which took Adams from the depths of discouragement in the opening months to heights of exaltation and mastery by summer, then with the approach of winter pulled him down once again to abysses of gloom and humiliation. This paralleled very closely the course of sentiment in the country at large with regard to relations with the French Republic. It began in a state of partisan malaise and division of purpose, followed by a tremendous soaring of patriotic unity, in turn undermined by a steady intrusion of new discontents and an ebbing away once more of national feeling. This same period would see the return to public life of Alexander Hamilton, with consequences profoundly significant for the fortunes of Federalism.

I

Second Phase: The Fever of 1798

Whatever the degree of attention the French may have been paying to signals coming from America between the summer of 1797 and the beginning of March 1798, those signals could spell but a single message: disunity. Republican leaders from Jefferson on down had never had any sympathy with the President's policy, had steadily refused to accept his definition of the problem of France, and had done everything they could to frustrate his program. Even Adams's own cabinet had given him no end of trouble over the appointment of a commission to negotiate with the French. The special session of Congress he had called in May 1797 had given him next to no support. The regular session which met in November, and to which he repeated his appeal for measures of defense, gave him even less. His call for a naval force capable of protecting American commerce was rejected by the Republican majority in the House, and he himself was charged with deliberately stirring up a warlike atmosphere which the circumstances in no way warranted. By the end of the year 1797, Consul Létombe could assure Talleyrand that Republican influence was rising. The Americans, it appeared, were more disunited and more disaffected from their government than ever. All this, of course, would change dramatically a few months later with the receipt and publication of the XYZ dispatches. But nobody, anywhere, could have predicted this before it happened, least of all John Adams.

By February 1798 Adams had about touched the depths. On the 5th, he informed the House and Senate that a British merchant ship had been attacked by a French privateer inside Charleston harbor. Jefferson could see in this nothing but more clumsy warmongering to provoke Congress into action, and in any case Congress paid little attention.[1] Indeed, most of the month was taken up with debating what to do about the Lyon-Griswold scuffle, in which one representative had spat in the face of another, who had then gone after his tormentor and beaten him with a hickory cane.[2] The House also considered the proposal of Representative Nicholas of Virginia to cut back the diplomatic establishment in Europe, and the Republicans even tried to repeal the tax passed in the previous session to provide for completion of the three frigates.[3] The fogs were further thickened by rumors drifting into Philadelphia since mid-January, though as yet without official confirmation, that Adams's commissioners in Paris had not been received. The President, wrote Abigail Adams to her sister, was being worn down "by continual opposition and by constant exertions," and they were both "sick, sick, sick of publicke life."[4]

At last, late in the evening of March 4, 1798, the first of the commissioners' dispatches from Paris arrived in Philadelphia. All but one being in cipher, they would require some days to be decoded. But two things were immediately apparent. The envoys had in fact not been received, which meant that the mission to all intents and purposes was a failure. Then a new decree of the Directory, more sweeping than any so far, had been approved by the French legislative councils to the effect that any neutral vessel carrying anything produced in England or in English possessions was declared good prize, and that French ports should be closed to any neutral ship, no matter what it carried, that had touched at an English port. This meant that virtually any American ship on the high seas—since they all carried something of British manufacture or production—was automatically subject to confiscation. Adams, with a covering message of three sentences, communicated the letter containing these facts to Congress on the following day.[5]

But what was now to be done, and what position should the President take? Adams had already addressed a circular letter to his cabinet six weeks earlier, requesting opinions on steps to be taken in the event of France's refusal to receive the envoys, and he addressed another on March 13, after the dispatches had been deciphered but while their contents were still a secret. How should the full news be communicated to Congress? What measures should he recommend? Should there be an immediate declaration of war? Should a closer connection with England be sought? (He himself evidently did not think so.) Not all of the cabinet replied in writing on either occasion, though there is reliable evidence for the views of each.[6] To complete the spectrum that they formed, we might add the views of Vice-President Jefferson—though of course Jefferson stood outside the executive circle and was not to know the full details of the case until some weeks later.

The most obvious and immediate question was whether the United States ought to go to war with France. Jefferson in his correspondence and conversation had insisted since the beginning of the crisis that war would be the ultimate calamity, to be avoided at almost any cost, and this had been the ground taken all along by the Republican opposition. Neither the earlier rumors nor the first actual news had done anything to alter it.[7] At the opposite end, Timothy Pickering, easily the most extreme member of the cabinet, seems to have wanted not only a declaration of war but as complete an alliance with England as was possible in order to prosecute it to the full.[8] The member ordinarily the most moderate, Attorney-General Charles Lee, also recommended—twice in writing—a formal declaration of war. In between, both Oliver Wolcott and James McHenry (McHenry prompted at every step by Hamilton) advised against such a step. They thought the American position would be more flexible in a state of limited hos-tilities, which appeared inevitable whether desired or not, and thus the way would be better kept open for an eventual negotiated peace. But all except Pickering believed it preferable to steer clear of any formal connection with England.[9] Adams, in his distracted search for balance, experimented with these various positions in fits and starts, in drafts of speeches he never made and warlike messages he would never send, before deciding not to call for war.

Today, the logic upon which war was seen as desirable or not desirable may not be wholly self-evident. Nobody then thought of warfare under anything like the categories that have rightfully come to dominate that idea in modern times: categories of totality, of mass involvement, of wholesale devastation and blood-shed. Those who resisted war in 1798 did not do so on those grounds. Even this late in the eighteenth century one could still think of war as an extension of diplomacy, as a measured response to challenges and dangers (whatever the pru-dence or folly of responding or not responding), as a device for achieving some more or less circumscribed purpose. So although changes in the traditional char-acter of warfare were already emerging with the wars of the French Revolution, and although war was certainly a towering inconvenience, the manner in which William T. Sherman would think of it some seventy years later was still no part of the common mentality. For that matter, *this* war, if it should ever occur, was bound to be even more limited in character than the one then being fought in Europe, because the forces that could be engaged at any given point in America or anywhere else were minimal.[10]

The most intensely held views for and against war with France, those of Pickering and Jefferson respectively, had something significant in common. The considerations animating each of them were wholly those of ideology; each indeed was enveloped in ideological nightmares. Pickering longed to mount a grand crusade against the hideous menace of jacobinism, licence, and disorder, and the logical way to do it was to make common cause with England, the more fully and explicitly the better. Jefferson's nightmare was Pickering's in reverse. For him, to move against France was to conjure up not the horrors of war as such, but the worse ones of driving us into the arms of England and delivering us over to the forces of anti-republicanism and monarchy that lurked, waiting to drop the mask and step forth, in our midst. Whereas staying clear and playing for time would allow the course of events—a general French military triumph in Europe and perhaps the collapse of England—to plant republicanism everywhere and make republicanism secure once and for all in America.[11]

Among Federalists in general there were variations of opinion on the specific question of going to war. But what they all did want more than anything else was national unity, and none more so than Adams himself. Some, however, were prepared to go to self-defeating lengths to secure it, and it was the strains that developed over this ground during the next year or so that would eventually bring the Federalists to ruin.

Initially, the advice Adams received from Hamilton, speaking through McHenry, might seem to have been the most rational of any—at least on the face of it. There was no doubt, McHenry told Adams, that the American people were disinclined toward war and that there was "a considerable part of them still peculiarly averse to a war with the French republic," even though "the late violent conduct of that nation has greatly alienated them from us." Nothing would be gained anyway by a formal war with France. "She has no trade; and as to Islands, if we could acquire such they are certainly not desirable in our present situation." The best policy, therefore, was to have "a truly vigorous defensive plan," while preserving an attitude of willingness to negotiate. Nor was there any point in being bound by a treaty of alliance with Great Britain. England's interests were such that America could get as much assistance from her without a treaty as with one, and if England's own future were precarious, as it might well be, it would take more than a treaty to save either of us. As to measures of defense, Hamilton urged not only a comprehensive naval program—arming merchant vessels, equipping some twenty sloops of war, procuring perhaps ten ships of the line, and completing the three frigates "as fast as possible"—but an extensive military one as well. He wanted to raise a regular force of 30,000 and an auxiliary "provisional army" of 30,000 to be used in case of invasion (McHenry circumspectly reduced these figures to 16,000 and 20,000), and to activate "all the sources of revenue." The President's language to Congress should be "cautious, solemn, grave," and devoid of "all asperity or insult," and while the urgency of the present danger should be stressed to the utmost, "the hope of an accommodation without proceeding to open rupture, ought not to be abandoned or precluded. . . ." Finally, he should proclaim a day of fasting and prayer, it being well "to oppose the honest enthusiasm of religious opinion to the phrenzy of political fanaticism."[12] So far so good, except that Hamilton's sweeping military plans would shortly take on a life of their own in his resourceful imagination, and would in time entirely pervert the prudent equilibrium he showed at this stage of the crisis.

Attorney-General Charles Lee, who lacked either the apocalyptic rage of Pickering or the nuanced perceptions of Hamilton, offered Adams a rather bleak and lawyer-like argument which did not contain a great deal of shading. Though he too was against any connection with England, Lee flatly asserted that with the non-reception of the envoys and the new French decree a formal declaration of war against France was the only alternative left. The decree meant the annihilation of American commerce and thus "national ruin"; to go no further than arming merchant ships meant greater danger to the lives of American seamen in cases of capture than would "a state of open war"; and war was the only way to arouse a public in which there was at present "no animation." Moreover, to "adhere to France in her present system" could not be defined as treasonable "until France is declared to be an enemy." He quoted Vattel to the effect that if by its "continued conduct one nation shows that it considers no right as sacred, the safety of the human race requires that it should be suppressed." Lee made only perfunctory reference to measures of defense, and without details. On the other hand, when it was a question of releasing the dispatches, about which Adams requested advice in his second circular of March 13, Lee thought that doing so might endanger the lives of the envoys if they had not yet departed. (Pickering at least saw that if one wanted war one had to release the dispatches and thus show the ground for it; Lee wanted it both ways.) On this particular question McHenry— this time without asking Hamilton's advice—saw no reason for withholding the dispatches, though he did not favor a declaration of war.[13]

As for the state of Adams's own mind, confronted as he was by these diverse exhortations, one discerns a condition of some turmoil. Adams seems to have snatched odd moments during the week beginning the 8th or 9th of March, 1798, scribbling out thoughts that might go into a message to Congress. The notes are preserved in his papers; they are, as usual, impulsive and not very connected. He had probably just read Lee's memorandum of the 8th, since he incorporated some of Lee's own language into his jottings, and he appears at first—with all his own efforts for an accommodation having come to nothing—to have found the idea of war strongly persuasive. The first page is one great snort of outrage. He lists the "continued Violences committed by the French" on the seas; their insult to Pinckney and "to the Nation which sent him"; "their unexampled arrogance" in refusing to receive the three envoys; and finally, the recent decree. "These all together form an accumulation of Injury outrage and Insult, which no nation which is not sunk below the Character of Man, ought or can submit to." And "in my opinion they demand on the Part of Congress an immediate Declaration of War against France."[14]

He then plunges into a disjointed lecture to his fellow-citizens which would be difficult to imagine anyone, even John Adams, seriously intending to say in a message to Congress. He deplores "too much hatred against some forms of government in Europe and too blind an attachment to others"; he discourses on the right of any people, including the French, to decide for themselves what form of government best suited them; then he denies that the French Revolution bears any resemblance to the American Revolution. He interrupts himself with baleful hints "that a Party in America though I hope a small one" had been plotting all along to engineer a rupture with France and then to take advantage of it in "hopes of rising upon French influence." The thought trails away, and next comes a string of historical references showing that "all great things [he has in mind the American Republic] have begun by being despised." But whatever may be said of our supposed divisions, it will be found that the American people are "too well united, impartial and independent . . . to submit ultimately to meditated Injuries and deliberate Insults. . . ."

By now Adams has about run out of steam, and the remainder of his notes are fitful and spasmodic. He allows for a hope that peace might still be possible. Then a flourish about what the Constitution now requires of him, and he considers once more a declaration of war and what measures this called for. But after a stab or two at such peripheral questions as letters of marque and the prohibition of all commerce with France, he simply throws down his pen and breaks off. The brief message he transmitted to Congress on the 19th of March was a model of restraint, containing not a word about war and bearing no resemblance to his candlelight epileptics.

We cannot know exactly what came over Adams, either at first or at last, though it was not an untypical bout with himself, lunging this way and that after "balance" as he was in his own remarkable manner. In the process of shaking himself down, Adams in his unique capacity as Chief Executive felt the logic of at least one gross proposition: that little was to be gained for the present by initiating a formal war with France. Signs of potential resistance to such a course were everywhere around him, and reasoned arguments against it had been laid before him by one member, and probably at least one other as well, of his own cabinet. A further deterrent, vexatious but for the time being difficult to reason out of the way, was the matter of releasing the full story told by the commissioners' dispatches. One cabinet member—and again, probably one other—had cautioned that to do this might be dangerous to the commissioners' personal safety. The evidence indicates that Adams was persuaded. Whatever he said, then, would have to remain between these boundaries. If there was one voice in the cabinet whose counsels of prudence—at least at this stage—most accurately reflected the position Adams himself finally arrived at, it appears to have been that of Oliver Wolcott. Wolcott on March 15 wrote out the draft of a short message, doubtless at Adams's own request, and Adams, altering no more than a word or two and adding a brief paragraph of his own, transmitted it to Congress on the 19th.[15]

The dispatches of the envoys had now been examined and considered, he said, and despite the envoys' "sincere and unremitted" efforts to adjust the two countries' differences, there now remained "no ground of expectation that the objects of their mission can be accomplished on terms compatible with the safety, the honor, or the essential interests of the nation." He therefore wished to "reiterate the recommendations which have been formerly made,"

> . . . for the protection of our seafaring and commercial citizens; for the defence of any exposed portions of our territory; for replenishing our arsenals, establishing foundries, and military manufactures; and to provide such efficient revenue as will

be necessary to defray extraordinary expenses, and supply the deficiencies which may be occasioned by depredations on our commerce.

He further observed that he no longer felt justified in restraining merchant vessels from sailing armed, and he concluded with the hope that Congress in its proceedings would show "zeal, vigor, and concert, in defence of the national rights, proportioned to the danger with which they are threatened."[16]

But moderate as such words may have been in view of the circumstances, Jefferson, wild with anxiety and not at the top of his judgment, called it an "insane message," and to his Republican friends he renewed his urging for delay. He wanted the House to remove the President's discretionary authority on the arming of merchant ships, and then, he thought, Congress should simply adjourn. Members might then "go home & consult their constituents" on the crisis in public affairs, and this would allow time for France's expected invasion of England to have its effect. (To "do nothing, & to gain time, is every thing with us. . . . ")[17] The congressional Republicans, shaken by the President's communication, were not prepared to take very seriously the idea of adjournment. But on March 27 one of them, Richard Sprigg of Maryland, offered a set of resolutions which were, perhaps unwittingly, full of potential mischief. They expressed the opinion "that under existing circumstances, it is not expedient for the United States to resort to war against the French Republic"; that there ought to be a law "restricting the arming of merchant vessels"; and that "adequate provision" should be made "for the protection of our seacoast, and for the internal defence of the country."[18]

It was the debate over the Sprigg resolutions that led to a call for the dispatches. The congressmen quickly began to realize that they could not deal with the second and third resolutions until they had disposed of the first (on whether it was expedient to go to war with France), whereas in order to do that they had either to determine in their own minds that the President's renewed call for comprehensive measures was justified, or to prove that he was unwarrantedly trying to rush the country into war. But in order to do either one, they would have to see the evidence on which the President's position was based. This logic, once set in motion, quickly became irresistible. It was first broached by Giles of Virginia, who speculated in the midst of a rambling speech on March 29 that the President was "pursuing hostile measures, and keeping back all information," and that there were grounds for suspicion, "which was the reason the expected papers were not sent."[19] Whereupon the next day John Allen of Connecticut, a very strong Federalist, proposed that the President be requested to send them, or rather "such parts thereof as considerations of public safety, in his opinion, may permit." Giles expostulated that nothing at all should be withheld; he wanted "not only to have the correspondence of our Ministers, but the instructions which were given to them."[20] There was no turning back. Some Federalists, suspecting that the documents might indeed contain sensational material, pressed for disclosure; others, such as Harrison Gray Otis, protested that confidentiality ought to be preserved. All of this only spurred the Republicans on. A large number of them believed there must be material that would show further negotiation to be still possible; even those who had misgivings, of whom Albert Gallatin was one (and Giles himself was said to have pulled back at the last minute), had no choice but to fall in. On April 2 the House voted by a very large majority to call for the papers. The House, observed Abigail Adams, wanted both the dispatches and the envoys' instructions, "and today *they will receive them.*"[21] They did, and no more was heard of the Sprigg resolutions. Within a week—though Adams urged in his covering message that "they be considered in confidence" until members could "deliberate on the consequences of their publication"—the papers were in print and were being read all over the country.[22]

At this point the world in which John Adams had functioned since the start of his presidency was stupendously transformed. It was during the months immediately to come that most of the actions occurred, performed both by himself and by great numbers of his fellow-citizens, that would set the terms for the remainder of his public service, and that he would be living with the recollection of to the end of his days. All was now going his way: *he* was finally in command, truly in charge of all his country's most vital concerns.

The opposition in Congress to all intents and purposes collapsed. Not that the Republicans changed their minds on first principles; great efforts were made to extenuate the tale told by the dispatches. Jefferson insisted that the papers did "not offer one motive the more for going to war." To be sure, it was "very possible" that Talleyrand, with his known leanings to corruption, had had something to do with the demand for bribes. "But that the Directory knew anything of it is neither proved nor provable." (Nine months later, Jefferson was still denouncing the "wicked use" made of the "X.Y.Z. dish cooked up by Marshall, where the swindlers were made to appear as the French government.") Nevertheless the voting margin whereby the Republicans had consistently blocked Adams's program over the past year now dissolved. There were enough "wavering characters" who went over to "the war party," according to Jefferson, in order to "wipe off the imputation of being French partisans," together with five members of the Virginia delegation who abruptly left for home, that the Federalists found themselves with a substantial working majority. "In this state of things," Jefferson predicted gloomily, "they will carry what they please." The Federalists would enjoy electoral gains throughout the remainder of the year and into 1799, most strikingly in the South.[23]

But in the surge of patriotic feeling that followed the disclosures the greatest single beneficiary was John Adams himself, who for a brief dizzying period became widely popular for the first and only time in his life. "I suppose the fact to be," wrote Robert Troup in amazement, "that since man was created and government was formed no public officer has stood higher in the confidence and affection of his countrymen than our present President now does."[24] The best evidence for this newfound glory could be read in the patriotic addresses of support that came pouring in on him from everywhere. Despite their great number, and despite all the other pressing business that claimed his attention, Adams spent a large portion of his time feasting upon these addresses, composing replies to each one himself, each adapted to the particular sentiments in the one before him, and each reply echoing the soaring feelings they inspired in his bosom.[25] His emotions tumbled over themselves in luxuriant chaos: wrath, self-righteousness, defiance, scorn, and delight. The tone of a good many of his responses is quite bellicose, and in two or three he actually intimates that war was all but certain. He rehearses many times the ways in which France had tried to destroy the independence of a sovereign people. ("Independence," a key word in Adams's own picture of himself, recurs in almost every reply.) There are expansive homilies on the lessons of history, on the fate of nations not governed by justice and virtue and that allowed themselves to be rent by faction: all have ended up as military despotisms. (Before Adams is through, most of his principles of political science have got themselves in somewhere.) He discourses frequently on the perversions of the French Revolution, schoolmastering any of his memorialists who appear not fully persuaded of this, even while praising them handsomely for their support of himself. He is benignly indulgent with the students of Princeton ("the innocence of your hearts and the purity of your intentions"), but admonishes them that the Borgias and the Catilines will always defeat well-meaning persons who have "little reading in the science of government."[26]

But the great preoccupation, transcending all else, is national unity. On the one hand, he exults in the thought of having achieved it; on the other, he is outraged when he thinks either of the foreign nation that has tried to destroy it or of the "wicked and designing men" who have tried to subvert it from within. This may account for much of the warlike tone that pervades these effusions. Adams is responding in case after case to symbolic offers of life and fortune in defense of the country's independence; and he is hardly disposed to damp such sentiments down. The unity they seem to promise, and for which he has so thirsted, is far too gratifying. So it was all very exhausting, but he loved it. Abigail thought he looked pale and had lost weight. But he slept well, his appetite was good, and she had seldom seen him in better spirits.[27]

Moreover, Congress was now giving him everything he had asked for. He could take particular satisfaction in the enactment of measures for naval defense and the protection of American commerce. Not only was final provision made for completion of the three large frigates already under construction and nearly finished, but Congress also authorized immediately the acquisition of twelve sloops of war of up to twenty-two guns each and ten galleys for the protection of the shallow coastal waters of the South. Twelve additional ships of war were authorized on June 30, and three more on July 16. Substantial sums were appropriated to fortify harbors and establish foundries for the production of cannon. An independent Navy Department was established to supervise the construction, maintenance, and operations of the new fleet about to come into being. Its first Secretary, who took office on June 24, was Benjamin Stoddert of Maryland, a successful shipping merchant and a man of substantial ability and sound judgment. An embargo was laid upon all trade with France and her colonies, and all treaties with France were formally abrogated. Naval vessels were now authorized to attack any armed French craft employed for preying on American shipping and to retake any American ships already captured. This sanction extended beyond American coastal waters to include the West Indies and in fact anywhere on the high seas. Merchant vessels might legally arm, resist attack, capture any attackers, and retake any captive American vessels. Short of privateering—which would in effect have been a declaration of war—the American merchant fleet now had the fullest protection the country's limited naval resources could provide.[28]

So it was no longer a question of Congress withholding anything of importance that Adams had asked for. The great difficulty now, which would increase in magnitude as the months passed, was with the things Congress gave him that he had not asked for. One was the Alien and Sedition Laws of June and July 1798; the other, the vastly expanded military establishment that was legislated during the same period, together with the taxes required for supporting it. It was these enactments and their consequences that would turn Adams's interval of triumph into ashes.

Referring to the Alien and Sedition Acts long after his retirement from public life, Adams would insist that these laws were not a part of his program and that he had "recommended no such thing." And although conceding that he believed the crisis called for some measures of the sort, which was why he consented to them, he still had misgivings "that a hurricane of clamor would be raised against them, as in truth there was, even more fierce and violent than I had anticipated." It may be suspected that in 1798 John Adams, no less than the protective Abigail, took relish in the thought of Bache and other opposition musketeers being punished for their abusive utterances, especially against himself.[29] Still, there is no evidence that a campaign against sedition was one of Adams's primary concerns. The sense of his own position as Chief Magistrate disposed him to prefer consent to coercion.

It is of some interest that the congressional Federalists themselves, the initiators of these inglorious measures, did not press their efforts with the kind of concerted conviction that has most often been attributed to them, and that the margins by which the laws passed were on the whole narrower than was the case with any of the other major legislation enacted in the crisis of 1798. The first steps toward what finally emerged as the Naturalization Act of June 18 were attempts to shut off or reduce the flow of aliens being admitted to United States citizenship, inordinate numbers of whom seemed disposed to support the Republican party, and to prevent all foreign-born persons from either voting or holding office. The latter effort was defeated by a two to one majority, while the main provision of the completed act, extending the period of residence required for naturalization to fourteen years from the previous five, passed the House and the Senate in each case by a single vote.[30]

As for resident aliens and domestic criticism of government, the most enthusiastic of the Federalists would have liked a single catch-all measure, as sweeping and summary as could be, enabling the Executive with a minimum of nicety to deal swiftly with the widest variety of menaces, from aliens of every sort as well as native citizens, and suspected plots as well as seditious utterances. Such impulses were amply enough expressed in the legislation that followed. But they were substantially chastened along the way from their original form, owing not only to the highly able opposition tactics of Albert Gallatin but also to a variety of misgivings within the Federalists' own ranks, and what they came out with in addition to the new naturalization law was not one measure but three.

The most precise and logical of the three, the Alien Enemies Act of July 6, would probably not have been passed at all had it not been for Republican insistence, and such were the modifications from the original that in its final stages it had become, as one authority has put it, "virtually a Republican measure." In the event of war—but only in the event of war, or invasion—the President had authority to designate as alien enemies any citizens or subjects of the hostile nation residing in the United States whose presence he regarded as dangerous, and to make regulations for their apprehension, restraint, or removal as the case might require. The procedures, which involved federal and state courts as well as enforcement officers, were defined by law rather than left to the President's discretion. But the law was never used against those for whom it was intended, since open war with France never took place. On the other hand, this was the only one of the four that survived as a permanent statute, two of them being of limited duration and the other being repealed a few years after its enactment.[31]

It could be argued that of all these laws the most farfetched and misbegotten was the Alien Act of June 25, 1798, which applied in peacetime as well as wartime not simply to aliens of an enemy nation but to any aliens upon whom for whatever reason the eye of disapproval might fall. Under it the President might expel any non-naturalized persons of foreign birth whom he judged "dangerous to the peace and safety of the United States," and this could be done without a hearing and without specifying any reason. If such persons failed to depart within the time specified, they could be imprisoned up to three years and barred permanently from becoming citizens. Arbitrary and unreasonable as all this was, it was substantially less draconic than the original Senate bill. The original idea was simply to get rid of as many aliens as possible through isolation and wholesale deportations, because the most numerous of them—the "wild Irish"—were of a naturally subversive temper, had pro-French sympathies, and were drawn into Republican politics in America, and because the presence of large numbers of aliens of any sort tended on general principles to threaten the purity of the national character. Originally there was to have been a vast system of registration, surveillance, and individual permits for persons to remain, obtainable only on proof of prior good behavior and restricting the holder to a particular locality. Nobody could "harbour, entertain, or conceal any alien" without giving written notice several days in advance to a federal judge. (This would have knocked out the entire tourist trade, such as it was, at one stroke.) Any alien who returned after having been expelled could be sentenced to life imprisonment at hard labor. All these provisions were struck out along the way, largely on Federalist initiative. Alexander Hamilton, seeing an earlier version of the bill, thought his friends must be running wild. The final bill passed the House by a margin of six votes. But the law was a dead letter from the first. Adams, determined upon the strictest of interpretations, never invoked it, and the Alien Act expired in June 1800 without a single alien having been deported under its provisions, though it certainly inspired some to leave on their own.[32]

The most notorious of the emerging measures, the one that had the widest variety of consequences and that caused by far the most discussion from the time of its enactment to the present day, was the Sedition Act of July 14, 1798. This law, as every student of American history knows, made it a crime to utter or publish "any false, scandalous, and malicious writing or writings against the Government of the United States, or either House of the Congress of the United States, with intent to defame . . . or to bring them . . . into contempt or disrepute. . . ." But this was sweet reason compared to what the more obsessed of the Federalist bedlamites first had in mind.

The House originally devised an omnibus alien and sedition bill so comprehensive that not simply defamation but even threats to defame were punishable; it would have virtually throttled any kind of opposition to the federal government. But in the course of June the sedition question was preempted by the Senate, and the bill upon which the completed act was based had its origin there rather than in the House. The proposed measure was exceedingly drastic. Its guiding light was James Lloyd of Maryland, as wrathful a spirit in the Senate as was John Allen in the House. Lloyd's bill dealt with treason as well as sedition. He had the novel idea that there was such a thing as treason in peacetime—or rather, that it was possible to have an "enemy" with whom one was not at war, that the enemy was France and should be named as such, and that giving aid and comfort and adhering to that enemy should be punishable by death. The sections on sedition were similar to those in the House omnibus bill. Seditious utterances could include anything that might cause a belief that the federal government had passed laws from motives "hostile to the constitution, or liberties and happiness of the people," which could cover almost anything in the way of opposition; and "libelous or scandalous" writings or expressions were punishable whether false or true. Expressions tending to justify the French government were also punishable. Hamilton emitted another groan when he saw this, and made predictions of trouble. Even the Senate, though generally of a more imperious temper than the House, had its second thoughts, and its members did not need Hamilton to tell them they had better pull back. They struck out the entire section relating to treason, and all references to France. The bill they then passed and sent to the House was one that more or less reflected traditional common-law practice in matters concerning sedition.[33]

But this was still too much for the House, where misgivings remained, and a number of further limitations were added, nearly all at the initiative of Federalist members. It was these amendments that have led a modern authority to comment that the Sedition Act of 1798 represented a substantial liberalization of the common law of seditious libel as it then stood. In the final version, malicious intent had to be proved; evidence of the truth of allegedly libelous utterances could be admitted as a defense; criticism of federal judges was eliminated from the scope of the law, leaving only criticism of Congress and the President; and the proviso was added that juries could determine not only the facts—as in traditional practice—but the law as well, which meant they could return general verdicts of guilty or not guilty. Representative Harper of South Carolina, who had proposed most of these amendments, also wanted the law limited to one year's duration. This was voted down, and the term was fixed at March 3, 1801, the day before the current administration was to end.[34]

But liberalized or not, the bill passed by the narrowest of margins, 44 to 41, and only four of the votes in favor came from south of the Potomac.[35] This certainly did not augur well for the immediate future. None of the four acts did anything to promote national unity, and this one in particular would do a great deal toward eroding away the considerable unity then existing. All things considered, the entire parcel was pure bad luck for John Adams.

The other piece of bad luck, and an even worse one, was the military program pushed through during this same period. It entailed an army far greater in size than anything Adams had asked for, or wanted, or thought was necessary, and that army would be commanded to all intents and purposes by the one man in the world he trusted less than any other, Alexander Hamilton. In the ideological climate of late eighteenth-century America an army of such magnitude would not have been thinkable were it not for the pitch of public feeling aroused by the crisis of 1798. Even so, it was just barely thinkable. The idea of armies was one which far transcended the current crisis; it was charged with the utmost significance in the minds of an entire people; and it was one whose immediate history went back at least to the close of the Revolution.

In 1783 the military committee of the Continental Congress, which happened to be chaired by Alexander Hamilton, reported the first plan for a peacetime army that would be under the control of the general government rather than of the several states. It consisted of a regular corps of a little over three thousand men, supplemented by a somewhat larger one which would be neither regulars nor militia but something in between, and having some of the advantages of both. This supplementary force would be a kind of elite reserve, recruited in cities and incorporated towns for greater convenience of assembly, of men otherwise liable to militia service but who were willing to volunteer for eight years and to train twenty-six days a year. It would be armed, paid, and maintained by the Confederation government and called into active service in case of war or invasion. (This was the first seed of the "provisional army" of 1798.) The entire plan was actually a rather imaginative one, providing as it did for a standing force that could be at least doubled immediately upon the outbreak of hostilities. This would be in addition to the state militias, which need no longer be solely relied upon at the moment of emergency, though here too there were possibilities for reform and greater efficiency.[36]

But nothing came of the plan. The revenue arrangements of the Confederation were endemically stultified by the requisition system, and the seaboard states were unwilling to spend money for protection of the frontier, which was the main justification for a peacetime force. As it was, military expenses accounted for over 40 percent of the entire budget. There were other reasons, such as the persisting antipathy to all centralizing tendencies.[37] But the basic reason was more pervasive. This was the odious specter of the traditional standing army of eighteenth-century Europe: the common soldiery gathered from the scum of society, officered by an insolent and imperious aristocracy, employed for arbitrary purposes, a tyrannical pestilence whenever it moved and wherever it was quartered. An abomination of standing armies had been a major component of the Country opposition literature of late seventeenth- and eighteenth century-England, and in the American colonies this sentiment, according to Lois Schwoerer, "became a basic assumption of almost every political leader."[38] New Englanders were particularly touchy after their experience with British garrisons in the 1770s, and it was the New England representatives, led by Elbridge Gerry, who were largely responsible for killing the plan of 1783. Under Gerry's goading, the Massachusetts General Court instructed the state's congressional delegation to "oppose, and by all ways and means . . . prevent the raising of a standing army of any number, on any pretence whatever, in time of peace." Some sort of force being needed in view of volatile conditions on the frontier, the Confederation had to make do with a very vaguely defined "army" of seven hundred men, not wholly under its own control since the men were contributed from the militias of the four states most concerned, on twelve-month enlistments.[39]

The Federal Constitution gave the United States government in theory the power to establish a regular peacetime army with no qualifications on the government's full control over it. This was accomplished only after considerable debate, and there was much "standing army" rhetoric both at the Convention and afterward. But this theoretical authority was no guarantee of an adequate force in fact. Its size was subject to continuous fluctuation at the pleasure of Congress, depending as it did upon appropriations, on which there was a two-year limit. Nobody yet dared advocate more than a small regular force; a classic "standing army" was out of the question; and to supplement this force the nation would still have to depend on militia and irregular levies in time of emergency. In practice the United States Army in the opening years of the Federal Republic amounted to little more than what it had been under the Confederation. The troops under Harmar and St. Clair with which the Washington administration in 1790, with great hesitation and reluctance, initiated its policy of force against the Indians in the Northwest consisted largely of state militia.[40]

Not until St. Clair's calamitous defeat in November 1791 was the Administration moved to press for an expanded regular army of five thousand men to cope with the situation in the Northwest, and only in such a setting was Congress persuaded to authorize it. The army's internal reorganization as a frontier "legion" under the vigorous leadership of Anthony Wayne represented a considerable step, apparently justified by Wayne's eventual success at Fallen Timbers in 1794. Yet the fact remained that no advances in military policy had been made since the end of the Revolution except under crisis conditions, from the direst necessity, and with the greatest reluctance. Moreover, after Wayne had achieved his objectives great efforts were again made either to reduce his force drastically or to dismantle it altogether. The Washington administration successfully resisted the worst of these pressures, and the principle of a peacetime army was eventually established by an act of 1796 which authorized a regular force of somewhat over three thousand men. But the principle was essentially a limited one. The army was conceived as a constabulary force to be dispersed in a string of outposts across the frontier, far removed from the principal centers and main currents of the national life, and the basic outlines and mission of the regular army would remain unaltered throughout the nineteenth century.[41]

Meanwhile the other objective envisioned by the committee report of 1783 — a plan for rapidly expanding the regular force in time of emergency, beyond sole reliance on state militia — remained no further realized than ever. During the crisis of 1794 when war with Great Britain appeared likely, the idea of an auxiliary reserve force had again been brought forward by Theodore Sedgwick. But because the ancient menace of a standing army seemed even greater than the menace of the ancient enemy England, this effort, as Madison assured Jefferson, "was strangled more easily . . . than I expected."[42] A similar attempt was made in 1797 during the initial phases of the crisis with France. In addition to the diplomatic rupture and the maritime depredations, the shadowy activities of General Victor Collot had aroused apprehensions of French designs in the Mississippi Valley. Even John Quincy Adams, not normally given to wild imaginings, was convinced that there was a French plan to send an invading army to detach the West and form a satellite republic with the aid of disaffected Americans there, not unlike those being set up in Europe. Once again, under the shadow of possible invasion, resolutions were brought in by William L. Smith proposing a provisional army of twenty thousand to serve in case of war, while strengthening the regular army with additional cavalry and artillery. But again, nothing came of it, and this was the way things stood at the moment of the XYZ revelations.[43]

The most extraordinary thing done in the extraordinary climate of the spring and summer of 1798 was the authorizing of a military establishment more formidable than anyone would have thought possible a few months before. The regular army was augmented by an "Additional Army" of twelve thousand men, and a "Provisional Army" of ten thousand men was to be activated by the President in the event of actual war or invasion, or "imminent danger" of invasion.[44] On the one hand, this went vastly beyond anything Adams himself had had in mind. But on the other hand, it fell a good deal short — in numbers, shape, and emphasis — of what had been projected by Alexander Hamilton earlier in the year through McHenry in response to the President's circular letter to the cabinet, or of what was pressed for by the Federalist leadership in Congress in the months of May, June, and July. So the question naturally arises of why the final legislation should have been so different from Adams's own conception of military requirements — even to the extent that one of the two bills whereby it was done was passed with overwhelming Republican support — and of what happened to Hamilton's original plan, with its emphasis on a large provisional army.

John Adams never believed, whatever anyone else may have thought, including his own son, that there was the least likelihood of France's sending an army to invade the United States. "Where is it possible for her to get ships to send thirty thousand men here? We are double the number we were in 1775. We have four times the military skill, and we have eight times the Munitions of War. What would 30,000 men do here?"[45] In his original call for defense measures the year before, he had dwelt at length on naval armaments while merely mentioning the need for some increase in the army to protect seaports from possible raids. He went little further in the report he had McHenry submit to Congress in April 1798. Hamilton had wanted a regular force of twenty thousand men and a provisional army of thirty thousand; Adams, in addition to his naval program, recommended an increase of three regiments in the regular army and a provisional force that could be called into service "in case of emergency." The latter he never took seriously at all, so it did not much matter what the numbers were since he did not expect that such a force would ever be used.[46] Even his most warlike outpourings in reply to the addresses that summer would contain no passages about glory on dry battlefields. "To arms, then, my young friends," he erupted in one of them, "to arms, *especially by sea*. . . ." He was even more explicit by September. "Floating batteries and wooden walls," he wrote in another, "have been my favorite system of warfare and defense for this country for three and twenty years. I have had very little success in making proselytes."[47]

At the beginning of the summer, war sentiment among Federalists, and indeed in public opinion generally, was considerable. Quite a few leading Federalists by now were all for an outright declaration of war. But though they all favored vigorous defense measures there were many reservations among Federalists themselves about taking the initiative for war, either because they thought the French would push matters to that point without it, or because public opinion was not quite ready for it, or even because war might still be avoided altogether. John Marshall landed in New York on June 17 and two days later was given a hero's welcome in Philadelphia. Yet for all the praise heaped upon him, and though in his replies to testimonials he urged support of the President's preparedness program, Marshall refrained from making any positive warlike statements. When a committee of New Jersey militia officers assured him they were resolved "to enforce by the sword, those injured rights which the milder means of negociation have failed to secure," he replied that "all honorable means of avoiding war should be essayed before the sword be appealed to." Marshall still did not believe France intended war, though some Federalists tried to represent him as thinking otherwise. "I apprehend," Jefferson remarked to Madison, "he is not hot enough for his friends."[48]

Hamilton, as has been noted, was not disposed to draw the sword either. "Shall we declare war? No—there are still chances for avoiding a general rupture which ought to be taken. Want of future success may bring the present despots to reason." Prepare for the worst, meet their aggressions at sea in "a limited and mitigated state of war, to grow into a general war or not at the election of France." Hamilton came to expect war—and probably even to desire it, though that is a later story—but he wanted France to be the initiator, and he never actually urged an immediate declaration. John Jay, with his usual circumspection, did not think it advisable "to declare war at present, for the public mind does not appear to me to be quite prepared for it."[49]

The high-water mark in the push for a declared war by Federalist radicals appears to have been reached, and then receded from, early in July. At a Federalist caucus held on the 1st or 2nd, moderates such as Joshua Coit of Connecticut and Samuel Sewall of Massachusetts succeeded in convincing them that they did not have the votes. John Allen pursued the matter anyway, and the closest thing to a test came with a resolution Allen offered on July 5, "That a committee be appointed to consider upon the expediency of declaring, by Legislative act, the state and relation subsisting between the United States and the French Republic." It was voted down the next day without a roll-call. So although some Federalists affected to believe that public opinion was far ahead of Congress on the war question, Congress as a whole seems to have thought otherwise.[50] Fisher Ames, condoling with Pickering over such "torpor and indecision," nevertheless intimated that a formal declaration might not, after all, be worth the "discords" it would arouse. Better to enact measures "*as if* we were in war," but without saying so. "Wage war and call it self-defence. . . ."[51]

As to where Adams himself should be located on this scale of opinion, his view seems in a way not to have been very different from that of Fisher Ames. If the people's representatives should resolve upon a declaration of war, well and good. That would be the strongest expression so far of national unity, and there is evidence that Adams—if his wife's opinions may be taken as in any way reflecting his own—would have found such an expression very gratifying. There was "one thing wanting," Abigail Adams wrote to her son as Congress was about to adjourn, ". . . a declaration of war ought undoubtedly to have been made." And to her sister: "Why, when we have the thing, should we boggle at the Name . . . ?"[52] But if Adams in his own mind welcomed—as he undoubtedly did—the thought of a declaration by Congress, to call for it himself was another matter. If he had "the thing," why risk the unity that was already there by reaching for "the Name"? On the naval side, nothing more was wanting in the way of energy that was not being done already; the frigates were now afloat, and with the capture of a French privateer by an American sloop of war off the New Jersey coast early in July, a state of limited hostilities on the sea had already begun.[53] Declared or undeclared, war for John Adams had always been ideally conceived in a naval vocabulary. It was this that marked him off from the main body of Federalists, Fisher Ames included. And by the same token a formal declaration of war, no matter how enticing and no matter where the initiative came from, was bound to force an increased degree of attention on the problems of a land army. This would almost certainly mean trouble. Unity, unity, balance, balance: how to resolve it? One way, of course, would be to pack up and be off for Quincy. But not before the trouble had already begun.

Among Republicans, there was no support whatever for a declaration of war, and the feeling against standing armies was as strong as ever. This would get into every debate on increasing the military force. But there was another variable that had a great deal to do with the anomalous outcome of these debates, and accounted as well for the Federalists' electoral gains of 1798 in the southern states. This was the spreading apprehension among many southern members that the French might invade the southern coast from St. Domingue with an army of blacks under Toussaint Louverture, or with a force under the villainous Victor Hugues (the Directory's freebooting commissioner in the West Indies), with the design of inciting a slave insurrection. Robert Goodloe Harper of South Carolina made the most of this in his speeches on military measures.[54]

Two major military bills were debated and enacted, one in May and the other in July. The outcome of the first effort was a keen discouragement to the advocates of a large army. A bill passed in the Senate on April 23 would have authorized a provisional army of twenty thousand men which the President might enlist "whenever he shall judge the public safety requires the measure" (that is, whenever he wished); he might also accept into national service any companies privately raised with their own arms and equipment. When the bill was brought into the House the next day, it met with a torrent of objections. The Constitution gave Congress the power to raise armies, but nowhere did it contemplate delegating such sweeping authority to the Executive. This would be the first step toward a standing army. As for the volunteer companies, these elite units would be drawn from "a certain class of citizens, such as merchants, lawyers, &c." and be placed at the President's disposal. (In other words they were sure to be all Federalists.) What security was there, Albert Gallatin demanded, that this force "would not be used for dangerous purposes?" Here was a reminder of Pitt's campaign against subversion in England five years earlier: a "system of alarm . . . which, day after day, brings forth motions calculated to spread fears of imaginary dangers; which one day produces an alien bill; on the next . . . an unconstitutional sedition bill; and . . . grants military associations of one part of the people, in order to suppress a supposed disaffection of the rest of the community." And finally, any danger of invasion could be met by militia. The militia, it was stoutly insisted, was "a support fully effectual without a recurrence to a standing army."[55]

The resulting bill, passed on May 18, 51–40, while retaining the volunteer companies and still authorizing a provisional army, cut that force in half and specified that the President could only bring it into being if war were declared against the United States, or in the event of actual or imminent invasion, "before the next session of Congress."[56] The act would thus be in force less than seven months.

But rumors and fears of invasion continued to mount during the next six weeks, and public opinion in the southern states, insisting on more vigorous measures of military defense, was apparently not to be turned aside. With the approach of the national patriotic holiday and in conjunction with the Federalists' final push for war, Robert Harper on July 3 was moved to have another try at creating what he and his friends saw as a fully suitable military force. Harper wanted to increase the provisional army to 50,000 men, 12,500 of whom would be mobilized immediately. The act that came out of this effort, though significantly modified from Harper's resolutions, was fashioned with Republican cooperation and passed on July 9, 60–11, with substantial Republican support. The provisional army was left as it had been set by the previous act, but the regular army was augmented by twelve new regiments and six troops of dragoons, to be organized at once. The shift of emphasis from a provisional army to regulars had been proposed by a Republican moderate, Samuel Smith of Maryland, and supported by Albert Gallatin. Why should the Republicans have regarded this as preferable? Because to them, what Harper had proposed was a kind of blank check, a huge army almost infinitely expansible under executive discretion, whereas this was a fixed number specified by Congress and under congressional control.[57] Nor was it even quite the same as a regular army, being enlisted only for the current emergency. Moreover, feeling in the South by this time was agitated enough that the Republicans did have to take account of it. Such, then, were the considerations that went into this vote. Congress adjourned a week later.

Alexander Hamilton, after more than three years of nominal outsidership, may now be observed edging once more toward the center of national events. What Congress had just done was not exactly what Hamilton had first envisioned. But it was more than suitable as a first step toward something he had long thought desirable: building a respectable armed force for the United States. He meant to take a personal part in it, and had begun to anticipate the form this would take almost from the moment the XYZ dispatches arrived. True, the additional force now authorized was to be in existence only "for and during the continuance of the existing differences between the United States and the French Republic." And although Hamilton was prudent enough not to press for a declaration of war, he seems to have assumed that these "differences" would exist for some time—time enough to create that force, possibly to augment it still further, and in any case to make manifest its value as an instrument of national power.

Though it was a new role he was imagining for himself, it was the old Hamilton all over again. Here once more was the grand projector, the man who thought he could perceive the whole vast picture regardless of intervening difficulties, who believed himself better able than anyone else to foresee all contingencies, manage all details, and anticipate all results. Ostensibly he was still a private citizen, as he had been since his retirement from the Treasury in January 1795, practicing his profession in New York and supporting a numerous family. But he had immense reserves of energy. Among leading Federalists at Philadelphia and elsewhere he still possessed enormous influence, and his opinions were listened to with profound respect. And he had already bounded into action. Between March 30 and April 21 he dashed off a series of articles for a New York newspaper depicting with much vividness France's imperial ambitions, her subjugation of Holland, Genoa, Venice, and the Swiss cantons, and her supposed plan to occupy Louisiana and other Spanish colonies in the New World and to dismember the United States. The nation must not simply resist but "resist with energy." Governor John Jay wanted to appoint Hamilton to a vacancy in the Senate, and wrote on April 19 urging him to accept. But Hamilton's vision was set on loftier things.

"There may arrive a crisis when I may conceive myself bound once more to sacrifice the interest of my family to public call."[58]

The kind of call Hamilton was thinking of became very explicit in an exchange of letters with Washington in May and early June, initiated by himself. He wrote Washington on May 19 to say that in "the present dangerous crisis of public affairs" it was "impossible not to look up to you," and warning him "that in the event of an open rupture with France, the public voice will again call you to command the armies of your Country. . . ." To be sure, he said, all will "deplore an occasion which should once more tear you from that repose to which you have so good a right—yet it is the opinion of all those with whom I converse that you will be compelled to make the sacrifice." Washington in his reply was reserved. He admitted his concern at "the outrageous conduct of France toward the United States" and that of France's "partisans among ourselves, who aid and abet their measures." But he was inclined to doubt that the French, though "capable of *any thing bad*," would attempt a "formidable Invasion" once they saw "the spirit, & policy of this country rising into resistance." He would leave his peaceful retirement only with the greatest reluctance. Still, if circumstances left him no choice, he would certainly want to know in advance "who would be my coadjutors, and whether you would be disposed to take an active part, if Arms are to be resorted to."[59]

One may almost picture Hamilton snapping to attention. He declared that he found it a great satisfaction to know that Washington would not withhold his services if the emergency were great enough. "There is no one but yourself that could unite the public confidence in such an emergency. . . ." As for himself, he proceeded briskly to the point. "If I am invited *to a station in which the service I may render may be proportioned to the sacrifice I am to make*—I shall be willing to go into the army. If you command, the place in which I should hope to be most useful is that of Inspector General with a command in the line. This I would accept." He took it for granted that "the services of all the former officers worth having may be commanded & that your choice would regulate the Executive. With decision & care in selection an excellent army may be formed."[60] He meant to form it himself, and within four months, despite the most furious resistance by no less than the Executive himself, he would be given his wish.

Hamilton was assured of cabinet support without having to ask for it. Aroused by stories about the British warship *Thetis* interfering with American commerce out of Charleston, Hamilton exclaimed in letters to Pickering that an American frigate ought to be dispatched there to put a stop to it. He thought the United States should "act with spirit and energy as well towards G Britain as France." Conceding that "no one, who does not see all the cards, can judge accurately," he would nonetheless deal out "the same measure to both of them," and by such conduct "our Citizens will be enthusiastically united to the government. It will evince that we are neither *Greeks* nor *Trojans*." Pickering, with a shudder of agitation at the very thought of getting embroiled in hostilities with England, intimated in his reply that all the trouble had been caused by dishonest American merchants falsifying cargoes in order to supply the French in the West Indies, then hastily changed the subject to military affairs. His conclusion was significant:

> I wish you were in a situation not only to "see all the cards," but to play them; with all my soul I would give you my *hand;* and engage in any other *game* in which I might co-operate, on the same side, *to win the stakes.*

The "game" Pickering had in mind was seeing that Hamilton was placed in effectual command of the new American army, second in rank only to Washington himself.[61]

On at least one question, that of Washington as head of whatever military force might eventually be authorized and raised, there was no disagreement between the President and any of his advisors. Indeed, Adams on July 2 sent in the nomination, confirmed at once, of Washington as "Lieutenant General and Commander in Chief of all the Armies raised or to be raised for the service of the United States," even before receiving Washington's reply to a previous letter requesting permission to do so. (The commission was then triumphantly dated the Fourth of July.)[62] But the main question—that of who Washington's chief subordinates were to be, their relative ranking, and most particularly who would be second in command and thus first in Washington's absence—was not settled until the end of September. The facts and the chronology, replete with intrigue and resulting in the deep disaffection of John Adams, are intricate enough to require extended consideration.

Pickering, with all the subtlety of a team of oxen, wrote Washington on July 6 that there was a "disinclination" on the President's part "to put Colonel Hamilton in what we think is his proper station, and that alone in which we suppose he will serve; the *second* to you, and the *chief* in your *absence.*" Besides, he added, if "any considerations should prevent your taking command of the army, I deceive myself extremely if you will not think it should be conferred on Colonel Hamilton." He hoped Washington would use his influence in either case to get the right result, and mentioned that McHenry was about to set off for Mount Vernon bearing Washington's commission.[63]

But Washington was not one to be jostled into any hasty decisions or dicta. In a series of letters to McHenry, Adams, and Pickering, all written prior to McHenry's arrival on July 11, he chose his words judiciously. To McHenry he repeated what he had already said to Hamilton, that he could not believe the French Directory, "intoxicated and abandoned as it is," would have the folly to undertake "a formidable Invasion." Yet if it did, or threatened to, and if his "declining years" were not an objection, "I should be ready to render every Service in my power to repel it. . . ." To Adams he said the same thing, and then indicated tactfully but pointedly that the general officers of any new army should be the best of those who had served in the Revolution, "without respect to Grade," and that they should be such "as the Commander in Chief can place entire confidence in." So far he had not mentioned a single name. But to Pickering he came down to business about "the abilities and fitness of the Gentleman you have named." On that question he had no doubts, and agreed that "his Services ought to be secured at *almost* any price." But he too, as well as the President, saw difficulty in what Pickering was proposing. Hamilton was greatly outranked at the end of the Revolution by Charles Cotesworth Pinckney, and Washington did not see how Pinckney could reasonably be expected to serve now as Hamilton's subordinate. "*If* the French should be so *mad*" as to attempt an invasion, they would "commence in the Southern quarter," in which case he saw the services "of so influential a character as Pinckney" as indispensable.[64]

It appears that the amiable McHenry, heavily coached before his departure by men of stronger minds and wills than his own, achieved at least partial success in easing Washington's misgivings as to whether Hamilton was quite the nation's choice after himself, and about the degree of Pinckney's reluctance to serve under him. Washington instructed McHenry to say, in the letter McHenry was about to write informing President Adams of having delivered the General's commission, that he would ask Washington for "the names of the persons he considers the best qualified for his confidential officers, without whom I think he would not serve." The list Washington gave him to take back was headed by three names for the three commissions as major-general authorized by the new act: Alexander Hamilton, Charles Cotesworth Pinckney, and Henry Knox. Washington had listed them in that order, though without yet claiming that the President might not rank them in some other.[65]

Hamilton had meanwhile told Pickering that he would be willing to serve under Knox "if *thought indispensable*," though he did not believe he should have to rank below Pinckney as well. "Nobody ever thought of such a thing," Pickering assured him with regard to Knox; and so in effect did Washington, who said that he himself had ranked Knox ("whom I love and esteem") below both Hamilton and Pinckney. The real difficulty was Pinckney, and Washington tried to explain his dilemma to Hamilton, which was that of "my wish to put you first, and my fear of loosing him." Then the ever-discreet Washington, recollecting himself, added, "But . . . after all it rests with the President to use his pleasure."[66]

Hamilton, a step closer to his heart's desire with Knox apparently no longer in the way, and not judging Washington's hint as strong enough to warrant his offering voluntarily to give way to Pinckney, did not do so. At the same time, Washington took another step toward shedding his misgivings about Pinckney (as it later turned out he need not have fretted, for when Pinckney arrived home from France in October he promptly let McHenry know he would be happy to serve under Hamilton), as well as toward persuading himself that his personal preference for Hamilton would meet with no serious difficulty either. He wrote a tactful letter to Knox, in which he said he hoped Knox would accept one of the three commissions as major-general. His list, he explained somewhat gingerly, consisted of "Colo. Hamilton, Genl. Chas. Cotesworth Pinckney and yourself. The first of these, in the public estimation, as declared to me, is designated to be second in command; with some fears, I confess, of the consequences; although I must acknowledge at the same time that I know not where a more competent choice could be made." Knox, though he opened his old chief's letter with "delightful sensations of affection," proceeded to read it with "astonishment," and finished it engulfed in disillusionment and bitterness.[67]

But for John Adams, Alexander Hamilton was the last person to be imagined as second in command or anywhere near it. "Oh no," he expostulated to Pickering when the latter first broached it to him, "it is not his turn by a great deal. I would sooner appoint Gates, or Lincoln, or Morgan." (When Pickering observed that Morgan had a "broken constitution," that Gates was an "old woman," and that Lincoln was "always asleep," Adams abruptly ended the conversation.) When McHenry arrived back from Mount Vernon on July 17 with Washington's list, Adams protested that he did not think Hamilton deserved to rank so high, or that Pinckney should be ranked over Knox. He continued to fidget the next day as he prepared to make out the nominations. He finally sent them in, with the names in the order Washington had listed them, upon McHenry's asserting "that any of the parties, if dissatisfied with the order of arrangement, might have their claim discussed and settled by a board of officers or the commander-in-chief." He left for Quincy on July 25.[68]

But Adams had gone off without signing any of the commissions, which meant that as long as they remained undated the relative ranks were still not finally settled. Pickering and the others, however, assumed by now that they had been, more or less, and so apparently did Washington. At the same time, everyone knew that Washington did not intend to take any more active part than he could help in getting the new army ready, so that the point of who should be second in command was vital. But Adams when he left was nursing a determination that it should not be Hamilton, and that he should appoint Knox in his place.[69]

The cabinet — and Washington himself, though not yet aware of Adams's obstinacy — had already determined otherwise. Washington replied to Knox's lamentations by telling him kindly but firmly that although he greatly hoped to have both his and Hamilton's services, "Colo. Hamilton was designated Second in command and first if I should decline acceptance, by the Federal characters of Congress; whence alone anything like a public sentiment thereto, could be deduced." He was passing the buck somewhat, but all the evidence being presented to him was confirming what he wanted to believe: that there would be no reasonable obstacles to his having Hamilton as his principal subordinate.[70]

The Hamiltonians hoped that they could get the matter finally closed by giving Adams, through McHenry, one more nudge by mail. Might not the Secretary of War call Hamilton and Knox into service at once? (With the commissions not yet made out, this would force Adams's hand.) But Adams, reversing the logic, replied that such a step would "be attended with difficulty, unless the rank were settled." He declared that in his opinion "General Knox is legally entitled to rank next to General Washington; and no other arrangement will give satisfaction." He added that Pinckney too "must rank before Hamilton." If Knox were made subordinate to either of them, the New England states would "not patiently submit to the humiliation that has been meditated for them." A further prod from McHenry, containing a reminder of the order in which the nominations had been submitted and confirmed, brought an explosion of wrath. (His nerves were on edge already over the state of Abigail's health, which was quite dangerous.) He wrote McHenry angrily that the order of the nominations was of no consequence, that it did not settle the question of rank, and that "officers appointed on the same day, in whatever order, have a right to rank according to antecedent services." He insisted on the Executive's authority, and asserted that however the persons concerned might agree or disagree among themselves the matter would eventually come back to him, "and I shall then determine it exactly as I should now;—Knox, Pinckney, and Hamilton." Besides, he added menacingly, "There has been too much intrigue in this business with General Washington and me. . . ."[71]

Asserting executive authority in these particular circumstances, however, was not so simple. McHenry agreed to make out the commissions as Adams instructed, but protested in hurt tones that he had not taken part in any intrigues, and that "should you not be convinced, I can immediately retire from a situation which demands a perfect and mutual confidence between the President and the person filling it." Adams, assuming he had won the battle, was now in a benevolent frame of mind. There, there, he said in effect; "the question being now settled, the responsibility for which I take upon myself, I have no hard thoughts concerning your conduct in this business, and I hope you will make your mind easy concerning it."[72]

But the question was *not* settled. Hamilton had let it be known he would not serve at all under those terms; Knox would not accept service if outranked by either Hamilton or Pinckney; Washington would shortly intimate that he would resign if the bickering went on much longer; McHenry had offered to resign; Adams himself had hinted at resigning. To stem (selectively) this threatened flood of resignations, the cabinet in a frenzy of exertion went to work. The great effort would be to rouse up Washington and bring Adams to reason.[73]

Oliver Wolcott, up to now the one least obviously involved in the "intrigues" Adams complained of, was delegated to make the case. He did so in a letter of September 17 bearing all the marks, in the way of research and consultation, of a state paper. Wolcott began with a precise outline of the events that had led Washington to propose the nominations of Hamilton, Pinckney, and Knox, and the Senate to confirm them, all in the expectation that Hamilton would be the second in command. He further pointed out that the only reservations intimated by Washington concerned Pinckney and not Knox, whatever his feelings of personal friendship for Knox might be. Knox based his own claims on his rank in the Revolution, but no rule made by the Continental Congress was then discoverable that could possibly apply to the current situation. Wolcott further stated that once Washington had consented to serve, it was "to be expected by all dispassionate men, that his reasonable wishes should be consulted." As for the idea that New England would insist on Knox, the President could be assured "that Gen. Knox has no popular character, even in Massachusetts; that in the other states his influence is a mere nullity." (This, together with Washington's view that Knox was simply not up to it, would be a hard point to get around.) And finally, if the President should try to be consistent and follow the precedents of the old army in all cases, he would find it "utterly impossible to make a distribution of the officers according to their real merits."[74]

Adams at last was trapped, and he knew it. He prepared one last thunderbolt of independent defiance. He was not persuaded that Washington had been initially committed to Hamilton, and as for himself:

> If I should consent to the appointment of Hamilton as second in rank, I should consider it as the most responsible action of my whole life, and the most difficult to justify. Hamilton is not a native of the United States, but a foreigner, and, I believe, has not resided longer, at least not much longer, in North America, than Albert Gallatin. His rank in the late army was comparatively very low. His merits with a party are the merits of John Calvin, —
>
> > "Some think on Calvin heaven's own spirit fell,
> > While others deem him instrument of hell."
>
> I know that Knox has no popular character, even in Massachusetts. I know, too, that Hamilton has no popular character in any part of America.

But this was all expostulation; it may be doubted whether Adams ever intended to send such a letter. At any rate he kept it, and simply wrote to McHenry on September 30: "Inclosed are the Commissions for the three Generals Signed and all dated on the Same Day."[75]

Many historians, beginning with Charles Francis Adams, have wanted to believe that Washington was not primarily responsible for Adams's humiliation, and have ascribed it instead to the plotting of Adams's cabinet. This may be literally true, but only literally. Just about everyone ganged up on Adams, Washington among them, and had it not been for Washington's influence—direct, indirect, and hanging in the very air—the order of the Major-Generals, and probably even their names, would have been quite different. After receiving a full account of McHenry's exchanges with Adams, Washington addressed a magisterial letter to the President which arrived at Quincy on October 8. He reminded Adams that his own appointment as commander had been made without his being given the opportunity beforehand either to accept or to state the conditions of his acceptance, that he had had to do all this afterward, but that he had done it and had supposed there to be no further ambiguity about his wishes. And now, he concluded with Olympian restraint, he requested "to be informed whether your determination to reverse the order of the three Major Generals is final. . . ."[76] Adams had already made up his mind two weeks before to swallow the dose, and had in effect done so with his returning of the commissions. So he could salvage what dignity remained to him by replying stiffly that he supposed Washington had already been informed about the commissions, and that any further controversies "will, of course, be submitted to you . . . and if, after all, any one should be so obstinate as to appeal to me, from the judgment of the Commander-in-chief, I was determined to confirm that judgment."[77] The President of the United States had been outmaneuvered; he had been obliged to give way before superior moral authority; and he would not soon forget it.

Alexander Hamilton now had his army. On the merits of the case he was probably entitled to it, since if an army were going to be organized there was little question of Hamilton's being better qualified than anyone else to do it. Little question, that is, except perhaps the basic one of whether such an army was necessary in the first place, and of what if anything it might be used for. Hamilton would go about his work of organizing the army without any overt interference from the President, but without a particle of assistance either. When McHenry in mid-October ventured to hope that the President might return to Philadelphia so things could move faster, Adams snapped back that because of his wife's health he could not think of it. He added ominously that regiments were "costly articles everywhere, and more so in this Country than any other under the sun." To what purpose? "At present there is no more prospect of seeing a French army here, than there is in Heaven."[78]

Adams's humiliation—the drastic curtailment of his independence of action on the military question—may be seen as a distinct turning point in the state of his overall views and intentions. It corresponds exactly—almost too exactly—with an emerging inclination on his part to consider new directions in policy toward France. Back in June, he had declared emphatically in a message to Congress: "I will never send another minister to France, without assurances that he will be received, respected, and honored as the representative of a great, free, powerful, and independent nation."[79] But things had happened to Adams in the meantime at the hands of his presumed subordinates and supporters, and now—say by early October—his mind was somewhat differently inclined. He was disposed to receive evidence, scanty though it might seem, that France had experienced a change of heart toward the United States.

But by the same token, most leading Federalists were no longer in a condition to think with much flexibility on this question. They had just made commitments which they would have had to abandon if peace were to be made with France. Or rather—to do them more justice—they had become convinced that a stable peace under current circumstances was simply not possible. There was certainly ground for such a view. Why should the French not continue to toy with the Americans in any further diplomatic moves that might be made on either side, just as they had persistently done for the past two years or more, treating us with ever more intricate forms of contempt while they went right on with their depredations—until and unless a stern show of force and determination should at last bring them to reason? These Federalists sensed that they could not have both their army and a new mission to France: either one in effect ruled out the other. And being now fully committed to the army, they could not be other than hostile to information that might require them to change their minds. Besides, it would become ever clearer that the President, who obviously was not so committed, was emerging as their greatest worry. Consequently every probe Adams made toward a change of policy in the coming months was resisted by the cabinet in every way possible, and when in the face of this Adams eventually reached the point of naming a new minister to France in February 1799, the entire Federalist phalanx would be thrown into consternation and fury.

The case of Elbridge Gerry is one instance of how these contrary tendencies had begun to work. Gerry arrived home from France on October 1, 1798, to be met with widespread ostracism by the Federalists of Boston. Nevertheless when Gerry rode out to Quincy on October 4 to call on the President and report on his doings in Paris—this was just four days after Adams had written his note of surrender to McHenry on the matter of Hamilton's commission—he found the President disposed to listen with interest to his version of the dealings he had had with Talleyrand after the departure of Marshall and Pinckney.[80] Whether Adams would have been so receptive a few weeks earlier is doubtful.

The first news that Gerry had divided the commission and was remaining in Paris had arrived at the beginning of June, and Adams was as angry as anyone when he heard it. This in fact was part of the reason for his outburst about not sending another minister. "The President is distresst beyond measure, but will not utter a word *as yet,*" wrote Abigail Adams to her cousin on June 4. "That vile intriguer Talleyrand I fear has entraped him whom I should have supposed the most wary—like the serpent he has charmed him, and like him, he will destroy his prey." The crowing of Bache in the *Aurora* must have tried Adams's self-restraint exceedingly. Bache took the line that it was Adams's provocations that had caused the crisis in the first place, that "our warlike President" had not wanted to negotiate anyway, that the envoys should have agreed to France's demands for money, and that Gerry, a "prophet of peace," had now sat down to "count the cost of war, and the result of his prudent calculation is, that we had better indemnify France for the losses occasioned by the British treaty, than fight her now and pay her hereafter."[81]

But if Adams fumed to himself (and to his wife) over Gerry's doings, Secretary Pickering shook with rage. Pickering believed what all other Federalists believed about the mischievous consequences of Gerry's remaining, only more so. Dispatches from William Vans Murray, the American minister in Holland, confirmed for him what he had already heard from Rufus King in London, that Gerry "with unpardonable arrogance and folly had determined to take upon himself the whole responsibility of the Mission agreeable to the *designation* of the *Executive Directory!*" Anyone could see that it was a move on France's part to immobilize us. There was not only the insult of the French government's presuming to decide for America which of her commissioners it would deal with and which ones would be sent away; Gerry's remaining would also discredit the work of Pinckney and Marshall, it would create new divisions in American public opinion (as in fact it did), and it would allow the French to go on with their procrastinations and deceptions while continuing their piracies on American commerce. Pickering, upon receipt of the commissioners' first dispatches in March, had already sent off a letter of recall to the three of them. He now sent Gerry another at the President's direction, in case he had not yet received and acted on the previous one. Another eleven weeks went by, at the end of which time he heard that Gerry was still in Paris. "Waiting the ultimatum of the French Government!!! Contemptible animal!"[82]

Actually Pickering for all his extravagant choler was but one among many. The American diplomatic representatives in Europe all seem to have thrown up their hands as soon as they heard what Gerry had done. "The extreme anger even to sickness into which this threw me may have darkened my vision," wrote Murray from The Hague, "but I see nothing but improper things in G's determination to separate and assume to himself in this way, and nothing but infernal consequences in America." According to King in London, "If we are the dupes of this repeated and bare-faced effort to deceive and divide us, we must shut our eyes to the fate of Switzerland and of the other victims of the pretended friendship of the great Nation. It must be the subject of perpetual regret that Mr. Gerry suffered himself to be separated from his Colleagues. . . ." John Quincy Adams in Berlin thought that the French in executing this maneuver had exactly achieved what suited them:

> 1st. They are now sure of having a man to deal with who dreads a rupture more than dishonor, disgrace, and vile indignity. 2dly. They have ascertained that they can drive him to any terms by threatening a rupture as the alternative. 3rdly. They know they can amuse him and keep him at bay as long as they think proper, and turn him off just when they please. 4thly. They have acquired too strong reasons to hope that they can make him consent to conditions of settlement which they know will not be ratified at home, but which will serve to foment the divisions upon which they rest their expectations, and to give *them* the appearance of being the injured party.[83]

John Adams of course was fully acquainted with all these views, and had in fact shared them. But by fall things looked different, certainly to him, and Gerry's story was at least worth listening to, especially now that he could hear it all from Gerry in person. Gerry had not remained behind willingly. He had stayed only because at that period he had thought it was the only way a complete rupture between France and America could be avoided. He had not assumed to himself any plenipotentiary powers. He had in fact continued to insist that he possessed no such powers and could go no farther than to hold informal conversations and be the informal carrier to his government of any propositions the Foreign Minister might informally make to him. When Pickering's first letter of recall reached him on May 12, he had replied that he would leave immediately, and he told Talleyrand the same thing, subject only to such delay as would be necessary to hear France's latest proposals. Talleyrand, however, insisted that Gerry surely did have plenipotentiary powers, and the French government, now that it had a friendly American representative to deal with, was ready to open negotiations. So why not begin? "Did you not come here, sir, to establish friendship between the two republics, and determined to spare nothing to attain this end, as desirable to the United States as to France? Do not the full powers given to the envoys authorize them to negotiate separately? . . . Ought you to [withdraw] when the French Government, superior to all resentments, and never listening to any thing but justice, manifests itself anxious to conclude a solid and mutually satisfactory agreement?"[84]

But Gerry would not budge, and the more obstinate he was in demanding his passports—repeating that if a basis for peace truly existed France might send a minister to the United States and conclude an agreement there—the more Talleyrand persisted in trying to keep him in Paris. And indeed it did appear that France's attitude was different; there did seem to be an urgency in Talleyrand's solicitations that was not there before. He kept promising changes in French maritime policy, and by July he was assuring Gerry that neither a loan to the Directory nor an explanation of Adams's speech would be required. All talk of a bribe had long since ceased. When the douceur story became public in May, Talleyrand piously denied having had anything to do with it, and made a show of demanding from Gerry the identities of the agents who had broached it. Gerry after some hesitation helped him out of his scrape by going through the motions and supplying the names of X, Y, and Z, even while he knew, and Talleyrand knew that he knew, that these agents were hardly imposters and that Talleyrand was as well aware as himself who they were. At length Talleyrand, abandoning his efforts to persuade Gerry to negotiate, granted him his passports. Gerry embarked on August 8, almost three months after he knew he had been ordered home.[85]

During the month of October while sojourning at Quincy, Adams, in addition to having some long talks with Gerry, received indications from two other sources that something new was afoot in France regarding American affairs. One such source was William Vans Murray, who described how he had been visited several times by Louis Pichon, a member of the French diplomatic corps at The Hague, assuring him that Talleyrand "was solicitous for accommodation." (Talleyrand, getting nowhere with Gerry, had clearly put Pichon up to this.) Murray thought the French were now "deeply alarmed," and that America's "energetic measures" had "stunned them." The other was Richard Codman, a Boston merchant living in Paris, who wrote insisting that the French "really appear anxious to convince America of their desire to redress her grievances" and that the moment was "extremely favourable for an accommodation."[86]

There were of course reasonable grounds for skepticism regarding any of these communications. Gerry's behavior, especially in the matter of the XYZ names, could be seen as something short of heroic, and Talleyrand's correspondence with him, some of which had already got into the newspapers, had done little to dispel the impression of the Foreign Minister as a sly trickster with anyone's guess as to what was up his brocaded sleeve. Murray in his letters had taken up far more space protesting his own determination not to be taken in than in expressing anything optimistic about the approaches now being made to him. The "motive . . . I believe to be merely to divide and bewilder, and to relax our energy. . . ."[87] All past performance clearly warned against anything but watchful pessimism. As for Codman, this man was a member of an American coterie in Paris that might best be described, with no injustice, as a gang of hustlers. There were upwards of two hundred of them there, drawn by the scent of speculative opportunities and the quick profits open to citizens of a nation officially both friendly and neutral, of which the United States was about the only one left. Many had acquired petty connections with insiders in the French government. They dealt in confiscated estates, confiscated furniture, and looted works of art; they imported foodstuffs at high markups, bought up for a pittance the claims of shippers victimized in the West Indies trade, and sold remote lands in America to credulous Frenchmen. For the most part they lived in very high style. And of course any threat of a rupture between the two countries made them turn pale with terror: a more ardent vested interest in not rocking this particular boat would be hard to envision. Before long, increasing numbers of this same group would be heard from.[88]

True enough, then, that the French scene was full of ambiguities, and any responsible American observing it did well, in view of past experience, to distrust anything he saw or heard there. The Federalists, in short, did have a case — up to a point. But beyond that point, where, if anywhere, were the cues to action, if any, to come from? Things were certainly in some kind of flux, and the Federalist imagination, having to a fair degree bound and shackled itself, was itself no longer quite to be trusted. The Republicans were in no better condition. They too had their commitments and were shackled by them; from the very first a full grasp of the picture had been largely beyond them. Nor had John Adams's own judgment been consistently dependable either. Still, what was happening to it now would be critical. A warlike atmosphere had been indispensable for animating public opinion, in order to present a determined face to the world and to produce any likelihood that America might in the smallest way affect the affairs of Europe. Adams had taken a leading part in creating this atmosphere, but events seemed now to have slipped from his control. Things had gone wrong; he was looking for a way out; and it had probably dawned on him by now that he could expect little assistance in finding it. The result seems to have been a curious kind of release. From here on, behavior that to the Federalists would be maddeningly erratic would be for Adams simply the Executive holding the scales and acting in his independent capacity.

There now seemed to be a kind of perverse detachment in Adams's relations with just about everyone. An important instance of this came with the question of what he should say in his annual message to Congress in December, especially regarding relations with France, a matter he had already begun to think about at the time of his talks with Gerry at Quincy. He addressed a short note to each of the cabinet on October 10 soliciting general suggestions, then a longer one to Pickering on October 20 containing certain more pointed questions which Pickering should discuss with his colleagues. One was whether it would be "expedient for the President to recommend to the consideration of Congress a declaration of war against France." Another, the really critical one, was "whether, in the speech, the President may not say, that in order to keep open the channels of negotiation, it is his intention to nominate a minister to the French republic, who may be ready to embark for France, as soon as he, or the President, shall receive from the

Directory satisfactory assurances that he shall be received and entitled to all the prerogatives and privileges of the general law of nations, and that a minister of equal rank and powers shall be appointed and commissioned to treat with him." Adams even mentioned the names of several possible candidates. And finally, he wondered whether Gerry's full correspondence might not be laid before Congress.[89] So it was not as though the cabinet had no clues, early on, to the direction in which Adams's mind was tending. Thus began another sequence of evasion, maneuver, and resistance that culminated in the speech itself and what Adams actually said.

They replied both as individuals and—in a long letter composed by Wolcott but evidently the result of concerted discussion—in a joint effort to speak with one voice. Lee and Stoddert, the two most moderate, largely confined themselves in their separate replies to questions concerning their own departments, though neither placed much faith in peaceful professions from France. McHenry, in his, was now all for "an immediate declaration of war." But he thought that to prevent any blame falling on the Executive it might be better if Congress took the initiative, after the President had furnished materials which would satisfy Congress as to "the necessity & propriety" of it. The President should say that he had seen nothing to persuade him that the French "had concluded on any radical change in their system toward this country," and should repeat his declaration of June 21 "not to send another minister to France, without assurances that he will be received, respected and honoured as the representative of a great powerful and independent nation." Pickering replied twice. A short note on November 5 hurriedly mentioned several items, the most important being relations with France. Gerry's correspondence should be released, "because probably the public will expect it," but it was evident from the context and from a remark in McHenry's letter that Pickering intended to annotate this correspondence himself to prevent any wrong interpretation of it. He avoided a direct answer on a new mission. But on November 27 he wrote at much greater length. He thought not only that the President should hold to his position of June 21 on not sending another minister, but also that the country now stood "on much higher ground" than it had then. "It now appears to me impossible for the United States to originate a third mission to the French Republic without humiliation and dishonor." As for recommending a declaration of war, he thought this "inexpedient" for the same reasons McHenry had given in his letter two days before. Nevertheless, he insisted, in "this middle state between peace and a formal war, our security lies wholly in vigorous preparations for the latter."[90]

Each member of the cabinet had undoubtedly seen what the others had written in response to the President's queries, and there had been a great deal of consultation prior to Adams's arrival in Philadelphia on November 23. There were really no sharp differences among them. But it was Wolcott's letter—longer, more comprehensive, and more deliberately drawn than the others—that most accurately reflected an agreed-upon effort to specify the content and expression of what Adams would say. It has since been assumed, from a remark dropped by Jefferson, that Hamilton had a hand in it too, which may well have been the case, though probably not directly.[91] Wolcott had Adams recalling the "failure of the measures which were taken by this government towards an amicable adjustment of differences" and conceding at the same time that the French government had, "in a qualified manner, declared itself willing to receive a new minister from us for restoring a good understanding." But Wolcott had him further say that he could "perceive nothing in the conduct of the French government which ought to change or relax our measures of defence; on the contrary, to invigorate them is, in my judgment, our true policy." To be sure, we should "give no room to infer that we abandon the desire of peace." But—here was the key phrase—"the sending another minister to make a new attempt at negotiation would be an act of humiliation to which the United States ought not to submit without extreme necessity; no such necessity exists, it must therefore be left with France, if she is desirous of accommodation, to take the requisite steps." He meant that if the French really wanted to negotiate, let them send a minister here. Pickering took the paper and gave it a last-minute polishing, added a preamble, and handed Adams as finished a manuscript as he could have wished for.[92]

When Adams came to deliver his speech on December 8, he actually did say all these things, in exactly the words that had been written for him—with one almost unnoticeable substitution. Sending another minister "without more determinate assurances that he would be received" was the qualification that made all the difference. It was the one point that either he or they cared about, and with it Adams reopened a door that his Secretaries wanted firmly closed. They did notice it, and were filled with displeasure.[93]

Still, what Adams said might not have mattered that much, simply as words, except for the discussions that had preceded it and that must have put them on the alert. Adams had called them together himself directly upon getting back to town, and they had gone over the principal questions. On that of a declaration of war, Adams showed no inclination to recommend one, or even a desire that Congress should do so. He later noted that judging from the look on their faces they seemed to be a bit disappointed. The other matter, which was harped upon a good deal more explicitly than appeared in the message, was the question of a new negotiation. The Pickering-Wolcott-McHenry view, advanced with great persistence, was that if the French were really serious about an accommodation American dignity required that they make the first move, that the negotiations could be carried on at Philadelphia, that another minister should not be sent to France for that purpose, and that the President should say so. Adams seems to have told them emphatically that "he would not commit himself." The Secretaries, he suspected, would not have held out such a condition had they not been fairly sure that the French would not accept it, especially if one of them had to come and deal with such as Timothy Pickering.[94]

So although the entire final draft of the speech, except for those few words, was Pickering's, Pickering and his friends were incensed, while the Republicans in general were agreeably surprised. "The papers will show you," Albert Gallatin wrote to his wife, "the speech of the President more moderate than we expected." But to Pickering it was "a subject of regret that he held out the most distant idea of sending another minister to France." Pickering told George Cabot that *"we wished it to be peremptory, not to send another; and we are unanimously of that opinion, but ———."*[95]

Another item in the speech about which Adams and Pickering had very different notions, though these seem not to have come to the surface until several weeks later, was the question of publishing Gerry's correspondence with Talleyrand. This, Adams had vaguely promised (again using Pickering's words), "would be the subject of a future communication." Adams's intention was simply to release the papers, with the idea that they would speak for themselves and substantially vindicate Gerry's conduct. Pickering's was to accompany them with a report to be written by himself which would discredit Gerry once and for all and expose Talleyrand's peaceable protestations as worthless. The origins of this episode went back to September, before Gerry arrived home and before he had sent Pickering all the correspondence with a long covering explanation of it.

Some of this material—including the exchange over the identities of X, Y, and Z, in which Talleyrand pretended to demand the names and Gerry pretended to supply them—had already appeared in the newspapers, Talleyrand having himself arranged for publication in America. Pickering made some contemptuous references to it in the course of a published reply to a memorial from the citizens of Prince Edward County, Virginia. When Gerry upon his return read Pickering's slurs he complained to Adams, and wrote a long and aggrieved letter to Pickering declaring that the facts had been distorted. He wanted to make this letter public, and Adams, then in Quincy, wrote to Pickering proposing that the latter release it since it would satisfy Gerry and do no harm. Pickering indignantly refused, protesting that if he did so he would also have to reply, and thus expose not only Gerry's "pusillanimity, weakness, and meanness alone, but his *duplicity* and *treachery*." Adams seems to have sensed upon second thought that Gerry would do better to let well enough alone, that a large part of his case—the way he made it—rested on quibbles and hair-splitting, and that if it came to testimony from Pinckney and Marshall that conflicted with Gerry's, Gerry would lose. He intimated as much to Gerry, and advised him to calm down "until you see the communications I shall make to Congress."[96]

It was certainly true that Gerry needed to be protected from himself. Abigail Adams, after receiving a call from Gerry in mid-January at Quincy and listening to his "round about & about manner" of talk, sighed that for a diplomatic representative she would as soon send a "voluable old woman." But although Gerry did stay out of print as Adams advised, at the same time making a great point in conversation of supporting the administration and its preparedness program, Secretary Pickering did not intend to let well enough alone. Adams, in order to carry out his version of the promise given in his speech to make the Gerry-Talleyrand correspondence public, sent his private secretary to Pickering's office several times during a period of about a month to get the papers, and was put off each time by excuses that they were needed for the report Pickering was preparing. (This was Pickering's version of the promise.) But with public opinion growing more and more impatient, Adams at last demanded the papers without delay, saying that he needed no such report and did not think Congress did either. Pickering, his report now almost ready, thereupon turned them over. Adams sent them to Congress on January 18, and the next day Pickering showed him his report. Adams only allowed it to go in after striking out whole passages, those especially derogatory to Gerry, despite Pickering's anguished entreaties to leave them in. How much difference the deletions made cannot of course be known, though Pickering thought they made a great deal, since he sent copies of them to all his friends, and would still be angry enough twenty-five years later to publish them himself.[97] What the episode did do was to make all but overt the growing tussle of cross-purposes between the President and the Secretary of State.

This period of ebbing peace, or of intramural cold warfare, was to last about a month more before Adams resolved at length to act: an event comparable to the arrival of the XYZ dispatches a year previously in marking the sharpest kind of turning point in the progress of his administration. But why was this decision— to appoint a new mission to France—made precisely when it was? The common-sense inference has generally been that the primary operative factor was a steady build-up of evidence that the French were at last prepared to negotiate in good faith, evidence that could no longer be ignored. There is a good case for charting Adams's movements with primary reference to this. But it was not quite the only factor.

The accumulating information was by no means all private and secret; a great deal of it was in fact generally known. A considerable portion, of course, was contained in the correspondence relating to Gerry's activities and in Gerry's own account of them, all of which became fully public in mid-January. These papers were sufficiently circumstantial that Pickering and his friends thought it of the utmost importance to see that they should be read in the proper way. Another channel was the American colony in Paris. A variety of reports and rumors from that source had been circulating for some time, especially in opposition newspapers.[98] Dr. George Logan, a leisured Quaker gentleman of Philadelphia, had gone to Paris the previous summer on a private peace mission of his own. Though he was at first mistaken for Logan, the Indian chief made famous in Jefferson's *Notes on Virginia,* he talked to persons highly placed in the French government, was toasted in Paris newspapers for his pacific sentiments ("le brave Logan"), and returned home in November convinced by what he had been told that the French were fully prepared to receive a new minister from America. Pickering gave him the cold shoulder, but Adams, when Logan came to call, at least received him civilly and listened to what he had to say. Logan also talked freely at public meetings, and the newspapers were full of his movements and opinions. Despite widespread criticism, and a law passed in Congress to prevent future unauthorized missions of this sort, the people of Logan's district promptly elected him to the state assembly by a large majority.[99]

And finally, Adams was given the most persuasive account of France's dispositions he had received thus far when his youngest son, Thomas Boylston

Adams, returned home in January 1799. Thomas had been serving at Berlin as the secretary of legation with his brother, John Quincy, the American minister there, and both brothers had been in close touch with William Vans Murray, who since the previous July had been the recipient of the overtures made by Talleyrand through Louis Pichon at The Hague. The President, overcome with emotion, welcomed his son on the evening of January 15. Thomas brought letters, dispatches, and all the latest news, and the two had some long talks in the days and evenings that followed. Thomas told his father how both Murray and John Quincy had changed their minds about the French advances; both were now persuaded that they were serious and ought to be responded to in some way—perhaps, as John Quincy Adams had suggested, with the opening of negotiations between Murray and a French representative in Holland.[100]

Was this the precipitant for the President's action? It was undoubtedly important. Yet Adams did nothing for another five weeks, and there was still, after all, a good case for not grasping the olive branch too eagerly and allowing the national will to relax itself too far. There *was* something else, and that something was Hamilton's army. The very idea of it had become a monster. The monster grew ever bigger during the months of December and January, and by early February Adams had had enough.

The invasion scare of the summer had dwindled as the weeks went by, and it seemed less imminent than ever when the news came in late November that the French fleet had been destroyed by Nelson on August 1 in the Battle of the Nile. Adams in October had already begun to mutter surly things to McHenry about what the army would cost, and to predict rising trouble if the nation should see "a great army to maintain, without an enemy to fight." The trouble was already apparent in November when Adams left Quincy for Philadelphia. He and his secretary William Shaw were met all across Massachusetts with the strongest expressions of resentment over the land tax that was being raised to finance military preparations. (Shaw even thought that if Elbridge Gerry had wanted to run for governor he could now have won easily.)[101] Nor was this the only evidence of discontent that had begun to emerge. The subsequently famous resolutions of protest by the legislatures of Virginia and Kentucky against the Alien and Sedition Acts became public knowledge in December.[102] In January and February petitions bearing thousands of signatures began coming in to Congress from everywhere, protesting against the whole Federalist program—Alien and Sedition Laws, the new taxes, and the military measures. Virtually every one of them included the tag-word "standing army."[103]

It was in this setting, then, that John Adams sullenly watched while the promoters of the new army pressed on with their plans. The hand of Hamilton was directly and indirectly discernible in every move they made. Though conceding that an invasion might now have become "less probable, or more remote,"[104] they would not hear of slowing down the effort or reducing the force. Quite the contrary. They wanted the recruitment of men and the appointment of officers to go forward with all possible speed. They wanted new legislation that would thoroughly reorganize, and in fact somewhat increase, the old regular army and with it the additional force of regulars that had been authorized by the law of July 16 to augment it. The authority to raise a provisional army had by this time expired. They wanted it revived in a form that would allow the raising of thirty thousand men, three times the previous number. These points were all embodied in a report submitted to the President by the Secretary of War on December 24. Adams sent it to the House of Representatives a week later without comment — at least not in writing. The report had been based on three lengthy memoranda, ostensibly from Washington but in fact all drafted by Hamilton. When bills for the desired legislation were introduced late in January, they too would be drafted by Hamilton. Moreover, although the New Army was by law to remain in being only for the duration of the current emergency, the precision of detail and the extraordinary amount of time and attention being devoted to the regulations for it gave every appearance of being the groundwork for a permanent army.[105]

Among those playing critical roles at the legislative end of military policy were James Gunn of Georgia, the chairman of the Senate's special committee on defense; Harrison Gray Otis, chairman of a similar committee of the House; and Senator Theodore Sedgwick of Massachusetts, one of the men most actively concerned in military affairs. During the period between late December and early February each of these men received letters from Alexander Hamilton containing detailed cues on the spirit in which, in Hamilton's view, they ought to proceed with their work.[106] These letters were shown around, and there is evidence that at least one of them came to the attention of John Adams. In addition to matters which Hamilton hoped to see embraced in the forthcoming legislation, they opened the prospect of other uses which might be contemplated for the new army besides simply preparing it as an instrument of defense. One was the possibility of a movement into Louisiana and Florida to prevent any design by France of taking possession of those provinces. Another would be to "detach South America from Spain which is only the Channel, through which the riches of *Mexico* and *Peru* are conveyed to France." A further thought was that if negotiations between the United States and France had not begun by August 1, 1799, the President should be empowered to declare war. And finally, the army should stand as a warning against insurrectionary tendencies in the United States itself, with particular reference to Virginia.[107] Any one of these letters could have made John Adams exclaim, as he later said he had done when he was shown it,

"this man is stark mad or I am." He knows nothing of the character the principles the feelings the opinions & prejudices of this nation. If congress should adopt this system it would produce an instantaneous insurrection of the whole nation from Georgia to New Hampshire.[108]

The last straw came on the evening of February 6, 1799, when Theodore Sedgwick called upon Adams to discuss military affairs. Sedgwick mentioned what he thought were dangerous signs in Virginia. "As to the Virginians, sir," Adams burst forth, "it is weakness to apprehend any thing from them, but if you must have an army I will give it to you, but remember it will make the government more unpopular than all their other acts. They have submitted with more patience than any people ever did to the burden of taxes ... *liberally laid on,* but their patience will not last always." There was a second explosion when Sedgwick mentioned that among the matters being considered in the reorganization bill then before the Senate was giving Washington the new title of "General," a military rank never previously conferred in America.

> "What," said he "are you going to appoint him general over the President?" "I have not been so blind but I have seen a combined effort, among those who call themselves the friends of government to annihilate the essential powers given by the president. This sir" (raising his voice) "my understanding has perceived and my heart felt."[109]

Who might inherit such an exalted title after Washington was gone? Not long thereafter, Adams told Elbridge Gerry with great intensity "that he thought Hamilton and a Party were endeavoring to get an army on foot to give Hamilton the command of it & then to proclaim a Regal Government, place Hamilton at the Head of it & prepare the way for a Province of Great Britain."[110]

Clearly Adams was all primed to move, and he had determined not to consult anyone beforehand. He knew what they would say; he knew they had a variety of resources for thwarting his intentions. They might actually persuade him to change his mind, and he did not want to be so persuaded.

There were still a few obstacles to what he intended to do, each of which was to his satisfaction removed during the first two weeks of February 1799. How explicit an assurance did he have, when all was said and done, that France's past treatment of American representatives would not be repeated—that not only would a new minister be received but that the French government would not presume, as it had in the case of Gerry, to dictate who he might be? But now here it was, in a dispatch newly received from Murray. It enclosed a letter from Talleyrand to Pichon, echoing in Adams's own words the proviso laid down in his message of June 21 and declaring that "*whatever* plenipotentiary the Government of the United States might send to France, to put an end to the existing differences between the two countries, would be undoubtedly *received with the respect due to the representative of a free, independent, and powerful nation.*" Pichon was ordered to "carry ... to Mr. Murray those positive expressions, in order to convince him of our sincerity, and prevail upon him to transmit them to his Government."[111] Further news arrived that the barbarous decree of October 29, 1798, threatening to treat as a pirate any American serving aboard a British ship, even if impressed, had been rescinded.[112]

And finally, there was the vexing riddle of Washington himself, the impassive facade behind which all Hamilton's plans for the army had been sanctioned and promoted. How would the patriarch respond to a sudden change of policy toward France? Providentially that question too was settled, at least for Adams's purposes, by a communication from the General with which was forwarded a letter from Joel Barlow, another of the American colony in Paris. Barlow was emphatic that "the French Directory is at present sincerely desirous of restoring harmony between this country and the United States, on terms honorable and advantageous to both parties," and he beseeched Washington's influence "in favor of a new attempt at negotiation before you draw your sword." He would be glad to reply, Washington wrote, if Adams should instruct him,

> . . . more especially if there is reason to believe that it would become a mean, however small, of restoring Peace and Tranquillity to the United States upon just, honorable and dignified terms: which I am persuaded is the ardent desire of all the friends of this rising Empire.[113]

Adams was not especially polite in his reply. Barlow's story was nothing new; it was one he had heard a dozen times already. Barlow himself was a "worthless fellow." Adams did not mention Washington's offer to answer the letter; he did not even thank him for sending it.[114] The main thing was that if Adams were now disposed to act, he would get no opposition from Mount Vernon. And he was most certainly aware that what he was about to do—besides, to be sure, opening the door to peace—would deal as mortal a stroke to Hamilton's army as any act he could think of.

On February 18, 1799, Adams's message was read to a gaping Congress. "Always disposed and ready to embrace every plausible appearance of probability of preserving or restoring tranquillity, I nominate William Vans Murray, our minister at the Hague, to be minister plenipotentiary of the United States to the French republic."[115]

2

February–October, 1799: Adams Temporizes

It was eight months between the time Adams so precipitately announced his appointment of a new mission to the French Republic and his issuing of final orders for the mission—by then enlarged from one member to three—to depart. Nobody has yet found a fully satisfactory explanation of why it took so long. There were certainly plausible grounds, at any of several junctures between February and October, for delaying the mission, or for not being in any great hurry about dispatching it. But whether they all quite add up, or why Adams should then have moved with as much impulsiveness at the end of this protracted interlude as he had at the beginning of it, are questions still full of riddles.

The word for everyone's reaction to the announcement of February 18, first voiced by Timothy Pickering and repeated by historians ever since, was "thunderstruck." "Yesterday," Pickering wrote to Rufus King on the 19th, "we were all thunderstruck by the President's nominating Mr. Murray Minister Plenipotentiary to the French Republic! We were of course all ignorant that the President had any such intention." The nomination, he told Washington two days later, was "solely the President's act and we were all thunderstruck when we heard of it." On the same day, the British minister Robert Liston informed Lord Grenville that "the federal party were thunderstruck with this step. . . . It was taken by Mr. Adams without the advice, indeed without the knowledge of the Secretary of State or the other members of the Administration, and without consultation with any of his own political friends." There was a similar response in Boston, the news having "electrified the public." It had been "so unexpected," Abigail Adams reported from Quincy, "that the whole community were like a flock of frightened pigions; nobody had their story ready; some called it a hasty measure; others condemned it as an inconsistent one; some swore, some curs'd. . . ." "Surprise, indignation, grief & disgust," according to George Cabot, "followed each other in quick succession in the breasts of the true friends of our country," and Theodore Sedgwick thought that "had the foulest heart & the ablest head in the world, been permitted to select the most embarrassing and ruinous measure, perhaps, it would have been precisely the one which has been adopted." It was another of "the misfortunes to which we are subjected by the wild & irregular starts of a vain, jealous, and half frantic mind." At the same time, Pickering was certain that the President was already "suffering the pains of purgatory" and the "torments of the damned" over what he had done, which may well have been true. Adams seldom did anything important without experiencing acute psychic consequences.[116]

In any case he soon amended his decision somewhat, though not without a few more "wild & irregular starts." A Senate committee headed by Sedgwick which had been appointed to consider the nomination called on the President on the evening of February 23. The Federalists would have liked to kill the entire mission out of hand, but had decided that their best strategy was to question the capacity and personal authority of Murray to manage it by himself, and to propose that two others be nominated to join him in a three-member commission. Adams in several outbursts of passion told the committee members that they were interfering in diplomatic affairs and in his own performance of his executive duties, that "there was a party who were determined to rule him, but he would disappoint them," that he would not send any such commission, and that although they might reject Murray if they chose, "it is upon your own responsibility." Yet he seems also to have intimated, according to Sedgwick's own account, that if the Senate did refuse to confirm Murray, *then* he might nominate a commission. The matter hung fire for two days, during which time the Federalist senators caucused and determined to reject the Murray nomination. But just as Sedgwick was about to submit his committee's report to this effect, Adams—having changed his mind again—sent another message to the Senate. In it were his nominations to a three-man commission to France: Murray, Chief Justice Oliver Ellsworth, and the venerable Patrick Henry of Virginia. They were confirmed by the Senate on February 27, and the Federalists agreed among themselves that under the circumstances this was the best they could get.[117]

The first of the subsequent delays in sending the mission on its way might be seen as unavoidable. Adams had promised in his message that the two additional commissioners would not embark "until they shall have received from the Executive Directory assurances, signified by their Secretary of Foreign Relations, that they shall be received in character; that they shall enjoy all the prerogatives attached to that character by the law of nations; and that a minister or ministers of equal powers shall be appointed and commissioned to treat with them."[118] But this meant that although such assurances had in effect already been given, they would have to be repeated with regard to the specific persons named; it also meant that although the commissioners might otherwise have proceeded forthwith to join Murray at The Hague and awaited their assurances there, they must now remain where they were for the duration of two ocean voyages—one for the demand and the other for the compliance—until such assurances were received in the United States. Then of course it would take still another voyage to get the ministers to their destination.

The American conditions were transmitted to Talleyrand through Murray, and Talleyrand responded promptly in accepting them. But he could not refrain from protesting that it was "certainly unnecessary to suffer so many months to elapse for the mere confirmation of what I have already declared to Mr. Gerry, and which after his departure I caused to be declared to you at The Hague. I sincerely regret that your colleagues await this answer at such a great distance." For all Murray's and Talleyrand's promptness, these assurances would not reach Philadelphia until July 30, long after the President had departed for Quincy. Meanwhile Patrick Henry had declined his appointment ("advanced age & encreasing debility"), and Adams had named Governor William R. Davie of North Carolina in his place.[119]

Adams's haste to get away from Philadelphia as soon as possible had some bearing on two other matters that required his attention. One was settling the question of what the envoys' instructions should consist of; the other was the tax rebellion that had just broken out in the German-populated counties of Bucks and Northampton north of Philadelphia. The latter affair in particular, and the manner in which Adams allowed it to be handled in his absence, certainly did him no good politically. Indeed, in all likelihood the damage was considerable. As for the instructions, Adams amid the bustle of his preparations to leave received from Pickering a paper he had requested eight weeks before, the draft of a treaty and consular convention with France such as might in Pickering's opinion be acceptable to the United States. Adams thereupon convened his cabinet on March 10, and with this draft as their agenda they quickly agreed upon an outline of the commissioners' instructions. They were stiffer in every way than those given to the Pinckney-Marshall-Gerry commission, notably in their insistence on full indemnities for French spoliations on American commerce. Adams made no difficulties, and after the final touches were added on the morning of the 11th he was off for Quincy the same day. Pickering had the satisfaction of telling Rufus King that he himself was "morally sure" France would never agree to such conditions, "and this has put us all much at our ease." He also reported sardonically: "In the midst of the great Executive business arising out of the late Session, and with an Insurrection begun, the President has left the Seat of Government."[120]

The tax rebellion was only another instance of the forces afoot in the spring of 1799 serving ever more inexorably to dampen what remained of the warlike spirit of 1798, the continuance of which Federalists saw, no doubt correctly, as their main hope of reinforcing a moral authority that was steadily ebbing away.

A direct victim of this diminishing patriotic ardor was the New Army, which persistently failed to heave itself into more than a halfway state of being. An administrative structure adequate for an undertaking of this magnitude did not exist, and the fashioning of one would have required a sense of common purpose and will that was nowhere present. Consequently coordination in matters of supply, recruitment, finance, and supervision was clogged with endless obstructions. The nominal head of the army was at Mount Vernon engaged in the affairs of his plantation. Out of lifetime habits of duty Washington was, as might be expected, continually concerned with the army's progress. Yet practically speaking his role, as understood from the first, was little more than a consultative one, and neither he nor anyone else could quite picture his actually taking the field with it. A further anomaly was the President of the United States at Quincy, betraying in every word and gesture his unconcern with the entire enterprise, if not his outright disapproval of it. At the War Department the well-meaning McHenry, try as he might, was simply not equal to the mass of detail daily engulfing him. Nor did it help, under the hectoring of Hamilton and Washington, that McHenry was made constantly aware of how thin their patience with him was and how little confidence either of them had in his capacities, even though the tasks facing him could probably not have been performed by a man of twice his competence. Even Hamilton, situated as he was in New York, and though laboring with demonic energy as always, found it impossible to keep his hands on everything at once. One unit might have money for bounties but no uniforms; another might have clothing but no money; there was neither an adequate payroll structure nor a supply system. All units suffered from inferior equipment: shoes that would not last through a day's march, weapons that could not be fired safely, and so on. And finally, the men themselves who were to make up the army never materialized. At no time did enlistments reach half the number authorized by Congress. "Had the Organization of the Augmented Corps," Washington wrote in March 1799, "and consequent instructions for raising it, tr[o]d as close on the passage of the Law, as the nature of the case would have permitted, a finer army for the size of it ... the World had never seen: but the golden opportunity is passed, and probably will never occur again. The zeal, enthusiasm, and indeed resentments, which warmed the breasts of the American youth ... is now no more; they are evaporated, and a listlessness has supplied its place."[121]

There was certainly a connection between the leaking away of the zeal needed to sustain the building of the New Army and Adams's projected new mission to France, holding out as this did the possibility of peace, and the baffled Federalists were all too aware of it. Another apparent victim of Adams's new policy was the informal cooperation with Great Britain, touching a number of mutual concerns, which since the year before had grown steadily but was now dropping off quite noticeably. For instance, soon after the publication of the XYZ dispatches the British government, ignoring its own restrictions against the export of military supplies, had provided the United States with a wide variety of items ranging from Indian saltpeter to naval guns for American warships and merchantmen. A number of cannon for harbor defense were even conveyed as an outright gift. American merchant ships were invited to join British convoys when convenient, and they did so in large numbers in all areas frequented by French raiders. The atmosphere of cooperation had become such that Alexander Hamilton, for his part, could entertain agreeable fancies about joint Anglo-American military movements against Louisiana and perhaps even in Latin America.[122]

Nevertheless by the late spring of 1799 this climate had begun to change. For one thing, the commission established by the Jay Treaty for settling the question of the prewar debts, sitting at Philadelphia, was moving toward an angry impasse. For another, there had been a definite upturn in British depredations on American commerce as commanders with a sharp eye for prize money, especially in the Gulf of Mexico, were defining contraband of war to the point of seizing entire cargoes if any portion of them included such items as four-penny nails or cotton cloth that could by any conception be put to warlike uses. How directly these particular developments were connected with Adams's policy regarding France is uncertain; nevertheless Rufus King thought that since the announcement of the Murray appointment he could discern "a coldness toward the U.S., an indifference to their affairs, a disposition to give unfavorable interpretations to their conduct, and in my ordinary intercourse with the Govt. . . . more difficulties than I had before been accustomed to experience."[123]

At any rate Timothy Pickering, under greater and greater strain as things seemed to be going wrong everywhere, at length gave way to a great explosion of impotent rage, vented upon the very man—William Vans Murray—whom Adams had designated to reopen negotiations with France. Murray in one of his dispatches from The Hague had innocently observed that although the President's message nominating the mission "was not expected here," the decision to do it was "considered a wise one," and that having taken firm measures the United States could now afford to meet French advances. This pulled the stopper from all Pickering's pent-up wrath. He replied on July 10 that the message had not been expected in Philadelphia either, and that in fact

> every man whom you knew and respected, every real patriot, every man who had steadily and faithfully supported his and his predecessor's administration was *thunderstruck,* it was *done* without any *consultation with any member of the* government, and for a reason *truly remarkable because he knew we should all be opposed to the measure!* . . . The truth is, that negociation for a treaty with a government so totally unprincipled, so shamelessly perfidious as that of France, would give us no security for peace or of compensation for injuries. . . . There will not be any safe treaty with France until its government (not the tyrants who successively administer it) shall be changed.[124]

This outburst still raises questions. Here was the Secretary of State, visiting his displeasure on a direct subordinate whom his own superior, the President of the United States, had chosen as the agent for his purposes, and denouncing without reserve the entire policy upon which the President's choice had been founded. He of all persons was telling Murray that no "real patriot" approved the mission Murray had been ordered to undertake, nor remotely believed that any agreement with the present government of France was possible. That a clear line of insubordination and disloyalty had marked Pickering's conduct for many months is hardly unknown; it has been noted and discussed by every writer who has touched the subject. But why? Pickering's was only the most extravagant example; the President's three principal cabinet officers, otherwise differing vastly in personality and temperament, were all in their way disloyal. Instead of resigning in disapproval of the President's policies, each had remained to act as accessory to the insubordination and disloyalty of the others. How is their behavior to be explained; what was the setting, what conditions can account for the part they played?

In the case of Timothy Pickering it might seem enough for most purposes to read his conduct here, as well as in both earlier and later phases of his public life, with reference to an exceedingly narrow and self-righteous personality. Few men with whom he was associated were disposed to rate his administrative capacities as being of more than routine quality, and what minimal influence he would later exert as a statesman in the Jeffersonian era can only be seen as destructive. Judging from his correspondence and other writings this was not for want of a certain intelligence; indeed, his mind was in some ways rather a sharp one. Yet he seems to have put it to somewhat specialized and parsimonious uses; it seldom took flight, and could be no more than partially engaged unless he was giving vent to some form of aggression. His was the kind of personality for which single-mindedness was functionally indispensable. Compromise was hateful, and the most logical sanction for anything he thought and did was "principle." Such traits and the "grim determination" they denoted led Henry Cabot Lodge in 1878 to declare that the character of Timothy Pickering could not be appreciated "without a constant recurrence to the marked and peculiar qualities, mental and moral, of the Puritan race from which he sprang and of which he was a type." Perhaps so, though how fair this was to the Puritans may be a nice question. The famous portrait of Pickering by Charles Willson Peale is indeed somewhat Puritan-like. But the one by Gilbert Stuart at the Essex Institute makes him look almost Satanic.[125]

Not unconnected with a pinched mind was being all his life pinched for money. There had been Pickerings in Salem since 1637, and all seem to have done well enough in farming and the acquisition of property. This certainly included Timothy Pickering's father, who acquired a substantial estate in land. But Timothy, born in 1745 the eighth of nine children, seems not to have got a very large share of it, though his father did see to it that he was educated at Harvard, an experience from which Timothy derived little satisfaction, intellectual or otherwise. Deacon Pickering was himself a self-righteous absolutist who affected plain habits, ruled as a tyrant in his own house, and was probably the most disagreeable man in town. (He thought few if any of the clergymen who called at the house "were sufficiently explicit in showing the people their sins.") His son Timothy junior was not very attractive either. He was furtively proud and ambitious; he read law and was admitted to the bar, but for some reason he did not do well at it. He craved standing and influence, which he pursued with a certain intensity; during his twenties he managed to get himself appointed to a number of local offices, though seldom without resistance from people who would have preferred somebody else. This came to be a pattern that would remain with him throughout most of his life. One that developed along with it, in the absence of private wealth, was his dependence on the fees and salaries of office for his livelihood, modest though these always were. This did not prevent him from erupting violently, whenever his private affairs became especially straitened, over the sacrifices he kept making for the public good. He acquired his most valuable and dependable asset at the age of thirty in his marriage to Rebecca White, who brought him no wealth but remained a devoted companion for over fifty years.[126]

Pickering held military as well as civil offices, and by the outbreak of the Revolution he had become colonel of the first regiment of Essex County militia. His zeal for the Revolution was strong, and when his unit was assigned to the main army at Morristown in 1777 Washington was sufficiently impressed with him to offer him a place on his staff as adjutant-general. But Washington's initially favorable impression of Pickering did not last. Pickering served in two other military jobs, a seat on the Board of War and then as quartermaster-general, and Washington's opinion of his abilities sank lower and lower as time went on. He had energy of a sort, but it was not very focused and he may actually have had rather too much of it. He could not bear to delegate authority to others, and he was forever distracted by details and trivia—spying out corruption, denouncing inefficiency, devising reforms—with the result that his supply system came alarmingly close to paralysis. (His predecessor, Nathanael Greene, seems to have understood that a margin of peculation had to be tolerated if the department were to function at all.) At one point Pickering wanted to use military force to impress transport and supplies; Washington, near the end of his patience, would have none of it. It was probably the intervention of Robert Morris in 1781, with his personal credit and influence, that rescued the supply system, making the Yorktown campaign possible and rescuing what remained of Timothy Pickering's frayed reputation.[127]

A return to private pursuits after the war was no more successful. A short venture as a commission merchant came to grief because of a glutted market and because too many others were engaged in the same business. Pickering only avoided bankruptcy through his and his partner's having managed to remain on the government payroll until 1785. They had meanwhile scraped up enough to buy several thousand acres of undeveloped land in backwoods Pennsylvania hoping for speculative profits, and when the lands proved unsalable Pickering tried his hand at farming some of them himself. The struggle exhausted him, financially and in all other ways, and by 1790 he was angling for some kind of appointment in the federal government. He had a few sympathetic supporters who badgered Washington on his behalf, and at length Washington with some reluctance appointed him as a special emissary to the Seneca Indians who were making trouble in the western Susquehanna country.

Indian diplomacy, as it turned out, was the one undertaking of Pickering's life that came close to being an unqualified success. He concluded a treaty with the Senecas that achieved their neutrality in the war that was threatening to break out between the United States and the tribes of the Northwest. He apparently persuaded them that he was one of the few persons in the world who had any true feeling for their interests, and having persuaded himself of the same thing he could pursue his mission with admirable single-mindedness. Forever thereafter he was a strong advocate of fair treatment and Indian rights. His work on this and several subsequent missions was much appreciated by the administration, and in 1791 Washington appointed him Postmaster-General, enabling him and his family to move back to Philadelphia and be again at the center of things. Since the War Department's concerns were at this period primarily with Indian affairs, when Henry Knox resigned as Secretary in 1794 Timothy Pickering now seemed the logical man to replace him—though not before Washington had asked three others first. He had served a little over seven months in that position when in August 1795 the Randolph affair occurred, brought about largely by Pickering's own efforts, and the part Pickering played in it, as we have seen, was character-istically censorious and vindictive. As a result, Washington was obliged to look for a new Secretary of State.

So far the performance of Timothy Pickering as a federal functionary, with minimal public exposure and duties that placed no great premium on political or diplomatic finesse, had been tolerably satisfactory. But the very idea of this glow-ering hack as custodian of the country's foreign relations was at first unthinkable. Though Washington asked Pickering to serve as Secretary of State *ad interim,* he had no intention of leaving him there. But he asked one man after another to take the position and was turned down each time. After the sixth refusal he wearily turned to Pickering. Pickering, who was no admirer of Washington and who could hardly have relished the knowledge of not even being on Washington's short list, made a show of declining, stiffly protesting his lack of competence. The occasion undoubtedly required some form of ceremonial rebuttal by Washington, which was really all Pickering wanted or needed. Actually he had no choice. He could not live without public office, psychologically or financially.

Pickering by now was a doctrinaire Federalist, persuaded that jacobinism lurked in every corner and must be hunted down without stint or mercy. This had not always been the case. He had earlier been a strong partisan of the French Revolution and had thought Louis XVI and Marie Antoinette had got just what they deserved; he was meanwhile possessed, George Hammond believed as late as 1795, of a "most blind and undistinguishing hatred of Great Britain."[128] These sentiments were simply transposed by the popular opposition to the Jay Treaty, which Pickering saw as indispensable to the success of his Indian policy, and by what he saw as the treasonable machinations of Edmund Randolph. His unclut-tered sense of truth and falsehood, of rectitude and wickedness, his trembling hatreds, his contempt for subtlety—except perhaps for a certain instinct for the word that could wound and destroy: these qualities had been there all along. But they emerged in the sight of the whole world with Pickering's accession to the Secretaryship of State. His abusive exchanges, for example, with Pierre Adet in 1796 and 1797—much as Adet may have had it coming—dismayed even his friends.[129] At any rate, by the time John Adams succeeded to the presidency Timothy Pickering had come to see it as altogether natural that his own continuance in office was indispensable to the safety of the United States government. Adams, for several reasons, did not seriously consider replacing Washington's cabinet with appointees of his own. But though Adams would never have admitted it, perhaps deep down he was more than a little intimidated by Timothy Pickering.

Though Pickering lived in good health for more than a quarter-century after the Adams administration departed from office (shortly following his own expulsion from it), his subsequent career amounted to little more than a long and bitter anticlimax. His Federalist friends believed, wrongly as it turned out, that Pickering might serve as a kind of bulwark and rallying point for the remnants of Federalism in New England. Accordingly a number of them subscribed funds for purchasing his still-worthless Pennsylvania lands and resettling him in his native Massachusetts, and they had sufficient influence in the Massachusetts legislature to get him placed in the United States Senate. But though he served two terms there, as an aging crank he did the Federalists little or no good, more often than not embarrassing them with his schemes of secession and his indiscriminate philippics against all the works of Jeffersonianism. There was one final moment, during the War of 1812 with the disaffection of New England at its height, when Timothy Pickering received the highest office to which he was ever chosen by popular vote, the people of Essex sending him to the United States House of Representatives. When the war was over they had little further use for him, and he retired to his farm to meditate for another twelve years over issues which to all but himself (and the Adamses) lay dead and buried. Nevertheless there remained to the end a contingent of those so specially constituted—among them, for example, the youthful William Lloyd Garrison—as to see in Colonel Timothy Pickering the very incarnation, in grand simplicity, of righteousness and principle.[130]

No two men could have been more different, in both appearance and personality, than Pickering and Oliver Wolcott. Pickering was tall, angular, and menacing; the contours of Wolcott, literally and figuratively, were all rounded. Wolcott, fifteen years Pickering's junior, was of medium height and rather on the plump side. Socially Pickering was awkward and austere, Wolcott easy and affable. Pickering's opinions were chronically intemperate and were seldom kept to himself; Wolcott was habitually the soul of discretion. But in other particulars there were certain parallels. Though both came from highly respectable families, neither was ever free from financial pressures. Neither could be said to possess more than superficial cultivation, and there was little that was creative in the mind of either. And for both, the formative stages of their careers were such as to make subsequent satisfactions and fulfillment largely dependent on their being employed in some form of public office.[131]

Oliver Wolcott was born in Litchfield in 1760; his great-grandfather had come to Connecticut in 1636; his grandfather served as governor of the province; his father was a general in the Revolution, signer of the Declaration of Independence, and later governor of the state. Oliver graduated from Yale in 1778 ("a good scholar, though not brilliant," as Noah Webster recalled), and studied law under Tapping Reeve at Litchfield. He was admitted to the bar in 1781, though he seems not to have engaged in any practice to speak of. Moving to Hartford with three dollars in his pocket, he was rescued by a clerkship with the state's Committee of the Pay Table. His service in the Revolution was at best attenuated. Once while he was home from college his militia unit was called out and engaged in a desultory skirmish; for a time he was employed in the quartermaster department looking after army stores at Litchfield; and on one occasion in his father's absence he extended the hospitality of the Wolcott house to General Washington and his aides, including Lieutenant-Colonel Hamilton, who happened to be passing through town.[132] Wolcott's first steps on the highway of adult life were not exactly brilliant ones, but they were patient, steady, and prudent. He was employed in state service all through the Confederation period; diligent discharge of his duties brought him increasing responsibilities, and in 1788 he was appointed to the newly created office of Comptroller of Public Accounts. In 1789 he was encouraged by Jeremiah Wadsworth and Oliver Ellsworth, both of whom probably also put in a word for him, to apply for a place in the United States Treasury. He was offered the post of Auditor; it was something short of what he would have liked, but he took it. Secretary Hamilton was subsequently much impressed with his work, and when the Comptroller died in 1791 Hamilton persuaded Washington to appoint Wolcott in his place.[133]

The men who composed the cabinet with which Washington began his presidency fully met Washington's definition of "first characters," and by the time the last of them had retired and been replaced by others, there was little doubt in anyone's mind—least of all Washington's—that the cabinet had undergone a considerable declension.[134] Ideally a suitable cabinet minister should meet two primary requirements. There should of course be administrative competence, but this tended to be the lesser consideration. More important was the man's public standing and what this brought to the Administration in the way of political weight. It was this element that was so visibly sacrificed in Washington's replacements, and he suffered many agonies as he made them. But it may still be worth noting that when Hamilton retired as Secretary of the Treasury, and when Oliver Wolcott became his successor on February 2, 1795, it was the first instance in which administrative merit was the only criterion, and in which no other candidate was considered.

Wolcott himself was fully aware that being a "first character" constituted no part of his qualifications, and he never expected to become one. When the appointment was still pending he wrote to his father: "Other qualifications than those which respect skill and capacity for the mere business of the Treasury will be desirable, and in these respects a successor to Col. Hamilton will not be found." If it should be offered to him, he continued, he would accept, and would perform its duties "in an orderly and proper manner." But the talent and influence required for persuading the public on matters of broad policy were qualities he did not possess, and in such matters "I shall be understood, if I am appointed, to have no responsibility."[135]

This was Wolcott's way of recognizing that he had arrived at the point where he now stood through scrupulous performance of a routine laid down by others. Hamilton had known him in no other connection than through what he had done under Hamilton's own eye and tutelage; both Hamilton and Washington were fully satisfied with the meticulous way in which he had mastered the administrative details of Hamilton's system. He aspired no further than to maintain it in good repair, and would henceforth write regularly to Hamilton for advice in his efforts to do so.

The logic of subordination was something that sat very easily with Oliver Wolcott, and it caused him few tensions. Conversely, few things disturbed his equanimity more in the early part of his secretaryship than an episode concerning someone under his own authority, Tench Coxe, who appeared quite devoid of any such fine sense. Coxe, the Commissioner of the Revenue, held an excessive view of his own talents, knew better than anyone else how things ought to be done, and followed his own rules and system. Wolcott put up with this for something over two years, whereupon Coxe found himself abruptly unemployed.[136] All of this makes certain aspects of Wolcott's own behavior under the Adams administration—some of which was astonishingly un-Wolcott-like—the more puzzling. One key to that puzzle may be that the system of subordination under which Adams's Secretaries had to function seemed so erratic, so little predictable, as to have no logic at all.

James McHenry, Adams's inherited Secretary of War, was very unwarlike. He was a touchingly affectionate man for whom life's fullest rewards seemed to lie in pleasing those grander than himself. McHenry, unlike Pickering and Wolcott, was not financially dependent on the office he held. But he may as well have been, being dependent on it in most other ways. Membership in the cabinet— the highest public station he would ever occupy—placed him in daily proximity to, and on confidential terms with, the inner circle of Federalist notables, a nourishment peculiarly essential to his being. The orthodoxy of McHenry's own Federalism was a matter that never occasioned any self-doubts. Distinction on his own independent merits was a thing always a step or two beyond him, and one of the many attractive traits of his character was the grace with which he seems to have understood this. Insidership was thus a fully acceptable, and indeed indispensable, functional substitute.[137]

James McHenry was born in 1753 in County Antrim, Ireland, of a family that had done well in trade there. They emigrated to America in 1772, and James's father and brother established a mercantile business in Baltimore that was highly successful. James would in time survive both parents and brother, and would fall heir to all the family property in 1790. He had a reasonably good education, first at a classical academy in Dublin and later at the academy of Newark in Delaware. He wrote verses after hours, none of which he ever got published. (They were actually rather pleasant, except that their rhymes always rang a bit off.)[138] He then went to study medicine under Dr. Benjamin Rush, who proved to be the first of a string of prominent friends he would acquire during his formative years. With the Revolution he volunteered for service in the Continental Army. He served briefly as a surgeon in the military hospital at Cambridge and later at Valley Forge, which seems to have been the first and last time he practiced his profession. There is no evidence that medicine interested him much, or even that he was especially good at it. In 1778 or perhaps earlier he came to the attention of Washington, probably through Rush's influence, and was taken on as Washington's secretary.[139]

If McHenry's life has one great theme, with a test that really should be applied to all he did, or failed to do, in his life, it was his extraordinary capacity for friendship. It does less than justice to James McHenry, who was genuinely liked by just about everyone, to dismiss him as a mere hanger-on. The thing his friends most valued in McHenry was, to be sure, not so much his talents, though these were at least respectable in their way; it was rather his willingness to give them his open-hearted devotion. One might begin with Washington, who became McHenry's hero and remained so forever after. McHenry's gaiety and good cheer made life at headquarters more tolerable for everyone, and certainly helped ease the cares of the great man himself, who could unbend more freely in McHenry's company than in almost any other. His notes and letters to McHenry "are marked," as one writer has observed, "by an affectionate, sometimes even a playful tone."[140] To the bright young men around Washington with whom McHenry associated during this period—Hamilton, Lafayette, Benjamin Tallmadge, they and he all roughly the same age—he gave his loyal friendship, as did they to him, friendships which in each case remained active and undiminished to the end of their lives. Hamilton in particular was both friend and model. Hamilton's superior capacities aroused in him no envy, only admiration. We see him impulsively urging Hamilton, as the war draws to an end, to write him about his plans in life, "that I may endeavor to follow your example."[141] McHenry ended his military service in the rank of major, and seems to have become well enough known in and around Baltimore that the state's electoral council chose him to a seat in the state senate. He remained there until 1786, part of the time doing double duty as a delegate in the Continental Congress, chosen to fill a vacancy. He was also elected as a delegate to the Philadelphia Convention in 1787. Of his legislative activities little has been recorded, though he was apparently busy enough with committee work. At the Convention he took little part in the debates, though he kept a conscientious record of the proceedings and strongly supported the finished document. William Pierce of Georgia wrote of him, "He is a man of Specious talents with nothing of genious to improve them. As a politician there is nothing remarkable in him, nor has he any of the graces of the Orator. He is however, a very respectable young Gentleman. . . ." He went back to the state legislature and remained there for the next seven years. He was still there when the Secretaryship of War fell vacant by reason of Timothy Pickering's becoming Secretary of State in January 1796.[142]

Washington appealed to one man after another to accept the position, in vain. When he finally offered it to McHenry he was quite candid about telling him he had been number four. Hamilton, in going over the possibilities with Washington beforehand, had remarked: "McHenry, you know. He would give no strength to the administration, but would not disgrace the office. His views are good." McHenry accepted happily and, after the customary ritual nonsense about the inner struggle between his private interests and the public good, announced that "the soothing idea of serving under you . . . has effectively and irresistibly silenced all opposition."[143]

There have been some differences among the authorities on the question of James McHenry's competence as Secretary of War. The most recent judgment appears to be that his performance was not as bad as has been claimed, though of course such words if carved in marble would do little to immortalize anyone. In the summer of 1798, with preparations for organizing the New Army no more than begun, Hamilton lamented to Washington that "my friend, McHenry, is wholly insufficient for his place," and that a number of members of Congress held the same view. To which Washington replied, "Your opinion . . . accords with mine, and it is to be regretted, *sorely,* at this time, that these opinions are so well founded. I early discovered, after he entered upon the Duties of his Office, that his talents were unequal to great exertions, or deep resources." Nevertheless Richard Kohn asserts that studying the War Department itself, "rather than listening to the complaints of Federalist leaders," shows McHenry's "personal weaknesses and administrative incompetence" to have been "overrated and overemphasized."[144] Perhaps so; one does feel an urge, after examining all the circumstances, to let McHenry off as lightly as possible. It is at least plausible to picture the War Department at some other period functioning quite smoothly under an administrator of talents no greater than McHenry's. His papers are more than merely workman-like, though we do not know how long it took him to turn them out; they show in their composition an admirable clarity, and one senses behind them an educated and serviceable intelligence. And the point that can hardly be avoided is that no Secretary of War could have been successful under the conditions McHenry was faced with; McHenry or no McHenry, the New Army never had a chance. When John Adams in effect dismissed McHenry in 1800, the primary reason was not incompetence.

After leaving the cabinet, McHenry never again held public office. He had ample means, and in the sixteen years that remained to him he could afford to live the life of a leisured gentleman at his country estate just outside Baltimore. His health had never been especially good, even in his youth, and his activities now were not extensive. Still, he kept himself well informed on public affairs, maintained an extensive correspondence, remained a Federalist to the end, and above all continued to cherish his friendships. Those with whom he had served in the cabinet were more than simply onetime colleagues; they remained forever his friends as well. To Timothy Pickering especially he was "my excellent friend," and at the last Christmas dinner McHenry partook of he was gladdened to have the old Colonel at his table. And so it was with those of his youth, Tallmadge and Lafayette in particular. More than thirty years after their first meeting, we find Lafayette writing, "Receive, my Dear McHenry, the Most Affectionate wishes and Sentiments of your old and Best friend." In 1784 James McHenry had married Margaret Caldwell of Philadelphia. Thirty-two years later she wrote, following his death, "In May 1816, my dearest and best earthly friend was taken from me. . . ."[145]

Pickering, Wolcott, and McHenry were all survivors of a previous administration, a regime whose executive standards and procedures had been more or less stable and predictable. Their usefulness was more bureaucratic than political; none were "first characters"; the status of each, and in two out of three cases their actual livelihood, depended on the positions they held rather than the other way around. These three certainly came to be the bane of John Adams's existence. But it should not go unnoted that he was the bane of theirs as well, and in all likelihood more so. As holdovers, they shared at least one feature of what would later be termed the civil service mentality: their own self-estimate required that they see themselves as bringing something of value to their new superior in the way of prior knowledge and experience, and that this in turn entitled them to a certain autonomy of movement as well as respect. Another maxim of civil service lore has it that an incoming regime needs, for its optimum functioning, to win the loyalty of an inherited bureaucracy—and, failing to make the effort, is asking for trouble. John Adams seems to have given the impression throughout most of his term that his cabinet members were at best a convenience, and at worst not of sufficient importance to warrant the bother of dismissing them.

It is frequently asserted that all three of these men were subservient to Alexander Hamilton, and that this was the root of all the troubles. This is in a way quite true. But it was distinctly less so at the beginning, and there is still the question of which was cause and which effect. What did such "subservience" mean, and how had it come about? For one thing, Alexander Hamilton, still the most authoritative voice in Federalist councils, was the most visible link with the previous administration and its standards and policies. And for another, his relation to all three was in no way either a disreputable or a casual one. Hamilton was the one man in public life whose capacities the ever-suspicious Pickering unqualifiedly admired; Wolcott owed everything—his very career—to Hamilton; and McHenry had been Hamilton's loyal friend since their army days together. John Adams, on the other hand, detested Hamilton and could fly into a temper at the very mention of his name. The resulting chronic rub of conflicting loyalties and interests was not so simple to resolve, and needs at least to be appreciated. Years later, Pickering observed in a letter to McHenry: "I do not subscribe to all Mr. Stoddert's opinions on the duty of Heads of Departments. Particularly that of *implicit obedience, or resignation.* On the contrary, I should think it their duty to prevent, as far as practicable, the mischievous measures of a wrong-headed president."[146] (All such "mischievous measures" had to do in one way or another with Hamilton and his army.) On the one hand, each was so situated that in the event of a rupture he had nowhere to go but down; on the other, they were confronted, as they saw it, not only with a "wrong-headed president," but with one who, for the greater part of the time, was not even there.

In touching on the character, personalities, and, as it were, the sociology of the Gang of Three, one is referring to the most written-about members of the Adams cabinet. There were of course not three but five members in all, and the two others—Charles Lee, the Attorney-General, and Benjamin Stoddert, the Secretary of the Navy—cannot in any way be made to fit, in either behavior or outlook, the categories just outlined. Leaving aside for the moment their personalities, what made them different? It might not be straining a modern analogy too much to view these two as "dollar-a-year men": men who were not dependent for their status on holding public office, and who were at the same time bringing a special form of knowledge and experience from private to public life.

"Mr. Lee," wrote Oliver Wolcott in 1799, "is a sensible man, and I think a candid man, who thinks much of Virginia . . . ; he frequently dissents to what is proposed by others, and approves of the sentiments of the President, but with respect to measures will rarely take an active part." The words of this character-ization of Charles Lee are more or less self-evident in their meaning—except for what is perhaps the key clause: *"who thinks much of Virginia."* Here Wolcott, in a long letter to Fisher Ames, is trying to explain what he sees as the condition of the Federalist party, the elements that made it up, and his own anxieties about the "state of the public councils." Charles Lee was, to be sure, a Federalist. But he was a Virginia Federalist, and Federalists in Virginia were different. Sur-rounded as they were by Jeffersonian Republicans, they tended to follow their own devices, and could not always be depended on to respond to the cues sent out from New York and New England. It might be added that Wolcott found John Marshall, another Virginia Federalist, similarly worrisome.[147]

Another thing that served to define Charles Lee—whatever he might or might not make of his life by his own exertions—was simply that he was a Lee, and the Lees had been a weighty presence in Virginia for some 150 years. Born in 1758, he was a fifth-generation descendant of Colonel Richard Lee ("gentleman") who arrived in 1641; he was a brother of Henry ("Lighthorse Harry") and Richard Bland Lee, a cousin of the "Stratford" Lees (Richard Henry, Arthur William, Philip Ludwell, and Francis Lightfoot Lee), and would in time be an uncle of Robert E. Lee, the third son of his brother Henry. His "great-great grandfather, his great-grandfather, and granduncle," Charles Royster notes, "had all served on the Virginia council."[148] Charles Lee's life as an individual, on the other hand, is scantily documented; we know disappointingly little about it. He went to college at Princeton and graduated in 1775 (his "application and genius" appear to have pleased President Witherspoon); he served as "naval officer of the S. Potomac" during the Revolution and through the Confederation, and was Collector of the Port of Alexandria between 1789 and 1793. At some point he read law and was admitted to practice, though it is not certain just when. He was elected to a term in the Virginia Assembly in 1793. In November 1795, following the death of William Bradford, he was appointed Attorney-General of the United States.[149]

Being a Lee carried a set of direct implications and consequences for the politics of Virginia. The Lee and Washington families were very close. And although the Lees, as Federalists, were somewhat independent and not altogether predictable, they never operated outside the field of force represented by George Washington. They could, for example, have strong suspicions of Hamilton's Treasury system, yet on anything involving direct loyalty to Washington they closed ranks without question, which tended to set them more and more at odds with the growing Jefferson-Madison-Monroe-Giles phalanx and their followers at Richmond. Charles Lee and his brother Henry in 1793 would hear of no nonsense about Washington's Neutrality Proclamation despite considerable opposition to it in Virginia. In October Henry Lee as governor opened the Assembly with an unprecedented request for a ringing declaration of support, and got it pushed through in the face of much pro-French grumbling, while his ailing kinsman and Charles's father-in-law, Richard Henry Lee, egged them on. They had less success two years later during the uproar over the Jay Treaty—the provision on prewar debts did not sit at all well in Virginia—when Charles Lee and John Marshall took the lead in pressing a resolution of "undiminished confidence" in the President after he had ratified the treaty. (Another was substituted in which the Republicans declared, after praising Senators Tazewell and Mason for voting against it, that they had not intended to censure Washington's "motives.") In January 1796, shortly after Charles Lee joined the cabinet, news was coming in of James Monroe's failure to represent vigorously the Administration's policy to the French government. Lee advised Washington most emphatically that Monroe ought to be recalled.[150]

In national affairs as well as Virginia politics Charles Lee, like his two brothers, steered his own course. Though he got on well enough with his cabinet colleagues, he "frequently," as Wolcott observed, disagreed with them. For instance, when Pickering, Wolcott, and McHenry unanimously insisted that Washington should not comply with the House's demand for the Jay Treaty papers, Lee conceded that he was not obliged to do so but thought it would do no harm if he did. He was largely impervious to Hamiltonian influence, as all the Lees were; if he had an intellectual mentor it was probably his close friend John Marshall.[151]

At the same time, there seems to have been a streak of literal-mindedness in Charles Lee. One sees this not only in the written opinions he delivered but also in his other relations with the President. Lee, having given his unquestioning loyalty to George Washington, seems not to have felt the least difficulty about transferring it to his new superior when Washington was succeeded by John Adams. He gave Adams no trouble whatever, which may be another reason we know so relatively little about him. And on at least one occasion he gave him considerable cheer. Just after the President went home to Quincy in March 1799, Lee forwarded to Adams a letter received "from my friend Marshall," containing a welcome variation on what Adams had been hearing from most Federalists, especially in New England. In it, Marshall expressed his strong approval of the Murray nomination. It was, Lee observed in his own note, "with no small pleasure I find his opinion correspondent with my own. . . ."[152]

Benjamin Stoddert was the only member of Adams's cabinet whom Adams had appointed himself, and Stoddert's sole motive in taking a temporary leave from his private affairs to accept was the thought of what he could make of the newly created Navy Department. After some two and a half years of observing Stoddert at work, Wolcott believed him to be "a man of great sagacity" and conceded— perhaps somewhat ruefully—that he had "more of the confidence of the President than any officer of the government." After noting the "success and energy" with which Stoddert ran his department, Wolcott went on to observe that "he professes to know less than he really knows, and to be unequal to the task of forming or understanding a political system; he will have much influence in the government, and avoid taking his share of the responsibility."[153] Here Oliver Wolcott, as with his characterization of Charles Lee, was saying more in a few words than he seemed to be saying. That is, whatever influence might accrue to Benjamin Stoddert—and by 1799 it promised to be substantial—would derive not from anything he represented politically (though he was certainly a good enough Federalist) but from the way he carried out the specific mission he had been asked to undertake, that of bringing a navy into being. And his estimate of his own capacity to perform it was secure enough that he could easily do his colleagues the courtesy of professing, as Wolcott put it with some irony, to know less than he really knew. Meanwhile he was sufficiently preoccupied as to have neither the time nor the urge—nor, as he saw it, the need—to assume the kind of "responsibility" for matters of great political moment that Wolcott, Pickering, and McHenry now thought it their duty to exercise on their own.

Stoddert was born in 1751 in Charles County, Maryland, some thirty miles south of Georgetown. His father and grandfather (the latter having emigrated from Scotland about 1675) had acquired substantial landholdings in the area along the Potomac shore. Though about to prepare for a life of business, with the outbreak of the Revolution Benjamin Stoddert joined the army, served as captain and major in the Pennsylvania line, was wounded at Brandywine, and was then made a member of the Board of War in 1779. He served until 1781, when he resigned and "returned to Maryland to marry, looking to commerce as the means by which I was to support a family." His new wife was Rebecca Lowndes, the daughter of a Bladensburg merchant. He established a shipping firm at Georgetown which was very successful, thanks in large part to his own intelligence and able management. He acted as one of Washington's confidential agents in the President's negotiations with the landholders of the newly designated Federal District in 1791. When John Adams was looking for a Secretary of the Navy in the spring of 1798, he offered the appointment first to George Cabot of Massachusetts. When Cabot declined, he turned to Benjamin Stoddert.[154]

Stoddert was of two minds about accepting. He thought at first that the odds were "about 30 to 1" he would not; still, the country was in a state of crisis, and he rather supposed, with his experience, that he was as capable of rising to it as anyone. "You know I have heretofore managed Peaceable ships very well," he wrote to his brother-in-law. "Why should I not be able to direct as well those of War?" When he arrived at Philadelphia in mid-June 1798 to take charge of his new department, the American navy had but one ship at sea. By the time he left it just short of three years later, having worked in a suite of two rooms and with a staff of four or five clerks, he had expanded that number to fifty-four.[155]

By mid-summer of 1799 John Adams—quite unlike Benjamin Stoddert—showed few signs of having a very clear vision of the future. Or if he had, it was not at all obvious to those around him. Back in February when he suddenly nominated his new mission to France, he had at least presented a picture, however it might be taken, of determination and purpose. But as the months went by, and most especially in the final six or eight weeks before he did at last dispatch the mission, there was no end of ambiguity as to just what was in Adams's mind. There were times when he seemed disposed to proceed with all promptness, others when he was apparently in no great hurry, and still other points at which he was to all appearances inclining toward the view of his Secretaries—three of them that is— that the mission should be delayed or suspended indefinitely. These uncertainties were greatly compounded by Adams's almost perverse determination to remain at Quincy as long as he possibly could, in the face of urgings by critics and well-wishers alike that he return to the seat of government to take personal charge of whatever was to be done. All these considerations, and their outcome and con-sequences, were to have a very direct bearing on the psychological state in which the Federalist party would find itself in 1800. The chronology of this period thus takes on somewhat more importance than it might normally have.

Talleyrand's assurances that the mission would be duly received, forwarded by Murray, finally arrived at Philadelphia on July 30. Pickering sent them on to Adams at Quincy, but observed sarcastically that Talleyrand was insulting the President with insinuations "that the President of the United States was wasting many months of precious time" in requiring such assurances. But Adams in his reply was all briskness and bustle. He would take no notice of Talleyrand's imper-tinences; he would not venture to say whether France's designs were "insidious and hostile" or not; any vengeful spirit that arose would be "conjured up by them, not me. In this spirit I shall pursue the negotiation, and I expect the cooperation of the heads of departments." Preparations on sea and land were not to be relaxed; they should in fact go forward "with great energy." At the same time he wanted all arrangements completed for the envoys' departure. Their instructions had been sufficiently considered and discussed that they needed only to be put in final form. He wanted this done promptly and sent to him "as soon as possible." His mind, he said, was sufficiently made up that he would need little time to look them over and send them back.[156] Adams wrote this on August 6; it was another six weeks before he had the finished instructions in his hands.

Charles Francis Adams asserts that the above-cited letter shows Adams to have been steadily settled upon a course from which he never deviated. Adams himself claimed a few years after leaving office that after the substance of the instructions had been agreed upon in Philadelphia just prior to his departure in March, he had then gone home to Quincy and thereafter looked for them in every mail. "Week after week passed away and no Instructions arrived. I was uneasy, because our Envoys ought to be upon their passage." Actually both of these assertions—the one about Adams's steady purpose, and the claim as to the instructions—are questionable. Adams would shortly begin saying things that would create all manner of doubts as to what his intentions really were. As for the instructions, there is no evidence that he was in any hurry about receiving them. He did not so much as mention them in any of his correspondence with Pickering for four and a half months after leaving Philadelphia, nor could the envoys have been "upon their passage" anyway until France's assurances (which Adams himself had stipulated) were in hand, which was not until the end of July. And it does seem apparent that Pickering, much as he may have disapproved of the mission itself, did get the instructions ready as soon as he could, considering that all government business had to be suspended while the government offices were moved from Philadelphia to Trenton in mid-August on account of the yellow fever.[157]

To be sure, Pickering and all his Federalist supporters and confidants were bitterly opposed to the mission from first to last, and the language of Pickering in particular accorded in no way with that of a public minister committed, by the very fact of his not resigning, to carrying out his superior's purposes. Yet it would be well to grant that the Federalists did at least have a case. It may not have been a very good case, but that has had to be judged from subsequent events. The mission was certainly a mortal threat to their military program, as we have seen: that was the unspoken aspect. But there was more to it than that. Ever since Nelson's destruction of the French fleet at Aboukir in August 1798, and especially after Suvarov's successes in Italy, among other things putting an end to Bonaparte's Cisalpine Republic in April 1799, there were good grounds for supposing that a general peace, dictated by the allies, was closer and closer at hand. Some Federalists believed that if the United States should become a party to the war on the allied side, this country would then have something to say about the peace as well, and it would be the best opportunity yet for the international object the American government had vainly groped for from the first: "to command respect from the british," as Stephen Higginson put it, "and to guard us against their domination, by good connections, and a respectable station, advantages which a timid temporising policy will lose." And in any case (so the argument ran), there was no point whatever in soliciting further dealings with the French now. It would gain us only contempt no matter how it came out—whether in a third instance of rejection and humiliation, or promises that under the circumstances could mean little or nothing—and "the British and Russian Governments, will have ample means to indulge their resentment at our deserting their Cause, which was in fact ours also by interest and principle."[158]

This reasoning seemed to receive further weight from news that arrived during the last week in August of the "coup of Prairial"—a turnover in the membership of the Directory due to the growing influence of the Legislative Councils sufficiently extensive as to raise doubts about how long the Directory itself would survive as the executive arm of the French government. Murray's imagination was greatly stirred by these events, and in forwarding the news he told Pickering he would not be surprised to see Louis XVIII restored to the throne of France in a few months.[159] (Pickering found Murray's views on many things displeasing, but not this one, and he put it to good use in the weeks to come.) If the present government fell, with whom would the American envoys be negotiating, and would they even be allowed to negotiate at all? Should not the mission be at least suspended until the future of the French government became more clearly discernible?

After the government offices had been settled in their emergency quarters in Trenton, Pickering transmitted the instructions for the envoys, based on the principles agreed on in March and then further discussed by the cabinet members, to the President as the latter had requested. This was on September 10. The following day, however, Pickering addressed another letter to Adams, signed by all four of the cabinet members then at Trenton, saying that the events described in the enclosed papers he was now forwarding from Murray had suggested to them "some doubts of the expediency of an immediate departure of the envoys." The President was asked to consider "the question of a temporary suspension of the mission," which "would seem to us to place the United States in a more commanding situation" and to allow the President to take account of any changes in the French government and what they might call for.[160] This letter appears to have been not without its effect on Adams, whatever he might later have said about it.

Timothy Pickering would certainly have done almost anything to frustrate the mission, and his correspondence with just about everyone from the moment of the Murray nomination leaves little doubt of this. The news from Europe stirred him to fresh exertions. He also tried to work through the now-senior member of the commission, Chief Justice Oliver Ellsworth. Actually Ellsworth needed no persuading, having never favored the mission in the first place and having reluctantly accepted his appointment only to prevent "a greater evil," meaning presumably a Republican appointee instead. He told Pickering his views on more than one occasion, and after the recent news from France he was especially hopeful, as he told Pickering and Wolcott (as well as George Cabot and no doubt others), that the President would see the wisdom of suspending the mission until there could be a clearer idea of whom the envoys would be dealing with. And in fact Ellsworth strongly intimated as much to Adams himself, when he wrote in mid-September inquiring whether he should proceed with his regular circuit court duties. Adams's reply was that he should. "The convulsions in France," he wrote, "the change of the Directory, and the prognostics of greater change, will certainly induce me to postpone for a longer or shorter time the mission to Paris."[161]

One great perplexity about this entire period derives from the mixed signals

Adams kept giving out with regard to his own intentions. He seems to have been unable to hold his tongue in social conversation, and his sayings were wildly inconsistent. Well before news of France's internal convulsions arrived, he was reported as saying that he had made the Murray nomination because he then thought the people still sufficiently attached to France and her cause that a further attempt to restore peace was required before they could be brought to support the strong measures "which he deemed necessary," but that he now thought popular sentiment was against any kind of treaty and any kind of connection with the present regime in France. But then why, expostulated Stephen Higginson, should he still be preparing to make such a treaty? "Strange man, whose words and actions are so often opposed, whose Opinions and conduct fluctuate with the gales of passion, and the feelings of the moment."[162]

Such confusion was made worse by Adams's continued absence. Robert Troup, extravagant in his praise of Adams the year before, was now saying, "All the measures of the government are retarded by this kind of abdication." The frail health of Abigail had been the reason in 1798. By now she was much improved, but the excuse was the same. General Uriah Forrest of Baltimore, a strong supporter, was concerned enough to be fairly blunt. "The public sentiment is very much against your being so much away. . . . The people elected you to administer the government. They did not elect your officers, nor do they . . . think them equal to govern, without your presence and control." Adams's answer, as his own grandson admits, "scarcely meets the argument." But "I do administer it here at Quincy," he protested, "as really as I could do at Philadelphia." All business was transmitted to him daily, and he answered everything by return mail "so that nothing suffers or is lost." Mrs. Adams, he conceded, was better, but her state was still sufficiently delicate that he did not think she should be moved before the heat of the summer was over.[163] By the end of August, Benjamin Stoddert was alarmed enough to take a hand on his own responsibility in urging the President to come to Trenton, and he kept the pressure on until Adams at last capitulated.

Stoddert appears to have been among those who assumed that the mission would duly depart; he had thought all along that it should, and in fact he and Adams had very recently corresponded on arrangements for carrying the envoys to their destination. He did at the same time see enough merit in Pickering's letter proposing at least a temporary suspension that he agreed to sign it. (Charles Lee, being absent, did not sign it; he sent a separate opinion that there should be no suspension and that the envoys ought to proceed "even if they should find a monarch on the throne of France," which he doubted would happen very soon.) But Stoddert's real concern was that, whatever was finally decided, it was a matter of sufficient importance that Adams ought to be there to oversee it. Adams's presence, he wrote on August 29, "would afford great satisfaction . . . to the great mass of good men all over the United States." Adams shuffled. The instructions, he said, had been fully attended to; if he came, it would "give more *éclat* to the business than . . . it deserves"; he was "perfectly willing" that the envoys' departure should be suspended if news came making it seem advisable (such news had in fact arrived, but Adams did not yet know of it); meanwhile he saw no need of his undertaking the journey.[164]

But Stoddert was not to be dislodged. Having "no motive unconnected with your honor and that of the government," he wrote in a long letter of September 13, "I hope you will pardon my freedom in adhering to my wish that you would join the officers here, before the departure of the mission to France." Adams, receiving this and Pickering's letter of the 11th accompanied by Murray's dispatches at about the same time, writhed in further discomfort, and then concluded that he had better go to Trenton after all. He thereupon wrote to Stoddert and Pickering on September 21, informing them he would be there some time "between the 10th and 15th of October."[165]

As to just what was in his mind as he set out, there is enough contradictory material in his correspondence to permit a variety of readings. It could be inferred that the actual dispatching of the mission—the question of whether such a mission should or should not be sent—had long since been determined and that he had never contemplated, even in his most undecided moments, a greater delay than two or three weeks, more or less, in sending the envoys on their way. There is plausible evidence for such a case; it may even be, with some qualifications, closest to the correct one. Nevertheless to some persons Adams also gave grounds for a very different inference. Ellsworth, for one, assumed from Adams's letter to him about proceeding with his circuit court duties, as well as from a direct conversation with the President on October 3 when the latter passed through Windsor on his way to Trenton, that the mission would indeed be suspended, and he so informed a number of his friends, including Pickering and Wolcott. Adams had already told Pickering on September 16: "The revolution in the Directory, and the revival of the clubs and private societies in France . . . seem to warrant a relaxation of our zeal for the sudden and hasty departure of our envoys." (Pickering might well have asked, *whose* zeal?) Stephen Higginson did not know what to think. "We are here all wondering at the new mission to France," he wrote Wolcott from Boston. "The language used by the President *and his lady,* is in direct opposition to such a measure, and she has expressed much surprise that the intimations given in the papers of preparations for the envoys should be believed. This singular opposition of sentiment perplexes people very much, and many will not believe that the President intends they shall go on."[166]

Adams arrived at Trenton on October 10. It is not clear how many meetings he had with his cabinet. But what is known is that although he had given the Secretaries good grounds for assuming that he was considering a suspension, or at the very least that the question would be fully canvassed when he got there, at no time did he bring this matter up for discussion at all, and he never told them face to face what he intended to do about it. Their business consisted only in going over the instructions and agreeing on their final form, which was completed at eleven o'clock on the night of October 15. At nine o'clock the following morning he sent Pickering a note ordering him to prepare copies of the instructions for all the envoys and to arrange for their departure aboard the frigate *United States* no later than November 1. He had decided that the case was closed.[167]

Why? Again, we cannot know. But two additional items are of some pertinence to this extraordinary event, which created such great and probably irreparable disaffection in the ranks of the entire Federalist party.

One is the story Adams himself told in later life, in three somewhat varying versions on three different occasions, about his meetings with the cabinet in Trenton. He claimed that the question of the mission and whether it should or should not be sent was in fact fully discussed. "I preserved my temper very happily," he wrote, "called my ministers together, heard all their reasons with the utmost coolness and candour, gave my reasons in answer to theirs, and decided that the instructions should be finished and the ambassadors embarked as soon as possible. . . ." In another version he gave a full account of the argument they made—similar to the one described above—and of his replies to it. The striking thing about this story is that it seems to have been fashioned almost entirely out of whole cloth. No such discussions occurred, and when Adams's purported account of them was published in the *Boston Patriot* it evoked astonished protests from those alleged to have taken part, both among each other and even to Adams himself.[168]

A clue, both to Adams's actual behavior at Trenton and to how he might have reported it otherwise than it really happened, may lie in still another episode, a meeting between John Adams and Alexander Hamilton which occurred some time between October 10 and 16. There is no account of it other than the one Adams himself gave, though in this case the main outlines of the story, except perhaps for an embellishment or two, appear to be more or less correct. Adams gave the impression that Hamilton had come to Trenton for the sole purpose of arguing him of out of the mission, and was grimly displeased to find him in town. Actually Hamilton was there in order to arrange with the War Department the details of General James Wilkinson's disposition of the western army, and was not even aware until he arrived that the President intended to be there also. Be that as it may, the conversation did take place, and Hamilton did present the case for suspending the mission. As Adams tells it, he worked himself up to a great pitch, while "I heard him"—as nearly always happens in stories about himself in which he is the narrator—"with perfect good humour." Pitt was determined, he reports Hamilton as saying,

> "to restore the house of Bourbon, the two imperial courts were also determined to restore the Bourbons, their [France's] enemies were triumphant, Louis 18th would be in glory at Versailles before my ministers could arrive there. Offence would be taken at my sending a mission to the Directory," and twenty other wild extravagancies in the same style of dogmatical confidence.

Adams answered all his points with his customary moderation and reason, but, he wrote, "never in my life did I hear a man talk more like a fool."[169]

At least one conclusion seems reasonable enough: that the cabinet conferences Adams described were a fictional transposition of the one he had with Hamilton. Benjamin Stoddert pointed this out to him a number of years later upon reading Adams's version of them. "The departments met you," he wrote, "to consider the instructions to the ministers, but never I think to discuss the propriety of sending on the mission; and I believe you have been mistaken in ascribing to the heads of departments language held with you by General Hamilton and others at Trenton."[170]

Another inference may not be quite as clear, but perhaps it should at least be mentioned as not out of keeping with the turnings of John Adams's mind and temper. If there were any one precipitant needed for resolving the multitude of doubts and hesitations Adams evidently still felt about dispatching the mission, it may well have been the unexpected appearance at Trenton of the one man in all the world he most detested, Alexander Hamilton.[171]

CHAPTER XIV

The Settlement

I

The Naval Quasi-War

Considering all the attention that has been given to the troubles with France in the 1790s, most general accounts have had surprisingly little to say about the actual hostilities that ensued from them, or the theater of action in which they occurred, or for that matter the general military, political, economic, and social setting out of which the conflict originated and which gave it the character it had. Exactly what kind of "war" was it, and how had it come about? The Jay Treaty with England — customarily taken as the starting point for explaining this course of events — actually did not have a great deal to do with it. More broadly, the official relations between the United States and metropolitan France were no more than a marginal factor in bringing matters to the crisis point. The real key has to be looked for in the French West Indies. There, conditions of social upheaval and revolution, together with invasion by British military forces, had created a dynamic of its own, one which the Directory in Paris showed itself either unable or disinclined to control, except in the most intermittent and desultory way. The consequences for American merchant shipping, as has already been seen, were little short of catastrophic. The main variables of this exceedingly complex situation have their own bearing on the full import of the pending Ellsworth-Murray-Davie mission to France.

If there were any single undertaking by the American government in the closing years of the eighteenth century that could be rated as something close to a full practical success — in the relation of means to ends, of intentions to outcome, and in obstacles surmounted — it was that of bringing the United States Navy into being and shaping the manner of its employment during the first two and a half years of its existence. The source of the effort — and its leading intelligence — was neither a fleet commander nor a naval careerist of any kind, but a civilian official: the first Secretary of the Navy, Benjamin Stoddert. By the nature of the case it fell upon Stoddert, fortunately a man of great energy and resourcefulness, to superintend everything. Unlike the army, which had at least survived in nominal form after the Revolution, the navy no longer existed, either in personnel or in ships, and for practical purposes all had to be made new.

For instance, the captains appointed to command the six frigates authorized by the Naval Armament Act of 1794 were all men whose primary experience lay in the merchant marine. True, all had seen service in the Revolution, either as privateersmen or aboard warships in the Continental Navy. But all returned to the merchant service when the Revolutionary naval force was disbanded, and during the fifteen years prior to 1798 none had done duty of any kind aboard an armed vessel. Indeed, none had ever commanded a ship comparable to the new heavy frigates, and the single officer of the six who would emerge as a figure of national prominence during the Quasi-War, Thomas Truxtun, had commanded privateers but had never held a naval commission at all.[1] All of this further meant that the Navy Department when organized in 1798 had nothing approaching an admiralty, or even a professional naval staff. Virtually every function such a staff would normally perform had to be assumed by Secretary Stoddert. Stoddert would take responsibility for the construction and purchase of additional ships, for choosing new officers to command them, and for the equipping and supply of the navy as a whole. Moreover, his would be the predominant voice in devising the navy's strategy and directing its operations.

Except for one converted merchant vessel that had been put into service less than four weeks earlier, the navy did not have a single ship at sea when Stoddert took office on June 18, 1798, though the three new frigates were by then almost ready. These frigates had originally been authorized by Congress in 1794 to resist the depredations of the Barbary powers in the Mediterranean. The act called for six of them, the construction, equipping, and manning of which would be under the charge of the War Department. Construction had begun on all six in 1795 but was suspended, in accordance with the same law, upon the conclusion of peace with Algiers in September of that year. (The bill could not have been passed at all without such a proviso.) President Washington was nevertheless greatly reluctant to abandon the program, and in 1796 a legislative compromise was effected whereby three of the six—*Constitution, United States,* and *Constellation*—would be brought to completion. These ships, for all the vicissitudes encountered in getting them built, proved to be of strikingly superior design and construction. Washington and Secretary of War Knox had been fortunate in obtaining the services of Joshua Humphreys, a master shipbuilder of Philadelphia, as chief naval constructor. Humphreys was a man of both good sense and imagination who had apparently given much thought to the problems of fighting ships. He had a simple but penetrating theory that if such ships were worth building they ought to be stronger, faster, heavier, and more efficient than all others of their class possessed by any foreign nation. Washington and Knox were willing to stretch the law to its limits in giving him the leeway to carry out this conception, and Humphreys meanwhile felt justified in claiming that his forty-four-gun frigate would be more than a match for any warship mounting fewer than sixty-four guns. *Constellation* got to sea on June 24, 1798, *United States* and *Constitution* on July 7 and July 23. Such was the potentially interesting but dauntingly small naval force with which Stoddert began his own work in the summer of 1798.[2]

As for building up that force, Congress in the crisis atmosphere following the XYZ disclosures had become unwontedly generous about granting the necessary means for doing it. Legislation was enacted throughout April, May, June, and July which authorized the building of three additional frigates and the acquisition by gift or purchase of six more, together with some forty-odd vessels of lesser rating, sloops, brigs, schooners, and galleys; the arming of merchantmen; the issuance of commissions to private armed vessels; and the establishment of a marine corps.[3] Stoddert lost no time in making maximum use of such authority, and by the end of 1798 he would already be forming plans for a permanent peacetime naval establishment which in addition to all other classes would include a force of seventy-four-gun ships of the line. Immediately upon taking office he set about establishing relations with the existing shipbuilding facilities, getting in touch with the five naval agents previously appointed in the leading Atlantic ports under the War Department and appointing a number of additional ones himself for the lesser centers. He gave the agents wide responsibility for the procurement of materials, the expediting of construction, the purchase and conversion of ships already built, and the recruitment of crews. At the same time, he drew on his own considerable experience as a merchant shipowner to make certain that proper construction standards would be met, that vessels should be competently manned, and that the government—just as he himself had generally managed to do in his own business—would get its full money's worth.[4]

The entire seaboard earlier that spring had been in a state approaching desperation. Since the beginning of the previous year French privateers had seized over 330 American ships. Both exports and imports had dropped dramatically, and insurance rates that had averaged no more than 6 percent for voyages in the summer of 1796 had since mounted to between 30 and 33 percent by early 1798. A voyage to Jamaica could run as high as 40 percent of the value of the ship and cargo.[5] By then French cruisers, no longer confining their activities to the Caribbean and outer Atlantic, were actually infesting American coastal waters, hovering off such places as Long Island Sound or the entrance to Delaware Bay, waiting to strike at any unarmed vessel that came out. Thus with no legal means of resistance and with no American naval vessels of any kind yet at sea, American merchantmen had no protection whatever. Nor was this horrid sense of helplessness confined to the maritime community. It had pervaded the entire southern coast, with thickening rumors of an actual invasion from the French West Indies. In April, Robert Goodloe Harper declared to the House of Representatives as an established fact that the infamous Victor Hugues, the French commander on Guadaloupe already renowned for his sweeping acts of brutality and sadism on that unhappy island, stood ready "with 5000 of his best troops . . . to make a blow upon Southern country whenever the word of command shall be given." Even an old soldier like Henry Knox was not immune to the fever. Knox warned President Adams in June that the French could quickly "convoy an army of ten thousand blacks and people of colour in vessels seized from our own citizens. They might land on the defenceless parts of South Carolina or Virginia. Under such circumstances, the slaves would instantly join them, & greatly encrease their force. I do not believe this picture is too highly coloured."[6]

That part of the picture was in fact "too highly coloured." That anybody in the West Indies would seriously contemplate a risky expedition which was certain to unite the whole of American society against France and all her dependencies, and probably bring in the assistance of Great Britain as well, was not very likely. True, it appears that General Gabriel-Théodore Hédouville, the recently arrived agent of the Directory in St. Domingue, did at some point seek to entice Toussaint Louverture with the idea of invading Jamaica and perhaps even the United States. But Toussaint, a man of exceptional astuteness who already had his hands full trying to consolidate his own control of the island, seems to have grasped at once that this was aimed not so much at France's enemies as at himself, being little more than a scheme to throw him to the wolves.[7]

Nevertheless the other side of the picture, that of the corsairs operating out of the French Antilles, was certainly real enough, and it was to this side that Benjamin Stoddert proceeded to address all his attention and efforts. Clearing the American coast could actually be managed more or less briskly as Stoddert moved to lay hold of the resources and authority which Congress was now making available to the Executive. The mounting of cannon aboard merchantmen and the purchase and conversion of quondam merchant vessels into heavily armed sloops of war soon began to make operations in American waters more and more dangerous and unprofitable for French privateers. A salutary example was the case of the schooner *Croyable,* lured into giving chase on July 7 to *Delaware,* Captain Stephen Decatur, Sr., off the Jersey coast, not perceiving at that distance that *Delaware* was a merchantman no longer and now mounted twenty guns. *Croyable* was handily captured and taken into the American navy. By mid-summer the three frigates and several supporting ships of war were at sea patrolling the entire coastline from Georges Bank to the St. Mary's River, in what amounted to a shakedown cruise for the small but growing fleet. Stoddert was now certain enough of America's control of her own coast that in early July he decided to order Captain John Barry of the newly commissioned *United States* to make a short cruise into the Caribbean. "By keeping up incessant attacks upon the French Cruisers on their own ground," he later observed to the President, "they will in a degree at least be prevented from coming on ours. . . ."[8]

The American navy would see little action of consequence during the summer and early fall of 1798. No more than a handful of French privateers were actually captured, and the problem of dealing with them "on their own ground" was only beginning to be worked out. But the panic of the spring and early summer was largely over. The presence of the heavy frigates, the awareness that an invasion from Guadaloupe or St. Domingue—whatever its ultimate likelihood—would be impossible in late fall or winter, and finally the news that Bonaparte's fleet had been destroyed by Nelson at Aboukir in August were all highly reassuring.

The "war," not having yet reached its serious phase, would go on for nearly two more years, all through 1799 and most of 1800. But was it a "real" war? It certainly was, though it was also a peculiarly special one, almost one of a kind, which makes it somewhat difficult to think about and classify satisfactorily from the viewpoint of either warfare itself or diplomacy. This one had few of those elements which give chronicles of martial conflict their principal structure and significance. It was undeclared; it was not undertaken to inflict defeat, nor retaliation; its strategy was not to give battle, not to seek out the "enemy" in the form of French national warships, except under special circumstances. There would be only three actual encounters between the public vessels of France and the United States in the entire course of the Quasi-War. Privateering against unarmed French vessels was forbidden by American law. The Quasi-War was undertaken for the measured and restricted purpose of effecting the safety of American overseas commerce. All of this meant that the test of its success, or lack of it, would have to be looked for not in numbers of French warships sunk or even of commerce raiders captured, but primarily in the movement of insurance rates.

Moreover, there is reason to conclude that strictly speaking the Quasi-War was not even the outcome of a diplomatic impasse between sovereign nations, though oftener than not that is the way it tends to be treated.

"I have detained them seven months from doing what they ought to have done at once," privately wrote James Monroe, then minister to France, to his friend Madison on September 1, 1796, after hearing that France intended to recall its own minister to the United States in protest against the Jay Treaty.[9] Monroe was referring to the edict of July 2, 1796—later to be followed by another, that of March 2, 1797—which constituted the authority for the massive assault upon American commerce from mid-1796 into 1798. From this it would seem to follow that these depredations were a direct consequence of, and in retaliation for, the insult and injury France believed herself to have suffered from America's having concluded a general understanding with France's enemy Great Britain. The evidence for such a causal connection is both plausible and extensive.

For instance, there was Fauchet's declaration to the Directory that the United States should be made to hear "the voice of France thundering against the treaty and demanding justice." Or Foreign Minister Charles Delacroix's brusque warning to Monroe that the French—as Monroe reported it—regarded the treaty with England "as having . . . annulled our treaty of alliance with them . . . that they had rather have an open enemy than a perfidious friend." The decree of July 2, 1796, announced that neutrals—meaning specifically Americans—would henceforth be treated by France "in the same manner as they shall suffer the English to treat them." In the instructions sent to Adet in August 1797 the Jay Treaty was denounced as "the equivalent of an alliance with their former oppressor . . . against a faithful ally, and a generous liberator." There followed the refusal of the French government to receive Minister-designate Pinckney, and finally there was the decree of March 2, 1797, which in addition to declaring enemy goods on neutral ships good prize, specified that any ship without a notarized list of its crew—the famous *rôle d'équipage,* which no American ship carried—would be subject to seizure and condemnation.[10]

All such actions and expressions—and many more could be cited—appear to indicate an intense resentment in France over the Jay Treaty and to confirm that a policy of retaliation was the direct consequence of it. In a sense this was true: there were without doubt Frenchmen who were greatly incensed over the treaty. But which Frenchmen? They appear for the most part to have been rather a select and even marginal category: disaffected functionaries who had done duty in America, who had had little luck advancing French interests there, and who most of the time could not even count on getting the attention of their superiors in Paris, whose minds were largely elsewhere. Fauchet, for instance, when he returned to France at the end of 1795 spent nearly two months trying to get an interview with the Foreign Minister, who at length confessed that he had not even read the mémoire on American affairs Fauchet had prepared for him, but would get to it as soon as he could. Adet, between spells of fervently wishing himself back home, believed that a demonstration of French displeasure with the treaty might persuade the American people to elect a President more sympathetic than Washington had been to France's cause in Europe: a thought that was encouraged, and probably even originated, by francophiles in America, including Monroe himself.[11]

In any case, as diplomatic policy the official French response to all this was surprisingly erratic and fitful. In January or February 1796 someone in the Foreign Office drew up a plan for a decree specifying a series of conditions for striking at American commerce—the "Pluviôse projet"—but the Directory failed to take any action on it.[12] The decree that finally was issued, that of July 2, 1796, was couched in the vaguest terms; "it created," in Professor Bowman's words, "the greatest confusion and was followed by general abuses." Nor was it a public declaration of anything, certainly not "the voice of France thundering against the treaty and demanding justice." It was issued in secret, and Monroe was not informed of it until October, the Minister of Marine having previously denied to him that such a decree existed.[13] But more to the point, these edicts appear to have followed rather than initiated the attacks on American shipping. The real initiative lay in the West Indies, not in Paris.

The commissioner in St. Domingue, Léger-Félicité Sonthonax, admitted— indeed boasted—to the Minister of Marine that American ships were regularly captured and condemned months before the decree of July 2, 1796, reached the West Indies.[14] Victor DuPont later told the same story to Talleyrand. "Long before the various laws and edicts restricting the commerce of neutrals were known in America, measures far more rigorous than the ones determined by these laws were put in force."[15] The scores of ships listed in American newspapers as captured and condemned in the summer and fall of 1796 may be taken as solid documentation of such reports. The traffic spread like an infectious fever; it was said that in Guadaloupe "practically every boat existing on the island" had been armed for privateering against the Americans. Few regulations were observed; much of the activity bordered on unabashed piracy, and it was engaged in by all classes, from the humblest "citizens of color" to officials acting in the name of the French Republic.[16] It was reaching such a scale by 1797 that the home authorities could probably not have controlled it even if they had wanted to.

It may be taken as an established historical principle that all through the Napoleonic wars, and indeed going back to the very onset of the wars of the French Revolution, neutral shipping was always fair game for belligerents, all but irresistibly so, no matter how well or how badly the neutrals might behave in the area of diplomacy. With each belligerent determined not only to secure the advantages of neutral trade for himself but also to deny them to his enemy—and with the neutral by definition both unwilling and unable to oblige him—the case overflowed with the most plausible pretexts, added to the lure of prize money, for assaults on unprotected property. This was nowhere more openly or extravagantly seen than in the French West Indies during the final years of the 1790s. But why especially there?

At least two gross factors combined to make it so. For one thing, the French sugar islands were just as ripe for revolution by 1789 as the society of metropolitan France, perhaps even more so. And for another, the British invasion of these islands which began in 1793 imposed a dimension of external warfare upon that of internal conflict, with scenes of disorder that ran almost beyond description. The turmoil, moreover, was in many ways aggravated rather than lessened by Britain's eventual decision to withdraw from a commitment that became more and more costly the longer it went on. Amid such conditions, which included not only social upheaval but stringencies of supplies of every sort, and given the type of freebooting local leadership that would emerge in these places, it was only to be expected that rules normally governing the conduct, even in wartime, of individuals and civilized states toward each other should be subject to unlooked-for transformations.

For France, St. Domingue up to the eve of the Revolution could be seen as the model Caribbean colony. It was the most efficient producer of sugar and coffee of all the West Indian islands, including the British, supplying two-thirds of France's tropical products and in fact constituting fully a third of her total overseas trade. American merchants were allowed to share in this bonanza commerce following the formation of the French alliance of 1778, and although the organized jealousy of French metropolitan merchants obliged the royal government to impose restrictions on American trade after 1783, the local demand for cheap fish and lumber, together with severe grain shortages in France in 1789, again forced the market wide open. American exports to St. Domingue thereupon mounted to $3 million in the following year, second only to the $6.9 millions' worth shipped to Britain and more than double the $1.4 million in American exports to metropolitan France.[17]

But if 1789 marked a new peak in St. Domingue's prosperity, it also marked the first tremors of a struggle for power among the various groups that made up St. Domingue's society, one that would eventually become so murderous as to shake it to pieces. The enormous profits wrung from the plantations since early in the century had produced a sharply layered social structure. At its apex were the royal officials who dominated the island's politics and social protocol. Directly beneath were the creole planters and wealthy merchants, known as the *grands blancs,* who resented the arrogance of the royal establishment but who in turn lorded it over the *petits blancs,* white storekeepers, craftsmen, and petty bureaucrats. A fourth class was the *gens de couleur,* the free mulattoes, often children of planters, sometimes substantial planters in their own right though much more typically small propertyholders and artisans. The *gens de couleur* were citizens and served in the militia; they nevertheless suffered the severest civic and social discrimination, probably more so than did mulattoes elsewhere in the West Indies. And finally at the bottom were the 400,000 black slaves who made up five-sixths of the island's population.[18]

Thus with the opening phases of the French Revolution there were materials in St. Domingue for much more than a faint echo of events in metropolitan France. The passions of every class were stirred into motion: those of the *grands blancs,* insistent on a greater share in the island's government; of the *petits blancs,* full of envy of the planters' prodigal wealth and increasingly captivated by Jacobin slogans of equality, yet determined that such equality not extend to the despised *gens de couleur;* and of the *gens de couleur* themselves, resolved to gain the full rights of citizenship implied in the sweeping promises of the Revolution. And as revolutionary rhetoric rang throughout the island, none of the groups echoing it quite appreciated until too late the effect it was having on the mass of largely African-born black slaves in their midst.

The great uprising of slaves that broke out in August 1791 was an occurrence virtually without warning. It involved the massacre of thousands, planter families and slaves alike, the burning of hundreds of plantations on the rich Northern Plain, and the emergence of a sizable force of black insurgents determined never again to live in slavery. It also touched off a general civil war of singular ferocity, almost a war of all against all, whose shifting alliances and cross-purposes—those of civil control, self-preservation, class hatred, and racial vengeance all mixed in together—were followed out to the accompaniment of blood and ruin. The struggle over the ensuing two years would lead variously to the destruction of Cap François and the flight of its surviving inhabitants to the United States; the emancipation of all slaves on St. Domingue by edict of the Jacobin commissioner Sonthonax; the invasion of the island by the British, urged on by a desperate planter remnant; and perhaps most remarkable and most important, the emergence of Toussaint Louverture and his black rebel troops as potentially the most effective military and political force on St. Domingue.

Americans, especially in the southern states, watched all this with a kind of hypnotized horror. American ships nevertheless continued to trade not only with St. Domingue but with any other of the Caribbean islands—French, British, Dutch, Danish, or Spanish—that were prepared to exchange sugar, coffee, and molasses for flour, meat, fish, and lumber. It was this trade, specifically that with the French colonies, that the British in preparing their own military plans for that quarter were determined to repress, at least temporarily, when they issued their notorious Order in Council of November 6, 1793. This was the Order that led to the condemnation of some 250 American vessels and to the crisis that eventuated in the Jay-Grenville settlement of 1794.

To Pitt and Henry Dundas, Secretary of State for War and the Colonies, an invasion of the French islands seemed on the face of it a logical response to the military situation that confronted Great Britain everywhere. They were still reluctant to commit British land resources unreservedly to the European continent, whereas a relatively limited effort in the West Indies might net proportionally sweeping dividends. The failure of French authorities to crush the slave uprising in St. Domingue and the anarchic conflict there among the whites and mulattoes presented not only a threat—to nearby Jamaica with its 300,000 slaves—but also an opportunity. Royalist planter representatives from St. Domingue and elsewhere had given the British assurances of full support in any military action they might take. With such assistance, a contingent of British regulars cooperating with Spanish forces from eastern Hispaniola could secure St. Domingue, Spain being still an ally of England, and a British expeditionary force might similarly go on to occupy all other French possessions in the Lesser Antilles. Moreover, by seizing the main ports out of which French privateers could operate, the British would assure the safety of their own considerable trade throughout the Caribbean.[19]

The first phase of the campaign went very satisfactorily. In the fall of 1793 the British seized a line of key ports on St. Domingue from Jérémie in the south to Môle St. Nicolas in the north, while their Spanish allies occupied most of the Northern Plain. Early in 1794 an expedition under Sir John Jervis proceeded to capture Martinique, Guadaloupe, and every other island in the Lesser Antilles except St. Barthélémy. Jervis then dispatched four of his battalions to St. Domingue for the final assault on Port-au-Prince, which fell on June 4, 1794. The British seemed on the verge of total victory in the West Indies.

Yet they had in fact fallen into the gravest military difficulties. Their forces everywhere, spread dangerously thin to begin with, were being undermined, in some units to the point of total incapacitation, by yellow fever. Then in June 1794 came the catastrophic descent of Victor Hugues. This fierce Jacobin commander had arrived with a contingent of troops from France in a small squadron that had escaped the British blockade at Rochefort, with the object of reinforcing the French garrison on Guadaloupe. The British could not scrape up sufficient force in time to challenge him, and by September Hugues was in control of the entire island. By rallying thousands of emancipated blacks to his troops and with further reinforcements from France he was able during the ensuing year to render the British foothold in the lesser islands exceedingly precarious. British fortunes took an equally bad turn on St. Domingue. Up to the spring of 1794 the forces of Toussaint Louverture had been at the disposal of the Spanish in their campaign against the French. But Toussaint had meanwhile become convinced that a total British victory would bring the return of slavery. In May he switched sides, carrying most of his followers with him, and by combining guerrilla and conventional tactics he was able to fight the British and Spanish to a standstill. By early 1796 Toussaint and his forces had gained control of most of North and West Provinces.

It was becoming more and more apparent to the British that the cost of their

West Indian campaign in money and manpower—nearly 100,000 casualties from all causes—had become prohibitive. The Spanish and Dutch, moreover, had changed sides and were now allied with France. The cabinet accordingly began laying plans for a withdrawal by stages from St. Domingue and a sharp curtailment of operations elsewhere in the Caribbean. There was the closest correlation between this decision and the unprecedented damage American shipping began suffering in the West Indies trade. Were it not for the British military failure there would have been no such depredations, certainly not on this scale, and in all probability no Quasi-War.[20]

Owing to the exploits of Victor Hugues, the French on Guadaloupe already had a secure base from which their privateers could go after American ships anywhere along the route they followed with the prevailing trade winds into the eastern Caribbean. Their sphere of activity would be greatly widened by the gradual British withdrawal from St. Domingue, enabling them to use the island's many coves and harbors as points from which to attack shipping in the Windward Passage, the normal route of exit from the Caribbean to the outer Atlantic. And with Dutch and Spanish bases now available as well, French corsairs could operate from an extensive string of small harbors all the way from Cuba, along the northern coast of Hispaniola, to Puerto Rico, Guadaloupe, and Martinique. To such as Victor Hugues, they need observe virtually no limits, and Hugues said as much in a sweeping decree issued from Guadaloupe on February 1, 1797. Declaring that "the Government and commerce of the United States have strangely abused the forbearance of the republic of France," the decree announced that any neutral vessel bound for any of the islands "evidently in a state of rebellion"—which of course included in some degree all the French colonies—would be subject to capture and sale, considering that it was "against every principle to treat a horde of insurgents, destitute of country, without government, and without a flag, with the same respect as civilized nations preserve towards each other during a war." And despite the insolent addendum that the Directory's edict of July 2, 1796, would continue to be executed "as far as shall not be contravened by the present decree," the Directory itself showed little inclination to restrain Hugues or any of his fellow commissioners. On the contrary, officials at all levels of the home government appeared to be more than glad to share in the plunder.[21]

The year 1797 was one of pure calamity for the American maritime community. Losses of ships, drops in both imports and exports, and the soaring of insurance costs all exceeded anything previous. Between the proclamations of Victor Hugues and Sonthonax, the edict of March 2, 1797, requiring the *rôle d'équipage,* and the order of January 18, 1798, declaring that any vessel loaded in whole *or in part* with English goods would henceforth be deemed good prize, it was a virtual certainty that no American merchant ship stopped by a French privateer would escape condemnation. So unless the Americans were willing to give up a trade that constituted a third of their foreign commerce, the new American navy would have to take responsibility for protecting its merchant marine all across a vast area dotted with islands and harbors and stretching in a two-thousand-mile arc from Havana to Trinidad and on to the coast of South America.

It was a very demanding assignment; if purposefully managed, however, it was not necessarily an impossible one, nor did Benjamin Stoddert so view it. French naval strength in that quarter was actually quite limited—one or two frigates at the most—and any effort on France's part to increase it would be challenged by Great Britain, whatever might be the British military situation on the islands. Moreover, should it come to the point of direct hostilities between opposing ships of war, the Americans already had the advantage. The American frigates, especially the heavier ones, *Constitution* and *United States,* outmatched anything the French were likely to have in that part of the world, or could send there. The problem that Stoddert confronted lay, rather, in the swarms of small corsairs operating in the area around the Windward Passage, along the northern coast of Hispaniola, and all around Guadaloupe in the Lesser Antilles.

By late summer and early fall of 1798, as more and more ships were becoming available, Stoddert had worked out a reasoned strategy for accomplishing the navy's overall mission. A small force would be dispatched to Havana to protect the growing American trade with Cuba and to deal with occasional privateers there. A second squadron would go to the Windward Passage, the scene of such severe trade losses the year before. But the bulk of American naval strength, including the three frigates then at sea, would be concentrated in the Lesser Antilles, out of which the great majority of French privateers operated. Once the entire force was in place, Stoddert was confident that "a State little short of perfect Security, may be given to our Commerce in those Seas." And "above all," he admonished his commanders, "your Efforts must be directed to relieve our Commerce, from the picaroons, and pirates, continually issuing from the Island of Guadaloupe."[22]

The greatest difficulty of this strategy, one requiring the most constant and painstaking attention to detail, lay not so much in the adequacy of available force as in the vast distances from home bases at which it would have to operate. The United States had no supply or repair facilities in the West Indies, which meant that there would have to be a regular sending out of supply ships to rendezvous with the several squadrons at previously designated locations, as well as maintenance of a carefully coordinated schedule of return voyages so that the warships might refit and receive fresh crews without overburdening the resources of any given part of the fleet. And although, predictably, such plans were never quite so precise in their execution as they were in emerging from Stoddert's mind, the system he laid out functioned with fair efficiency and brought very satisfactory results. Seizures by privateers dropped sharply in 1798 and would so continue the following year. The heavily armed American frigates and other warships would capture a number of French privateers in the winter and spring of 1798–99 and drastically inhibit the activities of many more.[23] Indeed, the United States Navy had more than paid for itself by the time it was eight months old. Insurance savings alone, according to the House Naval Affairs Committee report of January 17, 1799, already amounted to more than three times the total cost of the navy since the first appropriations of 1794, and such savings might be expected to increase as the navy continued to grow in strength.[24]

But the great moment for the American public at large came on February 9, 1799, when Captain Thomas Truxtun, commanding *Constellation* cruising off Nevis, "saw a Sail standing to the Westward, [and] gave Chase." The ship was *l'Insurgente,* said to be the fastest-sailing frigate in the French navy. *L'Insurgente,* with thirty-six guns, Captain Michel-Pierre Barreaut, had recently retaken the American ship of war *Retaliation* (originally the French privateer *Croyable* captured by Decatur); she had outrun all the British ships that had chased her, had eluded *Constitution* three weeks before, and was now cruising out of Guadaloupe. This time she was not so lucky. Unable to get away from *Constellation,* Barreaut was maneuvered into a ship-to-ship action which Truxtun conducted with skill and energy. Within an hour and a quarter *l'Insurgente* was reduced to helplessness, having taken two broadsides and a raking, her rigging in shreds, and suffering seventy casualties, twenty-nine fatal, to the Americans' five with only one killed. Barreaut had no choice but to surrender. Truxtun subsequently got his battered prize into St. Kitts for repairs and refitting, and *l'Insurgente* became a valuable addition to the United States Navy. There was great exultation in America, and Truxtun and his crew were cheered at patriotic celebrations all across the country. One Fourth of July toast was to "Captain Truxtun: our popular Envoy to the French, who was accredited at the first interview."[25]

A final segment remains to be fitted into the pattern of America's West Indies involvement of 1798–1800, one in which the navy may again be seen as an important variable. It concerns the immensely intricate sequence of informal three-sided diplomacy, the parties to which were seldom all on view at the same time, that stemmed directly from the British decision to withdraw from St. Domingue. The principals were Great Britain, the United States—not at first welcomed as a participant—and the emerging power on the island, Toussaint Louverture. Playing a critical part in it was the American Secretary of State, Timothy Pickering (heretofore not treated very handsomely in these pages), who acted with a considerable degree of resourcefulness and ingenuity. Each party had a sizable increment of self-interest to extract from the proceeding, and each pursued it with great pertinacity.

The various threads began coming together in mid-1798, even before British policy concerning St. Domingue was fully matured. The Americans had closely watched the rise of Toussaint Louverture and, as the British minister Robert Liston perceived it, no longer seemed very interested in seeing the French colonies under British control. Instead, as Liston wrote in some agitation to Grenville on June 12, Secretary Pickering had begun to hint approvingly at the possibility that the blacks of St. Domingue might soon "declare themselves independent and . . . erect the island into a sovereign State,—to which he seems to think it would not be inconsistent with the interests of America to consent." Grenville and the cabinet viewed such a possibility with "horror."[26] The example of a black republic in the West Indies would represent the gravest threat to Jamaica, with its large slave population, as well as to all the other British Caribbean possessions. The British were fully ready to deal with Toussaint, and were in fact already preparing to do so, but only for very circumscribed and immediate purposes. They would meet him in his character not as the acknowledged head of a government but simply as the strongest force on the island, a rebel against French authority as such authority then stood, in order to effect their own military withdrawal on conditions of greatest possible advantage to British interests. They wanted no less than a British monopoly for the time being on all St. Domingue's external trade, together with the fullest assurance that there would be no attempts of any kind from St. Domingue to stir up the affairs of Jamaica. Toussaint would be their temporary instrument, and if the future should bring altered conditions, say a general peace, they would not feel bound by prior informal engagements in responding to them.[27]

Actually Toussaint did not want to present himself as the head of an independent state either—not quite, and not yet—whatever part the Americans might have liked to mark out for him. He had his own reasons and his own purposes. Though his ties with metropolitan France were to become more and more tenuous, he continued to insist on his loyalty to the French Republic, a posture that suited his ends for the time being better than any other. He was the acknowledged leader of a population of blacks that had been formally emancipated from slavery by edict of a previous regime in France. But he was not yet by any means the master of the island, still in a state of civil war as well as a war to expel the invader; he was still surrounded by enemies, most of whom would have been glad to see his followers back in slavery and himself in Hell. Chief among them were the mulatto general André Rigaud, who with his army of *gens de couleur* in the south was contending for supremacy against whites and blacks alike, and the Directory's commissioner Hédouville, who was playing each against the other and willing to betray either one. And now with the British about to leave, Toussaint for his final grand effort to crush Rigaud was desperately in need of supplies and any other help he could get, no matter where it came from—England, France, or the United States. President Adams was only half right when he remarked of Toussaint, "All the rest of the World knows as little what to do with him as he knows what to do with himself."[28] Toussaint, given the position he was in, needed all the cunning of Machiavelli's prince, and in fact his military talents were well matched by astuteness in the essentials of statecraft.

As for the United States, the object of Pickering's diplomacy was parallel to that being pursued by the American navy, the full restoration of America's commercial position in the West Indies. Pickering was aware that this was not to be achieved without the cooperation of Great Britain—but not at the price of Britain's engrossing the lion's share of the St. Domingue trade, which had once been so rich and so profitable to American merchant enterprise. And the final key to success, as Pickering saw it, lay not in any new understanding with the French Directory—in which, as we have amply seen, he had no faith whatever—but in the rise to power of Toussaint Louverture.

Such, then, were the several positions from which the parties began their circlings about each other in 1798.

The British command on St. Domingue had devolved, by accident and attrition, upon an energetic young officer named Thomas Maitland, hastily promoted from lieutenant-colonel to brigadier, who welcomed large responsibilities and assumed a number of them on his own initiative. It was in fact Maitland and not the War Ministry who had determined that Britain's only sensible choice, rather than try to maintain any kind of presence at Jérémie and Môle St. Nicolas, was to deal directly with Toussaint and negotiate a total evacuation of the island. Accordingly he and the black general concluded a secret agreement on August 31, 1798. Great Britain would desist from any further attack on St. Domingue and any interference with its internal affairs; Toussaint made a similar promise with regard to Jamaica; and Maitland would see that provisions were allowed to reach the ports of St. Domingue without interference from British cruisers. Toussaint was not yet prepared to grant the British any exclusive trade privileges, and that question would be postponed until after Maitland's home government approved the present agreement, which it subsequently did. Maitland took it back to London himself.[29]

Toward the end of November, Rufus King, the American minister in London, got wind of the Maitland-Toussaint convention and immediately raised some difficulties with the Foreign Office. Had Great Britain recognized Toussaint as the head of an independent state? If so, then the United States had as much right to trade there as had England. But if not, the United States could not very well countenance Britain's sending supplies to the island as long as the American embargo of June 13, 1798, on shipments to French possessions remained in effect, inasmuch as such supplies would have had to originate in the United States, whoever might carry them. In any case, what assurance was there that such shipments would not be used for the supply of privateers preying on America's Caribbean commerce? King believed that the Maitland-Toussaint agreement should be amended before final ratification to include a guarantee that no privateers would be outfitted or allowed to sail from ports controlled by Toussaint, and he also indicated that if the article on supplies meant what it seemed to mean—exclusive trade privileges for Great Britain in St. Domingue—"Jealousies may be felt among our Merchants." Why not open it "to every Nation not at War with Great Britain"?[30]

King's objections occasioned some discomfiture within the Ministry. Pitt, Dundas, and Grenville were all agreed on the importance of British-American cooperation in any final arrangement on St. Domingue, and none wanted to treat Toussaint as the head of a sovereign state (though as to that point King rather inclined otherwise). Grenville was not entirely pleased with the latitude Maitland had assumed in making his convention with Toussaint, and was quite prepared to see it amended with regard to the suppression of privateers. But he was in full accord with Maitland's desire that the British engross as large a portion of St. Domingue's trade as they could, even though he conceded that they would probably have to accept the Americans' getting some share in it. He thought the best plan would be a joint Anglo-American trading company that would monopolize the entire commerce, the Americans supplying the produce and livestock and the British the manufactured goods, all controlled through a single port. But King pointed out that Americans did not like monopolies, that such an arrangement would be politically difficult if not impossible, and that he doubted whether

Congress had the power to set up such a company anyway. (King could well imagine how any American merchant not in on it, to say nothing of the Republican opposition, would take to a scheme like this.) Pitt and Dundas, anxious for cooperation, were disposed to be somewhat more flexible than Grenville. But not to the point of consenting to a trade open to both countries without restrictions.[31]

What they at length agreed on, with King taking part, was that a British representative should be sent to Philadelphia to work out the details of an equitable arrangement, which would then be taken to St. Domingue as the basis for a final understanding with Toussaint. The envoy would be Thomas Maitland. It was hoped and expected that the beleaguered black general would fall in with any reasonable plan they might devise. Maitland arrived at Philadelphia on April 2, 1799, there to experience at first hand the disposition of the Americans and the frugal hospitality of Secretary Pickering.[32]

But well before this, Pickering had already initiated a course of St. Domingue diplomacy on his own. Toussaint's forces were half starving for want of supplies, and under the American embargo he could not get them. Toussaint was willing, if the restriction were removed, to promise full protection against privateers and generous treatment of American merchants. Pickering, more than receptive, thought there was already a wide enough loophole. Since Toussaint had just forced Commissioner Hédouville off the island, and since the embargo applied to the possessions of France, and since the people of St. Domingue obviously no longer recognized France's authority, then the embargo no longer applied there. This was pushing things a bit too far even for Toussaint, who did not want to risk cutting connections entirely. But he still had to have those supplies, and he decided to send a personal representative, Joseph Bunel, to the United States to see what could be done. Bunel arrived in December in company with Jacob Mayer, the American consul at Cap François, and their lobbying with members of Congress and the cabinet seems to have been quite effective. An act of Congress signed on February 9, 1799, authorized the President, whenever he should judge American commerce sufficiently safe, to lift the embargo so far as it applied to St. Domingue, while American merchants rubbed their hands at the thought of the business that awaited them there. Pickering then prepared to dispatch Edward Stevens as the newly appointed consul-general to conclude an agreement with Toussaint face to face.[33] Captain Barry had meanwhile been ordered to show the flag at Cap François with the "greatest part" of his fleet as a mark of respect to General Toussaint, who had "a great desire to see some Ships of War belonging to America."[34]

The manner in which Pickering got the key South Carolina leaders to support his diplomacy with a rebel chieftain clearly on his way to the headship of a republic of liberated slaves was something of a virtuoso maneuver. He brought them together with Bunel and Mayer, who then described how the malevolent Hédouville had tried to induce Toussaint to mount invasions of Jamaica and the United States, and how Toussaint had refused to do it, subsequently driving the Commissioner out and shipping him back to France. Clearly the interests of America in that part of the world, including those of the slaveholding states, were safer in such hands as these than in any others. All this had occurred, and Stevens had already set sail for St. Domingue in a ship loaded with provisions for Toussaint, escorted by an American warship, before General Maitland set foot in the United States.[35]

President Adams had by then departed for Quincy, so Pickering took full charge of the negotiations with Maitland and Minister Liston. The bargain he drove with them was a very hard one. The British still wanted a monopoly on the export of all manufactured goods to St. Domingue and a free hand on any other products they might ship there; a single port of entry for all imports; and a complicated system of passports, issued only by British agents, for controlling the coasting trade. Pickering raised extensive objections to all of this, and in view of Pitt's instructions on conciliation and cooperation the British representatives were obliged to settle for a series of compromises. The goods of both countries should have free and equal access to Toussaint's domain; there would be two ports of entry instead of one (actually none of the negotiators considered it safe to have any more than two); and passports to control the coasting trade (both countries believing something of the sort to be necessary) could be issued by the agents of either one. Although Liston was inclined to be philosophical, believing that British interests would still derive substantial benefit from the agreement, Maitland departed burning with ire and muttering curses—perhaps unjustified, perhaps not—upon Americans in general. "I will venture to assert, there is but one principle which activates either the Government or the People of America, viz., the narrowest view of Commercial benefit. . . . Their only mode of viewing or arguing any point is merely on the score of Profit and loss, to every other feeling they are perfectly dead. . . ."[36]

Edward Stevens proved to be a very tactful diplomat, and he and Toussaint hit it off from the start. Despite Toussaint's lingering suspicions of the British, not lessened by their having allowed the details of his convention with Maitland the year before to become public, Stevens nevertheless persuaded him to approve the arrangement just concluded at Philadelphia and to take measures against future privateering in all places under his control.[37] Toussaint could now turn his full attention to Rigaud.

The American navy would remain fully employed until hostilities with France were officially ended in September 1800, and in fact for a short time afterward. Meanwhile it was fulfilling certain latent functions, in addition to the specific objects set forth for it by Secretary Stoddert. Its work was obviously producing an impression on the French, whose privateering activities were being made less and less profitable as a result of it. But less obvious, because of its indirectness, was the part it played in altering America's relationship with England. Even in the best of circumstances the United States in its previous dealings had had to approach the British somewhat in the character of a petitioner, whereas the Americans had entered into the transaction just concluded on St. Domingue not as petitioners but as participants, pursuing a course of common interest that was complicated by cross-currents of self-interest. It had occurred against a background which now contained something new, an American naval presence extending throughout the Caribbean. It is of course a well-known maxim that the availability of force has a range of uses in the realm of diplomacy; somewhat less apparent is that these need not include directly warlike uses, or even those of "deterrence." It applies not only with enemies, actual or potential, but with "friends" as well; the awareness of usable force, which can be welcome as well as unwelcome, has a way of greatly widening the scope of all diplomacy. It might be added that this principle was one to which succeeding American administrations in the Jeffersonian era would prove unusually insensitive.

There were some other and more direct uses to which American naval power found itself put which were neither intended nor anticipated. The turning point, probably decisive, in Toussaint's struggle against the forces of André Rigaud came in the winter of 1799–1800 when Toussaint's army laid siege to the port of Jacmel in South Province, where a major portion of Rigaud's troops were concentrated. Captain Raymond Perry, commanding the United States frigate *General Greene*, had been ordered to Jacmel to deal with privateers in that quarter, but upon his arrival Toussaint, lacking both the means to prevent Rigaud's being supplied by sea and adequate artillery for reducing the town, prevailed upon Perry to give him some very critical assistance. *General Greene* thereupon stood off the port, cutting out Rigaud's supply vessels, and in the final assault used her artillery to bombard Rigaud's harbor forts and compel their evacuation. Jacmel was taken on February 27, 1800. Rigaud's resistance was fully broken by August; he himself fled the island, and was captured at sea on October 1, 1800, by the American schooner *Experiment*.[38]

A similar case occurred at Curaçao in September 1800. The French had landed a contingent of some two thousand troops from Guadaloupe supported by seventeen ships, mostly privateers, and had delivered an ultimatum to the Dutch governor to turn over control of the island to them. An anguished appeal to the American squadron at St. Kitts brought two warships, *Merrimack* and *Patapsco*, to the harbor at Willemstad. Though the American commanders, Moses Brown and Henry Geddes, had no authority to operate against French forces on shore, *Patapsco* on the night of September 21 was brought within small-arms range of the waterfront; seventy marines were landed; and a three-hour battle ensued in which Geddes poured fire from his twenty-six guns into the French emplacements while the marines kept up a heavy musketry. The French took nearly a hundred casualties while only two Americans were wounded, and by morning the French began withdrawing to their ships. Over the next few days they evacuated Curaçao altogether.[39]

The American navy at the time of the Quasi-War's termination had by no means eliminated privateering in the Caribbean. Indeed, French corsairs took more American merchant ships in 1800 than they had in 1799, 101 as opposed to 78. Yet this did not indicate a lessening of the navy's effectiveness. Quite the contrary: on the one hand, with more and more merchantmen appearing in Caribbean waters in direct consequence of naval patrols having made them safer, it might have been expected that the remaining privateers should find more prizes to strike for. But on the other, American warships took more than twice as many French armed vessels in 1800 as they had in 1799, and during that same period they captured or recaptured more prizes from the French than were taken from Americans. Insurance rates, moreover, continued their steady decline.[40] The naval establishment Benjamin Stoddert had built by the time of his departure from office in 1801 would not be retained by the Jeffersonians in the form in which he left it, to say nothing of the augmented form which he hoped it might take on in the years ahead. Nevertheless the Jeffersonians, in all their zeal for frugality in military expenditures, would not go to the length of dismantling the navy altogether. Its institutional groundwork was already too solid; it had proven its value too persuasively; and it would shortly be called upon again, this time for service in the Mediterranean against the Barbary states of North Africa. Of additional note were certain technological and operational innovations, developed amid the urgency of quasi-wartime conditions under Stoddert's prompting, that would remain as a continuing asset. The copper sheathing required for protecting ship bottoms from barnacles and sea worms could not be imported after 1798, and techniques for rolling the sheets and turning them out domestically had to be devised. This was substantially accomplished by 1799. Another such case was the home manufacture of the carronade, a superior short-range gun invented by a British officer to smash and splinter wood rather than penetrate it, which was originally cast in a Scottish foundry. Carronades could not be obtained abroad for the American navy because of their being in too great demand elsewhere, so under the stimulation of generous government contracts carronade technology was adapted by the Foxall Furnace of Philadelphia and soon spread to other American foundries as well. Advances in hemp and canvas manufacture by home industry were likewise permanent legacies of Stoddert's encouragement.[41] Of similar note in Stoddert's policies on recruitment of naval leadership for the long term was his system of midshipmen, which he put into effect at once and expanded well beyond previous practice in this particular category of ship's personnel. The idea was to select youths of good education and family, preferably with no prior sea experience, and have them trained through direct service on a warship for naval careers, thereby laying the basis of a dependable elite corps for the future. A fair proportion of the highly capable young officers who went to sea in 1812 had started out as Stoddert's midshipmen.[42]

The diplomacy of the Quasi-War had so far reached its most direct form in Timothy Pickering's dealings with regard to St. Domingue. It had worked very well: almost too well for the liking of many onlookers both at home and abroad, based as it was in large part on the expectation of eventual independence for that island and the recognition of Toussaint Louverture as the head of a free republic. President Adams had his own reservations about that side of it, which were more than shared by the Republican opposition. The British certainly had theirs as well, and so also, most certainly, did Napoleon Bonaparte, who took power through the *coup d'état* of 18 Brumaire (November 9, 1799) as First Consul of the French Republic. To Adams, the St. Domingue policy had all along been something of a side issue, one which if pushed too far might bring embarrassments with the British, with no telling what other complications.[43] Pickering for his part was well aware that his own ideas of diplomacy and the President's, to put it mildly, were not compatible, and that the latter's decision to reopen negotiations with the French in Paris represented a mortal threat to what he himself had in mind for St. Domingue.[44] And he might well have wondered why, if Adams was so solicitous about concert and harmony with England, he should now be preparing to deal with England's enemy France. Conceivably such thoughts as these were coalescing in Pickering's mind to produce the thunderclap of wrath, already referred to, which he visited upon the astonished Murray in July 1799.[45]

Nevertheless there were other reasons why the St. Domingue policy had its limits in relation to the country's larger purposes. For one thing, the commercial possibilities there, though still lucrative, would never again be what they once had been. After nearly a decade of upheaval and civil war, the island's society and economy had been in large part wrecked, and its former position as a leading supplier of sugar and major market for American provisions and lumber was past regaining. And for another, though privateering out of St. Domingue had been for the most part suppressed, privateers continued to operate from Guadaloupe and other Caribbean ports, and controlling them would continue to require an ongoing and expensive vigilance on the part of the American navy. In the last analysis only a new understanding with France could bring about a satisfactory resolution of this problem, which was undoubtedly one of the reasons why Benjamin Stoddert felt no difficulty about supporting Adams's determination to send another mission to that country in 1799. Far from representing a threat to his navy, the reception of such a mission could be seen as marking the success of it.

As for France, Talleyrand, who had nimbly survived the downfall of the Directory and whose services were now at the disposal of Bonaparte, had for some time recognized that France's policy of countenancing aggressions upon American commerce had gone into diminishing returns. Profits from it had become marginal and the hazards beyond what had been expected; it was, in short, no longer worth it, and there was no point at all in driving the Americans closer to the English than they already were. The First Consul, for his own purposes, was inclined to agree that the time had come to make a settlement.

The principal loser, of course, would be Toussaint Louverture, who would shortly be abandoned by the powers of both worlds. The British made peace with France at Amiens in 1801, leaving Bonaparte free to turn his efforts to the subjugation of St. Domingue, the destruction of Toussaint, and perhaps even the restoration of slavery throughout the French colonies. The new President of the United States, Thomas Jefferson, expansively assured the French minister that "nothing would be easier than to furnish your army and fleet with everything, and to reduce Toussaint to starvation."[46] On June 7, 1802, Toussaint was lured through treachery and deception to a meeting with French officers in North Province. He was thereupon seized, sent to France, and thrown into a prison fortress high in the mountains near the Swiss border. He perished there, in cold and misery, on April 7, 1803.[47]

One more postscript may conclude this somewhat somber tale. In 1806 the blacks of St. Domingue were still refusing to be subjugated by the power of France, as in fact they never would be. But early in that year President Jefferson, hoping to oblige the newly proclaimed Emperor Napoleon, pushed through Congress a law prohibiting all commerce with that rebellious island. For this he received a letter, crackling with scorn, from one of the senators from Massachusetts. Could such an infamous measure be approved by him who had once praised the people of revolutionary France as "infuriated men . . . seeking . . . through blood and slaughter their long lost liberty"?

> If Frenchmen . . . could find in you an apologist for cruel excesses of which the world had furnished no example, — are the hapless, the wretched Haytians ("guilty," indeed, "of a skin not coloured like our own" but) *emancipated,* and by a great National Act declared Free . . . are these men, not merely to be abandoned to their own efforts, but to be deprived of those necessary supplies which . . . they have been accustomed to receive from the UStates, and without which they cannot subsist? . . . And what will be their *rights* under the law of nations? Seeing [that] we, by an act of Government, take part with their enemies, to reduce them to submission by *starving them!* . . . Save then your country, Sir, while you may, from such ignominy and thraldom.

The senator's name, of course, was Timothy Pickering.[48]

2

The Convention of 1800

The agreement which the American commissioners Oliver Ellsworth, William R. Davie, and William Vans Murray finally reached with the French government in late September 1800 after six months of exhausting negotiations was not — at least on the face of it — exactly a brilliant one. Nor was it so regarded at the time. The news of the Convention was not generally greeted with ringing of bells or outpourings of joy by throngs of either Federalist or Republican citizens. A Federalist-dominated Senate would, it is true, finally confirm it, but only with great reluctance and not before the attachment of a critical reservation. Some of Ellsworth's most loyal friends and supporters were dismayed. "You will read the treaty . . . with astonishment," privately wrote Oliver Wolcott. "I can account for it only on the supposition that the vigor of Mr. Ellsworth's mind has been enfeebled by sickness." Even Jefferson, though his nightmare of war with France was now dissipated, thought it had been "a bungling negotiation."[49]

Subsequent commentators have not found much to say for the Convention of 1800 either. There has, of course, been a fair amount of praise of John Adams for the intrepidity with which he sought peace with France, but the praise rather trails off when it comes to the peace itself and the terms upon which it was achieved. Indeed, some recent writers have been quite blunt about what they see as the Convention's deficiencies. "When the agreement ending the quasi-war was finally reached," asserts Forrest McDonald, "the United States had been removed as one of France's antagonists, had resumed the carrying of vital goods to France, and had sacrificed the valid spoliation claims of its citizens in the amount of $12 million. In exchange it received nothing except a cessation of hostilities that France had momentarily lost the capacity to sustain."[50] Nor for that matter—so the argument goes—would it have been in France's interest to continue these hostilities, quite aside from whether she had or had not kept the capacity to sustain them. France's attacks on American commerce were by then doing more damage to her own prosperity than to America's, and Talleyrand had had more than a fair inkling of this for some time. Moreover, had France kept up such attacks, another of Talleyrand's and Bonaparte's objectives—that of uniting Sweden, Denmark, Prussia, and Russia in a league of armed neutrality to resist British command of the seas and abuses of neutral shipping—would have been very seriously compromised. Finally, it could even be said that the entire negotiation was carried out against a background of deception. As subsequently became known, Bonaparte was all the while making every effort to cozen Spain into retroceding the province of Louisiana to France, a design which must obviously bring into question any interest he may have had in a long-term understanding with the United States. The very day after the signing of the Convention with the American negotiators, Bonaparte's minister to Spain did in fact conclude a secret agreement for the transfer of Louisiana, which according to Henry Adams "was equivalent to a rupture of the relations established four and twenty hours earlier."[51]

All such considerations are certainly persuasive, and should be weighed in whatever conclusions it is possible to reach regarding this somewhat ambiguous transaction. What was the great urgency about concluding it precisely then? The French appear to have been in as much of a hurry as the Americans, perhaps more so: why not take better advantage of this and temporize; why settle for something so minimal? Or, to reverse the question entirely, why not sooner? Why not act to end the Quasi-War, and the maritime depredations that had brought it about, upon receipt of the first signals, more than two years before, that the French were changing their tune? Either way, the settlement they did conclude, according to Jacob E. Cooke, "was more a French than an American diplomatic triumph."[52]

At best, historians have tended to treat the Convention of 1800 rather as they have the Jay Treaty—that is, equivocally. By and large, most of them have said in effect, the advantages of the Convention—peace, and an end to the entangling alliance—probably outweighed its disadvantages. A judicious assessment, perhaps, though somewhat left-handed. But conceivably the case could be made a good deal stronger than this, had not the categories of "diplomatic triumph" and "diplomatic defeat"—again, as with most discussions of the Jay Treaty—tended to preempt all others. Indeed, the value to the United States of the Convention of 1800—whether called a "triumph" or a "defeat"—may well have been such that its latent benefits were all but immeasurable.

For one thing, American diplomacy in general functioned under many constraints, most of them probably salutary, but owing to the very character of American society its diplomacy never had, and could not have, the kind of maneuverability possessed by every chancellery of eighteenth-century Europe, in which rulers and ministries could move as it suited them. For another, a settlement with France was in fact imperative and could not be put off any longer; there was little likelihood, on the other hand, that circumstances would have allowed it to occur much earlier. And for still another, receiving indemnities for spoliations on American commerce was not the principal thing the Americans wanted or needed, insistently as they may have pressed that question. There was never the least chance of obtaining them anyway—then, or earlier, or later on; the evidence for this is abundant, and the Americans themselves were more than a little aware of it. And finally, for reasons of both internal and external stability, a prime requirement of American diplomacy in the first decade or so of the new republic's existence was to arrive at some realistic definition of where America stood in relation to the two foremost powers of the Old World. With Great Britain this had been done, for better or worse, with the Jay Treaty of 1794, and the possible consequences of its not being done have seldom been contemplated. With regard to France, the Convention of 1800 permitted the United States to complete this process and wash its hands of a connection that had brought disruptions of every variety, internationally and domestically, from 1789 onwards.

Unlike any of the European powers, the United States was not truly free to move about at will on the diplomatic chessboard—declaring war, concluding a peace, or remaining in a state of suspended hostilities—with no more than a casual concern for public opinion. Anything the American government did in this realm was done in a newly formed republic that had a very large electorate, and whose political life and civic passions were bound up to an extraordinary degree with its foreign relations. At the same time, that public could not be expected to have an over-subtle response to international difficulties or a very refined sensitivity to "reasons of state" in dealing with them. The solutions it demanded tended to be straightforward, uncomplicated, and definitive—all, moreover, with an undercurrent of great touchiness as to the young nation's honor and self-esteem. It was in a setting of this sort that American diplomacy in this era had to operate; if American representatives abroad were kept honest, so to speak, by the public they served, by the same token whatever settlements they might achieve amid the complexities of European politics were more or less bound in the nature of things to be received at home with something less than universal satisfaction.

In any case, by 1800 the Quasi-War with France had come to place very strong demands on the patience of the American public. By then most Americans were tired of a state that was neither war nor peace, tired of the taxes for support of an army that served no apparent purpose, tired even of maintaining a navy that did have a clear purpose. The French commerce raiders in the West Indies had, to be sure, been brought under a measure of control. But what then? Even the merchants of New England were pulled in more than one direction. Some, in strong Federalist districts, would have liked a resolution through open and outright war. But what most of them wanted a great deal more was to resume a once-lucrative trade in provisions with metropolitan France. What just about everyone wanted, above all, was clarity. They wanted peace and a settlement.

Yet for such a peace to be negotiated, two things were essential. One was a French government with both the clear inclination and the recognized capacity to end the hostilities. The other was an American commission with sufficient political and moral authority to negotiate a settlement that a majority of the American public could be brought to accept, reluctantly or otherwise. These conditions, each requiring the other, could in no way be taken for granted, and they were simply not present prior to 1800.

The first change of the weather in Paris occurred in 1798, and the circumstances were fairly dramatic. In the late spring of that year Marshall's XYZ dispatches, with all their saucy implications of an Executive Directory and Foreign Ministry awash in corruption, were gleefully picked up from the New York press and reprinted in most of the London newspapers, translated into French, and spread all over Europe. It was the buzz of the cafés, and Talleyrand's discomfiture was hugely savored in the embassies. A bilingual cartoon circulating in Paris depicted the Directory itself as a five-headed hydra clutching a raised dagger and howling *"Money, money,"* as the three virtuous Americans stood fast, retorting "Assez, monstre, tu n'auras pas 6 pence."[53]

Talleyrand was in quite a scrape, and he did what he could to squirm his way out of it. In this he seems to have been more or less successful, or as much so as the case permitted. He made a show of demanding from Gerry, who was of course still in Paris, the names of X, Y, and Z, and Gerry obliged him by acting out the fiction of furnishing them. Talleyrand then submitted an interminable report to the Directory, so lengthy (twenty-three folio pages written in minuscule) and so laden with detail (some of which was tolerably true) that it may be doubted whether any of the Directors actually read it all through, much less bothered to correlate it with Marshall's narrative, upon which Talleyrand's concoction was being offered as critique and commentary. In it, he disavowed any connection with these "foreign intriguers" except for Hauteval, who had served him briefly as an interpreter, and declared that none of the "shocking propositions" described in the dispatches had come from him. At the same time, he caused to be published anonymously and in the same vein a defense of his own conduct, and with this he appears to have gone through whatever motions were required to save him from disgrace. Not, however, without a squeal of anguish from Bellamy, whose name had been disclosed and who rushed into print in his own defense, protesting that he had "done nothing, said nothing, and written nothing, without the orders of Citizen Talleyrand."[54]

Very likely nobody was at any point much deceived, and it remains to be conjectured why Talleyrand was not dismissed on the spot. One reason may have been that the Directors were sufficiently implicated themselves that it would have been imprudent to make a scapegoat of the Foreign Minister; and another, that the Directory was already on a shaky enough footing with both the Legislative Councils and the general public that an occasion for more questions and fresh criticism were on all counts best avoided.[55]

In any case, this episode did mark a turn of sorts in the management of American affairs. France had never intended war against the United States—as Marshall, for one, had correctly guessed all along—and now that the Americans were aroused to warlike preparations Talleyrand undertook a series of vigorous movements looking toward conciliation. He pressed Gerry mercilessly to conquer his hesitations and to assume the plenipotentiary authority with which, he insisted, the American had been clothed by his government and which he still retained, and to enter into negotiations which would lead to a peaceful settlement. Gerry, who by this time wanted nothing so much as to go home, would consent to no more than to receive whatever propositions the Minister might wish to make and to transmit them informally to the President. Meanwhile he kept on demanding, throughout their extensive exchange of letters, that he be given his passports. Talleyrand was at length obliged to give up on Gerry, and reluctantly delivered the passports on July 12, 1798. But concurrently, as previously noted, he had begun his confidential approaches to William Vans Murray through the agency of Louis Pichon at The Hague.[56]

At the same time, he undertook still another line of effort. This was a campaign to persuade the Directory that French depredations on American commerce had become an acute liability, and that France's own interests called for measures to stop them. His instrument for this purpose was Victor-Marie DuPont, who had served since 1795 as the French consul at Charleston. Earlier in 1798 DuPont had been promoted to Consul-General of the French Republic in America to replace Létombe, but he had been refused his exequatur by President Adams and had now returned to France, arriving at Bordeaux on July 3, 1798. He was full of news about the general ferment against France in the United States, and was especially well informed about the goings-on in the French West Indies, Charleston being the American port most favored by the privateers in their cruisings in and out of the Caribbean. Talleyrand perceived at once that a first-hand report on this subject could be very useful. He not only prevailed upon DuPont to give him such a report, but in all likelihood—given the resulting document's tone, its extraordinary length, fullness of detail, obvious care in preparation, and the implausible shortness of time between request and delivery—he himself was a prime contributor in the writing of it.[57]

The report begins on a note of pious fiction, pretending to assume that the Directors have up to now known nothing of the excesses of French, "or so-called French," cruisers in the Antilles and that the many dispatches from DuPont and his colleagues on these matters have somehow never reached them. DuPont then states categorically that such excesses had been a principal cause of "the gradual cooling of the Americans towards us," and there follows a four-thousand-word description, full of lively particulars, of the "acts of violence, of brigandage, of piracy committed in American seas by French cruisers, or under the French flag, principally directed at American commerce and which, far from being repressed by the Republic's agents at St. Domingue or Guadeloupe, are almost always encouraged or protected by them." He concludes with three recommendations which are obviously Talleyrand's own, forming as they would a basic theme in all the Minister's subsequent communications to the Directory on American affairs. The first is to revoke all existing privateers' commissions in the Antilles; the second, to revise the law of prizes and to so alter judicial procedures in prize cases as to rid them of their present prejudice; and finally, "to make known to the government of the United States that if it wishes to send new commissioners either to Paris or to Holland or Spain, we would be disposed to recognize them and treat with them."[58] All these steps would eventually be taken.

But not for another two years, and they would probably not have been taken then, had the Directory survived as France's executive power. The fact was that Talleyrand, for all his belated scurryings, was virtually impotent, and the Directory itself lacked either the will or the inclination, or indeed the very authority, to make the minimal engagements that would have had any meaning in the preparation of a mutually satisfactory settlement between France and the United States.

For one thing, Talleyrand, though allowed for reasons of expediency to remain in office after the XYZ scandal, was now kept more at arm's length than ever. His days of audience were cut by half; the most important diplomatic correspondence was drafted within the Directory itself by Merlin, Treilhard, and Reubell, copied at the General Secretariat, and confided to the Directory's own special couriers. Nominations of ambassadors and political agents were made without Talleyrand's advice and sometimes contrary altogether to his recommendations. Reubell if anything treated him more churlishly than before, incessantly calling him to order with thinly disguised insinuations of incompetence and even of treason. "Anyone else," observes Raymond Guyot, "would have been repelled by such contempt and would have resigned his place." But not the ex-Bishop of Autun, who was determined above all to hang on.[59]

But though Talleyrand was now all but excluded from any active part in France's European diplomacy, the Directors apparently saw little harm and perhaps some good in allowing him a sort of caretaker's role with regard to American affairs, in view of his familiarity with them and of their own lack of interest. Within those limits, which he was careful not to overstrain, he did what he could. The permission he had obtained back in the previous winter to hold Gerry in Paris while sending off Marshall and Pinckney was among other things—in principle at least—the authority to receive an accredited American minister. Yet he still felt obliged to toady to the Directors' short patience, prejudices, and preoccupations elsewhere in his communications on how such a minister should be dealt with. On July 10 Talleyrand submitted a very long summary of France's external relations, in which the United States was but one of twenty-three countries whose affairs were discussed. In that part of his report he was still saying that his object in detaining Gerry was simply

to engage him in a negotiation of which we may dictate a prolongation at will, because it would bring only the gravest inconvenience to break entirely with the

United States since our present position, half friendly, half hostile, is profitable to us in that our colonies continue to be provisioned by the Americans, and our privateers continue to enrich themselves by captures made on them.[60]

But eleven days later he had DuPont's report in hand, and with it he succeeded in persuading the hitherto bellicose Minister of Marine, Admiral Eustache Bruix, to use his influence with the Directory (he himself did not have much) for the issuance of a decree aiming at better control of the privateers. Talleyrand was able to place a copy of the decree in Gerry's hands just prior to the latter's embarkation for the United States on August 8. Louis Pichon was meanwhile well along in his informal conversations with Murray at The Hague. Primarily in consequence of these talks, President Adams was at length persuaded that the French were indeed now prepared to negotiate in good faith, and that—in Talleyrand's own words, transmitted to Pichon, who passed them to Murray, who in turn sent them to Adams—any plenipotentiary the United States might send to France "to terminate the differences which subsist between the two countries would unquestionably be received with the regard due the representative of a free, independent, and powerful nation."[61]

Well and good; yet it is more than likely that if such assurances had been acted upon as soon as they were received, and had such negotiations taken place as soon as an American mission could be dispatched to Paris to get them under way, little if anything would have come of them. The authority on which Talleyrand was making these assurances was tenuous at best. He was acting entirely on his own; the French minister at The Hague—in whose bureau Pichon was officially employed as a secretary—knew nothing of it; the Directory itself was not informed until months later, and then only in the most casual way, that anything of the sort was going on there.[62] In any case a settled, serious, and firm new French policy toward the United States (or any other country) would have to rest on something more substantial than the covert maneuverings of a Foreign Minister holding his office on bare sufferance.

A year later, in July 1799, as the Directory was eking out its final months of existence, Talleyrand himself saw the expediency of resigning. As things turned out, it was to be a short retirement, and he would be reappointed to office by Bonaparte less than two weeks following the latter's accession to power in November. Talleyrand's stand-in during this eighteen-week interim was Charles-Frédéric Reinhard, a friend and protégé who had served as the French minister to Hamburg, and who is referred to by Talleyrand's principal biographer as his "creature."[63] Yet if this "creature" continued his mentor's American policy, as has been more or less assumed by writers who have mentioned him, he certainly did it in a fitful and captious way. His one memorandum on American affairs shows little sign of instruction, and even less of prior knowledge of the subject. In a set of "Observations" dated October 1, Reinhard concedes that it is "in France's interest" to make peace with the United States. He further notes that the United States "are said to be sending new ministers to the French republic to negotiate." If they arrive, he says, "they can be listened to." But having somehow got it into his head that they were all "appointed under English influences," including "the one at The Hague" (Murray, the man with whom Talleyrand had so assiduously labored all through the summer of the previous year), he surmises that they should be for practical purposes by-passed, and France's effective negotiating be carried out under cover. He has the happy thought that "a confidential agent" should go to America clothed with full powers *"to negotiate and conclude,"* in a transaction requiring "neither correspondence nor replies," but that he should be "under the guise of a merchant going there on his own business." Before "revealing his character" he would have dealt secretly with Republicans who were sufficiently influential as to bring over majorities in the Senate and House of Representatives, and from there "the majority of the people." The only item for negotiation he specifically alludes to is the matter of indemnities, to the extent of working out a plan whereby France might appear willing to pay such indemnities without actually having to end up doing so. (This much he could conceivably have got from Talleyrand.) But what really inspires him is an entirely different object: that of arousing hopes of liberation in the Canadians and of bringing about "the revolution and independence of Canada, Nova Scotia, and Newfoundland, etc., under the protection of France"—which would have the additional merit of stirring up hostilities "between America and England." Such harebrained fancies had not been seriously entertained by any responsible French functionary since Genet's time.[64]

Such, then, was the state of diplomatic preparation in the French Foreign Office at the moment when the Ellsworth mission was receiving its orders to depart for Paris.

As for the Directory, the executive arm of the French government that would have had not only to support but to promote in an active and public way any meaningful steps toward a settlement, that body had been steadily losing credit in its own country for at least the previous two years. In the *coup d'état* of 18 Fructidor (September 4, 1797) the Directory had used military force to nullify the election of some two hundred new legislative deputies in the face of what was represented as a royalist plot to undermine and overthrow the Republic. But the result was a new resurgence of Jacobinism, which the Directory saw as equally if not more alarming. When in the following year, by the so-called coup of 22 Floréal, the Directory succeeded through obscure technicalities in getting over a hundred opposition candidates purged, its claim to be upholding republican stability had become exceedingly flimsy. Floréal was immediately followed by the XYZ sensation and by mounting attacks upon the Directory for abuse of power, corruption, and financial bungling. In the early fall of 1798 came news of the destruction of the French fleet at Aboukir. By the spring of 1799 a coalition of Jacobins and conservatives, united at least in their hatred of the Directory, had become sufficiently strong that the Council of Five Hundred could turn upon the executive body and bring about a purge of its own. After Reubell had drawn the short straw for annual replacement by lot (as managed by the ever-sinuous Barras), a legislative deputation found the means for pushing on and getting rid of the other three. They insisted that Treilhard had already been holding office on unconstitutional grounds and must go, and then browbeat Larevellière and Merlin into resigning under threat of indictment for illegal acts. This was the coup of 30 Prairial, June 18 1799. The four were replaced by Emmanuel Joseph Sieyès, who would shortly become the dominant voice—such as it was—of the new Directory, and by Roger Ducos, Louis Antoine Gohier, and Jean François Moulin.[65]

But though the new Directory bore little resemblance to the previous one, and though the Councils had decisively reasserted their constitutional authority, the stability of France's entire governmental structure continued to crumble. The military situation appeared desperate. The forces of the second coalition had retaken all of Italy; the Russians were moving upon Switzerland; the English had landed in Holland; and the very frontiers of France itself were exposed. Inside France there was enormous discontent on account of measures that bore on right and left alike: the extensive call-up of military conscripts on June 28, the law of hostages directed against the families of émigrés, the forced loan of August 6, and Sieyès' suppression under a new Minister of Police of the Paris Jacobin club as well as of the remaining royalist newspapers.

In September a democratic movement to seize power was narrowly aborted, as was an effort in the Council of Five Hundred to declare a state of national emergency. It was amid the most hopeless divisions that there came a dramatic break in the weather: a miraculous reversal of the military situation with French victories in Holland and Switzerland, and the return to France on October 9 of Napoleon Bonaparte, whose own credit had remained unimpaired by his misfortunes in Egypt and the Levant. Thereupon unfolded very quickly a design for the full reconstitution of the French government, of which the chief plotters were Sieyès and Talleyrand. Bonaparte was cast as their accessory, and it was consummated on November 9, 1799, in the *coup d'état* of 18 Brumaire, Year VIII of the French Republic.[66] At that moment the frigate bearing the American negotiators, Ellsworth and Davie, was in the first week of its passage in the North Atlantic.

At no time during the year and a half that preceded Brumaire had there been much of a chance that a new and genuine understanding between France and the United States could be achieved. The state of affairs that had brought about the Quasi-War in the first place—the depredations of the privateers in the West Indies—remained unchanged. Even if the Directory, the old one or the new, had been disposed to give Talleyrand its full support in altering that state, there was little or nothing the Directors alone could do about it. The stoutest bastion of resistance to any effort they might make in that direction was the Legislative Councils themselves. The Councils constituted the very heart of the privateering interest, which knew no ideological boundaries, embracing as it did the entire political spectrum from left to right. That interest, the Minister of Marine ruefully admitted in the summer of 1798, had "perverted public opinion" in all such matters; the Councils, back of which stood the port administrators and the tribunals of judgment, had turned a deaf ear to all proposals either to alter the current laws and regulations or even to enforce proper compliance with those that existed. This "new and already dominant power," Talleyrand vainly lamented in February 1799, "cannot be too much signaled to the Directory's attention, this power that grows by leaps and bounds in the very bosom of the Republic, that reduces to silence the timid voice of industry, the arts, and agriculture, that enriches a few men to the detriment of the entire nation. Perhaps it is too late!" One of the by-products of Brumaire was the sweeping away of the Councils. When the news reached William Vans Murray at The Hague, it brought him the deepest satisfaction. "I rejoice that the 500 are crushed," Murray wrote; "it was a nest of privateersmen."[67]

The three American envoys who had been designated to negotiate with France were very divergent types, and it does not appear that any one of them was greatly charmed by the other two. Yet none of the official documents conveys any hint of serious disharmony in their joint proceedings. Their prior and subsequent careers, moreover, contain elements sufficiently similar as to merit some note. Each was a man of higher than ordinary capacities, and each of their biographers has mused upon the anomaly of their having left no more of a mark on the historical record than any of them in fact did. Each was a solid Federalist, though none an extremist. Yet in each case, though the oldest was not quite fifty-five when the negotiation began, and the youngest had just turned forty, fashioning the Convention of 1800 would be the last act of any consequence in a public capacity that any of them performed.

Oliver Ellsworth, the head of the mission by virtue of both seniority and standing at home, held no less an office than that of Chief Justice. Such was the record of his public service, and such the respect he commanded in the inner circles at Philadelphia as well as in the state of Connecticut, that no one would have thought of disputing him the title of "Mr. Federalist."

He was born in 1745 in Windsor, Connecticut, where there had been Ellsworths almost since the colony's beginnings in the previous century. His father, a successful farmer, hoped his son might enter the ministry. But though Ellsworth would be actively connected with the Congregational Church all his life, would hold family prayers every morning and often serve as lay reader at the meeting house in Windsor, he turned instead to the study of law within a year of leaving college (Princeton '66) and was admitted to practice in 1771. After three impoverished years of little business and almost no fees, cases began coming his way and soon he was being sought after as one of the leading lawyers of the Hartford area. In 1775 he was sent to the General Assembly as one of the two deputies from Windsor.[68]

Contemporary reminiscences of Oliver Ellsworth give the impression of a stern and towering presence, a Demosthenes of the forum, an expositor of penetrating clarity, and a paragon of honor and sagacity who could do no wrong. All of which may have been true, though Ellsworth himself once let slip a clue to an alternative reading of his character: that of a powerful over-achiever who in native endowment was in fact not exceptionally bright. Soon after leaving college (he gravely reported of himself in later life) he made a "deliberate survey" of his understanding, which he found to be "weak." "I had no imagination and but little knowledge or culture." Whereupon he resolved "to take up but a single subject at a time, and to cling to that with an attention so undivided that if a cannon were fired in my ears I should still cling to my subject. That, sir, is all my secret." One senses here, aside from the cannon shot, a certain plausibility. Ellsworth could indeed be fearsomely single-minded; every topic he turned to came out with the look of having been overcome by force; he was much given to talking to himself; and in his powers of concentration he was from all accounts something of a prodigy. (A variant reading might be that of the bilious William Maclay, who tagged him "Endless Ellsworth.")[69] All such traits, in one form or another, were to have their bearing on the negotiations at Paris in 1800.

Ellsworth went there with a civic record that was in all ways formidable. Connecticut had been as hot for revolution in 1775 as any colony in America, and the young Ellsworth was prominent in the state's effort from the first, serving on the Council of Safety, the Committee of the Pay Table, the Assembly, and the Governor's Council. He was elected to the Continental Congress, where he served from 1777 to 1783 and was on each of the three most important standing committees, Marine, Treasury, and Judicial Appeals. Perhaps the closest he ever came to writing an emotional letter was one in which he pointed to the desperate need for "a sure establishment" of the public credit.[70] Though he did not at first share the ardent nationalism of Hamilton and Madison, the foundations of his Federalism were laid by what he saw of the many cross-purposes of the states, the deficiencies of the Articles of Confederation, and the drying up of the Confederation's revenues. Like Hamilton, he saw little point in vindictive measures against the erstwhile Loyalists; he held no rancor against England, and he thought the British for their part would be wise to concede America's independence "with grace, and *in a manner that shall also keep us independent of France.*"[71]

The Connecticut delegation to the Constitutional Convention, consisting of Ellsworth, William Samuel Johnson, and Roger Sherman, was one of the strongest, and in the part Ellsworth took he was one of the most prominent delegates there. He played a leading role in bringing about the so-called Connecticut Compromise on representation, and although he had to go home on business before the Convention adjourned and thus could not sign the completed instrument, before he left he had been a member of the committee of style that drew it up. When the new government began its functioning in 1789, the two senators from Connecticut were William Samuel Johnson and Oliver Ellsworth.

As a member of the first Senate and by virtue of his remaining in that body until nearly the end of Washington's second term, Ellsworth became the quintessential insider. He was on the committees most responsible for the critical precedents and procedures established during the first year, and his was the principal hand in shaping the Judiciary Act of 1789, the enabling law that organized the entire system of federal courts. All the main features of Hamilton's Treasury system—indeed all the measures most associated with what would come to be called Federalism—had Ellsworth's active support. Prior to the Jay mission to England, the self-appointed committee of influentials who helped persuade Washington to dispatch such a mission had Ellsworth as their spokesman, and

Ellsworth later supported the result with a special pertinacity. Early in 1796 Washington nominated Ellsworth as Chief Justice. He was confirmed at once, and exactly a year after receiving his commission he administered the oath of office to John Adams. Many years afterward, Adams was still grumbling that his own administration would have had a great deal more support in the Senate if Washington had left Ellsworth where he was.[72]

Oliver Ellsworth never had much enthusiasm for the French Revolution, and he had less and less the more he saw of it. When Adams in 1799 asked him to head a new mission to France he accepted only with the greatest reluctance, not trusting the Directory or the behavior of any of its agents. He only consented, as we have already seen, in order to prevent the "greater evil" of a Republican nominee. Nor could he have known, when he took that office, that he would never hold another.

William Richardson Davie, at the time of his appointment as the second member of the mission, had just been installed as Governor of North Carolina. To Andrew Jackson, who had served under him in the Revolution as an orderly and had known many other military officers by the time he reached the presidency, Davie remained the "model soldier." He was "swift but wary; bold in planning enterprises, but most cautious in execution; sleeplessly vigilant; untiringly active; one of those cool, quick men who apply master-wit to the art of war; who are good soldiers because they are earnest and clear-sighted men."[73] But it is probably less as a military figure that Davie is remembered in North Carolina than as one of the best criminal lawyers of his time and as the father of the university at Chapel Hill. He somehow rose to the front rank of North Carolina's public men as a Federalist despite his thinly veiled disdain for the democratic temper of the state's population and that of most of its other civic leaders.

Davie was born in 1756 at Egremont in Cumberland, just south of the Scottish border. Upon the urging of his childless uncle, William Richardson, who had emigrated a few years earlier, the boy was brought by his parents to the still-primitive settlement of the Waxhaws in South Carolina in 1763. Upon the death of his mother shortly after their arrival young Davie came under the care of his uncle, who saw to the youth's education and left him, still in his teens, with a fairly tidy legacy. He went to Princeton, then in the heyday of John Witherspoon, and graduated with the class of 1776, a few years behind Madison, Brackenridge, Burr, Bradford, Freneau, and Charles Lee, and a decade after Ellsworth. The place was popping with revolutionary ardor, and one day a coterie of students, Davie among them, abruptly formed themselves into a company of volunteers and dashed off to join Washington's army at Elizabethtown. But somebody seems to have persuaded them that their country's benefit would be better served for the time being if they went back to their studies, which they accordingly did. Directly after graduation, with first honors, Davie proceeded to Salisbury, North Carolina, to begin the study of law. Salisbury too was a nest of patriotic militancy, and again he interrupted his studies to take up arms in 1777.

One searches Davie's military record over the next five years in vain for the least sign of a blemish. True, a fair portion of what we know of it was written by himself, but the corroborative evidence is persuasive enough. Starting off as a lieutenant of cavalry attached to Pulaski's legion, he rose in the space of a year to the rank of brigade major. Badly wounded while leading a charge at Stone Ferry below Charleston, he spent his short convalescence qualifying for the bar, was licensed to practice in November 1779, and then returned to raise his own troop of cavalry and two troops of infantry. His exploits over the next year and a half as a partisan commander have led to his being ranked with Sumter, Pickens, and Marion in that kind of warfare, one writer claiming that Davie "possessed talents of a higher order and was much more accomplished, in education and manners, than either of his three competitors for fame."[74] He kept his own force intact despite Gates's rout and flight from Camden; he executed a daring raid on Tarleton's positions in the Waxhaws; and he maintained a persistent harassment of Cornwallis as the latter moved his forces into western North Carolina. General Nathanael Greene, taking command of the southern army for the Carolina campaign, was looking for a commissary-general in 1781 and pressed Davie to accept that duty. Davie, despite his loathing for drudgery of such a sort, his preference for an independent field command, and the army's lack of money, accepted and performed the most heroic labors in scratching up supplies and keeping the army subsisted. By the close of hostilities Davie, still in his twenties, had dealt with the leading civilian authorities in both the Carolinas and emerged with a reputation for energy, capability, and resourcefulness. He settled in Halifax, North Carolina, acquired property there, married the daughter of a former commanding officer, and resumed in earnest the practice of law. Success, given the uncontainability of his natural talents, was as inexorable as a snowslide in spring. Halifax, moreover, was about the only place in North Carolina that had any refinement or polish — for which the dashing would-be aristocrat had already acquired quite a taste.

Davie was elected nine times to the state assembly, where he sat from 1784 to 1798. During that time he performed a variety of public services. He was sent as a delegate to the Constitutional Convention in 1787 and gave some critical support to the Connecticut Compromise; Davie's vote in the committee that shaped the Compromise's final form was "without doubt" (his biographer somewhat grandly asserts) "the most decisive single vote cast in the convention."[75] North Carolina was one of the two states that refused to ratify, despite the exertions of Davie and James Iredell, the Constitution's two strongest defenders there. But their efforts over the following year to turn public opinion around were rewarded when a second ratifying convention in November 1789 finally brought the state in. Davie's work in establishing the University of North Carolina antedated by some years Thomas Jefferson's more famous association with the University of Virginia. He drafted the chartering act in 1789 and steered it through the Assembly, and then became the leading force in choosing the site, raising money for the endowment, overseeing the building, devising the curriculum, and selecting the faculty. In 1794, as trouble impended with Great Britain, Davie was commissioned a major-general of the state militia. In 1798, amid the more serious troubles with

France, he was placed in command of all the state's troops. When the legislators of North Carolina elected him as governor in November of that year, they were choosing their foremost and probably ablest citizen.

William R. Davie, face to face, made quite an impression. His "martial air" and "oratorical eloquence" were accompanied by a "beauty of person and graceful manner, rendered more attractive perhaps by a slight *hauteur* which was natural to him."[76] In a word, he was splendid. But given these superior attributes, and his keen appreciation of his own merits, North Carolina may not have been the best of all places to exercise them, especially as a Federalist. Foremost among the sources of his Federalism was a kind of standing negative reference group of uncouth fellow-citizens who were forever getting in his way, or saying "no" to their duty as he saw it. (They had given him no end of trouble in his wartime supplying efforts, they had refused to ratify *his* Constitution, and they kept putting up obstacles to his university.) Before their juries he defended Tories in his very first two law cases, both of which he lost; he later favored the return of Loyalist property and repeal of the state's confiscation laws, also without success. He had no use for the French Revolution, and heartily endorsed Edmund Burke's condemnation of it. He stood virtually alone in North Carolina in his strong support for the Jay Treaty.

But it was these very aspects of Davie's record and views that made him so logical a nominee for the French mission in 1799. When Patrick Henry declined, it was probably Oliver Ellsworth who first proposed Davie for his place, by reason, among other things, of his "dignified manners, extent of political information, and correctness of opinions."[77] Thus when Davie departed for France he was at the peak of his prestige, an eminence which his fellow-citizens had been obliged to concede him almost in spite of themselves. Yet in the fifteen months during which he was gone, they seem to have discovered that they could get along very well without him. In North Carolina after 1800 there was, for some reason, no longer any room for William R. Davie.[78]

William Vans Murray passed his entire life, which was unhappily not very long, in a state of juniority. The world in which he moved never quite allowed him to advance to the next logical phase of his career, the one beyond that in which the very bright young man, full of promise, wants only a little more seasoning, a touch more of stability and tempering of judgment, before he comes fully into his own. Thus although Murray was the only member of the American delegation with any experience in foreign diplomacy, and consequently had a direct acquaintance with European affairs which the others lacked, he was not seen by Federalists in America as carrying quite the kind of political or other kinds of weight that would justify his undertaking the mission by himself. President Adams, though privately and grudgingly, seems to have agreed with them. Murray took this outwardly in good grace; in the subsequent negotiation he played a full and able part, and more than held up his end in it. But although neither Ellsworth nor Davie left any record of what they thought of him, Murray privately imagined—perhaps correctly—that they never took him quite as seriously as they should have. Doubtless this was only natural, in the case of a man who had been demoted from number one to number three.[79]

Murray's Federalism, like that of the others, was unimpeachable, and he arrived at it more or less predictably. Born in 1760 in Dorchester County on the Eastern Shore of Maryland, Murray came of a family comfortably settled in commerce and the professions and having no great interest in agriculture. He did not see military service in the Revolution, as he probably would have if his health had been better, he and the rest of the family being all good Whigs. Whether his education came from private tutors or at some local academy is unknown, but in due course he took up the study of law, doing three years of it in London at the Middle Temple. He opened a practice at Cambridge, Maryland, in 1787. Yet he seems to have given more attention to politics than to law; under the aegis of an influential uncle he was elected to the Maryland House of Delegates, serving three terms; in 1790 he was elected to Congress and twice re-elected, always from a safe district. He took Federalist positions on the issues that counted most. He came to Hamilton's defense in the face of the Giles Resolutions; he was a strong supporter of the Jay Treaty; and he resisted the cheese-paring efforts of Gallatin and other Republicans to trim military appropriations to an even lower level than the skimpy one at which they already stood. One of Washington's last appointments was the naming of Murray as United States minister to the Netherlands, where he took up his duties in the late spring of 1797.

But somehow Murray never quite counted as a Federalist insider, one reason for which may have been a close and long-standing connection with the Adamses. He and John Quincy Adams had known each other since their London days in the 1780s, during which time Murray had written a book of political essays on American local governments under the elder Adams's encouragement. A decade later his "Short Vindication of Mr. Adams's 'Defence of American Constitutions,'" together with other newspaper pieces, was Murray's loyal response to the rumored plot to push John Adams aside in favor of Thomas Pinckney for the presidency in 1796.

Murray was slight of build, and his portrait by Mather Brown shows a man of strikingly delicate features. He was never entirely sure of himself; he was something of a hypochondriac, probably with cause; and was intellectually rather excitable, with a tendency to flit from one opinion to another. With the coming of the French Revolution, Murray, unlike Ellsworth and Davie, was at first full of enthusiasm. But he became heavily disillusioned by its excesses, and his correspondence from The Hague with John Quincy Adams overflows with distrust of the French in general and the Directory in particular. Valuing stability and order, Murray believed, or wanted to believe, that with 18 Brumaire the French nation had finally come to its senses. And in this state of mind he was profoundly impressed by what he saw, or thought he saw, in Napoleon Bonaparte.

The three Americans who met Napoleon Bonaparte for the first time on March 8, 1800, were all men who owed their careers to the combined circumstances of a successful revolution and the consequent establishment of a new national government. Yet the implied parallel is deceptive: there was nothing in the American experience that could have prepared them for Bonaparte. They themselves, and all the leading figures of their own civic universe, had made their way along a visible and generally ratified path. For all the turbulence of their times, each was the recognizable product of a regional culture; the aspirations of each were fully comprehensible to their fellow-citizens; and in turn they all took for granted that the scope of their ambitions and activities, however wide, would be delineated by an environing set of limits and prior expectations. Bonaparte, on the other hand, had only yesterday burst out of nowhere. His profoundest allegiance was not to a region, nor to a class, nor to a national culture, nor even to a revolutionary vision. It was secondarily to an obscure family clan, and primarily to a cosmic personal ambition, in a world as free of limits as he could make it.[80]

One could picture Ellsworth, Davie, and Murray, had each been a few years older, making fully respectable names for themselves in pre-Revolutionary America. But in the France of the *ancien régime* there would have been no room at all for a Napoleon Bonaparte. The Bonaparte family were of the impoverished minor nobility of Corsica, which had become French only through accident of conquest in 1768, the year before Napoleon was born. Though Corsicans were now accorded French citizenship, and although the youthful Bonaparte received an elite military education in France, he was reminded over and over of his own marginality there. He pursued his studies alongside the young men of France's noblest families while his own support came from scholarship funds for the sons of the poorer aristocracy; he was twitted on his provincial manners and Italian turns of speech; and he found himself somehow steered into the artillery, not a branch normally associated with dash and glory. He had thoughts of playing a part in the stirrings for independence in Corsica, which had to be abandoned when he found himself at odds with his sometime idol the patriot leader Pasquale Paoli. By 1793 it had become clear to him that he would have to make his career as a Frenchman, and as a soldier of France's own revolution. The ferocious energy that characterized the next three short years prior to his exploits in Italy—the parts he took in turning back revolt in the Midi, the defense of Toulon, suppressing the royalist Vendémiaire outbreak, and the rise in rank from captain to general of artillery—leaves the mind awhirl.

Historians of the French Revolution and the Napoleonic era never tire of pointing out the immense element of chance at every stage of Bonaparte's ascent, a wrong turn at any of which would have ruined him. Yet when one is limited to a mere swift survey, one has to be rather more impressed by the single-minded consistency with which he laid hold of each such "chance" that came his way. The conspirators of Brumaire—Sieyès in particular—had in their redrawing of the French constitution their own ideas of the role to be played by the popular hero just turned thirty. But they could have had little notion of how decisively Bonaparte, with his capacity for mastering detail and for working hours into the night during the weeks that followed the coup, would whisk the game out of their hands.

The initial response to Brumaire appears to have been somewhat muted and confused. To many a weary Frenchman it was simply another *coup d'état,* and it was not at all evident what this particular one signified. Indeed, for the first few weeks the new regime gave more the appearance of a modified Directory under a new name—the three-member provisional Consulate of Sieyès, Roger Ducos, and Bonaparte—than of a radically altered government. Moreover, Bonaparte saw it in his interest to retain this ambiguity for the time being and to foster an emphasis on returning order and moderation.

But in the daily consultations stretching into December on the drafting of a new constitution, it became more and more apparent to Sieyès—known as the "Oracle" because he had been meditating upon constitutions since the year 1789—that his ideas and Bonaparte's on that subject were profoundly different:

> Sieyès wanted a constitution under which no power in the state should predominate—a perfect division of political labor: Bonaparte was determined that one man should rule. But it would be dangerous to say so; and in all their conversations about ends he kept his own counsel about means.[81]

Nevertheless every turn that the process took was given its critical impulse by Bonaparte himself, and the instrument that resulted—brief and sketchy by intention—was completed by mid-December and promulgated on the 25th. The former Councils were eliminated; the two legislative assemblies created in their place could assent to laws but not initiate them; and all laws were henceforth to be framed by a Council of State presided over by the First Consul, who had to approve everything and could veto anything. Two of the provisional consuls, Sieyès and Ducos, were by Bonaparte's own wish replaced by Jean-Jacques Cambacères and Charles-François Lebrun, one a former regicide and the other an old royalist, neither of whom was to have more than a consultative voice.

Bonaparte was now the master of France—though he took care not to parade it, because there were still formidable pockets of opposition. He would move against them, in some cases with swift ruthlessness, in most others with guile and circumspection. And in any case, a significant harbinger of Bonaparte's support had come very early: a sharp rise on the Bourse in the price of the funds. Though Jacobins and royalists alike would have to wait a little to see just where they stood, the holders of state bonds were already wagering on what they saw as a steadying force in the nation's life.[82]

None of the American envoys had ever dealt with a man of this description— a military careerist on his way to assuming dictatorial powers over the most powerful state in Europe—and indeed two of them, when they began their transatlantic journey, had had little idea whom if anyone they would be dealing with at all. Ellsworth and Davie got their first news of Brumaire when they broke voyage at Lisbon on November 27, though they could as yet form little idea of what it implied. Because of bad weather and accidents it was three months more before they finally reached Paris. But when they arrived on March 2, Murray having preceded them by only a day, every sign relating to their particular business appeared favorable beyond all expectation. The new French government was to all intents and purposes firmly established, and it had already given ample indication that the American commission would be received with every mark of honor and respect.[83]

It might be observed that the fortunes of France and America were here intersecting at a brief and very special historical moment—the year 1800—which in the light of subsequent experience may be seen as one replete with ironies. There was as yet no way of imagining what would shortly befall France, Europe, and indeed half the world under the hand of this Napoleon Bonaparte. Nor could anyone yet be certain what changes were in store for America either: that Federalism, as a style of mind, as a system of principles to be taken as adequate and appropriate to the organization of society and government, was about to be overborne and eclipsed forever. The time was not far off, moreover, when the Federalists of New England, reduced to a forlorn remnant of protest, would be viewing France's imperial tyrant as the Antichrist of Europe. Still, Paris in 1800 was a special place at a special moment, one in which Frenchmen and Americans, or rather Brumairians and Federalists, could meet on something that resembled common ideological ground. Common, at least, in two respects if in no others. There was no real place in the Federalist mentality of 1800, any more than in that of 1789, for an organized partisan opposition. Nor did Consul Bonaparte have any use for opposition parties either. True, he took former Jacobins as well as former royalists into his advisory and ministerial circle, and he himself had mounted the first steps of his upward ladder as an ally of the Robespierres. But it has also been said of him that he hated the Jacobins most of all, and this may well have been on account of their having come closer, during the Directorate, than any other political grouping in France to constituting a coherent and responsible opposition.[84]

The other point of contact concerned popular participation, in government and in the choice of public officers. The highly articulated structure of local government in America had contributed to public careers' being relatively open there, and to an electorate that was relatively very wide. But this situation was not yet officially celebrated, even in America, and least of all by Federalists. And Bonaparte's attitude was more than simply a deep distrust of indiscriminate direct participation; it was a specific determination that such participation should never occur. Representative government under the new constitution was in effect eliminated by the device of having the adult males of each communal district pick a tenth of their number as communal notables; these would choose a tenth of their number; the resulting departmental notables would in turn choose a tenth of *their* number, and this would constitute the list of men eligible to be selected for public office by the national Senate, a body more or less handpicked by the Consuls.

The three Americans would undoubtedly have looked askance at any such system for their own country. Yet all in all, the face presented by the new French government, with what it seemed to imply for both France and America, could not but be viewed by them as auspicious. For one thing, "jacobinism" at home, which every Federalist in America saw as a spreading menace, could draw little inspiration from what was now happening in France. And for another, two of the watchwords of Federalism, stability and order, were receiving a heartening vindication here. And finally, for the first time in the federal republic's eleven-year existence a French government appeared to be taking America seriously. The First Consul himself welcomed the envoys at a "splendid levée" on March 8 in a manner very gratifying to all three, and by the time the negotiations were completed seven months later each of the Americans was left with the distinct impression that of the three it was himself of whom Bonaparte had particularly approved.[85] Before their final departure Bonaparte and Murray had a pleasant social chat, in the course of which the First Consul asked Murray how in America they had liked 18 Brumaire. Murray replied that the "friends of order and rational liberty" had "rejoiced"; that "the Jacobins c[oul]d not like it"; and as for Bonaparte himself, Murray observed afterward that "unless he w[oul]d give back his power to L[ouis XVIII], I wish for the peace of the world he may keep it as long as he lives!"[86] Murray and the others might well have remarked, had they thought of it, that at the very least Bonaparte had made the stagecoaches run on time.

Preparations in Paris for the forthcoming negotiations with the Americans had, for once, been pointed and purposeful. Talleyrand's return to the Foreign Office was settled four days after the coup of Brumaire; he was reinstalled, and Reinhard rusticated to Switzerland, on November 21; and in little more than a week Talleyrand was ready with a paper for Bonaparte on the American situation. This statement has about it an assurance, paralleling a sense of security in his own position being experienced for the first time since his having become Foreign Minister in 1797, that is missing from all the many previous memoranda on that subject submitted to the Directory. It is prefaced by a brief sketch, hardly more than a series of references, of the troubles between France and America. But aside from the customary platitudes about "English influence" and a perfunctory rap at Adams and Pickering, there is for the first time not a word about the Americans' being to blame for the current state of bad relations. The stereotyped whine over the Jay Treaty which Talleyrand had felt obliged to echo in all his previous reports is now dispensed with altogether, he having privately never taken that item very seriously anyway. On the contrary, he indicates, it was France's own handling of American affairs that must be held responsible for the accumulated evils, the basic source of which was "that fatality which entrusted every external mission to maladroit or quarrelsome men"; whereas there was in fact "no rivalry of views, no incompatibility of interests, no territorial disputes" between the two countries. Beginning in 1793 French agents in America, "swept away by the effervescence of the times," had demanded more privileges from the Franco-American treaties of 1778 than were really in them, and it was these men's version of America's conduct, culminating with the making of a treaty with England, upon which the Directory had acted in its decrees against American shipping—decrees which resulted in "a system of depredation and piracy . . . in the Antilles and along their own coasts."

There is no reason, Talleyrand urges, to let this go any further. The Americans "will achieve a destiny that we can no longer prevent, and the nation that hangs onto their friendship will be the last to retain colonies in the New World." The new American mission is on its way, and the sensible thing will be to make all preparations for receiving the ministers, to do so with "friendly dignity," to "abstain from all reproaches," to "express the intention to render them justice for justice," and to "put an end to differences that should never have arisen." In short, he briskly asserts,

> to dissipate by frank explanations the suspicions that have been reciprocally aroused; to agree on the meaning of the three treaties of alliance, commerce, and consular establishments; to restore to both sides the enjoyment of their rights; and to find the means of compensation for wrongs done: such are the grounds for the coming negotiations.[87]

Bonaparte, with characteristic swiftness of decision, agreed at once, whereupon Talleyrand had another happy thought. George Washington had died at Mount Vernon on December 14; the news of this reached Paris on February 1, 1800. Since Washington for all his virtues had not been noted as an enthusiast of the French Revolution, and the luster of his name in France had consequently become somewhat dimmed, there was at first a good measure of uncertainty as to just how this news should be responded to. It struck Talleyrand that here was a noble opportunity for the First Consul himself to give the nation its cue, to make a solemn occasion of it, and to do it up well. Again Bonaparte got the point with a minimum of prompting, and went into action. He decreed ten days of national mourning, with black crepe to be "hung upon all the flags and standards of the Republic" in memory of "that great man" who had "fought against tyranny" and "consolidated his country's freedom." He ordered the commissioning of a bust to be placed in the Tuileries amid those of Caesar, Hannibal, Condé, and Turenne. And finally, he arranged a tremendous ceremony, which was held on February 9, 1800, at the Temple of Mars. The original conception had been brilliant enough: a military occasion to dedicate the flags and other trophies captured from the Turks in Egypt; now it was to be climaxed by a funeral oration for the departed Washington. The orator was one Louis Fontanes, a former royalist now rumored to be the lover of Bonaparte's sister Elisa and presumably selected through her influence. Fontanes atop the high rostrum was perhaps not as imposing as another might have been, being very small and rather round, but he had dazzling white teeth, a melodious voice, and a true grasp of the nicely intertwined sentiments that were expected of him. The discourse he produced was a sonorous fugue of not-very-subtle parallels between the liberator of America and the present savior of France. "As a rule," he announced, "in the wake of great political crises an extraordinary personage must appear, one who by the very ascendancy of his glory shall restrain the audacity of parties and restore order in the midst of confusion." Washington "had triumphed over England; against the excesses of party he undertook a struggle no less arduous and no less glorious."

> Yes, thy counsels shall be heard, O Washington! O warrior! O legislator! O citizen without reproach! He who, still young, has surpassed thee on the field of battle, like thee shall heal with his triumphant hands his country's wounds.

The text was reprinted everywhere, and all accounts of Fontanes's life agree that it was this effort that assured his future. This ceremony, moreover, and other marks of homage to Washington, made a very good impression in America.[88] A final compliment to the Americans was the First Consul's choice of the negotiators who would shortly meet with them. The commission was headed by his own brother Joseph Bonaparte. The other two were Pierre-Louis Roederer and Charles-Pierre Claret de Fleurieu; all were Councillors of State; all were men of good reputation and ability; and all stood in the highest confidence of the First Consul. The industrious Louis Pichon, already known to Murray, would be the commission's secretary.[89]

The French government had thus taken every step to clothe the impending negotiation with a visible importance, and the evident determination on both sides that it should be successful gave much reason to expect that a mutually satisfactory accommodation would be reached without inordinate difficulty or delay.

Yet well-disposed as everyone was, this proved to be decidedly not the case. Neither side had fully anticipated that their instructions were so drawn, and their respective aims so contradictory, as almost to guarantee an unbreakable stalemate. The remarkable thing, indeed, about the negotiations of 1800 is that the Americans and their French counterparts could find themselves able in the face of these obstacles to hold onto their patience over a period of six months and conclude anything at all that could be regarded as a plausible settlement.

The basic incompatibility of aims sprang into view as soon as the negotiators exchanged their opening proposals as to procedure. They held their first joint meeting, amiably enough, on April 2 and agreed that in view of language obstacles the questions for discussion would be dealt with principally in writing. The Americans then presented a draft of the first six articles of a proposed new treaty, all six of which were concerned with methods of satisfying claims by American merchants for damages incurred through the irregular actions of French privateers. The remaining articles, they promised—on commerce, navigation, and other matters—would be presented later. This move was heavy with significance. It reflected an emphasis in the American instructions regarding the payment of indemnities that had not been present in those given to the Pinckney-Marshall-Gerry mission in 1797. It was now being insisted, as it had not been then, that a sine qua non of any accommodation between the two countries must be a settlement of claims for damages done to American commerce. Once the mode of settlement was agreed upon, the negotiators could proceed to the making of a new treaty. The idea of a new treaty was the other note of significance: the Americans were tacitly taking the ground that the old treaties, which had been declared by Congress in 1798 to be abrogated, were no longer in force and were not to be revived.[90]

This was not what the French had had in mind at all, and in their reply—though indirectly, and very politely—they said so. Far from contesting the principle of compensation, they freely agreed that "the first object" should be "to determine the rules, and the mode of procedure" for evaluating and indemnifying injuries. (It had been understood among themselves that a gesture—indeed more than just a gesture—would have to be made in that direction, and their instructions specified as much.) But they then added that "the second object" should be "to ensure the execution of the treaties of friendship and commerce now existing between the two nations," the implication being that with temporary misunderstandings removed, those treaties might now be regarded as having never ceased to be in effect at all. The French commissioners also threw in two additional points, both intended to deflect in some measure the momentum of the Americans' opening initiative. One was to qualify the principle of compensation by introducing the concept of national as well as individual injuries, the idea being that France too had suffered as a consequence of differing interpretations of the original treaties—such as in the matter of port privileges—and that these too should figure in the final settlement. The other was to ask for assurances that the President had ordered a suspension of those acts of Congress under which hostile steps had been taken against France—assurances which they undoubtedly knew the Americans were as yet in no position to give.[91]

This response on the part of the French, just as with the American proposal that brought it forth, was likewise full of significance. And it too reflected with an acute precision the instructions that stood back of it. For one thing, it was the opening signal of France's determination, which would be less and less disguised as the negotiations went on, to make the process of compensation as intricate and protracted as possible, if not to avoid it altogether. (Talleyrand's instructions were very specific here: that whatever engagement the French ministers might ultimately have to make, in view of France's "pecuniary position" they must "absolutely refuse any real or present recompense.") But just as significant was the question of the treaties. For France's present purposes in Europe, the symbolic importance of having the treaties of amity, commerce, and alliance of 1778 with the United States of America reaffirmed, with as much of their original luster as could be given them, constituted much of the main point of the negotiation.

These discordances, then, evident almost from the start, provide the key to the entire course taken by the joint proceedings as well as the answer to why it took so long to conclude them. Both sides wanted peace, and there would be few complications on that score. But the other aims were mutually exclusive, and there was no clear way to reach an accommodation on them. An accommodation was in fact arrived at, and under the circumstances a good one. But it had to be reached in *un*clear ways. Meanwhile every turn taken, every effort made by either side to adjust to the other's position while maintaining its own, occurred with reference to one or the other of the above-noted objects.

The first phase of the negotiation consisted primarily in a debate between the two delegations over whether the treaties of 1778 were in fact terminated as the Americans claimed they were; whether it was legally possible to abrogate them unilaterally, as Congress had presumed to do in its act of July 7, 1798; and whether, if the treaties were admitted to be no longer in effect, there remained any ground for the present negotiation insofar as it concerned reparations for past injuries. The French denied that a treaty could be annulled by a simple legislative act, under either the law of nations or America's own Constitution, except by mutual consent or by war. There had been no mutual consent, and if the Congressional measures of 1798 were taken to signify a state of war—as they certainly could be—then this would cancel any pretensions the United States might have to indemnities for injuries done to it beforehand. The American negotiators maintained, on the contrary, that the United States had not declared war on France; that the latter's extensive depredations on American commerce had constituted a clear violation of the treaties; that consequently the United States was fully justified under international law in announcing the treaties' termination, but that this hardly invalidated America's claim to compensation for such infractions; and that meanwhile the envoys had no authority to undo an act of their own government.

They were further limited, they claimed, by the Jay Treaty of 1794, whose obligations now took precedence over any subsequent engagements the United States might make. The critical provision here had to do with the reception of one party's warships, privateers, and prizes in the ports of the other. Article XVII of the Franco-American commercial treaty of 1778 specified that each party might bring such ships, with goods taken from its enemies, freely into the ports of the other without inspection or payment of duties and with no limit as to time of departure, and that similar privileges were denied to its enemies. Article XXV of the Jay Treaty contained the very same provisions, but with the reservation that they could not apply to France (if France should be one of Britain's enemies) because of America's prior treaty obligation to that country. This meant that as long as the French treaty remained in existence, France in wartime would have exclusive privileges in American ports, whereas with that treaty terminated the superior privileges became wholly England's.[92]

The French ministers understandably found such reasoning unacceptable, while the Americans felt themselves prevented by their instructions from proceeding on any other grounds. The negotiations were thus brought to a standstill.

The First Consul had departed for Italy on May 6 to take command of the army there, and would not be back until early in July. The French commissioners did not believe they could continue without fresh instructions, and Joseph Bonaparte personally undertook the journey to Italy to seek them. Meanwhile the Americans—Murray in particular, and especially after the news of Bonaparte's great victory over the Austrians at Marengo on June 14—were left to consider whether they could resume at all without breaking their own instructions, and if so, which ones.

The First Consul's thoughts were conveyed to them informally after a dinner at Joseph Bonaparte's on July 11. Compensation could occur on no other basis than the continued existence of the old treaties; he would make no treaty at all that surrendered France's once-exclusive rights to an enemy; and any treaty he did make must at the very least put France on an equal footing with Great Britain. This did not widen the ground very much, but it appeared to widen it a tiny bit. Both delegations thereupon undertook a series of efforts to make what they could of it.[93]

On July 15 Ellsworth offered a plan, warning that it was the farthest the

Americans could go within their instructions, whereby the extent of indemnities would be agreed upon in accordance with the treaty project earlier presented, but specifying that they need not be paid until the United States should offer within seven years the equivalent of the exclusive port privileges of Article XVII of the 1778 treaty. (The Jay Treaty would have expired by then.) But for the French this would emphatically not do: whatever they got in the way of port privileges—or more especially, what they were seen by the rest of Europe to have got—they wanted now, not sometime in the future.[94]

Then on the 24th, Pichon roused Ellsworth out of bed to inquire whether he and the others might be willing to revive Article XVII only to the extent of most-favored-nation treatment (not exclusive rights but at least equal rights), the hint being that conceivably this might be a way of salvaging the indemnities. But the hint could only have been greatly hedged, since Talleyrand had told the French negotiators two days before that "we are stretching as much as possible to set aside the indemnities." Nevertheless the Americans began persuading themselves, under Murray's goading, that the Jay Treaty was not after all a legal barrier—as they had earlier contended—to the granting of equal privileges, if by doing so they could hang onto the indemnities. Meanwhile the French minister Roederer in informal conversations with Murray was very helpful in digging up precedents from international law which would support this new position.[95]

Bonaparte cut all this short on August 11 when he let the Americans know, through his negotiators, that they could not have it both ways. Either reinstate the old treaties unimpaired (including France's exclusive privileges), or make a new treaty with no more than equal privileges (and he would sign nothing that did not include that), but do without the indemnities.

The penultimate phase of the negotiations stretched over the ensuing month, during which the Americans, with Ellsworth taking the initiative, made their final stand at keeping the indemnities question alive. One of their proposals was a scheme for a new treaty which would include every feature of the former ones except Article XVII of the commercial treaty (on port privileges) and Article XI of the treaty of alliance, the one in which the parties guaranteed "mutually . . . and forever" each other's possessions in the New World. Article XVII would be commuted to a cash payment of $1 million and a substitute article putting France on a most-favored-nation basis, and Article XI would be eliminated entirely, also for a $1 million payment—and the United States would have seven years in which to make the payments. The American claims for compensation would meanwhile remain intact.

The French counter-proposal, while not a flat rejection, might as well have been: that if at the end of the seven years (during which they must at least have most-favored-nation status) the United States had not offered, nor France accepted, the full restoration of the articles in question, France would have no further obligation to pay indemnities. (The handwriting on the wall, NO INDEMNITIES, was being writ larger and larger.) The Americans, finding this "altogether inadmissible," then advanced their final version of Ellsworth's pay-off plan on September 6. The old treaties would be revived, except for the guarantee of Article

XI (to be commuted by a $1 million payment); each party would indemnify the claimants of the other; but the United States government would reserve the choice, at the exchange of ratifications, of being released from the old treaties if it also agreed to renounce the indemnities.

But the French replied that they should have an equal right of choice, and repeated what they had said before: that they could agree to no settlement that included both indemnities and alterations of the old treaties. And they finally admitted openly that "their real object was to avoid, by any means, any engagement to pay indemnities," because of France's "utter inability . . . to pay, in the situation in which she would be left by the present war."[96] The negotiation was once more at an impasse. It might have ended then and there, had not all three of the Americans at last come to recognize—as Murray had already recognized for some time—that their own instructions required too much of them.

On the next day, September 13, they made their key decision. They would propose a postponement of the two main questions at issue, the indemnities and the old treaties, until such time in the future when discussion of them could be "resumed with fewer embarrassments," allowing the two delegations to proceed forthwith to a "temporary arrangement" which would bring their countries' everyday relations back to normal and adjust any other matters that might be immediately negotiable. The Americans were thus breaking their instructions without in so many words having to say so, and at length admitting, at least to themselves, that if they were going to get rid of the alliance, as they were determined to do no matter what, there was no chance of extracting so much as a penny in the way of compensation. "[We] defer—not abandon indemnity (tho' Lost in fact forever!!)."[97] If Oliver Ellsworth, who had kept his delegation dug in for twenty-two weeks while prying out every thinkable alternative, had at last come to such a reading as this, the likelihood of there being realistically any other could not have been very great. And by the same token, whatever chance there was of muting the cries of irreconcilables back home would derive much of its weight from the moral authority of "Mr. Federalist." He and his colleagues did what they did, Ellsworth later wrote, "to extricate the United States from a contest which it might be as difficult to relinquish with honour, as to pursue with a prospect of advantage."[98] They had been put in such a box in the first place not so much by France as by a set of all-or-nothing instructions, by conditions the authors of which had themselves more than half hoped the French would not even listen to.

The French delegation agreed to resume on this altered ground, and in less than two weeks the negotiators, meeting from day to day, reached a settlement more comprehensive than any of them, in light of the way things had stood in early September, could have anticipated. It provided for "a firm, inviolable, and universal peace"; the mutual restoration of property not yet condemned; the recovery of debts "as if there had been no misunderstanding"; rules for the prevention of future maritime abuses (including elimination of the notorious *rôle d'équipage*) and the settlement of disputes in cases of capture. Most provisions of the earlier treaties as well as of the Consular Convention of 1788 were restored, and port privileges were placed on a most-favored-nation basis. The French voluntarily added a bonus on neutral rights that the Americans had not even asked for, restoration of the "free ships, free goods" principle.

As for what the completed agreement should be called, the Americans had first proposed designating it as a "convention"; the French then tried to have it named a "treaty of amity and commerce"; the Americans, wanting something that sounded less permanent, insisted it should be no more than a "provisional treaty"; whereupon the First Consul himself proposed that it be a "convention" — to which they were glad enough to agree. It was signed amid great festivities at Môrtefontaine, Joseph Bonaparte's country chateau north of Paris, on October 3, 1800.[99]

Davie arrived home with copies of the Convention on December 11, and President Adams submitted it to the Senate on the 16th. It met with little enthusiasm among Republicans ("barely makes peace between the two republics," according to one of them), though they became more disposed to find merit in it when they observed the disgruntlement it aroused ("another chapter in the book of humiliation") among the Federalists. On January 23, 1801, the Convention, receiving 16 votes to 14, well short of the necessary two-thirds, was in effect rejected.[100]

But enough sentiment for acceptance had arisen in the meantime that the Senate agreed to reconsider. Alexander Hamilton had been advising his friends that it would be "better to close the thing where it is than leave it to a Jacobin Administration to do much worse." John Marshall — now Secretary of State — was inclined to agree, though he was "far very far from approving it." It had been thought by many that the most-favored-nation article would give umbrage to England, but reports from Rufus King arriving in mid-January (the Ministry had found nothing objectionable in it, and in fact Ellsworth, currently wintering in London, was being received with marks of distinction everywhere he went) took most of the wind out of that argument. By February 3 enough Federalist senators had changed their minds that a resolution to approve the Convention after striking out Article II (the one deferring the indemnities and the treaties questions), and inserting another limiting the Convention's duration to eight years, was agreed to by a vote of 22 to 9.[101]

The motives for their having done it this way were somewhat tortured and obscure. They wanted to register in some form their dissatisfaction but could not agree as to just how, at the same time realizing, as most of them did, that to turn down the Convention altogether was asking for trouble. Expunging Article II was the nicest balance among these impulses that they could think of. They could thereby pretend that the indemnities remained a live issue with or without such an article, whereas without it, the remaining provisions of the Convention together with the very fact of having made it, in preference to reaffirming the old treaties, had in effect killed these treaties forever. At the exchange of ratifications in Paris later that year, Bonaparte, readily penetrating this foggy maneuver, made his own ratification contingent on the understanding that the removal of Article II amounted to America's renunciation of all future claims to indemnity.[102] (Whether by that time anyone in America seriously supposed otherwise may well be doubted.) At any rate President Jefferson, the Adams administration having gone out of office the previous March, decided that any remaining ambiguity would be best settled by sending France's conditional ratification to the new Senate for "a second advice and consent . . . before I give it the last sanction, by proclaiming it to be a law of the land." He did so on December 11, 1801, and, as he evidently expected, such consent was obtained without further difficulty.[103]

The line between the material advantages and those of a more broadly symbolic kind for either nation in the Convention of 1800 may doubtless be traced in more than one way. But there were certainly both kinds, and each was of considerable weight, especially for the United States. On the one hand it might logically be supposed that there should have been a great clamor from the American mercantile community over the failure to obtain compensation for losses incurred through the actions of French commerce raiders. But in fact this was not the case at all; indeed the greatest single source of pressure for ratifying the Convention, from the moment its contents became known in America, was that same community. American merchants engaged in overseas shipping had never expected much in the way of indemnities anyway, at least not from the French, and what they wanted now above all else was an end to the Quasi-War and the resumption of a very profitable business.[104] Even the Federalist senators who wrangled over ratification in December and January 1800–1801 did not do so primarily on that ground. What seems to have galled them as much as any one other item in the Convention was something relatively minor: the provision in Article III that public ships taken in the course of hostilities were to be restored, meaning that the United States would have to give back Truxtun's trophy *L'Insurgente*.[105] (The American negotiators, however, could not very well have refused such an article if they were to hold the ground that the United States had never actually made war on France in the first place.) The difficulties raised over ratification — as had been the case with the Jay Treaty five years before — were concerned to an extraordinary degree with abstractions.

On the other hand, the Americans did derive material benefits from the Convention of 1800, some of which did not appear in the text at all. They consisted of a purposeful sequence of measures by France's Consular government — of a sort that its predecessor the Directory had been all but powerless to take — to suppress the many abuses of privateering. It had all been part of the effort to prepare the ground for conciliation and negotiation, to keep the negotiation going once it had begun, and to solidify its results once it was completed. Early in December 1799 Bonaparte had ordered the repeal of the law of 29 Nivôse (decreeing the condemnation of vessels wholly or in part laden with British-produced goods), which was thereupon replaced by the law of 23 Frimaire and the ordinance of 29 Frimaire (December 13 and 19) re-establishing the liberal principles of 1778. On March 27, 1800, he decreed the instituting at Paris of a new Council of Prizes, with wide-ranging authority to scrutinize every aspect of cases current and pending. When the Convention was completed, Talleyrand ordered the suspension of all such cases involving American vessels. By December the Council had released twelve ships, and when news arrived of the Senate's action, still more were restored to their owners. When Louis Pichon was appointed in November 1801 to be France's new chargé d'affaires in America, he was instructed to use all his efforts to suppress any more illegal privateering in the West Indies, and he subsequently did so.[106]

The greatest advantages sought by the French, aside from release from the indemnities, were those of a symbolic nature, and they exerted themselves to the utmost to obtain them. It would have suited their purposes best of all to have the old treaties with America revived in all their original vigor, not really because of any benefits they carried in the way of port privileges—these in themselves meant little to them, nor did they matter a great deal to the British either, who in effect said as much—but rather because the French might thus triumphantly exhibit to the neutral nations of Europe that they had clearly put themselves right with the world's leading neutral carrier. In this, of course, they fell short, owing to the obstinacy of the American negotiators. But simply to have reached an accord of any kind was an item of very high value, and they made the most of it. The great fête at Môrtefontaine, attended by the First Consul with 150 of the nation's dignitaries, and said to have been the most splendid occasion of its sort since the beginning of the Revolution, was an announcement to all the world of their satisfaction at having done so. The American negotiation had figured centrally in Bonaparte's strategy of uniting the nations of northern Europe in a league of armed neutrality based on liberal principles (including that of "free ships, free goods"), and in which the United States might itself be induced eventually to join, in order to place a check on British sea power. As it happened, the League, though duly formed, fell apart shortly afterward.[107] As for America's adherence to it, there was never, needless to say, the least chance of such a thing no matter how long it lasted or which party might be in control of the federal government.

Another of Bonaparte's aims was to complete France's reconciliation with the United States before his designs upon Louisiana became known there. Attempting to place the morality of this in the balance of benefits and disadvantages in the Convention of 1800 makes for a very ambiguous question, involving on the one hand the propriety of France's repossessing a territory that had once been hers but upon which the United States hoped to lay hands at some time in the future, and on the other that of Bonaparte's virtually giving us the entire province—which Spain would most certainly not have done—less than three years later.

Quite possibly the greatest benefit of all from the Convention, it too a symbolic one, was that which accrued to the United States. And here the American negotiators, in burying the treaties of 1778 for practical purposes once and for all, had in effect handed to their Republican successors what amounted to a free gift. It was not the obligations of an alliance, simply in itself, that had come to make these treaties such a burden. Few Americans, Republican or Federalist, had ever felt themselves bound by compulsions of that sort, even at the height of the enthusiasm in America for France's revolution in the delirious days of 1793. It was rather the ideological coercions surrounding the treaties, and the entire web of fraternal claims that connected them with America's own Revolution, that had come to play such havoc in the domestic politics of the United States. These coercions, which the Republicans had once joyfully accepted and which the Federalists had come more and more bitterly to resist, were now in large part removed. Still, the very poisonousness of American partisan politics prevented any real detachment in grasping the merits of the Convention of 1800. Most Federalists felt bound to find every kind of fault with an arrangement that appeared to make any palpable concessions to the detested French, while few Republicans could accord other than grudging approval to the work of any mission that had gone to France under Federalist auspices. Nor were the Republicans yet quite prepared to admit that their own ideological attachment to France, which had helped so much to bring their party into being and had once so fortified their claim to wide popular support, had by this time become a heavy embarrassment. They were now relieved from it, and without the additional burden of having to get rid of it for themselves, or even of having to say so.[108]

Nobody appreciated this more richly than Thomas Jefferson, as he prepared to assume the presidential chair in 1801. Jefferson was now serenely free to announce, with no reference at all to the Convention of 1800, a policy of "peace, commerce, and honest friendship with all nations, entangling alliances with none. . . ."[109]

The Mentality of Federalism in 1800

The year 1800 marked the end of Federalist predominance in the nation's public life, a predominance never to be reasserted. Whether Federalism had—or rather might have had—any kind of future after that time is a question that provokes the historical imagination. Could things conceivably have taken a different turn? Was there any likelihood that Federalism, as a party and as a persuasion, could have stabilized itself and survived as one side of a more or less settled polarity in the future life of American politics?

Thomas Jefferson, for one, believed that the "revolution of 1800"—a phrase he himself used, if he did not coin it[1]—had been in the nature of things bound to occur, and that the revolution would in all likelihood be a permanent one. Jefferson saw the defeat of the Federalists in that year as marking the definitive ascendancy of a natural republican majority over a minority faction whose hold on the powers of government had been maintained for twelve years through essentially artificial means. The influence and patronage of the Hamiltonian Treasury, the immense prestige of Washington, and the Federalists' willful exploitation of the crisis with France were all that had allowed them to hold on as long as they had. Yet sooner or later, as Jefferson saw it, the intrinsically republican temper of the American people was bound to repudiate—as it now had—the exclusivist, fiscalist, consolidationist, and perversely anglophile tendencies of Federalism. That decision, he thought, was final, and not likely to be reversed. Jefferson himself, moreover, was determined from the first see that this should be so, and to banish Federalism forever.[2]

To all intents and purposes he succeeded, and historical opinion well into our own time has remained largely satisfied with the Jeffersonian judgment. But a revival of interest in the Adams presidency, beginning in the mid-1950s, opened up the question again in a new and variant way. Some writers began pointing out that Federalism did, after all, have its moderate and reasonable side. A clear distinction, they urged, should be drawn between the irrational extremists and the moderates—the "Adams Federalists," as Manning Dauer called them—and from that viewpoint the turnover of 1800 might not look either as "revolutionary" or as foreordained as Jefferson and his successors, or indeed history itself, have pictured it. Adams himself, for instance, had little use for the extremists—the arch-Federalists, or "High Federalists," as they have been variously called—or for their main principles and policies. It was they who had carried the initiative for such measures as the extravagant build-up of the army, the Alien and Sedition Laws, and the burdensome program of federal taxation. (In matters of public finance, Adams was much closer to Jefferson than to Hamilton.) Whereas it was the moderates who gave Adams what Federalist support he had for his policy of liquidating the French crisis, and who worked for his re-election despite the covert and not-so-covert efforts of the Hamiltonians to slip Charles Cotesworth Pinckney in ahead of him. True, the Federalist party was badly split by Adams's sudden decision to dispatch the Ellsworth mission to France—that much has always been in some way noted in any review of these events—and this certainly had its effect on the fortunes of Federalism in 1800. Yet even so, the election was exceedingly close. Had it not been for the prodigious exertions of Aaron Burr in the pivotal state of New York, and switches of a few hundred votes for assemblymen in the city wards there, hitherto safely Federalist, Adams would have defeated Jefferson a second time for the presidency. The strength of moderate Federalism in 1800, then, for all the destructive mischief of the Hamiltonian extremists and despite the factor of bad luck in key places, must have been rather more solid than has traditionally been supposed.[3]

All of this may prompt conjectures as to a possible course of future developments in American politics, perhaps a very different one from what actually occurred. Might it not be conceivable to project the emergence after 1800 of a reconstituted and chastened Federalist party, tempered by experience and electoral success, toned down and divested of its apocalyptic accents, and proceeding under such leadership as that of Adams, John Marshall, Rufus King, Charles Cotesworth Pinckney, Oliver Ellsworth, Harrison Gray Otis, and others of like temper? A truly constructive future for Federalism? The consequences might have been salutary. They could have included, on the one hand, a sensible and balanced domestic program (a measured course of debt reduction but one that would not become an end in itself; modifying the excise structure but without wrecking it altogether); and on the other, a suitably peaceable but hard-headed foreign policy (a continuing naval presence intended not to challenge foreign nations but as an implicit resource both in diplomacy and for the security of American commerce) which might have made a clear difference in America's international bargaining power in the seven or eight years prior to 1812. But whatever the particulars, it might well be imagined that such a development could have meant the establishment of a responsible and intelligent conservatism as one of the standing alternatives—to embrace or not, as the times might call for it—when Americans in the advancing nineteenth century came periodically to make their political choices.[4]

An intriguing vision but—one fears—not a very likely one. Few indications are discernible that the Federalism of 1800, or any thinkable outgrowth of it, could ever really have served such a function, or perpetuated itself in any form as a serious force in the political future that was then unfolding. Federalism possessed none of the resources—of spirit, will, imagination, or responsiveness— that would enable it to play a role of that sort, or even to conceive of it. The Federalists of 1800 were all but paralyzed in their incapacity to think or act in a truly political way, in any of the senses that "political" would come more and more to be understood in the America of the nineteenth century. They could not picture themselves as an "alternative" to anything: more exactly, they could not function in a world that accepted, even on sufferance, the existence of parties, nor imagine a time when the idea of "party" might take on a morality of its own. They too, in spite of themselves, had become a party—a party and yet not a party—but it was a state they found scarcely tolerable, and would have given much to escape.

These men, moreover, imagined themselves in a state of siege. They, the friends of order, were menaced on every side by the forces of sedition, jacobinism, and insubordination. There was not even very much in their outlook by now that could be called authentically "conservative." A stable and judicious conservatism—which must perceive the future as well as the past—could not function at all in the the freeze of anxiety that penetrated every corner of these men's psychic landscape.

Nor, indeed, will the distinction between "High Federalists" and "Adams Federalists" carry the case very far either. Whether or not there was much to choose between them, which is itself debatable, John Adams as the successful leader of a rehabilitated Federalist party would have been so different from the actual Adams as to have been unrecognizable. Adams had less use for parties than almost any Federalist around, and spent much of his time declaring he would be bound by no party, including his own. To picture the Federalists as having been "split" over the Ellsworth mission is to see the end of a process, not the beginning of it. The party was not simply split, it was demoralized, Adams himself having been at least part of the problem all along, and the French mission was only one of the symptoms. In any case, if one had to select a public figure in 1800 who may have had some chance of setting Federalism to rights, one of the least likely choices for it would be John Adams.

There is more than a little reason, then, to concede that Jefferson was essentially right: that the "revolution of 1800" was an authentic one, and that the American people had spoken without ambiguity for *his* version of republicanism. They had done it, moreover, as opposed to something else: something they no longer saw, even, as quite American, something that had become *other* than true republicanism as they now understood it.

Federalism was to persist in regional pockets for another two decades, which should perhaps warn against too ready an assumption that it was essentially doomed by 1800. Yet there were already many signs that there was no longer room for anything resembling a Federalist national temper suited to the political life of the opening century. The older values of civic humanism—community harmony and civic virtue, public service above faction and party—which in Federalism now persisted in their least attractive form, were being attenuated not only by altering social perceptions but also by emerging novelties in political practice. True, partisanship as a mode of organizing majorities was not yet something that sat comfortably with the Jeffersonians either, and their vocabulary would continue to be rich with anti-party cant well into the future. But the Republicans' experience of opposition, and of the inhibitions that principled opposition had enabled them to overcome, had at least permitted them to take a decided step in that direction.

There were thus two markedly different states of mind in being, and the contrast between them may be discerned with particular sharpness at several points during the period just prior to the Republicans' assumption of power in 1801. The events that occurred at each of these points—some of which have been touched on already—have much to tell us about the mentality of Federalism in 1800. One is the alien and sedition issue; another is Hamilton's New Army; still another, the behavior of the parties—or quasi-parties—in the election of 1800.

I

The Aliens and the Seditious

The Naturalization Act of 1798 is in a way more striking than the Sedition Act as an indicator of how Federalists conceived their role toward large numbers of people with whom they might or might not form some kind of political relationship. It should be noted in passing that the leading advocate of this grotesquely restrictive and exclusionary law was not an arch-Federalist at all but a "moderate" Adams supporter, Harrison Gray Otis. Otis's particular target was the sizable influx of Irish that had begun arriving in American cities earlier in the 1790s, most of whom seemed to exhibit bitter anti-English and vigorous pro-French attitudes. He had already announced that he did "not wish to invite hordes of wild Irishmen, nor the turbulent and disorderly of all parts of the world, to come here with a view to disturb our tranquility, after having succeeded in the overthrow of their own Governments."[5] This cry was taken up and extended to include all foreigners, already resident or newly arriving, by the entire phalanx of congressional Federalists in the summer of 1798. The resulting legislation superseded the relatively mild naturalization law of 1795, which had required a five-year residence in the United States together with a declaration of intent made three years prior to admission to citizenship. The new act of 1798 now specified a fourteen-year period of residence and a declaration five years prior to admission. The idea, in no way concealed, was to exclude all such persons from political participation of any kind well into the future.

Actually they would have been excluded permanently if Otis and a number of others had had their way. Certain amendments to the original bill, forced by strong Republican opposition, afford with their consequences a gleam of insight into the respective mentalities at work. Not only was a Federalist move beaten down that would have made naturalized citizens forever ineligible either to vote or to hold public office, but there was a further modification that put some fairly wide loopholes in the finished act. The original notion had been to make it flatly retroactive. But the loosened version made it possible for aliens who had come in prior to the act of 1795 to have another year of grace in which to obtain naturalization, and for those who had declared their intention under the 1795 law of becoming citizens to complete their naturalization within four years of having done so. The result was that great numbers of resident immigrants, hitherto either ignorant of their rights or more or less casual about exercising them, immediately began lining up at the registry offices. The evidence is unmistakable that Republican organizers had a very large hand in getting them there. It is also evident that their votes played no insignificant part in the Republican majorities of 1800.[6]

True, it is easy to see why the Irish as a group might have been perceived as a special vexation for Federalism. Their memories of English oppression, and of French encouragement in the recent revolutionary uprisings in Ireland, made them natural recruits to Republicanism, and they were not at all backward about making their sentiments known when they got to America. Those who were politically minded tended to vote Republican from the start. Yet the least promising techniques that could have been thought of for getting them to change their ways were the very things the Federalists were now saying of them and doing to them.[7]

But whatever may have been the case with the Irish, the Federalists were no less obtuse and no less clumsy when it came to dealing with the Germans, who if anything could be seen as natural Federalists. In numbers of the ethnic-minority population in the 1790s the Germans were second only to the Irish. But by far the greatest numbers of Germans in America, mostly concentrated in the farming counties of southeastern Pennsylvania, were actually native-born, of families that had been there for a generation and more. True, most of them still spoke nothing but German and showed little inclination to adopt American ways. They kept largely to themselves; they had little liking for either the Irish or the French; and they had customarily shown slight interest in politics. It cannot be said that the Germans were people of large and venturesome views. But they seldom made any trouble, the principal things that concerned them being, according to a modern authority, "a good price for their grain at market, secure possession of their land, and fair taxes." And when they did vote, oftener than not they voted Federalist.[8]

The Pennsylvania Federalists throughout most of the 1790s decade could afford to take the Germans, or so they seem to have supposed, pretty much for granted. But meanwhile it was gradually penetrating the Germans' own minds that they were neither taken very seriously as a political force nor held in very high esteem as a social and cultural presence. They were thought to be "beasts of burden," "ignorant," and ready to believe anything. By 1797 a correspondent in one of the German newspapers was grumbling that the Federalists "boast that they always can do with the Germans whatever they want to, that they are patient asses."[9] Meanwhile the Philadelphia Republicans since about 1793 had been going after the ethnic minorities with greater and greater purposefulness, and were already by 1796 herding the immigrants to the naturalization offices. Even so, they appear to have been least successful with the country Germans—until, that is, sometime in 1798, when everything changed.[10]

The Federalists' war legislation of 1798—the military appropriations, the Alien and Sedition Laws, and most especially the taxes—struck the southeastern counties of Pennsylvania with a special force, hitting the Germans of that region both in their pocketbooks and in their prejudices. And their "ignorance"—about which current impressions were certainly not unfounded—was in this case anything but an asset to the Federalists. The whole countryside was astir in no time.

A majority of the population were "church Germans"—Lutheran or Reformed—and nearly all their congregations had been strongly attached to the Patriot cause in the Revolution, whereas the less numerous "sectarian" groups—Moravians, Mennonites, and Quakers—had tended to stand aside, thus giving the church Germans a convenient target for hostility ever since. Evils of any nature that arose could be, and were, regularly ascribed to these "tories." Now came the property taxes of 1798—for which nothing in the experience of these communities had thus far prepared them—and by winter Federalist assessors were appearing everywhere in their midst. The supervisor of revenue appointed in August for Northampton, Wayne, and Luzerne counties was a Moravian—who in turn chose other Moravians to assist him—and the one for Montgomery and Bucks was a Quaker. Republican propagandists had now been provided a setting in which they could hardly miss. Beginning in late summer they went about telling the farmers that the "tories" and the powers at Philadelphia were preparing to lay crushing taxes in order to possess themselves of their farms and send them all into serfdom. Before long, they were told, they would even need a license from the tax collector in order to kill a chicken. The October elections in Bucks, Northampton, Montgomery, and Berks brought decisive Republican victories, while Federalists sputtered over the "ignorance and credulity" of the Germans.[11] Meanwhile the Republicans had activated a tremendous petition campaign all around the country against the Alien and Sedition Laws, the taxes, and the military preparations, and by far the greatest numbers of signatures from any one area came from the southeastern counties of Pennsylvania. The people there, in greater measure than anywhere else, had been brought to see these acts as all of a piece, a horrid pattern of oppression, impoverishment, exclusion, and coercion. Yet a Federalist-dominated House committee loftily brushed them all aside, declaring that "innocent misconceptions" would "yield to reflection and argument," while the spirit of those petitions conceived in "vehement and acrimonious remonstrance" was one with which "the public councils cannot safely parley or temporize," and that consequently it would be "inexpedient" to repeal any of these laws.[12]

The Federalists never would wake up to the political effect they were having on these normally stolid people, and they continued to do one witless thing after another which would end only in their losing them forever. By January and February 1799 the Germans were both figuratively and literally up in arms. By means of noisy public meetings and then the actions of roving bands, in some cases mustered as local militia, they succeeded in intimidating the assessors and virtually halting their work. There seemed to be no room in their minds, such being their sense of persecution and the parochial view they had of the outside world, for any idea that there might be a day of reckoning for what they were doing, especially since many had got it into their heads that General Washington himself was opposed to the law and was ready with twenty thousand men to march to their aid in resisting it. But although no actual injuries were known to have been committed, the federal district judge concluded by late February that arrests would have to be made of those reported to be most prominent in obstructing the law. The United States Marshal thereupon rounded up a number of suspects and prepared to escort them to Philadelphia for examination. It was the subsequent action of March 7, 1799, of an armed assemblage of some 140 men under the leadership of John Fries, compelling the Marshal under threat of force to release his party of eighteen prisoners confined at the Sun Tavern in Bethlehem, that led to the sending of federal troops into the countryside of southeastern Pennsylvania.[13]

But whether the circumstances really called for military force of any kind remains an open question. No intermediate steps were taken—such as the commission of inquiry Washington had sent to the scene of the Whiskey Rebellion less than five years before—the only thought on heated Federalist minds now being to punish. Yet the fact was that on the cold light of the morrow Fries and his friends, as yet with no outside prompting, were themselves horrified at what they had done, while the entire area had sobered down in a matter of days. Before any news arrived of intended federal action, meetings were already being held at which there was general agreement that all further resistance must cease, that the law must be submitted to, and that the assessors should be allowed to resume their work without obstruction. Fries himself even declared that when they came to his house he would welcome them with a dinner.[14]

But no; it was as though the federal authorities at Philadelphia had stopped their ears and eyes to any extenuating signals that might henceforth come in; the time had come to cow, terrify, and humble. On March 12 President Adams, in his final hours of preparation for getting himself off to Quincy, was persuaded by his cabinet to issue a proclamation, news of the occurrences at Bethlehem having come in the day before. In it he declared that "combinations to defeat the execution of the laws" existed in the counties of Northampton, Montgomery, and Bucks, that acts had been perpetrated there "which, I am advised, amount to treason," and that he had determined "to call forth military force to suppress such combinations." But instead of remaining to oversee these important military proceedings the Commander-in-Chief departed the same day, leaving everything in the hands of his Secretaries.[15]

The troops when finally assembled did not begin their march until nearly four weeks after the President's proclamation, by which time a state of total peace had settled upon the disaffected counties. The force consisted of substantial units of both militia and regulars, Hamilton having lectured McHenry that "whenever the Government appears in arms it ought to appear like a *Hercules,*" and that "expence is of no moment compared to the advantages of energy."[16] The Federalist commander of the expedition, William McPherson, promoted at the last minute to brigadier-general, now issued a proclamation of his own to the people he was about to visit. This blustering manifesto contained both a long justification of the tax to which they had so unreasonably objected and information on what was about to befall those who had obstructed the law "in so treasonable a manner," in order that "their punishment may serve as an example." It admonished one and all to "return quietly to their homes" and listen no more to "the counsels of those malicious persons who . . . plume themselves upon being Republicans, while transgressing the most essential principles of Republican government." But since they had already returned "quietly to their homes," even before President Adams had commanded them to do so the previous month, these bellicose superfluities naturally set them on edge all over again.[17]

Then when the army hurled itself upon the populace and proceeded to hunt down suspects, rather than appearing "like a Hercules" it appeared more like an overgrown bully. The troops swarmed over the countryside making arrests, some based on little more than local rumor, gloating over their terrified captives and making themselves odious everywhere they went. Fries himself was crying an auction when he spied four companies of cavalry coming down the road after him, whereupon he took to the woods but was caught when the barking of his own dog gave away his hiding place. By the time it was over, many of the expedition's own officers were fully sick of what they had been brought there to do. "The scenes of distress which I have witnessed," one of them wrote, ". . . I cannot describe. . . . Conceive your home entered at the dead of night by a body of armed men, and yourself dragged from your wife and screaming children." Another complained that "these poor, well-meaning, but ignorant Germans" were "treated in no respect like citizens of the same country." Still another, writing from his camp in Bucks County, declared his opinion "that this expedition was not only unnecessary, but violently absurd," and that "a sergeant and six men might have performed all the service for which we have been assembled at so heavy an expense to the United States."[18]

Some sixty prisoners were taken back to Philadelphia, about half of whom were indicted and brought to trial for treason or lesser offenses. By the time the trials began, a comprehensive theory of the uprising and its significance, one that included all the menaces conceived to be confronting Federalism, had so fastened itself on every aspect of the proceedings as to leave scant hope for any kind of indulgence for the cowed and unhappy culprits. The Federalist newspapers of Philadelphia were insisting that the remedy for these menaces—which were all bound up with the spirit of French Jacobinism—must be a total one. "It is effecting but a partial purpose," according to John Ward Fenno's *Gazette of the United States,* "to put down the insurrection of a few counties, whilst a band of French mercenaries dispersed over the Commonwealth, are preparing an Insurrection of the whole state," with the design of "dismembering the Union, and . . . deliver[ing] us over, bound hand and foot, to the dominion of the Directory." The uprising in those counties, William Cobbett declared in *Porcupine's Gazette,* "is a weed that has poisoned the field; to crop off the stalk will only enable it to spring up again and to send out a hundred shoots instead of one. It must be torn up by the root; *the principle of insurrection must be eradicated,* or anarchy will ensue." At the trial of John Fries, which set the tone for all the others, the two presiding judges, both thorough Federalists, appeared to be imbued with this same theory.[19]

They began by denying a motion from Fries's counsel that the case should be tried in Northampton County in accordance with the language of the Judiciary Act of 1789 specifying "that in cases punishable with death, the trial shall be had in the county where the offence was committed; or where that cannot be done without great inconvenience, twelve petit jurors at least shall be summoned from thence." The judges, James Iredell and Richard Peters, held that since virtually the entire county had been in a state of insurrection, no fair trial could be held there.[20] Then after testimony was taken, the defense counsel, Alexander Dallas and William Lewis, argued at considerable length that whereas the acts committed by Fries and his companions (to which Fries had fully confessed) could be construed as sedition, riot, and jail rescue, they hardly fell within the legal definition of treason since no violence had been done and there had been no resistance to the armed force of the United States. But Iredell and Peters would have none of such reasoning, and in their charges to the jury laid down the most inclusive and at the same time literal-minded view of what the law of treason was: treason meant levying war against the United States by means of combining and conspiring with intent to prevent the operation of a public law. On this ground the jury had little choice but to bring in a verdict of guilty. Peter Porcupine exulted: "This is *liberty,* reader. This is the very *soul of liberty.* You shall never hear me inveigh against *republicanism,* if I find all the *Courts of Justice* like this."[21]

Fries had to be granted a second trial, since one of the jurors had talked too much out of doors during the first. But the second one turned out the same way, as the new presiding judge, Samuel Chase, was even more high-handed in his treatment of counsel and jury, and even more determined to see Fries hanged. President Adams, having by now examined the legal ground on which Dallas and Lewis had argued their case, had meanwhile become more and more uneasy over the judgments that had been given. On May 23, 1800, contrary to the strong opinions of his cabinet that the law should take its course, Adams issued a full pardon to Fries and the two others convicted of treason, and to all the rest under sentence for lesser crimes.[22]

But it was too late for any possible repair of the political damage that had been done in the German counties of southeastern Pennsylvania. One of the soldiers on the expedition that had been sent there predicted in a letter from camp that the local feeling aroused by the government's handling of the insurrection would "completely destroy the federal influence at the next election." And so it did. Those counties had been sweepingly converted to Republicanism, and so remained forever after. The Republicans already had the Irish; now they had the Germans. The Federalists, on the other hand, had shown with everything they said and did that their spirit was simply not a welcoming one. John Fries himself, hitherto a good Federalist, never cast another Federalist vote during the remaining eighteen years of his life.[23]

The Sedition Act of 1798 and its by-products may serve as yet another test of the strikingly divergent states of mind in which the Federalists and the Republicans faced their political future.

This measure—which made it a crime to utter or publish "any false, scandalous, and malicious writing or writings against the government of the United States, or the President of the United States, with intent to defame . . . or to bring them into contempt or disrepute"—has of course been much written about, most notably during the present century. The considerable wave of interest that arose in the 1950s over the entire subject of civil liberty produced among other things a view of the Sedition Act and the ensuing prosecutions under it which tended to picture the entire episode as a kind of lapse: an aberration, a betrayal of a libertarian tradition already established and in fact clearly embodied in the Bill of Rights. The governing assumption was that the English common law of seditious libel had been intentionally superseded by the First Amendment of the Constitution, for practical purposes removing all restraints upon freedom of the press, and that the Sedition Act, being "merely declaratory" of the English common law, was therefore unconstitutional.[24]

Subsequent writers have questioned such a view as being an unduly telescoped and present-minded reading both of the Framers' intentions and of the historical development of libertarian thought and practice in America. There is no evidence, they assert, that the First Amendment was designed to abolish the English common law of seditious libel; there is indeed reason to infer that the Framers took for granted the federal courts' jurisdiction over common-law crimes unless otherwise specified by federal statute. It could even be said that the Sedition Act was more than "merely declaratory" of the English common law; it represented a distinct liberalization of English common-law practice, allowing as the new law did for the truth of a statement to be accepted as a defense, for the jury rather than the judge to determine whether a statement was libelous, and for the prosecution's obligation to prove malicious intent. Thomas Jefferson himself, amid the initial Republican attack on the law, certainly did not deny the principle of seditious libel. He rather asserted that the federal government was not empowered with jurisdiction over that particular crime, such jurisdiction being reserved to the states.[25] Several years later in fact, Jefferson as President was to intimate to the Governor of Pennsylvania that "a few prosecutions" of the licentious "tory presses" of that state and others "would have a wholesome effect in restoring the[ir] integrity."[26] It would in reality take time before the problem of seditious libel was fully grasped, there being no settled theory ready to be laid hold of for opposition to the Alien and Sedition Laws of 1798. The most notable immediate protest came, of course, with the Virginia and Kentucky Resolutions of that same year, the principal message of which was a compact theory of government and the obligation to resist centralized tyranny. The first contributions to a specifically libertarian doctrine would be made not by Jefferson but by such other Republican theorists as Gallatin, Madison, Tunis Wortman, and John Nicholas. These men began pointing out that "truth" was no real protection for freedom of the press, there being no clear way of separating truth from falsehood, and that the "no prior restraints" doctrine of the common law was not an adequate protection either, since the press could hardly be free even without prior censorship if a writer could be punished afterward for something he had already said.[27]

Yet it may well be that the idea of civil liberty—civil liberty as counted then, or destined ultimately, among the self-evident and inalienable rights—is not the only key to why the Sedition Act should have raised such an uproar, and why it should have served as the point of departure for an eventual new way of thinking about the whole question of seditious libel. Another key, and perhaps a better one, is the relationship between the press and the state of political practice in America as it had evolved by the final two or three years of the eighteenth century. Along with the sheer proliferation of newspapers that had occurred in the 1790s went the taking for granted that a fair amount of free and easy language toward public figures was tolerable, and by no means all of it had to be respectful. So whatever the law might or might not say, the typical printer could be secure in knowing that public opinion allowed a very wide latitude for the press, and that grand juries were seldom likely to indict, or petit juries convict, for such a crime as seditious libel.

Such was the environment in which the Republican interest was taking shape as an organized opposition. Accordingly the freedom of the Republican press to pass judgment on officeholders—openly, aggressively, even abusively—was essential to the party's survival. In short, the very concept of seditious libel was flatly incompatible with party politics. The Republicans, if only by instinct and after the fact, were beginning to understand this, while the Federalists still had little or no inkling of it. Parties, in any modern sense, cannot function at all under such a principle, and parties by now—though nobody could yet admit it without some discomfort—were there. It might even be said that the Federalists now, in all their distracted movements, were doing something more than moving against "sedition"—more, even, than striking at their political opposition in the hope of suppressing it. Whether they knew it or not—perhaps nobody entirely knew it— they were striking out furiously at parties in general, in a desperate effort to turn back the clock.

To turn back the clock. This thought might well need some drawing out. Could it be that in the very fashioning of the Constitution itself, the Federalists of 1787 had done much the same thing as they were doing now, even though they might then have gone about it in rather a different spirit, and with a significantly higher degree of confidence? In devising the checks and balances of their "constitution against parties" (to use Richard Hofstadter's phrase) the Federalists in their role as founding statesmen had done their utmost to leave as little room in the structure of government for the growth and activity of parties as possible. In this of course they were acting in accordance with convictions still generally shared, and deeply embedded in the tradition of civic humanism that had shaped the value-system of eighteenth-century Anglo-American political discourse.

But the Federalists, who at that time still had no less a person than James Madison as their leading spokesman, appear to have had rather more in mind than "curing"—as Madison put it in the Tenth Federalist—"the mischiefs of faction." Back of this aim was something more comprehensive still, a profound anxiety over whether the right sort of men—men of enlightenment and virtue— would be chosen to occupy the seats of responsibility in the republic's new government. This concern too took its form from the same system of traditional civic humanist values, already threatened, as they saw it, by aggressive new forces afoot in American society that needed to be contained. And here too it was Madison who spoke for the Federalists, on behalf not of the new forces but of the old values.

Gordon Wood has suggested very persuasively that the Federalists, and Madison in particular, as they went about their work in the late 1780s were much more troubled over the irresponsibility and small-mindedness of the state legislatures in the years immediately following the Revolution than they were over the deficiencies of the Articles of Confederation.[28] What most offended them were such short-sighted actions as paper money laws, debtor relief laws, local tariffs, tax postponements, and a tendency to beat down court reforms and similar undertakings intended for the larger public benefit, all amid a babel of contending local demands, selfish private and parochial interests, and the pushing and shoving demagoguery of popular politics. Some general remedy seemed imperative. The Revolution itself had called such conditions into being. The extensive demands in food and military supplies generated by the eight-year war effort, and the newly mobilized entrepreneurial energies that went into supplying them, had effected immense transformations in American social and economic life, most significantly at the local level. The expansion and differentiation of internal trade had created a new acquisitiveness, new appetites, new habits of lending, borrowing, and consumption—whole new patterns of expectation—on a markedly higher plane of diversity and profusion than had been there before. "The Federalists in the 1780s," according to Professor Wood, "had a glimpse of what America was to become— a scrambling business society dominated by the pecuniary interests of ordinary people—and they did not like what they saw. The wholesale pursuit of private interest and private luxury were, they thought, undermining America's capacity for republican government."[29] Moreover, just as the society was becoming more broadly entrepreneurial, so also was it becoming more broadly and diversely political; questionable types who had previously tended to stay "in their place" were now elbowing their way more and more into local and state politics. It was the convergence, indeed the inseparability, of these two tendencies that most Federalists had in mind when they spoke of "faction."

Madison in *The Federalist* was inclined to see the terms "party" and "faction" as more or less interchangeable. But equally interchangeable, or at most barely distinguishable, were "faction" and "interest." There are, he announced, interests everywhere: debtors and creditors, "a landed interest, a moneyed interest, with many lesser interests"; they form themselves into contending parties and factions, full of "unfriendly passions" and "mutual animosity," and are "much more disposed to vex and oppress each other than to cooperate for their common good." The violence of faction (amid which "the public good is disregarded") distracts the harmony of the well-ordered republic, and the greatest danger of all is that of one such faction, through sinister arts and secret cabals, forming itself into a majority force thereupon able to oppress the entire community.[30]

The great object of the Tenth Federalist, as everyone knows, is to show that although the "*causes* of faction cannot be removed" without suppressing liberty itself, means may still be found for "controlling its *effects*," and they are more likely to exist in a large republic than in a small one. In a large and extended republic Madison discerns three great advantages. One is "a greater variety of parties, against the event of any one party being able to outnumber and oppress the rest"; another is the obstacles afforded by space and distance against concerting and accomplishing "the secret wishes of an unjust and interested majority." But the greatest advantage consists in the widened electoral districts out of which may be chosen *men of the right sort:* "representatives whose enlightened views and virtuous sentiments render them superior to local prejudices and to schemes of injustice." This principle—men of the right sort—comes close to holding the key to the entire Federalist idea.

The Tenth Federalist has often in modern times been read as a theory of broker politics in a pluralist national state, but such a reading had best be taken as an anachronism. There is reason to doubt that this was at all the function Madison had in mind for his men of "enlightened views and virtuous sentiments."[31] Such men were seen by him—and doubtless by all who called themselves Federalists, then or later—not as agents for the lateral mediation of private interests but rather as spirits of detachment able to see well beyond, and well above, such partial interests in the light of a higher public good. They were men apart, gentlemen who by birth, breeding, refinement, and independent circumstances were endowed with a special wideness of vision and were thus peculiarly fitted to dedicate talent and wisdom to disinterested public service.

James Madison himself, to be sure, was to form political connections in the course of the dozen years subsequent to his writing of the Tenth Federalist that would have the effect of attenuating, for him, certain of that paper's central assertions. But for the Federalists of 1800 this image—that of men of "enlightened views and virtuous sentiments"—had become an obsession. It applied to none other than themselves, a beleaguered company whose robes of authority were being smirched by the advancing forces of insolence, vulgarity, disorder, self-interest, faction, and demagoguery. And it was against these forces that the Federalists, with their sedition law, were now blindly striking back.

When they appear in historical accounts, the cases of prosecution under the Sedition Act (of which there were fourteen in all) are most often discussed, and appropriately so, with reference to their brutal high-handedness. But another aspect of these cases that is in some ways even more striking is the almost comic clumsiness, the sheer political ineptitude, with which the Federalists went about their work of trying to silence the opposition press. A few examples may show something of this.

One such might be the fruitless pursuit of William Duane, Benjamin Bache's successor as editor of the captious *Philadelphia Aurora*. Duane had to run one gauntlet after another, each time eluding his tormenters' grasp and each time covering them with public ridicule. Early in 1799 he and three recently arrived Irish friends were indicted for seditious riot after a scuffle had ensued from their having tried to circulate a petition against the Alien Act in the yard of a local Catholic church. The prosecutor claimed that foreigners had no right to petition "or to interfere in any respect with the government of this country." The jury needed no more than a half-hour to bring in a verdict of not guilty, as the courtroom erupted in cheers. Duane then went after the Administration in his paper, charging it with having been under corrupt British influence. When proceedings were instituted by Secretary of State Pickering for seditious libel in July 1799, Duane announced that he had not published a fact he could not prove. The "proof" was a letter he had got hold of, written by Adams himself several years before, complaining that there had been "much British influence" in the appointment of Thomas Pinckney as minister to London during the Washington administration, a letter Duane could be certain Adams would not now want to see made public. After an extended postponement, Duane could triumphantly inform his readers that the case had been "withdrawn by order of the President."[32]

But the chase continued. The final effort to pin Duane involved for practical purposes every Federalist member of the United States Congress. Duane had published a pending Federalist-inspired bill, leaked to him by three Republican senators, which would establish a "Grand Committee" to determine which electoral votes to count and which to throw out in the approaching presidential election. Denouncing it as a scheme to cook the election in secret, Duane in his editorial commentary got some of his facts mixed up, whereupon the Senate Federalists determined to close in on him. They devised a committee on privileges to discover grounds upon which the Senate might itself undertake punishment of the editor without risking the tedious procedure of a jury trial—the idea being that making a bill public before it had been passed was an illegal breach of Senate privilege (though this was hardly the first time such a thing had been done), and that Duane's editorial had contained false, defamatory, scandalous, and malicious assertions tending to bring the Senate into contempt.

But then everything began going wrong. The Federalist-dominated committee made up its verdict in advance without a hearing, sitting as prosecutor, judge, and jury, while the Republican press heaped derision on these "star chamber proceedings." Duane was then ordered to appear before the Senate to hear the charge and to say whatever he wished to say in "excuse or extenuation" of his utterances. He appeared and asked to be defended by counsel, but was told that although he might bring in counselors they could be heard only in denial of facts charged against him or in excuse or extenuation. (In other words they could not question the Senate's jurisdiction, or call witnesses, or undertake—as even the Sedition Law allowed—to prove the truth of any of the editor's statements.) The attorneys Duane had meanwhile engaged, Alexander Dallas and Thomas Cooper, thereupon refused to serve at all; Duane himself failed to reappear; the Senate declared him in contempt and issued a warrant for his detention; Duane went into hiding and stayed there until Congress adjourned, all the while continuing to publish the *Aurora* and broadcasting the details of his persecution.[33]

The rest was more or less damp fireworks that never went off. The Senate requested the Executive to initiate prosecution for seditious libel, but by the time an indictment was obtained the bill that had caused all the original stir had been killed by the House, and the government had moved to its new seat on the Potomac, which meant that most of the witnesses and accessories were now out of reach. After two postponements the case was finally set for trial in October 1801. Thomas Jefferson, who by that time had been President of the United States for seven months, promptly discontinued it.[34]

The case of Jedidiah Peck of Otsego County, New York, offers a little paradigm of how to convert a stout Federalist stronghold into a hive of Republicanism, with Federalists themselves doing most of the work. Peck was an odd little man, rustic in both dress and spelling, but he had a strong intelligence and a straightforward way of expressing himself when he chose to do so. He had been a good Federalist—fairly good, that is, until he began taking a line of his own on certain public issues. Peck had supported William Cooper, Otsego's leading Federalist grandee, when Cooper ran for Congress in 1796, and had been rewarded by an appointment as associate judge in the county court of common pleas. But Peck, when he was elected to the Assembly in 1798, began doing bad things. He opposed a motion to reject the Virginia and Kentucky Resolutions when they were debated in that body; he supported a Republican motion to declare the Alien and Sedition Acts unconstitutional; and he supported a move to have presidential electors chosen by popular vote rather than by the state legislature. The enraged Federalist insiders thereupon resolved to get the unreliable Peck removed from his judgeship, which they managed to do without leaving any record of the reasons, and then closed ranks in opposing Peck's re-election to the Assembly. He won anyway, by a strong majority.[35]

Thus despite his own previous inclinations, Peck had been turned into a Republican. The Federalists now swore to get Peck in any way they could, and thought their chance had come in the summer of 1799. Peck had been sent copies of a vigorously worded petition to Congress for repeal of the Alien and Sedition Acts, and had begun circulating it about the county. Cooper in his capacity as presiding county judge decided that it was seditious; he sent a copy to the district judge, who passed it on to the district attorney, who in turn recommended prosecution under the Sedition Act. Peck was accordingly indicted. He was arrested in late September, 1799 ("taken . . . at midnight," according to one of the Republican newspapers, "manacled, and dragged from his home'"), and his five-day journey in custody to New York turned into a triumphal progress. Jabez Hammond wrote:

> A hundred missionaries in the cause of democracy, stationed between New-York and Cooperstown, could not have done so much for the republican cause as this journey of Judge Peck, as a prisoner, from Otsego to the capital of the state. It was nothing less than the public exhibition of a suffering martyr for the freedom of speech and the press, and the right of petitioning, to the view of the citizens of the various places through which the marshal traveled with his prisoner.[36]

The trial was set for April 1800, by which time even the Federalists were aware that they had made a hash of it. For one thing, all the witnesses lived some two hundred miles away, and the trial was postponed the first time when none of them turned up; for another, the longer it dragged on, the stronger the Republican presence in Otsego became. Peck was again up for re-election, and the Federalists now realized they had better wash their hands of the affair as quietly as they could. But too late: Peck got more votes than any other candidate, and an honored place for him in the gallery of founding Republican elders in that part of the state was thenceforth assured.

2

The Apotheosis of Matthew Lyon

The Federalists would have done well to take all their warnings from the very first of the cases—that of Matthew Lyon—that were prosecuted under the Sedition Act. The lessons were there, for any who had eyes to read them. But few Federalists in this instance could have seen very steadily, because Lyon was the embodiment of everything in a public man that Federalists saw as most odious. Under normal circumstances probably few on either side, Republican or Federalist, could have found such a type very savory, least of all James Madison, and certainly not the James Madison of 1787. But the times were now anything but normal, and for the Republicans, though the man's redeeming qualities were few, it was nevertheless possible to make something tremendous out of them.

Matthew Lyon's uncouthness, his fractious insolence, and his instinct for responding to every circumstance with primary reference to his own self-interest all appear imprinted in the few details we have of his early youth. Born in Ireland in 1749, Lyon at the age of fifteen turned up in the province of Connecticut as an indentured servant, bound first to a dealer in pork, who soon sold him off to another master for a "Yoke of Bulls." Legend says of the new master that he believed in the rod "as an efficient instrument of discipline," that he felt himself obliged to give the surly lad frequent drubbings, but that he was at length rid of him, willingly or not, when "Matt threw a mallet at [his] head . . . and fled."[37] Whatever may have been the immediate consequences, Matt acquired enough wherewithal by the time he was twenty-three to buy a hundred acres in the frontier township of Cornwall and to marry the daughter of one of the settlers there, which may have brought him some additional property. At that very time, as it happened, men everywhere around him were buying up land at bargain prices and moving to the Hampshire Grants, in the country that later came to be called Vermont. Lyon felt the itch to go too. He sold his holdings in Connecticut, bought acreage in the township of Wallingford, and settled his new family there in 1773.

Lyon's activities in this new country—"unsettled" in every way—thereupon began giving hue and definition, touch by touch, to the character he would present when he made his sensational appearance in Philadelphia a quarter-century later. To note that he acquired extraordinary influence in local politics, did military service in the Revolution, and made a great deal of money in a variety of entrepreneurial dealings might convey something of the direction but little of the tone and texture.

He fell in right away with the Allen brothers, Ethan, Ira, and Levi, spirits very much compatible, though on a grander scale, with his own. The Allens' all-encompassing schemes and tortuous plottings formed the essential core of Vermont's beginnings. But the critical thing about every one of these schemes—the movement for statehood, or independence, and the various forms it took, or the organizing of the Green Mountain Boys and the part taken by Vermont in the Revolution, or the undercover dickerings with foreign governments—invariably referred back in some sense to ways and means of protecting and enhancing the vast holdings the Allens themselves were accumulating in that country and in which they had an enormous stake. The great advantage they had in organizing support for their doings was that every settler in the Hampshire Grants, large or small, lived in the shadow of insecure titles, the legitimacy of the Grants themselves having been for years a matter of dispute between the colonies of New Hampshire and New York. When the movement of speculators grew to a great rush following the French and Indian wars, New York's standing challenge to the grants that had previously been made by the governor of New Hampshire eventually came before the Privy Council, which then ruled in favor of New York. Thus a precarious situation was made endemic, and it persisted into the Revolution, past the achievement of independence, all through the Confederation period, and would not be resolved until a settlement was finally reached with the state of New York in 1790. Even so, traces of it remained, in the form of Loyalist claims against wartime confiscation and other issues, for years after that.[38]

Such, then, was the setting in which Matthew Lyon's own thirst for influence, standing, and gain could function with few limits and under the lightest of scruples. His participation in the Revolution, an outgrowth of his having joined one of the vigilante militias formed for the protection of settlers' property, is itself ambiguous, the record being less than clear as to his military exploits. (He underwent one court-martial, thrown back at him in later years.) In any case he left the army after Saratoga, having more pressing concerns elsewhere. Along with his ambition went qualities of persuasion that made for a haranguing kind of leadership, and by 1778 he was already serving, by election or appointment, as Councilman, Deputy Secretary of the Governor and Council, Assistant Treasurer, and

Clerk of the Court of Confiscation. In the latter capacity he used inside information to acquire choice Tory property for himself, and was eventually impeached in 1785 for ignoring an order by the Council of Censors to turn over his records for examination. He escaped any serious consequences through the protection of Governor Chittenden, who after Lyon's first wife's death the year before had become his new father-in-law.[39]

What really set him going was his own plan for the augmentation of government revenues through the granting of townships "to persons who could exert their good offices in behalf of the new state." As a member of the committee formed for this purpose he had five of them granted to himself as proprietor, and the fees he paid amounted to a speculative investment whereby he acquired his first substantial capital, which he then concentrated in the town of Fair Haven. There, as his biographer describes it, "by January 1781 he had possession of over four hundred contiguous acres rich in iron, lumber, and water power, resources that kindled Lyon's enterprising imagination." Lyon himself told a correspondent some thirty years later: "I had so attended to my affairs in the more advanced stages of the war, and towards its close, that I was able under the most favorable auspices to set agoing a number of mills and manufactures which made me rich. . . ."[40] In the 1790s his vision seemed to take on almost Hamiltonian dimensions with his advocacy of government aid in "promoting useful manufactures" — except that what he principally had in mind was assistance from the Vermont legislature for his own blast furnace, a scheme that was turned down by one vote.[41]

But what of the forces that made Matthew Lyon into the bombastic populist he became during that same period? Those forces had first made their appearance some years before in the form of a rival political presence in his own state, originally small but growing in influence, very different in outlook and values, a mounting challenge to everything the Allen-Chittenden-Lyon ring stood for, and a threat most especially to Lyon's own accelerating political ambitions. Its pivotal figure was a young man named Nathaniel Chipman, himself full of ambition, who had served under Washington at Valley Forge and had come out to Vermont to practice law in the closing years of the Revolution. Chipman, too, soon became involved in politics, and with the sense of order derived from his New England upbringing, Ivy League education, and Litchfield law training he found himself deeply offended by everything he saw around him. The nuclei of opposing parties thereupon took form as most of Chipman's colleagues in the legal community, lawyers and judges alike, became more and more confirmed in their opposition to what they saw as the free and easy irresponsibility of the state government in such matters as the rights of dispossessed loyalists, legal tender laws, and debtor relief, especially with the largest debtors happening to be the largest speculators. It was predictable that such critics should emerge as Federalists in the 1790s, during which period they gathered enough local support to gain control for a time of the state assembly. It was inevitable, too, that Matthew Lyon and Nathaniel Chipman should come face to face, and on one occasion actually to blows. The challenge Chipman represented was direct, personal, and total: to the legitimacy of the means whereby Lyon had made himself what he was, and to the right and fitness of Lyon and his sort to have any part in the functions of governing. The vocabulary with which Lyon thereupon armed himself, during the critical interlude in which the forces of Federalism and Republicanism were discovering themselves and each other, was the most logical one, indeed the only one available. When "the struggles commenced between aristocrats and democrats," as Lyon later explained it, "nature, reflection and patriotism led me to take the Democratic side."[42]

It was under these circumstances, and in this sort of ideological clothing, that Lyon launched his great drive to get himself elected to Congress. The effort began in 1791, lasted through the greater part of the decade, and was narrowly successful in 1797 only after annual failures and accumulating frustrations. He was held back on the one hand by the determined opposition of the Chipman forces with their grim charges of corruption, "unexampled turpitude," and a "conscience too callous for compunction," and on the other by the resentment he aroused in his own town of Fair Haven, letting it be understood that since the town owed its very existence to him, "it was his right to represent it as long as he should please."[43] At the same time, he started a weekly newspaper, the *Farmer's Library*, with his seventeen-year-old son as "publisher," devoted to the principles of republicanism, the interests of the "poor and midling people" and the "hardy yeomanry of Vermont," and serving above all as an electioneering vehicle for himself. He took advantage of the enthusiasm of 1793 for France, and called for the formation of Democratic Societies throughout the state. He was never an open member of any of them, though he sensed that with luck they could be useful in supporting his own aspirations. Things took a wrong turn when it leaked out that he had got involved in a French scheme for an insurrection against the British in Canada, whereupon he issued a plenary disclaimer:

> The stuff about my ever being President of a Democratic society, one of Genet's creatures, or having ever opposed the American government, or encouraged the Western Insurrection, are all as groundless as any lie ever conceived by the heart of the author.[44]

He seems to have been at least even-handed in his schemes of informal diplomacy, being at the same time implicated in a very different one, the object of which was to tie a detached and independent Vermont to Canada, not by conquest but through collusion with the British.[45]

But his determination was at last rewarded when he emerged with a majority of 396 in the congressional run-off election of 1797. He appeared in Philadelphia for the special session of May 1797, very full of himself and seething with aggressions. The rage with which he imbued the Federalists, from his first moments there, would put him behind bars within a year and a half.

Lyon's picturesque brawl with Roger Griswold on the floor of the House is probably better remembered than his later conviction for sedition. There seems to be an implicit rule always that a new member of any deliberative body who does not hold his tongue during at least his introductory sitting there will be regarded with suspicion. And so it was with Matthew Lyon. He had already set them all muttering when he burst out during the opening discussions about the customary reply to the President's address that he "did not come there prepared to approve all the former acts of government, but for other purposes," and then ridiculed the entire practice of addresses and replies, of making "obeisance to a magistrate." Otis's speech about the "wild Irish" touched him off again, for understandable reasons, and in no time he was the butt not only of mounting acrimony but of jibes and caricatures as well. ("I'm rugged Mat, the Democrat," captured in some Hibernian bog and sold for a yoke of bulls, and so on.) William Cobbett then raised a great titter through the cloakrooms when he printed a squib in *Porcupine's Gazette* about Lyon's court-martial for cowardice during the war, and how General Gates had sentenced him to wear a wooden sword for it.[46] One day during a recess Lyon was telling his hearers how the people of Connecticut were having their interests sold out by their (aristocratic) representatives, and how if he, Lyon, were to go in there with his newspaper he could set them all straight in six months; whereupon Roger Griswold of Connecticut asked if he intended to fight them with his wooden sword. Lyon spat in his face; Griswold went and bought a hickory cane, with which he gave Lyon a bad beating; and Matthew Lyon was now, in both senses, a marked man.

The Federalists' effort to expel Lyon, and thus be rid of him, fell short of the necessary two-thirds vote, so there he remained.[47] But after the Sedition Act became law five months later, two more of his exploits seemed exactly made to order for the language of Section 2: "intent to defame . . . or to bring . . . into contempt or disrepute." Lyon was just then replying in print to a bitter accusation in *Spooner's Vermont Journal* of criminal disloyalty in opposing the President's preparedness measures, in which he declared that "when I see every consideration of the public welfare swallowed up in a continual grasp for power, in an unbounded thirst for ridiculous pomp, foolish adulation, or selfish avarice . . . I shall not be their humble advocate." The other occasion was his reading passages of a letter from Joel Barlow, obtained on promise that he would not publish it, to crowds all across Vermont. Barlow had written from Europe that when the President told Congress the French "had turned pirates and plunderers; and it would be necessary to be perpetually armed against them, though they were at peace; We wondered that the answer of both Houses had not been an order to send him to a madhouse." Lyon was indicted for sedition on October 5, 1798, and brought to trial three days later. He was found guilty and sentenced to four months in jail, with a fine of $1,000.[48]

It was at this juncture, and in light of the treatment he subsequently received, that Matthew Lyon was transformed into something wholly new. He became a resplendent abstraction. The Federalists, with a precision which Lyon himself could never have accomplished on his own, had metamorphosed him into a martyr. He was imprisoned not in his own county of Rutland but in Vergennes, forty-four miles distant, and was paraded before the people of every settlement along the way. He was clapped in a freezing cell without glass in the windows or a stove, and with a stinking latrine that had to be shared with several vagrants occupying the same cell. And now, in place of the "Spitting Lyon" and "Paddy whack," he truly became the embodiment of his own picture of himself, the forthright man of the people, now made victim of all the malevolent works of Federalism. He conducted his own campaign for re-election from his prison cell with a new newspaper, *The Scourge of Aristocracy,* from which the narrative of his ordeal was reprinted in Republican papers all over the country. He was re-elected by margins he had never previously approached; at the same time, his plight inspired a movement among highly placed Republicans to raise a subscription for the payment of his fine.

The heart of the movement was located in that nursery of statesmen and citadel of refined manners, the gentry of Virginia. Senator Stevens T. Mason, informing Lyon of his and his friends' efforts on the prisoner's behalf which he thought were the least they could do for him, avowed that "the personal suffering to which you are exposed, is much more than the proportion you ought to bear in the common cause of Republicanism."[49] The man had been changed; his life rewritten, offered up to "the common cause of Republicanism."

3

Sedition and Subversion in England and America

Matthew Lyon and a few others, as we have seen, were made into martyrs in consequence of the Federalists' determination to hunt down and punish sedition. In England, on the other hand, a comparable drive against subversion and disloyalty was being carried out under the direction of William Pitt at that same period—Federalists and Republicans alike were in fact watching it closely—and with a degree of ruthlessness well beyond anything seen in the United States. Yet the English campaign created no martyrs. None of the victims there, though dealt with much worse, evoked any such outpouring of public sympathy as in America.[50] Why not?

Pitt's campaign had been launched as far back as 1792. It began with a royal proclamation warning the nation against "seditious writings that might cause tumult and disorder." Public response was hearty and favorable, and the September Massacres of that year in Paris gave the impetus for a very aggressive course of government action against any threat of domestic agitation.[51] For instance, two peers, Lord Sempill and Lord Edward Fitzgerald, were both summarily cashiered from their army commands, Sempill for signing an address to the French National Assembly on behalf of the Society for Constitutional Information, and Fitzgerald for conversations he was known to have had in Paris regarding French intervention in Ireland. But the attorney John Frost, who had uttered disloyal expressions while intoxicated in a coffee-house and been convicted of sedition for it, was "sentenced to six months' imprisonment at Newgate, an hour in the pillory at Charing Cross, to find sureties for good behavior for five years, and to be struck off the roll of attorneys." He was thus ruined for life. The reform societies were robbed of their most effective piece of propaganda when Thomas Paine's *Rights of Man* was condemned as a seditious libel and its author outlawed *in absentia* for having published it. Any printer or seller of Paine's work was thereupon exposed to certain prosecution.[52]

Irregularities and arbitrariness in legal procedure on the part of Federalist judges and other law officers in the United States are of course regularly brought up in almost any account of prosecutions under the Sedition Law. But such irregularities pale compared to the techniques resorted to in England by Treasury solicitors and the Attorney-General in their determination to suppress or drive out of business radical newspapers and booksellers. With the use of *ex officio* informations the prosecution, according to Albert Goodwin, "could dispense with grand juries . . . try cases before hand-picked special juries and . . . keep the threat of proceedings hanging over the heads of the accused for long periods."[53] Another element entirely missing from the American case was the formation, quite outside government auspices, of the "Association for the Preservation of Liberty and Property against Republicans and Levellers," a kind of vigilante league spread throughout England in which it has been estimated that as many as a third of all the adult males in the country participated.[54]

The English too had their alien and sedition laws. But whereas none of the American acts passed by more than the narrowest of margins, the support in Parliament for their English counterparts was overwhelming. An Aliens Act was passed in 1793, a Treasonable Practices Act late in 1795, and a Seditious Meetings and Assemblies Act also in 1795. The penalties for infraction of these and other such laws greatly exceeded in severity anything specified in the corresponding American legislation. For instance, Thomas Muir and the Reverend Thomas Fyshe Palmer, tried and convicted of sedition (which here consisted of advocating parliamentary reform and circulating Painite literature) were sentenced to transportation to Botany Bay, Palmer for seven years and Muir fourteen. There were ten times as many prosecutions for such offenses as there were in America. And even so, this says little as to the informal devices by which subversion of any sort was effectually stifled in England and Scotland during this same extraordinary period.[55]

But again: why the difference? There were, at first glance, a number of elements present in the American scene in the summer of 1798 that would seem to make the two situations at least roughly comparable. The Federalists, moreover, might well have had some basis for their conviction that Pitt's example, and the effectiveness of his campaign to stamp out all seditious activities, could be repeated in America. The threat of a French invasion, the surge of support for President Adams after the XYZ disclosures, the movement to mobilize a force of volunteers, recollection of the Democratic Societies and the Whiskey Rebellion, and the powerful urge to move against a scurrilous Republican press: all seemed to point in the same direction—draconian action, purposeful movement, swift and ruthless justice, a widely applauded assault upon all forms of disloyalty.

Yet none of this happened, except in caricature, because between the two scenes there were in fact few real analogies. British actions occurred against the backdrop of actual war with revolutionary France; the threat of invasion was never absent; and Pitt had behind him the sustained and undoubted weight of public opinion. The Federalists had no such advantages. An invasion of the American coast was never more than a transient illusion, which few took seriously for more than two or three months in mid-1798; and public opinion—judging simply from the flood of protest petitions in early 1799, as well as the growing number of Republican newspapers—was never other than deeply divided, and was by that time running more and more against Federalism with every passing week.

In England, on the other hand, there was in the radical opposition, such as it was, an element of extreme marginality. The leaders of the reform societies, with their addresses to the French National Convention and similar effusions, had a perverse genius for alienating not only British public opinion but even a good number of their own potential supporters. And in any case the greatest part of English society, and virtually the entire political nation, were intensely hostile to every aspect of the radical program, being deeply persuaded that such innovations as universal manhood suffrage and equal representation posed a mortal threat to the British constitution.[56]

In America, meanwhile, there was no longer any occasion for "radicalism" of this nature at all, as Thomas Paine himself had been among the first to point out, because constitutions had all been made new, and because in America the kinds of reforms so ardently but vainly called for in England had already been effected and were taken for granted. Radicalism consisted of something else. The "radicals" of America, who included tidewater grandees as well as scrambling entrepreneurs, were beginning to organize the entire political class—vastly wider and looser than that of Great Britain—in a new and unaccustomed way. They were organizing with the very specific object of challenging the right of incumbent magistrates and governments to go on governing. They now constituted a standing opposition: more precisely, an opposition party. The only instrument the Federalists could think of for defending themselves and striking back was the rusty principle of seditious libel—one which, even as a theoretical premise, had come to have little or no pertinence to the emerging state of political practice in America.

And finally, the point at which the parallel between Great Britain and America breaks down as much as it does anywhere is with the question of a governing elite. The claim of a greatly restricted political class in England to elite status was for practical purposes uncontested, whereas in America the Federalists' sole prop was their own picture of themselves as men of "enlightened views and virtuous sentiments." And although the status and authority that would accrue to a true governing elite was something to which they certainly had pretensions, the pretensions went ungratified: in such an immensely extended political class as there was here, such status and authority were close to meaningless. Indeed, the nearest thing to such an elite in America may well have existed not in the ranks of Federalism at all but in those of its "radical" opposition—at least in the state of Virginia, where radicals were masters of slaves and patrons of a still-deferential yeomanry.

4

Hamilton's Army

The Federalists' New Army, not unlike their campaign against sedition, was itself something of a caricature. The Federalists were, in a certain sense, endeavoring to repeat what they had so successfully done in 1787 when they set in motion the forces that culminated in the Federal Constitution. They were exploiting an immediate crisis — as they had done with Shays's Rebellion — for the momentum needed to fashion a permanent institutional structure that might ensure the strength and stability of the national government. But in the case of the New Army, the relation between the need as perceived and the solution projected did not seem to be visible to any but themselves.

To be sure, a military establishment of some sort need not have been regarded as a far-fetched object just in itself, and it is not impossible to make a case for this one. Simply on the level of general national policy, much could be said in support of a trained professional force, of moderate but adequate size, around which in time of emergency volunteers could rally and be mobilized. The insufficiency of an untrained militia had been made only too apparent to Washington in the Revolution, as it would be again to Madison a few years hence in the War of 1812, and in between, there ought logically to have been more than a casual lesson implied in the failure of St. Clair and the successes of Wayne in the Old Northwest. And from the viewpoint of immediate circumstances it might be conceded that no reasonable Federalist acquainted with the full scope of French-American relations in the 1790s could be entirely blamed for supporting some such force as the Federalists tried to bring into being in 1798. And yet the difficulty now was all too stark. This projected army was disconcertingly large, and once the momentary threat of invasion had passed, the American public simply did not want it.

There has been much speculation among historical writers regarding the specific uses the Federalists may have had in mind for their army. Its military uses need not have been limited to repelling a French invasion. Another possibility given consideration at the time was that of a movement in Latin America, in cooperation with Great Britain and local revolutionary forces under the leadership of Francisco Miranda, to liberate the Spanish colonies, assist in the establishment of friendly governments there, and thus prevent the likelihood of French client states in that region. Rufus King, the American minister in London, pressed such a project with some persistence, and Hamilton was more than receptive. An even more focused undertaking, with direct implications for American security, would involve occupation of Louisiana and the Floridas, with British cooperation if possible but without it if necessary. Various indications of French designs for repossessing Louisiana gave a considerable logic to this idea, one which Jefferson himself would articulate with great succinctness four years later. Neither of these notions need be seen as wholly irrational, even if, as many have pointed out, a strong factor in their attractiveness was the military glory that might thus accrue to Alexander Hamilton.[57]

Yet the fact was that neither scheme was ever more than a faint possibility, and nobody was more aware of this than Hamilton himself, much as he might have wished otherwise. Hamilton was exceedingly cautious in his correspondence with Miranda on the matter of action in South America. He was unwilling to make even the most tentative commitment without the support of the President, who was unlikely to want anything to do with British cooperation in an imperial incursion there. Even the more containable Louisiana project was a thing hedged about with difficulties. The Senate's reaction to the Blount conspiracy—which envisioned similar results—had made it clear that no such move, certain as it was to initiate armed conflict, would be made by the United States until evidence of French intentions was unmistakable. Moreover, as long as negotiations with France remained a live possibility (as of course they never ceased to be), an attack on Louisiana would be out of the question.[58]

Another line of historical conjecture, going as far back as the President's great-grandson Henry Adams, has been that the Federalists' true plan was to put the army to unabashed domestic uses: that they had no less a purpose than that of moving against their own political opposition.[59] And judging from things certain Federalists said at the time, evidence of such a purpose seems inescapable. At the very moment of the XYZ disclosures Theodore Sedgwick exclaimed, "It will afford a glorious opportunity to destroy faction. Improve it." A force of twenty thousand men, according to Robert Goodloe Harper, would "give us the flower of the country; and put arms into the hands of all our friends." The army, coupled with a declaration of war, James Lloyd hoped, would "enable us to lay our hands upon traitors"; while Uriah Tracy declared that "the only principle by which Democrats can be governed . . . is *fear*." And there was, of course, Hamilton's own subsequently famous outburst to Sedgwick: move a force toward the state of Virginia, and "then let measures be taken to act upon the laws & put Virginia to the Test of resistance."[60]

Yet implied in all this is a clarity of will and a specificity of intention that would probably have been hard to find anywhere in Federalist councils. The urges they may have felt in their sleepless hours, or blurted out in their private letters, was one thing; a readiness and commitment to act on them was quite another. Indeed, it may be suspected that the sort of group confidence and sense of group mission required for any specific policy of action with this army was simply not there. They would be lucky to find any real "traitors" to lay hands on, and if there were in fact "arms in the hands of all our friends," there would still be the very real question of just which way to point them. Hamilton himself in his right mind could hardly have supposed that there was any way to coerce an entire state with an army, least of all Virginia. Nor was there any real evidence that Virginia, as was charged, intended resistance to the Alien and Sedition Laws through force, the main determination all along of such leading Virginians as Jefferson, Madison, and Monroe in this regard being precisely that force *not* be used.[61] And it would take some stretch of fancy to picture George Washington leading an army of any kind against the state of Virginia.

What it came down to was that the Federalists did not know what they wanted of this army—*in particular*. About all they did know was simply that they wanted an army. It represented something out of another time and another country: authority, and the reassurance of authority—that, and little more. Perhaps they need not use it for anything at all—most of them may actually have hoped as much—but they wanted it, just to have it there. Throughout this entire interim period, from the time when the invasion threat had lost its urgency to that in which the New Army was clearly headed for extinction, Hamilton would persistently reject any compromise arrangement that might reduce the size of it or scale down the expense. When it finally was disbanded early in 1800, Hamilton was wracked by despondency and rage, the consequences of which would be a story in itself.[62]

It has been rightly pointed out that the Federalists in insisting on a disproportionately swollen military establishment were challenging a traditional and widely nurtured suspicion among Americans toward the very principle of standing armies. The origins of this hostility went well back into colonial times, and the attitude was in fact shared by the societies of both the colonies and the home country. The basic theory, of English origin, was first set forth in James Harrington's *Oceana* (1656) and then extended and modified by Radical Whigs in the Walpolean age. Roughly speaking, the theory had two premises. One was that a citizen militia in which all freeholders served was the best guarantee of free institutions in a free state, arms being thus "never lodged in the Hands of any who had not an Interest in preserving the public peace," and the citizenry thus not being dependent on government for their community's defense. The other was that a permanent, paid professional force—the result of the citizens' having delegated their military responsibilities elsewhere—was an instrument for tyranny and corruption and a standing threat to liberty and virtue. By the same token professional soldiers, dependent on government for their livelihood and having little in common with the larger community and its interests, could be manipulated by ambitious princes and made the auxiliaries of a tyrannical state.[63]

But in the advancing decades of the eighteenth century, attitudes in England regarding the management of military force began undergoing certain changes. Radical Whig theory had been primarily concerned with the moral consequences for civil society, and concerned only indirectly with the respective fighting capacities of militias and standing armies. A newer understanding emerged with the Moderate Whigs and such writers as Daniel Defoe, John Somers, and Adam Smith, who reversed the priorities in favor of military efficiency and dependable defense of the state. They argued that militias were incompatible with either modern warfare or the realities of modern society, that they were no match for trained and disciplined troops, and that under proper constitutional supervision and safeguards a permanent military establishment was much the more desirable.[64]

But though in England this view had superseded the older one and had become more or less dominant by the mid-eighteenth century, no such modification occurred in the colonies. Such Radical Whig pamphleteers as Trenchard and Gordon, who had a great influence in America, continued to press the older anti–standing army argument, which would persist there as the predominant conviction with regard to the maintenance and employment of military force. There may have been a streak of self-delusion in the colonials' insistence on the full adequacy of citizen militias, inasmuch as the protracted warfare with the French and Indians was largely conducted by British regulars and colonial volunteers rather than by militia. But then the use of redcoat regulars to coerce the colonies in the period just preceding the Revolution, together with the legends created by the militia at Lexington, Concord, and Bunker Hill, served to impart a certain inviolability to the citizen-soldier ideal and — despite repeated bad experience later on — to guarantee its preservation as one of the sacred fictions of the early republic.[65]

Now the Federalists were striking through this inherited web of belief. Here they were, straining to heave an enormous military machine into existence, with no clearly visible or acknowledged purpose. The traditional resort of an endangered community — should danger arise — was being snatched away from those most to be trusted for its well-being and placed in the hands of hired mercenaries, entirely dependent on the powers that paid them and wholly at their beck and call. And since their officers were to be none but reliable Federalists, what was to prevent their masters from using them as tools for whatever purpose they pleased? What assurance was there that the liberties of the citizen were not about to be done away, that this great engine was not to become the instrument of corruption, repression, and tyranny?

The ideological resistance, then, was formidable. The Federalists did get their army — on paper. But a process of special interest is the convergence of forces that served to snatch it back away from them, and the Federalists' incapacity to grasp the implications of it. They should perhaps have been warned straight off by the narrowness of the vote on the military bill, and should have perceived that what they did get was obtained at the optimum time when anything in that line could have been had before or since. Yet now they had it; opposition no longer mattered; they had been given it by law; they could move as they saw fit. But no: they did not have it; opposition did matter; and this was true for two reasons, neither of which they ever quite took in. One was that the political class in America was of a proportion that had no precedent in a modern state, constituting for practical purposes the entire adult white male public, and the Federalists, whatever they might deem themselves entitled to, were not accorded any special standing within it. The other, more important still, was a principle that has held from that day to this: when such a state attempts a major military undertaking, it cannot do so with any hope of success without the approval and support of an overwhelming majority of its entire society. Anything much short of that spells failure, if not from one cause then from some other. The New Army was a failure from a variety of apparently unconnected causes. But disparate as they were, the causes all flowed in some way from the same source: this society did not want this army, was determined not to have it, and was in effect delegating one agent after another to tell all the rest that it need not exist.

Well might Hamilton berate McHenry for delay after delay in the procurement of supplies and for the scandalous condition most of them were in when they did arrive, or for the payroll system that had no more than begun to function, or for the mutinous troops, some of whom had gone as many as nine months without being paid. Yet McHenry's "incompetence" is far from a sufficient explanation for what was happening. It was rather that an administrator of no more than average energies was being signaled in a variety of ways by everyone he dealt with that the environing society was not taking seriously what he was asking of them and saw little urgency in it. In a true crisis, generally acknowledged as such, a political class this extensive would have tapped energies that nobody knew existed, nor would it have tolerated those piles of worthless shoes, rusty muskets, mismatched uniforms, ridiculous-looking hats, and threadbare tents, or the callous avarice of those who furnished them.[66] But the signals now, coming in from everywhere, contained little that would inspire that sort of energy, and ranged only between indifference and downright disapproval of the entire New Army idea.

They came not only from Republican newspapers, petitions, and public meetings; some actually came from the ranks of Federalism itself. Noah Webster suspected that a "principal object" in raising such an army was merely "to overawe and repress the opposition to government." The Secretary of the Treasury, a High Federalist insider whom McHenry saw every day, had misgivings on different grounds, but they came to the same thing: Oliver Wolcott felt that "the expense of supporting idle men" should be "avoided as much as possible." And if anyone had the authority, at least *ex officio,* to send signals on behalf of the whole political nation, it ought to have been the President himself. Here is one of those he gave, altogether typical. McHenry had sent for his approval (he was then summering at Quincy, as usual) a plan drawn up by Hamilton for improvement of the supply system. Adams did not comment on it one way or the other; he simply replied that he would keep it "in order to recur to it upon occasion," that he presumed it would require an act of Congress (whether he really thought so may be doubted), and that meanwhile the cabinet officers should consider it among themselves, even though he almost certainly knew they had already done so.[67]

In short, the Federalists were discovering—as with the Sedition Law, and as they shortly would again with the election of 1800—that in a political society of this nature and extent a "mandate" for anything requires a great deal more than backstairs plotting, manipulation, and the margin of a few votes. And that society would find many ways of saying so. In this case, no more basic a way could have been found than the one eventually taken. By law this army, should there be an actual declaration of war, could have contained as many as fifty thousand men. Of these, fifteen thousand had been authorized to be raised at once; this was the "New Army" Hamilton and McHenry were dealing with. But authorization was one thing, actual enlistments quite another: the recruiting officers could persuade barely a fourth of that number that their country really wanted or needed them. The rest, of course, failed to answer at all.[68]

Congress eventually did see the futility of hanging onto this sorry force. It voted in late January 1800 to halt enlistments, and in May to disband the New Army altogether. Alexander Hamilton tried at the end, as he told his wife, to play "the game of good spirits—but . . . it is a most artificial game—and at the bottom of my soul there is a more than usual gloom."[69]

5

Virginia and Kentucky Resolutions

The famous Resolutions of 1798, adopted by the legislatures of Kentucky and Virginia on November 13 and December 24 respectively, were drafted in secret by Thomas Jefferson and James Madison and formally introduced by two others, John Breckinridge for Kentucky and John Taylor for Virginia. They were designed as a non-violent protest against the Alien and Sedition Acts. The Resolutions became famous because, among other reasons, of their distinguished authorship (though this would not become known until some years later), and because of the unusual fact that the protest was taken up in a formal way by no less a power than the constituted legislatures of two states against an act of the national government.

Other questions as well have made the Resolutions a continued object of interest. One concerns the extensive use to which the Resolutions, as text and example, were put by state-rights spokesmen in the South throughout the entire ante-bellum era, long after the specific occasion for them had ceased to be an issue. Another is the question of how the Resolutions are to be read as statements of constitutional doctrine, and how compatible they are with the idea of a federated national state. Historically, in other words, the immediate context of the Resolutions came to be overshadowed by implications that far outlived the occasion which inspired them and for which they were designed.[70]

But that same occasion, to Jefferson and Madison, seemed sufficiently critical that they sought to establish their position on the widest ground of principle, the ground on which the Constitution itself, as they saw it, derived its ultimate sanction. Jefferson's view, as embodied in the much lengthier Kentucky Resolutions, appears to be the more extreme beside the relatively more cautious and compressed Virginia statement. But though the variations between them subsequently proved to be of some significance, their conclusions were for practical purposes interchangeable. Both sets of resolutions were argued on a strict-construction basis and a view of the Constitution as a compact among the several states, a compact that had been violated by recently enacted federal legislation. They asserted—as Jefferson and Madison had each done as individuals seven years before with reference to Hamilton's proposal for a national bank—that the Constitution to which the contracting states had assented delegated certain powers to the federal government, specifically enumerated, all others not so delegated being reserved to the states; that "in case of a deliberate, palpable, and dangerous exercise of other powers not granted by the said compact, the states . . . are in duty bound to interpose for arresting the progress of the evil" (Virginia Resolutions); and that with the Alien and Sedition Acts the federal government had exercised a power not only undelegated but "expressly and positively forbidden" in the First Amendment. Both sets of resolutions concluded with an appeal to the other states to join with them "in declaring these acts void and of no force" (Kentucky), or, as with the Virginia Resolutions, simply "unconstitutional."[71]

In the period of roughly a year following the issuance of the Virginia and Kentucky Resolutions, none of the other fourteen state legislatures so invited prove willing to lend their concurrence to them. Ten emphatically rejected the Resolutions; the other four took no action at all.[72] But to conclude from this that the Resolutions failed of their purpose would not only be misleading but would end the story almost before it begins. The story is in fact rather a tangled one, full of complexities and powerful consequences both delayed and immediate.

One line of consequences, in some ways the more visible and momentous, stems from the fact that the Resolutions as statements of constitutional theory were to have a career far more protracted than either of their authors intended for them. It was a career, moreover, fraught with no small degree of mischief, though that aspect of it is not our primary concern here, nor should it obscure certain of the significant functions the Resolutions appear to have effected for the Republican party in 1800.

It should nevertheless not be overlooked that their theoretical side proved more a liability than an asset, both then and later on. The doctrinal implications are anything but clear-cut, owing in large measure to the part Jefferson played, even with Madison's moderating influence, in the movement that produced them, and to the ambiguities and fluctuations of Jefferson's own mind during the period of their formulation. Actually neither Jefferson's nor Madison's version was acceptable to any of the states that replied to them, and in the case of all who gave their reasons the principal objection was everywhere the same. "It belongs not to state legislatures [as the Vermont reply to Virginia phrased it] to decide on the constitutionality of laws made by the general government; this power being exclusively vested in the judiciary courts of the Union."[73] Madison, whose mind, as usual, worked with greater precision than Jefferson's, had couched his version in language decidedly less prolix and less menacing than that of the Kentucky Resolutions. Not that this mattered much for immediate purposes; the responding states saw little or no difference between them. Yet Jefferson, to a far greater degree than Madison, had left some ill-omened hostages to an unforeseen future.

The secret of Jefferson's authorship of the Kentucky Resolutions would eventually become known. So also, a number of years later, would papers come to light containing his unamended drafts of them. This occurred in 1832, at the height of the nullification movement in South Carolina, and Jefferson's conception of state rights, expressed in terms that were a mixture of the extravagant, the threatening, and the vague, were exactly suited to the nullifiers' purposes. The "principles of '98" thereupon became their rallying cry and would be a bible of state-rights particularism down to the Civil War, with Jefferson as its prophet. Yet Jefferson himself never did quite say whether a single state could properly judge the constitutionality of a federal law: he seems to have thought that it could, though it is also possible he did not entirely know what he thought. Nor was it clear whether, if so, such action could be taken by the legislature; here too he seems to have thought that it could, whereas Madison tried to persuade him otherwise, perhaps successfully. What exactly, then, might a state, or states, do in defense of their violated rights? Jefferson insisted in a second set of Kentucky resolutions in 1799, though not in the first, and with much greater bellicosity privately than in their final form—which suggests that Madison or Breckinridge may have persuaded him to tone it down—that the "rightful remedy" was "nullification." Yet there remains some doubt whether Jefferson (in theory) meant the same thing by "nullification" as the South Carolinians did, or whether (again in theory) his meaning was more extreme than theirs, or less. He seems not to have believed, as they did, that a state could nullify a federal law and yet remain in the Union. That he did conjure with the idea of secession is implied in a letter to Madison containing the phrase "determined . . . to sever ourselves from that union we so much value, rather than give up the rights of self government which we have reserved. . . ." In any case, a new edition of the Resolutions published in 1859 gave southern spokesmen a renewed warrant for construing from them a complete theory of state sovereignty accompanied by the right of peaceable secession. "Generally," according to Merrill Peterson, ". . . the secession movement was a remarkable testament to the compact theory of government, which Jefferson, more than anyone, had fixed upon the American political mind."[74]

But this is something of a digression, serving perhaps as a kind of counterpoint to the immediate significance of what the two leading spirits of Republicanism were engaged in during what would prove to be the closing months of the Federalist ascendancy. On this level vagueness and miscalculation dissolve, and in their place one perceives precision, purpose, and an assurance about the Republican future that had no counterpart in Federalist circles, an assurance that was about to be borne out by events. This aspect of the case emerges with a special clarity when the Virginia and Kentucky Revolutions are viewed in their character not as expositions of constitutional theory but as a powerful piece of party propaganda, and most particularly when the strategy of their issuance and dissemination is seen as the opening shot—nearly two years in advance, and in circumstances not on their face encouraging—in the election campaign of 1800.[75]

The very concept of a "campaign"—not simply as a contest between rival candidates for election to a public office but, much more portentous, between opposing political parties for possession of the national government—was an idea that had not yet penetrated the vocabulary of the founding generation, much less its understanding. So if there were to be one now, it would have to manifest itself as something else, or something more. And a certain psychological protection would be required in order that large numbers of men—Republicans at least, if not Federalists—might make the transition.

There seems to have been little doubt by now in Jefferson's mind that he wanted the presidency and was ready to assume it, as had decidedly not been the case in 1796.[76] There was a more or less general assumption too, not only in Jefferson's own circle but in the Republican aggregations in the various states (however loosely knit, or even fully aware of themselves, they may have been), that Jefferson was indeed the man, that Jefferson's claim and no other was the one to be pressed in the election of 1800, and that his claim was their claim. They would have to do "party" things, think something like party thoughts, and mobilize themselves in party ways. But there was still a sense in which they would have to do it without saying so, and perhaps not even knowing it with more than half their minds. This applied from Jefferson on down, the very idea of party having still little more than a halfway authenticity, even for them, and for the Federalists even less so. But this was where Jefferson's mind could combine with his instincts to reach a tactical accuracy perhaps even beyond Madison's—a by-product of which was that the Republicans, for all the ups and downs of the ensuing two years, would take scarcely a false step and would succeed in doing all the important things right. Meanwhile the Federalists, as we have already begun to see, would somehow manage at each turn to do everything wrong.

The Sedition Act in particular would serve the Republicans in a dual function: as an all-encompassing menace, and as a providential opportunity. It was a threat to the entire idea of party, and thus to be resisted, on whatever ground, with every resource they had; while in the very course of resistance that same idea could be submerged, never mentioned—placed, almost, beyond their own awareness—under the higher urgency of principle.

Thomas Jefferson already had something of a reputation for intrigue,[77] going as far back as his scheme of 1791 to employ Philip Freneau in the State Department as part of the inducement for setting up a newspaper of the right tendency in Philadelphia. The reputation was in a way unfair, or rather would have been if it had been acquired at a later stage in the emergence of American party politics. It was just that Jefferson had a singularly refined sense, probably a degree ahead of his time, of how a given political situation felt and looked, and of just which pins on the map needed to be moved in order to make it look different. Some of this may have been gained a little the hard way, such as when a private letter of his would find its way into the newspapers, or fall into the wrong hands. But considering the amazing number of such letters to which this did not happen, letters teeming with political observation and analysis, or in view of certain of his own personal choices—such as lying low in 1796 in full awareness of the foreign mess he would have on his hands should he take high office at that time—the overall impression is one of caution, perceptivity, and sureness of step. All such qualities came into ample play in the summer of 1798 as Jefferson took in the full import of the Sedition Act and how it might bear on the fortunes of the Republican party.

For the manifestoes of protest envisioned by Jefferson to be set in motion in the right way and in the right direction, secrecy as to origin was indispensable. Otherwise the anomaly of Jefferson's position as Vice-President of the United States under a Federalist administration, and of Madison's as his closest friend and political associate, would have been too great a liability to survive any such effort as they were now preparing. And indeed they covered their tracks so carefully that we still do not know, except in a general way, the course of their movements between midsummer of 1798 and the introduction of the Kentucky and Virginia Resolutions, by those who had agreed to do it, in the legislatures of those states at the beginning of winter.[78]

Jefferson's instincts, no doubt modified along the way by Madison's sharp eye and quiet stubbornness, led them to touch every right point in the political logic that was unfolding before them. Republican influence on the level of national affairs had been fearfully undermined by the XYZ disclosures and by the patriotic fever that had followed them. But shoring it up on the state level, where in certain places (and who could tell how many others?) a clear working base could be counted upon, was an undertaking that held out some real promise. (This was certainly the case with Virginia, and was similarly so, as John Breckinridge assured them some time in the early fall, with Kentucky as well.)[79] The logic further ordained that in the resulting resolutions the state-rights line was to be pushed for all it was worth. Neither Jefferson nor Madison could have felt much strain there; they had been doing this in one way or another ever since Madison's conversion early in the decade to a strict-construction theory under the exigencies of resisting Hamilton's Treasury program.

But whatever the outcome, there must be no appearance of anything disorderly or illegal; there must be no ground on which individuals could be got at for seditious utterances; and there must on no account be anything like a resort to force. "This," as Jefferson emphatically put it, "is not the kind of opposition the American people will permit. But keep away all show of force, and they will bear down the evil propensities of the government, by the constitutional means of election & petition."[80]

Though the Resolutions were clothed in the idiom of state rights, the mother language was that of highest republican principle—of principle guaranteed, so they argued, by the already-sacred Constitution itself, and now violated through the exercise of an unsanctioned and oppressive power. The Virginia Resolutions recalled that when that state ratified the Constitution its convention had expressly declared that "the liberty of conscience and of the press cannot be cancelled, abridged, restrained or modified by any authority of the United States," and that "an amendment for that purpose . . . was in due time annexed to the Constitution."[81] The Kentucky Resolutions added something with reference to foreign arrivals (whose inherent republicanism presumably ought not to be discouraged), insisting "that alien friends are under the jurisdiction and protection of the laws of the State wherein they are;" that "no power over them has been delegated to the United States, nor prohibited to the individual States distinct from their power over citizens"; but that through the Alien Act (unconstitutional on five different grounds, as explained in Resolutions IV, V, and VI) "a very numerous and valuable description of the inhabitants of these States" were "reduced as outlaws to the absolute dominion of one man [the President]," meaning in effect that "the barrier of the Constitution [was] thus swept away from us all."[82] In short, the Alien and Sedition Acts together struck both indirectly and directly at every one of the rights and liberties that the people constitutionally enjoyed, and were but another evidence of that spirit which was ever leading the federal government to "enlarge its powers" (Virginia again) "so as to consolidate the states, by degrees, into one sovereignty" and to "transform the present republican system of the United States into an absolute, or, at best, a mixed monarchy."[83]

These were ringingly familiar Republican sentiments, and they could sound echoes of one sort or another in every Republican ear that heard them. Nor could they be mistaken for anything else, despite the remarkable fact that "party" was never so much as mentioned, in either set of Kentucky Resolutions, nor in those of Virginia, nor even in the twenty-thousand-word report on the Resolutions and their reception, running to more than sixty printed pages, that was subsequently prepared by James Madison for a special committee of the Virginia legislature in 1800.[84] It hardly needed to be: a key phrase in the Virginia Resolutions had made the whole point without having to state it in other than muted words. The Sedition Act ought to arouse "universal alarm," because

> it is levelled against the right of freely examining public characters and measures, and of free communication among the people thereon, which has ever been justly deemed the only effectual guardian of every other right.[85]

And perhaps as striking as anything about this entire two-year period, as inflamed passions swirled everywhere around him, was the essentially settled state of Jefferson's mind with regard to the future. He may have been vague and oscillating as to particular points of theory and doctrine. But overriding it all was a kind of lofty optimism, a persisting confidence that all would come right, and since it was now the figure of Jefferson upon whom all Republican eyes were fixed, this could not have failed to be inspiriting. There certainly were discouragements. The elections in the fall of 1798 and spring of 1799 did not go at all badly for the Federalists, who increased their control of the New York Assembly by electing all thirteen of the New York City members, did very well in both North and South Carolina, and even picked up four more seats than they had previously held in the congressional delegation of Virginia. In Congress they beat down a Republican movement to get the Alien and Sedition Laws repealed, and managed to pass bills for further increases in both the army and navy. And finally, of course, not a single state legislature anywhere proved willing to give the official concurrence that the Resolutions of Kentucky and Virginia had asked of them.

But none of this seems to have made much of a dent in the intrinsically sanguine temper of Jefferson. The XYZ frenzy, with which it had all begun, was unreal, "not the natural state." "A little patience, and we shall see the reign of witches pass over, their spells dissolved, and the people recovering their true sight, restoring their government to its true principles." This was because the fever was temporary, and the body sound. "This disease of the imagination will pass over, because the patients are essentially republican. Indeed, the Doctor is now on his way to cure it, in the guise of a tax gatherer." As for those elections, no need for alarm: they could even be seen "on the whole as rather in our favor"; and in the Virginia case the result came from "accidental combinations of circumstances, & not from an unfavorable change of sentiment." In short: take heart, one and all, and be "fully confident that the good sense of the American people, and their attachment to those very rights we are now vindicating, will, before it shall be too late, rally with us round the true principles of our federal compact."[86]

And indeed it all began to work out as he said, while Republican morale took a steady rise in the course of 1799 and into 1800. The petition movement was in full flood by February ("wonderful & rapid change"; Congress "daily plied with petitions against the alien & sedition laws & standing armies"), in the midst of which came the President's nomination of William Vans Murray for a new mission to France ("a great event . . . yesterday"), letting still more wind out of High Federalist talk of a French invasion. Meanwhile the state of Pennsylvania was looking better and better ("even the German counties . . . changing sides"), and with the elections of October 1799, it fell at last into Republican hands ("a subject of real congratulation & hope"), with similar possibilities now discernible in New Jersey and New York.[87]

Somewhere along the way Jefferson found the time to write out for one of his well-wishers a long and detailed catalogue of his principles, added to which was his conviction that "they are unquestionably the principles of the great body of our fellow citizens."[88] There, of course, was the great point: it was above all else a question of principle, upon which it was as certain as could be that Thomas Jefferson and that "great body" stood as one. But perhaps not the whole point. How and when might such a certainty be fully revealed? In the letters that went off in every direction during these two dozen months (most of them accompanied by cautions not unlike the one in the "principles" letter, that since there were prying eyes in post offices and everywhere, "our correspondence must be as secret as if we were hatching [our country's] destruction"),[89] there are glimpses of another side of things. We see Jefferson busily urging his spokesmen to find their voices, volunteering materials that might be useful in this or that place, calculating the electoral vote, balancing possibilities, weighing the respective merits of general tickets and election by districts, locating the bellwether states, and projecting the swing vote. As early as February 1799 he is telling Madison that the forthcoming summer must be a season of hard work. ("Every man must lay his purse & his pen under contribution.")[90]But then, in the midst of a surprisingly technical outline of all such matters to Monroe, Jefferson innocently interrupts himself. "Perhaps," he ventures,

> it will be thought I ought in delicacy to be silent on this subject. But you, who know me, know that my private gratifications would be most indulged by that issue, which should leave me most at home. If anything supersedes this propensity, it is merely the desire to see this government brought back to it's republican principles.[91]

"Merely" indeed! But with this, we are brought back once more to the eighteenth century.

To all intents and purposes the Federalist measures of 1798, foremost among them the odious Alien and Sedition Acts, had furnished all those in any way attached to the Republican cause not only with an "issue" but with a vast release. It was a release from a whole series of inhibitions erected by the values and assumptions under which their entire generation had come to maturity, inhibitions having to do with the "baneful spirit"—as Washington had called it—of party. They could now unite, not as a mere faction in pursuit of office and emolument but as a band of patriots in resistance to encroaching tyranny and arbitrary power. They could join on the ground of principle to do what had to be done in the achievement of what they and everyone else might otherwise see as mere party ends.

And the Virginia and Kentucky Resolutions, the first counter-stroke in that effort, had done as much as, and perhaps more than, anything that came after them to set the tone and to point the way. Historians have from time to time puzzled themselves over just what effect they could have had, if any, on the "revolution of 1800," and have rightly concluded that there can be no straight-forward answer.[92] But it can at least be suspected that the Resolutions performed, at a critical time, a vigorous latent function. Something or other had to be done about them, or so it was thought, and not at some distant center where the national affairs were transacted but much closer to home, in each of ten separate state legislatures. It may actually have been fortunate for the Republicans in those places that they were in every case surrounded by Federalist majorities, because the challenge was not exactly an easy one, requiring as it did some nice discrimina-tions. But what it did do was present them with an occasion for taking a long step in their own awareness of themselves as a party, and for striking a very satisfactory balance between party and principle. Few Republicans appear to have had any doubts about the principles embodied in the Resolutions in general. Yet a good many shied away from the implied remedy—that a state legislature might officially declare an act of Congress unconstitutional—and a number of them said so. Nevertheless when it came down to the question of how the Resolutions were to be disposed of, in each known case where the yeas and nays were recorded, it was settled by a strict party vote.[93] Party and principle may not have been *entirely* merged, and that may have been just as well. The Republicans now knew a little more about where their work lay, where the help might come from, and what the arguments were, than they had beforehand.

6

Federalism and the "Campaign" of 1800

There are turns of luck in all things, and it is conceivable that the Federalists, as late as the opening of the Sixth Congress in December 1799, still possessed the means of effecting repairs of some sort, some purposeful arrest to the course of deterioration their fortunes were now evidently taking. It was still a Federalist Congress; indeed more so than the Fifth Congress that had preceded it. Its members had been elected while the surge of patriotic support for the Administration, reaching its meridian in mid-summer of 1798, was still very much in being, and the result had brought the Federalists even greater majorities than they had had then. True, the Republican victory in Pennsylvania had been a setback, as were Republican gains in southern legislatures. But it could still be supposed that with Federalist control of the House and Senate, and with a Federalist Executive, there ought to have been more than a fair possibility that with exertions in the right direction the Federalists might still face the test that lay before them in the all-important election of 1800 and emerge from it with success.[94]

On the face of it, their true strategy could be seen as self-evident — or would have been so seen, say, by a later political generation. The great theme that had brought such a heightened degree of national unity in 1798 — the encroaching menace of revolutionary France, the clear need of defense preparations for resisting it, the urgency of means for preventing the spread of subversive jacobinical principles at home — must now be substantially abandoned, or at least significantly modified. With the Ellsworth mission at last on its way, and with public opinion generally inclined to approve the President's decision to send it, the French threat in the all-or-nothing form which the Federalists had given it could no longer be counted on as a sufficient rallying point for the citizenry. A peaceful settlement was now a possibility that must at least be allowed for, and a place made in their minds for the rewards that might accrue from it. With the likelihood of an actual French invasion having long since faded, and with popular exasperation at high taxes, the Alien and Sedition Laws, and an expensive army becoming every day more manifest, there was little to be gained from a continuing sole preoccupation with the specter of jacobinism. The time had come to turn it around: to exploit the growing popular support for the President's peace initiative, to insist that it was *their* firm and forthright policy that had made it possible, forcing the French to accept fresh negotiations on American terms, and to close the ranks of Federalism with a new and higher call for national unity in the name of peace and prosperity, to be reaffirmed and ratified by the re-election of the current administration.

On the other hand, the liabilities they would have to overcome, residing less in their environment than in themselves, were so gross as to be all but immovable. The jacobin menace, at home and abroad, had become a consuming obsession. The other obsession, vastly more complex, was their self-image as men of "enlightened views and virtuous sentiments." They recoiled from any notion of themselves as agents of a partisan coalition with a diverse constituency, a party whose continuing vitality required a readiness to entice new and disparate aggregations of people to come inside and find a welcome. That was no part of their mission. Theirs was not to accommodate but to stand as examples and to point the way: not to mirror public opinion but to lead and correct it. Adjusting to popular passions was to play the demagogue, pander to the unenlightened, and set another example altogether — one of cowardice, hypocrisy, opportunism.

The President's action, then, in dispatching the Ellsworth mission left in them little room for anything but confusion and rage. Adams had deliberately cut away the one issue that had enabled them to rise in vindication of the public honor, arm the nation, arouse the people to their danger, and move against the lurking menace at home. In response to what they could only see as this willful folly, a number of leading Federalists were now furtively looking for a way to push Adams aside and replace him with a more suitable candidate in 1800.

As it happened, there was at least one Federalist recently come into prominence who saw all these things differently. One of the newly elected members in the Virginia delegation to the Sixth Congress was John Marshall, who would take a highly active hand in the proceedings that opened in December 1799. One way to view these proceedings and their significance would be to do so through Marshall's eyes.

When Marshall arrived at Philadelphia for the beginning of the session he was disturbed at much of what he saw and heard. "The eastern people," he wrote to his brother,

> are very much dissatisfied with the President on account of the late mission to France. They are strongly disposd to desert him & to push some other candidate. King or Ellsworth with one of the Pinckneys—most probably the general [Charles Cotesworth], are thought of. If they are deterd from doing this by the fear that the attempt might elect Jefferson I think it not improbable that they will vote generally for Adams & Pinckney so far as to give the latter gentleman the best chance if he gets the southern vote to be the President. Perhaps this ill humor may evaporate before the election comes on—but at present it wears a very serious aspect.[95]

In other words, if the "ill humor" should *not* evaporate, there could be only one outcome: instead of drawing their lines against the opposition, the Federalists would end up drawing them against each other.

The southern Federalists were generally of a more moderate temper than those in much of the North, especially New England. On the question of electing a Speaker, Marshall thought that as one step toward a measure of party harmony it would be a good idea to choose a Southerner, two of the three previous Speakers having been from the middle states and the other from New England. A leading candidate, able and respected, was John Rutledge of South Carolina, and Marshall undertook to handle the case for electing him. But the New Englanders insisted on Theodore Sedgwick of Massachusetts, and after three caucuses without any giving of ground it was evident to Rutledge that there was little point in drawing it out any further. He thereupon submitted with grace, and to prevent the Republicans from taking advantage of a Federalist division to elect one of their own, he told his supporters to cast their votes for Sedgwick. Sedgwick was as rigid an ideologue, and as bitter an opponent of Adams's French policy, as any High Federalist around.[96]

Marshall's talents were certainly well understood by Federalists of all complexions, and a number of them said so. They even recognized, moreover, that Marshall was a presence that could matter if there were to be anything like a workable reconciliation within their own ranks. Theodore Sedgwick himself acknowledged as much. "He possesses great powers and has much dexterity in the application of them. He is highly & deservedly respected by the friends of Government from the South. In short, we can do nothing without him."[97] Nevertheless there was something about Marshall that made a Federalist of Sedgwick's sort uneasy. For one thing, he paid rather too much attention to public opinion. "He is disposed . . . to express great respect for the sovereign people and to quote their opinions as an evidence of truth."[98] And for another, very little that was coming out of the state of Virginia nowadays could be seen as unmixed good news, even such a power as Marshall. "I believe his intentions are perfectly honorable, & yet I do believe he would have been a more decided man had his education been on the other side of the Delaware. . . ." For all Marshall's moral weight ("In Congress, you see Genl. M. is a leader"),[99] it would never be quite enough to turn the scales of reason, though certainly not for want of trying, or for Marshall's not fully knowing what he was about.

By common consent, the choice of who should prepare the House's customary reply to the President's annual message fell upon Marshall. The resulting address, though suitably elevated in tone, was the product of some sweating. It politely echoed the President's sentiments on all the topics of his speech, on measures taken and others desirable, though there had to be shadings of emphasis here and there to ensure that it would get through the House without an eruption of unseemly debate on the floor. For instance, Adams had been singularly perfunctory about the need for continued measures of defense, with a rather pointed hint about taking thought for "an exact economy." Marshall, aware of what any High Federalist would make of that, put the case for defense on a distinctly more spirited plane, saying nothing about economy (except "commensurate with our resources"), and prudently avoiding any distinction between military and naval appropriations. And of course the touchiest of all the topics was the Ellsworth mission to France, and the obvious freedom from doubt in the President's mind as to his own wisdom in having sent it. Marshall's reply made a great deal of Adams's sincerity of purpose (consistent with "your conduct through a life useful to your fellow-citizens, and honorable to yourself"), but qualified with a touch of irony by the hope "that similar dispositions may be displayed on the part of France." That ought to have done it: except that everyone knew, or would soon find out, that Marshall himself had personally approved Adams's decision, and that Adams knew it as well. So the outcome was rather a sullen stand-off. The address passed, according to Oliver Wolcott, "with silent dissent."[100]

One of Marshall's worst liabilities in the eyes of most northern Federalists (besides generally "thinking too much of Virginia") was his known disapproval of the Sedition Act. This was because they could not face the thought that the Sedition Act had itself become one of *their* worst liabilities. Marshall in his campaign for Congress in Virginia had made it clear that he was "not an advocate for the alien and sedition bills" and that had he been in Congress at the time he would "certainly have opposed them," thinking them "useless" and "calculated to create, unnecessarily, discontents and jealousies." Sedgwick thought this "a mean & paltry electioneering trick," and Fisher Ames declared, "Excuses may palliate,—future zeal in the cause may partially atone,—but his character is done for." Still, this was John Marshall, a man they knew they needed: perhaps he could be redeemed. "Marshall has not yet learned his whole lesson," cautioned George Cabot. But they ought to believe that he would. "Some allowance too should be made for the influence of the Atmosphere of Virginia. . . ."[101]

Commendable indulgence, though it might have been more so had "some allowance" been made for Marshall's taking a hand in redeeming *them*. The Sedition Act did in fact come up for repeal in January 1800. Marshall supported the motion for doing it, which thereby passed by a margin of two votes. But then an adroit Federalist parliamentary maneuver, an amendment replacing the repealed act with the even more obnoxious common law of seditious libel, gave Marshall no choice but to reverse himself and vote against it. The entire Republican contingent did so as well. The Sedition Act thus had to remain where it stood.[102]

Still another giddy measure came before the House in the course of the session, the Ross Election Bill for a "Grand Committee" of House and Senate to pass upon the validity of electoral votes from the several states in the coming presidential election. Marshall moved against this too, this time with success. But although he thereby helped save his Federalist colleagues from more short-wittedness, they were hardly disposed to thank him for it. The joint committee envisioned by the Ross bill was to have the final determination on any question concerning the election; any "irregularity" would be whatever the committee said it was; and so it would rest with this body of thirteen men, chosen by a Federalist-dominated Congress, to decide who should be the next President of the United States. Nor was it any secret that the bill had been especially shaped to deal with what the state of Pennsylvania was likely to do in the election, that state's government having just turned Republican, or that such a committee would be peculiarly receptive to any plausible ground for counting out Thomas Jefferson. Marshall had as little use for Jefferson as any Federalist in the House. But this scheme as he saw it was not only unconstitutional, it was disreputable, and politically demented. What he then did with his influence, on the floor and in committee, was to get the bill altered to a form in which it could no longer carry out the function its originators had designed it for, whereupon the Senate would have no more to do with it.[103]

One more issue upon which such a temper as Marshall's could have made some difference was the distracted question of what now to do about the army. The army was in deep difficulty, and it was not as though the Federalists were not all too disagreeably aware of it. Sedgwick himself, probably its most passionate supporter in the House, had to admit privately "that the army everywhere to the southward is very unpopular, and is growing, daily, more so."[104] Moreover, a shortfall in tax collections, leaving a gap of some $5 million between estimated revenue and what would be needed to support the country's expanded program of armaments, meant that the difference could only be made up by borrowing. The Republicans were making a very big point of this.[105] The best thing would undoubtedly have been simply to disband the New Army and to let the southern Federalists be given the credit for having done it.

But it could not be quite that simple. The Federalist position had become so impacted, and that of the Republicans at such a distance from it, as to tax the mind of the most conciliatory Federalist in sight. What further complicated it was that with the Hamiltonians' grim commitment to a permanent army, and in the absence as yet of any information on how the American mission would be greeted in Paris, such a step as demobilization, however politically effective it might be, was not yet thinkable, even to such as Marshall.

Marshall's was nevertheless a vanguard mind, nearly always a step ahead of the others, and probably better able than any to see into what was for most of them a hopelessly opaque political future. Marshall at the beginning of the session resisted a Republican move to disband the army, which if successful would probably have brought even more demoralization to Federalism than if things had been allowed for the time being to go on as they were. He did, however, put his weight behind a compromise whereby the New Army would remain in being but with further recruitments suspended. Yet there was no provision for commencing demobilization should the news from France be favorable, which would have allowed the Federalists some flexibility of movement when reports began trickling in that the American envoys were in fact to be received with due honors by the Bonaparte regime. By then, support for the New Army was crumbling, and even the most warlike Federalists now saw that the only way to keep credit away from the Republicans for what was inevitable would be to do it themselves. Robert G. Harper so moved on May 7, with the provision—proposed by John Marshall— that the demobilization be carried out at the discretion of the President as soon as in his judgment the diplomatic situation warranted it.[106] Marshall probably had a fair idea that the President had already so concluded some time before.

But it was too little and too late. Had Adams been given such authority three months earlier, the Federalists would have had a stopper to Republican talk of a great military machine to be kept in perpetual being, and they might thus have seized the benefit from the first encouraging news from France. As it was, they managed to kick away even the little good this eleventh-hour gesture might have done them. Three days after Harper's motion passed, Adams dismissed Secretary of State Pickering, and on the same day announced the immediate demobilization of the New Army. The enraged Federalists in the Senate, determined that Adams should not now be allowed the satisfaction of dismantling Hamilton's army, there-upon withdrew such authority from the House motion and voted to exercise it themselves, to take effect on or before June 15, 1800.[107]

So as Federalist congressmen, full of black thoughts, departed from Philadelphia for the last time, and the brooding Adams was off to inspect the new Federal City of Washington before journeying home to Quincy, the chasm between them had become unbridgeable. But that hardly meant that they had run out of ways to do themselves mischief, or indeed that they were not to find yet new capacities for ensuring that the curtain would be brought down upon Federalism forever.

Only one man would be truly spared. John Marshall had left early, to attend to his diminishing law practice in Richmond, and meanwhile the President had decided he needed a new Secretary of War. The man he determined to appoint was Marshall, whose loyalty to him throughout had been above question, even while Marshall had been doing all one individual could do to set his tottering party to rights. Marshall politely declined, owing to the demands of his affairs at home. A few days later the President was looking for a Secretary of State as well. Again he wanted Marshall, who this time accepted. He took up his duties on June 8, 1800, and would discharge them with due competence until the end of Adams's term.[108] Just before that, on January 20, 1801, he would be nominated as Chief Justice. He was thus diverted from a highly promising but probably doomed career as a politician.

By May 1800 the covert movement whose beginnings John Marshall had discerned with such foreboding the previous December—the Federalist cabal to prevent John Adams from succeeding himself—had taken on a life of its own. What followed throughout the summer and fall was a sequence of political madness. The madness, to be sure, was not exactly one-sided. There was a distinct aspect of it for which John Adams could have had no other to blame but himself. But in another sense it was all mixed in together.

The final stage of self-destruction and demoralization began with the spring elections in New York for seats in the state assembly. It had been evident for some time that this would be a critical test, since the new legislature that resulted from it would be the one to choose New York's twelve electors by a joint vote of both houses. The situation in Pennsylvania made it even more critical, because of the deadlock that had developed in the legislature there as to the manner in which that state's fifteen electors would be chosen—whether by general election, election by districts, or by the legislature itself—and there was a real possibility that it would not be resolved in time for Pennsylvania's electoral votes to be cast at all.[109] Thus since Jefferson had received fourteen of those fifteen votes in 1796, and since Adams in 1796 had carried all of New York's twelve, there was now a clear likelihood that the New York vote could decide the election of 1800. Everything thus depended on whether the New York Assembly was to come under Federalist or Republican control.

And it was generally recognized that this in turn depended on something else, that with a relatively close balance in the country districts the key to the outcome would be the way things went in New York City. While the city had been safely Federalist from 1789 to 1796, the Republicans had carried the assembly elections there in 1797 and 1798. But the city's Federalists were then able in 1799 to benefit from a strictly municipal issue—public hostility to some sharp dealings over the chartering of a Republican-dominated bank—to elect their entire slate of Assembly candidates by good majorities.[110] So for 1800 it was anyone's guess: given candidates of strong caliber, it could go either way. For the Republicans, the work that lay before them had a self-evident clarity of outline. The Federalists, in a congestion of divided purposes, approached theirs with a singular lack of direction.

One of New York's most decided Federalists was Robert Troup, a longtime friend and close associate of Alexander Hamilton who had regularly taken an active hand in city politics. Troup certainly knew what the Federalists had to do if they expected to win this one, and he said as much in a letter to Rufus King two months beforehand. The coming election, he said, "to choose a Legislature to appoint electors" would be "all important." "We are full of anxiety here. . . . It is next to an impossibility to get men of weight and influence to serve. . . . We must bring into action all our energies; if we do not the election is lost—and if our Legislature should give us anti-federal electors, Jefferson will be in."[111]

Yet it did not occur to Troup that there was a very good reason why all those energies could not be brought into action, and why it was proving so difficult "to get men of weight and influence to serve." He gave the game away himself when he asserted his conviction, and that of others who saw the case as he did, that "the federal cause essentially depends on removing Mr. Adams and appointing a more discreet man to the Presidency."[112] With anything short of an all-out mission, proclaiming the importance above all else of reelecting a Federalist administration, they were without a wholehearted cause with which to rally the voters.

And such indeed was the way it worked out. A nominating committee of city Federalists, rent by internal factions, spent the month of March and half of April trying to patch together a slate of Assembly candidates. All New York knew of their differences, which were aired once more at the public meeting of April 15 at which the sum of their efforts was announced. The slate included, according to a jubilant Republican stalwart who was among the first to know of it, "two grocers, a ship chandler, a baker, a potter, a bookseller, a mason, and a shoemaker." The only others with any claim to visibility were Cadwallader Colden and Gabriel Furman, both less than popular with the city's voters. When the ticket was published, "all was Joy & Enthusiasm" among the Republicans.[113]

They, meanwhile, had seen to every detail. Aaron Burr had been quietly at work for many weeks on the party's Assembly slate and had succeeded in persuading three authentic notables—ex-Governor George Clinton, the distinguished lawyer and future Supreme Court justice Brockholst Livingston, and General Horatio Gates, the hero of Saratoga—to head the list. Burr and his lieutenants, working in total harmony with the Republican committees, and with a new and lively Republican newspaper, the *American Citizen,* to aid in preparing public opinion, had one uncomplicated object: to bring down all the works of Federalism in order to bring about the election of Thomas Jefferson. They addressed meetings, distributed literature, and stationed themselves in force at the polls on all three days of the election. The returns, announced on May 3, 1800, showed that the city Republicans had elected all twelve of their Assembly candidates, as well as their nominees for the state senate and the United States Congress. They now had a majority of the legislature, which would meet in November and cast New York's twelve electoral votes for Jefferson.[114]

The Federalists were of course profoundly shaken. Alexander Hamilton now flailed out in two directions in an effort to shore up the damage. He wrote to

Governor John Jay imploring him to reconvene the existing legislature and persuade it to enact a new law for choosing electors by district, which he thought might bring a Federalist majority. Jay, aware that such a far-fetched maneuver could well cause a major upheaval in the state, silently chose to do nothing.[115] Hamilton's other move was to call for the full activation, through his confidants in Congress, of the undercover plan that had been in ferment for some months to ease Adams out in favor of Charles Cotesworth Pinckney. The essentials of the plan were in fact adopted by a nominating caucus of congressional Federalists on May 3.[116] Whatever appeared to be straightforward in it was counter-balanced by unavowed or disavowed intentions, which required telling some men one thing and assuring others of the opposite, and it was anything but a trumpet call to the people. On the contrary, its success depended in a real sense not on uniting the people but on dividing them.

The idea in its simplest form was that Federalist electors North and South were to support Adams and Pinckney for President and Vice-President, and to support them equally. On the face of it this could simply be seen as a precaution against a scattering of wasted second votes which would benefit the opposition, with the expectation that a judicious dropping of one or more Pinckney votes would be enough to permit Adams's re-election and still ensure against an opposition Vice-President. (This was in fact the exact strategy the Republicans would adopt with regard to Jefferson and Burr.) But that was not really what the Hamiltonian plotters had in mind. Their expectations all hinged ultimately on what they hoped would happen in Pinckney's home state of South Carolina. If New England and certain of the middle states were all to cast their votes equally for Adams and Pinckney, Pinckney's popularity in South Carolina would then give him the extra votes needed to make him President, even if the South Carolina electors gave their other votes to Jefferson. Adams had to be the ostensible head of the ticket, much as the insiders might have wished otherwise, because he had more support among the rank and file in the North, and in New England especially, than any other Federalist. So the logic of equal support was not to undermine Adams in those places but rather to take advantage of Adams's strength there by keeping Pinckney's vote abreast of his so that the resulting balance might be tipped in Pinckney's favor elsewhere. "The plot of an old Spanish play," observed Fisher Ames, "is not more complicated with underplot."[117]

The New Englanders in general, and the unqualified Adams supporters in particular, were uneasy and suspicious from the start. Samuel Dexter of Massachusetts, who was present at the caucus meeting, objected that since "Mr. Adams, as he is viewed by the great majority of Federalists[,] . . . is the most popular man in the U.S. and deemed best qualified to perform the duties of President," such an arrangement would be seen as the "insidious intention . . . to displace him from the office," and that this would "crumble the federal party to atoms." Harrison Gray Otis felt the same way, and his sentiments had been known for some time.[118] Hamilton undertook a tour through New England in June, ostensibly for a final inspection of military posts but with a particular view to testing the state of political opinion there. He discovered, as he himself conceded, that though the greatest number of strong minded men in New England are not only satisfied of the expediency of supporting *Pinckney,* as giving the best chance against Jefferson, but even prefer him to *Adams;* yet in the body of that people there is a strong personal attachment to this gentleman, and most of the leaders of the second class are so anxious for his re-election that it will be difficult to convince them that there is as much danger of its failure as there unquestionably is, or to induce them faithfully to cooperate in Mr. Pinckney, notwithstanding their common and strong dread of Jefferson.

He was also said to have been told by Governor Fenner of Rhode Island, "Sir I see what you are after. you mean to bring in Gen'll pinckney. I will not engage in any Such jockeying trick."[119]

And mixed in with the distrust being spread by those who did not conceal their designs were the falsehoods resorted to by those who did. One of the "jockeys" was Robert Goodloe Harper, who had recently transferred his residence from South Carolina to Maryland and was in close touch with political affairs in both states. Harper tried to soothe Otis's suspicions by telling him that the Adams supporters had nothing to fear in either state so long as New England remained steady in equal support of Pinckney. The South Carolina Federalists, he prevaricated, were actually more solid for Adams than for Pinckney. "There is no doubt that every federal Nerve in the state, will be exerted in support of Mr. Adams and that no people in the Union would more decidedly reject any attempt to supersede him." No one "to the Southward, including South Carolina," saw Pinckney as a competitor to Adams. "They intend him, solely, as a prudent mariner does a spare yard, which he wishes to have on board, lest that on which he places his chief reliance should fail him in a storm." Meanwhile, of course, the New England insiders were insinuating assurances to the South Carolina insiders as to *their* labors on behalf of Pinckney.[120]

The least consulted, in any of this, were the interests or self-respect of the candidates themselves. By the end of the summer it had penetrated even the essentially innocent mind of Charles Cotesworth Pinckney that there were disreputable forces afoot from which he really ought to dissociate himself. He therefore gave a promise to the New England Federalists that he would accept no votes for himself that were not also pledged to Adams. This would pull out the props from the Hamilton-Sedgwick-Harper strategy for South Carolina, which counted on Pinckney's popularity extending across party lines and thus enabling him to pick up votes there even if the state went Republican—but not if Pinckney refused to accept the vote of any elector whose other vote would be cast for Jefferson.[121]

The other candidate, John Adams, had seen through the equal-support scheme the instant he heard what the Federalist caucus of May 3 had done. He thereupon gave himself over to a torrent of rage whose after-effects, by the end of the year 1800, were to leave the ruins of Federalism in even smaller fragments than they were in already. Two days after the caucus meeting, which had occurred on the same day the results from New York were made public, Adams summoned an unsuspecting James McHenry away from a dinner party, ostensibly to settle a minor item of department business. His abomination of Hamilton, which now occupied most of his waking hours, was steaming within him. The matter in question was quickly settled; then without warning came the explosion. Hamilton had worked against him in New York and had caused him to lose the election there, and McHenry had been his tool from the beginning, what with having played upon Washington to insist on Hamilton as first in rank of the major-generals in 1798, then scheming at Trenton to get the mission to France suspended, and endless other things. Hamilton, he ranted, was an intriguer, "the greatest intrigu[er] in the World—a man devoid of every moral principle—a Bastard, and as much a foreigner as Gallatin. Mr. Jefferson is an infinitely better man. . . . You are subservient to Hamilton, who ruled Washington, and would still rule if he could." When McHenry tried to defend himself, Adams let loose another tirade at the ineptness with which he claimed the Secretary had managed his department. The broken McHenry saw he had no choice but to offer his resignation, which was promptly accepted.[122] Whether Adams intended this in advance, or simply lost control of himself, or whether he did indeed intend it but needed to work himself up before he could do it, cannot of course be known. In all likelihood he had been agitating himself with the thought in one form or another for some time. Five days later he sent Pickering a brief note requesting his resignation as well. When Pickering declined to give it Adams dismissed him, effective immediately.[123]

McHenry drew up a record of his remarkable interchange with the President, and sent the latter a copy of it. He also sent one to Hamilton, who received it a day or two before starting off on his tour of New England.[124] The emotions it stirred in him must have been lively indeed, and undoubtedly tinged what Hamilton said to every Federalist he encountered there. They may also have inspired the initial thoughts of what he would eventually do some months later, issue a manifesto under his own name denouncing in every detail the character and conduct of John Adams, and thus commit the most lunatic political act of his life. Not that he lacked provocation. Even among Adams's own supporters, who outnumbered those for any other potential Federalist candidate, few who knew him were now wholly free from misgivings as to his hold on himself and on the responsibilities of his office, while those whom he had alienated believed him quite unhinged. Theodore Sedgwick, who had once sat regularly as an intimate at the Adams family table, had of course long since given him up. "Every tormenting passion rankles in the bosom of that weak and frantic old man. . . ."[125]

There were two items in Adams's unguarded talk during this period that gave deep offense to Federalists of whatever complexion. One was the declaration, repeatedly made, that there was a "British faction" entrenched in their midst.[126] It would have been as well for the Chief Executive to leave this kind of thing to the "jacobinical" Republicans, who were making such charges every day anyway. The other, equally serious for the suspicions it raised, was what he had said to McHenry about Jefferson: that he was "an infinitely better man" than Hamilton, that "if President, [he] will act wisely," and that "I . . . would rather be Vice President under him . . . than indebted to such a being as Hamilton for the

Presidency." This and similar sayings gave rise to rumors, untrue but widely believed, that Adams and Jefferson had in fact concluded a secret alliance for sharing power in the forthcoming administration.[127]

As the summer wore on, the Federalists' movements, in contrast to the élan and single-mindedness of the Republican drive, gave a deepening impression of drift, blurred purpose, divided conviction, and harried furtiveness. For one thing, it was becoming more and more evident that no plan for bringing Pinckney to the presidency had any substantial support outside Hamilton's circle of irreconcilables. Oliver Wolcott even wondered whether it might not be better to put aside all disguise of equal support, to drop Adams and promote Pinckney freely and openly. (Hamilton's own disguise was thin enough already.) But such Massachusetts Federalists as George Cabot and Fisher Ames protested that such a course could only make things worse. Ames, whose super-heated High Federalism did not preclude occasional fits of good sense, declared that unless the party's sole aim were that of keeping the enemy out, it was lost:

> That, instead of analyzing the measures of the man who has thus brought the cause into jeopardy, you must sound the tocsin about Jefferson; that the hopes and fears of the citizens are the only sources of influence; and surely we have enough to fear from Jefferson; by thus continually sounding our just alarms we remain united with the people, instead of separated from them. . . .[128]

But Alexander Hamilton was a driven man. John Adams had taken away his army, and now with his ravings about British factions and the intrigues of a bastard foreigner, the President of the United States was striking not only at his patriotism but at his total picture of himself as a leading founder of the republic. He wrote to Adams with a direct request for confirmation of whether he had in fact said what he was reported to have said about "the existence of a *British Faction*," and whether he had "plainly alluded to me" as a member of it.[129] Receiving no reply, Hamilton set to work on the subsequently famous *Letter from Alexander Hamilton, Concerning the Public Conduct and Character of John Adams, Esq., President of the United States.* Cabot and Ames knew he was preparing such a document — which Hamilton had said he intended for private circulation only — and both were uneasy, each hoping that if he did anything of the sort he would do it anonymously. Even Wolcott was "clearly of opinion that you ought to publish nothing with your signature *at present.*" What they would all have preferred was that he simply drop it altogether.[130]

But Hamilton, not to be deterred, had his letter printed in the form of a pamphlet, dated October 24, 1800, which came to fifty-four octavo pages in a limited edition of two hundred copies. Of course it would take no more than one of them, falling into Republican hands, for it to be spread all over the country in no time, which naturally was just what happened.[131] There is every likelihood that this was exactly what Hamilton wanted to happen. Why? The best clue may lie in the very structure of the *Letter* itself.

Hamilton began with what he said was his object. Since the President's closest friends were disparaging the motives of all Federalists who advocated equal support of the incumbent and General Pinckney, and since this was being accompanied by a growing list of slanders as to the particular part he, Hamilton, was taking in the effort, he felt himself obliged not only to repel such slanders but to acknowledge that there was in fact a difference between his own motives and most of the others with regard to John Adams, and he proceeded to state what it was. It was nothing less than "the conviction that he does not possess the talents adapted to the *Administration* of Government, and that there are great and intrinsic defects in his character, which unfit him for the office of Chief Magistrate." In the early stages of the Revolution, Hamilton said, he had begun with "a high veneration for Mr. ADAMS," but with time and observation he had come to

> an opinion, which all my subsequent experience has confirmed, that he is a man of an imagination sublimated and eccentric; propitious neither to the regular display of sound judgment, nor to steady perseverance in a systematic plan of conduct; and I began to perceive what has since been too manifest, that to this defect are added the unfortunate foibles of a vanity without bounds, and a jealousy capable of discoloring every object.[132]

Hamilton's case, had it stopped there, might well have represented the judgment which history itself ought to have settled upon with regard to John Adams. The subsequent judgment has turned out somewhat otherwise, for various reasons, and perhaps the remainder of Hamilton's own pamphlet should be counted as one of them.

The greatest portion of it was taken up with a critical commentary on Adams's entire public career, dotted at every point with instances of his fatuities, his inconsistencies, his blunders, and his foolishness, most of them occurring in his presidency. The central charge there was his handling of the Ellsworth mission, and it was based on the premise that the mission ought not to have gone at all. After France's repeated outrages, America's dignity required France not only to make the first overtures for a new negotiation but to send a minister to the United States to carry it out.[133] But that premise was by then hopelessly out of date, and for some time had been contrary to the drift of public opinion. And thus the rest of the list—Adams's not consulting his advisors, the irresponsible pardoning of the Fries rebels, the precipitate dismissal of Pickering, the brutal treatment of McHenry, and so on—never quite added up.[134]

The concluding section of the *Letter,* which should doubtless be read not as a series of afterthoughts but as Hamilton's true peroration, was a bitterly passionate defense of his own honor. Adams had aimed at the heart of it with his calumny of him as "a man destitute of every moral principle" and with his "British faction" bombast. If, Hamilton protested, he had been a partisan of Great Britain at the expense of his own country's interests, he could hardly have taken the part he did take in the preliminaries to the Jay mission. He had urged a "negociation, to be followed, if unsuccessful, by a declaration of war," and had called for preparations "by land and sea for the alternative." Moreover, when relations with France had reached a crisis in 1797 he had proposed a commission, with Jefferson or Madison as a member of it, and was "disposed to go greater lengths to avoid rupture with France than with Great Britain. ...." Must he not have found it shocking then, he demanded, "to have to combat a slander so vile, after having sacrificed the interests of his family to the service of th[is] country, in counsel and in the field"?[135]

If there is indeed an afterthought, it would appear to be Hamilton's closing insistence that whatever his opinion of Adams, he was still "finally resolved not to advise the withholding from him a single vote."[136] It might well be wondered what anyone who read it was to make of that.

All of Hamilton's friends, as well as Federalists everywhere, were appalled. The Letter had both revealed confidential knowledge of a fragmented administration and exposed the distracted state of the party at large for all the world to see; it had created the widespread impression that revenge for Hamilton's own injured vanity had overridden any consideration of the public interest that he professed; and it led to the sad conclusion that Hamilton's once-formidable influence in the councils of Federalism was at an end.[137] The Republicans were jubilant. To James Madison the *Letter* was a "Thunderbolt." "I rejoice with you," he exulted to Jefferson, "that Republicanism is likely to be so *completely* triumphant. ...." The *Aurora* announced:

> The pulsation given to the body politic, by *Hamilton's* precious letter, is felt from one end of the union to the other. Never was there a publication so strange in its structure, more destructive in its purposed end. It has confirmed facts that were before known, but held in doubt. It has displayed the treachery, not only of the *writer,* but of his *adherents* in the public counsels; and while it has thrown much false glare on the character of Mr. Adams, it has given some new and faithful traits also; but it has thrown a blaze of light on the real character and designs of the writer and his partizans.[138]

The episode revealed in addition to everything else a good many things about the individual character of both John Adams and Alexander Hamilton, most of it less than attractive. The two hated each other to a degree exceeded by no comparable enmity in the early life of the republic. But between the lines, as it were, are glimpsed certain affinities which may be taken as a kind of augury for Federalism itself in the hour of its eclipse. The main one was a towering defiance to anything that might be called a morality of partisanship.

Here were two men who at their best had lived by the loftiest of civic humanist ideals, the pursuit of the public good as they had perceived and understood it. Now, at their worst, they were perverting the very force—virtue, the "positive passion for the public good," as Adams himself had once phrased it—that was seen to inspire that same pursuit. And in so doing they had exposed the concept of virtue itself for what it was, the most fragile element, the greatest single liability, of the entire civic humanist tradition. They had allowed the public good to become so intertwined with their own sulks, spites, and rages as to blind them to what might have been an intermediary loyalty, a loyalty to the joint venture they had seen into being in 1789. Since that time each had persuaded himself that his own virtue transcended any requirements of a body of like-minded men who, for better or worse, had accomplished extraordinary things and might as a body conceivably accomplish still more. Here was John Adams, holding up to contempt any claim that mere party might have on him, and giving it out that any Federalist who had not seen the public good as he did was the servant of a "British faction." And here was Alexander Hamilton, hardly less blind to party claims than Adams, imagining that through the manipulation of two or three electoral votes his version of the public good might somehow be imposed on the entire political nation.

Moreover, there was something self-destructive about both of them, as seen in the attitude each had come to take with regard to Jefferson. Hamilton had told Sedgwick, "I will never more be responsible for [Adams] by my direct support — even though the consequence should be the election of *Jefferson*. If we must have an enemy at the head of the Government, let it be one whom we can oppose & for whom we are not responsible. . . ."[139] In preference to Adams, Hamilton would take even Jefferson; Adams too would take Jefferson, in preference to anyone but himself. Hamilton had now thrown away what pretensions he may once have had as a party influential; Adams had never felt obliged to have such pretensions at all. A Federalist newspaper in Baltimore retrospectively made much the same point nine years later: "Mr. Adams *never was* a favorite with the leading men of the federal party . . . for they were sensible that he had neither abilities nor discretion to *lead a party*, much less to govern a nation. . . ."[140]

The Republican party was by 1800 united in a version of the public good very different from that which had animated Federalism since 1789. And although they too were still dependent on the vocabulary of civic humanism for the words, at least, of most of what they thought and said, somehow for them the concept of "virtue" had slipped a notch or two from the primacy it had once held in the value-system of the founding generation. Their commitment, a collective determination to become the official custodians of the public good as *they* conceived it, had an integrity of its own that went a step beyond the conflicting claims of individual virtue. They would not yet do the things to each other that the Federalists were doing to themselves in 1800.

The support given to the Republicans' nominees must be as unambiguous and straightforward as the still-cumbersome electoral system allowed them to make it. They too had their congressional caucus meeting, held on May 11, 1800, at which they unanimously agreed that Aaron Burr, whose work in the New York election had been critical, should be their choice for Vice-President. Burr had been a candidate for that office in 1796, but only the leading one among several, and he still resented having got next to no support from the electors of Virginia. Jefferson himself was determined that this should not happen again, and went out of his way to see that the Virginians stayed in line. And now the "jacobins," as the Boston Federalist Theophilus Parsons sarcastically observed, "appear to be completely organized throughout the United States. The principals have their agents dispersed in every direction; and the whole body act with a union to be *expected* only from men, in whom no moral principles exist to create a difference of conduct resulting from a difference in sentiment."[141]

Their discipline and *esprit de corps* did, at any rate, hold. When the returns were finally in, they showed Jefferson and Burr tied with 73 votes each, Adams with 65, and Pinckney with 64.

These results became known only with maddening gradualness, drawn out over a period of more than seven months beginning in early May, when New York's choice became clear, to well into December; as late as the 20th of that month there was still no news in Philadelphia from Georgia, Kentucky, or Tennessee.[142] This and the ambiguity of the figures themselves were owing, for one thing, to the anomalous provision in the Constitution (shortly to be amended in 1804) for presidential elections; for another, to the variations of practice embodied in the electoral laws of the several states; and for still another, to the fact that the states held their elections at widely differing times. Moreover, the final count, for all its apparent closeness, concealed a fact of the most vital historic significance: the political nation had spoken resoundingly for Jefferson, and Adams was actually not entitled to the vote he did get.

Thanks primarily to the Constitution itself, and secondarily to state election laws, the popular voice with regard to the choosing of a President could not yet be clearly sounded in the year 1800. In ten of the sixteen states electors were chosen by a majority vote of the legislature; in three, by district elections; in two, by statewide election on a general ticket; and in one, by a curious combination of district and legislative choice. And the laws could be changed at any time as expediency might call for it, and in several cases they were. District elections could produce a split electoral vote, as they did in 1800 in the case of both Maryland and North Carolina. Either this method or that of legislative choice could result in a real perversion of the popular preference. It certainly did so in both Pennsylvania and New Jersey. Pennsylvania's lower house fell under Republican control in 1799 while the senate retained a narrow Federalist majority, and the two houses came to an impasse over the method to be followed in choosing electors for 1800, broken only by an eleventh-hour compromise whereby the Republican house appointed eight electors and the Federalist senate seven. All fifteen of those votes should have gone to Jefferson. The New Jersey legislature, with a Federalist majority, also chose the state's electors. But all three of New Jersey's most populous counties were overwhelmingly Republican, and a statewide election would have given Jefferson the seven electoral votes that went to Adams instead. In any case the clearest indicator of the popular will in the country at large was the congressional elections of 1800. They brought for the first time a sizable Republican majority of 65–41 in the House of Representatives, more than reversing the Federalist majority of 63–43 in the previous Congress.[143]

South Carolina turned out to be the pivotal state in 1800, just as the Hamiltonians guessed that it might. But it was pivotal in an opposite way from what they had hoped. South Carolina, as Charles Cotesworth Pinckney's biographer has aptly put it, "was in a twilight era of mixed political systems."[144] The Federalist preponderance there had been slipping away, and the recently elected legislature now had a Republican majority. Yet this greatly oversimplifies a political situation in which party divisions had always been vague and had only in the past two or three years taken on much of a discernible outline. These in turn were overlaid by factors—family, wealth, geography, and personal connections—which made for other kinds of divisions and an elusive fluidity of political behavior.[145]

Such was the setting in which the new legislature met at Columbia in November 1800 to choose the state's presidential electors. On one side was a still-formidable Federalist presence, though there were nine absences—all from the rich Low Country, where Federalist strength had been greatest, one of various indications that the grandees of that region were already beginning to ease themselves out of politics and retreating to other areas of civic life.[146] And on the other side was the new Republican majority, though nobody yet knew the exact size of it or could tell how its members would act on the choices that lay before them. This was because in between lay the very broad shadow of Charles Cotesworth Pinckney, probably the most popular man in South Carolina, who commanded loyalties, influence, and affections that transcended a wide range of party considerations on either side. In that setting, the choice of electors could very well go in any of several ways. One of them would have made Pinckney President; another, Vice-President under Adams; another, Vice-President under Jefferson. Still another would leave him nothing at all.[147]

But the other strategic figure in this extraordinary picture was a man who had come to Columbia with the sole purpose of preventing every one of these outcomes except the last, and determined to use every resource of persuasion and intrigue in order to bring that one about in order to elevate Thomas Jefferson to the presidency. This was Charles Pinckney, a second cousin of Charles Cotesworth Pinckney, who had some years before turned the course of his ambitions into opposition politics after having been passed over by President Washington for the ministerial appointment to London which went instead to his cousin Thomas Pinckney, Charles Cotesworth's brother. He had alienated a sizable portion of that extended family by becoming a prime mover within the growing Republican interest in South Carolina, and was now familiarly known on the Federalist side as "Blackguard Charley."[148] He had obtained one of the state's two seats in the United States Senate in 1798, and would have been on hand for the opening of the winter session at Washington on November 17 but for the supreme urgency, for him, of what needed to be done in Columbia. Charles Pinckney thereupon became, as it were, the Aaron Burr of South Carolina.

As for all the arts he used and how they were applied, this is still a subject of conjecture. But we do know in more than a general way the results they achieved. The number of Federalist legislators was almost equal to the number of those committed to Jefferson and Burr, though neither side had quite enough for the majority required to carry their ticket. In between were some dozen to sixteen waverers, more or less Republican but whose party attachments were qualified by an equal or greater attachment to Charles Cotesworth Pinckney. The internal struggle that surged back and forth during the ten days prior to the final balloting on December 2 was one in which a variety of cross-pressures were brought to bear upon this knot of irresolutes. The Federalists tried to detach some of them for their ticket, while temporary groupings of Jefferson men, working at odds with Charles Pinckney's aim for a straight Republican ticket, made at least two efforts for a compromise that would result in a divided slate of Jefferson-Pinckney electors, one version of which would have given Pinckney the vice-presidency, and the other the presidency.

In the end Charles Pinckney's labors—a mixture of appeals for Republican unity and inducements of influence in a Jefferson administration—prevailed, and the eight electors chosen on the final day were all committed to Jefferson and Burr. Charles Pinckney would subsequently be assiduous in the claims he made to Jefferson as to his own primary role in effecting the outcome, and Jefferson would be gracious in accepting his recommendations for federal offices in South Carolina. Charles Pinckney for his part would be rewarded with appointment as the new United States minister to Spain.

And yet it may well be that in the deciding of things at Columbia in those closing days of November 1800, the really critical figure was after all Charles Cotesworth Pinckney himself, and not his renegade cousin. He too had been present, sitting as a state senator from the Charleston district. Temptations, it appears, had twice been dangled before him, and both times he had repelled them. Having already made his promise to the New Englanders, he did not intend to break it now. He would have nothing to do with a ticket that linked his name with Jefferson's, nor would he accept any votes for himself that were not pledged equally to Adams. He certainly knew that the vice-presidency would make him an anomaly in a Republican administration, and that the presidency, should it rest on no wider ground than the favor of a small Federalist faction, would bring him little honor. It was by this conviction, and this promise, that he himself had made possible the final triumph of "Blackguard Charley."

7

Burr and the Revolution of 1800

No public man of less than the first rank in the Republic's founding generation continues to be written about more amply or more often—or with a greater conviction on the part of each author that the job needed to be done all over again—than Aaron Burr. In one sense this would seem superfluous: the record of Burr's comings and goings is actually fairly complete, certainly as much so as that of any representative man of the time. We seem nevertheless not content to leave it at that. Few who have undertaken Burr's case have failed to make the point in some form that his story remains an "enigma."[149]

There are certainly reasons for this. Much of what we are still curious to know about Burr's after-dark thoughts, movements, and purposes has eluded the record, voluminous though the record may otherwise be. But more pertinently, Aaron Burr was *not* a representative man of his time. He was clearly a deviant type;

whether he represented anything or anyone beyond himself is at best debatable. At the same time Burr's undoubted charm, his considerable talents, and the picaresque quality of his life—combined with the all but universal odium that hung over him throughout the latter half of his days—have rightly made him a perennial object of interest. Yet what keeps eluding us is a standard of justice, if indeed there is one, to be applied to this unusual man who so narrowly missed becoming our third President.

Aaron Burr was born in 1756 into what might have been a nurturing academic milieu. Both his father, Aaron Burr, Sr., and his grandfather, the great Jonathan Edwards, had briefly held the presidency of the newly established college at Princeton. But he never knew either of them, both having died within months of each other while he was still an infant. His mother died during that same year, leaving him and his sister orphans at the ages of two and four. Aaron and Sarah Burr were thereupon handed about to various family members, and though they appear to have been well enough looked after, they led a somewhat nomadic existence in New Jersey, Pennsylvania, and Massachusetts. Aaron himself was eventually sent to Princeton, and graduated with distinction at sixteen. His commencement oration was on "Building Castles in the Air." He then considered theology, though not for very long; his study of that subject ceased after a few months. At the outbreak of the Revolution he was reading law at Litchfield, Connecticut, with Tapping Reeve, who had recently married Burr's sister Sarah.

Burr served with merit as an officer in the Continental line and later built a thriving law practice in New York City. His career as a womanizer, somewhat abnormal for those times, began early. He also loved luxury, abhorred boredom, and was never good at managing money. Much of his ingenuity, to the end of his life, was expended in eluding creditors.

He had both a taste and a talent for politics. He was elected to the New York Assembly in 1784, appointed Attorney-General of New York in 1789, and in 1791 chosen by the Assembly as a United States senator. This was an intricate maneuver in which rival factions were persuaded to combine in unseating Philip Schuyler, the father-in-law of Alexander Hamilton. Hamilton's untrusting eye thereafter followed Aaron Burr down to the day not of Burr's death but of his own. Burr's fortunes, meanwhile, together with his ambitions and energies, became mingled with those of the Republican interest in both state and national affairs.

The election of 1800 may well be thought of as the true turning point in both his career and his reputation, though perhaps only retrospectively so in view of the more dramatic transitions that occurred later on. For his work in the New York City elections he was rewarded, as we have seen, with the Republican party's designation of him as its choice for the vice-presidency, and an unforeseen unity of party discipline, and insufficient attention to the dropping of one or two Burr votes,[150] had resulted in the tie vote in the Electoral College between himself and Jefferson. The tie, as will be noted in more detail below, would finally be broken in Jefferson's favor.

But meanwhile we may skip ahead somewhat. To Hamilton's distrust would shortly be added Jefferson's as well, and Burr would not again be the Republican vice-presidential candidate when the time came for Jefferson's successful run for re-election in 1804. Thus frozen out of Administration councils and with no future there, Burr let himself be supported for the governorship of New York by Federalists who were contemplating a scheme of disunion, though he gave no promises that he would abet such designs; very probably he would not have. But he was defeated, and it was Hamilton's frantic warnings against Burr during that campaign that brought on Burr's challenge and Hamilton's death on the dueling ground in 1804.

When his vice-presidential term ended in 1805, Burr set out for the West, full of plans that were both grand and dim. The "Burr Conspiracy" took on a variety of forms, depending on whom he approached for money and support. The main outline of it appears to have been a projected armed expedition into Spanish Mexico to carve out a vast domain, to be ruled over by himself. A minor variation, probably never very seriously intended, was rumored to involve detaching a portion of the American Southwest to add to it. He was betrayed by a co-conspirator, delivered into federal custody, tried for treason before John Marshall in the circuit court at Richmond, and acquitted for want of evidence. President Jefferson, though once indebted in some degree to Burr for the office he held, had been exceptionally anxious to secure Burr's conviction.

After four years in Europe, where he vainly tried to stir up interest in Latin American filibustering schemes, Burr returned to America in 1812 and resumed his old practice of law in New York City, shunned by most of his former friends. His last great exploit, at the age of seventy-seven, was marrying the rich widow Eliza Jumel, who promptly brought suit for divorce when he began running through her property. The decree was awarded on the day of Burr's death in his eighty-first year, 1836.

The predominant impulse of all who have written about Burr has been to insist that he was really not that bad. And indeed there is no denying that when today we view the whole span of Burr's story in a mood of detachment, the badness in it takes on a certain mistiness of outline. The story does not repel us; rather it tantalizes, and sets us to musing. Burr's private life was far more interesting than that of any other man of his time of whom much is known, most of them having lived theirs out in settings devoid of decor or scenery. His fascination with women included their minds, another thing that set him off from most of his contemporaries. His devotion to his daughter Theodosia and to his young grandson, both of whom met tragic deaths, appears as a shaft of light from a troubled spirit.

True, he cadged thousands of dollars from others, which they never saw again, but he was a soft touch himself. He was a man of genuine culture, and he read everything. Everything he said and wrote—even when lying, which he did often and with great finesse—showed a lively and piquant intelligence. He may have been crafty and designing, but not diabolically so. His judgment of people and circumstances was really not very good, and his schemes for riches and power kept blowing up in his face. He was not vindictive and held few grudges. Even the duel with Hamilton may have been less a matter of revenge than of desperation, of turning upon a grim pursuer.[151] As for Jefferson's urge to get Burr, his thirst for the man's very life on the flimsiest of grounds: we are naturally disposed to take Burr's side there. But why should the man have been so pursued?

"Burr's 'sins,'" writes his most recent biographer, "existed for the most part in the eyes of the beholders."[152] But that may be the whole point, unintended though it probably is. We are now a long way off from those beholders, and have in some measure lost touch with them. What exactly did they see, and, more important, what did they make of what they could *not* see? Aaron Burr lived at a unique time in the Republic's life, and it is not the easiest thing to say why he did not fit into it, or why it chose in the end to set him at a distance. Burr's private life is almost certainly not the key to this question. To be sure, a combined appetite for money, women, and power, at any time, whether exercised in malevolence (of which Burr actually had little) or careless narcissism, carries a heavy potential for damage to others. Of that, Burr in his blithe progress left plenty. But when all was said and done it was the "power" side of that equation, rather than his private morals, that most struck the sensibilities of the age. The private side merely made it look more of a piece.

One is brought back once more to the two great contending abstractions in the world-view of an inordinately political-minded age. These were, of course, "liberty" and "power," power in any form being perceived as the crouching menace to liberty, whose vigilance must be its only protector. A trustworthy man was not even supposed to desire power, but when he was seen to reach for it, other men needed at the very least some idea of what he thought about its acceptable uses and limits. Aaron Burr was the only man of prominence in his time who disdained to provide, through either word or example, any such information or even misinformation. Burr's "political correspondence is large," observes his biographer, "but one combs it in vain for so much as a single sentence that can be cited as pointing to a political philosophy." Burr, it seems, preferred a more private code, that of Lord Chesterfield, and he admitted as much. "A gentleman is free to do whatever he pleases so long as he does it with style" — and "so long as no ill-will was intended."[153]

The matter might be put in a somewhat variant way, in the light of that other great abstraction of the eighteenth century's value-system, "virtue." It bore little resemblance, as we have seen, to the meaning attached to that term today. This "passion for the public good," an idea that went as far back as the Roman Republic, was in some sense a fiction, as enveloping abstractions always must be. But it occupied a disproportionate place in the consciousness of a generation of nation-builders, and the people of that age looked for some approximation of it in the figures they chose to regard as exemplary. It was questions of this sort, involving in some way the uses of power and the clothing of virtue, that they were asking of Aaron Burr in the closing days of 1800.

The tie with Jefferson would throw the election into the House of Representatives, each state casting one vote, to be decided by a majority of that state's delegation for one or the other candidate, and the balloting would begin on February 11,

1801. The Federalists now prepared to play their most desperate game yet. (This was still the Federalist-dominated Sixth Congress; the Republican Seventh would not meet for nearly another year.) They had got it into their heads that there was still a way of snatching the Republicans' victory away from them if they could organize enough support to break the tie in Burr's favor rather than Jefferson's. The logic was that Burr, whose Republican principles might be regarded as adjustable, and who would be aware that whatever weight his presidency might have was dependent on the Federalist movement that gave it to him, would therefore see little choice but to put himself in their hands when he took office. Only eight of the sixteen states had delegations with Republican majorities. Jefferson could thus be denied the nine he needed in either of two ways. If the Federalists could bring in the other eight for Burr, and detach a vote or two from Jefferson to Burr so as to reverse the balance in one of the others, Burr would be in. Or, failing a majority for Burr, they might still prevent one for Jefferson if the doubtful states remained deadlocked, which might in turn open the way to deciding the presidency by some other means.[154]

The one prominent Federalist who viewed this scheme with profound horror when he heard of it was Alexander Hamilton, who had of course known Burr for many years. "For heaven's sake," he implored Theodore Sedgwick, "let not the Foederal party be responsible for the elevation of this Man."[155] Letters from Hamilton thereupon went out in all directions. Burr, he told Gouverneur Morris, "in my judgment has no principle public or private—could be bound by no agreement—will listen to no monitor but his ambition. . . ." To Otis: "Burr loves nothing but himself; thinks of nothing but his own aggrandizement, and will be content with nothing, short of permanent power in his own hands."[156] Better, he urged, to seek some assurances from Jefferson: that he would preserve the established system of finance and public credit, maintain the navy, hold to a strict neutrality toward the belligerent powers, and keep in office "all our Foederal friends except in the Great Departments. There and in other matters he ought to be free."[157] Whereas should any such promises be extracted from Burr, "he will laugh in his sleeve when he makes them and he will break them the first moment it may serve his purpose." And finally: "As to his theory, no mortal can tell what it is."[158]

Nor did any mortal have a very clear sense of Burr's thoughts and intentions during the eight-week period between mid-December 1800 and mid-February 1801. The letter he wrote to Congressman Samuel Smith of Maryland on December 16 implies one thing; after that, both his letters and his silences suggest others. He had not at first believed there would be a tie after all, because he had heard there would be an extra Jefferson vote from Vermont, and he said renunciatory things to Smith in that belief. If a tie should happen he would "utterly disclaim all ambition," and he appointed Smith as his proxy "to declare these sentiments if the occasion shall require." A few days later he was assuring Jefferson himself of his "unremitted Zeal" in support of his forthcoming administration and hinting that he would be happy to resign the vice-presidency if he could "be more useful in any Active station."[159]

Other stirrings, however, appear to have been aroused in him by the end of

December. By that time the tie had been confirmed, and Jefferson had not got that vote from Vermont after all. Burr had meanwhile been getting letters asking what his intentions were, and he seemed to find them rather irritating. If chosen President, would he engage to resign? To this, he now informed Samuel Smith, he had made no answer; moreover, "if I had made any I should have told that at present advised, I should not." To Smith this was disturbing, as well it might be; he had already given Burr's previous high-minded declaration to the press, a gesture, it was now being rumored, at which Burr had "expressed his displeasure." Rumors of the sort reached Jefferson himself, who professed to take no stock in them.[160]

At the same time, Burr received a piece of advice from Robert Goodloe Harper, one of those most prepared to do anything to keep Jefferson out. It was being "whispered," Harper said, that Republican overtures were being made to persuade Burr to yield in favor of Jefferson. However, he counseled, "I advise you to take no step whatever by which the choice of the house of Representatives can be impeded or embarrassed. Keep the game perfectly in your hand; but do not answer this letter, or any other that may be written to you by a federalist; nor write to any of that party."[161] Whether or not Burr needed such advice, no further word of his intentions would escape him until the balloting was all but over. He had resolved, for whatever reason, not to do what the virtuous Charles Cotesworth Pinckney had done in South Carolina.

Theodore Sedgwick's case for electing Burr shows something of the pass to which the mentality of Federalism had now come. There was "no disagreement," Sedgwick insisted to Hamilton, "as to his character."

> He is ambitious—selfish—profligate. His ambition is of the worst kind—it is a mere love of power. . . . This is agreed, but then it is known that his manners are plausible, that he is dextrous in the acquisition & use of the means necessary to effect his wishes. . . . He holds to no pernicious theories. . . . His very selfishness prevents his entertaining any mischievous predilections for foreign nations. The situation in which he lives has enabled him to justly appreciate the benefits result-ing from our commercial & other national systems; and this same selfishness will afford some security that he will not only patronize their support but their invig-oration. . . . Burr must depend on good men for his support & that support he cannot receive but by a conformity to their views.[162]

Hamilton's supreme effort on behalf of Jefferson was made on January 16 to the Federalist Congressman James A. Bayard of Delaware. For himself, Hamilton said, it was too late to become Jefferson's apologist. "Nor can I have any dispo-sition to do it."

> I admit that his politics are tinctured with fanaticism, that he is too much in earnest in his democracy, that he has been a mischevous enemy to the principle measures of our past administration, that he is crafty & persevering in his objects, that he is not scrupulous about the means of success, not very mindful of truth, and that he is a contemptible hypocrite.

"But" (pausing for breath),

> it is not true as is alleged that he is an enemy to the power of the Executive. . . .
> I have more than once made the reflection that viewing himself as the reversioner,
> he was solicitous to come into a Good Estate. Nor is it true that Jefferson is zealot
> enough to do anything in pursuance of his principles which will contravene his
> popularity, or his interest. He is as likely as any man I know to temporize—to
> calculate what will be likely to promote his own reputation and advantage; and
> the probable result of such a temper is the preservation of systems, though orig-
> inally opposed, which . . . could not be overturned without danger to the person
> who did it. . . . Add to this that there is no fair reason to suppose him capable of
> being corrupted, which is a security that he will not go beyond certain limits.[163]

Bayard never did say what he thought of Hamilton's letter, nor does the letter
seem to have been a direct influence on the part Bayard took when he arrived in
Washington for the balloting. Bayard had fallen in with the Federalist determination to elect Burr, and was uniquely situated to have a controlling voice in the
outcome. This was because he, as Delaware's sole representative, could at any
point decide which way the whole vote of one state would go.[164]

Thirty-six ballots were required through six days of continuous voting. The
scene was heavy with portent, or so it would appear: ponderous forces teetering
in a fragile balance, all too liable to be tilted either way. The first ballot produced
a deadlock which left Jefferson one state short of the nine he needed, and which
would not be broken until the final day. Eight were for Jefferson, six for Burr,
and two were tied. It would have taken but one man's crossover in each of three
states' delegations to make Burr President.[165]

But this, seen in retrospect, made for something of an illusion. For all the
suspense and exhaustion of those six days it can almost certainly be concluded
that from the first ballot on, Burr never actually had a chance. At least one
Republican state would have had to be turned around (New York or New Jersey
were the only ones in which there was any likelihood of doing it), as would both
of the two that were tied (Maryland and Vermont), so that what the deadlock
really meant was that the Federalists, heave as they might, simply could not bring
it off. They could do nothing more without some move from Burr. But Burr was
of course immobilized. Meanwhile inauguration day drew closer.[166]

Circumstances had made James Bayard the key figure, because Bayard controlled not only his own state's vote but in effect those of two others as well. He
and the Federalist delegates of the tied states—Maryland and Vermont—had
agreed that however they acted they would do so in concert, and the agreement
held through thirty-five ballots. But each ballot had made Bayard's nerves another
degree less steady, and they frayed out altogether on February 14. ("I was chiefly
influenced," he later admitted, "by the current of public sentiment, which I
thought it neither safe nor politic to counteract.") On that evening he announced
at a hastily called caucus that he would cast Delaware's vote for Jefferson on the
following Monday. He was persuaded to delay a day because of expected letters
from Burr. The letters came, though they have not survived. Burr resigned his

pretensions, and the two tied states went over to Jefferson, giving him one more than he needed. The Federalist holdouts in those states simply refrained from voting, which now gave them Republican majorities, and Bayard cast a blank ballot for Delaware.[167]

So although they had in effect given in, not one Federalist in the House was obliged in the end to do the graceful thing, and change his vote to Jefferson. As for Aaron Burr, one of two things had happened. It could be that the voice of virtue had belatedly roused him to his duty. Or, he had at last perceived that the game was up.

8
"We are all Republicans . . ."

The first major transfer of power in the life of the Federal Republic, momentous enough to many minds for it to be thought of as a "revolution," was effected peaceably and under the law. The event continues to be marveled at and perennially celebrated. The tone, however, is taken not from the defeated but from the victorious, and in particular from the benign accents of Jefferson's First Inaugural. The other side of the picture is neither benign nor very attractive. The Federalists, from whose hands the power was taken, did not, to be sure, resist the transfer by any resort to force. They nevertheless played a miserable part, and this may justify a final effort to fathom the state of mind that had brought them to it.

It is true that the Federalists could not conceive the accession of Thomas Jefferson without sensations of horror. Jefferson might well pull down everything they had built. He might do away with the Bank, dismantle the navy, perhaps even in some way destroy the entire system of public credit. He might commit the American government to the cause of France in Europe, expose the country to a ruinous war with Great Britain, and end by returning its affairs to the anarchy in which they had floundered in the worst days of the Confederation.[168]

But although the specter of Jefferson may have been the most formidable single item in the Federalists' line of sight as they looked out over the world at the dawn of the nineteenth century, and may have served as their readiest notation for all the ills they perceived there, it cannot account for quite everything. What Jefferson and his followers had already done to that world, and might further do, was fearsome enough. But that was only one side of the Federalists' affliction. What had demoralized and undone them was the cloud that had settled over *them*—the doubts which that world had cast on the place they themselves held in it, or ought to hold, or indeed ever had held. It was a crisis of soul and spirit of a sort that would never again be undergone by any such group in the subsequent course of the nation's life, over no less a question than that of where exactly they did fit, in space or in time, or in the memory of those that came after them.

The Federalists by and large, as we have seen, were men who had ascribed to themselves the status of a social and civic elite, and their political enemies had made much of their "aristocratic" pretensions. Nor is it very difficult to see the connection between this and their dread that Jefferson, as one of them put it, "would begin by democratizing the people & end with throwing every thing into their hands."[169] Yet there are elites and elites, and this one was of a special sort. For one thing, the term "aristocrat" comes under some strain when applied to the Federalists of the 1790s, those in the North at least, insofar as it might denote family connections and the deference accorded to standing acquired over time. A striking number of these men were self-made: one thinks of such as Theodore Sedgwick, Robert Morris, William Cooper, even George Cabot, not to mention Alexander Hamilton and a good many others—"aristocrats," that is, fashioned by no hand but their own.[170] And for another, elites that are not quite secure, in either their own eyes or those of the community at large, do not behave in the same way as those that are. An intriguing sidelight of public life after the Revolution is seen in the numbers of men, later counted as Federalists, who as legal counsel or in other ways came to the aid and support of persons known to have been Loyalists in wartime. This could not have been altogether owing to inherent promptings of fair play, or even to commercial interests which might inspire anglophile leanings. Large numbers of Loyalists in New York, Pennsylvania, and New England had been men of prominence and standing in their prewar communities who subsequently found themselves stripped of their property, roughly handled, and in many cases driven out altogether, either by popular hostility or by what amounted to outright mob action. Any man with elite aspirations of his own, however different his political principles may have been, could hardly have observed such action without a shudder. An orderly state, in whose affairs he might picture himself taking part, was not likely to prosper with such forces afoot in it. Indeed the time might even come, and altered circumstances be such, that he could see himself served in the same way. Such disorderly scenes, and the emotions they aroused, appear to have occurred with some regularity throughout the middle and northern states. But they did not occur very often in places like Virginia and South Carolina. There, the ruling elites, overwhelmingly Whig, were entrenched and secure, while the Tory class was both very small and socially marginal.[171]

But there was still something else, the most important of all, that set the Federalists apart in their own estimation as a chosen few, and such would have been the case quite aside from any claims based on worldly success or social preeminence. This was their picture of themselves as first comers, that select circle who had been present at a unique historical moment, those statesmen who had taken a hand in bringing forth and setting in motion a miraculous prodigy, a new government, a New Republic.

According to Douglass Adair, the reward craved above all else by these men of the founding generation, these first makers of law and government, was something that went beyond riches and beyond popularity. It was fame: the kind of honor and glory that is reached by a road other than passing acclaim and popular fancy, and is made finally secure in something akin to immortality. The standards were there, in a kind of hierarchy, for those who could recognize and meet them. They had been set in antiquity by the heroes of Plutarch—Lycurgus and Solon, Romulus and Theseus—and reaffirmed in the pages of Montesquieu, Bacon, Rousseau, and Hume.[172] "Of all men, that distinguish themselves by memorable atchievements," Hume had written,"the first place of honour seems due to LEGISLATORS and founders of states, who transmit a system of laws and institutions to secure the peace, happiness, and liberty of future generations."[173]

And to this standard of fame, Hume added another of ill fame, one that could not have failed to strike the Federalists of 1800 with a special force: the example of other men whose factious movements could undo the Legislator's noblest work.

> As much as legislators and founders of states ought to be honoured and respected among men, as much ought the founders of sects and factions to be detested. . . . Factions subvert government, render laws impotent, and beget the fiercest animosities among men of the same nation. . . . And what should render the founders of parties more odious is, the difficulty of extirpating these weeds, when once they have taken root in any state.[174]

Fame: well and good. Yet there was one element in the legendary examples of Lycurgus and Solon to which the Federalists of 1800 were deaf and blind, as has been many a first comer in other states from antiquity to the present. It was the maxim that he who gave the law should not remain to administer it. For "he who has command over the laws," as Rousseau put it, "ought not any more to have it over men; or else his laws would be ministers of his passions and . . . his private aims would inevitably mar the sanctity of his work." Lycurgus, when he gave laws to his country, "began by resigning the throne." That example, Rousseau might have added, is one that all too few have followed.[175]

The first comers and insiders in any new or revolutionary state do not let go easily, because their association with the building of it has given them to imagine, perhaps rightly, that it is all theirs: they own it. And so it was with the Federalists of 1800. Worse, they had now corrupted that very principle—the sovereignty of the people—that had enabled them a dozen years before to ride down the opposition to their new Constitution.[176] These men had themselves thus imparted to the sovereignty of the people—previously a hackneyed platitude—a vitality and a meaning it had hitherto never possessed.[177]

What the Federalists of 1800 could not now face, or even admit, was that the sovereign people had spoken for Jefferson, and not for them.

Jefferson's inaugural address, pronounced on the fourth of March, 1801, was full of conciliation. The new Chief Magistrate began with becoming modesty, professing his awareness "that the task is above my talents," and that he approached it "with those anxious and awful presentiments which the greatness of the charge and the weakness of my powers so justly inspire." There was no talk of doing away with banks or navies, and he made rather a point of the "honest payment of our debts and sacred preservation of the public faith." Moreover, he intended peace with all nations and "entangling alliances with none," and at home, "the preservation of the general government in its whole constitutional vigor."[178]

But the most extended single passage, coming before any of this, concerned the open expression of political opinion, the topic which may well have stood above all the others in Jefferson's thoughts. This part too was conciliatory and reassuring, though how reassuring might depend somewhat on the way it was read, for it was not without its ambiguities. The recent "contest of opinion," he said, had had an "animation" that might have been perplexing to "strangers unused to think freely and speak and write what they think." But although the issue had been "decided by the voice of the nation . . . according to the rules of the constitution," and although the majority will "is in all cases to prevail, [yet] that will, to be rightful, must be reasonable." That is, the minority too have their equal rights, to be protected by equal laws, and to violate them "would be oppression." Little is gained if after banishing religious intolerance we should countenance a political intolerance equally "despotic" and "wicked." And on the really important things, we mostly think alike anyway: "every difference of opinion is not a difference of principle. We have called by different names brethren of the same principle." Then, in eight words, comes what is probably the most famous single sentence Jefferson ever uttered. "We are all republicans—we are all federalists."

One way of reading these mollifying words would be to conclude that Jefferson was here coming as close as he could, short of saying it outright, to pronouncing an official benediction on party politics. He, after all, had just led an opposition party to victory over an incumbent one, and the legitimacy of it had been "decided by the voice of the nation" in full accordance with "the rules of the constitution." He had, moreover, been forthright in his assertion that political intolerance had no place in this free republic, where men must be at liberty "to speak and write what they think."

But these were individuals, who in that character could do no harm to the community's health—as individuals. If they wanted to "dissolve this Union" or "change its republican form," they might "stand undisturbed as monuments to the safety with which error of opinion may be tolerated where reason is left free to combat it." This, to be sure, was saying something important and saying it officially, which in view of what some free speakers had recently undergone was saying a very great deal. Nevertheless he did not say it of parties, nor did he intend to; nor, it seems, did he even think it.[179] There was still something about parties that fell short of true legitimacy; in particular, he could not imagine "the voice of the nation" calling the Federalists back.

Jefferson in his private character was more specific as to what he did mean. His idea had always been "that the mass of our countrymen, even of those who call themselves Federalists, are republicans."[180] All would be set right if these persons could simply be made to see where they had gone wrong, and be induced to cross over. "If we can hit on the true line . . . which may conciliate the honest part of those who were called Federalists," he wrote to Horatio Gates, ". . . I shall hope to ... obliterate, or rather [perhaps he should not have said "obliterate"] to unite the names of federalists & republicans."[181] The bane of party might then be banished altogether! "The greatest good we can do our country is to heal it's party divisions & make them one people."[182]

But if this should actually happen, would not new parties eventually arise? Probably so, Jefferson conceded. Yet it would have to be "under another name," because "that of federalism is to become so scouted that no party can rise under it."[183] He himself would see to that. "I shall ... by the establishment of republican principles ... sink federalism into an abyss from which there shall be no resurrection for it."[184]

ABBREVIATIONS

AC	*Annals of Congress*
AECPE-U	Archives Etrangères, Correspondance Politique, Etats-Unis
AHA:AR	*American Historical Association Annual Report*
AHR	*American Historical Review*
AP:AFC	Lyman H. Butterfield, ed., *The Adams Papers: Adams Family Correspondence* (Cambridge, Mass., 1963–).
AP:DAJA	Lyman H. Butterfield, ed., *The Adams Papers: Diaries and Autobiography of John Adams* (Cambridge, Mass., 1961), 4v.
APM	Adams Papers Microfilm
AQ	*American Quarterly*
ASP:CN	*American State Papers: Commerce and Navigation*
ASP:F	*American State Papers: Finance*
ASP:FR	*American State Papers: Foreign Relations*
ASP:IA	*American State Papers: Indian Affairs*
ASP:MA	*American State Papers: Military Affairs*
ASP:Misc	*American State Papers: Miscellaneous*
ASP:NA	*American State Papers: Naval Affairs*
CFM	Frederick J. Turner, ed., "Correspondence of the French Ministers to the United States, 1791–1797," *Annual Report of the American Historical Association for the Year 1903,* Vol. II (Washington, 1904).
CPJJ	Henry P. Johnston, ed., *The Correspondence and Public Papers of John Jay* (New York, 1890–93), 4v.
CUL	Columbia University Library
DAB	Allen Johnson et al., eds., *Dictionary of American Biography* (New York, 1928–36), 20v.
DGW	Donald Jackson and Dorothy Twohig, eds., *The Diaries of George Washington* (Charlottesville, Va., 1976–79), 6v.
DHFFC	Linda G. DePauw et al., eds., *Documentary History of the First Federal Congress of the United States of America* (Baltimore, 1972–).
FO	Foreign Office
IBM	Bernard Mayo, ed., "Instructions to the British Ministers to the United States, 1791–1812," *Annual Report of the American Historical Association for the Year 1936,* Vol. III (Washington, 1941).

JAH	*Journal of American History*
L&B	Andrew A. Lipscomb and Ellery Bergh, eds., *The Writings of Thomas Jefferson* (Washington, 1903), 20v.
LC	Library of Congress
MHS	Massachusetts Historical Society
MVHR	*Mississippi Valley Historical Review*
NEQ	*New England Quarterly*
NYUL	New York University Library
PAH	Harold C. Syrett et al., eds., *The Papers of Alexander Hamilton* (New York, 1961–81), 27v.
PCAB	Mary-Jo Kline, ed., *The Political Correspondence and Public Papers of Aaron Burr* (Princeton, N.J., 1983), 2v.
PJM	William T. Hutchinson et al., eds., *The Papers of James Madison* Chicago, 1962–).
PJnMl	Herbert A. Johnson et al., eds., *The Papers of John Marshall* (Chapel Hill, N.C., 1974–).
PMHB	*Pennsylvania Magazine of History and Biography*
PRO	Public Record Office
PSQ	*Political Science Quarterly*
PTJ	Julian P. Boyd et al., eds., *The Papers of Thomas Jefferson* (Princeton, N.J., 1950–).
WFA	Seth Ames, ed., *The Works of Fisher Ames* (Boston, 1854), 2v.
WGW	John C. Fitzpatrick, ed., *The Writings of George Washington* (Washington, 1931–41), 39v.
WJA	C. F. Adams, ed., *The Works of John Adams, Second President of the United States . . .* (Boston, 1850–56), 10v.
WJM	Stanislaus M. Hamilton, ed., *The Writings of James Monroe* (New York, 1898–1903), 7v.
WJQA	W. C. Ford, ed., *The Writings of John Quincy Adams* (New York, 1913–17), 7v.
WMQ	*William and Mary Quarterly*
WTJ	Paul L. Ford, ed., *The Writings of Thomas Jefferson* (New York, 1892–99), 10v.

Short Titles Used

Brant, *Madison*	Irving Brant, *James Madison* (Indianapolis, 1941–61), 6v.
Freeman, *Washington*	Douglas S. Freeman, *George Washington: A Biography* (New York, 1948–57), 7v. (Vol. VII by John A. Carroll and Mary W. Ashworth.)
Gibbs, *Memoirs*	George Gibbs, *Memoirs of the Administrations of Washington and John Adams, Edited from the Papers of Oliver Wolcott* (New York, 1846), 2v.
King, *King*	Charles R. King, ed., *The Life and Correspondence of Rufus King* (New York, 1894–1900), 6v.
Malone, *Jefferson*	Dumas Malone, *Jefferson and His Time* (Boston, 1948–80), 6v.
Mitchell, *Hamilton*	Broadus Mitchell, *Alexander Hamilton* (New York, 1957–62), 2v.

NOTES

INTRODUCTION
Modes of Thought and Feeling in the Founding Generation

1. E.g., Charles Beard, referring to "the Fathers of the American Constitution" as being "among the great practicing statesmen of all ages," in *An Economic Interpretation of the Constitution of the United States* (New York, 1913, 1935), p. xvii; or Richard Hofstadter, affirming a "common agreement among modern critics that the debates over the Constitution were carried on at an intellectual level that is rare in politics, and that the Constitution itself is one of the world's masterpieces in practical statecraft," in *The American Political Tradition and the Men Who Made it* (New York, 1949), p. 15. Most of these "great practicing statesmen" who continued in their practicing through the 1790s were of course Federalists. By the end of that decade, according to John C. Miller, "they had made a parchment into a workable instrument of government; they had proved themselves to be conscientious, honest, and efficient administrators; they had proved that republicanism was compatible with stability," etc. *The Federalist Era, 1789–1801* (New York, 1960), p. 277.

2. Marshall Smelser, "The Federalist Period as an Age of Passion," *AQ,* X (Winter 1958), 391–419; also *idem,* "The Jacobin Phrenzy: Federalism and the Menace of Liberty, Equality, and Fraternity," *Review of Politics,* XIII (Oct. 1951), 457–482; and "The Jacobin Phrenzy: The Menace of Monarchy, Plutocracy, and Anglophobia, 1789–1798," *ibid.,* XXI (Jan. 1959), 239–258; John R. Howe, Jr., "Republican Thought and the Political Violence of the 1790s," *AQ,* XIX (Summer 1967), 147–165 (passage qu. is on pp. 150–151).

3. Though some features of this literature are examined in the present chapter, for an extensive listing and historiographical discussion of it the reader is referred to two essays by Robert E. Shalhope, "Toward a Republican Synthesis: The Emergence of an Understanding of Republicanism in American Historiography," *WMQ,* 3rd Ser., XXIX (Jan. 1972), 49–80; and "Republicanism and Early American Historiography," *ibid.,* XXXIX (Apr. 1982), 334–356. In an effort to reconcile the diverse points of view represented in this body of writing, Professor Shalhope has offered a synthesis of his own, *The Roots of Democracy: American Thought and Culture, 1760–1800* (Boston, 1990).

4. Most prominently, e.g., in Abraham S. Eisenstadt, ed., *Reconsidering Tocqueville's Democracy in America* (New Brunswick, N.J., 1988).

5. Sean Wilentz would make the transition even shorter. "Even if we concede that every historical moment is, in some sense, a moment of transition, there are ample grounds for describing the half-decade from 1828 to 1833—and even more specifically the period immediately surrounding Tocqueville's brief stay in 1831—as a turning point in American

history. The sheer pace and drama of events, crowding in upon each other, reinforces that impression. . . ." "Many Democracies: On Tocqueville and Jacksonian America," *ibid.,* pp. 213–214.

6. An earlier and somewhat less developed version of this book appeared as the General Introduction to Bailyn, ed., *Pamphlets of the American Revolution* (Cambridge, Mass., 1965), I. Subsequently published in separate form in 1967 as *Ideological Origins,* it was awarded both the Bancroft and Pulitzer prizes.

7. See, of course, James A. Henretta et al., eds., *The Transformation of Early American History: Society, Authority, and Ideology* (New York, 1991) on the ways in which (as is rightly stated on the cover) "the writings and influence of Bernard Bailyn have changed our understanding of the American past."

8. The term itself had acquired an earlier currency in Renaissance studies with the work of Hans Baron, esp. *The Crisis of the Early Italian Renaissance* (Princeton, 1955), 2v., to which Pocock gives ample acknowledgment.

9. We take some liberty with chronology in placing *The Creation of the American Republic, 1776–1787* (Chapel Hill, N.C., 1969) after Pocock's work in our discussion, its actual publication having antedated *The Machiavellian Moment* by six years. But not, we believe, too grave a liberty. Pocock's main emphasis was on a historical era that came much earlier than that on which Wood centered his attention, while his earlier essays and other writings, which gave a full foretaste of what he would subsequently do, were well known to Wood when the latter began his own work.

10. On this point see Pocock, "States, Republics, and Empires: The American Founding in Early Modern Perspective," Terence Ball and J. G. A. Pocock, eds., *Conceptual Change and the Constitution* (Lawrence, Kans., 1988), pp. 61–62.

11. Madison's phrase, in Federalist 10, Jacob E. Cooke, ed., *The Federalist* (Cleveland, 1961), p. 64.

12. J. G. A. Pocock, "Virtue and Commerce in the Eighteenth Century," *Journal of Interdisciplinary History,* III (Summer 1972), 122. A somewhat diffuse statement of this principle is Clifford Geertz, "Ideology as a Cultural System," David E. Apter, ed., *Ideology and Discontent* (Glencoe, Ill., 1964), pp. 47–76; more succinct ones are two essays by Gordon S. Wood, "Intellectual History and the Social Sciences," John Higham and Paul Conkin, eds., *New Directions in American Intellectual History* (Baltimore, 1979), pp. 27–41; and "Ideology and the Origins of Liberal America," *WMQ,* 3rd Ser., XLIV (July 1987), 628–640.

13. An excellent example is Quentin Skinner, "The Principles and Practice of Opposition: The Case of Bolingbroke versus Walpole," Neil McKendrick, ed., *Historical Perspectives: Studies in English Thought and Society in Honour of H. J. Plumb* (London, 1974), pp. 93–128. Skinner's point is that Bolingbroke's ideological weapons were limited to values which the Walpolean Whigs themselves might be expected to accord some sort of recognition, though the cynical Bolingbroke did not really believe them. (We rather suspect he did believe them, at least while voicing them, but that is a point that does not alter the argument either way. A more positive version of Bolingbroke may be found in Isaac Kramnick, *Bolingbroke and His Circle: The Politics of Nostalgia in the Age of Walpole* [Cambridge, Mass., 1968].) A comparable case, if Cecelia Kenyon is correct, is that of the debates over ratification of the United States Constitution in which, as she asserts, "the factors that united the Federalists and Anti-Federalists were stronger than those that divided them." Kenyon, ed., *The Antifederalists* (Indianapolis, 1966), p. xcvii.

14. One way (among several) to read the symposium on Wood's *Creation of the*

American Republic in *WMQ,* 3rd Ser., XLIV (July 1987), 549–640, might be as a corroboration of this point.

15. E.g., Pocock, *Machiavellian Moment,* pp. 508–509; H. T. Dickinson, *Liberty and Property: Political Ideology in Eighteenth-Century Britain* (London, 1977), p. 95.

16. On the financial revolution see P. G. M. Dickson, *The Financial Revolution in England: A Study of the Development of Public Credit, 1688–1756* (London, 1967); and John Brewer, *The Sinews of Power: War, Money, and the English State, 1688–1783* (New York, 1990).

17. The Whig ascendancy and the new forms of order it imposed on political and administrative practice are discussed in J. H. Plumb, *The Growth of Political Stability in England, 1660–1730* (London, 1967); H. T. Dickinson, *Walpole and the Whig Supremacy* (London, 1973); and *idem, Liberty and Property.* We have found Chs. 3–5 of the last-named especially useful for our own understanding of Court-Country ideological divisions in eighteenth-century England.

18. It is true that the gentry would manage by the late eighteenth century to pass much of the tax burden on to other classes; they nevertheless continued to feel much put upon. See Brewer, *Sinews of Power,* p. 206.

19. Lance Banning, *The Jeffersonian Persuasion: Evolution of a Party Ideology* (Ithaca, N.Y., 1978), p. 125.

20. Drew R. McCoy, *The Elusive Republic: Political Economy in Jeffersonian America* (Chapel Hill, N.C., 1980). The above paragraphs constitute our reading of McCoy's argument.

21. John M. Murrin, "The Great Inversion, or Court versus Country: A Comparison of the Revolution Settlements in England (1688–1721) and America (1776–1816)," J. G. A. Pocock, ed., *Three British Revolutions, 1641, 1688, 1776* (Princeton, N.J., 1980), pp. 368–453.

22. Cooke, ed., *Federalist,* pp. 384–385. This elitist slant has been noted by John Zvesper, *Political Philosophy and Rhetoric: A Study of the Origins of American Party Politics* (Cambridge, 1977), pp. 24–25; and by Richard Hofstadter in the essay cited in n. 1 above, mentioning such men as Edmund Randolph, Elbridge Gerry, William Livingston, and Charles Pinckney (all of whom eventually crossed over to the Country side) as deploring "the turbulence and follies of democracy." *American Political Tradition,* p. 4. On Publius' rhetorical strategy see Albert Furtwangler's excellent *The Authority of Publius: A Reading of the Federalist Papers* (Ithaca, N.Y., 1984).

23. Cooke, ed., *Federalist, passim.* The points noted here may be checked through the excellent index to this edition, which lists all the topics in any way touched on by Publius throughout. Also useful for this purpose is Thomas Engeman et al., eds., *The Federalist Concordance* (Chicago, 1988).

24. Stanley Elkins and Eric McKitrick, "The Founding Fathers: Young Men of the Revolution," *PSQ,* LXXVI (June 1961), 181–216, discusses this "Continentalist" aspect. But see also E. James Ferguson, "The Nationalists of 1781–1783 and the Economic Interpretation of the Constitution," *JAH,* LVI (Sept. 1969), 241–261.

25. On the Court defense in England, see again Dickinson, *Liberty and Property,* pp. 121–162. We know of no comparable movement in America, on this scale of self-assurance, to justify to the public a broad Federalist conception in Hamiltonian terms, or of anything in the modern literature on the divisions of the 1790s that seeks to discern such an effort. Richard Buel, Jr., *Securing the Revolution: Ideology in American Politics, 1789–1815* (Ithaca, N.Y., 1972) is very useful on the actual clash of issues at the point, as it were, of contact;

Zvesper, *Political Philosophy* (cited in n. 22 above) is good on the world-view of Federalism prior to its coming under persistent challenge from Jeffersonian Republicanism. Neither, however, considers the question of a systematic Federalist polemical counter-challenge, or whether in fact there was one.

26. This refers of course to the assumption, once given currency principally through the writings of Charles Beard, that the economic basis for the Federalist-Republican division was a kind of fundamental antagonism between commercial and agricultural interests.

27. Sean Wilentz, *Chants Democratic: New York City and the Rise of the Working Class, 1788–1850* (New York, 1984), esp. pp. 62–103.

28. See again Elkins and McKitrick, "Young Men of the Revolution," cited in n. 24 above.

29. It might be noted that of the 55 delegates to the Philadelphia Convention, 24 served either in Congress or in high executive or judicial office in the new federal government, and of the 95 men who served in the First Congress, 58 could be described as Federalists, 41 of whom would remain so throughout their careers. See, e.g., Clinton Rossiter, *1787: The Grand Convention* (New York, 1966); Kenneth C. Martis, ed., *The Historical Atlas of Political Parties in the United States, 1789–1989* (New York, 1988); and individual entries in *DAB*.

30. The three were Madison (initially the Administration's all-but-official spokesman in Congress), Jefferson, and Edmund Randolph. Suggestive clues to what we are calling the "Virginia principle" might also be found in Lance Banning, "James Madison and the Nationalists, 1780–1783," *WMQ*, 3rd Ser., XL (Apr. 1983), 227–255; and esp. Herbert Sloan, *Principle and Interest: Thomas Jefferson and the Problem of Debt* (New York, 1994).

31. Joyce Appleby has argued that liberal capitalism, in both theory and practice, was a primary goal of Jeffersonian Republicanism. While this is not our reading (the persistent animus in Jefferson's own writings, as well as in his principal public acts, against most aspects of what is commonly understood as entrepreneurship suggests if anything the reverse), we would nevertheless concede that with some rearrangement, aided by certain historical ironies, the argument could have a special kind of validity. As an economic design the free-swinging laissez-faire capitalism of nineteenth-century America was the last thing the Jeffersonians envisioned or would have wanted. But as the product of political exigencies and political choices it could hardly have turned out otherwise. It was of course the centralizing, high-finance, big-mercantile implications of Hamiltonian Federalism, dependent for support on close commercial relations with Great Britain (seen as contaminating to public virtue and a threat to republican liberty) that inspired the formation of the Jeffersonian opposition. The Republicans came to office in 1801 determined to remove the hand of government from all such concerns (and to do away with the taxes required to support them), to steer clear of foreign connections, and to interfere as little as possible in the daily pursuits of the citizenry. In addition, the Jeffersonians in building their own party, starting with an opposition, could afford no constraints against reaching out everywhere for support—the result being a politics of welcome that had room for everyone. A more auspicious setting for the unrestrained individualism that subsequently characterized the great cycles of economic expansion in the nineteenth century could hardly be imagined, no matter what form of economic theory may have been in the minds of those who first opened the door to it.

Professor Appleby's ideas have occasioned a fair amount of debate, which has also involved the related issue of how important a place should be accorded the influence of John Locke upon the world-view that accompanied the transition to modernity in both American and British societies. See Joyce Appleby, "Commercial Farming and the 'Agrarian Myth' in the Early Republic," *JAH*, LXVIII (Dec. 1981), 833–849; "What is Still American in the Political Philosophy of Thomas Jefferson?" *WMQ*, 3rd Ser., XXXIX (Apr. 1982), 287–309; "Republicanism and Ideology," *AQ*, XXXVII (Fall 1985), 461–473; "Republicanism in Old and New Context," *WMQ*, 3rd Ser., XLIII (Jan. 1986), 20–34 (all reprinted in *Liberalism and Republicanism in the Historical Imagination* [Cambridge, Mass., 1992]); and *Capitalism and a New Social Order: The Republican Vision of the 1790s* (New York, 1984). See also Isaac Kramnick, *Republicanism and Bourgeois Radicalism: Political Ideology in Late Eighteenth-Century England and America* (Ithaca, N.Y., 1990), esp. Chs. 1 and 6; Sloan, *Principle and Interest,* Introduction; Lance Banning, "Jeffersonian Ideology Revisited; Liberal and Classical Ideas in the New American Republic," *WMQ*, 3rd Ser., XLIII (Jan. 1986), 3–19; and James T. Kloppenberg, "The Virtues of Liberalism: Christianity, Republicanism, and Ethics in Early American Political Discourse," *JAH*, LXXIV (June 1987), 9–33.

32. Murrin makes a strong point of this in "Great Inversion," p. 429.

33. The evidence as to elite control of local and provincial government in the colonial era is very extensive. Among the studies illustrating this are Richard L. Bushman, *Puritan to Yankee: Character and the Social Order in Connecticut, 1690–1765* (Cambridge, Mass., 1967); Edward M. Cook, *The Fathers of the Towns: Leadership and Community Structure in Eighteenth-Century New England* (Baltimore, 1976); Robert Zemsky, *Merchants, Farmers, and River Gods: An Essay on Eighteenth-Century American Politics* (Boston, 1971); Gary B. Nash, *Quakers and Politics: Pennsylvania, 1681–1726* (Princeton, N.J., 1968); and Rhys Isaac, *The Transformation of Virginia, 1740–1790* (Chapel Hill, N.C., 1982).

34. The most comprehensive account so far written of the emergence in America of a democratic society "unlike any that had ever existed" is Gordon Wood, *The Radicalism of the American Revolution* (New York, 1991). Wood discusses at length many of the critical challenges to an older civic humanist value-system that occurred in the 1790s, recognizing that although the victory of the Jeffersonians in 1800 did not in itself mark the ascendancy of a democratic order—that was still a generation in the future—it did signal the fading of a conviction, shared by most of the Constitution-makers, that the norms of civic life were to be more or less exclusively set by a disinterested elite (as Madison himself had put it in the Tenth Federalist) of "enlightened views and virtuous sentiments."

CHAPTER I

Legitimacy

1. *Journals of the Continental Congress* (Washington, 1904–57), XXXIV, 599–601. There was no formal adjournment, but no quorum could be obtained after October 10, 1788.

2. Resolution of Feb. 21, 1787, *ibid.,* XXXII, 74.

3. C. O. Paullin, "The First Elections Under the Constitution," *Iowa Journal of History and Politics,* II (Jan. 1904), 3–33; for greater detail, see the pertinent volumes of Merrill Jensen et al., eds., *The Documentary History of the First Federal Elections, 1788–1790* (Madison, Wis., 1976–89), 4v. St. John de Crevecoeur to Jefferson, Oct. 20, Nov. 20, 1788, *PTJ,* XIV, 29, 274.

4. Edward Stanwood, *A History of the Presidency* (Boston, 1901), pp. 20–30. In New Hampshire, one of the five states in which popular election of electors was prescribed, no

candidate received a majority of votes. The law provided that in such a case a full list be appointed by the legislature, which was duly done. More and more states adopted the mode of popular election as time went on, until by 1832 all but one were using it. The exception was South Carolina, whose electors continued to be appointed by the legislature down to 1860. Also by 1832 all but Maryland and South Carolina were using the general ticket, voted upon throughout the state, as opposed to election by districts. This had not been the case in the first presidential election. At that time, in every state that provided for any form of popular election, the voting was done by districts, which made it possible that the electoral vote of a state could be divided. The first general-ticket election law was that adopted by Virginia in 1800, in order to ensure that that state's entire electoral vote would go to one or the other of the candidates. *Ibid.,* pp. 21, 38, 47, 59, 60, 83, 93, 103, 133, 164.

5. The material in this section is largely drawn from Douglas S. Freeman, *George Washington* (New York, 1948–57), 7v. It also profits from the many insights in Marcus Cunliffe, *George Washington: Man and Monument* (Boston, 1958).

6. The fullest study of this subject is Rick W. Sturdevant, "Quest for Eden: George Washington's Frontier Land Interests" (Unpub. diss., U. of Calif., Santa Barbara, 1982).

7. Cf. entries in *Oxford English Dictionary* (Oxford, 1933), II, 280–281; and Bergen and Cornelia Evans, *A Dictionary of American Usage* (New York, 1957), pp. 90, 366, on "character" and "personality."

8. See Bernard Bailyn, "Politics and Social Structure in Virginia," James M. Smith, ed., *Seventeenth-Century America: Essays in Colonial History* (Chapel Hill, N.C., 1959), pp. 90–115.

9. Charles S. Sydnor, *Gentlemen Freeholders: Political Practices in Washington's Virginia* (Chapel Hill, N.C., 1952), esp. Chs. 7–8; Bernard Bailyn, *The Origins of American Politics* (New York, 1970), p. 77; Rhys Isaac, *The Transformation of Virginia, 1740–1790* (Chapel Hill, N.C., 1982), esp. Chs. 5–6.

10. *Virginia Gazette,* Oct. 25, 1765, qu. in Thomas J. Wertenbaker, *Give Me Liberty: The Struggle for Self-Government in Virginia* (Philadelphia, 1958), p. 228; Jack P. Greene, *The Quest for Power: The Lower Houses of Assembly in the Southern Royal Colonies, 1689–1776* (Chapel Hill, N.C., 1963), pp. 364ff.

11. Marvin Kitman's (not wholly serious) *George Washington's Expense Account* (New York, 1970) made something of a splash with the claim, based on a facsimile edition of Washington's wartime accounts published in 1833, that Washington's refusal of a salary was more than counter-balanced by the bill of $449,261 he submitted in 1783 for out-of-pocket headquarters expenses. According to a subsequent estimate, however, allowing for the collapse in value of the Continental currency over the seven-year period of Washington's command, this in hard dollars would have come to less than $20,000. See Marshall Smelser, "A Cool Half Million," *Book World,* July 19, 1970; and Marcus Cunliffe's review, *JAH,* LVIII (June 1971), 138.

12. The distinction here between "administrative" and "executive" is important. The executive function in government, according to Edward S. Corwin, is "the power . . . that is the most spontaneously responsive to emergency conditions; conditions, that is, which have not attained enough of stability or recurrence to admit of their being dealt with according to rule." *The President: Office and Powers, 1787–1957* (New York, 1957), p. 3.

13. For example, Congress was more willing to use the power of impressing supplies than Washington was. See *Journals of the Continental Congress,* IX, 1013–1015, Dec. 10, 1777; Brant, *Madison,* I, 319; II, 114–115.

14. Thomas Balch, ed., *Journal of Claude Blanchard, Commissary of the French Aux-*

iliary Army . . . 1780–1783 (Albany, N.Y., 1876), p. 93, qu. in Freeman, *Washington,* V, 267; see also Gilbert Chinard, ed., *George Washington as the French Knew Him* (Princeton, N.J., 1940), *passim.*

15. Salvador de Madariaga, in his *Bolívar* (New York, 1952), shrewdly suggests that neither Bolívar nor San Martín would be comprehensible without the example of Napoleon. See p. xviii and *passim.*

16. *WGW,* XXVII, 393.

17. Washington to James Warren, Oct. 7, 1785, *ibid.,* XXVIII, 290.

18. *PTJ,* VII, 592.

19. The "official" source on the proceedings of the Convention is Max Farrand, ed., *The Records of the Federal Convention of 1787* (New Haven, Conn., 1937), 4v., with Vol. IV (containing additions and corrections to I–III) having been replaced by James Hutson, ed., *Supplement to Max Farrand's . . . Records . . .* (New Haven, Conn., 1987). Several of the delegates kept notes, the most complete set of which was that of James Madison. These are printed as written in *Records,* I–II. A somewhat more usable version of Madison's notes—because of corrected spelling and more convenient arrangement—is in Jonathan Elliot, ed., *Debates on the Adoption of the Federal Constitution,* 2nd ed. (Philadelphia, 1836), Vol. V of Elliot's series on the proceedings of the state ratifying conventions. On Washington at Philadelphia, Arthur N. Holcombe, "The Role of Washington in the Framing of the Constitution," *Huntington Library Quarterly,* XIX (Aug. 1956), is suggestive, as is Frederick Byrne, "The Model Chief Executive: George Washington and the Establishment of the Executive" (Unpub. M.A. thesis, Columbia U., 1989).

20. Benjamin Rush to Timothy Pickering, Aug. 30, 1787, Lyman Butterfield, ed., *Letters of Benjamin Rush* (Princeton, N.J., 1951) I, 440; [William Lewis to Thomas Lee Shippen], Oct. 11, 1787, *PTJ,* XII, 230; Pierce Butler to Weedon Butler, May 5, 1788, Farrand, *Records,* III, 302; Freeman, *Washington,* VI, 117n.

21. *New-Jersey Journal,* Apr. 29, 1789, qu. in *ibid.,* p. 183.

22. Edgar S. Maclay, ed., *Journal of William Maclay* (New York, 1890), pp. 1–10; *AC,* 1 Cong., 1 Sess., 24, 29. A new edition of Maclay's diary appeared in 1988 as Vol. IX of Linda G. DePauw et al., eds., *Documentary History of the First Federal Congress of the United States of America, March 4, 1789–March 3, 1791* (Baltimore, 1972–). It is a direct transcription of Maclay's notes exactly as he wrote them, and is accompanied by a highly useful set of editorial annotations. But since the earlier Edgar Maclay edition regularizes the spelling and punctuation of the original, we have found it preferable for purposes of quotation, and the references in these pages will be to that edition.

23. *AC,* 1 Cong., 1 Sess., 24, 29–31, 191, 213; Maclay, *Journal,* pp. 1, 10–12, 14, 15–16, 18, 21–22.

24. *Ibid.,* pp. 22–29; *AC,* 1 Cong., 1 Sess., 31, 33–35, 247. Maclay's version of the resolution, somewhat more mouth-filling than the one reported in *AC,* was "His Highness the President of the United States of America and Protector of the Rights of the Same."

25. Maclay, *Journal,* pp. 30–38; *AC,* 1 Cong., 1 Sess., 36, 294, 318–324; Fisher Ames to George Minot, May 14, 27, 1789, *WFA,* I, 36–37, 46; Washington to David Stuart, July 26, 1789, *WGW,* XXX, 362–363 and n. See also James Hart, *The American Presidency in Action, 1789* (New York, 1948), pp. 34–40. There is a legend that Washington himself would actually have liked a title, and that his preference was for "His High Mightiness." The legend appears to be without foundation. It was first given general currency in Rufus W. Griswold's *The Republican Court; or, American Society in the Days of Washington* (New York, 1854), pp. 153–154. Griswold had picked it up from Henry A. Muhlenberg's then recently published *Life of Major-General Peter Muhlenberg, of the Revolutionary Army*

(Philadelphia, 1849), pp. 317–318. As the story went, Peter Muhlenberg, then a representative from Pennsylvania, was invited to dine at the President's with several other congressmen including at least one other Pennsylvanian; Washington during dinner consulted him about the title "High Mightiness," whereupon Muhlenberg turned him off with a joke, later voting against all titles. The story has all the marks of a family legend that grew with the telling. Three considerations make its truth unlikely: (1) Maclay's lack of knowledge of it (he was in close touch with his fellow-Pennsylvanians and would have been the first — as he said himself — to hear such a tidbit and to record it if it had really happened); (2) Washington's letter to Stuart, cited above; and (3) Muhlenberg's own grievance against Washington at not having been appointed to the command of the Indian army, a command that went instead to Arthur St. Clair. (This point is rather strikingly juxtaposed with the titles story in Muhlenberg's *Life,* p. 318.)

26. Richard M. Gummere, *The American Colonial Mind and the Classical Tradition: Essays in Comparative Culture* (Cambridge, Mass., 1963), esp. Chs. 1–2, 4, 6, 10–11; Howard Mumford Jones, *O Strange New World; American Culture: The Formative Years* (New York, 1964), pp. 227–272; Chares F. Mullett, "Classical Influences on the American Revolution," *Classical Journal,* XXXV (Nov. 1939), 92–104; Gilbert Chinard, "Polybius and the American Constitution," *Journal of the History of Ideas,* I (Jan. 1940), 38–58; Bernard Bailyn, *The Ideological Origins of the American Revolution* (Cambridge, Mass., 1967), pp. 23–26. On the extent to which one member found congressional behavior not up to the Roman standard (as he had taken for granted it would be), see Fisher Ames to George Minot, May 23, 27, July 8, 1789, *WFA,* I, 35, 45, 64. The remark about Madison is in J.-P. Brissot de Warville, *New Travels in the United States of America, 1788,* ed. Durand Echeverria (Cambridge, Mass., 1964), p. 147; for Madison's speech on titles see *PJM,* XII, 155.

27. Samuel E. Morison, "The Young Man Washington," *By Land and by Sea: Essays and Addresses* (New York, 1953), pp. 168–171; Cunliffe, *George Washington,* pp. 16–17, 190–197; Fredric M. Litto, "Addison's Cato in the Colonies," *WMQ,* 3rd Ser., XXIII (July 1966), 431–449; Albert Matthews, "Some Sobriquets Applied to Washington," *Publications of the Colonial Society of Massachusetts,* VIII (1906), 275–287; Frank Monaghan, *Supplementary Notes on the Inaugural Journey and the Inaugural Ceremonies of George Washington . . .* (New York, privately distributed, 1939), p. 9; Brissot de Warville, *New Travels,* pp. 342–343; Chinard, *Washington as the French Knew Him,* pp. 93–94 and *passim.* Garry Wills, *Cincinnatus: George Washington and the Enlightenment* (Garden City, N.Y., 1982), is a learned and splendidly realized examination of the Cincinnatus theme in Washington's public image.

28. "Queries on a Line of Conduct to Be Pursued by the President," *WGW,* XXX, 319–321; Washington to Madison, May 12, 1789, and to David Stuart, July 26, 1789, *ibid.,* 322–323, 361–362; Hamilton to Washington, May 5, 1789, *PAH,* V, 335–337; Adams to Washington, May 17, 1789, *WJA,* VIII, 491–493; Freeman, *Washington,* VI, 199–203; William Sullivan, *The Public Men of the Revolution: Including Events from the Peace of 1783 to the Peace of 1815* (Philadelphia, 1847), p. 120.

29. Freeman, *Washington,* VI, 202.

30. Louis de Fontanes, in his funeral oration on Washington at the Hôtel des Invalides in 1800, said: "Washington was born in an opulence which he has nobly enhanced amidst agricultural pursuits, as the heroes of ancient Rome. Although he was an enemy of vain ostentation, he wished that republican customs be clad with dignity." Chinard, *Washington as the French Knew Him,* p. 135.

31. Maclay, *Journal,* pp. 23, 24; Benjamin Rush to Adams, July 21, 1789, Butterfield,

Letters, I, 523; Adams to Rush, July 28, 1789, *Old Family Letters; Copied from the Originals for Alexander Biddle* (Philadelphia, 1892), pp. 47–51.

32. Jones, *O Strange New World,* p. 259; John R. Howe, Jr., *The Changing Political Thought of John Adams* (Princeton, N.J., 1977), Chs. 5–6.

33. *AC,* 1 Cong., 1 Sess., 368–383, 456–585, 590–591; Hart, *American Presidency,* pp. 155–184; Leonard D. White, *The Federalists: A Study in Administrative History* (New York, 1948), pp. 20–25; *PJM,* XII, 170–174. Hamilton, in Federalist 77, had clearly stated that the consent of the Senate "would be necessary to displace as well as to appoint." But it appears that Madison, having considered the implications of this, became convinced that without such a power the executive authority might easily be eroded away by an aggressive Senate. Madison to Edmund Randolph, May 31, 1789, *PJM,* XII, 189–190. See also Joseph P. Harris, *The Advice and Consent of the Senate: A Study of the Confirmation of Appointments by the United States Senate* (Berkeley, Calif., 1953), pp. 17–43.

34. Maclay, *Journal,* pp. 97, 103–104, 106, 109–117.

35. Hart, *American Presidency,* pp. 214–239; *AC,* 1 Cong., 1 Sess., 71–72, 384–396, 592–607, 612–615, 778.

36. *Ibid.,* 78–79, 90. Accompanying Jefferson's nomination were those of Edmund Randolph of Virginia and Samuel Osgood of New York, for Attorney-General and Post-master-General respectively.

37. See J. H. Plumb, *The Growth of Political Stability in England, 1675–1725* (London, 1967).

38. Bailyn, *Origins of American Politics,* pp. 31–58, 143–146.

39. E.g., Oliver M. Dickerson, *The Navigation Acts and the American Revolution* (Philadelphia, 1951), pp. 208–265, on colonial response to the "customs racketeering" carried on by royal appointees. For evidence that the example of Walpole was still very much a looming presence in the America of 1789 see Maclay, *Journal,* p. 123: "When Walpole debauched the British Senate (House of Lords), was it either morally or politically different whether he did it by court favor, loans, jobs, lottery-tickets, contracts, offices, or expectancy of them, or with the clinking guinea? The motive and effect were certainly the same. But Walpole was a villain. What, then, must be the man that follows his footsteps."

40. Washington to Samuel Vaughan, Mar. 21, 1789, *WGW,* XXX, 240; Timothy Pickering to Ebenezer Bowman, Oct. 10, 1791, qu. in White, *Federalists,* p. 260. On administrative procedure during this period Carl E. Prince, *The Federalists and the Origins of the U.S. Civil Service* (New York, 1977), is a thorough and highly useful study, though Professor Prince imputes to the early civil service a kind of party-oriented professionalism which we do not believe it could have acquired until some years later.

41. Gaillard Hunt, "Office-Seeking During Washington's Administration," *AHR,* I (Jan. 1896), 270–283; *WGW,* XXX, 371. See also White, *Federalists,* pp. 253ff.

42. July 27, 1789, *WGW,* XXX, 366.

43. E. Neville Williams, *The Eighteenth-Century Constitution, 1688–1815: Documents and Commentary* (Cambridge, 1960), p. 129.

44. The only contemporary description of this episode is Maclay, *Journal,* pp. 128–133. The other quotation is from an entry in John Quincy Adams's diary for Nov. 10, 1824, repeating two versions of the same story (turning on whether Washington "said he would be damned" or whether he simply "swore"), both told by William H. Crawford, and which Crawford in turn had probably heard from Monroe. Monroe himself, however, had it on hearsay. He did not take his seat in the Senate until December 6, 1790. C. F. Adams, ed., *Memoirs,* VI, 427.

45. Not only had Congress been furnished the relevant information well in advance,

but it had also provided for the expenses of making the treaty, and the Senate had approved the nominations of the commissioners who would negotiate it. *AC*, 1 Cong., 1 Sess., 58–59, 65, 684–688, 690–703, 763–766; Ralston Hayden, *The Senate and Treaties, 1789–1817: The Development of the Treaty-Making Functions of the United States Senate During the Formative Period* (New York, 1920), pp. 16–29.

46. *WGW*, XXX, 369–375; *AC*, 1 Cong., 1 Sess., 65.

47. See *ibid.*, 66–71; and Hart, *American Presidency*, pp. 80–97; in addition to Maclay, *Journal*.

48. *WGW*, XXX, 295.

49. Farrand, *Records*, II, 637–640; Robert A. Rutland, *The Birth of the Bill of Rights* (Chapel Hill, N.C., 1955), pp. 115–120; Madison to Jefferson, Oct. 24, 1787, and Washington to Madison, Oct. 10, 1787, *PJM*, X, 215, 190. For other expressions of Washington's annoyance with Mason, see letters to Bushrod Washington, Nov. 10, 1787, and to David Stuart, Nov. 30, 1787, *WGW*, XXIX, 309–312, 323–324.

50. Rutland, *Bill of Rights*, pp. 126–189; Madison to Hamilton, [July 20, 1788], *PAH*, V, 184–185; Robert B. Semple, *A History of the Rise and Progress of the Baptists in Virginia* (Richmond, 1810), pp. 76–77. Helen E. Veit et al., *Creating the Bill of Rights: The Documentary Record from the First Federal Congress* (Baltimore, 1991), is a useful collection covering the legislative history, the congressional debates, and the correspondence and other documents concerning the proposed amendments.

51. Brant, *Madison*, II, 264; Washington to John Armstrong, Apr. 25, 1788, *WGW*, XXIX, 464–467; Madison to George Eve, Jan. 2, 1789, *PJM*, XI, 404–405; *AC*, 1 Cong., 1 Sess., 247.

52. *Ibid.*, 424–449.

53. *Ibid.*, 74–88, 660–665, 703–763, 765–778, 903, 905, 913–914, 916; Rutland, *Bill of Rights*, pp. 190–218.

54. Madison to Jefferson, Oct. 17, 1788; Jefferson to Madison, Mar. 15, 1789; *PTJ*, XIV, 16–21, 659–662.

55. Gov. John Collins to Washington, Sept. 26, 1789, Veit, *Bill of Rights*, p. 298; Griffith J. McRee, *Life and Correspondence of James Iredell* (New York, 1857–58), II, 270–273; Walter Clark, ed., *State Records of North Carolina* (Winston, Goldsboro, Charlotte, Raleigh, 1895–1914), XXII, 43–52.

56. The above account is based on Charles Warren, "New Light on the History of the Judiciary Act of 1789," *Harvard Law Review*, XXXVII (Nov. 1923), 49–132; Julius Goebel, Jr., *History of the Supreme Court of the United States: I, Antecedents and Beginnings to 1801* (New York, 1971), 457–508; *AC*, 1 Cong., 1 Sess., 18, 46, 47, 49, 50, 659, 782–785, 796–834, 892, 894; Maclay, *Journal*, pp. 85–109, 117–118; and *Statutes at Large*, I, 73–93.

57. Such an argument was made by William W. Crosskey, *Politics and the Constitution in the History of the United States* (Chicago, 1953), esp. I, 610–674; II, 754–764.

58. Farrand, *Records*, I, 124–125. For Hamilton's thoughts on the judiciary see Federalist 82, Cooke ed., pp. 553–557. Gouverneur Morris, who as chairman of the Committee on Style had been responsible for the phraseology of the Constitution, wrote many years later that the judiciary article, unlike the others, had to be worded somewhat equivocally. "On that subject, conflicting opinions had been maintained with so much professional astuteness, that it became necessary to select phrases, which expressing my own notions would not alarm others, nor shock their selflove, and to the best of my recollection, this was the only part which passed without cavil." To Timothy Pickering, Dec. 22, 1814, Farrand, *Records*, III, 420. According to Abraham Baldwin, another delegate, there were

a few things that had been "left a little unsettled," the judiciary being one of them. *Ibid.,* 370.

59. For a discussion of the colonial legal systems, in direct challenge to the Crosskey assumption that the Framers felt themselves free to start from *tabula rasa,* see Julius Goebel, Jr., *"Ex Parte* Clio," *Columbia Law Review,* LIV (Mar. 1954); and *idem, Supreme Court,* I, 1–95.

60. Cf. *Journals of the Continental Congress,* XXIV, 195–201, 257–261; and *AC,* 1 Cong., 1 Sess., 102–104.

61. On the background of the Tariff of 1789 see William Hill, "The First Stages of the Tariff Policy of the United States," *Publications of the American Economic Association,* VIII (1893), 455–614.

62. *AC,* 1 Cong., 1 Sess., 106, 115, 156, 158, 224–225, 295–296 (italics in Tucker qu. added); Ames to Minot, May 14, 1789, *WFA,* I, 37.

63. *Ibid.,* 49; Ames to Minot, July 2, 1789, *ibid.,* 58; *AC,* 1 Cong., 1 Sess., 110ff.

64. *Ibid.,* 103.

65. *Ibid.,* 108, 234–247, 252–265, 272–290.

66. *Ibid.,* 608–610, 615–619; Maclay, *Journal,* pp. 47–48, 51–52, 76–78, 89, 91, 96–97; *WFA,* I, 38–39, 48–49, 57–60. Evidence that the influence of the New York mercantile community had much to do with the Senate's rejection of discrimination is scanty but persuasive. Alexander Hamilton told Major George Beckwith in October: "Whilst the Revenue and Tonnage Bills were under discussion, I was decidedly opposed to those discriminating Clauses, that were so warmly advocated by some gentlemen. I was at pains to obtain information from our mercantile body here upon this subject, who with a few Exceptions were against Every species of distinction, upon the principle that it would be productive of a War of Commerce." *PAH,* V, 488–489. The chief opponent of discrimination in the House was John Laurance of New York, himself a merchant, whom Hamilton had actively promoted as a candidate for Congress earlier in the year. *Ibid.,* 268–269, 274–277, 283–286. (Maclay in his *Journal,* p. 47, refers to Laurance as "a mere tool for British agents and factors.") Madison, writing to Jefferson on May 9, 1789, speaks of the opposition to discrimination as "chiefly abetted by the spirit of this City, which is steeped in Anglicism." *PJM,* XII, 143. Maclay in this same connection refers on June 17 to "the influence of this city," and on July 1 says: "But mark the influence of the city of New York, or let me call it British influence. To work they set in the Senate, and, before the Impost got up, they had secured a majority to reject the discrimination." *Journal,* pp. 78, 96.

67. Vernon G. Setser, *The Commercial Reciprocity Policy of the United States, 1774–1829* (Philadelphia, 1937), pp. 52–98; Lawrence S. Kaplan, *Jefferson and France: An Essay on Politics and Political Ideas* (New Haven, Conn., 1967); Malone, *Jefferson,* II, Chs. 1–10; Merrill D. Peterson, "Thomas Jefferson and Commercial Policy," *WMQ,* 3rd Ser., XXII (Oct. 1965), 584–610; Jacob M. Price, *France and the Chesapeake: A History of the French Tobacco Monopoly, 1674–1791, and of Its Relationship to the British and American Tobacco Trades* (Ann Arbor, Mich., 1973), II, 756–787.

68. Lord Sheffield, *Observations on the Commerce of the United States* (London, 1784), 6th ed. [pub. originally 1783], pp. 264–265.

69. Phyllis Deane, *The First Industrial Revolution* (Cambridge, 1965, 1979), pp. 56–58; T. S. Ashton, *Economic Fluctuations in England, 1700–1800* (Oxford, 1959), pp. 62–63; Phyllis Deane and W. A. Cole, *British Economic Growth, 1688–1959: Trends and Structure* (Cambridge, 1962), p. 87.

70. John F. Stover, "French-American Trade During the Confederation, 1781–1789,"

North Carolina Historical Review, XXXV (Oct. 1958), 399–414; Carl L. Lokke, *France and the Colonial Question: A Study of Contemporary French Opinion, 1763–1801* (New York, 1932), pp. 63–67; Setser, *Commercial Reciprocity,* pp. 81–92. French legislators, according to William Short, took for granted that "commerce with the United States is a losing commerce. They are supported in this opinion by many of their merchants who tell them there is no instance of a French house having undertaken that commerce without having lost by it." Short to Jefferson, Oct. 21, 1790, *PTJ,* XVII, 609.

71. J. F. Bosher, *The Single Duty Project: A Study of the Movement for a French Customs Union in the Eighteenth Century* (London, 1964), pp. 72–83; Henri See, "Commerce Between France and the United States, 1783–1784," *AHR,* XXXI (July 1926), 732–752; Lokke, *Colonial Question,* pp. 65–66; Kaplan, *Jefferson and France,* pp. 31–32.

72. Louis Gottschalk, *Lafayette Between the American and the French Revolution, 1783–1789* (Chicago, 1950), pp. 202–258. Jefferson to Richard Henry Lee, Apr. 22, 1786; to Lafayette, Nov. 3, 1786; *PTJ,* IX, 397–389; X, 505. It appears that Jefferson's efforts to break the tobacco monopoly actually had the opposite effect from what he had hoped. "After the Morris contract was ended," according to Professor Stover, "England quickly took over the bulk of the American tobacco crop. In 1789–1790 British imports of American tobacco were over seven times those of France." "French-American Trade," p. 409.

73. For a discussion of the Montagnard reaction against the economic liberalism of the Old Regime (and later of the Gironde), culminating in the restrictionary legislation of the National Convention, see Frederick L. Nussbaum, *Commercial Policy in the French Revolution: A Study of the Career of G. J. A. Ducher* (Washington, 1923). In this as well as in the works of Stover, Lokke, and Bosher cited above, one sees the essential fragility of the concessions made by the French to Jefferson.

74. Federalist 11 [Hamilton], Cooke ed., pp. 66–67; Hill, "First Stages," 592–594; Adams to Jefferson, Aug. 7, 1785, *PTJ,* VIII, 354–355; Editorial Note, *ibid.,* VII, 468–469; Setser, *Commercial Reciprocity,* pp. 97–98. For the tone of Jefferson's and Madison's references to England and the English during the 1780s see, e.g., *PTJ,* VII, 122, 421, 506; VIII, 39–40, 460–461; X, 233.

75. Edward Channing, *A History of the United States* (New York, 1905–32), III, 408–423; Dec. 21, 1789, "Letters of Stephen Higginson, 1783–1804," *AHA:AR, 1896,* I, 772.

76. *AC,* 1 Cong., 1 Sess., 181–182, 185, 239–240; Maclay, *Journal,* p. 97.

77. *AC,* 1 Cong., 1 Sess., 234–236; *WFA,* I, 35, 42.

78. *Ibid.,* 45–46; *AC,* 1 Cong., 1 Sess., 903; *Statutes at Large,* I, 24–27.

79. William S. Baker, *Washington After the Revolution* (Philadelphia, 1898), pp. 15–160; *DGW,* V, 474–475.

80. Jan. 9, 1790, *WGW,* XXX, 496–497.

CHAPTER II
Finance and Ideology

1. On this problem see, e.g., Seymour M. Lipset, *The First New Nation: The United States in Historical and Comparative Perspective* (New York, 1963), pp. 61–66.

2. T. V. Smith, "Saints: Secular and Sacerdotal—James Madison and Mahatma Gandhi," *Ethics,* LIX (Oct. 1948), 52.

3. Opinions of Martha Bland and Thomas Shippen, qu. in Brant, *Madison,* II, 33; Gaillard Hunt, ed., *The First Forty Years of Washington Society, portrayed by the Family Letters of Mrs. Samuel Harrison Smith* (New York, 1906), pp. 235–236.

4. On Madison's early life see Brant, *Madison,* I, Chs. 1–7.

5. Madison to James Madison, Sr., July 23, 1770, *PJM,* I, 50; Mark A. Noll, *Princeton and the Republic, 1768–1822* (Princeton, N.J., 1989), pp. 3–58.

6. *PJM,* I, 7–17, 61–68; Jacob N. Beam, *The American Whig Society of Princeton University* (Princeton, N.J., 1933), pp. 1–61; Brant, *Madison,* I, 84–89.

7. *Ibid.,* 106–108. Joseph Breuer and Sigmund Freud, *Studies in Hysteria* (New York, 1936), p. 9. Madison to Bradford, Nov. 9, 1772, Apr. 28, 1773; Bradford to Madison, Mar. 1, 1772; *PJM,* I, 75, 80, 84.

8. Madison to Bradford, Jan. 24, 1774, *ibid.,* 106, 170ff.; Douglass Adair, ed., "James Madison's Autobiography," *WMQ,* 3rd Ser., II (Apr. 1945), 198–199; Brant, *Madison,* II, 301.

9. *Ibid.,* 159; Madison to Mazzei, July 7, 1781, *PJM,* III, 180.

10. Farrand, *Records,* I, 529.

11. *Princeton* (9): Bedford, Davie, Dayton, Ellsworth, Houston, Madison, Alexander Martin, Luther Martin, Paterson; *Yale* (4): Baldwin, Ingersoll, Johnson, Livingston; *William and Mary* (4): Blair, McClure, Mercer, Randolph; *Harvard* (3): Gerry, King, Strong; *King's* (2) Hamilton, G. Morris; *College of Philadelphia* (2): Mifflin, Williamson; *Oxford* (1); C. C. Pinckney; *St. Andrews* (1): Wilson. Clinton Rossiter, *1787: The Grand Convention* (New York, 1966), pp. 146–147.

12. Irving Brant, "Madison on the Separation of Church and State," *WMQ,* 3rd Ser., VIII (Jan. 1951), 3–24; Francis Alison to Ezra Stiles, Aug. 1, 1769, qu. in Varnum L. Collins, *President Witherspoon: A Biography* (Princeton, N.J., 1925), I, 124; Madison to Bradford, Jan. 24, 1774, *PJM,* I, 105; Brant, *Madison,* I, 68; Olive H. G. Leigh et al., eds., *The Works of Voltaire,* (Akron, Ohio, 1903), XII, 295, XXXIX, 218–219.

13. Thomas J. Wertenbaker, *Princeton, 1746–1896* (Princeton, N.J., 1946), pp. 48–117; "John Witherspoon," Willard Thorp, ed., *The Lives of Eighteen from Princeton* (Princeton, N.J., 1946), pp. 68–85; Donald R. Come, "The Influence of Princeton on Higher Education in the South Before 1825," *WMQ,* 3rd Ser., II (Oct. 1945), 359–396; Francis L. Broderick, "Pulpit, Physics, and Politics: The Curriculum of the College of New Jersey, 1746–1794," *ibid.,* VI (Jan. 1949), 42–68; Collins, *Witherspoon,* I, 109ff. and *passim;* Noll, *Princeton,* pp. 16–27.

14. Henry Hamilton, *An Economic History of Scotland in the Eighteenth Century* (Oxford, 1963), *passim;* David Kettler, *The Social and Political Thought of Adam Ferguson* (Columbus, Ohio, 1965), pp. 15–41; John Clive and Bernard Bailyn, "England's Cultural Provinces: Scotland and America," *WMQ,* 3rd Ser., XI, (Apr. 1965), 200–213; Caroline Robbins, "'When It Is That Colonies May Turn Independent': An Analysis of the Environment and Politics of Francis Hutcheson (1694–1746)," *ibid.,* 214–251. Other useful works include Anand C. Chitnis, *The Scottish Enlightenment: A Social History* (London, 1976); Istvan Hont and Michael Ignatieff, *Wealth and Virtue: The Shaping of Political Economy in the Scottish Enlightenment* (Cambridge, 1983); Richard B. Sher and Jeffery Smitten, eds., *Scotland and America in the Age of the Enlightenment* (Princeton, N.J. 1990).

15. Robbins, "When It Is That Colonies May Turn Independent"; Collins, *Witherspoon* I, 28, II, 203, 205; Ralph A. Ketcham, "James Madison and the Nature of Man," *Journal of the History of Ideas,* XIX (Jan. 1958), 62–76; I. Woodbridge Riley, *American Philosophy: The Early Schools* (New York, 1907), p. 489; Broderick, "Pulpit, Physics, and Politics," pp. 65–66n.; Douglass Adair, "James Madison," Thorp, ed., *Eighteen from Princeton,* pp. 137–157.

16. Douglass Adair, "'That Politics May Be Reduced to a Science': David Hume, James Madison, and the Tenth *Federalist,*" *Huntington Library Quarterly,* XX (Aug. 1957), 343–360.

17. Collins, *Witherspoon,* II, 208, 211. A valuable discussion of the Scots as social scientists is Gladys Bryson, *Man and Society: The Scottish Inquiry of the Eighteenth Century* (Princeton, N.J., 1945). See also Richard B. Sher, *Church and University in the Scottish Enlightenment* (Princeton, N.J. 1985), pp. 160–162, 267–268; Chitnis, *Scottish Enlightenment,* pp. 91–123; Roy Branson, "James Madison and the Scottish Enlightenment," *Journal of the History of Ideas,* XL (Apr.–June 1979), 235–250.

18. David Hume, "The Idea of a Perfect Commonwealth," T. H. Green and T. H. Grose, eds., *Essays Moral, Political, and Literary* (London, 1882), I, 481.

19. Federalist 10, Cooke ed., p. 57.

20. "So strong is this propensity of mankind to fall into mutual animosities, that when no substantial occasion presents itself, the most frivolous and fanciful distinctions have been sufficient to kindle their unfriendly passions, and excite their most violent conflicts." *Ibid.,* pp. 58–59. The sequence and logic of Madison's intentions might have been rendered a little clearer if he had transposed this sentence to follow rather than precede the thoughts which conclude the paragraph. Many an argument over the Tenth Federalist might have been avoided had it been unmistakable that differing property interests were only among the most frequent motives for the forming of factions, along with a series of others, but that Madison's most basic conviction on this point was that if people had no immediate motives for factious aggression, they would be sure to find them. "What Madison is here suggesting," according to T. V. Smith, "means, in the depth of his thought, that economic interest, which bulks so large because so visible, is but the outward stain of an inward acidity that tends to eat away the fibers of fraternity." "Saints: Secular and Sacerdotal," p. 50. Hume wrote: "Men have such a propensity to divide into personal factions, that the smallest appearance of real difference will produce them. What can be imagined more trivial than the difference between one colour of livery and another in horse races? Yet this difference begat two most inveterate factions in the GREEK empire, the PRASINI and VENETI, who never suspended their animosities, till they ruined that unhappy government." "Of Parties in General," *Essays,* I, 128.

21. *Essays,* I, 492; Adair, "Hume and the Tenth *Federalist,*" 351.

22. *Federalist,* Cooke ed., pp. 63–65.

23. Smith, "Saints: Secular and Sacerdotal"; Ralph L. Ketcham, "James Madison and T. V. Smith: A Study in the Politics of Privacy," *Antioch Review,* XX (Fall 1960), 261–282.

24. Ames to George R. Minot, May 29, 1789, *WFA,* I, 49. Samuel Whitcomb, Jr., an itinerant book salesman, wrote: "Mr. Madison has nothing in his looks, gestures, expression or manners to indicate anything extraordinary in his intellect or character, but the more one converses with him, the more his excellences are developed and the better he is liked. . . . *His mind is his all.*" William Peden, ed., "A Book Peddler Invades Monticello," *WMQ,* 3rd Ser., VI (Oct. 1949), 636.

25. See above, pp. 67–78.

26. *WFA,* I, 48.

27. "Money," *PJM,* I, 302–310.

28. *Ibid.,* 309. See also Janet A. Riesman, "The Origins of American Political Economy, 1690–1791" (Unpub. diss., Brown U., 1983), pp. 390–397, for a discussion of Madison's argument.

29. The system of marketing and exchange underwent considerable alteration from mid-century on, mostly in the direction of greater efficiency, and one of the results was that many more of its retail operations came to be located in Virginia. This was not, however, accomplished through Virginia initiative, nor was it accompanied by the devel-

opment of an indigenous merchant class. It was rather the work of Scottish firms and resulted in the multiplication of resident Scottish factors constituting a kind of extraterritorial community with interests and attitudes distinct in many ways from those of the native agricultural population. This development could only have accented the planters' sense of their own passivity in the workings of the system as a whole. Jacob M. Price, *Capital and Credit in British Overseas Trade: The View from the Chesapeake, 1770–1776* (Cambridge, Mass., 1980), pp. 84–203; Timothy H. Breen, *Tobacco Culture: The Mentality of the Great Tidewater Planters on the Eve of the Revolution* (Princeton, N.J., 1985), pp. 84–203.

30. E.g., Charles A. Beard, *Economic Origins of Jeffersonian Democracy* (New York, 1915), p. 270; and Isaac S. Harrell, *Loyalism in Virginia: Chapters in the Economic History of the Revolution* (Durham, N.C., 1926), pp. 26ff. For a full discussion of this argument see Emory G. Evans, "Planter Indebtedness and the Coming of the Revolution in Virginia," *WMQ*, 3rd Ser., XIX (Oct. 1962), 511–533.

31. Washington to George Mason, Apr. 5, 1769, *WGW*, II, 502. On the Robinson affair see Donald J. Mays, *Edmund Pendleton, 1721–1803: A Biography* (Cambridge, Mass., 1952), I, 174–208; and Joseph A. Ernst, "The Robinson Scandal Redivivus: Money, Debts, and Politics in Revolutionary Virginia," *Virginia Magazine of History and Biography*, LXXVII (Apr. 1969), 146–173.

32. Robert Carter Nicholas, qu. in Mays, *Pendleton*, I, 188.

33. Qu. in Evans, "Planter Indebtedness," 519. See also Gordon S. Wood, "Rhetoric and Reality in the American Revolution," *WMQ*, 3rd Ser., XXIII (Jan. 1966), 3–32.

34. Emory G. Evans, "The Rise and Decline of the Virginia Aristocracy in the Eighteenth Century: The Nelsons," Darrett B. Rutman, ed., *The Old Dominion: Essays for Thomas Perkins Abernethy* (Charlottesville, Va., 1964), p. 77.

35. Jack P. Greene, ed., *The Diary of Colonel Landon Carter of Sabine Hall, 1752–1778* (Charlottesville, Va., 1965), I, 373, II, 813; *PTJ*, X, 27; Jefferson to Lucy Ludwell Paradise, Aug. 27, 1786, *ibid.*, 304–305. On the touchiness of the gentry at having their credit questioned, and the hazards of alienating a class knit by ties of kinship, see Evans, "Planter Indebtedness," pp. 522–523. An additional element in the anglophobia of Virginia was the destruction of property by Cornwallis's army in 1781. Elizabeth Cometti, "Depredations in Virginia During the Revolution," Rutman, ed., *Old Dominion*, pp. 135–151; Madison to Mazzei, July 7, 1781, *PJM*, III, 180; Jefferson to William Jones, Jan. 5, 1787, *PTJ*, XI, 14–18. See also Breen, *Tobacco Culture*, pp. 124–203.

36. An excellent discussion of the differing views of Hamilton is the first chapter of Clinton Rossiter, *Alexander Hamilton and the Constitution* (New York, 1964), pp. 3–33.

37. The imperious and uncompromising side of Hamilton is discussed in Cecelia M. Kenyon, "Alexander Hamilton: Rousseau of the Right," *PSQ*, LXXIII (June 1958), 161–178.

38. We have very little information about Hamilton's boyhood and early life in the West Indies. For the best gleanings of what is extant in official records, contemporary recollections, and other scraps see Broadus Mitchell, *Alexander Hamilton: Youth to Maturity, 1755–1788* (New York, 1957), I, Chs. 1–3.

39. This correspondence, with Nicholas Cruger, Tileman Cruger, William Newton, and others, is in *PAH*, I, 9–30.

40. *Ibid.*, 80; Nathan Schachner, ed., "Alexander Hamilton Viewed by his Friends: The Narratives of Robert Troup and Hercules Mulligan," *WMQ*, 3rd Ser., IV (Apr. 1947), 203–225; Brant, *Madison*, I, 105.

41. Mitchell, *Hamilton*, I, 53–64; Schachner, "Narratives," pp. 212–215. There is a

story in John C. Hamilton's *Life of Alexander Hamilton* (New York, 1840), I, 21–23, that Hamilton first came to the notice of the New York Patriot leadership with an impromptu speech made at a public meeting in the Fields (now City Hall Park) on July 6, 1774, at which Alexander McDougall, the leader of the New York radicals, presided. There is no other authentication for the story, though Mitchell regards it as plausible. A hitherto unknown Hamilton letter (undated, but probably written sometime in 1774) came to light in 1968 which shows not only that Hamilton was acquainted with McDougall while still a student, but also that the latter thought sufficiently well of him to lend him books. *New York Times*, Feb. 19, 1968.

42. Samuel Seabury, *Letters of a Westchester Farmer*, ed. Clarence H. Vance (White Plains, N.Y., 1930). This includes four pamphlets: *Free Thoughts, The Congress Canvassed, A View of the Controversy*, and *An Alarm to the Legislature*. Hamilton's *Full Vindication* and *The Farmer Refuted* are repr. in *PAH*, I, 45–78, 81–165. For the conditions in New York that provided the background for this controversy see Carl L. Becker, *The History of Political Parties in the Province of New York, 1760–1776* (Madison, Wis., 1910), pp. 142ff. and *passim*.

43. See also Moses C. Tyler, *The Literary History of the American Revolution, 1763–1783* (New York, 1897), I, 384, 391; and William H. Nelson, *The American Tory* (Oxford, 1961), pp. 74–78.

44. Mitchell, *Hamilton*, I, 77–105; Washington to Joseph Reed, Jan. 23, 1776, *WGW*, IV, 269, VII, 218.

45. Hamilton to John Hancock, Sept. 18, 1777, and to Elias Boudinot, Sept. 8, 1775, *PAH*, I, 326–328, 347–365, 545–547; Mitchell, *Hamilton*, I, 125–142, 158–173; "Proceedings of a General Court-Martial . . . for the Trial of Major-General Lee, July 4, 1778 . . . ," *Collections of the New-York Historical Society for the Year 1873, Lee Papers*, III, 201.

46. Mitchell, *Hamilton*, I, 175–177; Hamilton to Jay, Mar. 14, 1779, *PAH*, II, 17–19; to New York Committee of Correspondence, Apr. 20, Aug. 18, 1777, *ibid.*, 233–234, 316; to George Clinton, Dec. 22, 1777, Feb. 13, 1778, *ibid.*, 368, 425–428; to Duer, June 18, 1778, *ibid.*, 499–500; to Boudinot, July 26, 1778, *ibid.*, 528–529; to Jay, Mar. 14, 1779, *ibid.*, II, 191.

47. To Duane, Sept. 3, 1780, *ibid.*, 400–418; to R. Morris, Apr. 30, 1781, *ibid.*, pp. 604–635. *The Continentalist* is repr. in *ibid.*, II, 649–652, 654–657, 660–665, 669–674; III, 75–82, 99–106.

48. It is true that Hamilton would venture an occasional piece of political trickery in the course of his career, most notably his electoral intrigues against John Adams (discussed in Chs. XI and XV below). But these rashly transparent maneuvers were among the clumsiest things he ever did, and all of them backfired.

49. Hamilton to Philip Schuyler, Feb. 18, 1781, *PAH*, II, 563–568, is the chief source on Hamilton's rupture with Washington. On the romance with Elizabeth Schuyler, Mitchell's discussion in *Hamilton*, I, 196–208 is both genial and judicious, in contrast to the rather arch treatment in John C. Miller, *Alexander Hamilton: Portrait in Paradox* (New York, 1959), pp. 62–66. Hamilton to Elizabeth Hamilton, Oct. 16, 1781, *PAH*, II, 682.

50. *Ibid.*, III, 87, 89, 93–94, 98, 117, 122, 189. Hamilton resigned his receivership to Thomas Tillotson on Nov. 10, 1782; *ibid.*, III, 195. Mitchell, *Hamilton*, I, 261–284; Brant, *Madison*, II, 188.

51. Hamilton to George Clinton, Mar. 12, 1778.; to Duane, Sept. 3, 1780; *PAH*, I, 439–442; II, 400–418.

52. E. James Ferguson, *The Power of the Purse: A History of American Public Finance*,

1776–1790 (Chapel Hill, N.C., 1961), pp. 146–176; Brant, *Madison,* II, 209–253; Mitchell, *Hamilton,* I, 283–326; *PAH,* III, 420–426.

53. Madison, "Debates in the Congress of the Confederation," *PJM,* VI, 143–145, 265–266; Hamilton to Washington, Feb. 13, Mar. 17, Mar. 25, 1783, *PAH,* III, 253–55, 290–293, 305–308; Washington to Hamilton, Mar. 12, Apr. 4, 1783, *ibid.,* 286–288, 315–316; Richard H. Kohn, *Eagle and Sword: The Federalists and the Creation of the Military Establishment in America, 1783–1802* (New York, 1975), pp. 17–35.

54. "Address of the Annapolis Convention," Sept. 14, 1786, *PAH,* III, 686–690. Authorship of certain numbers of *The Federalist* remained in doubt for many years, and it was not until relatively recent times that the above enumeration was finally established. For an account of this controversy, and the eventual settling of it first by historical analysis and finally by statistical techniques see Douglass Adair, "The Authorship of the Disputed Federalist Papers," *WMQ,* 3rd Ser., I (Apr. 1944), 97–122, and (July 1944), 235–264; Frederick Mosteller and David L. Wallace, *Inference and Disputed Authorship: The Federalist* (Reading, Mass., 1964), esp. pp. 1–15, 263–267; and Adair, "The Federalist Papers: A Review Article," *WMQ,* 3rd Ser., XXII (Jan. 1965), 131–139. The question of authorship is also discussed in *PAH,* IV, 287–301; and *PJM,* X, 259–263. On Madison in the Virginia ratifying convention see Brant, *Madison,* III, 185–228. The complexities of the New York situation are still being debated. In addition to Mitchell, *Hamilton,* I, 426–465, see Linda G. DePauw, *The Eleventh Pillar: New York State and the Federal Constitution* (Ithaca, N.Y., 1966), and esp. review of same by Alfred F. Young, *WMQ,* 3rd Ser., XXV (Apr. 1968), 286–289; Young, *The Democratic Republicans of New York: The Origins, 1763–1797* (Chapel Hill, N.C., 1967), pp. 109–128; and Robin Brooks, "Alexander Hamilton, Melancton Smith, and the Ratification of the Constitution in New York," *WMQ,* 3rd Ser., XXIV (July 1967).

55. The principal exponents of this argument are Douglass Adair, "Disputed Authorship"; Alpheus T. Mason, "The Federalist: A Split Personality," *AHR,* LVII (Apr. 1952), 625–643; and, to a lesser degree, Benjamin F. Wright, "Editor's Introduction," *The Federalist* (Cambridge, Mass., 1961), pp. 1–86. The statement by John Quincy Adams was made in his *Eulogy on the Life and Character of James Madison* (Boston, 1836), p. 32.

56. *PAH,* IV, 178–211. These remarks on "corruption" were made in a short speech a few days later. *Ibid.,* 217.

57. Such a case is strongly implied in Rossiter, *Hamilton and the Constitution.*

58. Hamilton to Duane, Sept. 3, 1780, *PAH,* II, 400–418; Madison to Jefferson, Apr. 16, 1781, *PJM,* III, 71–72; VI, 312–313, 493; Brant, *Madison,* II, 233, 245; *PAH,* III, 213–223; *Continentalist* (see above, n. 47); I. Brant, ed., "Two Neglected Madison Letters" [*North American* I and II], *WMQ,* 3rd Ser., III (Oct. 1946), 569–587. Madison's authorship of *North American* has been questioned by the editors of *PJM,* who think it more likely that the writer was Richard Peters of Philadelphia, who became a close friend of Madison when they served together in the Continental Congress. In any case Madison's views and those of "North American" were very similar. VII, 319–346.

59. The argument that Hamilton's speech was made for tactical purposes is noted and considered in Rossiter, *Hamilton and the Constitution,* pp. 46, 277n.

60. Hume's influence on Madison has been discussed by Douglass Adair (see above, p. 86 and n. 16); the same thinker's influence on Hamilton is noted in Rossiter, *Hamilton and the Constitution,* Chs. 4 and 5, *passim,* and in Gerald Stourzh, *Alexander Hamilton and the Idea of Republican Government* (Stanford, Calif., 1970), pp. 77–80.

61. E.g., the bemused remarks of John Mercer: "He who studies it [*The Federalist*]

with attention, will perceive that it is not only argumentative, but that it addresses different arguments to different classes of the American public, in the spirit of an able and skillful disputant before a mixed assembly. Thus from different numbers of this work, and sometimes from the same numbers, may be derived authorities for opposite principles and opinions. For example, nothing is easier to demonstrate by the numbers of Publius than that the government, which it was written not to expound merely, but to recommend to the people, is, or is not a National Government; that the State Legislatures may arraign at their respective bars, the conduct of the Federal Government or that no state has any such power." *Proceedings and Debates of the Virginia State Convention of 1829–1830* (Richmond, 1830), p. 187.

62. Hume's discussion of "corruption" as a counterweight to Parliament and as a means of maintaining the Executive's independence is in "Of the Independency of Parliament," *Essays,* I, 120–121; it might also be noted that Hamilton's comments in Federalist 71 on the disparity between the people's intentions and their judgment—usually attributed to Rousseau—were just as likely to have been derived from Hume. See *Essays,* I, 97, 113, 287–288, 365, 376; also John B. Stewart, *The Moral and Political Philosophy of David Hume* (New York, 1963), p. 199. On Madison and the removal power see above, p. 151 and n. 33.

63. The most useful summing-up on the origins of Hamilton's economic ideas are the editors' introductions to the Report on Public Credit and Report on Manufactures, *PAH,* VI, 51–65; X, 1–15.

64. Benjamin F. Wright says, "Hamilton was a mercantilist." John C. Miller is more balanced; "he owed more to Colbert, the exponent of mercantilism, than to Adam Smith, the apostle of laissez faire." But Clinton Rossiter protests that "all the mercantilists and neo-mercantilists in England and France could not have spoiled his taste for the commonsense views of Adam Smith." On the other hand, according to Broadus Mitchell, "he refused and refuted laissez-faire teachings ... and found surer guidance in the maxims that had made strong nations in Europe." For Joseph Dorfman, Hamilton may have been a mercantilist, "but he had his own way of handling the logic." However, after quoting a passage from Hamilton's *Continentalist* No. V, Russell Kirk exclaims: "This is mercantilism. Hamilton had read Adam Smith with attention, but his heart was in the seventeenth century." But Louis Hacker will have none of this. "His ... preferences are clear. He follows Adam Smith so plainly and completely that one can only express wonder that the Hamilton text has been misunderstood for so long." Paul Studenski disagrees. "His outlook was ... mercantilistic rather than laissez-faire." Hacker again: "Mercantilism ... Hamilton rejects again and again in all his famous reports." Mercantilist or advocate of laissez faire? "The answer," suggests Rossiter judiciously, "... is that he was both, that his eclectic, undogmatic mind had room for the best teachings of both Colbert and Adam Smith." Wright, *Federalist,* p. 21; Miller, *Hamilton,* p. 290; Rossiter, *Hamilton and the Constitution,* pp. 119, 179; Mitchell, *Hamilton,* I, 248; Joseph Dorfman, *The Economic Mind in American Civilization, 1606–1865* (New York, 1946), I, 410; Russell Kirk, *The Conservative Mind from Burke to Santayana* (Chicago, 1953), p. 68; Louis M. Hacker, *Alexander Hamilton in the American Tradition* (New York, 1957), pp. 12, 166; Paul Studenski and Herman E. Kroos, *Financial History of the United States,* 2nd ed. (New York, 1963), p. 45.

65. H. R. Trevor-Roper, in D. F. Pears, ed., *David Hume: A Symposium* (London, 1963), p. 89. Hume, according to Stuart Hampshire, is "of all philosophers who have written in English, the most admired in British universities at the present time." *Ibid.,* p. 3.

66. Eugene Rotwein, *David Hume: Writings on Economics* (Madison, Wis., 1955), pp. cx–cxi.

67. See Peter F. Drucker, "On the 'Economic Basis' of American Politics," *The Public Interest,* No. 10 (Winter 1968), 30–42.

68. See above, pp. 84–85.

69. David Hume (1711–76) was twelve years the senior of Adam Smith (1723–90), but in a sense it could be said that the two were separated intellectually by nearly a generation. Hume's first book, *A Treatise of Human Nature,* was published in 1739, whereas Smith's first, *The Theory of Moral Sentiments,* did not appear until 1759. All of Hume's economic essays except one were brought out in 1752; Smith's *Wealth of Nations* was published in 1776, twenty-four years later.

70. They are contrasted in Rotwein, *Hume,* pp. cvi–cx.

71. In 1752 Hume published *Political Discourses,* a volume of twelve essays, seven of which were on economic subjects (eight if one counts, as Rotwein does, "Of the Populousness of Ancient Nations"). They are "Of Commerce," "Of Refinement in the Arts" (entitled, in the first edition and in one subsequent one, "Of Luxury"), "Of Money," "Of Interest," "Of the Balance of Trade," "Of Taxes," and "Of Public Credit." Another, "Of the Jealousy of Trade," was added in 1758. They are all reprinted, with an introductory analysis of Hume's economic thought that constitutes a brief book in itself, in Rotwein, *Hume.* The edition cited in the present work is that of Green and Grose, 1882, *Essays Moral, Political, and Literary.*

72. "Of Refinement in the Arts," *ibid.,* I, 301–302.

73. See below, p. 201 and n. 11.

74. "Of Public Credit," *Essays,* I, 371.

75. See Donald F. Swanson and Andrew P. Trout, "Alexander Hamilton, 'the Celebrated Mr. Néckar,' and Public Credit," *WMQ,* 3rd Ser., XLVII (July 1990), 422–430. The frequency of references to Hume in Hamilton's writings has certainly been noticed by more than one writer, and such references may be readily checked throughout the indexes of *PAH,* as well as in the prefatory notes to Hamilton's Treasury reports in that same edition. The present authors have become convinced, however, that with regard to Hume's economic ideas Hamilton did more than simply cite Hume on particular points: at an early stage in his reading he had internalized Hume's entire vision of commercial and industrial development. It is known that he was familiar with the *Essays* and *Treatises on Several Subjects* (which contained all the essays in question) while still at college, and that he referred to them in his pamphlet controversy with Seabury in 1774–1775. In preparing his letter to Robert Morris, dated Apr. 30, 1781, he asked Timothy Pickering for a copy of the *Essays,* whose contents he already knew, to use as reference. (The work also appears in a partial list of books in his library given by Allen McLane Hamilton, *The Intimate Life of Alexander Hamilton* [New York, 1910], p. 74.) This letter, which occupies thirty-one printed pages in *PAH,* II, 604–635, is the best single piece of testimony to how fully Hamilton had absorbed Hume's basic economic assumptions. A careful reading of the essays cited in n. 71 above, followed by a reading of this letter, makes this strikingly evident. On the other hand, the philosophical framework, which is quite prominent in the letter to Morris, is less so in the Report on the Public Credit and Report on a National Bank, in view of the more technical nature of these reports and their concentration on immediate detail. (On the latter report, indeed, Hamilton got little from Hume, who did not favor public banks.) It reappears, however, in the Report on Manufactures, especially in Hamilton's remarks on the relative degree of exertion and enterprise to be observed between artisans and farmers (*PAH,* X, 241, 255–256), which reflects Hume's "Of Refine-

ment in the Arts"; on carelessness in the accumulation of debt (*ibid.*, 282; cf. "Of Public Credit"); and on the perniciousness of poll taxes (*PAH*, X, 312; cf. "Of Taxes"). Garry Wills, *Explaining America: The Federalist* (Garden City, N.Y., 1981), pp. 66–71, is one of the few modern accounts that make a point of Hume's influence on Hamilton's economic thought.

76. Hamilton to Madison, Oct. 12, 1789, in response to a letter from Madison (subsequently lost); Madison to Hamilton [Nov. 20–28, 1789], *PAH*, V, 439, 531; John C. Hamilton, *History of the Republic of the United States of America, as Traced in the Writings of Alexander Hamilton and of His Contemporaries* (New York, 1857–64), IV, 29n.

77. On the general character of New York City in the year 1789, and the daily routine of people at that time and place, see Thomas E. V. Smith, *The City of New York in the Year of Washington's Inauguration* (New York, 1889), which has an excellent map; Isaac N. Phelps Stokes, *The Iconography of Manhattan Island* (New York, 1915–28), 6v.; Sidney I. Pomerantz, *New York: An American City, 1783–1803: A Study of Urban Life* (New York, 1938); Stephen Decatur, Jr., *The Private Affairs of George Washington, From the Records and Accounts of Tobias Lear, Esquire, His Secretary* (Boston, 1933); and Margaret M. Christman, *The First Federal Congress, 1789–1791* (Washington, 1989).

78. On the tempo of Hamilton's first days in office—especially that first Sunday—his correspondence speaks for itself: *PAH*, V, 366ff.

79. Ferguson, *Power of the Purse*, pp. 271–272.

80. The expression "a national blessing" first appears in Hamilton's letter to Robert Morris, Apr. 30, 1781; in his Report on Public Credit of Jan. 9, 1790, it reappears as "the proper funding of the present debt, will render it a national blessing." *PAH*, II, 635; VI, 106. The best source for the precedents for Hamilton's report is the Introductory Note in *ibid.*, VI, 51–58. See also Donald F. Swanson, *The Origins of Hamilton's Fiscal Policies* (Gainesville, Fla., 1963). The most lucid account of Hamilton's financial program is Forrest McDonald, *Alexander Hamilton: A Biography* (New York, 1979), pp. 117–188.

81. On the argument for discrimination see Introductory Note, *PAH*, VI, 60–61; and Hamilton's own discussion, 73–78.

82. *Ibid.*, 74, 76.

83. McDonald, *Hamilton*, pp. 152–160.

84. The principle of concentration, central to the economic thought of David Hume and the guiding concept of present-day growth economics (the mobilization of scarce resources), was understood by Hamilton, Robert Morris, and a number of others as early as the Confederation period. A stable national government could, they believed, through a funded debt and perhaps a national bank, help provide the conditions under which concentration of capital could be achieved and could exert its salutary effect on the community's enterprise. Hamilton touched on the principle in his letter to Morris of Apr. 30, 1781, referring to the need "to erect a mass of credit that will supply the defect of monied capitals and answer all the purposes of cash," which would not only be of advantage to individual investors but would have "the most beneficial influence upon [the country's] future commerce and be a source of national strength and wealth." *PAH*, II, 617. "Since interest on investing capital in the United States," as E. James Ferguson puts it, "was higher than the interest payments required to support the debt, the new capital created by funding, if properly invested, would bring a net increase in national income. Moreover, since the securities were held by propertied men, the gains from an increase in security values would go to persons in a position to use them not for consumption but for investment." "The Nationalists of 1781–1783 and the Economic Interpretation of the Constitution," *JAH*, LVI (Sept. 1969), 248. Robert Morris wrote in 1782 that funding, "by

distributing property into those hands, which could render it most productive," would increase the national revenues "while the original stock continued the same." Report to the President of Congress, July 29, 1782, E. James Ferguson et al., *The Papers of Robert Morris* (Pittsburgh, 1973–), VI, 63. The principle of concentration appears discreetly in Hamilton's Report on Public Credit; a funded debt answering "most of the purposes of money" is a stimulus to trade and manufacturing "because there is a larger capital to carry it on," and because the merchant "has greater means for enterprize." *PAH*, VI, 70–71. He would develop it further in his Report on a National Bank, Dec. 13, 1790, emphasizing "the active capital of the country." "This, it is, which generates employment; which animates and expands labor and industry. Every addition, which is made to it, by contributing to put in motion a greater quantity of both, tends to create a greater quantity of the products of both." *Ibid.,* VII, 317. By the time he wrote his Report on Manufactures the following year, Hamilton would virtually repeat Morris's statement of a decade earlier. Referring to a funded debt as "an engine of business, or as an instrument of industry and Commerce," he declared that "though a funded debt is not in the first instance, an absolute increase of Capital, or an augmentation of real wealth; yet by serving as a New power in the operation of industry, it has within certain bounds a tendency to increase the real wealth of a Community, in like manner as money borrowed by a thrifty farmer, to be laid out in the improvement of his farm may, in the end, add to his Stock of real riches." (For "thrifty farmer" one should probably read "enterprising merchant capitalist.") *Ibid.,* X, 281–282. In his essay "Of Money," Hume spelled out the process whereby an increase of money—or credit—brought about a real increase in the wealth of the community. The key was concentration. "When any quantity of money is imported into a nation, it is not at first dispersed into many hands, but is confined to the coffers of a few persons, who immediately seek to employ it to advantage." It was these men, merchants and manufacturers, who would use such funds to extract more labor, produce more goods, and generally enhance the community's well-being. *Essays,* I, 313. Albert Gallatin, on the other hand, who was to serve both Jefferson and Madison as Secretary of the Treasury on fiscal principles very different from Hamilton's, not only recognized the theoretical assumptions behind Hamilton's system but challenged them directly. There was no reason, Gallatin insisted, to assume that the credit resources produced by funding would in fact become investment capital. Rather, he argued, capital "acquired suddenly by individuals . . . has been applied in the same manner as every other sudden acquisition of wealth; it has enabled those individuals to consume, to spend more, and they have consumed and spent extravagantly." "A Sketch of the Finances of the United States" (1796), Henry Adams, ed., *The Writings of Albert Gallatin* (Philadelphia, 1879), III, 147.

85. Report, *PAH*, VI, 78–81.

86. *Ibid.,* 81–83. The only fully satisfactory discussion of this problem and its bearing on assumption of state debts is Ferguson, *Power of the Purse,* pp. 203–219 and 308ff.

87. Report, *PAH*, VI, 82.

88. Hamilton calculated about $27 million for the domestic debt, $13 million for accrued interest, $2 million for unliquidated Continental currency still in the hands of the states, and about $12 million for the foreign debt. He estimated that the state debts to be assumed would total about $25 million. As of Sept. 30, 1791, the total debt either funded or registered amounted to about $50.2 million, and it appeared unlikely that it would go much beyond $52 million in the final accounting. Report, *PAH* VI, 86–119; *ASP:F,* I, 149–150. Of the $21.5 million in state debts that Congress agreed to assume, only $18.2 million was actually subscribed. The additional $4 million paid to the creditor states after the final settlement made a total of about $22 million. The grand total of the federal debt would

come to about $74 million, not far below Hamilton's original estimate of $79 million. Ferguson, *Power of the Purse,* pp. 330, 332–333; Whitney K. Bates, "The Assumption of State Debts, 1783–1793" (Unpub. diss., U. of Wisconsin, 1951), pp. 226, 228–229.

89. Higginson to Hamilton, Nov. 11, 1789; Bingham to Hamilton, Nov. 25, 1789; *PAH,* V, 507–511; 538–557; see also James O. Wettereau, "Letters from Two Business Men to Alexander Hamilton on Federal Fiscal Policy, November, 1789," *Journal of Economic and Business History,* III (Aug. 1931), 667–672.

90. It is true that some of the language as well as certain of the sentiments of the Bingham and Higginson letters are paralleled in passages of Hamilton's report. The same might be said of Madison's suggestion that an excise on domestic spirits be levied according to the size of stills, or the argument of John Witherspoon against discrimination between classes of creditors. Madison to Hamilton, Nov. 19, 1789; Witherspoon to Hamilton, Oct. 26, 1789; *PAH,* V, 525–527, 464–465. The emphasis in the present account, however, is on the way in which Hamilton had to steer a path between differing conceptions of how interest on the debt ought to be paid, and on the characteristic way in which he made up his own mind on this question. For his discussion of interest see Report, *ibid.,* VI, 85–99; on the sinking fund, 196; for the remark about "probabilities," 88.

91. Report, *ibid.,* 90–97. Hamilton proposed seven separate plans, including partial payment in western lands, or a bonus in land to compensate for a reduction in interest, among which each creditor might take his choice. The immediate interest would have averaged between 4 and 5 percent. Congress in the Funding Act of Aug. 4, 1790, reduced the options to one: $66\frac{2}{3}$ percent in 6 percent stock and $33\frac{1}{3}$ percent in deferred stock bearing 6 percent after 1800. Accrued interest—or indents—was funded at 3 percent, contrary to Hamilton's recommendation that indents be treated on equal terms with other securities. Other departures from Hamilton's plan included the rating of Continental currency at 100 to 1 in specie, rather than the recommended 40 to 1, and the payment of a slightly lower rate of interest on state than on federal securities. Ferguson, *Power of the Purse,* pp. 296–297; *AC,* 1 Cong., 2 Sess., 2303–2311; or *Statutes at Large,* I, 138–144.

92. Report, *PAH,* VI, 89.

93. *Ibid.;* Hume, "Of Interest," *Essays,* I, 323.

94. See above. n. 91.

95. The basic source for this episode is Douglas Brymner, *Report on Canadian Archives, 1890* (Ottawa, 1891), in which the documents describing Beckwith's conversations with Hamilton and others were first brought to light and published. The code numbers Beckwith assigned to each of his informants are listed in Brymner's introduction, pp. xli–xliii.

96. Beckwith to Dorchester [1788], *ibid.,* p. 101; Samuel F. Bemis, *Jay's Treaty: A Study in Commerce and Diplomacy,* rev. ed. (New Haven, Conn., 1962), pp. 57–59.

97. Beckwith to Henry Dundas, June 20, 1792, qu. in *ibid.,* p. 378; Brymner, *Canadian Archives,* pp. 121–123.

98. *Ibid.,* pp. 125–129; also *PAH,* V, 482–490.

99. *Ibid.,* 483, 485, 486.

100. Julian Boyd, *Number 7: Alexander Hamilton's Secret Attempts to Control American Foreign Policy* (Princeton, N.J., 1964), is in the present authors' judgment over-wrought, casting an aura of conspiracy and deceit over the Hamilton-Beckwith conversations that is unwarranted by the evidence. A similar conclusion has been reached by two other students of the diplomacy of this period: see Charles R. Ritcheson, *Aftermath of Revolution: British Policy Toward the United States, 1783–1795* (Dallas, Tex., 1969), p. 431n., and review of *Number 7, Journal of Southern History,* XXXI (Feb. 1965), 202–203;

and Jerald A. Combs, *The Jay Treaty: Political Battleground of the Founding Fathers* (Berkeley, Calif., 1970), pp. 52–56.

101. Bemis, *Jay's Treaty*, p. 6.

102. *Ibid.*, pp. 1–27, 148–153. Major-General Arthur St. Clair, Governor of the Northwest Territory, spent the entire spring and summer of 1789 in New York promoting various kinds of legislative and executive action on behalf of the Territory, and was on intimate terms with the President during this time. He gave Washington considerable information on the instability of Indian affairs, and the latter fully shared his sense of the problem's gravity. St. Clair had been aware for some time that British retention of the posts, the warlike state of the Indian tribes, and British intrigues among the Kentuckians (stirring up secessionism and encouraging hopes for assistance against the Spanish, who controlled navigation of the Mississippi) were closely related. Washington to Beverley Randolph, July 15, 1789, *WGW*, XXX, 355–356; St. Clair to Washington, Sept. 14, 1789, William H. Smith, ed., *The St. Clair Papers* ... (Cincinnati, 1882), II, 123–124; St. Clair to John Jay, Dec. 13, 1788, *ibid.*, 101–105. Several times during the 1789 session Washington sent Congress messages and documents on the Indian problems of the Northwest: *ASP:IA*, I, 5–54, 57–58; and at one time during the summer he considered an outright demand for the surrender of the posts. Washington to Madison, [Aug. 1789], *WGW*, XXX, 394.

103. *Ibid.*, 439–442.

104. *DGW*, V, 456; Boyd, *Number 7*, pp. 15–19.

105. See above, n. 102.

106. *PAH*, IV, 192–193; Rossiter, *Hamilton and the Constitution*, pp. 153–156; Louise B. Dunbar, *A Study of "Monarchical" Tendencies in the United States from 1776 to 1801* (Urbana, Ill., 1922), pp. 85–88.

107. Mitchell, *Hamilton*, I, 74–75, 219, 239–240, 341–345; Brant, *Madison*, II, 181–182; Hamilton to Henry Knox, June 7, 1782, *PAH*, III, 92; on Hamilton and honor see Combs, *Jay Treaty*, pp. 55–57.

108. Beckwith, in correspondence with Grenville in January and March 1791, strongly urged the advantages of a trade agreement. See *ibid.*, pp. 52–53, 89; and Ritcheson, *Aftermath of Revolution*, pp. 118–119. Judging from what Beckwith had written to Dorchester on the same subject in 1788, it is probably safe to assume that he had favored such an arrangement all along, and that this must have been apparent to Hamilton. Brymner, *Canadian Archives*, p. 101.

109. See above, pp. 69–70

110. These estimates are for combined imports and exports. In imports from Britain to America, however, the proportions are much more dramatic: these constitute about 90 percent of America's total imports and about 17 percent of Britain's total exports. See Bemis, *Jay's Treaty*, pp. 45–49.

111. See above, pp. 70–72.

112. See below, pp. 215–222.

CHAPTER III

The Divided Mind of James Madison, 1790
Nationalist Versus Ideologue

1. Madison to Jefferson, Oct. 8, Nov. 1, 1789; to Washington, Nov. 20, 1789; *PJM*, XII, 433, 439, 451–453.

2. The fullest account of the "residence question" (as the locating of the capital was called) is Kenneth Bowling, "Politics in the First Congress, 1789–1791" (Unpub. diss., U. of Wisconsin, 1968), pp. 152–199.

3. Madison to Washington, Nov. 20, 1789, *PJM*, XII, 451–453.

4. *Ibid.;* same to same, Dec. 20, 1789, *ibid.*, 458–459, Hardin Burnley to Madison, Nov. 28, Dec. 5, 1789, *ibid.*, 455–456, 460. Edmund Randolph to Washington, Nov. 26, Dec. 6, 15, 1789; Richard Henry Lee and William Grayson to His Excellency the Governor of Virginia, Sept. 28, 1789; the same to The Honorable the Speaker of the House of Representatives in Virginia, Sept. 28, 1789; David Stuart to Washington, Dec. 3, 1789; Edward Carrington to Madison, Dec. 20, 1789; all in *Documentary History of the Constitution of the United States of America, 1786–1870* (Washington, 1894–1905), V, 214–225, 227–230. Madison to Washington, Jan. 4, 1790; Henry Lee to Madison, Nov. 25, 1789; *PJM*, XII, 466–467, 454–455.

5. Robert A. Rutland, *The Birth of the Bill of Rights, 1776–1791* (Chapel Hill, N.C., 1955), p. 215. Virginia finally ratified the amendments on Feb. 15, 1791. For the debate over an amendment that would have denied the federal government the power to levy direct taxes see Helen Veit et al., eds., *Creating the Bill of Rights: The Documentary Record from the First Federal Congress* (Baltimore, 1991), pp. 206–213.

6. See above, pp. 127–128. Madison, memorandum dated Oct. 8, 1789; Madison to Jefferson, Oct. 8, 1789; *PJM*, XII, 433–434.

7. Malone, *Jefferson*, II, 241–249; Brant, *Madison*, III, 287–289; Jefferson to Washington, Dec. 15, 1789, *PTJ*, XVI, 34–35; Madison to Washington, Jan. 4, 1790, *PJM*, XII, 466–467; Washington to Jefferson, Jan. 21, 1790; Madison to Jefferson, Jan. 24, 1790, *PTJ*, XVI, 116–118, 125–126, 184.

8. E. James Ferguson, *The Power of the Purse: A History of American Public Finance, 1776–1790* (Chapel Hill, N.C., 1961), pp. 297–299. Hamilton to Edward Carrington, May 26, 1792, *PAH*, XI, 428.

9. Ferguson, *Power of the Purse*, pp. 251–257, 270; Joseph S. Davis, *Essays in the Earlier History of American Corporations* (Cambridge, Mass., 1917), I, 339–341.

10. *Ibid.;* Maclay, *Journal*, p. 179 (Jan. 18, 1790); Madison to Jefferson, Jan. 24, 1790, *PJM*, XIII, 4; Whitney K. Bates, "Northern Speculators and Southern State Debts: 1790," *WMQ*, 3rd Ser., XIX (Jan. 1962), 30–48.

11. Speeches of James Jackson (Ga.), Jan. 28, 1790, *AC*, 1 Cong., 2 Sess., 1095, 1096; Maclay, *Journal*, pp. 177–178; Hamilton to Henry Lee, Dec. 1, 1789, *PAH*, VI, 1; Ferguson, *Power of the Purse*, pp. 271–272; Davis, *American Corporations*, I, 174ff. Robert F. Jones, "William Duer and the Business of Government in the Era of the American Revolution," *WMQ*, 3rd Ser., XXXII (July 1972), 393–416; Cathy Matson, "Public Vices, Private Benefit: William Duer and his Circle, 1776–1792," William Pencak, ed., *New York and the Rise of American Capitalism* (New York, 1989), pp. 72–123.

12. Brant, *Madison*, III, 290–305; Ferguson, *Power of the Purse*, pp. 298, 302.

13. Madison to Jefferson, May 9, 1789; to Henry Lee, Apr. 13, 1790; *PJM*, XII, 143, XIII, 148. Henry Lee to Hamilton, Nov. 16, 1789; Hamilton to Lee, Dec. 1, 1789; *PAH*, V, 517, VI, 1. Lee to Madison, Apr. 3, 1790, *PJM*, XIII, 137.

14. Madison to Jefferson, Jan. 24, 1790, *PJM*, XIII, 4.

15. *AC*, 1 Cong., 2 Sess., 1094, 1099–1100; 1139–1143.

16. *Ibid.*, 1145–1147; Maclay, *Journal*, pp. 200–201.

17. *AC*, 1 Cong., 2 Sess., 1131–1137, 1143–1144, 1149–1155.

18. *Ibid.*, 1191–1197, 1182, 1191.

19. *Ibid.,* 1182–1191, 1197–1205; Donald L. Robinson, *Slavery and the Structure of American Politics, 1765–1820* (New York, 1971), pp. 302–304.

20. *AC,* 1 Cong., 2 Sess., 1191–1196.

21. *Ibid.,* 1206–1240.

22. *Ibid.,* 1270–1296, 1298; Brant, *Madison,* III, 298; Maclay, *Journal,* p. 202.

23. Madison to Hamilton, Nov. 19, 1789, *PJM,* XII, 449–451.

24. Madison to Jefferson, Feb. 14, 1790; to Edward Carrington, Mar. 14, 1790; *PJM,* XIII, 41, 104.

25. See above, p. 121.

26. This and the previous paragraph draw on Ferguson, *Power of the Purse,* pp. 203–219.

27. *Ibid.,* p. 304.

28. Albert Gallatin, "A Sketch of the Finances of the United States," Henry Adams, ed., *The Writings of Albert Gallatin* (Philadelphia, 1879), III, 70–203.

29. *AC,* 1 Cong., 2 Sess., 1338–1342, 1384.

30. *Ibid.,* 1384–1392.

31. *Ibid.,* 1392–1393, 1403; White's motion had been made on February 25 and was voted down the next day (1345–1377); 1406, 1408.

32. Maclay, *Journal,* p. 209; *AC,* 1 Cong., 2 Sess., 1478–1480, 1525.

33. *Ibid.,* 1544.

34. The petitions are printed in *ibid.,* 1182–1183, 1197–1198.

35. *AC,* 1 Cong., 2 Sess., 1473–1474; see also Robinson, *Slavery in Politics,* pp. 304–306. The significance of the year 1808 in the committee's report derives, of course, from the provision in Article I, Section 9 of the Constitution that the importation of slaves might legally continue until that year.

36. *Ibid.,* pp. 306–311; *AC,* 1 Cong., 2 Sess., 1450–1473; Madison to Randolph, Mar. 21, 1790, *PJM,* XIII, 110.

37. *Ibid.*

38. *AC,* 1 Cong., 2 Sess., 1534; Brant, *Madison,* III, 309.

39. *AC,* 1 Cong., 2 Sess., 1513, 1525–1526, 1532–1544; Madison to Monroe, Apr. 17, 1790, *PJM,* XIII, 151.

40. *AC,* 1 Cong., 2 Sess., 1557, 1570–1572; italics added.

41. *Ibid.,* 1572–1581; Jefferson to Thomas Mann Randolph, May 30, 1790, *PTJ,* XVI, 450; see also Madison to Monroe, June 1, 1790, *PJM,* XIII, 233–234.

42. *AC,* 1 Cong., 2 Sess., 992–993, 997, 1006, 1653–1655, 1656–1657, 2240–2241; Maclay, *Journal,* p. 310; *New York Daily Advertiser,* June 29, 1790. Sketchy reporting of this measure in *AC* makes it extremely difficult to follow. It seems that on July 1, 1790, Elbridge Gerry moved that the House agree to the Senate amendments eliminating discrimination, and the House voted 31-19 to accept the motion. See *DHFFC,* VI, 1951.

43. "Documents on American Commercial Policy", and Washington to Jefferson, June 19, 1790, with enclosures, *PTJ,* XVI, 513–535.

44. *AC,* 1 Cong., 2 Sess., 1656–1657.

45. The above, an undated memorandum written about 1792 and repr. in *PTJ,* XVII, 205–207, is one of two accounts Jefferson left of the assumption-residence affair; the other is contained in the introduction written in 1818 to the collection of memoranda called "Anas," repr. in *WTJ,* I, 161–164. He also refers to it briefly in a letter to Washington, Sept. 9, 1792, declaring that on that occasion he had been "duped . . . by the Secretary of the Treasury, and made a tool for forwarding his schemes, not then sufficiently understood

by me; and of all the errors of my political life, this has occasioned me the deepest regret." *PTJ*, XXIV, 352.

46. Jacob E. Cooke, "The Compromise of 1790," *WMQ*, 3rd Ser., XXVII (Oct. 1970), 523–545.

47. The present discussion is indebted to Kenneth Bowling's well-documented "Politics in the First Congress," Ch. 6, and assumes, as Bowling does, that Jefferson's dinner occurred on June 20, 1790. We have somewhat modified Bowling's conception of two voting coalitions and are considering the Pennsylvania delegation separately as constituting in certain respects a third, based on such statements as Thomas FitzSimons's that Pennsylvania "holds the balance." (Cooke, "Compromise," 525, n. 6.) For references to "centrality" and "convenience" see *AC*, 1 Cong., 2 Sess., 1660–1679. "In a representative body on a question arousing the most parochial loyalties, the 'center' of the nation could be agreeably defined only as an abstract theoretical center such as the cartographer, the surveyor, or the demographer would construct." James S. Young, *The Washington Community: 1800–1828* (New York, 1966), p. 16. For Bowling's criticism of Cooke, "Compromise," and Cooke's reply, see "Dinner at Jefferson's: A Note on Jacob E. Cooke's 'The Compromise of 1790'", *WMQ*, 3rd Ser., XXXIII (Apr. 1976), 314. See also Norman K. Risjord, *Chesapeake Politics, 1781–1800* (New York, 1978), pp. 363–393; Forrest McDonald, *Alexander Hamilton: A Biography* (New York, 1979), pp. 181–188; and Charlene B. Bickford and Kenneth R. Bowling, *Birth of the Nation: The First Federal Congress, 1789–1791* (Madison, Wis., 1989), pp. 67–75.

48. See above, pp. 133–134; Maclay, *Journal*, p. 190; Bowling, "Politics," p. 173. The preference of South Carolina and the other two states of the Lower South for New York was based not only on New York's greater convenience by sea but also on the Southerners' awareness of Philadelphia's hostile climate regarding slavery, as evidenced both in the Quaker petitions and in the Pennsylvania law requiring manumission of any slave remaining within the state after six months. Kenneth R. Bowling, *The Creation of Washington, D.C.: The Idea and Location of the American Capital* (Fairfax, Va., 1991), pp. 89, 176, 191, 212.

49. Bowling, "Politics," pp. 173–174; Cooke, "Compromise," 528–529; Maclay, *Journal*, pp. 271–275.

50. *AC*, 1 Cong., 2 Sess., 1622, 1625–1626; Madison to Monroe, June 1, 1790, *PJM*, XIII, 233–234; Maclay, *Journal*, pp. 278–282; Richard Henry Lee to Thomas Lee Shippen, June 5, 1790, James C. Ballagh, ed., *The Letters of Richard Henry Lee* (New York, 1914), II, 521–522; Bowling, "Politics," p. 174.

51. Maclay, *Journal*, pp. 284–286; Bowling, "Politics," pp. 175–177; *AC*, 1 Cong., 2 Sess., 1660–1663; Jefferson to George Mason, June 13, 1790, *PTJ*, XVI, 493.

52. Maclay, *Journal*, pp. 292–295.

53. *Ibid.*, p. 294; Bowling, "Politics," p. 182; Peter Muhlenberg to Benjamin Rush, June 17, 1790, qu. in *ibid.*, p. 183.

54. Writing to Monroe about assumption on June 17, 1790, Madison said: "I suspect that it will yet be unavoidable to admit the evil in some qualified shape"; Jefferson had written much the same thing to George Mason on June 13, adding, "In general I think it necessary to give as well as take in a government like ours." *PJM*, XIII, 247; *PTJ*, XVI, 493.

55. King, *King*, I, 384.

56. Cooke refers to the switch of votes in the Senate on June 29 as "inexplicable," inasmuch as the Massachusetts senators switched back against Philadelphia on a later vote.

But the inexplicability would be largely removed by the simpler explanation that the emergent understandings on residence and assumption were in fact connected after all. The Massachusetts men appear to have been persuaded by Hamilton that they would never get assumption without a Philadelphia-Potomac bargain, which makes their original switch (as well as that of Butler of South Carolina) quite comprehensible. They did it reluctantly, however, being loath to desert New York, and their subsequent reversal is probably to be explained by their belief that the Philadelphia-Potomac arrangement (which on the first June 29 vote had a 16-9 majority) would now be carried without their votes. The bill finally passed the Senate on July 1 and the House on July 9. Cooke, "Compromise," 537; King, *King*, I, 384–385; *AC*, 1 Cong., 2 Sess., 994–1001, 1660–1680, 1681–1682; Bowling, "Politics," pp. 190–194.

57. *AC*, 1 Cong., 2 Sess., 1005–1011, 1686–1712; Ferguson, *Power of the Purse*, pp. 321–322. The settlement of accounts was provided for by a separate act which passed the House June 22 and the Senate on July 9. *Ibid.*, p. 322; *AC*, 1 Cong., 2 Sess., 1005, 1646, 2306–2307.

58. *Ibid.*, 1661–1662, 1665–1666.

59. Risjord, *Chesapeake Politics*, p. 385, esp. n. 93.

CHAPTER IV
The Republic's Capital City

1. Joseph J. Ellis, *After the Revolution: Profiles of Early American Culture* (New York, 1979), pp. 4, 9. The "profiles" in Ellis's subtitle are of four representative figures—Charles Willson Peale, Hugh Henry Brackenridge, William Dunlap, and Noah Webster—which illustrate the kinds of disillusionment that ensued from such hopes' failure to materialize. This, as Neil Harris has put it, could be called "The Revolution That Never Was" ("The Making of an American Culture: 1750–1800," Charles F. Montgomery and Patricia E. Kane, eds., *American Art, 1750–1800, Towards Independence* [Boston, 1976], p. 31); and it was this same failed expectation that Emerson referred to in the lecture cited in n. 4 below.

2. Perhaps by Thomas Wentworth Higginson, in "A Plea for Culture," *Atlantic Monthly*, XIX (Jan. 1867), 29–37; see also discussion of this article in Lawrence W. Levine, *Highbrow/Lowbrow: The Emergence of Cultural Hierarchy in America* (Cambridge, 1988), pp. 213–214. Van Wyck Brooks reported in 1915: "I have proposed these terms ['Highbrow' and 'Lowbrow'] to a Russian, an Englishman, and a German, asking each in turn whether in his country there was anything to correspond with the conceptions implied in them. In each case they have been returned to me as quite American, authentically our very own. . . ." *America's Coming-of-Age* (New York, 1915), p. 6.

3. E.g., Neil Harris, *The Artist in American Society: The Formative Years, 1790–1860* (New York, 1966), esp. Chs. 2–5. Lillian B. Miller, *Patrons and Patriotism: The Encouragement of the Fine Arts in the United States, 1790–1860* (Chicago, 1966) makes a good case for what vitality there was in this realm, but everywhere in the author's own evidence the wasteland quality of the artistic terrain keeps peeping through. See also David Grimsted, *Melodrama Unveiled: American Theater and Culture, 1800–1850* (Chicago, 1968), esp. Ch. 7.

4. Edward Waldo Emerson, ed., *The Complete Works of Ralph Waldo Emerson* (Cambridge, Mass., 1903), I, 156–157.

5. George Santayana, *The Genteel Tradition: Nine Essays,* ed. Douglas L. Wilson (Cambridge, Mass., 1967), pp. 39–40.

6. *Coming-of-Age,* pp. 7–8.

7. *Genteel Tradition,* p. 40; *Coming-of-Age,* p. 4.

8. *Genteel Tradition,* p. 78.

9. *Coming-of-Age,* p. 94. This derivativeness had in fact been a recurrent complaint throughout most of the nineteenth century. Orestes Brownson: "We are now the literary vassals of England, and continue to do homage to the mother country. Our literature is tame and servile, wanting in freshness, freedom, and originality. We write as Englishmen, not as Americans." Cornelius Mathews: "Our writers . . . slavishly adhere to old and foreign models . . . ; they are British, or German, or something else than American." Herman Melville: "Let us away with this leaven of literary flunkeyism toward England." Qu. in Richard Ruland, ed., *The Native Muse: Theories of American Literature* (New York, 1972), I, 272, 301, 324.

Santayana: "The American Will inhabits the sky-scraper; the American Intellect inhabits the colonial mansion. The one is the sphere of the American man; the other, at least predominantly, of the American Woman." Brooks: "In fact we have in America two publics, the cultivated public and the business public[,] . . . the one largely feminine, the other largely masculine." *Genteel Tradition,* p. 40; *Coming-of-Age,* p. 111.

10. *Ibid.,* pp. 8–14; *Genteel Tradition,* pp. 40–44. A subsequent outpouring of such statements, much less temperate than those of either Brooks or Santayana, included H. L. Mencken, "Puritanism as a Literary Force," *A Book of Prefaces* (Garden City, N.Y., 1917), pp. 197–283; Randolph Bourne, "The Puritan's Will to Power," *Seven Arts,* I (Apr. 1917), 631–637; Waldo Frank, *Our America* (New York, 1919), pp. 45–46, 75; James Truslow Adams, *The Founding of New England* (Boston, 1921), pp. 64–85; Ernest A. Boyd, "Puritan: Modern Style," *Portraits: Real and Imaginary* (New York, 1924), pp. 106–117; Harvey O'Higgins and Edward H. Reede, M.D., *The American Mind in Action* (New York, 1924), pp. 1–25, 132–140; and *passim;* Langdon Mitchell, *Understanding America* (New York, 1927), pp. 110–111; and Vernon L. Parrington, *Main Currents in American Thought: An Interpretation of American Literature from the Beginnings to 1920* (New York, 1927), I, 85. Some of these writings are discussed in Frederick J. Hoffman, "Philistine and Puritan in the 1920s: An Example of the Misuse of the American Past," *AQ,* I (Fall 1949), 247–263. After the work of Perry Miller, of course, references to "Puritan influence" became much more sophisticated; e.g., Robert E. Spiller et al., eds., *Literary History of the United States,* 3rd ed. (New York, 1963), I, 54–81; Max Savelle, *Seeds of Liberty: The Genesis of the American Mind* (New York, 1948), pp. 5, 10, 27, 360–369, 586; Richard Chase, *The American Novel and Its Tradition* (New York, 1957), p. 11; John C. Gerber, ed., *Twentieth-Century Interpretations of the Scarlet Letter: A Collection of Critical Essays* (Englewood Cliffs, N.J., 1968); and Sacvan Bercovitch, *The Puritan Origins of the American Self* (New Haven, Conn., 1975), pp. 136–186. On the other hand we recall Lionel Trilling's remarking, as a casual aside in one of his lectures on American literature at Columbia in the early 1950s: "If you want to 'explain' American culture, don't start with 'Puritanism.' Try everything else first."

11. Lewis P. Simpson, ed., *The Federalist Literary Mind: Selections from The Monthly Anthology and Boston Review* (Baton Rouge, La., 1962), p. 68; Van Wyck Brooks, *The Ordeal of Mark Twain* (London, 1922), pp. 94, 212; Emerson, *Complete Works,* I, 173–174.

12. Ruland, *Native Muse,* I, 71, 343.

13. Henry James, *Hawthorne* (New York, 1879), pp. 42–43, 3. James was here elab-

orating on Hawthorne's own complaint that "no author, without a trial, can conceive of the difficulty of writing a romance about a country where there is no shadow, no antiquity, no mystery, no picturesque and gloomy wrong, nor anything but a commonplace prosperity, in broad and simple daylight, as is happily the case in my dear native land." James Fenimore Cooper had said something strikingly similar thirty years before Hawthorne: "There are no annals for the historian; no follies (beyond the most vulgar and commonplace) for the satirist; no manners for the dramatist; no obscure fictions for the writer of romance; no gross and hardy offences against decorum for the moralist; nor any of the rich artificial auxiliaries of poetry." Qu. in Ruland, *Native Muse*, I, 224–225.

14. Ann Douglas, *The Feminization of American Culture* (New York, 1976; rev. ed., 1988). For a case study of how this new allocation of social roles worked, containing also a concrete instance of the feminine-clerical alliance discussed by Douglas (see below), see Paul E. Johnson, *A Shopkeeper's Millennium: Society and Revivals in Rochester, New York, 1815–1837* (New York, 1978). See also Jessica S. E. Young, "Rocking the Cradle: The First Generation of Nineteenth-Century American Career Women" (Unpub. diss., Columbia U., 1988); and of course Barbara Welter's now-classic "The Cult of True Womanhood: 1820–1860," *AQ*, XVIII (Summer 1966), 151–174.

15. *Feminization*, pp. 103, 234–235. "It is worth remembering that the sales of all the works by Hawthorne, Melville, Thoreau, and Whitman in the 1850s did not equal the sales of one of the more popular domestic novels." *Ibid.*, p. 96.

16. *Ibid.*, p. 44. "I think . . . it is from the clergy only," wrote Frances Trollope, "that the women receive that sort of attention which is so dearly valued by every female heart throughout the world. With the priests of America, the women hold that degree of influential importance which, in the countries of Europe, is allowed them throughout all orders and ranks of society . . . and in return for this they seem to give their hearts and souls into their keeping." *Domestic Manners of the Americans* [orig. pub. 1832], ed. Donald Smalley (New York, 1949), p. 75.

17. It seems odd that there has been so little critical writing that takes up this question (which neither Brooks nor Santayana so much as mentions) as a possible variable in the evaluation of America's cultural past. But there have been exceptions. Cooper remarked in 1838 that "without a social capital," the American people, "who are really more homogeneous than any other of the same numbers in the world perhaps, possess no standard for opinion, manners, social maxims, or even language." Brownson in the same year wrote: "We have never yet felt that we are a nation, with our own national metropolis. Washington is only a village where are the government offices, and where congress meets; it gives no tone to our literature, and only partially even to our politics." Robert Herrick in 1914 observed that "instead of our having as yet evolved into a fairly homogeneous nation, such as England or France, we inhabit the broad section of a continent with no central metropolis of such indisputable prominence as would serve to unify the social, economic, and political life of the varied peoples that have gathered in it—as London holds together a scattered empire and Paris typifies to every Frenchman the mother land." And because of the "army-like" conditions of urban life, Herrick added, "never has an American city got itself expressed imaginatively as have London and Paris and Rome. For the novelist our cities are like huge hotels where his characters eat and sleep—hotels with meaningless names." Ruland, ed., *Native Muse*, I, 230, 403–404; *idem*, ed., *A Storied Land: Theories of American Literature*, II (New York, 1976), 343, 349. Very suggestive as to the consequences of a separation of a society's political, economic, and cultural pursuits is R. P. Blackmur, "The American Literary Expatriate," David F. Bowers, ed., *Foreign Influences in American Life* (Princeton, N.J., 1944), pp. 126–145.

18. Fiske Kimball, *Thomas Jefferson, Architect* (Boston, 1916), pp. 31–33, 38, 40–43, 142–148; the qu. is from Merrill D. Peterson, *Thomas Jefferson and the New Nation* (New York, 1970), p. 175.

19. "Documents Concerning the Residence of Congress," *PTJ*, VI, 361–370.

20. *Ibid.*, 362, 364–365; Jefferson to George Gilmer, June 27, 1790, *ibid.*, XVI, 574–575.

21. A discussion which argues that there was an intended correspondence between the Constitution and the layout of the capital city is in James S. Young, *The Washington Community, 1800–1828* (New York, 1966), pp. 1–10.

22. Kimball, *Jefferson, Architect*, p. 51; L'Enfant, "Observations Explanatory of the Plan," Elizabeth S. Kite, ed., *L'Enfant and Washington, 1791–1792: Published and Unpublished Documents Now Brought together for the First Time* (Baltimore, 1929), Charles Moore, Foreword to *ibid.*, p. vi; F. Kimball, "The Origin of the Plan of Washington," *Architectural Review*, VII (Sept. 1918), 41–45; Elbert Peets, "The Genealogy of L'Enfant's Washington," *Journal of the American Institute of Architects*, XV (April, May, June 1927), 115–119, 151–154, 187–191; John W. Reps, *Monumental Washington: The Planning and Development of the Capital Center* (Princeton, N.J., 1967), pp. 1–25; F. Kimball, "L'Enfant, Pierre Charles," *DAB*, XI, 165–169. "The Capitol corresponds in position to the palace, the President's house to the Grand Trianon, the Mall to the *parc*, East Capitol Street, Pennsylvania and Maryland Avenues on the east to the Avenue de Paris, de Sceaux, and de St. Cloud. On the west, Pennsylvania Avenue corresponds essentially with the Avenue de Trianon." *Ibid.*, 167.

23. J. McManners, "France," in Albert Goodwin, ed., *The European Nobility in the Eighteenth Century: Studies in the Nobilities of the Major European States in the Pre-Reform Era* (New York, 1967), p. 25; Orest Ranum, "The Court and Capital of Louis XIV: Some Definitions and Reflections," in John C. Rule, ed., *Louis XIV and the Craft of Kingship* (Columbus, Ohio, 1969), pp. 265–285; Jacques Chastenet, "Paris, Versailles, and the 'Grand Siècle,'" in Sir Ernest Barker, ed., *Golden Ages of the Great Cities* (London, 1952), pp. 213–239; Alexis de Tocqueville, *The Old Regime and the French Revolution*, tr. Stuart Gilbert (Garden City, N.Y., 1952), p. 75. It has been argued that Louis XIV did not, strictly speaking, want a "capital"; he simply wanted a seat of government. He nevertheless wanted to make Versailles France's social, intellectual, and artistic center as well, which proved impossible.

In using the term "boggy squalor" we are not unmindful of Kenneth Bowling's effort to dispel the "myth," perpetuated by numerous early visitors, of Washington as a city built on swampland—"swamp," as he correctly points out, being a reference to terrain with trees standing in water most of the time, of which there was very little. There were, on the other hand, tidal marshes, and the low-lying land around the main government buildings in what is now southwest Washington was plagued with problems of drainage that persisted down to the twentieth century. Bowling, *Creating the Federal City, 1774–1800: Potomac Fever* (Washington, 1988), pp. 94–95; see also Don Alexander Hawkins, "The Landscape of the Federal City: A 1792 Walking Tour," *Washington History*, III (Spring/Summer 1991), 10–33.

24. J.-J. Jusserand, Introduction to Kite, ed., *L'Enfant and Washington*, pp. 1–30 (qu. from Ampère on p. 28); Margaret Truman Daniel, as told to the authors by Clifton Daniel.

25. Wilhelmus B. Bryan, *A History of the National Capital; From its Foundation Through the Period of the Adoption of the Organic Act* (New York, 1914), I, 108–115; Washington to Jefferson, Jan. 4, 1791, and Proclamation, Jan. 24, 1791, *WGW*, XXXI, 191, 202–204.

26. Draft of Agenda for the Seat of Government, Aug. 29, 1790 (once erroneously assumed to be of date Nov. 29, 1790), *PTJ*, XVII, 460–461; see also Editorial Note, *ibid.*, 452–460.

27. Washington, Commission Appointing Commissioners, Jan. 22, 1791; to Jefferson, Feb. 1, 1791; *WGW*, XXXI, 200, 206–207; Bryan, *National Capital*, I, 125–127; *Georgetown Weekly Ledger*, Mar. 12, 1791; Jefferson to Ellicott, Feb. 2, 1791; to L'Enfant, Mar. 1791, Apr. 10, 1791; to Washington, Apr. 10, 1791; Ellicott to Jefferson, Feb. 14, 1791; L'Enfant to Jefferson, Mar. 10, 11, 1791; all in Saul K. Padover, ed., *Thomas Jefferson and the National Capital: Containing Notes and Correspondence exchanged between Jefferson, Washington, L'Enfant, Ellicott, Hallett, Thornton, Latrobe, the Commissioners, and others, relating to . . . the City of Washington, 1783–1818* (Washington, 1946), pp. 40–47, 58–61.

28. Washington to Jefferson, Mar. 31, 1791, *WGW*, XXXI, 256–258; Bryan, *National Capital*, I, 154; Ellicott to L'Enfant, Sept. 12, 1791, Kite, ed., *L'Enfant and Washington*, p. 73.

29. Notes on Commissioners' Meeting, Sept. 8, 1791, Padover, ed., *Jefferson and National Capital*, pp. 70–74.

30. Jefferson described these efforts to Washington in a letter of Apr. 10, 1791, with which he enclosed copies of the Pennsylvania Assembly debates; *ibid.*, pp. 60–61. For Washington's constant agitation on this point see *WGW*, XXXI, 262–264, 372–374, 376–377, 381, 422–423, 495, 504; Bryan, *National Capital*, I, 139–141; Freeman, *Washington*, VI, 324n.

31. James S. Young has called attention to this point in *Washington Community*, pp. 27, 256–257, n. 20. Washington did consider it, though it seems not seriously. Washington to Commissioners, Nov. 17, 1792, *WGW*, XXXII, 226.

32. L'Enfant to Washington, Aug. 19, 1791, Kite, ed., *L'Enfant and Washington*, pp. 67–72.

33. David Stuart to Washington, Oct. 19, 1791, *ibid.*, p. 78; Bryan, *National Capital*, I, 159–160; *WGW*, XXXI, 400.

34. Washington to Commissioners, Sept. 29, Nov. 17, 1792; Fourth Annual Address to Congress, Nov. 6, 1792; *ibid.*, XXXII, 170–171, 205–212, 225–226. Bryan, *National Capital*, I, 204 (date of sale incorrectly given), 213–214. There are descriptions of the festivities in *Columbian Mirror and Alexandria Gazette*, Sept. 25, 1793, and recollections of George Watterston in *National Intelligencer*, Aug. 26, 1847. Washington, Fifth Annual Address to Congress, Dec. 3, 1793; to Arthur Young, Dec. 12, 1793; *WGW*, XXXIII, 163–169, 176. Andrew Ellicott, in running the District line through the area south of Alexandria, was appalled at both the poverty of the inhabitants and the thinness of the soil, but was quite aware of how strong was Washington's will to believe. "As the President is so much attracted to this country," Ellicott wrote to his wife, "I would not be willing that he should know my real sentiments about it." June 26, 1791, qu. in Bryan, *National Capital*, I, 173. On the three public sales see also Bob Arnebeck, *Through A Fiery Trial: Building Washington, 1790–1800* (Lanham, Md., 1991), pp. 70, 132–137, 174–175.

35. Tobias Lear to L'Enfant, Oct. 6, 1791; L'Enfant to Lear, Oct. 19, 1791; Kite, ed., *L'Enfant and Washington*, pp. 74–78. Washington would not believe that L'Enfant himself was responsible for the delay, but he did think there had been "something very unaccountable in the conduct of the Engraver." Washington to David Stuart, Nov. 20, 1791, *WGW*, XXXI, 419–423.

36. The final phase of L'Enfant's association with the Federal City—the demolition of the house of Daniel Carroll of Duddington (a nephew of one of the Commissioners), the discharge and imprisonment of Roberdeau, and the fruitless efforts by Washington,

Jefferson, and the Commissioners to have the Major hasten the engraving of the city plan—
is described in Bryan, *National Capital*, I, 165–169, 173–176, and more succinctly in Malone,
Jefferson, II, 378–382. The pertinent correspondence is in Kite, ed., *L'Enfant and Washington*, pp. 79–155.

37. L'Enfant to Jefferson, Feb. 26, 1792; Jefferson to L'Enfant, Feb. 27, 1792; *ibid.*,
pp. 147, 150, 151–152. L'Enfant promptly declared that "the same Reasons which have
driven me from the establishment, will prevent any man of capacity . . . from engaging in
a work that must defeat his sanguin hopes and baffle every exertions. . . ." To Jefferson,
Feb. 27, 1792, *ibid.*, pp. 152–153. The following year, strained relations between Ellicott
and the Commissioners resulted in their discharging him and his entire corps of assistants.
Washington restored him on April 9, 1793, but about a week later Ellicott received an
appointment to survey a road in Pennsylvania, which he promptly accepted. Samuel Blodgett was appointed as superintendent in charge of construction in January 1793 and dismissed a year later. Bryan, *National Capital*, I, 193–194, 209–211, 226–227. Washington to
Commissioners, Apr. 3, 1793, *WGW*, XXXIII, 404–406. Washington to David Stuart, Apr.
8, Nov. 30, 1792; to Benjamin Stoddert, Nov. 14, 1792; to Thomas Johnson, Jan. 23, 1794;
ibid., XXXII, 19, 223–224, 244–245, XXXIII, 250–252. After L'Enfant's dismissal the
Commissioners offered to re-employ Roberdeau. "Considering him a misguided young
man, we have felt more compassion than resentment towards him." Roberdeau, with broad
irony, said he was sensible of having been forgiven "as a misguided young man, but I am
fearful that I should not behave as well in future, therefore, as there may be a *possibility*
to exist independent of such honors, I decline." Kite, ed., *L'Enfant and Washington*, p.
161n.

38. David Stuart to Washington; L'Enfant to Jefferson, Feb. 26, 1792; *ibid.*, pp. 147,
149. Washington to Stuart, Mar. 8, 1792, *WGW*, XXXI, 504, 506.

39. Washington to William Deakins, Jr., and Benjamin Stoddert (partially drafted by
Jefferson), Mar. 2, 1791; to Jefferson, Mar. 31, 1791; *ibid.*, XXXI, 226–227, 256–258. Bryan,
National Capital, I, 128–129, 131–134, 138–147. *DGW*, VI, 103–106, 164–166 (Mar. 28–30,
June 27–30, 1791).

40. Kite, ed., *L'Enfant and Washington*, pp. 167–181; Jefferson to Thomas Johnson,
Feb. 29, 1792; to George Walker, Mar. 1, 1792, Padover, ed., *Jefferson and the National
Capital*, pp. 100–102; Bryan, *National Capital*, I, 178–180.

41. *Ibid.*, pp. 189–190, 211, 237, 255 and n. Washington to Thomas Johnson, Jan. 23,
Feb. 23, 1794; to Commissioners, Apr. 27, 1794; to Johnson, June 27, 1794; to Tobias Lear,
Aug. 28, 1794, *WGW*, XXXIII, 250–252, 277, 343, 415, 481–482. Washington to Johnson,
Mar. 6, 1795, *ibid.*, XXXIV, 134. *Ibid.*, 177, 186, 196–197.

42. Malone, *Jefferson*, II, 384–385; Bryan, *National Capital*, I, 195, 376–377, 405, 458–
460; II, 238.

43. *Ibid.*, I, 195–202; Malone, *Jefferson*, II, 385–387; Kimball, *Jefferson, Architect*, pp.
54–56; Jefferson to Daniel Carroll, Feb. 1, 1793, Padover, ed., *Jefferson and National
Capital*, p. 171.

44. Bryan, *National Capital*, I, 202–204, 241–242, 259–260, 314–319, 377–378, 449–
454, 456, 618, II, 433–434. Washington to Jefferson, June 30, 1793; to Commissioners, July
25, 1793; *WGW*, XXXII, 510–512, XXXIV, 29–30.

45. Bryan, *National Capital*, I, 187, 205–208, 214–221, 224–225, 227–231, 233–236,
243–246, 256–259, 281, 283–285, 295–298, 553.

46. *Ibid.*, I, 264–270; *WGW*, XXXIV, 420; *ASP:Misc*, I, 134.

47. Bryan, *National Capital*, I, 270–272, 278; Gibbs, *Memoirs*, II, 377; Kite, ed., *L'Enfant and Washington*, p. 165n.

48. This portion of our discussion draws on Lewis Mumford's formulations of baroque as set forth in *The Culture of Cities* (New York, 1938), esp. pp. 77–139.

49. *Idem, The City in History: Its Origins, Its Transformations, and its Prospects* (New York, 1961), p. 405.

50. *Ibid.*, pp. 404–405 (Mumford's "sixty thousand" acres was probably intended to read "six thousand"); see also *Culture of Cities*, pp. 94–98.

51. Kite, ed., *L'Enfant and Washington*, pp. 55, 65. The Potomac Company, organized under Washington's auspices in 1785, built canals around the falls and tried to improve the river bed by the removal of rocks. Yet after thirty-five years and considerable expense, the Company still had little to show for its efforts, since the only navigation possible despite these improvements was during the time of floods and freshets. According to the report of a commission examining its affairs in 1823, "The whole time when goods and produce could be stream borne on the Potomac in the course of an entire year did not exceed forty-five days." The Chesapeake and Ohio Canal, the Potomac Company's successor, began work in 1828. By 1850, after an expenditure of nearly $10 million, the canal had reached Cumberland. "But the original purpose of a waterway to the Ohio," according to Carter Goodrich, "had been tacitly abandoned. The canal reached only the foot of the mountains, and that at a time when the railroad had already taken most of its prospective trade." Bryan, *National Capital*, I, 69–70; Goodrich, *Government Promotion of American Canals and Railroads, 1800–1890* (New York, 1960), pp. 76–81. On the hazards of navigation and loading at Georgetown see Bryan, *National Capital*, I, 497–498 and n.; Young, *Washington Community*, p. 22. For a geographer's view of the Potomac as a navigable river see Harry R. Merrens, "The Locating of the Federal Capital of the United States" (Unpub. M.A. thesis, U. of Maryland, 1957), pp. 52–54.

52. Young, *Washington Community*, p. 24, citing Augustus J. Foster, Thomas Hamilton, Frances Trollope, and E. A. Cooley.

53. Bryan, *National Capital*, I, 231–232, 323; John C. Miller, *The Federalist Era, 1789–1801* (New York, 1960), p. 253; Young, *Washington Community*, pp. 25–26, 28–31; Gibbs, *Memoirs*, II, 377–378.

54. John H. Mundy and Peter Riesenberg, *The Medieval Town* (Princeton, N.J., 1958), p. 25.

55. Robert S. Lopez, "The Crossroads Within the Wall," Oscar Handlin and John Burchard, eds., *The Historian and the City* (Cambridge, Mass., 1963), pp. 27–43; Richard L. Meier, "The Organization of Technological Innovation in Urban Environments," *ibid.*, p. 75.

56. Mundy and Riesenberg, *Medieval Town*, pp. 36–66; on Genoa see Lopez, "Crossroads," pp. 36–39.

57. Fritz Rörig, *The Medieval Town* (Berkeley, Calif., 1967), p. 172. See also Mumford, *City in History*, pp. 299–314; Mundy and Riesenberg, *Medieval Town*, pp. 40–41 (and ordinance from Costumes et reglemens ... d'Avignon qu. in *ibid.*, p. 157); and esp. descriptions of such great civic projects in Florence as building the "third circle" (city wall); the campanile of Santa Marie del Fiore—supervised by the artist Giotto and initiated by a grand procession headed by the Bishop; and the rebuilding of the Ponte Vecchio with shops in stone at either end numbering forty-three, "from which the commune drew an annual rental of eighty and more gold florins"; Ferdinand Schevill, *History of Florence: From the Founding of the City Through the Renaissance* (New York, 1936), pp. 252–256.

58. See Mumford, *City in History*, pp. 225, 299, 311, 322, and Notes to Plates 21, 25, 26. That the city did see itself as possessing a "soul"—the combined vision of a corporate self in the present, a mythic past, and a civic mission—is made quite evident in Donald

Weinstein, "The Myth of Florence," Ch. 1 of *Savonarola and Florence: Prophecy and Patriotism in the Renaissance* (Princeton, N.J., 1970).

59. Thomas C. Chubb, *Dante and His World* (Boston, 1966), p. 451.

60. The material for this and the following paragraphs is drawn from Ian Grey, *Peter the Great: Emperor of Russia* (Philadelphia, 1960), and Christopher Marsden, *Palmyra of the North: The First Days of St. Petersburg* (London, 1942).

61. *Ibid.*, pp. 51–52.

62. *Ibid.*, p. 56. The figure on population is from William B. Steveni, *Petrograd Past and Present* (Philadelphia, 1916), p. 39.

63. James Holston, *The Modernist City: An Anthropological Critique of Brasilia* (Chicago, 1989); Alan Riding, "Brasilia: A City of the Future Grapples with a Troubled Present," *New York Times,* Jan. 3, 1988; Kurt F. Fischer, "The Golden Age of Planning and Its End: A Cultural Perspective on Canberra," *Ekistics,* LII (July/Aug. 1985), 290–300; Peter Musson, "Capitalist Utopias," *Geographical Magazine,* LXIII (Aug. 1991), 26–28; Jean Gottmann, ed., "Capital Cities" [a symposium], *Ekistics,* L (Mar./Apr. 1983), 86–152.

64. Denis Brogan, "Implications of Modern City Growth," Handlin and Burchard, eds., *Historian and the City,* p. 54; Gwyn A. Williams, *Medieval London: From Commune to Capital* (London, 1963), p. 311 and *passim;* D. W. Robertson, *Chaucer's London* (New York, 1968), pp. 313–314.

65. John W. Reps, *The Making of Urban America: A History of City Planning in the United States* (Princeton, N.J., 1965), pp. 147–154; Fred R. Frank, "The Development of New York City, 1600–1900" (Unpub. M.A. thesis, Cornell U., 1955), pp. 1–24; Bayrd Still, *Mirror for Gotham: New York as Seen by Contemporaries from Dutch Days to the Present* (New York, 1956), pp. 3–36.

66. *Ibid.*, pp. 37, 54–55, 66–67; Sidney I. Pomerantz, *New York: An American City, 1783–1803: A Study of Urban Life* (New York, 1938). pp. 21–22, 158–159.

67. *Ibid.*, pp. 233–236.

68. On relative distances and convenience see Robert G. Albion, *The Rise of New York Port, 1815–1860* (New York, 1939), pp. 107, 416.

69. Augustus J. Foster, *Jeffersonian America* (San Marino, Calif., 1954), p. 9.

70. Ellis, *After the Revolution,* pp. 113–158; George C. D. Odell, *Annals of the New York Stage* (New York, 1927–49), I, 232ff.

71. Pomerantz, *New York,* pp. 474–480; Paul L. Ford, *Washington and the Theatre* (New York, 1899), pp. 35–43 and *passim;* for more on Dunlap and his activities see Oral S. Coad, *William Dunlap: A Study of His Life and Works and of His Place in Contemporary Culture* (New York, 1917); and Grimsted, *Melodrama Unveiled,* pp. 1–21.

72. Charles F. Montgomery and Patricia E. Kane, eds., *American Art, 1750–1800: Toward Independence* (New Haven, Conn., 1976), pp. 68–143; Harold Dickson, *Arts of the Early Republic: The Age of William Dunlap* (Chapel Hill, N.C., 1968), pp. 24–41; Richard McLanathan, *Gilbert Stuart* (New York, 1988), pp. 86–87.

73. Still, *Mirror for Gotham,* p. 147; Richard Hofstadter, *Anti-Intellectualism in American Life* (New York, 1963), p. 145 and ff.

74. On Irving see Stanley T. Williams, *The Life of Washington Irving* (New York, 1935), 2v.; on Cooper, George Dekker, *James Fenimore Cooper: The American Scott* (New York, 1967); on Bryant, Charles H. Brown, *William Cullen Bryant* (New York, 1971).

75. Arthur Livingston, ed., *Memoirs of Lorenzo da Ponte* (New York, 1959), pp. 213–256; April Fitzlyon, *The Libertine Librettist: A Biography of Mozart's Librettist Lorenzo da Ponte* (London, 1955), pp. 239–278; Henry E. Krehbiel, *Chapters of Opera: Being Historical*

and Critical Observations and Records Concerning the Lyric Drama in New York from Its Earliest Days down to the Present Time (New York, 1909, 1980), pp. 1–52; Howard Shanet, *Philharmonic: A History of New York's Orchestra* (Garden City, N.Y., 1975), pp. 54–76.

76. Actually the University of Geneva scheme was not as harebrained as it might seem—or rather would not have been, had the geographical context for it not been what it was. A new and hostile political regime in the city of Geneva had placed the entire faculty in jeopardy, and it was one of their own spokesmen, François d'Ivernois, who in 1794 broached to Jefferson the idea of their migrating to America as a body if they could be assured of the necessary support there. But Jefferson's soundings, both in the Virginia legislature and with Washington himself, made it starkly evident that no such support was conceivable, facilities for accommodating them in the Potomac area being non-existent and the youth of that region being in no way prepared to receive the caliber of instruction offered by that learned company. The case might have turned out quite differently had it been enacted in an urban setting such as New York. D'Ivernois to Jefferson, Sept. 5, 23, 1794, Jefferson Papers, LC; Jefferson to Wilson Cary Nicholas, Nov. 22, 1794, *WTJ*, VI, 513–515; to John Adams, Feb. 6, 1795, Lester J. Cappon, ed., *The Adams-Jefferson Letters: The Complete Correspondence Between Thomas Jefferson and Abigail and John Adams* (Chapel Hill, N.C., 1939), I, 256–257; to d'Ivernois, Feb. 6, 1795, *WTJ*, VII, 2–6; to Washington, Feb. 23, 1795, Jared Sparks, ed., *Correspondence of the American Revolution: Being Letters of Eminent Men to George Washington* (Boston, 1853), IV, 464–469; Washington to Jefferson, Mar. 15, 1795, *WGW*, XXXIV, 146–149. On Columbia College see David C. Humphrey, *From King's College to Columbia, 1746–1800* (New York, 1976), esp. pp. 208–228, 269–305; and John S. Whitehead, *The Separation of College and State: Columbia, Dartmouth, Harvard, and Yale, 1776–1876* (New Haven, Conn., 1973), pp. 21–31.

CHAPTER V

Jefferson and the Yeoman Republic

1. Thomas P. Abernethy, ed., *Notes on the State of Virginia* (New York, 1964), pp. 157–158; see also Roland Van Zandt, *The Metaphysical Foundations of American History* (The Hague, 1959), pp. 170–180; on the anti-urban Jeffersonian influence among American intellectuals see Morton and Lucia White, *The Intellectual versus the City: From Thomas Jefferson to Frank Lloyd Wright* (Cambridge, Mass., 1962, esp. Chs. 3–4. The literature on Jefferson himself is of course enormous, especially that of the "Thomas Jefferson and . . ." variety. The less patient reader might thus welcome Merrill D. Peterson, ed., *Thomas Jefferson: A Reference Biography* (New York, 1986), a collection of essays by various authorities covering virtually every activity with which Jefferson was associated. And John C. Foley, ed., *The Jeffersonian Cyclopedia* (New York, 1900), is still a very useful standby.

2. Jefferson to John Banister, Jr., Oct. 15, 1785, *PTJ*, VIII, 635–637.

3. Jefferson to Washington, Apr. 10, 1791, *ibid.,* XX, 88; to Rush, Sept. 23, 1800, *WTJ*, VII, 458–459; Merrill D. Peterson, *Thomas Jefferson and the New Nation* (New York, 1970), p. 268.

4. "There were deep ambiguities in his thinking, which made any effort of consistency impossible." Richard Hofstadter, *The American Political Tradition, and the Men Who Made It* (New York, 1948), p. 24. "Ever since Jefferson's death scholars have been trying to discern order in—or to impose it upon—his elusive, unsystematic thought, but without much success. It simply does not lend itself to ordinary standards of consistency." Leo

Marx, *The Machine in the Garden: Technology and the Pastoral Ideal in America* (New York, 1964), p. 135.

5. Jefferson to the Rev. Charles Clay, Jan. 27, 1790, *PTJ*, XVI, 129.

6. Jefferson to G. K. van Hogendorp, Oct. 13, 1785, *ibid.*, VIII, 633; to DuPont de Nemours, Jan. 18, 1802, *WTJ*, VIII, 125–127; A. Whitney Griswold, *Farming and Democracy* (New York, 1948), p. 35.

7. A good discussion of Jefferson's reform activities during this period is in Peterson, *Jefferson*, pp. 97–165. On Jefferson and his gradualist approach to slavery see John C. Miller, *The Wolf by the Ears: Thomas Jefferson and Slavery* (New York, 1977), esp. pp. 39–40, 120–121, 206–207; William W. Freehling, "The Founding Fathers and Slavery," *AHR*, LXXVII (Feb. 1972), 81–93; and David B. Davis, *The Problem of Slavery in the Age of Revolution* (Ithaca, N.Y., 1975), pp. 171–175. The sentence quoted is in "Autobiography," *WTJ*, I, 68.

8. "Thus we see the fate of millions unborn hanging on the tongue of one man," he wrote, "and heaven was silent in that awful moment." Jefferson to Jean Nicolas Démeunier, June 22, 1786, *PTJ*, X, 58. "Jefferson's practical activity," comments Richard Hofstadter, "was usually aimed at some kind of minimum program that could be achieved without keen conflict or great expenditure of energy. He hated vigorous controversy, shrank from asserting his principles when they would excite the anger of his colleagues or neighbors." *American Political Tradition*, p. 25.

9. "The exigencies of Indian warfare, and the excitement of land speculation, with its lure of large and easy profits, were decidedly demoralizing. The absence of any established form of social life, and the recourse to such rough sports as fighting, wrestling, gouging, and running, and to gambling and heavy drinking, further weakened the appeal of the moral and religious life." Niels H. Sonne, *Liberal Kentucky, 1780–1828* (New York, 1939), p. 12.

10. For the material in this and the following paragraph we are indebted to Professor Marx's brilliant study. *The Machine in the Garden*, pp. 88–105.

11. "But there also was a curious strain of extravagance running through their cult, a seemingly neurotic tendency that these rational theories [of the political economists] cannot explain. After the middle of the century, among the upper classes, the taste for the bucolic rose to an extraordinary pitch of faddish excitement. A passion for gardening and playing farmer cropped up in remote villages of English as well as at the court of Louis XVI." *Ibid.*, p. 98.

12. "Not content to lay down the law in a general way, Jefferson liked to offer practical advice whenever the spirit moved him. He often drew his ideas from the architectural works of his large library." Paul F. Norton, *Latrobe, Jefferson, and the National Capitol* (New York, 1977), p. 73.

13. Malone, *Jefferson*, I, 3; Jefferson, "Autobiography," *WTJ*, I, 2.

14. *Ibid.*, 1n., 2; Malone, *Jefferson*, I, 7–33. Inquiry into the family background, according to Professor Malone, shows "that the early Jeffersons were rather more prosperous and prominent than has commonly been supposed." I, 426.

15. *Ibid.*, I, 21–22, 37–48.

16. *Ibid.*, I, 49–74.

17. "Autobiography," *WTJ*, I, 4; Malone, *Jefferson*, I, 75–87; Jefferson to L. H. Girardin, Jan. 15, 1815, L&B, XIV, 231–232.

18. Malone, *Jefferson*, I, 88ff.

19. What we have said about Jefferson's personality in these pages is based, except

otherwise noted, on information in *ibid.*, I, which for completeness leaves little to be desired; and an entry in the Index, "Personal Qualities and Characteristics," is very helpful.

20. Peterson, *Jefferson,* pp. 30–31; to Martha Jefferson, Nov. 28, Dec. 22, 1783, *PTJ,* VI, 360, 417.

21. *American Political Tradition,* p. 25. The General Court and the Governor's Council actually consisted of the same men, and it was to this group—Jefferson's social familiars, and all insiders—rather than to juries, that Jefferson argued his cases. Frank L. Dewey, *Thomas Jefferson, Lawyer* (Charlottesville, Va., 1986), pp. 18–20.

22. Jefferson to John Banister, Jr., Oct. 15, 1785, *PTJ,* VIII, 637.

23. A convenient account of Jefferson's war governorship is in Peterson, *Jefferson,* pp. 166–240; see also, of course, Malone, *Jefferson,* I, 301–369.

24. Jefferson to Steuben, Mar. 10, 1781, *PTJ,* V, 120; original italicized.

25. *Ibid.,* VI, 135–136.

26. Richard Hofstadter and Michael Wallace, eds., *American Violence: A Documentary History* (New York, 1970), p. 36.

27. Rosemarie Zagarri, "Representation and the Removal of State Capitals, 1776–1812," *JAH,* LXXIV (Mar. 1988), 1239–1256.

CHAPTER VI

Jefferson as Secretary of State

1. "The experiment," according to Merrill Peterson, "would have lasting consequences for Jefferson's career. He became a convert to the principle and the strategy of commercial coercion not only in the Revolutionary struggle against the mother country but in the larger campaign for national independence in the decades ahead." *Thomas Jefferson and the New Nation* (New York, 1970), p. 36. Two other recent works, each seeing Jefferson's preoccupation with commercial coercion as central to his entire perception of America's foreign relations, are Robert W. Tucker and David C. Hendrickson, *Empire of Liberty: The Statecraft of Thomas Jefferson* (New York, 1990); and Doron Ben-Atar, *The Origins of Jeffersonian Commerical Policy and Diplomacy* (London, 1993).

2. See above, p. 70.

3. Aug. 9, 1788, *PTJ,* XIII, 489.

4. See above, p. 72.

5. John Holland Rose, *William Pitt and National Revival* and *William Pitt and the Great War* (London, 1911). The first two volumes of a new biography, John Ehrman, *The Younger Pitt: The Years of Acclaim* and *The Younger Pitt: The Reluctant Transition* (London, 1969, 1983), carry Pitt's career through 1796. Ehrman has examined American materials which Holland Rose either did not know about or did not regard as pertinent to his subject.

6. Ehrman, *Younger Pitt,* I, 520–551.

7. The most complete study is William R. Manning, "The Nootka Sound Controversy," *AHA:AR 1904,* 279–478; see also John M. Norris, "The Policy of the British Cabinet in the Nootka Crisis," *English Historical Review,* LXX (Oct. 1955), 562–580; and Lennox Mills, "The Real Significance of the Nootka Sound Incident," *Canadian Historical Review,* VI (March 1925); 110–122. King Ferdinand II persuaded Pope Alexander VI, a Spaniard, to issue a bull in 1493 which proclaimed that all lands west and south of a line

drawn at one hundred leagues from the Azores and Cape Verde Islands were to belong to Spain.

8. Ehrman, *Younger Pitt,* I, 554-571.

9. The first move in the Nootka affair had been clumsily handled by Leeds, which was the point at which Pitt decided to take charge himself. But as early as the Holland crisis the French Foreign Minister, Montmorin, had observed, "Lord Carmarthen . . . n'est que le prête-nom de M. Pitt." *Ibid.,* 536, 555.

10. Jerald A. Comb's observation that Pitt "tended to ignore American problems, and British policy toward the United States was left in the hands of subordinate officials" seems indisputable. *The Jay Treaty: Political Battleground of the Founding Fathers* (Berkeley, Calif., 1970), p. 87. On Hawkesbury's private encouragement of British merchants to express, through memorials to his Committee, their discontent over America's tonnage duties in 1789, see *ibid.,* p. 102.

11. Washington to Morris, Oct. 13, 1789, *WGW,* XXX, 440-442.

12. Beatrix Cary Davenport, ed., *A Diary of the French Revolution, by Gouverneur Morris, 1752-1816* (Boston, 1939), I, 464-466.

13. Leeds to Morris, Apr. 28, 1790; Morris to Washington, May 1, 1790; *ibid.,* 495, 499.

14. Authorities have differed in their assessments of which was the dominating motive—the fur trade or the protection of their Indian allies—in the retention of the posts of the British. The former is emphasized in Samuel F. Bemis, *Jay's Treaty: A Study in Commerce and Diplomacy,* rev. ed. (New Haven, Conn., 1962), pp. 6-10; whereas Alfred L. Burt, *The United States, Great Britain, and British North America: From the Revolution to the Establishment of Peace After the War of 1812* (New Haven, Conn., 1940), pp. 82-105, stresses the latter; neither, however, denies that to a significant extent the two were inseparable. For an appraisal of this controversy see Combs, *Jay Treaty,* pp. 191-192.

15. See below, n. 19.

16. See below, n. 28.

17. Charles R. Ritcheson, *Aftermath of Revolution: British Policy Toward the United States, 1783-1795* (Dallas, Tex., 1969), pp. 147-150. On the eventual debt settlement see Bradford Perkins, *The First Rapprochement: England and the United States, 1795-1805* (Philadelphia, 1955), pp. 138-149.

18. Grenville to Dorchester, Dispatches 22, 23, 24 (Secret), May 6, 1790, Douglas Brymner, ed., *Report on Canadian Archives, 1890* (Ottawa, 1891), pp. 131-133.

19. Samuel F. Bemis, "Relations between the Vermont Separatists and Great Britain, 1789-1791," *AHR,* XXI (Apr. 1916), 547-560; Ritcheson, *Aftermath of Revolution,* pp. 152-159; Frederick J. Turner, "English Policy Toward America in 1790-1791," *AHR,* VII (July 1902), 706-735, VIII (Oct. 1902), 78-86; Douglas Brymner, ed., "Vermont Negotiations," *Report on Canadian Archives, 1889* (Ottawa, 1890), pp. 53-58. The Spanish were carrying on their own intrigues with the Westerners; in addition to the documents repr. by Turner in the foregoing, see William R. Shepherd, "Wilkinson and the Beginnings of the Spanish Conspiracy," *AHR,* IX (Apr. 1904), 490-506.

20. Davenport, ed., *Morris Diary,* I, 520-523; Morris to Washington, May 29, 1790, *ASP:FR,* I, 123-125. Morris certainly overestimated British concern over the possibility of America's becoming a belligerent. The Undersecretary at the Foreign Office, James Bland Burges, did say that "before we know where we are, we shall have the Americans, and possibly the Russians on our backs, if we lose a week commencing the war with Spain by some vigorous and decisive stroke, which may crush their naval power, and incapacitate

them from standing against us at sea." But America was not Burges's real concern here, being used rather as one item in his case for going to war without further ado. Burges was taking the side of his friend and patron Leeds, who opposed the more deliberate course being conducted by Pitt. Burges to Leeds, June 27, 1790, qu. in Norris, "British Cabinet in Nootka Crisis," p. 575n.

21. *Canadian Archives, 1890,* pp. 134–143. The part of Beckwith's report relating to conversations with Hamilton is that from pp. 134–136; according to Julian Boyd, the archivist erroneously headed this section with a number 1 (code for William Samuel Johnson), whereas it should be 7 (Hamilton). *Number 7,* p. 33n. Beckwith to Grenville, Apr. 7, 1790, qu. in Bemis, *Jay's Treaty,* p. 790.

22. Beckwith was given two sets of instructions ("secret" and "less secret") by Dorchester, repr. in *Canadian Archives, 1890,* pp. 143–144. The only record of his conversation with Hamilton on July 8 is Hamilton's own memorandum of that date to Washington, *PAH,* VI, 484–485. Boyd tries to show that Beckwith did not say what Hamilton reported him as saying, the argument resting, however, not on a comparison of Beckwith's report and Hamilton's (Beckwith did not make one), but on inferences drawn from Dorchester's instructions as to what Beckwith ought to have said. Actually the instructions and Hamilton's memorandum—except for the prospect of an alliance, which Hamilton, with his will to believe, obviously magnified—tally quite closely. Interested readers may wish to check this for themselves; the documents are also repr. in Boyd, *Number 7,* pp. 143–149. Dorchester apparently wanted to excuse the British government's not taking Morris as seriously as they might have by mentioning not only the difficulties over the treaty but also Morris's not being a regularly accredited minister. (See also below, n. 27.) This awkward effort seems not to have sat well with Washington.

23. *DGW,* VI, 94–95; Jefferson's suggestions of July 12 as to what Hamilton should say to Beckwith are in *PTJ,* XVII, 110. Reports of Hamilton's further conversations with Beckwith are in *PAH,* VI, 493–498, 546–549, 550–551; VII, 70–74, 111–115, 440–442; VIII, 41–45, 342–343, 475–477, 544–545; IX, 29–30. See also *Canadian Archives, 1890,* pp. 145–146, 148–151, 158–159, 161–168, 172.

24. *Ibid.,* p. 161. Hamilton to Washington, July 15, 1790, *PAH,* VI, 495. Jefferson to William Carmichael, Aug. 2, 1790, and "Outline of Policy on the Mississippi Question," same date; to Washington, Aug. 27, 1790; *PTJ,* XVII, 111–116, 129–130. Hamilton to Washington, Sept. 15, 1790, *PAH,* VII, 36–57.

25. *Canadian Archives, 1890,* pp. 148–149; *PAH,* VI, 497.

26. Davenport, ed., *Morris Diary,* I, 597–604. Morris to Leeds, Sept. 10, 1790; Morris to Washington, Sept. 18, 1790, *ASP:FR,* I, 125–127.

27. The point of whether Morris did or did not end his mission as *persona non grata* is an intriguing example of how differently the same evidence can be read depending on how the context is perceived. Bemis, assuming that the Morris mission could have made some difference and that American interests might have been better served by someone else, concludes: "Morris's untactful behavior made him *persona non grata* both to the Government and the Court." Ritcheson, believing there was a real possibility of mutual understanding which Morris bungled, deplores Morris's confidences to La Luzerne, his association with Fox, and his high demeanor with Leeds and Pitt: he was "too stiff and unbending"; he "overplayed his hand and ruined his usefulness in London." (Hamilton's own response was quite similar.) Boyd, with the object of exhibiting everywhere the duplicity and deceit of Hamilton, devotes a chapter to arguing that the story of Morris's behavior was really fabricated by Hamilton and put into Beckwith's mouth in Hamilton's report of conversations in which Morris's mission had been mentioned. Combs, while

open-minded, is skeptical of so elaborate a theory (which seems to assume that Beckwith's reports were complete—whereas they were fragmentary—and which depends on what Beckwith did not say rather than what he did say) and doubts that Hamilton made the story up. It almost certainly came through Beckwith, and Hamilton was only too ready to believe Morris had botched something otherwise promising. Common sense strongly suggests that Combs is right. Bemis, *Jay's Treaty*, p. 84; Ritcheson, *Aftermath of Revolution*, p. 102; Boyd, *Number 7*, pp. 66–72; Combs, *Jay Treaty*, pp. 52–55.

In any case *persona non grata* is much too strong a term. Morris with his airs was undoubtedly irritating. But whether he was or was not probably made no more than a marginal difference, except to give the British one more reason for temporizing. On this point Morris himself is probably his own best defense. Writing to Robert Morris some time later, he said: "I will suppose it to be a very good Reason to be given to America for not conferring a *Favor* on her that the Man sent to ask it was disagreeable, no Matter from what Cause, but I trust they will never avow to the british Nation a Disposition to make Sacrifice of their Interests to please a pleasant Fellow." Davenport, ed., *Morris Diary*, I, 616.

28. Grenville on May 31 consulted Sir Frederick Haldimand, Dorchester's predecessor as Governor of Canada, about surrendering the posts, and was told that it could be done with safety; "if the Americans insisted upon having the posts," Haldimand said, "a merit should be made of giving them up." *Canadian Archives, 1889,* p. 287; Burt, *U.S., Great Britain, British North America,* pp. 111–112. Morris himself quickly got wind of these and similar inquiries about the posts. Davenport, ed., *Morris Diary,* I, 530, 542–543; Morris to Washington, May 29, 1790, *ASP:FR,* I, 125. Grenville still wanted, however, to provide guarantees for the fur trade and for a peaceful frontier, and it was with reference to these concerns that he devised his Indian barrier state idea. On this project see Bemis, *Jay's Treaty,* Ch. 6.

29. Morris returned to London in December for another visit, and was unable to see Leeds at all. He did, however, confer with the Undersecretary, James Bland Burges, who told him that it had been decided to send a minister but that this in turn depended on Hawkesbury's forthcoming report. "When received, no time would be lost in setting all the different engines at work. Hoped we would soon have residents with each other, &c. &c. &c." Morris to Jefferson, Dec. 28, 1790, *PTJ,* XVIII, 367–368.

30. The most extreme statement is Boyd, *Number 7.*

31. This is the argement of Ritcheson, *Aftermath of Revolution.*

32. Conversations with Beckwith in which these matters were raised may be found in *Canadian Archives, 1890,* pp. 126, 127, 150, 161, 163, 164, 171, 172. Hamilton did not directly refer to the separationist movements, but in emphasizing the United States' need for access to the Mississippi, which he did repeatedly, he made it clear that this was important in order to hold the western provinces. He also made it clear on several occasions that the United States would tolerate no outside interference in its efforts to make peace with the Indians.

33. Malone, *Jefferson,* II, 319, 331–332; Report on Relations with Great Britain, Dec. 15, 1790, *PTJ,* XVIII, 302.

34. Malone, *Jefferson,* II, 337.

35. *ASP:FR,* I, 13–15; *AC,* 1 Cong., 3 Sess., 1789, 1791, 1792–1797; Washington to Madison, Dec. 11, 1790; *PJM,* XIII, 311–314, 316–318.

36. *PTJ,* XVIII, 301–303, 423–436, 565–570; XIX, 206–220.

37. *PTJ,* XVIII, 232–233; *DHFFC,* III, 728; *PTJ,* XVIII, 304–307, 237; *ASP:FR,* I, 128; *PTJ,* XVIII, 237; *DHFFC,* III, 734.

38. *PAH,* VII, 210–236, 256–342.

39. Cf. Madison to Hamilton, Nov. 9, 1789, *ibid.,* V, 525–527; *DHFFC,* I, 656; Maclay, *Journal,* pp. 381–383, 385–391, 398–399, 401. The debate is discussed in Kenneth Bowling, "Politics in the First Congress, 1789–1791" (Unpub. diss., U. of Wisconsin, 1968), pp. 237–240.

40. See above, pp. 117–118. As long as securities were significantly below par they remained a speculation, and a holder who sold them gave up the benefits of further appreciation. Once they reached par, however, their speculative value would drop sharply. They might continue to appreciate, but no more than marginally and temporarily, and would now become a good investment paying dependable interest. They could thereupon be readily exchanged in the European money market for specie if one wished to invest one's capital in a mercantile or industrial venture.

41. For details of the bank's charter as Hamilton conceived it see Report, *PAH,* VII, 334–337. The combined capital of the three state banks then in existence was hardly over $2 million. See Forrest McDonald, *Alexander Hamilton: A Biography* (New York, 1979), pp. 189–210.

42. David Hume, *Essays Moral, Political and Literary,* T. H. Green and T. H. Grose, eds. (London, 1882), I, 311–312, 339–340; cf. Report, *PAH,* VII, 306–307, and Adam Smith, *An Inquiry into the Nature and Causes of the Wealth of Nations* (New York, Modern Library ed., 1937), pp. 304–305; Charles F. Dunbar, *Economic Essays* (New York, 1904), p. 92; Bray Hammond, *Banks and Politics in America, from the Revolution to the Civil War* (Princeton, N.J., 1957), pp. 128–134. The best and most comprehensive discussion of the influences behind Hamilton's plan is the editors' introductory note in *PAH,* VII, 236–256. The ratio paid by private subscribers was three-fourths federal securities to one-fourth specie, but the government's contribution was to be entirely in specie, which changed the proportion of securities in the total capital from three-fourths to three-fifths.

43. E.g., the tontine and sinking fund proposed in his first Report on the Public Credit of Jan. 9, 1790. See Dunbar, *Economic Essays,* pp. 77–79, 82–88.

44. However, "in the conduct of the affairs of this country," as Pitt himself once said to Henry Dundas, "there should be an avowed and real minister possessing the chief weight in council and the principal place in the confidence of the King. . . . That power must rest with the person generally called the First Minister; and that Minister ought . . . to be at the head of the finances." Qu. in Ehrman, *Pitt,* I, 281. "It is worth while to remark," observes Dunbar, ". . . that, under the early practice of our government, the Secretary of the Treasury occupied a position more nearly like that of an English Chancellor of the Exchequer than the present spirit of Congress would allow." *Economic Essays,* p. 71.

45. Ehrman, *Pitt,* I, 157–158. William Bingham to Hamilton, Nov. 25, 1789; Samuel Paterson to Hamilton, Sept. 30, 1790; *PAH,* V, 547–548, VII, 81–82.

46. Ehrman, *Pitt,* I, 239–275.

47. *PAH,* V, 488. "It struck me," wrote a Scottish admirer to Hamilton in sending him some materials on British finance, "that Great Genius, Might like to See the Works of their Cotemporrys. Mr. Pitt many in Britain think, to be too desirous of Ruling among the Nations, to be able to reduce the Nationall Debts, tho the Resources of this Country are very great. I am happy to have the opinions I had of the Resources of your Country Confirmed by the Perusall of your Speech." Samuel Paterson to Hamilton, Sept. 30, 1790, *ibid.,* VII, 82.

48. *DHFFC,* I, 516, 522, 536; Maclay, *Journal,* pp. 364, 368–374; *AC,* 1 Cong., 3 Sess., 1738, 1739, 1741, 1745, 1746, 1748, 1873, 1875, 1891–1894. There is a convenient reprinting

of the congressional proceedings, together with other material, in Matthew St. C. Clarke and D. A. Hall, eds., *Legislative and Documentary History of the Bank of the United States, Including the Original Bank of North America* (New York, 1967). See also *DHFFC*, IV, 164–215.

49. *AC*, 1 Cong., 3 Sess., 1891, 1936; Maclay, *Journal*, p. 368. For the debate on the Bank see Benjamin B. Klubes, "The First Federal Congress and the First National Bank: A Case Study in Constitutional Interpretation," *Journal of the Early Republic*, X (Spring 1990), 19–41.

50. Bowling, "Politics in the First Congress," pp. 233–236; Fisher Ames to George R. Minot, Feb. 17, 1791, *WFA*, I, 95–96; William L. Smith, *The Politicks and Views of a Certain Party, Displayed* (Philadelphia, 1792), pp. 16–17.

51. *AC*, 1 Cong., 3 Sess., 1894–1902. A supplementary act passed in the closing days of the session delayed the opening of subscriptions until July 4, 1791, and made 3 percent federal securities, as well as 6 percents, receivable for subscriptions. Contrary to Hamilton's own recommendations, the original Senate bill included a provision for branches—though Madison did not regard this as meeting his objections to a single bank. Stuart W. Bruchey, "Alexander Hamilton and the State Banks," *WMQ*, 3rd Ser., XXVII (July 1970), 349–378; *PAH*, IX, 538–539; *PJM*, XIII, 372–381. Contrary to Madison's prognostications, all federal securities began to rise about June 1; their price was sharply stimulated when Bank scrip went on sale July 4; and the 6 percents reached par by the beginning of August and continued upward. "Madison here reveals himself weak," observes Joseph S. Davis, "both as psychologist and as economist." *Essays in the Earlier History of American Corporations* (Cambridge, Mass., 1917), I, 202n. See esp. graphs in *ibid.*, 187, 210.

52. *AC*, 1 Cong., 3 Sess., 1903–1909.

53. Sedgwick's speech was made on Feb. 4, Gerry's on Feb. 7. *Ibid.*, 1910, 1914, 1945–1954.

54. *Ibid.*, 1919–1928. See also *Federalist*, Cooke ed., pp. 303–305.

55. *AC*, 1 Cong., 3 Sess., 1956–1960; Elizabeth Fleet, ed., "Madison's 'Detached Memoranda,'" *WMQ*, 3rd Ser., III (Oct. 1946), 542; *PJM*, XIII, 383–388.

56. Clarke and Hall, eds., *Documentary History*, pp. 86–91.

57. *Ibid.*, pp. 91–94; *PTJ*, XIX, 275–280.

58. Washington had enclosed them both with his letter of request; Washington to Hamilton, Feb. 16, 1791, *PAH*, VIII, 50.

59. *Ibid.*, 63–134.

60. Neither Jefferson's nor Madison's biographer makes any effort to defend their opinions; see Malone, *Jefferson*, II, 341–344; Brant, *Madison*, III, 331–332. But see also Klubes, cited in n. 49 above.

61. Madison to Jefferson, May 1, 1791, *PJM*, XIV, 16.

62. The text of Jefferson's 1784 plan is in *PTJ*, VII, 194–202. *Journals of the Continental Congress*, XXXI, 876–878.

63. C. Doris Hellman, "Jefferson's Efforts Toward the Decimalization of U.S. Weights and Measures," *Isis*, XVI (Nov. 1931), 266–314; Malone, *Jefferson*, II, 276–281; Broadus Mitchell, *Alexander Hamilton* (New York, 1957, 1962), II, 118–122; *PTJ*, XVI, 650–655; Jefferson to Hamilton, Dec. 29, 1790, Jan. 24, 1791, *PTJ*, XVIII, 459–460.

64. Report on the Establishment of a Mint, Jan. 28, 1791, *PAH*, VII, 570–607.

65. *Ibid.*, 573ff.

66. Jefferson to Hamilton, Jan. 24, 1791, *PTJ*, XVIII, 460.

67. Hamilton to Edward Carrington, May 26, 1792, *PAH*, XI, 434–435; *WGW*, XXXI, 403; *Statutes at Large*, I, 246–251.

68. Cf. *PAH*, VII, 389–390, 408, 423–424, 425–426, 451–452; VIII, 26, 179–180, 234–235, 268, 278–279, 284–286, 289–290, 330, 450, 503–504.

69. Jefferson to Mason, Feb. 4, 1791; to Innes, Mar. 7, 13, 1791; *PTJ*, XIX, 241–242, 521–522, 542–543.

70. Malone, *Jefferson*, II, 354–359.

71. "Colo. Hamilton & Colo. Beckwith are open-mouthed against me, taking it in another view, as likely to give offence to the court of London. H. adds further that it makes my opposition to the government. Thus endeavoring to turn [upon] the government itself those censures I meant for the enemies of the government, to wit those who want to change it into a monarchy." Jefferson to Madison, May 9, 1791, *PTJ*, XX, 293–294.

72. Jefferson to Washington, May 8, 1791; to Adams, July 17, Aug. 30, 1791; Adams to Jefferson, July 29, 1791; *ibid.*, 291–292, 302–303, 310–312, 305–307. Madison had already told Jefferson, having heard it from Beckley, that "Publicola" was John Quincy Adams. Madison to Jefferson, June 23, July 13, 1791, *PJM*, XIV, 35–36, 46–47; Malone, *Jefferson*, II, 363–370.

73. Jefferson to Washington, Sept. 9, 1792, *PTJ*, XXIV, 356; see also Editorial Note and correspondence, *ibid.*, XX, 718–759.

74. Lewis Leary, *That Rascal Freneau: A Study in Literary Failure* (New Brunswick, N.J., 1941), p. 84.

75. *Ibid.*, pp. 113, 115.

76. *Ibid.*, p. 189.

77. Jefferson to Freneau, Feb. 28, 1791; Freneau to Jefferson, Mar. 5, 1791; *PTJ*, XX, 351, 416–417. Madison to Jefferson, May 1, 1791, *PJM*, XIV, 14–16. Jefferson to Madison, May 9, 1791; to Thomas Mann Randolph, May 15, 1791; *PTJ*, XX, 293, 414–416. Madison to Jefferson, July 10, 1791, *PJM*, XIV, 42–44. Jefferson to Madison, July 21, 1791, *PTJ*, XX, 657. Madison to Jefferson, July 24, 1791; Freneau to Madison, July 25, 1791; Madison to Charles Simons and Mann Page, Aug. 1, 1791; *PJM*, XIV, 52–53, 57, 72–73. Freneau to Jefferson, Aug. 4, 1791, *PTJ*, 754. Madison to James Madison, Sr., Nov. 13, 1791; to Henry Lee, Dec. 18, 1791; *PJM*, XIV, 106–107, 154–155. Malone, *Jefferson*, II, 423–427. Brant, *Madison*, III, 334–336.

78. Jefferson to Madison, July 10, 1791, *PTJ*, XX, 616. Madison wrote: "I wish you success with all my heart in your efforts for Payne. Besides the advantage to him which he deserves, an appointment for him, at this moment would do public good in various ways." To Jefferson, July 13, 1791, *PJM*, XIV, 47. On August 12 Timothy Pickering of Massachusetts was appointed to replace the retiring Samuel Osgood as Postmaster-General.

79. Jefferson to Livingston, Feb. 4, 1791; Livingston to Jefferson, Feb. 20, 1791; *PTJ*, XIX, 240–241, 295–296.

80. Claude G. Bowers, *Jefferson and Hamilton* (Boston, 1925), p. 108. Bowers made nothing of this particular trip, but he devoted a whole chapter ("Jefferson Mobilizes," pp. 140–160) to creating an impression of purposeful state-to-state organizing by Jefferson and his "lieutenants" during the early 1790s. An example of the results, in a popular textbook: "On a 'botanizing excursion' that led Jefferson and Madison up the Hudson in the summer [sic] of 1791, they undoubtedly found occasion to study *Clintonia borealis* and other hardy perennials in Ulster County and the neighborhood of Albany." Samuel E. Morison and Henry S. Commager, *The Growth of the American Republic* (New York, 1942), I, 343.

81. See discussion in Alfred F. Young, *The Democratic Republicans of New York: The Origins, 1763–1797* (Chapel Hill, N.C., 1967), pp. 194–201; see also editorial note, *PTJ*, XX, 434–445.

82. They had in fact discussed such subjects in their epistolary exchange of February. (See n. 79 above.)

83. George Dangerfield, *Chancellor Robert R. Livingston of New York, 1746–1813* (New York, 1960), pp. 241–255.

84. Troup to Hamilton, June 15, 1791, *PAH*, VIII, 478–479; Bemis, *Jay's Treaty*, p. 115 and nn.

85. Davis, *American Corporations*, I, 202–212. Except, that is, for a brief dip in March 1792, which Hamilton remedied with purchases from the sinking fund.

86. Jefferson to Monroe, July 10, 1791; to Pendleton, July 24, 1791; to Madison, July 24, 1791; *PTJ*, XX, 298, 669–670, 666–667. Jefferson arrived at his figure of "13 per cent" by adding 7 percent (the dividend he assumed the Bank would pay) and 6 percent (the interest on one of the classes of federal securities receivable for Bank stock) and concluding that this combined amount was what the public would be paying for circulation of the Bank's notes. But the 6 percent was an incident not of banking and currency but of the public debt, which was there already and would not have been altered one way or the other by a bank, while the 7 percent represented profits from the Bank's commercial activities. Another way of putting this would be that the convenience of a circulating medium (the Bank's notes) was being paid for not by the public at large but by those specific persons who borrowed money from the Bank.

In this connection it might be noted that the Bank itself probably never received anywhere near the amount of actual specie which the embodying act specified for payment of its shares. By the time subsequent installments were due, the Bank had already opened for business, and since the Bank's notes were defined as the equivalent of specie it would be logical that those notes should have constituted the bulk of what was accepted for that portion of the payment (one-fourth) not covered by federal securities (three-fourths) in payment for Bank stock. See Hammond, *Banks and Politics*, pp. 123–143.

87. Madison to Jefferson, July 10, Aug. 4, 8, 1791, *PJM*, XIV, 42–43, 65, 69.

88. Jefferson to Rutledge, Aug. 25, 1791, *PTJ*, XXII, 73–75.

89. There is no biography of George Hammond. See the brief article by Sidney Lee in *Dictionary of National Biography*, ed. Sir Leslie Stephen and Sir Sidney Lee (Oxford, 1885–1901), VIII, 1125–1126; "King George's First Envoy," in Beckles Willson, *Friendly Relations: A Narrative of Britain's Ministers and Ambassadors to America (1791–1930)* (Boston, 1934), pp. 3–18; and Leslie Reade, "'George III to the United States Sendeth Greeting . . . ,'" *History Today*, VIII (Nov. 1958), 770–780. On Thornton, see S. W. Jackman, ed., "A Young Englishman Reports on the New Nation: Edward Thornton to James Bland Burges, 1791–1793," *WMQ*, 3rd Ser., XVIII (Jan. 1961), 85–121. The "rosey-faced" characterization is that of Williamina Bond Cadwalader (sister of P. Bond) in a letter to her sister, cited in Beckles Willson, p. 6. On Hammond's relations with Bond see Joanne L. Neel, *Phineas Bond: A Study in Anglo-American Relations, 1786–1812* (Philadelphia, 1968), pp. 85ff.

90. Liston to Henry Cunningham, qu. in Willson, *Friendly Relations*, p. 19.

91. Qu. in *ibid.*, p. 17.

92. See above, pp. 216–217, 221; Ritcheson, *Aftermath of Revolution*, pp. 138ff.; and editorial note, *PTJ*, XVIII, 220–283.

93. There was a limited printing of this report, subsequently recalled; it was, however, later repr. in *Collection of Interesting and Important Reports and Papers on the Navigation and Trade of Great Britain, Ireland, and the British Colonies in the West Indies and America* (London, 1807). An abstract of it found its way into Jefferson's hands and is preserved in his papers. It was this abstract (not the original) that was later repr. by Worthington C.

Ford under the title *Report of a Committee of the Lords of the Privy Council on the Trade of Great Britain with the United States* (Washington, 1888). See also *PTJ*, XVIII, 267–272. Hawkesbury's draft instructions and Grenville's final ones are printed in IBM, pp. 2–19.

94. On the differences between Hawkesbury's and Grenville's points of view see Ritcheson, *Aftermath of Revolution*, pp. 141–142.

95. See, e.g., Brymner, *Report on Canadian Archives, 1890*, p. 140; Hammond to Grenville, Apr. 2, 1793, PRO:FO 5/1.

96. Same to same, Oct. 23, Nov. 1, 16, 1791 (Dispatches 1, 2, 4), PRO:FO 4/11, II; same to same, Nov. 1, 1791 (private), *Manuscripts of J. B. Fortescue, Esq., Preserved at Dropmore* (London, 1894), II, 223.

97. Jefferson to Hammond, Nov. 29, 1791, *PTJ*, XXII, 352–353; Thornton to James B. Burges, Dec. 5, 1791, Jackman, ed., "Young Englishman," p. 95.

98. Hammond to Jefferson, Nov. 30, 1791, *PTJ*, XXII, 356–357.

99. Jefferson to Hammond, Dec. 5, 1791, *ibid.*, 378–379.

100. Hammond to Jefferson, Dec. 6, 1791; Jefferson to Hammond, Dec. 13, 1791; Hammond to Jefferson, Dec. 14, 1791; *ibid.*, 380–381, 399, 402–403.

101. Hammond to Grenville, Dec. 6, 19, 1791 (Dispatches 8, 13), PRO:FO 4/11, III.

102. Benjamin Hawkins to Jefferson, Mar. 26, 1792, *PTJ*, XXIII, 342–343.

103. Even after it had become evident that a minister would shortly be on his way, Jefferson told Edward Rutledge that the British had "no serious view of treating or fulfilling treaties," and his sayings to this effect reached the ears of Hammond and Thornton soon after they arrived. Meanwhile he continued to hope that a navigation act against British commerce could be passed, and had requested American representatives in Europe to do what they could to persuade the governments of France, Spain, and Portugal to take similar action. Jefferson had his report on commerce with Great Britain (with its recommendations of measures the United States ought to take) largely ready by December 1791, but at a cabinet meeting during that month Hamilton successfully urged that the report be withheld on the ground that it would embarrass the negotiations Jefferson was about to begin with Hammond. Jefferson to Rutledge, Aug. 25, 1791, *PTJ*, XXII, 73–75; Hammond to Grenville, Nov. 16, 1791 (Private), *Dropmore*, II, 229; Thornton to Burges, Dec. 5, 1791, Jackson, ed., "Young Englishman," 95–96; Hammond to Grenville, Dec. 6, 19, 1791, Jan. 9, 1792 (Dispatches 8, 13, 3), PRO:FO 4/11, II–III, 4/14, I; Jefferson to David Humphreys, Mar. 15, 1791, and to William Carmichael, Mar. 17, 1791, *PTJ*, XIX, 572–574, 574–575; Jefferson to Speaker of House of Representatives, Feb. 22, 1792, and Jefferson, Memorandum of Mar. 11, 1792, *ibid.*, XXIII, 143, 258–262. On Jefferson's hopes for an arrangement with France, see "Questions to be Considered Of," Nov. 26, 1791, *ibid.*, XXII, 344.

104. Jefferson to Hammond, Dec. 15, 1791; Hammond to Jefferson, Dec. 19, 1791; *PTJ*, XX, 409–411, 422.

105. *ASP:IA*, I, 137–138.

106. Hammond to Grenville, Dec. 19, 1791 (Dispatch 13), PRO:FO 4/11, III; also *PAH*, X, 373–374; "Conversation with George Beckwith, May 15, 1791," *ibid.*, VIII, 342–343, and Brymner, *Report on Canadian Archives, 1890*, p. 388.

107. Hammond to Grenville, Jan. 9, 1792 (Dispatch 3), PRO:FO 4/14, II; also *PAH*, X, 493–496.

108. Hammond to Jefferson, Mar. 5, 1792, *PTJ*, XXIII, 196–212.

109. Jefferson to Hammond, May 29, 1792, *ibid.*, 551–601; Bemis, *Jay's Treaty*, pp. 140, 144; Peterson, *Jefferson*, p. 453; Malone, *Jefferson*, II, 412, 414.

110. Hamilton to Jefferson, May [20–27], 1792, *PAH,* XI, 408–414; Madison's Notes on Jefferson's Letter to Hammond [ca. May 16, 1792], *PTJ,* XXIII, 514–516.

111. Hammond to Jefferson, June 2, 1792, *PTJ,* XXIV, 17–18. Hammond to Grenville, June 8, 1792 (Dispatch 22), PRO:FO 4/15; excerpt repr. in *PAH,* XI, 454–455.

112. No British debts were collected in Virginia until 1793. An arbitration committee was established under the Jay Treaty of 1794, and the United States government would eventually pay £600,000 in 1802 to settle these claims. Ritcheson, *Aftermatch of Revolution,* pp. 238–241; Charles F. Hobson, "The Recovery of British Debts in the Federal Circuit Court of Virginia, 1790 to 1797," *Virginia Magazine of History and Biography,* XCII (Mar. 1984), 176–200. See also *PJnMl,* V, 259–263.

113. Malone, *Jefferson,* II, 410; *PTJ,* XXIV, 301.

114. Hammond to Grenville, June 8, 1792 (Dispatch 22), PRO:FO 4/15; Jefferson to Madison, June 4, 1792, *PJM,* XIV, 314–315.

115. Grenville to Hammond, Mar. 17, 1792, IBM, pp. 25–26; Hammond to Grenville, June 8, 1792 (Dispatch 23), PRO:FO 4/15; *PAH,* XI, 446–447.

116. Grenville, in acknowledging receipt of Jefferson's letter, said he would "defer entering into any particular Consideration of that Paper at present," inasmuch as he was turning it over to Phineas Bond (then in London on leave) for his comments. He assured Hammond meanwhile "of His Majesty's gracious and entire Approbation of the prudent Conduct you have held upon this Occasion. . . ." Bond submitted his report to Grenville in the fall of 1792. War broke out between Great Britain and France on February 1, 1793, and the questions under discussion were not resumed until the arrival of John Jay in England in June 1794. Grenville to Hammond, Aug. 4, 1792, IBM, pp. 30–31; Bond to Grenville, Oct. 12, 1792, J. Franklin Jameson, ed., "Letters of Phineas Bond to the Foreign Office, 1787–89," *AHA:AR 1896,* I, 512.

117. [Oliver Wolcott], *British Influence on the Affairs of the United States, Proved and Explained* (Boston, 1804), pp. 14–15.

CHAPTER VII

The Emergence of Partisan Politics

1. Washington, First Annual Message to Congress, Jan. 8, 1790, *WGW,* XXX, 493; *House Journal,* I, 141–142.

2. Report on the Subject of Manufactures, *PAH,* X, 230–231.

3. *Ibid.,* 231–235.

4. *Ibid.,* 236–259.

5. *Ibid.,* 261–263.

6. *Ibid.,* 266–269.

7. *Ibid.,* 274–282.

8. *Ibid.,* 293–296.

9. *Ibid.,* 296–340.

10. See above, pp. 107–108.

11. Peter F. Drucker, "On the 'Economic Basis' of American Politics," *The Public Interest,* No. 10 (Winter 1968), 35; *PAH,* X, 260. For a modern formulation in certain ways reminiscent of the report, see the discussion of "backward and forward linkage" in Albert O. Hirschman, *The Strategy of Economic Development* (New Haven, Conn., 1958), 98–119.

12. On Coxe's role in the preparation both of the Society's prospectus and of the *Report on Manufactures* see Joseph S. Davis, *Essays in the Earlier History of American Corporations* (Cambridge, Mass., 1917), I, 349–357; Introductory Note, *PAH*, X, 10–12; and Jacob E. Cooke, *Tench Coxe and the Early Republic* (Chapel Hill, 1978), pp. 182–200.

13. *PAH*, IX, 144ff.; Davis, *Essays*, I, 360.

14. *Ibid.*, 372–375.

15. *Ibid.*, 377–378.

16. *Ibid.*, 408.

17. Richard Hofstadter, *The Idea of a Party System: The Rise of Legitimate Opposition in the United States, 1780–1840* (Berkeley, Calif., 1970), p. 3.

18. *Ibid.*, pp. 8–10ff.

19. See above, pp. 86–87.

20. "Thoughts on the Cause of the Present Discontents" (1770), *The Works of the Right Honorable Edmund Burke*, 5th ed. (Boston, 1877), I, 526.

21. For a good discussion of this phase in the the political life of Virginia see Richard P. Beeman, *The Old Dominion and the New Nation, 1788–1801* (Lexington, Ky., 1973), esp. pp. 56–118.

22. Mason to Jefferson, Jan. 10, 1791; Jefferson to Mason, Feb. 4, 1791; *PTJ*, XVIII, 484, XIX, 242.

23. The complete series of eighteen essays, with titles and the dates on which they appeared, are repr. in *PJM*, XIV, 117–122, 137–139, 170, 178–179, 191–192, 197–198, 201–202, 206–208, 217–218, 233–234, 244–246, 257–259, 266–268, 274–275, 370–372, 426–427; I, 302–309; XVII, 559–560; see also Editorial Note, XIV, 110–112. For another discussion of two of these essays, "Parties," and "A Candid State of Parties," see Hofstadter, *Idea of a Party System*, pp. 80–86.

24. *PJM*, XIV, 197–198.

25. *Ibid.*, 274–275.

26. *Ibid.*, 370–372.

27. "Republican Distribution of Citizens," *ibid.*, 244–246.

28. *Ibid.*, 426–427.

29. Ames to George R. Minot, Feb. 16, 1792, *WFA*, I, 112.

30. Freeman, *Washington*, VI, 336–341; *ASP:FR*, I, 137–138; Francis P. Prucha, *The Sword of the Republic: The United States Army on the Frontier, 1783–1846* (New York, 1969), pp. 22–27; Henry Lee to Madison, Dec. 8, 1791, Madison to Lee, Dec. 18, 1791, *PJM*, XIV, 144, 155.

31. *National Gazette*, Dec. 19, 22, 1791; William H. Smith, ed., *The St. Clair Papers: The Life and Public Service of Arthur St. Clair* (Cincinnati, 1882), II, 267–269.

32. *Philadelphia American Daily Advertiser, Newark Gazette, Connecticut Courant,* all repr. in *National Gazette*, Jan. 9, 12, 26, 1792; *Boston Gazette*, Dec. 26, 1791, qu. in Donald R. Stewart, *The Opposition Press of the Federalist Period* (Albany, N.Y., 1969), pp. 58–59. See also *ibid.*, pp. 65, 359–360; and speeches in Congress, *AC*, 2 Cong., 1 Sess., 337–338. Another useful summary of opinion as found in newspapers and other writings is in Freeman, *Washington*, VI, 340–341, fn. 91.

33. Letter from Albany, repr. in *National Gazette*, Jan. 9, 1792; *AC*, 2 Cong., 1 Sess., 338–342; Stewart, *Opposition Press*, p. 361.

34. *National Gazette*, Jan. 9, 19, 23, Feb. 2, 1792; *AC*, 2 Cong., 1 Sess., 343–355; Jefferson to Washington, Apr. 17, 1791, *PTJ*, XX, 145. To Monroe Jefferson wrote, "I hope we shall drub the Indians well this summer & then change our plan from war to bribery." Apr. 17, 1791, *PTJ*, XX, 234. Stewart, *Opposition Press*, pp. 360–361, appears to

be mistaken in asserting, "Federalists urged a larger regular force for protection, but Eastern Democrats were fiercely opposed." Sentiment on this question did not divide along "party" lines, as may be seen from the *National Gazette* and from the congressional debates. Freneau gave space in his paper to all viewpoints on the Indian war, but his own seems to have been similar to those of the Virginians and of his former Princeton classmate, the ultra-hawkish Brackenridge. On the other hand, though Freeman's statement (*Washington*, VI, 340) that "no sharp political issue developed from this debate" is technically correct, it is being argued here that while the debate itself was not a partisan one, its side-effects and the climate of recrimination it created did much to prepare the partisan atmosphere that followed, with regard not only to the tariff act of 1792 (raising additional revenue for military purposes) but to a range of other issues as well.

35. To Mrs. Pickering, Jan. 7, 1792, Octavius Pickering and Charles W. Upham, *The Life of Timothy Pickering* (Boston, 1867–1873), III, 23. ("For my own part," Pickering added, "I, from the beginning, regretted the *commencement* of the war, as a thing not of *inevitable* necessity. But perhaps I am mistaken.") "The foes of the Secretary at War," wrote Fisher Ames, "have not been idle." Ames to Thomas Dwight, Jan. 13, 1792, *WFA*, I, 109. "Poor honest Knox seems to be seriously struck at," Henry Lee observed, though he added that to some extent Knox had it coming: "repeated heavy calamitys demand on the part of govt. minute enquiry into the conduct of those entrusted with the preparation & execution of the measures which have terminated in disaster." Lee to Madison, Jan. 17, 1792, *PJM*, XIV, 189. Stewart, *Opposition Press*, pp. 61, 360; Davis, *Essays*, I, 259–263; House Committee Report, "Causes of the Failure of the Expedition Against the Indians," May 8, 1792, and supplementary report, Feb. 15, 1793, *ASP:MA*, I, 36–44. On Washington's handling of St. Clair's resignation and the appointment of Wayne see Freeman, *Washington*, VI, 341–342; and *St. Clair Papers*, II, 282–286.

36. Davis, *Essays*, I, 113–114; Robert F. Jones, *"The King of the Alley": William Duer, Politician, Entrepreneur, and Speculator, 1768–1799* (Philadelphia, 1992), pp. 1–15.

37. Davis, *Essays*, I, 114–117.

38. *Ibid.*, 118–123.

39. Miniature by Charles Willson Peale, painted in 1780; reproduced in Clarence Bowen, ed., *History of the Centennial Celebration of the Inauguration of George Washington* ... (New York, 1892); a line drawing made from it is in *National Cyclopaedia of American Biography*, VII, 503.

40. Manasseh Cutler, qu. in Davis, *Essays*, I, 126. Jones (*Duer*, pp. 129–134) estimates that Duer realized somewhere between $250,000 and $370,000 in federal dollars from his speculations in government securities while employed in the Treasury.

41. "The Deane Papers," iv, *Collections of the New-York Historical Society* (New York, 1890), XXII, 168; Davis, *Essays*, I, 129.

42. *Ibid.*, 124–150, 213–253.

43. *Ibid.*, 259–263.

44. *Ibid.*, 205–207; Hamilton to Duer, Aug. 17, 1791, *PAH*, IX, 74–75.

45. *AC*, 2 Cong., 1 Sess., 51, 362; Henry Cabot Lodge, *Life and Letters of George Cabot* (Boston, 1877), pp. 38–39, 40–42, 46–54.

46. *AC*, 2 Cong., 1 Sess., 363–364.

47. *Ibid.*, 376.

48. *Ibid.*, 381.

49. *Ibid.*, 369.

50. *Ibid.*, 383.

51. *Ibid.*, 385–389.

52. *Ibid.*, 374, 400–401. From the original language of the bill it would seem that the term "bounty" with respect to the fisheries was not an innovation at all but had been in use, at least informally, since the Revenue Act of 1789. That Act had provided for a unit payment on fish exported from the United States "in lieu of a drawback of the duties imposed on the importation of salt employed and expended therein," and the payment was increased by the Act of Aug. 10, 1790. The intent of the present measure was simply to benefit the fishermen more directly by transferring "the bounty *now allowed*" (our italics) from the fish exported to the vessels employed. *Ibid.*, 362; William H. Michael and Pitman Pulsifer, eds., *Tariff Acts Passed by the Congress of the United States from 1789 to 1895, Including All Acts, Resolutions, and Proclamations Modifying or Changing Those Acts* (Washington, 1896), pp. 11, 13. Ames to Thomas Dwight, Jan. 30, 1792, *WFA*, I, 112.

53. *AC*, 2 Cong., 1 Sess., 437, 439–440, 442, 452; Hamilton to Edward Carrington, May 26, 1792, *PAH*, XI, 433.

54. "Report Relative to the Additional Supplies for the Ensuing Year," Mar. 16, 1792, *ibid.*, 139–149; *AC*, 2 Cong., 1 Sess., 349–354. This speech is mistakenly reported under the date of Jan. 27; it could only have been delivered sometime between Apr. 17 and 21, 1792.

55. *Ibid.*, 569, 572.

56. Davis, *Essays*, I, 279–289.

57. *Ibid.*, 290–295. Duer to Hamilton, Mar. 12, 1792; Hamilton to Duer, Mar. 14, 23, 1792; Robert Troup to Hamilton, Mar. 19, 1792, *PAH*, XI, 126, 131–132, 155–158. Jones, *Duer*, pp. 176–178.

58. Seth Johnson to Andrew Craigie, Mar. 25, 1792; H. M. Colden to Jeremiah Wadsworth, Apr. 18, 1792; qu. in Davis, *Essays*, I, 296, 304. "It was reported here last night that there had been a collection of people round the place of Duer's confinement of so threatening an appearance as to call out the Governor and militia. . . ." Jefferson to Henry Remsen, Apr. 14, 1792, *PTJ*, XXIII, 426.

59. Davis, *Essays*, I, 310–315. Actually the program never did have much of a chance. Hamilton's agrarian opponents, in Virginia and in the South generally, were of course solidly against it on grounds of both ideology and interest. Meanwhile there was as yet no "manufacturing interest," in the sense that would come to characterize northern industry in the nineteenth century, though the masters of the numerous artisan establishments in the northern cities certainly favored a protective tariff for their products. Nevertheless the largest entrepreneurs of the day, those in shipping and overseas trade, and in whose business British manufactures played a very large part, tended to be less than wholeheartedly enthusiastic. Jacob E. Cooke, *Alexander Hamilton* (New York, 1982), pp. 101–102.

60. Material in this par. is drawn from Davis, *Essays*, I, 454–503.

61. Johnson to Craigie, Aug. 20, 1791, qu. in *ibid.*, 208, Oliver Wolcott to Oliver Wolcott, Sr., Jan. 30, 1792, Gibbs. *Memoirs*, I, 72.

62. Hirschman, *Strategy of Economic Development*, pp. 20–21.

63. On Holyoke, Lowell, Chicopee, Waltham, and other centers of manufacturing enterprise in early nineteenth-century New England see, e.g., Caroline F. Ware, *The Early New England Cotton Manufacture: A Study in Industrial Beginnings* (Boston, 1931); Vera Shlakman, *Economic History of a Factory Town: A Study of Chicopee, Mass.* (Northampton, 1935); and esp. Robert F. Dalzell, Jr., *Enterprising Elite: The Boston Associates and the World They Made* (Cambridge, Mass., 1987).

64. *National Gazette*, Jan. 12, 1792, Dec. 1, 1791.

65. *Ibid.*, Nov. 17, 24, 28, Dec. 1, 1791.

66. *Ibid.*, Dec. 26, 29, 1791, Jan. 2, 5, 9, 12, 1792.

67. See above, n. 23.

68. *National Gazette,* Mar. 15, 1792. Other "Brutus" papers appeared Mar. 19, 22, 26, Apr. 5, 9, 1792.

69. The "Farmer" appears to have been Dr. George Logan, a Philadelphia Republican and a strong opponent of Hamiltonian policies. His essays appeared intermittently in the *National Gazette* in March and April 1792 and were published in pamphlet form as *Five Letters addressed to the Yeomanry of the United States: Containing some Observations on the Dangerous Scheme of Governor Duer and Mr. Secretary Hamilton, to establish National Manufactories. By a Farmer* in August of that year.

70. The "Sidney" pieces appeared in the issues of Apr. 23, 26, 30, May 3, 7, 10, 17, 21, 24, 1792, of the *National Gazette.*

71. *Ibid.,* June 7, Apr. 26, May 7, 1792.

72. *Ibid.,* June 11, 1792. See also the elaborate "Rules for changing a limited Republican Government into an unlimited hereditary one," July 4, 7, 1792.

73. *Gazette of the United States,* June 9, 1792; *National Gazette,* June 11, 1792.

74. *Ibid.,* July 28, 1792; *Gazette of the United States,* Aug. 4, 8, 1792. Hamilton's third "T.L." letter appeared in *ibid.,* August 11, 1792.

75. There were three "American" letters (Aug. 4, 11, 18, 1792), six signed "Catullus" (Sept. 15, 19, 29, Oct. 17, Nov. 24, Dec. 22, 1792), and a single "Metellus" letter (Oct. 24, 1792), all in *Gazette of the United States.*

Other newspaper pieces published during this period have been attributed by Philip Marsh—though it seems mistakenly—to Hamilton: "Original Communications," June 27, 1792; "Detector," July 28, Aug. 23, 1792; "Candor," Aug. 18, 1792; "Scourge," Sept. 22, 1792; "Americanus," Oct. 20, 1792; and "C," Nov. 10, 1792; all in *ibid.* See Marsh, "Hamilton's Neglected Essays, 1791–1793," *New-York Historical Society Quarterly,* XXXII (Oct. 1948), 280–300; *idem,* "Further Attributions to Hamilton's Pen," *ibid.,* XL (Oct. 1956), 351–360; Malone, *Jefferson,* II, 470–473. The editors of *PAH,* however, find no evidence that Hamilton wrote any of these, and in the case of "Scourge" they have shown that the author was William Loughton Smith. See XI, 581–582; XII, 123, 225, 266, 411–412, 558; XIII, 33.

76. Jefferson to Edmund Randolph, Sept. 17, 1792, *PTJ,* XXIV, 387. Randolph wrote as "Aristides" in *Gazette of the United States,* Sept. 8, 1792, and perhaps in *National Gazette,* Sept. 26, 1792 (though the second "Aristides" letter may have been by someone else); Monroe and Madison collaborated on a series entitled "Vindication of Mr. Jefferson," which ran in the Philadelphia *American Daily Advertiser,* Sept. 22, Oct. 10, 13, 20, 30, Nov. 8, Dec. 3, 31, 1792, and which was reprinted in both the *National Gazette* and *Gazette of the United States.* The texts have been edited and published as a pamphlet by Philip Marsh, *Monroe's Defense of Jefferson and Freneau against Hamilton* (Oxford, Ohio, 1948). For the story of the "Vindication," and Jefferson's part in it, see Marsh, "'The Vindication of Mr. Jefferson,'" *South Atlantic Quarterly,* XLV (Jan. 1946), 61–67; *idem,* "Madison's Defense of Freneau," *WMQ,* 3rd Ser., III (Apr. 1946), 269–280; *idem,* "Monroe's Draft of the Defense of Freneau," *PMHB,* LXXI (Jan. 1947), 73–76; Malone, *Jefferson,* II, 475–476; Brant, *Madison,* III, 362–363.

77. *National Gazette,* Sept. 5, 12, Oct. 17, 1792. As "Amicus" Hamilton defended himself against the charge of having advocated monarchy at the Constitutional Convention. *Ibid.,* Sept. 12, 1792. *PAH,* XII, 320–327, 354–357, 570–571.

78. Jefferson to Washington, Sept. 9, 1792, *PTJ,* XXIV, 356.

79. *Gazette of the United States,* Aug. 8, 1792; *PAH,* XII, 188–189.

80. Jefferson to Washington, Sept. 9, 1792, *PTJ,* XXIV, 357.

81. *Ibid.*, 356; see above, n. 79. Over half a century later, Rufus Griswold published a story to the effect that Freneau in his old age had confessed in great remorse to having written articles in the *Gazette* against Washington which had been "dictated" by Jefferson. The story seems highly questionable, and Philip Marsh has persuasively discredited it. "The Griswold Story of Jefferson and Freneau," *AHR*, LI (Oct. 1945), 68–73.

82. Elisha Boudinot to Hamilton, Aug. 16, 1792. "This I know," Boudinot quoted his niece's husband, William Bradford, as saying, "that at the time I was in New-York, and was informed of Mr. J.'s writing him [Freneau] a letter, which he took in dudgeon, as striking at his independence, &c., and wrote a very insulting answer, which he showed to Mr. Childs, who prevented his sending it, &c.; and in fact related the whole story as I had it." *PAH*, XII, 210–211. Later on, after the *National Gazette* had been well launched, Jefferson seems on one occasion to have sent Freneau a clipping from Fenno's paper, perhaps with a hint that some comment on it might be in order. Freneau condescendingly replied that he might do so later, "when nothing more interesting offers." Lewis Leary, *That Rascal Freneau: A Study in Literary Failure* (New Brunswick, N.J., 1941), p. 389n.

83. E.g., Jefferson to Washington, Sept. 9, 1792, *PTJ*, XXIV, 354.

84. Particulars on Jefferson and the proposal to transfer the French loan are in Malone, *Jefferson*, II, 188–189, 470–471.

85. Hamilton to Carrington, May 26, 1792, *PAH*, XI, 426–445.

86. The quotations, in order, are from "Conversations with the President," Feb. 28, 29, July 10, 1792, and Jefferson to Washington, May 23, 1792, *WTJ*, I, 174, 177, 177–178, 200, XXIII, 537.

87. Washington to Hamilton, July 29, 1792, *PAH*, XII, 129–134. Hamilton acknowledged receipt of it on Aug. 3, 1792, *ibid.*, 139.

88. Qu. in Noble E. Cunningham, Jr., *The Jeffersonian Republicans: The Formation of Party Organization, 1789–1801* (Chapel Hill, 1957), p. 29.

89. *Ibid.*, pp. 33–49; on the Jay-Clinton election see Alfred F. Young, *The Democratic Republicans of New York: The Origins, 1763–1797* (Chapel Hill, N.C., 1967), pp. 304–323; and Carol R. Berkin, "The Disputed 1792 Gubernatorial Election in New York" (Unpub. M.A. thesis, Columbia U., 1966); Jefferson to Madison, June 21, 1792, and to Monroe, June 23, 1792, *PTJ*, XXIV, 105, 114–115; Brant, *Madison*, III, 364.

90. William Page to William Plumer, June 26, 1792, qu. in Cunningham, *Jeffersonian Republicans*, p. 34.

91. *Ibid.*, pp. 38ff.

92. Jefferson to Pinckney, Dec. 3, 1792, *PTJ*, XXIV, 696.

93. "Conversations with the President," July 10, 1792, *WTJ*, I, 199–200.

94. Memoranda of Conversations with the President, May 5, 9, 1792; Madison to Washington, June 20, 1792; *PJM*, XIV, 299–304, 319–324.

95. Washington to Jefferson, Aug. 23, 1792, *PTJ*, XXIV, 317; Hamilton, Aug. 26, 1792, *PAH*, XII, 276–277.

96. Hamilton to Washington, Sept. 9, 1792, *ibid.*, 347–349.

97. Jefferson to Washington, Sept. 9, 1792, *PTJ*, XXIV, 351–359.

98. Same to same, May 23, 1792, *ibid.*, XXIII, 539; Hamilton to Washington, July 30–Aug. 3, 1792, *PAH*, XII, 139.

99. Freeman, *Washington*, VI, 371, 378–379, 383–384.

100. Every detail presently known about the Reynolds affair is contained in *PAH*, XXI, 121–144, 215–285 and *passim*, in the form of (1) the pertinent correspondence of all the parties, with editorial annotation; (2) the original draft of Hamilton's "Reynolds Pamphlet," in which Hamilton offers his own account of the affair, together with the printed

version issued in 1797 (both also annotated); and (3) most useful of all, an impressive scholarly essay by Barbara Chernow, an Introductory Note of twenty-four closely printed pages, which performs the valuable service of examining all the evidence for every variation of the story that has been advanced from that time to the present. Less successful in this respect is a similar though somewhat curious undertaking by Julian Boyd in *PTJ*, XVIII, 611–688 (curious, in that Jefferson had nothing directly to do with the episode), whose principal object seems to be that of proving Hamilton guilty of financial misconduct. An earlier discussion is Broadus Mitchell, *Alexander Hamilton: The National Adventure, 1788– 1804* (New York, 1962), II, 399–422, which assumes that the story's main outlines were more or less what Hamilton said they were. Dr. Chernow's scrutiny of the evidence tends to bear out Mitchell's view of the case, that Hamilton's transgressions were limited to frailties of the flesh, a view which the present authors take to be the one most plausible.

101. *PAH*, XIII, 116n.; XXI, 278–279.

102. "Reynolds Pamphlet," *ibid.*, XXI, 250–256.

103. *Ibid.*, XIII, 116n.; XXI, 278–279.

104. *Ibid.*, XXI, 128–129; Richard Folwell to Edward Jones, Aug. 12, 1797, *ibid.*, XXI, 190n.

105. *Ibid.*, XXI, 121–122n. Boyd, cited in n. 100 above, substantially adopts Callender's theory as true. Dr. Chernow's essay (cited in same n.) points out a number of the difficulties raised by the Boyd-Callender version.

106. *PAH*, XXI, 131–138. The affair nearly brought on a duel between Hamilton and Monroe.

107. Dumas Malone, "William Branch Giles," *DAB*, VII, 283; *idem, Jefferson*, III, 15–18.

108. *AC*, 2 Cong., 2 Sess., 759; *PAH*, XIII, 451–462, 475–477.

109. *AC*, 2 Cong., 2 Sess., 835–840; Introductory Note, *PAH*, XIII, 532–541.

110. Report of Feb. 4, 1793, *ibid.*, 548–549; Mitchell, *Hamilton*, II, 251.

111. *PAH*, XIII, 549–552; Mitchell, *Hamilton*, II, 251–252.

112. Report of Feb. 13, 1793, *PAH*, XIV, 26–32.

113. *Ibid.*, 35n., 43–46; Report of Feb. 19, 1793, *ibid.*, 113–114.

114. *Ibid.*, 46–49, 103–110.

115. *AC*, 2 Cong., 2 Sess., 899–900.

116. *PAH*, XIII, 539; Mitchell, *Hamilton*, II, 260–261; Malone, *Jefferson*, III, 27–28, 30–33. See also Eugene R. Sheridan, "Thomas Jefferson and the Giles Resolutions," *WMQ*, 3rd Ser., XLIX (Oct. 1992), 589–608.

117. *AC*, 2 Cong., 2 Sess., 900–905, 907–963 (the qu. are from Giles's remarks introducing the Resolutions, and the text of Resolution 8, *ibid.*, 895, 900); Mitchell, *Hamilton*, II, 261–266.

118. Jefferson to Thomas Mann Randolph, Mar. 3, 1793, *WTJ*, VI, 194–195.

CHAPTER VIII

The French Revolution in America

1. Stanley Hoffman, "Old Whine, New Bottles," *New York Times*, May 19, 1976. A notable exception, however, to the "mutual ignorance" theme on the French side is Patrice Higonnet, *Sister Republics: The Origins of French and American Republicanism* (Cambridge, Mass., 1988), an elegant and learned study of the profound differences, rooted in

the character and prior experience of the two societies, between the American and French Revolutions and their respective consequences.

2. Three random, trifling, but nonetheless interesting symptoms of this situation struck us the day we began investigating it. One was a copy of Elizabeth B. White's excellent *American Opinion of France from Lafayette to Poincaré*, published in 1927, which had sat on the shelves of the Smith College Library for nearly fifty years with its pages uncut; a second was E. Malcolm Carroll's *French Public Opinion and Foreign Affairs, 1870–1914*, which contains not a single reference to the United States; and the third was *The French American Review*, a quarterly which was founded in 1948 with high hopes of furthering mutual understanding, but expired with the completion of the third volume. According to the closing announcement, "While local historical societies are supported by comparatively large memberships, there seems to be no large public for a periodical like ours which aims to be national. It was consequently agreed that the publication of the *French American Review* be suspenced."

3. Qu. in Frank Monaghan, *French Travellers in the United States, 1765–1932: A Bibliography* (New York, 1933), ix.

4. The "mirage" motif is a recurrent one in the writings of Gilbert Chinard, especially *L'Exotisme américain dans la littérature française au XVIe siècle* (Paris, 1911) and *L'Amérique et le rêve exotique dans la littérature française au XVIIe et au XVIIIe siècle* (Paris, 1913); and it is fully realized in Durand Echeverria, *Mirage in the West: A History of the French Image of American Society to 1815* (Princeton, N.J., 1957), to which we are indebted for some of the formulations that follow.

5. *Ibid.*, pp. 3–14.

6. *Ibid.*, pp. 21–22, 26, 67.

7. "Eripuit fulmen coelo sceptrumque tyrannis." *Ibid.*, p. 50.

8. *Ibid.*, pp. 24–25, 29, 31–34, 48, 75, 152–161.

9. *Ibid.*, p. 183. Except, that is, for the later case of the Statue of Liberty, which coincided in time with an intense need on the part of political leaders of the Third Republic in the 1880s to enhance and solidify France's republican character, America once more serving as the model. They gave strong support to the movement to raise money for a monument which would once again symbolically unite the sister republics. See Sanford Elwitt, *The Making of the Third Republic: Class and Politics in France, 1868–1884* (Baton Rouge, La., 1975), pp. 136–169.

10. Echeverria, *Mirage in the West*, pp. 177–178, 180, 183, 188–205, 219–220; Frances S. Childs., *French Refugee Life in the United States, 1790–1800: An American Chapter of the French Revolution* (Baltimore, 1940), pp. 74–75.

11. Echeverria, *Mirage in the West*, p. 144.

12. André Siegfried, "France and the United States: What Each Can Learn from the Other," *American Society Legion of Honor Magazine*, XX (Winter 1949), 297–306; J.-J. Servan-Schreiber, *The American Challenge* (New York, 1968); Georges Duhamel, *America the Menace: Scenes from the Life of the Future* (Boston, 1931); James F. Marshall, "Stendhal and America," *French American Review*, II (Oct.–Dec. 1949), 240–267. See also C. E. Andrews, "French Authors Take Revenge," *Bookman*, LXXIII (Mar. 1931), 15–21; and Grace Flandran, "On What It Is to Be French," *AQ*, I (Spring 1949), 9–22.

13. Phillips Bradley, Introduction to Alexis de Tocqueville, *Democracy in America* (New York, 1945), I, esp. xl-lii; Elizabeth B. White, *American Opinion of France, From Lafayette to Poincaré* (New York, 1927), pp. 277, 285. It should be noted that Lafayette, at the time of his triumphal visit to the United States in 1824–25, was officially out of favor

in France, and news of his successes in America was excluded from French newspapers. Thus he did not really represent France at all, only the Americans' version of France. It might then be added that six years later Tocqueville and Beaumont, both of royalist families, went about in dread that they might have to drink toasts in public to Lafayette, the republican. See *ibid.,* pp. 79–85, and George W. Pierson, *Tocqueville and Beaumont in America* (New York, 1938), pp. 89–90, 146.

14. Howard Mumford Jones, *America and French Culture, 1750–1848* (Chapel Hill, N.C., 1927), esp. pp. 569–572; Lowell qu. in White, *American Opinion,* p. 211.

15. This was because the French universities would not award higher degrees unless the candidate held a lower one from a French institution; the German universities, on the other hand, put very few restrictions on foreign students wishing to obtain such degrees, and a substantial number of Americans did. *Ibid.,* pp. 235–236.

16. Jones, *America and French Culture,* pp. 300–309; Eliot G. Fay, "Henry James as a Critic of French Literature," *French American Review,* II (July–Sept. 1949), 184–193; Gay Wilson Allen, ed., *Walt Whitman Abroad* (Syracuse, N.Y., 1955), pp. 56–60; Harry Levin, "Some European Views of Contemporary American Literature," Margaret Denny and William H. Gilman, eds., *The American Writer and the European Tradition* (Minneapolis, 1950), pp. 177–180. The French were aware that these writers were not to be mistaken for intellectuals, and that their work "lacked art"; yet they seemed to feel, in their currently exhausted state, that the Americans with their raw virility and their stories full of punch and action, provided something French fiction could do with a dash of. Thus a certain amount of self-flagellation was probably inevitable, amid which the customary note of condescension almost disappeared. Almost, but not quite. "The writers of the New World," announced Henri Peyre in 1947, "have taught the French a refreshing disregard for composition, a total detachment from such rules as unity of plot, a youthful freedom from artistic restraint." "American Literature Through French Eyes," *Virginia Quarterly Review,* XXIII (Summer 1947), 421–438. Actually it seems that for many decades there was a segment of French youth, fretting under lycée discipline, who sought relief in American penny dreadfuls. Howard C. Rice recalls a lawyer who told him at a Rotary Club meeting in a southern French city about how as a boy he had devoured contraband translations of Nick Carter and Buffalo Bill. "I had been brought up," he confessed, " on the Comtesse de Ségur and the Bibliothèque Rose—and here for the first time I had something else, *action* (though bad literature!) and fresh air!" Howard C. Rice, "Seeing Ourselves as the French See Us," *French Review,* XXI (May 1948), 432–441.

17. *The Education of Henry Adams: An Autobiography* (Boston, 1918), p. 96. It was not until more than thirty years after his first visit that Adams came to appreciate the cathedrals of France. Richard L. Shoemaker, "The France of Henry Adams" *French Review,* XXI (Feb. 1948), 292–299.

18. Lafayette to Washington, Mar. 17, 1790, Louis Gottschalk, ed., *The Letters of Lafayette to Washington, 1777–1790* (Philadelphia, 1976), p. 348; Paine to Washington, May 1, 1790, Philip S. Foner, ed., *The Complete Writings of Thomas Paine* (New York, 1945), II, 1303; Catharine Macaulay Graham to Washington, Oct. 1789, Jared Sparks, ed., *Correspondence of the American Revolution; Being Letters of Eminent Men to George Washington from the Time of His Taking Command of the Army to the End of His Presidency* (Boston, 1853), IV, 328; Louis M. Sears, *George Washington and the French Revolution* (Detroit, 1960), pp. 76–77. Lafayette sent the key to Paine in London, who transmitted it to Washington with a letter of his own. Catharine Macaulay Graham was the sister of a Lord Mayor of London and had made a name for herself as a historian. Lucy

M. Donnelly, "The Celebrated Mrs. Macaulay," *WMQ*, 3rd Ser., VI (Apr. 1949), 173–207.

19. Robert R. Palmer makes a special point of the parallelism with the Virginia Declaration in *The Age of the Democratic Revolution: A Political History of Europe and America, 1760–1800* (Princeton, N.J. 1959–64), I, 487–488, 518–521.

20. This *américanisme*, however, was hardly as spontaneous and wholehearted as it appeared in America. It happened to serve a clear factional strategy in Assembly politics, and a determination to overpower the *anglomane* party, who wanted to reproduce in the French constitution certain elements of the English. This posture was not without its embarrassments for the *américanistes*, inasmuch as one of their principal objectives, a unicameral legislature, had little sanction in American precedents. Joyce Appleby, "America as a Model for the Radical French Reformers of 1789," *WMQ*, 3rd Ser., XXVIII (Apr. 1971), 267–286.

21. *AC*, 1 Cong., 3 Sess., 1791–1792, 1798, 1883, 1968–1969, 2116–2118 (Dec. 1790–Feb. 1791); *ibid.*, 2 Cong., 1 Sess., 100, 456–457 (Mar. 1792). R. R. Palmer, conjecturing on why Hamilton should have been given honorary citizenship and not Jefferson, suggests that since Jefferson had been intimate with the by-then-proscribed Lafayette, the Assembly may have imagined Hamilton to be sounder on the Revolution than Jefferson. *Age of the Democratic Revolution*, II, 55.

22. *Gazette of the United States*, Oct. 10, 1789; John Jay to M. Grand, Mar. 1, 1790, and to Robert G. Harper, Jan. 19, 1796, *CPJJ*, III, 386, IV, 198–203; John S. Adams, ed., *An Autobiographical Sketch by John Marshall* . . . (Ann Arbor, Mich., 1937), p. 13; John Marshall, *The Life of George Washington* (Philadelphia, 1804–07), V, 186, 389–391; Chauncey Goodrich to Oliver Wolcott, Feb. 9, 1793, Gibbs. *Memoirs*, I, 87; Robert Goodloe Harper, *Select Works* . . . (Baltimore, 1814), I, 50–51; Gilbert L. Lycan, *Alexander Hamilton and American Foreign Policy: A Design for Greatness* (Norman, Okla., 1970), pp. 134, 136–137; John C. Miller, *Alexander Hamilton: Portrait in Paradox* (New York, 1959), pp. 363–364; Harry R. Warfel, *Noah Webster: Schoolmaster to America* (New York, 1936), p. 226; Gary B. Nash, "The American Clergy and the French Revolution," *WMQ*, 3rd Ser., XXII (July 1965), 392–412. Ruth H. Bloch makes the useful point that most Americans were not deists and freethinkers even though a few of their leaders may have been, that for a great many of them these events had a strong religious significance, and that they saw the Revolution as "moving towards the establishment of the millennial kingdom." *Visionary Republic: Millennial Themes in American Thought, 1756–1800* (Cambridge, 1985), p. 156.

23. Charles D. Hazen, *Contemporary American Opinion of the French Revolution* (Baltimore, 1897), pp. 164–171.

24. Appleby, "America as a Model," *passim*; see also above, n. 20.

25. "LOI. Qui confère le titre de Citoyen François a plusieurs Etrangers. Du 26 Août 1792, l'an quatrième de la Liberté," *PAH*, XII 545–546; Brant, *Madison*, III, 373.

26. A French edition of Paine's *Common Sense*—attributed, however, to Samuel Adams—had recently been published in Paris. *AP:DAJA*, II, 351–352.

27. Edward Handler, *America and Europe in the Political Thought of John Adams* (Cambridge, Mass., 1964), p. 40. This study has been of great assistance in shaping the following discussion.

28. *Ibid.*, p. 129.

29. *Ibid.*, pp. 6–7.

30. *Ibid.*, p. 158.

31. There is a considerable literature on Adams's views about aristocracy, much of it taking as its starting point Adams's anachronistic application of the English constitution to American conditions, where it could never quite be made to fit. See, e.g., John R. Howe, Jr., *The Changing Political Thought of John Adams* (Princeton, N.J., 1966); and Gordon S. Wood, *The Creation of the American Republic, 1776–1787* (Chapel Hill, N.C., 1969), esp. pp. 567–592; in addition to the Handler work cited above. It appears to us, however, that the point might equally well be turned around: that Adams's ideas on aristocracy, considering the American setting in which they were formed, were even less applicable to "real" aristocracies as they existed in Europe than to the synthetic ones he postulated for the United States.

32. Jefferson to Adams, Aug. 30, 1787, *PTJ*, XII, 68.

33. Robert R. Palmer, "The Dubious Democrat: Thomas Jefferson in Bourbon France," *PSQ*, LXXII (Sept. 1957), 396.

34. Jefferson to Monroe, Aug. 9, 1788, *PTJ*, XIII, 489.

35. Jefferson to Thomas Lee Shippen, Sept. 29, 1788, *ibid.*, 642. Malone, *Jefferson*, II, 217–219. Jefferson to Lafayette, May 6, 1789; to Rabaut de St. Etienne, June 3, 1789, *PTJ*, XV, 98, 166–168.

36. "The king is honest and wishes the good of his people, but the expediency of an hereditary aristocracy is too difficult a question for him. On the contrary his prejudices, his habits and his connections decide him in his heart to support it." Jefferson to John Jay, June 17, 1789, *ibid.*, 189.

37. Jefferson to Paine, Sept. 13, 1789, *ibid.*, 424.

38. Jefferson to Madison, Aug. 28, 1789, *ibid.*, 366–367; Adet to Minister of Foreign Relations, Dec. 31, 1796, CFM, 983.

39. To Mason, Feb. 4, 1791; to Lafayette, June 16, 1792; *PTJ*, XIX, 241, XXIV, 85–86.

40. "Anas," Mar. 12, 1792, *WTJ*, I, 187–188.

41. Short to Jefferson, July 20, 31, Aug. 15, 24, 1792, *PTJ*, XXIV, 243, 271, 298, 322, 324.

42. Jefferson to Short, Jan. 3, 1793, *WTJ*, VI, 153–156.

43. Jefferson to Thomas Mann Randolph, Jan. 7, 1793, *ibid.*, 157.

44. Works which emphasize the high perspicacity of Morris's observations on the Revolution include Hazen, *Contemporary American Opinion*, pp. 54–119; Hippolyte Taine, *Derniers essais de critique et d'histoire* (Paris, 1923), p. 307; Adhémar Esmein, *Gouverneur Morris, un témoin américain de la révolution française* (Paris, 1906); Daniel Walther, *Gouverneur Morris, témoin de deux révolutions* (Lausanne, 1932); Sears, *George Washington and the French Revolution*, esp. pp. 188, 205; and Jean-Jacques Fiechter, *Un diplomate américain sous la Terreur: les années européennes de Gouverneur Morris, 1789–1798* (Paris, 1983).

45. E.g., Alexander DeConde, *Entangling Alliance: Politics and Diplomacy Under George Washington* (Durham, N.C., 1958), pp. 311–341; Albert H. Bowman, *The Struggle for Neutrality: Franco-American Diplomacy During the Federalist Era* (Knoxville, Tenn., 1974), pp. 99–122.

46. The best single source on Morris for this period is Beatrix C. Davenport, ed., *A Diary of the French Revolution by Gouverneur Morris* (Boston, 1939), 2v., largely superseding (though not for other periods in Morris's life) Anne C. Morris, ed., *The Diary and Letters of Gouverneur Morris* (New York, 1888), 2v., and Jared Sparks, ed., *The Life of Gouverneur Morris, with Selections from His Correspondence and Miscellaneous Papers* (Boston, 1832), 3v. There is no satisfactory modern biography of Morris. Max M. Mintz,

Gouverneur Morris and the American Revolution (Norman, Okla., 1970) is useful but brief. Mary-Jo Kline, "Gouverneur Morris and the New Nation, 1775–1778" (Unpub. diss., Columbia U., 1970) is scholarly and complete, but covers only the period prior to his departure for Europe in 1789. The qu. from Hamilton is in Davenport, ed., *Diary*, I, xii.

47. This point should be underlined. Morris was certainly not among those who, like Hamilton, were willing to bend over backward to avoid offending England. Quite the contrary; his pro-French attitude and hostility toward England during his mission to London in 1790 gave Hamilton occasion for positive annoyance. Indeed, Morris would have liked to see the French make war on Great Britain, and actually engaged in some undercover efforts to egg them on. See Davenport, ed., *Diary*, I, 506–509; Mintz, *Morris*, pp. 211–226. It was not until his alienation from revolutionary France that he concluded that Britain was, after all, America's best friend.

48. Davenport, ed., *Diary*, I, 137; Morris to Washington, July 31, 1789, Jan. 24, 1790, *ibid.*, 170–172, 379–387.

49. With perhaps a nudge from Hamilton; Morris to Hamilton, Mar. 21, 1792, *PAH*, XI, 162.

50. Morris to Short, Apr. 7, 1790, Davenport, ed., *Diary*, I, 470.

51. *Ibid.*, II, 53.

52. Morris to Montmorin, July 30, 1791, *ibid.*, 230.

53. *Ibid.*, 249–252.

54. *Ibid.*, 264–269.

55. *Ibid.*, 321–323.

56. Washington to Morris, Jan. 28, 1792, *WGW*, XXXI, 468–470; Morris to Washington, Apr. 6, 1792, Davenport, ed., *Diary*, II, 403, 429.

57. A good modern biography of Paine is David F. Hawke, *Paine* (New York, 1974), upon which we have drawn heavily for details, though it does not entirely supersede Moncure D. Conway, *The Life of Thomas Paine: With a History of His Literary, Political, and Religious Career in America, France, and England* (New York, 1908), 2v.

58. Hawke, *Paine*, pp. 7–17.

59. *Ibid.*, pp. 17–18.

60. *Ibid.*, pp. 19–25.

61. Eric Foner, *Tom Paine and Revolutionary America* (New York, 1976), is good on the setting of Philadelphia politics in which *Common Sense* made its appearance.

62. Hawke, *Paine*, pp. 57–147.

63. *Ibid.*, p. 168.

64. *Ibid.*, p. 107.

65. *Common Sense*, Foner, ed., *Complete Writings*, I, 32.

66. E. Foner, *Tom Paine*, pp. 183–209; Hawke, *Paine*, 149–159, 184.

67. E.g., Paine to Jefferson, Sept. 9, 1788, *PTJ*, XIII, 587–590; on Paine and the artisans of Philadelphia see E. Foner, *Tom Paine*, pp. 99–100.

68. Paine had an arch built at his own expense which was exhibited for a time at Paddington and aroused much interest, though not to the point of anyone's offering to buy it. However, the famous Sunderland bridge later erected over the River Wear was built on Paine's basic design, and the work was supervised by the same man whom Paine had in effect trained at the Walker iron works in Yorkshire. Though Paine himself received no financial reward from the Sunderland bridge, his pioneering role in working out the principles upon which it and many other iron bridges were subsequently constructed has been recognized by authorities on the subject. See W. H. G. Armytage, "Thomas Paine and the Walkers: An Early Episode in Anglo-American Cooperation," *Pennsylvania His-*

tory, XVIII (Jan. 1951), 16–30; and references in Audrey Williamson, *Thomas Paine: His Life, Work and Times* (London, 1973), pp. 105–106; and Hawke, *Paine,* pp. 212–213. Even in his portentous letter of transmittal to Washington that accompanied Lafayette's gift of the key to the Bastille (see above p. 309), Paine could not resist changing the subject in order to tell Washington about his bridge. Foner, ed., *Complete Writings,* II, 1303.

69. Hawke, *Paine,* pp. 175–187.

70. *Ibid.,* pp. 188–202.

71. Paine to Burke, Jan. 17, 1790, and Burke to Paine, n.d., qu. in R. R. Fennessy, *Burke, Paine and the Rights of Man: A Difference of Political Opinion* (The Hague, 1963), pp. 103–104; Paine to Thomas Walker, Apr. 14, 1790, Armytage, "Paine and the Walkers," 25.

72. "Preface," *Rights of Man,* II, Foner, ed., *Complete Writings,* I, 349; Fennessy, *Burke, Paine,* pp. 108–159.

73. *Ibid.,* 160–180.

74. The foregoing paragraph is based on Fennessy's analysis of British public opinion in *ibid.,* Chs. 6 and 7. The qu. is from *Rights of Man,* II, Foner, ed., *Complete Writings,* I, 360.

75. E. P. Thompson, *The Making of the English Working Class* (New York, 1964), pp. 90–95.

76. Hawke, *Paine,* pp. 258–264.

77. *Ibid.,* pp. 270–276; the texts of Paine's speeches of Jan. 15 and 19 are in Foner, ed., *Complete Writings,* II, 551–558.

78. An eleborated version of this argument is presented in Michael Walzer, ed., *Regicide and Revolution: Speeches at the Trial of Louis XVI* (Cambridge, 1974), pp. 1–89.

79. Winthrop D. Jordan, "Familial Politics: Thomas Paine and the Killing of the King, 1776," *JAH,* LX (Sept. 1973), 294–308.

80. Samuel Adams to Paine, Nov. 30, 1802, Foner, ed., *Complete Writings,* II, 1433n.; Patrick Henry to his daughter (Mrs. William Aylett), Aug. 20, 1796, William Wirt Henry, *Patrick Henry: Life, Correspondence and Speeches* (New York, 1891), II, 570; George Morgan, *The True Patrick Henry* (Philadelphia, 1907), 366n. Benjamin Rush declared that the *Age of Reason* was "so offensive to me that I did not wish to renew my intercourse with him." Qu. in G. Adolf Koch, *Republican Religion: The American Revolution and the Cult of Reason* (New York, 1933), p. 135. *The Age of Reason* seems to have been widely read in America, but for reasons more of notoriety and a desire to condemn it than from any effectiveness it may have had in turning Christians into deists. See *ibid.,* pp. 134–137; Herbert M. Morais, *Deism in Eighteenth-Century America* (New York, 1934), pp. 120–122, 153, 163, 164, 168.

81. Hawke, *Paine,* p. 48; see also n. 26 above.

82. The most complete accounts in print of Genet's family and his early career are Jules Jusserand, "La jeunesse du Citoyen Genet, d'après des documents inédits," *Revue d'histoire diplomatique,* XLIV (1930), 237–268; and Meade Minnegerode, *Jefferson, Friend of France, 1793: The Career of Edmond Charles Genet, Minister Plenipotentiary from the French Republic to the United States, as Revealed by His Private Papers, 1763–1834* (New York, 1928), pp. 3–161. Though the latter's prose and the style of mind it reflects are fatuous in the extreme, and most of the documents used are neither dated nor fully identified, the book is the closest thing to a biography that exists. Extensive materials for a good one, however, are in the Genet Papers, LC. On Genet's mission to America see Harry Ammon, *The Genet Mission* (New York, 1973); Maude H. Woodfin, "Citizen Genet and His Mission" (Unpub. diss., U. of Chicago, 1928); and William F. Keller, "American

Politics and the Genet Mission" (Unpub. diss., U. of Pittsburgh, 1951). One of the best-known sources on the affairs of the royal household in the closing years of the Old Regime was written by Genet's sister Jeanne Louise Henriette Campan, who was a lady-in-waiting to the Queen, but Mme. Campan's memoirs contain only a few passing (though revealing) references to the activities of her brother Edmond. G. F. Fortescue, ed., *Memoirs of Madame Campan on Marie Antoinette and her Court* (Boston, 1909), II, 123–125.

83. Woodfin, "Citizen Genet," pp. 119–161. There are some useful details on Genet's appointment in Frederick A. Schminke, *Genet: The Origins of His Mission to America* (Toulouse, 1939).

84. Brissot was the prime example of the Frenchman mesmerized at a distance by the American idea. He had made up his mind about America in advance (he did go there for a few months' visit in 1788–89), and had written a blistering critique of Chastellux's *Voyages* because he liked Crèvecoeur's idealized *Lettres* much better. On this, as well as Brissot's universalism and optimism, see Eloise Ellery, *Brissot de Warville: A Study in the History of the French Revolution* (Boston, 1915), esp. pp. 57–60. For a recently uncovered aspect of Brissot's pre-Revolutionary past, see Robert Darnton, "A Spy in Grub Street," *The Literary Underground of the Old Regime* (Cambridge, Mass., 1982), pp. 41–70.

85. Ellery, *Brissot,* pp. 226–227. On some of the sources from which Brissot may have picked up these notions, see Felix Gilbert, "The 'New Diplomacy' of the Eighteenth Century," *World Politics,* IV (Oct. 1951), 1–38.

86. Qu. in Ellery, *Brissot,* p. 238.

87. Hippolyte Taine, *The French Revolution* (New York, 1881), II, 99. But Brissot's sympathetic biographer holds much the same view; see Ellery, *Brissot,* p. 257; also T. C. W. Blanning, *The Origins of the French Revolutionary Wars* (London, 1986), pp. 99–119. There is a discussion of the Girondins' American policy in Bowman, *Struggle for Neutrality,* pp. 39–55.

88. Louis-Guillaume Otto wrote of Genet in 1797 that "He was charged with drawing up his own instructions." Gilbert Chinard, ed., "Considérations sur la conduite du Gouvernement américain envers la France, depuis le commencement de la Révolution jusqu'en 1797," *Bulletin de l'Institut Français,* No. XVI (Dec. 1943), 19. It is to be doubted, however, whether this extended beyond the opening rhetorical declarations. Otto was not employed in the Foreign Office at the time the instructions were prepared. See Frédéric Masson, *Le département des affaires etrangères pendant la révolution, 1787–1804* (Paris, 1877), p. 244.

89. The instructions are printed in CFM, pp. 201–211. But these were not the only instructions Genet received; an additional set dated Jan. 4, 1793, relating to the financing of his mission, are in *ASP:FR,* I, 142–146. Also serving in some sense as instructions are a series of letters from Lebrun, the Minister of Foreign Affairs, to Genet numbered 1 through 10, dated Feb. 1, 3, 24, Mar. 10, 31, Apr. 10, 11, 23, May 29, and June 19, 1793; two (those of Feb. 24 and Mar. 10) are printed in Cornelis De Witt, *Thomas Jefferson: étude historique sur la démocratie américaine* (Paris, 1861), pp. 516–519. The only part of the instructions made public were the first two paragraphs of the "Mémoire pour servir d'instruction," CFM, 202–203, in the form of a speech by Lebrun to the National Convention, Dec. 20, 1792, AECPE-U 36, 470–471, which was reprinted in American newspapers. See *Philadelphia Daily Advertiser,* May 6, 1793.

90. CFM, p. 204; Lebrun to Genet, Feb. 24, 1793, *ibid.,* 215n., and De Witt, *Jefferson,* p. 516.

91. Lebrun to Genet, Feb. 3, 1793, AECPE-U 37, 100–103.

92. CFM, p. 204.

93. *Ibid.,* p. 210.

94. *Ibid.*, p. 209; see also above, p. 124.

95. *ASP:FR*, I, 142–146.

96. Genet to Minister of Foreign Affairs, Apr. 16, 1793, CFM, pp. 211–212; "Rapport du citoyen Genet . . . sur son voyage et sa réception populaire dans les Etats-Unis d'Amérique," DeWitt, *Jefferson*, p. 542. Others have suspected reasons less straightforward than contrary winds; on this question see Charles M. Thomas, *American Neutrality in 1793: A Study in Cabinet Government* (New York, 1931), pp. 79–80.

97. Minnegerode, *Jefferson*, pp. 186–189; writings of Genet cited in n. 96 above; Jefferson, "Note given to the President, July 26, 1793," *WTJ*, I, 248–249.

98. On Mangourit and the Florida project see Richard K. Murdoch, "Citizen Mangourit and the Projected Attack on East Florida in 1794," *Journal of Southern History*, XIV (Nov. 1948), 522–540; Frederick J. Turner, "The Origin of Genet's Projected Attack upon the Floridas," *AHA:AR, 1897*, 575–679.

99. Minnegerode, *Jefferson*, pp. 191–197; "Rapport," De Witt, *Jefferson*, pp. 542–547; a good account, based on newspaper reports, of Genet's reception in Charleston and his overland journey to Philadelphia is Keller, "American Politics and the Genet Mission," pp. 114–141. An equally good one is Woodfin, "Citizen Genet," pp. 86–132.

100. Though many authorities on international law (Grotius, Bynkershoek, Vattel, and others) had asserted that nations not involved in war *ought* to observe a strict impartiality in their relations with the belligerents (and members of Washington's cabinet would naturally ransack their writings to support the position the United States government took in 1793), there was little in the international practice of the eighteenth century to indicate general acceptance of such an assumption. It was not regarded as incompatible with neutral status that a nation might give very material assistance to one or more of the belligerents. On this point see Charles S. Hyneman, *The First American Neutrality: A Study of the American Understanding of Neutral Obligations During the Years 1792 to 1815* (Urbana, Ill., 1934), pp. 14–19. "Indeed, it has been suggested by careful students that, at a period not long prior to the first American neutrality, a nation would have been hard put to it to show that it had even a legal right to be impartial during a war." *Ibid.*, p. 16.

101. Jefferson to Washington, Apr. 7, 1793; to Madison, Apr. 7, 1793, *WTJ*, VI, 212–213. Jefferson, "Anas," Apr. 18, 1793, *ibid.*, I, 226. Washington to Jefferson, Apr. 12, 1793; "Questions Submitted to the Cabinet," Apr. 18, 1793; Washington to Heads of Departments, Apr. 18, 1793; *WGW*, XXXII, 415–416, 419–421. Carroll and Ashworth, *Washington*, VII, 44. Jefferson was almost certainly right about Hamilton's having been for practical purposes the author of the thirteen questions, though he omits to add that he himself might have prepared such a list had he so wished. In all likelihood he did not so wish, and for reasons similar to those for avoiding authorship of the Neutrality Proclamation. See also Thomas, *American Neutrality*, pp. 28–30.

102. Jefferson, "Anas," Apr. 18, 1793, *WTJ*, I, 226–227; "Cabinet Opinion on Proclamation and French Minister," Apr. 19, 1793, *ibid.*, VI, 217; Jefferson to Madison, June 23, 1793, *ibid.*, 315–316; Hamilton, "Pacificus," Nos. I, VII, *PAH*, XV, 33–43, 130–135. Hamilton, according to Jefferson, repeated the same arguments in his "Pacificus" papers on these points as he had used in the cabinet discussions. Jefferson to Madison, June 29, 1793, *WTJ*, VI, 327. On the lack of evidence for, or the unlikelihood of, Great Britain's asking the United States for its neutrality at this time, see Malone, *Jefferson*, III, 70.

103. E.g., DeConde, *Entangling Alliance*, p. 195; Harry Ammon, *The Genet Mission* (New York, 1973), p. 51.

104. Apr. 28, 1973, *WTJ*, VI, 232.

105. "Cabinet Opinion," *ibid.*, 217.

106. Jefferson to Madison, May 19, June 29, Aug. 11, 1793; to Monroe, July 14, 1793; *ibid.*, 259, 328, 369, 346. Washington, Proclamation, *WGW*, XXXII, 430–431.

107. Hamilton and Knox to Washington, May 2, 1793; Hamilton to Washington, May 2, 1793; *PAH*, XIV, 367–396, 398–408.

108. Jefferson to Washington, Apr. 28, 1793, "Opinion on French Treaties," Apr. 28, 1793, *WTJ*, VI, 218–231. Though Jefferson had not seen Hamilton's written opinion, and probably never would, he explicitly addressed himself in this paper to the same arguments Hamilton had already made verbally.

109. "Anas," Apr. 18, Mar. 30, 1793, *ibid.*, I, 227, 224. The entry of Apr. 18 was written on May 6.

110. Letter of Credence, Jan. 13, 1793, F.-Alphonse Aulard, ed., *Recueil des actes du Comité de Salut Public; avec la correspondance officielle des représentants en mission et le régistre due Conseil Executif Provisoire* (Paris, 1889), I, 478–480; English translation in National Archives Microfilm Publications, M53 (France), Roll 1; Genet's powers to negotiate new treaty, Jan. 4, AECPE-U 37, 22–23; Address of National Convention to United States of America, Dec. 22, 1792, AECPE-U 36, 473–474vo. For Genet's speech to Washington see Jefferson to Madison, May 19, 1793, *WTJ*, VI, 260–261.

111. It is not likely that Washington was effusive. But only later, in making up his defense for the failure of his mission, did Genet conclude that he had been coldly received. This was because Washington, as he claimed, was "profoundly wounded" at the contrast in public opinion between the address presented to the President by "300 merchants, mostly English," and the "six thousand citizens who came to felicitate me upon my arrival." Genet to Minister of Foreign Affairs, Oct. 7, 1793, CFM, p. 245. See also Genet to Jefferson, July 4, 1797, Minnegerode, *Jefferson*, p. 417, in which he referred to it as "a perfectly neutral and insignificant reception."

112. Keller, "Genet Mission," pp. 142–148; *Philadelphia American Daily Advertiser,* May 17, 18, 20, 1793; J. S. Biddle, ed., *Autobiography of Charles Biddle . . . 1745–1821* (Philadelphia, 1883), pp. 251–253; Hazen, *Contemporary Opinion,* pp. 176–182; Genet, "Rapport," De Witt, *Jefferson,* pp. 544–546.

113. "His principles, his experience, his talents, his devotion to the cause we are defending inspire me with the greatest confidence, and give me to hope that we shall arrive at that glorious end which the general interest of mankind should make us desire to attain." Genet to Minister of Foreign Affairs, May 18, 1793, CFM, p. 215.

114. Genet to Jefferson, May 22, 1793, *ASP:FR,* I, 142.

115. *Ibid.,* 147.

116. Jefferson to Ternant, May 15, 1793; Genet to Jefferson, May 27, 1793; *ibid.,* 147–150.

117. Genet to Minister of Foreign Affairs, May 31, 1793, CFM, p. 216; Keller, "Genet Mission," pp. 215–216; Minnegerode, *Jefferson,* p. 418; *National Gazette,* June 1, 1793. Jefferson, Genet reported, "has published in the papers under the name of *Veritas* three letters [there were actually four] against the system of these gentlemen. . . ." He referred in another letter to Jefferson's "anonymous writings." Genet to Minister of Foreign Affairs, Oct. 7, Aug. 15, 1793, CFM, pp. 245, 241.

118. Same to same, Oct. 7, 1793, *ibid.,* p. 245; to Jefferson, July 4, 1797, Minnegerode, *Jefferson,* p. 418. "Thus initiated by you in the foibles and secrets of your Cabinet, in the political divisions of your country, seeing mine in danger . . . I could only give myself up to you who seemed so well disposed, to the people which appeared so warm, and derive every possible advantage from my position. . . . I did so." *Ibid.* Genet told Jefferson that he, unlike Jefferson, did not have it in his character "to speak . . . in one way, and act in

another; to have an official language, and a language confidential." Same to same, Sept. 18, 1793, *ASP:FR*, I, 172–174.

119. The disinclination to enter into new treaty negotiations with France seems to have been generally shared, occasioning no basic disagreements within the cabinet, and here the tone was probably established at the outset by Washington himself. When Jefferson first described to him Genet's offers on this question and on that of the debt, even before the Minister's letters had been translated, Washington's instinct was to avoid doing anything hasty. "In general, I observed to the Secretary," he noted, "that in the present posture of French Affairs, I thought we ought to consider very deliberately on all these measures before we acted—for it was impossible to decide with precision what would be the final issue of the contest—consequently, that the Governmt. ought not to go faster than it was obliged; but to walk on cautious ground." Journal of the Proceedings of the President, May 24, 1793, Washington Papers, LC. See also Woodfin, "Citizen Genet," pp. 406–413.

There are two versions of how Jefferson handled this matter with Genet, one his and the other Genet's. Jefferson told the cabinet "that having observed from our conversns that the proposns to treat might not be acceded to immedty. I had endeavored to prepare Mr. Genet for it by taking occasion in conversns to apprize him of the controul over treaties which our consn had given to the Senate, that tho' this was indirectly done (because not having been authorized to say anything official on the subject, I did not venture to commit myself directly) yet on some subsequent conversn, I found it had struck him exactly as I had wished, for speaking on some other matter, he mentd. incidentally his propositions to treat, and said 'however as I know now that you cannot take up that subject till the meeting of the Senate, I shall say no more about it now,' and so proceeded with his other subject, which I do not now recollect." "Anas," Aug. 23, 1793, *WTJ*, I, 262. Genet, on the other hand, reported, "Mr. Jefferson seemed convinced of the usefulness of this negotiation and of the need to contract new political and commercial ties with us, but meanwhile he does not conceal from me that he will encounter many obstacles from the partisans of England and of the system introduced into the United States government, after the fashion of England's [celui de cette vieille puissance], a system that is today the principal foundation of its revenues and the sole mortgage of its debt. The enemies of that corrupting system are the philosophers, the friends of unlimited liberty, the farmers whose virtuous industry is the basis of all wealth; its defenders are all the capitalists, all the speculators in the funds, all the creatures of the Federal government in Congress, in the lower legislatures, and in the government, for the art of buying men is already pushed very far among our brothers." Genet to Minister of Foreign Affairs, Oct. 5, 1793, CFM, p. 258. For a general survey of the problem see Randolph to Monroe, June 1, 1795, *ASP:FR*, I, 705–712, in which Randolph quotes (though inaccurately, 708–709) from Genet's instructions; on background see George F. Zook, "Proposals for New Commercial Treaty Between France and the United States, 1778–1793," *South Atlantic Quarterly*, VIII (July 1909), 267–283. On Jefferson's state of mind during this period see below, pp. 357ff.

120. CFM, pp. 203, 206.

121. Genet to Jefferson, June 1, 1793; Jefferson to Genet, June 1, 1793; *ASP:FR*, I, 151. Jefferson's original draft had closed with: "no doubt need be entertained that his case will have the favorable issue you desire. The forms of law involve certain necessary delays; of which however he will assuredly experience none but what are necessary. It will give me great pleasure to be able to communicate to you that the laws (which admit of no controul) on being applied to the actions of Mr. Henfield, shall have found in them no cause for animadversion," *WTJ*, VI, 274n.

122. *ASP:FR*, I, 150.

123. *Ibid.*, 156. Hamilton's paper would have been even more brusque had not Washington asked him to rewrite it. "This not according altogether with my ideas," he noted, "as being rather too dry & abrupt an answer—I sent it to the Secretary of State for his remarks thereon." Journal of Proceedings of the President, June 6, 1793, Washington Papers, LC; Jefferson to Washington, June 6, 1793, *WTJ*, VI, 287–289. For a full discussion of the French debt see Robert R. LaFollette, "The American Revolutionary Foreign Debt and Its Liquidation" (Unpub. diss., George Washington U., 1931); Samuel F. Bemis, "Payment of the French Loans to the United States, 1777–1795," *Current History*, XXIII (Mar. 1926), 824–836; Alphone Aulard, "La dette américaine envers la France," *Revue de Paris*, III (May 15, June 1, 1925), 319–338, 524–550.

124. On benevolent neutrality see Hyneman, *First American Neutrality*, pp. 15–16, 153–154. Article XXII of the Treaty of Amity and Commerce of 1778 had stated, "It shall not be lawful for any foreign Privateers . . . who have Commissions from any other Prince or State in enmity with either Nation to fit their Ships in the Ports of either the one or the other of the aforesaid Parties," and Jefferson himself (judging from notes he made for a debate in cabinet over what to do about Genet's privateers fitted out at Charleston) seems to have thought there was some implication that it might be lawful for France to do this. "So understood universally, by everyone here—by ourselves at Charleston—by Genet. Still true it is not expressly permitted—may be forbidden. But till forbidden must be slight offense." Hunter Miller, ed., *Treaties and Other International Acts of the United States of America* (Washington, 1931), II, 19–20; "Anas," May 20, 1793, *WTJ*, I, 229. The first federal statute explicitly forbidding such activity was the Neutrality Act of 1794, though the cabinet meanwhile concluded that it could be forbidden on other grounds. See below, pp. 352–354.

125. On March 5, 1795, Congress passed an act which did in effect liquidate the remaining portion of the French debt. LaFollette, "Foreign Debt," pp. 118–119.

126. "Conversation with George Hammond," [Apr. 2–May 17, 1793], *PAH*, XIV, 273–274.

127. Genet to Jefferson, June 8, 1793, *ASP:FR*, I, 151.

128. Same to same, June 14, 1793, *ibid.*, 156–157.

129. Same to same, June 14, 1793, *ibid.*, 152.

130. Jefferson to Genet, June 17, 1793, *ibid.*, 158.

131. Same to same, June 17, 1793, *WTJ*, VI, 311–312.

132. Same to same, June 19, 1793, *ASP:FR*, I, 157.

133. "Reasons for the Opinion of the Secretary of the Treasury and the Secretary at War Respecting the Brigantine *Little Sarah*," July 8, 1793, *PAH*, XV, 75.

134. Genet to Jefferson, June 22, 1793, *ASP:FR*, I, 158–159.

135. *Ibid.*

136. Genet to Minister of Foreign Affairs, Aug. 15, 1793, CFM. p. 241.

137. "Anas," July 5, 1793, *WTJ*, I, 235–237.

138. Genet to Minister of Foreign Affairs, July 25, 1793, CFM, p. 221.

139. Carroll and Ashworth, *Washington*, VII, 102n. When Washington on July 25 asked Jefferson to prepare a statement of Genet's verbal communications, this conversation was not mentioned in the resulting paper Jefferson submitted the following day. *Ibid.*, 109–110; "Note Given to the President," July 26, 1793, *WTJ*, I, 248–250. The basic materials on the Louisiana plan are Frederick J. Turner, "The Origins of Genet's Projected Attack on Louisiana and the Floridas," *AHR*, III (July 1898), 650–671; and "The Policy of France Toward the Mississippi Valley in the Period of Washington and Adams," *ibid.*,

X (Jan. 1905), 249–279; Turner, ed., "Selections [on] . . . the Proposed French Expedition Under General George Rogers Clark against Louisiana, in the Years 1793–94," *AHA:AR, 1896*, I, 930–1107; and "Documents on the Relations of France to Louisiana, 1792–95," *AHR*, III (Apr. 1898), 499–516; "Journal of André Michaux, 1793–1796," Reuben G. Thwaites, ed., *Early Western Travels, 1748–1846* (Cleveland, 1904), III, esp. 27–53; F. R. Hall, "Genet's Western Intrigue, 1793–1794," *Illinois State Historical Society Journal*, XXI, no. 3, (1928), 359–381; Archibald Henderson, "Isaac Shelby and the Genet Mission,"*MVHR*, VI (Mar. 1920), 445–469; and Regina K. Crandall, "Genet's Projected Attack on Louisiana and the Floridas, 1793–1794" (Unpub. diss., U of Chicago, 1928). Mildred S. Fletcher, "Louisiana as a Factor in French Diplomacy from 1763 to 1800," *MVHR*, XVII (Dec. 1930), 367–376, is critical of Turner's assumptions as to the seriousness of France's desire to recover Louisiana.

140. Thomas, *American Neutrality*, pp. 137–143; Jefferson, "Anas," July 5, 10, 1793, *WTJ*, I, 235, 237–241.

141. *Ibid.*, 237–241; Jefferson to Madison, July 7, 1793, *ibid.*, VI, 338–339.

142. Carroll and Ashworth, *Washington*, VII, 100.

143. July 10, 1793, cited in nn. 140, 141 above.

144. "Cabinet Opinion on 'Little Sarah,'" *WTJ*, VI, 339–340. See also n. 133 above, and "Reasons for his Dissent," *ibid.*, 340–344.

145. Genet to Jefferson, July 9, 1793, *ASP:FR*, I, 163.

146. *WGW*, XXXIII, 4; Carroll and Ashworth, *Washington*, VII, 102–103; "Anas," July 13, 23, Aug. 1, 2, 20, 1793, *WTJ*, I, 243, 247, 252–254, 259–261.

147. Jefferson to Chief Justice and Judges, July 18, 1793, *ibid.*, VI, 351–352; Washington to Justices, July 23, 1793, *WGW*, XXXIII, 28; Jay and Justices to Washington, Aug. 8, 1793, *CPJJ*, III, 488–489; the twenty-nine questions are reprinted in *WTJ*, VI, 352–354. Jefferson to Genet, July 12, 1793, *ASP:FR*, I, 163 (on detaining *Little Democrat* in port). The exact date of the ship's departure is unknown (see Thomas, *American Neutrality*, p. 142); but it is interesting that the British should take it so mildly. Hammond simply observed (after noting that the captain had been ordered to repel by force any effort to detain her), "The privateer then sailed, and the government, from the want of having any cannon or military in readiness, was compelled to submit to the Belligerents." Aug. 3, 1793, *WTJ*, VI, 358–359.

148. *Ibid.*; Thomas, *American Neutrality*, pp. 152–153.

149. Francis Wharton, *State Trials of the United States During the Administrations of Washington and Adams* (Philadelphia, 1849), pp. 49–89; Hyneman, *First Neutrality*, pp. 129–132; Thomas, *American Neutrality*, pp. 170–176, 185–188; Jefferson to Isaac Shelby, Aug. 29, 1793, *ASP:FR*, I, 455. See also A. Henderson, cited in n. 139 above; and Samuel L. Wilson, *A Review of "Isaac Shelby and the Genet Mission" by Dr. Archibald Henderson* (Lexington, Ky., 1920). Sections 1 and 2 of the Neutrality Act of June 5, 1794, define recruiting and enlistment of American citizens in the service of a foreign belligerent as a "high misdemeanor." *Statutes at Large*, I, 381–383.

150. Thomas, *American Neutrality*, pp. 109–112; Jefferson to Genet, Nov. 8, 1793, *ASP:FR*, I, 183.

151. Thomas, *American Neutrality*, pp. 206–220; Hyneman, *First Neutrality*, pp. 118–127.

152. *Ibid.*, pp. 145–150; Thomas, *American Neutrality*, pp. 247–257; on "free ships, free goods" see *ibid.*, pp. 257–260. The text of the June 8, 1793, Order in Council is in *ASP:FR*, I, 240; Jefferson to Genet, July 24, 1793, *ibid.*, 166–167.

153. R. Therry, ed., *Speeches of the Right Honorable George Canning, with a Memoir*

of His Life (London, 1836), V, 50 (in opposition to a motion to repeal the Foreign Enlistments Bill, Apr. 16, 1823).

154. Such is the impression given by Carroll and Ashworth, *Washington*, VII, 88, and there seems in general little reason to doubt it. Yet inasmuch as opposition did arise, some of it very sharp, a careful analysis of public opinion on the Proclamation would be useful. To our knowledge, none has been attempted.

155. Jefferson to Morris, Apr. 20, 1793; to Madison, Apr. 28, 1793; *WTJ*, VI, 217, 232.

156. This point is made in Harry Ammon, "The Genet Mission and the Development of American Political Parties," *JAH*, LII (Mar. 1966), 725–741, upon which Ch. 10 of Professor Ammon's *Genet Mission* is based.

157. *National Gazette*, June 1, 5, 8, 12, 1793. No one has yet discovered who "Veritas" really was. John Beckley, for whom a daily ration of gossip seems to have been necessary for health, told Jefferson that it was one William Irvine, "a clerk in the treasury, an Irishman," and that he, Beckley, "had it from Swaine the printer to whom the pieces were delivd.," but "would not permit the name of his informer to be men[tione]d." This was the very kind of thing Jefferson was most ready to believe. "I had long before suspected this excessive foul play in that party, of writing themselves in the character of the most exaggerated democrats, & incorporating with it a great deal of abuse on the President to make him believe it was that party who were his enemies, & so throw him entirely into the scale of the monocrats." But Beckley's stories, as Jefferson had occasion to know, were not always reliable. It seems somewhat far-fetched to imagine Hamilton risking such a thing, or even thinking of it; one wonders, on the other hand, what was to prevent Jefferson—if he was bent on finding out—from simply asking Freneau who "Veritas" was. Carroll and Ashworth mention that Washington received a note dated June 13, 1793 and signed only "G.H." (possibly George Hammond) saying that it was one "Stockdon of Richmond." They conclude, however, that "editor Freneau was directly responsible." It is quite probable that they are right, though they cite as their authority a "thoughtful interpretation," Samuel E. Forman, *The Political Activities of Philip Freneau* (Baltimore, 1902), which is in fact neither very thoughtful nor very dependable. (For instance, Forman quotes on p. 68 a passage from the *Gazette* which he attributes to Freneau, and on p. 71 another which he says "was most certainly not written by Freneau," and yet both are from "Veritas.") The mystery, it might be added, is deepened by Hamilton's failure even to mention "Veritas" in any of his public or private writings. Philip Marsh, "The Griswold Story of Freneau and Jefferson," *AHR*, LI (Oct. 1945), 68–73, has a theory that "Veritas" may have been Thomas McKean, a leading Republican in Pennsylvania politics. Jefferson, "Anas," June 12, July 18, 1793, *WTJ*, I, 235, 244–245; Carroll and Ashworth, *Washington*, VII, 86n. On Genet's opinion see n. 117 above.

158. Jefferson to Madison, Mar. [n.d.], 1793, *WTJ*, VI, 192; Hammond to Grenville, No. 11, Apr. 2, 1793, PRO:FO 5/1.

159. *National Gazette*, Apr. 20, 1793; on public opinion regarding the King's execution see Hazen, *Contemporary Opinion*, pp. 253–257. There is a story, since frequently reprinted, that at one of the civic feasts in Philadelphia celebrating the French Revolution in 1793, a pig (representing Louis XVI) was decapitated and the head passed around to the guests, each of whom exclaimed "Tyrant!" as he plunged his knife into it. This hallucinated scene—of which no witnesses have ever come to light—was almost certainly the invention of William Cobbett, a man whose extravagance of mind gave a lively tone to all his writings, and who was at this period of his life a violent francophobe. See William Playfair, *The History of Jacobinism . . . With an Appendix by Peter Porcupine, Containing*

a History of the American Jacobins, Commonly Denominated Democrats (Philadelphia, 1796), II, Appendix, 25–26. See also Hazen, *Contemporary Opinion,* p. 183 and n.; Kenneth R. Rossman, *Thomas Mifflin and the Politics of the American Revolution* (Chapel Hill, N.C., 1952), p. 216.

160. Jefferson to _____, Mar. 18, 1793, L & B, IX, 45; Madison to Jefferson, Apr. 12, 1793, *PJM,* XV, 7. But in 1821 Jefferson wrote that he would not have voted for execution. "I should have shut up the Queen in a Convent, putting harm out of her power, and placed the king in his station, investing him with limited powers, which I verily believe he would have honestly exercised, according to the measure of his understanding. In this way no void would have been created, courting the usurpation of a military adventurer [Napoleon Bonaparte], nor occasion given for those enormities which demoralized the nations of the world, and destroyed, and is yet to destroy millions and millions of it's inhabitants." *WTJ,* I, 141. A typically balanced Republican reaction was that of Benjamin Rush. "His execution," Rush wrote, "was unjust, unconstitutional, illegal, impolitic, and cruel in the highest degree. . . . Ninety-nine of our citizens out of a hundred have dropped a tear to his memory." As for France herself, however, Rush insisted that "the noble cause in which she is engaged, though much disgraced by her rulers, must finally prevail." Similarly, James Monroe wrote, "In my route I scarcely find a man unfriendly to the French revolution as now modified. Many regret the unhappy fate of the King. But they seem to consider these events as incidents to a much greater one, & which they wish to see accomplished." According to the Republican clergyman William Bentley: "The melancholy news of the beheading of the Roi de France is confirmed in the public opinion, & the event is regretted most sincerely by all thinking people. The french loose much of their influence upon the hearts of the Americans by this event." Rush to John Coakley Lettson, Apr. 26, 1793, Lyman H. Butterfield, ed., *Letters of Benjamin Rush* (Princeton, N.J., 1951), II, 635; Monroe to Jefferson, May 8, 1793, *WJM,* I, 252; *The Diary of William Bentley, D.D., Pastor of the East Church, Salem, Massachusetts* (Salem, 1907), II, 13, Mar. 25, 1793.

161. Jefferson to Monroe, May 5, 1793 (he wrote similarly to Thomas Mann Randolph and John Wayles Eppes, May 6, 23); to Madison, Apr. 28, 1793; *WTJ,* VI, 232, 238, 241, 264.

162. Jefferson to Thomas Mann Randolph, May 6, 1793; to Brissot de Warville, May 8, 1793; to Monroe, June 4, 1793; to same, May 5, 1793; *ibid.,* 241, 249, 281–282, 238.

163. Madison to Jefferson, June 19, 1793, *PJM,* XV, 33.

164. Jefferson to Madison, May 12, 19, Aug. 11; to Monroe, May 5, 1793; "Anas," Apr. 18, 1793. *WTJ,* VI, 250–251, 259; *ibid.,* I, 227; *PJM,* XV, 57–58.

165. Jefferson to Madison, May 19, 27, June 2, 1793, *WTJ,* VI, 261, 268–269, 278.

166. Madison to Jefferson, May 27, 1793; Jefferson to Madison, June 9, 1793; *PJM,* XV, 22, 26–27.

167. "Anas," July 13, 1793, *WTJ,* I, 243.

168. *PAH,* XIV, 475, 193.

169. Hamilton to _____, May 18, 1793; "Defense of the President's Neutrality Proclamation," May 1793, *ibid.,* 473–476, 503.

170. *National Gazette,* May 15, June 1, 8, 1793. "But most," according to Donald H. Stewart, "eschewed any idea of war with Britain at this time. . . ." *The Opposition Press of the Federalist Period* (Albany, N.Y., 1969), p. 700.

171. *PAH,* XV, 33–43 (June 29), 55–63 (July 3), 65–69 (July 6), 82–86 (July 10), 90–95 (July 13–17), 100–106 (July 17), 130–133 (July 27).

172. Jefferson, "Anas," Aug. 2, 1793, *WTJ*, I, 254.

173. "No Jacobin," No. I; David Ross to Hamilton, Aug. 30, 1793; *PAH*, XV, 145, 309–310.

174. Jefferson to Madison, July 7, June 29, 1793, *WTJ*, VI, 338, 328. Madison to Jefferson, July 18, 30, 1793; "Letters of Helvidius"; *PJM*, XV, 44, 66–73, 80–87, 95–103, 106–110, 113–120.

175. Jefferson, "Anas," Aug. 2, 1793, *WTJ*, I, 253; to Madison, Aug. 11, 1793, *PJM*, XV, 57.

176. "Anas," Aug. 6, 1793; to Washington, Aug. 11, 1793; *WTJ*, I, 256–259, VI, 366–367.

177. Jefferson to Madison, Aug. 3, 1793, *ibid.*, VI, 361.

178. For circumstances surrounding the preparation of this paper (post-dated Aug. 16, through not finally approved until Aug. 20), memoranda from other cabinet members, and the text itself, see "Anas," Aug. 1, 2, 20, 1793; Jefferson to Morris, Aug. 16, 23, 1793; to Madison, Aug. 18, 1793; *ibid.*, I, 252–254, 259–261, VI, 371–397. (Text also in *ASP:FR*, I, 167–172.) Jefferson transmitted a copy of it to Genet sometime in September, with a covering letter, to which Genet replied heatedly and at length on Sept. 18. *WTJ*, VI, 429–430; *ASP:FR*, I, 172–174.

179. Jefferson to Madison, Aug. 11, 1793, *PJM*, XV, 56–57.

180. The typical sequence of ideas, together with the quotations, in the above paragraph are drawn from the Caroline County (Virginia) resolutions of Sept. 10, 1793, which are in turn a modified version of Madison's "train of Ideas" sent to Jefferson on Sept. 2. Most of the Virginia meetings followed Madison's and Monroe's model, with many identically worded passages. The "our beloved president" phrase is from the Amelia County (Virginia) resolutions of Oct. 24. Boston *Independent Chronicle*, Oct. 10, 1793; *PJM*, XV, 79–80; *Baltimore Daily Intelligencer*, Nov. 11, 1793. For Washington's replies, see *WGW*, XXXIII, *passim*. The best published treatment of these meetings is Ammon, "Genet Mission and Political Parties," which contains a very complete set of newspaper references. In one respect our interpretive emphasis differs a little from Professor Ammon's; he stresses the difference between "Republican" and "Federalist" resolutions, whereas we were rather more struck by the similarities. Another very full account of the resolutions campaign is in Woodfin, "Citizen Genet," pp. 323–338, 348–360.

181. Jefferson to Madison, Sept. 1, 1793, *WTJ*, VI, 401–402; *ASP:FR*, I, 240.

182. Even the doctors had violently differing theories of the cause of the disease, which reflected in an uncanny way their political views. Republican doctors tended to claim that it arose from noxious local origins, whereas Federalist doctors thought it had been brought in from the outside (the thousands of Frenchmen fleeing from St. Domingue). The most notorious Republican cure, that of Benjamin Rush, required drawing extraordinary amounts of blood, more than most patients possessed. (Somewhat reminiscent of the guillotine, the treatment was frequently lethal.) Martin S. Pernick, "Politics, Parties, and Pestilence: Epidemic Yellow Fever in Philadelphia and the Rise of the First Party System," *WMQ*, 3rd Ser., XXIX (Oct. 1972), 559–586. The two Republican leaders referred to above who died in the epidemic were James Hutchinson and Jonathan Dickinson Sergeant. Jefferson, in the letter referred to in n. 181 above, implied that Freneau, in being among the very last to adhere to Genet (who had "totally overturned the Republican interest in Philadelphia"), had become politically rather isolated.

183. "Anas," Nov. 28, 1793, *WTJ*, I, 270–272; *AC*, 3 Cong., 1 Sess., 14–16, 17–18, 138–139. The message referred to was one on the state of relations with France and Great

Britain, transmitted to both houses on Dec. 5, 1793. The papers accompanying it are in *ASP:FR,* I, 141–246. On Jefferson's report and Madison's proposals for retaliatory legislation, see Ch. IX below.

184. See, e.g., calendar of ministers' correspondence for constant complaints from Ternant, Fauchet, and Adet at having no instructions from home; CFM, pp. 20ff.

185. Genet to Minister of Foreign Affairs, May 31, June 19, 1793 (received July 31, 30), CFM, pp. 216–218; Deforgues to Genet, July 30, 1793, *ibid.,* pp. 228–231.

186. *Ibid.*

187. "Etats-Unis," AECPE-U 39, 466–469vo. Paine to Barère, Sept. 5, 1793; to Monroe, Oct. 20, 1794; Foner, ed., *Complete Writings,* II, 1332–1333, 1364–1374. De V. Payen-Payne, ed., *Memoirs of Bertrand Barère, Chairman of the Committee of Public Safety During the Revolution* (London, 1896), II, 114.

188. *Ibid.,* 114; Aulard, ed., *Actes du Comité de Salut Public,* VI, 461.

189. Deforgues to Genet, Sept. 28, 1793, AECPE-U 38, 277–277vo.

190. Thomas, *American Neutrality,* Appendix II ("Genet's Financial Difficulties"), pp. 272–274; Genet to Jefferson, Nov. 11, 14, 1793, *ASP:FR,* I, 185–186. A convenient summary of Genet's activities regarding the St. Domingue fleet is in Ammon, *Genet Mission,* pp. 111–131. Genet to Minister of Foreign Affairs, July 22, 1793, AECPE-U 38, 62–67; see also Bowman, *Struggle for Neutrality,* p. 91 and n.

191. The Executive Council "shall review [*épurer,* a word which literally means "purify" and "purge"] the selection of diplomatic agents already sent to various parts of the globe; such review to be submitted for the approval of the Committee of Public Safety with the instructions to be given." Aulard, ed., *Actes du Comité de Salut Public,* VI, 461, in connection with the order cited in n. 188 above.

192. "Exposé succinct de la conduite du Citoyen Genet dans les Etats Unis de l'Amérique," CFM, pp. 283–286. The archivist's annotation ("vers Octobre 1793"), however, seems to be mistaken. Paul Mantoux asserts, persuasively it seems to us, that the report was prepared sometime "in the course of September at the latest." "Le Comité de Salut Public et la mission de Genet aux Etats-Unis," *Revue d'histoire moderne et contemporaine,* XIII (Jan.–Feb. 1909), 12–13.

193. Morris to Jefferson, Oct. 10, 1793; to Deforgues, Oct. 8, 1793; Deforgues to Morris, Oct. 10, 1793; *ASP:FR,* I, 372–373, 375. "Etat des Agens politiques, Etats unis," AECPE-U 39, 193. Order of Oct. 11, Aulard, ed., *Actes du Comité de Salut Public,* VII, 359–360. There is no evidence that this was other than a routine committee decision, or that Robespierre had made it his particular business, as implied in Bowman, *Struggle for Neutrality,* p. 94. Nor are the notations in the margins of Otto's memorandum in Robespierre's handwriting. This paper too ("Etat des Agens politiques") seems to have been misattributed as to date ("Brumaire"); it could not have been prepared after Oct. 11, and probably not before Oct. 8. See again Mantoux, "Comité de Salut public," 18 and n.

194. A. G. J. [*sic*] Ducher, *Les deux hémispheres* (Paris, Oct. 28, 1793), AECPE-U 39, 201–204vo. Roland and Condorcet also committed suicide.

195. *Rapport . . . sur la situation politique de la République,* Nov. 17, 1793, AECPE-U 39, 279–293vo.; also in Henri Calvet, ed., *Les grands orateurs républicains: Robespierre* (Monaco, 1950), pp. 149–168.

196. Instructions to Commissioners, Nov. 15, 1793, CFM, p. 293. On Ducher's economic dogmas see Frederick L. Nussbaum, *Commercial Policy in the French Revolution: A Study of the Career of G. J. A. Ducher* (Washington, 1923).

197. Louis Didier, "Le Citoyen Genet," *Revue des questions historiques,* XCII (July 1912), 73.

198. Instructions to Commissioners, Nov. 15, 1793; Fauchet and Commissioners to Minister of Foreign Affairs, May 20, 1794; CFM, pp. 292, 345. Murdoch, "Citizen Mangourit," 537–539.

199. Fletcher, "Louisiana as a Factor in French Diplomacy," pp. 361, 370–373; E. Wilson Lyon, *Louisiana in French Diplomacy, 1759–1804* (Norman, Okla., 1934), pp. 61–65, 69. See also n. 139 above.

200. King, *King,* I, 478–479; Minnegerode, *Jefferson,* pp. 361ff. The qu. from Martha Genet is in *ibid.,* p. 403.

201. George Clinton Genet, *Washington, Jefferson, and "Citizen" Genet, 1793* (New York, 1899), pp. 50–51.

CHAPTER IX

America and Great Britain

1. Jefferson, "Anas," Nov. 28, 1793, *WTJ,* I, 271–272; *ASP:FR,* I, 141–246 (the Order in Council of June 8, 1793, repr. on p. 240); Hammond to Grenville, No. 2, Feb. 22, 1794, FO 5/4; Charles R. Ritcheson, *Aftermath of Revolution: British Policy Toward the United States, 1783–1795* (Dallas, Tex., 1969), p. 292.

2. Carroll and Ashworth, *Washington,* VII, 144 and n.

3. Jefferson, Report on Privileges and Restrictions, *WTJ,* VI, 470–484. A useful treatment of the report's background is Merrill D. Peterson, "Thomas Jefferson and Commercial Policy, 1783–1793," *WMQ,* 3rd Ser., XXII (Oct. 1965), 584–610. Peterson (*ibid.,* 609), Vernon G. Setser (*Commercial Reciprocity,* p. 114), and Dumas Malone (*Jefferson,* III, 159) are inclined to think that Jefferson intended his report to be simply a kind of valedictory, and that he expected nothing to come of it. But the evidence seems to show otherwise. The timing of the report, the circumstances in which it was issued, and the elaborate use Madison made of it in his resolutions campaign early in 1794 all point to the conclusion that both he and Jefferson were in dead earnest.

4. John Lord Sheffield, *Observations on the Commerce of the United States* 2nd ed. (London, 1784), p. 87.

5. The report is printed in *Collection of Interesting and Important Reports and Papers on the Navigation and Trade of Great Britain, Ireland, and the British Colonies in the West Indies and America, with Tables of Tonnage and of Exports and Imports, &c. &c. &c.* (London, 1807), pp. 47–154. The version that Jefferson saw in abstract form and filed with his papers is printed as *Report of a Committee of the Lords of the Privy Council on the Trade of Great Britain with the United States, January, 1791,* Worthington C. Ford, ed. (Washington, 1888). On the circumstances under which he came by it, see *PTJ,* XVIII, 267–272.

6. Report, *WTJ,* VI, 481–484.

7. *AC,* 1 Sess., 3 Cong., 157 (Jan. 3, 1794).

8. The great drop in the legal trade between the United States and the British West Indies, emphasized in the Hawkesbury Report, was for the most part offset by smuggling, by trade authorized under temporary proclamations from hard-pressed island governors, and by a very extensive indirect trade conducted through Dutch and French ports in the Caribbean. With the outbreak of war in 1793, British shipowners began shifting their tonnage to the more profitable and less risky European and Far Eastern trade, and the governors opened their ports more and more freely to all manner of American products

for extended periods of time. According to U.S. Treasury statistics, in the year ending Sept. 30, 1794 (the very time during which the Madison resolutions were being debated), 58,989 tons of American shipping had made at least one trip to the British West Indies (repeated voyages were not counted), whereas for 1790 the figure had been only 3,620 tons. This meant—since the tonnage in the Dutch and French West Indies trade dropped only slightly—that the Americans had completely absorbed the trade with the West Indies: British, Dutch, and French combined. On this and other matters referred to in the above paragraph see *ASP:CN*, I, 329–330; Alice B. Keith, "Relaxations in the British Restrictions on the American Trade with the British West Indies, 1783–1802," *Journal of Modern History*, XX (Mar. 1948), 1–18; and Gordon C. Bjork, "The Weaning of the American Economy: Independence, Market Changes, and Economic Development," *Journal of Economic History*, XXIV (Dec. 1964), 541–560.

9. This estimate is in John G. B. Hutchins, *The American Maritime Industries and Public Policy, 1789–1914* (Cambridge, Mass., 1941), p. 185. Though statistics for this period are erratic, evidence that a tremendous upturn in shipbuilding began in 1793, a point of particular importance for the events being discussed above, is scarcely to be doubted. "It can be demonstrated," according to the *Columbian Centinel* of Boston on June 21, 1794, "that the quantity of shipping owned in this town has increased more than double within the last eighteen months," and Edmond Genet noted similar activity in Philadelphia. Writing home on May 18, 1793, Genet reported that he had promises of 600,000 barrels of American grain and flour but that ships were scarce; they were, however, "being built everywhere." *CFM*, p. 215. Robert Goodloe Harper in a circular letter to his constituents (Mar. 22, 1795) stated that in 1789 "the ships built in the United States amounted to between 17,000 and 18,000 tons. In 1790, to 32,000 tons, which was an increase of nearly double in one year. In the year 1793 and in the first six months of 1794, the United States built vessels to the amount of 80,000 tons, without including the ports of Boston, Nantucket, Baltimore, Alexandria, Edenton, and the two Wilmingtons—these are ship-building ports. If the returns from them were completed, it would probably appear that the ship building of the United States in 1793, and the first part of 1794, amounted to at least 100,000 tons. This is at the rate of 70,000 tons which is more than four times what it was in the year 1789." *Newport Mercury*, qu. in Maude H. Woodfin, "Citizen Genet and his Mission" (Unpub. diss., U. of Chicago, 1928), p. 292n. Alexander Hamilton reported a total of 289,394 tons of shipping as of Sept. 30, 1792, and 367,734 tons as of Dec. 30, 1793. Subtracting about 15,000 tons for "ghost tonnage" (shipping still registered but having been lost or otherwise destroyed during the previous year), and adding roughly the same amount for ships sold to foreigners (the formula used by Albert Gallatin in his accounting of 1812), Harper's estimate of a 70,000-ton increase in shipbuilding for 1793 would seem about right. *ASP:CN*, I, 252, 897.

On the other hand, Douglass North's table in "U.S. Balance of Payments," p. 595, appears to show a drop in registered tonnage between 1792 and 1793 (and thus by implication a drop in shipbuilding), but this is almost certainly mistaken. For the years 1790–1792 North seems to have used "entering tonnage" rather than "registered tonnage" ("entering tonnage" is in effect a ship's tonnage multiplied by as many times as that ship entered port during a given year), whereas from 1793 on, he used the official figures for registered tonnage (which is counted only once). This created the anomaly of a higher figure for 1792 than for 1793.

10. On this point see *PAH*, XIII, 407.

11. *AC*, 3 Cong., 1 Sess., 189 (Jan. 13, 1794).

12. *Ibid.*, 191.

13. *Ibid.*, 197; see also above, pp. 248–249.

14. *Ibid.*, 206.

15. *Ibid.*, 211 (Jan. 14, 1794).

16. *Ibid.*, 212–213; see also table, p. 382 above, and n. 11.

17. *Ibid.*, 215.

18. *Ibid.*, 262–263 (Jan. 22, 1794).

19. *Ibid.*, 406–407 (Jan. 29, 1794).

20. *Ibid.*, 333 (Jan. 27, 1794).

21. *Ibid.*, 334.

22. *Ibid.*, 348–349 (changed from 3rd to 1st person in *WFA*, II, 37).

23. *Ibid.*, 338–339.

24. *Ibid.*, 368–369 (Jan. 29, 1794).

25. *Ibid.*, 393; on the powers of Joseph Fauchet, see above, p. 371.

26. *Ibid.*, 386.

27. *Ibid.*, 390.

28. Ames to Gore, Jan. 28, 1794 (probably misdated; it was more likely the 29th), *WFA*, I, 133–134.

29. *AC*, 3 Cong., 1 Sess., 422.

30. *Ibid.*, 431–432; Madison to Jefferson, Mar. 2, 1794, *PJM*, XV, 270. It was believed, according to George Hammond, that Madison and his friends, fearing "that they should be deserted by a part of their majority . . . deemed it more expedient to postpone the final decision for a few weeks, and to take the chance of fresh causes of irritation against Great Britain arising in that period." Hammond to Grenville, No. 2, Feb. 22, 1794, FO 5/4.

31. Christopher Gore to Rufus King, Mar. 3, 1794, King, *King*, I, 547; Ritcheson, *Aftermath of Revolution*, p. 299; also mentioned in Madison to Jefferson, letter cited in n. 33 above.

32. Alfred F. Young, *The Democratic Republicans of New York: The Origins, 1763–1797* (Chapel Hill, N.C., 1967), pp. 373–374; Laurance to King, Mar. 8, 1794, King, *King*, I, 549.

33. Hammond to Grenville, No. 4, Mar. 7, 1794, FO 5/4; *PAH*, XVI, 132 and note. The vote does not appear in *AC*.

34. E.g., "Probably the outstanding point in connection with the negotiation of the treaty, however, is the extent to which a small group of Federalist Senators, who were also among Washington's most trusted advisers, dominated the entire proceeding. These men suggested the mission; they secured its acceptance by the President, and practically directed the selection of the envoy; they secured his confirmation by the Senate; they sent him out fully cognizant of their views as to what sort of treaty should be striven for and under very flexible instructions from the Department of State." Ralston Hayden, *The Senate and Treaties, 1789–1817: The Development of the Treaty-Making Functions of the United States Senate During Their Formative Period* (New York, 1920), and qu. with approval in Edgar A. Robinson, *The Evolution of American Political Parties: A Sketch of Party Development* (New York, 1924), pp. 65–66.

35. *PAH*, XVI, 131; *ASP:FR*, I, 430.

36. Hamilton to Washington, Mar. 8, 1794, *PAH*, XVI, 134–136.

37. King, *King*, I, 517–518.

38. *AC*, 1 Sess., 3 Cong., 485, 500–504. (The debate on the frigates bill is in *ibid.*, 432–441, 444–451, 459, 485–498.) Madison to Jefferson, Mar. 12, 1794, *PJM*, XV, 279.

39. Same to same, Mar. 9, 14, 1794, *ibid.*, 274, 284. Madison's arguments against building warships were made on Feb. 6, 7, and 11, 1794, *AC*, 3 Cong., 1 Sess., 433, 438, 441, 449–451.

40. *Ibid.*, 521–522 (Mar. 14, 1794). Madison's letters of Mar. 9, 12, and 14 to Jefferson, and to his father, Mar. 10, 1794, reflect the course of his thinking on both the commercial resolutions and the possibilities of an embargo. *PJM*, XV, 276–277, and citations in nn. 41–42 above.

41. Pinckney to Randolph, Nov. 25, 1793, qu. in *PAH*, XVI, 130–131. The Order in Council of Nov. 6 was still a secret, but Pinckney had heard rumors that "they meditate fresh embarrassments to our trade."

42. King, *King*, I, 518. "The President," according to King, "was at first reserved [one could probably read "glacial"]—finally more communicative and apparently impressed with Ellsworth's representation."

43. Madison to Jefferson, Mar. 24, 1794, *PJM*, XV, 288. The debate, held behind closed doors, was not reported in *AC*.

44. "We are continually receiving information of the capture, dentention & condemnation of our vessels," Christopher Gore wrote to Rufus King from Boston on Mar. 15. The merchants there, he said, were for the time being opposed to punitive action against British property. "But such a temper cannot be expected to continue for any length of time, in those, who, from the most exalted state of affluence, are thrown into poverty and bankruptcy. . . ." The Salem merchants, he added, "have not that spirit of forbearance which operates on those of this place." King, *King*, I, 552–553. According to the Federalist *Gazette of the United States*, "The unparalleled depredations on commerce by the British nation, has provoked universal indignation. . . . Indeed what is their conduct but universal piracy!" Mar. 26, 1794.

45. Skipwith to Randolph, Mar. 1, 7, 1794, *ASP:FR*, I, 428–429. According to the endorsement on the originals in the National Archives, they were received at Baltimore on Mar. 20, though there is no indication of when they reached Philadelphia.

46. Clinton to Washington, Mar. 20, 1794, enclosing copy of Dorchester's speech, Washington Papers, LC. The text of the speech was printed in *Gazette of the United States*, Mar. 26, 1794, and headed "By this Day's mail NEW-YORK, March 24," which suggests that Washington received his copy no later than that date, and that this and the Skipwith dispatches must have reached him at nearly the same time, certainly no more than a day or two apart. For a discussion of how the speech became public see Samuel F. Bemis, *Jay's Treaty: A Study in Commerce and Diplomacy*, rev. ed. (New Haven, 1962), p. 267n. The text of it is also printed in Ernest A. Cruikshank, ed., *The Correspondence of Lieutenant Governor John Graves Simcoe* (Toronto, 1923–1931), II, 149–150.

47. *ASP:FR*, I, 428: *AC*, 3 Cong., 1 Sess., 75–76, 529–530; John J. Reardon, *Edmund Randolph: A Biography* (New York, 1975), p. 444, n. 63.

48. *AC*, 3 Cong., 1 Sess., 535–541; Jerald A. Combs, *The Jay Treaty: Political Battleground of the Founding Fathers* (Berkeley Calif., 1970), pp. 121–122. The point about Washington's conviction that the British intended war assumes that if he had not been so convinced he would not even have considered transmitting the Dorchester speech before making an effort to confirm its authenticity.

49. *Gazette of the United States*, Mar. 28, 1794; Herman LeRoy to Rufus King, Mar. 30, 1794, King, *King*, I, 557.

50. *Gazette of the United States*, Mar. 28, 1794; Washington to Clinton, Mar. 31, 1794, *WGW*, XXXIII, 310–311. (Although Washington's inference that the speech had been made on orders from London proved unfounded, there were good grounds for it in the

speech itself and in the references Dorchester made therein to having recently returned from a stay in England.) Pinckney to Randolph, Jan. 9, 1794, *ASP:FR*, I, 430–431.

51. *Ibid.*, 429. The rumors had been current among Federalists for two or three weeks (see John Alsop to Rufus King, Apr. 4, 1794, King, *King*, I, 559); the Nicholas and Monroe letters cited below indicate that by now they had reached the Republicans as well.

52. Randolph to Washington, Apr. 6, 1794, Jared Sparks, ed., *Correspondence of the American Revolution: Being Letters of Eminent Men to George Washington from the Time of His Taking Command of the Army to the End of His Presidency* (Boston, 1853), IV, 448–451; Nicholas to Washington, Apr. 6, 1794, qu. in *PAH*, XVI, 263, and *WJM*, I, 292n.; Monroe to Washington, Apr. 8, 1794, *ibid.*, I, 291–292; Washington to Monroe, Apr. 9, 1794, *WGW*, XXXIII, 320–321; Reardon, *Randolph*, pp. 263–264.

53. *Ibid.*, p. 264; King, *King*, I, 518–519; Jay to Mrs. Jay, Apr. 9, 10, 1794, *CPJJ*, IV, 2–3.

54. *AC*, 3 Cong., 1 Sess., 561–603.

55. Hamilton to Washington, Apr. 14, 1794, *PAH*, XVI, 266–279 (see 265n. on date of confirmation). King, *King*, I, 520–521. Washington to Jay, Apr. 15, 1794; to Randolph, Apr. 15, 1794; to Senate, Apr. 16, 1794; *WGW*, XXXIII, 329–330, 332–333. *AC*, 3 Cong., 1 Sess., 88–90, 675–683, 731–734. Combs, *Jay Treaty*, pp. 134–135. The Jay appointment, according to Madison, "has had the effect of impeding all legislative measures for extorting redress from G.B." To Jefferson, May 11, 1794, *PJM*, XV, 327.

56. *Philadelphia General Advertiser*, Apr. 28, 1794; see also Donald H. Stewart, *The Opposition Press of the Federalist Period* (Albany, N.Y., 1969), pp. 188–190 for a summary of the various newspaper arguments against the mission.

57. *Boston Independent Chronicle*, Apr. 28, 1794.

58. Madison to Jefferson, May 11, Apr. 28, 1794, *PJM*, XV, 328, 316. On Jay's views regarding debts and Peace Treaty violations see Bemis, *Jay's Treaty*, pp. 283–285; and Ritcheson, *Aftermath of Revolution*, p. 86.

59. *Ibid.*, pp. 310–312; Bemis, *Jay's Treaty*, pp. 239–241. Hammond on Apr. 7 had told Rufus King "in confidence that Dorchester was not authorized to have made the speech. . . ." King, *King*, I, 524.

60. *Ibid.*, 523; *PAH*, XVI, 319n.

61. *Ibid.*, XVI, 319–323; Frank Monaghan, *John Jay, Defender of Liberty* (Indianapolis, 1935), p. 368.

62. This supposition was based on the British Order in Council of Jan. 8, 1794, which confined seizures to ships sailing directly between European ports and the French West Indies (in addition to those carrying French property or military contraband). The operative word is "directly," the implication being that island cargoes first landed in the United States and then trans-shipped would not be subject to seizure. Hamilton to Washington, Apr. 23, 1794; to Jay, May 6, 1794; *PAH*, XVI, 320, 382–383. The Order is repr. in *ASP:FR*, I, 431.

63. *PAH*, XVI, 322–323, 357–358.

64. *ASP:FR*, I, 472–474.

65. *PAH*, XVI, 381.

66. Bemis, *Jay's Treaty*, p. 297, asserts that this "conflicted with the mandate in Jay's instructions not to let the question of the spoliations be connected in the negotiation with that of the old treaty disputes." Such was not, however, what the instructions said. They specified that "no adjustment of the [inexecution and infraction of the treaty] is to *be influenced* by the [vexations and spoliations]." *ASP:FR*, I, 473; italics added.

67. Bemis, *Jay's Treaty*, p. 298.

68. *PAH,* XVI, 383.

69. Grenville, according to Bemis, "shrewdly manipulated Jay during the negotiations"; Jay was "outplayed" by a "more able and experienced diplomat." Ritcheson, on the other hand, stoutly insists that whatever advantages Grenville secured, "they outweighed not a whit those won by John Jay." "The wheel had come full circle," he writes of the treaty's completion, "and Pitt, Grenville, and many of their countrymen caught at least a glimpse of Shelburne's vision: a working, harmonious, and mutually beneficial Anglo-American partnership." Bemis, *Jay's Treaty,* pp. 282, 370, 371; Ritcheson, *Aftermath of Revolution,* pp. 351, 352.

70. E.g., according to Bemis "the diplomatic situation, as it would have been viewed by a shrewd diplomatist who knew all the cards, all the players, all the stakes in the great international game, would have been pronounced favorable to the United States." (Except, of course, that "the great international game" did not include the United States.) *Jay's Treaty,* p. 316. And Ritcheson declares: "The stark truth in 1794 was that Britain simply could ill afford a war with America." (In principle this was probably more or less true, though one might hesitate to say how "stark" it was.) *Aftermath of Revolution,* p. 350.

71. Hawkesbury to Grenville, June 19, 1794, qu. in *ibid.,* p. 324; Pitt and Grenville, it will be remembered, had been prepared in principle to consider evacuation of the posts since the Nootka Sound crisis of 1790. See also Bemis, *Jay's Treaty,* pp. 78, 128, 206, 318.

72. Ritcheson, *Aftermath of Revolution,* pp. 299–303.

73. On the St. Domingue undertaking see John W. Fortescue, *A History of the British Army* (London, 1899–1930), IV, 326–349, 457–459, 466–476, 545–566; see also David P. Geggus, *Slavery, War, and Revolution: The British Occupation of Saint Domingue 1793–1798* (Oxford, 1982).

74. John Ehrman, *The Younger Pitt: The Reluctant Transition* (London, 1983), II, 327–361; Georges Lefebvre, *The French Revolution from 1793 to 1799* (New York, 1964), pp. 14–15, 19–20, 129.

75. Philip A. Brown, *The French Revolution in English History* (London, 1965), pp. 75–122; Ehrman, *Younger Pitt,* pp. 385–402.

76. Francis O'Gorman, *The Whig Party and the French Revolution* (London, 1967), pp. 139–208; Ehrman, *Younger Pitt,* pp. 402–419.

77. Combs, *Jay Treaty,* pp. 143–144; IBM, pp. 57–58.

78. Strictly speaking, two; the bulk of Hammond's dispatches came in on the 10th (Nos. 2–15, between Feb. 22 and Apr. 17), with two final ones (Nos. 17 and 18, dated Apr. 28 and May 8) arriving on the 12th. *Ibid.,* p. 58n.; Bemis, *Jay's Treaty,* p. 300n.

79. Hammond to Grenville, Feb. 22, 1794, No. 2, FO 5/4.

80. Same to same, Apr. 17, 1794, No. 15, FO 5/4. A portion of this dispatch is repr. in *PAH,* XVI, 281–286.

81. Same to same, Apr. 28, 1794, No. 17, FO 5/4. Jay had, according to Hammond, "assured me of his sincere personal disposition to remove by fair and candid explanation every obstacle that may be opposed to the amicable adjustment of the points in discussion between Great Britain and the United States; and added that the hope of effecting so great a benefit to his country was the sole consideration which could have induced him to accept the trust that had been committed to him, in the execution of which he had required that much should be left to his own discretion, and that for this reason he had explicitly expressed to this government his determination of relinquishing his appointment, if any of the measures of hostility against Great Britain which have been so much agitated in the house of representatives, should be passed by the legislature, and finally receive the sanction of the President under the existing circumstances."

82. See n. 74 above.

83. Jay to Randolph, June 23, 1794, No. 2, *ASP:FR*, I, 476, and *CPJJ*, IV, 28; Jay to Washington, June 23, 1794, *ibid.*, IV, 26; Jay to Randolph, July 6, 1794, No. 4, *ASP:FR*, I, 476; Dundas to Simcoe, July 4, 1794, and Dundas to Dorchester, July 5, 1794, *Michigan Pioneer and Historical Society Historical Collections*, XXIV (1895), 678–682; Ritcheson, *Aftermath of Revolution*, pp. 319–320.

84. Jay to Randolph, July 6, 9, 1794, Nos. 4 and 5, *ASP:FR*, I, 477, 479; Jay to Hamilton, July 11, 1794, *PAH*, XVI, 608–609. See also Bemis, *Jay's Treaty*, p. 320n.

85. Jay to Randolph, July 12, 1794, No. 6, *ASP:FR*, I, 479.

86. Same to same, Sept. 13, 1794, No. 15, July 6, 1794, No. 4, *ibid.*, 486, 477; on exclusion of the secretaries, see Combs, *Jay Treaty*, p. 151.

87. Jay to Randolph, Sept. 13, 1794, No. 15, *ASP:FR*, I, 485–486.

88. Jay to Grenville, July 30, 1794; Grenville to Jay, Aug. 1, 1794, *ibid.*, 481–482. The two Orders are repr. in *ibid.*, 482, and in Josiah T. Newcomb, "New Light on Jay's Treaty," *American Journal of International Law*, XXVIII (Oct. 1934), 686n., respectively.

89. Jay to Randolph, Aug. 8, 1794, No. 11, *ASP:FR*, I, 483.

90. Jay to Grenville, Aug. 6, 1794, *ibid.*, 486–487.

91. The point was made in Hamilton's memorandum of Apr. 23, 1794, to Washington, having been agreed upon in cabinet meetings and conceded by Jefferson in his correspondence with Hammond the year before. *PAH*, XVI, 320–321. See esp. Jefferson to Hammond, Sept. 5, 1793, *ASP:FR*, I, 174–175.

92. Grenville to Jay, Aug. 30, 1794, *ibid.*, 487–490. See also "Project of Heads of Proposals to be made to Mr. Jay," undated ms. in Grenville's private papers, pr. as Appendix in Bemis, *Jay's Treaty*, pp. 381–390.

93. Jay to Grenville, Sept. 1 and 4, 1794, *ASP:FR*, I, 490–492. Grenville had actually proposed two possible lines which would rectify this alleged "boundary gap," resulting from a "geographical error" at the time of the Peace Treaty, subsequently discovered by George Hammond, and Jay in his letter of Sept. 4 to Grenville enclosed two maps showing in square miles the territorial losses which the United States would incur from either of the proposed adjustments. They are reproduced in *ibid.*, 492. For a discussion of the boundary gap question see Bemis, *Jay's Treaty*, pp. 329–332, and "Jay's Treaty and the Northwest Boundary Gap," *AHR*, XXVII (Apr. 1922), 465–484.

94. Jay to Grenville, Sept. 4, 1794; Grenville to Jay, Sept. 5, 1794; "Notes" on Grenville's projet in preparation for meeting of Sept. 6, enclosed in Jay to Randolph, Sept. 13, No. 15; same to same, Oct. 29, 1794, No. 19; *ibid.*, 490–493, 500.

95. Grenville to Jay (private), Sept. 7, 1794; Jay to Grenville (private), Sept. 7, 1794 (on the indiscretions of Monroe and the two letters from Randolph to the Committee of Public Safety, likewise rather giddy, which Monroe presented at the same time), FO 95/512. "I do not believe," Grenville wrote, "that you personally will much envy Mr. Monroe the honour of the fraternal kiss which he has received; and if such an exhibition is thought not to degrade an American Minister I know not why it should become matter of complaint on the part of the British Government." "But," he continued, referring to both Monroe and Randolph, "it is not consistent with neutrality to make Ministerial declarations of favour and preference, nor can it lead to the maintenance of good order in any Country that its Government should give official sanction and adherence to acts at which all Religion and all Humanity revolt." Jay in his reply wrote, "Had I been in Mr. Randolph's place, I should not have written exactly such a Letter." Bemis calls this "a pious exchange of epistles" (*Jay's Treaty*, p. 333), which it certainly was. Jay to Washington, Sept. 13, 1794; to Randolph, Sept. 13 (private); to Hamilton, Sept. 11, 1794; *CPJJ*, IV, 58–60; National

Archives Microfilm, Diplomatic Dispatches, Series M39, Great Britain. Jay was exceedingly blunt with Randolph, telling him of the "uneasy Sensation" the affair had created in London. "It is not pleasant for me to say these Things, but so is the fact, and it is proper that you should know it." The texts of Monroe's speech and Randolph's letters are in *ASP:FR,* I, 674–675.

96. Jay to Grenville, Sept. 30, 1794, pr. as Appendix III in Bemis, *Jay's Treaty,* pp. 391–433.

97. Bemis calls this a "stupendous retreat" on Jay's part from the positions he had taken in his Sept. 30 draft, with which Ritcheson strongly disagrees. The evidence seems somewhat to favor Ritcheson's view here, though Ritcheson's further argument that Jay's reason for not transmitting the draft home with his other papers was that it consisted merely of "a set of working notes" appears somewhat strained. *Ibid.,* p. 334; *Aftermath of Revolution,* p. 332 and n.; The text of the treaty is in each of these works, as well as in *ASP:FR,* I, 520–525; and Hunter Miller, ed., *Treaties and Other International Acts of the United States of America* (Washington, 1931–48), II, 245–267.

98. Jefferson to Genet, July 24, 1793. *ASP:FR,* I, 166–167; to Robert R. Livingston, Sept. 9, 1801, *WTJ,* VIII, 92. "And I believe we may safely affirm," Jefferson continued, "that not a single instance can be produced where any nation of Europe, acting professedly under the law of nations alone, unrestrained by treaty, has, either by it's executive or judiciary organs, decided on the principle of 'free bottoms, free goods.'"

99. On the question of free trade across the border, see esp. Grenville to Jay, Aug. 30, 1794, Art. 1 of treaty projet, *ASP:FR,* I, 488; Jay to Randolph, Sept. 13, 1794, No. 15 ("Notes," Note 4), and same to same, Oct. 29, 1794, No. 19 ("It was proposed that goods for the Indian trade should pass from Canada to the Indians within the United States, *duty free;* to this I could not consent"); *ibid.,* 488, 492, 500.

On tonnage duties, Art. IV of the treaty reserved to the British government "the right of imposing on American Vessels entering into the British Ports in Europe a Tonnage Duty, equal to that which shall be payable by British Vessels in the Ports of America." This was equalization, in that each would pay the same tonnage duties in the other's ports, but it did not do away with the discrimination in American ports between American and foreign ships as established by the Tonnage Act of 1789; six cents a ton on American-built and American-owned ships, thirty cents on ships built in America but partly or wholly owned by foreigners, and fifty cents on all others. (*U.S. Statutes at Large,* I, 27). This discrimination, on the other hand, was not the same kind Madison had in mind when he first devised the measure; Madison's original bill would also have discriminated between British and French shipping by requiring the former to pay a higher duty. The treaty prohibited this form of discrimination. Jay wrote Randolph on Oct. 29, 1794, "It has been proposed that alien tonnage and impost should cease; to this there . . . appeared to me to be very strong objections." (*ASP:FR,* I, 500.) The "strong objections" held, inasmuch as Art. IV of the completed treaty provided that "the United States will not impose any *new or additional* Tonnage Duties on British Vessels, nor increase the now subsisting difference between the Duties payable on the importation of any articles in British or in American Vessels." (Italics added.) See also Jay to Randolph, Nov. 19, No. 22, *ASP:FR,* I, 503. It is true, on the other hand (turning again to the "equalization" referred to above), as Combs points out, that "the lighthouse and Trinity fees charged American ships in British ports exceeded the tonnage duties charged British ships in American ports." *Jay Treaty,* p. 152.

100. Jay to Randolph, Sept. 13, 1794, No. 15; same to same, Feb. 6, 1795, No. 31, *ASP:FR,* I, 485, 518. Jefferson to Monroe, May 10, 1786, *PTJ,* IX, 501. On the difficulties of presenting evidence, see Ritcheson, *Aftermath of Revolution,* pp. 70–74.

101. Bemis, *Jay's Treaty*, p. 339.

102. It speaks for Bemis's scrupulousness as a scholar that his own evidence, from which conclusions very different from his own may be drawn, is so complete. See *ibid.*, pp. 299–315, 337–344; "The United States and the Abortive Armed Neutrality of 1794," *AHR*, XXIV (Oct. 1918), 26–47; and Ritcheson, *Aftermath of Revolution*, pp. 352–353.

103. On the benefits to the United States of the East India article see Holden Furber, "The Beginnings of American Trade with India, 1784–1812," *NEQ*, XI (June 1938), 235–265; and G. Bhagat, "The Jay Treaty and the Indian Trade," *Essex Institute Historical Collections*, CVII (Apr. 1972), 153–172.

104. Jay to Washington, Mar. 6, 1795, *CPJJ*, IV, 163; Jay to Randolph, June 1, 1795, *ASP:FR*, I, 520.

105. Ritcheson makes the most of this; see *Aftermath of Revolution*, pp. 345–350, and "Lord Hawkesbury and Article Twelve of Jay's Treaty," *Studies in Burke and his Time*, XV (Winter 1973–74), 155–166; see also Perkins, "Lord Hawkesbury and the Jay-Grenville Negotiations," and Combs, *Jay Treaty*, p. 154.

106. Grenville, "Heads of Proposals," Bemis, *Jay's Treaty*, p. 389; Buckingham to Grenville, Aug. 6, 1794, Historical Manuscripts Commission, *The Manuscripts of J. B. Fortescue, Esq., Preserved at Dropmore* (London, 1894), II, 611.

107. See above, nn. 11–12.

108. Monroe to Madison (and subsequently to Edmund Randolph), Dec. 18, 1794. Monroe wanted Madison to consider this letter and decide whether it should be passed on to Randolph. *PJM*, XV, 416–418; *WJM*, II, 154–161.

109. Jay to Hamilton, July 18, 1794, *PAH*, XVI, 609.

110. Stewart, *Opposition Press*, pp. 190–191; "Peter Porcupine" [William Cobbett], *A Little Plain English, Addressed to the People of the United States, on the Treaty . . .* (Philadelphia, 1795), p. 105; John B. McMaster, *A History of the People of the United States, from the Revolution to the Civil War* (New York, 1885), II, 213.

111. "An American," *Boston Independent Chronicle*, Nov. 3, 1794; "A", repr. from *ibid.*, Nov. 10, 13, 1794, from *New York Journal.* Whereas the Federalist *New York Minerva* declared that the "spirited and manly, as well as decent tone of Mr. Jay's note to the British minister, does him much honor," the Republican *Philadelphia Aurora*, discussing the same note, referred to "the servile language of Mr. Jay's humble address to Lord Grenville." Repr. in *Aurora*, Oct. 25, 1794; *ibid.*, Nov. 19, 1794. Likewise James Madison, who called it a "humiliating memorial." To Jefferson, Nov. 16, 1794, *PJM*, XV, 381. The Americans' exaggerated defensiveness and touchiness in matters of etiquette and ceremony is interestingly shown by "Philo-Republicanus" in the *Aurora*, Nov. 18, 1794. The "genuine republican," he wrote, "conceives it beneath the dignity of Man, to either give or receive the smallest degree of unmerited respect. His candid soul disdains the mask of hypocritical politeness. . . ." (Under this rule, of course, diplomacy as conventionally conducted would be out of the question.)

112. The fourteen essays appeared in the *Philadelphia Independent Gazetteer* from March 11 to June 10, 1795, and were collected in pamphlet form as *Letters of Franklin on the Conduct of the Executive, and the Treaty Negociated, by the Late Chief Justice of the United States, with the Court of Great-Britain* (Philadelphia, 1795). References here are to the pamphlet, the direct quotations being from pp. 11, 20, 51. William Cobbett suspected that "Franklin" was none other than the French minister, Joseph Fauchet. But if he had been, Fauchet would have needed some local assistance, for he wrote no English—though the gallicism "combatting," quoted above, suggests that the *Letters* could have been a translation from French. When Cobbett's *A Little Plain English* was republished by his

children in 1835, they ignored their father's (plausible, we believe) conjectures as to Fauchet, referring now to the *Letters* as "supposed to be written by Mr. [Alexander J.] Dallas, Secretary of the State of Pennsylvania, but published under the assumed name of *Franklin.*" The difficulty here is that in writing Dallas's life, his son, George M. Dallas, while referring freely to his father's activities against the treaty, including the authorship of a very influential pamphlet entitled *Features of Mr. Jay's Treaty* which the junior Dallas reprinted as an appendix, made no reference whatever to "Franklin." In tone and texture the two works do not appear similar. *Plain English* (1795 ed.), pp. 89–90; John M. Cobbett and James P. Cobbett, eds., *Selections from Cobbett's Political Works . . .* (London, 1835), I, 53; George M. Dallas, *Life and Writings of Alexander James Dallas* (Philadelphia, 1871), pp. 50–54, 160–210. But it would be a safe guess that "Franklin," whoever he was, must have had close connections with the Democratic Society of Philadelphia.

113. Carroll and Ashworth, *Washington,* VII, 236–239.

114. Stewart, *Opposition Press,* p. 192. Josiah Parker declared that "if we do not get all we ask it must be the fault of our Negociator at the Court of London." Parker to Thomas Smith, Dec. 28, 1794, qu. in Combs, *Jay Treaty,* p. 159.

115. *WFA,* I, 166. Ames seems to have been fairly shrewd on this; he was almost certainly referring to a set of suspiciously honeyed predictions in the *Philadelphia Aurora,* Feb. 2, 1795, of the wonderful benefits shortly forthcoming with the treaty; only five days later, Feb. 7, 1795, the *Aurora* was denouncing "so ignoble, so dishonorable a treaty as that said to have been concluded."

116. News that a treaty had actually been signed reached Boston about Jan. 27, and New York about Jan. 31. It was first published in the Philadelphia papers Feb. 2. (See *Gazette of the United States* of that date, et seq.) Fragmentary details from various sources thereupon began making their appearance. See also Carroll and Ashworth, *Washington,* VII, 233–234 and nn.

117. E.g., to James Madison, Sr., Feb. 8, 1795, *PJM,* XV, 469.

118. R. R. Livingston to Madison, Jan. 30, 1795; Madison to Livingston, Feb. 8, 1795; Madison to Jefferson, Feb. 15, 1795; *ibid.,* 459–461, 468–469, 473.

119. *Ibid.,* 121.

120. Another was "Sidney" and his series of five essays which appeared in the *Aurora* June 17, 19, 22, and 26, 1795. The message was very similar to that of "Franklin."

121. *Philadelphia Aurora,* June 22, 1795. See also Stewart, *Opposition Press,* pp. 193–194; James D. Tagg, *Benjamin Franklin Bache and the Philadelphia Aurora* (Philadelphia, 1991), pp. 244–245; *Letters of Franklin,* pp. 38–41; "Sidney," No. III, *Aurora,* June 22, 1795. The reason for the secrecy (and for flouting the sovereignty of the people) was obviously that the treaty was bad; otherwise "it would not be concealed." New York *Journal,* May 20, 1795. See also Daniel L. Hoffman, *Government Secrecy and the Founding Fathers: A Study in Constitutional Controls* (Westport, Conn., 1981), pp. 145–147.

122. King, *King,* II, 9–10; Hamilton to King, June 11, 1795, *PAH,* XVIII, 370–371; *AC,* 3 Cong., 3 Sess., 853–868. Strictly speaking, there would have been twenty-one Federalists and nine Republicans, but the defection of Pierce Butler, until then nominally a Federalist, made it twenty and ten.

123. *Ibid.;* Hayden, *Senate and Treaties,* p. 78; Eugene F. Kramer, ed., "Senator Pierce Butler's Notes of the Debates on Jay's Treaty," *South Carolina Historical Magazine,* LXII (Jan. 1961), 1–9. "I understand they have determined not to countenance a publication," wrote Oliver Wolcott to his wife, "though they have reserved the right of conversing generally about it." June 25, 1795, Gibbs, *Memoirs,* I, 199.

124. *AC,* 3 Cong., 3 Sess., 863.

125. Some of these questions are discussed in Hayden, *Senate and Treaties,* pp. 74–76, though more succinctly in Reardon, *Randolph,* pp. 294–295.

126. Washington to Hamilton, July 13, 1795, *PAH,* XVIII, 461–463.

127. Hamilton left office Jan. 31, 1795, and was succeeded by Oliver Wolcott, Jr., Comptroller of the Treasury since 1789. Henry Knox had also resigned as Secretary of War, effective Dec. 31, 1794. Knox's successor was Timothy Pickering, who had ably negotiated several Indian treaties for the federal government and had served as Postmaster-General since 1791. Carroll and Ashworth, *Washington,* VII, 228–229, 232–233.

128. Randolph to King, July 6, 1795, King, *King,* II, 15; Hamilton to Wolcott, June 26, 1795. *PAH,* 388–389; Edmund Randolph, *A Vindication of Mr. Randolph's Resignation* (Philadelphia, 1795), p. 28.

129. Tagg, *Bache,* pp. 246–247. Randolph was unable to get the treaty officially into print sooner because he had lent his only copy to Adet. As Tagg points out, however, Adet could not tell Randolph that he already had a copy. Adet's version is in his dispatch to Committee of Public Safety, July 3, 1795, CFM, pp. 741–742.

130. There are many descriptions of these public demonstrations. Documented accounts of those which occurred in Philadelphia, Baltimore, New York, and Boston may be found in William S. Wheeler, "Urban Politics in Nature's Republic: The Development of Political Parties in the Seaport Cities in the Federalist Era" (Unpub. diss., U. of Virginia, 1967), pp. 97–99, 173, 268–273, 368–372. See also Carroll and Ashworth, *Washington,* VII, 268–273; McMaster, *History,* II, 216–229. Broadus Mitchell in his *Alexander Hamilton,* II, 342–343, has thrown doubt on the story of Hamilton's having been stoned at the July 18 meeting in New York, and these doubts have been picked up by Alfred F. Young, *The Democratic Republicans of New York: The Origins, 1763–1797* (Chapel Hill, N.C., 1967), p. 451, and the editors of *PAH,* XVIII, 485n. Probably Hamilton did not retire "with blood streaming down his face" (McMaster, II, 219), but there is evidence enough that at least one stone made contact with Hamilton's head; the question appears to be not whether he was hit, but simply how hard. The incident was referred to in a number of newspapers at the time, and there is an account of the meeting signed by its chairman, W. S. Smith, which mentions it, in *Gazette of the United States,* July 21, 1795. On Philadelphia, see also Roland M. Baumann, "The Democratic-Republicans of Philadelphia: The Origins, 1776–1797" (Unpub. diss., Pennsylvania State U., 1970), pp. 517–522. The originals of the various petitions and addresses, of which there were about fifty, are in the Washington Papers, LC; some half of these were published by Mathew Carey, ed., *The American Remembrancer: or an Impartial Collection of Essays, Resolves, Speeches, &c. Relative, or Having Affinity, to the Treaty with Great Britain* (Philadelphia, 1795), 3v.

131. That is, nobody in America. The text of the Order remained unpublished until the twentieth century; it was rediscovered in the British Record Office, published, and analyzed by Josiah T. Newcomb in "New Light on Jay's Treaty," cited in n. 88 above. It is not known exactly when the first clear news of the Order and the seizures reached America. An item, somewhat tentative, appeared in the *Philadelphia Aurora* as early as June 25, but it seems that Washington did not take the reports seriously until they were confirmed by letters from Hamilton and Jay on the 6th and 7th of July, respectively. Randolph, however, tells a slightly different story in his *Vindication,* pp. 29–30; see also Carroll and Ashworth, *Washington,* VII, 262n.

132. Newcomb, "New Light," 691–692; Earl Spencer to Captain Sidney Smith, June 7, 1795, qu. in Perkins, *First Rapprochement,* p. 35; J. Stevenson, "Food Riots in England,

1792–1818," R. Quinault and J. Stevenson, eds., *Popular Protest and Public Order: Six Studies in British History, 1790–1920* (London, 1974), pp. 33–74; John Bassett Moore, ed., *International Adjudications . . .* (New York, 1931), IV, 28–29, 121–123.

133. On Grenville's responses to American complaints, see Newcomb, "New Light," 689–691; IBM, 88, 97–98; J. Q. Adams to Secretary of State, Dec. 5, 1795, *WJQA*, I, 434–449. (Adams wrote this from London, having been detailed there on a temporary mission from his regular post in the Netherlands to clear up unfinished details relating to the treaty.)

134. It is still not known exactly when or in what manner the Order was withdrawn. E.g., on Apr. 22, 1796, Samuel Smith of Maryland said in the House of Representatives that the British "had withdrawn that order since the ratification" (the exchange of ratifications occurred in London Oct. 28, 1795), but it had certainly been withdrawn well before then. The American chargé d'affaires in London, acting in Pinckney's absence, had written home twice that the Order "had a few days previous" to the 15th of September, 1795, "been rescinded," but adding that "as these Orders have not yet [as of Oct. 13] reached all the Cruizers, American Vessels are still sent in." *AC,* 4 Cong., 1 Sess., 1155; William A. Deas to Secretary of State, Sept. 15, Oct. 13, 1795, Diplomatic Dispatches, Great Britain, Series M30, National Archives. Adams, in the letter cited in n. 136 above, also refers to the Order as "revoked," sardonically adding that it would "not be revived so long as the costs of their captures will evidently mount higher than their value to the captors." *WJQA,* I, 447.

135. To these would shortly be added some fresh incidents of impressment, of which the most flagrant involved the activities of Captain Rodham Home, commanding the British cruiser *Africa,* off the coast of Rhode Island. See Carroll and Ashworth, *Washington,* VII, 301–302.

136. Randolph, *Vindication,* p. 28.

137. See above, pp. 393–394.

138. See esp. Randolph to Jay, Dec. 15, 1794 (which if taken at face value would virtually have required Jay to start over), and subsequent correspondence. *ASP:FR,* I, 509–512 *et seq.*

139. Randolph sent Washington three separate memoranda on this subject in the space of two days, the first two on June 24 and the third on June 25. The first and third are printed in W. C. Ford, ed., "Edmund Randolph on the British Treaty, 1795," *AHR,* XII (Apr. 1907), 589–590 and 587–588; the second in Jared Sparks, ed., *The Writings of George Washington . . .* (Boston, 1836), XI, 477–478. On the dating of them (unclear in both Sparks and Ford), see Reardon, *Randolph,* p. 457, nn. 74–75.

140. Washington to Secretaries of State, Treasury, and War, and Attorney-General, June 29, 1795, *WGW,* XXXIV, 224–225; Reardon, *Randolph,* pp. 296–297. On the opinion of Bradford, who was ill and may have given it informally, see *ibid.,* p. 458, n. 88.

141. "I do myself the honor of enclosing to you a letter from Colo. H. It proves, what I suspected, that the first opinion was not maturely weighed. But there is something in the business that is a little mysterious to me. . . ." Randolph to Washington, July 20, 1795, Washington Papers, LC.

142. Same to same (private), July 7, 1795, Moncure D. Conway, *Omitted Chapters in the History Disclosed in the Life and Papers of Edmund Randolph* (New York, 1888), pp. 265–267. See also Reardon, *Randolph,* pp. 297–299.

143. Sparks, ed., *Writings of Washington,* XI, 477; Ford, ed., "Randolph on British Treaty," 590–599.

144. *Ibid.*, 598.

145. Randolph, *Vindication*, pp. 31–32.

146. Washington to Hamilton, July 14, 1795, *PAH*, XVIII, 467; to Randolph, July 18, 1795, *WGW*, XXXIV, 243; Randolph to Washington, July 25, 31, 1795 (enclosing drafts of reply to Boston Selectmen), Washington Papers, LC; "To the Boston Selectmen," July 28, 1795, *WGW*, XXXIV, 252–253. (Replies to the other addresses, except to a few regarded as "too indecent" to merit one, were generally couched in the same language as the preceding.) During the period (July 15–Aug. 10) when Washington was absent from Philadelphia, Randolph wrote him a total of thirteen letters, all of which are in Washington Papers, LC. His own letters for that period are chronologically printed in *ibid.* The correspondence is discussed in Carroll and Ashworth, *Washington*, VII, 265–278, and Reardon, *Randolph*, pp. 303–308.

147. Washington to Randolph, July 22, 1795, *WGW*, XXXIV, 244.

148. Randolph to Washington, July 20, 1795, Washington Papers, LC; Washington to Randolph, July 24, 1795, *WGW*, XXXIV, 246–247.

149. Same to same, July 29, 1795, *ibid.*, 254–257.

150. Washington to Hamilton, July 29, 1795, *PAH*, XVIII, 525.

151. Randolph to Washington, July 29, 1795, Washington Papers, LC.

152. Randolph in his *Vindication* presents the evidence that he had converted Washington to his point of view and that the President was intending to act on it. To us the evidence is convincing. *How* firm Washington's intentions were, however (and thus how readily they might have been dislodged), may be another matter, and eminently debatable. There is no question but that while he was at Mount Vernon his apprehensions about France had gained considerable ground against those he already entertained regarding Britain (a point which seems to us insufficiently appreciated in other writings about the case), or that the implications of a delay in ratification were giving him more and more uneasiness. (Note the long "Sylla and charibdas" passage in his letter of July 31 to Randolph.) True, he assures Randolph, or seems to be reassuring him, that he still intends to do things his way—but not without a full, final canvassing of the whole question. The peculiar construction "It is not to be inferred from hence that I am, or shall be disposed to quit the ground I have taken, unless . . . but" occurs twice in his final letters. Washington to Randolph, July 31 and (slightly varied) Aug. 3, 1795, *WGW*, XXXIV, 266, 269. Nor was Randolph correct in claiming that Washington had "approved" his draft of the memorial to Hammond. He may have intended to—again, in principle—but he had not yet done it. Rather, he had cautiously written that it "*seems* well designed, to answer the end proposed" (without saying what he thought of "the end proposed"), and then referred to its being "revised, and new dressed." *Ibid.*, 267; *Vindication*, p. 40. (Italics added.)

153. Same to same, July 29, 1795, *WGW*, XXXIV, 255.

154. Randolph to Washington, July 31, 1795, Washington Papers, LC (2nd of 2 of that date); Pickering to Washington, July 31, 1795, Charles W. Upham, *The Life of Timothy Pickering* (Boston, 1873), III, 188–189.

155. *Ibid.*, 217; Gibbs, *Memoirs*, I, 233, 243.

156. *Ibid.*, 232–233, 243; Grenville to Hammond, May 9, 1795, IBM, 83; Hammond to Grenville, July 27, 1795, PRO:FO 5/9. Fauchet's dispatch in the original French is in CFM, pp. 444–455 (the other two referred to, Nos. 3 and 6, are also in *ibid.*, pp. 372–377, 411–418); an English translation is printed in Randolph, *Vindication*, pp. 41–48.

157. Upham, *Pickering*, III, 218.

158. Hammond to Grenville, Aug. 14, 1795, No. 33, PRO:FO 5/9. The pertinent

sections of both draft and final version of the memorial are repr. in Randolph, *Vindication*, pp. 33–34; and Newcomb, "New Light," 690n., respectively. A copy of the latter, dated Aug. 14, 1795, is in State Department Domestic Letters, National Archives.

159. Randolph, *Vindication*, pp. 5–9; Gibbs, *Memoirs*, I, 244–245; Upham, *Pickering*, III, 218. Bradford, in the last stages of his illness, was not present. He died only a few days later, on Aug. 23.

160. The chief contemporary writings and reminiscences on which our knowledge rests are those of Randolph, Wolcott, and Pickering cited above. Later writings are Conway, *Omitted Chapters*, pp. 237–357; Carroll and Ashworth, *Washington*, VII, 277–336; and Reardon, *Randolph*, pp. 307–334. Irving Brant's somewhat blustering "Edmund Randolph, Not Guilty!" *WMQ*, 3rd Ser., VII (Apr. 1950), 179–198, made a stir at the time of its appearance but looks rather less impressive now, in view of the flimsiness of two main assumptions on which its argument rests. One of these is that Randolph was deliberately framed by Pickering and Wolcott through their suppression of Dispatches 3 and 6, whereas it is now known that neither Pickering nor Wolcott (nor Hammond nor Grenville) had ever seen those dispatches. The other is the assumption that awkwardness of translation in the version Washington read altered the sense of it in significant ways. This seems greatly overdrawn, inasmuch as Pickering's translation and the one which Randolph (who knew French) thought acceptable enough to print differed very slightly, and in no instance were the words used by Pickering actually wrong. For instance, Brant makes much of the difference between the transliterated "precious confessions" ("précieuses confessions") and "valuable disclosures" (which comes closer to the writer's intentions); yet one cannot imagine Washington's state of mind being in the least altered by either one's having been used rather than the other. Indeed, he might well have seen "valuable disclosures" as the more sinister. For further discussion of these and other aspects of the case see Jerald Combs, *Jay Treaty*, Appendix II, pp. 193–196; and W. Allen Wilbur, "Oliver Wolcott, Jr., and Edmund Randolph's Resignation, 1795; An Explanatory Note on an Historic Misconception," *Connecticut Historical Society Bulletin*, XXXVIII (Jan. 1973), 12–16. A viewpoint similar to Brant's is Mary K. Bonsteel Tachau, "George Washington and the Reputation of Edmund Randolph," *JAH*, LXXIII (June 1986), 15–34, which argues that Washington "acquiesced in the sacrifice of Randolph's reputation in order to preserve his own." (p. 34).

161. Washington to Hamilton, July 29, 1795; to Randolph, July 31, 1795; *WGW*, XXXIV, 263, 266.

162. On the various extant translations, see *PAH*, XVIII, 528–529.

163. As is evident from the undated memorandum he sent to Wolcott and Pickering sometime between his return to Philadelphia and the scene of Aug. 19, 1795 (*WGW*, XXXIV, 275–276), asking their opinions on how Randolph ought to be confronted and the "measures proper to be taken." No one who reads through all the materials on the case can avoid some distress at the brutality of Washington's proceeding on the 19th. But this memorandum at least shows the nature of the dilemma he knew himself to be in, believing as he evidently did that the question of Randolph's "guilt" (of corruption, or whatever) was actually less important than the likelihood that no "Investigation of this subject" would be "so clear as to restore confidence and a continuance in Office." He had never removed a cabinet officer before, and was painfully embarrassed by the lack of a precedent, but what he did know was that he did not want the man around any longer, whatever extenuating details might eventually turn up. Yet there was no way this could be effected—either through outright dismissal or by a private effort to persuade Randolph to leave quietly—without ugly and mortifying public disclosures, because in either case

Randolph was bound to insist on vindicating his conduct, and Washington could not honorably place obstacles in the way of his doing so. Washington was thus forced, at least as he saw it, to cut off his options in advance, to stage it in such a way as to give Randolph no choice, to get it over with, and then to take the consequences, which were bound to be bad no matter what.

164. Randolph to Monroe [circular to all American representatives abroad], July 21, 1795, *ASP:FR,* I, 719; Randolph to Monroe, July 29, 1795, Monroe Papers, NYPL; also in Conway, *Omitted Chapters,* pp. 254–255. Carroll and Ashworth (*Washington,* VII, 289) take for granted that the letter of the 29th was among the papers Randolph showed to Washington, since Conway reported having seen, and in fact quoted from, an abstract in Washington's handwriting, even though the abstract is no longer to be found in the Washington papers. Reardon (*Randolph,* pp. 461–462) nonetheless argues that Randolph in fact did not show this letter to Washington, otherwise "he would have been obliged to mention it in his *Vindication.*" This reasoning, however, does not seem as plausible as the common-sense supposition that Conway had no reason to "invent" the abstract or to lie about Washington's handwriting, and that Randolph would not have been likely to conceal from the President a communication sent him in his capacity as an officer of the Executive.

165. Washington to Randolph, Oct. 21, 1795, *WGW,* XXXIV, 339–342.

166. Madison to Monroe, Jan. 26, 1796, *PJM,* XVI, 204; Carroll and Ashworth, *Washington,* VII, 329–336; Reardon, *Randolph,* pp. 332–334; Combs, *Jay Treaty,* pp. 169–170.

167. Upham, *Pickering,* III, 226–227. Presumably the account is Pickering's own, though this is not clear from the context. Conway (*Omitted Chapters,* p. 356) does not believe such an interview ever took place, claiming that the account contained "inaccuracies no Virginian could have uttered" regarding the background of the Randolph-Washington relationship. Conway's suspicions appear justified to the extent that Pickering in all likelihood put into Washington's mouth a whole string of reasons for his disillusionment that were more his own than Washington's. We would guess, however (given this qualification), that a scene in some way resembling the one referred to probably did occur. For comment on the evidence for other such scenes, see Carroll and Ashworth, *Washington,* VII, 332nn.

168. Robert R. Livingston's sixteen "Cato" essays appeared in the *New York Argus, or Greenleaf's New Daily Advertiser* between July 15 and Sept. 30, 1795; Brockholst Livingston wrote five as "Decius" and six as "Cinna" in the same paper, July 10–16 and Aug. 1–18, 1795, respectively; all are reprinted in Carey, *American Remembrancer* (see n. 130 above). With two or three notable exceptions, almost all the controversial writings on the treaty are collected in this valuable work. Alexander J. Dallas's "Features of Mr. Jay's Treaty" is one of the exceptions; it was published in five parts in *Dunlap and Claypoole's American Daily Advertiser* of Philadelphia, July 18–Aug. 7, 1795, and reprinted seventy-six years later in George M. Dallas, *Life and Writings of Alexander James Dallas.* Noah Webster published twelve essays signed "Curtius" in the New York *American Minerva,* July 18–Aug. 5, 1795, and reprinted them in N. Webster, *A Collection of Papers on Political, Literary and Moral Subjects* (New York, 1843), pp. 179–224; two of them were written by James Kent and the remainder by himself. Hamilton's "The Defence," thirty-eight pieces under the signature "Camillus," ran from July 22, 1795, to Jan. 9, 1796. The first twenty-one numbers appeared in the *New York Argus,* the remainder in the *New York Herald, a Gazette for the Country.* Hamilton wrote in addition four "Philo-Camillus" papers, July

17–Aug. 19, 1795, also published in the *Argus*. All are repr. in *PAH,* XVIII–XIX, except for the ten "Camillus" numbers written by Rufus King (though previously read and occasionally edited by Hamilton), repr. in Henry C. Lodge, ed., *The Works of Alexander Hamilton* (New York, 1885–86), V–VI.

169. Concluding phrase of a harangue delivered by McClenachan at the mass meeting of July 25, 1795, at Philadelphia; on the variant reported versions of the outburst see Carroll and Ashworth, *Washington,* VII, 272 and n.

170. "Observations on Mr. Jay's Treaty," No. I (July 15, 1795), Carey, ed., *American Remembrancer,* I, 114–119.

171. "Observations," Nos. II, III, IV (July 17, 22, 25, 1795), *ibid.,* 119–122, 147–156.

172. "The Defence," No. I (July 22, 1795), *PAH,* XVIII, 479–489.

173. No. II (July 25, 1795), *ibid.,* 493–501.

174. Nos. III, IV (July 29, Aug. 1, 1795), *ibid.,* 513–523; XIX, 77–85. On the various criticisms that had been made of the treaty's preamble see *ibid.,* XVIII, 514n.

175. Nos. VII, VIII, IX (Aug. 12, 15, 21, 1795), *ibid.,* XIX, 115–124, 134–145, 163–171.

176. "Observations," No. XV (Sept. 23, 1795), *American Remembrancer,* II, 13; "Juricola" [Tench Coxe], "An Examination of the Pending Treaty with Great Britain," No. IV (Aug. 12, 1795), *ibid.,* II, 88; "Cinna," No. V (Aug. 15, 1795), *ibid.,* III, 226; Dallas, "Features," *Life and Writings,* p. 196; Jefferson to Madison, Sept. 21, 1795, *WTJ,* VII, 192–193. "Even his enemies," said Brockholst Livingston (who was one of them), "must allow him to write well." *American Remembrancer,* III, 102.

177. Nos. I–V defend the treaty in general terms; the first ten articles are taken up in Nos. VI–XXII, five essays being devoted to Article X alone. In these five, Hamilton mounts a comprehensive attack on the entire principle of commercial coercion as debated in Congress in the spring of 1794, especially sequestration of debts, which he argues was contrary to all modern usages of international law. Most of the commercial articles are discussed by Rufus King in Nos. XXIII–XXX; Hamilton resumes with Articles XVII and XVIII in Nos. XXXI–XXXIII; and King concludes the substantive discussion with Nos. XXXIV and XXXV. The last three numbers, XXXVI–XXXVIII, argue the constitutionality of the treaty. In refuting the treaty's critics, Hamilton confined his attention almost entirely to the ablest of them, the two Livingstons and Dallas, though others are occasionally mentioned. The separate "Philo-Camillus" series of four essays is the rebuttal to a specific attack on "Camillus" made by "Cinna" (Brockholst Livingston). For another article-by-article defense of the treaty by Hamilton, see his long memorandum to Washington, "Remarks on the Treaty of Amity Commerce and Navigation lately made between the United States and Great Britain," July 9–11, 1795, *PAH,* XVIII, 404–454.

178. Ames to Jeremiah Smith, Jan. 18, 1796, *WFA,* I, 183.

179. See, e.g., below, pp. 446–447. Petition from Western Counties, Mar. 8, 1796 (wrongly dated Mar. 21), Gallatin Papers Microfilm, NYUL (also pr. in *Pittsburgh Gazette,* Mar. 12, 1796); "From the Western Telegraphe," *Gazette of the United States,* Apr. 5, 1796. Every expression of western opinion—in newspaper correspondence, petitions, or speeches in Congress—in support of the treaty made the same argument.

On the Greenville treaty terms and description of the boundaries see Reginald Horsman, *Expansion and American Indian Policy, 1783–1812* (East Lansing, Mich., 1967), pp. 101–102; and Beverley W. Bond, Jr., *The Foundations of Ohio* (Columbus, Ohio, 1941), pp. 247–248, 321. On the treaties of Ft. Stanwix, Ft. McIntosh, Ft. Finney, and Ft. Harmar see *ibid.,* pp. 244–247; and Horsman, *Expansion,* p. 48.

180. *ASP:IA,* I, 12–14; see also Francis P. Prucha, *The Great Father: The United States Government and the American Indians* (Lincoln, Neb., 1984), I, 61–71; and Dorothy V. Jones, *License for Empire: Colonialism by Treaty in Early America* (Chicago, 1984), pp. 137–186.

181. Bernard W. Sheehan, *Seeds of Extinction: Jeffersonian Philanthropy and the American Indian* (Chapel Hill, 1973), p. 10; Richard H. Kohn, *Eagle and Sword: The Beginnings of the Military Establishment in America, 1783–1802* (New York, 1975), pp. 95–96.

182. *Ibid.,* pp. 96–116; Jefferson to Monroe, Apr. 17, 1791, *WTJ,* V, 319; Randolph C. Downes, *Council Fires on the Upper Ohio: A Narration of Indian Affairs in the Upper Ohio Valley Until 1795* (Pittsburgh, 1940), pp. 320–322.

183. Kohn, *Eagle and Sword,* pp. 116–126.

184. *Ibid.,* pp. 148–155.

185. Reginald Horsman, "The British Indian Department and the Resistance to General Anthony Wayne, 1793–1795," *MVHR,* XLIX (Sept. 1962), 269–290; J. Leitch Wright, Jr., *Britain and the American Frontier, 1783–1815* (Athens, Ga., 1975), p. 96.

186. Horsman, "Resistance," 284–289; Wright, *Britain and the American Frontier,* p. 102.

187. Bond, *Foundations of Ohio,* pp. 321, 393.

188. The treaty is conveniently printed as Appendix V in Samuel F. Bemis, *Pinckney's Treaty: America's Advantage from Europe's Distress, 1783–1800,* rev. ed. (New Haven, Conn., 1960), pp. 343–362. The background of Spanish policy toward the United States regarding the Mississippi is discussed at length in *ibid.* and in Arthur P. Whitaker, *The Spanish-American Frontier, 1783–1795: The Westward Movement and the Spanish Retreat in the Mississippi Valley* (Boston, 1927), two works which complement each other and should be used together.

189. *Ibid.,* pp. 174–177.

190. Evarts B. Greene and Virginia D. Harrington, *American Population Before the Federal Census of 1790* (New York, 1932), pp. 192–194; Donald B. Dodd and Wynelle S. Dodd, *Historical Statistics of the South, 1790–1970* (University, Ala., 1973), pp. 22, 50; James G. M. Ramsey, *The Annals of Tennessee to the End of the Eighteenth Century* (Kingsport, Tenn., 1853), p. 648. The above figure for Kentucky is an estimate; since a census was taken for Tennessee in 1795 for purposes of admission to statehood, and since the proportion of increase from 1790 to 1800 for both states was almost identical, the estimate could be arrived at by linear interpolation:

	Tennessee	Kentucky
1790	35,691	73,677
1795	77,262	$[x = 161,252]$
1800	105,602	220,955

191. Whitaker, *Spanish-American Frontier,* p. 156.

192. *Ibid.,* pp. 180–222; Bemis, *Pinckney's Treaty,* pp. 218–284. A gentlemanly debate persisted for many years between Bemis and Whitaker (and was never settled) over the question of whether Godoy had actually seen the text of Jay's treaty before concluding his negotiations with Pinckney. For details, see Carroll and Ashworth, *Washington,* VII, 345–346n.

In view of the section which follows, and in conjunction with the point made above,

p. 439, on the abrupt expansion in 1796 of settlements in Ohio, it should be noted that the implications of Pinckney's treaty (in addition to those of Jay's) were immediately grasped by speculators. Navigation of the Mississippi, remarked Robert Morris, "doubles or trebles the value of lands bordering upon the Western Waters of the Ohio." Qu. in *ibid.*, 346n.

193. See pp. 381–382 and n. 9 above. Item from *Columbian Centinel* qu. in Walter B. Smith and Arthur H. Cole, *Fluctuations in American Business, 1790–1860* (Cambridge, Mass., 1935), p. 15.

194. From 1790 to 1796, money wages doubled and real wages rose 20 percent for laborers and 30 percent for ship carpenters. Before the rising cost of living began to reduce these gains in 1795, the Philadelphia ship carpenter had seen his real wages increase by over 40 percent, and the laborer's had risen by 58 percent, from 1790 to 1794.

Daily Wage and Real Wage Rates in Philadelphia, 1790–1796

	Ship carpenters		Laborers	
	Daily wage	Real wage	Daily wage	Real wage
1790	1.06	1.06	.50	.50
1791	1.16	1.204	.53	.550
1792	1.20	1.217	.66	.669
1793	1.50	1.379	.80	.735
1794	1.86	1.470	1.00	.790
1795	2.00	1.318	1.00	.659
1796	2.13	1.304	1.00	.612

Donald R. Adams, Jr., "Wage Rates in the Early National Period: Philadelphia, 1785–1830," *Journal of Economic History*, XXVIII (Dec. 1968), 404–426. Cost of living index for this period is in *ibid.*, 324.

195. The following tables show the movement of export and import values between 1790 and 1796:

Exports and Imports, 1790–1796

	Value of domestic exports (1000s of dollars)	Export price index (Base 1790)	Import price index (Base 1790)	Terms of trade (Base 1790)
1790	19,905	100	100	100
1791	18,512	85.8	109.8	78.1
1792	19,753	81.7	118.8	68.8
1793	24,360	97.8	108.4	90.2
1794	26,544	103.6	129.2	80.2
1795	39,689	153.6	124.3	123.6
1796	40,764	172.6	132.8	130.0

Douglass C. North, *The Economic Growth of the United States, 1790–1860* (Englewood Cliffs, N.J., 1961), pp. 221, 229.

Export Commodity Prices, 1790–1796

	Price of Rice[a] Charleston (per cwt.)	Price of Wheat[b] Philadelphia (per bu.)	Price of Flour[b] Philadelphia (per bl. superfine)	Price of Tobacco Philadelphia (per cwt.)
1790	$2.30	$1.34	$6.86	$6.30
1791	2.21	.99	5.24	4.63
1792	—	.96	5.05	4.67
1793	2.68	1.11	6.16	4.67
1794	2.71	1.20	7.76	4.83
1795	3.59	1.82	11.23	6.16
1796	4.16	1.95[c]	12.54[c]	7.26

a. Arthur H. Cole, *Wholesale Commodity Prices in the United States, 1700–1861* (Cambridge, Mass., 1938), I, 154.

b. *Ibid.*, II, 93–111. Monthly prices have been averaged and reduced to dollars.

c. In April, 1796 (in the midst of the House debate over the Jay Treaty) wheat reached $2.25 per bu. and flour $14 per bl., a peak that would not again be reached until 1817.

Value of Imports for Domestic Consumption, 1790–1796

1790	$23,500,000
1791	30,000,000
1792	31,500,000
1793	30,800,000
1794	29,500,000
1795	63,000,000
1796	56,636,164

North, *Economic Growth*, p. 228. On the grain fleet, see Bowman, *Struggle for Neutrality*, 159.

196. John S. Littell, ed., *Memoirs of his Own Times: With Reminiscences of the Men and Events of the Revolution, by Alexander Graydon* (Philadelphia, 1846), p. 377.

197. Stephen G. Kurtz, *The Presidency of John Adams: The Collapse of Federalism, 1795–1800* (Philadelphia, 1957), p. 20, takes for granted (we believe rightly) a direct connection between the Republicans' attack on the treaty and their hopes of electing Jefferson to the presidency. Dumas Malone, *Jefferson*, III, 253n., and Thomas J. Farnham, "The Virginia Amendments of 1795: An Episode in the Opposition to Jay's Treaty," *Virginia Magazine of History and Biography*, LXXV (Jan. 1967), 85n., both protest, on the ground that Jefferson himself took no part in these various movements. That much appears to be true, but it hardly invalidates Kurtz's point. John Beckley, indeed, seems to have had little else on his mind. "If the Treaty is rejected," he wrote to DeWitt Clinton in the midst of the House debate, "it will doubtless operate well in those States where the appointment of Electors is given to the people and does not come on speedily. In other cases, the friends of republicanism must redouble their exertions to counteract their opponents. The British Treaty defeated, and a republican president to succeed Mr. Washington, and our country is yet safe, prosperous, and happy" (Apr. 11, 1796). And ten days later: "I think . . . that a major vote once obtained & recorded *vs* the Treaty, it will be extremely difficult

to change, and in this view, your elections which I am told come on next Tuesday, will be greatly important, and from the influence it must have as well upon the Treaty, as upon the future choice of a president, it will I hope and trust call forth all the energies of patriotism." Same to same, Apr. 21, 1796, DeWitt Clinton Papers, CUL. That Jefferson would be the Republican candidate was generally understood. "The republicans," wrote Madison to Monroe in cipher, "knowing that Jefferson alone can be started with hope of success mean to push him. I fear much that he will mar the project . . . by a peremptory and public protest." Feb. 26, 1796, *PJM*, XVI, 232–233. "Mr. Jefferson's election becomes a matter of extreme importance to republicanism and to the southern states. You ought therefore to begin to look out for an elector in your district. . . ." Henry Tazewell to Bishop James Madison, Mar. 6, 1796, qu. in Edmund and Dorothy Smith Berkeley, *John Beckley: Zealous Partisan in a Nation Divided* (Philadelphia, 1973), pp. 135–136. The British chargé, Phineas Bond, even assumed (wrongly) that Jefferson himself was directing the campaign against the treaty "for the double purpose of promoting the interests of France and of advancing his candidacy for President." Bond to Grenville, May 4, 1796, qu. in DeConde, *Entangling Alliance,* p. 458.

198. Draft of Petition, *PJM*, XVI, 75–76.

199. Jefferson to Monroe, Sept. 6, 1795; to Edward Rutledge, Nov. 30, 1795; *WTJ,* VIII, 188, 200.

200. Baumann, "Democratic-Republicans of Philadelphia," pp. 523–524; Young, *Democratic Republicans of New York,* p. 458; Arthur I. Bernstein, "The Rise of the Democratic-Republican Party in New York City, 1789–1800" (Unpub. diss., Columbia U., 1964), p. 168.

201. Farnham, "Virginia Amendments of 1795," pp. 83–85.

202. R. R. Livingston to Edward Livingston, Jan. 5, 1796, qu. in Young, *Democratic Republicans,* p. 460.

203. Baumann, "Democratic-Republicans," pp. 524–525; Walters, *Dallas,* p. 73.

204. Farnham, "Virginia Amendments of 1795," 85–88; Jones to Madison, Oct. 20, 1795, *Massachusetts Historical Society Proceedings,* 2nd Ser., XXV (1901–1902), 151.

205. William Constable Letterbook, II, 184, Constable-Pierrepont Collection, NYPL; Fisher Ames to Thomas Dwight, Sept. 13, 1795, *WFA,* I, 174; Henry Van Schaak to Theodore Sedgwick, Dec. 14, 1795, qu. in Young, *Democratic Republicans,* p. 460; *WGW,* XXXIV, 389.

206. Madison to Monroe, Dec. 20, 1795; to Jefferson, Dec. 13, 1795; *PJM,* XVI, 170, 163.

207. Rush to John R. Coxe, Jan. 16, 1796, Lyman H. Butterfield, ed., *Letters of Benjamin Rush* (Princeton, N.J., 1951), II, 769.

208. Madison to Jefferson, Dec. 27, 1795, *PJM,* XVI, 173.

209. The Treaty of Grenville was agreed to by the Senate Dec. 22, 1795, and sent to the House Feb. 16, 1796; the Pinckney Treaty was agreed to by the Senate Feb. 26 and sent to the House Mar. 3, 1796; and the treaty with Algiers agreed to by the Senate Mar. 2 and sent to the House Mar. 8, 1796. The Jay Treaty was proclaimed Feb. 29 and sent to the House Mar. 1. *Senate Executive Journal,* I, 197, 202, 203; *AC,* 4 Cong., 1 Sess., 328, 394, 784, 821; *WGW,* XXXIV, 481.

210. Rush to Griffith Evans, Mar. 4, 1796, *Letters,* II, 773.

211. *AC,* 4 Cong., 1 Sess., 400–401.

212. Madison thought Livingston's motion "so questionable that he will probably let it sleep or withdraw it." But Livingston did not withdraw it, and Madison was outvoted when he proposed to tone it down by excepting from the call "so much of said papers as

in his [the President's] judgment, it may not be consistent with the interest of the United States, at this time, to disclose." Livingston had meanwhile amended his own resolution with the words, "Excepting such of said papers as any existing negotiation may render improper to be disclosed." Madison twice admitted his misgivings publicly, once when offering his amendment on Mar. 7, and the other time in the course of his speech of Mar. 10 in which he had supported the resolution. Madison to Jefferson, Mar. 6, 1796 (another reference in same to same, Mar. 13, 1796), *PJM,* XVI, 247, 264; *AC,* 4 Cong., 1 Sess., 438, 426, 494.

213. *Ibid.,* 438–444 (Mar. 8, 1796).

214. *Ibid.,* 464–474 (Mar. 9, 1796).

215. *Ibid.,* 487–495 (Mar. 10, 1796).

216. *Ibid.,* 495–500 (Mar. 10, 1796).

217. *Ibid.,* 642–650 (Mar. 18, 1794).

218. *Ibid.,* 759–760.

219. *Ibid.,* 760–762; *WGW,* XXXV, 2–5 (Mar. 30, 1796).

220. *AC,* 4 Cong., 1 Sess., 782–783.

221. As recollected many years later by Gallatin; see *PAH,* XX, 112n.

222. Beckley to DeWitt Clinton, Apr. 11 (also Apr. 21), 1796, Clinton Papers, NYPL.

223. Madison to Monroe, Apr. 18, 1796; to Jefferson, Apr. 23, 1796; *PJM,* XVI, 333–334, 331.

224. E.g., Philip Van Cortlandt of New York, one of Beckley's "waverers" who finally did give way, explained his vote for the treaty in a circular letter to his constituents by saying that "as it appeared during the course of the debates from memorials and other sources of information, to be the general wish of the people of the northern and eastern states, that it ought to be carried into effect; and taking into view all the existing circumstances, I upon the whole conceived it most advisable to give an affirmative vote on the occasion." May 20, 1796, Van Cortlandt–Van Wyck Papers, NYPL.

225. Washington referred to "the torrent of Petitions, and remonstrances which were pouring in from all the Eastern and middle states, and were beginning to come pretty strongly from that of Virginia," in writing to Thomas Pinckney, May 22, 1796, *WGW,* XXXV, 62; petitions and memorials in favor of the treaty from Norfolk, Portsmouth, King William, Accomack, Northampton, Augusta, Williamsburg, and Alexandria were printed or described in *Gazette of the United States,* May 6, 11, 18, 20, 21, and June 3, 1796, and *Philadelphia American Daily Advertiser,* Apr. 27, 1796. Those from New England in particular are extensively reported in *Columbian Centinel,* from about Apr. 27 through mid-May 1796. According to a grammatically ambiguous item of Apr. 30, "Latter accounts say there are more than one hundred petitions in favour of carrying the treaty into effect, than there are against it."

226. Young, *Democratic Republicans,* p. 465.

227. Madison to Jefferson, May 9, 1796, *PJM,* XVI, 352.

228. Philadelphia *American Daily Advertiser,* Apr. 28, 1796; *Columbian Centinel,* extra, Apr. 28, 1796.

229. Young, *Democratic Republicans,* p. 465.

230. Petitions from Allegheny, Westmoreland, and Fayette Counties, Mar. 8, 14, and 29, 1796, *Pittsburgh Gazette,* Mar. 12, 19, 1796; *Gazette of the United States,* Apr. 9, 1796. One of Gallatin's correspondents warned him that more were on the way; Alexander Addison to Gallatin, Apr. 7, 1796, Gallatin Papers Microfilm, NYUL. David Redick, a Republican leader of Washington County, told Gallatin, "I believe it is the earnest wish of a verry great Majority here that the Treaty should be Executed with all fidelity. . . . It

is believed that this can be done without giving up any true Constitutional ground. I have conversed with divers of the personal as well as the Political Friends of our immediate Representatives in Congress, and with little variation in sentiment all have declared their wish that the Treaty may not be defeated. . . ." Redick to Gallatin, Apr. 7, 1796, Gallatin Papers Microfilm, NYUL. The Allegheny petition was originated by Hugh Henry Brackenridge, a Republican, and Alexander Addison, a Federalist. On the politics of the Jay Treaty in western Pennsylvania see Russell J. Ferguson, *Early Western Pennsylvania Politics* (Pittsburgh, 1938), pp. 136–138.

231. Addison to Gallatin, May 4, 1796, Gallatin Papers Microfilm, NYUL; *Pittsburgh Gazette,* May 7, 1796.

232. *AC,* 4 Cong., 1 Sess., 941–943, 969.

233. *Ibid.,* 1065–1077 (Apr. 19, 1796); 1095–1097 (Apr. 20, 1795).

234. *Ibid.,* 1153–1157 (Apr. 22, 1796).

235. *Ibid.,* 1183–1202 (Apr. 26, 1796).

236. *Ibid.,* 1239–1263 (Apr. 28, 1796); *WFA,* II, 37–71.

237. John Adams to Abigail Adams, Apr. 30, 1796, *Letters of John Adams Addressed to His Wife* (Boston, 1841), II, 225–227; *AC,* 4 Cong., 1 Sess., 1263–1264.

238. *Ibid.,* 1273–1280; Theodore Sedgwick to Loring Andrews, Apr. 5, 1796, qu. in Combs, *Jay Treaty,* p. 185.

239. *AC,* 4 Cong., 1 Sess., 1280.

240. *Ibid.,* 1280–1291. Republican members who had switched their votes are listed in Carroll and Ashworth, *Washington,* VII, 375n.

241. Joshua Coit, Apr. 22, *AC,* 4 Cong., 1 Sess., 1151; Madison to Jefferson, Apr. 23, 1796, *PJM,* XVI, 335. Madison's apparent loss of leadership, and perhaps of nerve, was widely noted at the time. "Mr. Madison looks worried to death. Pale, withered, haggard." John to Abigail Adams, Apr. 28, 1796, APM, reel 381; Combs, *Jay Treaty,* p. 178; Carroll and Ashworth, *Washington,* VII, 376n. "Every real patriot must be grieved, and filled with resentment, to see such a majority in the House listed under Madison and Gallatin, or rather Gallatin and Madison, for the latter has become so changed, as to be only a second to the former. . . ." "From a Federal Republican," *Columbian Centinel,* Apr. 27, 1796. Madison himself told Jefferson, "The progress of this business throughout has to me been the most worrying & vexatious that I ever encountered. . . ." May 1, 1796, *PJM,* XVI, 343.

242. Qu. in Baumann, "Democratic-Republicans," p. 538.

243. *Gazette of the United States,* May 5, 1796.

CHAPTER X

The Populist Impulse

1. Oscar and Mary Handlin, "Voluntary Associations," in *The Dimensions of Liberty* (Cambridge, Mass., 1961), pp. 89–112, brief though it is, remains the ablest and most satisfactory effort at a historical synthesis. Stuart M. Blumin, *The Emergence of the Middle Class: Social Experience in the American City, 1760–1900* (Cambridge, Mass., 1989), pp. 192–229, contains a good discussion of the development of voluntary associations in early nineteenth-century America, but does not deal with the transitional phase that followed the Revolution. Other discussions of various aspects of the subject are cited in the notes that follow, esp. n. 9.

2. Arthur M. Schlesinger, "Biography of a Nation of Joiners," *AHR,* L (Oct. 1944),

1–25; Charles W. Ferguson, *Fifty Million Brothers: A Panorama of American Lodges and Clubs* (New York, 1937); Mark C. Carnes, *Secret Ritual and Manhood in Victorian America* (New Haven, Conn., 1989).

3. Michael Zuckerman, *Peaceable Kingdoms: New England Towns in the Eighteenth Century* (New York, 1970), *passim,* and esp. pp. 62, 69, 191.

4. *Ibid.,* pp. 47, 70–71, 140.

5. Richard D. Brown, "The Emergence of Voluntary Associations in Massachusetts, 1760–1830," *Journal of Voluntary Action Research,* II (Apr. 1973), 64–65.

6. Handlin, "Voluntary Associations," pp. 92–94; Schlesinger, "Nation of Joiners," 2–3; Sidney E. Mead, *The Lively Experiment: The Shaping of Christianity in America* (New York, 1963), pp. 103–133.

7. Handlin, "Voluntary Associations," pp. 90–97.

8. Brown, "Voluntary Associations in Massachusetts," p. 71; Robert A. Gross, *The Minute-Men and Their World* (New York, 1976), pp. 173–175; Anne Farnam, "A Society of Societies: Associations and Voluntarism in Early Nineteenth-Century Salem," *Essex Institute Historical Collections,* CXIII (July 1977), 181–190. For Salem, the impulse may to a fascinating extent be traced through the entries in *The Diary of William Bentley, D.D.* (Salem, 1914), 4v., esp. I–II.

9. E.g., Richard D. Brown, *Modernization: The Transformation of American Life, 1600–1865* (New York, 1976); *idem,* "Modernization and the Modern Personality in Early America, 1600–1865: A Sketch of a Synthesis," *Journal of Interdisciplinary History,* II (Winter 1972), 201–228; *idem,* "The Emergence of Urban Society in Rural Massachusetts, 1760–1820," *JAH,* LXI (June 1974), 29–51; David H. Smith, "Modernization and the Emergence of Volunteer Organizations," *International Journal of Comparative Sociology,* XIII (June 1972), 113–134; Stuart M. Blumin, *The Urban Threshhold: Growth and Change in a Nineteenth-Century American Community* (Chicago, 1976), esp. pp. 150–165; Walter S. Glazer, "Participation and Power: Voluntary Associations and the Functional Organization of Cincinnati in 1840," *Historical Methods Newsletter,* V (Sept. 1972), 151–168; Gregory H. Singleton, "Protestant Voluntary Organizations and the Shaping of Victorian America," *AQ,* XXVII (Dec. 1975), 549–560; Don H. Doyle, "The Social Functions of Voluntary Associations in a Nineteenth-Century American Town," *Social Science History,* I (Spring 1977), 333–355. The most perceptive discussion of modernization and related theories of community transformation currently available is Thomas Bender, *Community and Social Change in America* (New Brunswick, N.J., 1978).

10. Alexis de Tocqueville, *Democracy in America,* Phillips Bradley, ed. (New York, 1945), II, 115; William E. Channing, "Remarks on Associations" (1829), in *Works* (Boston, 1875), p. 139. The "main cause" of the associational activity he saw everywhere around him, Channing thought, was "the immense facility given to intercourse by modern improvements, by increased commerce and travelling, by the post-office, by the steamboat, and especially by the press,—by newspapers, periodicals, tracts, and other publications."

11. "Associations, A Vital Form of Social Action" (1838), in William H. Channing, ed., *The Memoir and Writings of Thomas Handasyd Perkins* (Cincinnati, 1851), pp. 170–171; Page Smith, *As a City Upon a Hill: The Town in American History* (New York, 1966), p. 169.

12. Subsequent judicial constructions as to the right of association have been derived not from explicit constitutional guarantees but from the related rights of assembly and petition or remonstrance, together with the right of religious expression. Both Charles E. Rice, *Freedom of Association* (New York, 1962), and Robert A. Horn, *Groups and the*

Constitution (Stanford, Calif., 1956), have some difficulty grasping the historical circumstances which prevented this "right" from emerging more clearly or less ambiguously than it did in the latter part of the eighteenth century. Associations, most especially political ones, were not then seen as uniformly innocent or desirable. They were factions, and they could use the strength of their numbers for purposes not in the public interest, representing a kind of private power which might actually inhibit the free expression of public opinion. Madison was not defending such groups in Federalist 10, except negatively; even in objecting to Washington's denunciation of the Democratic Societies in 1794, Madison was not upholding the right of association. He was simply saying that government should not censure opinions that were not in themselves illegal. Even Tocqueville, greatly impressed by the importance of associational life in America, was not quite prepared to hold that the right of association should be unrestricted. *Democracy in America*, II, 119. Glenn Abernathy, *The Right of Assembly and Association*, rev. ed. (Columbia, S.C., 1981), recognizes the Founders' concern with factions, but his primary interest for the period from the late eighteenth century through the early nineteenth is in the ending of restrictions on religious associations and early trade unions.

13. There were only 28 post offices in 1776; by 1790 these had increased to 75 (about three-fold); in the decade 1790–1800 the number leaped from 75 to 903. John B. McMaster, *A History of the People of the United States, From the Revolution to the Civil War* (New York, 1885), II, 59n.; U.S. Dept. of Commerce, *Historical Statistics of the United States: Colonial Times to 1970* (Washington, 1975), II, 805. The number of newspapers during that decade increased from 92 to 235; meanwhile the speed with which news flowed between the major cities—Boston, New York, Philadelphia, and Baltimore—increased by about 50 percent between 1790 and 1794. During that four-year period the time-lag in the movement of news between Philadelphia and New York dropped from 4 to 1.6 days. Allan R. Pred, *Urban Growth and the Circulation of Information: The United States' System of Cities, 1790–1840* (Cambridge, Mass., 1973), pp. 19, 39–42.

14. Eugene P. Link, *Democratic-Republican Societies, 1790–1800* (New York, 1942), pp. 19–24. Our contention is that such groups as the Sons of Liberty and the Committees of Correspondence represented a principle quite different from that of the "voluntary association" as we are considering it here. Their participants thought of themselves not as a club, nor as an opposition force, nor as a mere contingent, but as representing the real community—even to the point of exercising certain governmental or quasi-governmental functions in the community's name, and in most places that assumption was more or less ratified by general consent. To put it another way: the key differentiating principle, as seen at the time, between the Revolutionary and post-Revolutionary situations was that of the sovereignty of the people. One the one hand, the Sons of Liberty could claim to represent the people's real sentiments—those of the whole community—as against the pretensions of the Crown and its minions, who had obscured and perverted the community's true will. On the other, the Democratic Societies arose in communities where all constituted authority had already been put there by the people, and thus when the societies took it upon themselves to monitor and censor the conduct of those so placed in authority, they themselves were usurping authority to which—according to the logic of popular sovereignty as still construed by the civic values of the late eighteenth century—they were not wholly entitled. Such activity can be acceptable only after the community has conceded the legitimacy of the voluntary association for political as well as other purposes, and with the numbers involved being largely irrelevant. In the mid-1790s that time, we believe, had not yet arrived.

15. Philip S. Foner, ed., *The Democratic-Republican Societies, 1790–1800: A Docu-*

mentary Sourcebook of Constitutions, Declarations, Addresses, Resolutions, and Toasts (Westport, Conn., 1976), pp. 10, 67, 153.

16. Link, *Democratic-Republican Societies*, p. 16.

17. Foner, ed., *Democratic-Republican Societies*, p. 180.

18. *Ibid.*, pp. 255, 359.

19. *Ibid.*, pp. 69, 259, 335, 382.

20. Link, *Democratic-Republican Societies*, pp. 13–15.

21. Foner, ed., *Democratic-Republican Societies*, pp. 69, 319, 359.

22. *Ibid.*, pp. 238, 320.

23. Roland M. Baumann, "The Democratic-Republicans of Philadelphia: The Origins, 1776–1797" (Unpub. diss., Pennsylvania State U., 1970), pp. 448–451. The qu. is on p. 450. Foner, ed., *Democratic-Republican Societies*, pp. 439–441.

24. Raymond Walters, Jr., *Alexander James Dallas: Lawyer—Politician—Financier* (Philadelphia, 1943), pp. 14–26; Baumann, "Democratic-Republicans," pp. 222–224; William B. Wheeler, "Urban Politics in Nature's Republic: The Development of Political Parties in the Seaport Cities in the Federalist Era" (Unpub. diss., U. of Virginia, 1967), p. 60 and n.

25. James D. Tagg, *Benjamin Franklin Bache and the Philadelphia Aurora* (Philadelphia, 1991), pp. 1–170; J. Philip Gleason, "A Scurrilous Colonial Election and Franklin's Reputation," *WMQ*, 3rd Ser., XVIII (Jan. 1961), 68–84; Wheeler, "Urban Politics," pp. 56–57. A sympathetic account of Bache's relations with his grandfather is Jeffrey A. Smith, *Franklin and Bache: Envisioning the Enlightened Republic* (New York, 1990).

26. David F. Hawke, *Benjamin Rush: Revolutionary Gadfly* (Indianapolis, 1971), pp. 182, 385, 392; George W. Corner, ed., *The Autobiography of Benjamin Rush: His "Travels Through Life" together with his Commonplace Book for 1789–1813* (Princeton, 1948), pp. 78–79; Wheeler, "Urban Politics," pp. 60–61. Rush too, like Bache and Swanwick, had hoped for federal patronage when the government moved to Philadelphia in 1790, but was disappointed. Hawke, *Rush*, p. 385.

27. Harry E. Wildes, *Lonely Midas: The Story of Stephen Girard* (New York, 1943), *passim.*

28. William B. Clark, "That Mischievous Holker: The Story of a Privateer," *PMHB*, LXXIX (Jan. 1955), 27–62; Margaret B. Tinkcom, "Cliveden: The Building of a Philadelphia Countryseat, 1763–1767," *ibid.*, LXXXVIII (Jan. 1964), 35; Hubertis Cummings, "Items from the Morris Family Collection of Robert Morris Papers," *ibid.*, LXX (Apr. 1946), 187; Henry Simpson, *The Lives of Eminent Philadelphians Now Deceased* (Philadelphia, 1859), pp. 736–737; John H. Campbell, *History of the Friendly Sons of St. Patrick and of the Hibernian Society for the Relief of Emigrants from Ireland* (Philadelphia, 1892), p. 126.

29. Roland W. Baumann, "John Swanwick: Spokesman for 'Merchant-Republicanism' in Philadelphia, 1790–1798," *PMHB*, XCVII (Apr. 1973), 131–182. The qu. is on p. 142.

30. Still other motives have been ascribed to groups and individuals for joining the societies. One conjecture is that such men as Girard, Swanwick, Peter Barrière, and Peter Duponceau were influenced by their French business connections; another is that the Pennsylvania Society was formed expressly to influence state elections. Wheeler, "Urban Politics," p. 86 and n.; Baumann, "Democratic-Republicans," pp. 444–445.

31. "Many important leaders of the period," according to Philip Foner, "belonged to these popular societies." *Democratic-Republican Societies*, p. 8. Professor Foner does not, however, produce a very long list of them.

32. Qu. in Link, *Democratic-Republican Societies*, p. 13n.

33. Qu. in Foner, ed., *Democratic-Republican Societies*, p. 154.

34. *Ibid.*, p. 162. The delegates at a Federalist state convention at Lancaster, Pa., in 1792 were referred to by A. J. Dallas as "self-created." Walters, *Dallas*, p. 39.

35. Foner, ed., *Democratic-Republican Societies*, pp. 257, 275, 279–281. The Chittenden Society quoted Nathaniel Chipman's *Sketches of the Principles of Government* in support of its argument, whereupon Judge Chipman published an open letter protesting that his book had been improperly used and that he had never approved of "self created societies and clubs." *Ibid.*, pp. 290–293.

36. E.g., Richard Hofstadter, *The Idea of a Party System: The Rise of Legitimate Opposition in the United States, 1780–1840* (Berkeley, Calif., 1969), p. 92, characterizes these societies as "lively pressure groups functioning on [the Republican party's] left wing." See also Noble E. Cunningham, Jr., *The Jeffersonian Republicans: The Formation of Party Organization, 1789–1801* (Chapel Hill, N.C., 1957), p. 65.

37. Foner, ed., *Democratic-Republican Societies*, pp. 66, 69, 75–76, 134, 379, 393; Judah Adelson, "The Vermont Democratic-Republican Societies and the French Revolution," *Vermont History*, XXXII (Jan. 1964), 3–23.

38. Foner, ed., *Democratic-Republican Societies*, pp. 75–78, 267, 283, 387, 396.

39. *Ibid.*, pp. 104–105, 134, 246, 353, 400.

40. *Ibid.*, pp. 108, 240, 322, 362.

41. *Ibid.*, pp. 80, 88–91, 106, 146–147, 184, 243.

42. *Ibid.*, pp. 77–78; Harry M. Tinkcom, *The Republicans and Federalists in Pennsylvania, 1790–1801: A Study in National Stimulus and Local Response* (Harrisburg, Pa., 1950), pp. 85–86; Baumann, "Democratic-Republicans," pp. 479–480.

43. Link, *Democratic-Republican Societies*, pp. 135–137.

44. E. Merton Coulter, "The Efforts of the Democratic Societies of the West to Open the Navigation of the Mississippi," *MVHR*, XI (Dec. 1924), 376–389; Foner, ed., *Democratic-Republican Societies*, pp. 127, 360, 371, 375.

45. E.g., the organization meeting of the Republican Society of Newark was full of persons who opposed the forming of such a society; the Portland Society could not get the local press to carry notices of its meetings; the Philadelphia Society referred to the "clamour raised against this and similar institutions" as being "proof of the utility of them." *Ibid.*, pp. 85, 143; Link, *Democratic-Republican Societies*, p. 59.

46. *PAH*, XVII, 29n.

47. Henry Adams, ed., *The Writings of Albert Gallatin* (Philadelphia, 1879), III, 7.

48. George Clymer to Alexander Hamilton, Oct. 10, 1792, *PAH*, XII, 540–542.

49. Hamilton to Washington, Aug. [4], 1794, *ibid.*, XVII, 24–58.

50. *Ibid.*, XVII, 27, 30–31, 40–41, 42.

51. *Ibid.*, XVII, 34, 37, 41–43.

52. Pauline Maier, *From Resistance to Revolution: Colonial Radicals and the Development of American Opposition to Britain, 1765–1776* (New York, 1972), pp. 3–48; the Hutchinson remarks are qu. in John Lax and William Pencak, "The Knowles Riot and the Crisis of the 1740's in Massachusetts," *Perspectives in American History*, X (1976), 163. See also Paul A. Gilje, *The Road to Mobocracy: Popular Disorder in New York City, 1763–1834* (Chapel Hill, N.C., 1987), pp. vii–viii, 5–35; Dirk Hoerder, *Crowd Action in Revolutionary Massachusetts, 1765–1780* (New York, 1977), pp. 1–15 and *passim*.

53. William Findley, *History of the Insurrection in the Four Western Counties of Pennsylvania in the year MDCCXCIV . . .* (Philadelphia, 1796), pp. vi–viii, 41. Other accounts by contemporaries which touch on the injustice of the excise are Hugh H. Brackenridge, *Incidents of the Insurrection in the Western Parts of Pennsylvania in the Year 1794* (Phil-

adelphia, 1795), 3v. in 1, III, 6; Henry M. Brackenridge (son of the foregoing), *History of the Western Insurrection in Western Pennsylvania, Commonly Called the Whiskey Insurrection, 1794* (Pittsburgh, 1859), pp. 16–18; James Carnahan, "The Pennsylvania Insurrection of 1794, Commonly Called the 'Whiskey Insurrection,'" *New Jersey Historical Society Proceedings,* VI (1853), 115–152, esp. 117–120.

54. Findley, *History,* pp. 41–50.

55. *Ibid.,* pp. 56–57; Washington to Burges Ball, Sept. 25, 1794, *WGW,* XXXIII, 506.

56. Findley, *History,* pp. 69–71, 77–92.

57. *Ibid.,* pp. 129–139, 309–313.

58. See, e.g., Charles A. Beard, *Economic Origins of Jeffersonian Democracy* (New York, 1915), pp. 248–267 (esp. p. 250: "This opposition is explicable on purely economic grounds."); Harold U. Faulkner, *American Economic History* (New York, 1924), pp. 230–231, 313 (for acceptance of the argument that reduction of bulk was the main reason for converting grain to whiskey; also for the assumption that whiskey was made from "corn"); William Miller, "The Democratic Societies and the Whiskey Insurrection," *PMHB,* LXII July 1938), 324–349; Link, *Democratic-Republican Societies,* p. 80 (for the assertion that "the excise . . . tended to impoverish the West"); and Leland D. Baldwin, *Whiskey Rebels: The Story of a Frontier Uprising* (Pittsburgh, 1939).

59. Jacob E. Cooke, "The Whiskey Insurrection: A Re-Evaluation," *Pennsylvania History,* XXX (July 1963), esp. 329–336; David O. Whitten, "An Economic Inquiry into the Whiskey Rebellion of 1794," *Agricultural History,* XLIX (July 1975), 491–504; William D. Barber, "'Among the Most *Techy Articles of Civil Police':* Federal Taxation and the Adoption of the Whiskey Excise," *WMQ,* 3rd Ser., XXV (Jan. 1968), 58–84.

60. Madison to Edmund Pendleton, Jan. 2, 1791, *WJM,* XIII, 344. Each of the three articles cited above, especially Barber's, deals in some way with this point.

61. Cooke, "Whiskey Insurrection," pp. 327–329.

62. *Ibid.,* 336–345.

63. Edwin G. Burrows, "Albert Gallatin and the Political Economy of Republicanism, 1761–1800" (Unpub. diss., Columbia U., 1974), pp. 335–350.

64. Carnahan, "Pennsylvania Insurrection," pp. 119–120; Brackenridge, *Incidents,* III, 6; Baldwin, *Whiskey Rebels,* pp. 23–25, 56–61.

65. *Ibid.,* pp. 107–108, 284–286; Carnahan, "Pennsylvania Insurrection," p. 118.

66. Dorothy Fennell, "From Rebelliousness to Insurrection: A Social History of the Whiskey Insurrection" (Unpub. diss., U. of Pittsburgh, 1981), pp. 98–122.

67. *Ibid.,* pp. 227–258; as opposed to the case made in Whitten, "Economic Inquiry," following Hamilton's argument.

68. Mary K. Bonsteel Tachau, "The Whiskey Rebellion in Kentucky: A Forgotten Episode of Civil Disobedience," *Journal of the Early Republic,* II (Fall 1982), 239–259; and "A New Look at the Whiskey Rebellion," Steven R. Boyd, ed., *The Whiskey Rebellion: Past and Present Perspectives* (Westport, Conn., 1985), pp. 97–118; Jeffrey J. Crow, "The Whiskey Rebellion in North Carolina," *North Carolina Historical Review,* LXVI (Jan. 1989), 1–28; Thomas P. Slaughter, *The Whiskey Rebellion: Frontier Epilogue to the American Revolution* (New York, 1986), pp. 119–120, 256, n. 24.

There was arguably, on the other hand, a significant difference between western Pennsylvania and the other frontier areas with regard to resistance to the excise. The law was probably not consistently enforced in any of them. But in such places as Kentucky and North Carolina the resistance tended for the most part to take a passive form—legal maneuvers, unwillingness of local juries to convict, etc.—rather than that of riot, intimidation, and violence.

69. *Ibid.*, pp. 146–149.

70. *Ibid.*, pp. 152–154; Fennell, "Rebelliousness to Insurrection," p. 124; Russell J. Ferguson, *Early Western Pennsylvania Politics* (Pittsburgh, 1938), pp. 113–115; Neville B. Craig, *The History of Pittsburgh* (Pittsburgh, 1851), pp. 229–230.

71. From late 1791 through June 1794, Neville repeatedly insisted that the excise law could not be enforced in western Pennsylvania unless the government were prepared to take military measures. Neville to George Clymer, Nov. 11, Dec. 22, 1791, June 7, 21, 1793, June 13, 20, 1794, Wolcott Papers, XIX, Connecticut Historical Society.

72. The word "rabble" is used in same to same, Sept. 1791, Wolcott Papers, XIX. The first historian to suggest the significance of the "Neville Connection" was Jacob E. Cooke, "Whiskey Insurrection," cited in n. 59 above; see also Fennell, "Rebelliousness to Insurrection," pp. 124–128; and Slaughter, *Whiskey Rebellion*, pp. 152–153. For the background of the Neville Connection see Craig, *Pittsburgh*, pp. 229–230; and Ferguson, *Western Pennsylvania*, pp. 113–115.

73. Robert E. Harper, "The Class Structure of Western Pennsylvania in the Late Eighteenth Century" (Unpub. diss., U. of Pittsburgh, 1969), pp. 77–79, 125–126, 220; James A. Henretta, "Economic Development and Social Structure in Colonial Boston," *WMQ*, 3rd Ser., XXII (Jan. 1965), 86.

74. Kenneth R. Rossman, *Thomas Mifflin and the Politics of the American Revolution* (Chapel Hill, N.C., 1952), pp. 232–248.

75. Harper, "Class Structure," pp. 223–235; Arthur P. Whitaker, *The Mississippi Question, 1795–1803: A Study in Trade, Politics, and Diplomacy* (New York, 1934), pp. 84–85; Pearl Edna Wagner, "The Economic Conditions in Western Pennsylvania During the Whiskey Insurrection" (Unpub. M.A. thesis, U. of Pittsburgh, 1926); "Judge Addison's Charge to the Grand Jury of Allegheny," *Pennsylvania Archives: Second Series,* IV (Harrisburg, 1876), 243.

76. *ASP:Misc,* I, 88.

77. The most perceptive discussion of Brackenridge and his career is Joseph J. Ellis, *After the Revolution: Profiles in Early American Culture* (New York, 1981), pp. 73–110. The only full biography is Claude M. Newlin, *The Life and Writings of Hugh Henry Brackenridge* (Princeton, N.J., 1932); Daniel Marder, *Hugh Henry Brackenridge* (New York, 1967) is a brief treatment. Professor Marder has also edited a modern printing of Brackenridge's *Incidents of the Insurrection* (New Haven, 1972). Since it is somewhat abridged, the citations given below will refer to the original edition of 1795.

78. Brackenridge, *Incidents,* I, 5–70. The letter to Coxe is printed in *ibid.,* III, 128–131; also in *Pennsylvania Archives,* IV, 140–144.

79. Brackenridge, *Incidents,* I, 70–107.

80. *Ibid.,* I, 116.

81. *Ibid.,* I, 31.

82. *Ibid.,* I, 116. When Bradford boasted of defeating "the first army that comes over the mountains," a Colonel Crawford, who was a seasoned Indian fighter and who happened to be sitting in the gallery, remarked, "Not so easy, neither."

83. *Ibid.,* I, 42–43.

84. *Ibid.,* II, 11.

85. *Ibid.,* II, 20.

86. *Pennsylvania Archives,* IV, 396–397.

87. Brackenridge, *Incidents,* I, 101–102.

88. Richard H. Kohn, *Eagle and Sword: The Federalists and the Creation of the Military Establishment in America, 1783–1802* (New York, 1975), p. 161; *ASP:IA,* I, 487–488; Carroll

and Ashworth, *Washington,* VII, 199 (Wayne's dispatch of July 7, 1794, describing the Indian attack on Fort Recovery had not yet reached Philadelphia, and Washington would not get the news of Fallen Timbers until Sept. 30); Randolph to Jay, Aug. 18, 1794, *ASP:FR,* I, 483; Carroll and Ashworth, *Washington,* VII, 179–180; *PAH,* XVI, 588n.

89. Kohn, *Eagle and Sword,* p. 161; Hamilton to Tench Coxe, Aug. 1, 1794, *PAH,* XVII, 1.

90. "Conference Concerning the Insurrection in Western Pennsylvania," Aug. 2, 1794, *ibid.,* XVII, 9–14.

91. James Wilson to Washington, Aug. 4, 1794, *ASP:Misc,* I, 85.

92. "Memorandum of an Executive Conference," *Pennsylvania Archives,* IV, 82.

93. Hamilton to Washington, Aug. 2, 1794, *PAH,* XVII, 15–19.

94. Knox to Washington, Aug. 4, 1794, Washington Papers, LC.

95. Bradford to Washington, Aug. [4 or 5], 1794, Washington Papers, LC.

96. Randolph to Washington, Aug. 5, 1794, Washington Papers, LC; also repr. in Randolph, *A Vindication of Mr. Randolph's Resignation* (Philadelphia, 1795), pp. 100–103, and Francis Wharton, *State Trials of the United States During the Administrations of Washington and Adams* (Philadelphia, 1849), p. 156. For the date of Randolph's conversation with Fauchet, see *Vindication,* p. 84.

97. Mifflin to Washington, Aug. 5, 1794, *ASP:Misc,* I, 97–99.

98. *WGW,* XXXIII, 457–461; *ASP:Misc,* I, 86–87.

99. Randolph to Mifflin, Aug. 7, 1794, *ASP:Misc,* I, 99–101.

100. Kohn, *Eagle and Sword,* p. 164; Hamilton to Washington, Aug. 5, 6, 1794, *PAH,* XVII, 24–59, 61; Bradford to Elias Boudinot, Aug. 7, 1794, J. J. Boudinot, ed., *The Life, Public Services, Addresses and Letters of Elias Boudinot* (Boston, 1896), II, 86–89.

101. *Ibid.,* II, 87.

102. Kohn, *Eagle and Sword,* pp. 165–167; *Pennsylvania Archives,* IV, 103–106.

103. "Minutes of a Meeting Concerning the Insurrection in Western Pennsylvania," Aug. 24, 1794, *PAH,* XVII, 135–138.

104. Kohn, *Eagle and Sword,* pp. 167–169; *Pennsylvania Archives,* IV, 218–219.

105. Kohn, *Eagle and Sword,* p. 169; *Philadelphia General Advertiser,* Sept. 10, 11, 1794; Foner, ed., *Democratic-Republican Societies,* pp. 59, 91–93, 147–148, 183–184, 243, 339, 378.

106. *Ibid.,* p. 339.

107. *ASP:Misc,* I, 90.

108. Kohn, *Eagle and Sword,* pp. 169–170; *PAH,* XVII, 268; Baldwin, *Whiskey Rebels,* pp. 220–258, 262–264.

109. Foner, *Democratic-Republican Societies,* p. 147.

110. Jefferson, "Anas," Aug. 2, 1793, *WTJ,* I, 254.

111. Findley, *History,* p. 187.

112. *Pittsburgh Gazette,* Oct. 4, 1794, July 18, Sept. 5, Oct. 3, 1795, Mar. 12, 1796.

113. *Pittsburgh Gazette,* Nov. 21, 1795. We are indebted to Dorothy Fennell for bringing this choice item to our attention.

114. Washington to Burges Ball, Sept. 25, 1794; to Henry Lee, Aug. 26, 1794; to Daniel Morgan, Oct. 8, 1794; *WGW,* XXXIII, 506, 476, 523. For other references see *ibid.,* XXXIII, 133, 321–322, 464, XXXIV, 3–4, 17.

115. Moncure D. Conway, *Omitted Chapters of History Disclosed in the Life and Papers of Edmund Randolph . . .* (New York, 1888), p. 195.

116. *WGW,* XXXIV, 29.

117. *AC,* 3 Cong., 2 Sess., 794.

118. Findley, *History*, pp. 56–57; Brackenridge, *Incidents*, III, 25–27; *AC*, 3 Cong., 2 Sess., 920.

119. Link, *Democratic-Republican Societies*, pp. 146–147; Foner, ed., *Democratic-Republican Societies*, p. 130. William Miller, in "Democratic Societies," p. 325, believes the societies were "only indirectly responsible" for the insurrection.

120. Findley, *History*, p. 56; Baldwin, *Whiskey Rebels*, p. 118 and n.

121. Madison to Monroe, Dec. 4, 1794, *PJM*, XV, 406.

122. *AC*, 3 Cong., 2 Sess., 899.

123. *Ibid.*, 920–932 (Nov. 26, 1794).

124. *Ibid.*, 934–935 (Nov. 27, 1794).

125. *Ibid.*, 935–947; Madison to Jefferson, Nov, 30, 1794, *PJM*, XV, 396–398.

126. Dec. 4, 1794, *Ibid.*, 406.

127. For resolutions of protest, see Foner, *Democratic-Republican Societies*, pp. 60–63, 98–102, 137–139, 148–149, 192–198, 260–264, 304–318, 324–334, 339–343; on the societies' rapid expiration see Miller, "Democratic Societies," pp. 341–342; and Link, *Democratic-Republican Societies*, pp. 200–209. We are contending that despite (or perhaps as a reflection of) their resolutions of self-justification, the societies themselves were far from secure in the sense of their own legitimacy. A letter from David Redick, a leading member of the Washington Democratic Society and a man of some importance in the local politics of western Pennsylvania, to the editor of the *Pittsburgh Gazette*, Dec. 28, 1794 (printed Jan. 23, 1795), declared that "at a time when it becomes all to give every possible evidence of their attachment to the lately violated laws and government . . . I withdraw myself from the Society; and I do recommend to the Society to dissolve themselves entirely if they think as I do." Qu. in Foner, *Democratic-Republican Societies*, pp. 136–137. Brackenridge refers to the "account given me by Mr. M'Donald, the secretary [of the Mingo Creek club], *or rather the apology made,* for instituting this society. . . ." *Incidents*, III, 26. (Our italics.)

128. E.g., Horn, *Groups and the Constitution* (cited in n. 12 above), pp. 17–18, 155; Hofstadter, *Idea of a Party System*, pp. 92–96.

129. Very suggestive regarding the "wicked councillors" principle, as well as related matters, is Edmund S. Morgan, *Inventing the People: The Rise of Popular Sovereignty in England and America* (New York, 1988), pp. 30–31.

CHAPTER XI

The Retirement of Washington

1. On contemporary opinion see Victor H. Paltsits, *Washington's Farewell Address* . . . (New York, 1935), pp. 55–74, 327–360. A number of later writings are collected in Burton I. Kaufman, ed., *Washington's Farewell Address: The View from the 20th Century* (Chicago, 1969). See also Arthur A. Markowitz, "Washington's Farewell and the Historians: A Critical Review," *PMHB*, XCIV (Apr. 1970), 173–191.

2. Paltsits, *Farewell Address*, and *PAH*, XX, 169–183, 237–240, 247, 264–288, 293–303, 307–309, 311–314, 316–319, provide between them a complete documentary record—successive drafts, pertinent correspondence, and editorial commentary—of every stage in the Address's evolution. The text of the Address cited in the following paragraphs is that of *WGW*, XXV, 214–238.

3. *Ibid.*, 214–218.

4. *Ibid.,* 218–226.

5. *Ibid.,* 226–227.

6. *Ibid.,* 227–228.

7. *Ibid.,* 228–233.

8. *Ibid.,* 233–235.

9. *Ibid.,* 235–238.

10. *Ibid.,* 234. See also n. 1 above.

11. Samuel F. Bemis, "Washington's Farewell Address: A Foreign Policy of Independence," *AHR,* XXXIX (Jan. 1934), 250–268.

12. Felix Gilbert, *To the Farewell Address: Ideas of Early American Foreign Policy* (Princeton, N.J., 1961), esp. pp. 115–136.

13. Burton I. Kaufman, "Washington's Farewell Address: A Statement of Empire," *idem,* ed., *Farewell Address,* pp. 169–187.

14. Richard Hofstadter, *The Idea of a Party System: The Rise of Legitimate Opposition in the United States, 1780–1840* (Berkeley, Calif., 1969), pp. 96, 99.

15. Joseph Charles, *The Origins of the American Party System: Three Essays* (Chapel Hill, N.C., 1956), p. 44; Alexander DeConde, *Entangling Alliance: Politics and Diplomacy Under George Washington* (Durham, N.C., 1958), p. 469.

16. *WGW,* XXXV, 224–225.

17. E.g., Fisher Ames's quip about "party racers" (see below, p. 513); [William Duane], *Letter to George Washington ... Concerning Strictures on his Address of the Seventeenth of September, 1796 ...* (Philadelphia, 1796); John B. McMaster, *A History of the People of the United States* (New York, 1883–1913), II, 290–291.

18. *WGW,* XXXV, 227.

19. Hofstadter, *Idea of a Party System,* p. 99.

20. *WGW,* XXXV, 310–311.

21. See below, pp. 510–511, 520–521.

22. Carroll and Ashworth, *Washington,* VII, 320–322. See also above, p. 40 and n. 11.

23. Washington to Jefferson, July 6, 1796, *WGW,* XXXV, 120.

24. Paltsits, *Farewell Address,* p. 171; Washington to Hamilton, Aug. 25, 1796, *PAH,* XX, 307–308.

25. Washington to Jefferson, July 6, 1796, *WGW,* XXV, 119.

26. *Ibid.,* 119.

27. DeConde, *Entangling Alliance,* pp. 342–344; Albert H. Bowman, *The Struggle for Neutrality: Franco-American Diplomacy During the Federalist Era* (Knoxville, Tenn., 1974), pp. 118–119, 172–173; Harry Ammon, *James Monroe: The Quest for National Identity* (New York, 1971), pp. 113–116. These, taken together, largely supersede the older work of Beverly W. Bond, *The Monroe Mission to France* (Baltimore, 1907). The three others whom Washington had asked prior to nominating Monroe were Thomas Pinckney, Robert R. Livingston, and James Madison.

28. Randolph to Monroe, June 10, 1794, *ASP:FR,* I, 668–669.

29. *Ibid.,* 672–674; Randolph to Monroe, Dec. 2, 1794, *ibid.,* 689–690; Monroe to Madison, Sept. 2, 1794, *WJM,* II, 37–41; Washington to Jay, Dec. 18, 1794, *WGW,* XXXIV, 61.

30. Monroe to Committee of Public Safety, Sept. 3, 1794; Randolph to Monroe, Dec. 2, 1794; *ASP:FR,* I, 677, 689–690. See also n. 53 below.

31. *ASP:FR,* II, 685–686.

32. Monroe to Randolph, Nov. 20, Dec. 2, 1794, *ibid.,* 685, 688.

33. *Ibid.,* 688.

34. Monroe to Randolph, Dec. 18, 1794 (private), *WJM,* II, 160–161; Ammon, *Monroe,* p. 142.

35. *ASP:FR,* I, 668–669. Monroe to Madison, Nov. 30, 1794; to Randolph, Dec. 8, 1794; Committee of Public Safety to Monroe, Dec. 27, 1794; *WJM,* II, 136–137, 154–158, 169n., 162–163. Randolph to Monroe, June 1, 1795, *ASP:FR,* I, 711–712.

36. Monroe to Committee of Public Safety, Dec. 27, 1794; Jay to Monroe, Nov. 24, 25, 1794; *WJM,* II, 163, 169–170n., 180–181. *ASP:FR,* I, 517. *WGW,* XXXVI, 203, 221.

37. Monroe to Randolph, Sept. 10, 1795, *ASP:FR,* I, 721–722. See also Monroe to Madison, Sept. 8, 1795, *WJM,* II, 357.

38. J. Q. Adams to John Adams, Sept. 12, 1795, *WJQA,* I, 411.

39. Pickering to Monroe, Sept. 12, Nov. 23, 1795, June 13, Aug. 22, 1796, *ASP:FR,* I, 596–598, 727, 737–738, 741–742; Monroe to Madison, July 5, 1796, *WJM,* III, 22–23. Among the first to conclude that Monroe ought to be recalled was Oliver Wolcott, who wrote Hamilton that "we must stop the channels by which foreign poison is introduced into our Country." June 17, 1796, *PAH,* XX, 231.

40. DeConde, *Entangling Alliance,* pp. 368–369.

41. Monroe to Charles Delacroix, Feb. 17, 1796, AECPE-U 45, 145–146vo.; Ammon, *Monroe,* p. 148; M. A. Thiers, *Histoire de la révolution française* (Paris, 1842), IX, 41. The nature and date of the document from which Thiers quotes (a portion of which is qu. above) are unknown.

42. Monroe to George Logan, June 24, 179[5]; to Jefferson, June 23, 1795; *WJM,* III, 6–7; II, 292–304. Ammon, *Monroe,* p. 152.

43. Secretaries of Departments to Washington, July 2, 1796; Charles Lee to Washington, July 7, 1796; Sparks, ed., *Writings of Washington,* XI, 483–487.

44. Monroe to Randolph, Mar. 6, 17, 1795, *ASP:FR,* I, 698, 701; to William Short, May 30, 1795, *WJM,* II, 289–290; DeConde, *Entangling Alliance,* pp. 366–367. The instructions to François Barthélemy, far from saying anything about assisting the United States, included among the arguments for Spain's retroceding Louisiana that it would form a useful barrier between the United States and Spain's other colonies. May 12, 1795, *Papiers de Barthélemy, ambassadeur de France en Suisse, 1792–1797* (Paris, 1910), VI, 25. The completed treaty, which did not include such retrocession, is in *ibid.,* pp. 81–87.

45. George W. Kyte, "A Spy on the Western Waters: The Military Intelligence Mission of General Collot in 1796," *MVHR,* XXXIV (Dec. 1947), 427–442; Gibbs, *Memoirs,* I, 350–355.

46. Durand Echeverria, ed., "General Collot's Plan for a Reconnaissance of the Ohio and Mississippi Valleys, 1796," *WMQ,* 3rd Ser., IX (Oct. 1952), 512–520. The qu. is in Gibbs, *Memoirs,* I, 354.

47. Monroe to Secretary of State, Aug. 27, 1796, *ASP:FR,* I, 742. Pickering's letter of recall is dated Aug. 22, 1796, *ibid.,* 741–742.

48. Jefferson to Madison, Jan. 30, 1787, *PTJ,* XI, 97.

49. Washington, "Remarks on Monroe's 'View of the Conduct of the Executive,'" Mar. 1798, *WGW,* XXXVI, 194; Randolph to Monroe, Sept. 25, 1794, *ASP:FR,* I, 678; Monroe, "A View, &c.," *WJM,* III, 450–451, in which Monroe asserts that he had been given to understand, with regard to Jay's instructions, that "if the existence of a power to form a commercial treaty was not positively denied, yet *it* was withheld, and the contrary evidently implied." And according to Fauchet, Randolph "positively assured me that there was no question of a treaty, only of simple demands. . . ." Randolph to Monroe, June 1,

1795, *ASP:FR*, I, 711–712; Fauchet to Committee of Public Safety, Feb. 16, 1795, CFM, p. 578; Declaration of Edmund Randolph, July 8, 1795, *ASP:FR*, I, 711–712.

50. E.g., such characterizations as these in Fauchet's dispatches: "This Mr. Randolph is undoubtedly an excellent man, very much a partisan of our revolution, but I believe him to be of weak character; it is very easy to penetrate his secrets once you get him agitated; besides which I do not give him mine except when I want him to know them." Or: "I have rightly guessed that Mr. Randolph, pressed in cabinet councils between Mr. Hamilton's influence and the force of our rights which are ever heightened in his eyes by his attachment to our Republic, never makes his official communications with sufficient coldness but what at bottom he feels the emptiness of the means of satisfaction he is charged with offering me." To Minister of Foreign Affairs, May 7, Nov. 15, 1794, CFM, pp. 376, 472.

51. As Professor Ammon wryly observes, "Histories of France during this era do not contain any references to the United States or to Monroe. Of all the diplomatic problems facing France, that presented by the United States was one of the least significant." Ammon, *Monroe*, p. 601n.; see also 604n. (Though an exception, the work of Thiers, is cited in n. 42 above.)

52. *Ibid.*, pp. 118–120. Monroe to Randolph, Aug. 25, 1794; to Madison, Sept. 2, 1794; *WJM*, II, 32–33, 37–40.

53. This was done in two stages, an Order of Nov. 15, 1794 which made some trifling concessions but left the 1793 decree essentially intact, and a subsequent one, Jan. 3, 1795, which restored the "free ships, free goods" principle of the commercial treaty of 1778. *ASP:FR*, I, 642–643, 689, 752. (Date of Nov. 15 misreported as Nov. 18 on p. 689.)

54. Ammon, *Monroe*, p. 129; DeConde, *Entangling Alliance*, pp. 399–404; Bowman, *Struggle for Neutrality*, pp. 228–231. See also Ch. VIII above, n. 123.

55. *WJQA*, I, 353–362, 408–409n.; CFM, p. 728; Bowman, *Struggle for Neutrality*, pp. 236–238.

56. Report to Executive Directory, Jan. 16, 1796, AECPE-U 45, 41–53; Bowman, *Struggle for Neutrality*, pp. 236–238.

57. Jefferson to R. R. Livingston, Apr. 18, 1802, *WTJ*, VIII, 145.

58. Frances S. Childs, "French Opinion of Anglo-American Relations 1795–1805," *French American Review*, I (Jan.–Mar. 1948), 22–23; Adet to Committee of Public Safety, Dec. 2, 1795, CFM, p. 798.

59. "I take it . . . for granted," Monroe assured the Committee of Public Safety, "that the report [of a treaty "derogatory to the treaties of alliance" between France and the United States] is without foundation; for I cannot believe that an American minister would ever forget the connections between the United States and France, which every day's experience demonstrates to be the interest of both Republics still further to cement." Dec. 27, 1794, *WJM*, II, 163. Fauchet's dispatches to his government, beginning well before any news from either London or Paris had reached America, were full of information on how the friends of France in America were viewing the Jay mission, starting with Monroe himself. "If Mr. Monroe is vested with the necessary powers," he wrote as early as May 17, 1794, "you will find it more advantageous to treat with him, and he will be the first to so invite you, in order to thwart Jay's mission, upon which he has very real fears, probably only too well founded." And again on Sept. 16, 1794: "Mr. Monroe . . . opened his heart to me on that subject before his departure. His zeal for our interests will probably inspire him to give you his views on how we may ensure an effective reaction against the influence of that mission. . . ." Fauchet has an occasional word for Randolph as well, with whom

he talked after the news arrived of Monroe's effusive debut in Paris: "He told me (just between ourselves, as he himself put it) that he was delighted with the conduct of his friend Mr. Monroe, but feared that he might have gone beyond his instructions and that this might cause irritation." A private talk with Madison early in February 1795 had elicited that Madison had fears similar to Monroe's as to Jay's doings and, though as yet ignorant of the treaty's actual provisions, believed it would be "altogether disadvantageous to the United States." CFM, pp. 344, 422, 490, 573. See also dispatches of Oct. 22, 31, Nov. 15, 19, Dec. 27, 1794, Feb. 2, 4, 16, Mar. 8, 16, Apr. 3, 9, May 3, 1795, *ibid.,* pp. 440–441, 455, 473–474, 482, 520–524, 551–557, 559–564, 578–580, 601–609, 619, 628–634, 674–675, 707–710.

John Churchman, a scientist from Maryland, was the carrier of Monroe's final dispatches from Bordeaux, delivering them to the State Department on July 29, 1796. In the course of conversation with Secretary Pickering, Churchman was asked about the state of opinion in France as to Jay's treaty. "He answered that . . . very little was said by *Frenchmen* about the treaty—tho' much was said against it by the *American Citizens* in Paris." Pickering to Washington, July 29, 1796, *WJM,* II, 494n. According to Uriah Tracy: "Information from the Hague [J. Q. Adams] . . . is full, that the French Directory were governed entirely by advice of Americans who were in Paris, and by information received there from Americans on this side of the water, in all their movements respecting America." Tracy to Wolcott, Jan. 7, 1797, Gibbs, *Memoirs,* I, 415–416. See also *WJQA,* I, 481. When Monroe published his defense of his mission in 1797 (*View of the Conduct of the Executive,* repr. in *WJM,* III, 383–457), he said that as soon as the American newspapers appeared in Paris in mid-August, 1795, with the text of the treaty, opinion in the French government "openly and severely censure[d] it." On his copy Washington wrote in the margin, "They were predetermined to do so and took the tone from their partisans on this side the water." *Ibid.,* 421; *WGW,* XXXVI, 205.

60. Marvin R. Zahniser, *Charles Cotesworth Pinckney: Founding Father* (Chapel Hill, N.C., 1967), pp. 142–149; *ASP:FR,* II, 6–7; "Observations on the note of T. Payne relative to the unconstitutionality of the nomination of Mr. Pinckney," Dec. 6, 1796, AECPE-U 46, 427–428.

61. Bowman, *Struggle for Neutrality,* pp. 239, 241, 244–245, 250, 253–254; *ASP:FR,* I, 583.

62. *Ibid.,* I, 579–583; DeConde, *Entangling Alliance,* pp. 456–458, 471–478; Dec. 31, 1796, CFM, p. 983.

63. Georges Lefebvre, *The Directory,* tr. Robert Baldick (London, 1965), pp. 1–14, 72–77; Robert R. Palmer, *The Age of the Democratic Revolution: A Political History of Europe and America, 1760–1800* (Princeton, N.J., 1958–1964), II, 214–228, 270–275; Louis Madelin, *The French Revolution* (London, 1933), pp. 478–516. (The qu. is on p. 515.)

64. Monroe to Madison, Sept. 1, 1796, *WJM,* III, 53.

65. Same to same, Jan. 1, 1797, Ammon, *Monroe,* p. 155.

66. Ames to Wolcott, Sept. 26, 1796, Gibbs, *Memoirs,* I, 384.

67. Calculations on the party composition of the Fourth and Fifth Congresses are in Rudolph M. Bell, *Party and Faction in American Politics: The House of Representatives, 1789–1801* (Westport, Conn., 1973), pp. 255–257. The most accurate listing presently available of individual members of the First through Seventh Congresses, with their party identification, is in John F. Hoadley, *Origins of American Political Parties, 1789–1803* (Lexington, Ky., 1986), 192–219. On politics in the states mentioned above see Alfred F. Young, *The Democratic Republicans of New York: The Origins, 1763–1797* (Chapel Hill,

N.C., 1967); Harry M. Tinkcom, *The Republicans and Federalists in Pennsylvania, 1790–1801: A Study in National Stimulus and Local Response* (Harrisburg, Pa., 1950); Bernard Faÿ, "Early Party Machinery in the United States: Pennsylvania in the Election of 1796," *PMHB*, LX (Oct. 1936), 375–390; Roland M. Baumann, "Philadelphia's Manufacturers and the Excise Taxes of 1794: The Forging of the Jeffersonian Coalition," *PMHB*, CVI (Jan. 1982), 3–39; Paul Goodman, *The Democratic-Republicans of Massachusetts: Politics in a New Republic* (Cambridge, Mass., 1964); George R. Lamplugh, *Politics on the Periphery: Factions and Parties in Goergia, 1783–1806* (Newark, Del., 1986); and Lisle A. Rose, *Prologue to Democracy: The Federalists in the South, 1789–1800* (Lexington, Ky., 1968).

68. Hofstadter, "A Constitution Against Parties," *Idea of a Party System*, pp. 40–73. On the methods whereby electors were chosen in the several states in 1796, see table in Stephen G. Kurtz, *The Presidency of John Adams: The Collapse of Federalism, 1795–1800* (Philadelphia, 1957), 409.

69. Noble E. Cunningham, *The Jeffersonian Republicans: The Formation of Party Organization, 1789–1801* (Chapel Hill, N.C., 1957), pp. 91–92, 163–164.

70. *Ibid.*, pp. 107–108; Malone, *Jefferson*, III, 274–276.

71. Adams to H. Knox, Mar. 30, 1797, *WJA*, III, 535 (see also 524n.). The movement to slip Pinckney in ahead of Adams in 1796 was less concentrated and purposeful than a similar movement under similar auspices on behalf of Pinckney's brother Charles Cotesworth in 1800. But that such a movement existed seems to have been more or less common knowledge. Pierre Adet, for one, knew all about it and so reported to his home government. To Minister of Foreign Relations, Dec. 15, 1796, *CFM*, p. 978. See also Stephen Higginson to Hamilton, Jan. 12, 1797, *PAH*, XX, 465; and there are a number of clues and allusions scattered through Hamilton's correspondence during this period: *ibid.*, 158–159, 372, 376, 377–378, 403–404, 406, 418, 437–438, 445.

72. "One man alone—Benjamin Franklin Bache—either wrote or published the vast majority of the attacks. The more astute Republican leadership . . . shunned any connection with the assault on the President. Almost all notoriety for the defamation of Washington belonged to Bache and the *Aurora*." James D. Tagg, "Benjamin Franklin Bache's Attack on George Washington," *PMHB*, C (Apr. 1976), 194.

73. Jefferson to Monroe, June 12, 1796; to Madison, Mar. 27, 1796; *WTJ*, VII, 80, 69.

74. Evidence for this is quite widespread. E.g., Baumann, "Philadelphia Manufacturers," *passim;* Young, *Democratic Republicans of New York*, p. 581; Joyce Appleby, *Capitalism and a New Social Order* (New York, 1984), pp. 48–49 and n.; Gordon S. Wood, *The Radicalism of the American Revolution* (New York, 1992), p. 281.

75. Kurtz, *Presidency of John Adams*, p. 141.

76. *Ibid.*, pp. 412–414.

77. Tinkcom, *Republicans and Federalists*, pp. 159–162; Richard G. Miller, *Philadelphia—The Federalist City: A Study of Urban Politics, 1789–1801* (Port Washington, N.Y., 1976), pp. 22–24, 74–77.

78. Tinkcom, *Republicans and Federalists*, pp. 163–164.

79. *Ibid.*, pp. 166–168; Kurtz, *Presidency of John Adams*, pp. 177–181.

80. *Ibid.*, pp. 181–186. It is true that Madison, for one, was greatly disturbed by Adet's paper, and he so wrote to Jefferson on Dec. 5, 1796: "Adéts Note which you will have seen, is working all the evil with which it is pregnant. Those who rejoice at its indiscretions & are taking advantage of them, have the impudence to pretend that it is an electioneering

manoevre, and that the French Govt. have been led to it by the opponents of the British Treaty." *PJM,* XVI, 422. Professor Cunningham concludes from this that "there seems to be no evidence that Republican leaders were implicated." *Jeffersonian Republicans,* p. 101. Adet's own correspondence, however, strongly suggests otherwise. Describing a visit to New England in one of his dispatches, Adet mentions having consulted with the "most influential" of "our friends" there, reporting that "they have all told me France must adopt measures that will cause the merchants to fear for their property, and to make them see the need to place at the head of the government a man whose known character would inspire confidence in the [French] Republic and thus put him in a position to play the mediator between it and the United States." To Minister of Foreign Relations, Sept. 24, 1796, CFM, p. 948. From this, and in view of his local connections—and especially of the arrangements he made with Bache for publication—it is hard to imagine Adet's not having had similar conversations in Philadelphia.

81. Delayed returns from one of the counties, had they arrived in time, would have meant the election of all fifteen. Tinkcom, *Republicans and Federalists,* p. 172.

82. *Ibid.,* pp. 271–272; Kurtz, *Presidency of John Adams,* pp. 186–187; Miller, *Philadelphia,* pp. 85, 150. On the presumed effect of Adet's activities see *ibid.,* pp. 89–90; Kurtz, pp. 189–190; and Oliver Wolcott to O. Wolcott, Sr., Nov. 27, 1796, Gibbs, *Memoirs,* I, 400–401.

83. The material for this and the two succeeding paragraphs is drawn from Miller, *Philadelphia,* Chs. 3–5.

84. Qu. in Cunningham, *Jeffersonian Republicans,* pp. 100–101.

85. *Ibid.,* p. 98.

86. *Idea of a Party System,* p. 216.

87. Mark D. Kaplanoff, "Making the South Solid: Parties and the Structure of Society in South Carolina, 1790–1815 (Unpub. diss., Cambridge U., 1979), pp. 6–14. Other works on which we have drawn for the section that follows are George C. Rogers, Jr., *Evolution of a Federalist: William Loughton Smith of Charleston, 1758–1812* (Columbia, S.C., 1962); Zahniser, *Pinckney;* Rose, *Prologue to Democracy;* Joseph W. Cox, *Champion of Southern Federalism: Robert Goodloe Harper of South Carolina* (Port Washington, N.Y., 1972); and Richard B. Clow, "Edward Rutledge of South Carolina, 1749–1800: Unproclaimed Statesman" (Unpub. diss., U. of Georgia, 1976).

88. Rogers, *Smith,* p. 290.

89. Hamilton to King, May 4, 1796, *PAH,* XX, 158.

90. See n. 71 above.

91. Cox, *Harper,* pp. 73–74; Ulrich B. Phillips, ed., "South Carolina Federalist Correspondence, 1789–1797," *AHR,* XIV (July 1909), 782.

92. Clow, "Rutledge," pp. 287–288; Rose, *Prologue to Democracy,* p. 135; Rogers, *Smith,* p. 291.

93. Kaplanoff, "Making the South Solid," pp. 7–8, 140.

94. Rogers, *Smith,* pp. 203–207, 226–227; Clow, "Rutledge," pp. 261–264.

95. Rogers, *Smith,* pp. 264–267, 276–278, 281.

96. *Ibid.,* pp. 279–280; Zahniser, *Pinckney,* pp. 127–128n., 129, 133–134; Kaplanoff, "Making the South Solid," p. 156.

97. Smith to Gabriel Manigault, Dec. 22, 1796, Rogers, *Smith,* p. 294.

98. Clow, "Rutledge," pp. 290–299.

99. To Abigail Adams, Mar. 5, 1797, C. F. Adams, ed., *Letters of John Adams, Addressed to His Wife* (Boston, 1841), II, 244.

100. Jefferson to Walter Jones, Jan. 2, 1814, *WTJ,* IX, 448–449.

CHAPTER XII

John Adams and the Dogma of "Balance"

1. E.g., Gilbert Chinard, *Honest John Adams* (Boston, 1933); Manning J. Dauer, *The Adams Federalists* (Baltimore, 1953); Stephen G. Kurtz, *The Presidency of John Adams: The Collapse of Federalism, 1795–1800* (Philadelphia, 1957); Page Smith, *John Adams* (Garden City, N.Y., 1962), 2v.; John M. Allison, *Adams and Jefferson: The Story of a Friendship* (Norman, Okla., 1966), pp. 193–196; Richard B. Morris, *Great Presidential Decisions: State Papers that Changed the Course of History* (Philadelphia, 1967), pp. 48–51; Ralph A. Brown, *The Presidency of John Adams* (Lawrence, Kans., 1975). Here we refer only to a tendency, upon which there are as many variations as authors. (Kurtz and Dauer, for example, do not concede that Adams's policies made his loss of the 1800 election inevitable.) Gerard H. Clarfield, *Timothy Pickering and American Diplomacy, 1795–1800* (Columbia, Mo., 1969) neither defends Pickering nor challenges the pro-Adams view. Adams's own version is to be found principally in E. M. Cunningham, ed., *Correspondence between the Hon. John Adams . . . and the Late Wm. Cunningham, Esq., . . . Beginning in 1803, and Ending in 1812* (Boston, 1823); and *Correspondence of the Late President Adams, Originally Published in the Boston Patriot . . .* (Boston, 1809), the latter reprinted in *WJA*, IX, 241–311. To these might be added the biographical portion of *ibid.*, I, 500–598.

2. Jacob E. Cooke, "Country Above Party: John Adams and the 1799 Mission to France," Edmund Willis, ed., *Fame and the Founding Fathers: Papers and Comments Presented at the Nineteenth Conference on Early American History . . .* (Bethlehem, Pa., 1967), pp. 53–79; Peter Shaw, *The Character of John Adams* (Chapel Hill, N.C., 1976), pp. 250–265; Forrest McDonald, *Alexander Hamilton: A Biography* (New York, 1979), pp. 329–352.

3. No major study of Adams has gone so far in associating his thought with reactionary principles as does Correa M. Walsh, *The Political Science of John Adams: A Study in the Theory of Mixed Government and the Bicameral System* (New York, 1915), a work which had wide influence among historians in the Progressive Era and subsequently; on the other hand Adams was much praised by such "new conservative" writings of the 1950s as Russell Kirk, *The Conservative Mind, from Burke to Santayana* (Chicago, 1953); and Peter Viereck, *Conservatism: From John Adams to Churchill* (Princeton, N.J., 1956); whereas Edward Handler, *America and Europe in the Political Thought of John Adams* (Cambridge, Mass., 1964), asserts that "what is called American conservatism, when considered within the wider context of European political ideas, is itself a variant of the liberal creed," and that Adams was well within that tradition (p. 191 and *passim*). Others have come to a similar judgment; e.g., George M. Dutcher, "The Rise of Republican Government in the United States," *PSQ*, LV (June 1940), 199–216; Richard B. Morris, *Seven Who Shaped Our Destiny: The Founding Fathers as* Revolutionaries (New York, 1973), p. 110; Randolph G. Adams, *Political Ideas of the American Revolution: Britannic-American Contributions to the Problem of Imperial Organization, 1765–1775*, 3rd ed. (New York, 1958), pp. 107–127.

4. The most explicit argument for a periodization of Adams's thought in distinct phases is John R. Howe, Jr., *The Changing Political Thought of John Adams* (Princeton, N.J., 1966); but there are similar assumptions in other works: Walsh, *Political Science of John Adams*, pp. 3–4; Dauer, *Adams Federalists*, pp. 36–37; Joseph Charles, *The Origins of the American Party System* (Chapel Hill, N.C., 1956), pp. 55–56; Gordon S. Wood, *The Creation of the American Republic, 1776–1787* (Chapel Hill, N.C., 1969), pp. 570–572; and Joyce Appleby, "The New Republican Synthesis and the Changing Political Ideas of John

Adams," *AQ,* XXV (Dec. 1973), 578–595. For the contrary argument, that of an essential sameness, or at least consistency, see Zoltán Haraszti, *John Adams and the Prophets of Progress* (Cambridge, Mass., 1952), p. 27; Smith, *John Adams,* I, 273–274; Richard M. Gummere, "The Classical Politics of John Adams," *Boston Public Library Quarterly,* IX (Oct. 1957), 167–182; Morris, *Seven Who Shaped Our Destiny,* p. 110; and *WJA,* IV, 181.

5. On Adams's writing as a reflection in large part of fluctuating moods see *WTJ,* I, 273 ("he never acted on any system, but was always governed by the feeling of the moment"); Frank W. Grinnell, "The Constitutional History of the Supreme Judicial Court of Massachusetts from the Revolution to 1813," *Massachusetts Law Quarterly,* II (1916–1917), 394–405; Bernard Bailyn, "Butterfield's Adams: Notes for a Sketch," *WMQ,* 3rd Ser., XIX, 253; and Shaw, *Character of John Adams,* pp. 210–212. On the disorganization of Adams's writing and his extensive copying of other authors, see Haraszti, *Prophets of Progress,* esp. pp. 46–48, 155–164. A correspondence between theory and behavior is suggested by Stephen G. Kurtz, "The Political Science of John Adams, A Guide to His Statecraft," *WMQ,* 3rd Ser., XXV (Oct. 1968), 605–613.

6. Page Smith's *John Adams* is a narrative account of Adams's life and career; Peter Shaw's *Character of John Adams* is an admirable effort to exhibit what is implied in its title. We have found both helpful, especially the latter, upon whose suggestions we have drawn for some of our own formulations in this and the following paragraphs.

7. Where Adams would have stood by modern academic standards is unclear, though probably not first. He himself evidently regarded Moses Hemmenway and Samuel Locke as the top scholars of the class, though William Browne was chosen as valedictorian, which at that time was an honor given for oratory rather than scholarship. Still, each of the graduates had some forensic part to play at commencement, and Adams's performance seems to have been impressive enough to attract the notice of the Rev. Thaddeus Maccarty of Worcester, who invited him to come there and serve as schoolmaster. Clifford K. Shipton, ed., *Sibley's Harvard Graduates,* XIII (Boston, 1965), 514, 551, 609, 620.

8. The *Dissertation* is reprinted in *WJA,* III, 447–464; the Braintree Instructions in *ibid.,* 465–468. Thomas Hutchinson, *The History of the Colony of Massachusetts-Bay,* ed. Lawrence S. Mayo (Cambridge, 1936), III, 284.

9. *Thoughts on Government, WJA,* IV, 189–200; *Defence, ibid.,* IV, 270–588, V, and VI, 3–220. Page Smith doubts that the first volume of the *Defence* could have had great influence on the deliberations at the Philadelphia Convention (*John Adams,* II, 701), though there is persuasive evidence that it did: Haraszti, *Prophets of Progress,* pp. 31, 38; Wood, *Creation of the American Republic,* pp. 581–582; and esp. Merrill Jensen, ed., *The Documentary History of the Ratification of the Constitution* (Madison, Wis., 1976), II, 160–161, 167n., 205, 505, 507n., 509, 511, 512–513, 683, 686.

10. *AP:DAJA,* II, 362–363; to Abigail Adams, Apr. 7, 1783, APM, reel 360; Shaw, *Character of John Adams,* p. 12; to Abigail Adams, Dec. 3, 1778, *AP:AFC,* III, 129–130.

11. *AP:DAJA,* I, 6, 7–8, 31; to Abigail Adams, Dec. 7, 1796, APM, reel 382; Shaw, *Character of John Adams,* pp. 22, 33.

12. To Benjamin Waterhouse, Aug. 19, 1812, Worthington C. Ford, ed., *Statesman and Friend: Letters to John Adams to Benjamin Waterhouse, 1784–1822* (Boston, 1927), p. 86; Shaw, *Character of John Adams,* pp. 97, 117; from *Boston Gazette,* Aug. 29, 1763, in *WJA,* III, 432.

13. To James Warren, July 17, 1774, *Warren-Adams Letters* (Boston, 1917–23), I, 29. "The Science of Government it is my Duty to study, more than all other Sciences. . . ." To Abigail Adams, May 12, 1780, *AP:AFC,* III, 342.

14. Wood, *Creation of the American Republic,* p. 568; Charles, *Origins,* p. 54.

15. We here follow the line of analysis advanced in Howe, *Changing Political Thought*, despite the reservations concerning it in Shaw, *Character of John Adams*, pp. 210–216.

16. The most perceptive sense of the disjunction between Adams's view of the Federal Constitution and that of most of his countrymen is in Wood, *Creation of the American Republic*, pp. 567–592.

17. The "balance" theme is present in everything Adams wrote on government. It might be added that Adams invariably filled the margins of his books with notes as he read, but he read Shakespeare through twice in 1805 without making any marginalia at all—except the one comment that in Shakespeare's time a balance of powers was lacking. Shaw, *Character of John Adams*, p. 313.

18. *AP:DAJA*, I, 335; iii, 284; to Mercy Warren, Apr. 16, 1776, *Warren-Adams Letters*, I, 222; Howe, *Changing Political Thought*, pp. 28–58.

19. *Ibid.*, pp. 89–101. During this period Adams was entirely concerned with the forming of state constitutions, his principal ideas for which were first embodied in *Thoughts on Government*. He took little interest and played no part (being out of the country) in the nationalist movement of the 1780s that resulted in the Philadelphia Convention—though as noted above, he became a strong supporter of the new Constitution.

20. *Ibid.*, pp. 102–103 ff., 137–140, 147–155, 164; Wood, *Creation of the American Republic*, pp. 571–574.

21. Adams to Jefferson, Nov. 15, 1813, Lester J. Cappon, ed., *The Adams-Jefferson Letters: The Complete Correspondence between Thomas Jefferson and John Adams* (Chapel Hill, 1959), II, 398; to John Taylor, *WJA*, VI, 456; Howe, *Changing Political Thought*, pp. 167–176; Wood, *Creation of the American Republic*, pp. 574–580. A discussion of the immediate stimuli for writing the *Defence* is Appleby, "New Republican Synthesis" (n. 4 above); on the concept of "ostracism," see Shaw, *Character of John Adams*, p. 209n. The *Discourses on Davila* is reprinted in *WJA*, VI, 223–403.

22. On the titles controversy see Ch. I above.

23. The question of Adams's alleged "monarchism" and of his various denials of it is discussed in Haraszti, *Prophets of Progress*, pp. 39–42; and Dauer, *Adams Federalists*, pp. 53–54.

24. *Creation of the American Republic*, esp. pp. 580–582.

25. *AP:DAJA*, I, 37.

26. Smith, *John Adams*, I, 121–125; Shaw, *Character of John Adams*, pp. 58, 77–78.

27. *Ibid.*, pp. 109–111; Smith, *John Adams*, I, 402–406, 422; Bailyn, "Butterfield's Adams," 246–249. "But what is all this to me? I receive but little Pleasure in beholding all these Things, because I cannot but consider them as Bagatelles, introduced by Time and Luxury in Exchange for the great Qualities and hardy manly Virtues of the human Heart. I cannot help suspecting that the more Elegance, the less Virtue in all Times and Countries." To Abigail Adams, Apr. 12, 1778, *AP:AFC*, III, 10. Or: "I could fill volumes with Descriptions of Temples and Palaces, Paintings, Sculpture, Tapestry, Porcelains, &c., &c., &c.—but I could not do this without neglecting my duty." To same, May 12, 1780, *ibid.*, 342.

28. Qu. in Adrienne Koch, *Power, Morals, and the Founding Fathers: Essays in the Interpretation of the American Enlightenment* (Ithaca, N.Y., 1967), p. 82.

29. Adet to Pickering, Oct. 27, 1796, *ASP:FR*, I, 576–577; Monroe to Pickering, Aug. 4, 15, 1796, *ibid.*, 741. Washington did not arrive in Philadelphia from Mount Vernon until the afternoon of the 31st, by which time Adet's communication had been made public. Carroll and Ashworth, *Washington*, VII, 412–413.

30. J. Q. Adams to John Adams, Aug. 13, 1796, *WJQA*, II, 19, 24; R. King to Monroe, Aug. 11, 1796, King, *King*, II, 78.

31. Samuel F. Bemis, "Washington's Farewell Address: A Foreign Policy of Independence," *AHR*, XXXIX (Jan. 1934), 252–253n.

32. Albert H. Bowman, *The Struggle for Neutrality: Franco-American Diplomacy During the Federalist Era* (Knoxville, Tenn., 1974), pp. 108–117, 185–186. For a detailed account of how American shipping fared amid these many shifts of French policy, with lists of individual cases (including one story of how a group of influential French privateer owners could effect the repeal of the May 23, 1793, decree in order to keep a rich American prize they had captured), see Pickering's report to Congress, Feb. 28, 1797 (misdated 1798), *ASP:FR*, I, 748–760. Adet's two notes, Oct. 27 and Nov. 15, 1796, are in *ibid.*, 576–577, 579–583. See also n. 34 below.

33. *ASP:FR*, I, 578.

34. E.g., *WJQA*, II, 112, 121, 143, 151; Alexander Hamilton, "The Warning," I–VI (series of essays published in *Gazette of the United States* between Jan. 27 and Mar. 27, 1797), *PAH*, XX, esp. 491–493, 551–556. Most of the supporting documents in the report cited above (n. 32) were prepared by Fulwar Skipwith, American consul-general in Paris during the Monroe mission, whose lists of French spoliations were compiled before the Jay Treaty was negotiated. Aspersions were cast by Frenchmen themselves upon the good faith in which this and other maritime decrees were issued. A long speech to this effect was delivered by Claude E. J. P. Pastoret in the Council of Five Hundred on June 20, 1797, *Gazette National, ou le Moniteur Universel*, June 25, 26, 1797; also published in *Gazette of the United States*, Sept. 19, 1797. See also Alexander DeConde, *The Quasi-War: The Politics and Diplomacy of the Undeclared War with France, 1797–1801* (New York, 1966), pp. 390–391, n. 4.

35. Pickering to Adet, Nov. 1, 1796 (published in *Aurora* and *Claypoole's American Daily Advertiser* Nov. 3); the other reply was in the form of an extended letter of instruction to C. C. Pinckney, Jan. 16, 1797 (communicated to Congress Jan. 19 and published in *Gazette of the United States*, Jan. 20, 23, 24, 25, 26, 27, 28, 30, 1797); *ASP:FR*, I, 578, 559–576. Hamilton to Washington, Jan. 19, 1797, *PAH*, XX, 469; Madison to Jefferson, Jan. 8, 1797, *PJM*, XVI, 447; "Report of the Secretary of State respecting the depredations committed on the commerce of the United States, since the last of October, 1796," June 21, 1797, *ASP:FR*, II, 28–65. A definitive report of Pinckney's non-reception did not reach the American government until late in March 1797, but romors and suspicions of it had been current six or seven weeks before. Henry Tazewell mentioned reading one such rumor as early as Feb. 1 in a letter to Jefferson of that date, Jefferson Papers, LC. See also DeConde, *Quasi-War*, pp. 383–384n.

36. Jefferson, "Anas," *WTJ*, I, 272–273.

37. "Pickering and all his colleagues are as much attached to me as I desire. I have no jealousies from that quarter." Adams to Elbridge Gerry, Feb. 13, 1797, *WJA*, VIII, 523. "When I came into office," Adams later wrote to Benjamin Lincoln, "it was my determination to make as few removals as possible—not one from personal motives, not one from party considerations." Mar. 10, *ibid.*, IX, 47. See also Kurtz, *Presidency of John Adams*, pp. 268–270; and Shaw, *Character of John Adams*, pp. 254–255. Adams's attitude here need not, of course, be seen as inconsistent with James McHenry's subsequent complaint that the President considered "the heads of departments little more than mere clerks." To Pickering, Feb. 23, 1811, Henry C. Lodge, *Life and Letters of George Cabot* (Boston, 1877), p. 208.

38. This distinction has been astutely made by Peter Shaw in *Character of John Adams,* p. 247.

39. *WTJ,* VII, 91–92.

40. John Adams to Abigail Adams, Jan. 3, 1797; same to same, Jan. 1, 1797; APM, reel 383. Rush to Jefferson, Jan. 4, 1797, Jefferson Papers, LC. Adams to Tristram Dalton, Jan. 19, 1797, *WTJ,* VII, 108n. The entire question of exactly when Adams became aware of Hamilton's election maneuverings is complicated in that his private response did not correspond to the face he put on the matter in his letters to others. Though he certainly knew about these efforts by early December, he continued for the next three months to profess either not to believe the stories, or to believe that such activities were not primarily directed at depriving him of the presidency, or that even if they were, it was for motives of the public good. What he may occasionally have blurted out in private can probably be inferred, e.g., from Rush's remark to Jefferson, qu. above, about Adams's viewing the case "in its proper light," or in his outburst to Abigail, Jan. 9, 1797, that "his [Hamilton's] intrigues in the election I despise." It is of course well known that the net product of his relations with Hamilton—in which this episode certainly constituted a turning point—was a hatred of the man which lasted all his life and which was perpetuated in Adams family tradition. Epistolary evidence bearing on the question includes John Adams to Abigail Adams, Dec. 12, 1796, *WJA,* I, 496; same to same, Dec. 16, 18, 1796, APM, reel 382; Elbridge Gerry to Abigail Adams, Dec. 28, 1796, Gerry Papers, LC; same to same, Jan. 7, 1797, Dauer, *Adams Federalists,* pp. 113–114; Abigail Adams to Gerry, Dec. 31, 1796, James T. Austin, *The Life of Elbridge Gerry* (Boston, 1829), II, 144–145; John Adams to Abigail Adams, Jan. 9, 1797, APM, reel 383; Gerry to Adams, Feb. 3, 1797, *WJA,* VIII, 524; Adams to Rush, Feb. 13, 1797, APM, reel 117; Adams to Gerry, Feb. 13, 1797, *WJA,* VIII, 524; Elkanah Watson to Adams, Mar. 5, 1797, APM, reel 383; Adams to Thomas Welsh, Mar. 10, 1797, qu. in Brown, *Adams Presidency,* p. 20; Adams to Henry Knox, Mar. 30, 1797, *WJA,* VIII, 535. See also Brown, *Adams Presidency,* pp. 18–20; Shaw, *Character of John Adams,* pp. 250–252; and Lynn H. Parsons, "Continuing Crusade: Four Generations of the Adams Family View of Alexander Hamilton," *NEQ,* XXXVII (Mar. 1964), 43–63.

41. Jefferson to Madison, Jan. 1, 1797, *WTJ,* VII, 95–96.

42. Jefferson to Adams, Dec. 28, 1796 (not sent), *ibid.,* 95–96.

43. Madison to Jefferson, Jan. 15, 1797, *PJM,* XVI, 455–456.

44. Jefferson to Madison, Jan. 30, 1797, *ibid.,* 479.

45. Both Jefferson and Adams left accounts of this episode, Jefferson's in his "Anas," based largely on notes made at the time, *WTJ,* I, 272–273; and Adams in his *Boston Patriot* letters written in 1809, a dozen years after the event, *WJA,* IX, 284–285.

46. *WJA,* I, 508; *WTJ,* I, 272–273.

47. *WJA,* IX, 105–111; *Aurora,* Mar. 14, 1797; McMaster, *History,* II, 310–311.

48. *WJA,* IX, 286.

49. *Ibid.,* 285; *WTJ,* I, 272–273.

50. This is the tendency in most works primarily sympathetic to Adams (Kurtz, *Presidency,* p. 238; Dauer, *Adams Federalists,* p. 124; Smith, *Adams,* II, 922); though as we argue below, the case has its other side.

51. Gibbs, *Memoirs,* I, 456, 462, 468. A degree of respect to this view of Adams's character, as mentioned in n. 2 above, has been accorded in the works by Cooke, Shaw, and McDonald therein cited.

52. Marvin R. Zahniser, *Charles Cotesworth Pinckney, Founding Father* (Chapel Hill, N.C., 1967), pp. 134–135.

53. E.g., Washington wrote to Adams on Feb. 20, 1797, of his *"strong hope* that you will not withhold merited promotion for Mr. John [Quincy] Adams because he is your Son. For without intending to compliment the father or the mother, or to censure any others, I give it as my decided opinion that Mr. Adams is the most valuable public character we have abroad, and that he will prove himself to be the ablest of all our Diplomatic Corps." Washington added that the country would "sustain a loss" if young Adams's "talents and worth" were "checked by over delicacy on your part." *WGW,* XXXV, 394. Abigail Adams wrote to her son on Nov. 3, 1797: "That you would not have been sent to Berlin at this time, if Mr. Washington had continued in office, I fully believe. But I can tell you where you would have been employed—as one of the envoys to France. This was the desire and opinion of all the ministers, and nothing but your near connection with the chief Magistrate prevented your being nominated. He had a delicacy upon the subject, and declined it." *WJQA,* II, 253n. See also Wolcott to Hamilton, Mar. 31, 1797, *PAH,* XX, 573.

54. Hamilton to Washington, Nov. 4, 5, 11, 1796; to Wolcott, Nov. 9, 22, 1796; *ibid.,* XX, 373, 374, 389, 380, 412.

55. Hamilton to Washington, Jan. 19, [25-31], 1797; Washington to Hamilton, Jan. 22, 1797; *ibid.,* XX, 470, 480-481, 477.

56. Hamilton to W. L. Smith, Jan. 19, Apr. 5, 10, 1797; to T. Sedgwick, Jan. 20, Feb. 26, 1797; to Pickering, Mar. 22, 29, May 11, 1797; to McHenry, Mar. [22], Apr. 29, 30, 1797; to Wolcott, Mar. 30, Apr. 5, 1797; *ibid.,* XX, 468, XXI, 20-21, 29-41, XX, 474, 521-522, XX, 545, 556-557, XXI, 81-82, XX, 575, XXI, 61-68, 72-75, XX, 567-568, XXI, 22-23. For reaction to Hamilton's ideas see Tracy to Hamilton, Mar. 23, Apr. 6, 1797; Pickering to Hamilton, Mar. 26, Apr. 29, 1797; Wolcott to Hamilton, Mar. 31, 1797; McHenry to Hamilton, Apr. 14, 1797; Smith to Hamilton, May 1, 1797; McHenry to Pickering, May 28, 1797; *ibid.,* XX, 547, XXI, 24-26, XX, 549, XXI, 68-71, XX, 569, XXI, 48, 75-76; Bernard C. Steiner, *The Life and Correspondence of James McHenry* (Cleveland, 1907), pp. 224-226; Richard E. Welch, Jr., *Theodore Sedgwick, Federalist: A Political Portrait* (Middletown, Conn., 1965), pp. 165-166. On Ames, see n. 58 below.

57. Wolcott informed Hamilton that "by means of my most earnest sincere & urgent expostulations nay supplications, it was postponed." Mar. 31, 1797, *PAH,* XX, 570. According to Jefferson, "Charles Lee [the Attorney-General] consulted a member from Virginia to know whether Marshall would be agreeable. He named you, as more likely to give satisfaction. The answer was, 'Nobody of mr. Madison's way of thinking will be nominated.'" To Madison, June 1, 1797, *WTJ,* VII, 132.

58. Fisher Ames, persuaded that the course Hamilton advocated was the right one, urged it upon Adams on Mar. 3 before departing for Massachusetts; Uriah Tracy, though not agreeing with Hamilton, nonetheless presented the latter's views to Adams a number of weeks later. Instead of welcoming such support for his own plan, Adams was decidedly irritated, and seems to have given them both rather short shrift. Hamilton wrote in 1800 that the expediency of a new mission to France "was suggested to Mr. ADAMS, through a Federal channel, a considerable time before he determined to take it." *WJA,* IX, 282-283, 288-290; Gibbs, *Memoirs,* I, 483-484; Winfred B. A. Bernhard, *Fisher Ames: Federalist and Statesman, 1758-1808* (Chapel Hill, N.C., 1965), pp. 292-293; *Letter . . . Concerning the Public Conduct and Character of John Adams . . . , PAH,* XXV, 206. See also Adams's exchange in March 1797 with Henry Knox, *WJA,* VIII, 532-536.

59. Jefferson to Madison, Dec. 17, 1796; to Rutledge, Dec. 27, 1796; to Madison, Jan. 8, 1797; *WJT,* VII, 91-92, 94, 104.

60. Same to same, Jan. 22, 1797, *ibid.,* VII, 107-108.

61. James D. Tagg, *Benjamin Franklin Bache and the Philadelphia Aurora* (Philadelphia, 1991), pp. 315–316; circular letters of Samuel Cabell (Va.), Jan. 12, 1797, and John Clopton (Va.), Jan. 24, 1797, Noble E. Cunningham, Jr., ed., *Circular Letters of Congressmen to Their Constituents, 1789–1829* (Chapel Hill, N.C., 1978), I, 68–69, 77; *Aurora*, Jan. 24, 26, Feb. 14, 17, 1797; Washington to Hamilton, Jan. 22, 1797, *PAH*, XX, 477; Madison to Jefferson, Jan. 22, 1797, *PJM*, XVI, 471; Abigail Adams to John Adams, Jan. 27, 1797, APM, reel 383.

62. Federalist response is documented in n. 56 above, as is Hamilton's response to Federalist objections. He and they were not, however, in disagreement as to evils that could issue from such negotiations—except that Hamilton believed they could be guarded against through the presence of a Federalist on the commission.

63. Kurtz, *Presidency of John Adams*, pp. 211–212; Dauer, *Adams Federalists*, pp. 116–119.

64. Madison to Jefferson, Dec. 19, 1796, Jan. 29, Feb. 5, 1797, Jan. 15, 1797, *PJM*, XVI, 433, 476, 484, 456.

65. Same to same, Jan. 22, 1797, *ibid.*, 471.

66. Jefferson to Madison, Jan. 22, 1797, *WTJ*, VII, 108; Adams to Abigail Adams, Mar. 17, 1797, C. F. Adams, ed., *Letters of John Adams Addressed to his Wife* (Boston, 1841), II, 252.

67. Madison to Jefferson, Apr. 15, 1798, *PJM*, XVII, 113; Jefferson to Edmund Pendleton, Jan. 29, 1799, *WTJ*, VII, 336. The chapter in Bowman, *Struggle for Neutrality*, which deals with the episode is entitled "'The X.Y.Z. Dish.'"

68. Marshall in particular, it appears, was greatly taken by Paris and quite enjoyed himself there. See esp. Marshall to Pinckney, Apr. 21, 1798, *PJnMl*, III, 463, 84. One of the sidelights of the XYZ affair concerns "a lady" who, according to one of the dispatches, approached Pinckney in December 1797, perhaps at a party, and tried to wheedle him into a more receptive attitude about an American loan to France—but who, in a subsequent effort by Talleyrand to discredit the story, was referred to by him as "a lady known to be connected with Mr. Pinckney." The story has been spun out into several variations (some of them prurient), and is still a subject of speculation. According to one version the lady was a Madame de Villette, in whose large house Marshall and Gerry had their lodgings. She was an attractive widow of considerable charm who delighted them both, and with whom they spent a great deal of time, including at least one extended weekend at her country residence outside Paris. After the envoys returned home from France, rumors were set afoot in America under Republican auspices which imputed various boudoir exploits to Marshall and Pinckney, but for some reason not to Gerry. See John C. Miller, *Crisis in Freedom: The Alien and Sedition Acts* (Boston, 1951), pp. 148–149, for a description of the story and details of its provenance. Some of this continues to rub off in modern accounts (E.g., Bowman, *Struggle for Neutrality*, p. 317; DeConde, *Quasi-War*, pp. 51–52; Zahniser, *Pinckney*, pp. 175–176), though more recently William Stinchcombe has argued that Madame de Villette and the "lady" of the dispatches were probably not the same person. *The XYZ Affair* (Westport, Conn., 1980), pp. 75–76; *PJnMl*, III, 318n. As for the fascination of Marshall and Gerry with their landlady, about which they themselves were quite open (and aside from the question of whether Madame de Villette was the one who approached Pinckney about the loan, or whether that lady was an agent of Talleyrand), how far it extended has never been settled and probably never will be. Actually there is very little in what evidence does exist to suggest that it was other than innocent. (Had it been otherwise, somebody would almost certainly have told on somebody, or at least dropped innuendoes; somebody in the American colony in Paris would at least have

gossiped about Madame's morals. But so far as is known, nobody did.) *PJnMl*, III, 300 and n.; Marshall to Fulwar Skipwith, Apr. 21, 1798, *ibid.*, 464; George A. Billias, *Elbridge Gerry: Founding Father and Republican Statesman* (New York, 1976), p. 268. A further item, probably not related to any of the foregoing, is Pinckney's reference, in his letters to Pickering from Amsterdam during the spring and summer of 1797, to "a lady" in Paris with whom he was in correspondence and who was supplying him with information. Zahniser, *Pinckney*, p. 155n.

69. This is the approach taken in Stinchcombe, *XYZ Affair*, and "A Neglected Memoir by Talleyrand on French-American Relations, 1793–1797," *Proceedings of the American Philosophical Society*, CXXI (June 1977), 195–208.

70. Pinckney to Pickering, Dec. 20, 1796, *ASP:FR*, II, 5–10, 18; Zahniser, *Pinckney*, pp. 141–149. Zahniser reports this news as having officially reached Adams on March 21, 1797, *ibid.*, p. 149.

71. *ASP:FR*, I, 747; a slightly variant translation of Barras's speech is in *ibid.*, II, 12; Ammon, *Monroe*, pp. 155–156.

72. King to Hamilton, Feb. 6, 1797, *PAH*, XX, 507–508; Washington to McHenry, Apr. 3, 1797, *WGW*, XXXV, 430.

73. The version of the decree which was transmitted among the papers accompanying Adams's message, printed in *ASP:FR*, II, 12–13, is incomplete; the full text is in *ibid.*, II, 30–31. DeConde, *Quasi-War*, p. 17; Bowman, *Struggle for Neutrality*, pp. 275–278; Gardner W. Allen, *Our Naval War with France* (Boston, 1909), pp. 32–33.

74. *WJA*, IX, 111–119; Dauer, *Adams Federalists*, p. 129 and n.; *Aurora*, May 18, 19, 1797; Adams to Abigail Adams, Dec. 12, 1796, *WJA*, I, 495; *AC*, 5 Cong., 1 Sess., 364; Jefferson to Peregrine Fitzhugh, June 4, 1797; to Aaron Burr, June 17, 1797, *WTJ*, VII, 136, 146.

75. Adams submitted two sets of questions to members of the cabinet, dated Apr. 14, and 15, 1797, the first ranging over the entire situation and the second applying particularly to what he might say in his special message. They are printed in *WJA*, VIII, 540–541, and Gibbs, *Memoirs*, I, 500–502. Wolcott's reply is in *ibid.*, 502–517. Pickering's (dated May 1, 1797), McHenry's (one undated, the other Apr. 29), and Lee's (Apr. 30 and May 5) are in APM, reel 384. There is a brief commentary on the replies by Adams's grandson and editor C. F. Adams in *WJA*, VIII, 541–543. McHenry asked Hamilton for advice on the questions, and Hamilton gave it to him in two papers, one dated Apr. 29 and the other undated, *PAH*, XXI, 61–68, 72–75. Much of what McHenry then wrote to Adams was simply copied verbatim from what Hamilton had written to him, though not all of it. In each case McHenry did a certain amount of editing and added material of his own.

76. Jefferson to Horatio Gates, May 30, 1797, *WTJ*, VII, 131.

77. Malone, *Jefferson*, III, 315–317, 322.

78. May 13, 1797, *WTJ*, VII, 121–122.

79. Since a good many of the Scots who had kept stores in the Chesapeake region returned to do business there with the resumption of peace, a number of them becoming American citizens, Jefferson might be excused for imagining that the tobacco trade was still a British monopoly. But by 1797, with competition from American merchants having steadily increased, particularly since the outbreak of war in Europe, this was no longer the case. See Jacob M. Price, *France and the Chesapeake: A History of the French Tobacco Monopoly, 1674–1791, and of its Relationship to the British and American Tobacco Trades* (Ann Arbor, Mich., 1973), II, 773; *idem*, "The Last Phase of the Virginia-London Consignment Trade: James Buchanan & Co., 1758–1768," *WMQ*, 3rd Ser., XLIII (Jan. 1986), 64–98; Edward C. Papenfuse, *In Pursuit of Profit: The Annapolis Merchants in the Era of the American Revolution, 1763–1803* (Baltimore, 1975), pp. 35–75; and Charles G. Steffen,

"The Rise of the Independent Merchant in the Chesapeake: Baltimore County, 1660–1769," *JAH*, LXXVI (June 1989), 9–33. It is also true that during this same period federal securities and stock in the Bank of the United States were increasingly attractive to investors both in Great Britain and on the Continent, thanks to the strong credit of the American government. But that is not to say that such investors had any measurable influence on federal financial policy.

80. "As to going to war with France lightly," Adams wrote to Gerry on May 3, "I know of nobody who is willing for it. . . ." APM, reel 117. George Cabot wrote, in a letter to the *Columbian Centinel*, May 3, 1797: "But it will be asked, must we make war on France? I answer, *No*. War might be just, but is not expedient: it is a great calamity, and should always be avoided, *except when necessary to prevent a greater evil than itself.*" Qu. in Henry C. Lodge, *Life and Letters of George Cabot* (Boston, 1878), p. 583. Robert Goodloe Harper, in a circular letter to his constituents, July 30, 1797, wrote that peace would be "a great happiness to our country." Cunningham, ed., *Circular Letters*, I, 104. Certainly none of the cabinet desired war at this stage, as is evident in the material cited in n. 75 above, and of course the entire effort of Hamilton with regard to a new mission to France, begun well before Adams took office, was in the hope of avoiding war. On Cobbett ("Peter Porcupine"), Fisher Ames declared that Porcupine "might do more good if directed by men of sense & experience—his ideas of an *intimate* connection with G Britain justly offend correct thinkers—& still more the multitude." To Hamilton, Jan. 26, 1797, *PAH*, XX, 488–489 and n.

81. E.g., to Madison, May 18, 1797; to Thomas Pinckney, May 29, 1797; to Peregrine Fitzhugh, June 4, 1797; to French Strother, June 8, 1797; to Madison, June 8, 15, 1797; to Burr, June 17, 1797; to Gerry, June 21, 1797; to Edward Rutledge, June 24, 1797; to Edmund Randolph, June 27, 1797; *WTJ*, VII, 124–130, 134–140, 142–156. The two principal themes in all these letters are, one the one hand, the warlike intentions of the Administration and, on the other, the desirability of thwarting them by delay and inaction on all defense legislation while awaiting the course of military events in Europe—the outcome of which, Jefferson hoped, would be a great triumph for France. In the letter to Randolph cited above, he referred to "Buonaparte's victories, the victories on the Rhine, the Austrian peace, Irish insurgency, English bankruptcy, insubordination in the fleet, &c." as "miraculous events," and declared that "nothing can establish firmly the republican principles of our government but an establishment of them in England. France will be the apostle for this." On Jefferson's talks with Letombe, see below, pp. 566–567.

82. Malone, *Jefferson*, III, 320–322; Adams to Uriah Forrest, June 20, 1797, *WJA*, VIII, 546–547. This was the second time in less than two months that Jefferson had got into trouble of this sort. Early in May, a letter he had written over a year before to Philip Mazzei, an Italian emigrant who had once lived in Virginia and had since returned to Italy, found its way into the newspapers. There was a heated passage in it about the "Anglican monarchical, & aristocratical party" whose object was to bring the United States over to "the substance, as they have already done to the forms of the British government," followed by one that pointed directly at Washington: "It would give you a fever were I to name to you the apostates who have gone over to these heresies, men who were Samsons in the field & Solomons in the council, but who have had their heads shorn by the harlot England." Apr. 24, 1796, *WTJ*, VII, 72–78; for details see Malone, *Jefferson*, III, 266–268, 302–308.

83. Jefferson's long letter of June 17, 1797 to Burr, with its discussion of all the issues, is rightly seen by Professor Malone as something of a Republican policy paper. At about

the same time, Samuel A. Otis wrote: "Our new V. President is very active, and I think his influence visibly increasing." *Ibid.,* 322–324; qu. in Carroll and Ashworth, *Washington,* VII, 463n. On the dinner for Monroe, see Malone, *Jefferson,* III, 324–325; and Ammon, *Monroe,* p. 158.

84. Most of Letombe's political dispatches through July 15, 1797 (by which time the special session had adjourned), had been received in Paris by the end of September. CFM, p. 1043n. The American commissioners arrived the first week in October. Before setting off for Paris from Holland, Marshall and Pinckney were told about a dinner conversation of an assorted company of bankers in which it was taken for granted that there was "a strong party amongst us, at least equal to counteract the operations of our Government. . . ." Francis Childs to William Vans Murray, Sept. 11, 1797, qu. in *PJnMl,* III, 257n.

85. Clarfield, *Pickering and American Diplomacy,* pp. 104, 109–110; Billias, *Gerry,* 259–260; Stinchcombe, *XYZ Affair,* p. 31, n. 27; *WJA,* IX, 286–287; Gibbs, *Memoirs,* I, 467–469, 531; McHenry to Pickering, Feb. 23, 1811, Lodge, *Cabot,* pp. 204–205 (also qu. in Steiner, *McHenry,* p. 224).

86. The items upon which we have most depended in the paragraphs that follow are Billias, *Gerry,* which is based on thorough scholarship, and Samuel E. Morison, "Elbridge Gerry, Gentleman-Democrat," *NEQ,* II (Jan. 1929), 6–33, and repr. in Morison, *By Land and by Sea: Essays and Addresses* (New York, 1953), and "Elbridge Gerry" in *DAB.* A discussion of other literature on Gerry is in Billias, *Gerry,* pp. 342–343. The proposition that Gerry's career and personality be considered within the framework of classical republicanism is in *ibid.,* pp. xiii–xviii and *passim.*

87. Qu. in *ibid.,* p. 292. The parallel with Randolph is suggested by Robert Dawidoff's brilliant study, *The Education of John Randolph* (New York, 1979).

88. Billias, *Gerry,* p. 58.

89. Austin, *Life of Elbridge Gerry,* II, 307.

90. Qu. in *Billias,* Gerry, p. 67.

91. Charles Thomson to Richard Peters, Jan. 19, 1784, E. C. Burnett, ed., *Letters of Members of the Continental Congress* (Washington, 1934), VII, 422.

92. Billias, *Gerry,* p. 195; ——— to Jefferson, Oct. 11, 1787, Max Farrand, ed., *The Records of the Federal Convention of 1787* (New Haven, Conn., 1911), III, 104.

93. Billias, *Gerry,* p. 262; Jefferson to Gerry, May 13, June 21, 1797, *WTJ,* VII, 119–124, 149–151. The anglophobic ferocity of both these letters is striking; in the second, Jefferson urges Gerry to accept appointment to the mission, the character of which he felt depended entirely on him, and insists that Gerry's nomination had given "a spring to hope, which was dead before."

94. To J. Q. Adams, Mar. 31, 1797, *WJA,* VIII, 537.

95. No modern biography of Marshall has as yet superseded Albert J. Beveridge's *Life of John Marshall* (Boston, 1916–19), 4v.; Leonard Baker, *John Marshall: A Life in Law* (New York, 1974) falls well short of that object. One reason for the deficiency, aside from the still-daunting durability of Beveridge's work, may be that Marshall's very long and innovative career as Chief Justice has led the best-qualified writers to direct their studies of it to aspects which fall more readily into the realm of legal and constitutional history than biography. Edward S. Corwin's extended article on Marshall in *DAB* is, however, very good and useful.

96. John Stokes Adams, ed., *An Autobiographical Sketch by John Marshall . . .* (Ann Arbor, Mich., 1937), p. 4.

97. *Ibid.,* pp. 9–10.

98. Jefferson to Madison, Nov. 26, 1975, *WTJ,* VII, 38.

99. *DAB*, XII, 318.

100. King to C. C. Pinckney, Oct. 17, 1797, King, *King*, II, 235.

101. The best source for Pinckney's life and career is Zahniser, *Pinckney*, cited in n. 52 above. The qu. is from Eliza Pinckney to C. C. Pinckney [late 1767], *ibid.*, p. 18.

102. *Ibid.*, pp. 13–14, 20, 24–25, 34.

103. Qu. in *ibid.*, p. 98.

104. C. C. Pinckney to Thomas Pinckney, Jan. 7, 1793, qu. in *ibid.*, p. 117n.

105. The body of Talleyrand scholarship is immense. Those items found to be most useful for our purposes were Georges Lacour-Gayet, *Talleyrand: 1754–1838* (Paris, 1928–34), 4v., still the most complete, and full of quotations from letters and other documents; J. F. Bernard, *Talleyrand: A Biography* (New York, 1973) an ample and intelligently written work, without footnote references but with a very full bibliography; Crane Brinton, *The Lives of Talleyrand* (New York, 1936), suggestive but superficial and persistently arch in tone; and Louis Madelin, *Talleyrand: A Vivid Biography of the Amoral, Unscrupulous, and Fascinating French Statesman*, tr. Rosalie Feltenstein (New York, 1948), by a noted French historian, originally published in Paris, 1944, without the above lurid (though not inaccurate) subtitle. Pieter Geyl, "The French Historians and Talleyrand," *Debates with Historians* (The Hague, 1955) is not, as the title might suggest, a critical essay on the Talleyrand literature but a series of interesting though somewhat disjointed reflections on Talleyrand's statecraft. A new biography is in progress as of the present writing, though the sequence of volumes appearing so far has not accorded with the actual chronology of Talleyrand's career, resulting in some repetition: Michel Poniatowski, *Talleyrand aux Etats-Unis, 1794–1796* (Paris, 1967); *Talleyrand et le Directoire* (Paris, 1982); *Talleyrand et le Consulat* (Paris, 1986); and *Talleyrand et l'ancienne France, 1754–1789* (Paris, 1988). The story about Adalbert, the tenth-century Count of Périgord, is in all Talleyrand biographies; the qu. about being forced into the priesthood is from Madelin, *Tallyerand*, p. 16.

106. The story about Hamilton is in Nathan Schachner, *Alexander Hamilton* (New York, 1946), p. 345; for Talleyrand's otherwise high opinion of Hamilton see Duc de Broglie, ed., *Memoirs of the Prince de Talleyrand*, tr. R. Ledos de Beaufort (New York, 1891), I, 181–182. Other material on Talleyrand's sojourn in America includes Hans Huth and Wilma J. Pugh, eds., *Talleyrand in America as a Financial Promoter, 1794–1796* (Washington, 1942); John L. Earl III, "Talleyrand in Philadelphia, 1794–1796," *PMHB*, XCI (July 1967), 282–298; *idem*, "Talleyrand in America: A Study of His Exile, 1794–1796" (Unpub. diss., Georgetown U., 1964); Richard M. Brace, "Talleyrand in New England: Reality and Legend," *NEQ*, XVI (Sept. 1943), 397–406; Edwin R. Baldridge, Jr., "Talleyrand in the United States, 1794–1796" (Unpub. diss., Lehigh U., 1963).

107. Madelin, *Talleyrand*, p. 56. "Il faut y faire une fortune immense, une immense fortune, une immense fortune, une fortune immense." Poniatowski, *Talleyrand et le Directoire*, p. 161.

108. Henry J. Ford, in "Timothy Pickering," S. Bemis, ed., *The American Secretaries of State and Their Diplomacy* (New York, 1927), II, 217, believes that the principal author of the instructions was Marshall; Beveridge, *Marshall*, II, 218, does not claim this but does imply that the coincidence of Marshall's and Hamilton's both being in Philadelphia during the early part of July "may or may not have been significant"; Bowman, *Struggle for Neutrality*, p. 286, suggests that the two probably collaborated on the instructions. A more common-sense likelihood could be that they were drafted by the Secretary of State himself, who by this time was in more or less full agreement with the principles they embodied, as was taken for granted by Pickering's early biographers in the 1860s when they referred to the instructions as one of Pickering's "celebrated State Papers." Pickering and Upham,

Pickering, III, 371. Stinchcombe, *XYZ Affair,* pp. 22–23, 31, n. 29, also assumes Pickering's authorship, but plausibly suggests that Hamilton's ideas were at the same time influential, and that Adams was aware of where they came from. He cites an undated set of notes in Adams's handwriting headed "H Ideas" (APM, reel 387) which do in fact tally with the suggestions Hamilton made to McHenry (n. 75 above). It should be added, however, that ideas from all the Secretaries, as set forth in the above-cited papers, found their way into the instructions. They are printed in *ASP:FR,* II, 153–157; and *PJnMl,* III, 102–119.

109. *Ibid.,* 117. In addition to the subjects summarized above, the envoys were to seek a revision, in the interests of greater clarity, of the Consular Convention concluded between the United States and France in 1788. The main point at issue here was whether judicial decisions of consuls regarding their own nationals should be executed by officials of the host country, as France contended was allowed by the Convention. This did not, however, as DeConde (*Quasi-War,* p. 45) mistakenly asserts, include prize court jurisdiction by one party in the ports of the other, which no treaty or convention had ever permitted. The text of the Consular Convention is in Hunter Miller, ed., *Treaties and Other International Acts of the United States of America* (Washington, 1931), II, 228–241.

110. *Gazette National, ou le Moniteur Universel,* June 25, 26, 1797. This version omitted the excerpts from treaties, laws, and decrees cited by Pastoret in his speech; but the complete text in an English translation was published in *Gazette of the United States,* Sept. 19, 1797. One is struck by the circumstantial detail and evident authenticity of Pastoret's facts, until one discovers how readily accessible such facts were: Pinckney in Amsterdam had had a thousand copies printed of Pickering's powerful report of Jan. 16, 1797 (in the form of a dispatch to himself), on French-American relations (see *ASP:FR,* I, 559–576) and had sent one to every member of France's legislative body. That body, before being decimated by the *coup d'etat* of Fructidor (Sept. 4, 1797), was already disaffected from the Directory and thus more than ordinarily disposed to listen to such philippics. Several weeks before Pastoret's speech, Louis-Philippe Ségur had made a similar argument in two very strong articles in *Nouvelles Politiques,* Apr. 25, May 17, 1797. Zahniser, *Pinckney,* p. 156; Clarfield, *Pickering and American Diplomacy,* p. 112; Bernard Faÿ, *The Revolutionary Spirit in France and America: A Study of Moral and Intellectual Relations Between France and the United States at the End of the Eighteenth Century,* tr. Ramon Guthrie (New York, 1955), pp. 392–393.

111. Gilbert Chinard, ed., "Considérations sur la conduite du Gouvernement américain envers la France, depuis le commencement de la Révolution jusqu'en 1797, par Louis-Guillaume Otto," *Bulletin de l'Institut Français,* No. XVI (Dec. 1943), 9–37.

112. Joseph Fauchet, *A Sketch of the Present State of our Political Relations with the United States of North-America,* tr. Benjamin F. Bache (Philadelphia, 1797), pp. 5, 13, 18, 28, 30; first published in Paris in the summer of 1797.

113. Adet to Talleyrand, Sept. 22, 1797, AECPE-U 48, 258–264vo.; sentences qu. are on 263–263vo.

114. Talleyrand to Létombe, Aug. 4, Sept. 1, 1797, AECPE-U 48, 154–155, 214–215vo.

115. Talleyrand to Bourdieu and others, Jan. 15, 1795, Huth and Pugh, eds., *Talleyrand in America,* p. 92; Georges Pallain, ed., "Les Etats-Unis et l'Angleterre en 1795: Lettre de M. de Talleyrand [to Lord Lansdowne, Feb. 1, 1795]," *Revue d'histoire diplomatique,* III (1889), 76; Talleyrand, *Memoir Concerning the Commercial Relations of the United States with England . . .* (Boston, 1809), p. 13, an English translation of a paper read at the National Institute, Apr. 4, 1797.

116. "Objects which should figure in the forthcoming negotiations with the United States," Oct. 2, 1797, AECPE-U 48, 278–286vo. There has been some question concerning

this paper. Bowman, *Struggle for Neutrality,* p. 312, assumes it to have been prepared by Talleyrand, as by implication does E. Wilson Lyon, "The Directory and the United States," *AHR,* XLIII (Apr. 1938), 520–521—with which, judging from internal evidence, we are inclined to agree. Stinchcombe, *XYZ Affair,* p. 49, however, contends that it must have been written by someone else in the Foreign Office, because (a) "Talleyrand did not accept any of this report's recommendations on indemnities, cessation of hostilities, and the revision of treaties during the next nine months"; and (b) he "specifically rejected a number of the report's suggestions in his margin notes." But it would be more accurate to say he did not *act* on any of them during that time, not being, for any number of reasons, free to do so. Moreover, this was a preliminary memorandum, as the author makes clear in several places. Nor are the two or three marginal jottings rejections of anything; they are simply additions, in Talleyrand's handwriting, of words that had been inadvertently omitted by the clerk who transcribed the document. On the other hand there is a section of this paper, 284–286vo., headed "Indemnities—Negotiations with the United States," which Lyon and Bowman take to be a separate memorandum; we are treating the entire sequence as a single piece. In all likelihood it was never actually submitted to the Directory as a formal report.

117. Stinchcombe, "Neglected Memoir by Talleyrand," pp. 206–207. This paper seems to have been prepared later in October and did serve, as later evidence corroborates, as a report to the Directory. As we know, the hint contained in it about an "explanation" of President Adams's message, and with the question of money, were then emerging as prerequisites to any kind of negotiation. The tactics on the indemnities question were outlined in "Objects which should figure in the forthcoming negotiations," pp. 284–286vo.

118. Frances S. Childs, "A Secret Agent's Advice on America," Edward M. Earle, ed., *Nationalism and Internationalism: Essays Inscribed to Carlton J. H. Hayes* (New York, 1950), pp. 18–44, is a good-humored summary, with many excerpts, of this extremely tedious correspondence. The phrases quoted are on pp. 33, 35, 38.

119. Létombe to Minister of Exterior Relations, June 7, 1797, CFM, p. 1030. During the period of the special session when Jefferson was in Philadelphia, Létombe refers in four of his dispatches to having seen him: May 16, 30, June 5, 7, *ibid.,* pp. 1018, 1025, 1027, 1029–1031. In a later one the following winter there is mention of Jefferson's having once more urged that Létombe "not hesitate to drop in on him any time I liked." Jan. 17, 1798, AECPE-U 49, 145. Hauterive in a letter of July 16, 1797, reported that the Republican party in America (the "friends of France and liberty") did not then favor an immediate or final accommodation with France: "wisdom and patriotism seem to unite to counsel the way of a prorogation until a time when the maritime destinies of the European states will be more settled." Qu. in Childs, "Secret Agent," p. 38.

120. To Minister of Exterior Relations, May 30, June 7, 1797, Jan. 17, 1798; CFM, pp. 1024–1025, 1031; AECPE-U 49, 145.

121. See n. 117 above; as for the "hint" there referred to, the entire course of the American commissioners' dealings with Talleyrand's agents, as described below, is evidence of how the hint was developed.

122. "Objects which should figure in the forthcoming negotiations," AECPE-U 48, 284–286vo.

123. The most circumstantial first-hand accounts are George Duruy, ed., *Memoirs of Barras: Member of the Directorate* (New York, 1895), II, 530–573 (much the fullest); *Memoirs of Talleyrand,* I, 188–190; Baroness de Staël, *Considerations on the Principal Events of the French Revolution,* ed. Duc de Broglie and Baron de Staël (New York, 1818), I, 381–382; Robert d'Angers, ed., *Mémoires de Larevellière-Lépeaux . . .* (Paris, 1895), II, 114–115;

a Rashomon-like situation in which each of the parties concerned gives a particular version of the truth. For an appraisal of this problem see Bernard, *Talleyrand*, pp. 179–186.

124. Hippolyte Carnot, *Mémoires sur Carnot, par son fils* (Paris, 1863), II, 116; Talleyrand, *Memoirs*, I, 191; Paul Bailleu, ed., *Preussen und Frankreich von 1795 bis 1807, Diplomatische Correspondenzen* (Leipzig, 1880), I (disp. of Oct. 25, 1797), 155.

125. On Reubell's treatment of Talleyrand, see Barras, *Memoirs*, III, 218–220, and Lacour-Gayet, *Talleyrand*, I, 288–290, for some entertaining examples. On the state of France's foreign relations after Fructidor, see Raymond Guyot, *Le Directoire et la Paix de l'Europe: des traités de Bâle à la deuxième coalition* (1795–99) (Paris, 1911), pp. 548–553.

126. *Ibid.*, pp. 553–557; Geyl, "French Historians and Talleyrand," pp. 198–203. The qu. is from an obsequiously laudatory circular Talleyrand addressed to all foreign agents of the Republic, Sept. 6, 1797, Georges Pallain, ed., *Le Ministère de Talleyrand sous le Directoire* (Paris, 1891), p. 138.

127. Jean-Baptiste H. R. Capefigue, "Talleyrand," *Biographie universelle, ancienne et moderne . . .* , new ed. (Paris, 1870–73), XL, 610.

128. Bailleu, ed., *Preussen und Frankreich*, I, 168; Capefigue, "Talleyrand," 611.

129. Louis Bastide, *Vie politique et religieuse de Talleyrand-Périgord* (Paris, 1838), p. 227; Lacour-Gayet, *Talleyrand*, I, 237–238; Whitelaw Reid, "Introduction," *Memoirs of Talleyrand*, I, xviii.

130. Georges Lefebvre, *The Directory*, tr. Robert Baldick (New York, 1967), pp. 95–119. What the Directors wrote about each other was picturesque to say the least. Carnot said of Larevellière-lépeaux that "nature, when creating him deformed and stinking," did so to warn others "against the falseness of his character and the profound corruption of his heart," and of Reubell, that he was "the protector of men charged with thefts and peculations." "This Monsieur Reubell," said Sieyès, "must needs *take* something for his health every morning." (He even pocketed wax candles when leaving sessions of the Directory.) Barras, according to Larevellière, was surrounded at the Luxembourg only by "the most crapulous brawlers, the most corrupted aristocrats, abandoned women, men of ruined reputation, jobbers and fixers, mistresses and lover-boys. . . . A lie costs him nothing; calumny is but a game. He is faithless and without morals. . . ." Duruy, "Preface," *Memoirs of Barras*, III, xiii; *Mémoires de Larevellière-Lépeaux*, I, 338–339. Barras himself in his *Memoirs*, esp. III, is full of anecdotes involving the "cold, treacherous, narrow, perfidious" Merlin (p. 311), the "hard-hearted" Treilhard, "coarse and insolent" (pp. 323, 417), Neufchâteau, "a libertine of old, whom neither infirmities nor years had reformed" (p. 212), and so on.

131. Evidence of any kind of sustained attention to, or concern with, or policy toward the United States on the part of the Directory up to the time of Adams's special mission is so fragmentary as to be all but meaningless. This is not to deny a kind of endemic hostility toward the United States all during this period—the decrees against American shipping and the treatment of Pinckney are sufficient evidence of that—but these actions must be seen as a function of France's very *un*concern with American affairs, and have to be explained in a particular context, that of France's military involvements in Europe and the problem, to which all else was subordinate and for which no pretext was too far-fetched, of resources with which to sustain them. For example, the Prussian minister Sandoz-Rollin, after listening to a tirade from Carnot against the city of Hamburg ("Those people are too rich, and it's indispensable that they should pay dearly for their neutrality"), noted on May 6, 1796: "You see it and you hear it: the opportunity for extortion and for gathering up a bit of money makes every other consideration give way here, and becomes the mainspring of their enterprises and, I venture to say, of their policy." Bailleu, ed.,

Preussen und Frankreich, I, 67. The pretext in the case of the United States was of course the Jay Treaty, a formula which the individual Directors—when they mentioned it at all, which was seldom—repeated almost mindlessly.

But beyond this, the Directors showed virtually no interest in the United States. There is scarcely a reference to America in all of Barras's memoirs (by far the most detailed of any); even with regard to the Jay Treaty, Barras does not get around to mentioning it until March 1796, and then only to note that it had aroused discontent *in America* (II, 97). Reubell never wrote anything about America until 1799, when he prepared a "mémoire justicatif" defending himself from a whole series of charges made against the Directory in the Council of Five Hundred, a minor one of which was breaking off relations with the United States. To this, Reubell devoted three sentences in a paper filling thirty-four printed pages, and managed to get his facts wrong in all three. (He said the Jay Treaty had been made by John Adams, "the President of Congress.") Gerlof D. Homan, *Jean-François Reubell: French Revolutionary, Patriot, and Director (1747-1807)* (The Hague, 1971), p. 153; Bernard Nabonne, ed., "Le Mémoire justicatif de Reubell, chef de la diplomatie du Directoire," *Revue d'histoire diplomatique,* LXIII (1949), 85-86. Larevellière too was one of the accused Directors in the denunciation of 1799, without which the United States would probably not have made its way into his memoirs at all. He professes great esteem for Monroe (Monroe was President of the United States by the time he wrote them, and he himself a private citizen), and he too gets his chronology all muddled up. (He has Monroe counseling patience against "the unjust proceedings of John Adams's government," whereas Monroe had been recalled well before Adams took office.) Larevellière also accuses Carnot (whom he hated) of wanting to declare war against the United States and of taking Monroe for a tiresome bore. The first charge is doubtful; the second is rather more plausible since the only mention of the United States in Carnot's own biography, prepared by his son, is a patronizing reference to Monroe as being more of a French revolutionary than Carnot himself, followed by a footnote which has Monroe, Jefferson, and Adams all dying on the same day to commemorate the Declaration of Independence. Larevellière-lépeaux, *Mémoires,* II, 257-260; III, 179-189; *Mémoires sur Carnot,* II, 133. Merlin de Douai, one of the two new Directors installed after Fructidor, is briefly associated with America for having written a "treatise" (referred to below, Ch. XIV, n. 21) on the *rôle d'équipage* while serving as Minister of Justice. We may well imagine the circumstances. Merlin, according to the ever-malicious Barras, "sought to make war, politics, and revolution subject to all the chicanery of the law," and was once the subject of a "dessert joke" told by Bonaparte. "Whenever I commit any arbitrary act," the latter recounted, "and have been obliged to overstep my functions, I go the next morning to Merlin, and beg him to be good enough to point out to me some ancient or modern law under which I can shelter myself. He reflects awhile, and in a very few minutes he finds the answer in his head, or he puts his hand on the volume and his finger on the page. Never does this good Merlin leave me in the lurch. He is Merlin the Magician." Barras, *Memoirs,* II, 590, 413-414. François Barthelemy, the other Director purged with Carnot after Fructidor, protests that his own feelings toward the United States were entirely peaceable and asserts that it "was not believed that the Americans' treaty with the court of London was a sufficient motive" for the undeclared war set off by the decree of March 2, 1797. Jean L. G. Soulavie, ed., *Mémoires historique et diplomatique de Barthelemy depuis le 14 juillet jusqu'au 30 prairial An 7* (Paris, 1799), p. 60. This is probably more or less authentic, even though the *Mémoires* themselves are said to be apocryphal. (Guyot, *Le Directoire et la paix de l'Europe,* p. 27.)

The three brief references to the United States in the Directory's minutes from the time of the American commissioners' arrival in October 1797 to the end of the year are quite perfunctory. One concerns the Directory's authorizing the Minister of Exterior Relations to demand an "explanation" of President Adams's speech; another mentions the capture of an American merchant ship lacking a *rôle d'équipage;* and the third involves a verbal order to the Minister to confer with envoys from the United States and from Hamburg about taking some shares in the Dutch loan ("Batavian rescriptions"). Sittings of Oct. 17, Nov. 17, Dec. 24, 1797, AF III, 8, 9, Archives Nationales, Paris. We are indebted to Isser Woloch for this bit of negative evidence.

132. Stinchcombe, *XYZ Affair,* p. 35; Pinckney to Pickering, Dec. 20, 1796, *ASP:FR,* II, 8.

133. See below, p. 596.

134. Marshall, Paris Journal, Oct. 8, 14, 18–19, 1797; Envoys to Pickering, Oct. 22, 1797, *PJnMl,* III, 159–165, 255–258. The journal kept by Marshall frequently gives a fuller account of the commission's proceedings than do the dispatches sent home by the envoys, though not invariably so. Parallel references to both sources will be given here wherever possible. When this material was transmitted to Congress and subsequently released for publication the letters "X," "Y," and "Z" were substituted by Secretary Pickering for the names of the individuals given in the dispatches and journal. There was actually a "W" who made a very brief early appearance, Nicholas Hubbard of the Amsterdam firm of Van Staphorst and Hubbard; technically, then, it could be called the "WXYZ" affair, though it seldom is. *Ibid.,* 256n.

135. *Ibid.,* 165–168, 258–261.

136. *Ibid.,* 261–262.

137. *Ibid.,* 168.

138. *Ibid.,* 263–265.

139. *Ibid.,* 265.

140. *Ibid.,* 170–173; Envoys to Pickering, Nov. 8, 1797 (here begins the sequel to events occurring between Oct. 22 and this date), 276–279. The envoys did of course transmit further dispatches after this one. There were eight altogether, through Apr. 3, 1798. Numbers 1 and 2, those that caused the great upheaval of feeling in America, were transmitted to Congress by President Adams on Apr. 3; he sent the remainder of them May 4, June 5, and June 18, 1798. *ASP:FR,* II, 157–163, 169–182, 185–188, 188–189.

141. *PJnMl,* III, 174–178, 280–283.

142. *Ibid.,* 178–180, 283–285.

143. *Ibid.,* 181–182, 286–287.

144. *Ibid.,* 182–184, 287–289.

145. *Ibid.,* 185–194, 293–295, 305–307, 331–382.

146. *Ibid.,* 195–197.

147. Talleyrand in a report to the Directory, probably in late January, wrote: "Messrs. Pinckney and Marshall are devoted to the ideas reigning at Philadelphia, and they have already let them appear more than once. . . . I propose that the Directory authorize me to bypass these two ministers. . . . There remains Mr. Gerry." Marshall and Pinckney, he concluded, should "be invited to withdraw." Pluviôse, Year VI [Jan. 20–Feb. 18, 1798, but probably before Feb. 4], AECPE-U 49, 174–187vo.

148. *PJnMl,* III, 197–203.

149. *Ibid.,* 203–205.

150. *Ibid.,* 205–228.

151. *ASP:FR,* II, 188–191.

152. "He believes," Marshall wrote in his journal, "that Genl. Pinckney and myself

are both determined to remain no longer, unless we can be accredited." Marshall was further persuaded that Talleyrand did not think Gerry shared this determination. Feb. 4, 1798, *PJnMl*, III, 197.

153. *Ibid.*, 231–232. Envoys to Talleyrand, Apr. 3, 1798, *ibid.*, 428–459, esp. 459.

154. *Ibid.*, 233.

155. *Ibid.*, 232–242, 461–462; Zahniser, *Pinckney*, pp. 188–190.

156. *PJnMl*, III, 236–238; Marshall to Pinckney, Apr. 21, 1798, *ibid.*, 464; Billias, *Gerry*, p. 265.

157. See below, pp. 608–609.

CHAPTER XIII

Adams and Hamilton

1. *AC*, 5 Cong., 2 Sess., 963–964; Jefferson to Madison, Feb. 8, 1798, *WTJ*, VII, 196. The dispatch of Létombe to Talleyrand above referred to is in *CFM*, pp. 1094–1096.

2. On Matthew Lyon and his doings see Ch. XV below.

3. On the debates in the House over the Lyon-Griswold affair, and the efforts to reduce the diplomatic corps and repeal the stamp tax, see *AC*, 5 Cong., 2 Sess., 955–969, 961–962, 964–1029, 1034, 1036–1043, 1048–1058, 1063–1068 (Lyon-Griswold); 849–945, 1058, 1083–1143, 1145–1200 (Foreign Intercourse); 1069–1083, 1097–1098 (Stamp Duty).

4. Abigail Adams to Eliza Peabody, Feb. 13, 1798, Shaw Family Papers, LC.

5. *ASP:FR*, II, 151–152.

6. Adams to Heads of Department, Jan. 24, Mar. 13, 1798, *WJA*, VIII, 561–562, 568. The replies are summarized in *ibid.*, 562–563n. and 568–569n. See also n. 9 below.

7. Malone, *Jefferson*, III, 370–371.

8. Gerard H. Clarfield, *Timothy Pickering and American Diplomacy, 1795–1800* (Columbia, Mo., 1969), pp. 144–147.

9. McHenry to Adams, Feb. 14, Mar. 14, 1798; Charles Lee to Adams, Mar. 8, 14, 1798; Wolcott to Adams, Mar. 15, 1798 (wrongly dated Mar. 19 in Gibbs, *Memoirs*, II, 14–15); APM, reel 387. McHenry's letter of Feb 15 closely parallels the ideas and actual wording of Hamilton to McHenry, [Jan. 27–Feb. 11, 1798], *PAH*, XXI, 341–346.

10. See, e.g., Reginald C. Stuart, *War and American Thought: From the Revolution to the Monroe Doctrine* (Kent, Ohio, 1982), a treatment of what the author calls "The Limited-War Mentality."

11. This was more or less the view of Republicans generally. See John W. Kuehl, "The XYZ Affair and American Nationalism: Republican Victories in the Middle Atlantic States," *Maryland Historical Magazine*, LXVII (Spring 1972), 2; Jefferson to Burr, June 17, 1797; to Gerry, June 21, 1797; to Edmund Randolph, June 27, 1797; to Arthur Campbell, Sept. 1, 1797; all in *WTJ*, VII, 145–149, 151, 155–156, 169–171, 218–221, 227–230.

12. McHenry to Adams, Feb. 15, 1798, APM, reel 387; Hamilton to McHenry, [Jan. 27–Feb. 11, 1798], *PAH*, XXI, 341–346.

13. Charles Lee to Adams, Mar. 8, 14, 1798; McHenry to Adams, Mar. 14, 1798; APM, reel 387.

14. Notes for Message to Congress [undated, but probably after Mar. 8 and before Mar. 19, 1798], APM, reel 387.

15. Wolcott to Adams, Mar. 15, 1798, Gibbs, *Memoirs*, II, 14–15; Adams, Message to Congress, Mar. 19, 1798, *ASP:FR*, II, 152.

16. *Ibid.*

17. Jefferson to Madison, Mar. 21, 1798, *WTJ*, VII, 219.

18. *AC*, 5 Cong., 2 Sess., 1319–1320.

19. *Ibid.*, 1349.

20. *Ibid.*, 1357–1358.

21. *Ibid.*, 1359–1371. Abigail Adams to J. Q. Adams, Apr. 4, 1798, APM, reel 388. On Giles and Gallatin, see Abigail Adams to Mary Cranch, Apr. 4, 1798, *New Letters*, p. 151. The resolution was passed 65–27; every Republican voted for it, and all twenty-seven against were Federalists, with the possible exception of Tillinghast of Rhode Island. Rudolph M. Bell, *Party and Faction in American Politics: The House of Representatives, 1789–1801* (Westport, Conn., 1973), pp. 166, 256–257.

22. *ASP:FR*, II, 153; DeConde, *Quasi-War*, pp. 72–73 and nn.

23. Jefferson to Madison, Apr. 6, 19, 26, 1798; to Peter Carr, Apr. 12, 1798; to Monroe, Apr. 19, 1798; to E. Pendleton, Jan. 29, 1799; *WTJ*, VII, 234–236, 238–246, 337. "The Democrats in neither House of Congress make much opposition; and out of doors the French Devotees are rapidly quitting the worship of their idol." Pickering to Washington, Apr. 14, 1798, Pickering Papers, XXXVII, MHS. On Federalist electoral gains, see John W. Kuehl, "Southern Reaction to the XYZ Affair: An Incident in the Emergence of American Nationalism," *Kentucky State Historical Society Register*, LXX (Jan. 1972), 21–49.

24. Robert Troup to Rufus King, June 3, 1798, King, *King*, II, 329.

25. "The numerous addresses," Abigail Adams wrote to her sister, "... load the President with constant application to his pen, as he answers all of them and by this means has an opportunity of diffusing his own sentiments, more extensively & probably where they will be more read and attended to than they would be through any other channel." The British minister Robert Liston reported, "Mr. Adams spends the whole morning from 6 o'clock till 12 or 1, in writing these answers, which are frequently as long as the addresses to which they apply." For more than two months, Abigail told her son in mid-July, "upon an average he has replied to 4 or 5 addresses every day with his own hand." Abigail Adams to Mary Cranch, May 18, 1798, *New Letters*, p. 175; Liston to Grenville, May 20, 1798, qu. in DeConde, *Quasi-War*, p. 403, n. 15; Abigail Adams to J. Q. Adams, July 14, 1798, APM, reel 390.

26. A generous selection of these replies is reprinted in *WJA*, IX, 180–231. A great many of the addresses themselves, as well as the replies, were published in the newspapers, and a collection of them was brought out in book form: *A Selection of the Patriotic Addresses to the President of the United States. Together with the President's Answers ...* (Boston, 1798). The originals of both the addresses and replies are in APM, reels 388–390 and 119.

27. Abigail Adams to Eliza Peabody, June 22, 1798, Shaw Family Papers, LC; to Mary Cranch, May 21, 1798, *New Letters*, p. 178. "The numerous addresses which pour in daily in abundance give him much additional writing. They are however a grateful and pleasing testimony of the satisfaction of the publick mind...." To Mary Cranch, May 13, 1798, *ibid.*, p. 173. Though the burden was considerable, it was "a gratefull and pleasing employment as it assures him of the approbation confidence and satisfaction of the people in his conduct and administration." To Eliza Peabody, June 22, 1798, Shaw Family Papers, LC.

28. *ASP:MA*, I, 120; *AC*, 5 Cong., 2 Sess., 2127, 3717, 3722–3727, 3733, 3747–3755; Smelser, *Congress Founds the Navy*, pp. 150–159; DeConde, *Quasi-War*, pp. 90–91.

29. *WJA*, IX, 291. Abigail Adams's letters certainly leave little doubt as to where her own sentiments lay. She declared that "nothing will have an Effect untill congress pass a

Sedition Bill, which I presume they will do before they rise," adding that there was not an issue of Bache's paper or of the *Boston Chronicle* "but what might have been prosse-cuted as libels upon the President and Congress." To Mary Cranch, Apr. 26, 1798, *New Letters*, p. 165. "And in any other Country Bache & all his papers would have been seazd and ought to be here, but congress are dilly dallying about passing a Bill enabling the President to seize suspisious persons, and their papers." To same, June 19, 1798, *ibid.*, p. 193. See also *ibid.*, pp. 172, 179, 196. When Congress finally adjourned, she thought "their last deeds may be marked amongst their best, an Alien Bill a Sedition Bill and a Bill declaring void, all our Treaties and conventions with France. . . ." To Thomas Boylston Adams, July 20, 1798, APM, reel 390.

30. *AC*, 5 Cong., 2 Sess., 1571, 1580, 1778; James Morton Smith, *Freedom's Fetters: The Alien and Sedition Laws and American Civil Liberties* (Ithaca, N.Y., 1956), pp. 27–33.

31. *Ibid.*, p. 48. For Gallatin's speeches against the original bill, and his later insistence on bringing the final version to a vote, see *AC*, 5 Cong., 2 Sess., 1788–1790, 1792–1796, 2034–2035, 2049.

32. *Aurora*, May 8, 1798; Smith, *Freedom's Fetters*, pp. 59–93; Hamilton to Pickering, June 7, 1798, *PAH*, XXI, 495; *AC*, 5 Cong., 2 Sess., 1973–2029.

33. *Ibid.*, 596; *Aurora*, June 6, 1798; Smith, *Freedom's Fetters*, pp. 94–130; Hamilton to Wolcott, June 29, 1798, *PAH*, XXI, 522.

34. See below, Ch. XV, n. 25; *AC*, 5 Cong., 2 Sess., 2093–2116, 2133–2171.

35. The roll-call is in *ibid.*, 2171. The texts of the four acts are in *ibid.*, 3739–3742, 3744, 3746, 3753–3754, 3776–3777, and Smith, *Freedom's Fetters*, pp. 435–442.

36. *PAH*, III, 378–397; Richard W. Kohn, *Eagle and Sword: The Beginnings of the Military Establishment in America* (New York, 1975), pp. 47–48.

37. *Ibid.*, pp. 73–88.

38. Lois G. Schwoerer, *"No Standing Armies!" The Antiarmy Ideology in Seventeenth-Century England* (Baltimore, 1974), p. 195.

39. Kohn, *Eagle and Sword*, pp. 60–62 (the qu. is on p. 61).

40. *Ibid.*, pp. 73–88.

41. *Ibid.*, pp. 91–127, 139–157, 174–189.

42. Madison to Jefferson, June 1, 1794, *PJM*, XV, 340.

43. J. Q. Adams to John Adams, Aug. 3, 1797, *WJQA*, II, 155–157; Kohn, *Eagle and Sword*, pp. 222–224.

44. "An Act to augment the Army of the United States, and for other purposes," approved July 16, 1798; "An Act authorizing the President of the United States to raise a Provisional Army," approved May 28, 1798; *AC*, 5 Cong., Appendix, 3785–3787, 3729–3733.

45. Adams to Elbridge Gerry, May 3, 1797, APM, reel 117.

46. *ASP:MA*, I, 120–123.

47. *WJA*, IX, 194, 221. Italics added.

48. *PJnMl*, III, 470–471; Jefferson to Madison, June 21, 1798, *WTJ*, VII, 272.

49. "The Stand," No. VI, Apr. 19, 1798, *PAH*, XXI, 437–438; Gilbert E. Lycan, *Alexander Hamilton and American Foreign Policy: A Design for Greatness* (Norman, Okla., 1970), pp. 360–362; John Jay to William North, June 25, 1798, *CPJJ*, IV, 244–245.

50. DeConde, *Quasi-War*, pp. 103–106, 343, 411, n. 63, 412, n. 67; Kohn, *Eagle and Sword*, pp. 390–391n.; *AC*, 5 Cong., 2 Sess., 2114, 2120. Nevertheless, Abigail Adams insisted that "the people throughout the United States, with few exceptions, would have heartily joined in the most decided declaration which Congress could have made . . . but

the majority in Congress did not possess firmness and decision enough to boldly make it." To J. Q. Adams, July 20, 1798, APM, reel 390. This is undoubtedly an overstatement.

51. Ames to Pickering, July 10, 1798, Ames, *Ames,* I, 233–234.

52. Abigail Adams to J. Q. Adams, July 14, 1798, APM, reel 390; to Mary Cranch, July 9, 1798, *New Letters,* p. 201.

53. Gardner W. Allen, *Our Naval War with France* (Boston, 1909), pp. 64–65.

54. Kuehl, "Southern Reaction to the XYZ Affair," esp. 25–26; *AC,* 5 Cong., 2 Sess., 1529–1531, 1646–1648, 1691–1692 (Harper's speeches on the danger of a French invasion).

55. Kohn, *Eagle and Sword,* pp. 224–226; *AC,* 5 Cong., 2 Sess., 542–544, 546, 559–561, 1525–1545, 1561, 1594, 1631–1707, 1725–1772. The qu. from Gallatin and Thomas Sumter are in *ibid.,* 1743–1744, 1668.

56. *Ibid.,* 3729–3733.

57. *Ibid.,* 605, 609, 611, 613–614, 2084, 2088–2093, 2114, 2128–2132, 3785–3787; Kohn, *Eagle and Sword,* pp. 227–228.

58. "The Stand," all numbers of which were originally published in the *New York Commercial Advertiser,* are reprinted in *PAH,* XXI, 386, 390–396, 402–408, 412–432, 434–447. Jay to Hamilton, Apr. 19, 1798; Hamilton to Jay, Apr. 24, 1798; *ibid.,* 433, 447. Robert G. Harper had a scheme, to which he had apparently obtained the President's agreement in principle, whereby Hamilton would replace McHenry as Secretary of War, but nothing came of that either. Harper to Hamilton, Apr. 27, 1798, *ibid.,* 449.

59. Hamilton to Washington, May 19, 1798; Washington to Hamilton, May 27, 1798; *ibid.,* 494, 500–506.

60. Hamilton to Washington, June 2, 1798, *ibid.,* 479. Italics in original.

61. Hamilton to Pickering, June 7, 8, 1798; Pickering to Hamilton, June 9, 1798; *ibid.,* 494, 500–506.

62. Adams to Washington, June 22, 1798, *WJA,* VIII, 572–573; Carroll and Ashworth, *Washington,* VII, 517–519.

63. Pickering to Washington, July 6, 1798, Sparks, ed., *Washington's Writings,* XI, 530–531.

64. Washington to McHenry, July 4, 1798; to Adams, July 4, 1798; to Pickering, July 11, 1798; *WGW,* XXXVI, 304–315, 323–327.

65. Washington to McHenry, July 5, 1798, *ibid.,* 318; McHenry to Adams, July 12, 1798, Sparks, ed., *Washington's Writings,* XI, 533–534; Carroll and Ashworth, *Washington,* VII, 519–524; Steiner, *McHenry,* pp. 309–312.

66. Hamilton to Pickering, July 17, 1798; Pickering to Hamilton, July 18, 1798; Washington to Hamilton, July 14, 1798; *PAH,* XXII, 24–25, 17–21. Pickering later admitted to Hamilton that in order to avoid muddying the waters he had "concealed" the letter of July 17 in which Hamilton had said he would serve under Knox if necessary. Pickering to Hamilton, Aug. 21–22, 1798, *ibid.,* 148.

67. Hamilton to Washington, [July 29–Aug 1, 1798], *ibid.,* 36–40. Washington to Knox, July 16, 1798; Knox to Washington, July 29, 1798; *WGW,* XXXVI, 345–349. Pinckney to McHenry, Oct. 31, 1798, *PAH,* XXII, 202n.

68. Pickering to Washington, Sept. 13, 1798, Pickering Papers, IX, MHS; McHenry to Washington, Sept. 19, 1798, Sparks, ed., *Washington's Writings,* XI, 542–543.

69. Charles Francis Adams (the able editor of his grandfather's papers) gives the impression that had it not been for cabinet machinations to influence Washington, the latter would really have preferred Knox as second in command. But this appears to be largely wishful thinking. Washington's letter of Aug. 9 to Hamilton indicates that Washington might have been persuaded to have Knox ranked above Pinckney, but not above

Hamilton, and he had already told Hamilton on July 9 that he had ranked Knox "below you both." *PAH*, XXII, 62, 20; *WJA*, VIII, 590n. Another of Adams's afflictions was the Senate's rejection on July 19, principally through Pickering's influence, of his son-in-law, Col. William S. Smith, as adjutant-general, on the grounds of Smith's reputation for irresponsible business dealings. Adams did not discover Pickering's part in the affair until some time later, though exactly when is unknown. Details are in Kohn, *Eagle and Sword*, pp. 233–234, and *WJA*, VIII, 618–619n.

70. Washington to Knox, Aug. 9, 1798, *WGW*, XXXVI, 396–401.

71. McHenry to Adams, Aug. 4, 20, 1798, APM, reel 390 (also summarized at length in Sparks, ed., *Washington's Writings*, XI, 543–544); Adams to McHenry, Aug. 14, 29, 1798, *WJA*, VIII, 580, 587–589.

72. McHenry to Adams, Sept. 6, 1798, Sparks, ed., *Washington's Writings*, XI, 546; Adams to McHenry, Sept. 13, 1798, *WJA*, VIII, 593–594.

73. For these various threats of resignation or refusal of service (veiled or otherwise), see Hamilton to McHenry, Sept. 8, 1798, *PAH*, XXII, 177; Knox to Washington, July 29, 1798, *WGW*, XXXVI, 347–349; Knox to McHenry, Aug. 5, 1798, *PAH*, XXII, 69–71; Knox to Washington, Aug. 26, 1798, Sparks, ed., *Washington's Writings*, XI, 538–540; Washington to Adams, Sept. 25, 1798, and Washington to McHenry, Sept. 26, 1798 (in which he refers to the possible necessity "for me to proceed to the final step"), *WGW*, XXXVI, 453–463; McHenry to Adams, Sept. 6, 1798, Sparks, ed., *Washington's Writings*, XI, 546; *WJA*, VIII, 588.

74. Wolcott to Adams, Sept. 17, 1798, Gibbs, *Memoirs*, II, 93–99.

75. Adams to Wolcott, Sept. 24, 1798 (not sent), *WJA*, 601–604; to McHenry, Sept. 30, 1798, Steiner, *McHenry*, p. 341.

76. McHenry to Washington, Sept. 19, 1798, Sparks, ed., *Washington's Writings*, XI, 542–547; Washington to Adams, Sept. 25, 1798, *WGW*, XXXVI, 453–462.

77. Adams to Washington, Oct. 9, 1798, *WJA*, VIII, 600–601.

78. Adams to McHenry, Oct. 22, 1798, *ibid.*, 612–613.

79. June 21, 1798, *ibid.*, IX, 159.

80. Billias, *Gerry*, pp. 290, 294–295.

81. The first intimations that Gerry intended to remain came on June 1 with the arrival of dispatches from Rufus King enclosing a letter from Pinckney, a correct report of which found its way into the newspapers. King to Pickering, Apr., 16, 1798; Pinckney to King, Apr. 4, 1798; King, *King*, II, 317, 303–304 (the originals are endorsed as having been received June 1; Pickering Papers, XXII, MHS); *Philadelphia Aurora*, June 4, 5, 1798; Abigail Adams to William Smith, June 4, 1798, Smith-Carter Collection, MHS. The quotation from Bache is in *Aurora*, June 6, 1798. Other letters of Abigail Adams which refer to the President's and her sentiments on Gerry's behavior are to Mary Cranch, June 4, 13, 19, 25, 1798, *New Letters*, 186, 192, 194, 196; to William Smith, June 9, 1798, Smith-Carter Collection, MHS; to Eliza Peabody, June 22, 1798, Shaw Family Papers, LC.

82. Pickering to King, June 12, 1798, King, *King*, II, 347; Pickering to Commissioners, Mar. 3, 1798, *PJnMl*, III, 422–424 (also in *ASP:FR*, II, 200–201); Pickering to Gerry, June 25, 1798, *ASP:FR*, II, 204; Pickering to Benjamin Goodhue, Sept. 11, 1798, Pickering Papers, IX, MHS.

83. Murray to J. Q. Adams, Worthington C. Ford, ed., "Letters of William Vans Murray to John Quincy Adams, 1797–1803," *AHA:AR 1912*, 393; King to Pickering, June 14, 1798, King, *King*, II, 349; J. Q. Adams to Murray, Apr. 27, 1798, *WJQA*, II, 281–282.

84. Gerry to Pickering, Oct. 1, 1798; Talleyrand to Gerry, June 27, 1798; *ASP:FR*, II, 204–206, 215.

85. Gerry to Pickering, Oct. 1, 1798, *ibid.,* 206–208; see also accompanying correspondence, 208–227.

86. Murray to Adams, July 17, 1798, *WJA,* VIII, 680–684; Richard Codman to H. G. Otis, Aug. 26, 1798, Samuel E. Morison, *Life and Letters of Harrison Gray Otis, Federalist, 1765–1848* (Boston, 1913), I, 168–170.

87. This correspondence was not officially received in the United States until October, when Gerry transmitted it to Pickering together with his own report of Oct. 1, but Talleyrand had already sent copies to Létombe with instructions to have them published. Portions appeared in the *Aurora,* Aug. 31 and Sept. 1, 1798; more appeared Nov. 1, the date on which the paper resumed publication after having been suspended from Sept. 10 because of Bache's death, and more still on Nov. 3. The quotation from Murray's letter of July 17 is in *WJA,* VIII, 682; other private letters of same to same (July 22, Aug. 3), each featured by much skepticism, are in *ibid.,* 685–687. To Pickering, Murray wrote to much the same effect, Aug. 10, 1798, "Letters of Murray," 452.

88. Stinchcombe, *XYZ Affair* (Ch. 5, "A Member of the American Club"), esp. pp. 81–88.

89. Adams to Members of Cabinet, Oct. 10, 1798; to Pickering, Oct. 20, 1798; *WJA,* VIII, 602–604, 609–610.

90. Wolcott to Adams, Nov. 26, 1798, Gibbs, *Memoirs,* II, 168–171; McHenry to Adams, Nov. 25, 1798; Lee to Adams, Oct. 27, Nov. 1, 1798; Stoddert to Adams, Nov. 23, 25; Pickering to Adams, Nov. 5, 27, 1798; APM, reels 391, 392. Stoddert's letter of Nov. 23 is in Gibbs, *Memoirs,* II, 115–117.

91. Jefferson to Madison, Jan. 3, 1799, *WTJ,* VII, 313. It seems obvious, from evidence later exhibited in Adams's "Letters to the Boston *Patriot*" and C. F. Adams's accompanying notes, that Hamilton, who was in Philadelphia at the time, knew just about everything that went on in cabinet meetings. *WJA,* IX, 304–308 and nn. But whether the Secretaries needed any specific advice from him about what Adams should say in his message (comparable to what he had given McHenry on previous occasions), or whether he felt any special urgency about giving it here, seems doubtful. On this particular point we have found no evidence. Our inference that the cabinet members showed each other their replies to Adams's letter of Oct. 10 is drawn from Stoddert's note to Wolcott, Nov. 27, 1798, in Gibbs, *Memoirs,* II, 115, and on the coincidence between Pickering's and McHenry's ideas both on the Gerry question and on that of recommending a declaration of war.

92. Historians have generally assumed, following Charles Francis Adams (*WJA,* IX, 131n.), that Adams's message as finally delivered was primarily based on Wolcott's letter. Though we are reluctant to assert otherwise, the fact remains that the Pickering draft, which contains a number of alterations from that of Wolcott, was the one Adams actually used—except, of course, for Adams's much-discussed modification regarding assurances that a minister would be received. The draft, in Pickering's handwriting and with some very minimal editing by Adams, is in APM, reel 392.

93. *WJA,* IX, 128–134.

94. *Ibid.,* 305–309 and nn. The unlikelihood of the French government's being disposed to send a minister to negotiate at Philadelphia had been referred to in the Codman letter mentioned above. Despite efforts to persuade the French to do this, Codman wrote, "there seems to be a fear that from the present temper of the American Govt he would not be received, they are therefore not inclined to risque it." Morison, *Otis,* I, 169.

95. Gallatin to his wife, Dec. 14, 1798, Adams, *Gallatin,* p. 223; Pickering to Murray, Dec. 11, 1798, Pickering Papers, X, MHS; Pickering to Cabot, Feb. 4, 1799, Lodge, *Cabot,*

p. 216. See also Stephen Higginson to Pickering, Jan. 1, 1799 (the President had "committed himself too far"), Pickering Papers, XXIV, MHS; Higginson to Wolcott, Feb. 14, 1799, Gibbs, *Memoirs*, II, 179–180; Pickering to Cabot, Feb. 26, 1799, Lodge, *Cabot*, pp. 223–224. Jefferson conceded Adams's message to have been "so unlike himself in point of moderation," and even the *Aurora* offered congratulations on the "*brevity and comparative moderation* of the speech." Jefferson to Madison, Jan. 3, 1799, *WTJ*, VII, 313; *Philadelphia Aurora*, Dec. 10, 1798. "The Jacobins here," wrote William Shaw to his Aunt Abigail, "say that the speech—the answer of the Senate and house are the most moderate they ever remember to have heard—they don't say much against them. I can tell you the reason. Knowing the firm and intrepid policy which the president has always recommended and pursued and moreover convinced of what ought to be done, the jacobins here thought & I believe expected that a declaration of war between America and France would be recommended by the president and echoed back by the two houses—they are very agreeably disappointed and to be sure they have reason to be pleased—they can now still pursue their tampering and lullaby policy." William Shaw to Abigail Adams, Dec. 20, 1798, APM, reel 392.

96. This memorial, dated Aug. 21, 1798, had been addressed to the President. But unlike virtually all the other addresses this one was critical of Administration policy toward France, and Pickering undertook to reply to it himself in Adams's absence, on the ground that he could not forward anything "calculated to insult the chief magistrate of my country." In his reply (published on Sept. 29 and widely reprinted) he denounced both the French government and its American defenders, in the course of which he made some sarcastic references to its recent dealings with Gerry. Upham, *Pickering*, III, 471–478. The spokesman for the freeholders, understandably goaded, thereupon replied to the reply; *Aurora*, Nov. 22, 1798. For Gerry's part in the controversy see Gerry to Adams, Oct. 20, 1798; Adams to Pickering, Oct. 26, 1798; Pickering to Adams, Nov. 5, 1798; *WJA*, VIII, 610–612, 614, 616. The particular points at issue (such as whether the dinner at which Talleyrand's agents repeated their demands for money was a "private" or a "public" one) are too trifling to be recounted here. Suffice it to say that Pickering, for all his vindictiveness, appears at least to have got his facts straight, while Gerry, making mountains out of molehills as he frequently did, does not show up well in the squabble. (Though for a contrary view see Billias, *Gerry*, pp. 293–294.) Marshall, whose Paris journal had provided the basis for much of Pickering's information, was reluctant to be drawn into the dispute, and he eventually wrote to Gerry himself urging him to drop it. Pickering to Marshall, Nov. 5, 1798; Marshall to Pickering, Nov. 12, 1798; Marshall to Gerry, Nov. 12, 1798; *PJnMl*, III, 520–528.

97. Abigail Adams to John Adams, Jan. 25, 1799, APM, reel 393; Billias, *Gerry*, p. 295; William Shaw to Abigail Adams, Jan. 15, 1799, APM, reel 393; Gerry, Minutes of a Conference with the President, Mar. 26, 1799, Gerry Papers, LC; Adams to William Cunningham, Mar. 20, 1809, APM, reel 118 (partially quoted in Clarfield, *Pickering and American Diplomacy*, p. 198); Pickering to Adams, Jan. 18, 1799, *WJA*, VIII, 621–623. The Gerry-Talleyrand correspondence and Pickering's report, transmitted to Congress on Jan. 18 and 21 respectively and immediately published, are in *ASP:FR*, II, 204–238. The aggrieved Pickering immediately wrote to Washington, Marshall, Jay, Cabot, and Jedidiah Morse about the way Adams had altered his report (Upham, *Pickering*, III, 386–390, Pickering Papers, X, MHS; Lodge, *Cabot*, p. 215); see also Pickering, *A Review of the Correspondence between the Hon. John Adams . . . and the late William Cunningham, Esq., . . . Beginning in 1803, and Ending in 1812* (Salem, 1824), pp. 128–132, for the passages deleted.

98. E.g., *Philadelphia Aurora,* Nov. 7, 16, 22, 30, 1798, Jan. 9, Feb. 1, 1799; Nathaniel Cutting to Jefferson, Aug. 27, 1798 (received Nov. 22), Jefferson Papers, LC. The published letters are without signatures but are presented as being from "a respectable American in France, to his friend, a merchant in this city," or "an American gentleman in Paris to a merchant of Baltimore," and so on. They are dated Aug. 24, 26, 27, 30, Sept. 10, and Nov. 5, 1798. Judging from these dates (perhaps excepting the last one or two), there must have been quite a bustle among this group during the last week of August, probably inspired by the peace-seeking efforts being made at that time by Dr. Logan (see below).

99. Frederick B. Tolles, *George Logan of Philadelphia* (New York, 1953), pp. 153–204.

100. Samuel F. Bemis, *John Quincy Adams and the Foundations of American Foreign Policy* (New York, 1949), pp. 99–101. William Shaw to Abigail Adams, Jan. 15, 1799; John Adams to Abigail Adams, Jan. 16, 1799; APM, reel 393.

101. Early rumors of Nelson's victory were dismissed by the *Aurora* as "apocryphal" (Nov. 16); an American brig arriving at Gloucester Nov. 21 brought confirmation of early reports; official news arrived at New York Nov. 30, and a full account was published in Philadelphia Dec. 3. *Aurora,* Nov. 30, Dec. 3, 1798. Adams to McHenry, Oct. 22, 1798, *WJA,* VIII, 613; William Shaw to Abigail Adams, Nov. 25, 1798, APM, reel 392.

102. Richard R. Beeman, *The Old Dominion and the New Nation, 1788–1801* (Lexington, Ky., 1972), pp. 188–194; Malone, *Jefferson,* III, 399–407; *PAH,* XXII, 454n.

103. Some of these petitions were printed in *Philadelphia Aurora,* Jan. 22, 30, Feb. 12, 1799; see also *AC,* 5 Cong., 2 Sess., 2807, 2817, 2906, 2934, 2955, 2959, 2985.

104. McHenry's Report on Reorganization of the Army, Dec. 24, 1798, *ASP:MA,* I, 124.

105. *Ibid.,* 124–129. Washington to McHenry, three letters, all dated Dec. 13, 1798, *PAH,* XXII, 351–366; Kohn, *Eagle and Sword,* p. 245.

106. Hamilton to Gunn, Dec. 22, 1798; to Otis, Dec. 27, 1798, Jan. 26, 1799; to Sedgwick, Feb. 2, 1799; *PAH,* XXII, 388–390, 393–394, 440–441, 452–453.

107. *Ibid.,* 440–441, 453.

108. The expression quoted is from a letter written many years later in Adams's old age to Harrison Gray Otis, May 9, 1823, APM, reel 124. He refers to a letter of Hamilton's "to a member of the house containing a dissertation [with] a complete system of administration foreign & domestic." The reference is tantalizing, since the old man is either hazy about some of his facts or else has telescoped two or more of Hamilton's letters into one, or both (his description does not quite fit any one letter of Hamilton's that has survived); yet he obviously remembers something. S. E. Morison's mention of it in *Otis,* I, 162, is sufficiently oblique that historians continue to be misled as to when the scene actually occurred.

109. Sedgwick to Hamilton, Feb. 7, 1799, *PAH,* XXII, 469–471.

110. Gerry, Minutes of a Conference with the President, Mar. 26, 1799, Gerry Papers, LC. Adams continued to believe this to the end of his life. He wrote three other letters to Otis to the same effect besides the one cited in n. 108 above: Mar. 16, 29, Apr. 4, 1823, APM, reel 124.

111. Murray to Adams, Oct. 7, 1798, enclosing Talleyrand to Pichon, Sept. 28, 1798, *WJA,* VIII, 688–691; translation of Talleyrand's letter in *ASP:FR,* II, 239–240. The exact date received is unknown; C. F. Adams, *WJA,* VIII, 688n., says "it must have been received by the early part of February"; DeConde, *Quasi-War,* p. 174, says "apparently on February 1"; Bowman, *Struggle for Neutrality,* p. 366, thinks it "probable" that it arrived "between

February 15 and 18." The paper was in any case transmitted with Adams's message of Feb. 18, 1799.

112. *ASP:FR*, II, 238–239.

113. Barlow to Washington, Oct. 2, 1798, Sparks, ed., *Washington's Writings*, XI, 561; Washington to Adams, Feb. 1, 1799, *WGW*, XXXVII, 120.

114. Adams to Washington, Feb. 19, 1799, *WJA*, VIII, 624–626.

115. *ASP:FR*, II, 239.

116. Pickering to King, Feb. 19, 1799, Pickering Papers, X, MHS; Pickering to Washington, Feb. 21, 1799, Washington Papers, LC; Liston to Grenville, Feb. 22, 1799, *PAH*, XXII, 494–495; Abigail Adams to John Adams, Mar. 3, 1799, APM, reel 393; Cabot to King, Mar. 10, 1799, King, *King*, II, 551 (similar sentiments by Cabot to Pickering, Mar. 7, 1799, Lodge, *Cabot*, p. 224); Sedgwick to Hamilton, Feb. 22, 1799, *PAH*, XXII, 494; Gibbs, *Memoirs*, II, 203. On Adams's private torments in these and similar circumstances see Shaw, *Character of John Adams*, esp. Ch. 10.

117. Sedgwick to Hamilton, Feb. 25, 1799, *PAH*, XXII, 503; Sedgwick to John Rutherfurd, Mar. 1, 1799, Welch, *Sedgwick*, pp. 188–189n.; Upham, *Pickering*, III, 439–443; *ASP:FR*, II, 240; DeConde, *Quasi-War*, pp. 184–185, 432, n. 11.

118. *ASP:FR*, II, 240.

119. *Ibid.*, 244; Patrick Henry to Pickering, Apr. 16, 1799, *ibid.*, 241; DeConde, *Quasi-War*, pp. 187, 432–433nn.

120. *Ibid.*, p. 186; Adams to Pickering, Jan. 15, 1799, *WJA*, VIII, 621; *ibid.*, IX, 251n.; Gibbs, *Memoirs*, II, 248; Pickering to King, Mar. 12, 1799, King, *King*, II, 558.

121. Kohn, *Eagle and Sword*, pp. 246–249; Washington to McHenry, Mar. 25, 1799, *WGW*, XXXVII, 159.

122. Bradford Perkins, *The First Rapprochement: England and the United States, 1795–1805* (Philadelphia, 1955), pp. 95–98; Maitland to Henry Dundas, Apr. 20, 1799, qu. in *ibid.*, p. 109; Hamilton to H. G. Otis, Jan. 26, 1799, *PAH*, XXII, 440–441.

123. Clarfield, *Pickering and the American Republic*, pp. 195–196; King to Pickering, Oct. 11, 1799, King, *King*, III, 123–124.

124. Murray to Pickering, Apr. 23, 1799, "Letters of Murray," *AHA:AR 1912*, p. 543; Pickering to Murray, July 10, 1799, *ibid.*, 574.

125. H. C. Lodge, "Timothy Pickering," *Atlantic Monthly*, XLI (June 1878), 751. The Peale portrait, better known, is reproduced in many places, among them Alexander DeConde's *Quasi-War;* the Stuart appears in Gerard Clarfield's *Timothy Pickering and American Diplomacy*, as well as in the same author's full biography, *Timothy Pickering and the American Republic.*

126. The best and most convenient works on Pickering are the two volumes by Clarfield cited above, and we have drawn heavily on the second of these for the profile offered here. Others are the 4-volume *Life of Timothy Pickering* by his son, Octavius Pickering, and Charles W. Upham (Boston, 1867–73), which is long on documentary materials but very short on Pickering's own life and personality (one would hardly guess from it that there was any real friction between him and Adams); the article in *DAB* by William A. Robinson; and an unpublished doctoral dissertation, Edward H. Phillips, "The Public Career of Timothy Pickering, Federalist, 1745–1802" (Harvard, 1950). The great mass of Pickering papers is at the Massachusetts Historical Society, to which the Society published an excellent 580-page calendar index, *Collections of the Massachusetts Historical Society*, 6th ser., VIII (Boston, 1896). There is also a microfilm edition of these papers, arranged in the same order as the originals are filed at MHS. The qu. about Pickering's father and the clergyman is in T. Pickering to James McHenry, Jan. 5, 1811, Steiner, *McHenry*, p. 561.

127. Clarfield, *Pickering and the American Republic,* pp. 16–74, *passim.* The following three paragraphs are based on *ibid.,* pp. 85–164.

128. *Ibid.,* p. 154; Hammond to Grenville, Jan. 5, 1795, Bernard Mayo, ed., "Instructions to British Ministers," *AHA:AR 1936,* III, 83n.

129. E.g., Hamilton to Washington, Mar. 5, 1796, asserting that "Mr. Pickering, who is a very worthy man, has nevertheless something warm and angular in his temper & will require . . . a vigilant moderating eye," and adding in a subsequent letter, "These opinions are not confined to me." Same to same, Nov. 11, 1796, *PAH,* XX, 374, 390.

130. On the young Garrison's devotion to Pickering and his principles see John L. Thomas, *The Liberator: William Lloyd Garrison, A Biography* (Boston, 1963), pp. 30, 32–34, 40, 42.

131. There is no published biography of Oliver Wolcott, though his public life, especially his service to the federal government, is reasonably well documented. Available materials include Gibbs's *Memoirs* (1846), repeatedly cited here, an immensely useful compilation with intelligent (if understandably biased) commentary by Wolcott's grandson; and three unpublished dissertations: Frederick H. Schmauch, "Oliver Wolcott: His Political Role and Thought Between 1789 and 1800" (St. John's, 1969); James Bland, "The Oliver Wolcotts of Connecticut: The National Experience, 1775–1800" (Harvard, 1970); and William C. Dennis, "A Federalist Persuasion: The American Ideal of the Connecticut Federalists" (Yale, 1971), containing two chapters on Wolcott.

132. Samuel Wolcott, *Memorial of Henry Wolcott and Some of His Descendants* (New York, 1881), p. 228; Schmauch, "Wolcott," pp. 6–8.

133. *Ibid.,* pp. 10–17, *et seq.*

134. "In short, what with the non-acceptance of some, the known deriliction of those who are most fit; the exceptionable draw backs from others; and a wish (if it were practicable) to make a geographic distribution of the *great* offices of the Administration, I find the selection of proper characters an arduous duty." Washington to Hamilton, Oct. 29, 1795, *PAH,* XIX, 358. Earlier that year William Vans Murray (then a member of the House of Representatives) was writing that "we certainly are retrograding as to characters." To James McHenry, Jan. 1, 1795, Steiner, *McHenry,* p. 158. "The offices are once more filled," John Adams wrote to Abigail, Feb. 6, 1796, "but how differently than when Jefferson, Hamilton, Jay, etc., were here!" C. F. Adams, ed., *Letters of John Adams, Addressed to His Wife* (Boston, 1848), p. 195.

135. To O. Wolcott, Sr., Jan. 6, 1795, Gibbs, *Memoirs,* I, 178.

136. Jacob E. Cooke, *Tench Coxe and the Early Republic* (Chapel Hill, N.C., 1978), pp. 300–307.

137. Bernard C. Steiner's *Life and Correspondence of James McHenry* (1907) is the only biography available. It has many virtues, though a modern scholarly treatment, with an effort to supply some interpretive dimension, would be welcome. McHenry's performance as Secretary of War is discussed with understanding in M. Howard Mattsson-Boze, "James McHenry, Secretary of War, 1796–1800" (Unpub. diss., U. of Minn., 1965); and in the pertinent sections of Richard H. Kohn's *Eagle and Sword,* esp. Ch. 12.

138. "Dull is Plato, dry his morals,/ To the forest's floating carols," Steiner, *McHenry,* p. 3.

139. *Ibid.,* pp. 1–18.

140. Frederick J. Brown, *A Sketch of the Life of Dr. James McHenry* (Baltimore, 1877), p. 12.

141. McHenry to Hamilton, Aug. 11, 1782, *PAH,* III, 129.

142. Steiner, *McHenry,* pp. 41–60.

143. Hamilton to Washington, Nov. 5, 1795, *PAH,* XIX, 397; Washington to

McHenry, Jan. 20, 1796, *WGW*, XXXIV, 423–424; McHenry to Washington, Jan. 21, 24, 1796, Steiner, *McHenry*, pp. 163–164.

144. Hamilton to Washington, July 29, 1798; Washington to Hamilton, Aug. 9, 1798; *PAH*, XXII, 35, 62–63. Kohn, *Eagle and Sword*, pp. 395, n. 12, 248.

145. Wolcott to McHenry, Apr. 9, 1804 ("my friends, among whom, I rank you in the first class"), Steiner, *McHenry*, p. 529; T. Pickering to Rebecca Pickering, Dec. 19, 1815, Upham, *Pickering*, IV, 269–270; Lafayette to McHenry, Dec. 22, Steiner, *McHenry*, pp. 573, 615.

146. Pickering to McHenry, Feb. 3, 1811, *ibid.*, p. 568.

147. Wolcott to Ames, Dec. 29, 1799, Gibbs, *Memoirs*, II, 315.

148. What is known of Charles Lee goes little beyond the sketches in Richard A. Harrison, ed., *Princetonians, 1769–1775: A Biographical Dictionary* (Princeton, N.J., 1980), pp. 493–499 by Wesley F. Craven, and in *DAB* by Maude H. Woodfin. Anything else has to be gleaned from writings about the Lee family, which are fairly numerous, the most recent being Paul C. Nagel, *The Lees of Virginia: Seven Generations of an American Family* (New York, 1990). The quotation is from Charles Royster, *Light-Horse Harry Lee and the Legacy of the American Revolution* (New York, 1981), p. 118.

149. Woodfin, "Charles Lee," 101; Washington to Lee, Nov. 19, 1795, *WGW*, XXXIV, 365–366.

150. Norman K. Risjord, *Chesapeake Politics, 1781–1800* (New York, 1978), pp. 432, 457–458; R. H. Lee to Richard Bland Lee, Feb. 4, 1794, James C. Ballagh, ed., *The Letters of Richard Henry Lee* (New York, 1914), II, 564; Carroll and Ashworth, *Washington*, VII, 393–394.

151. Wolcott to Ames, Dec. 29, 1799, Gibbs, *Memoirs*, II, 315; Carroll and Ashworth, *Washington*, VII, 354.

152. Lee to Adams, Mar. 14, 1799, *WJA*, VIII, 628.

153. Wolcott to Ames, Dec. 29, 1799, Gibbs, *Memoirs*, II, 315.

154. Harriot S. Turner, "Memoirs of Benjamin Stoddert, First Secretary of the United States Navy," *Columbia Historical Society Records*, XX (1917), 141–166; Stoddert to John Templeman [c. 1804], Wilhelmus B. Bryan, *A History of the National Capital* (New York, 1914), I, 98.

155. Stoddert to Francis Lowndes, May 26, 1798, Turner, "Memoirs," 152.

156. Talleyrand to Murray, May 12, 1799, *ASP:FR*, II, 243–244; Pickering to Adams, July 31, 1799; Adams to Pickering, Aug. 6, 1799, *WJA*, IX, 10–12.

157. C. F. Adams, *ibid.*, IX, 12n.; Adams to William Cunningham, Nov. 7, 1808, E. M. Cunningham, ed., *Correspondence Between the Hon. John Adams . . . and the Late Wm. Cunningham, Esq., Beginning in 1803, and Ending in 1812* (Boston, 1823), p. 46; Jacob E. Cooke, "Country Above Party: John Adams and the 1799 Mission to France," Edmund P. Willis, ed., *Fame and the Founding Fathers* (Bethlehem, Pa., 1967), pp. 66–67.

158. Higginson to Pickering, Aug. 7, 1799, "Letters of Stephen Higginson," *AHA:AR, 1896*, I, 822. See also memorandum of George Cabot, Sept. 22, 1799, Lodge, *Cabot*, pp. 238–240.

159. Peter P. Hill, *William Vans Murray, Federalist Diplomat: The Shaping of Peace with France, 1797–1801* (Syracuse, N.Y., 1971), p. 155; Gibbs, *Memoirs*, II, 264–265. News of the Directorial upheaval appeared in the *Gazette of the United States* on Aug. 26, and in the *Philadelphia Aurora* Aug. 27, 1799.

160. Pickering to Adams, Sept. 11, 1799, *WJA*, IX, 23–25.

161. Ellsworth's views on the mission, and the manner in which he communicated them to the various persons named, may be traced in the following correspondence: Pickering to Cabot, Feb. 26, Sept. 13, 29, 1799, Lodge, *Cabot*, pp. 224, 235–237, 243;

Cabot to Pickering, Sept. 23, Oct. 16, 1799, *ibid.,* pp. 242, 247; Ellsworth to Pickering, Sept. 19, 20, 26, Oct. 1, 5, 1799, Pickering Papers, XXV, MHS; Ellsworth to Wolcott, Sept. 20, Oct. 1, 1799, Gibbs, *Memoirs,* II, 265–267; Ellsworth to Adams, Sept. 18, 1799, and Adams to Ellsworth, Sept. 22, 1799, *WJA,* IX, 31, 34–35.

162. Higginson to Pickering, Aug. 22, 1799, "Letters of Higginson," pp. 823–824.

163. Troup to King, Apr. 19, 1799, King, *King,* II, 597. Uriah Forrest to Adams, Apr. 28, 1799; Adams to Forrest, May 13, 1799; *WJA,* VIII, 637–638, 645–646. C. F. Adams in *ibid.,* I, 551, VIII, 638n.

164. Lee to Adams, Oct. 6, 1799; Stoddert to Adams, Aug. 29, 1799; Adams to Stoddert, Sept. 4, 1799; *ibid.,* IX, 38, 18–19.

165. *Ibid.,* IX, 25–29, 33–34.

166. *Ibid.,* IX, 30; Higginson to Wolcott, Sept. 16, 1799, Gibbs, *Memoirs,* II, 262–263. See also Higginson to Pickering, Sept. 20, Oct. 3, 1799, "Letters of Higginson," pp. 827–828.

167. Cooke, "Country Above Party," pp. 68–69.

168. The three versions are (1) a paper intended by Adams as a reply to Hamilton's *Letter . . . Concerning the Public Conduct and Character of John Adams* (Oct. 24, 1800) and quoted by C. F. Adams in *WJA,* IX, 255–256n.; (2) Letter VI of "Letters to the Boston *Patriot*," published in 1809 and reprinted in *ibid.,* IX, 253–255; and (3) Adams to William Cunningham, Jr., Nov. 7, 1808, Cunningham, *Correspondence,* pp. 47–48. On cabinet reactions to the *Patriot* letters see McHenry to Pickering, Feb. 23, 1811, Lodge, *Cabot,* p. 208; Stoddert to Adams, Oct. 12, 1809, *ibid.,* pp. 200–203; Stoddert to McHenry, Apr. 14, 1810, Steiner, *McHenry,* p. 557. That Adams in their meetings never asked their opinions on suspending the mission was amply confirmed at the time, long before the *Patriot* letters made an issue of it. E.g., Wolcott to Hamilton, Oct. 2, 1800, *PAH,* XXV, 141; Wolcott, "Notes on the negotiation with France, written January, 1800"; Pickering to Washington, Oct. 24, 1799; Gibbs, *Memoirs,* II, 279–280.

169. The quotation is from Adams to William Cunningham, Jr., Nov. 7, 1808, Cunningham, *Correspondence,* p. 48; a similar version is Letter VI of the *Patriot* series, *WJA,* IX, 254–255; Abigail Adams mentions the interview in A. Adams to Mary Cranch, Dec. 30, 1799, *New Letters,* p. 224; and Hamilton himself refers to it in *Letter on John Adams, PAH,* XXV, 219. The evidence for Hamilton's having gone to Trenton solely on army business, and with no knowledge of the President's intentions, is fairly persuasive: *Letter on John Adams, ibid.,* 221; McHenry to Pickering, Feb. 3, 1811, Lodge, *Cabot,* pp. 209–210; Cooke, "Country Above Party," pp. 69–70n.

170. Stoddert to Adams, Oct 12, 1809, Lodge, *Cabot,* p. 203.

171. Cf. Gibbs: "Again had HAMILTON risen up like a spectre in his path. To meet *him,* the intriguer, there . . . had roused the lurking demon of suspicion in his breast, and from that moment he was ungovernable." *Memoirs,* II, 276.

CHAPTER XIV

The Settlement

1. Dudley W. Knox, *A History of the United States Navy* (New York, 1936), p. 6; Eugene S. Ferguson, *Truxtun of the Constellation* (Baltimore, 1956), p. 102.

2. Passage of the legislation of 1794 and its subsequent modification are described at length in Marshall Smelser, *The Congress Founds the Navy, 1787–1798* (Notre Dame, Ind., 1959), pp. 48–86; and more briefly in Craig L. Symonds, *Navalists and Antinavalists:*

The Naval Policy Debate in the United States, 1789–1827 (Newark, Del., 1980). On Humphreys, see Howard I. Chapelle, *The History of the American Sailing Navy: The Ships and Their Development* (New York, 1949), pp. 119–127 and *passim;* Michael A. Palmer, *Stoddert's War: Naval Operations During the Quasi-War with France, 1798–1801* (Columbia, S.C., 1989), pp. 27–28; Humphreys to Knox, Dec. 23, 1794, *ASP:NA,* I, 8. The currently prevailing view on Humphreys appears to be that his influence was more important in the realm of naval thought than in that of design; aspersions on Humphreys's draftsmanship and doubts about which ships' plans should or should not be attributed to him, broached by Chapelle and picked up by subsequent authors, have succeeded to some degree in lowering Humphreys's historical reputation. Whatever the merits of this revisionism, we assume here what nobody has denied, that as a force for creative ingenuity at a critical point in the progress of naval shipbuilding, Humphreys's influence was salutary.

3. A chronological listing of these acts is in Robert G. Albion, "The First Days of the Navy Department," *Military Affairs,* XII (Spring 1948), 6; texts of them are in Dudley W. Knox, ed., *Naval Documents Related to the Quasi-War Between the United States and France* (Washington, 1935), I, 58, 64, 87–88, 127, 135–137, 181–183, 188–189, 211; and their passage is described in Smelser, *Congress Founds the Navy, passim.* In Gardner W. Allen, *Our Naval War with France* (Boston, 1909), Appendixes IV–V, pp. 301–305, there are lists of all vessels in naval service between 1798–1801 (totaling fifty-four) with their ratings and commanders, and of all officers of the first three grades appointed in that same period. Additional information about each of these ships may be found in Chapelle, *History of the Sailing Navy.*

4. Albion, "First Days," 6–9; Palmer, *Stoddert's War,* pp. 14–17. Charles O. Paullin, "Early Naval Administration Under the Constitution," *United States Naval Institute Proceedings,* XXXIII (1906), 1008, has a table of the first constructors and agents and the ports of their employment. On Stoddert's plans for the future see Stoddert to Josiah Parker, Dec. 29, 1798, *ASP:NA,* I, 65–66; and Robert F. Jones, "The Naval Thought and Policy of Benjamin Stoddert, First Secretary of the Navy, 1798–1801," *American Neptune,* XXIV (Jan. 1964), 61–69.

5. Alexander DeConde, *The Quasi-War: The Politics and Diplomacy of the Undeclared War with France, 1797–1801* (New York, 1966), pp. 124–125; Robert G. Albion and Jennie M. Pope, *Sea Lanes in Wartime: The American Experience, 1775–1942* (New York, 1942), pp. 70, 83; Palmer, *Stoddert's War,* p. 6.

6. *AC,* 5 Cong., 2 Sess., 1531; Henry Knox to Adams, June 26, 1798, D. W. Knox, ed., *Naval Documents,* I, 140.

7. Thomas O. Ott, *The Haitian Revolution, 1789–1804* (Knoxville, Tenn., 1973), p. 103.

8. Palmer, *Stoddert's War,* pp. 18–19, 30–31, 35–36, 56; Albion, "First Days," 10; Stoddert to Barry, July 11, 1798, and to Adams, July 30, 1798, *Naval Documents,* I, 189–191, 256.

9. *WJM,* III, 53.

10. Albert H. Bowman, *The Struggle for Neutrality: Franco-American Diplomacy During the Federalist Era* (Knoxville, Tenn., 1974), pp. 234, 255; Monroe to Madison, Feb. 25, 1796, *WJM,* II, 460–461; *ASP:FR,* II, 12–13.

11. Carl L. Lokke, ed., "Mémoire sur les Etats-Unis d'Amérique," *AHA:AR, 1936,* I, 85–119; Bowman, *Struggle for Neutrality,* pp. 234–235, 238. Fauchet's mémoire was itself in no small part an extended lament over how little interest officials of the French government had shown in American affairs, their failure to take seriously—or even to read—the voluminous reports sent to them from America by France's agents there, and how he

and his predecessors had had to go for months (in his own case a whole year) "without receiving anything that could be called a dispatch" from Paris. On cues from Monroe and others as to how the French ought to respond to the treaty, and Monroe's counsel to be patient and await the election of a Republican President, see Ch. XI, above.

12. Bowman, *Struggle for Neutrality,* pp. 243–244.

13. Monroe to Pickering, Aug. 15, 1796; Delacroix to Monroe, Oct. 7, 1796; *ASP:FR,* I, 741, 745.

14. Sonthonax to Minister of Marine, Feb. 24, 1797, Archives de la Marine, Sous-section Colonies, Archives Nationales, Paris.

15. Samuel E. Morison, ed., "DuPont, Talleyrand, and the French Spoliations," *MHS Proceedings,* XLIX (Oct. 1915–June 1916), 69.

16. Ulane Bonnel, *La France, les Etats-Unis, et la guerre de course (1797–1815)* (Paris, 1961), p. 96; Morison, ed., "DuPont," p. 68.

17. Ott, *Haitian Revolution,* p. 8; Rayford W. Logan, *The Diplomatic Relations of the United States with Haiti* (Chapel Hill, N.C., 1941), pp. 3 and n., 26–30; *ASP:CN,* I, 134.

18. Ott, *Haitian Revolution,* pp. 9–13. The succeeding three paragraphs draw heavily on this highly useful work.

19. The British campaign in the West Indies is fully treated in John W. Fortescue, *A History of the British Army* (London, 1899–1930), IV; and David P. Geggus, *Slavery, War, and Revolution: The British Occupation of Saint Domingue, 1793–1798* (Oxford, 1982).

20. Palmer specifically makes this point in an earlier version of *Stoddert's War,* "The Quasi-War and the Creation of the American Navy, 1798–1801" (Unpub. diss., Temple U., 1981), p. 63.

21. *ASP:FR,* I, 759. That there was a direct interest in the profits of the privateering traffic within the French government appears to have been a matter of common knowledge. For instance John Marshall noted in his journal (and in the dispatch of Nov. 8, 1797, which was subsequently made public) that according to Conrad Hottinguer, one of the "XYZ" agents currently soliciting a bribe from the American commissioners, not all of the Directors expected to share in the douceur since one of them, Merlin de Douai, "was paid from another quarter." Pinckney thereupon remarked that he understood Merlin's money came from "the owners of the Privateers," and Hottinguer "nodded an assent to that fact." It was Merlin who, as Minister of Justice, had obliged these men by thinking up the *rôle d'équipage* pretext and writing a "treatise" on that subject, for which they had rewarded him with a present of four thousand louis. Talleyrand himself profited from the same sources, according to estimates later made of the corrupt revenues received by him during the first three years of his ministry. Moreover, it appears that the Legislative Council of Five Hundred continued to stifle any effort to reform the prize law because, as William Vans Murray put it, the Council was itself "a nest of privateersmen." *PJnMl,* III, 172, 247, 262, 278; Louis Bastide, *Vie politique et religieuse de Talleyrand Périgord* (Paris, 1838), p. 227; Duc de Broglie, ed., *Memoirs of the Prince de Talleyrand,* tr. Raphael Ledos de Beaufort and Mrs. Angus Hall (Paris, 1895), I, xviii; Murray to J. Q. Adams, Dec. 10, 1799, Worthington C. Ford, ed., "Letters of William Vans Murray to John Quincy Adams, 1797–1803." *AHA:AR, 1912,* p. 630; Hill, *Murray,* pp. 164–165.

22. Stoddert to Barry, Dec. 7, 1798, *Naval Documents,* II, 70–72.

23. Palmer, *Stoddert's War,* pp. 84–87, 235–236.

24. Josiah Parker, chairman of the Naval Affairs Committee, made these claims in support of Stoddert's proposal for an expanded naval building program, and thus wanted to make the case as strong as he could. Albert Gallatin, who opposed such a program,

challenged Parker's figures and argued that the drop in maritime insurance rates, being worldwide and due to a variety of factors including changes in British and French naval policy, could hardly be ascribed simply to the existence of the United States Navy. As to particulars, Gallatin's assertions were not without substance. Nevertheless Parker's basic argument, that the navy had saved American merchants considerable sums in insurance costs, was a sound one, and if its scope is limited to the West Indies, where the navy's role in reducing premiums was obvious, the evidence is clear and convincing. In the summer of 1796 before the French began their attacks on American commerce, the normal rate for a West Indies voyage was 6 percent of the value of ship and cargo; by the end of the year it had doubled, and would rise to between 15 and 25 percent during 1797, reaching a peak of between 30 and 33 percent in the summer of 1798; whereas by 1800 the rate would fall to 10 percent. Thus if one estimated about $100 million in West Indies trade during 1799 and 1800 and calculated an average of 12 percent savings during this period, the total savings on insurance alone would come to some $12 million, almost twice the cost of the navy during the Quasi-War. Of equal significance to both merchants and producers was that American exports of wheat, flour, lumber, salt beef, and fish to the West Indies rose from $19.7 million in 1797 and $19.75 million in 1798 to $27.4 million in 1799 and $23.5 million in 1800. No matter how the calculation is made, there appears little question that the navy paid for itself several times over, nor was there any serious question of it at the time. *ASP:NA,* I, 69–70; *AC,* 5 Cong., 3 Sess., 2823–2827; Albion and Pope, *Sea Lanes in Wartime,* p. 83; Palmer, *Stoddert's War,* pp. 130–131; *ASP:CN,* I, 384, 417, 431, 453.

25. Ferguson, *Truxtun,* pp. 160–171; *Naval Documents,* II, 326–338.

26. Charles C. Tansill, *The United States and Santo Domingo, 1789–1873: A Chapter in Caribbean Diplomacy* (Baltimore, 1938), p. 33; Rufus King to Pickering, July 14, 1798, King, *King,* II, 368.

27. Tansill, *U.S. and Santo Domingo,* pp. 38–39.

28. Adams to Pickering, July 2, 1799, *WJA,* VIII, 661.

29. Tansill, *U.S. and Santo Domingo,* pp. 23–29; Logan, *U.S. and Haiti,* pp. 64–66.

30. King to Pickering, Dec. 7, 1798; to Dundas, Dec. 8, 1798; Dundas to King, Dec. 9, 1798; King to Pickering, Dec. 11, 1798; King, *King,* II, 475–477, 483–488.

31. Grenville to King, Jan. 9, 1799; King to Pickering, Jan. 10, 16, 1799; *ibid.,* II, 499–505, 511–512.

32. Bradford Perkins, *The First Rapprochement: England and the United States, 1795–1805* (Philadelphia, 1955), p. 108; Tansill, *U.S. and Santo Domingo,* p. 47.

33. *Ibid.,* p. 45; Logan, *U.S. and Haiti,* pp. 73–74; Toussaint to Adams, Nov. 6, 1798, J. Franklin Jameson, ed., "Letters of Toussaint Louverture and of Edward Stevens, 1796–1800," *AHR,* XVI (Oct. 1910), 65–66.

34. Stoddert to Barry, Jan. 16, 1799, *Naval Documents,* II, 242.

35. Logan, *U.S. and Haiti,* pp. 75, 179; Pickering to King, Mar. 12, 1799, King, *King,* II, 557–558; Robert G. Harper to constituents, Mar. 20, 1799, Noble Cunningham, ed., *Circular Letters of Congressmen to their Constituents, 1789–1829* (Chapel Hill, N.C., 1978), I, 171.

36. Tansill, *U.S. and Santo Domingo,* pp. 47–57; Maitland to Dundas, Apr. 20, 1799, qu. in *ibid.,* p. 56; Perkins, *First Rapprochement,* pp. 108–109.

37. Tansill, *U.S. and Santo Domingo,* pp. 58–64.

38. Palmer, *Stoddert's War,* pp. 162–164, 217.

39. *Ibid.,* pp. 196–201.

40. *Ibid.,* p. 235; see also above, n. 24.

41. *Ibid.,* pp. 34–35, 121.

42. Palmer, "Quasi-War," pp. 356–360; W. D. Puleston, *Annapolis: Gangway to the Quarterdeck* (New York, 1942), pp. 2–3, 19–22.

43. Logan, *U.S. and Haiti,* pp. 85–88; Tansill, *U.S. and Santo Domingo,* pp. 68–69; Adams to Pickering, Apr. 17, 1799, *Works,* VIII, 634–635.

44. Pickering to King, Feb. 19, 1799, Pickering Papers, MHS, X. "Among ourselves and on our West India prospects the consequences will be pernicious. By West India prospects I mean the opening of the commerce of St. Domingo and its independence of the French Republic, which Toussaint would in all probability have soon declared. He I believe only waited to know what was to be expected from the U.S."

45. Adams to Pickering, July 2, 1799, *WJA,* VIII, 661. It is quite possible that Pickering had this letter before him, having just received it, when he got off his blast of July 10 to Murray (referred to in Ch. XIII above).

46. Louis Pichon to Talleyrand, July 22, 1801, qu. in Tansill, *U.S. and Santo Domingo,* p. 81.

47. Ott, *Haitian Revolution,* pp. 171–172.

48. Pickering to Jefferson, Feb. 24, 1806, Jefferson Papers, LC.

49. Wolcott to Pickering, Dec. 28, 1800, Gibbs, *Memoirs,* II, 468; Jefferson to Madison, Dec. 19, 1800, *WTJ,* VII, 471.

50. Forrest McDonald, *Alexander Hamilton: A Biography* (New York, 1979), p. 347.

51. *Ibid.,* pp. 347–348; Jacob E. Cooke, "Country Above Party: John Adams and the 1799 Mission to France," Edmund Willis, ed., *Fame and the Founding Fathers* (Bethlehem, Pa., 1967), pp. 72ff.; Henry Adams, *History of the United States of America During the Administrations of Jefferson and Madison* (New York, 1889–91), I, 370.

52. Cooke, "Country Above Party," p. 75n. The mission, according to McDonald, "resulted in a brilliant diplomatic triumph for France." *Hamilton,* p. 347.

53. R. King to Pickering, June 6, 1798, King, *King,* II, 336; Bernard Faÿ, *The Revolutionary Spirit in France and America: A Study of Moral and Intellectual Relations Between France and the United States at the end of the Eighteenth Century,* tr. Ramon Guthrie (New York, 1955), pp. 426–427; Georges Lacour-Gayet, *Talleyrand: 1754–1838* (Paris, 1928–1934), I, 238–239; Raymond Guyot, *Le Directoire et la paix de l'Europe: des traités de Bâle à la deuxième coalition (1795–1799)* (Paris, 1911), pp. 563–564n.; Bonnel, *Guerre de course,* p. 61n. On May 31, 1798, the Prussian minister Sandoz-Rollin reported to his government: "Talleyrand spoke to me of the damaging particulars being spread about in the American newspapers regarding his ministry and published by order of Congress, and presented in such a way as to influence his ministerial fate. The distraught and disconcerted air with which he referred to this latter circumstance led me to guess that there was truth in the account; I told him the thirst for money will have dragged him through a great deal of dirt. . . . I believe him lost for the foreign ministry. Mr. Truguet has arrived from Spain with proofs of his venality in the treaty with Portugal." Paul Bailleu, ed., *Preussen und Frankreich von 1795 bis 1807: Diplomatische Correspondenzen* (Osnabrück, 1965), I, 210.

54. *ASP:FR,* II, 206, 210–211 (Gerry's account, and his correspondence with Talleyrand on the subject); Talleyrand, Report to Directory, May 31, 1798, AECPE-U 49, 393–404; *Talleyrand's Defence: Strictures on the American State Papers . . .* (London, 1798); the same material in a slightly different translation is reprinted in *ASP:FR,* II, 224–227. Bellamy's protest, dated June 25, was first published in *L'Ami des loix* in answer to the story

of the dispatches that appeared in that paper on 21 Prairial (June 9, 1798); his letter was translated and republished the following month in the London newspapers, then picked up by the *Philadelphia Gazette,* Sept. 20; the *Boston Columbian Centinel,* Sept. 22; *Porcupine's Gazette,* Oct. 10; and by various other American papers.

55. Guyot, *Le Directoire et la paix de l'Europe,* pp. 562–563.

56. *ASP:FR,* II, 209–219; Hill, *Murray,* pp. 103–115.

57. Morison, "DuPont," pp. 63–66.

58. *Ibid.,* pp. 66–78.

59. *Le Directoire et la paix de l'Europe,* pp. 564–565.

60. Georges Pallain, ed., *Le ministère de Talleyrand sous le Directoire* (Paris, 1891), p. 309.

61. E. Wilson Lyon, "The Directory and the United States," *AHR,* XLIII (Apr. 1938), 527; Talleyrand to Bruix, July 27, 1798; Bruix to Directory, July 11, 1798; to Talleyrand, July 31, Aug. 18, 1798, AECPE-U 50, 34, 132, 134, 178–179; *ASP:FR,* II, 222–223, 242; Hill, *Murray,* pp. 122–128; *WJA,* VIII, 688–691. Bruix, according to Sandoz-Rollin, seems to have acted as something of a go-between during this period. Bailleu, ed., *Preussen und Frankreich,* I, 213.

62. DeConde, *Quasi-War,* p. 148; the first reference Talleyrand makes to the Pichon-Murray talks is in that of Feb. 14, 1799, AECPE-U 51, 40–50.

63. Lacour-Gayet, *Talleyrand,* I, 343. A biographical sketch of Reinhard is in *Nouvelle Biographie générale, depuis les temps les plus reculés jusqu'à 1850–60* (Copenhagen, 1968), XLI, 928.

64. Oct. 1, 1799, AECPE-U 51, 240–241VO. Bowman (*Struggle for Neutrality,* p. 387n.) correctly points out that a second paper, mistakenly attributed to Reinhard by other authors because of its having been misfiled in the Archives as pp. 244–247 in Vol. 51, was actually not his at all but originated in an earlier ministry, prior even to Talleyrand's. Charles Delacroix, or someone in his bureau, seems to have toyed briefly with similar thoughts, though probably not very seriously. See above, p. 508.

65. These events are described in Alphonse Aulard, *The French Revolution: A Political History, 1789–1804,* tr. Bernard Miall (London, 1910), IV, 115–126; and Leo Gershoy, *The French Revolution and Napoleon* (New York, 1964), pp. 329–331, 340–341.

66. *Ibid.,* pp. 340–347; Aulard, *French Revolution,* IV, 127–151.

67. Bruix to Talleyrand, Aug. 18, 1798, AECPE-U 50, 178–179; Albert DuCasse, ed., *Histoire des négociations diplomatiques relatives aux traités de Mortfontaine, de Lunéville at d'Amiens* (Paris, 1855), I, 187; Talleyrand, Report to Directory, Feb. 14, 1799, AECPE-U 51, 40–50; Murray to J. Q. Adams, Dec. 10, 1799, "Letters of Murray," p. 630.

68. The principal source for Ellsworth's life and career, old but serviceable, is William G. Brown, *The Life of Oliver Ellsworth* (New York, 1905), upon which we have largely drawn for the following paragraphs.

69. *Ibid.,* p. 26n.; *Journal of William Maclay,* p. 133.

70. Brown, *Ellsworth,* pp. 76–77.

71. *Ibid.,* p. 100; italics in original.

72. Adams to James Lloyd, Jan. 1815, *WJA,* X, 112–113.

73. James Parton, *Life of Andrew Jackson* (New York, 1861), I, 72. The only full account of Davie's life is Blackwell P. Robinson, *William R. Davie* (Chapel Hill, N.C., 1957).

74. Charles Caldwell, *Memoirs of the Life and Campaigns of the Hon. Nathaniel Greene* (Philadelphia, 1819), p. 113.

75. Robinson, *Davie,* p. 186.

76. *Ibid.,* pp. 39, 117, 226, 230, 354.

77. *Ibid.,* p. 322.

78. What was left of Federalism in North Carolina had been for practical purposes snuffed out once and for all under the Jeffersonian tide of 1800. None of the state's four Federalist congressmen would be re-elected, and when Davie himself, the party's titular head, ventured to run for Congress in 1802 he was defeated by the crushing margin of two to one. He thereupon moved out of the state altogether and retired to his holdings in South Carolina. *Ibid.,* pp. 359–375.

79. William Vans Murray, who died prematurely at forty-three, has been handsomely served by Peter P. Hill's correspondingly brief but highly intelligent and stylish biography, *William Vans Murray,* cited above in n. 56. Largely superseded by Hill's work, but still useful, are two articles by Alexander DeConde, "The Role of William Vans Murray in the Peace Negotiations Between France and the United States, 1800," *Huntington Library Quarterly,* XV (Feb. 1952), 185–194; and "William Vans Murrary and the Diplomacy of Peace: 1797–1800," *Maryland Historical Magazine,* XLVIII (Mar. 1953), 1–26. Also of interest is the same author's "William Vans Murray's *Political Sketches:* A Defense of the American Experiment," *MVHR,* XLI (Mar. 1955), 623–640.

A show of irritation in one entry of Murray's private diary (qu. in Hill, *Murray,* p. 170) is the ground for an impression given in some accounts of an endemic state of friction within the American commission throughout the negotiations of 1800. In it, Murray says he did not believe his colleagues had "a good or respectful opinion of me," and indeed that "not *one* liked the *other!*" They were "but on terms of decent civility," and the other two were "too conceited, particularly Davie, to borrow any idea w[it]h complacency from me, the third named, & youngest of the mission." Still, it would be misleading, we think, to place too great an emphasis on this passage, written more than a year after the envoys' first meeting, or to read any of it into their working relations. There is no evidence in the day-to-day journal Murray kept during the proceedings to indicate any such "friction," and although their personal terms may well not have exceeded those of "decent civility," and although they did not always agree as to means, there is repeated evidence of a lively *esprit de corps* in their pursuit of the common end. At one point, for instance, Murray refers to Ellsworth's being "heart and soul occupy'd to make it succeed. So is D. So am I." Immediately after the mission concluded its work, Murray told J. Q. Adams, "My colleagues have acted from the first jump with the clearest and most pressing sincerity." And a few weeks later, with reference to Ellsworth, "I profoundly admired the neatness and accuracy of his mind," and regarding Davie: "General D is a firm, soldierly, and well-informed man." He added: "We certainly did all in our power, and with one spirit." "Letters of Murray," pp. 654, 658–659.

80. There is, of course, a vast literature on Napoleon Bonaparte. We have drawn our principal impressions from James M. Thompson, *Napoleon Bonaparte: His Rise and Fall* (New York, 1951); and Georges Lefebvre, *Napoleon: From 18 Brumaire to Tilsit, 1799–1807,* tr. Henry F. Stockhold (New York, 1969).

81. Thompson, *Bonaparte,* pp. 140–141.

82. Aulard, *French Revolution,* IV, 153.

83. Pertinent details of the envoys' voyage, the various delays that obstructed both their sea passage and their overland journey to Paris, and the courtesies extended to them when they arrived there, are all contained in the dispatches and other papers reprinted in *ASP:FR,* II, 307–310.

84. There is a perceptive discussion in Isser Woloch, *Jacobin Legacy: The Democratic*

Movement under the Directory (Princeton, N.J., 1970), pp. 272–277 *et seq.*, of the precarious state of the party idea with specific reference to the comparative experience of France and America in the late 1790s. To our knowledge no other writer has thought to make such a comparison, one which we have found greatly suggestive. Professor Woloch's account also includes an illuminating anecdote (pp. 276–277) that illustrates Bonaparte's attitude on this subject long before Brumaire had even been thought of.

85. The "splendid levée" is described by Murray to J. Q. Adams, Mar. 7, 1800 (evidently misdated: the levee was held on the 8th), "Letters of Murray," p. 644. Ellsworth's biographer cites a "tradition" that Bonaparte, on the occasion of his first meeting with the Chief Justice, had been so struck with his "grave, firm face" that he "said to some one, 'We must make a treaty with this man.'" But according to Davie's secretary, "Bonaparte, in addressing the American legation at his levees, seemed for the time to forget that Governor Davie was *second* in the commission, his attention being more particularly directed to him." And yet it is probable that Murray, the only one of the three who spoke any French, actually got more of Bonaparte's attention than did either of the other two. Murray's detailed description of the lavish two-day entertainment at Joseph Bonaparte's chateau that marked the final signing of the Convention, and of his extended conversations there with the First Consul (solicited by the latter), certainly gives that impression. Brown, *Ellsworth*, p. 284; Robinson, *Davie*, pp. 354–355. George F. Hoar, ed., "A Famous Fête," *Proceedings of the American Antiquarian Society*, XII (Apr. 1898), 240–259, is a full transcription of Murray's account of the doings at Môrtefontaine.

86. *Ibid.*, 253–254.

87. Emile Dard, *Napoleon et Talleyrand* (Paris, 1935), p. 37; Report to the Consuls of the Republic, Nov. 30, 1799, AECPE-U 51, 260–262vo.

88. A. Aulard, ed., *Paris sous le Consulat: recueil de documents pour l'histoire de l'esprit public à Paris* (Paris, 1903), I, 144, 149, 267; Henri Plon, ed., *Correspondance de Napoleon Ier, publiée par ordre de l'Empereur Napoléon III* (Paris, 1858–1870), VI, 118; Louis A.-P. Bourrienne, *The Life of Napoleon Bonaparte* (Philadelphia, 1832), pp. 199–200; H. Noel Williams, *The Women Bonapartes: The Mother and Three Sisters of Napoleon I* (New York, 1909), pp. 268–269; Faÿ, *Revolutionary Spirit,* pp. 431–436. The official newspaper, *Le Moniteur,* announced Washington's death, in two sentences and without comment, in its issue of Feb. 2, 1798, and on Feb. 4 reported the previous day's session of the Corps Legislatif, in which a kind of embarrassed indecision prevented that body from taking any kind of action in response to the news despite some urging by one of the deputies that it do so. But within a few days, as noted above, the climate had dramatically changed in consequence of the First Consul's orders of Feb. 7. *Le Moniteur* devoted a "Supplement" on Feb. 19 to the full text of Fontanes's oration, which was also circulated in pamphlet form. For a brief account of Fontanes's career, see M. Prevost et al., *Dictionnaire de biographie française* (Paris, 1979), IV, 325–327.

89. Hill, *Murray,* p. 174; E. Wilson Lyon, "The Franco-American Convention of 1800," *Journal of Modern History,* XII (Sept. 1940), 310–311; *ASP:FR,* II, 310.

90. DuCasse, ed., *Histoire des négotiations,* I, 224–225, 229–230, 233–243; *ASP:FR,* II, 314–317. The Americans' instructions are in *ibid.,* 301–306.

91. *Ibid.,* 314–315; DuCasse, *Histoire,* I, 186–213 (Talleyrand's instructions to the French negotiators), 230–231; "Some remarks on the status of our negotiations at Paris" (Murray's journal, kept throughout the proceedings), LC, entries of Apr. 9, 15, 16, 18, 1800.

92. *ASP:FR,* II, 319–326; DuCasse, *Histoire,* I, 247–256 (report from Pichon, May 5, 1800, on the state of the negotiations up to that date), 256–272; DeConde, *Quasi-War,*

pp. 229–237; Bowman, *Struggle for Neutrality,* pp. 394–400; Murray, "Some remarks," entries of May 15, 23, 25, 1800.

93. *ASP:FR,* II, 326–328; DuCasse, *Histoire,* I, 272–277; Bowman, *Struggle for Neutrality,* pp. 402–403; Hill, *Murray,* pp. 182–183.

94. *ASP:FR,* II, 328–330; DuCasse, *Histoire,* I, 277–286; Murray, "Some Remarks," entries of July 15, 20, 21, 22, 23, 1800.

95. *Ibid.,* July 25, 1800; Hill, *Murray,* pp. 183–185; Talleyrand to French commissioners, n.d. (but on or shortly after July 27, 1800), AECPE-U 52, 187.

96. References for the foregoing four paragraphs are *ASP:FR,* II, 330–339; DuCasse, *Histoire,* I, 291–308.

97. *ASP:FR,* II, 339; Murray, "Some remarks," entry of Sept. 20, 1800.

98. Ellsworth to Pickering (date unknown; original not in Pickering Papers), quoted in Pickering to Wolcott, Jan. 3, 1801, Gibbs, *Memoirs,* II, 463. As Murray later observed, "Indemnities it is true sleep. . . . That they ever should have been made a point so important in this negociation, was, because the wisdom of government commanded it, not because we considered them as of first-rate consequence." Murray to J. Q. Adams, Nov. 7, 1800, "Letters of Murray," p. 658.

99. *ASP:FR,* II, 339–343. The completed Convention is in *ibid.,* 295–301; also in various other works including James B. Scott, ed., *The Controversy over Neutral Rights Between the United States and France, 1797–1800: A Collection of American State Papers and Judicial Decisions* (New York, 1917), pp. 487–510; and DeConde, *Quasi-War,* pp. 351–372. See also Hill, *Murray,* pp. 192–197; Hoar, ed., "Famous Fête," 245–259. The reader wishing to consult more fully detailed descriptions of the proceedings which eventuated in the Convention's reaching its final form may find them in the works by Hill, DeConde, Bowman, and Lyon cited in the foregoing notes. In the interest of clarity many such details have been omitted from the present account.

100. Robinson, *Davie,* pp. 356–357; H. G. Otis to Hamilton, Dec. 17, 1800; James Gunn to Hamilton, Dec. 18, 1800, *PAH,* XXV, 260, 263; *AC,* 6 Cong., 2 Sess., 775–776.

101. Hamilton to Sedgwick, Dec. 22, 1800; Marshall to Hamilton, Jan. 1, 1801, *PAH,* 270, 291. King to Secretary of State, Oct. 31, Nov. 22, 1800, *ASP:FR,* II, 343–344. *AC,* 6 Cong., 2 Sess., 777–778.

102. Hill, *Murray,* pp. 210–212; *ASP:FR,* II, 344.

103. *Ibid.,* 345.

104. DeConde, *Quasi-War,* pp. 290, 292; A. Gallatin to his wife, Jan. 15, 29, 1801, Henry Adams, *The Life of Albert Gallatin* (Philadelphia, 1879), pp. 254–255, 258. "As to indemnification for spoliations," according to Hamilton, "that was rather to be wished than expected. . . . The people of this country will not endure that a definitive rupture with France shall be hazarded on this ground." Hamilton to Gouverneur Morris, Dec. 24, 1800, *PAH,* XXV, 272.

105. "The French treaty will be violently opposed by the Feds; the giving up the vessels is the article they cannot swallow." Jefferson to Madison, Dec. 26, 1800, *WTJ,* VII, 473–474. "We lose our honor by restoring the Ships we have taken. . . ." John Rutledge, Jr. to Hamilton, Jan. 10, 1801, *PAH,* XXV, 309. On the other hand, as William Vans Murray pointed out, "had we been at war they could have had no right to demand a restoration of the public ships, but as it was not war, and as we would not restore their former treaty of commerce and alliance, etc., etc., we had the less ground to resist a proposition for a *mutual* restoration of public ships." Murray to J. Q. Adams, Mar. 23, 1801, "Letters of Murray," p. 691.

106. Eli F. Heckscher, *The Continental System: An Economic Interpretation* (Oxford,

1922), p. 50. Bonnel, *Guerre de course,* pp. 141–144. Murray to Pickering, No. 111, Dec. 26, 1799; to Marshall, No. 121, Dec. 28, 1800; No. 126, Jan. 30, 1801, Netherlands Dispatches, I, National Archives. Hill, *Murray,* pp. 198–199, 213–214.

107. Arthur A. Richmond, "Napoleon and the Armed Neutrality of 1800: A Diplomatic Challenge to British Sea Power," *Journal of the Royal United Service Institution,* CIV (May 1959), 186–194.

108. The growing discomfiture of Virginia Republicans (including Jefferson) over their pro-French attachments, in the light of Bonaparte's accession to power, is described in Joseph I. Shulim, *The Old Dominion and Napoleon Bonaparte: A Study in American Opinion* (New York, 1952), Ch. 3.

109. First Inaugural Address, Mar. 4, 1801, James D. Richardson, ed., *A Compilation of the Messages and Papers of the Presidents, 1789–1897* (Washington, 1896–1899), I, 323.

CHAPTER XV
The Mentality of Federalism in 1800

1. For information on how this term came into existence and who used it, see Daniel Sisson, *The American Revolution of 1800* (New York, 1974).

2. Jefferson to Levi Lincoln, Oct. 25, 1802, *WTJ,* VIII, 175–176.

3. The line of thought here being referred to was set afoot most notably by Manning Dauer, *The Adams Federalists* (Baltimore, 1953), and Stephen G. Kurtz, *The Presidency of John Adams* (New York, 1957); with a number of others finding a similar approach highly congenial, among them Page Smith, *John Adams* (Garden City, 1962), 2v.; Clinton Rossiter, "The Legacy of John Adams," *Yale Review,* XLV (Summer 1957), 528–550; and Ralph A. Brown, *The Presidency of John Adams* (Lawrence, Kan., 1975).

4. A tempting analogy might be the resource for England that Churchill represented in 1940 (though not, say, in 1945).

5. *AC,* 5 Cong., 1 Sess., 429–430 (July 1, 1797).

6. Edward C. Carter II, "A 'Wild Irishman' Under Every Federalist's Bed: Naturalization in Philadelphia, 1789–1806," *PMHB,* XCIV (July 1970), 331–346; James M. Smith, *Freedom's Fetters: The Alien and Sedition Laws and American Civil Liberties* (Ithaca, N.Y., 1956), pp. 22–34. Another factor that seems to have contributed substantially to Jeffersonian majorities in 1800 was the considerable number of newspapers established by these onetime immigrants, especially the Irish. See Michael Durey, "Thomas Paine's Apostles: Radical Emigrés and the Triumph of Jeffersonian Republicanism," *WMQ,* 3rd Ser., XLIV (Oct. 1987), 661–688.

7. It is a pity there is no way of measuring the numbers of Irish votes that must have been lost by Otis's "Wild Irishmen" speech alone. For instance, the Republican *Boston Chronicle* declared that "the 'wild Irish' of that city would choose a new representative and never cast their votes for *'Young Harry'* again." Carter, "Wild Irishman," 334.

8. Quoted in Kenneth W. Keller, "Diversity and Democracy: Ethnic Politics in Southeastern Pennsylvania, 1788–1799" (Unpub. diss., Yale U., 1971), p. 47. This and the same author's "Rural Politics and the Collapse of Pennsylvania Federalism," *Transactions of the American Philosophical Society,* LXXII (1982), were indispensable in shaping the thoughts of the above paragraphs.

9. Keller, "Diversity and Democracy," p. 214; *idem,* "Rural Politics," p. 20.

10. Keller, "Diversity and Democracy," pp. 130–133, 177–178, 185.

11. *Ibid.,* pp. 16–18, 231–233, 235–237; Keller, "Rural Politics," pp. 12–13, 26–28.

12. Keller, "Diversity and Democracy," pp. 234–235; *AC*, 5 Cong., 3 Sess., 2992–2993. See also 2795, 2807, 2955, 2958–2959, 2985.

13. There is no complete modern scholarly study of the Fries Rebellion. Still serviceable, however, is William W. H. Davis, *The Fries Rebellion, 1798–99* (Doylestown, Pa., 1899), the research for which had been done some forty years previously while many of the participants were still living. The principal documentary sources for the rebellion and subsequent legal proceedings are Thomas Carpenter, comp., *The Two Trials of John Fries, on an Indictment for Treason; Together with a Brief Report of the Trials of Several Other Persons . . .* (Philadelphia, 1800); and Francis Wharton, *State Trials of the United States During the Administrations of Washington and Adams; with References, Historical and Professional, and Preliminary Notes on the Politics of the Times* (Philadelphia, 1849). Also useful is Russel B. Nye, *A Baker's Dozen: Thirteen Unusual Americans* (East Lansing, Mich., 1956), pp. 3–26. Peter Levine, "The Fries Rebellion: Social Violence and the Politics of the New Nation," *Pennsylvania History*, XL (July 1973), 241–258, examines the rebellion from the viewpoint of crowd-behavior theory. The rumor about Washington and his "20,000 men" is noted in Wharton, *State Trials*, p. 130.

14. Davis, *Fries Rebellion*, pp. 67–69; Wharton, *State Trials*, p. 551.

15. See above, n. 6 to Ch. XIII.

16. *PAH*, XXII, 552–553.

17. Davis, *Fries Rebellion*, pp. 62–86.

18. Quoted in *ibid.*, pp. 102, 111, 139.

19. Nye, *Baker's Dozen*, p. 18; Carpenter, *Two Trials*, pp. 209–213, 226; *Gazette of the United States*, Apr. 26, 1799; *Porcupine's Gazette*, Mar. 30, 1799.

20. And instead of twelve petit jurors from Northampton, only two from that place were selected. Davis, *Fries Rebellion*, pp. 118–119; Wharton, *State Trials*, pp. 487–490.

21. Wharton, *State Trials*, pp. 539–548, 565–577, 584–598; *Porcupine's Gazette*, May 10, 1799.

22. Adams, *Works*, IX, 178–179.

23. Nye, *Baker's Dozen*, p. 25.

24. John C. Miller, *Crisis in Freedom: The Alien and Sedition Acts* (Boston, 1951), p. 83; Smith, *Freedom's Fetters*, p. 431.

25. Mark DeWolfe Howe, review of *Freedom's Fetters*, *WMQ*, 3rd Ser., XIII (Oct. 1956), 573–576; Leonard W. Levy, *Legacy of Suppression: Freedom of Speech and Press in Early American History* (Cambridge, Mass., 1960), pp. 221–225. English practice was itself partially liberalized with Fox's Act (1792), which permitted the jury to decide facts and law in seditious libel cases. On Jefferson, see L. W. Levy, *Jefferson and Civil Liberties: The Darker Side* (Cambridge, Mass., 1963), pp. 46, 56–58.

26. *Ibid.*, pp. 57–61; Jefferson to Thomas McKean, Feb. 19, 1803, *WTJ*, VIII, 218.

27. E.g., the speeches of Nicholas and Gallatin against the resolution to prevent Matthew Lyon from resuming his seat after having been convicted of sedition, and that of Nicholas favoring repeal of the Sedition Law, *AC*, 5 Cong., 3 Sess., 2961–2966, 2969–2974, 3002–3014; Madison's "Report of 1800," *PJM*, XVII; and Tunis Wortman, *A Treatise Concerning Political Enquiry, and the Liberty of the Press* (New York, 1800).

28. Gordon S. Wood, "Interests and Disinterestedness in the Making of the Constitution," Richard Beeman et al., eds., *Beyond Confederation: Origins of the Constitution and American National Identity* (Chapel Hill, N.C., 1987), p. 73.

29. *Ibid.*, p. 81. Janet A. Riesman, "The Origins of American Political Economy, 1690–1781" (Unpub. diss., Brown U., 1983), pp. 302–377, contains a brilliant account of the new entrepreneurial climate created by the Revolution.

30. *Federalist,* Cooke ed., pp. 56–65.

31. Paul Bourke, "The Pluralist Reading of James Madison's Tenth *Federalist,*" *Perspectives in American History,* IX (1975), 271–295; and Robert J. Morgan, "Madison's Theory of Representation in the Tenth Federalist," *Journal of Politics,* XXXVII (Nov. 1974), 852–885; in addition to Wood, "Interests," cited above, strike us as conclusive on this point. Another suggestive statement as to the true status and function of such men is G. S. Wood, "The Democratization of Mind in the American Revolution," Library of Congress Symposia on the American Revolution, *Leadership in the American Revolution* (Washington, 1974), pp. 63–88.

32. Smith, *Freedom's Fetters,* pp. 277–287; Raymond Walters, Jr., *Alexander James Dallas: Lawyer—Politician—Financier, 1759–1817* (Philadelphia, 1943), pp. 78–79; Wharton, *State Trials,* pp. 345–391. The letter referred to is Adams to Tench Coxe, May 1792, Gibbs, *Memoirs,* II, 424–425. Duane's editorial concerning it appeared in the *Philadelphia Aurora* July 24, 1799, unambiguously titled "BRITISH INFLUENCE."

33. Smith, *Freedom's Fetters,* pp. 288–300; the proceedings against Duane are reported in *AC,* 6 Cong., 1 Sess., 68–96, 104–105, 111–124.

34. Smith, *Freedom's Fetters,* pp. 301–305.

35. *Ibid.,* pp. 390–392; Throop Wilder, "Jedidiah Peck: Statesman, Soldier, Preacher," *New York History,* XXII (July 1941), 290–300; Alfred F. Young, *The Democratic-Republicans of New York: The Origins, 1763–1797* (Chapel Hill, N.C., 1967), 508–517.

36. Smith, *Freedom's Fetters,* pp. 392–398; Jabez D. Hammond, *The History of Political Parties in the State of New York* (Syracuse, N.Y., 1852), I, 132.

37. Aleine Austin, *Matthew Lyon: "New Man" of the Democratic Revolution, 1749–1822* (University Park, Pa., 1981), pp. 7–11. This work, upon which we have drawn for the main outlines of the profile that follows, has among its merits that of having been consciously designed (*vide* the subtitle) to exhibit an archetype, newly fashioned as it were out of the hazards and opportunities of the Revolution, and constituting the direst threat to the central values of Federalism.

38. *Ibid.,* pp. 14–63; for a more detailed and comprehensive survey of early Vermont politics in its economic setting see Chilton Williamson, *Vermont in Quandary, 1763–1825* (Montpelier, Vt., 1949).

39. Austin, *Lyon,* pp. 15–19, 22, 23–24, 25, 57–59.

40. *Ibid.,* p. 26; Lyon to Armisted C. Mason, Jan. 16, 1817, qu. in J. Fairfax McLaughlin, *Matthew Lyon, the Hampden of Congress: A Biography* (New York, 1900), p. 500.

41. Austin, *Lyon,* pp. 42–43.

42. *Ibid.,* pp. 45–54. On Chipman, see Daniel Chipman, *The Life of Hon. Nathaniel Chipman, L.L.D., Formerly Member of the United States Senate, and Chief Justice of the State of Vermont, with Selections from his Miscellaneous Papers* (Boston, 1846). See also Gordon Wood, *The Radicalism of the American Revolution* (New York, 1991), pp. 242–243. The quotation is in McLaughlin, *Lyon,* pp. 500–501.

43. Austin, *Lyon,* p. 69.

44. *Ibid.,* pp. 76–85.

45. *Ibid.,* p. 86.

46. *Ibid.,* pp. 91–95; *AC,* 5 Cong., 1 Sess., 194, 234–235, 425–426. When Lyon intimated that the proposed twenty-dollar tax on naturalization certificates (the occasion for Otis's speech) "was introduced on the suggestion of a certain foreign minister," the Speaker ruled him out of order. *Ibid.,* 426.

47. The full record of the Lyon-Griswold affair, with the testimony of all parties relative to the effort to expel Lyon from the House, is in *AC*, 5 Cong., 2 Sess., 959–1058, 1063–1067.

48. Smith, *Freedom's Fetters*, pp. 221–246; Wharton, *State Trials*, pp. 333–344.

49. Austin, *Lyon*, pp. 119–127 (quotation on p. 120); McLaughlin, *Lyon*, pp. 375–382. It might be added that another such effort by Republican notables of Virginia (Jefferson, John Taylor of Caroline, Philip Norborne Nicholas, William Wirt, William B. Giles, and Governor James Monroe) was undertaken on behalf of the impecunious journalist James T. Callender, an even less savory character than Lyon, who was tried and convicted of seditious libel in 1800 and who, willing to defame anyone, would later turn upon Jefferson and do it to him. Malone, *Jefferson*, III, 466–472; IV, 207–220; Smith, *Freedom's Fetters*, pp. 345–346; and Michael Durey, *"With the Hammer of Truth": James Thomson Callender and America's Early National Heroes* (Charlottesville, Va., 1990), pp. 127–137, 156–163.

50. There is a good body of literature on the radical societies and the British government's dealings with them; e.g., Albert Goodwin, *The Friends of Liberty: The English Democratic Movement in the Age of the French Revolution* (Cambridge, Mass., 1979); Robert R. Dozier, *For King, Constitution, and Country: The English Loyalists and the French Revolution* (Lexington, Ky., 1983); and Ian R. Christie, *Stress and Stability in Late Eighteenth-Century Britain: Reflections on the British Avoidance of Revolution* (Oxford, 1984). See also Malcolm I. Thomis and Peter Holt, *Threats of Revolution in Britain, 1789–1848* (Hamden, Conn., 1977); and John Ehrman, *The Younger Pitt: The Reluctant Transition* (London, 1983). Evidence of how news of English actions against subversion was received in America may be found in Dauer, *Adams Federalists*, pp. 157–159; and two examples, one Federalist and one Republican, of how that subject made its way into congressional debates are Robert Goodloe Harper's speech of June 19, 1798 on the Alien Enemies Bill, and that of Albert Gallatin, May 16, 1798 on the Provisional Army Bill. *AC*, 5 Cong., 2 Sess., 1992, and 1744–1745.

51. Dozier, *King and Country*, p. 1. It appears that the tendency of English radicals to extenuate the slaughter of priests and aristocrats in Paris prisons in the late summer of 1792 gave a powerful push for a general inclination to close in on them. Goodwin, *Friends of Liberty*, pp. 230n., 241.

52. *Ibid.*, pp. 270–271.

53. *Ibid.*, pp. 271–273.

54. Dozier, *King and Country*, p. 63.

55. Ehrman, *Younger Pitt*, II, 225, 238, 390, 455–459; Goodwin, *Friends of Liberty*, pp. 266, 287–289, 387–388.

56. *Ibid.*, pp. 266–267; Christie, *Stress and Stability*, pp. 50–53.

57. That King took the idea of a movement in South America very seriously is evident in King to Pickering, Feb. 7, 26, Apr. 6, Aug. 17, and Oct. 20, 1798, King, *King*, II, 281, 283–284, 305–306, 393–394, 453–454. Hamilton's interest is expressed, though guardedly, in Hamilton to King, Aug. 22, 1798, *PAH*, XXII, 154–155. As for Louisiana and the Floridas, there is no doubt that Hamilton found the idea of an undertaking in that quarter very attractive: Hamilton to Otis, Jan. 26, 1799; to McHenry, June 27, 1799; *ibid.*, XXII, 441, XXIII, 227.

58. Hamilton to Miranda, Aug. 22, 1798, *ibid.*, XXII, 155–156, is quite equivocal. Adams, meanwhile, was fully aware of the South America idea but showed no interest in it. Miranda to Adams, Mar. 24, Aug. 17, 1798; Pickering to Adams, Aug. 21, 1798; Adams to Pickering, Oct. 3, 1798; *WJA*, VIII, 569–572, 581–582 and n., 600. The reference to the "Blount conspiracy" concerns the case of William Blount, formerly Governor of the South-

west Territory and then a senator from Tennessee, who in 1799 was discovered to have plotted a filibustering expedition into Spanish Louisiana with British support, and who was subsequently expelled from the Senate. Thomas P. Abernethy, *The South in the New Nation, 1789–1819* (Baton Rouge, La., 1961), pp. 169–216.

59. E.g., Henry Adams, *The Life of Albert Gallatin* (Philadelphia, 1879), pp. 199, 211; Dauer, *Adams Federalists,* p. 210; Kurtz, *Presidency of John Adams,* pp. 313–314; Smith, *Freedom's Fetters,* p. 20n.

60. Sedgwick to _____, Mar. 7, 1798, qu. in *ibid.,* p. 21; Harper to Hamilton, Apr. 27, 1798, *PAH,* XXI, 449; Lloyd to Washington, July 4, 1798, qu. in Dauer, *Adams Federalists,* p. 199; Tracy to Jeremiah Wadsworth, Jan. 29, 1799, qu. in Kohn, *Eagle and Sword,* p. 252; Hamilton to Sedgwick, Feb. 2, 1799, *PAH,* XXII, 453.

61. Federalist charges that Virginia was planning to oppose the Alien and Sedition Acts with force were based on the legislature's having voted measures for reorganizing the state militia and for building an armory in Richmond. Philip G. Davidson, "Virginia and the Alien and Sedition Laws," *AHR,* XXXVI (Jan. 1931), 336–342, concludes, however, that such charges were not warranted: that these measures, having antedated the Alien and Sedition Acts, had no connection with them. Richard R. Beeman, *The Old Dominion and the New Nation, 1788–1801* (Lexington, Ky., 1972), also takes this position (though cf. Kohn, *Eagle and Sword,* p. 399, n. 50); see also William Heth to Hamilton, Jan. 18, 1799, *PAH,* XXII, 423, and esp. 424, n. 6. Jefferson's opposition to any resort to force is amply documented in his correspondence: e.g., to Madison, Jan. 30, 1799; to Archibald Stuart, Feb. 13, 1799; to Edmund Pendleton, Feb. 14, 1799; to Madison, Nov. 26, 1799, *WTJ,* VII, 341, 354, 356; Adrienne Koch and Harry Ammon, "The Virginia and Kentucky Resolutions: An Episode in Jefferson's and Madison's Defense of Civil Liberties," *WMQ,* 3rd Ser., V (Apr. 1948), 170.

62. Hamilton to Otis, Dec. 27, 1798; to Jonathan Dayton, [Oct.–Nov.] 1799; to King, Jan. 5, 1800; *PAH,* XXII, 394, XXIII, 602, XXIV, 169. See also below, p. 719 and n. 69, and Kohn, *Eagle and Sword,* p. 255, for Hamilton's state of mind over the collapse of the New Army. A striking example of this Federalist urge for an army without any clear sense of what they wanted it for is Fisher Ames to Wolcott, Jan. 12, 1800, Gibbs, *Memoirs,* II, 318–321. See also Kohn, *Eagle and Sword,* p. 252.

63. Two very useful studies on this question, one concerning its origins in England and the other the form it took in America, are Lois G. Schwoerer, *"No Standing Armies!" The Antiarmy Ideology in Seventeenth-Century England* (Baltimore, 1974), and Lawrence D. Cress, *Citizens in Arms: The Army and the Militia in American Society to the War of 1812* (Chapel Hill, N.C., 1982). The qu. is in Cress, p. 19.

64. *Ibid.,* pp. 25–33.

65. *Ibid.,* pp. 34–93.

66. A sampling of such difficulties is abundantly available throughout Vols. XXII, XXIII, and XXIV of *PAH:* XXII, 453, 470, 483, 567, 586; XXIII, 88, 122, 160, 180, 184, 185, 187, 193, 214, 229, 243, 257–258, 307, 310, 320, 345–346, 391, 399, 430, 537; XXIV, 21, 35–36, 38, 50ff., 57–58, 100, 123–124, 182, 233.

67. Webster as qu. in Dauer, *Adams Federalists,* p. 220; Wolcott to F. Ames, Dec. 29, 1799, Gibbs, *Memoirs,* II, 317; *PAH,* XXIII, 100n.; McHenry to Hamilton, Sept. 20, 1799, *ibid.,* XXIII, 447–448.

68. The maximum number of enlistments was about four thousand. Kohn, *Eagle and Sword,* p. 263.

69. To Elizabeth Hamilton, May 24, 1800, *PAH,* XXIV, 525.

70. The most circumstantially detailed modern study of the Resolutions is that of Koch and Ammon (cited in n. 61 above), the great merit of which lies in the authors'

effort to clear up the several obscurities that still hung over the story of the Resolutions' origins, and probably exhausts whatever can now be known of them. Ch. 7 of A. Koch, *Jefferson and Madison: The Great Collaboration* (New York, 1950), is largely a repetition of that essay. See also Editorial Notes in *PJM*, XVII, 199–206, 303–307. Another study, much older but still exceedingly useful and suggestive, is Frank M. Anderson, "Contemporary Opinion of the Virginia and Kentucky Resolutions," *AHR*, V (Oct. 1899) and (Jan. 1900), 45–63 and 225–252, which examines the way in which the Resolutions were received in the various states that acted on them. A very perceptive discussion of how public men as well as successive generations of historical writers have used and thought about the Resolutions is in Merrill D. Peterson, *The Jefferson Image in the American Mind* (New York, 1960), pp. 32–39, 51–66, 202–218, 296–300.

71. Texts of the Resolutions, as well as the replies of the other states, are reproduced in Jonathan Elliot, ed., *Debates . . . on the Adoption of the Federal Constitution . . . Together with . . . Virginia and Kentucky Resolutions of '98–99 . . .* (Philadelphia, 1836), IV, 528–545.

72. Ten, that is, took action, though only seven of these (Delaware, New York, Connecticut, Rhode Island, Massachusetts, New Hampshire, and Vermont) sent actual replies; the others (Maryland, Pennsylvania, and New Jersey) dismissed them by resolution after debate, without then officially transmitting the result to the legislatures of Kentucky and Virginia. Anderson, "Contemporary Opinion," 45–55. The remaining four states, whose legislatures took no action at all, were North and South Carolina, Tennessee, and Georgia.

73. Elliot, *Debates*, IV, 539.

74. Jefferson to Madison, Aug. 23, 1799, qu. in Koch and Ammon, "Virginia and Kentucky Resolutions," 166; Peterson, *Jefferson Image*, p. 213. See also *ibid.*, pp. 51–56; and William W. Freehling, *Prelude to War: The Nullification Controversy in South Carolina, 1816–1836* (New York, 1965), pp. 207–210.

75. These aspects have certainly not gone unperceived by previous writers: e.g., Hofstadter, *Idea of a Party System*, p. 112; Koch and Ammon, "Virginia and Kentucky Resolutions," 147; and Noble E. Cunningham, *The Jeffersonian Republicans: The Formation of Party Organization, 1789–1801* (Chapel Hill, N.C., 1957), p. 129.

76. His biographer, Dumas Malone, appears to take this point more or less for granted in the closing chapters of his third volume, *Jefferson and the Ordeal of Liberty*. (And the letter of Jan. 12, 1800 to Monroe, qu. on p. 725 below, would seem to be rather a giveaway.) Cunningham states flatly: "With the drafting of the Kentucky Resolutions, Jefferson began his campaign for the presidency." *Jeffersonian Republicans*, p. 128.

77. This is noted (with regret) in Malone, *Jefferson*, III, 317.

78. Koch and Ammon, "Virginia and Kentucky Resolutions," 154.

79. *Ibid.*, p. 155. Prior to this, Jefferson seems to have had North Carolina rather than Kentucky in mind.

80. Jefferson to Edmund Pendleton, Feb. 14, 1799, *WTJ*, VII, 356.

81. Elliot, *Debates*, IV, 529.

82. *Ibid.*, 541–543.

83. *Ibid.*, 528.

84. "The Report of 1800," *PJM*, XVII, 307–351.

85. Elliot, *Debates*, IV, 528.

86. Jefferson to John Taylor, June 1, Nov. 26, 1798; to Monroe, Jan. 23, 1799; to Tench Coxe, May 21, 1799; to Wilson C. Nicholas, Sept. 5, 1799; *WTJ*, VII, 265, 310, 322, 380, 390–391.

87. Jefferson to Archibald Stuart, Feb. 13, 1799; to Edmund Pendleton, Feb. 19, 1799; to Aaron Burr, Feb. 11, 1799; *ibid.*, VII, 354, 364, 349.

88. Jefferson to Elbridge Gerry, Jan. 26, 1799, *ibid.,* VII, 329.

89. *Ibid.,* 336.

90. To Madison, Feb. 5, 1799, *ibid.,* 344.

91. Jefferson to Monroe, Jan. 12, 1800, *ibid.,* 402–403.

92. E.g., Anderson, "Contemporary Opinion," p. 244; Edward Channing, *History of the United States* (New York, 1917), IV, 232. ("It is impossible," Channing thought, "to trace any connection. . . .")

93. Anderson, "Contemporary Opinion," pp. 52, 53, 57. In Connecticut and New Hampshire most of the Republican members, in both cases few in number, simply absented themselves from the final vote.

94. The Federalist majority in the House of Representatives had been 56–49 in the Fifth Congress; in the Sixth it was increased to 63–43. Dauer, *Adams Federalists,* pp. 316, 326. On Republican gains in the South see Lisle A. Rose, *Prologue to Democracy: The Federalists in the South, 1789–1800* (Lexington, Ky., 1968), pp. 229–230.

95. Marshall to James M. Marshall, Dec. 16, 1799, *PJnMl,* IV, 44–45.

96. Patrick J. Furlong, "John Rutledge, Jr., and the Election of a Speaker of the House in 1799," *WMQ,* 3rd Ser., XXIV (July 1967), 432–436.

97. Sedgwick to King, Dec. 29, 1799, King, *King,* III, 163.

98. Same to same, May 11, 1800, *ibid.,* III, 237.

99. Same to same (as per n. 97 above); George Cabot to King, Jan. 20, 1800, *ibid.,* III, 184. See also Wolcott to Ames, Dec. 29, 1799, Gibbs, *Memoirs,* II, 314.

100. *Ibid.,* 314; Albert J. Beveridge, *The Life of John Marshall* (Boston, 1916), II, 433–436; "Speech to Both Houses of Congress," *WJA,* IX, 136–140; "Address," ca. Dec. 6, 1799, *PJnMl,* IV, 39–43.

101. "To a Freeholder," Oct. 2, 1798, *ibid.,* III, 505–506; Sedgwick to Pickering, Oct. 23, 1798, qu. in Richard E. Welch, *Theodore Sedgwick, Federalist: A Political Portrait* (Middletown, Conn., 1965), p. 97; Ames to C. Gore, Dec. 18, 1798, *WFA,* I, 246; Cabot to King, Apr. 26, 1799, King, *King,* III, 9.

102. *AC,* 6 Cong., 1 Sess., 404–419; Beveridge, *Marshall,* II, 451; *PJnMl,* IV, 37.

103. *Ibid.,* IV, 36–37, 121–124; Beveridge, *Marshall,* II, 452–458; *AC,* 6 Cong., 1 Sess., 29–33, 47, 126–146, 649, 670, 673–674, 678, 692, 694–697, 709–710, 713.

104. Sedgwick to King, Dec. 29, 1799, King, *King,* III, 163.

105. Kohn, *Eagle and Sword,* pp. 260–261.

106. *Ibid.,* 262–263, 266; Beveridge, *Marshall,* II, 476–481; *PJnMl,* IV, 33, 53–58.

107. Kohn, *Eagle and Sword,* pp. 266–267.

108. Adams to Pickering, May 10, 1800; Pickering to Adams, May 12, 1800; Adams to Pickering, May 12, 1800; *WJA,* IX, 53–55. *PJnMl,* IV, 148–149, 156–161.

109. Harry M. Tinkcom, *The Republicans and Federalists in Pennsylvania, 1790–1801: A Study in National Stimulus and Local Response* (Harrisburg, Pa., 1950), pp. 243–245.

110. Arthur I. Bernstein, "The Rise of the Democratic-Republican Party in New York City, 1789–1800" (Unpub. diss., Columbia U., 1964), pp. 341–362.

111. Troup to King, Mar. 9, 1800, King, *King,* III, 208–209.

112. *Ibid.,* 208.

113. *PCAB,* I, 423; Bernstein, "Democratic-Republican Party," pp. 390–399.

114. *Ibid.,* pp. 400–414; *PCAB,* I, 423–425. See also *PAH,* XXIV, 452–453n.

115. Hamilton to Jay, May 7, 1800, *ibid.,* XXIV, 464–466. Jay wrote at the bottom of this letter: "Proposing a measure for party purposes wh. I think it wd. not become me to adopt." *Ibid.,* 467n.

116. Hamilton to Sedgwick, May 4, 1800, *ibid.,* XXIV, 452–453. This letter was actu-

ally dated the day after the caucus was held, which suggests that Sedgwick and his friends needed no prompting. See also *ibid.*, 446.

117. Ames to King, July 15, 1800, King, *King*, III, 275.

118. Sedgwick to Hamilton, May 7, 1800, *PAH*, XXIV, 467; Samuel E. Morison, *The Life and Letters of Harrison Gray Otis, Federalist, 1765–1848* (Boston, 1913), I, 189.

119. Hamilton to Charles Carroll of Carrollton, July 1, 1800, *PAH*, XXV, 2. Abigail Adams to Thomas B. Adams, July 12, 1800, *ibid.*, XXIV, 576; see also Arthur Fenner to [Christopher G. Champlin?], June 25–26, 1800, *ibid.*, XXIV, 595–597; and Introductory Note, *ibid.*, 574–585.

120. Harper to Otis, June 25, Oct. 10, 1800, Morison, *Otis*, I, 192, 197; Joseph W. Cox, *Champion of Southern Federalism: Robert Goodloe Harper of South Carolina* (Port Washington, N.Y., 1972), p. 198, n. 21.

121. Marvin R. Zahniser, *Charles Cotesworth Pinckney: Founding Father* (Chapel Hill, N.C., 1967), pp. 221–22.

122. McHenry to John McHenry, Jr., May 20, 1800; McHenry to Adams, May 31, 1800; *PAH*, XXIV, 507–512, 551–565. The qu. is on p. 557. It should be added that Adams had received two anonymous letters several weeks before, dated Mar. 11 and 19, 1800, to which he referred in his conversation with McHenry. The first of them warned him, "Hamilton says you will not have a vote in N York *in any event*," and the other reported its being said that "the southern States will unite [with] the Hamilton party when they are *shown* that you stand no chance of succeeding." APM, reel 397. The letter of Mar. 19 is repr., except for the opening paragraph, in Welch, *Sedgwick*, pp. 214–215n.

123. See n. 108 above.

124. McHenry to Hamilton, June 2, 1800; Hamilton to McHenry, June 6, 1800; *PAH*, XXIV, 550, 573.

125. Welch, *Sedgwick*, p. 105; Sedgwick to Hamilton, May 13, 1800, *ibid.*, XXIV, 482. "Oh mad! mad! mad!" Hamilton to McHenry, May 23, 1800, *ibid.*, XXIV, 520. "The people," according to Oliver Wolcott, "believe their President is Crazy." Wolcott to Hamilton, Sept. 3, 1800, *ibid.*, XXV, 108.

126. The "British faction" charge seems to have been made widely and freely. Hamilton to Wolcott, July 1, Aug. 3, 1800; Wolcott to Hamilton, Sept. 3, 1800; *ibid.*, XXV, 5, 54, 106–107. Even John Marshall, loyal to Adams though he was, observed that "the hardest thing for federalists to bear was the charge of British influence." Fisher Ames to Christopher Gore, Dec. 29, 1800, *WFA*, I, 287.

127. *PAH*, XXIV, 557. See also the extended discussion of these rumors in *ibid.*, 483–486, n. 3.

128. Ames to Wolcott, June 12, 1800, Gibbs, *Memoirs*, II, 368.

129. Hamilton to Adams, Aug. 1, Oct, 1, 1800, *PAH*, XXV, 51, 125–126.

130. Cabot to Hamilton, Aug. 21, 1800; Ames to Hamilton, Aug. 26, 1800; Wolcott to Hamilton, Sept. 3, 1800; *ibid.*, XXV, 75, 87–88, 106.

131. A discussion of the possible circumstances under which the *Letter* became public is in *ibid.*, XXV, 173–178.

132. See *ibid.*, 186–234 for complete text of the *Letter*. The qu. are on pp. 186, 187, 190.

133. *Ibid.*, 210–211.

134. *Ibid.*, 214–228.

135. *Ibid.*, 230, 232–233.

136. *Ibid.*, 233.

137. Introductory Note, *ibid.*, 178–185.

138. Nov. 5, 1800, qu. in *ibid.*, 181–182.

139. Hamilton to Sedgwick, May 10, 1800, *ibid.*, XXIV, 475.

140. *Federal Republican & Commercial Gazette*, Mar. 31, 1809, qu. in *ibid.*, XXV, 183–184.

141. Cunningham, *Jeffersonian Republicans,* pp. 162–164, 240; Parsons to Jay, May 5, 1800, *CPJJ*, IV, 270.

142. *PAH,* XXIV, 446.

143. The Jefferson-Burr tie itself was of course the result of the Constitution's failure (Art. II, Sec. 1) to allow the electors to discriminate between their choices for President and Vice-President by voting separately for those offices. It simply provided that the candidate with the greatest number of votes (if that number were a majority of the electors) "shall be the President," and the next greatest, Vice-President. (Another way of putting the difficulty would be that the Constitution in its original form did not anticipate parties.) The defect was corrected by the Twelfth Amendment, adopted in 1804. On the Pennsylvania situation see Tinkcom, *Republicans and Federalists,* pp. 247–253; on New Jersey, Carl E. Prince, *New Jersey's Jeffersonian Republicans: The Genesis of an Early Party Machine, 1789–1817* (Chapel Hill, N.C., 1967), pp. 61–65. On changes in state electoral laws see Cunningham, *Jeffersonian Republicans,* pp. 144–147, 189–190.

Most of the other matters referred to in the above paragraph are represented in the following consolidated tabulation:

State	Electoral votes 1800					Method of choosing electors	6th Cong. HR		7th Cong. HR	
	Jefferson	Burr	Adams	Pinckney	Jay		Fedlst.	Repub.	Fedlst.	Repub.
Conn			9	9		legisl.	7	0	7	0
Dela.			3	3		legisl.	1	0	1	0
Ga.	4	4				legisl.	2	0	0	2
Ky.	4	4				distr.	0	2	0	2
Md.	5	5	5	5		distr.	5	3	3	5
Mass.			16	16		legisl.	12	2	8	6
N.H.			6	6		legisl.	4	0	4	0
N.J.			7	7		legisl.	2	3	0	5
N.Y.	12	12				legisl.	4	6	3	7
N.C.	8	8	4	4		distr.	5	5	5	5
Pa.	8	8	7	7		legisl.	5	8	4	9
R.I.			4	3	1	genl. ticket	2	0	0	2
S.C.	8	8				legisl.	5	1	3	3
Tenn.	3	3				legisl. & distr.	0	1	0	1
Vt.			4	4		legisl.	1	1	1	1
Va.	21	21				genl. ticket	8	11	2	17
TOTAL	73	73	65	64	1		63	43	41	65

Information drawn from Dauer, *Adams Federalists*, pp. 257, 326; *PAH*, XXIV, 445, 452. Tables on relative party strength in the Senate, plus much other useful material, are provided in John F. Hoadley, *Origins of American Political Parties, 1789–1803* (Lexington, Ky., 1986), esp. pp. 215–219.

144. Zahniser, *Pinckney*, p. 224.

145. *Ibid.*, pp. 222–225; Rose, *Prologue to Democracy*, pp. 51–59, 179–186.

146. That there was by this time a growing tendency on the part of South Carolina's planter aristocracy to wash their hands of politics is persuasively argued in Mark D. Kaplanoff, "Making the South Solid: Parties and the Structure of Society in South Carolina, 1790–1815" (Unpub. diss., Cambridge U., 1979), esp. pp. 200–201.

147. Zahniser, *Pinckney*, pp. 224–233, is the most perceptive and analytical treatment of the doings at the South Carolina state capitol in November and December 1800; but see also Cunningham, *Jeffersonian Republicans*, pp. 231–237; John H. Wolfe, *Jeffersonian Democracy in South Carolina* (Chapel Hill, N.C., 1940), pp. 135–165 (but cf. Zahniser, p. 232n., on Wolfe's version); and J. F. Jameson, ed., "South Carolina in the Presidential Election of 1800," *AHR*, IV (Oct. 1898), 111–129.

148. These paragraphs are based primarily on the above-cited pages in Zahniser, *Pinckney*.

149. E.g., J. C. A. Stagg, "The Enigma of Aaron Burr," *Reviews in American History*, XII (Sept. 1984), 378–382. A sampling of the Burr literature may include Matthew L. Davis, *Memoirs of Aaron Burr; With Miscellaneous Selections from his Correspondence* (New York, 1836–37), 2v.; James Parton, *The Life and Times of Aaron Burr* (New York, 1858); Nathan Schachner, *Aaron Burr: A Biography* (New York, 1937); Herbert S. Parmet and Marie B. Hecht, *Aaron Burr: Portrait of an Ambitious Man* (New York, 1967); Gore Vidal, *Burr: A Novel* (New York, 1973); Charles J. Nolan, *Aaron Burr and the American Literary Imagination* (Westport, Conn., 1980); Milton Lomask, *Aaron Burr* (New York, 1979–83), 2v.; Mary-Jo Kline, ed., *Political Correspondence and Public Papers of Aaron Burr* (Princeton, N.J., 1983), 2v. (elsewhere cited as *PCAB*); Gordon S. Wood, "The Revenge of Aaron Burr," *New York Review of Books*, Feb. 2, 1984, pp. 23–26; and R. Jackson Wilson, "The Foundling Father (Aaron Burr was not the villain you think)," *New Republic*, June 13, 1983, pp. 25–31. The profile offered above is adapted from Eric L. McKitrick, "Confounding Father," *New York Times Book Review*, Jan. 23, 1983, pp. 6, 23.

150. Cunningham, *Jeffersonian Republicans*, pp. 239–240.

151. There has been some speculation on such questions as the extent to which Burr was driven beyond the point of choice, or even whether Hamilton, in refusing to extenuate himself while there was still a chance of averting a duel, may have come close to willing his own destruction. See Thomas P. Slaughter, "Conspiratorial Politics: The Public Life of Aaron Burr," *New Jersey History*, CIII (Spring–Summer 1985), 69–81.

152. Lomask, *Burr*, jacket copy.

153. *Ibid.*, I, 69; II, xvii.

154. On the House election see Morton Borden, *The Federalism of James A. Bayard* (New York, 1955), pp. 73–95; Kline, "The Electoral Tie of 1801," *PCAB*, I, 481–487; Elizabeth Donnan, ed., "The Papers of James A. Bayard, 1796–1815," *AHA:AR 1913*, II. The possibility that other means of designating a President might be found—e.g., appointing a president pro tempore of the Senate, who might then take power in the event of a continued deadlock, or passing a special law—was removed when Jefferson showed he intended to remain in his seat as the Senate's presiding officer until the end of the session, and when the House resolved to do no business until a President should be chosen. *PCAB*, I, 485–486.

155. Hamilton to Sedgwick, Dec. 22, 1800, *PAH*, XXV, 270.

156. To Morris, Dec. 24, 1800; to Otis, Dec. 23, 1800; *ibid.*, 271–272.

157. To McHenry, Jan. 4, 1801, *ibid.*, 292–293.

158. To James Ross, Dec. 29, 1800, *ibid.*, 280–281.

159. Burr to Samuel Smith, Dec. 16, 1800; to Jefferson, Dec. 23, 1800; *PCAB*, I, 471, 474.

160. Burr to Smith, Dec. 29, 1800, *ibid.*, 479. Burr and Smith met in Philadelphia on the weekend of Jan. 3–4, at which time Burr appears to have repeated what he had already said in this letter, and according to a local newspaper, "Mr. Burr was heard to insinuate that he felt as competent to the exercise of the Presidential functions as Mr. Jefferson," *Ibid.*, 483–484. Burr's "displeasure" at the publication of his Dec. 16 letter to Smith is noted in Sedgwick to Hamilton, Jan. 10, 1801, *PAH*, XXV, 312. Benjamin Hichborn reported to Jefferson from Philadelphia on Jan. 5, 1801: "I could not leave this place without intimating to you a Circumstance, which gives me some little uneasiness. Colo. Burr is in the house with me & Genl. Smith from Baltimore has been here. I am convinced that some of our Friends, as they call themselves are willing to join the other party in Case they shou'd unite in favor of Colo. Burr." Jefferson Papers, LC. On the question of whether Jefferson's suspicions of Burr may or may not have been aroused this early see Kline, "Electoral Tie," *PCAB*, I, 483; and Malone, *Jefferson*, III, 494–495; also Jefferson to Mary Jefferson Eppes, Jan. 4, 1801, *WTJ*, VII, 478.

161. Harper to Burr, Dec. 24, 1800, *PCAB*, I, 474.

162. Sedgwick to Hamilton, Jan. 10, 1801, *PAH*, XXV, 311.

163. Hamilton to Bayard, Jan. 16, 1801, *ibid.*, 319–320.

164. Borden, *Bayard*, pp. 87–88.

165. *PAH*, XXV, 258n., 346, n. 7.

166. *PCAB*, I, 485–486. On the one hand, the continuing deadlock had made it obvious to the Federalists that the majorities in the eight pro-Jefferson delegations had solidified their positions and were determined to keep them that way; consequently the only chance left of bringing over the votes necessary to convert them would be a clear signal of cooperation from Burr—notwithstanding Harper's earlier counsel to Burr that he was best off keeping quiet. But on the other hand, the likelihood of anything at all happening at this point to turn the vote in Burr's favor had become exceedingly remote, no matter what he might do. Thus when it should become known—as it would of course have to be—that Burr had intrigued with the Federalists and failed (and with the odds of failure as great as they were), Burr's political future would have been wrecked then and there. Burr would have had to be dull indeed not to sense this. Bayard's subsequent anger at Burr's immobility ("He will never have another chance of being President . . . and the little use he has made of the one which has occurred gives me but a humble opinion of the talents of an unprincipled man") thus strikes one as both ironic and grossly unreasonable. Bayard to Hamilton, Mar. 8, 1801, *PAH*, XXV, 345. See also John S. Pancake, "Aaron Burr: Would-be Usurper," *WMQ*, 3rd Ser., VIII (Apr. 1951), 204–213.

167. Borden, *Bayard*, pp. 88–95; *PCAB*, I, 486–487. Bayard's torments may be followed in the numerous letters he wrote during this brief period. Donnan, ed., "Bayard Papers," pp. 122–132. The quotation is from a deposition Bayard made in 1805, reprinted a half-century later in *Congressional Globe*, 33 Cong., 2 Sess., Appendix, 136 (Jan. 1855).

168. E.g., John Marshall: "To Mr. Jefferson . . . I have felt almost insuperable objections. His foreign prejudices seem to me totally to unfit him for the chief magistracy of a nation which cannot indulge those prejudices without sustaining debt & permanent injury." James Bayard: "There would be really cause to fear that the government would

not survive the course of moral & political experiments to which it would be subjected at the hands of Mr. Jefferson." Theodore Sedgwick: "[He is] hostile to all those great systems of Administration, the combined effect of which is our national prosperity, and all we possess of character & respectability . . . [and] he is known to be devoted to the views of those men . . . whose unceasing efforts it has been & is to reduce, in *practice,* the administration of this government to the *principles* of the old confederation. . . ." Marshall to Hamilton, Jan. 1, 1801; Bayard to Hamilton, Jan. 7, 1801; Sedgwick to Hamilton, Jan. 10, 1801; *PAH,* XXV, 290, 301, 310–311. The assurances which Hamilton urged should be sought from Jefferson—regarding the financial system, the navy, and relations with foreign governments—reflected those items about which Federalist fears had been most consistently expressed.

169. John Rutledge, Jr., to Hamilton, Jan. 10, 1801, *PAH,* XXV, 309.

170. David H. Fischer offers many sketches of such types in an extended Appendix and elsewhere throughout his *Revolution of American Conservatism: The Federalist Party in the Era of Jeffersonian Democracy* (New York, 1965), pp. 227–412 and *passim.* Gordon Wood likewise makes a point of the striking number of Revolutionary leaders who were "first-generation gentlemen." *Radicalism of the American Revolution,* p. 197.

171. The incidence of prominent figures in the northern and middle states who had been Whigs in the Revolution and became Federalists after 1789, and who tended to advocate mild treatment for former Loyalists, is quite striking. The names of Hamilton, Jay, Ellsworth, Sedgwick, Ames, and Higginson come readily to mind, and there were undoubtedly a great many more. On Loyalism in Virginia, according to Wallace Brown, "unlike Massachusetts there is here a distinct dearth of talent and representatives of leading families." In South Carolina it was much the same, with "a solid Whig front of the . . . ruling class," Loyalism being "largely an immigrant phenomenon." Brown, *The King's Friends: The Composition and Motives of the American Loyalist Claimants* (Providence, 1966), pp. 185, 219.

172. Trevor Colbourn, ed., *Fame and the Founding Fathers: Essays by Douglass Adair* (New York, 1974), pp. 3–26. For the writers above mentioned, the uppermost category in this hierarchy of figures most deserving of fame and immortality is occupied by the law-givers and founders of states, ranking well above wise rulers and military conquerors. (Though Bacon—who, as Adair notes, had originally subscribed to this ordering—later changed his mind and urged an additional category superior to all the others, that of philosophers and inventors whose "Divine gift of Reason" had benefited mankind. Thomas Jefferson found this reformulation especially attractive.) *Ibid.,* p. 16.

173. "Of Parties in General," T. H. Green and T. H. Grose, eds., *Essays Moral, Political, and Literary by David Hume* (London, 1882), I, 127.

174. *Ibid.,* 127–128.

175. Jean-Jacques Rousseau, *The Social Contract, and Discourses,* tr. by G. D. H. Cole (New York, 1950), p.39.

176. In the world of our own day, of course, cases abound of revolutionary elites grimly hanging on beyond their time.

177. The development of this point on popular sovereignty is of course one of the many insights in Gordon Wood's *Creation of the American Republic,* esp. pp. 530–532.

178. The text of Jefferson's (admirably brief) First Inaugural is in James D. Richardson, ed., *A Compilation of the Messages and Papers of the Presidents* (Washington, 1911), I, 309–312; or, more conveniently, Adrienne Koch and William Peden, eds., *The Life and Selected Writings of Thomas Jefferson* (New York, 1944), pp. 321–325.

179. More exactly, he seems to have toyed with the thought and then rejected it. His

papers contain jottings for a passage in which he allowed that "whenever there are men there will be parties," but in "cases of danger or commotion . . . consider the laws as the standard to which you are to rally." *WTJ*, VIII, 1 n.

180. To Thomas McKean, July 24, 1801, *ibid.,* 78.

181. To Gates, Mar. 8, 1801, *ibid.,* 11–12.

182. To John Dickinson, July 23, 1801, *ibid.,* 76.

183. To Joel Barlow, May 3, 1802, *ibid.,* 150.

184. To Levi Lincoln, Oct. 25, 1802, *ibid.,* 175–176.

INDEX